Allez, viens!

Your passport to proficiency

Sans frontières

Plan your itinerary for success

What's your **Destination?**

Communication!

Allez, viens! takes your classroom there.

It's even possible that **"What's next?"** becomes your students' favorite question!

Communication and culture in context

The clear structure of each chapter makes it easy for students to present, practice, and apply language skills—all in the context of the location where the chapter takes place!

Grammar support and practice in every lesson

Allez, viens! builds a proven communicative approach on a solid foundation of grammar and vocabulary so students become proficient readers, writers, and speakers of French. With the *Travaux pratiques de grammaire*, Grammar Tutor, and the CD-ROM and DVD Tutors, students can practice the way they learn best.

Technology that takes you there

Bring the world into your classroom with integrated audio, video, CD-ROM, DVD, and Internet resources that immerse students in authentic language and culture.

Assessment for state and national standards

To help you incorporate standardized test practice, the Standardized Assessment Tutor provides reading, writing, and math tests in French that target the skills students need. The Joie de lire Reader and Reading Strategies and Skills Handbook offer additional reading practice and reading skills development.

Easy lesson planning for all learning styles

Planning lessons has never been easier with a Lesson Planner with Substitute Teacher Lesson Plans, an editable One-Stop Planner® CD-ROM, and a Student Make-Up Assignments with Alternative Quizzes resource.

Travel a balanced program that's easy to navigate.

Le monde à votre portée!

Allez, viens!

Program components

Texts
- Pupil's Edition
- Annotated Teacher's Edition

Middle School Resources
- Middle School Teaching Resources
- Exploratory Guide

Planning and Presenting
- One-Stop Planner CD-ROM with Test Generator
- Lesson Planner with Substitute Teacher Lesson Plans
- Student Make-Up Assignments with Alternative Quizzes
- Teaching Transparencies

Grammar
- Travaux pratiques de grammaire
- Grammar Tutor for Students of French

Reading and Writing
- Reading Strategies and Skills Handbook
- Joie de lire Reader
- Cahier d'activités

Listening and Speaking
- Audio CD Program
- Listening Activities
- Activities for Communication
- TPR Storytelling Book (Levels 1 and 2)

Assessment
- Testing Program
- Alternative Assessment Guide
- Student Make-Up Assignments with Alternative Quizzes
- Standardized Assessment Tutor

Technology
- One-Stop Planner CD-ROM with Test Generator
- Audio CD Program
- Interactive CD-ROM Tutor
- Video Program
- Video Guide
- DVD Tutor (Levels 1 and 2)

Internet
- go.hrw.com
- www.hrw.com
- www.hrw.com/passport

Allez, viens!®

HOLT FRENCH

LEVEL
3

220792

HOLT, RINEHART AND WINSTON

A Harcourt Education Company

Austin • Orlando • Chicago • New York • Toronto • London • San Diego

T 72828

For permission to reprint copyrighted material in the Annotated Teacher's Edition, grateful acknowledgment is made to the following sources:

National Standards in Foreign Language Education Project: "National Standards Report" from *Standards for Foreign Language Learning: Preparing for the 21st Century.* Copyright © 1996 by National Standards in Foreign Language Education Project.

In the *Annotated Teacher's Edition,*

Cover and Title Page Photography Credits
Front Cover and Title Page: (background), © John Elk III, (students), HRW Photo/Steve Ewert Photography

Back Cover: © Ping Amranand/ Superstock, (frame) © 1998 Image Farm, Inc.

Illustration Credits
All art, unless otherwise noted, by Holt Rinehart & Winston.

Photography Credits
All photos HRW Photo/Marty Granger except:
Technology border: Digital imagery® © 2003 PhotoDisc, Inc.
Clock for pacing tips: Digital imagery® © 2003 PhotoDisc, Inc.
Chess piece for games feature: Digital imagery® © 2003 PhotoDisc, Inc.
House for Community Link feature: Courtesy Ellen Boelsche
Jeux interactifs computer: Digital imagery® © 2003 PhotoDisc, Inc.
All euros: © European Communities
All globes: Mountain High Maps® Copyright ©1997 Digital Wisdom, Inc.
Recipe card fabric: HRW Photo/Victoria Smith
Sage for recipe card: Corbis Images; Remaining herbs: Digital imagery® © 2003 PhotoDisc, Inc.

Front Matter: T1(t), Corbis Images; T1 (bl), (bc), (br), T2 (tr), (br), HRW Photo/Marty Granger/Edge Productions; T2 (l), HRW Photo/Sam Dudgeon; T3 (tl), Creatas; T3 (tc), HRW Photo/Marty Granger/Edge Productions; T3 (tr), Courtesy Neel Heisel; T3 (tc), HRW Photo/Marty Granger/Edge Productions; T3 (tc), Corbis Images; T8, HRW Photo by Marty Granger / Edge Productions; T27, Courtesy Neel Heisel ; T41, HRW Photo/Lance Schriner; T45, HRW Photo by Michelle Bridwell; T55, P.J. Sharpe/Superstock; T56, Pierre Berger/ Photo Researchers; T57, © The Purcell Team / Corbis; T58(t), Eric Beggs; T58(b), Michael Newman / PhotoEdit; T59, © Beryl Goldberg Photography; T60, © Lineair/R. Giling/Peter Arnold; T61, © David Cimino / International Stock Photography; T62, © Roberto M. Arakaki/ International Stock Photography; T63, Wolfgang Kaehler Photography; T64, Kit Kittle / Viesti Collection, Inc.; T65, Joseph Schuyler/ Stock Boston; T66, © Bongarts Photography/ SportsChrome USA; T67, Pierre Berger / Photo Researchers; T69, Kit Kittle / Viesti Collection; T70, HRW Photo/ Patrice Maurin-Berthier; 3D (l), © Owen Franken/CORBIS; 3D (r), © Robert Fried; 3E(t), both HRW Photos/Edge Productions; 3E (b), Courtesy Neel Heisel ; 3F, Digital imagery® © 2003 PhotoDisc, Inc.; 7,15, HRW Photo/Edge Productions ; 31D, © Robert Fried; 31E (t), both HRW Photos /Edge Productions; 31E (b), Courtesy Neel Heisel ; 31F, Digital imagery® © 2003 PhotoDisc, Inc.; 35, 43, HRW Photo/Edge Productions; 61D(l), Digital imagery® © 2003 PhotoDisc, Inc.; 61D(r), © Robert Fried; 61E(t), both HRW Photos /Edge Production; 61E (b), Courtesy Neel Heisel ; 61F, Digital imagery® © 2003 PhotoDisc, Inc.; 65, 73, HRW Photo/Edge Productions; 91D(l), HRW Photo/Sam Dudgeon; 91D(r), © Robert Fried; 91E(t), both HRW Photos / Edge Productions; 91E(b), Courtesy Neel Heisel ; 91F, Digital imagery® © 2003 PhotoDisc, Inc.; 95, 105, HRW Photo/Edge Productions; 125D(l), © José Nicolas/Hémisphères; 125D(r), © Robert Fried; 125E(t), both HRW Photos/Edge Productions; 125E(b), Courtesy Neel Heisel 1; 125F, Digital imagery® © 2003 PhotoDisc, Inc.;129, 137, HRW Photo/ Edge Productions; 155D(l), Jean Whitney/Tony Stone Images; 155D(r), HRW Photo/Sam Dudgeon; 155E(t), both HRW Photos, / Edge Productions; 155E(b), Courtesy Neel Heisel ; 155F, Digital imagery® © 2003 PhotoDisc, Inc.; 159, 167, HRW Photo/Edge Productions; 185D, © Robert Fried; 185E(t), both HRW Photos/Edge Productions; 185E(b), Courtesy Neel Heisel ; 185F, Digital imagery® © 2003 PhotoDisc, Inc.; 189, 199, HRW Photo/Edge Productions; 215D(l), © Philippe Dannic/Photononstop/DIAF; 215D(r), © Robert Fried; 215E(t), both HRW Photos/Edge Productions; 215E(b), Courtesy Neel Heisel ; 215F, Digital imagery® © 2003 PhotoDisc, Inc.; 219, 229, HRW Photo/Edge Productions; 249D(l), © Philippe Renault/Hémisphères; 249D(r), © Robert Fried; 249E (t), both HRW Photos/Edge Productions; 249E(b), Courtesy Neel Heisel; 249F, Digital imagery® © 2003 PhotoDisc, Inc.; 253, 263, HRW Photo/Edge Productions; 279D(l), © Hémisphères/Jean Boisberranger; 279D(r), © Robert Fried; 279E(t), both HRW Photos/Edge Productions; 279F, Digital imagery® © 2003 PhotoDisc, Inc.; 283, 293, HRW Photo/Edge Productions; 309D(l), © D. Donne Bryant/DDB Stock Photo; 309D, © Robert Fried; 309E (t), both HRW Photos/Edge Productions; 309E(b), Courtesy Neel Heisel; 309F, Digital imagery® © 2003 PhotoDisc, Inc.; 313, 321, HRW Photo/Edge Productions; 339D(l), © AFP/Corbis; 339D(r), © Robert Fried; 339E (t), both HRW Photos/Edge Productions; 339E(b), Courtesy Neel Heisel ;339F, Digital imagery® © 2003 PhotoDisc, Inc.; 343, 351, HRW Photo/Edge Productions.

ACKNOWLEDGMENTS continued on page R113, which is an extension of the copyright page.

Allez viens! Level 3
Annotated Teacher's Edition

CONTRIBUTING WRITERS

Jennie Bowser Chao
Consultant
Oak Park, IL
Ms. Chao was the principal writer of the Level 3 Annotated Teacher's Edition.

Judith Ryser
San Marcos High School
San Marcos, TX
Ms. Ryser contributed teaching suggestions and notes for the reading and writing sections of the Level 3 Annotated Teacher's Edition.

Jayne Abrate
The University of Missouri
Rolla Campus
Rolla, MO
Ms. Abrate contributed teaching suggestions, notes, and background information for the Location Openers of the Level 3 Annotated Teacher's Edition.

Margaret Sellstrom
Consultant
Austin, TX
Ms. Sellstrom contributed answers to activities of the Level 3 Annotated Teacher's Edition.

FIELD TEST PARTICIPANTS

Marie Allison
New Hanover High School
Wilmington, NC

Gabrielle Applequist
Capital High School
Boise, ID

Jana Brinton
Bingham High School
Riverton, UT

Nancy J. Cook
Sam Houston High School
Lake Charles, LA

Rachael Gray
Williams High School
Plano, TX

Katherine Kohler
Nathan Hale Middle School
Norwalk, CT

Nancy Mirsky
Museum Junior High School
Yonkers, NY

Myrna S. Nie
Whetstone High School
Columbus, OH

Jacqueline Reid
Union High School
Tulsa, OK

Judith Ryser
San Marcos High School
San Marcos, TX

Erin Hahn Sass
Lincoln Southeast High School
Lincoln, NE

Linda Sherwin
Sandy Creek High School
Tyrone, GA

Norma Joplin Sivers
Arlington Heights High School
Fort Worth, TX

Lorabeth Stroup
Lovejoy High School
Lovejoy, GA

Robert Vizena
W.W. Lewis Middle School
Sulphur, LA

Gladys Wade
New Hanover High School
Wilmington, NC

Kathy White
Grimsley High School
Greensboro, NC

REVIEWERS

Khaled Bendakhlia
Consultant
Austin, TX

Jeannette Caviness
Mount Tabor High School
Winston-Salem, NC

Robert H. Didsbury
Consultant
Raleigh, NC

Joseph F. Herney
Briarcliff High School
Briarcliff Manor, NY

Patricia Rebac
Clarksville High School
Clarksville, TN

Jo Anne Wilson
Consultant
Glen Arbor, MI

Tony Zaunbrecher
Calcasieu Parish School Board
Lake Charles, LA

PROFESSIONAL ESSAYS

Bringing Standards into the Classroom
Paul Sandrock
Foreign Language Consultant
Department of Public Instruction
Madison, WI

Reading Strategies and Skills
Nancy A. Humbach
Miami University
Oxford, OH

Using Portfolios in the Language Classroom
Jo Anne S. Wilson
J. Wilson Associates
Glen Arbor, MI

Teaching Culture
Nancy A. Humbach
The Miami University
Oxford, OH

Dorothea Brushke, retired
Parkway School District
Chesterfield, MO

Learning Styles and Multi-Modality Teaching
Mary B. McGehee
Louisiana State University
Baton Rouge, LA

Multi-Level Classrooms
Dr. Joan H. Manley
The University of Texas
El Paso, TX

To the Teacher

Principles and Practices

As nations become increasingly interdependent, the need for effective communication and sensitivity to other cultures becomes more important. Today's youth must be culturally and linguistically prepared to participate in a global society. At Holt, Rinehart and Winston, we believe that proficiency in more than one language is essential to meeting this need.

The primary goal of the Holt, Rinehart and Winston World Languages programs is to help students develop linguistic proficiency and cultural sensitivity. By interweaving language and culture, our programs seek to broaden students' communication skills while at the same time deepening their appreciation of other cultures.

We believe that all students can benefit from foreign language instruction. We recognize that not everyone learns at the same rate or in the same way; nevertheless, we believe that all students should have the opportunity to acquire language proficiency to a degree commensurate with their individual abilities.

Holt, Rinehart and Winston's World Languages programs are designed to accommodate all students by appealing to a variety of learning styles.

We believe that effective language programs should motivate students. Students deserve an answer to the question they often ask: "Why are we doing this?" They need to have goals that are interesting, practical, clearly stated, and attainable.

Holt, Rinehart and Winston's World Languages programs promote success. They present relevant content in manageable increments that encourage students to attain achievable functional objectives.

We believe that proficiency in another language is best nurtured by programs that encourage students to think critically and to take risks when expressing themselves in the language. We also recognize that students should strive for accuracy in communication. While it is imperative that students have a knowledge of the basic structures of the language, it is also important that they go beyond the simple manipulation of forms.

Holt, Rinehart and Winston's World Languages programs reflect a careful progression of activities that guide students from comprehensible input of authentic language through structured practice to creative, personalized expression. This progression, accompanied by consistent re-entry and spiraling of functions, vocabulary, and structures, provides students with the tools and the confidence to express themselves in their new language.

Finally, we believe that a complete program of language instruction should take into account the needs of teachers in today's increasingly demanding classrooms.

At Holt, Rinehart and Winston, we have designed programs that offer practical teacher support and provide resources to meet individual learning and teaching styles.

We have seen significant advances in modern language curriculum practices:

1. a redefinition of the objectives of foreign language study involving a commitment to the development of proficiency in the four skills and in cultural awareness;

2. a recognition of the need for longer sequences of study;

3. a new student-centered approach that redefines the role of the teacher as facilitator and encourages students to take a more active role in their learning;

4. the inclusion of students of all learning abilities.

The new Holt, Rinehart and Winston World Languages programs take into account not only these advances in the field of foreign language education but also the input of teachers and students around the country.

ANNOTATED TEACHER'S EDITION
Contents

Pacing and Planning

Traditional Schedule

Days of instruction: 180

Location Opener	2 days per Location Opener x 6 Location Openers	12 days
Chapter	13 days per chapter x 12 chapters	156 days
		168 days

If you are teaching on a traditional schedule, we suggest following the plan above and spending 13 days per chapter. A complete set of lesson plans in the interleaf provides detailed suggestions for each chapter. For more suggestions, see the **Lesson Planner with Substitute Teacher Lesson Plans.**

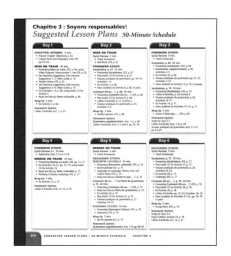

Block Schedule

Blocks of instruction: 90

Location Opener	1/2 block per Location Opener x 6 Location Openers	3 blocks
Chapter	7 blocks per chapter x 12 chapters	84 blocks
		87 blocks

If you are teaching on a block schedule, we suggest following the plan above and spending seven blocks per chapter. A complete set of lesson plans in the interleaf provides detailed suggestions for each chapter. For more suggestions, see the **Lesson Planner with Substitute Teacher Lesson Plans.**

One-Stop Planner CD-ROM

Use the **One-Stop Planner CD-ROM with Test Generator** to aid in lesson planning and pacing.

- Editable lesson plans with direct links to teaching resources
- Printable worksheets from resource books
- Direct launches to the HRW Internet activities
- Video and audio segments
- Test Generator
- Clip Art for vocabulary items

Pacing Tips
At the beginning of each chapter, you will find a Pacing Tip to help you plan your lessons.

Articulation Across Levels

The following chart shows how topics are repeated across levels in *Allez, viens!* from the end of Level 1 to the beginning of Level 3.

- In each level, the last chapter is a review chapter.
- In Levels 2 and 3, the first two chapters review the previous level.

LEVEL 1

CHAPTER 12
Review of Level 1

- Contractions with **de** and **à**
- The partitive
- The **passé composé**
- Possessive adjectives
- Asking for and giving directions
- Asking for advice
- Expressing need
- Family vocabulary
- Inviting
- Making requests
- Making suggestions
- Making excuses
- Pointing out places; things

LEVEL 2

CHAPTER 1

- Adjective agreement
- **Avoir** and **être**
- **Choisir** and other **–ir** verbs
- The imperative
- The future with **aller**
- Asking for information
- Asking for and giving advice
- Asking for, making, and responding to suggestions
- Clothing and colors
- Describing yourself and others
- Expressing likes and dislikes
- Family vocabulary
- Relating a series of events
- Pronunciation: **liaison**

CHAPTER 2
Review of Level 1

- Using **tu** and **vous**
- Question formation
- Adjectives that precede the noun
- Contractions with **de** and **à**
- Prepositions of location
- Asking for and giving directions
- Asking how someone is feeling and telling how you are feeling
- Making suggestions
- Pointing out where things are
- Paying compliments
- Pronunciation: intonation

CHAPTER 12
Review of Level 2

- The **passé composé** and the **imparfait**
- Asking for and giving information
- Asking for and giving advice
- Clothing vocabulary
- Complaining
- Describing people and places
- Expressing discouragement and offering encouragement
- Giving directions
- Making and responding to suggestions
- Relating a series of events
- Sports and activities

LEVEL 3

CHAPTER 1

- The **passé composé** and the **imparfait**
- Definite, indefinite, and partitive articles
- Question formation
- Describing what a place was like
- Exchanging information
- Expressing indecision
- Food vocabulary
- Inquiring; expressing enthusiasm and dissatisfaction
- Making recommendations
- Ordering and asking for details

CHAPTER 2
Review of Level 2

- The future with **aller**
- The imperative
- Pronouns and their placement
- Asking for and giving directions
- Asking about and telling where things are
- Expressing enthusiasm and boredom
- Expressing impatience
- Making, accepting, and refusing suggestions
- Reassuring someone

CHAPTER 12
Review of Level 3

- The future tense
- The subjunctive
- **Si** clauses
- Prepositions with countries
- Expressing anticipation
- Expressing certainty and doubt
- Expressing excitement and disappointment
- Greeting and introducing people
- Inquiring
- Making suppositions
- Offering encouragement

Allez, viens! French Level 1
Scope and Sequence

FUNCTIONS	GRAMMAR	VOCABULARY	CULTURE	RE-ENTRY
CHAPITRE PRELIMINAIRE *Allez, viens!, Pages xxvi–11*				
• Introducing yourself • Spelling • Counting • Understanding classroom instructions	• French alphabet • French accent marks	• French names • French numbers 0–20 • French classroom expressions	• The French-speaking world • Famous French-speaking people • The importance of learning French • French gestures for counting	
Poitiers **CHAPITRE 1** *Faisons connaissance!, Pages 16–45*				
• Greeting people and saying goodbye • Asking how people are; telling how you are • Asking someone's name and age and giving yours • Expressing likes, dislikes, and preferences about things • Expressing likes, dislikes, and preferences about activities	• **Ne...pas** • The definite articles **le, la, l'**, and **les** • The connectors **et** and **mais** • Subject pronouns • **-er** verbs	• Things you like or don't like • Activities you like or don't like to do	• Greetings and goodbyes • Hand gestures • Leisure time activities	• Introductions • Numbers 0–20 • Expressing likes, dislikes, and preferences about things
Poitiers **CHAPITRE 2** *Vive l'école!, Pages 46–73*				
• Agreeing and disagreeing • Asking for and giving information • Telling when you have class • Asking for and expressing opinions	• Using **si** instead of **oui** to contradict a negative statement • The verb **avoir**	• School subjects • School-related words • Class times • Parts of the school day • Numbers 21–59	• The French educational system/**le bac** • **L'heure officielle** • Curriculum in French schools • The French grading system	• Greetings • The verb **aimer** • Numbers for telling time

Poitiers

CHAPITRE 3 Tout pour la rentrée, *Pages 74–101*

FUNCTIONS	GRAMMAR	VOCABULARY	CULTURE	RE-ENTRY
• Making and responding to requests • Asking others what they need and telling what you need • Telling what you'd like and what you'd like to do • Getting someone's attention • Asking for information • Expressing thanks	• The indefinite articles **un, une,** and **des** • The demonstrative adjectives **ce, cet, cette,** and **ces** • Adjective agreement and placement	• School supplies • Things you might buy for school and fun • Colors • Numbers 60–201	• Bagging your own purchases • Buying school supplies in French-speaking countries • French currency (euros)	• The verb **avoir** • Expressing likes and dislikes • Numbers

Québec

CHAPITRE 4 Sports et passe-temps, *Pages 106–135*

FUNCTIONS	GRAMMAR	VOCABULARY	CULTURE	RE-ENTRY
• Telling how much you like or dislike something • Exchanging information • Making, accepting, and turning down suggestions	• Expressions with **faire** and **jouer** • Question formation • **De** after a negative verb • The verb **faire** • The pronoun **on** • Adverbs of frequency	• Sports and hobbies • Weather expressions • Months of the year • Time expressions • Seasons	• Old and new in Quebec City • Celsius and Fahrenheit • Sports in francophone countries • **Maison des jeunes et de la culture**	• Expressing likes and dislikes • The verb **aimer;** regular **-er** verbs • Agreeing and disagreeing

Paris

CHAPITRE 5 On va au café?, *Pages 140–167*

FUNCTIONS	GRAMMAR	VOCABULARY	CULTURE	RE-ENTRY
• Making suggestions and excuses • Making a recommendation • Getting someone's attention • Ordering food and beverages • Inquiring about and expressing likes and dislikes • Paying the check	• The verb **prendre** • The imperative	• Foods and beverages	• Food served in a café • Waitpersons as professionals • **La litote** • Tipping	• Accepting and turning down a suggestion • Expressing likes and dislikes • Numbers 20–100

	FUNCTIONS	GRAMMAR	VOCABULARY	CULTURE	RE-ENTRY

Paris

CHAPITRE 6 Amusons-nous!, *Pages 168–197*

FUNCTIONS	GRAMMAR	VOCABULARY	CULTURE	RE-ENTRY
• Making plans • Extending and responding to invitations • Arranging to meet someone	• Using **le** with days of the week • The verb **aller** and **aller** + infinitive • Contractions with **à** • The verb **vouloir** • Information questions	• Places to go • Things to do	• Going out • Dating in France • Conversational time	• Expressing likes and dislikes • Days of the week • Making, accepting, and turning down suggestions • Sports and hobbies • **L'heure officielle**

Paris

CHAPITRE 7 La famille, *Pages 198–225*

FUNCTIONS	GRAMMAR	VOCABULARY	CULTURE	RE-ENTRY
• Identifying people • Introducing people • Describing and characterizing people • Asking for, giving, and refusing permission	• Possession with **de** • Possessive adjectives • Adjective agreement • The verb **être**	• Family members • Adjectives to describe and characterize people	• Family life • Pets in France	• Asking for and giving people's names and ages • Adjective agreement

Abidjan

CHAPITRE 8 Au marché, *Pages 230–259*

FUNCTIONS	GRAMMAR	VOCABULARY	CULTURE	RE-ENTRY
• Expressing need • Making, accepting, and declining requests • Telling someone what to do • Offering, accepting, or refusing food	• The partitive articles • **Avoir besoin de** • The verb **pouvoir** • **De** with expressions of quantity • The pronoun **en**	• Food items • Expressions of quantity • Meals	• The Ivorian market • Shopping for groceries in francophone countries • The metric system • Foods of Côte d'Ivoire • Mealtimes in francophone countries	• Food vocabulary • Activities • The imperative

Arles

CHAPITRE 9 Au téléphone, *Pages 265–291*

FUNCTIONS	GRAMMAR	VOCABULARY	CULTURE	RE-ENTRY
• Asking for and expressing opinions • Inquiring about and relating past events • Making and answering a telephone call • Sharing confidences and consoling others • Asking for and giving advice	• The **passé composé** with **avoir** • Placement of adverbs with the **passé composé** • The **-re** verb: **répondre** • The object pronouns **le, la, les, lui,** and **leur**	• Daily activities	• History of Arles • The French telephone system • Telephone habits of French-speaking teenagers	• Chores • Asking for, giving, and refusing permission • **Aller** + infinitive

Arles

CHAPITRE 10 Dans un magasin de vêtements, *Pages 292–321*

FUNCTIONS	GRAMMAR	VOCABULARY	CULTURE	RE-ENTRY
• Asking for and giving advice • Expressing need; inquiring • Asking for an opinion; paying a compliment; criticizing • Hesitating; making a decision	• The verbs **mettre** and **porter** • Adjectives used as nouns • The **-ir** verbs: **choisir** • The direct object pronouns **le, la,** and **les** • **C'est** versus **il/elle est**	• Articles of clothing	• Clothing sizes • Fashion in francophone countries • Responding to compliments	• The future with **aller** • Colors • Likes and dislikes

Arles

CHAPITRE 11 Vive les vacances!, *Pages 322–349*

FUNCTIONS	GRAMMAR	VOCABULARY	CULTURE	RE-ENTRY
• Inquiring about and sharing future plans • Expressing indecision; expressing wishes • Asking for advice; making, accepting, and refusing suggestions • Reminding; reassuring • Seeing someone off • Asking for and expressing opinions • Inquiring about and relating past events	• The prepositions **à** and **en** • The **-ir** verbs: **partir**	• Vacation places and activities • Travel items	• **Colonies de vacances** • Vacations	• **Aller** + infinitive • Asking for advice • Clothing vocabulary • The imperative • Weather expressions • The **passé composé** • The verb **vouloir**

Fort-de-France

CHAPITRE 12 En ville, *Pages 354–383*

REVIEW CHAPTER

FUNCTIONS	GRAMMAR	VOCABULARY	CULTURE	RE-ENTRY
• Pointing out places and things • Making and responding to requests • Asking for advice • Making suggestions • Asking for and giving directions	• The pronoun **y** • Contractions with **de**	• Buildings • Things to do or buy in town • Means of transportation • Locations	• Store hours in France and Martinique • Making "small talk" in francophone countries • Getting a driver's license in francophone countries • **DOMs** and **TOMs** • Public areas downtown	• Contractions with **à** • The partitive • Contractions with **de** • Family vocabulary • Possessive adjectives • The **passé composé** • Expressing need • Making excuses • Inviting

Allez, viens! French Level 2
Scope and Sequence

	FUNCTIONS	GRAMMAR	VOCABULARY	CULTURE	RE-ENTRY

Environs de Paris

CHAPITRE 1 Bon séjour!, *Pages 4–31*

REVIEW CHAPTER

FUNCTIONS	GRAMMAR	VOCABULARY	CULTURE	RE-ENTRY
• Describing and characterizing yourself and others • Expressing likes, dislikes, and preferences • Asking for information • Asking for and giving advice • Asking for, making, and responding to suggestions • Relating a series of events	• The verbs **avoir** and **être** • Adjective agreement • The interrogative adjective **quel** • **Choisir** and other **-ir** verbs • The imperative • The future with **aller**	• Travel items	• Travel documents for foreign countries • Studying abroad • Ethnic restaurants	• Adjectives to characterize people • Regular **-er** verbs • Pronunciation: **liaison** • Family vocabulary • Clothing and colors • Weather expressions and seasons

Environs de Paris

CHAPITRE 2 Bienvenue à Chartres!, *Pages 32–59*

REVIEW CHAPTER

FUNCTIONS	GRAMMAR	VOCABULARY	CULTURE	RE-ENTRY
• Welcoming someone and responding to someone's welcome • Asking about how someone is feeling and telling how you're feeling • Pointing out where things are • Paying and responding to compliments • Asking for and giving directions	• Using **tu** and **vous** • Question formation • Adjectives that precede the noun • Contractions with **à**	• Furniture and rooms • Places in town	• Polite behavior for a guest • Teenagers' bedrooms in France • Paying and receiving compliments • **Notre-Dame de Chartres** • Houses in francophone countries	• Pronunciation: intonation • Prepositions of location • Contractions with **de** • Making suggestions

Environs de Paris

CHAPITRE 3 Un repas à la française, *Pages 60–89*

FUNCTIONS	GRAMMAR	VOCABULARY	CULTURE	RE-ENTRY
• Making purchases • Asking for, offering, accepting, and refusing food • Paying and responding to compliments • Asking for and giving advice • Extending good wishes	• The object pronoun **en** • The partitive articles • The indirect object pronouns **lui** and **leur**	• Places to shop • Food items to buy • Meals • Gift items	• Neighborhood stores • Typical meals in the francophone world • Courses of a meal • The euro • Special occasions	• Giving prices • Expressions of quantity • Food vocabulary • The verbs **vouloir** and **pouvoir**

	FUNCTIONS	GRAMMAR	VOCABULARY	CULTURE	RE-ENTRY

Martinique

CHAPITRE 4 Sous les tropiques, *Pages 94–123*

FUNCTIONS	GRAMMAR	VOCABULARY	CULTURE	RE-ENTRY
• Asking for information and describing a place • Asking for and making suggestions • Emphasizing likes and dislikes • Relating a series of events	• Recognizing reflexive verbs • The reflexive pronouns **se** and **me** • The relative pronouns **ce qui** and **ce que** • The present tense of reflexive verbs • Adverbs of frequency	• Places, flora, and fauna • Vacation activities • Daily activities	• **La ville de Saint-Pierre** • Places to visit in different regions • **Yoles rondes** • The **créole** language • **Carnaval** • Music and dance in Martinique	• **De** with adjectives and plural nouns • Connectors for sequencing events • Adverbs of frequency • Pronunciation: **e muet** • Sports vocabulary • Weather expressions

Touraine

CHAPITRE 5 Quelle journée!, *Pages 128–155*

FUNCTIONS	GRAMMAR	VOCABULARY	CULTURE	RE-ENTRY
• Expressing concern for someone • Inquiring; expressing satisfaction and frustration • Sympathizing with and consoling someone • Giving reasons and making excuses • Congratulating and reprimanding someone	• The **passé composé** with **avoir** • Introduction to the **passé composé** with **être**	• School day vocabulary	• **Carnet de correspondance** • Meals at school • French grades and report cards • School life in francophone countries	• Connector words • Sports and leisure activities • Pronunciation: the nasal sound [$\tilde{\varepsilon}$] • Question words • Reflexive verbs

Touraine

CHAPITRE 6 A nous les châteaux!, *Pages 156–183*

FUNCTIONS	GRAMMAR	VOCABULARY	CULTURE	RE-ENTRY
• Asking for opinions; expressing enthusiasm, indifference, and dissatisfaction • Expressing disbelief and doubt • Asking for and giving information	• The phrase **c'était** • The **passé composé** with **être** • Formal and informal phrasing of questions • The verb **ouvrir**	• Weekend activities • Verbs that use **être** in the **passé composé**	• Types of châteaux in France • Studying historical figures in school • Buses and trains in France	• Pronunciation: [y] versus [u] • The **passé composé** with **avoir** • Expressing satisfaction and frustration • Telling time

Touraine

CHAPITRE 7 En pleine forme, *Pages 184–213*

FUNCTIONS	GRAMMAR	VOCABULARY	CULTURE	RE-ENTRY
• Expressing concern for someone and complaining • Giving advice; accepting and rejecting advice • Expressing discouragement and offering encouragement • Justifying your recommendations; advising against something	• Reflexive verbs in the **passé composé** • The pronoun **en** with activities • The verb **devoir** • The verb **se nourrir**	• Health expressions • Parts of the body • Injuries • Staying fit • Good and bad eating habits	• Pharmacies in France • Figures of speech • Teenagers' exercise habits • Staying healthy • Mineral water	• Expressing doubt • Telling how often you do something • Pronunciation: the [r] sound • Sports activities

Côte d'Ivoire

CHAPITRE 8 C'était comme ça, *Pages 218–247*

FUNCTIONS	GRAMMAR	VOCABULARY	CULTURE	RE-ENTRY
• Telling what or whom you miss; reassuring someone • Asking and telling what things were like • Reminiscing • Making and responding to suggestions	• The **imparfait** of **avoir** and **être** • Formation of the **imparfait** • **Si on** + the **imparfait**	• Describing places • Childhood activities • Things to see and buy in Côte d'Ivoire	• Village life in Côte d'Ivoire • Ethnic groups in West Africa • High school in Côte d'Ivoire • Félix Houphouët-Boigny • City versus country living • Abidjan	• Pronunciation: the [ɛ] sound • Adjectives of physical traits and personality • Chores • Places in a city

Provence

CHAPITRE 9 Tu connais la nouvelle?, *Pages 252–279*

FUNCTIONS	GRAMMAR	VOCABULARY	CULTURE	RE-ENTRY
• Wondering what happened; offering possible explanations • Accepting and rejecting explanations • Breaking some news; showing interest • Beginning, continuing, and ending a story	• **Avoir l'air** + adjective • The **passé composé** vs. the **imparfait** • The **passé composé** and the **imparfait** with interrupted actions • Using **être en train de** and the **imparfait**	• Feelings • Personal happenings	• The **cours Mirabeau,** Aix-en-Provence • Friendship • **Histoires marseillaises**	• School-related mishaps • The **passé composé** of reflexive verbs • Accidents and injuries • The relative pronouns **ce qui** and **ce que** • Explanations and apologies

Provence

CHAPITRE 10 Je peux te parler?, *Pages 280–307*

FUNCTIONS	GRAMMAR	VOCABULARY	CULTURE	RE-ENTRY
• Sharing a confidence • Asking for and giving advice • Asking for and granting a favor; making excuses • Apologizing and accepting an apology; reproaching someone	• Object pronouns and their placement • Direct object pronouns with the **passé composé** • Object pronouns before an infinitive	• Apologetic actions • Party preparations	• Paul Cézanne • Roman ruins in Aix-en-Provence • **Provençale** cuisine • Talking about personal problems	• Accepting and refusing advice • Personal happenings • Pronunciation: the nasal sound [ã] • Making excuses

Provence

CHAPITRE 11 Chacun ses goûts, *Pages 308–337*

FUNCTIONS	GRAMMAR	VOCABULARY	CULTURE	RE-ENTRY
• Identifying people and things • Asking for and giving information • Giving opinions • Summarizing	• The verb **connaître** • **C'est** versus **il/elle est** • The relative pronouns **qui** and **que**	• Songs and singers • Types of music • Types of movies • Types of books	• **La Fête de la musique** • Musical tastes • Movie theaters in France • The **Minitel**	• Emphasizing likes and dislikes • Making and responding to suggestions

Québec

CHAPITRE 12 A la belle étoile, *Pages 342–371*

REVIEW CHAPTER

FUNCTIONS	GRAMMAR	VOCABULARY	CULTURE	RE-ENTRY
• Asking for and giving information; giving directions • Complaining; expressing discouragement and offering encouragement • Asking for and giving advice • Relating a series of events; describing people and places	• The verb **emporter** • The **passé composé** and the **imparfait**	• Animals • Outdoor activities • Camping equipment • Rules related to nature	• **Le parc de la Jacques-Cartier** • Ecology in Canada • Endangered animals • French-Canadian expressions	• Sports and activities • Clothing vocabulary • Making and responding to suggestions

Allez, viens! French Level 3
Scope and Sequence

FUNCTIONS	GRAMMAR	VOCABULARY	CULTURE	RE-ENTRY
la France — **CHAPITRE 1** France, les régions, *Pages 4–31*				
REVIEW CHAPTER • Renewing old acquaintances • Inquiring; expressing enthusiasm and dissatisfaction • Exchanging information • Asking and describing what a place was like • Expressing indecision • Making recommendations • Ordering and asking for details	• The **passé composé** • The **imparfait**	• French menu	• Traditional regional clothing • Regional specialties • Regional foods	• Sports and activities • Food vocabulary • Definite, indefinite, and partitive articles • Question formation
la Belgique — **CHAPITRE 2** Belgique, nous voilà!, *Pages 32–61*				
REVIEW CHAPTER • Asking for and giving directions • Expressing impatience • Reassuring someone • Expressing enthusiasm and boredom • Asking and telling where things are	• The verb **conduire** • The imperative • Pronouns and their placement	• At the gas station • Adjectives	• Languages in Belgium • Favorite comic book characters • Overview of Belgium	• The future with **aller** • Making, accepting, and refusing suggestions
la Suisse — **CHAPITRE 3** Soyons responsables!, *Pages 62–91*				
• Asking for, granting, and refusing permission • Expressing obligation • Forbidding • Reproaching • Justifying your actions and rejecting others' excuses	• The subjunctive • **Ne...pas** + infinitive	• Household chores • Personal responsibilities • Social responsibilities	• Swiss work ethic • Switzerland's neutrality • Overview of Switzerland • Environmental issues • **La minuterie**	• The verb **devoir** • Complaining • Chores • Negative expressions

	FUNCTIONS	GRAMMAR	VOCABULARY	CULTURE	RE-ENTRY
la France	**CHAPITRE 4** Des goûts et des couleurs, *Pages 92–121*				
	• Asking for and giving opinions • Asking which one(s) • Pointing out and identifying people and things • Paying and responding to compliments • Reassuring someone	• The interrogative and demonstrative pronouns • The causative **faire**	• Clothing and styles • Describing clothing and hairstyles • Hair and hairstyles	• French clothing stores • Fashion and personal style • French sense of fashion	• Clothing vocabulary • Adjectives referring to clothing • Family vocabulary • Chores
le Sénégal	**CHAPITRE 5** C'est notre avenir, *Pages 126–155*				
	• Asking about and expressing intentions • Expressing conditions and possibilities • Asking about future plans • Expressing wishes • Expressing indecision • Giving advice • Requesting information • Writing a formal letter	• The future • The conditional • Question formation with inversion	• Future choices and plans • Careers	• Careers and education in Senegal • Overview of Senegal • Planning for a career • Types of job training	• The subjunctive • Giving advice • The **passé composé** • The imperfect • Making a telephone call • Expressing likes and preferences
le Maroc	**CHAPITRE 6** Ma famille, mes copains et moi, *Pages 156–185*				
	• Making, accepting, and refusing suggestions • Making arrangements • Making and accepting apologies • Showing and responding to hospitality • Expressing and responding to thanks • Quarreling	• Reciprocal verbs • The past infinitive	• Family relationships	• Bargaining in North Africa • Values of francophone teenagers • Overview of Morocco • Hospitality in Morocco	• Reflexive verbs • Expressing thanks

	FUNCTIONS	GRAMMAR	VOCABULARY	CULTURE	RE-ENTRY
La République centrafricaine	**CHAPITRE 7 Un safari-photo,** *Pages 186–215*				
	• Making suppositions • Expressing doubt and certainty • Asking for and giving advice • Expressing astonishment • Cautioning someone • Expressing fear • Reassuring someone • Expressing relief	• Structures and their complements • Using the subjunctive • Irregular subjunctive forms	• Rainforest and savannah • Packing for a safari • African animals	• Overview of the Central African Republic • Animal conservation in the Central African Republic • Stereotypical impressions of francophone regions	• The subjunctive • Travel items • The conditional
la Tunisie	**CHAPITRE 8 La Tunisie, pays de contrastes,** *Pages 216–245*				
	• Asking someone to convey good wishes • Closing a letter • Expressing hopes or wishes • Giving advice • Complaining • Expressing annoyance • Making comparisons	• **Si** clauses • The comparative	• Traditional life • City life	• Overview of Tunisia • Traditional and modern life in Tunisia • Carthage • Modernization in francophone countries • Traditional and modern styles of dress in Tunisia	• The imperfect • Intonation • Adjective agreement • Describing a place
le Canada	**CHAPITRE 9 C'est l'fun!,** *Pages 250–279*				
	• Agreeing and disagreeing • Expressing indifference • Making requests • Asking for and making judgments • Asking for and making recommendations • Asking about and summarizing a story	• Negative expressions • The expression **ne...que** • The relative pronouns **qui, que,** and **dont**	• Television programming • The television • Types of movies	• Multilingual broadcasting in Canada • Overview of Montreal • Favorite types of movies • The Canadian film industry	• Expressing opinions • Quarreling • Agreeing and disagreeing • Types of films • Summarizing a story • Continuing and ending a story • Relating a series of events • Relative pronouns

FUNCTIONS	GRAMMAR	VOCABULARY	CULTURE	RE-ENTRY

la Guadeloupe

CHAPITRE 10 Rencontres au soleil, *Pages 280–309*

FUNCTIONS	GRAMMAR	VOCABULARY	CULTURE	RE-ENTRY
• Bragging; flattering; teasing • Breaking some news; showing interest • Expressing disbelief; telling a joke	• The superlative • The past perfect	• Sea life • Everyday life	• Climate and natural assets of Guadeloupe • Overview of Guadeloupe • **La fête des Cuisinières** • Daily routines of francophone teenagers • Greetings in Guadeloupe	• Forms of the comparative • Reciprocal verbs • Adjective agreement • Breaking some news

la Louisiane

CHAPITRE 11 Laissez les bons temps rouler!, *Pages 310–339*

FUNCTIONS	GRAMMAR	VOCABULARY	CULTURE	RE-ENTRY
• Asking for confirmation • Asking for and giving opinions • Agreeing and disagreeing • Asking for explanations • Making observations • Giving impressions		• Musical instruments • Kinds of music • Cajun food	• **Mardi gras** and festivals in Louisiana • Cajun French • Cajun music • History of Louisiana • Parties and celebrations in francophone countries	• Renewing old acquaintances • Food vocabulary • Types of music • Agreeing and disagreeing • Asking for and giving opinions • Emphasizing likes • Making suggestions • Expressing opinions • The relative pronouns **ce qui** and **ce que**

Autour du monde

CHAPITRE 12 Echanges sportifs et culturels, *Pages 340–367*

REVIEW CHAPTER

FUNCTIONS	GRAMMAR	VOCABULARY	CULTURE	RE-ENTRY
• Expressing anticipation • Making suppositions • Expressing certainty and doubt • Inquiring • Expressing excitement and disappointment	• The future after **quand** and **dès que**	• Sports and equipment • Places of origin	• International sporting events in francophone countries • Stereotypes of people in francophone countries	• Sports vocabulary • Making suppositions • **Si** clauses • Expressing certainty and doubt • The future • Prepositions with countries • Greeting people • Introducing people • Asking someone's name and age and giving yours • Offering encouragement

Pupil's Edition

Allez, viens! offers an integrated approach to language learning. Presentation and practice of functional expressions, vocabulary, and grammar structures are interwoven with cultural information, language learning tips, and realia to facilitate both learning and teaching. The technology, audiovisual materials, and additional print resources are integrated throughout each chapter.

Allez, viens! Level 3

Allez, viens! Level 3 consists of twelve instructional chapters. To facilitate articulation from one level to the next, Chapters 1, 2, and 12 are review chapters and Chapter 11 introduces minimal new material.

Following is a description of the various features in *Allez, viens!* and suggestions on how to use them in the classroom.

Starting Out...

Location Opener In *Allez, viens!,* chapters · · · · ▸ are arranged by location. Each new location is introduced by four pages of colorful photos and information about the region.

Chapter Opener These two pages provide a visual introduction to the theme of the chapter and include a list of objectives students will be expected to achieve. · · · · · · · · · · · · · · ▸

Setting The Scene...

◂ · · · Language instruction begins with the **Mise en train** and the **Remise en train,** the comprehensible input that models language in a culturally authentic setting. Accompanied by the audio compact disc recording, the highly visual presentation ensures success as students practice their receptive skills and begin to recognize some of the new functions and vocabulary they will encounter in the chapter. Following the **Mise en train** and the **Remise en train,** is a series of activities that can be used to help guide students through the story and check comprehension.

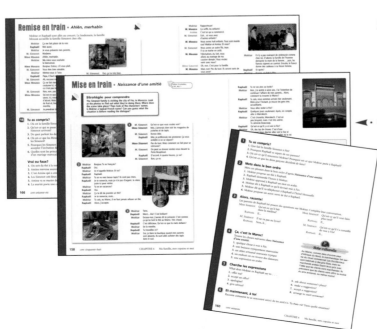

Building Proficiency Step By Step...

Première and **Deuxième étape** are the core instructional sections · · · · ▶
where most language acquisition will take place. The communicative
goals in each chapter center on the functional expressions presented
in **Comment dit-on...?** boxes. These expressions are supported by material in the **Vocabulaire, Grammaire,** and **Note de grammaire** sections.
Activities following the above features are designed to practice recognition or to provide closed-ended practice. Activities then progress from
controlled to open-ended practice where students are able to express
themselves in meaningful communication.

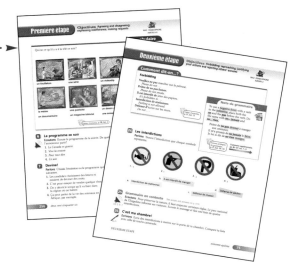

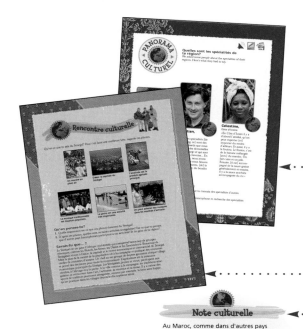

Discovering the People and the Culture...

There are also two major cultural features to help students
develop an appreciation and understanding of the cultures of
French-speaking countries.

· · · · · **Panorama Culturel** presents interviews conducted throughout
the French-speaking world on a topic related to the chapter theme.
The interviews may be presented on video or done as a reading
supplemented by the compact disc recording. Culminating activities on this page verify comprehension and encourage students to
think critically about the target culture as well as their own.

· · · · · · · · · · · · · · · · · ▶ **Rencontre culturelle** invites students to compare and contrast
other cultures with their own.

◀ · · · · **Note culturelle** helps students gain knowledge and
understanding of other cultures.

Note culturelle

Au Maroc, comme dans d'autres pays
d'Afrique du Nord, le marchandage fait partie du rituel commercial. Les Occidentaux
sont habitués à des prix fixes, mais les
marchands arabes fixent leurs prix avec
l'idée que les clients vont marchander. Ils
prévoient que les clients vont offrir la moitié
du prix annoncé, ou même moins!

Understanding Authentic Documents...

Lisons! presents reading strategies that help students · · · · · · · · ▶
understand authentic French documents and literature
presented in each chapter. The accompanying prereading,
reading, and postreading activities develop students'
overall reading skills and challenge their critical
thinking abilities.

Ecrivons! presents writing strategies that help stu- · · · · · ▶
dents develop their writing skills. The strategies are
integrated with prewriting, writing, and postwriting
tasks designed to develop students' expressive and
creative writing abilities in French.

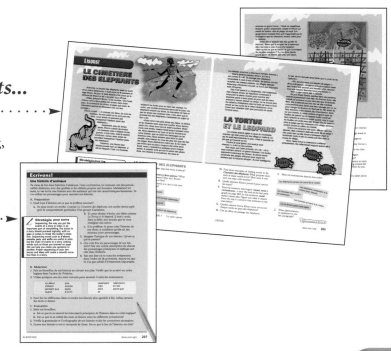

A la française

You've already learned that French speakers drop certain words and letters when they speak informally.

**C'est pas vrai!   J'le trouve hyper-cool!
Je crois pas!   T'as pas l'temps?**

They also tend to run certain syllables and words together. Look at the pronunciation of these common phrases:

/shsai pa/   (Je ne sais pas.)
/y'en a/   (Il y en a.)
/kes tu/   (Qu'est-ce que tu... ?)
/wes que tu/   (Où est-ce que tu... ?)
/ifait/   (Il fait...)

Remember, though, that it is not correct to write this way.

Vocabulaire à la carte

un pattes d'eph	*bell bottoms*
un débardeur	*a tank top*
un coupe-vent	*a windbreaker*
des bretelles (f.)	*suspenders. straps*
des bottines (f.)	*ankle boots*
des mocassins (m.)	*loafers*
à manches courtes/ longues	*short/long-sleeved*
en toile	*linen*
en daim	*suede*
à carreaux	*checked*
imprimé(e)	*printed*
bleu clair	*light blue*
bleu foncé	*dark blue*

Si tu as oublié
the forms of the comparative
va à la page 232

Tu te rappelles?

Do you remember the forms of the subjunctive that you learned in Chapter 3? Take the **-ent** off of the present tense **ils/elles** form of the verb and add the endings **-e, -es, -e, -ions, -iez, -ent**. Remember that some verbs have irregular stems, but use the regular endings. Have you noticed some new uses of the subjunctive?

Travaux pratiques de grammaire, pp. 43–44, Act. 5–7

Targeting Students' Needs...

In each **étape** several special features may be used to enhance language learning and cultural appreciation.

De bons conseils suggests effective ways for students to learn a foreign language.

A la française provides students with tips for speaking more natural-sounding French.

Vocabulaire à la carte presents optional vocabulary related to the chapter theme.

Tu te rappelles? is a re-entry feature that lists and briefly explains previously learned vocabulary, functions, and grammar that students might need to review at the moment.

Si tu as oublié is a handy page reference to either an earlier chapter where material was presented or to a reference section in the back of the book.

Wrapping It All Up...

Grammaire supplémentaire provides additional practice on the grammar concepts presented in the chapter.

Mise en pratique gives students the opportunity to review what they have learned and to apply their skills in new communicative contexts. Focusing on all four language skills as well as cultural awareness, the **Mise en pratique** can help you determine whether students are ready for the Chapter Test.

Que sais-je? is a checklist that students can use on their own to see if they have achieved the goals stated on the Chapter Opener.

Vocabulaire presents the chapter vocabulary grouped by **étape** and arranged according to function or theme.

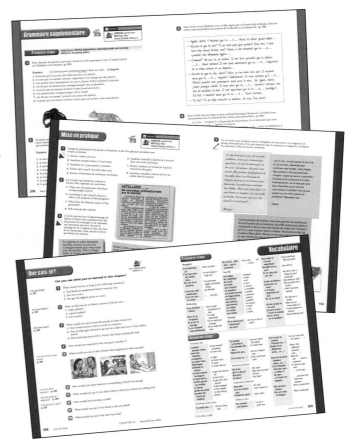

Technology Resources

Video Program

The *Video Program* provides the following video support:

- **Location Opener** documentaries
- **Camille et compagnie** episodes
- **Panorama Culturel** interviews on a variety of cultural topics
- **Vidéoclips** which present authentic footage from target cultures

The *Video Guide* contains background information, suggestions for presentation, and activities for all portions of the *Video Program*.

Interactive CD-ROM Tutor

The *Interactive CD-ROM Tutor* offers:

- a variety of supporting activities correlated to the core curriculum of **Allez, viens!** and targeting all five skills
- a Teacher Management System (TMS) that allows teachers to view and assess students' work, manage passwords and records, track students' progress as they complete the activities, and activate English translations
- features such as a grammar reference section and a glossary to help students complete the activities

Internet Connection

Keywords in the *Pupil's Edition* provide access to two types of online activities:

- **Jeux interactifs** are directly correlated to the instructional material in the textbook. They can be used as homework, extra practice, or assessment.
- **Activités Internet** provide students with selected Web sites in French-speaking countries and activities related to the chapter theme. A printable worksheet in PDF format includes pre-surfing, surfing, and post-surfing activities that guide students through their research.

For easy access, see the keywords provided in the *Pupil's* and *Teacher's Editions.* For chapter-specific information, see the F page of the chapter interleaf.

One-Stop Planner CD-ROM with Test Generator

The *One-Stop Planner CD-ROM* is a convenient tool to aid in lesson planning and pacing.

Easy navigation through menus or through lesson plans allows for a quick overview of available resources. For each chapter, the *One-Stop Planner* includes:

- Editable lesson plans with direct links to teaching resources
- Printable worksheets from resource books
- Direct launches to the HRW Internet activities
- Video and audio segments
- Test Generator
- Clip Art for vocabulary items

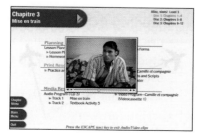

Ancillaries

The *Allez, viens!* French program offers a comprehensive ancillary package that addresses the concerns of today's teachers and is relevant to students' lives.

Lesson Planning

One-Stop Planner
with Test Generator

- editable lesson plans
- printable worksheets from the resource books
- direct link to HRW Internet activities
- entire video and audio programs
- Test Generator
- Clip Art for vocabulary items

Lesson Planner with Substitute Teacher Lesson Plans

- complete lesson plans for every chapter
- block scheduling suggestions
- correlations to Standards for Foreign Language Learning
- a homework calendar
- chapter by chapter lesson plans for substitute teachers
- lesson plan forms for customizing lesson plans

Student Make-Up Assignments

- diagnostic information for students who are behind in their work
- copying masters for make-up assignments

Listening and Speaking

Listening Activities

- print material associated with the *Audio Program*
- Student Response Forms for all Pupil's Edition listening activities
- Additional Listening Activities
- scripts, answers
- lyrics to each chapter's song

Audio Compact Discs

Listening activities for the *Pupil's Edition,* the Additional Listening Activities, and the *Testing Program*

Activities for Communication

- Communicative Activities for partner work based on an information gap
- Situation Cards to practice interviews and role-plays
- Realia: reproductions of authentic documents

Grammar

Travaux pratiques de grammaire

- re-presentations of major grammar points
- additional focused practice
- *Teacher's Edition* with overprinted answers

Grammar Tutor for Students of French

- presentations of grammar concepts in English
- re-presentations of French grammar concepts
- discovery and application activities

Reading and Writing

Reading Strategies and Skills Handbook
- explanations of reading strategies
- copying masters for application of strategies

Joie de lire 3
- literary readings
- cultural information
- additional vocabulary
- interesting and engaging activities

Cahier d'activités
- activities for practice
- *Teacher's Edition* with overprinted answers

Teaching Transparencies
- Colorful transparencies that help present and practice vocabulary, grammar, culture, and a variety of communicative functions
- **Grammaire supplémentaire** Answers
- **Travaux pratiques de grammaire** Answers

Assessment

Testing Program
- Grammar and Vocabulary quizzes
- **Etape** quizzes that test the four skills
- Chapter Tests
- Speaking Tests
- Midterm and Final Exams
- Score sheets, scripts, answers

Alternative Assessment Guide
- Suggestions for oral and written Portfolio Assessment
- Performance Assessment
- CD-ROM Assessment
- rubrics, portfolio checklists, and evaluation forms

Student Make-Up Assignments
Alternative Grammar and Vocabulary quizzes for students who missed class and have to make up the quiz

Standardized Assessment Tutor
Reading, writing, and math tests in a standardized, multiple-choice format

Annotated Teacher's Edition

Using the Chapter Interleaf

Each chapter of the **Allez, viens!** *Annotated Teacher's Edition* includes the following interleaf pages to help you plan, teach, and expand your lessons.

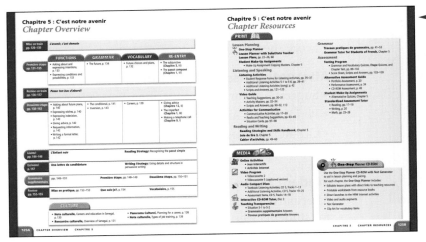

Chapter Overview

The Chapter Overview chart outlines at a glance the functions, grammar, vocabulary, re-entry, and culture featured in the chapter. You will also find a list of corresponding print and audiovisual resources organized by listening, speaking, reading, and writing skills, grammar, and assessment.

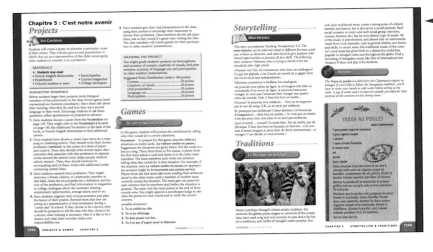

Projects/Games/ Storytelling/Traditions

Projects allow students to personalize and expand on the information from the chapter. Games reinforce the chapter content. In the Storytelling feature, you will find a story related to a *Teaching Transparency*. The Traditions feature concentrates on a unique aspect of the culture of the region. A recipe typical for the region accompanies this feature.

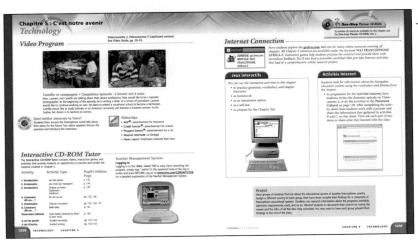

Technology

These pages assist you in integrating technology into your lesson plans. The Technology page provides a detailed list of video, CD-ROM, and Internet resources for your lesson. You will also find an Internet research project in each chapter.

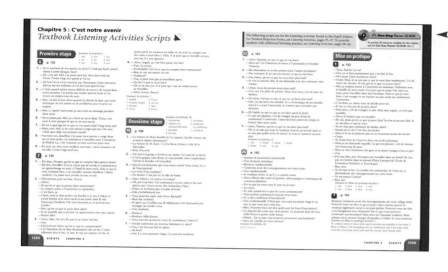

Textbook Listening Activities Scripts provide the scripts of the chapter listening activities for reference or for use in class. The answers to each activity are provided below each script for easy reference.

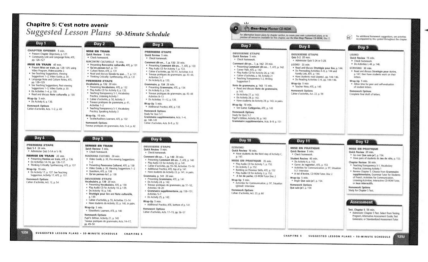

Suggested Lesson Plans— 50-Minute Schedule

This lesson plan is used for classes with 50-minute schedules. Each lesson plan provides a logical sequence of instruction along with homework suggestions.

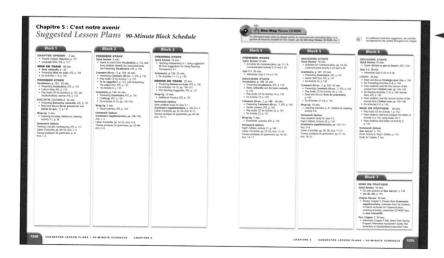

Suggested Lesson Plans— 90-Minute Schedule

This lesson plan is used for classes with 90-minute schedules. Each lesson plan provides a logical sequence of instruction along with homework suggestions.

Using the Wrap-Around Teacher Text

Resource boxes · · · · · · · · · · · provide a quick list of all the resources you can use for each chapter section.

Presenting boxes · · · · · · · · · · offer useful suggestions for presenting new material.

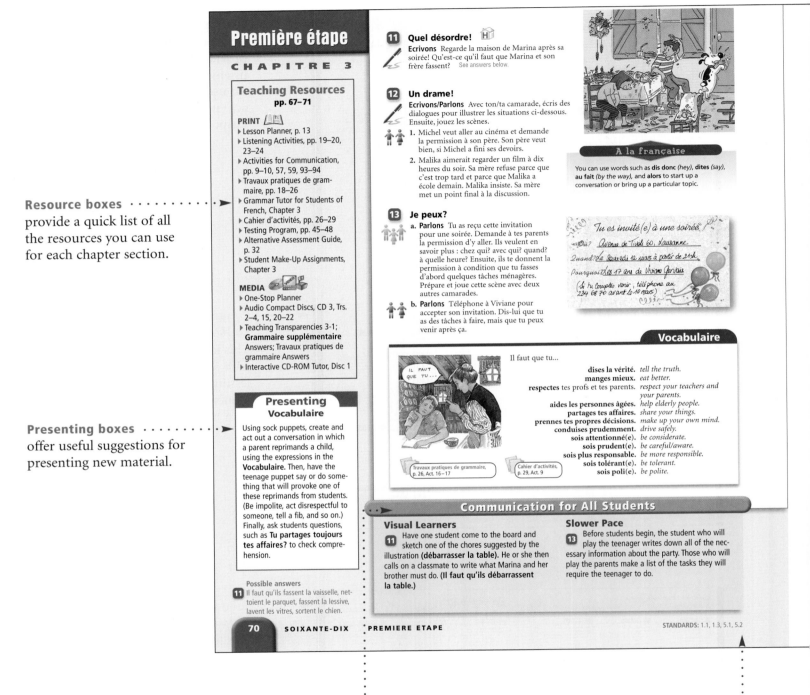

Communication for All Students
Under this head you will find helpful suggestions for students with different learning styles and abilities.

Correlations to the Standards for Foreign Language Learning are provided for your reference.

Première étape

CHAPITRE 3

Teaching Resources
pp. 67–71

PRINT
▸ Lesson Planner, p. 13
▸ Listening Activities, pp. 19–20, 23–24
▸ Activities for Communication, pp. 9–10, 57, 59, 93–94
▸ Travaux pratiques de grammaire, pp. 18–26
▸ Grammar Tutor for Students of French, Chapter 3
▸ Cahier d'activités, pp. 26–29
▸ Testing Program, pp. 45–48
▸ Alternative Assessment Guide, p. 32
▸ Student Make-Up Assignments, Chapter 3

MEDIA
▸ One-Stop Planner
▸ Audio Compact Discs, CD 3, Trs. 2–4, 15, 20–22
▸ Teaching Transparencies 3-1; **Grammaire supplémentaire** Answers; Travaux pratiques de grammaire Answers
▸ Interactive CD-ROM Tutor, Disc 1

Presenting Vocabulaire

Using sock puppets, create and act out a conversation in which a parent reprimands a child, using the expressions in the **Vocabulaire**. Then, have the teenage puppet say or do something that will provoke one of these reprimands from students. (Be impolite, act disrespectful to someone, tell a fib, and so on.) Finally, ask students questions, such as **Tu partages toujours tes affaires?** to check comprehension.

Possible answers
11 Il faut qu'ils fassent la vaisselle, nettoient le parquet, fassent la lessive, lavent les vitres, sortent le chien.

---

11 Quel désordre!
Ecrivons Regarde la maison de Marina après sa soirée! Qu'est-ce qu'il faut que Marina et son frère fassent? See answers below.

12 Un drame!
Ecrivons/Parlons Avec ton/ta camarade, écris des dialogues pour illustrer les situations ci-dessous. Ensuite, jouez les scènes.
1. Michel veut aller au cinéma et demande la permission à son père. Son père veut bien, si Michel a fini ses devoirs.
2. Malika aimerait regarder un film à dix heures du soir. Sa mère refuse parce que c'est trop tard et parce que Malika a école demain. Malika insiste. Sa mère met un point final à la discussion.

13 Je peux?
a. **Parlons** Tu as reçu cette invitation pour une soirée. Demande à tes parents la permission d'y aller. Ils veulent en savoir plus : chez qui? avec qui? quand? à quelle heure? Ensuite, ils te donnent la permission à condition que tu fasses d'abord quelques tâches ménagères. Prépare et joue cette scène avec deux autres camarades.
b. **Parlons** Téléphone à Viviane pour accepter son invitation. Dis-lui que tu as des tâches à faire, mais que tu peux venir après ça.

À la française
You can use words such as **dis donc** (hey), **dites** (say), **au fait** (by the way), and **alors** to start up a conversation or bring up a particular topic.

Vocabulaire

Il faut que tu...

dises la vérité.	*tell the truth.*
manges mieux.	*eat better.*
respectes tes profs et tes parents.	*respect your teachers and your parents.*
aides les personnes âgées.	*help elderly people.*
partages tes affaires.	*share your things.*
prennes tes propres décisions.	*make up your own mind.*
conduises prudemment.	*drive safely.*
sois attentionné(e).	*be considerate.*
sois prudent(e).	*be careful/aware.*
sois plus responsable.	*be more responsible.*
sois tolérant(e).	*be tolerant.*
sois poli(e).	*be polite.*

Travaux pratiques de grammaire, p. 26, Act. 16–17

Cahier d'activités, p. 29, Act. 9

Communication for All Students

Visual Learners
11 Have one student come to the board and sketch one of the chores suggested by the illustration (**débarrasser la table**). He or she then calls on a classmate to write what Marina and her brother must do. (**Il faut qu'ils débarrassent la table.**)

Slower Pace
13 Before students begin, the student who will play the teenager writes down all of the necessary information about the party. Those who will play the parents make a list of the tasks they will require the teenager to do.

STANDARDS: 1.1, 1.3, 5.1, 5.2

14 **C'est pas bien, ça!** *Possible answers:*

Parlons Ces gens n'ont pas une attitude très responsable. Dis-leur ce qu'il faut qu'ils fassent.

1. Il faut que tu partages tes affaires.
2. Il faut que vous mangiez mieux.
3. Il faut que vous soyez attentionnés.
4. Il faut que tu respectes ta mère.

15 **Il faut que tu...**

Ecrivons Parlons Quelles sont les choses que tes parents te rappellent souvent? Fais-en une liste et compare-la avec celle de ton/ta camarade.

16 **Voilà ce qu'il faut faire**

Parlons Ton ami(e) te téléphone pour discuter des problèmes suivants. Dis-lui ce qu'il/elle doit faire, à ton avis.

Il/Elle s'est foulé la cheville.

Il/Elle s'est fâché(e) parce que sa sœur a voulu emprunter son nouveau jean.

Il/Elle a eu une mauvaise note à une interro et l'a caché à ses parents.

Son grand-père ne peut plus conduire.

Il/Elle s'est disputé(e) avec ses parents.

Il/Elle a grossi.

Fumer, c'est pas ma nature!

17 **Que c'est compliqué, tout ça!**

Ecrivons/Parlons D'après toi, quelles sont les responsabilités et obligations d'un(e) adolescent(e)? Fais-en une liste et compare ta liste à celle de ton/ta camarade.

CHAPITRE 3

Music Link

Play the song *Sur le pont de Nantes* (Level 2, Audio CD 5, Track 25). Have students listen carefully and tell what they think the song is about. You might copy the lyrics of the song on a transparency and have students read or sing along as you play the song. Ask students what the moral of the song is (you should not disobey your parents; otherwise, you'll probably get in trouble). For additional practice, have small groups create a conversation in which the mother gives the daughter unconditional or conditional approval.

Language Note

Affaires refers to a person's belongings in general. A parent might tell a child **Range tes affaires!** *(Put away your things!)* It can also mean *business* or *dealings*. Students might want to use the expressions **Ce n'est pas tes/mes affaires** *(It's none of your/my business)* or **Mêle-toi de tes affaires** *(Mind your own business).*

Assess
▶ Testing Program, pp. 45–48
Quiz 3-1A, Quiz 3-1B,
Audio CD 3, Tr. 15

▶ Student Make-Up Assignments
Chapter 3, Alternative Quiz

▶ Alternative Assessment Guide,
p. 32

The Annotated Teacher's Edition Wrap-Around Text offers helpful suggestions and information at point-of-use. You will also find annos, cultural information, correlations to the Standards for Foreign Language Learning, and references to other ancillaries.

Assessment
At the end of every **étape** and again at the end of the chapter, you will find references to all the assessment material available for that section of the chapter.

Cultures and Communities

Culture Note
Point out to students that the phone number on the invitation consists of one group of three digits and two groups of two digits each. Phone numbers in Switzerland all have seven digits. Ask students to recall how French phone numbers are composed (five sets of two digits: 04.42.13.76.23, the first set being an area code) and what Canadian phone numbers look like (like American phone numbers, two sets of three digits and one set of four digits: 512–243–3982, the first set being an area code).

Cultures and Communities
Under this head you will find helpful cultural information and suggestions that relate the content to students' families and communities.

Bringing Standards into the Classroom

by Paul Sandrock, Foreign Language Consultant, Wisconsin Department of Public Education

The core question that guided the development of the National Standards and their accompanying goals was simply: what matters in instruction?

Each proposed standard was evaluated. Did the standard target material that will have application beyond the classroom? Was the standard too specific or not specific enough? Teachers should be able to teach the standard and assess it in multiple ways. A standard needs to provide a target for instruction and learning throughout a student's K–12 education.

In the development of standards, foreign languages faced other unique challenges. The writers could not assume a K–12 sequence available to all students. In fact, unlike other disciplines, they could not guarantee that all students would experience even any common sequence.

From this context, the National Standards in Foreign Language Education Project's task force generated the five C's, five goals for learning languages: communication, cultures, connections, comparisons, and communities. First presented in 1995, the standards quickly became familiar to foreign language educators across the US, representing our professional consensus and capturing a broad view of the purposes for learning another language.

To implement the standards, however, requires a shift from emphasizing the means to focusing on the ends. It isn't a matter of grammar versus communication, but rather how much grammar is needed to communicate. Instead of teaching to a grammatical sequence, teaching decisions become based on what students need to know to achieve the communicative goal.

The Focus on Communication

The first standard redefined communication, making its purpose **interpersonal, interpretive,** and **presentational** communication. Teaching to the purpose of interpersonal communication takes us away from memorized dialogues to spontaneous, interactive conversation, where the message is most important and where meaning needs to be negotiated between the speakers. Interpretive communication is not an exercise in translation, but asks beginners to tell the gist of an authentic selection that is heard, read, or viewed, while increasingly advanced learners tell deeper and deeper levels of detail and can interpret based on their knowledge of the target culture. In the presentational mode of communication, the emphasis is on the audience, requiring the speaker or writer to adapt language to fit the situation and to allow for comprehension without any interactive negotiation of the meaning.

Standards challenge us to refocus many of the things we've been doing all along. The requirements of speaking and our expectation of how well students need to speak change when speaking is for a different purpose. This focus on the purpose of the communication changes the way we teach and test the skills of listening, speaking, reading, and writing.

Standards help us think about how to help students put the pieces of language to work in meaningful ways. Our

Standards for Foreign Language Learning

Communication Communicate in Languages Other than English	**Standard 1.1**	Students engage in conversations, provide and obtain information, express feelings and emotions, and exchange opinions.
	Standard 1.2	Students understand and interpret written and spoken language on a variety of topics.
	Standard 1.3	Students present information, concepts, and ideas to an audience of listeners or readers on a variety of topics.
Cultures Gain Knowledge and Understanding of Other Cultures	**Standard 2.1**	Students demonstrate an understanding of the relationship between the practices and perspectives of the culture studied.
	Standard 2.2	Students demonstrate an understanding of the relationship between the products and perspectives of the culture studied.
Connections Connect with Other Disciplines and Acquire Information	**Standard 3.1**	Students reinforce and further their knowledge of other disciplines through the foreign language.
	Standard 3.2	Students acquire information and recognize the distinctive viewpoints that are only available through the foreign language and its cultures.
Comparisons Develop Insight into the Nature of Language and Culture	**Standard 4.1**	Students demonstrate understanding of the nature of language through comparisons of the language studied and their own.
	Standard 4.2	Students demonstrate understanding of the concept of culture through comparisons of the cultures studied and their own.
Communities Participate in Multilingual Communities at Home and Around the World	**Standard 5.1**	Students use the language both within and beyond the school setting.
	Standard 5.2	Students show evidence of becoming life-long learners by using the language for personal enjoyment and enrichment.

standards answer *why* we are teaching various components of language, and we select *what* we teach in order to achieve those very standards.

The 5 C's

Originally the five C's were presented as five equal circles. During the years since the National Standards were printed, teachers implementing and using the standards to write curriculum, texts, and lesson plans have come to see that communication is at the core, surrounded by four C's that influence the context for teaching and assessing.

The four C's surrounding our core goal of **Communication** change our classrooms by bringing in real-life applications for the language learned:

- **Cultures:** Beyond art and literature, learning occurs in the context of the way of life, patterns of behavior, and contributions of the people speaking the language being taught.

- **Connections:** Beyond content limited to the culture of the people speaking the target language, teachers go out to other disciplines to find topics and ideas to form the context for language learning.

- **Comparisons:** Foreign language study is a great way for students to learn more about native language and universal principles of language and culture by comparing and contrasting their own to the target language and culture.

- **Communities:** This goal of the standards adds a broader motivation to the context for language learning. The teacher makes sure students use their new language beyond the class hour, seeking ways to experience the target culture.

Implementation at the Classroom Level: Assessment and Instruction

After the publication of the standards, states developed more specific performance standards that would provide evidence of the application of the national content standards. Standards provide the organizing principle for teaching and assessing. The standards-oriented teacher, when asked what she's teaching, cites the standard "students will sustain a conversation." With that clear goal in mind, she creates lessons to teach various strategies to ask for clarification and to practice asking follow-up questions that explore a topic in more depth.

Textbook writers and materials providers are responding to this shift. Standards provide our goals; the useful textbooks and materials give us an organization and a context. Standards provide the ends; textbooks and materials can help us practice the means. Textbooks can bring authentic materials into the classroom, real cultural examples that avoid stereotypes, and a broader exposure to the variety of people who speak the language being studied. Textbooks can model the kind of instruction that will lead students to successful demonstration of the knowledge and skill described in the standards.

To really know that standards are the focus, look at the assessment. If standards are the target, assessment won't consist only of evaluation of the means (grammatical structures and vocabulary) in isolation. If standards are the focus, teachers will assess students' use of the second language in context. The summative assessment of our target needs to go beyond the specific and include open-ended, personalized tasks. Regardless of how the students show what they can do, the teacher will be able to gauge each student's progress toward the goal.

Assessment is like a jigsaw puzzle. If we test students only on the means, we just keep collecting random puzzle pieces. We have to test, and students have to practice, putting the pieces together in meaningful and purposeful ways. In order to learn vocabulary that will help students "describe themselves," for example, students may have a quiz on Friday with an expectation of close to 100% accuracy. But if that is all we ever do with those ten words, they will quickly be gone from students' memory, and we will only have collected a puzzle piece from each student. It is absolutely essential to have students use those puzzle pieces to complete the puzzle to provide evidence of what they "can do" with the language.

During this period of implementing our standards, we've learned that the standards provide a global picture, the essence of our goals. But they are not curriculum, nor are they lesson plans. The standards influence how we teach, but do not dictate one content nor one methodology. How can we implement the standards in our classrooms? Think about the targets; think about how students will show achievement of those targets through our evaluation measures; then think about what we need to teach and how that will occur in our classrooms. Make it happen in your classroom to get the results we've always wanted: students who can communicate in a language other than English.

Reading Strategies and Skills

by Nancy Humbach, Miami University

Reading is the most enduring of the language skills. Long after a student ceases to study the language, the ability to read will continue to provide a springboard to the renewal of the other skills. We must consider all the ways in which our students will read and address the skills needed for those tasks.

How can we accomplish this goal? How can we, as teachers, present materials, encourage students to read, and at the same time foster understanding and build the student's confidence and interest in reading?

Selection of Materials

Reading material in the foreign language classroom should be relevant to students' backgrounds and at an accessible level of difficulty, i.e., at a level of difficulty only slightly above the reading ability of the student.

Authentic materials are generally a good choice. They provide cultural context and linguistic authenticity seldom found in materials created for students, and the authentic nature of the language provides a window on a new world. The problem inherent in the selection of authentic materials at early levels is obvious: the level of difficulty is frequently beyond the skill of the student. At the same time, however, readers are inspired by the fact that they can understand materials designed to be read by native speakers.

Presenting a Selection/ Reading Strategies

We assume that students of a second language already have a reading knowledge in their first language and that many of the skills they learned in their "reading readiness" days will serve them well. Too often, however, students have forgotten such skills as activating background knowledge, skimming, scanning, and guessing content based on context clues. Helping students to reactivate these skills is part of helping them become better readers.

Teachers should not assume their students' ability to transfer a knowledge set from one reading to another. Students use these skills on a regular basis, but often do not even realize they are doing so. To help students become aware of these processes, they need to be given strategies for reading. These strategies offer students a framework for the higher-level skills they need to apply when reading. Strategies also address learners of different learning styles and needs.

Advance Organizers

One way to activate the student's background knowledge is through advance organizers. They also serve to address the student's initial frustrations at encountering an unfamiliar text.

Advance organizers call up pertinent background knowledge, feelings, and experiences that can serve to focus the attention of the entire group on a given topic. In addition, they provide for a sharing of information among the students. Background information that includes cultural references and cultural information can reactivate in students skills that will help them with a text and provide for them clues to the meaning of the material.

A good advance organizer will provide some information and guide students to think about the scenarios being presented. An advance organizer might include photographs, drawings, quotations, maps, or information about the area where the story takes place. It might also be posed as a question, for example, "What would you do if you found yourself in….?" Having students brainstorm in advance, either as a whole class or in small groups, allows them to construct a scenario which they can verify as they read.

Prereading Activities

Prereading activities remind students of how much they really know and can prepare students in a number of ways to experience the language with less frustration. While we know that we must choose a reading selection that is not far beyond students' experience and skill level, we also know that no group of students reads at the same level. In the interest of assisting students to become better language learners, we can provide them with opportunities to work with unfamiliar structures and vocabulary ahead of time.

Preparing students for a reading selection can include a number of strategies that may anticipate but not dwell on potential problems to be encountered by students. Various aspects of grammar, such as differences in the past tenses and the meanings conveyed, can also cause problems. Alerting students to some of the aspects of the language allows them to struggle less, understand more quickly, and enjoy a reading selection to a greater degree.

Grouping vocabulary by category or simply choosing a short list of critical words for a section of reading is helpful. Providing an entire list of vocabulary items at one time can be overwhelming. With a bit of organization, the task becomes manageable to the point where students begin to master words they will find repeated throughout the selection.

Having students skim for a particular piece of information or scan for words,

phrases, indicators of place or time, and names, and then asking them to write a sentence or two about the gist of a paragraph or story, gives them a sense of independence and success before they begin to read.

Getting into the Assignment

Teachers can recount the times they have assigned a piece of reading for homework, only to find that few students even attempted the work. Therefore, many teachers choose to complete the reading in class. Homework assignments should then be structured to have the student return to the selection and complete a assignment that requires critical thinking and imagination.

During class, several techniques assist students in maintaining interest and attention to the task. By varying these techniques, the teacher can provide for a lively class, during which students realize they *are* able to read. Partners can read passages to each other or students can take turns reading in small groups. The teacher might pose a question to be answered during that reading. Groups might also begin to act out short scenes, reading only the dialogue. Students might read a description of a setting and then draw what they imagine it to be. Of course, some selections might be silent reading with a specific amount of time announced for completion.

Reading aloud for comprehension and reading aloud for pronunciation practice are two entirely unrelated tasks. We can all recall classes where someone read aloud to us from weary lecture notes. Active engagement of the readers, on the other hand, forces them to work for comprehension, for the development of thought processes, and for improvement of language skills.

Postreading Activities

It is important to provide students with an opportunity to expand the knowledge they have gained from the reading selection. Students should apply what they have learned to their own personal experiences. How we structure activities can provide students more opportunities to reflect on their reading and learn how much they have understood. We often consider a written test the best way to ensure comprehension; however, many other strategies allow students to keep oral skills active. These might include acting out impromptu scenes from the story and creating dialogues that do not exist in a story, but might be imagined, based on other information. Consider the possibility of debates, interviews, TV talk show formats, telephone dialogues, or a monologue in which the audience hears only one side of the conversation.

Written assignments are also valid assessment tools, allowing students to incorporate the vocabulary and structures they have learned in the reading. Students might be encouraged to write journal entries for a character, create a new ending, or retell the story from another point of view. Newspaper articles, advertisements, and other creations can also be a means of following up. Comparisons with other readings require students to keep active vocabulary and structures they have studied previously. Encourage students to read their creations aloud to a partner, to a group, or to the class.

Conclusion

Reading can be exciting. The combination of a good selection that is relevant and rates high on the interest scale, along with good preparation, guidance, and postreading activities that demonstrate to the students the level of success attained, can encourage them to continue to read. These assignments also allow for the incorporation of other aspects of language learning, and incorporate the Five C's of the National Standards. Communication and culture are obvious links, but so are connections (advance organizers, settings, and so on), comparisons (with other works in the heritage or target language), and communities (learning why a type of writing is important in a culture).

Allez, viens!

offers reading practice and develops reading skills and strategies in the following ways:

THE PUPIL'S EDITION

▶ Provides an extensive reading section in each chapter called **Lisons!** Each **Lisons!** section offers a strategy students apply to an authentic text, as well as activities to guide understanding and exploration of the text.

THE ANNOTATED TEACHER'S EDITION

▶ Provides teachers with additional activities and information in every **Lisons!** section. Additional suggestions are provided for Pre-reading, Reading, and Postreading activities.

THE ANCILLARY PROGRAM

▶ *Joie de lire* This component offers reading selections of various formats and difficulty levels. Each chapter has a prereading feature, a reading selection with comprehension questions, and two pages of activities.

▶ The *Reading Strategies and Skills Handbook* offers useful strategies that can be applied to reading selections in the *Pupil's Edition*, *Joie de lire*, or a selection of your choosing.

▶ The *Cahier d'activités* contains a reading selection tied to the chapter theme, and reading activities for each chapter in *Allez, viens!*

Using Portfolios in the Language Classroom

by Jo Anne S. Wilson, J. Wilson Associates

Portfolios offer a more realistic and accurate way to assess the process of language teaching and learning.

The communicative, whole-language approach of today's language instruction requires assessment methods that parallel the teaching and learning strategies in the proficiency-oriented classroom. We know that language acquisition is a process. Portfolios are designed to assess the steps in that process.

What Is a Portfolio?

A portfolio is a purposeful, systematic collection of a student's work. A useful tool in developing a student profile, the portfolio shows the student's efforts, progress, and achievements for a given period of time. It may be used for periodic evaluation, as the basis for overall evaluation, or for placement. It may also be used to enhance or provide alternatives to traditional assessment measures, such as formal tests, quizzes, class participation, and homework.

Why Use Portfolios?

Portfolios benefit both students and teachers because they:

- **Are ongoing and systematic.** A portfolio reflects the real-world process of production, assessment, revision, and reassessment. It parallels the natural rhythm of learning.

- **Offer an incentive to learn.** Students have a vested interest in creating the portfolios, through which they can showcase their ongoing efforts and tangible achievements. Students select the works to be included and have a chance to revise, improve, evaluate, and explain the contents.

- **Are sensitive to individual needs.** Language learners bring varied abilities to the classroom and do not acquire skills in a uniformly neat and orderly fashion. The personalized, individualized assessment offered by portfolios responds to this diversity.

- **Provide documentation of language development.** The material in a portfolio is evidence of student progress in the language learning process. The contents of the portfolio make it easier to discuss their progress with the students as well as with parents and others.

- **Offer multiple sources of information.** A portfolio presents a way to collect and analyze information from multiple sources that reflects a student's efforts, progress, and achievements in the language.

Portfolio Components

The language portfolio should include both oral and written work, student self-evaluation, and teacher observation, usually in the form of brief, nonevaluative comments about various aspects of the student's performance.

The Oral Component

The oral component of a portfolio might be an audio- or videocassette. It may contain both rehearsed and extemporaneous monologues and conversations. For a rehearsed speaking activity, give a specific communicative task that students can personalize according to their individual interests (for example, ordering a favorite meal in a restaurant). If the speaking activity is extemporaneous, first acquaint students with possible topics for discussion or even the specific task they will be expected to perform. (For example, tell them they will be asked to discuss a picture showing a sports activity or a restaurant scene.)

The Written Component

Portfolios are excellent tools for incorporating process writing strategies into the language classroom. Documentation of various stages of the writing process—brainstorming, multiple drafts, and peer comments—may be included with the finished product.

Involve students in selecting writing tasks for the portfolio. At the beginning levels, the tasks might include some structured writing, such as labeling or listing. As students become more proficient, journals, letters, and other more complicated writing tasks are valuable ways for them to monitor their progress in using the written language.

Student Self-Evaluation

Students should be actively involved in critiquing and evaluating their portfolios and monitoring their own progress.

The process and procedure for student self-evaluation should be considered in planning the contents of the portfolio. Students should work with you and their peers to design the exact format. Self-evaluation encourages them to think about what they are learning (content), how they learn (process), why they are learning (purpose), and where they are going in their learning (goals).

Teacher Observation

Systematic, regular, and ongoing observations should be placed in the portfolio after they have been discussed with the student. These observations provide feedback on the student's progress in the language learning process.

Teacher observations should be based on an established set of criteria that has been developed earlier with input from the student. Observation techniques may include the following:

- Jotting notes in a journal to be discussed with the student and then placed in the portfolio

- Using a checklist of observable behaviors, such as the willingness to take risks when using the target language or staying on task during the lesson

- Making observations on adhesive notes that can be placed in folders

- Recording anecdotal comments, during or after class, using a cassette recorder.

Knowledge of the criteria you use in your observations gives students a framework for their performance.

Electronic Portfolios

Technology can provide help with managing student portfolios. Digital or computer-based portfolios offer a means of saving portfolios in an electronic format. Students can save text, drawings, photographs, graphics, audio or video recordings, or any combination of multimedia information. Teachers can create their own portfolio templates or consult one of the many commercial software programs available to create digital portfolios. Portfolios saved on videotapes or compact discs provide a convenient way to access and store students' work. By employing technology, this means of alternative assessment addresses the learning styles and abilities of individual students. Additionally, electronic portfolios can be shared among teachers, and parents have the ability to easily see the students' progress.

Logistically, the hypermedia equipment and software available for students' use determine what types of entries will be included in the portfolios. The teacher or a team of teachers and students may provide the computer support.

How Are Portfolios Evaluated?

The portfolio should reflect the process of student learning over a specific period of time. At the beginning of that time period, determine the criteria by which you will assess the final product and convey them to the students. Make this evaluation a collaborative effort by seeking students' input as you formulate these criteria and your instructional goals.

Students need to understand that evaluation based on a predetermined standard is but one phase of the assessment process; demonstrated effort and growth are just as important. As you consider correctness and accuracy in both oral and written work, also consider the organization, creativity, and improvement revealed by the student's portfolio over the time period. The portfolio provides a way to monitor the growth of a student's knowledge, skills, and attitudes and shows the student's efforts, progress, and achievements.

How to Implement Portfolios

Teacher-teacher collaboration is as important to the implementation of portfolios as teacher-student collaboration. Confer with your colleagues to determine, for example, what kinds of information you want to see in the student portfolio, how the information will be presented, the purpose of the portfolio, the intended purposes (grading, placement, or a combination of the two), and criteria for evaluating the portfolio. Conferring among colleagues helps foster a departmental cohesiveness and consistency that will ultimately benefit the students.

The Promise of Portfolios

The high degree of student involvement in developing portfolios and deciding how they will be used generally results in renewed student enthusiasm for learning and improved achievement. As students compare portfolio pieces done early in the year with work produced later, they can take pride in their progress as well as reassess their motivation and work habits.

Allez, viens!

supports the use of portfolios in the following ways:

THE PUPIL'S EDITION

▶ Includes numerous oral and written activities that can be easily adapted for student portfolios, such as **Mon journal, Ecrivons!,** and **Jeu de rôle.**

THE ANNOTATED TEACHER'S EDITION

▶ Suggests activities in the Portfolio Assessment feature that may serve as portfolio items.

THE ANCILLARY PROGRAM

▶ Includes criteria in the *Alternative Assessment Guide* for evaluating portfolios.

▶ Provides Speaking Tests in the *Testing Program* for each chapter that can be adapted for use as portfolio assessment items.

▶ Offers several oral and written scenarios on the *Interactive CD-ROM Tutor* that students can develop and include in their portfolios.

Teaching Culture

by Nancy A. Humbach, Miami University, and Dorothea Bruschke, Parkway School District

We must integrate culture and language in a way that encourages curiosity, stimulates analysis, and teaches students to hypothesize.

The teaching of culture has undergone some important and welcome changes in recent years. Instead of teaching the standard notions of cultures, language and regions, we now stress the teaching of analysis and the critical thinking skills required to evaluate a culture, by comparing it to one's own, but within its own setting. The setting includes the geography, climate, history, and influences of peoples who have interacted within that cultural group.

The National Standards for the Teaching of Foreign Languages suggests organizing the teaching of culture into three categories: products, practices, and perspectives. Through the presentation of these aspects of culture, students should gain the skill to analyze the culture, evaluate it within its context, compare it to their culture and develop the ability to function comfortably in that culture.

Skill and practice in the analysis of cultural phenomena equip students to enter a cultural situation, assess it, create strategies for dealing with it, and accepting it as a natural part of the people. The ultimate goal of this philosophy is to reduce the "we vs. they" approach to culture. If students are encouraged to accept and appreciate the diversity of other cultures, they will be more willing and better able to develop the risk-taking strategies necessary to learn a language and to interact with people of different cultures.

There are many ways to help students become culturally knowledgeable and to assist them in developing an awareness of differences and similarities between the target culture and their own. Two of these approaches involve critical thinking, that is, trying to find reasons for a certain behavior through observation and analysis, and putting individual observations into larger cultural patterns. We must integrate culture and language in a way that encourages curiosity, stimutates analysis, and teaches students to hypothesize.

First Approach: Questioning

The first approach involves questioning as the key strategy. At the earliest stages of language learning, students begin to learn ways to greet peers, elders, and strangers, as well as the use of **tu** and **vous.** Students need to consider questions such as: "How do French-speaking people greet each other? Are there different levels of formality? Who initiates a handshake? When is a handshake or kisses on the cheeks (**la bise**) appropriate?" Each of these questions leads students to think about the values that are expressed through word and gesture. They start to "feel" the other culture, and at the same time, understand how much of their own behavior is rooted in their cultural background.

Magazines, newspapers, advertisements, and television commercials are all excellent sources of cultural material. For example, browsing through a French magazine, one finds a number of advertisements for food items and bottled water. Could this indicate a great interest in eating and preparing healthy food? Reading advertisements can be followed up with viewing videos and films, or with interviewing native speakers or people who have lived in French-speaking countries about customs involving food selection and preparation. Students might want to find answers to questions such as: "How much time do French people spend shopping for and preparing a meal? How long does a typical meal **en famille** last? What types of food and beverages does it involve?" This type of questioning might lead students to discover different attitudes toward food and mealtimes.

An advertisement for a refrigerator or a picture of a French kitchen can provide an insight into practices of shopping for food. Students first need to think about the refrigerator at home, take an inventory of what is kept in it, and consider when and where their family shops. Next, students should look closely at a French refrigerator. What is its size? What could that mean? (Shopping takes place more often, stores are within walking distance, and people eat more fresh foods.)

Food wrappers and containers also provide good clues to cultural insight. For example, since bread is often purchased fresh from a **boulangerie,** it is usually carried in one's hand or tote bag, with no packaging at all. Since most people shop daily and carry their own groceries home, heavier items like sodas often come in bottles no larger than one and one-half liters.

Second Approach: Associating Words with Images

The second approach for developing cultural understanding involves forming associations of words with the cultural images they suggest. Language and culture are so closely related that one might actually say that language *is* culture. Most words, especially nouns, carry a cultural connotation. Knowing the literal equivalent of a word in another

language is of little use to students in understanding this connotation. For example, **ami** cannot be translated simply as *friend,* **pain** as *bread,* or **rue** as *street.* The French word **pain,** for instance, carries with it the image of a small local bakery stocked with twenty or thirty different varieties of freshly-baked bread, all warm from a brick oven. At breakfast, bread is sliced, covered with butter and jam, and eaten as a **tartine;** it is eaten throughout the afternoon and evening meals, in particular as an accompaniment to the cheese course. In French-speaking countries, "bread" is more than a grocery item; it is an essential part of every meal.

When students have acquired some sense of the cultural connotation of words—not only through teachers' explanations but, more importantly, through observation of visual images—they start to discover the larger underlying cultural themes, or what is often called deep culture.

These larger cultural themes serve as organizing categories into which individual cultural phenomena fit to form a pattern. Students might discover, for example, that French speakers, because they live in much more crowded conditions, have a great need for privacy (cultural theme), as reflected in such phenomena as closed doors, fences or walls around property, and sheers on windows. Students might also discover that love of nature and the outdoors is an important cultural theme, as indicated by such phenomena as flower boxes and planters in public places—even on small traffic islands—well-kept public parks in every town, and people going for a walk or going hiking.

As we teach culture, students learn not only to recognize elements of the target culture but also of their American cultural heritage. They see how elements of culture reflect larger themes or patterns. Learning what constitutes American culture and how that information relates to other people throughout the world can be an exciting journey for a young person.

As language teachers, we are able to facilitate that journey into another culture and into our own, to find our similarities as well as our differences from others. We do not encourage value judgments about others and their culture, nor do we recommend adopting other ways. We simply say to students, "Other ways exist. They exist for many reasons, just as our ways exist due to what our ancestors have bequeathed us through history, traditions, values, and geography."

Allez, viens!
develops cultural understanding and awareness in the following ways:

THE PUPIL'S EDITION

▸ Informs students about French-speaking countries through photo essays, maps, almanac boxes, and **Notes culturelles** that invite comparison with the students' own cultural experiences.

▸ Engages students in analysis and comparison of live, personal interviews with native speakers in the **Panorama Culturel** sections.

▸ Uses the **Rencontre culturelle** section to expose students to cross-cultural situations that require observation, analysis, and problem-solving.

▸ Helps students integrate the language with its cultural connotations through a wealth of authentic art, documents, and literature.

THE ANNOTATED TEACHER'S EDITION

▸ Provides the teacher with additional culture, history, and language notes, background information on photos and almanac boxes, and multicultural links.

▸ Suggests problem-solving activities and critical thinking questions that allow students to hypothesize, analyze, and discover larger underlying cultural themes.

THE ANCILLARY PROGRAM

▸ Includes additional realia to develop cultural insight by serving as a catalyst for questioning and direct discovery.

▸ Offers activities that require students to compare and contrast cultures.

▸ Provides songs, short readings, and poems as well as many opportunities for students to experience regional variation and idioms in the video, audio, and CD-ROM programs.

Learning Styles and Multi-Modality Teaching

by Mary B. McGehee, Louisiana State University

Incorporating a greater variety of activities to accommodate the learning styles of all students can make the difference between struggle and pleasure in the foreign language classroom.

The larger and broader population of students who are enrolling in foreign language classes brings a new challenge to foreign language educators, calling forth an evolution in teaching methods to enhance learning for all our students. Educational experts now recognize that every student has a preferred sense for learning and retrieving information: visual, auditory, or kinesthetic. Incorporating a greater variety of activities to accommodate the learning styles of all students can make the difference between struggle and pleasure in the foreign language classroom.

Accommodating Different Learning Styles

A modified arrangement of the classroom is one way to provide more effective and enjoyable learning for all students. Rows of chairs and desks must give way at times to circles, semicircles, or small clusters. Students may be grouped in fours or in pairs for cooperative work or peer teaching. It is important to find a balance of arrangements, thereby providing the most comfort in varied situations.

Since visual, auditory, and kinesthetic learners will be in the class, and because every student's learning will be enhanced by a multi-sensory approach, lessons must be directed toward all three learning styles. Any language lesson content may be presented visually, aurally, or kinesthetically.

Visual presentations and practice may include the chalkboard, charts, posters, television, overhead projectors, books, magazines, picture diagrams, flash cards, bulletin boards, films, slides, or videos. Visual learners need to see what they are to learn. Lest the teacher think he or she will never have the time to prepare all those visuals, Dickel and Slak (1983) found that visual aids generated by students are more effective than ready-made ones.

Auditory presentations and practice may include stating aloud the requirements of the lesson, oral questions and answers, paired or group work on a progression of oral exercises from repetition to communication, tapes, CDs, dialogues, and role-playing. Jingles, catchy stories, and memory devices using songs and rhymes are good learning aids. Having students record themselves and then listen as they play back the cassette allows them to practice in the auditory mode.

Kinesthetic presentations entail the students' use of manipulatives, chart materials, gestures, signals, typing, songs, games, and role-playing. These lead the students to associate sentence constructions with meaningful movements.

A Sample Lesson Using Multi-Modality Teaching

A multi-sensory presentation on greetings might proceed as follows:

For Visual Learners

As the teacher begins oral presentation of greetings and introductions, he or she simultaneously shows the written forms on transparencies, with the formal expressions marked with an adult's hat, and the informal expressions marked with a baseball cap.

The teacher then distributes cards with the hat and cap symbols representing the formal and informal expressions. As the students hear taped mini-dialogues, they hold up the appropriate card to indicate whether the dialogues are formal or informal. On the next listening, the students repeat the sentences they hear.

For Auditory Learners

A longer taped dialogue follows, allowing the students to hear the new expressions a number of times. They write from dictation several sentences containing the new expressions. They may work in pairs, correcting each other's work as they "test" their own understanding of the lesson at hand. Finally, students respond to simple questions using the appropriate formal and informal responses cued by the cards they hold.

For Kinesthetic Learners

For additional kinesthetic input, members of the class come to the front of the room, each holding a hat or cap symbol. As the teacher calls out situations, the students play the roles, using gestures and props appropriate to the age group they are portraying. Non-cued, communicative role-playing with props further enables the students to "feel" the differences between formal and informal expressions.

Helping Students Learn How to Use Their Preferred Mode

Since we require all students to perform in all language skills, part of the assistance we must render is to help them develop strategies within their preferred learning modes to carry out an assignment in another mode. For example, visual students hear the teacher assign an oral exercise and visualize what they must do. They must see themselves carrying out the assignment, in effect watching themselves as if there were a movie going on in their heads. Only then can they also hear themselves saying the right things. Thus, this assignment will be much easier for the visual learners who have been taught this process, if they have not already figured it out for themselves. Likewise, true auditory students, confronted with a reading/writing assignment, must talk themselves through it, converting the entire process into sound as they plan and prepare their work. Kinesthetic students presented with a visual or auditory task must first break the assignment into tasks and then work their way through them.

Students who experience difficulty because of a strong preference for one mode of learning are often unaware of the degree of preference. In working with these students, I prefer the simple and direct assessment of learning styles offered by Richard Bandler and John Grinder in their book *Frogs into Princes,* which allows the teacher and student to quickly determine how the student learns. In an interview with the student, I follow the assessment with certain specific recommendations of techniques to make the student's study time more effective.

The following is an example of an art-based activity from *Allez, viens!*

It is important to note here that teaching students to maximize their study does not require that the teacher give each student an individualized assignment. It does require that each student who needs it be taught how to prepare the assignment using his or her own talents and strengths. This communication between teacher and student, combined with teaching techniques that reinforce learning in all modes, can only maximize pleasure and success in learning a foreign language.

References

Dickel, M.J. and S. Slak. "Imaging Vividness and Memory for Verbal Material." *Journal of Mental Imagery* 7, i (1983):121–126.

Bandler, Richard, and John Grinder. *Frogs into Princes.* Real People Press, Moab, UT. 1978.

Allez, viens!

accommodates different learning styles in the following ways:

THE PUPIL'S EDITION

▸ Presents basic material in audio, video, print, and online formats.

▸ Includes role-playing activities and a variety of multi-modal activities, including an extensive listening strand and many art-based activities.

THE ANNOTATED TEACHER'S EDITION

▸ Provides suggested activities for visual, auditory, and kinesthetic learners as well as suggestions for slower-paced learning and challenge activities.

▸ Includes Total Physical Response activities.

THE ANCILLARY PROGRAM

▸ Provides additional reinforcement activities for a variety of learning styles.

▸ Presents a rich blend of audiovisual input through the video program, audio program, CD-ROM Tutor, transparencies, and blackline masters.

Multi-Level Classrooms

by Joan H. Manley

There are positive ways, both psychological and pedagogical, to make this situation work for you and your students.

So you have just heard that your third-period class is going to include both Levels 2 and 3! While this is never the best news for a foreign language teacher, there are positive ways, both psychological and pedagogical, to make this situation work for you and your students.

Relieving student anxieties

Initially, in a multi-level class environment, it is important to relieve students' anxiety by orienting them to their new situation. From the outset, let all students know that just because they "did" things the previous year, such as learn how to conjugate certain verbs, they may not yet be able to use them in a meaningful way. Students should not feel that it is demeaning or a waste of time to recycle activities or to share knowledge and skills with fellow students. Second-year students need to know they are not second-class citizens and that they can benefit from their classmates' greater experience with the language. Third-year students may achieve a great deal of satis-faction and become more confident in their own language skills when they have opportunities to help or teach their second-year classmates. It is important to reassure third-year students that you will devote time to them and challenge them with different assignments.

Easing your own apprehension

When you are faced with both Levels 2 and 3 in your classroom, remind yourself that you teach students of different levels in the same classroom every year, although not officially. After one year of classroom instruction, your Level 2 class will never be a truly homogeneous group. Despite being made up of students with the same amount of "seat time," the class comprises multiple layers of language skills, knowledge, motivation, and ability. Therefore, you are constantly called upon to make a positive experience out of a potentially negative one.

Your apprehension will gradually diminish to the extent that you are able to . . .

- make students less dependent on you for the successful completion of their activities.
- place more responsibility for learning on the students.
- implement creative group, pair, and individual activities.

How can you do this? Good organization will help. Lessons will need to be especially well-planned for the multi-level class. The following lesson plan is an example of how to treat the same topic with students of two different levels.

Teaching a lesson in a multi-level classroom

Lesson objectives

Relate an incident in the past that you regret.

Level 2: Express surprise and sympathy.

Level 3: Offer encouragement and make suggestions.

Lesson plan

1. **Review and/or teach the past tense.** Present the for-mation of the past tense. Model its use for the entire class or call upon Level 3 students to give examples.

2. **Practice the past tense.** Have Level 3 students who have mastered the past tense teach it to Level 2 students in pairs or small groups. Provide the Level 3 student instructors with several drill and practice activities they may use for this purpose.

3. **Relate your own regrettable past experience.** Recount a personal regrettable incident—real or imaginary—to the entire class as a model. For example, you may have left your automobile lights on, and when you came out of school, the battery was dead and you couldn't start your car. Or you

may have scolded a student for not doing the homework and later discovered the student had a legitimate reason for not completing the assignment.

4. Prepare and practice written and oral narratives. Have Level 2 students pair off with Level 3 students. Each individual writes about his or her experience, the Level 3 partner serving as a resource for the Level 2 student. Partners then edit each other's work and listen to each other's oral delivery. You might choose to have students record their oral narratives.

5. Present communicative functions.
A. Ask for a volunteer to recount his or her own regrettable incident for the entire class.
B. Model reactions to the volunteer's narrative.
(1) Express surprise and sympathy (for Level 2): "Really! That's too bad!"
(2) Offer encouragement and make suggestions (for Level 3): "Don't worry. You can still..."

6. Read narratives and practice communicative functions. Have Level 2 students work together in one group or in small groups, listening to classmates' stories and reacting with the prescribed communicative function. Have Level 3 students do the same among themselves. Circulate among the groups, listening, helping, and assessing.

7. Assess progress. Repeat your personal account for the entire class and elicit reactions from students according to their level. Challenge students to respond with communicative functions expected of the other level if they can.

Every part of the above lesson plan is important. Both levels have been accommodated. The teacher has not dominated the lesson. Students have worked together in pairs and small groups, while Level 3 students have helped their Level 2 classmates. Individual groups still feel accountable, both within their level and across levels.

Any lesson can be adapted in this way. It takes time and effort, but the result is a student-centered classroom where students share and grow, and the teacher is the facilitator.

Allez, viens!

facilitates work in a multi-level classroom in the following ways:

THE PUPIL'S EDITION

▸ Provides creative activities for pair and group work that allow students at different levels to work together and learn from one another.

THE ANNOTATED TEACHER'S EDITION

▸ Offers practical suggestions for Projects and Cooperative Learning that engage students of different levels.

▸ Provides Communication for All Students teaching suggestions throughout the program. Second-year students will benefit from the Slower Pace activities, while third-year students will take advantage of the Challenge exercises.

▸ Provides a clear, comprehensive outline of the functions, vocabulary, and grammar that are recycled in each chapter. The Chapter Overview of each chapter is especially helpful to the teacher who is planning integrated or varied lessons in the multi-level classroom.

THE ANCILLARY PROGRAM

▸ Provides a variety of materials and activities to accommodate different levels in a multi-level classroom.

▸ Facilitates collective learning so that groups of students at different learning levels may work together, pacing an activity according to their specific abilities.

Professional References

This section provides information about several resources that can enrich your French class. Included are addresses of government offices of francophone countries, pen pal organizations, subscription agencies, and many others. Since addresses change frequently, you may want to verify them before you send your requests. You may also want to refer to the HRW web side at http://www.hrw.com for current information.

CULTURAL AGENCIES

For historic and tourist information about France and francophone countries, contact:

French Cultural Services
972 Fifth Ave.
New York, NY 10021
(212) 439-1400

French Cultural Services
540 Bush St.
San Francisco, CA 94108
(415) 397-4330

TOURIST OFFICES

French Government Tourist Office
444 Madison Ave.
New York, NY 10022
(212) 838-7800

Délégation du Québec
53 State Street
Exchange Place Bldg., 19th floor
Boston, MA 02109
(617) 723-3366

Caribbean Tourism Association
20 E. 46th St., 4th floor
New York, NY 10017
(212) 682-0435

INTERCULTURAL EXCHANGE

American Field Service
198 Madison Ave.
New York, NY 10016
(212) 299-9000

CIEE Student Travel Services
205 East 42nd St.
New York, NY 10017
(212) 661-1414

PEN PAL ORGANIZATIONS

For the names of pen pal groups other than those listed below, contact your local chapter of AATF. There are fees involved, so be sure to write for information.

**Student Letter Exchange
(League of Friendship)**
211 Broadway, Suite 201
Lynbrook, NY 11563
(516) 887-8628

World Pen Pals
PO BOX 337
Saugerties, NY 12477
(914) 246-7828

PERIODICALS

Subscriptions to the following cultural materials are available directly from the publishers. See also the section on Subscription Services.

- *Phosphore* is a monthly magazine for high school students.
- *Okapi* is a bimonthly environmentally-oriented magazine for younger teenagers in France.
- *Le Monde* is the major daily newspaper in France.
- *Le Figaro* is an important newspaper in France. Daily or Saturday editions are available by subscription.
- *Elle* is a weekly fashion magazine for women.
- *Paris Match* is a general interest weekly magazine.
- *Le Point* is a current events weekly magazine.
- *L'Express* is a current events weekly magazine.

SUBSCRIPTION SERVICES

French-language magazines can be obtained through subscription agencies in the United States. The following companies are among the many that can provide your school with subscriptions.

EBSCO Subscription Services
5724 Hwy 280 E
Birmingham, AL 35242
(205) 991-6600

Continental Book Company
8000 Cooper Ave., Bldg. 29
Glendale, NY 11385
(718) 326-0560

PROFESSIONAL ORGANIZATIONS

The two major organizations for French teachers at the secondary-school level are:

The American Council on the Teaching of Foreign Languages (ACTFL)
6 Executive Blvd.
Upper Level
Yonkers, NY 10701
(914) 963-8830

The American Association of Teachers of French (AATF)
Mailcode 4510
Southern Illinois University
Carbondale, IL 61820

A Bibliography for the French Teacher

This bibliography is a compilation of several resources available for professional enrichment.

SELECTED AND ANNOTATED LIST OF READINGS

I. Methods and Approaches

Cohen, Andrew D. *Assessing Language Ability in the Classroom,* **(2nd ed.).** Boston, MA: Heinle, 1994.
- Assessment processes, oral interviews, role-playing situations, dictation, and portfolio assessment.

Hadley, Alice Omaggio. *Teaching Language in Context,* **(2nd ed.).** Boston, MA: Heinle, 1993.
- Overview of the proficiency movement and a survey of past language-teaching methods and approaches; application of the five skills in language education; includes sample activities, teaching summaries, and references.

Lafayette, R. (Ed.). *National Standards: A Catalyst for Reform.* Lincolnwood, IL: National Textbook Co., 1996.
- Outline and implications of the National Standards for the modern language classroom; addresses technology, teacher training, materials development, and the changing learning environment.

Lee, James F., and Bill VanPatten. *Making Communicative Language Teaching Happen.* New York: McGraw-Hill, 1995.
- Task-based approach to language education, includes activities and test sections to encourage communicative interaction in the classroom.

II. Second-Language Theory

Brown, H. Douglas. *Principles of Language Learning and Teaching* **(3rd. ed.).** Englewood Cliffs, NJ: Prentice Hall Regents, 1994.
- Addresses the cognitive, psychological, and sociocultural factors influencing the language-learning process; also includes theories of learning, styles and strategies, motivation, and culture; as well as assessment, error analysis, communicative competence, and theories of acquisition.

Ellis, Rod. *The Study of Second Language Acquisition.* Oxford: Oxford University Press, 1994.
- Provides an overview of second language acquisition: error analysis, acquisition orders, social factors, affective variables, individual differences, and the advantages and disadvantages of classroom instruction.

Krashen, Stephen. *The Power of Reading.* New York: McGraw, 1994.
- Updates Optimal Input Theory by incorporating the reading of authentic texts.

III. Technology-Enhanced instruction

Bush, Michael D., and Robert M. Terry, (Eds.), in conjunction with ACTFL. *Technology Enhanced Language Learning.* Lincolnwood, IL: National Textbook Co., 1997.
- Articles deal with the application of technology in the modern language classroom, including: computer-mediated communication, electronic discussions, hyper-media, the Internet, multimedia, videos, and the WWW.

Muyskens, Judith Ann. (Ed.). *New Ways of Learning and Teaching: Focus on Technology and Foreign Language Education.* Boston: Heinle and Heinle, 1997.
- Compilation of articles on the use of technology in the classroom; techniques for applying technology tools to the four skills and culture; also discusses implementation, teacher training, and language laboratories.

Steen, Douglas R., Mark R. Roddy, Derek Sheffield, and Michael Bryan Stout. *Teaching With the Internet: Putting Teachers before Technology.* Bellevue, WA: Resolution Business Press, Inc., 1995.
- Designed for K–12 teachers and based on educational theory, provides tips and strategies for using the Internet in and out of the classroom, cites specific case studies; topics include the Internet, e-mail, mailing lists, newsgroups, the WWW, creating a Web page, and other research services.

IV. Professional Journals

Calico
(Published by the Computer Assisted Language Instruction Consortium)
- Dedicated to the intersection of modern language learning and high technology. Research articles on videodiscs, using computer-assisted language learning, how-to articles, and courseware reviews.

The Foreign Language Annals
(Published by the American Council on the Teaching of Foreign Languages)
- Consists of research and how-to-teach articles.

The French Review
(Published by the American Association of Teachers of French)
- Articles on French-language literature.

The IALL Journal of Language Learning Technologies
(Published by the International Association for Learning Laboratories)
- Research articles as well as practical discussions pertaining to technology and language instruction.

The Modern Language Journal
- Primarily features research articles.

Allez, viens!®

HOLT FRENCH

LEVEL 3

HOLT, RINEHART AND WINSTON

A Harcourt Education Company

Austin • Orlando • Chicago • New York • Toronto • London • San Diego

ASSOCIATE DIRECTOR
Barbara Kristof

EXECUTIVE EDITOR
Priscilla Blanton

SENIOR EDITORS
Marion Bermondy
Jaishree Venkatesan

MANAGING EDITOR
Chris Hiltenbrand

EDITORIAL STAFF
Annick Cagniart
Yamilé Dewailly
Virginia Dosher
Ruthie Ford
Serge Laîné
Géraldine Touzeau-Patrick
Leigh Marshall, *Intern*
Mark Eells,
  Editorial Coordinator

EDITORIAL PERMISSIONS
Carrie Jones, *CCP Supervisor*
Nicole Svobodny,
  Permissions Editor

Brigida Donohue,
  Interpreter-Translator

ART, DESIGN, & PHOTO
  BOOK DESIGN
Richard Metzger,
  Design Director
Marta L. Kimball,
  Design Manager
Lisa Woods
Andrew Lankes
Alicia Sullivan
Ruth Limon

IMAGE SERVICES
Joe London, *Director*
Jeannie Taylor, *Photo Research*
  Supervisor
Elisabeth McCoy
Michelle Rumpf, *Art Buyer*
  Supervisor
Coco Weir

DESIGN NEW MEDIA
Susan Michael, *Design Director*
Amy Shank, *Design Manager*

Kimberly Cammerata,
  Design Manager
Czeslaw Sornat,
  Senior Designer
Grant Davidson

MEDIA DESIGN
Curtis Riker, *Design Director*
Richard Chavez

GRAPHIC SERVICES
Kristen Darby, *Manager*
Linda Wilbourn
Jane Dixon
Dean Hsieh

COVER DESIGN
Richard Metzger,
  Design Director
Candace Moore,
  Senior Designer

PRODUCTION
Amber McCormick,
  Production Supervisor

Colette Tichenor,
  Production Coordinator

MANUFACTURING
Shirley Cantrell, *Supervisor,*
  Inventory & Manufacturing
Deborah Wisdom, *Senior*
  Inventory Analyst

NEW MEDIA
Jessica Bega,
  Senior Project Manager
Lydia Doty,
  Senior Project Manager
Elizabeth Kline,
  Senior Project Manager

VIDEO PRODUCTION
Video materials produced by
Edge Productions, Inc.,
Aiken, S.C.

COVER AND TITLE PAGE PHOTOGRAPHY CREDITS

FRONT COVER AND TITLE PAGE: (background), © John Elk III, (students), HRW Photo/Steve Ewert Photography.

BACK COVER: © Ping Amranand/Superstock, (frame) © 1998 Image Farm, Inc.

Acknowledgments appear on page R111, which is an extension of the copyright page.

ALLEZ, VIENS! is a trademark licensed to Holt, Rinehart and Winston, registered in the United States of America and/or other jurisdictions.

Printed in the United States of America

ISBN 0-03-056596-0

1 2 3 4 5 6 7   48   06 05 04 03 02 01

AUTHOR

Emmanuel Rongiéras d'Usseau
Le Kremlin-Bicêtre, France

Mr. Rongiéras d'Usseau contributed to the development of the scope and sequence for the chapters, created basic material and listening scripts, selected realia, and wrote activities.

CONTRIBUTING WRITERS

Jayne Abrate
The University of Missouri
Rolla Campus
Rolla, MO

Judith Ryser
San Marcos High School
San Marcos, TX

CONSULTANT

John DeMado
Washington, CT

REVIEWERS

Deana Allert
U.S. Peace Corps volunteer
Senegal, 1991-1992
Berkeley, CA

Donna Clementi
Appleton West High School
Appleton, WI

Donald Doehla
Vallejo Senior High School
Vallejo, CA

Amina Elaisammi
Embassy of the Kingdom of Morocco
Washington, DC

Zohra Ben Hamida
Tunisian Information Office
Washington, DC

Joseph F. Herney
Briarcliff High School
Briarcliff Manor, NY

Sam Leone
Freehold Township High School
Freehold, NJ

Patricia Norwood
University of Texas at Austin
Austin, TX

Joann K. Pompa
Mountain Pointe High School
Phoenix, AZ

Marc Prévost
Austin Community College
Austin, TX

FIELD TEST PARTICIPANTS

Marie Allison
New Hanover High School
Wilmington, NC

Gabrielle Applequist
Capital High School
Boise, ID

Jana Brinton
Bingham High School
Riverton, UT

Nancy J. Cook
Sam Houston High School
Lake Charles, LA

Rachael Gray
Williams High School
Plano, TX

Katherine Kohler
Nathan Hale Middle School
Norwalk, CT

Nancy Mirsky
Museum Junior High School
Yonkers, NY

Myrna S. Nie
Whetstone High School
Columbus, OH

Jacqueline Reid
Union High School
Tulsa, OK

Judith Ryser
San Marcos High School
San Marcos, TX

Erin Hahn Sass
Lincoln Southeast High School
Lincoln, NE

Linda Sherwin
Sandy Creek High School
Tyrone, GA

Norma Joplin Sivers
Arlington Heights High School
Fort Worth, TX

Lorabeth Stroup
Lovejoy High School
Lovejoy, GA

Robert Vizena
W.W. Lewis Middle School
Sulphur, LA

Gladys Wade
New Hanover High School
Wilmington, NC

Kathy White
Grimsley High School
Greensboro, NC

TO THE STUDENT

Some people have the opportunity to learn a new language by living in another country. Most of us, however, begin learning another language and getting acquainted with a foreign culture in a classroom with the help of a teacher, classmates, and a textbook. To use your book effectively, you need to know how it works.

Allez, viens! (*Come along!*) is organized to help you learn French and become familiar with the cultures of people who speak French. Each chapter presents concepts in French and strategies for learning a new language. This book also has three Location Openers set throughout the francophone world.

Location Opener Three four–page photo essays called Location Openers introduce different French-speaking places. You can also see these locations on video and on the *Interactive CD-ROM Tutor.*

Chapter Opener The Chapter Opener pages tell you the chapter theme and goals.

Mise en train (*Getting started*) and **Remise en train** (*Getting started again*) These illustrated stories show you French-speaking people in real-life situations, using the language you'll learn in the chapter.

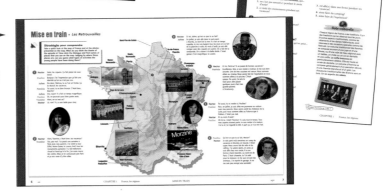

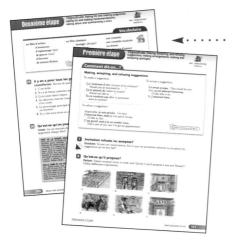

Première and **Deuxième étape** (*First and Second Part*) the chapter is divided into two sections called **étapes**. At the beginning of each **étape,** there is a reminder of the goals for this part of the chapter. Within the **étape** are **Comment dit-on... ?** (*How do you say . . . ?*) boxes that contain the French expressions you'll need to communicate and **Vocabulaire** and **Grammaire/Note de grammaire** boxes that give you the French words and grammatical structures you'll need to know. Activities in each **étape** enable you to develop your skills in listening, reading, speaking, and writing.

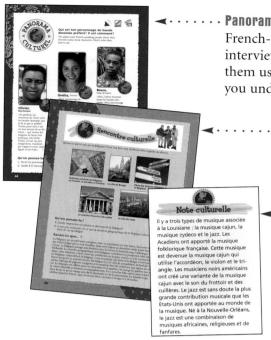

Panorama Culturel (*Cultural Panorama*) On this page are interviews with French-speaking people from around the world. You can watch these interviews on video or listen to them on audio CD. You can also watch them using the *Interactive CD-ROM Tutor*, then check to see how well you understood by answering some questions about what the people say.

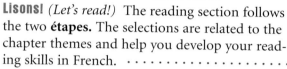

Rencontre culturelle (*Cultural Encounter*) This section, found in nine of the chapters, gives you a firsthand encounter with some aspect of a French-speaking culture.

Note culturelle (*Culture Note*) In each chapter, there are notes with more information about the cultures of French-speaking people.

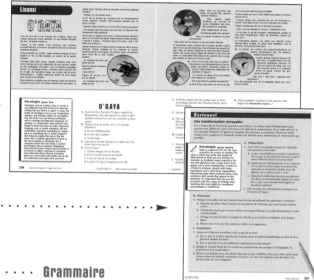

Lisons! (*Let's read!*) The reading section follows the two **étapes.** The selections are related to the chapter themes and help you develop your reading skills in French.

Ecrivons! (*Let's write!*) will develop your writing skills. Each chapter will guide you to write a composition related to the themes of the chapter.

Grammaire supplémentaire (*Additional grammar practice*) This section begins the chapter review. You will find four pages of activities that provide additional practice on the grammar concepts you learned in the chapter. For each activity, you will find the page number where the grammar concept you are practicing is presented.

Mise en pratique (*Review*) The activities on these pages practice what you've learned in the chapter and help you improve your listening, reading, and communication skills. You'll also review what you've learned about culture.

Que sais-je? (*Let's see if I can . . .*) This page at the end of each chapter contains a series of questions and short activities to help you see if you've achieved the chapter goals.

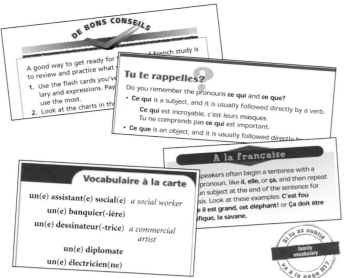

DE BONS CONSEILS

A good way to get ready for ~~f~~ French study is
to review and practice what ~~~~
1. Use the flash cards you've ~~~~
   lary and expressions. Pa~~~~
   use the most.
2. Look at the charts in th~~~~

Tu te rappelles? ❓

Do you remember the pronouns **ce qui** and **ce que**?

• **Ce qui** is a subject, and it is usually followed directly by a verb.

   Ce qui est incroyable, c'est leurs masques.
   *Tu ne comprends pas **ce qui** est important.*

• **Ce que** is an object, and it is usually followed directly b~~~~

À la française

~~~~ speakers often begin a sentence with a
~~~~ pronoun, like **il, elle,** or **ça,** and then repeat
~~~~ subject at the end of the sentence for
~~~~sis. Look at these examples: **C'est fou**
~~~~ il est grand, cet éléphant! or **Ça doit être**
~~~~fique, la savane.

Vocabulaire à la carte

un(e) **assistant(e) social(e)** *a social worker*

un(e) **banquier(-ière)**

un(e) **dessinateur(-trice)** *a commercial artist*

un(e) **diplomate**

un(e) **électricien(ne)**

Si tu as oublié
family vocabulary
va à la page P17.

You'll also find special features in each chapter that provide extra tips and reminders.

De bons conseils *(Helpful advice)* offers study hints to help you succeed in a language class. **Tu te rappelles?** *(Do you remember?)* and **Si tu as oublié** *(If you forgot)* remind you of expressions, grammar, and vocabulary you may have forgotten.

À la française *(The French way)* gives you additional expressions to add more color to your speech.

Vocabulaire à la carte *(Additional Vocabulary)* lists extra words you might find helpful. These words will not appear on the quizzes and tests unless your teacher chooses to include them.

Vocabulaire *(Vocabulary)* On the French-English vocabulary list on the last page of the chapter, the words are grouped by **étape.** These words and expressions will be on the quizzes and tests.

You'll also find French-English and English-French vocabulary lists at the end of the book. The words you'll need to know for the quizzes and tests are in boldface type.

At the end of your book, you'll find more helpful material, such as:
- a summary of the expressions you'll learn in the **Comment dit-on...?** boxes
- a list of review vocabulary
- additional vocabulary words you might want to use
- a summary of the grammar you'll study
- a grammar index to help you find where structures are presented

Allez, viens! Come along on an exciting trip to new cultures and a new language!

Bon voyage!

Explanation of Icons in *Allez, viens!*

Throughout **Allez, viens!,** ***you'll see these symbols, or icons, next to activities and presentations. The following key will help you understand them.***

 Video Whenever this icon appears, you'll know there is a related segment in the *Allez, viens!* Video Program.

 Listening Activities

 Pair Work/Group Work Activities

 Writing Activities

 CD-ROM Activities Whenever this icon appears, you'll know there is a related activity on the *Allez, viens!* Interactive CD-ROM Tutor.

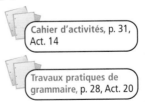

Cahier d'activités, p. 31, Act. 14

Travaux pratiques de grammaire, p. 28, Act. 20

Practice Activities These icons tell you which activities from the *Cahier d'activités* and the *Travaux pratiques de grammaire* practice the material presented.

Grammaire supplémentaire, p. 86, Act. 7 →

Grammaire supplémentaire This reference tells you where you can find related additional grammar practice in the review section of the chapter.

 Internet Activities This icon provides the keyword you'll need to access related online activities at **go.hrw.com.**

en Europe francophone !

LOCATION • CHAPITRES 1, 2, 3, 4 XXVIII

CHAPITRE 1

France, les régions 4

CHAPITRE 2

Belgique, nous voilà! 32

CHAPITRE 3

Soyons responsables! 62

CHAPITRE 4

Des goûts et des couleurs 92

en Afrique francophone!

LOCATION • CHAPITRES 5, 6, 7, 8 122

CHAPITRE 5

C'est notre avenir 126

CHAPITRE 6

Ma famille, mes copains et moi 156

CHAPITRE 7

Un safari-photo 186

CHAPITRE 8

La Tunisie, pays de contrastes.....216

en Amérique francophone!

CHAPITRE 9

C'est l'fun!..... 250

CHAPITRE 10

Rencontres au soleil 280

CHAPITRE 11

Laissez les bons temps rouler! 310

CHAPITRE 12

Echanges sportifs et culturels 340

REFERENCE SECTION

Cultural References

*Page numbers referring to material in the **Pupil's Edition** appear in regular type. When the material referenced is located in the **Annotated Teacher's Edition**, page numbers appear in boldface type.*

Maps

LA FRANCE

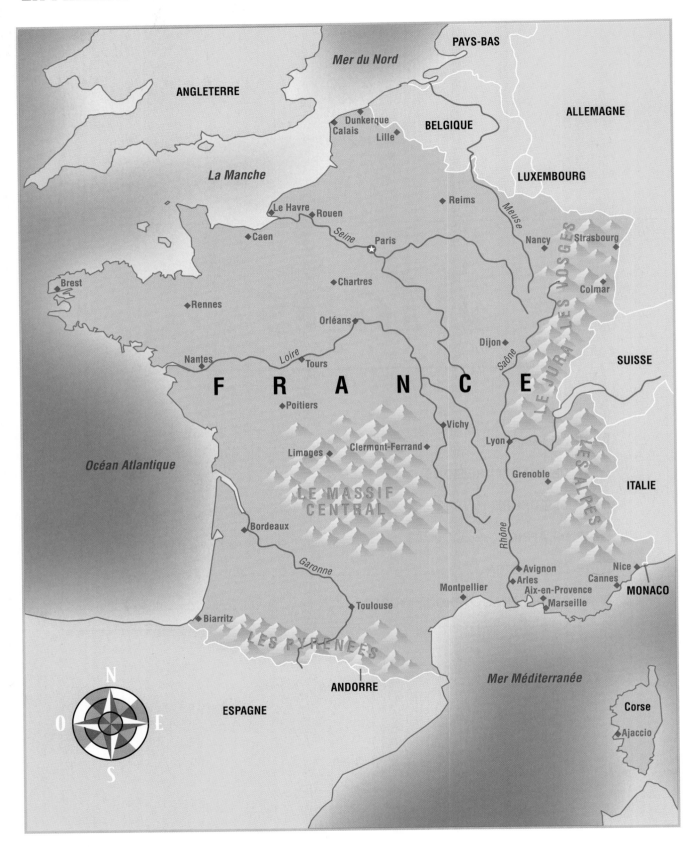

PAYS-BAS

Mer du Nord

ANGLETERRE

ALLEMAGNE

Dunkerque
Calais
Lille

BELGIQUE

La Manche

LUXEMBOURG

Le Havre
Rouen
Reims
Meuse
Caen
Seine
Nancy
Strasbourg
Paris

Brest
Chartres
Colmar

Rennes

Orléans
Dijon
Saône
SUISSE

Nantes
Loire
Tours
LE JURA LES VOSGES

F R A N C E

Poitiers
Vichy
Lyon
LES ALPES

Limoges
Clermont-Ferrand
Grenoble

Océan Atlantique
ITALIE

LE MASSIF
CENTRAL

Bordeaux
Rhône

Garonne
Avignon
Nice
Arles
Cannes
Montpellier
Aix-en-Provence
MONACO
Toulouse
Marseille

Biarritz

LES PYRÉNÉES

ANDORRE
Mer Méditerranée

N
O   E
S

ESPAGNE
Corse

Ajaccio

FRANCE, LES RÉGIONS

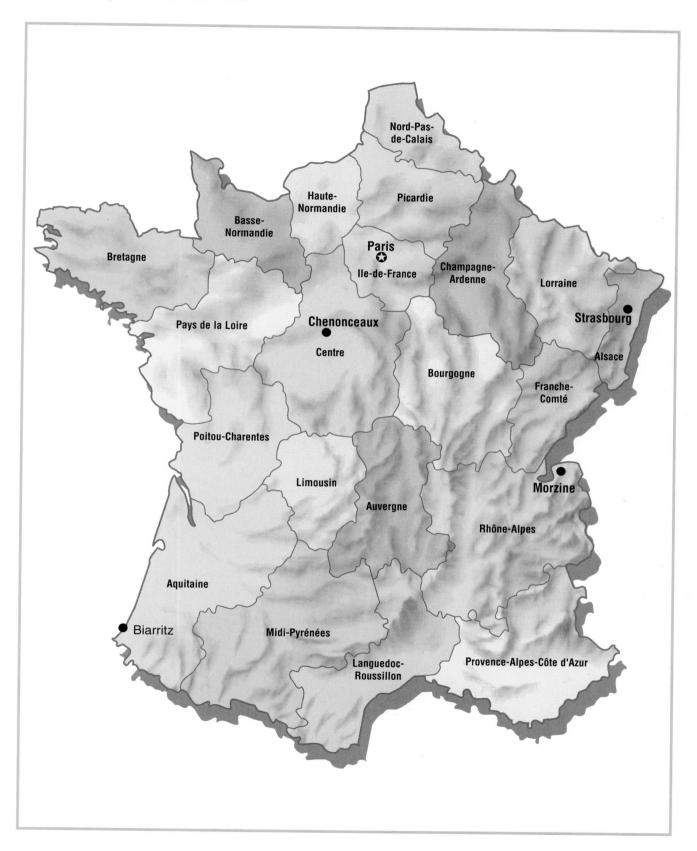

Nord-Pas-de-Calais

Haute-Normandie

Picardie

Basse-Normandie

Bretagne

Paris

Ile-de-France

Champagne-Ardenne

Lorraine

Strasbourg

Pays de la Loire

Chenonceaux

Centre

Alsace

Bourgogne

Franche-Comté

Poitou-Charentes

Limousin

Morzine

Auvergne

Rhône-Alpes

Aquitaine

Biarritz

Midi-Pyrénées

Languedoc-Roussillon

Provence-Alpes-Côte d'Azur

L'EUROPE FRANCOPHONE

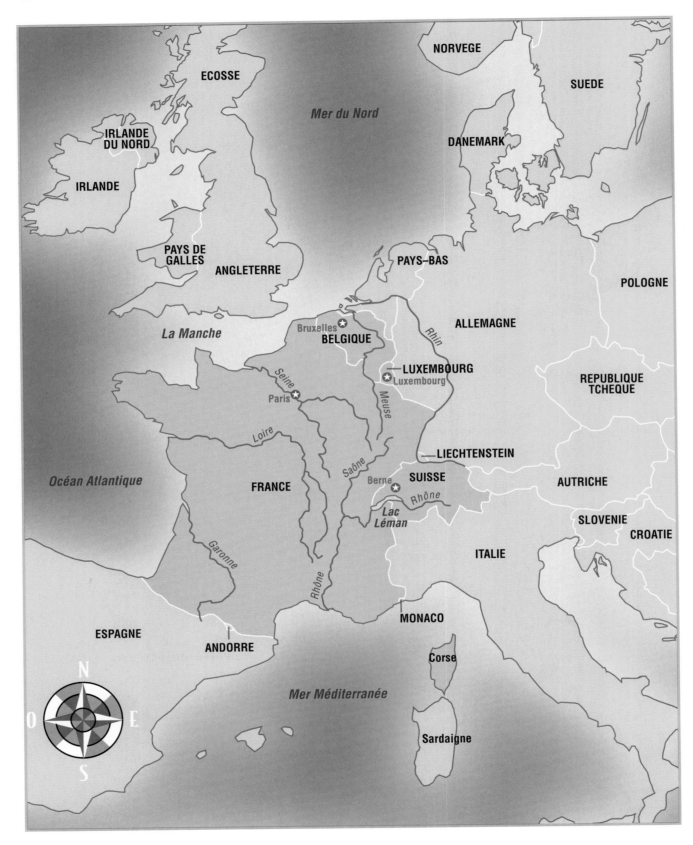

NORVEGE

ECOSSE

Mer du Nord

SUEDE

DANEMARK

IRLANDE
DU NORD

IRLANDE

PAYS DE
GALLES

PAYS-BAS

POLOGNE

ANGLETERRE

La Manche

Bruxelles

BELGIQUE

Rhin

ALLEMAGNE

LUXEMBOURG

Luxembourg

REPUBLIQUE
TCHEQUE

Seine

Paris

Meuse

Loire

Océan Atlantique

LIECHTENSTEIN

Saône

FRANCE

Berne

SUISSE

AUTRICHE

Rhône

Lac
Léman

SLOVENIE

Garonne

CROATIE

ITALIE

Rhône

MONACO

ESPAGNE

ANDORRE

Corse

N

O   E

Mer Méditerranée

S

Sardaigne

L'AFRIQUE FRANCOPHONE

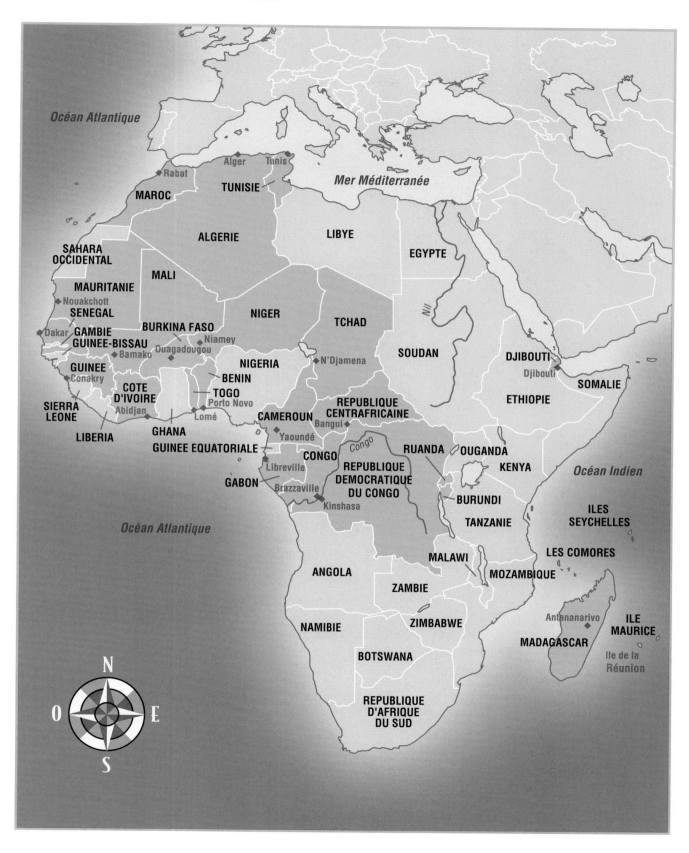

Océan Atlantique

MAROC

Rabat

Alger Tunis

TUNISIE

Mer Méditerranée

ALGERIE

LIBYE

EGYPTE

SAHARA OCCIDENTAL

MAURITANIE

Nouakchott

SENEGAL

MALI

NIGER

TCHAD

Dakar

GAMBIE

GUINEE-BISSAU

BURKINA FASO

Niamey

Ouagadougou

Bamako

Nil

SOUDAN

DJIBOUTI

Djibouti

GUINEE

Conakry

NIGERIA

BENIN

TOGO

Porto Novo

N'Djamena

SOMALIE

ETHIOPIE

COTE D'IVOIRE

Abidjan

SIERRA LEONE

LIBERIA

GHANA

Lomé

CAMEROUN

Bangui

REPUBLIQUE CENTRAFRICAINE

GUINEE EQUATORIALE

Yaoundé

Congo

CONGO

RUANDA

OUGANDA

KENYA

Océan Indien

GABON

Libreville

Brazzaville

Kinshasa

REPUBLIQUE DEMOCRATIQUE DU CONGO

BURUNDI

TANZANIE

ILES SEYCHELLES

Océan Atlantique

MALAWI

LES COMORES

ANGOLA

ZAMBIE

MOZAMBIQUE

Antananarivo

ILE MAURICE

NAMIBIE

ZIMBABWE

MADAGASCAR

Ile de la Réunion

BOTSWANA

REPUBLIQUE D'AFRIQUE DU SUD

N
O E
S

L'AMÉRIQUE FRANCOPHONE

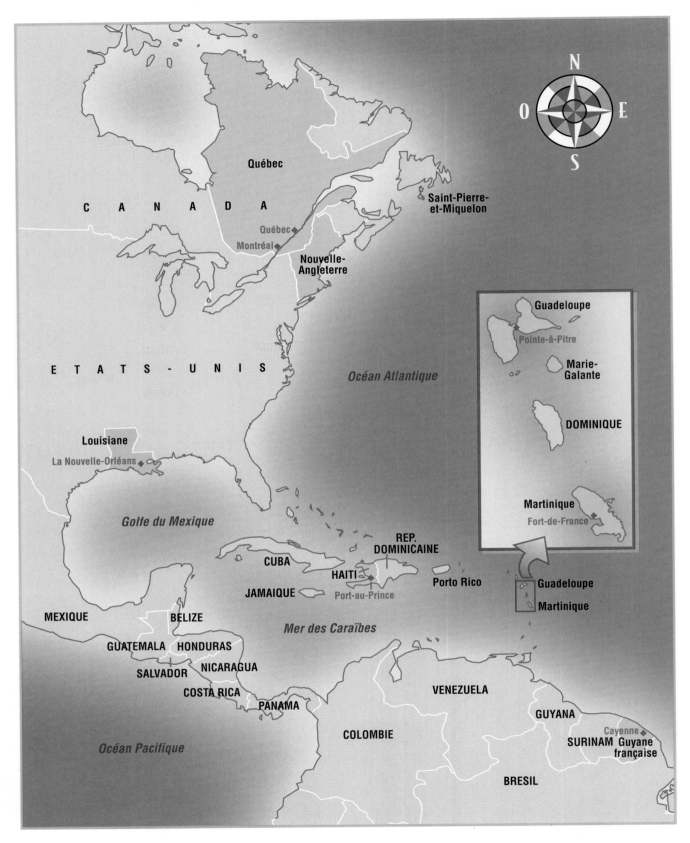

LE MONDE FRANCOPHONE

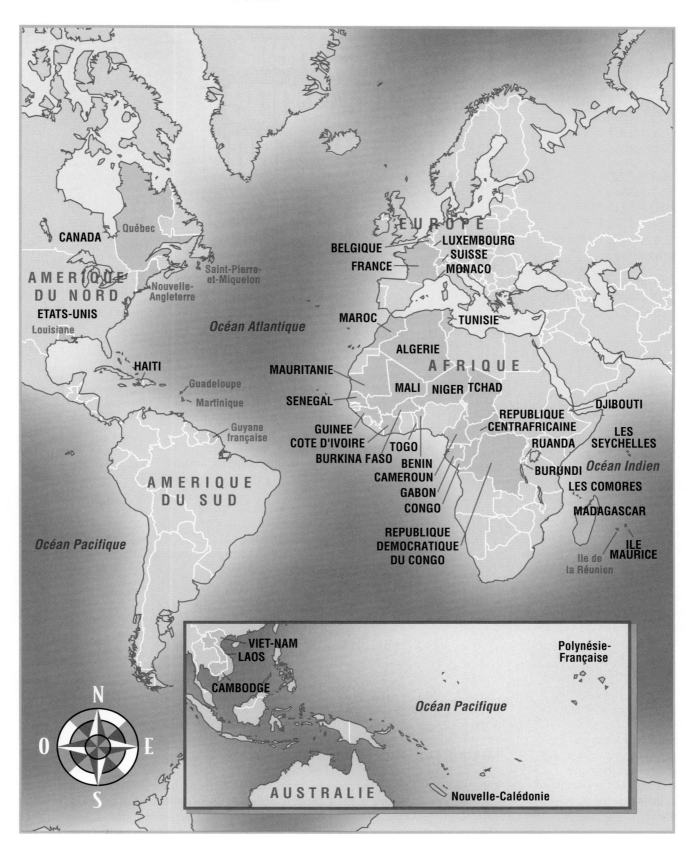

CANADA
Québec
Saint-Pierre-et-Miquelon
AMERIQUE DU NORD
Nouvelle-Angleterre
ETATS-UNIS
Louisiane
Océan Atlantique
HAITI
Guadeloupe
Martinique
Guyane française
AMERIQUE DU SUD
Océan Pacifique

EUROPE
BELGIQUE
LUXEMBOURG
SUISSE
FRANCE
MONACO
MAROC
TUNISIE
ALGERIE
AFRIQUE
MAURITANIE
MALI
NIGER
TCHAD
SENEGAL
DJIBOUTI
GUINEE
REPUBLIQUE CENTRAFRICAINE
COTE D'IVOIRE
LES SEYCHELLES
TOGO
RUANDA
BURKINA FASO
BENIN
CAMEROUN
BURUNDI
Océan Indien
GABON
LES COMORES
CONGO
MADAGASCAR
REPUBLIQUE DEMOCRATIQUE DU CONGO
Ile de la Réunion
ILE MAURICE

VIET-NAM
LAOS
Polynésie-Française
CAMBODGE
Océan Pacifique
AUSTRALIE
Nouvelle-Calédonie

N O S E

T77

Teaching Resources
pp. T78–3

PRINT
▶ Lesson Planner, p. 1
▶ Video Guide, pp. 1–2

MEDIA
▶ One-Stop Planner
▶ Video Program
  Videocassette 1, 1:03–6:23
▶ Interactive CD-ROM Tutor, Disc 1
▶ Map Transparency 3

 go.hrw.com
WA3 FRANCOPHONE
EUROPE

 Using the Almanac and Map

Terms in the Almanac

• **Bruxelles,** the capital of Belgium, is also the site of the headquarters of NATO and the EU. It is famous for its beautiful tapestries woven with golden thread (**tapis d'or**).

• **Anvers** is a Flemish city on the Escaut River. A famous legend tells how this town was terrorized by a giant whose hand was cut off and thrown into the river by the local hero.

• **Paris** was named after the Celtic tribe that first inhabited the area, the **Parisii.** It has been the capital of France since the advent of the Capetian dynasty (987).

• **Marseille,** founded by the Greeks as **Massilia** in 600 B.C., is one of France's largest cities and a major port.

• **Genève** was once known as the "Rome of Protestantism" because Jean Calvin came here in the sixteenth century to try to apply his principles during the Protestant Reformation.

• **Bâle** is a major port on the Rhine River. In 1521, it became the home of the Dutch humanist Erasmus, who preached tolerance.

Allez, viens en Europe francophone!

	La Belgique	**La France**	**La Suisse**
Population	10.241.000	59.300.000	7.262.000
Superficie (km²)	30.527	543.965	41.285
Capitale	Bruxelles	Paris	Berne
Autres villes importantes	Liège	Lyon	Zurich
	Anvers	Marseille	Genève
	Charleroi	Bordeaux	Lausanne
	Mons	Nice	Bâle
	Gand	Strasbourg	

Autres états francophones : Le Luxembourg,
La principauté de Monaco

WA3 FRANCOPHONE
EUROPE

La ville de Genève au bord du lac Léman ▶

Cultures and Communities

Background Information
France, Belgium, and Switzerland are francophone countries because the land these countries now occupy was at one time under the control of the Franks. Charlemagne, a Frankish king and emperor, formed a huge empire that included not only these areas, but parts of northern Spain, Italy, Germany, Austria, and even Denmark.

Language Note
Have students look up the origins of the various place names. Sources include the Greek names **Massilia** (Marseilles) and **Nikaia** (Nice); Celtic tribal names such as the **Parisii** (Paris); Roman names such as **Lugdunum** (Lyons) and **Belgica Prima** (Belgium); and Germanic names such as **Francs** (France) and **Burgondes** (Burgundy).

Using the Map
Have students look at the map and describe France's borders with its neighbors (the ocean, rivers, mountains).

Map Activity
Have students name different regions of the United States and tell what they know about them. Then, show *Map Transparency 3* (**L'Europe francophone**) and ask students what they already know about the different regions of France.

Connections and Comparisons

History Link
The current borders of France were fixed in 1860, when Nice and Savoie were annexed. The provinces of Alsace and Lorraine, however, have changed hands several times between France and Germany. Germany controlled the areas from 1871–1918 and from 1940–1945. After World War II, Alsace and Lorraine were returned to France and have remained French ever since.

However, the influence of German culture is still evident throughout these regions.

Art Link
The Flemish artist Peter Paul Rubens painted for many of the monarchs of Europe. Some of his paintings are on display in the Louvre in Paris. When Rubens died in 1640, he was buried in Anvers.

Using the Photo Essay

1 Brussels' historic **Grand-Place** is the site of a flower market where vendors carpet the square with their colorful blooms to form the **tapis de fleurs.**

2 **Mont Cervin,** located near the Swiss border with the Italian province of Aosta, is 4,478 meters high. A British climber was the first to scale it in 1865.

3 Known for its thirteenth-century Gothic abbey, **Mont-Saint-Michel,** an island in the Gulf of Saint-Malo between Normandy and Brittany, has been the destination of pilgrims since the Middle Ages. In the past, the island was accessible only at low tide, when the receding waters revealed a passage to the island. Since the tides in the bay would come in dangerously fast, many pilgrims lost their lives trying to outrun them. Today, the island is connected to the mainland by a mile-long causeway.

Construction is planned to replace half of the causeway that connects **Mont-Saint-Michel** to the mainland with a bridge to allow the tide to flow freely, thereby restoring the natural ecology.

L'Europe francophone

L'Europe de l'Ouest n'est pas très grande, mais elle présente beaucoup de régions différentes qui ne correspondent pas exactement aux frontières politiques. La langue contribue à accentuer ces différences parce qu'elle correspond à une culture. Par exemple, en Belgique, on parle français dans le sud et flamand dans le nord. En Suisse, on parle français, italien et allemand et au Luxembourg, on parle français, luxembourgeois et allemand. Il y a environ six millions de francophones en Europe qui vivent dans des pays autres que la France.

📶 internet

ADRESSE: go.hrw.com
MOT-CLE: WA3
FRANCOPHONE EUROPE

1 Bruxelles
Bruxelles est la capitale de la Belgique et sa population est bilingue français-flamand.

2 Le Mont Cervin
«Matterhorn» est le nom allemand du Mont Cervin dans les Alpes suisses. Il domine la célèbre station de sports d'hiver de Zermatt, un village où les automobiles ne sont pas autorisées.

3 Le Mont-Saint-Michel
En Normandie, dans le nord-ouest de la France, l'abbaye gothique du Mont-Saint-Michel est un grand lieu touristique.

Cultures and Communities

Culture Notes

In Luxembourg, French is the language of government, while German is the business language and **Letzeburgesch (Luxembourgeois),** the official language. Operating under a constitutional monarchy similar to Belgium's, Luxembourg is a highly industrialized country with a high standard of living and an extremely low illiteracy rate.

5 Legend has it that in the Middle Ages, Carcassonne was running low on food as it was besieged by Charlemagne. The leader of the city, Dame Carcas ordered that the last bit of wheat be fed to the only remaining pig, and that the pig be tossed over the town wall. The pig landed at Charlemagne's feet and burst open. Believing that the inhabitants had plenty of food, since the pig was so well fed, Charlemagne decided to withdraw.

4 Les Ardennes
La région des Ardennes est partagée entre la France, le Luxembourg et la Belgique.

5 La ville de Carcassonne
Les fortifications de cette ville sont un bel exemple d'architecture médiévale.

Aux chapitres 1, 2, 3 et 4, tu vas visiter trois pays d'Europe francophone. Le chapitre 1 va te faire visiter la France. Ensuite, tu vas faire un tour en Belgique, petit pays situé au nord de la France. Au chapitre 3, tu vas connaître un peu la Suisse, où l'environnement tient une place importante dans la vie de tous les jours.

6 Les chemins de fer
En Europe, les chemins de fer sont très développés et permettent d'aller partout et de visiter un maximum de régions.

7 La ville de Strasbourg
C'est la capitale de l'Alsace, à la frontière franco-allemande. Sa culture est partagée entre les deux pays.

4 Les Ardennes, a rugged forest where Charlemagne once hunted, covers northern France, eastern Belgium, and Luxembourg. It was the site of the final German offensive in World War II, the Battle of the Bulge, which took place in December of 1944 and January of 1945.

5 Carcassonne is one of the most spectacular fortified cities in Europe. It is surrounded by an inner wall and an outer wall that connects the towers. The current structure dates from the thirteenth century, when Carcassonne came into French hands. The Romans established an encampment here as a trading center between the Mediterranean Sea and the city of Toulouse. About 1,000 people presently live in the old fortified city, and thousands more live in the more modern city **(la ville basse)** outside the ramparts.

6 The construction of roads and railroads into the mountainous areas of France and Switzerland has eased the previous isolation of the inhabitants. Although the mountains did not prevent major invasions over the centuries, they did isolate the people from much of the outside world.

7 Strasbourg is located near the Rhine River, which forms the border with Germany. An important commercial, manufacturing, and transportation center, Strasbourg has a long and eventful history. It was occupied by the Huns in the fifth century, and after the Franks helped rebuild the city, it became part of the Holy Roman Empire. Strasbourg became a part of France during the reign of Louis XIV.

7 Science Link
Johannes Gensfleisch, known as Gutenberg, developed his revolutionary printing press in Strasbourg in 1438.

Connections and Comparisons

Geography Link
3 The Couesnon River empties into the bay near **Mont-Saint-Michel.** Once known for its severe flooding, it is now controlled by dams and dikes. The flood control projects, however, have yielded an unexpected consequence for the island. The dams prevent the flooding that flushed out sand and sediment from the bay. Without this flooding, sediment remains in the bay and Mont-Saint-Michel is truly an island only during high tides.

Multicultural Link
Have students compare the regional differences in francophone Europe with those in the United States. Have them list the different nationalities and languages in francophone Europe and the United States.

Chapitre 1 : France, les régions

Chapter Overview

Mise en train pp. 6–8	*Les Retrouvailles*			

	FUNCTIONS	**GRAMMAR**	**VOCABULARY**	**RE-ENTRY**
Première étape pp. 9–13	• Renewing old acquaintances, p. 9 • Inquiring; Expressing enthusiasm and dissatisfaction, p. 9 • Exchanging information, p. 10 • Asking and describing what a place was like, p. 12	• The **passé composé**, p. 11 • The **imparfait**, p. 13		• Chapters 1 and 2 are a global review of Holt French, Levels 1 and 2.

Remise en train pp. 14–15	*Bon appétit!*			

Deuxième étape pp. 16–19	• Expressing indecision; making recommendations, p. 17 • Ordering and asking for details, p. 18		• A French menu, p. 17	

Lisons! pp. 20–22	**Il faut être raisonnable**	**Reading Strategy:** Identifying the point of view of the narrator
Ecrivons! p. 23	**Une brochure touristique**	**Writing Strategy:** Defining your purpose
Grammaire supplémentaire	**pp. 24–27**	**Première étape,** pp. 24–26	**Deuxième étape,** p. 27
Review pp. 28–31	**Mise en pratique,** pp. 28–29	**Que sais-je?,** p. 30	**Vocabulaire,** p. 31

CULTURE

• **Note culturelle,** Traditional regional clothing, p. 8
• **Panorama Culturel,** Regional specialties, p. 16
• **Note culturelle,** Regional foods, p. 18

Chapter Resources

 PRINT

Lesson Planning

 One-Stop Planner

Lesson Planner with Substitute Teacher Lesson Plans, pp. 2–6, 64

Student Make-Up Assignments
- Make-Up Assignment Copying Masters, Chapter 1

Listening and Speaking

Listening Activities
- Student Response Forms for Listening Activities, pp. 3–5
- Additional Listening Activities 1-1 to 1-6, pp. 7–9
- Additional Listening Activities (song), p. 10
- Scripts and Answers, pp. 101–105

Video Guide
- Teaching Suggestions, pp. 4–5
- Activity Masters, pp. 6–8
- Scripts and Answers, pp. 80–82, 112

Activities for Communication
- Communicative Activities, pp. 1–4
- Realia and Teaching Suggestions, pp. 51–53
- Situation Cards, pp. 89–90

Reading and Writing

Reading Strategies and Skills Handbook, Chapter 1

Joie de lire 3, Chapter 1

Cahier d'activités, pp. 1–12

Grammar

Travaux pratiques de grammaire, pp. 1–8

Grammar Tutor for Students of French, Chapter 1

Assessment

Testing Program
- Grammar and Vocabulary Quizzes, **Etape** Quizzes, and Chapter Test, pp. 1–14
- Score Sheet, Scripts and Answers, pp. 15–21

Alternative Assessment Guide
- Portfolio Assessment, p. 16
- Performance Assessment, p. 30
- CD-ROM Assessment, p. 44

Student Make-Up Assignments
- Alternative Quizzes, Chapter 1

Standardized Assessment Tutor
- Reading, pp. 1–3
- Writing, p. 4
- Math, pp. 25–26

 **MEDIA**

Online Activities
- Jeux interactifs
- Activités Internet

Video Program
- Videocassette 1
- Videocassette 5 (captioned version)

Audio Compact Discs
- Textbook Listening Activities, CD 1, Tracks 1–15
- Additional Listening Activities, CD 1, Tracks 21–27
- Assessment Items, CD 1, Tracks 16–20

Interactive CD-ROM Tutor, Disc 1

Teaching Transparencies
- Situation 1-1 to 1-2
- **Grammaire supplémentaire** Answers
- **Travaux pratiques de grammaire** Answers

  One-Stop Planner CD-ROM

Use the **One-Stop Planner CD-ROM with Test Generator** to aid in lesson planning and pacing.

For each chapter, the **One-Stop Planner** includes:

- Editable lesson plans with direct links to teaching resources
- Printable worksheets from resource books
- Direct launches to the HRW Internet activities
- Video and audio segments
- Test Generator
- Clip Art for vocabulary items

Chapitre 1 : France, les régions

Projects ··········

Les Régions de la France

Groups of students will research the history, specialties, products, and traditional dress of a region of France, display their information on a poster, and give a short oral presentation.

MATERIALS

✂ **Students may need**
- Posterboard
- Colored pencils or markers
- Scissors
- Glue
- Travel brochures and encyclopedias
- Travel guide books

SUGGESTED SEQUENCE

1. In groups of four, students choose a region of France to research. Then, group members decide who will be the writer, illustrator, proofreader, and presenter.

2. All group members do research. Each member may choose a specific topic (traditional clothing, food specialties, products, geographic features, language/dialect). Group members then share their information with one another and decide what to include in the final project.

3. The writer organizes and writes a rough draft of the oral presentation. The proofreader edits the information and proposes the final draft. With the other group members, the illustrator determines the visuals that will be used for the poster, assembles the necessary materials, and makes the visuals. The presenter assists the other group members and begins to plan out the presentation.

4. The group organizes and assembles their poster. They should all help the presenter prepare. Finally, the presenter conveys the group's findings to the class, using the poster as a visual aid.

5. You might display students' posters around the classroom or school.

GRADING THE PROJECT

Suggested Point Distribution (total = 100 points)
Content	25 points
Language use	25 points
Appearance of visuals	25 points
Effort/participation	25 points

Games ··········

Le Mot juste

This game will help your students develop the skill of circumlocution, the linguistic art of communicating when a person doesn't know the precise word he or she needs. Explain to students that they will learn to paraphrase, use synonyms, describe essential elements, and apply key phrases to communicate when they find themselves at a loss for the exact word.

Materials To play this game, you will need index cards.

Preparation Create a list of words related to the vocabulary presented in the chapter or **étape**. On each card, write one word from the list. Arrange four desks at the front of the room so that the two partners from each team can face each other. Place the cards face down where they can easily be reached by the players from any of the desks. On the board or a transparency, write the following key phrases:

C'est un(e)...
C'est un(e) truc, personne, animal que/qui...
Il/Elle est grand(e)/âgé(e). (C'est... rouge/grand.)
Ça ressemble à...
C'est le contraire de...
C'est un endroit où...
Il/Elle a...
... est fait(e) en plastique/bois/verre/coton.
On l'utilise pour...

Procedure Divide the class into two teams and select a scorekeeper and a timekeeper. Have two players from each team sit at the desks. A player from Team A selects a card and shows it to one of the players from Team B. Using circumlocution, the Team A player makes a statement about the vocabulary word without saying the word itself. (For an elephant, one could say **C'est un animal gris.**) If his or her partner guesses the word, Team A receives five points. (Allow 30 seconds per guess.) If not, the Team B player in turn gives a clue to his or her partner. If the partner guesses correctly, Team B receives four points. Play alternates between the two teams, with point value dropping by one after each incorrect guess. If no team scores a point after five clues, any student on Team A may guess to earn one point. If Team A can't guess correctly, a student from Team B is given the same opportunity. Announce the answer if no one guesses correctly. After four words, select four new players to go to the front for the next round.

Storytelling

Mini-histoire

This story accompanies Teaching Transparency 1-1. The mini-histoire can be told and retold in different formats, acted out, written as dictation, and read aloud to give students additional opportunities to practice all four skills. The following story relates Marion's vacation last summer.

Les vacances de Marion ont mal commencé. Au mois de juillet, elle est partie faire du camping à la montagne avec des amis, Patrick et Virginie. Avant de partir, ils se sont répartis les rôles : Virginie devait faire les courses, Patrick, la vaisselle et Marion, la cuisine. Tout était bien organisé mais il a plu pendant toute la semaine et Marion déteste la pluie. En plus de cela, elle devait faire la cuisine et donc allumer un feu. Ce n'est pas facile d'allumer un feu quand tout est mouillé. Mais elle n'avait pas le choix car Virginie n'avait acheté que de la nourriture qu'il fallait faire cuire.

Heureusement, la deuxième partie des vacances de Marion s'est mieux passée. Elle est allée au Canada avec sa famille. Et ça, c'était génial. Elle a visité les villes de Québec, Montréal et Toronto, où elle a pu pratiquer son anglais. Et il a fait beau tout le temps!

Traditions

Les Plats régionaux

One of France's most important traditions is its regional cooking. Recipes featuring local ingredients are handed down from one generation to the next and savored at home or in regional inns and restaurants. Each region has its own specialty depending on the products found or produced in the area. For example, Normandy is famous for dishes that feature butter, cream, cheese, and apple cider, while Provence is known for dishes made with olives, herbs, garlic, and tomatoes. Perhaps two of France's most famous regional dishes are **foie gras** and **truffes** *(truffles)* from the Périgord region. **Foie gras** is baked liver from fattened ducks or geese. **Truffes** are black, nutty-flavored fungi that grow at the base of oak and hazelnut trees. Specially trained pigs and dogs are used to find truffles, which are often added to sauces, pâtés, and other dishes. Have students find a recipe for a French regional dish and prepare it for the class.

Recette

*The **Clafoutis** originated in the Limousin region, in France. It has become a popular dish throughout the country. When the French prepare a **clafoutis**, they sometimes leave the pits in the cherries. If you do so, make sure to let your guests know!*

CLAFOUTIS AUX CERISES

pour 6 personnes

1 livre de cerises bien mûres

4 œufs

1/2 tasse de farine

1/2 tasse de sucre

1 cuillère à café de beurre

2 tasses de lait

1 sachet de sucre vanillé ou 1 cuillère à café d'extrait de vanille

1 pincée de sel

Mettre la farine dans un grand bol. Ajouter le sel, le beurre fondu, le sucre et les œufs battus.

Mélanger en ajoutant le lait petit à petit. Ajouter les cerises à la pâte. Beurrer un moule. Verser la pâte dans le moule et mettre au four à 350 F pendant 40 minutes. Servir encore tiède.

Technology

Video Program

Videocassette 1, Videocassette 5 (captioned version)
See Video Guide, pp. 3–8.

Camille et compagnie • Premier épisode : *Les Retrouvailles*

Camille is working at her parents' restaurant for the summer. Max, a former friend from **collège**, walks into the restaurant, wearing a cap and dark sunglasses to disguise himself. When Camille tries to take Max's order, he pretends to be indecisive and very picky. When Camille starts to get impatient, Max reveals his identify. The two are happy to see each other again and talk about their summer activities. Then, Camille's friend Sophie arrives and tells about her summer vacation. Finally, another customer arrives, acting much like Max, but not as a joke.

Quelles sont les spécialités de ta région?

Students from France and the Côte d'Ivoire describe dishes typical of their area. Two native speakers discuss the **Panorama Culturel** question and introduce the interviews.

Vidéoclips

- **Cousteron®**: advertisement for cheese
- **News report:** Interview with French chef Joël Robuchon

Interactive CD-ROM Tutor

The **Interactive CD-ROM Tutor** contains videos, interactive games, and activities that provide students an opportunity to practice and review the material covered in Chapter 1.

Activity	Activity Type	Pupil's Edition Page
1. Comment dit-on... ?	Jeu des paires	p. 10 (©2000/©2003 only)
2. Grammaire	Les mots qui manquent	p. 11
3. Grammaire	Le bon choix	pp. 11, 13 (p. 13 ©2000/©2003 only)
4. Vocabulaire	Chacun à sa place	p. 17
5. Comment dit-on... ?	Chacun à sa place	pp. 17, 18
6. Comment dit-on... ?	Du tac au tac	pp. 9, 10, 12, 17, 18 (p. 12 ©2000/©2003 only)
Panorama Culturel	Quelles sont les spécialités de ta région? Le bon choix	p. 16
A toi de parler	*Guided recording*	pp. 28–29
A toi d'écrire	*Guided writing*	pp. 28–29

Teacher Management System

Logging In

Logging in to the *Allez, viens!* TMS is easy. Upon launching the program, simply type "admin" in the password area of the log-in screen and press RETURN. Log on to **www.hrw.com/CDROMTUTOR** for a detailed explanation of the Teacher Management System.

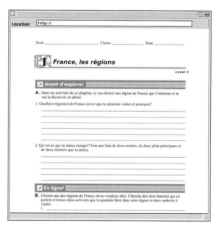

One-Stop Planner CD-ROM

To preview all resources available for this chapter, use the **One-Stop Planner CD-ROM,** Disc 1.

Internet Connection ....

*Have students explore the **go.hrw.com** Web site for many online resources covering all chapters. All Chapter 1 resources are available under the keyword **WA3 FRANCOPHONE EUROPE-1.** Interactive games help students practice the material and provide them with immediate feedback. You'll also find a printable worksheet that provides Internet activities that lead to a comprehensive online research project.*

Jeux interactifs

You can use the interactive activities in this chapter

- to practice grammar, vocabulary, and chapter functions
- as homework
- as an assessment option
- as a self-test
- to prepare for the Chapter Test

Activités Internet

Students look on line for information about a French region and record activities to do there and dishes from the area, using the vocabulary and phrases from the chapter.

- In preparation for the **Activités Internet,** have students review the dramatic episode on Video-cassette 1, or do the activities in the **Panorama Culturel** on page 16. After completing the activity sheet, have students work with a partner and share the information they gathered in Activities B and C on that sheet. Then ask each of the partners to share what they learned with the class.

Projet

Have a group of students create a virtual guided tour of one of the places the young people mentioned in **Mise en train.** You might assign a different place to each group, and specific roles within the groups. Students will search for maps, pictures, and historical information about their assigned region or town. Have them also include dishes typical of the area. Students will then take their class on a virtual tour. They should document their sources by noting the names and URLs of all the sites they consulted.

Première étape

8   **p. 9**   Answers to Activity 8
1. b   2. a   3. d

1. —Salut! Comment vas-tu? Ça fait longtemps qu'on s'est pas vus!
—Oui, ça fait bien deux ans! Qu'est-ce que tu deviens?
—Oh, toujours la même chose.

2. —Tiens, Jean-Paul! Je suis contente de te revoir!
—Oui, moi aussi. Ça fait combien de temps qu'on s'est pas vus?
—Ça fait trois mois au moins. Ça va?
—Oui, super.

3. —Quoi de neuf?
—Oh, tu sais, toujours la même chose. Et toi?
—Rien de spécial. Dis donc, ça fait combien de temps qu'on s'est pas vus?
—Depuis le mois de juin, je crois.

10   **p. 10**   Answers to Activity 10
1. contente   2. non   3. non   4. non   5. contente   6. contente

1. —Alors, c'était comment, tes vacances à la mer?
—Génial. Je me suis bien amusée.

2. —C'était comment, ce voyage?
—Pas trop bien. Ça s'est mal passé.

3. —Tu t'es bien amusée chez tes cousins?
—Pas du tout. C'était vraiment pas terrible comme vacances.

4. —Tiens, Véronique. Ça s'est bien passé, ce week-end?
—Non, je me suis ennuyée.

5. —Raconte-moi un peu ce séjour. C'était comment, la Martinique?
—Super. On a passé des vacances formidables.

6. —Comment ça s'est passé, cette journée à la campagne?
—Ça s'est très bien passé. On a fait un pique-nique.

13   **p. 11**   Answers to Activity 13
1. passé   3. futur   5. passé   7. passé
2. futur   4. passé   6. futur   8. futur

1. —Alors, ces vacances?
—Super! On s'est beaucoup amusées.
—Quel temps est-ce qu'il a fait?
—Magnifique! Il a fait beau tous les jours.

2. —Et en juillet alors?
—Oh, je ne sais pas. J'ai envie de rester ici pour travailler un peu.
—Ah oui? Tu vas faire quoi?
—Je vais être réceptionniste à l'hôtel de mon oncle.

3. —Paul y va début juillet, mais moi, je ne peux pas y aller avant le quinze.
—Pourquoi?
—J'ai promis à mon frère de l'aider au magasin.
—C'est pas de chance, ça!

4. —La Côte d'Azur, ça doit être chouette, non?
—Oui, c'est super. J'y suis allée avec mes parents il y a quelques années.
—Vous avez de la famille là-bas?
—Non, non, on a dormi à l'hôtel.

5. —Dis donc, Laurence, tu n'es pas très bronzée!
—Oh, ne m'en parle pas. J'ai passé des vacances horribles.
—Qu'est-ce qui s'est passé?
—Il a plu tout le temps. Pas un jour de soleil, tu te rends compte!

6. —Salut, Coralie. Comment ça va?
—Oh, pas mal. J'essaie de choisir où je vais aller en vacances cet été.
—Ah oui? Avec qui est-ce que tu pars? Tes parents?
—Non, cette année, je pars avec mes cousins.
—Vous devriez aller faire du camping.
—Bonne idée! Je vais leur en parler.

7. —Tiens, tu es déjà de retour?
—Oui. Je devais revenir fin août, mais j'ai voulu rentrer plus tôt.
—Pourquoi? Ça s'est mal passé chez tes amis?
—On n'a pas arrêté de se disputer! La prochaine fois, je dors à l'hôtel.

8. —Et Martine, qu'est-ce qu'elle fait?
—Elle va aller en Egypte.
—Ouah! Super! Elle part comment? En avion?
—En bateau, je crois.
—Et combien de temps est-ce qu'elle reste?
—Dix jours, je crois.

15   **p. 12**   Answers to Activity 15
1. b   2. a   3. c

1. Salut! C'est Annick. Je viens juste de rentrer de vacances. C'était super, là-bas. Je me suis vraiment bien amusée. C'était mieux que l'Auvergne l'année dernière. Il y avait des tas de choses à faire. Il faisait super beau et je me suis baignée tous les jours. Notre camping était situé à dix minutes de la plage seulement, alors j'en ai vraiment profité. Il faut que je te raconte. Alors, téléphone-moi quand tu rentres.

2. Bonjour, c'est Joséphine. Ça va? Qu'est-ce que tu deviens? Tu peux venir chez moi ce soir? Je veux te

The following scripts are for the Listening Activities found in the *Pupil's Edition*. For Student Response Forms, see *Listening Activities*, pages 3–5. To provide students with additional listening practice, see *Listening Activities*, pages 7–10.

One-Stop Planner CD-ROM

To preview all resources available for this chapter, use the **One-Stop Planner CD-ROM**, Disc 1.

raconter mes vacances à tout prix. J'étais à Sion, une petite ville qui se trouve dans les Alpes. Il y avait des pistes de ski incroyables, là-bas. J'ai pris des cours. Il y avait plusieurs écoles et j'en ai trouvé une pas trop chère. Si tu me voyais sur les pistes maintenant! Bon, je te laisse. A plus!

3. Salut, c'est Pierre. Je t'appelais pour te dire que je t'ai ramené les posters que tu voulais. Paris, c'était pas terrible. Il faisait mauvais et il a même plu plusieurs fois. Bien sûr, il y avait des musées super à visiter, mais je n'étais pas trop en forme, alors je n'ai pas pu faire grand-chose. Appelle-moi quand tu peux. Salut.

Mise en train

24   p. 15

HECTOR   Toi, Julien, tu as pris la quiche à cinq euros... et tu as bu de l'eau. Avec ton plat et ton dessert, ça fait neuf euros. Pauline... le plat du jour à huit euros, les crudités à six euros et un coca... Ça fait seize euros. Et toi, Patricia... tu as pris le potage, la truite, l'assiette de crudités et la crème brûlée. Ça te fait vingt-sept euros. Yasmine, ton presskopf et ta choucroute, ça te fait vingt euros. Moi, j'ai pris le plat du jour, les crudités et un dessert. Alors, pour moi, ça fait dix-huit euros.

Answers to Activity 24
1. Julien: neuf euros (9 €)
2. Pauline: seize euros (16 €)
3. Patricia: vingt-sept euros (27 €)
4. Yasmine: vingt euros (20 €)
5. Hector: dix-huit euros (18 €)

Deuxième étape

26   p. 17

1. —Hum. Fromage ou dessert? Je n'arrive pas à me décider.

2. —Je ne sais pas quoi prendre. Tout a l'air si bon!

3. —Pourquoi tu ne prends pas la tarte aux pommes? Elle est très bonne ici.

4. —J'ai tellement faim. Tout me tente. Qu'est-ce que je pourrais bien prendre?

5. —A mon avis, tu devrais boire plus de jus de fruits. C'est excellent pour la santé.

6. —Voyons... J'hésite entre le poisson et le poulet.

28   p. 18   Answer to Activity 28
b

—Excusez-moi, monsieur, qu'est-ce que vous avez pris comme entrée?

—Comme entrée, attendez... Ah oui, j'ai pris une salade de tomates.

—Et comme plat?

—Du poulet.

—Avec des frites?

—Non, avec des haricots verts. Voyons... mon fromage... et comme dessert, j'ai pris une tarte aux pommes.

—C'est noté. Merci, monsieur.

30   p. 19

1. —Vous avez choisi?

2. —Que voulez-vous comme entrée?

3. —Et comme boisson?

4. —Comment désirez-vous votre viande?

5. —Que voulez-vous comme dessert?

Answers to Activity 30
1. Oui, je vais prendre le steak-frites.
2. Les crudités.
3. De l'eau minérale.
4. A point.
5. La crème caramel, s'il vous plaît.

Mise en pratique

5   p. 29

Answers to Mise en pratique Activity 5
1. Collège Molière
2. Institution Saint-Jean
3. Cité Technique
4. Lycée Camille Sée
5. Collège Berlioz

1. —Qu'est-ce qu'on mange aujourd'hui?
—Des raviolis au gratin et une glace.

2. —Tu as choisi?
—Non, j'hésite entre les spaghettis et le veau aux petits pois.

3. —Quel dilemme! Je n'arrive pas à me décider. La raie ou le coq au riesling?
—Tu devrais prendre le poisson. C'est bon pour la mémoire.

4. —Je voudrais manger du caviar et du filet mignon.
—Pas de chance. Aujourd'hui, c'est spaghettis ou raviolis.

5. —Qu'est-ce que c'est, le filet de lingue avec des blettes?
—Je ne sais pas, mais c'est le plat du jour.

Answers to Activity 26
1. hésite
2. hésite
3. recommande quelque chose
4. hésite
5. recommande quelque chose
6. hésite

Chapitre 1 : France, les régions
Suggested Lesson Plans 50-Minute Schedule

Day 1

CHAPTER OPENER 5 min.
- Present Chapter Objectives, p. 5.
- Geography Link, ATE, p. 4
- Thinking Critically: Comparing and Contrasting and Culture Note, ATE, pp. 4–5

MISE EN TRAIN 40 min.
- Presenting **Mise en train,** ATE, p. 6
- Preteaching Vocabulary and Culture Notes, ATE, pp. 6–7
- Do Activities 1–6, p. 8.
- Language Note, ATE, p. 8
- Do Activity 7, p. 8, orally.

Wrap-Up 5 min.
- Read and discuss **Note culturelle,** p. 8.

Homework Options
Cahier d'activités, Act. 1, p. 1

Day 2

MISE EN TRAIN
Quick Review 5 min.
- Check homework.
- Bell Work, ATE, p. 9

PREMIERE ETAPE
Comment dit-on... ?, p. 9 20 min.
- Presenting **Comment dit-on... ?,** ATE, p. 9
- Play Audio CD for Activity 8, p. 9.
- Cahier d'activités, p. 2, Activity 2
- Have students do Activity 9, p. 9, in pairs.

Comment dit-on... ?, p. 9 20 min.
- Presenting **Comment dit-on... ?,** ATE, p. 9
- Play Audio CD for Activity 10, p. 10.
- Complete Activity 11, p. 10.
- Visual Learners, ATE, p. 10

Wrap-Up, 5 min.
- Have volunteers share their conversations from Visual Learners.

Homework Options
Cahier d'activités, Act. 3, p. 2

Day 3

PREMIERE ETAPE
Quick Review 5 min.
- Check homework.

Comment dit-on... ?, p. 10 20 min.
- Presenting **Comment dit-on... ?,** ATE, p. 10
- Do Activity 12, p. 10.
- Game: **Mémoire,** ATE, p. 11

Grammaire, p. 11 20 min.
- Presenting **Grammaire,** ATE, p. 11
- Play Audio CD for Activity 13, p. 11.
- **Grammaire supplémentaire,** pp. 24–25, Activities 1–3
- Cahier d'activités, p. 4, Activity 6
- Complete Activity 14, p. 12.

Wrap-Up 5 min.
- Read and discuss **De bons conseils,** p. 11.

Homework Options
Travaux pratiques de grammaire, Acts. 1–4, pp. 1–3

Day 4

PREMIERE ETAPE
Quick Review 5 min.
- Check homework.

Comment dit-on... ?, p. 12 15 min
- Presenting **Comment dit-on... ?,** ATE, p. 12
- Play Audio CD for Activity 15, p. 12.
- Cahier d'activités, p. 4, Activity 7

Grammaire, p. 13 25 min.
- Presenting **Grammaire,** ATE, p. 13
- Travaux pratiques de grammaire, pp. 4–5, Activities 5–7
- Complete Activity 16, p. 13.
- Travaux pratiques de grammaire, p. 5, Activity 8
- Have students do Activity 17, p. 13, in pairs.
- Complete Activity 18, p. 13.

Wrap-Up 5 min.
- Have students do Tactile Learners suggestion, p. 13, ATE, using journals from Activity 18.

Homework Options
Study for Quiz 1-1
Grammaire supplémentaire, Acts. 4–5, p. 25
Cahier d'activités, Act. 8, p. 5

Day 5

PREMIERE ETAPE
Quiz 1-1 20 min.
- Administer Quiz 1-1A or 1-1B.

REMISE EN TRAIN 25 min.
- Presenting **Remise en train,** ATE, p. 14
- Preteaching Vocabulary and Teacher Notes, ATE, pp. 14–15
- Do Activities 20–24, pp. 14–15.
- Thinking Critically: Comparing and Contrasting, ATE, p. 14

Wrap-Up 5 min.
- Activity 25, p. 15

Homework Options
Cahier d'activités, Act. 9, p. 6

Day 6

REMISE EN TRAIN
Quick Review 5 min.
- Check homework.

DEUXIEME ETAPE
PANORAMA CULTUREL 10 min.
- Presenting **Panorama Culturel,** ATE, p. 16
- **Qu'en penses-tu?,** p. 16
- Questions, ATE, p. 16

Comment dit-on… ? and Vocabulaire, p. 17 30 min.
- Presenting **Comment dit-on… ?,** ATE, p. 17
- Play Audio CD for Activity 26, p. 17.
- Cahier d'activités, p. 7, Activity 11
- Presenting **Vocabulaire,** ATE, p. 17
- Do Activity 27, p. 18.
- Play Audio CD for Activity 28, p. 18.
- Travaux pratiques de grammaire, pp. 6–7, Activities 9–11
- Have students do Activity 29, p. 18, in pairs.

Wrap-Up 5 min.
- Have volunteers do Activity 29 for the class.

Homework Options
Cahier d'activités, Acts. 12–13, p. 8
Travaux pratiques de grammaire, Acts. 12–13, p. 8

For alternative lesson plans by chapter section, to create your own customized plans, or to preview all resources available for this chapter, use the **One-Stop Planner CD-ROM**, Disc 1.

For additional homework suggestions, see activities accompanied by this symbol throughout the chapter.

Day 7

DEUXIEME ETAPE

Quick Review 5 min.
- Check homework.

Comment dit-on... ?, p. 18 25 min.
- Presenting **Comment dit-on... ?,** ATE, p. 18
- Culture Notes, ATE, p. 18
- Read and discuss **Note culturelle,** p. 18.
- Play Audio CD for Activity 30, p. 19.
- Cahier d'activités, p. 9, Activity 15
- Have students do Activity 31, p. 19, in pairs.
- Complete Activity 32, p. 19.
- Read and discuss **Tu te rappelles?,** p. 19.

Wrap-Up 20 min.
- Teaching Suggestion, ATE, p. 19

Homework Options
Study for Quiz 1-2.
Pupil's Edition, Activity 33, p. 19
Grammaire supplémentaire, Acts. 8–9, p. 27

Day 8

DEUXIEME ETAPE

Quiz 1-2 20 min.
- Administer Quiz 1-2A or 1-2B.

LISONS! 25 min.
- Motivating Activity, ATE, p. 20
- Read and discuss **Stratégie pour lire,** p. 20.
- Do Prereading Activities A–B, p. 20.
- Have students read **Il faut être raisonnable,** pp. 20–22.
- Complete Activities C–M, pp. 20–22.

Wrap-Up 5 min
- Thinking Critically: Comparing and Contrasting, ATE, p. 22

Homework Options
Cahier d'activités, Act. 18, p. 11

Day 9

LISONS!

Quick Review 5 min.
- Check homework.

LISONS! 15 min.
- Do Activities N–Q, p. 22.
- Challenge/Tactile Learners, ATE, p. 22

ECRIVONS! 25 min.
- Discuss the **Stratégie pour écrire,** p. 23, and then allow students to work on their brochures.

Wrap-Up 5 min.
- Allow time for peer review of brochures.

Homework Options
Complete brochures for **Ecrivons!**

Day 10

ECRIVONS!

Quick Review 5 min.
- Allow volunteers to share their brochures with the class.

MISE EN PRATIQUE 40 min.
- Complete Part A of Activity 1, p. 28.
- Have students do Part B of Activity 1, in groups.
- Have students do Activity 2, p. 28, in pairs.
- Do Activity 3, p. 28.
- Language Note, ATE, p. 28
- **A toi de parler,** CD-ROM Tutor, Disc 1

Wrap-Up 5 min.
- Career Path, ATE, p. 28

Homework Options
Cahier d'activités, Acts. 19–21, p. 12

Day 11

MISE EN PRATIQUE

Quick Review 5 min.
- Go over homework.

MISE EN PRATIQUE 40 min.
- Complete Activity 4, p. 29.
- Play Audio CD for Activity 5, p. 29.
- Activities for Communication, Situation Card (global): Interview, pp. 89–90
- **A toi d'écrire,** CD-ROM Tutor, Disc 1

Wrap-Up 5 min.
- Thinking Critically: Analyzing, p. 29

Homework Options
Que sais-je?, p. 30

Day 12

MISE EN PRATIQUE

Quick Review 15 min.
- Go over **Que sais-je?,** p. 30
- Have groups do **Jeu de rôle,** p. 29.

Chapter Review 35 min.
- Review Chapter 1. Choose from **Grammaire supplémentaire,** Grammar Tutor for Students of French, Activities for Communication, Listening Activities, Interactive CD-ROM Tutor, or **Jeux interactifs.**

Homework Options
Study for Chapter 1 Test.

Assessment

Test, Chapter 1 50 min.
- Administer Chapter 1 Test. Select from Testing Program, Alternative Assessment Guide, Test Generator, or Standardized Assessment Tutor.

Chapitre 1 : France, les régions

Suggested Lesson Plans *90-Minute Block Schedule*

Block 1

CHAPTER OPENER 5 min.
- Present Chapter Objectives, p. 5.
- Geography Link and Culture Note, ATE, pp. 4–5
- Thinking Critically: Comparing and Contrasting, ATE, p. 4

MISE EN TRAIN 45 min.
- Preteaching Vocabulary, ATE, p. 6
- Presenting **Mise en train**, ATE, p. 6
- Culture Notes, ATE, p. 7
- Do Activities 1–6, p. 8.
- **Note culturelle**, p. 8

PREMIERE ETAPE
Comment dit-on... ?, p. 9 20 min.
- Presenting **Comment dit-on... ?**, ATE, p. 9
- Play Audio CD for Activity 8, p. 9.
- Do Activity 9, p. 9.

Comment dit-on... ?, p. 9 15 min.
- Presenting **Comment dit-on... ?**, ATE, p. 9
- Play Audio CD for Activity 10, p. 10.
- Do Activity 11, p. 10.

Wrap-Up 5 min.
- Teaching Transparency 1-1, using suggestion #2 on Suggestions for Using Teaching Transparency 1-1

Homework Options
Cahier d'activités, pp. 1–2, Acts. 1–3

Block 2

PREMIERE ETAPE
Quick Review 5 min.
- Ask students questions and have them respond with the appropriate expressions from the **Comment dit-on... ?** boxes on page 9.

Comment dit-on... ?, p. 10 20 min.
- Presenting **Comment dit-on... ?**, ATE, p. 10
- Do Activity 12, p. 10.
- Game: **Mémoire**, ATE, p. 11

Grammaire, p. 11 40 min.
- Presenting **Grammaire**, ATE, p. 11
- Play Audio CD for Activity 13, p. 11.
- Reteaching: Reflexive verbs, ATE, p. 11
- Do Activity 14, p. 12.
- Teaching Transparency 1-1, using suggestion #1 from Vocabulary Practice Using Teaching Transparency 1-1

Comment dit-on... ?, p. 12 20 min.
- Presenting **Comment dit-on... ?**, ATE, p. 12
- Play Audio CD for Activity 15, p. 12.

Wrap-Up 5 min.
- Geography Link, ATE, p. 12

Homework Options
Grammaire supplémentaire, pp. 24–25, Acts. 1–3
Cahier d'activités, pp. 3–4, Acts. 4–7
Travaux pratiques de grammaire, pp. 1–3, Acts. 1–4

Block 3

PREMIERE ETAPE
Quick Review 10 min.
- Write six infinitives on the board. Have students write a sentence for each verb using **passé composé**.

Grammaire, p. 13 30 min.
- Presenting **Grammaire**, ATE, p. 13
- Do Activities 16–17, p. 13.

REMISE EN TRAIN 45 min.
- Presenting **Remise en train**, ATE, p. 14
- Do Activities 20–23, pp. 14–15.
- Do Activity 24, using Teaching Suggestion, ATE, p. 15.

Wrap-Up 5 min.
- Listening Activities, p. 7, Additional Listening Activity 1-1

Homework Options
Have students study for Quiz 1-1.
Grammaire supplémentaire, pp. 25–26, Acts. 4–7
Cahier d'activités, p. 5, Acts. 8–9
Travaux pratiques de grammaire, pp. 4–5, Acts. 5–8

3K   SUGGESTED LESSON PLANS • 90-MINUTE SCHEDULE   CHAPITRE 1

One-Stop Planner CD-ROM

For alternative lesson plans by chapter section, to create your own customized plans, or to preview all resources available for this chapter, use the **One-Stop Planner CD-ROM,** Disc 1.

For additional homework suggestions, see activities accompanied by this symbol throughout the chapter.

Block 4

PREMIERE ETAPE
Quick Review 10 min.
- Activities for Communication, pp. 1–2, Communicative Activity 1-1A and 1-1B

Quiz 1-1 20 min.
- Administer Quiz 1-1A or 1-1B.

DEUXIEME ETAPE
PANORAMA CULTUREL 20 min.
- Presenting **Panorama Culturel,** ATE, p. 16
- Questions, ATE, p. 16
- **Qu'en penses-tu?,** p. 16

Comment dit-on... ?, p. 17 15 min.
- Presenting **Comment dit-on... ?,** ATE, p. 17
- Play Audio CD for Activity 26, p. 17.

Vocabulaire, p. 17 20 min.
- Presenting **Vocabulaire,** ATE, p. 17
- Do Activity 27, p. 18.
- Play Audio CD for Activity 28, p. 18.

Wrap-Up 5 min.
- Listening Activities, p. 8, Additional Listening Activity 1-4

Homework Options
Cahier d'activités, pp. 6–8, Acts. 10–12

Block 5

DEUXIEME ETAPE
Quick Review 10 min.
- Teaching Transparency 1-2, using suggestion #1 on Vocabulary Practice Using Teaching Transparency 1-2

Vocabulaire, p. 17 15 min.
- Building on Previous Skills, ATE, p. 17
- Do Activity 29, p. 18.

Comment dit-on... ?, p. 18 60 min.
- Presenting **Comment dit-on... ?,** ATE, p. 18
- **Note culturelle,** p. 18
- Play Audio CD for Activity 30, p. 19.
- Do Activity 31, p. 19.
- Read and discuss **Tu te rappelles?,** p. 19.
- Do Activity 32, p. 19.
- Teaching Transparency 1-2, using suggestion #3 from Suggestions for Using Teaching Transparency 1-2

Wrap-Up 5 min.
- Culture Notes, ATE, p. 18

Homework Options
Have students study for Quiz 1-2.
Grammaire supplémentaire, p. 27, Acts. 8–9
Cahier d'activités, pp. 8–10, Acts. 13–17
Travaux pratiques de grammaire, pp. 6–8, Acts. 9–13

Block 6

DEUXIEME ETAPE
Quick Review 10 min.
- Activities for Communication, pp. 3–4, Communicative Activities 1-2A and 1-2B

Quiz 1-2 20 min.
- Administer Quiz 1-2A or 1-2B.

LISONS!, pp. 20–22 30 min.
- Motivating Activity, ATE, p. 20
- Do Prereading Activities A–B, p. 20.
- Read **Lisons!,** pp. 20–22.
- Culture Note, ATE, p. 20
- Teaching Suggestions, ATE, p. 21

MISE EN PRATIQUE 30 min.
- Play Audio CD for Activity 5, using Slower Pace, ATE, p. 29.
- Do Activities 2–4, pp. 28–29.

Homework Options
Que sais-je?, p. 31
Interactive CD-ROM Tutor: Games
Study for Chapter 1 Test

Block 7

MISE EN PRATIQUE
Quick Review 10 min.
- Check homework.
- Have groups do **Jeu de rôle,** p. 29.

Chapter Review 35 min.
- Review Chapter 1. Choose from **Grammaire supplémentaire,** Grammar Tutor for Students of French, Activities for Communication, Listening Activities, Interactive CD-ROM Tutor, or **Jeux interactifs.**

Test, Chapter 1 45 min.
- Administer Chapter 1 Test. Select from Testing Program, Alternative Assessment Guide, Test Generator, or Standardized Assessment Tutor.

CHAPITRE 1

 One-Stop Planner CD-ROM

For resource information, see the **One-Stop Planner,** Disc 1.

Pacing Tips
The first and second **étapes** have approximately the same amount of material to cover. In the second **étape,** you might make use of the cultural content in the **Panorama Culturel,** whose topic is closely related to the theme of the **étape** (regional foods). For Lesson Plans and timing suggestions, see pages 3I–3L.

Meeting the Standards

Communication
- Renewing old acquaintances, p. 9
- Inquiring; expressing enthusiasm and dissatisfaction, p. 9
- Exchanging information, p. 10
- Asking and describing what a place was like, p. 12
- Expressing indecision; making recommendations, p. 17
- Ordering and asking for details, p. 18

Cultures
- Culture Notes, pp. 5, 7, 18, 20
- Notes culturelles, pp. 8, 18
- Panorama Culturel, p. 16

Connections
- Community Link, p. 16
- Geography Link, p. 4
- Multicultural Links, pp. 8, 16
- Music Link, p. 16
- Literature Link, p. 22

Comparisons
- Thinking Critically, pp. 4, 14, 22, 29

Communities
- Career Path, p. 28
- De l'école au travail, p. 19

Connections and Comparisons

Geography Link
Have students locate Alsace and Colmar on a map of France (see *Map Transparencies 1* and *2*). Have them draw or trace a map of France on a piece of posterboard and label the different regions. Have them recall what they know about the different regions of France and draw illustrations of the various regional specialties and costumes in the appropriate areas on their maps.

Thinking Critically
Comparing and Contrasting In Levels 1 and 2, students got acquainted with various types of architecture. Have them look at the photo above and compare the houses of Colmar to those found in the Paris region, Touraine, Quebec, Provence, Martinique, and Côte d'Ivoire. You might tell them that Colmar is located in the northeast of France, very close to the German border.

CHAPITRE

1
France, les régions

Objectives

In this chapter you will review and practice how to

Première étape

- **renew old acquaintances**
- **inquire**
- **express enthusiasm and dissatisfaction**
- **exchange information**
- **ask and describe what a place was like**

Deuxième étape

- **express indecision**
- **make recommendations**
- **order and ask for details**

internet

ADRESSE: go.hrw.com
MOT-CLE: WA3 FRANCOPHONE
EUROPE-1

◀ **La belle ville alsacienne de Colmar**

CHAPITRE 1

Focusing on Outcomes

Have students read the list of objectives and tell in what situations they might use each one. Then, have them suggest words and expressions they already know in French to accomplish these objectives. You may want to use the video to support the objectives.

NOTE: The self-check activities in **Que sais-je?** on page 30 help students assess their achievement of the objectives.

Teacher Note

Some activities suggested in the *Annotated Teacher's Edition* ask students to contact various people, businesses, and organizations in the community. Before assigning these activities, it is advisable to request parental permission. In some cases, you may also want to obtain permission from the parties the students will be asked to contact.

Cultures and Communities

Culture Note

This photo shows Colmar's **Quai de la Poissonnerie,** with its half-timbered houses decorated with multicolored flowers. Such houses are typical of Alsace, Normandy, Champagne, and the Basque country. In this construction, the areas in between the timbers are filled with *wattle* and *daub,* or interwoven poles and twigs covered with plaster or clay.

Colmar is known as **petite Venise** because of its picturesque waterways. The canals that go through the heart of the city were used as early as the sixteenth century for transporting and selling goods. The historic district of Colmar remains to this day the city's business district, as well as its cultural center. Nowadays, Colmar hosts various cultural events, such as a music festival, and international businesses.

Teaching Resources
pp. 6–8

PRINT
▸ Lesson Planner, p. 2
▸ Video Guide, pp. 4, 6
▸ Cahier d'activités, p. 1

MEDIA
▸ One-Stop Planner
▸ Video Program
Camille et compagnie
Videocassette 1, 06:26–13:46
Videocassette 5 (captioned version), 00:22–07:42
▸ Audio Compact Discs, CD 1, Tr. 1

Presenting
Mise en train

Have students look at the photos to determine what the conversation is about. Then, play the audio recording and have them follow along in their books. After each person's account of his or her vacation, ask a few comprehension questions, such as **Où est-ce qu'il/elle a passé les vacances? Qu'est-ce qu'il/elle a fait?**

CD 1 Tr. 1

> **Stratégie pour comprendre**
> Take a quick look at the map of France and at the photos presented on the map. What do you think the theme of the episode is? Now skim the dialogue and find names of places that you see on the map. Judging by where those places are, can you guess what types of activities the young people have been doing there?

1 Hector   Salut, les copains. Ça fait plaisir de vous revoir.

Pauline   Bonjour. J'ai l'impression que ça fait une éternité qu'on ne s'est pas vus.

Julien   Dis donc, Patricia, tu as l'air en forme. Ça te réussit, les vacances.

Patricia   Toi aussi, tu es bien bronzé. C'était bien, Biarritz?

Julien   Oui, super! Il a fait un temps magnifique.

Pauline   Eh, on pourrait aussi bien parler assis.

Yasmine   Alors, on se met où?

Hector   Là, non? Il y a une table pour cinq.

2 Hector   Alors, Yasmine, c'était bien, tes vacances?

Yasmine   Oui, pas mal. J'ai passé une semaine à Paris avec mes parents. J'ai visité la tour Eiffel, Notre-Dame, le Louvre, bref, tous les monuments parisiens! Il a fait tellement chaud et lourd qu'à la fin, j'en avais marre des visites. Mais je ne connaissais pas Paris et je suis ravie d'y être allée.

Nord-Pas-de-Calais

Haute-Normandie

Basse-Normandie

Paris

Bretagne

Pays de la Loire

Chenonceaux

Centre

Poitou-Charentes

Limousin

Aquitaine

Biarritz

Languedoc-Roussillon

Midi-Pyrénées

PARIS   MUSÉE DU LOUVRE

Preteaching Vocabulary

Using Prior Knowledge
Point out that in this story, the young people are telling each other where they went and what they did on their summer vacation. Ask students to recall expressions they already know for talking about vacations (**Ça s'est bien passé? Comment se sont passées tes vacances? Excellent!**). Form several groups and ask each group to find a specific category of expressions. One group should find

phrases for inquiring about vacations or expressing enthusiasm and dissatisfaction about vacations (**C'était bien, tes vacances? Oui, pas mal.**); another group must find expressions about the sports characters did on their vacation (**J'ai fait de la planche à voile.**). You might assign the same category to several groups. The groups with the highest number of expressions win!

3 Hector Et toi, Julien, qu'est-ce que tu as fait?

Julien En juillet, je suis allé dans le sud-ouest, à Biarritz, au bord de la mer. Il a fait un temps superbe. Je me suis baigné tous les jours et j'ai fait de la planche à voile. Au mois d'août, je suis allé camper avec des copains en Lozère. On a fait de la randonnée. On a dormi à la belle étoile. C'était génial. C'est magnifique, la Lozère.

Ile-de-France
Picardie

Champagne-Ardenne

Lorraine

4 Hector Et toi, Patricia? Tu as passé de bonnes vacances?

Patricia Excellentes. Moi, je suis restée à Colmar. Je me suis bien amusée. Une de mes cousines est venue. Nous sommes allées au cinéma. Nous avons fait de l'équitation et nous sommes allées à la piscine. C'était sympa. Fin août, j'ai pris le train pour aller passer quelques jours chez mes grands-parents à Strasbourg.

Strasbourg ●

Alsace

Franche-Comté

Bourgogne

5 Hector Toi aussi, tu es restée ici, Pauline?

Pauline Non, en juillet, je suis allée me promener en voiture avec mes parents. Nous avons visité les châteaux de la Loire, puis nous sommes allés au Futuroscope à Poitiers. C'était pas mal.

Hector Et au mois d'août?

Pauline Oh là là, c'était l'horreur! Il a plu tout le temps. Tous mes copains étaient partis. Je suis restée à la maison. J'ai lu et j'ai regardé la télé. A part ça, je n'ai rien fait.

Auvergne

Rhône-Alpes

Morzine

Provence-Alpes-Côte d'Azur

6 Pauline Qu'est-ce que tu as fait, Hector?

Hector Je suis parti trois semaines en camp de vacances à Morzine, en Savoie. C'était super. Nous avons fait du vélo et du rafting. J'ai adoré. Après, en août, je suis allé chez mon oncle. Il a une ferme à Saint-Quentin, au nord-est de Paris. C'était chouette. Je l'ai aidé pour la moisson. Je me suis occupé des animaux. J'ai repeint le garage. Je ne me suis pas ennuyé une seconde!

Using the Captioned Video

Culture Notes

• **Biarritz,** in southwestern France, is a fashionable beach resort. Known as "the queen of resorts and the resort of kings," Biarritz has boasted visits by Queen Victoria, Edward VII, and Alfonse XIII of Spain.

• The controversial modern glass pyramid in the Louvre courtyard was built in the late 1980s by the Chinese-American architect I. M. Pei. Some feel that its modern style clashes with the Louvre's classic construction.

• The **Futuroscope** is a cinematic theme park in Poitiers that offers a circular-screen theater, 3-D movies, a hemispherical theater, a large movie screen (**le kinémax**), and a computerized audiovisual spectacle shown on ten screens.

• **Savoie,** on the Italian border, and **Haute-Savoie,** on the Swiss border, are popular ski areas. Their snow-capped mountains are some of the highest peaks in Europe.

Camille et compagnie

You may choose to show students Episode 1: *Les Retrouvailles* now or wait until later in the chapter. In the video, Camille is working at her parents' restaurant. Her friend Max walks into the restaurant in disguise and pretends to be a difficult customer. When Camille starts to get impatient, Max reveals his identity. Another friend of Camille's, Sophie, arrives and they all talk about their summer vacation. A customer sits at the next table and acts much like Max at the beginning of the episode.

Language Note

Sabot is the root of the French word **sabotage,** which is also used in English. The word was used in the nineteenth century when factory workers protested poor working conditions by throwing their wooden shoes **(sabots)** into the machinery. It came to mean deliberately poor workmanship or intentional damage to equipment.

Multicultural Link

Have students investigate the traditional clothing, music, food, and dances of different ethnic groups around the world. As an added challenge, you might have them find out why particular clothing is worn or on what occasions special food is served.

Answers

1
1. in a restaurant
2. fall; They are just back from summer vacation.
3. all summer
4. Yasmine: Paris; Julien: Biarritz et Lozère; Patricia: Colmar et Strasbourg; Pauline: les châteaux de la Loire et le Futuroscope à Poitiers; Hector: Morzine et Saint-Quentin
5. *Possible answers:*
   sightseeing, swimming, windsurfing, camping, hiking, going to the movies, horseback riding, visiting relatives, reading, watching TV, biking, rafting, helping with the harvest, repainting the garage

6
1. Ça fait plaisir de vous revoir. Ça fait une éternité qu'on ne s'est pas vus.
2. ... tu as l'air en forme. Ça te réussit, les vacances. ... tu es bien bronzé.
3. Eh, on pourrait aussi bien parler assis.
4. ... j'en avais marre des visites. C'était l'horreur.
5. Je suis ravie d'y être allée. Je me suis bien amusée. Je ne me suis pas ennuyé une seconde! C'était génial/sympa/pas mal/super.

1 **Tu as compris?** See answers below.

1. Où est-ce que ces jeunes se réunissent?
2. A quelle époque de l'année ils se réunissent? Comment tu le sais?
3. Depuis quand ils ne se sont pas vus?
4. Où est-ce que ces jeunes sont allés en vacances?
5. A quelles activités est-ce qu'ils ont participé?

These activities check for comprehension only. Students should not yet be expected to produce language modeled in **Mise en train.**

2 **Vrai ou faux?**

1. C'était la première fois que Yasmine visitait Paris.   vrai
2. Pendant l'été, Julien a fait du camping.   vrai
3. Patricia est partie en camp de vacances.   faux
4. Pendant ses vacances, Pauline a voyagé avec ses parents.   vrai
5. L'oncle d'Hector habite à Morzine.   faux

3 **C'est qui?**

Parmi les jeunes dans *Les Retrouvailles,* qui...

1. ne s'est pas amusé(e) pendant le mois d'août?   Pauline
2. a visité des monuments pendant ses vacances?   Yasmine
3. est allé(e) dans une ferme pendant ses vacances?   Hector
4. aime faire du camping?   Julien
5. aime faire de l'équitation?   Patricia

4 **Content ou pas content?**

Qui est très content(e) de ses vacances?

Qui est moins content(e)?

Très content(e): Julien, Patricia, Hector
Moins content(e): Yasmine, Pauline

5 **Qu'est-ce qu'on peut y faire?**

D'après *Les Retrouvailles,* où est-ce qu'on peut...

1. se baigner dans l'océan?   à Biarritz
2. visiter des musées?   à Paris   3. à Morzine
3. trouver des rivières avec des torrents?
4. voir de magnifiques châteaux?
   dans la vallée de la Loire

6 **Cherche les expressions**

What do the young people in *Les Retrouvailles* say to . . .   See answers below.

1. greet one another after a long absence?
2. compliment someone?
3. make a suggestion?
4. express dissatisfaction with a vacation?
5. express enthusiasm for a vacation?

7 **Et maintenant, à toi**

Regarde les cartes postales aux pages 6 et 7. Où est-ce que tu aimerais aller en vacances? Pourquoi?

Note culturelle

Chaque région de France a ses traditions. Il y a des traditions qu'on observe tous les jours. D'autres aspects traditionnels, comme les vêtements et les danses folkloriques, sont réservées à des occasions spéciales comme les festivals. Le costume traditionnel des femmes se compose souvent d'une jupe et d'une blouse, ou d'une robe de tissu régional avec un tablier, un châle ou un col en dentelle et une coiffe. **La coiffe bretonne** est particulièrement célèbre. Elle est haute et ornée de dentelle. Le costume d'homme se compose généralement d'un pantalon décoré, d'une chemise blanche et d'un gilet. Les chaussures traditionnelles des Bretons sont en bois. On les appelle des **sabots.**

Bretagne

Comprehension Check

Additional Practice

2 For each true statement, have students cite proof from the text.

4 Have students tell whether they would feel the same or differently if they had taken the same vacations as the French teenagers.

Building on Previous Skills

6 List on the board or on a transparency the expressions students find. Then, have them recall previously learned expressions that accomplish the same purposes.

Première étape

Objectives Renewing old acquaintances; inquiring; expressing enthusiasm and dissatisfaction; exchanging information; asking and describing what a place was like

WA3 FRANCOPHONE
EUROPE-1

Comment dit-on...?

Renewing old acquaintances

To greet someone you haven't seen recently:

Ça fait longtemps qu'on ne s'est pas vu(e)s. *It's been a long time since we've seen each other.*
Je suis content(e) de te revoir. *I'm glad to see you again.*
Qu'est-ce que tu deviens? *What's going on with you?*
Quoi de neuf? *What's new?*

To respond:

Ça fait deux mois. *It's been . . .*
Depuis l'hiver. *Since . . .*

Moi aussi.

Toujours la même chose! *Same old thing!*

Rien (de spécial). *Nothing (special).*

> Cahier d'activités, p. 2, Act. 2

---

8 Ça fait combien de temps? See scripts on p. 3G.

Ecoutons Ecoute les dialogues et choisis la phrase qui correspond à chaque dialogue. Ils ne se sont pas vus depuis: 1. b   2. a   3. d

a. trois mois   **b.** deux ans   **c.** janvier   **d.** le mois de juin

CD1 Tr. 2

9 Il y a belle lurette... !

Parlons Ça fait longtemps que tu n'as pas vu un(e) de tes ami(e)s. Qu'est-ce que vous vous dites? Avec ton/ta camarade, crée une conversation.

Comment dit-on...?

Inquiring; expressing enthusiasm and dissatisfaction

To inquire about someone's trip or vacation:

C'était comment, tes vacances?
Ça s'est bien passé?

Comment ça s'est passé?
Tu t'es bien amusé(e)?

To express enthusiasm:

C'était chouette!
Ça s'est très bien passé.
Super!
Je me suis beaucoup amusé(e).
   I had a lot of fun.

To express dissatisfaction:

C'était pas terrible.
Ça ne s'est pas très bien passé.
Pas trop bien. *Not too good/well.*
Je me suis ennuyé(e). *I was bored.*

> Cahier d'activités, p. 2, Act. 3

Communication for All Students

Language Notes

• Remind students to use **à** with most cities, **en** with feminine countries, and **au** with masculine countries. **En** Arles is one exception.

• Remind students that to form a question, they can put a question word at the beginning (using

est-ce que) or the end of a statement, or use intonation. (**Tu es parti(e) quand?**) To ask a yes-no question, students can also put **est-ce que** before a statement. (**Est-ce que tu es parti(e) à midi?**)

Teaching Resources
pp. 9–13

PRINT
▶ Lesson Planner, p. 3
▶ Listening Activities, pp. 3–4, 7–8
▶ Activities for Communication, pp. 1–2, 51, 53, 89–90
▶ Travaux pratiques de grammaire, pp. 1–5
▶ Grammar Tutor for Students of French, Chapter 1
▶ Cahier d'activités, pp. 2–5
▶ Testing Program, pp. 1–4
▶ Alternative Assessment Guide, p. 30
▶ Student Make-Up Assignments, Chapter 1

MEDIA
▶ One-Stop Planner
▶ Audio Compact Discs, CD 1, Trs. 2–5, 16, 21–23
▶ Teaching Transparencies: 1-1; **Grammaire supplémentaire** Answers; Travaux pratiques de grammaire Answers
▶ Interactive CD-ROM Tutor, Disc 1

   Bell Work

Have students choose a location from *Les Retrouvailles* and list two activities available there.

Presenting
Comment dit-on... ?

• Create a skit in which two people, who haven't seen each other in a long time, meet. Use the new expressions with gestures and facial expressions to convey meaning.

• Tell students about an imaginary vacation, miming or showing pictures of activities. Express enthusiasm about some activities and boredom about others, using facial expressions.

Teaching Resources
pp. 9–13

PRINT
▶ Lesson Planner, p. 3
▶ Listening Activities, pp. 3–4, 7–8
▶ Activities for Communication, pp. 1–2, 51, 53, 89–90
▶ Travaux pratiques de grammaire, pp. 1–5
▶ Grammar Tutor for Students of French, Chapter 1
▶ Cahier d'activités, pp. 2–5
▶ Testing Program, pp. 1–4
▶ Alternative Assessment Guide, p. 30
▶ Student Make-Up Assignments, Chapter 1

MEDIA
▶ One-Stop Planner
▶ Audio Compact Discs, CD 1, Trs. 2–5, 16, 21–23
▶ Teaching Transparencies: 1-1; **Grammaire supplémentaire** Answers; Travaux pratiques de grammaire Answers
▶ Interactive CD-ROM Tutor, Disc 1

Presenting
Comment dit-on... ?

Act out one side of a phone conversation in which a friend asks you about a trip. Repeat your friend's questions. Then answer, giving details about your vacation.

Possible answers

11 **a.** —Comment ça s'est passé, ton week-end?
   —Ça ne s'est pas très bien passé. J'ai eu un accident.
b. —C'était comment, ton week-end?
   —Super!
c. —C'était comment, tes vacances?
   —C'était pas terrible. Je me suis ennuyé.
d. —Comment ça s'est passé, le week-end au ski?
   —Pas trop bien. Je me suis cassé le bras.

---

10 **C'était comment, tes vacances?** See scripts and answers on p. 3G.

Ecoutons Ecoute ces dialogues. Est-ce que ces personnes sont contentes ou non?
CD 1 Tr. 3

11 **Qu'est-ce qu'ils disent?**

Parlons/Ecrivons Christophe téléphone à ses amis pour savoir comment leur week-end s'est passé. Utilise les expressions dans **Comment dit-on...?,** à la page 9, pour recréer leurs conversations. See answers below.

a.   b.   c.   d.

Comment dit-on...?

Exchanging information

To ask about someone's vacation:

Est-ce que tu es resté(e) ici?
Did you stay here?

Quand est-ce que tu y es allé(e)?

Avec qui est-ce que tu y es allé(e)?

Tu es parti(e) comment?
How did you get there?
Quel temps est-ce qu'il a fait?

Où est-ce que tu as dormi?

To answer:

Oui, je suis resté(e) ici **tout le temps.**
   . . . the whole time.
Non, je suis parti(e) dix jours en août.
   No, I went away for . . .
J'y suis allé(e) début/fin juillet.
   I went there at the beginning/end of . . .
J'y suis allé(e) seul(e)/avec mes parents.
   I went alone/with . . .
Je suis parti(e) en train. *I went by . . .*

Il a fait un temps magnifique.
   The weather was . . .
Il a plu. *It rained.*
A l'hôtel. *In the hotel.*

Cahier d'activités, p. 3, Act. 5

12 **Cherche la bonne réponse**

Lisons Choisis la bonne réponse à chaque question.

1. Où est-ce que tu es allé?
2. Quand est-ce que tu y es allé?
3. Avec qui est-ce que tu y es allé?
4. Vous êtes partis comment?
5. Quel temps est-ce qu'il a fait?

a. Super beau! 5
b. Avec un groupe de jeunes. 3
c. Fin août. 2
d. Dans les Alpes. 1
e. En train. 4

Communication for All Students

Kinesthetic Learners

10 Students might respond by writing plus or minus signs, or by making thumbs-up or thumbs-down gestures.

Auditory Learners

11 Create and read aloud conversations suggested by the illustrations and have students match them to the illustrations.

Visual Learners

11 Have students draw illustrations of a good or bad situation, exchange drawings, and write conversations based on them.

The *passé composé*

To tell what happened in the past, you use the **passé composé**. Remember that the passé composé has two parts: a present-tense form of a helping verb, **avoir** or **être**, and the past participle of the main verb.

You use **avoir** as the helping verb with most French verbs.

Vous **avez acheté** des souvenirs.

Other verbs require **être** as their helping verb. These include . . .

1. verbs that indicate motion: **aller, sortir, partir, retourner, venir, arriver, entrer, monter, descendre, tomber, rentrer,** and **revenir.**

   Je **suis tombé(e).**

2. verbs that indicate a state or condition, like **mourir, naître,** and **rester.**

   Tu **es resté(e)** jusqu'à dix heures.

3. all reflexive verbs, like **se lever, s'amuser, se laver,** and **se promener.**

   Elle **s'est amusée** avec ses amis.

Do you remember how to form the past participle of regular verbs?

-er verbs	drop **-er** from the infinitive and add **-é:** emporter → emport → **emporté**
-ir verbs	drop **-ir** from the infinitive and add **-i:** finir → fin → **fini**
-re verbs	drop **-re** from the infinitive and add **-u:** perdre → perd → **perdu**

As you already know, some verbs have irregular past participles. You use **avoir** as the helping verb with those listed here.

dire	**dit**	prendre	**pris**	voir	**vu**	boire	**bu**
écrire	**écrit**	être	**été**	lire	**lu**	pouvoir	**pu**
mettre	**mis**	faire	**fait**	avoir	**eu**	vouloir	**voulu**

Remember that when you use **être** as the helping verb, the past participle agrees in gender and number with the subject, unless it is followed by a direct object.

Elle **s'est lavée.** *but* Elle **s'est lavé** les cheveux.

Grammaire supplémentaire, pp. 24–25, Act. 1–3

Cahier d'activités, p. 4, Act. 6

Travaux pratiques de grammaire, pp. 1–3, Act. 1–4

See scripts and answers on p. 3G.

13 Grammaire en contexte

Ecoutons Ecoute ces gens qui parlent de leurs vacances. Est-ce qu'ils parlent du passé ou du futur?

CD 1 Tr. 4

DE BONS CONSEILS

A good way to get ready for this year of French study is to review and practice what you learned before.

1. Use the flash cards you've made to review vocabulary and expressions. Pay close attention to those you use the most.
2. Look at the charts in the back of this book to refresh your memory on important grammar points.
3. With a classmate, practice short conversations on the topics you learned about last year.

Communication for All Students

Game

Mémoire Draw a 12-square grid on a transparency. Write questions from **Comment dit-on... ?** in some of the squares and their answers in others. Cover the squares. Form teams. The first player uncovers two of the squares. If the exposed squares reveal a question and its answer, the player earns a point for the team. If not, he or she covers the squares again, and the next team takes a turn.

Building on Previous Skills

De bons conseils You might suggest that students find and organize old vocabulary cards, go over last year's portfolio, and view posters or projects from last year's class. You might display posters from last year's projects.

Teaching Resources
pp. 9–13

PRINT
▸ Lesson Planner, p. 3
▸ Listening Activities, pp. 3–4, 7–8
▸ Activities for Communication, pp. 1–2, 51, 53, 89–90
▸ Travaux pratiques de grammaire, pp. 1–5
▸ Grammar Tutor for Students of French, Chapter 1
▸ Cahier d'activités, pp. 2–5
▸ Testing Program, pp. 1–4
▸ Alternative Assessment Guide, p. 30
▸ Student Make-Up Assignments, Chapter 1

MEDIA
▸ One-Stop Planner
▸ Audio Compact Discs, CD 1, Trs. 2–5, 16, 21–23
▸ Teaching Transparencies: 1-1; **Grammaire supplémentaire** Answers; Travaux pratiques de grammaire Answers
▸ Interactive CD-ROM Tutor, Disc 1

Presenting
Comment dit-on... ?

Draw five columns on the board and write one of the following questions as a head for each column: **Où ça se trouve?/Qu'est-ce qu'il y avait à faire là-bas?/Qu'est-ce qu'il y avait à voir?/C'était comment?/Quel temps il a fait?** After modeling answers to the questions you wrote on the board, have students supply answers based on a place they visited.

Answers
14
1. sont partis
2. avons pris
3. est arrivées
4. a fait
5. ont dormi
6. a préféré
7. est allées
8. s'est baignées
9. a joué
10. a visité
11. ai vu
12. avons rencontré

---

14 Grammaire en contexte

Lisons/Ecrivons Complète la carte postale que ton amie Elodie t'a envoyée avec le passé composé des verbes entre parenthèses. See answers below.

> Une petite carte postale pour te dire bonjour de Cannes où nous passons des vacances super. Mes parents ___1___ (partir) en voiture début juillet, mais ma sœur et moi, nous ___2___ (prendre) le train. On ___3___ (arriver) le 16 juillet. Il ___4___ (faire) un temps magnifique toute la semaine. Mes parents ___5___ (dormir) chez nos amis. Nous, on ___6___ (préférer) faire du camping. Cette semaine, Sophie et moi, on ___7___ (aller) à la plage tous les jours. On ___8___ (se baigner) et on ___9___ (jouer) au volley. Hier, on ___10___ (visiter) le musée maritime. J' ___11___ (voir) des bateaux superbes. Et nous ___12___ (rencontrer) des garçons sympas. Et toi, qu'est-ce que tu fais? A bientôt.
>
> Elodie

Comment dit-on...?

Asking and describing what a place was like

To ask what a place was like:

Où se trouve la Côte d'Azur?

Qu'est-ce qu'il y avait à voir?
What was there to see?
Qu'est-ce qu'il y avait à faire?
What was there to do?
Il y avait des gens sympas?
C'était comment?

Il faisait beau/chaud?
Was the weather . . . ?

To describe what a place was like:

La Côte d'Azur **se trouve** au bord de la Méditerranée.
La Côte d'Azur **est située** dans le sud de la France. . . . *is located . . .*
Il y avait de belles plages.

Il y avait des tas de choses à faire.

Il y avait beaucoup de jeunes.
C'était génial/mieux que Paris/**super.**
Il faisait beau.
The weather was . . .

Cahier d'activités, p. 4, Act. 7

15 Ils sont allés où? See scripts on p. 3G.

CD1 Tr. 5

Ecoutons Tes amis Annick, Joséphine et Pierre viennent juste de rentrer de vacances. Ils t'ont laissé des messages sur ton répondeur. Ecoute leurs messages et choisis l'endroit où chaque personne est allée.

Joséphine
a.

Annick
b.

Pierre
c.

Connections and Comparisons

Geography Link

Bring a world map to class. After presenting **Comment dit-on... ?** place the map on the board and ask students where various countries and regions are. You might just use a map of the United States and ask them to name the states where various cities are located. (**Où se trouve Orlando? / Orlando se trouve en Floride.**) Or you might have students review parts of the French-speaking world they studied in Levels 1 and 2. (**Où se trouve Québec? / Québec se trouve au Canada.**) You might expand on the activity by having students imagine that they just spent their vacation at the locations you mention. Use other questions presented in **Comment dit-on... ?** to ask students what there was to see and do, what the weather was like, etc.

Grammaire

The *imparfait*

To describe what things used to be like or to talk about repeated actions in the past, you use the imperfect tense. To form the **imparfait,** use the **nous** form of the verb in the present tense without **-ons** (partir → nous **partons** → part-). Add the following endings to the stem: **-ais, -ais, -ait, -ions, -iez,** and **-aient.**

Je **partais** vers sept heures.   Nous **allions** à la montagne tous les ans.

To describe things in the past, you will often need to use the imperfect forms of **avoir** and **être.** Just as for other verbs, you add the imperfect endings to the stems. The stem of **avoir** is **av-.**

Tu **avais** les cheveux blonds.

Remember that **être** has the irregular stem **ét-.**

Ils **étaient** en vacances au bord de la mer.

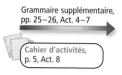

Grammaire supplémentaire, pp. 25–26, Act. 4–7

Cahier d'activités, p. 5, Act. 8

Travaux pratiques de grammaire, pp. 4–5, Act. 5–8

16 ### Grammaire en contexte

Lisons/Ecrivons Qu'est-ce que Cédric faisait pendant les vacances quand il était plus jeune? Complète son journal avec des verbes à l'imparfait.   *See answers below.*

| aller | nager | faire | partir | s'ennuyer | rester | dormir | être | danser | se promener |

Quand j'étais petit, mes parents et moi, nous ___1___ à la Martinique tous les ans pour rendre visite à mes grands-parents. On ___2___ en avion de l'aéroport de Paris. On ___3___ là-bas tout l'été. J'adorais aller à la Martinique parce que là-bas, il ___4___ toujours beau! Mes parents dormaient chez mes grands-parents, mais moi, je ___5___ dans une tente dans le jardin. C'___6___ chouette! Nous ___7___ sur la plage le matin. L'après-midi, moi, je ___8___ dans la mer. Et le soir, on ___9___ le zouk. On faisait beaucoup de choses et on ne ___10___ jamais. C'était vraiment bien, les vacances à la Martinique.

17 ### Qu'est-ce que tu as fait?

Parlons Demande à ton/ta camarade ce qu'il/elle a fait pendant ses vacances. Puis, changez de rôle.

18 ### Mon journal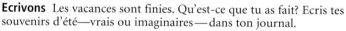

Ecrivons Les vacances sont finies. Qu'est-ce que tu as fait? Ecris tes souvenirs d'été—vrais ou imaginaires—dans ton journal.

Si tu as oublié — sports — *va à la page R18.*

19 ### Interview

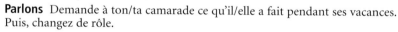

a. Parlons Avec un(e) camarade, pense à une personne célèbre. Il/Elle rentre de vacances. Tu es journaliste et tu l'interviewes sur ses vacances. Tu es payé(e) à la ligne, donc pose beaucoup de questions pour écrire ton article. Jouez cette scène et changez de rôle.

b. Ecrivons Ecris ton article. Avant publication, tu le soumets à l'éditeur (ton/ta camarade), qui en fait la critique et fait quelques petites corrections, si nécessaire.

Communication for All Students

Tactile Learners

In groups of four or five, have each student write a sentence on a piece of paper, describing an imaginary past event or person, using the **imparfait.** Each student should fold the piece of paper to hide his or her sentence, and pass it to the next person, who adds a sentence, folds the paper, and passes it on. When the piece of paper has been passed around the group a couple of times, ask for a volunteer in each group to read the entire description. You might want to give each group a specific topic or context to write about (**un écrivain célèbre, ce que tu faisais quand tu étais enfant, les rues d'une ville ancienne).**

Presenting Grammaire

The imparfait Prepare two sets of large index cards. On one set, write the subject pronouns and on the other, the various **imparfait** forms of a verb of your choice. Tape the second set of cards to the board in random order. Ask students if they recognize this verb tense. Go over the **Grammaire** with students. Then, show the cards with the subject pronouns one at a time, and have students come to the board and place each card next to the appropriate verb form.

Teacher Note
To respect students' privacy, you might give an alternate assignment in which students may substitute fictitious information.

Assess
▸ Testing Program, pp. 1–4
  Quiz 1-1A, Quiz 1-1B,
  Audio CD 1, Tr. 16

▸ Student Make-Up Assignments
  Chapter 1, Alternative Quiz

▸ Alternative Assessment Guide,
  p. 30

Answers
16
1. allions
2. partait
3. restait
4. faisait
5. dormais
6. était
7. nous promenions
8. nageais
9. dansait
10. s'ennuyait

Teaching Resources
pp. 14–15

PRINT
▸ Lesson Planner, p. 4
▸ Video Guide, pp. 4, 6
▸ Cahier d'activités, p. 6

MEDIA
▸ One-Stop Planner
▸ Video Program
▸ **Camille et compagnie**
   Videocassette 1, 06:26–13:46
   Videocassette 5 (captioned version), 00:22–07:42
▸ Audio Compact Discs, CD 1, Tr. 6

Presenting
Remise en train

Before playing the audio recording, have students read the questions in Activity 20 and scan the menu and dialogue for words related to food. Then, play the recording, pausing after each person orders to ask **Qu'est-ce qu'il/elle va prendre?**

Thinking Critically
Comparing and Contrasting
Have students compare what the teenagers in *Bon appétit!* ordered with what they might order in an American restaurant. Have them compare how the food is ordered as well.

Remise en train · *Bon appétit!*

CD 1 Tr. 6

Regarde la carte. Est-ce que tu reconnais certains de ces plats? Lesquels?

20 **Tu as compris?**
1. De quoi les jeunes parlent dans *Bon appétit!?* what to order
2. Qui a des difficultés à prendre une décision? Patricia
3. Qu'est-ce que les jeunes demandent à la serveuse? bread and water
4. Pourquoi est-ce qu'ils ne peuvent pas diviser l'addition de façon égale? Pauline and Yasmine didn't have dessert.

21 **Vrai ou faux?**
1. D'habitude, Yasmine prend du poulet et des frites. vrai
2. Pauline n'a jamais mangé de presskopf. faux
3. Hector a pris le plat du jour. vrai
4. Tout le monde a pris un dessert. faux
These activities check for comprehension only. Students should not yet be expected to produce language modeled in **Remise en train**.

22 **Entrée ou fromage?**
Regarde la carte de L'Auberge et dis si ces plats sont des entrées, des poissons, des viandes ou des desserts.

Preteaching Vocabulary

Recognizing Cognates
Have students look at the menu on this page and identify words that are used in English or words that look like those used in English (**entrée, menu, spécialités, desserts, omelette, quiche, sauce, vinaigrette, salade, sorbet, café, crème brûlée**). You might ask them why they think so many French words are used in English to describe food and food-related products. (French cuisine has had a strong influence on the Western world for centuries.) Make students aware that just because French words and English words look alike, they don't necessarily mean the same thing. There are false cognates (**faux amis** in French). Have student guess the **faux ami** on the menu (**entrée**), based on its location (**entrée** comes first on the menu, and means *appetizer*).

Midi et quart...

Patricia	Qu'est-ce que vous allez prendre? Je n'arrive pas à me décider.
Julien	Moi non plus, tout me tente. Comme entrée, j'hésite entre une bouchée à la reine et de la quiche. Et toi, Yasmine?
Yasmine	Aucune idée. Je ne sais pas quoi prendre.
Julien	Toi, évidemment, si tu n'as pas ton poulet rôti et tes frites, tu préfères mourir de faim.
Yasmine	Oh, ça suffit, les sarcasmes.
Pauline	Essaie le presskopf. C'est un plat alsacien délicieux.
La serveuse	Vous avez décidé?
Hector	Non, pas encore. Un instant, s'il vous plaît.

Midi vingt-cinq...

La serveuse	Vous avez choisi, maintenant?
Pauline	Oui, je crois. Comme entrée, je vais prendre l'assiette de crudités. Et ensuite, le plat du jour.
Hector	Moi aussi, la même chose.
Patricia	Je voudrais la choucroute... ou, non, donnez-moi plutôt l'entrecôte grillée. Ou bien...

Julien	Bon, tu te décides!
Patricia	OK, OK! Je vais prendre... Ah, non! Voilà, j'ai trouvé! La truite!

Une heure...

Pauline	Alors, il est comment, ton presskopf?
Yasmine	Pas mal... Euh, passe-moi le sel, s'il te plaît. Et la moutarde.
Patricia	Madame, est-ce qu'on pourrait avoir du pain, s'il vous plaît? Ah! Et une carafe d'eau!
La serveuse	Oui, tout de suite.

Deux heures et quart...

Patricia	Bon, on y va?
Hector	D'accord... Madame? L'addition, s'il vous plaît?
La serveuse	Oui, tout de suite... Voilà.
Julien	Ça fait combien?
Hector	90 €. Divisé par cinq, ça fait... 18 € par personne.
Pauline	Eh, moi, j'ai pas pris de dessert! Et Yasmine non plus!
Hector	C'est vrai, tu as raison. Bon, eh bien, chacun paie sa part.

Cahier d'activités, p. 6, Act. 10

---

23 **Cherche les expressions**

Look back at *Bon appétit!* to find ways to . . .   See answers below.

1. ask someone what he or she is going to have.
2. express indecision.
3. tell what you're going to have.
4. ask someone to pass you something.
5. ask a server to bring you something.
6. ask how much the check is.

24 **Ça fait combien?**   See scripts and answers on p. 3H.

CD 1 Tr. 7

Ecoutons Ecoute le dialogue. Combien est-ce que chaque personne doit payer?

Julien	Pauline	Hector
	Yasmine	Patricia

25 **Et maintenant, à toi**

Pense à des plats américains. Qu'est-ce que tu préfères manger comme entrée, poisson, viande et dessert?

Teacher Notes

- The term **à la carte** refers to items chosen from anywhere on the menu. **Le menu** usually refers to a fixed-price menu (**un prix fixe**), where the diner may choose from among several specified dishes for each course. Eating **à la carte** is usually more expensive.

- To request tap water in a French restaurant, ask for **une carafe d'eau,** which is usually free of charge.

Teaching Suggestion

24 Before playing the recording, review higher numbers with flash cards.

Teacher Note

24 Remind students that the tip is usually included in the price (**service compris**), so they don't need to figure the tip in their calculations.

VIDEO   **Camille et compagnie**

As an alternative or in addition to the **Remise en train,** you may wish to show Episode 1 of *Camille et compagnie.* For suggestions and activities, see the *Video Guide.*

Comprehension Check

Challenge

21 Instead of having students respond with **faux,** encourage them to make complete statements, using the expressions they have learned so far. (**2. C'est faux. Pauline a déjà mangé du presskopf. Elle aime beaucoup ça. 4. C'est faux. Pauline et Yasmine n'ont pas pris de dessert.)**

Additional Practice

Have small groups create a skit in which a group of friends sits at a café and orders from a menu on page 14. One person in the group is the server. First the group brainstorms the dialogue. When they are ready, the groups perform their skits.

Answers

23 1. Qu'est-ce que vous allez prendre?
2. Je n'arrive pas à me décider. J'hésite entre... et... ; Je ne sais pas quoi prendre.
3. Je vais prendre... ; Je voudrais... ; Donnez-moi...
4. Passe-moi...
5. Est-ce qu'on pourrait avoir... ?
6. Ça fait combien?

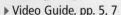

Teaching Resources
p. 16

PRINT
▸ Video Guide, pp. 5, 7
▸ Cahier d'activités, p. 12

MEDIA
▸ One-Stop Planner
▸ Video Program
  Videocassette 1, 13:47–18:13
▸ Audio Compact Discs, CD 1, Trs.
  8–11
▸ Interactive CD-ROM Tutor, Disc 1

Presenting
Panorama Culturel

Have students recall food specialties they've learned about (**pissaladière, ratatouille, attiéké, foutou**). Then, play the video. Write the specialties mentioned on a transparency and have volunteers write the name of the interviewee who mentions each one next to it. Then, ask the **Questions** below.

Questions

1. **La bouillabaisse est une spécialité de quelle région?** (la Provence, Marseille)

2. **Quelles sont les spécialités de Cherbourg?** (des petits homards) **de Normandie?** (du cidre, de la crème fraîche, du boudin, du thon)

3. **Quelles sont les spécialités de la Côte d'Ivoire?** (l'attiéké, le foutou, la sauce graine, la sauce arachide)

4. **Comment est-ce qu'on prépare le foutou?** (On mélange la banane avec du manioc. On le fait cuire et on pile.)

Quelles sont les spécialités de ta région?

We asked some people about the specialties of their regions. Here's what they had to say.

Marie,
France

«La bouillabaisse. C'est un plat provençal surtout marseillais... C'est une soupe de poissons... On fait ça avec divers poissons et du pain, des petits croûtons de pain... Voilà.» Tr. 9

Christian,
France

«Euh... les spécialités [de Cherbourg, ce] sont des petits homards que nous appelons «les demoiselles de Cherbourg» et qui sont des grosses crevettes... En Normandie, nous avons du cidre que nous faisons avec des pommes, [de] la crème fraîche, du boudin et du thon.» Tr. 10

Célestine,
Côte d'Ivoire

«En Côte d'Ivoire il y a d'abord l'attiéké, qu'on peut exporter [et] importer du moins d'ailleurs. Et aussi, il y a le foutou. Le foutou, c'est de la banane mélangée [avec] du manioc. On fait cuire et on pile. Ensuite, [il est] accompagné de la sauce graine généralement et ensuite, il y a la sauce arachide accompagnée du riz.» Tr. 11

1. la bouillabaisse, "les demoiselles de Cherbourg,"
   le cidre, la crème fraîche, le boudin, le thon, l'attiéké,
   le foutou, la sauce graine, la sauce arachide

Qu'en penses-tu?

1. De quelles spécialités est-ce que ces gens parlent?

2. Quelles sont les spécialités de ta région? Est-ce que tu connais des spécialités d'autres états?

3. Choisis une région de France ou d'un autre pays francophone et recherche des spécialités de cet endroit.

Connections and Comparisons

Community Link
Ask if there are local stores or restaurants that offer ethnic specialties.

 Multicultural Link
Have students plan a multicultural and ethnic food-tasting for the class.

Music Link
Play the song *Ma Normandie* (Level 2, Audio CD 3, Track 27). Tell students that the song is about an area mentioned in the **Panorama Culturel**. Have students research additional information about Normandy.

WA3 FRANCOPHONE
EUROPE-1

Comment dit-on...?

Expressing indecision; making recommendations

A server might ask:

> **Qu'est-ce que vous allez prendre?**

To express indecision:

Je ne sais pas.
Tout me tente.
Everything looks tempting.
Je n'arrive pas à me décider.
I can't make up my mind.
J'hésite entre le saumon **et** la truite fumée.
I can't decide between . . . and . . .

To make recommendations:

Tu devrais prendre les côtelettes d'agneau.
Pourquoi tu ne prends pas l'escalope de veau à la crème?
Essaie les tomates farcies.
Try . . .
Prends le saumon.

Cahier d'activités,
p. 7, Act. 11

26 **Au restaurant** See scripts and answers on p. 3H.

Ecoutons Ecoute les phrases suivantes. Est-ce que les personnes hésitent ou recommandent quelque chose?

CD 1 Tr. 12

Vocabulaire

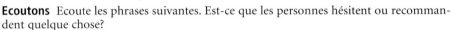

Voici un menu français traduit en anglais:

CD-ROM
DISC **1**

Le Routier Sympa
Menu à 10 euros

LES ENTREES
APPETIZERS
les carottes râpées
grated carrots with vinaigrette
le céleri rémoulade
grated celery root with mayonnaise and vinaigrette
l'assiette de crudités
plate of raw vegetables with vinaigrette
l'assiette de charcuterie
plate of pâté, ham, and cold sausage

LES PLATS PRINCIPAUX
MAIN DISHES
le steak-frites
steak with French fries
le poulet haricots verts
roasted chicken with green beans
l'escalope de dinde purée
sliced turkey breast with mashed potatoes
le filet de sole riz champignons
filet of sole with rice and mushrooms
la côtelette de porc pâtes
porkchop with pasta

LA SALADE VERTE
SALAD

L'ASSIETTE DE FROMAGES
A SELECTION OF CHEESES
camembert
brie
roquefort
fromage de chèvre
goat cheese

LES DESSERTS
DESSERTS
les tartes aux fruits
fruit pies/tarts
la crème caramel
caramel custard

Travaux pratiques de grammaire, pp. 6–7, Act. 9–11

Cahier d'activités, p. 8, Act. 12–13

Communication for All Students

Building on Previous Skills
Ask students to point out expressions in the **Comment dit-on... ? box** they remember seeing before. (**Je ne sais pas, Tu devrais prendre... , Pourquoi tu ne... ,**) They might recall other expressions to use when they order in a café. (**Vous avez choisi? Vous prenez? Je voudrais... , Je vais prendre... , Qu'est-ce que vous avez** **comme... ?, Prends...**) Have students recall food-related vocabulary that they would find in a French café or restaurant. Then have them form groups and act out a situation where they are ordering food, hesitate on what to order, advise each other, ask the server questions, and finally order drinks and food.

Teaching Resources
pp. 17–19

PRINT
▶ Lesson Planner, p. 5
▶ Listening Activities, pp. 4–5, 8–9
▶ Activities for Communication, pp. 3–4, 52–53, 89–90
▶ Travaux pratiques de grammaire, pp. 6–8
▶ Grammar Tutor for Students of French, Chapter 1
▶ Cahier d'activités, pp. 7–10
▶ Testing Program, pp. 5–8
▶ Alternative Assessment Guide, p. 30
▶ Student Make-Up Assignments, Chapter 1

MEDIA
▶ One-Stop Planner
▶ Audio Compact Discs, CD 1, Trs. 12–14, 17, 24–26
▶ Teaching Transparencies: 1-2, **Grammaire supplémentaire** Answers; Travaux pratiques de grammaire Answers
▶ Interactive CD-ROM Tutor, Disc 1

Bell Work
Have students write out an "order" of five things they'd like to have for dinner, using food and drink items they already know.

Presenting
Comment dit-on... ?

Act out the new expressions, using appropriate facial expressions. Ask students whether you are expressing indecision or making a recommendation.

Vocabulaire

Tape pictures of the food items to the board. Point to each one and ask either-or questions. (**C'est un steak-frites ou du camembert?**)

Teaching Resources
pp. 17–19

PRINT
▶ Lesson Planner, p. 5
▶ Listening Activities, pp. 4–5, 8–9
▶ Activities for Communication, pp. 3–4, 52–53, 89–90
▶ Travaux pratiques de grammaire, pp. 6–8
▶ Grammar Tutor for Students of French, Chapter 1
▶ Cahier d'activités, pp. 7–10
▶ Testing Program, pp. 5–8
▶ Alternative Assessment Guide, p. 30
▶ Student Make-Up Assignments, Chapter 1

MEDIA
▶ One-Stop Planner
▶ Audio Compact Discs, CD 1, Trs. 12–14, 17, 24–26
▶ Teaching Transparencies: 1-2; **Grammaire supplémentaire** Answers, Travaux pratiques de grammaire Answers
▶ Interactive CD-ROM Tutor, Disc 1

Presenting
Comment dit-on... ?

To present the new expressions, play the first part of *Les Retrouvailles* on Videocassette 1 6:26–8:42. Pause the video after each new expression is modeled, say the expression aloud, and have students repeat. Then, go over the **Comment dit-on... ?** box with students. Finally, write sentences from a conversation that might take place at a restaurant in random order on a transparency, and have students number them in the correct order.

---

27 **Pas américain, ça!**

Parlons Regarde le menu à la page 17. A ton avis, quels plats est-ce qu'on ne trouve pas normalement aux Etats-Unis?

Possible answers: les carottes râpées, le céleri rémoulade, l'assiette de crudités, l'assiette de fromages, la crème caramel

Si tu as oublié foods va à la page R18.

28 **Quelle est la bonne commande?**   See scripts on p. 3H.

 CD 1 Tr. 13

Ecoutons Ecoute ce dialogue. Le serveur a mélangé les commandes et demande à son client ce qu'il a mangé. Laquelle des commandes suivantes est la bonne?

Travaux pratiques de grammaire, p. 8, Act. 12–13

salade de tomates
poulet frites
salade verte
tarte aux pommes

a.

salade de tomates
poulet haricots verts
assiette de fromages
tarte aux pommes

b.

salade de tomates
poulet haricots verts
salade verte
tarte aux prunes

c.

29 **Vous désirez?**

Parlons Et toi, qu'est-ce que tu prends? Regarde la carte du **Routier Sympa** et choisis une entrée, un plat et un dessert. Ensuite, demande à un(e) camarade de classe ce qu'il/elle prend.

Comment dit-on...?

Ordering and asking for details

 CD-ROM DISC 1

A server might ask:

Vous avez choisi?
Have you made your selection?
Vous avez décidé?
Que voulez-vous comme entrée?
What would you like for an appetizer?
Et comme boisson? *And to drink?*
Comment désirez-vous votre viande?
How do you like your . . . cooked?

To respond to the server:

Non, pas encore.
Un instant, s'il vous plaît.
Oui, je vais prendre la soupe à l'oignon.
Comme entrée, j'aimerais le pâté de campagne.
De l'eau, s'il vous plaît.
Saignant(e). *Rare.*
A point. *Medium rare.*
Bien cuit(e). *Well-done.*

To ask for details:

Qu'est-ce que vous avez comme spécialités? *What kind of . . . do you have?*
Qu'est-ce que vous me conseillez?
What do you recommend?
Qu'est-ce que c'est, le presskopf?
What is . . . ?

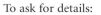
Cahier d'activités, p. 9, Act. 15

 Note culturelle

Dans chaque région de France, on peut manger des plats traditionnels variés; par exemple, **la bouillabaisse** en Provence, **le foie gras** dans le Périgord, **les crêpes** en Bretagne, **le cassoulet** dans le Languedoc et **la choucroute** en Alsace.

Cultures and Communities

Culture Notes
• Many French people prefer their meat less cooked than Americans. They might even ask for it to be served **bleue** (with only the outside layer browned). If you prefer your meat more thoroughly cooked, ask specifically for it to be **à point** or **bien cuite**.

• **Bouillabaisse** is a type of seafood soup from Marseilles. **Foie gras** is duck or goose liver pâté

often served as an **entrée** with small pieces of toast. **Crêpes** resemble thin pancakes and are usually rolled up and stuffed with sugar, jam, or other fillings, such as ham and cheese. **Cassoulet** is a casserole of white beans, various meats, vegetables, and herbs. **Choucroute** is *sauerkraut,* chopped cabbage that is salted and fermented in its own juice, and served with sausages, ham, and boiled potatoes.

30 **A votre service!**   See scripts on p. 3H.

Ecoutons Tu es au restaurant. Le serveur te pose des questions. Choisis la meilleure réponse.

CD 1
Tr. 14

a. A point.   4
b. De l'eau minérale.   3
c. La crème caramel, s'il vous plaît.   5
d. Les crudités.   2
e. Oui, je vais prendre le steak-frites.   1

31 **Méli-mélo!**

Lisons/Parlons Mets dans l'ordre ce dialogue entre un serveur et un client. Ensuite, joue la scène avec ton/ta camarade.

7 «Bon, je reviens.»

2 «Non, pas encore... euh... Qu'est-ce que vous avez comme spécialités?»

3 «Nous avons notre choucroute maison.»

4 «OK, une choucroute.»

5 «Bon, c'est tout?»

6 «Ah non, finalement, je vais prendre le poulet haricots verts et une carafe d'eau.»

1 «Vous avez choisi?»

32 **Au dîner**

Lisons Choisis des mots et expressions dans la boîte suivante pour compléter cette conversation entre un serveur et un client.

qu'est-ce que		dessert	boisson
comme	du	des	saignante
de l'	comment	de la	un
	s'il vous plaît		

— Bonjour, vous avez choisi?   **1.** comme
— Oui, __1__ entrée, j'aimerais les crudités.
— D'accord. Et comme plat principal?
— Je vais prendre un steak-frites.
— __2__ désirez-vous votre viande?   Comment
— Bien cuite, s'il vous plaît.
— Et comme __3__ ?   dessert
— Qu'est-ce que vous avez comme gâteaux?
— Nous avons __4__ tarte aux poires et __5__ gâteaux au chocolat.   **4.** de la   **5.** des
— Euh... non, je vais plutôt prendre __6__ fromage.   du
— Très bien. Et comme __7__ ?   boisson
— Eh bien, __8__ eau minérale, s'il vous plaît.   de l'

Tu te rappelles?

Use the definite articles **le, la,** and **les** *(the)* when you are referring to a specific item and with the verb **aimer,** for example, **J'aime les escargots.** The indefinite articles **un, une** *(a, an)* and **des** *(some)* are used to refer to whole items. Remember to use the partitive articles **du, de la,** and **de l',** *(some)* when you refer to a portion of an item. **Je voudrais de la salade et de l'eau minérale.**

Grammaire supplémentaire, p. 27, Act. 8–9

33 **De l'école au travail**

Parlons This summer, you're going to work at a fancy French restaurant in your town. To impress your French-speaking patrons, you should speak their language with them. Make small talk, tell them about the specialties, and take their orders, if they wish. Act out this scene with two classmates, who will act very demanding. Then, change roles.

Communication for All Students

Visual/Kinesthetic Learners

30 Give pictures of the food items to five students, who stand in front of the class. As students hear the waiter's questions, they should write the name of the student holding the picture they would choose to answer the question. Then, as you play the recording again, have the students at the front step forward as they hear the question that corresponds to their picture. The class confirms or corrects.

Kinesthetic Learners

31 In groups of seven, each student writes one of the sentences on a sheet of paper and holds it up. Group members arrange themselves in the proper order and read the dialogue aloud.

Writing Assessment

33 You might use the following rubric when grading your students on this activity.

Speaking Rubric	Points			
	4	3	2	1
Content (Complete– Incomplete)				
Comprehension (Total–Little)				
Comprehensibility (Comprehensible– Incomprehensible)				
Accuracy (Accurate– Seldom accurate)				
Fluency (Fluent–Not fluent)				

| 18–20: A | 14–15: C | Under |
| 16–17: B | 12–13: D | 12: F |

Teaching Suggestion

List the courses of a meal on the board (**entrée, plat principal, fromage, dessert,** and **boisson**). Ask students **Qu'est-ce que vous voulez comme... ?** Have them hesitate, make recommendations, and then order a dish for that course.

Assess

▶ Testing Program, pp. 5–8 Quiz 1-2A, Quiz 1-2B, Audio CD 1, Tr. 17

▶ Student Make-Up Assignments Chapter 1, Alternative Quiz

▶ Alternative Assessment Guide, p. 30

Lisons!

CHAPITRE 1

Teaching Resources
pp. 20–22

PRINT 📖
▸ Lesson Planner, p. 6
▸ Cahier d'activités, p. 11
▸ Reading Strategies and Skills Handbook, Chapter 1
▸ Joie de lire 3, Chapter 1
▸ Standardized Assessment Tutor, Chapter 1

MEDIA 💿
▸ One-Stop Planner

Prereading
Activities A–B

Motivating Activity
Ask students to list famous little boys or girls from movies, television, or comics (Calvin of *Calvin and Hobbes*®, Dennis the Menace, Lucy of *Peanuts*®). Have them think of words or expressions to describe them. Why are these children funny?

Teaching Suggestions
A. You might remind students that scanning involves looking over a text quickly to find specific information. Have them find clues in the story to determine the speaker's approximate age.

B. Have students also look at the illustrations and anticipate what the story might be about.

Answers
B. *Possible answer:*
The story will probably be an account of a child talking with his parents.

E. Alceste : Périgord ; manger des truffes
Geoffroy : au bord de la mer
Agnan : Angleterre ; apprendre à parler anglais

Il faut être raisonnable

C e qui m'étonne, c'est qu'à la maison on n'a pas encore parlé des vacances ! Les autres années, Papa dit qu'il veut aller quelque part, Maman dit qu'elle veut aller ailleurs, ça fait des tas d'histoires. Papa et Maman disent que puisque c'est comme ça ils préfèrent rester à la maison, moi je pleure, et puis on va où voulait aller Maman. Mais cette année, rien.

Pourtant, les copains de l'école se préparent tous à partir. Geoffroy, qui a un papa très riche, va passer ses vacances dans la grande maison que son papa a au bord de la mer.

Agnan, qui est le premier de la classe et le chouchou de la maîtresse, s'en va en Angleterre passer ses vacances dans une école où on va lui apprendre à parler l'anglais. Il est fou, Agnan.

Alceste va manger des truffes en Périgord, où son papa a un ami qui a une charcuterie. Et c'est comme ça pour tous : ils vont à la mer, à la montagne ou chez leurs mémés à la campagne. Il n'y a que moi qui ne sais pas encore où je vais aller, et c'est très embêtant, parce qu'une des choses que j'aime le mieux dans les vacances, c'est d'en parler avant et après aux copains.

Alors, je suis allé dans le jardin et j'ai attendu Papa, et quand il est arrivé de son bureau, j'ai couru vers lui ; il m'a pris dans ses bras, il m'a fait « Oupla ! » et je lui ai demandé où nous allions partir en vacances. Alors, Papa a cessé de rigoler, il m'a posé par terre et il m'a dit qu'on allait en parler dans la maison, où nous avons trouvé Maman assise dans le salon.

- Je crois que le moment est venu, a dit Papa.
- Oui, a dit Maman, il m'en a parlé tout à l'heure.

chouette!

Stratégie pour lire
Identifying the point of view of the narrator of a story is a key to understanding the story itself. A foreign tourist, a small child, and an eighty-year-old woman would probably relate the same incident very differently. When you read, think about the person who is telling the story. Who is he? Where does he live? What is his age? What kind of person does he seem to be? Answering these kinds of questions will help you to understand the narrator's point of view, and so get more out of the story.

A. Scan the first paragraph. From whose point of view is the story told? How old would you say this person is?   *a child; around seven or eight*

B. Knowing who the narrator is, what do you think you'll read about in the story?   See answer below

C. What is the narrator's relationship to . . .   *classmate*
  1. Geoffroy, Agnan, and Alceste?
  2. Maman and Papa?   *son*

D. What is Nicolas concerned about at the beginning of the story?   *uncertain vacation plans*

E. Match Nicolas's schoolfriends with their vacation destinations and planned activities. See answers below.

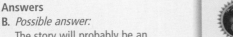
apprendre à parler anglais
Périgord
Angleterre
manger des truffes
au bord de la mer

Alceste
Geoffroy
Agnan

Cultures and Communities

Culture Note
In 1954, the humorist René Goscinny began his collaboration with the illustrator Jean-Jacques Sempé. The result was the publication of *Le Petit Nicolas*. Nicolas shares his world with a child's typical innocence and simplicity. Besides writing *Le Petit Nicolas,* René Goscinny collaborated with cartoonist Albert Uderzo on the famous comic book series *Astérix le Gaulois*®. Jean-Jacques Sempé has produced many humorous books for almost forty years. His cartoons have been published in many international magazines.

- Alors, il faut le lui dire, a dit Papa.

- Eh bien, dis-lui, a dit Maman.

Alors, Papa s'est assis dans le fauteuil, il m'a pris par les mains et il m'a tiré contre ses genoux.

- Mon Nicolas est un grand garçon raisonnable, n'est-ce pas ? a demandé Papa.

Moi, j'aime pas trop quand on me dit que je suis un grand garçon, parce que d'habitude, quand on me dit ça, c'est qu'on va me faire des choses qui ne me plaisent pas.

- Et je suis sûr, a dit Papa, que mon grand garçon aimerait bien aller à la mer !

- Oh ! oui, j'ai dit.

- Aller à la mer, nager, pêcher, jouer sur la plage, se promener dans les bois, a dit Papa.

- Il y a des bois, là où on va ? j'ai demandé. Alors c'est pas là où on a été l'année dernière ?

- Ecoute, a dit Maman à Papa. Je ne peux pas. Je me demande si c'est une si bonne idée que ça. Je préfère y renoncer. Peut-être, l'année prochaine...

- Non ! a dit Papa. Ce qui est décidé est décidé. Un peu de courage, que diable ! Et Nicolas va être très raisonnable ; n'est-ce pas, Nicolas ?

Moi j'ai dit que oui, que j'allais être drôlement raisonnable.

- Et on va aller à l'hôtel ? j'ai demandé.

- Pas exactement, a dit Papa. Je... je crois que tu coucheras sous la tente. C'est très bien, tu sais...

Alors là, j'étais content comme tout.

- Sous la tente, comme les Indiens dans le livre que m'a donné tante Dorothée ? j'ai demandé.

- C'est ça, a dit Papa.

- Chic ! j'ai crié. Tu me laisseras t'aider à monter la tente ? Et à faire du feu pour

F. How do you know that Nicolas's parents don't want to tell him something? Find five things they say that show you this. Then find three actions or gestures that illustrate their nervousness. *See answers below.*

G. Which of the following sentences do they say to make him accept the idea? *See answers below.*

> Ce qui est décidé est décidé.

> Ce soir, pour le dessert, il y aura de la tarte.

> C'est la première fois que tu seras séparé de nous...

> Tu iras seul, comme un grand.

> Mon Nicolas est un grand garçon raisonnable, n'est-ce pas?

H. Pourquoi est-ce que Nicolas n'aime pas que ses parents l'appellent «grand garçon»? *See answers below.*

I. Where do Nicolas's parents plan for him to go on vacation? What will he do there? Where will he sleep? *See answers below.*

J. Associe ces mots de vocabulaire avec leurs synonymes.

1. cesser de   b
2. des tas de   f
3. ce qui m'étonne, c'est que   e
4. leurs mémés   a
5. puisque   g
6. ailleurs   c
7. rigoler   d

a. leurs grands-mères
b. s'arrêter de
c. autre part
d. rire
e. je suis surpris que
f. beaucoup de
g. parce que

Communication for All Students

Building on Previous Knowledge

G. Ask for examples of words or expressions in English that a parent might say to placate a child. Have a volunteer read aloud the choices for this activity, one at a time, as the class decides which ones correspond to the English phrases they listed.

Slower Pace

J. Have students find each expression in the story and write the sentence in which it appears. Then, have them substitute the synonyms in the second column until they find one that logically completes the sentence.

Reading
Activities C–P

Teaching Suggestions

C.–E. Have partners or small groups of students read the story and answer the questions in these activities. You might have students give quotations from the story to support their answers.

H. Ask students if they would have the same reaction as Nicolas. Is there an expression that they've heard adults use in English to preface something unpleasant they are about to say?

J. Remind students that they don't need a dictionary for this activity. If they're uncertain, encourage them to go back to the story and use the context to try to guess the meaning of the word.

Answers

F. *Possible answers:*
They hesitate to tell Nicolas the news. They try to break the news to him gently. They act nervous.
1. —Je crois que le moment est venu.
2. —Alors, il faut le lui dire, a dit Papa.
3. —Ecoute, a dit Maman à Papa. Je ne peux pas.
4. —Non! a dit Papa... Un peu de courage, que diable!
5. —Il faut que tu sois très raisonnable.
Papa a cessé de rigoler. Papa s'est essuyé la figure avec son mouchoir. Papa a toussé un peu dans sa gorge.

G. —Tu iras seul, comme un grand.
—Mon Nicolas est un grand garçon raisonnable, n'est-ce pas?
—Ce soir, pour le dessert, il y aura de la tarte.

H. This usually means they are going to do something he won't like.

I. summer camp; swim, fish, play on the beach, walk in the woods; in a tent

Postreading
Activity Q

Challenge/Tactile Learners
Bring in several comic strips from the Sunday newspaper. Have students choose a strip, cut blank speech bubbles out of construction paper, and paste the blank bubbles over the originals. Then, have them create new French dialogues and write them in the blank speech bubbles.

cuire le manger ? Oh ! ça va être chic, chic, chic !

Papa s'est essuyé la figure avec son mouchoir, comme s'il avait très chaud, et puis il m'a dit :

- Nicolas, nous devons parler d'homme à homme. Il faut que tu sois très raisonnable.

- Et si tu es bien sage et tu te conduis comme un grand garçon, a dit Maman, ce soir, pour le dessert, il y aura de la tarte.

Alors Papa a toussé un peu dans sa gorge, il m'a mis ses mains sur mes épaules et puis il m'a dit :

- Nicolas, mon petit, nous ne partirons pas avec toi en vacances. Tu iras seul, comme un grand.

- Comment, seul ? j'ai demandé. Vous ne partez pas, vous ?

- Nicolas, a dit Papa, je t'en prie, sois raisonnable. Maman et moi, nous irons faire un petit voyage, et comme nous avons pensé que ça ne t'amuserait pas, nous avons décidé que toi tu irais en colonie de vacances. Ça te fera le plus grand bien, tu seras avec des petits camarades de ton âge et tu t'amuseras beaucoup...

- Bien sûr, c'est la première fois que tu seras séparé de nous, Nicolas, mais c'est pour ton bien, a dit Maman.

> **Pourtant, je ne sais pas, moi, mais je crois que j'ai été raisonnable, non?**

- Alors, Nicolas, mon grand... qu'est-ce que tu en dis ? m'a demandé Papa.

- Chouette ! j'ai crié, et je me suis mis à danser dans le salon. Parce que c'est vrai, il paraît que c'est terrible, les colonies de vacances : on se fait des tas de copains, on fait des promenades, des jeux, on chante autour d'un gros feu, et j'étais tellement content que j'ai embrassé Papa et Maman. Ce qui est drôle, c'est que Papa et Maman me regardaient avec des gros yeux ronds. Ils avaient même l'air un peu fâché.

K. Recherche ces mots de vocabulaire et ces expressions dans le texte ci-dessus. Utilise le contexte et les images pour deviner leur sens.

> the teacher's pet
> **le chouchou de la maîtresse**

> He pulled me against his knees.
> **Il m'a tiré contre ses genoux.**

> **Papa s'est essuyé la figure.**
> Papa wiped his face.

> **Je préfère y renoncer.**
> I'd rather give up on the idea.

> **Je me suis mis à danser...**
> I started to dance . . .

L. What is Nicolas's reaction to his parents' news? Why?   He dances around; He's excited.

M. How do Nicolas's parents feel about his reaction? Are they really relieved that he took it so

well? How do you know?   See answers below.

N. What is the significance of the title **Il faut être raisonnable?** Why is the title ironic, in light of the story?   See answers below.

O. En te référant au texte ci-dessus, comment pourrais-tu décrire Nicolas? Et ses parents?

P. This story is told from a child's point of view. Find five examples in the text of language typical of the way a child would express himself.

Q. Quels seraient tes sentiments si tu étais à la place de Nicolas?
See answers below for letters O and P.

Cahier d'activités, p. 11, Act. 18

Answers

M. They feel surprised, a bit angry, and a little hurt; No; "... Papa et Maman me regardaient avec de gros yeux ronds. Ils avaient même l'air un peu fâché."

N. Nicolas' parents tell him he must be reasonable, and then they are surprised when he is.

O. *Possible answers:*
Nicolas has a sense of adventure and doesn't understand his parents' annoyance at his eagerness to attend camp alone. Nicolas' parents worry about his feelings, thinking he is more dependent than he is.

P. *Possible answers:*
Il est fou, Agnan; ... chez leurs mémés... ; ... j'allais être drôlement raisonnable; ...
j'étais content comme tout; Sous la tente, comme les Indiens... ? Chic! j'ai crié; Chouette! j'ai crié... ; Il paraît que c'est terrible, les colonies de vacances...

Connections and Comparisons

Literature Link
N. You might explain to students that the word *ironic* describes an event or situation that is contrary to what was expected or intended. Ask them for examples of irony from books they've read or movies or TV programs they've seen.

Thinking Critically
O. Comparing and Contrasting   Have students list adjectives or phrases to describe Nicolas. Then, have them compare this list to the one they created to describe famous boys and girls from American cartoons (see Motivating Activity on page 20). How is Nicolas similar to them? How is he different? If *Le Petit Nicolas* were translated into English, do students think it would be popular?

Ecrivons!

Une brochure touristique

Dans l'histoire que tu as lue, Nicolas parle d'endroits où ses amis passent leurs vacances. En Amérique aussi, il y a beaucoup de régions différentes. Dans l'activité suivante, tu vas sélectionner une région d'Amérique où tu voudrais passer tes vacances. Ensuite, tu vas écrire une brochure touristique pour cette région. Inclus toutes les informations utiles aux touristes.

Stratégie pour écrire
You always have a purpose for writing. You may want to explain something to someone, to relate a funny incident, to create, or just to put your thoughts down on paper. Whatever your reason is, it will influence the way you write. You will determine the tone, the language, and even the organization of your writing according to your purpose.

A. Préparation

1. Connais-tu bien la région que tu as choisie? Commence par écrire ce que tu sais déjà.

2. Si tu as besoin de plus d'informations, renseigne-toi à la bibliothèque. Essaie de trouver des renseignements sur les activités, les points d'intérêt, les spécialités régionales et la géographie de la région que tu vas décrire.

3. Réfléchis un peu. Dans quel but *(purpose)* est-ce que tu écris?

4. Pense à des mots que tu vas utiliser dans ta brochure pour atteindre ton but.
   a. Fais une liste d'adjectifs emphatiques comme «formidable» ou «extraordinaire» pour décrire la région.
   b. Maintenant, fais une liste de mots ou d'expressions qui décrivent les caractéristiques de ta région; par exemple, «montagneux» ou «Il y a beaucoup de soleil».

B. Rédaction

1. Fais un brouillon *(rough draft)* de ta brochure. N'oublie pas de diviser ta présentation en trois parties :
   a. une brève introduction où l'on apprend de quelle région tu parles
   b. toutes les informations sur les aspects les plus intéressants de la région
   c. une partie finale qui puisse convaincre les gens de venir découvrir la région

2. Pour illustrer ta brochure, trouve des photos dans des magazines ou fais tes propres dessins.

C. Evaluation

1. Est-ce que ta brochure peut vraiment convaincre quelqu'un de choisir cet endroit pour y passer ses vacances? Montre-la à un(e) camarade de classe et demande-lui son opinion.

2. Vérifie l'orthographe *(spelling)* et la grammaire de ton brouillon. Fais les révisions nécessaires. Mets ta brochure au propre.

Teaching Resources
p. 23

PRINT
▶ Lesson Planner, p. 6
▶ Cahier d'activités, p. 145
▶ Alternative Assessment Guide, p. 16
▶ Standardized Assessment Tutor, Chapter 1

MEDIA
▶ One-Stop Planner
▶ Test Generator, Chapter 1
▶ Interactive CD-ROM Tutor, Disc 1

Process Writing

Prewriting

Motivating Activity
Pass several travel brochures around the class. Have students identify techniques the designers use to attract people to a particular area (content of photos, layout, language, special offers).

Visual Learners
A. 1. Have students begin by drawing sketches or gathering photos and pamphlets of their chosen region.

Teaching Suggestion
A. 3. Have students brainstorm reasons for writing (personal expression, to inform, to persuade). Then, have them decide which purposes apply to a travel brochure. Have them also consider the audience they're targeting.

Writing

Visual/Tactile Learners
B. 1. Have students organize their brochures by rewriting the words they listed in Activity A.4. on colored paper, using a different color for each part of the presentation (introduction, body of information, conclusion).

Apply and Assess

Postwriting

Teaching Suggestion
Remind students that peer evaluation should focus on content and organization, as well as on spelling and grammar. Partners should point out both strengths and weaknesses and make specific suggestions to help the writer improve the brochure.

You might have students consult the Peer Editing Rubric found on page 8 of the *Alternative Assessment Guide* for content evaluation guidelines and a proofreader's checklist.

CHAPITRE 1

For **Grammaire supplémentaire** Answer Transparencies, see the *Teaching Transparencies* binder.

Grammaire supplémentaire

internet

ADRESSE: go.hrw.com
MOT-CLE: WA3
FRANCOPHONE EUROPE-1

Première étape

Objectives Renewing old acquaintances; inquiring; expressing enthusiasm and dissatisfaction; exchanging information; asking and describing what a place was like

1 Complète les phrases avec le passé composé du verbe entre parenthèses. (**p. 11**)

1. Yasmine _____ (monter) dans la tour Eiffel.
2. Eric _____ (visiter) les châteaux de la Loire.
3. Paul et Pascal _____ (boire) des menthes à l'eau dans un café du cours Mirabeau.
4. Alissa _____ (se perdre) dans le jardin de Monet.
5. Valérie et moi, nous _____ (acheter) des papayes au marché de Treichville.
6. Julien _____ (se promener) à Fort-de-France.
7. Perrine et Mariyam _____ (se baigner) dans l'océan Atlantique.
8. Ariane et toi, vous _____ (déguster) des spécialités alsaciennes.

2 Mets les verbes entre parenthèses au passé composé. Fais l'accord du participe passé, s'il y a lieu. (**p. 11**)

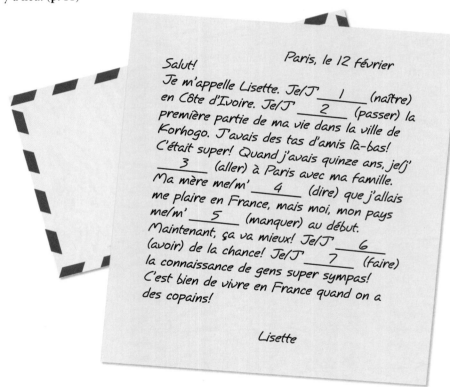

Paris, le 12 février

Salut!
Je m'appelle Lisette. Je/J' __1__ (naître) en Côte d'Ivoire. Je/J' __2__ (passer) la première partie de ma vie dans la ville de Korhogo. J'avais des tas d'amis là-bas! C'était super! Quand j'avais quinze ans, je/j' __3__ (aller) à Paris avec ma famille. Ma mère me/m' __4__ (dire) que j'allais me plaire en France, mais moi, mon pays me/m' __5__ (manquer) au début. Maintenant, ça va mieux! Je/J' __6__ (avoir) de la chance! Je/J' __7__ (faire) la connaissance de gens super sympas! C'est bien de vivre en France quand on a des copains!

Lisette

Answers
1
1. est montée
2. a visité
3. ont bu
4. s'est perdue
5. avons acheté
6. s'est promené
7. se sont baignées
8. avez dégusté

2
1. suis née
2. ai passé
3. suis allée
4. a dit
5. a manqué
6. ai eu
7. ai fait

Grammar Resources for Chapter 1

The **Grammaire supplémentaire** activities are designed as supplemental activities for the grammatical concepts presented in the chapter. You might use them as additional practice, for review, or for assessment.

For more grammar presentations, review, and practice, refer to the following:
• Travaux pratiques de grammaire
• Grammar Tutor for Students of French

• Grammar Summary on pp. R29–R54
• Cahier d'activités
• Grammar and Vocabulary quizzes (Testing Program)
• Test Generator
• Interactive CD-ROM Tutor
• **Jeux interactifs** at <u>go.hrw.com</u>

3 Demande si tes amis ont fait ce qu'ils aiment faire pendant les vacances. (**p. 11**)

EXEMPLE   Ce qui me plaît, c'est de me lever tard.
            Tu t'es levée tard pendant les vacances?

1. Ce que j'aime bien, c'est me mettre en condition.
2. Ce qui nous plaît, c'est de nous habiller à la martiniquaise.
3. Ce que nous aimons bien, c'est nous coucher à minuit.
4. Ce qui plaît à mes copines, c'est de se promener en bateau sur la mer des Caraïbes.
5. Ce que je préfère, c'est m'amuser avec mes amis.
6. Ce qui plaît à mes frères, c'est de s'entraîner à la natation.

4 Tes amis et toi, vous ne savez pas quoi faire. Suggère les activités suivantes. Utilise **si on** et l'imparfait. (**p. 13; II, p. 209**)

EXEMPLE   prendre un café sur la place Plumereau
            Si on prenait un café sur la place Plumereau?

1. faire un circuit des châteaux de la Loire
2. assister à un spectacle son et lumière au château de Chenonceau
3. monter dans les tours du château d'Ussé
4. aller voir les inventions de Léonard de Vinci au manoir du Clos-Lucé
5. se promener dans le parc du château d'Azay-le-Rideau
6. descendre dans les passages souterrains du château d'Amboise

5 Tes amis te disent ce qu'ils ont fait et ont mangé pendant leurs séjours dans différents pays francophones. Mets les verbes entre parenthèses à l'imparfait. (**p. 13**)

CELINE   C'est pas vrai! Quand tu ___1___ (être) en Arles, tu ___2___ (amener) parfois ton chien dans un restaurant pour les chiens?

HECTOR   Quand mes copains ___3___ (rendre) visite à leur ami marseillais, ils allaient au restaurant et ils ___4___ (manger) toujours de la bouillabaisse au déjeuner!

EVE   Quand je/j'___5___ (être) petite, je ___6___ (partir) en camp de vacances en Normandie tous les étés. Je/J'___7___ (adorer) ça! On ___8___ (manger) du boudin, du thon et du fromage! Moi, je/j' ___9___ (prendre) toujours du cidre comme boisson!

Answers

3 1. Tu t'es mis(e) en condition pendant les vacances?
2. Vous vous êtes habillé(e)s à la martiniquaise pendant les vacances?
3. Vous vous êtes couché(e)s à minuit pendant les vacances?
4. Elles se sont promenées en bateau sur la mer des Caraïbes pendant les vacances?
5. Tu t'es amusé(e) avec tes amis pendant les vacances?
6. Ils se sont entraînés à la natation pendant les vacances?

4 1. Si on faisait... ?
2. Si on assistait... ?
3. Si on montait... ?
4. Si on allait voir... ?
5. Si on se promenait... ?
6. Si on descendait... ?

5 1. étais
2. amenais
3. rendaient
4. mangeaient
5. étais
6. partais
7. adorais
8. mangeait
9. prenais

For **Grammaire supplémentaire** Answer Transparencies, see the *Teaching Transparencies* binder.

Grammaire supplémentaire

WA3 FRANCOPHONE EUROPE-1

6 Mets les phrases dans un ordre logique pour créer une histoire. (**p. 13**)

___ Elle est rentrée tellement vite qu'elle a laissé une de ses pantoufles sur le chemin.

___ Elle passait toute la journée à nettoyer la maison pendant que ses deux demi-sœurs s'amusaient.

___ Elle s'est lavée et elle a mis la belle robe et les pantoufles.

___ Elle voulait aller à ce bal, mais elle était trop sale.

___ Un après-midi, pendant qu'elle nettoyait la cuisine, une fée est apparue.

___ Il était une fois une jeune fille qui s'appelait Cendrillon. Elle vivait avec sa belle-mère et ses deux demi-sœurs qui étaient méchantes avec elle.

___ Au bal, elle s'amusait bien avec le prince quand elle a entendu minuit sonner.

___ Le lendemain, tout le village a appris que le beau prince cherchait celle qui portait les pantoufles de verre...

___ Un jour, elle a appris que ses demi-sœurs allaient aller au bal du village.

___ La fée lui a donné une robe et des pantoufles en verre pour aller au bal. La fée lui a dit qu'elle devait revenir du bal avant minuit.

7 Complète les phrases suivantes avec les mots proposés dans la boîte. Ensuite, dis si l'histoire que chaque phrase raconte est croyable (**C'est vrai?**) ou incroyable (**Mon œil!**). (**p. 13**)

portait	a décidé	voulait
j'ai vu	était	est partie
a beaucoup travaillé	a commencé	

1. Hier _____ la tante d'Alexis au supermarché avec son caniche, Riquiqui.
2. Le chien _____ des lunettes de soleil et un petit chapeau de cow-boy.
3. Il _____ à danser comme une ballerine.
4. La tante d'Alexis _____ en train d'acheter un gros bifteck.
5. Elle _____ le préparer pour le chien.
6. «Il danse bien», ai-je dit. «Il _____. Il le mérite bien.»
7. Elle _____ avec le chien et le bifteck.
8. Riquiqui _____ de conduire la voiture jusqu'à la maison.

Answers

6 Sentences should be numbered as follows: 9, 2, 7, 4, 5, 1, 8, 10, 3, 6

7
1. j'ai vu ; C'est vrai?
2. portait ; Mon œil!
3. a commencé ; Mon œil!
4. était ; C'est vrai?
5. voulait ; C'est vrai?
6. a beaucoup travaillé ; Mon œil!
7. est partie ; C'est vrai?
8. a décidé ; Mon œil!

Communication for All Students

Challenge
Have students write a few sentences on a card, telling where they went for a real or imaginary vacation, how they got there, where they stayed, and what it was like. Collect and distribute the cards. Have students circulate, asking one another questions to try to find the student who wrote the description on the card that they were assigned.

(Où est-ce que tu es allé(e)? Tu es parti(e) comment?)

Group Work
In groups of three or four, have students write and act out a scene similar to *Les Retrouvailles,* on pages 6–7. Have students greet one another and ask about one another's vacation. You might have groups turn in their written scripts.

Deuxième étape

Objectives Expressing indecision; making recommendations; ordering and asking for details

8 Trouve l'image qui correspond à chaque phrase et puis, récris les phrases sur une feuille de papier. (**p. 19**)

a.

b.

c.

d.

e.

1. Je dois dire que j'adore _____. Ils sont mignons comme tout!
2. _____ sont à côté de la salle de bains.
3. _____, c'est pratique pour apprendre l'anglais.
4. Encore _____? Tu as l'air d'avoir soif.
5. Ça te dit de commander _____?

9 Lis ces conversations et ajoute les articles définis, indéfinis ou partitifs qui conviennent. (**p. 19**)

BELLA	Excusez-moi, monsieur, qu'est-ce que vous avez comme entrées?
LE SERVEUR	___1___ carottes râpées et ___2___ céleri rémoulade, mademoiselle.
BELLA	Eh bien, je vais prendre ___3___ carottes râpées, s'il vous plaît!
MAX	Dis, Loïc, tu as choisi?
LOÏC	Non. J'hésite entre ___4___ côtelette de porc et ___5___ escalope de dinde.
OMAR	J'ai envie de manger ___6___ poisson!
FATIMA	Alors, prends ___7___ filet de sole! Il est très bon ici!
ANNE	Qu'est-ce que tu prends comme dessert aujourd'hui?
KARIM	Hmm... Je n'arrive pas à me décider. ___8___ crème caramel me tente, mais je fais un régime.
ANNE	Alors, c'est très simple! Tu devrais boire ___9___ eau et manger ___10___ pomme!

Review and Assess

You may wish to assign the **Grammaire supplémentaire** activities as additional practice or homework after presenting material throughout the chapter. Assign Activities 1–3 after **Grammaire** (p. 11), Activities 4–7 after **Grammaire** (p. 13), and Activities 8–9 after **Tu te rappelles?** (p. 19).

To prepare students for the **Etape** Quizzes and Chapter Test, we suggest doing the **Grammaire supplémentaire** activities in the following order. Have students complete Activities 1–7 before taking Quiz 1-1A or 1-1B; and Activities 8–9 before Quiz 1-2A or 1-2B.

Answers

8 1. Je dois dire que j'adore les chiens/les caniches; match to photo of poodle
2. Les toilettes sont à côté de la salle de bains; match to photo of bathroom
3. Un dictionnaire, c'est pratique pour apprendre l'anglais; match to photo of dictionary
4. Encore de la limonade?; match to photo of lemon soda
5. Ça te dit de commander une pizza?; match to photo of pizza

9 1. Des
2. du
3. les
4. la
5. l'
6. du
7. le
8. La
9. de l'
10. une

Mise en pratique

CHAPITRE 1

The **Mise en pratique** reviews and integrates all four skills and culture in preparation for the Chapter Test.

Teaching Resources
pp. 28–29

PRINT
- Lesson Planner, p. 6
- Listening Activities, p. 5
- Video Guide, pp. 5, 7–8
- Grammar Tutor for Students of French, Chapter 1
- Standardized Assessment Tutor, Chapter 1

MEDIA
- One-Stop Planner
- Video Program Videocassette 1, 18:16–21:31
- Audio Compact Discs, CD 1, Tr. 15
- Interactive CD-ROM Tutor, Disc 1

Career Path

A career in international affairs provides opportunities to live, work, and travel abroad. Many international organizations are located in Europe. The headquarters of NATO and the European Union (EU) are located in Brussels, the World Health Organization is in Geneva, and UNESCO (United Nations Educational, Scientific and Cultural Organization) is located in Paris. Ask students why French might be an important language to know for someone who wanted to pursue a career in international affairs. Ask students if they can name an international organization that is located in the U.S. (the United Nations in New York).

Language Note

Une salade au gruyère is an appetizer consisting only of shredded **gruyère** cheese (similar to Swiss cheese) served with a light dressing. **Spaetzlé** is an Alsacian dish of handmade egg noodles, usually served with a sauce as a side dish.

CD-ROM DISC 1

🖳 internet

ADRESSE: go.hrw.com
MOT-CLE: WA3
FRANCOPHONE EUROPE-1

 1
a. Prépare un questionnaire sur les vacances des jeunes Américains.
b. Pose tes questions aux autres élèves pour savoir où ils sont allés, comment, avec qui, etc.

2 C'est le premier jour d'école. Tu rencontres un(e) ami(e) qui te demande comment tes vacances se sont passées, ce que tu as fait, mangé, etc. Joue cette scène avec ton/ta camarade.

3 Regarde les menus et fais une liste de deux entrées, trois plats principaux et trois desserts.

3. *Possible answers*
Entrées: assiette de charcuterie, potage
Plats: aile de raie, filet de poisson, spaghettis à la bolognaise
Desserts: cône glacé, orange, salade de fruits

▬ A LA SOUPE LES POTACHES ▬

Les menus suivants seront servis mardi à midi dans les cantines scolaires:

CITÉ TECHNIQUE: aile de raie, sauce aux câpres, pommes vapeur ou coq au riesling et spaetzlé, entrée au choix, dessert au choix.

LYCÉE BARTHOLDI: assiette de charcuterie, filet de poisson sauce nantua, riz, orange.

LYCÉE CAMILLE SÉE: spaghettis à la bolognaise ou gratin de raviolis au poulet, entrée et dessert au choix.

COLLÈGE BERLIOZ: choux-fleurs ou brocolis en salade, filet de lingue, blettes et pommes de terre à la crème, Danette.

COLLÈGE MOLIÈRE: potage, raviolis au gratin, salade verte, cône glacé.

COLLÈGE SAINT-ANDRÉ: côte de porc, gratin de choux-fleurs ou émincé de dinde, pâtes, entrée, fromage et dessert au choix.

INSTITUT DE L'ASSOMPTION: omelette-frites, entrée, fromage et dessert au choix.

INSTITUTION SAINT-JEAN: spaghettis bolognaise ou émincé de veau, petits pois à la française, entrée, fromage et dessert au choix.

ÉCOLES MATERNELLES: salade au gruyère, rôti de bœuf, choux-fleurs au gratin, salade de fruits.

Un petit mot de ta correspondante à Colmar. Je t'envoie les menus scolaires qui sont publiés dans l'Alsace, notre journal régional. Les spécialités comme les spaetzlé (ce sont des pâtes alsaciennes) et la salade au gruyère, c'est typique de chez nous. En général, on a deux heures pour manger. On peut manger à la cantine ou rentrer à la maison. Moi, je préfère manger au lycée. Écris-moi pour me dire comment ça se passe, les repas du midi chez vous.
Salut,
Martine

Apply and Assess

Slower Pace
2 You might have students write out their questions before they interview their partner.

Additional Practice
3 Have students read Martine's letter and point out some differences between her school in France and their own school. Students should consider: a) specialty foods served, b) the amount of time students have for lunch, and c) where students are allowed to eat their lunches on school days.

4 Réponds à ta correspondante Martine et explique-lui comment le repas de midi se passe dans ton école. N'oublie pas de donner des exemples de menus typiques.

5 Écoute les lycéens suivants. Décide dans quelle école ils vont en t'aidant des menus à la page 28 de ton livre.   See scripts and answers on p. 3H.

CD 1 Tr. 15

Le Cygne

Les Entrées

Potage du jour	3 €
Salade de crudités	6 €
Escargots maison Dz. .12, -1/2 Dz.	6 €
Champignons frais sautés à l'ail	7 €
Salade frisée au chèvre chaud	8 €
Salade de foie de veau	8 €

Les Viandes

Faux-filet au poivre	14 €
Filet mignon	12 €
Steak Tartare	13 €
Émincé de veau au curry	14 €
Steak de saumon grillé, sauce à l'oseille	14 €

Les Plats Régionaux et les Petits Plats

Tarte flambée gratinée	6 €
Tripes au vin blanc	11 €
Rognons de porc aux champignons	11 €
Foies de lapins sautés	12 €

Cervelle d'agneau	12 €
Brochette garnie	12 €
Steak foie de veau lyonnaise	13 €
Pâté en croûte garni	10 €
Salade de bœuf garnie	11 €

Les fromages

Assortiment de fromages	5 €
Munster	4 €
Camembert	3 €
Gruyère	3 €
Chèvre	4 €
Bleu	4 €

Les desserts

Assiette de sorbets	6 €
Gâteau au chocolat, aux deux sauces	5 €
Soupe de kiwis à la sauce menthe	6 €
Pommes Grand-Mère au miel	5 €
Brochette de fruits	6 €
Tarte flambée aux pommes ou bananes	5 €

---

6 **Jeu de rôle**

You're at a restaurant with friends. One of you plays the server. The others, playing the customers, look at the menu from **Le Cygne** but are unsure about what to order. Ask each other questions, make recommendations, and order.

Apply and Assess

Kinesthetic Learners

6 Have students stage the scene, using a table, chairs, menus, props, and costumes. To extend the scene, they might enter the restaurant one at a time, greet one another as if they haven't met for a long time, get seated, ask for menus, order their food, eat, and pay the check.

Game

L'addition, s'il vous plaît! Copy the items and prices from the **Le Cygne** menu onto a transparency. Divide the class into teams. Read an order from the menu. The players find each item on the menu, note the prices, race to add up the cost of the meal, and give the total. The first player to give the correct total in French wins a point for his or her team.

Teaching Suggestion

4 Remind students to mention whether or not they usually go home for lunch. They might also discuss the pros and cons of an open campus for lunch.

Portfolio

4 **Written** This activity is appropriate for students' written portfolios. For suggestions, see *Alternative Assessment Guide*, page 16.

Slower Pace

5 Before you play the recording, have students compare the school menus. You might also pause the recording after each conversation and have students decide which school the speakers attend.

6 Have students note the foods they like and don't like.

Thinking Critically

6 **Analyzing** Have students consider the advantages of a long, relaxing meal spent with friends and family (more time to develop social relationships, better digestion). What are the disadvantages? (It can be more expensive; it takes time from work and school.)

Language Note

Students might want to know the following words from the menu: **lapin** *(rabbit)*; **brochette** *(shish kebob)*; **miel** *(honey)*; **cervelle** *(brains)*.

Que sais-je?

Teaching Resources
p. 30

PRINT
▶ Grammar Tutor for Students of French, Chapter 1

MEDIA
▶ Interactive CD-ROM Tutor, Disc 1
▶ Online self-test

Teaching Suggestions

4 5 6 Have students write a short description of their last vacation, real or imaginary, using the **passé composé** and the **imparfait**.

5 Students might interview one another, using the questions they've written.

Answers

6 *Possible answers:*
1. Je suis allé(e)...; Je suis partie en...
2. J'y suis allé(e) seul(e)/avec...
3. A l'hôtel; il a fait un temps magnifique. Il a plu tout le temps.

7 Qu'est-ce qu'il y avait à voir? Qu'est-ce qu'il y avait à faire? Il faisait... ?/Il faisait... est situé(e)...

11 1. Un café, s'il vous plaît.
2. Je vais prendre du poulet.
3. Comme dessert, j'aimerais de la glace aux fraises.

Que sais-je?

Can you use what you've learned in this chapter?

Can you renew old acquaintances? p. 9

1 How would you . . .
1. Ça fait longtemps qu'on ne s'est pas vu(e)s. Je suis content(e) de te revoir.
1. greet a friend you hadn't seen in a while?
2. inquire about your friend's activities? Qu'est-ce que tu deviens? Quoi de neuf?

2 How would you respond if . . .
1. a friend you hadn't seen in a while greeted you? Ça fait... ; Depuis...
2. your friend wanted to know what you've been doing?
Toujours la même chose! Rien (de spécial).

Can you inquire and express enthusiasm and dissatisfaction? p. 9

3 How would you ask a friend how his or her vacation was? C'était comment, tes vacances?

4 How might these people describe their vacations? *Possible answers:*

1. C'était pas terrible.
2. Pas trop bien. J'ai vu un ours.
3. Super! Ça s'est très bien passé.
4. C'était chouette! Je me suis beaucoup amusée.

Can you exchange information? p. 10

5 What questions would you ask to find out . . .
1. where your friend went on vacation and how he or she got there? Où est-ce que tu es allé(e)? Tu es parti(e) comment?
2. who he or she went with? Avec qui est-ce que tu es allé(e)?
3. where he or she stayed and what the weather was like? Où est-ce que tu as dormi? Quel temps qu'il a fait?

Can you ask and describe what a place was like? p. 12

6 How would you answer the questions in number 5? See answers below.

7 How would you ask what a place was like? How would you describe a place? See answers below.

Can you express indecision? p. 17

8 What would you say if you couldn't decide what to order in a restaurant? *Possible answers:* Je ne sais pas. Tout me tente. Je n'arrive pas à me décider. J'hésite entre... et...

Can you make recommendations? p. 17

9 How would you recommend that someone order a certain dish? Tu devrais prendre... ; Pourquoi tu ne prends pas... ? ; Essaie... ; Prends...

10 How do you ask the server . . .
1. what the restaurant's specialties are? Qu'est-ce que vous avez comme spécialités?
2. what kinds of appetizers there are? Qu'est-ce que vous avez comme entrées?
3. for a recommendation? Qu'est-ce que vous me conseillez?

Can you order and ask for details? p. 18

11 How would you order each of the following items? See answers below.
1. un café 2. du poulet 3. de la glace aux fraises

Review and Assess

Additional Practice
9 Have students list three or four of their favorite French or Alsatian dishes and recommend them to a partner.

Kinesthetic Learners
10 You might have partners act out the roles of server and customer, using the questions as a guide.

Additional Practice
11 You might also have students tell what the server would ask to elicit these orders.

Première étape

Renewing old acquaintances

Ça fait longtemps qu'on ne s'est pas vu(e)s.	It's been a long time since we've seen each other.
Je suis content(e) de te revoir.	I'm glad to see you again.
Ça fait...	It's been . . .
Depuis...	Since . . .
Qu'est-ce que tu deviens?	What's going on with you?
Quoi de neuf?	What's new?
Toujours la même chose!	Same old thing!
Rien (de spécial).	Nothing (special).

Inquiring; expressing enthusiasm and dissatisfaction

C'était comment, tes vacances?	How was your vacation?
Tu t'es bien amusé(e)?	Did you have fun?
Je me suis beaucoup amusé(e).	I had a lot of fun.
C'était pas terrible.	It wasn't so great.
Je me suis ennuyé(e).	I was bored.
Pas trop bien.	Not too good/well.

Exchanging information

Est-ce que tu es resté(e) ici?	Did you stay here?
Oui, je suis resté(e) ici tout le temps.	Yes, I stayed here the whole time.
Non, je suis parti(e)...	No, I went away for . . .
J'y suis allé(e) début/fin...	I went at the beginning/end of . . .
J'y suis allé(e) seul(e)/avec...	I went alone/with . . .
Tu es parti(e) comment?	How did you get there?
Je suis parti(e) en...	I went by . . .

Où est-ce que tu as dormi?	Where did you stay?
A l'hôtel.	In a hotel.
Quel temps est-ce qu'il a fait?	What was the weather like?
Il a fait un temps...	The weather was . . .
Il a plu.	It rained.

Asking and describing what a place was like

... est situé(e)...	. . . is located . . .
Qu'est-ce qu'il y avait à voir?	What was there to see?
Qu'est-ce qu'il y avait à faire?	What was there to do?
Il faisait… ?	Was the weather . . . ?
Il faisait…	The weather was . . .

Deuxième étape

Expressing indecision

Tout me tente.	Everything looks tempting.
Je n'arrive pas à me décider.	I can't make up my mind.
J'hésite entre... et...	I can't decide between . . . and . . .

Making recommendations

Tu devrais prendre...	You should have . . .
Essaie...	Try . . .

French menu

les entrées (f.)	appetizers
l'assiette (f.) de charcuterie	plate of pâté, ham, and cold sausage
l'assiette de crudités (f.)	plate of raw vegetables with vinaigrette
les carottes râpées	grated carrots with vinaigrette dressing
le céleri rémoulade	grated celery root with mayonnaise and vinaigrette
les plats (m.) principaux	main dishes
la côtelette de porc pâtes	porkchop with pasta
l'escalope (f.) de dinde purée	sliced turkey breast with mashed potatoes
le filet de sole riz champignons	filet of sole with rice and mushrooms
le poulet haricots verts	roasted chicken with green beans
la salade verte	salad
l'assiette de fromages	a selection of cheeses
le fromage de chèvre	goat cheese
la crème caramel	caramel custard
les tartes (f.) aux fruits	fruit pies/tarts

Ordering and asking for details

Que voulez-vous comme entrée?	What would you like for an appetizer?
Comme entrée, j'aimerais...	For an appetizer, I would like . . .
Et comme boisson?	And to drink?
Comment désirez-vous votre viande?	How do you like your meat cooked?
Saignante.	Rare.
A point.	Medium rare.
Bien cuite.	Well-done.
Qu'est-ce que vous avez comme... ?	What kind of . . . do you have?
Qu'est-ce que vous me conseillez?	What do you recommend?
Qu'est-ce que c'est,... ?	What is . . . ?

Vocabulaire

CHAPITRE 1

Game

Réponse-Question Create a grid on a transparency with these categories across the top: *Renewing old acquaintances, Vacations,* and *Ordering.* Down the left-hand side, write point values from 100 to 500. In the squares, write answers to questions that might be asked in each category. Then, cover each square with an adhesive note. Form two teams. Have a member of one team choose a category and a point value. Remove the adhesive note to reveal the answer (**Rien de spécial.**) The student has ten seconds to ask a question that would elicit that response (**Qu'est-ce que tu as fait pendant les vacances?**) Have teams take turns.

Chapter 1 Assessment

▸ **Testing Program**
Chapter Test, pp. 9–14
Audio Compact Discs, CD 1, Trs. 18–20
Speaking Test, p. 295

▸ **Alternative Assessment Guide**
Portfolio Assessment, p. 16
Performance Assessment, p. 30
CD-ROM Assessment, p. 44

▸ **Interactive CD-ROM Tutor, Disc 1**
A toi de parler
A toi d'écrire

▸ **Standardized Assessment Tutor**
Chapter 1

▸ **One-Stop Planner, Disc 1**
Test Generator
Chapter 1

Review and Assess

Circumlocution

Have partners take turns playing the role of an American exchange student who recently ate dinner at a French restaurant, and a French friend from school. The exchange student is trying to tell the friend about the meal, but is having difficulty remembering the French words for the dishes and must use circumlocution skills to communicate.

Have students switch roles after the friend has correctly guessed two items. Students can use the phrase **une sorte de** *(a kind of)* to describe the dishes. For example, **Comme plat principal, j'ai mangé une sorte de viande avec une pomme de terre coupée en longs morceaux (un steak-frites).**

Chapitre 2 : Belgique, nous voilà!
Chapter Overview

Mise en train pp. 34–36	*En route pour Bruxelles*

	FUNCTIONS	GRAMMAR	VOCABULARY	RE-ENTRY
Première étape pp. 37–41	• Asking for and giving directions, p. 37 • Expressing impatience; reassuring someone, p. 40	• The verb **conduire**, p. 39 • The imperative, p. 41	• At the gas station, p. 39	• Extending invitations (**Chapitre 6**, I) • The imperative (**Chapitre 1**, II) • **Aller** plus an infinitive (**Chapitre 1**, II)

Remise en train pp. 42–43	*Au Centre de la B.D.*

Deuxième étape pp. 44–49	• Expressing enthusiasm and boredom, p. 45 • Asking and telling where things are, p. 47	• Pronouns and their placement, p. 46	• Adjectives, p. 45	• Direct and indirect object pronouns (**Chapitre 10**, II) • The imperfect (**Chapitre 1**, III)

Lisons! pp. 50–52	**Julie, Claire, Cécile—Destinations avariées**	**Reading Strategy:** Previewing
Ecrivons! p. 53	**Ma propre bande dessinée**	**Writing Strategy:** Identifying your audience
Grammaire supplémentaire	pp. 54–57	**Première étape,** pp. 54–55	**Deuxième étape,** pp. 55–57
Review pp. 58–61	**Mise en pratique,** pp. 58–59	**Que sais-je?,** p. 60	**Vocabulaire,** p. 61

CULTURE

• **Note culturelle,** Languages in Belgium, p. 37
• Realia: Map of area around Liège, Belgium, p. 38

• **Panorama Culturel,** Favorite comic-book characters, p. 44
• **Rencontre culturelle,** Overview of Belgium, p. 48

PRINT

Lesson Planning

 One-Stop Planner

Lesson Planner with Substitute Teacher Lesson Plans, pp. 7–11, 65

Student Make-Up Assignments
- Make-Up Assignment Copying Masters, Chapter 2

Listening and Speaking

Listening Activities
- Student Response Forms for Listening Activities, pp. 11–13
- Additional Listening Activities 2-1 to 2-6, pp. 15–17
- Additional Listening Activities (song), p. 18
- Scripts and Answers, pp. 106–110

Video Guide
- Teaching Suggestions, pp. 10–11
- Activity Masters, pp. 12–14
- Scripts and Answers, pp. 82–84, 112

Activities for Communication
- Communicative Activities, pp. 5–8
- Realia and Teaching Suggestions, pp. 54–56
- Situation Cards, pp. 91–92

Reading and Writing

Reading Strategies and Skills Handbook, Chapter 2

Joie de lire 3, Chapter 2

Cahier d'activités, pp. 13–24

Grammar

Travaux pratiques de grammaire, pp. 9–17

Grammar Tutor for Students of French, Chapter 2

Assessment

Testing Program
- Grammar and Vocabulary Quizzes, **Etape** Quizzes, and Chapter Test, pp. 23–36
- Score Sheet, Scripts and Answers, pp. 37–43

Alternative Assessment Guide
- Portfolio Assessment, p. 17
- Performance Assessment, p. 31
- CD-ROM Assessment, p. 45

Student Make-Up Assignments
- Alternative Quizzes, Chapter 2

Standardized Assessment Tutor
- Reading, pp. 5–7
- Writing, p. 8
- Math, pp. 25–26

 **MEDIA**

 Online Activities
- Jeux interactifs
- Activités Internet

Video Program
- Videocassette 1
- Videocassette 5 (captioned version)

Audio Compact Discs
- Textbook Listening Activities, CD 2, Tracks 1–12
- Additional Listening Activities, CD 2, Tracks 18–24
- Assessment Items, CD 2, Tracks 13–17

 Interactive CD-ROM Tutor, Disc 1

Teaching Transparencies
- Situation 2-1 to 2-2
- **Grammaire supplémentaire** Answers
- **Travaux pratiques de grammaire** Answers

  One-Stop Planner CD-ROM

Use the **One-Stop Planner CD-ROM with Test Generator** to aid in lesson planning and pacing.

For each chapter, the **One-Stop Planner** includes:
- Editable lesson plans with direct links to teaching resources
- Printable worksheets from resource books
- Direct launches to the HRW Internet activities
- Video and audio segments
- Test Generator
- Clip Art for vocabulary items

Projects

Le Code de la route

Students will create a poster promoting safe driving habits.

> **MATERIALS**
>
> ✂ **Students may need**
> - Posterboard
> - Glue
> - Scissors
> - Pens
> - Colored markers
> - French-English dictionary

SUGGESTED SEQUENCE

1. Have students decide which safety rules they will feature. Students might contact local defensive-driving schools or the Department of Transportation for brochures and information on safe-driving tips.

2. Have students look up any unfamiliar words. They might also research French and Belgian traffic signs. Have them create a slogan or a promotional character to feature on their poster.

3. Have students write out the slogans, captions, and safety tips they intend to use on their posters. They should exchange and edit papers with a partner.

4. Have students organize and sketch the layout of their posters. You might have them exchange papers at this point to get advice from their peers on how to make the layout and message more attractive and attention-getting.

5. Students should incorporate their peers' suggestions and corrections into the final text and arrangement of the illustrations for the poster.

6. You might display students' posters around the classroom or the school.

> **GRADING THE PROJECT**
> To evaluate the project, you might base students' grades on appropriate content, language use, creativity, and appearance of the poster.
>
> Suggested Point Distribution (total = 100 points)
> Content...25 points
> Language use....................................25 points
> Creativity..25 points
> Appearance.......................................25 points

Games

Sentence Scrambler

In this game, students will practice word order by unscrambling words to form sentences.

Procedure To prepare for this game, write the individual words of various sentences on strips of transparency. Several sentences are suggested below. Put the transparency strips for each sentence in a separate bag. To play the game, divide the class into two teams. Scatter the transparency strips for the first sentence on the overhead projector. Have two students from the first team come to the overhead and try to rearrange the words in the correct order within ten or twenty seconds. If they form the sentence within the allotted time, they win a point for their team. Then, the opposing team takes a turn. Award a point for each correct sentence. You might play until one team has earned five or ten points.

SUGGESTED SENTENCES:

1. **Ça ne va pas prendre longtemps!**
2. **Comment on va à Bruxelles?**
3. **Vous allez voir un panneau qui indique l'entrée de l'autoroute.**
4. **Après Bruxelles, vous allez tomber sur un petit village.**
5. **Cette route va vous conduire au centre-ville.**

Charades

In this game, students will practice service-station vocabulary and expressions for giving directions.

Procedure To prepare for this game, write words and expressions from the chapter on index cards and place them in bags according to categories. Then, write the categories on the board, such as **à la station-service** and **les indications.** You might include additional categories related to the vocabulary. Divide the class into two teams. To play the game, have one player from the first team choose a category. He or she then draws a card from the corresponding bag and acts out the word or expression. The player's team has 30 seconds to try to guess the word or expression. If the player's team does not guess correctly, the other team has a chance to guess. The turn then passes to the second team. You might play until one team wins a given number of points.

Storytelling

Mini-histoire

This story accompanies Teaching Transparency 2-2. The **mini-histoire** *can be told and retold in different formats, acted out, written as dictation, and read aloud to give students additional opportunities to practice all four skills. The following story concerns a delivery man who delivers to the wrong address.*

Olivier, Morgane, Céline et Pierre sont au café. Ils sont en train de regarder des photos. Une des photos rappelle à Céline une histoire qu'elle a lue dans un magazine la semaine précédente :

«C'est l'histoire d'un coursier qui doit livrer des fleurs chez une certaine Madame Duchamp. Quand il arrive devant l'immeuble, il sonne chez Madame Duchamp et lui annonce à l'interphone qu'il vient pour livrer des fleurs. Madame Duchamp lui ouvre la porte de l'immeuble et lui indique qu'elle habite au quatrième étage. Le coursier monte les quatre étages. Quand il arrive sur le palier, en face de lui, il voit une porte sur laquelle les lettres D.U.C.H.A.M.P. sont écrites en majuscules. Il frappe à la porte. Une charmante vieille dame lui ouvre, toute surprise de recevoir des fleurs. Mais en fait, quand le coursier se retourne, une jeune femme le regarde très mécontente. Derrière elle, il aperçoit les lettres D.U.C.H.A.M.P. se détacher sur la porte. Il se rend compte qu'il a livré les fleurs à la mauvaise adresse!».

Traditions

Les Langues en Belgique

Due to its history, close political and commercial ties with neighboring countries, and its excellent transportation system, Belgium has become known as the crossroads of Europe. As a result, Belgians have traditionally learned to speak more than one or two languages. In fact, all children in Belgium are required to learn at least a second language in school. Since Brussels is officially a bilingual city, students must learn French and Flemish there. However, in other parts of the country, students may choose to learn German, English, Spanish, or Italian as their second or third language. English and German are the most popular choices because English is important for advanced study at universities and Germany is a neighbor and important trading partner. Ask students if they think people should study a second or third language in the United States and why.

Recette

Waterzoï *is a Flemish dish. While comparable to the typical Marseilles dish* **bouillabaisse,** *it substitutes cream, eggs and sage for garlic, tomatoes, and saffron. The main ingredient of* **waterzoï** *is either fish or chicken.*

WATERZOÏ

pour 6 personnes

1 tasse de branches de céleri

1 gros poireau

3 carottes

1 oignon

4 pommes de terre

1 cuillère à soupe de beurre

1 poulet coupé en morceaux

4 tasses d'eau bouillante

sauge

1/2 tasse de persil

sel

poivre

1 cuillère à soupe de farine

1 tasse de crème fraîche

2 jaunes d'œufs

1 baguette coupée en tranches

Couper en petits morceaux le céleri, le poireau, les carottes et l'oignon.

Dans une marmite, faire revenir les légumes avec le beurre pendant 5 minutes. Ajouter l'eau. Quand l'eau bout, ajouter le poulet coupé en morceaux. Ajouter le persil, le sel et le poivre. Laissez mijoter pendant 45 minutes. A mi-cuisson, ajouter les pommes de terre épluchées.

A la fin de la cuisson, prendre 1 1/2 tasse de bouillon pour préparer la sauce.

Pour la sauce, ajouter la farine, la crème fraîche et les jaunes d'œufs au bouillon. Quand la sauce a épaissi, la verser dans la marmite avec le poulet et les légumes.

Servir bien chaud avec le pain.

Technology

Video Program

Videocassette 1, Videocassette 5 (captioned version)
See Video Guide, pp. 9–14.

Camille et compagnie • Deuxième épisode : *Allez, en route!*

Camille, Max, and Sophie are ready to go to the Nostradamus art gallery in Camille's car, but Camille decides to play a trick on Max. She calls her friend Laurent, who works at a gas station, and asks him to help her. At the gas station, Max asks Laurent directions to the art gallery. As part of the trick, Laurent's directions are very confusing, and Max doesn't understand any of them. When the three friends are finally ready to leave, Camille's car won't start.

Qui est ton personnage de bande dessinée préféré? Il est comment?

Students from France and the Côte d'Ivoire describe their favorite cartoon characters. Two native speakers discuss the Panorama Culturel question and introduce the interviews.

Vidéoclips

- **Gepy®**: advertisement for shoes
- **Citroën GSA®**: advertisement for automobiles
- **Vynex®**: advertisement for hardware
- **News report**: Interviews with French comic strip artists

Interactive CD-ROM Tutor

The **Interactive CD-ROM Tutor** contains videos, interactive games, and activities that provide students an opportunity to practice and review the material covered in Chapter 2.

Activity	Activity Type	Pupil's Edition Page
1. Vocabulaire	Jeu des paires	p. 39
2. Comment dit-on… ?	Les mots qui manquent	pp. 37, 40
3. Grammaire	Le bon choix	pp. 38, 41
4. Vocabulaire	Chacun à sa place	p. 45
5. Grammaire	Méli-mélo	p. 46
6. Comment dit-on… ?	Chasse au trésor Explorons! Vérifions!	p. 47
Panorama Culturel	Qui est ton personnage de bande dessinée préféré? Il est comment? Le bon choix	p. 44
A toi de parler	*Guided recording*	pp. 58–59
A toi d'écrire	*Guided writing*	pp. 58–59

Teacher Management System

Logging In

Logging in to the *Allez, viens!* TMS is easy. Upon launching the program, simply type "admin" in the password area of the log-in screen and press RETURN. Log on to **www.hrw.com/CDROMTUTOR** for a detailed explanation of the Teacher Management System.

One-Stop Planner CD-ROM

To preview all resources available for this chapter, use the **One-Stop Planner CD-ROM,** Disc 1.

Internet Connection

ADRESSE: go.hrw.com
MOT-CLE: WA3 FRANCOPHONE EUROPE-2

*Have students explore the **go.hrw.com** Web site for many online resources covering all chapters. All Chapter 2 resources are available under the keyword **WA3 FRANCOPHONE EUROPE-2.** Interactive games help students practice the material and provide them with immediate feedback. You'll also find a printable worksheet that provides Internet activities that lead to a comprehensive online research project.*

Jeux interactifs

You can use the interactive activities in this chapter

- to practice grammar, vocabulary, and chapter functions
- as homework
- as an assessment option
- as a self-test
- to prepare for the Chapter Test

Activités Internet

Students look for information about comic-book characters, using the vocabulary and phrases from the chapter.

- In preparation for the **Activités Internet,** have students review the dramatic episode on Video-cassette 1, or do the activities in the **Panorama Culturel** on page 44. After completing the activity sheet, have students work with a partner and share the information they gathered in activities B and C on that sheet. Then ask each pair of students to share what they learned with the class.

Projet

Have groups of students create a virtual guided tour of their imaginary comic book museum. You might assign different sections of the museum to each group, and roles within the group. Students will search sites on famous cartoons and historical information about their assigned authors and characters. (They should document their sources by noting the names and the URLs of all the sites they consulted.) Students will then take their class on a virtual tour, using the expressions for giving directions they are learning in this chapter.

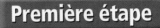

Première étape

7 **p. 37**

—Bon, bien. Vous continuez tout droit. Vous allez voir le panneau qui indique l'entrée de l'autoroute. C'est la N. soixante-trois. Suivez l'autoroute pendant à peu près cinq kilomètres et sortez à Court St-Etienne. C'est un petit village. Après le village, vous traversez un grand pont. Prenez la première route à gauche. Vous allez arriver à un carrefour. Là, vous tournez à droite, et cette route vous conduira au centre du village. Vous ne pouvez pas le manquer.

—D'accord. Je crois que je comprends. Merci, monsieur.

—Je vous en prie.

Answer to Activity 7
Malmédy

11 **p. 39**

1. Le plein de super, s'il vous plaît.

2. Vous avez besoin d'huile, madame.

3. Vous pourriez vérifier les pneus?

4. Oh là là! Je suis tombé en panne d'essence! Il y a une station-service près d'ici?

5. Vous pourriez me nettoyer le pare-brise, s'il vous plaît?

6. Voilà. J'ai mis de l'air dans les pneus et j'ai vérifié l'huile. Ça va.

7. Eh bien, le plein de super, ça vous fait trente-cinq euros.

8. Et les freins ne marchent pas très bien. Vous pouvez les vérifier?

Answers to Activity 11
1. chauffeur
2. pompiste
3. chauffeur
4. chauffeur
5. chauffeur
6. pompiste
7. pompiste
8. chauffeur

16 **p. 40**

1. Mais qu'est-ce que tu fais? Le film va commencer dans dix minutes!

2. Et moi aussi, j'ai faim, mais on n'a pas le temps d'aller manger. On va rater le train!

3. Attends! Je dois trouver mes lunettes de soleil. Ça ne va pas prendre longtemps.

4. Mais on va arriver, il n'y a pas le feu!

5. Eh bien, tu m'embêtes, là. Grouille-toi! On a encore un tas de choses à faire.

6. Le musée n'ouvre pas avant dix heures de toute façon. On a largement le temps!

7. Eh, du calme, du calme. On peut changer le pneu.

8. Tu peux te dépêcher un peu? Moi aussi, j'ai besoin du téléphone.

Answers to Activity 16
1. impatiente
2. impatiente
3. calme
4. calme
5. impatiente
6. calme
7. calme
8. impatiente

One-Stop Planner CD-ROM

To preview all resources available for this chapter, use the **One-Stop Planner CD-ROM**, Disc 1.

Deuxième étape

25 p. 45

1. Tu as lu ça? Lucky Luke®, c'est ma B.D. préférée. C'est marrant comme tout.

2. Eh regarde! Tintin®! Ce que c'est bien, Tintin. Tu sais, lire Tintin, ça me branche!

3. Tu vois? C'est Spirou®. Tu aimes, toi? Moi, non. C'est mortel!

4. Et voilà un album de Boule & Bill®. Tu vas le lire? Moi, je trouve que c'est ennuyeux à mourir. Je vais chercher autre chose.

5. Tu n'as jamais lu Tif et Tondu®? Tu devrais en lire. C'est rigolo comme tout!

6. Tu l'as trouvé, ton Gaston®? Oh, c'est rasant, Gaston. Je ne sais pas pourquoi tu aimes tant ça.

7. Tiens! Les Mousquetaires®! Tu vois? Qu'est-ce qu'ils sont dingues!

8. Dis donc, tu n'as pas dit que tu préférais Jojo®? Moi, ça m'embête. Et c'est tellement bébé!

Answers to Activity 25
1. s'amuse
2. s'amuse
3. s'ennuie
4. s'ennuie
5. s'amuse
6. s'ennuie
7. s'amuse
8. s'ennuie

28 p. 47

1. —Vous pourriez me dire où est le café?
　　—Oui. Prenez l'escalier, montez au premier étage et c'est tout de suite à gauche.

2. —Excusez-moi, où sont les toilettes?
　　—Elles sont tout au fond, à droite, à côté de l'entrée.

3. —Excusez-moi, vous savez où est la fusée de Tintin?
　　—Bien sûr. Prenez l'escalier, et elle sera juste en face de vous, au premier étage.

4. —Excusez-moi, je cherche l'ascenseur.
　　—Il est sur votre gauche, après l'escalier, à côté des téléphones.

5. —Pardon, madame, où se trouve la bédéthèque, s'il vous plaît? En haut ou en bas?

　　—Au rez-de-chaussée. Elle est au fond, à gauche, après l'ascenseur.

6. —Pour aller à la boutique de souvenirs, s'il vous plaît?
　　—C'est en haut, sur votre droite, juste après la fusée de Tintin.

Answers to Activity 28
1. d
2. b
3. e
4. c
5. a
6. f

Mise en pratique

3 p. 58

1. —Ecoute! Tu viens ou pas? On n'a pas le temps de s'arrêter!
　　—Oh! Tu as raison! Le spectacle va bientôt commencer!

2. —Tu peux te dépêcher? J'ai faim!
　　—Du calme, du calme. On y arrive.

3. —Mais qu'est-ce que tu fais?! Allons-y!
　　—Je dois vérifier le plan du parc. Ça ne va pas prendre longtemps.

4. —Je suis vraiment impatient de voir les feux d'artifice!
　　—Moi aussi! Ça va être super!

5. —Plus vite! Je dois téléphoner à ma mère à une heure!
　　—Du calme, du calme. On a largement le temps!

Answers to Mise en pratique Activity 3
1. impatiente
2. essaie de rassurer
3. essaie de rassurer
4. impatiente
5. essaie de rassurer

Chapitre 2 : Belgique, nous voilà!

Suggested Lesson Plans 50-Minute Schedule

Day 1

CHAPTER OPENER 5 min.
- Present Chapter Objectives, p. 33.
- Culture Note, ATE, p. 33
- Thinking Critically: Comparing and Contrasting, ATE, p. 33

MISE EN TRAIN 40 min.
- Presenting **Mise en train**, ATE, p. 34; using Video Program, Videocassette 1, see ATE, p. 35
- See Teaching Suggestions, Viewing Suggestions 1–2, Video Guide, p. 10.
- Culture Notes and Math Link, ATE, p. 35
- See Teaching Suggestions, Post-viewing Suggestions 1–2, Video Guide, p. 10.
- Do Activities 1–5, p. 36.

Wrap-Up 5 min.
- Do Activity 6, p. 36.

Homework Options
Cahier d'activités, Act. 1, p. 13

Day 2

PREMIERE ETAPE
Quick Review 5 min.
- Check homework.
- Bell Work, ATE, p. 37

Comment dit-on... ?, p. 37 20 min.
- Presenting **Comment dit-on... ?**, ATE, p. 37
- Play Audio CD for Activity 7, p. 37.
- Cahier d'activités, pp. 14–15, Activities 2–3
- Read and discuss **Note culturelle**, p. 37.
- Have students do Activities 8–9, p. 38, in pairs.

Vocabulaire, p. 39 20 min.
- Presenting **Vocabulaire**, ATE, p. 39
- Play Audio CD for Activity 11, p. 39.
- Travaux pratiques de grammaire, p. 10, Activities 2–3
- Do Activity 12, p. 39.

Wrap-Up, 5 min.
- TPR, ATE, p. 38

Homework Options
Pupil's Edition, Activity 10, p. 38
Grammaire supplémentaire, Act. 1, p. 54
Cahier d'activités, Act. 4, p. 15
Travaux pratiques de grammaire, Act. 1, p. 9

Day 3

PREMIERE ETAPE
Quick Review 5 min.
- Check homework.

Grammaire, p. 39 20 min.
- Presenting **Grammaire**, ATE, p. 39
- Language Notes, ATE, p. 39
- Do Activity 13, p. 40.
- Travaux pratiques de grammaire, p. 11, Activity 4
- **Grammaire supplémentaire**, p. 54, Activity 2
- Complete Activities 14–15, p. 40.

Comment dit-on... ?, p. 40 20 min.
- Presenting **Comment dit-on... ?**, ATE, p. 40
- Play Audio CD for Activity 16, p. 40.
- Cahier d'activités, p. 16, Activity 7
- Complete Activity 17, p. 41.

Wrap-Up 5 min.
- Have students finish letters from Activity 15, p. 40.

Homework Options
Cahier d'activités, Act. 6, p. 16

Day 4

PREMIERE ETAPE
Quick Review 5 min.
- Check homework.

Grammaire, p. 41 30 min.
- Presenting **Grammaire**, ATE, p. 41
- Travaux pratiques de grammaire, pp. 11–12, Activities 5–7
- Cahier d'activités, p. 17, Activity 9
- Have students do Activity 18, p. 41, in pairs.
- Game: **Jacques a dit**, ATE, p. 41

Wrap-Up 15 min.
- Game: Sentence Scrambler, ATE, p. 31C

Homework Options
Study for Quiz 2-1
Grammaire supplémentaire, Acts. 3–6, pp. 54–55
Cahier d'activités, Act. 8, p. 17

Day 5

PREMIERE ETAPE
Quiz 2-1 20 min.
- Administer Quiz 2-1A or 2-1B.

REMISE EN TRAIN 25 min.
- Presenting **Remise en train**, ATE, p. 42
- Culture Notes, ATE, p. 43
- Do Activities 19–23, pp. 42–43.
- Thinking Critically: Drawing Inferences, ATE, p. 43

Wrap-Up 5 min.
- Do Activity 24, p. 43.

Homework Options
Cahier d'activités, Acts. 10–11, p. 18

Day 6

REMISE EN TRAIN
Quick Review 5 min.
- Check homework.

DEUXIEME ETAPE
PANORAMA CULTUREL 10 min.
- Presenting **Panorama Culturel**, ATE, p. 44
- Multicultural Link and Language Note, ATE, p. 44
- **Qu'en penses-tu?**, p. 44
- Questions, ATE, p. 44

Comment dit-on… ? and Vocabulaire, p. 45 30 min.
- Presenting **Comment dit-on… ?**, ATE, p. 45
- Presenting **Vocabulaire**, ATE, p. 45
- Play Audio CD for Activity 25, p. 45.
- Cahier d'activités, p. 19, Activities 12–13
- Do Activity 26, p. 45.

Wrap-Up 5 min.
- Read and discuss **A la française**, p. 45.

Homework Options
Travaux pratiques de grammaire, Acts. 8–9, pp. 13–14

 **One-Stop** Planner CD-ROM

For alternative lesson plans by chapter section, to create your own customized plans, or to preview all resources available for this chapter, use the **One-Stop Planner CD-ROM**, Disc 1.

 For additional homework suggestions, see activities accompanied by this symbol throughout the chapter.

Day 7

DEUXIEME ETAPE
Quick Review 5 min.
- Check homework.

Grammaire, p. 46 20 min.
- Presenting **Grammaire**, ATE, p. 46
- Do Activity 27, p. 46.
- Travaux pratiques de grammaire, pp. 14–17, Activities 10–15
- Cahier d'activités, pp. 20–21, Activities 15–16

Comment dit-on... ?, p. 47 20 min.
- Presenting **Comment dit-on... ?**, ATE, p. 47
- Play Audio CD for Activity 28, p. 47.
- Do Activity 29, p. 47.
- Cahier d'activités, p. 22, Activity 18
- Have students do Activities 30–31, p. 49, in pairs.

Wrap-Up 5 min.
- Go over **Tu te rappelles?**, p. 49.

Homework Options
Study for Quiz 2-2
Pupil's Edition, Activity 33, p. 49
Grammaire supplémentaire, Acts. 7–11, pp. 55–57

Day 8

DEUXIEME ETAPE
Quiz 2-2 20 min.
- Administer Quiz 2-2A or 2-2B.

RENCONTRE CULTURELLE 10 min.
- Presenting **Rencontre culturelle**, ATE, p. 48
- History Link and Geography Link, ATE, p. 48
- Read and discuss **Savais-tu que… ?,** p. 48.

LISONS! 15 min.
- Read and discuss **Stratégie pour lire**, p. 50.
- Do Prereading Activities A–B, with Teaching Suggestions, ATE, p. 50.
- Have students read *Destinations avariées*, pp. 50–52.

Wrap-Up 5 min
- Career Path, ATE, p. 50

Homework Options
Pupil's Edition, Activities C–K, pp. 51–52

Day 9

LISONS!
Quick Review 5 min.
- Check homework.

LISONS! 15 min.
- Do Postreading Activity L, using Group Work, ATE, p. 52.

ECRIVONS! 25 min.
- Discuss the strategy for **Ecrivons!,** p. 53, and then allow students to work on their comic strips.

Wrap-Up 5 min.
- Allow time for peer and self-evaluation of comic strips.

Homework Options
Complete comic strips for **Ecrivons!,** Pupil's Edition, p. 53.

Day 10

ECRIVONS!
Quick Review 5 min.
- Allow volunteers to share their comic strips with the class.

MISE EN PRATIQUE 40 min.
- Do Activity 1, p. 58.
- Do Activity 2, p. 58.
- Play Audio CD for Activity 3, p. 58.
- Do Activity 4, p. 59.
- Have students do Activity 5, p. 59, in pairs.
- **A toi de parler,** CD-ROM Tutor, Disc 1

Wrap-Up 5 min.
- Additional Practice, ATE, p. 59

Homework Options
Cahier d'activités, Act. 21, p. 24.

Day 11

MISE EN PRATIQUE
Quick Review 5 min.
- Go over homework.

MISE EN PRATIQUE 40 min.
- Play Videocassette 1, then Videocassette 5 (captioned version). See Challenge, ATE, p. 59.
- **A toi d'écrire,** CD-ROM Tutor, Disc 1
- Activities for Communication, Situation Cards (Global), pp. 91–92

Wrap-Up 5 min.
- Have volunteers present a situation from each **étape** for the class.

Homework Options
Que sais-je?, p. 60

Day 12

MISE EN PRATIQUE
Quick Review 15 min.
- Go over **Que sais-je?**, p. 60.
- Have pairs do **Jeu de rôle**, p. 59.

Chapter Review 35 min.
- Review Chapter 2. Choose from **Grammaire supplémentaire**, Grammar Tutor for Students of French, Activities for Communication, Listening Activities, Interactive CD-ROM Tutor, or **Jeux interactifs.**

Homework Options
Study for Chapter 2 Test.

Assessment

Test, Chapter 2 50 min.
- Administer Chapter 2 Test. Select from Testing Program, Alternative Assessment Guide, Test Generator, or Standardized Assessment Tutor.

Chapitre 2 : Belgique, nous voilà!

Suggested Lesson Plans 90-Minute Block Schedule

Block 1

CHAPTER OPENER 10 min.
- Present Chapter Objectives, p. 33.
- Culture Note, ATE, p. 33

MISE EN TRAIN 30 min.
- Presenting **Mise en train**, ATE, p. 34, using Audio CD
- Math Link, ATE, p. 35
- Culture Notes, ATE, pp. 35–36
- Do Activities 2–5, p. 36.

PREMIERE ETAPE

Comment dit-on...?, p. 37 40 min.
- Presenting **Comment dit-on...?**, ATE, p. 37
- Play Audio CD for Activity 7, p. 37.
- **Note culturelle**, p. 37
- TPR, ATE, p. 38
- Read and discuss **Tu te rappelles?**, p. 38
- Do Activity 8, p. 38.

Wrap-Up 10 min.
- Listening Activities, p. 15, Additional Listening Activity 2-1

Homework Options
Pupil's Edition, Activity 10, p. 38
Grammaire supplémentaire, p. 54, Act. 1
Cahier d'activités, pp. 13–15, Acts. 1–3
Travaux pratiques de grammaire, p. 9, Act. 1

Block 2

PREMIERE ETAPE

Quick Review 10 min.
- Teaching Transparency 2-1, using suggestion #3 from Suggestions for Using Teaching Transparency 2-1

Vocabulaire, p. 39 20 min.
- Presenting **Vocabulaire**, ATE, p. 39
- Play Audio CD for Activity 11, p. 39.
- Do Activity 12, p. 39.

Grammaire, p. 39 40 min.
- Presenting **Grammaire**, ATE, p. 39
- Language Notes, ATE, p. 39
- Do Activities 13–15, p. 40.

RENCONTRE CULTURELLE 15 min.
- Presenting **Rencontre culturelle**, ATE, p. 48
- Read and discuss **Savais-tu que...?**, p. 48.

Wrap-Up 5 min.
- Teaching Transparency 2-1, using suggestion #1 from Vocabulary Practice Using Teaching Transparency 2-1

Homework Options
Grammaire supplémentaire, p. 54, Act. 2
Cahier d'activités, pp. 15–16, Acts. 5–6
Travaux pratiques de grammaire, pp. 10–11, Acts. 2–4

Block 3

PREMIERE ETAPE

Quick Review 5 min.
- Using Teaching Transparency 2-1 or another illustration of a car, have students call out the names for the car parts, as you point them out.

Comment dit-on...?, p. 40 20 min.
- Presenting **Comment dit-on...?**, ATE, p. 40
- Play Audio CD for Activity 16, p. 40.
- Do Activity 17, p. 41.

Grammaire, p. 41 60 min.
- Presenting **Grammaire**, ATE, p. 41
- Game: **Jacques a dit**, ATE, p. 41
- Do Activity 18, p. 41.
- Have students work in pairs to present their conversations from Activity 18, p. 41.

Wrap-Up 5 min.
- Call out expressions from **Comment dit-on...?**, p. 40, in random order and have students tell whether each phrase is expressing impatience or reassuring.

Homework Options
Have students study for Quiz 2-1.
Grammaire supplémentaire, pp. 54–55, Acts. 3–6
Cahier d'activités, pp. 15–17, Acts. 4, 7–9
Travaux pratiques de grammaire, p. 12, Acts. 5–7

One-Stop Planner CD-ROM

For alternative lesson plans by chapter section, to create your own customized plans, or to preview all resources available for this chapter, use the **One-Stop Planner CD-ROM**, Disc 1.

For additional homework suggestions, see activities accompanied by this symbol throughout the chapter.

Block 4

PREMIERE ETAPE
Quick Review 10 min.
- Activities for Communication, pp. 5–6, Communicative Activity 2-1A and 2-1B

Quiz 2-1 20 min.
- Administer Quiz 2-1A or 2-1B.

REMISE EN TRAIN 40 min.
- Presenting **Remise en train,** ATE, p. 42
- Do Activities 19–23, pp. 42–43.

DEUXIEME ETAPE
Comment dit-on...?, p. 45 15 min.
- Presenting **Comment dit-on...?,** ATE, p. 45
- **A la française,** p. 45

Wrap-Up 5 min.
- Thinking Critically: Drawing Inferences, ATE, p. 43

Homework Options
Cahier d'activités, pp. 18–19, Acts. 10–12

Block 5

DEUXIEME ETAPE
Quick Review 5 min.
- Randomly call out expressions from **Comment dit-on...?,** page 45, and have students tell whether each expression is expressing enthusiasm or boredom.

Vocabulaire, p. 45 15 min.
- Presenting **Vocabulaire,** ATE, p. 45
- Play Audio CD for Activity 25, p. 45.
- Do Activity 26, p. 45.

Grammaire, p. 46 30 min.
- Presenting **Grammaire,** ATE, p. 46
- **Grammaire supplémentaire,** pp. 55–56, Acts. 7–8
- Do Activity 27, p. 46.

Comment dit-on...?, p. 47 30 min.
- Presenting **Comment dit-on...?,** ATE, p. 47
- Play Audio CD for Activity 28, p. 47.
- Do Activity 29, p. 47.
- Do Activity 30, p. 49.

Wrap-Up 10 min.
- TPR, ATE, p. 47

Homework Options
Have students study for Quiz 2-2.
Pupil's Edition, Activity 33, p. 49
Grammaire supplémentaire, p. 57, Acts. 9–11
Cahier d'activités, pp. 19–22, Acts. 13–19
Travaux pratiques de grammaire, pp. 13–17, Acts. 8–15

Block 6

DEUXIEME ETAPE
Quick Review 10 min.
- Activities for Communication, pp. 7–8, Communicative Activity 2-2A or 2-2B

Quiz 2-2 20 min.
- Administer Quiz 2-2A or 2-2B.

PANORAMA CULTUREL 15 min.
- Presenting **Panorama Culturel,** ATE, p. 44
- Answer Questions, ATE, p. 44.
- Discuss **Qu'en penses-tu?,** p. 44.

LISONS!, pp. 50–52 30 min.
- Do Prereading Activities A–B, Teaching Suggestions, ATE, p. 50.
- Read *Destinations avariées,* ATE, pp. 50–52.
- Language-to-Language, ATE, p. 52

MISE EN PRATIQUE 15 min.
- Play Audio CD for Activity 3, p. 58.
- Do Activity 4, p. 59.

Homework Options
Pupil's Edition, Activity 2, p. 58
Que sais-je?, p. 60
Interactive CD-ROM Tutor: Games
Study for Chapter 2 Test

Block 7

MISE EN PRATIQUE
Quick Review 10 min.
- Check homework.
- **Jeu de rôle,** p. 59

Chapter Review 35 min.
- Review Chapter 2. Choose from **Grammaire supplémentaire,** Grammar Tutor for Students of French, Activities for Communication, Listening Activities, Interactive CD-ROM Tutor, or **Jeux interactifs.**

Test, Chapter 2 45 min.
- Administer Chapter 2 Test. Select from Testing Program, Alternative Assessment Guide, Test Generator, or Standardized Assessment Tutor.

Chapter Opener

One-Stop Planner CD-ROM

For resource information, see the **One-Stop Planner**, Disc 1.

Pacing Tips
The first **étape** has more content to cover than the second **étape.** You might keep that in mind when planning your lessons. For Lesson Plans and timing suggestions, see pages 31I–31L.

Meeting the Standards
Communication
- Asking for and giving directions, p. 37
- Expressing impatience; reassuring someone, p. 40
- Expressing enthusiasm and boredom, p. 45
- Asking and telling where things are, p. 47

Cultures
- Culture Notes, pp. 33, 35, 36, 40, 43
- Note culturelle, p. 37
- Panorama Culturel, p. 44
- Rencontre culturelle, p. 48

Connections
- History Link, p. 48
- Geography Links, pp. 48, 51
- Language Arts Link, p. 52
- Math Link, p. 35
- Multicultural Links, pp. 37, 44
- Reading/Writing Link, p. 53

Comparisons
- Language-to-Language, p. 52
- Thinking Critically, pp. 33, 43, 52

Communities
- Career Path, p. 50
- Community Links, pp. 37, 44
- De l'école au travail, p. 49

Connections and Comparisons

Architecture Link
The historical **Grand-Place**, at the congruence of seven major streets in the center of Brussels, is famous for its richly decorated Gothic and Baroque façades. Dating back to the Middle Ages, the square was reconstructed after being bombarded by Louis XIV's army in 1695. Many beautiful houses (**hôtels particuliers**) and former medieval guild halls, which are now restaurants and cafés, define the square's perimeter. The magnificent **Hôtel de Ville**, constructed in the fifteenth century in the elaborate High Gothic style, is the square's hallmark.

Objectives

In this chapter you will review and practice how to

Première étape

- ask for and give directions
- express impatience
- reassure someone

Deuxième étape

- express enthusiasm and boredom
- ask and tell where things are

internet

go.hrw.com
ADRESSE: go.hrw.com
MOT-CLE: WA3 FRANCOPHONE
EUROPE-2

◀ **La Grand-Place, cœur de la ville de Bruxelles**

Chapter Opener

Focusing on Outcomes

Have students read the list of objectives and tell in what situations they might use each one. Then, have them list French words and expressions they already know that accomplish these functions. (*Asking for and giving directions:* **Je cherche... , s'il vous plaît. Tournez à...** *Reassuring someone:* **Ça va aller mieux.** *Expressing enthusiasm and boredom:* **C'est sensass/mortel/sinistre.** *Asking and telling where things are:* **Où se trouve... ? C'est à gauche de...**)

NOTE: The self-check activities in **Que sais-je?** on page 60 help students assess their achievement of the objectives.

Thinking Critically

Comparing and Contrasting

Have students look at this photo of the center of Brussels and compare what they see with the center of their own city or town.

Cultures and Communities

Culture Note

Call students' attention to the lace shown on the border of page 33 of their textbook. In the early seventeenth century, lace became a popular fabric and luxury item in Europe. Handmade lace was worn and coveted by both men and women. In the seventeenth and eighteenth centuries, Flanders, now part of Belgium, was one of the major centers of lace production, along with France and Italy. In later centuries, cotton clothing became more popular, and electric bobbins made handmade lace expensive and less practical than more durable fabrics. However, traditional handmade lace is still proudly produced in the town of Bruges and is quite popular with tourists.

Teaching Resources
pp. 34–36

PRINT 📖
▶ Lesson Planner, p. 7
▶ Video Guide, pp. 10, 12
▶ Cahier d'activités, p. 13

MEDIA 💿📼
▶ One-Stop Planner
▶ Video Program
Camille et compagnie
Videocassette 1, 21:48–27:41
Videocassette 5 (captioned version), 07:48–13:41
▶ Audio Compact Discs, CD 2, Tr. 1

Presenting
Mise en train

Play the audio recording, stopping after each scene. Have students tell what they understood. Ask questions 1–3 of Activity 1 on page 36 after the first scene and questions 4–5 after the fourth scene.

Teaching Suggestion

• Have students scan *En route pour Bruxelles* to find two services a gas station attendant might perform, three things to see in Brussels, two roads, and a tool one might carry in a car (**faire le plein, vérifier l'huile et les pneus; la Grand-Place, le palais, le musée de l'Armée; la N. 89, la E. 411; le cric**).

Language Notes

• **Le type** is slang for *guy*.
• Tell students that **Oh là là!** is an expression of dismay or annoyance, not admiration.

Stratégie pour comprendre

CD 2 Tr. 1

What are Stéphane and Hervé doing? Before reading this episode, look at the photos and try to guess what is happening to the two boys. Then, as you read the dialogue, try to find the words and phrases that best describe what is represented in the photos.

Cahier d'activités, p. 13, Act. 1

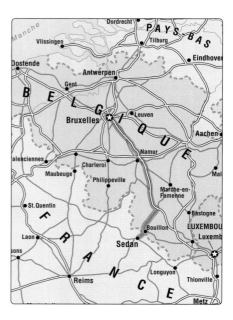

1 Le pompiste — Bonjour!

Stéphane — Le plein de super, s'il vous plaît.

Hervé — A quelle heure tu crois qu'on va arriver à Bruxelles?

Stéphane — Bruxelles, c'est à environ 170 kilomètres d'ici. Donc, ça va nous prendre une heure et demie au plus et le Centre ouvre à dix heures. On a largement le temps.

Hervé — Chouette! Je suis vachement content d'aller au Centre de la B.D.

Le pompiste — Voilà. Ce sera tout?

Hervé — Euh... Vous pourriez vérifier l'huile, s'il vous plaît? Ah! Et les pneus aussi!

2 Le pompiste — Oui, bien sûr.

Stéphane — Qu'est-ce qu'on va faire après la visite du Centre?

Hervé — On pourrait aller à la Grand-Place, au palais, au musée de l'Armée...

Stéphane — Hé! N'oublie pas qu'on doit rentrer ce soir.

Le pompiste — L'huile, ça va. J'ai mis de l'air dans les pneus. Ça fait 35 euros.

Stéphane — Hervé, tu me passes 15 euros?

Hervé — Euh... Moi, j'ai juste assez pour Bruxelles...

Stéphane — Oh, tu pousses, quand même! C'est toujours la même chose!

Preteaching Vocabulary

Guessing Words from Context

Have students look at the photos on pages 34 and 35. Ask them to make predictions about what is going on in this story. Have them guess what the word **essence** in the second photo on page 34 might mean, based on where the characters are. What do they think the older man in the second photo on page 35 is doing? Finally, what is happening in the last photo? Once students have answered these questions, ask them to skim the reading and find expressions that might describe or relate to the events they just described. (**Le plein de super; Pardon, monsieur; La route pour...; On a un pneu crevé!**)

Ils traversent la ville de Bouillon...

3 **Stéphane** Tiens, tu as vu le château? Super! On s'arrête?

Hervé Oh, non, écoute! On n'a pas le temps!

Stéphane En tout cas, on doit s'arrêter pour demander comment on arrive à l'autoroute.

4 **Stéphane** Pardon, monsieur. La route pour Bruxelles, s'il vous plaît?

Le monsieur Alors, pour Bruxelles... Vous suivez la N. 89 pendant à peu près 12 kilomètres. Là, vous allez voir un panneau qui indique l'entrée de l'autoroute. Prenez la direction de Bruxelles. C'est la E. 411. Elle vous conduira tout droit au centre-ville. Vous ne pouvez pas le manquer.

Stéphane Ah ben, ça n'a pas l'air compliqué. Merci, monsieur.

Sur la E. 411, près de Namur...

5 **Hervé** Je suis vraiment impatient d'arriver! Va plus vite, bon sang! Tu n'avances pas!

Stéphane Du calme, du calme! Il n'y a pas le feu! Il est seulement neuf heures. Tu es toujours... Oh là là! Qu'est-ce qui se passe?

Hervé On a un pneu crevé! Arrête-toi! Arrête-toi!

Stéphane Zut, alors!

Hervé Euh, tu sais changer les pneus, toi?

Stéphane Ouais, mais tu vas m'aider quand même!

Hervé Euh, ouais. Mais je ne sais pas comment on fait.

Stéphane Tu es vraiment nul comme type! Bon, je vais chercher la roue de secours. Prends la boîte à outils et le cric.

Hervé Grouille-toi! On va être en retard! Je voulais arriver à l'heure d'ouverture pour éviter la foule.

Stéphane Oh, écoute. Ça ne va pas prendre longtemps.

Using the Captioned Video

As an alternative, you might want to show the captioned version of *Camille et compagnie : Allez, en route!* on Videocassette 5. Some students may benefit from seeing the written words as they listen to the target language and watch the gestures and actions in context. This visual reinforcement of vocabulary and functions will facilitate students' comprehension and help reduce their anxiety before they are formally introduced to the new language in the chapter.

Math Link
Have students figure out the distance between Sedan and Brussels (about 170 km) in miles. To convert kilometers to miles, multiply by .62 (105 miles).

Visual/Auditory Learners
On the board or on a transparency, draw a gas pump, the Bouillon castle, and a flat tire, and number them from 1–3. Then, play excerpts of the audio recording and have students call out the number of the corresponding illustration.

Culture Note
In France, gasoline costs about as much per liter as it does per gallon (about 4 liters) in the United States. For this reason, **diesel/gazole,** or diesel fuel, has become popular.

Camille et compagnie

You may choose to show students Episode 1: *Allez, en route!* now or wait until later in the chapter. In the video, Camille, Max, and Sophie are getting ready to go to an art gallery in Camille's car. Camille decides to play a trick on Max. She calls her friend Laurent, who works at a gas station, and asks him to help her. At the gas station, Max asks Laurent for directions to the art gallery. As part of the trick, Laurent's directions are confusing, and Max doesn't understand any of them! When the three friends are finally ready to go, Camille's car won't start.

3 Ask individuals to suggest additional quotes and have the class try to guess who the speakers were.

4 Have students support their answers with quotations from *En route pour Bruxelles.* Have them suggest other adjectives to describe Stéphane and Hervé.

6 Have partners ask each other these questions. Students might then volunteer information about their partner. **(Suzanne est allée en Californie en voiture.)**

Culture Note
Roads in France and Belgium are identified by both a letter and number. The letters indicate the type of road: **N** designates a **route nationale,** while **D** signifies a **route départementale. E** indicates international highways that cross several European countries. An **A** road is an **autoroute,** which often requires a toll.

Answers
5 1. Le plein de super, s'il vous plaît.
2. Vous pourriez vérifier l'huile, s'il vous plaît?
3. On pourrait aller à...
4. Tiens, tu as vu... ?
5. Oh, non, écoute! On n'a pas le temps! Je suis vraiment impatient d'arriver! Va plus vite, bon sang! Tu n'avances pas! Grouille-toi! On va être en retard!
6. La route pour... , s'il vous plaît?
7. Oh, tu pousses, quand même! C'est toujours la même chose. Tu es vraiment nul comme type.
8. On a largement le temps. Du calme, du calme! Il n'y a pas le feu. Oh, écoute. Ça ne va pas prendre longtemps.

---

1 ## Tu as compris?

These activities check for comprehension only. Students should not yet be expected to produce language modeled in **Mise en train.**

1. Où vont Stéphane et Hervé? Brussels
2. Qu'est-ce qu'ils veulent y faire? visit the Comic Book Center
3. Où est-ce qu'ils s'arrêtent? Pourquoi? service station, for gas, oil, and air for their tires; Bouillon, to ask directions
4. Qui a l'air impatient? Pourquoi? Hervé; He keeps telling Stéphane to hurry.
5. Qu'est-ce qui se passe à la fin de l'histoire? flat tire

2 ## Mets dans le bon ordre
Mets ces phrases dans le bon ordre d'après *En route pour Bruxelles.* 6, 3, 2, 5, 1, 4

1. Ils ont un pneu crevé.
2. Stéphane dit qu'il veut visiter le château.
3. Le pompiste vérifie l'huile.
4. Stéphane va chercher la roue de secours.
5. Ils s'arrêtent pour demander la route.
6. Le pompiste fait le plein de super.

3 ## Qui dit quoi?

Hervé — **Stéphane** **Hervé** Hervé **le pompiste** Stéphane **le monsieur**

Grouille-toi! On va être en retard! *Hervé*

Le Centre ouvre à dix heures. On a largement le temps. *Stéphane*

Moi, j'ai juste assez pour Bruxelles. *Hervé*

Ah ben, ça n'a pas l'air compliqué. *Stéphane*

Vous allez voir un panneau qui indique l'entrée de l'autoroute. *le monsieur*

Voilà. Ce sera tout? *le pompiste*

Tu es vraiment nul comme type! *Stéphane*

L'huile, ça va. Ça fait 35 euros. *le pompiste*

4 ## Comment sont-ils?
Comment est Stéphane? Et Hervé? Choisis les adjectifs qui les décrivent le mieux.

Hervé impatient — *Stéphane* sûr de lui — *Stéphane* patient — *Hervé* embêtant

Stéphane calme — grippe-sou *(stingy)* *Hervé* — *Hervé* énervé — *Hervé* égoïste

5 ## Cherche les expressions
What do the young people in *En route pour Bruxelles* say to . . . See answers below.

1. have the gas tank filled?
2. have the oil checked?
3. suggest places they should visit?
4. point out something?
5. express impatience?
6. ask for directions?
7. express annoyance?
8. reassure someone?

6 ## Et maintenant, à toi
Est-ce que tu as déjà fait un long voyage en voiture? Où est-ce que tu es allé(e)? Avec qui? Est-ce que vous vous êtes arrêté(e)s en route? Pourquoi?

Comprehension Check

Tactile Learners
2 Have students write these and additional sentences on strips of paper and arrange them in the correct order.

Kinesthetic Learners
2 Have six students act out the sentences and have the class put them in order.

Auditory Learners
3 Have students close their books. Write **Stéphane, Hervé, le pompiste,** and **le monsieur** on the board. Then, read the quotes aloud and have students match each one to the correct speaker.

Comment dit-on...?

Asking for and giving directions

To ask for directions:

La route pour Bruxelles, **s'il vous plaît?** *Could you tell me how to get to . . .?*
Comment on va à Namur?
Où se trouve... ?

To give directions:

Pour (aller à) Bruxelles, **vous suivez la** N. (Nationale) 89 **pendant à peu près** 35 **kilomètres.** *To get to . . . , follow . . . for about . . . kilometers.*
Vous allez voir un panneau qui indique l'entrée de l'autoroute. *You'll see a sign that points out the freeway entrance.*
Vous allez traverser un grand pont.
Après le pont, **vous allez tomber sur** un petit village. *After . . . , you'll come across . . . .*
Cette route va vous conduire au centre-ville. *This road will lead you into the center of town.*
Vous allez continuer tout droit, jusqu'au carrefour/au feu rouge. *. . . up to the intersection/stop light.*

> Cahier d'activités, pp. 14–15, Act. 2–3

7 **Les directions pour aller à...** See scripts on p. 31G.

Ecoutons Ecoute cette conversation. Est-ce que cette jeune fille va à Spa, Malmédy ou Verviers? *Malmédy*

CD 2 Tr. 2

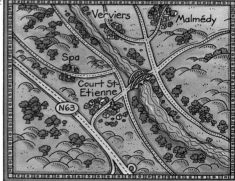

Note culturelle

La Belgique a trois langues officielles: le français, le flamand et l'allemand. Le flamand est un dialecte dérivé du hollandais qu'on parle en Flandre, la partie nord de la Belgique. Dans le sud de la Belgique, en Wallonie, on parle français. Dans l'est, on parle aussi l'allemand. Cette division linguistique a toujours causé des disputes entre les Wallons et les Flamands. C'est pourquoi en 1971, une réforme constitutionnelle a créé des régions linguistiques distinctes. La capitale, Bruxelles, est devenue officiellement bilingue (français et flamand). Les cartes géographiques belges contiennent les noms des villes dans les deux langues; par exemple, Anvers/Antwerpen et Bruges/Brugge.

Connections and Comparisons

Multicultural Link

Have students name bilingual countries, regions, or states (Morocco, Florida), and then find out what each culture has contributed to the community.

Community Link

Ask students to give detailed directions in English from the school to their house or to a grocery store or movie theater. Then, have them list French expressions they've already learned for giving directions.

Teaching Resources
pp. 37–41

PRINT

▶ Lesson Planner, p. 8
▶ Listening Activities, pp. 11–12, 15–16
▶ Activities for Communication, pp. 5–6, 54, 56, 91–92
▶ Travaux pratiques de grammaire, pp. 9–12
▶ Grammar Tutor for Students of French, Chapter 2
▶ Cahier d'activités, pp. 14–17
▶ Testing Program, pp. 23–26
▶ Alternative Assessment Guide, p. 31
▶ Student Make-Up Assignments, Chapter 2

MEDIA

▶ One-Stop Planner
▶ Audio Compact Discs, CD 2, Trs. 2–4, 13, 18–20
▶ Teaching Transparencies: 2-1; **Grammaire supplémentaire** Answers; Travaux pratiques de grammaire Answers
▶ Interactive CD-ROM Tutor, Disc 1

Bell Work

Have students use the following direction words they've already learned to tell where a classmate is seated in relation to their own seat: **à droite, à gauche, près de, loin de, devant, derrière.** (**Il est derrière moi, à gauche.**)

Presenting
Comment dit-on...?

Have students recall expressions they've learned for giving directions. Draw a city map on a transparency. Bring in a toy car and move it along the map as you say the various directions. Then, have a volunteer come to the overhead and move the car as you give directions.

Teaching Resources
pp. 37–41

PRINT
- Lesson Planner, p. 8
- Listening Activities, pp. 11–12, 15–16
- Activities for Communication, pp. 5–6, 54, 56, 91–92
- Travaux pratiques de grammaire, pp. 9–12
- Grammar Tutor for Students of French, Chapter 2
- Cahier d'activités, pp. 14–17
- Testing Program, pp. 23–26
- Alternative Assessment Guide, p. 31
- Student Make-Up Assignments, Chapter 2

MEDIA
- One-Stop Planner
- Audio Compact Discs, CD 2, Trs. 2–4, 13, 18–20
- Teaching Transparencies: 2-1; **Grammaire supplémentaire** Answers; Travaux pratiques de grammaire Answers
- Interactive CD-ROM Tutor, Disc 1

 TPR To review prepositions of location, direct students to stand or sit in various places in the classroom (**Phil, mets-toi derrière Simone. Lisa, assieds-toi à côté de moi.**) and have them respond accordingly.

8 Méli-mélo!

Parlons Mets ce dialogue entre Adrienne et Mme Zidan dans le bon ordre. Ensuite, joue la scène avec ton/ta camarade.

10 «Au revoir, mademoiselle.»

6 «Eh bien, le panneau pour la N. 44.»

7 «Ah bon, très bien. Je vous remercie beaucoup, madame.»

4 «Ensuite, vous allez continuer pendant à peu près 10 kilomètres et vous allez tomber sur une vieille église. Juste après l'église, vous allez voir le panneau.»

1 «Pardon, madame. Où se trouve la N. 44, s'il vous plaît?»

3 «Bon, très bien. Et ensuite?»

2 «Eh bien, vous allez suivre cette route jusqu'au feu rouge. Au feu rouge, vous allez tourner à droite.»

9 «Au revoir, madame.»

5 «Quel panneau?»

8 «Je vous en prie.»

9 La route pour Liège, s'il vous plaît?

Parlons Tu voyages en Belgique près de Salmchâteau. Tu t'arrêtes à une station-service pour demander la route pour Liège. Joue cette scène avec ton/ta camarade.

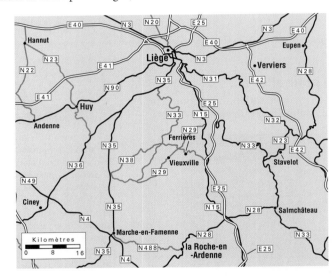

10 Devine!

Ecrivons Regarde la carte et choisis une ville autre que Liège. Ecris un mot à un camarade pour lui expliquer comment aller de cette ville à Liège sans nommer la ville. Ton camarade doit lire ton mot et deviner quelle ville tu as choisie. Ensuite, changez de rôle.

Tu te rappelles?

Do you remember how to tell that something is going to happen? Use a form of the verb **aller** plus the infinitive of another verb. **Demain, je vais visiter la ville de Bruxelles.**

Travaux pratiques de grammaire, p. 9, Act. 1 → Grammaire supplémentaire, p. 54, Act. 1

Communication for All Students

Slower Pace
8 Have students first identify the sentences spoken by Adrienne and those spoken by Mme Zidan. Then, have them copy the girl's lines onto strips of paper of one color and the woman's lines onto strips of a different color, and put the dialogue in order.

Challenge
10 After students have written directions to another city, collect the papers and redistribute them. Students should follow the directions on the paper they receive and write where they lead at the bottom. Return the papers to the original writers, who verify the answer.

avoir un pneu crevé — *to have a flat tire*
faire la vidange — *to change the oil*
faire le plein — *to fill it up*
vérifier ... — *to check . . .*
les freins (m.) — *the brakes*
l'huile (f.) — *the oil*
la pression des pneus — *the tire pressure*
mettre de l'air dans les pneus — *to put air in the tires*
mettre de l'huile dans le moteur — *to put oil in the motor*
mettre la roue de secours — *to put on the spare tire*
nettoyer le pare-brise — *to clean the windshield*
tomber en panne (d'essence) — *to break down (run out of gas)*

la station-service
l'essence (f.)
du super (sans plomb)
le réservoir
le pompiste
un pneu

Travaux pratiques de grammaire, p. 10, Act. 2–3

Cahier d'activités, p. 15, Act. 4

11 A la station-service See scripts and answers on p. 31G.

Ecoutons Est-ce que c'est le pompiste ou le chauffeur qui parle?
CD 2 Tr. 3

12 Qu'est-ce qui se passe?

Parlons Qu'est-ce qui se passe sur ces images? *Possible answers:*

1.
Il vérifie l'huile.

2.
Elle a un pneu crevé.

3.
La pompiste nettoie le pare-brise.

4.
Il est tombé en panne.

Grammaire

The verb *conduire*

Conduire is an irregular verb. Here are the present-tense forms.

Grammaire supplémentaire, p. 54, Act. 2

conduire	
je **conduis**	nous **conduisons**
tu **conduis**	vous **conduisez**
il/elle/on **conduit**	ils/elles **conduisent**

Cahier d'activités, p. 16, Act. 6

Travaux pratiques de grammaire, p. 11, Act. 4

• The past participle of **conduire** is **conduit:** Il **a conduit** trop vite.

Presenting
Vocabulaire

Act out the new expressions as you say them. Then, give students commands (**Vérifiez l'huile! Nettoyez le pare-brise!**) and have them respond by performing the actions. You might also call on individuals to perform an action and have the others try to identify the action.

Grammaire

The verb conduire Bring in photos of different makes of cars from magazines and hold them up as you introduce the verb forms. (**Je conduis une (Peugeot). Elle conduit une...**) Then, give the pictures to individual students and ask the class **Qu'est-ce qu'il/elle conduit?** Next, point to two boys or two girls together and ask **Qu'est-ce qu'ils/elles conduisent?** Then, ask two or more students **Qu'est-ce que vous conduisez?** to elicit **Nous conduisons...** Finally, ask students if they know how to drive (**Tu sais conduire?**) and if they drive well or badly. (**Tu conduis bien ou mal?**)

Communication for All Students

Slower Pace

11 Before they listen to the recording, have students give examples of what a gas station attendant and a customer might say.

Language Notes

• **Une** is used with the makes of all cars (**une Peugeot**) because **voiture** is feminine.

• When discussing driving at a certain speed, the verb **rouler** is used. (**On roule à 60 kilomètres à l'heure.**)

Teaching Resources
pp. 37–41

PRINT
▸ Lesson Planner, p. 8
▸ Listening Activities, pp. 11–12, 15–16
▸ Activities for Communication, pp. 5–6, 54, 56, 91–92
▸ Travaux pratiques de grammaire, pp. 9–12
▸ Grammar Tutor for Students of French, Chapter 2
▸ Cahier d'activités, pp. 14–17
▸ Testing Program, pp. 23–26
▸ Alternative Assessment Guide, p. 31
▸ Student Make-Up Assignments, Chapter 2

MEDIA
▸ One-Stop Planner
▸ Audio Compact Discs, CD 2, Trs. 2–4, 13, 18–20
▸ Teaching Transparencies: 2-1; **Grammaire supplémentaire** Answers; Travaux pratiques de grammaire Answers
▸ Interactive CD-ROM Tutor, Disc 1

Presenting
Comment dit-on... ?

Ask students to describe situations that make them impatient. **(Quand est-ce que tu es impatient(e)?)** Then, pace back and forth, looking repeatedly at your watch. Call out some of the expressions of impatience out the door to an imaginary person. Do the same for the expressions of reassurance, standing on the other side of the doorway as if responding to the impatient person.

---

13 **Grammaire en contexte**

Parlons Est-ce que ces chauffeurs conduisent bien ou mal?

1. M. Martin conduit mal. **2. Elles** conduisent bien. **3. Tu** conduis mal. **4. Vous** conduisez mal.

14 **Des problèmes de voiture**

Parlons Qu'est-ce qu'il faut faire dans chacun des cas suivants? Propose une solution à chaque problème.

1. L'huile de ma voiture est trop vieille. d
2. On est tombés en panne d'essence. a
3. Ma voiture ne s'arrête pas assez vite. b
4. J'ai un pneu crevé. c
5. Je ne vois pas bien la route. f

a. Il faut faire le plein de super.
b. Tu devrais vérifier les freins.
c. Il faut mettre la roue de secours.
d. Tu devrais faire la vidange.
e. Vérifie la pression des pneus!
f. Il faut nettoyer le pare-brise.

15 **Viens chez moi!**

Ecrivons Ton ami habite à Stavelot. Ecris-lui une lettre pour l'inviter à passer un week-end chez toi à Hannut. Ton ami n'est jamais venu chez toi et il ne conduit pas souvent. Explique-lui comment venir à Hannut. Rappelle-lui aussi ce qu'il doit faire avant de partir pour éviter d'avoir des problèmes de voiture en route. Utilise la carte à la page 38.

Comment dit-on...?

Expressing impatience; reassuring someone

To express impatience:

Mais qu'est-ce que tu fais?
Tu peux te dépêcher? *Can you hurry up?*
Grouille-toi! *Get a move on!*
On n'a pas le temps!
Je suis vraiment impatient(e) d'arriver!

To reassure someone:

Ça ne va pas prendre longtemps! *It won't take long!*
Sois patient(e)! *Be patient!*
On a largement le temps. *We've got plenty of time.*
Il n'y a pas le feu. *Where's the fire?*
Du calme, du calme. *Calm down.*

Cahier d'activités, p. 16, Act. 7

16 **Du calme!** See scripts and answers on p. 31G.

Ecoutons Est-ce que ces personnes sont impatientes ou plutôt calmes?

CD 2 Tr. 4

Cultures and Communities

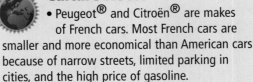

Culture Notes

• Peugeot® and Citroën® are makes of French cars. Most French cars are smaller and more economical than American cars because of narrow streets, limited parking in cities, and the high price of gasoline.

• The highest legal speed limit in Belgium is 120 kilometers per hour. You might have students convert this into miles per hour (1 km = .62 miles, so 120 km equals about 75 miles).

---

17 Qu'est-ce qu'ils sont énervés!

Parlons Rassure ces gens. *Possible answers:*

1. Sois patiente!
2. Du calme, du calme.
3. Il n'y a pas le feu.
4. On a largement le temps!

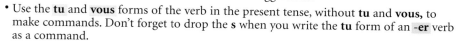
Grammaire

The imperative

Do you remember how to make commands and suggestions?

- Use the **tu** and **vous** forms of the verb in the present tense, without **tu** and **vous,** to make commands. Don't forget to drop the **s** when you write the **tu** form of an **-er** verb as a command.

  Faites le plein! **Mets** de l'huile dans le moteur!
  Regarde! **Vérifie** la pression des pneus!

- To make suggestions, use the **nous** form of the verb, without **nous.**

  Allons à Bruxelles! **Tournons** à droite!

- Place reflexive or object pronouns after the verb in a positive command or suggestion. Place a hyphen between the verb and the pronoun when writing. In negative commands and suggestions, place the pronouns before the verb.

  Grouille-toi! **Dépêchons-nous!** Ne **vous** inquiétez pas!

- While almost all verbs follow this pattern, the verb **être** has irregular imperative forms.

  Sois gentil! **Soyez** patients! **Soyons** à l'heure!

Grammaire supplémentaire, pp. 54–55, Act. 3–6

Cahier d'activités, p. 17, Act. 9

Travaux pratiques de grammaire, p. 12, Act. 5–7

18 Grammaire en contexte

Ecrivons/Parlons Utilise les expressions de la boîte à droite pour écrire une conversation dans laquelle vous êtes enfin parti(e)s pour un concert avec un(e) ami(e). Tu ne sais pas comment y arriver, donc tu demandes des indications à ton ami(e). En route, vous tombez en panne d'essence. Comme vous êtes déjà en retard, tu es très impatient(e)! Ton ami(e) va te rassurer et proposer une solution.

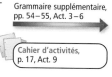

être patient(e)

regarder la carte   se grouiller

ne... pas avoir le temps

faire le plein

Communication for All Students

Game
Jacques a dit Form small groups. On slips of paper, write various activities, using infinitives, and put them into several bags, one for each group. The group leader draws a slip (**regarder à droite**) and tells the other members to do the activity. (**Regardez à droite!**) If the leader says **Jacques a dit** before the command, the members should perform the activity. If not, the players should remain still. A player who moves when the leader does not say **Jacques a dit** is out, but remains involved by acting as a judge.

Presenting
Grammaire

The imperative Make a copy of the lyrics of the following songs: *Il pleut bergère, Au clair de la lune, Dansons la capucine, Vent frais, Trois jeunes tambours,* and *Nous n'irons plus au bois.* (See *Listening Activities,* Level 1, page 42; Level 2, pages 58, 66; Level 3, pages 18, 50.) Ask students how to form the imperative and when to use it. Then, form small groups and distribute copies of the songs. Play the songs and have groups find the imperative forms that appear in their copy. For each verb in the imperative they find, they should write down the imperative form, the infinitive of the verb, whether it is used as a command or a suggestion, and anything else they notice about the verb in question (irregular imperative, whether it is used with a pronoun and if so, where the pronoun is placed, and so on). You might have each group give a short report to share their findings.

Assess
▶ Testing Program, pp. 23–26
Quiz 2-1A, Quiz 2-1B,
Audio CD 2, Tr. 13

▶ Student Make-Up Assignments
Chapter 2, Alternative Quiz

▶ Alternative Assessment Guide,
p. 31

Teaching Resources
pp. 42–43

PRINT
▸ Lesson Planner, p. 9
▸ Video Guide, pp. 10, 12
▸ Cahier d'activités, p. 18

MEDIA
▸ One-Stop Planner
▸ Video Program
  Camille et compagnie
  Videocassette 1, 21:48–27:41
  Videocassette 5 (captioned version), 07:48–13:41
▸ Audio Compact Discs, CD 2, Tr. 5

Presenting
Remise en train

Have students tell all they can about the comic-book center from the illustrations. Have them look at the book covers and tell which one(s) they might like to read. Then, play the audio recording. After the first scene, ask **Comment est le Centre de la B.D.? Qu'est-ce que les garçons voient là-bas?** Next, play the second scene. Read aloud the titles of the comic books mentioned and have students tell whether Stéphane or Hervé liked them.

Answers
19 1. Comic-book Center
2. Tintin
3. **les Schtroumpfs** *(the Smurfs);* Yes
4. a comic-book library; **Bédéthèque** is formed from **bédé** *(B.D., bandes dessinées)* and **-thèque** (as in **bibliothèque**).

Remise en train • *Au Centre de la B.D.*

CD 2 Tr. 5

CENTRE BELGE DE LA BANDE DESSINEE
ouvert tous les jours (sauf lundi) de 10 à 18 heures
20 rue des Sables - B- 1000 Bruxelles
Tél.: 02/219.19.80
Fax : 02/219.23.76

BELGISCH CENTRUM VAN HET BEELDVERHAAL
open alle dagen behalve op maandag van 10 tot 18 uur.
Zandstraat 20 - B.1000 Brussel
Tel.: 02/219.19.80
Fax : 02/219.23.76

A l'accueil...

Stéphane Tu as vu ça? C'est grandiose ici. Je n'imaginais pas ça comme ça. Regarde un peu cet escalier.

Hervé «1905. Art nouveau. Architecte Horta. C'est un ancien magasin qui... »

Stéphane Arrête, ça suffit. Une vraie encyclopédie, ce garçon. Tu as les billets? Tu viens?

Hervé Attends, je voudrais demander quelque chose. Pardon, mademoiselle, on n'est jamais venus ici. On commence par où?

L'hôtesse Vous pouvez commencer où vous voulez, mais surtout ne manquez pas la bédéthèque. C'est là, juste en face.

Hervé Merci, mademoiselle.

Stéphane Alors, on monte?

19 Tu as compris? See answers below.
1. Où sont Hervé et Stéphane?
2. Quelle B.D. est-ce qu'Hervé collectionne?
3. Qu'est-ce que Stéphane décide de lire? Est-ce qu'il aime ce qu'il lit?
4. Qu'est-ce que c'est que la **bédéthèque?** Est-ce que tu peux deviner l'origine du mot **bédéthèque?***

20 Trouve... *Possible answers:* *On a marché sur la lune,*
1. le nom d'un album de B.D. *Le Sceptre d'Ottokar*
2. le nom d'un personnage de B.D. Tintin
3. le nom d'un architecte. Horta

These activities check for comprehension only. Students should not yet be expected to produce language modeled in **Remise en train.**

21 Vrai ou faux?
1. Stéphane a déjà visité le Centre de la B.D. faux
2. La bédéthèque est au premier étage. faux
3. Hervé a lu tous les Tintin. faux
4. D'habitude, Stéphane lit de la science-fiction. vrai
5. *Le Sceptre d'Ottokar* est un album de Tintin. vrai
6. Le Centre est fermé le lundi. vrai
7. Le Centre est ouvert jusqu'à huit heures du soir. faux

* On appelle souvent les bandes dessinées **B.D.** (prononcé "bédé"). Le mot **bédéthèque** fait partie du jargon des amateurs de bandes dessinées. Il vient de l'abbréviation **bédé** et du suffixe **thèque** (comme dans **bibliothèque**) et décrit un endroit où on peut lire et emprunter des bandes dessinées.

Preteaching Vocabulary

Using Prior Knowledge
Point out that Hervé and Stéphane are now inside the **bédéthèque** in Brussels. Have students skim through the text for familiar words and words they learned in the **Première étape.** You might write words students suggest on the board and ask for a translation. They might suggest:

magasin	*store*
garçon	*boy*
billet	*ticket*
en face	*across*
regarde	*look*
lire	*read*
Tu devrais	*you should*
Ça t'a plu?	*Did you like it?*

Stéphane Eh, regarde. C'est la fusée de Tintin dans *On a marché sur la lune.* Tu l'as lu?

Hervé Bien sûr. J'ai lu tous les Tintin, sauf *Le Sceptre d'Ottokar.*

A la bédéthèque...

Stéphane Regarde toutes ces bandes dessinées! Je pourrais passer toute la journée ici.

Hervé Moi, je vais chercher le Tintin que je n'ai pas encore lu. Et toi, qu'est-ce que tu vas lire?

Stéphane Je ne sais pas. Tu as une idée?

Hervé Tiens, regarde! On est juste devant toute la série des Schtroumpfs, les petits hommes bleus. Tu en as déjà lu?

Stéphane Non, jamais.

Hervé Tu devrais. C'est rigolo comme tout.

Stéphane Bon, donne. Ça me changera de la science-fiction.

Plus tard...

Stéphane Alors, ça t'a plu, ton *Sceptre d'Ottokar?*

Hervé Oui, c'était drôle et plein d'action. Et toi, les Schtroumpfs, qu'est-ce que tu en penses?

Stéphane J'ai «schtroumpfé» que c'était bien!

Cahier d'activités, p. 18, Act. 10–11

22 Mets dans le bon ordre

Mets les activités de Stéphane et d'Hervé dans le bon ordre d'après *Au Centre de la B.D.* 5, 6, 3, 2, 4, 1

1. Hervé cherche le Tintin qu'il n'a pas lu.
2. Ils voient la fusée de Tintin.
3. Stéphane veut monter au premier étage.
4. Hervé conseille à Stéphane de lire un album des Schtroumpfs.
5. Ils se trouvent à l'accueil.
6. Hervé demande à l'hôtesse par où commencer la visite.

23 Cherche les expressions

What do the people in *Au Centre de la B.D.* say to . . . See answers below.

1. point out something?
2. tell where something is?
3. give advice?
4. ask an opinion?
5. express enthusiasm?

24 Et maintenant, à toi

Quel est ton personnage de bande dessinée préféré? Pourquoi?

Comprehension Check

Thinking Critically

Drawing Inferences Have students look at the covers of the comic books shown on pages 42 and 43 and try to guess what the main characters are like. Have them make a list of adjectives in French and/or English to describe them.

Language Note

Stéphane says **J'ai "schtroumpfé" que c'était bien!,** imitating the language of the Smurfs, who often substitute a form of the word **schtroumpf** for various parts of speech. Ask your students what Stéphane meant (**J'ai trouvé**). Students might enjoy **"schtroumpfing"** their own sentences.

 Culture Notes

• Victor Horta was an outstanding architect of the Art Nouveau style in Belgium. His organic, curvilinear forms adorn several of Brussels' public buildings. The building in which the **Centre Belge de la Bande Dessinée** is housed, the former Waucquez department store (1903), was designed by Horta in his later, simplified style.

• The first **Tintin** comic book, *Tintin au pays des Soviets,* appeared in 1929. **Tintin** is currently published in over forty languages. Several of the books have even been made into full-length cartoon films, such as *Le Mystère de la toison d'or* and *Le Temple du soleil.*

VIDEO **Camille et compagnie**

As an alternative or in addition to the **Remise en train,** you may wish to show Episode 2 of *Camille et compagnie.* For suggestions and activities, see the *Video Guide.*

Answers

23 1. Tu as vu ça? Regarde un peu... Tiens, regarde!
2. C'est là, juste en face.
3. Tu devrais...
4. ... ça t'a plu,... ? Qu'est-ce que tu en penses?
5. Je pourrais passer toute la journée ici. C'est rigolo comme tout. ... c'était drôle et plein d'action. ... que c'était bien!

CHAPITRE 2

Teaching Resources
p. 44

PRINT 📖
▸ Video Guide, pp. 10–11, 13
▸ Cahier d'activités, p. 24

MEDIA 💿📼
▸ One-Stop Planner
▸ Video Program
  Videocassette 1, 27:44–32:27
▸ Audio Compact Discs, CD 2, Trs. 6–9
▸ Interactive CD-ROM Tutor, Disc 1

Presenting
Panorama Culturel

On the board, write in two columns the names of the comic-book characters and adjectives describing them from the interviews. Play the video and have students match the characters with their descriptions. Then, ask students the **Questions** below. Have partners or groups read the interviews together.

Questions

1. **Quelle bande dessinée est-ce qu'Olivier préfère?** (Tintin)

2. **Comment est Tintin, d'après Olivier?** (un peu maigrichon, intelligent et très futé)

3. **Comment est *Le Calife qui voulait devenir...*, d'après Onélia?** (très drôle, un peu cynique)

4. **Comment est oncle Picsou?** (très avare, très rigolo)

Qui est ton personnage de bande dessinée préféré? Il est comment?

We asked some French-speaking people about their favorite comic book characters. Here's what they had to say.

Olivier, Martinique

«En général, *Les Aventures de Tintin* sont les bandes dessinées que je lis et que je préfère. Tintin, pour moi, c'est un bon moyen de se distraire… qui trouve des énigmes de façon très loufoque, très drôle. Tintin, [il est] un peu maigrichon, vraiment, par rapport à moi, intelligent et très futé.» Tr. 7

Onélia, France

«Mon personnage de bande dessinée préféré, c'est Iznogoud. Le titre de la bande dessinée, c'est *Le Calife qui voulait devenir…* Il est assez méchant, mais très drôle. Il y a beaucoup d'humour dans cette bande dessinée. Et je trouve ça très drôle, même si c'est un peu cynique comme histoire. J'aime beaucoup.» Tr. 8

Bosco, Côte d'Ivoire

«Moi, j'adore énormément les bandes dessinées. Mon personnage préféré de bande dessinée est Donald. C'est un canard. Il est toujours dans les bandes dessinées de Walt Disney. Ce qui me plaît beaucoup dans ce personnage-là, c'est que… il a… c'est surtout à lui qu'arrivent les malheurs par rapport à Gontran, et oncle Picsou qui est très avare. J'adore beaucoup celui-là parce que vraiment il est très strict et puis il se met beaucoup en colère et puis, enfin, il est très rigolo, quoi.» Tr. 9

Qu'en penses-tu?

1. Parmi les personnages de B.D. mentionnés, lesquels est-ce que tu connais?
2. Quelle B.D. francophone est-ce que tu voudrais lire? Pourquoi?

Connections and Comparisons

Community Link
Ask students to describe their favorite comic book or cartoon characters and tell why they like them.

Language Note
You might have students say **"Iznogoud"** aloud to determine the English phrase that sounds like it *(Is no good)*. From this pun, have students imagine what Iznogoud's character is like.

Multicultural Link
Ask students what American cartoonist(s) and cartoon characters the interviewees mention. Tell them that American cartoons are very popular in French-speaking countries. Ask students if they read foreign comic books and why they think American cartoons are so popular in other countries.

Deuxième étape

Objectives Expressing enthusiasm and boredom; asking and telling where things are

go.
hrw
.com

WA3 FRANCOPHONE
EUROPE-2

Comment dit-on...?

Expressing enthusiasm and boredom

To express enthusiasm:

Qu'est-ce que c'est... ! *That is so . . . !*
Ce que c'est bien! *Isn't it great!*
C'est... comme tout! *It's as . . . as anything!*
Ça me branche! *I'm crazy about that!*

To express boredom:

C'est mortel!
Ça me casse les pieds! *That's so boring/annoying!*
Ça m'embête! *That bores me!*
Ça m'ennuie à mourir! *That bores me to death!*

Cahier d'activités, p. 19, Act. 12

Vocabulaire

rigolo (rigolote) *funny, hysterical*
fou (folle) *crazy, funny*
dingue *wild, crazy, funny*
marrant(e) *funny*

rasant(e) *boring*
mortel (mortelle) *deadly boring*
de mauvais goût *in poor taste*
bébé *childish, stupid*

CD-ROM
DISC 1

Travaux pratiques de grammaire, pp. 13–14, Act. 8–9   *Cahier d'activités, p. 19, Act. 13*

25 **A la bédéthèque**   See scripts and answers on p. 31H.

Ecoutons Stéphane et Hervé visitent la bédéthèque. Est-ce qu'ils s'amusent ou s'ennuient?

 CD 2 Tr. 10

26 **Des goûts et des couleurs**

Parlons Qu'est-ce que tu penses de ces bandes dessinées? Utilise les expressions et mots du **Vocabulaire** et du **Comment dit-on...?** pour donner ton opinion.

EXEMPLE   Corto Maltèse®, ce que c'est bien!

Snoopy®   Garfield®
Superman®   Tintin®   Calvin et Hobbes®
Astérix®

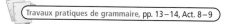
A la française

Look at these gestures that French speakers commonly use to express enthusiasm or boredom. Can you tell which is which?

Communication for All Students

Building on Previous Skills
Have students list expressions they already know for giving opinions of books or movies. (**C'est drôle/bête/un navet/du n'importe quoi.**)

Visual Learners
Divide students into groups. The A groups cut out pictures from magazines to illustrate the vocabu-lary on this page (**rigolo/marrant, fou/dingue/rasant/mortel, de mauvais goût, bébé**). The B groups write the vocabulary words on pieces of paper. Then, pair A groups with B groups to play a Concentration® game. A groups lay out their pic-tures on the table and B groups match their cards to the pictures they see.

Teaching Resources
pp. 45–49

PRINT
▶ Lesson Planner, p. 10
▶ Listening Activities, pp. 12–13, 16–17
▶ Activities for Communication, pp. 7–8, 55–56, 91–92
▶ Travaux pratiques de grammaire, pp. 13–17
▶ Grammar Tutor for Students of French, Chapter 2
▶ Cahier d'activités, pp. 19–22
▶ Testing Program, pp. 27–30
▶ Alternative Assessment Guide, p. 31
▶ Student Make-Up Assignments, Chapter 2

MEDIA
▶ One-Stop Planner
▶ Audio Compact Discs, CD 2, Trs. 10–11, 14, 21–23
▶ Teaching Transparencies: 2-2; **Grammaire supplémentaire** Answers; Travaux pratiques de grammaire Answers
▶ Interactive CD-ROM Tutor, Disc 1

Bell Work
Have students give directions in French to a nearby city.

Presenting
Comment dit-on... ?

Hold up two comic books and, using facial expressions to con-vey enthusiasm or boredom, describe each book with the new expressions.

Vocabulaire

Say each expression, using appropriate facial expressions and intonation. Then, list movies and ask either-or questions about them. (**C'est rigolo ou rasant?**)

Teaching Resources
pp. 45–49

PRINT

▶ Lesson Planner, p. 10
▶ Listening Activities, pp. 12–13, 16–17
▶ Activities for Communication, pp. 7–8, 55–56, 91–92
▶ Travaux pratiques de grammaire, pp. 13–17
▶ Grammar Tutor for Students of French, Chapter 2
▶ Cahier d'activités, pp. 19–22
▶ Testing Program, pp. 27–30
▶ Alternative Assessment Guide, p. 31
▶ Student Make-Up Assignments, Chapter 2

MEDIA

▶ One-Stop Planner
▶ Audio Compact Discs, CD 2, Trs. 10–11, 14, 21–23
▶ Teaching Transparencies: 2–2; **Grammaire supplémentaire** Answers; Travaux pratiques de grammaire Answers
▶ Interactive CD-ROM Tutor, Disc 1

Presenting
Grammaire

Pronouns and their placement Write the following question and answer on the board: **Est-ce que tu regardes le chien? Oui, je regarde le chien.** Then, cross out the noun in the answer and rewrite it, using the appropriate pronoun. (**Oui, je le regarde.**) Ask students what you did and have volunteers tell what type of pronoun you used.

Answers
27 1. y   5. les
2. l'   6. en
3. leur   7. t'
4. m'   8. lui

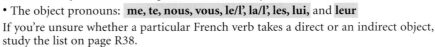

Pronouns and their placement

You've already learned several pronouns commonly used in French.

• The object pronouns: **me, te, nous, vous, le/l', la/l', les, lui,** and **leur**

If you're unsure whether a particular French verb takes a direct or an indirect object, study the list on page R38.

• The pronouns **en** and **y:**

En replaces **de +** a thing or things that have already been mentioned.

    Tu veux **des B.D.** pour Noël?   Oui, j'**en** voudrais trois.

Y replaces a phrase meaning *to, at,* or *in* + a place that has been mentioned.

    Tu es allé **au Centre de la B.D.?**   Oui, j'**y** suis allé hier.

• Pronouns are usually placed before the conjugated verb.

    Je **la** regarde.   Elle **en** parle.   Je **leur** ai donné de l'argent.

• In affirmative commands, put the pronoun after the verb, connected by a hyphen in writing. Remember that in this position, **me** and **te** change to **moi** and **toi.**

    Allons-**y!**   Cherchons-**la!**   Ecris-**moi!**

• If an infinitive follows the verb, put the pronoun before the infinitive.

    Il ne veut pas **le** lire.   Tu devrais **en** acheter.

• Use the table below to help you remember how to order pronouns if you have more than one in a sentence.

me	le			
te	la	lui	y	en
se	l'	leur		
nous	les			
vous				

    Nous **le lui** avons donné.   Tu **leur en** as parlé?

Grammaire supplémentaire, pp. 55–57, Act. 7–11

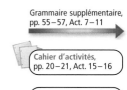

Cahier d'activités, pp. 20–21, Act. 15–16

Travaux pratiques de grammaire, pp. 14–17, Act. 10–15

27 **Grammaire en contexte**   See answers below.

Ecrivons Tu viens de recevoir un message électronique d'un ami qui te raconte sa visite au Centre belge de la bande dessinée. Complète son message avec les pronoms qui manquent.

> Samedi, j'ai visité le Centre de la B.D. C'était très chouette. Je ne regrette pas d'___1___ être allé! D'abord, en arrivant, je suis allé en haut pour voir la fusée de Tintin. Je ___2___ ai trouvée vraiment super. Après, je me suis promené dans le Centre avec mes parents, mais ils ne voulaient pas rester trop longtemps à la bédéthèque, alors je ___3___ ai demandé de ___4___ attendre au café, au premier étage. J'ai trouvé des tas de B.D. de Tintin. Comme je ne ___5___ ai pas toutes à la maison, j'___6___ ai lu plusieurs. C'est marrant comme tout, Tintin! Ensuite, je suis allé à la boutique de cadeaux. Je ___7___ ai acheté un Astérix parce que je sais que ça te branche, Astérix. J'ai aussi acheté quelque chose pour ton frère. Il va trouver ça très rigolo. Dis-___8___ que c'est une surprise! Bon, je te laisse. A la semaine prochaine.
>
>   Victor

Communication for All Students

Auditory Learners

In order to familiarize students with the order of pronouns, you might have them sing or recite the following formula: **me le me la me les, te le te la te les, se le se la se les, le lui la lui les lui, le leur la leur les leur, y en!**

Challenge

27 Have students write e-mail messages about a place they visited recently, replacing the pronouns used with blanks. Have students exchange their messages with a partner and fill in the missing pronouns.

Comment dit-on...?

Asking and telling where things are

To ask where something is:

Vous pourriez me dire où il y a un téléphone?

Pardon, vous savez où se trouve l'ascenseur?
Tu sais où sont les toilettes?

To tell where something is:

Par là, au bout du couloir. *Over there, at the end of the hallway.*
Juste là, à côté de l'escalier. *Right there, next to . . .*
En bas. *Downstairs.*
En haut. *Upstairs.*
Au fond. *Towards the back.*

Au rez-de-chaussée. *On the ground floor.*
Au premier étage. *On the second floor.*
En face du guichet. *Across from . . .*
A l'entrée de la bédéthèque. *At the entrance to . . .*

Cahier d'activités, p. 22, Act. 18

Cahier d'activités, p. 22, Act. 18

28 Au Centre de la B.D. See scripts on p. 31H.

Ecoutons Ecoute ces personnes qui demandent des renseignements à l'accueil du Centre de la B.D. Regarde le plan du Centre et choisis la lettre qui correspond à leur destination.

CD 2
Tr. 11

1. d   **2.** b   **3.** e   **4.** c   **5.** a   **6.** f

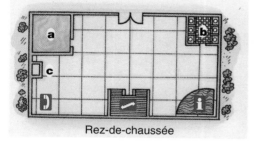

Rez-de-chaussée   Premier étage

29 Pardon, vous savez où...

Lisons Mets cette conversation entre un visiteur et un employé du Centre de la Bande Dessinée dans le bon ordre.

2 — Oui, bien sûr. Elles sont au premier étage, à côté de la boutique de cadeaux.

4 — Ah, non, elle est en bas, en face du guichet, au bout du couloir.

6 — Alors, voyons... il y en a un au rez-de-chaussée, en face de la bédéthèque. Et il y en a aussi au premier étage, près de l'escalier.

3 — Et la bédéthèque? Elle est bien en haut?

7 — Bon, très bien. Merci.

5 — Ah, oui, je vois. Et je dois aussi téléphoner. Vous savez où se trouvent les téléphones?

8 — Je vous en prie. Bonne visite!

1 — Pardon, Monsieur, vous pourriez me dire où sont les toilettes?

Presenting
Comment dit-on... ?

Draw the floor plan of your school on butcher paper and tape it to the board. Ask questions, such as **Vous pourriez me dire où est la cantine?**, and answer them yourself, pointing to the floor plan. Then, ask students where things are (**Où est la cantine, en haut ou en bas?**). Point to the floor plan as you give the choices. You might also ask yes-no questions, such as **Les toilettes sont au fond du couloir?**

TPR Stack two boxes with the open ends facing the students. Position a stuffed animal in a box and ask questions about it, such as **M. Flouflou est en haut ou en bas? Il est au fond ou à l'entrée?** Then, have a student reposition the animal and ask the class to describe its location. (**Où est M. Flouflou?**) Then give individual students commands (**Mets M. Flouflou en haut!**) and have them move the animal accordingly.

Communication for All Students

Group Work

Have groups draw a plan of their ideal school on butcher paper. Each group member, in turn, places a stuffed animal or other object on the plan and then gives directions to the other group members, who move the animal accordingly.

Visual Learners

29 After students have unscrambled the dialogue, form groups and have them draw the floor plan according to the directions in the dialogue. You might assign roles to students: One student should read out loud the directions given in the dialogue. Another student should draw the floor plan. Another student might review the final floor plan while someone else reads the dialogue again.

Rencontre culturelle

Qu'est-ce que tu sais sur la Belgique? Pour t'en faire une meilleure idée, regarde ces photos.

Quelques produits de Belgique :
le chocolat, la dentelle et l'endive

La ville de Bruges

Deux des langues officielles de
la Belgique

Le quartier financier à Bruxelles

La ville de Liège

Qu'en penses-tu?

1. Quelle impression ces photos te donnent de la Belgique?
2. A ton avis, comment est-ce que la situation géographique de la Belgique influence le style de vie des Belges? *Possible answers: Due to its central location, Belgium is influenced by the political and economic fluctuations of its neighboring countries. Its proximity to France and the Netherlands has resulted in two language groups (French and Dutch).*

Savais-tu que... ?

La Belgique est un petit pays européen, mais sa population est très dense. Son nom vient des tribus belgae qui se sont installées dans cette région au deuxième siècle avant Jésus-Christ. La Belgique partage une frontière avec la France, le Luxembourg, l'Allemagne et la Hollande. La situation géographique de la Belgique contribue à sa prospérité. Mais dans le passé, cette situation a aussi causé des problèmes car les pays voisins se sont souvent battus en Belgique. Aujourd'hui, la Belgique a une économie très forte et les Belges vivent bien. Parmi les sports et activités favoris des Belges, il y a le vélo de compétition, le football, la pêche, l'élevage de pigeons voyageurs et le camping dans les Ardennes, une région du sud-est. La Belgique est célèbre pour ses chocolats et ses gaufres. On mange les gaufres avec de la crème chantilly et d'autres accompagnements. Il y a aussi les frites qu'on peut acheter dans la rue et qu'on mange avec de la moutarde ou de la mayonnaise. La dentelle belge, célèbre depuis le Moyen-Age, est encore faite à la main à Bruges et à Bruxelles.

Connections and Comparisons

30 **Dis-moi où se trouve...**

 Parlons Ton ami(e) belge passe sa première journée dans ton école. Il/Elle te demande où se trouvent certains endroits. Joue cette scène avec ton/ta camarade.

Tu te rappelles?

Do you remember how to make, accept, and refuse suggestions?

To make a suggestion:	*To accept:*	*To refuse:*
Si on allait à la Grand-Place?	**Bonne idée.**	**Je n'ai pas envie.**
On pourrait voir la cathédrale.	**Pourquoi pas?**	**Ça ne me dit rien.**
Ça te dit d'aller à Bruges?	**Je veux bien.**	**Non, je préfère...**

---

31 **Qu'elle est belle, la ville de Bruxelles!**

 Parlons Tu fais la visite de Bruxelles avec ton ami(e). Regarde les activités sur les photos suivantes. Dis ce que tu veux faire. Ton ami(e) va accepter ou refuser et dire s'il/si elle trouve ces activités amusantes ou ennuyeuses.

| aller au théâtre de marionnettes de Toone | acheter de la dentelle | aller voir la Grand-Place | goûter du chocolat belge |

---

32 **De l'école au travail**

 Parlons Tu travailles comme guide dans un musée de Bruxelles. Réponds aux questions de tes camarades qui jouent le rôle de visiteurs qui te demandent où sont certains endroits. Regarde le plan du musée et explique-leur où aller.

33 **Le guide du musée**

Ecrivons Utilise le plan de l'activité 32 pour créer une brochure pour les visiteurs du musée. Explique où se trouvent la bibliothèque, les salles d'exposition, le restaurant et la boutique de cadeaux. N'oublie pas aussi d'indiquer où il y a des toilettes et des téléphones.

Rez-de-chaussée

Toilettes · Bibliothèque · Boutique de cadeaux · Escalier · Ascenseur · Restaurant · Renseignements · Entrée

Premier étage

Salle d'expositions 3 · Salle d'expositions 1 · Téléphones · Escalier · Ascenseur · Salle d'expositions 2 · Bureaux · Toilettes

---

Teaching Suggestions

30 You might have students use places such as their locker (**mon casier**), the water fountain (**la fontaine d'eau potable**), or the parking lot (**le parking**).

32 Have students choose a point of departure before they give their directions.

Writing Assessment

33 You might use the following rubric when grading your students on this activity.

Writing Rubric	Points			
	4	3	2	1
Content (Complete– Incomplete)				
Comprehensibility (Comprehensible– Incomprehensible)				
Accuracy (Accurate– Seldom accurate)				
Organization (Well organized– Poorly organized)				
Effort (Excellent–Minimal)				

18–20: A	14–15: C	Under 12: F
16–17: B	12–13: D	

Assess

▸ Testing Program, pp. 27–30 Quiz 2-2A, Quiz 2-2B, Audio CD 2, Tr. 14

▸ Student Make-Up Assignments Chapter 2, Alternative Quiz

▸ Alternative Assessment Guide, p. 31

Teaching Resources
pp. 50–52

PRINT
▶ Lesson Planner, p. 11
▶ Cahier d'activités, p. 23
▶ Reading Strategies and Skills Handbook, Chapter 2
▶ Joie de lire 3, Chapter 2
▶ Standardized Assessment Tutor, Chapter 2

MEDIA
▶ One-Stop Planner

Prereading
Activities A–B

Teaching Suggestions
A. Have students identify the cognate in the title of the comic strip (**destinations**) and predict what the story will be about (deciding on a vacation destination).

A. You might have students work in small groups or with a partner to answer the questions in Activity A. Remind them not to read the text, but to infer the answers to the questions from the illustrations.

B. Have students give examples of types of language they would expect to find in a comic book (sound effects, exclamations, slang words, narration).

B. Ask students what predictions they can make about the tone and plot of the story.

Possible Answers
A. 1. a friend, a boyfriend
2. books, brochures, papers; a vacation, leisure activities
3. excitement, anger, amusement, happiness, satisfaction; Yes.
4. One girl will be happy, and the other two won't be quite as happy with the outcome.

Lisons!

Stratégie pour lire
Previewing lets you get an idea of what's going to happen before you begin to read. When you preview, you take note of such things as the title, subheadings, pictures, captions, charts, and graphs in order to see how the text is organized and what its function is. Once you've done that, you'll be able to predict the kinds of information and vocabulary you will encounter. Taking time to preview a text will make a new reading easier and more fun.

For Activity A, see answers below.

A. Preview the comic strip and make predictions about what's going to happen.
1. A girl is talking on the phone. Who might she be talking to?
2. Two other girls arrive. What are they carrying? What might the girls be planning?
3. What emotions do the girls display during their discussion? Do the emotions change as the story progresses?
4. What can you predict about the outcome of the story based on the girls' expressions in the last frame?

B. What predictions can you make about the language you'll find in the comic strip?
Possible answers: informal, slang

Cultures and Communities

Career Path
Translators have many opportunities to use their language skills in a wide variety of career fields. Translators may work on books, advertisements, movies, TV shows, business or government documents, or music lyrics. Translating is a very precise skill that requires a high level of fluency in the languages involved. Ask students if they think it would be easy or difficult to translate a comic book and why (difficult slang, puns, cultural context, sound effects). Have students try to translate a frame from *Destinations avariées.* You might provide dictionaries for the students to use for this activity.

Reading
Activities C–K

Geography Links
D. Have students locate the three suggested countries on a map of Europe or on *Map Transparency 3* (**L'Europe francophone**). Which of the three countries is closest to Belgium? Which one is farthest away?

D. Have students name countries, states, or regions that have the same characteristics as those mentioned in the comic strip. (**les plages:** la Côte d'Azur, Florida, California; **les montagnes:** Colorado, les Alpes)

Teaching Suggestion
G. You might have students give English equivalents of some of these slang expressions.

C. Now, read the dialogue in the first frame. Is the comic strip about friends getting together to . . .
a. leave for vacation?
b. talk about a vacation they took?
c. talk about where to go on vacation?

D. Associe chaque pays avec ce qu'on y trouve. See answers below.

| l'Irlande | l'Espagne | la Suisse |

| les plages | vert | les montagnes |
| sauvage | le soleil | moins de monde |

For Activities D, E and F, see answers below.

E. What words and phrases in the text express the girls' disagreement about where to go?

F. Why do Claire and Cécile change their minds about where they want to go? What causes them to get angry once again?

G. Trouve dans la colonne de droite l'équivalent des expressions de la colonne de gauche.
1. une tonne de   c
2. se marrer   d
3. faire la nouba   a
4. terrible   e
5. c'est dingue   b

a. faire la fête
b. c'est incroyable
c. beaucoup de
d. s'amuser
e. merveilleux

Answers
D. *l'Irlande:* vert, sauvage
   l'Espagne: les plages, le soleil
   la Suisse: les montagnes, moins de monde

E. ... faudra discuter! Y a pas à discuter: pour moi, c'est l'Espagne. Y a des plages terribles. Ah, non! Flûte! La Suisse, c'est mieux! Il y a des montagnes et aussi moins de monde! Moins de monde! Et moi, je ne veux pas aller chez... C'est fini, oui? Tu rêves? Tandis que l'Irlande, c'est vert, peu peuplé, sauvage!

F. They change their minds because Julie insists that they compromise. They get angry again because they still disagree.

Communication for All Students

Challenge
D. Have students suggest additional reasons for going to each country. Collect their suggestions and read them aloud. Have the class guess to which country they refer.

Building on Previous Skills
E. Have students first list expressions they already know for expressing disagreement. (**Pas question!**) Ask them what facial expressions and gestures they associate with these expressions. Then, have them look for those gestures and expressions in the comic strip to find the frames in which the characters are disagreeing.

Lisons!

Teaching Suggestion

H. You might have students work with a partner to find the clues to these expressions. Remind them not to look them up in a dictionary, but to use the context to determine their meaning.

Teaching Suggestion

Have students review the predictions they made for Activity A on page 50. Were they confirmed? How accurate were their predictions?

Postreading
Activity L

Group Work

L. Have small groups create and act out a skit involving a disagreement. They might choose one of the following topics: deciding on a movie to see, choosing a restaurant, selecting a vacation destination, or assigning household chores.

Answers

H. Et tout et tout. *(And so on and so forth.)* C'est bien parce que c'est toi. *(Just because it's you.)* Mener quelqu'un par le bout du nez. *(To lead someone by the nose.)* Assez ri. *(Enough joking around.)*

I. 1. ... t'as pas oublié... ; Ça va pas être facile... ; Y a pas à discuter... ; ... j'veux pas aller...
2. ... t'as pas oublié...
3. ... y a des questions plus désagréables... ; Y a pas à discuter... ; Y a des plages terribles; ... en Suisse, y a des gens aussi!
4. ... j'veux pas aller...

J. Julie is happy because they are going where she wanted to go. The other girls realize that Julie "won" without having to fight for her choice of destination by encouraging the others to compromise.

K. "Ruined Destinations"; The girls' vacation plans were almost ruined (**avariées**) because their destinations were varied (**variées**).

H. Retrouve les expressions ci-dessous dans le texte. Réfère-toi au contexte pour deviner leur sens. For Activities H–K, see answers below.

> Et tout et tout.   C'est bien parce que c'est toi.
>
> Mener quelqu'un par le bout du nez.   Assez ri.

I. Some dialogues are written to represent the way people speak in everyday language. How are **ne, tu, il y a,** and **je** abbreviated in this comic strip? Can you think of a general rule these writers used to represent spoken language?

J. Why is Julie so happy at the end of the story? Why are the other two girls suspicious?

K. If **avarié** means *ruined*, what does the title mean? How is this a play on words?

L. Est-ce qu'il t'est déjà arrivé de te disputer avec tes amis? Comment est-ce que ça s'est terminé?

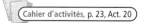
Cahier d'activités, p. 23, Act. 20

Connections and Comparisons

Language-to-Language
I. Have students think of expressions in English where sounds are dropped or words are run together *(gonna, hafta, gotta, I dunno).* You might have groups make lists and then compile a class list.

Thinking Critically
J. Analyzing Have students look at the emotional changes pictured on this page. As they look at the last frame of the comic strip, have them suggest who or what might be the reason for the girls' change in attitude.

Language Arts Link
K. Ask students what a play on words is called in English (a pun) and if they can think of any examples.

Ecrivons!

Ma propre bande dessinée

Est-ce que tu as déjà créé une bande dessinée? C'est difficile de raconter toute une histoire avec quelques dessins. Il n'y a pas beaucoup de place pour le dialogue, donc il faut faire très attention aux mots qu'on choisit. Maintenant, tu vas créer ta propre bande dessinée. Imagine des personnages et crée une situation amusante ou intéressante. Ensuite, raconte ton histoire sans la rendre trop longue!

> **Stratégie pour écrire**
> Just as the way you talk depends on whom you're talking to, the way you write should also be directed by the people who will be reading your writing, your audience. Before you begin to write, ask yourself the following questions: For what audience is this intended? How much does my audience know about this topic? What strong feelings might the audience have about the topic? Should I use formal or informal language in addressing the audience? How can I make my message interesting to this particular audience? Your writing will be much more effective and meaningful if you tailor it to fit the interests, knowledge, and experience of the people for whom it is intended.

A. Préparation

Avant d'écrire ta B.D., n'oublie pas de suivre les étapes suivantes.

1. Réfléchis bien à ces questions.
   a. A quel public est-ce que tu t'adresses? A des enfants? A tes camarades de classe?
   b. Quel ton est approprié à ton sujet? Sérieux? Amusant?
   c. Quels types de personnages et quel genre d'histoire est-ce que tu veux créer?

2. Ecris une description de tes personnages et de ce qui leur arrivera.

3. Pense au nombre d'images nécessaires pour raconter ton histoire.

B. Rédaction

1. Pour créer tes illustrations, dessine des images ou découpe-les dans un magazine ou une autre B.D.

2. Ecris les dialogues dans les bulles de ta B.D.

C. Evaluation

1. Fais une évaluation de ta B.D. Pose-toi ces questions.
   a. Est-ce que ta B.D. est amusante ou intéressante?
   b. Est-ce que chaque image montre la progression de l'histoire?
   c. Est-ce que tu as utilisé un vocabulaire approprié à tes lecteurs?
   d. Est-ce que tu as raconté toute l'histoire sur le même ton?

2. Fais les révisions nécessaires. N'oublie pas de vérifier l'orthographe et la grammaire.

Apply and Assess

Postwriting

Teaching Suggestion

C. 1. Once students have evaluated their comic strips according to these criteria, have them exchange papers with a partner and evaluate each other's work. Remind them to make specific suggestions for improving the comic strip. You might have students consult the Peer Editing Rubic found on page 8 of the *Alternative Assessment Guide* for content evaluation guidelines and a proofreader's checklist.

Teaching Resources
p. 53

PRINT
- Lesson Planner, p. 11
- Cahier d'activités, p. 146
- Alternative Assessment Guide, p. 17
- Standardized Assessment Tutor, Chapter 2

MEDIA
- One-Stop Planner
- Test Generator, Chapter 2
- Interactive CD-ROM Tutor, Disc 1

Process Writing

Prewriting

Motivating Activity

Ask students if they have ever clipped a comic strip from the paper or recounted a cartoon episode to a friend. Have them give examples.

Reading/Writing Link

A. 1. Have students also consider the level of language that they plan to use in their comic strips. They might look back at Activity G on page 51 and decide if they would like to use any of these slang expressions.

Writing

Teaching Suggestion

Have students look back at the second frame of *Destinations avariées* on page 51. Point out the use of the caption in the second frame on page 51. Explain that comic book writers often use captions because speech bubbles alone cannot always show when and where a new scene is taking place. Students might use similar captions in their comic strips to make it easier for the reader to understand the story.

Grammaire supplémentaire

CHAPITRE 2

For **Grammaire supplémentaire** Answer Transparencies, see the *Teaching Transparencies* binder.

Première étape

Objectives Asking for and giving directions; expressing impatience; reassuring someone

1 Demain, Noël va faire ce que Nora a fait aujourd'hui. Complète les phrases suivantes en utilisant **aller** et l'infinitif du verbe qui convient. (**p. 38**)

> **EXEMPLE**　　Ce matin, j'ai visité le Centre de la B.D.
> **Demain, je vais visiter le Centre de la B.D. aussi!**

1. Je suis arrivée à l'heure d'ouverture.
2. Je suis allée à la bédéthèque.
3. J'ai fait le tour du Centre de la B.D.
4. J'ai vu la fusée de Tintin.
5. J'ai lu tous les Tintin.
6. J'ai acheté *Le Sceptre d'Ottokar*.
7. J'ai créé ma propre bande dessinée.
8. J'ai écrit des dialogues dans les bulles de ma B.D.

2 Complète les phrases avec le présent de **conduire**. (**p. 39**)

1. Du calme, du calme! Les freins ne marchent pas très bien! Tu _____ trop vite!
2. Qu'est-ce que vous _____ comme voiture?
3. Les Anglais _____ à gauche.
4. Cette route _____ bien à Bruges?
5. De temps en temps, je _____ la Citroën® de ma mère.
6. Ma sœur et moi, nous _____ toujours très prudemment.

3 Tu es en vacances en France avec des amis. Vous allez faire un voyage en voiture. Complète ce petit mot que votre famille d'accueil vous a laissé avec la deuxième personne du pluriel de l'impératif des verbes entre parenthèses. (**p. 41**)

> Surtout, ___1___ (être) prudents! ___2___ (conduire) doucement et ___3___ (faire) attention sur la route. ___4___ (s'arrêter) dans une station-service et ___5___ (vérifier) les freins et l'huile avant de partir. Et ___6___ (téléphoner) à Marc au bureau quand vous arriverez à Lyon. ___7___ (prendre) assez d'argent et ___8___ (s'amuser) bien!

Answers

1
1. Demain, je vais arriver à l'heure d'ouverture aussi.
2. Demain, je vais aller à la bédéthèque aussi.
3. Demain, je vais faire le tour du Centre de la B.D. aussi.
4. Demain, je vais voir la fusée de Tintin aussi.
5. Demain, je vais lire tous les Tintin aussi.
6. Demain, je vais acheter *Le Sceptre d'Ottokar* aussi.
7. Demain, je vais créer ma propre bande dessinée aussi.
8. Demain, je vais écrire des dialogues dans les bulles de ma B.D. aussi.

2
1. conduis
2. conduisez
3. conduisent
4. conduit
5. conduis
6. conduisons

3
1. soyez
2. Conduisez
3. faites
4. Arrêtez-vous
5. vérifiez
6. téléphonez
7. Prenez
8. amusez-vous

Grammar Resources for Chapter 2

The **Grammaire supplémentaire** activities are designed as supplemental activities for the grammatical concepts presented in the chapter. You might use them for additional practice, for review, or for assessment.

For more grammar presentations, review, and practice, refer to the following:

• Travaux pratiques de grammaire

• Grammar Tutor for Students of French

• Grammar Summary on pp. R29–R54
• Cahier d'activités
• Grammar and Vocabulary quizzes (Testing Program)
• Test Generator
• Interactive CD-ROM Tutor
• **Jeux interactifs** at **go.hrw.com**

STANDARDS: 1.2

4 Stéphane et Hervé sont sur la route et ont besoin de s'arrêter dans une station-service. Complète les phrases suivantes et emploie l'impératif. Utilise la forme familière ou formelle selon le cas. (**p. 41**)

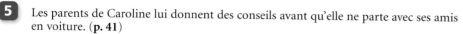

1. _____ (tourner) à gauche à la station-service, s'il te plaît.
2. _____ (faire) le plein, s'il vous plaît.
3. _____ (passer)-moi le plan, s'il te plaît.
4. _____ (mettre) de l'air dans les pneus, s'il vous plaît.
5. _____ (vérifier) l'huile aussi, s'il vous plaît.
6. On n'a pas le temps. _____ (grouiller)-toi, Stéphane.
7. Du calme. _____ (être) patient.

5 Les parents de Caroline lui donnent des conseils avant qu'elle ne parte avec ses amis en voiture. (**p. 41**)

EXEMPLE Il ne faut pas parler aux gens que vous ne connaissez pas.
Ne parlez pas aux gens que vous ne connaissez pas.

1. Tu devrais faire attention sur la route.
2. Tu devrais conduire prudemment.
3. Vous devriez rester tous ensemble.
4. Il faut être prudentes, les filles.
5. Vous devriez nous appeler si vous avez des problèmes.
6. Vous devriez rentrer à l'heure.

6 Qu'est-ce que tu dirais dans les situations suivantes? Utilise l'impératif dans tes réponses. (**p. 41**)

1. Il n'y a presque plus d'essence dans notre voiture.
2. Tu veux que tes amis et toi, vous alliez au Centre de la B.D.
3. Ton ami Martin conduit beaucoup trop vite.
4. Le pare-brise de votre voiture est très sale.
5. Il n'y a pas assez d'air dans les pneus de la voiture de Sophie et Etienne.
6. Ton ami Luc est toujours en retard.

Deuxième étape
Objectives Expressing enthusiasm and boredom; asking and telling where things are

7 Félicité et Luc vont aller en Belgique. Ecris leurs réponses en utilisant un pronom direct ou indirect, **y** ou **en** dans chaque réponse. (**p. 46**)

EXEMPLE —Vous allez lire *Astérix chez les Belges* avant de partir?
—Oui, on va le lire avant de partir.

1. Vous allez prendre la E. 411 pour aller à Bruxelles?
2. Vous allez vous arrêter à Bouillon?
3. Vous allez visiter le château?
4. Vous allez manger des gaufres?
5. Vous allez poser une question au gardien du musée de l'Armée?
6. Vous allez rapporter un album des Schtroumpfs à vos petits frères?
7. Vous allez acheter de la dentelle pour votre mère?

Communication for All Students

Slower Pace
6 You might have students proceed step by step in this activity. Organize them by three. Student A reads the statement out loud. (**Il n'y a presque plus d'essence dans notre voiture.**) Student B provides the expression in the infinitive. (**faire le plein**) Student C uses Student B's response in the imperative. (**Faisons le plein!**)

Challenge
7 Before students write their answers to this activity, have them practice orally with a partner. One student reads the statement, and the other answers as fast as possible, using pronouns. You might pair up students with different ability levels and have Student A model for Student B. Then have them exchange roles.

Answers

4
1. Tourne
2. Faites
3. Passe
4. Mettez
5. Vérifiez
6. Grouille
7. Sois

5
1. Fais attention sur la route.
2. Conduis prudemment.
3. Restez tous ensemble.
4. Soyez prudentes.
5. Appelez-nous si vous avez des problèmes.
6. Rentrez à l'heure.

6 *Possible answers:*
1. Faites le plein.
2. Allons au Centre de la B.D.
3. Conduis moins vite.
4. Nettoyons le pare-brise.
5. Mettez de l'air dans les pneus.
6. Sois à l'heure.

7
1. Oui, on va la prendre.
2. Oui, on va s'y arrêter.
3. Oui, on va le visiter.
4. Oui, on va en manger.
5. Oui, on va lui poser une question.
6. Oui, on va leur rapporter un album des Schtroumpfs. Oui, on va en rapporter un à nos petits frères.
7. Oui, on va lui en acheter.

CHAPITRE 2

For **Grammaire supplémentaire** Answer Transparencies, see the *Teaching Transparencies* binder.

8 Complète les phrases suivantes avec le pronom qui convient. (**p. 46**)

— Corinne, ça ___**1**___ dit d'aller au Musée du costume et de la dentelle?
— Oui, j'aimerais bien ___**2**___ aller.

— Milo et Mireille, je voudrais ___**3**___ poser une question.
— Vas- ___**4**___! On ___**5**___ écoute!
— Que pensez-vous de la Grand-Place?
— On ___**6**___ trouve magnifique!

— Mes frères aimeraient bien goûter du chocolat belge.
— Dis- ___**7**___ d'aller aux Galeries St-Hubert!

— Excusez-moi, madame. Je voudrais acheter des Tintin. Vous savez où on peut ___**8**___ trouver?
— Vous ___**9**___ trouverez au Centre belge de la bande dessinée.

CENTRE BELGE DE
LA BANDE DESSINÉE
ouvert tous les jours (sauf
lundi) de 10 à 18 heures
20 rue des Sables - B- 1000 Bruxelles
Tél.: 02/219.19.80
Fax : 02/219.23.76

BELGISCH CENTRUM
VAN HET BEELDVERHAAL
open alle dagen behalve op maandag
van 10 tot 18 uur.
Zandstraat 20 - B.1000 Brussel
Tel.: 02/219.19.80
Fax : 02/219.23.76

— Janine et moi, nous voudrions bien aller au théâtre de marionnettes de Toone. Qu'est-ce vous ___**10**___ pensez? Ça ___**11**___ dirait de/d' ___**12**___ aller avec nous?

— Je dois téléphoner à Christophe!
— Alors, téléphone- ___**13**___! Je ___**14**___ attendrai à l'entrée du Musée de cire. On se/s' ___**15**___ retrouve dans dix minutes. D'accord?

Answers

8 *Possible answers:*
1. te
2. y
3. vous
4. y
5. t'
6. la
7. leur
8. en
9. en
10. en
11. vous
12. y
13. lui
14. t'/vous
15. y

Communication for All Students

Group Work

Divide up the class in small groups. Have students prepare strips of paper with a single pronoun written on each of them. Each student should have a complete set of pronouns. Distribute Activity 8 on a large piece of paper for students to share within a group. They should place their strips of paper in the appropriate blanks. Give each group a limited amount of time to complete the activity. (Five minutes should be sufficient.) Verify the answers in class, orally or on a transparency.

9 Lis cette conversation entre Solange et Prosper et complète-la avec le pronom qui convient. (**p. 46**)

SOLANGE   Il paraît qu'en Belgique, c'est comme en Suisse : il y a plusieurs langues officielles.

PROSPER   Oui, c'est vrai. Mais il ___1___ en a moins qu'en Suisse. En Belgique, il n'y ___2___ a que trois.

SOLANGE   J'aimerais bien savoir parler toutes les langues officielles de la Belgique!

PROSPER   Bon, le français, tu ___3___ parles déjà. L'allemand, c'est facile. Et le flamand, tu ___4___ apprendras vite. Tu n'as qu'à passer quelques mois en Flandre! Ma sœur ___5___ habite. Elle ___6___ logera!

SOLANGE   Super! Si elle veut bien ___7___ loger, moi, je vais ___8___ offrir des Astérix. Tu sais que je/j' ___9___ ai beaucoup.

PROSPER   Oui, je sais. Malheureusement, ma sœur n'aime pas les B.D. Ça ne ___10___ dit rien. Elle préfère lire des romans.

10 Simon dit la même chose que Fabien, mais il s'exprime d'une façon un peu différente. Complète les passages suivants en utilisant le pronom qui convient. (**p. 46**)

EXEMPLE   **FABIEN**   On s'est arrêtés à la station-service au nord de Namur.
                        SIMON   **Oui, on s'y est arrêtés.**

1. On a demandé au pompiste de vérifier l'huile.

2. Le pompiste nous a conseillé de faire la vidange.

3. Puis, il a voulu vérifier la pression des pneus.

4. Il a mis de l'air dans les pneus.

5. Il nous a nettoyé le pare-brise.

6. Ensuite, il a fait le plein.

7. Il a rechargé la batterie.

8. Finalement, il a vérifié les freins.

11 Complète les passages suivants en utilisant les pronoms qui conviennent. (**p. 46**)

EXEMPLE   Rachid et Samir, demandez la route au pompiste!
                        Demandez-la-lui!

1. Rachid, donne la boîte à outils à Fatima!

2. Fatima et Aïcha, apportez-moi la roue de secours!

3. Aïcha, explique à Rachid et Samir comment changer le pneu!

4. Gilles et Ahmed, mettez la roue de secours dans le coffre!

5. Claire, envoie les directions à tes cousines!

Answers

9 1. y   6. te
2. en   7. me
3. le   8. lui
4. l'   9. en
5. y   10. lui

10 1. Oui, on lui a demandé de la vérifier *or* on le lui a demandé.
2. Oui, il nous a conseillé de la faire *or* il nous l'a conseillé.
3. Oui, il a voulu la vérifier *or* il a voulu en vérifier la pression.
4. Oui, il y en a mis.
5. Oui, il nous l'a nettoyé.
5. Oui, il l'a fait.
7. Oui, il l'a rechargée.
8. Oui, il les a vérifiés.

11 1. Donne-la-lui!
2. Apportez-la-moi!
3. Explique-le-leur!
4. Mettez-la dans le coffre.
5. Envoie-les-leur!

Review and Assess

You may wish to assign the **Grammaire supplémentaire** activities as additional practice or homework after presenting material throughout the chapter. Assign Activity 1 after **Tu te rappelles?** (p. 38), Activity 2 after **Grammaire** (p. 39), Activities 3–6 after **Grammaire** (p. 41), and Activities 7–11 after **Grammaire** (p. 46).

To prepare students for the **Etape** Quizzes and Chapter Test, we suggest doing the **Grammaire supplémentaire** activities in the following order. Have students complete Activities 1–6 before taking Quiz 2-1A or 2-1B; and Activities 7–11 before Quiz 2-2A or 2-2B.

Mise en pratique

The **Mise en pratique** reviews and integrates all four skills and culture in preparation for the Chapter Test.

Teaching Resources
pp. 58–59

PRINT
▶ Lesson Planner, p. 11
▶ Listening Activities, p. 13
▶ Video Guide, pp. 9, 14
▶ Grammar Tutor for Students of French, Chapter 2
▶ Standardized Assessment Tutor, Chapter 2

MEDIA
▶ One-Stop Planner
▶ Video Program
   Videocassette 1, 32:28–35:43
▶ Audio Compact Discs, CD 2, Tr. 12
▶ Interactive CD-ROM Tutor, Disc 1

Writing Assessment
2 You might use the following rubric when grading your students on this activity.

Writing Rubric	Points			
	4	3	2	1
Content (Complete– Incomplete)				
Comprehensibility (Comprehensible– Incomprehensible)				
Accuracy (Accurate– Seldom accurate)				
Organization (Well organized– Poorly organized)				
Effort (Excellent–Minimal)				

18–20: A 14–15: C Under
16–17: B 12–13: D 12: F

Mise en pratique

1 Lis les lettres suivantes et réponds aux questions.

Aimez-vous la B.D. ?

«Je voudrais vous poser une question : que pensez-vous des bandes dessinées ? Aimez-vous Tintin, Astérix, Gaston et les autres ? Lisez-vous plus de BD que de romans? D'avance, merci ! » Marie-Céline, Le Chesnay

«Buenos días, Marie-Céline ! Ta question est très intéressante. Personnellement, je trouve que si l'histoire est bien tournée et les dessins sont bien faits, les BD feront exploser les librairies.
   Mais je pense qu'on devrait s'en servir pour expliquer aux enfants et aux adolescents la vie ou la politique ; parfois on ne comprend plus rien ! Et peut-être que les BD pourront nous apprendre plein de choses faciles ou compliquées, tout en rigolant ! On pourrait apprendre la vie de Napoléon ou celle de César !
   Entre nous, ça serait plus drôle que les explications de nos parents, non? Enfin, je t'ai donné mon avis là-dessus. Vive les bandes dessinées et vive le dessin artistique !»

Bénédicte, Pontoise

«Moi, je préfère les romans aux bandes dessinées.
   D'abord parce que je suis un rêveur et que les romans chassent les idées noires de notre tête et peuplent celle-ci de songes merveilleux.
   J'ai peu de BD, mais je lis tout de même quelques BD : Tintin, Astérix, Boule et Bill, Gaston et d'autres.
   Je voudrais laisser un message : «Ceux qui n'ont pas encore découvert les romans ne doivent pas avoir peur de ceux-ci, car une BD ne remplacera jamais un roman !» Bonne lecture ! Plongez-vous vite dans Alexandre Dumas, Jules Verne, Victor Hugo !»

Julien, Alès

«Salut Marie-Céline ! Moi, j'adore les bandes dessinées. Je bouquine beaucoup. Mais dans les BD, il n'y a pas ce qu'il y a dans les autres livres. Même si on ne sait pas lire, les images nous aident à comprendre le thème, et si on n'aime pas lire, rien ne vaut de feuilleter les BD.
   J'ai toute la collection Tintin, Lucky Luke, et Astérix. Quand on n'a pas envie de se plonger dans des romans mieux vaut lire une bande dessinée.»

Aurélie, Toulouse

1. D'après toi, ces lettres sont de quel genre?   teen forum

2. Ces jeunes répondent à quelle question?   What is your opinion of comic books?

3. Combien de jeunes aiment lire les bandes dessinées? Combien préfèrent les romans?   2; 1

4. Pourquoi certains jeunes préfèrent les bandes dessinées? Pourquoi certains préfèrent les romans?   Comics can be used to explain difficult subjects with humor; Comics are amusing, with illustrations that aid understanding; Novels stimulate the imagination and the intellect.

2 Ecris ta réponse à la question posée par Marie-Céline. Est-ce que tu lis souvent des bandes dessinées? Plus souvent que des romans? Pourquoi ou pourquoi pas?

See scripts and answers on p. 31H.

3 Ecoute les conversations de ces jeunes qui se trouvent dans un parc d'attractions. Est-ce que la personne qui répond est impatiente ou est-ce qu'elle essaie de rassurer l'autre?
CD 2 Tr. 12

Apply and Assess

Auditory Learners
1 Before students open their books, write the questions submitted by Marie-Céline on the board. Make sure students understand them. Then, tell students to listen carefully for the gist of the responses as you read the letters aloud. Finally, discuss each one with students.

Additional Practice
1 For additional reading and speaking practice, have students take turns choosing lines from the letters to read aloud to a partner, who tries to name the person who wrote them.

---

4 Donne le nom de quelques produits typiques de la Belgique. Qu'est-ce que tu voudrais acheter si tu allais en Belgique? *Possible answers:* le chocolat, la dentelle, les gaufres

5 Avec ton/ta camarade, choisissez un de ces endroits pour y passer la journée. N'oubliez pas de donner votre opinion sur chaque endroit.

PARC DE RECREATION MONT MOSAN
Huy ⒷＦ8

Il y a toujours du nouveau au Mont Mosan ! Enfin un vrai parc de récréation à la portée de toutes les bourses.
Le spectacle des otaries (trois espèces différentes), les phoques, l'exposition sur les mammifères marins, la vaste plaine de jeux, les châteaux gonflables, la cafétéria et sa petite restauration, etc...
Pour une journée de détente, pensez Mont Mosan.
Ouvert du 2/4 au 31/10/94 : de 10h00 à 20h00 • Prix : 2,50€ Grp 1,75€ • p, P • B-4500 Huy, Plaine de la Sarte • Tél.: 085/23.29.96 • Fax : 085/21.30.61.

CHATEAU FORT DE LOGNE
Vieuxville-Ferrières F9

L'un des plus fameux châteaux de la vallée de l'Ourthe (IXᵉ - XVᵉ siècles) et néanmoins injustement méconnu !
Antique forteresse des abbés de Stavelot, le Château de Logne devint au XVᵉ siècle une base importante des de la Marck, les "Sangliers des Ardennes".
Sur place, le guide vous fera revivre le Moyen Age avec ses coutumes et ses guerres; il vous mènera dans de mystérieux souterrains que hante encore la Gatte d'Or, gardienne d'un fabuleux trésor. Du haut de son enceinte, le Château vous offrira un point de vue unique.

A proximité, le Musée du Comté de Logne présente les objets découverts lors des fouilles au Château.

Ouvert du 1/7 au 31/8, tous les jours de 10.00 à 18.00 h + W.E. de mai à octobre : de 13.00 à 18.00 h. • Prix : ad. 2,50 € , enf. 1,75 €; grp. : ad. 1,99 € , enf. 1,45 € • V : 45 min. Visites guidées en F, NL (GB sur demande) • p, P • B-4190 Vieuxville, La Bouverie 1 • Tél.: 086/21.20.33 ou 086/21.24.12.

6 ## Jeu de rôle

You've chosen where to go, but you don't know how to get there! You have to call the tourist bureau to ask where the town is and how to get there from Stavelot. Your friend will play the role of the tourist bureau employee. He/She can use the map on page 38. Write the directions that he/she gives you. Don't forget to repeat them to make sure you understood. Ask the employee what he/she thinks of the attraction you plan to visit.

Apply and Assess

Challenge
As a chapter review, write out the conversation from a section of *Allez, en route!* (for scripts, see *Video Guide*) and leave out targeted expressions that students have learned in the chapter. Play the video and have students fill in the blanks. Then, play the captioned version on Videocassette 5 and have students check their answers.

Additional Practice
5 Have students take turns imagining they went to one of the places pictured and describing to a partner one of the activities they did there, without naming the place. (**J'ai vu des otaries.**) The partner names the place (**Parc de récréation Mont Mosan**).

STANDARDS: 1.1, 1.2, 1.3, 5.1

Teaching Suggestion
4 You might also ask students the following questions: **Qu'est-ce que tu voudrais voir en Belgique? Quelles villes est-ce que tu voudrais visiter? Pourquoi?**

Group Work
5 You might have students do this activity in small groups. Students might also suggest other places in Brussels mentioned in the chapter.

Speaking Assessment
5 You might use the following rubric when grading your students on this activity.

Speaking Rubric	Points			
	4	3	2	1
Content (Complete– Incomplete)				
Comprehension (Total–Little)				
Comprehensibility (Comprehensible– Incomprehensible)				
Accuracy (Accurate– Seldom accurate)				
Fluency (Fluent–Not fluent)				

18–20: A   14–15: C   Under 16–17: B   12–13: D   12: F

Teaching Suggestion
6 You might have students do this activity with toy phones, sitting back-to-back to simulate a phone conversation.

Teaching Resources
p. 60

PRINT
▶ Grammar Tutor for Students of French, Chapter 2

MEDIA
▶ Interactive CD-ROM Tutor, Disc 1
▶ Online self-test

 go.hrw.com
WA3 FRANCOPHONE
EUROPE-2

Auditory/Visual Learners

2 You might have students record the directions on audiocassette or draw a map to accompany their written directions.

Teaching Suggestions

5 Encourage students to vary their responses and use as many expressions as they can recall.

8 Have volunteers read their directions aloud as their classmates try to guess the destination.

Answers

3 *Possible answers:*
1. Grouille-toi! Tu peux te dépêcher?
2. On n'a pas le temps.
3. Mais, qu'est-ce que tu fais? Tu peux te dépêcher?

5 Qu'est-ce que c'est rigolo! Ce que c'est bien! C'est marrant comme tout! Ça me branche!

6 C'est mortel! Ça me casse les pieds! Ça m'embête! C'est rasant! Ça m'ennuie à mourir!

7 *Possible answers:*
1. Vous pourriez me dire où il y a un téléphone?
2. Tu sais où sont les toilettes?
3. Pardon, vous savez où se trouve l'ascenseur?

Can you use what you've learned in this chapter?

Can you ask for and give directions?
p. 37

1 How would you ask someone for directions to Brussels?
La route pour Bruxelles, s'il vous plaît? Comment on va à Bruxelles?

2 How would you give someone directions from your home to . . .
1. your school?
2. your best friend's house?
3. the nearest grocery store?

Can you express impatience?
p. 40

3 How would you express your impatience if . . .   See answers below.
1. you wanted to leave, but your friend wouldn't get ready?
2. your friend wanted to stop and look in a music store on the way to the movies?
3. you were hurrying to a class with a friend who suddenly stopped to talk to someone?

Can you reassure someone?
p. 40

4 For each of the situations in number 3, what would the other person say to reassure you?   *Possible answers:*   1. Il n'y a pas le feu. Sois patient(e)!
2. Ça ne va pas prendre longtemps.   3. Du calme, du calme! On a largement le temps!

Can you express enthusiasm and boredom?
p. 45

5 How would you express your enthusiasm for your three favorite TV shows and comic strips to a friend?   See answers below.

6 How would you express boredom with these activities?   See answers below.

> playing golf
> doing homework
> cleaning the house
> listening to a lecture
> watching a documentary

Can you ask and tell where things are?
p. 47

7 What questions would you ask to find . . .   See answers below.
1. a telephone?
2. a bathroom?
3. the elevator?

8 How would you tell a new student at your school where to find . . .
1. the bathroom?
2. the cafeteria?
3. the science lab?
4. the principal's office?

ET LE SOLEIL SE COUCHE. FIN DE L'ÉPISODE. IL VA SE REMETTRE À CHANTER QU'IL EST UN COW-BOY SOLITAIRE...

Review and Assess

♟ Game

La voilà!   Write the questions from **Que sais-je?** on one set of cards and the answers on another set. Tape the question cards on the board at random and place the answer cards in a bag. Then, form two or more teams. Have the first player from each team come to the front. On your cue, the players each select one card from the bag, find the matching question on the board, and call out **La voilà!** The first player to find the correct question wins a point for his or her team. Repeat the process with the next two players. Play until one team has earned ten or fifteen points.

STANDARDS: 1.2

Première étape

Asking for and giving directions

La route pour... , s'il vous plaît?	Could you tell me how to get to . . .?
Comment on va à... ?	How can I get to . . .?
Pour (aller à)... , vous suivez la... pendant à peu près... kilomètres.	To get to . . . , follow . . . for about . . . kilometers.
Vous allez voir un panneau qui indique l'entrée de l'autoroute.	You'll see a sign that points out the freeway entrance.
Vous allez traverser...	You'll cross . . .
Après... , vous allez tomber sur...	After . . . , you'll come across . . .
Cette route va vous conduire au centre-ville.	This road will lead you into the center of town.
Vous allez continuer tout droit, jusqu'au carrefour/au feu rouge.	You'll keep going straight ahead, up to the intersection/the stop light.
conduire	to drive

At the gas station

avoir un pneu crevé	to have a flat tire
l'essence (f.)	gas
faire le plein	to fill it up
faire la vidange	to change the oil
mettre de l'air dans les pneus	to put air in the tires
de l'huile dans le moteur	oil in the motor
la roue de secours	to put on the spare tire
nettoyer le pare-brise	to clean the wind-shield
le/la pompiste	the gas station attendant
le réservoir	the gas tank
une station-service	a gas station
du super (sans plomb)	premium gas
tomber en panne (d'essence)	to break down (run out of gas)
vérifier...	to check . . .
les freins (m.)	the brakes
l'huile (f.)	the oil
la pression des pneus	the tire pressure

Expressing impatience

Mais qu'est-ce que tu fais?	What are you doing?
Tu peux te dépêcher?	Can you hurry up?
Grouille-toi!	Get a move on!
On n'a pas le temps!	We don't have time!
Je suis vraiment impatient(e) de... !	I'm really anxious to . . . !

Reassuring someone

Ça ne va pas prendre longtemps!	It's not going to take long!
Sois patient(e)!	Be patient!
On a largement le temps.	We've got plenty of time.
Il n'y a pas le feu.	Where's the fire?
Du calme, du calme.	Calm down.

Deuxième étape

Expressing enthusiasm and boredom

Qu'est-ce que c'est... !	That is so . . . !
Ce que c'est bien!	Isn't it great!
C'est... comme tout!	It's as . . . as anything!
Ça me branche!	I'm crazy about that!
Ça me casse les pieds!	That's so boring!
Ça m'embête!	That bores me!
Ça m'ennuie à mourir!	That bores me to death!

Adjectives

rigolo (rigolote)	funny, hysterical
fou (folle)	crazy, funny

dingue	wild, crazy, funny
marrant(e)	funny
rasant(e)	boring
mortel (mortelle)	deadly boring
de mauvais goût	in poor taste
bébé	childish, stupid

Asking and telling where things are

Vous pourriez me dire où il y a... ?	Could you tell me where I can find . . . ?
Pardon, vous savez où se trouve... ?	Excuse me, do you know where . . . is?
Tu sais où sont... ?	Do you know where . . . are?

Par là, au bout du couloir.	Over there, at the end of the hallway.
Juste là, à côté de...	Right there, next to . . .
En bas.	Downstairs.
En haut.	Upstairs.
Au fond.	Towards the back.
Au rez-de-chaussée.	On the ground floor.
Au premier étage.	On the second floor.
A l'entrée de...	At the entrance to . . .

Review and Assess

Game

Lève-toi! Prepare a stack of yellow and blue cards and form two teams. Call out a category from the **Vocabulaire** (*Asking for and giving directions, At the service station*). Tell students to stand if they can give a word or expression in that category. Call on the first person to stand. If the student gives an appropriate response, his or her team wins a point, and he or she receives a yellow card. If the answer is not correct, the other team may try to answer. The second time a student answers correctly, he or she gets a blue card and may no longer answer questions for the team. Students with blue cards help keep score, determine who stood first, and judge the accuracy of the answers. The team with the most points wins.

Vocabulaire

CHAPITRE 2

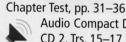

Circumlocution
Have students imagine that they are on a road trip through Belgium and that they have stopped at a gas station for service. The driver is trying to explain to the gas station attendant what needs to be done to the car, but is having difficulty remembering the exact words in French. Have partners take turns playing the roles of the driver and the gas station attendant. The driver needs to use circumlocution skills to communicate what he or she needs. The gas station attendant will try to guess what the driver is trying to say.

Chapter 2 Assessment

▸ **Testing Program**
Chapter Test, pp. 31–36
Audio Compact Discs, CD 2, Trs. 15–17

Speaking Test, p. 295

▸ **Alternative Assessment Guide**
Portfolio Assessment, p. 17
Performance Assessment, p. 31
CD-ROM Assessment, p. 45

▸ **Interactive CD-ROM Tutor, Disc 1**

A toi de parler
A toi d'écrire

▸ **Standardized Assessment Tutor**
Chapter 2

▸ **One-Stop Planner, Disc 1**
Test Generator
Chapter 2

Chapitre 3 : Soyons responsables!
Chapter Overview

Mise en train pp. 64–66	**Je peux sortir?**

	FUNCTIONS	**GRAMMAR**	**VOCABULARY**	**RE-ENTRY**
Première étape pp. 67–71	• Asking for, granting, and refusing permission, p. 68 • Expressing obligation, p. 68	• The subjunctive, p. 69	• Household chores, p. 67	• Chores (**Chapitre 7**, I) • The verb **devoir** (**Chapitre 7**, II) • Asking for, giving, and refusing permission (**Chapitre 7**, I)

Remise en train pp. 72–73	**Laissez-les vivre!**

Deuxième étape pp. 74–79	• Forbidding, p. 75 • Reproaching, p. 78 • Justifying your actions and rejecting others' excuses, p. 78	• **Ne... pas** + infinitive, p. 75	• Social responsibilities, p. 77	• **Ne... pas** (**Chapitre 1**, I) • **Ne... jamais** (**Chapitre 4**, I)

Lisons! pp. 80–82	**Albert Nez en l'air; Julie Boum**	**Reading Strategy:** Deriving meaning from context
Ecrivons! p. 83	**Ta fable à toi**	**Writing Strategy:** Making an outline
Grammaire supplémentaire	**pp. 84–87**	**Première étape,** pp. 84–86 **Deuxième étape,** pp. 86–87
Review pp. 88–91	**Mise en pratique,** pp. 88–89 **Que sais-je?,** p. 90 **Vocabulaire,** p. 91	

CULTURE

• **Note culturelle,** Swiss work ethic, p. 66
• Realia: Party invitation, p. 70
• Realia: Anti-smoking ad, p. 71
• **Note culturelle,** Switzerland's neutrality, p. 73

• **Rencontre culturelle,** Overview of Switzerland, p. 74
• **Panorama Culturel,** Environmental issues, p. 76
• **Note culturelle, La minuterie,** p. 78

Chapitre 3 : Soyons responsables!
Chapter Resources

PRINT

Lesson Planning

One-Stop Planner

Lesson Planner with Substitute Teacher Lesson Plans, pp. 12–16, 66

Student Make-Up Assignments
- Make-Up Assignment Copying Masters, Chapter 3

Listening and Speaking

Listening Activities
- Student Response Forms for Listening Activities, pp. 19–21
- Additional Listening Activities 3-1 to 3-6, pp. 23–25
- Additional Listening Activities (song), p. 26
- Scripts and Answers, pp. 111–115

Video Guide
- Teaching Suggestions, pp. 16–17
- Activity Masters, pp. 18–20
- Scripts and Answers, pp. 84–87, 112–113

Activities for Communication
- Communicative Activities, pp. 9–12
- Realia and Teaching Suggestions, pp. 57–59
- Situation Cards, pp. 93–94

Reading and Writing

Reading Strategies and Skills Handbook, Chapter 3

Joie de lire 3, Chapter 3

Cahier d'activités, pp. 25–36

Grammar

Travaux pratiques de grammaire, pp. 18–28

Grammar Tutor for Students of French, Chapter 3

Assessment

Testing Program
- Grammar and Vocabulary Quizzes, **Etape** Quizzes, and Chapter Test, pp. 45–58
- Score Sheet, Scripts and Answers, pp. 59–65

Alternative Assessment Guide
- Portfolio Assessment, p. 18
- Performance Assessment, p. 32
- CD-ROM Assessment, p. 46

Student Make-Up Assignments
- Alternative Quizzes, Chapter 3

Standardized Assessment Tutor
- Reading, pp. 8–9
- Writing, p. 10
- Math, pp. 25–26

MEDIA

Online Activities
- Jeux interactifs
- Activités Internet

Video Program
- Videocassette 1
- Videocassette 5 (captioned version)

Audio Compact Discs
- Textbook Listening Activities, CD 3, Tracks 1–14
- Additional Listening Activities, CD 3, Tracks 20–26
- Assessment Items, CD 3, Tracks 15–19

Interactive CD-ROM Tutor, Disc 1

Teaching Transparencies
- Situation 3-1 to 3-2
- **Grammaire supplémentaire** Answers
- **Travaux pratiques de grammaire** Answers

One-Stop Planner CD-ROM

Use the **One-Stop Planner CD-ROM with Test Generator** to aid in lesson planning and pacing.

For each chapter, the **One-Stop Planner** includes:
- Editable lesson plans with direct links to teaching resources
- Printable worksheets from resource books
- Direct launches to the HRW Internet activities
- Video and audio segments
- Test Generator
- Clip Art for vocabulary items

Chapitre 3 : Soyons responsables!

Projects

L'Environnement

Groups of students will create posters in French that describe an environmental problem and propose solutions. They will also give an oral presentation to the class, based on their posters.

MATERIALS

✂ **Students may need**
- Posterboard
- Colored markers or pens
- Scissors
- Glue
- Recent current-events magazines

SUGGESTED SEQUENCE

1. Have students form small groups and select a topic related to the environment. Students might choose to feature a local environmental concern, or one unique to a certain area of the world.

2. Students should research the problem using current magazines and newspapers to find relevant statistics and popular opinions about the issue. They should also find or draw pictures to illustrate the problem.

3. Have group members share and compile their research and propose a solution and plan the graphics and layout. They might create a slogan or a symbol, such as Woodsy Owl. Encourage them to create charts and graphs to present the statistics that they've gathered.

4. Have groups exchange their rough drafts and layouts to check French spelling and grammar as well as the content and design of the poster. They might make suggestions for additional or alternative graphics and illustrations.

5. Have groups plan the final layout. They should arrange their illustrations and copy the text onto the poster.

6. Have group members present their poster to the class. Each member should take part in describing the environmental problem and explaining the proposed solution.

GRADING THE PROJECT

Suggested Point Distribution (total = 100 points)

Inclusion of requirements	20 points
Language use	20 points
Creativity/overall appearance	20 points
Effort/participation	20 points
Oral presentation	20 points

Games

Jeu de société

In this game, students will practice expressing obligation and social responsibilities.

Procedure In small groups, students will make and play their own board game. They will need construction paper, markers, and dice. Students should draw a path or a road divided into 20–30 squares. They should mark a starting point (**Départ**) and an ending point (**Arrivée**). In the squares, have them write examples of both pro- and anti-environmental behavior and a positive or negative point value for each. For example, they might write **Tu jettes des ordures dans la rue** (−3) or **Tu prends une douche de 3 minutes** (+4). They should also create "free" squares with environmental messages, such as **Sauvons les forêts tropicales!** To start the game, students place playing pieces such as coins or paper clips at the starting point. Then, each player rolls a die and moves his or her playing piece the number of spaces indicated. When a student lands on a square with a negative point value (**Tu jettes des ordures dans la rue**), the other players must reproach him or her (**Il ne faut pas que tu jettes des ordures dans la rue!**) in order for the points to be deducted from the player's score. When a player lands on a square with a positive point value (**Tu prends une douche de trois minutes**), he or she must tell the other players to do that activity in order to earn the points. (**Vous devriez prendre des douches de trois minutes!**) appoint a scorekeeper in each group to keep track of each player's points. The player with the most points at the end of the game wins.

Storytelling

Mini-histoire

This story accompanies Teaching Transparency 3-2. The mini-histoire can be told and retold in different formats, acted out, written as dictation, and read aloud to give students additional opportunities to practice all four skills. The following story concerns a park ranger who has to deal with people who don't respect the park's rules.

Notre pauvre garde champêtre a bien des problèmes aujourd'hui. D'habitude, il doit bien réprimander un ou deux promeneurs. Comme, par exemple, il y a celui qui marche sur la pelouse, ou encore celui qui jette son papier sale par terre. Mais aujourd'hui, il ne peut pas en croire ses yeux. Il ne sait pas par où commencer : d'abord, il y a ces deux jeunes qui se font les yeux doux au milieu des fleurs. En plus, l'homme a osé cueillir des fleurs! Ensuite, il y a cet homme avec sa cigarette... Mais, il va mettre le feu, avec ses cendres! Et c'est sans compter qu'il est interdit de marcher, de s'asseoir et de s'allonger sur la pelouse. Et cette famille en train de pique-niquer... A l'entrée du parc, il y a pourtant bien un panneau indiquant qu'il est interdit de pique-niquer! Si encore ils faisaient attention à leurs papiers gras. Et il est interdit de donner à manger aux animaux. Après mûre réflexion, notre garde champêtre décide d'agir en criant à pleins poumons : «Tout le monde dehors, vite! Il y a un tigre dans le parc!».

Traditions

Traditions écologistes

The Swiss have a long-standing tradition of environmental protection, dating back to 1876 when they enacted a federal forestry law protecting timber against overcutting. Even Swiss industry reflects the country's desire to preserve its natural resources. For example, one of Switzerland's most important industries is clock and watch making, a trade that uses few raw materials. First fostered in the seventeenth century by French religious **émigrés** called **Huguenots,** the Swiss clock and watch industry today comprises a large portion of the world's trade in timepieces. Other important industries that reflect the Swiss penchant for using resources other than nature's raw materials are banking and pharmaceuticals. Have students investigate Switzerland's top five industries and determine the resources they require. Then have them compare their findings with the top five industries in the United States and/or France.

Recette

Raclette is a cheese produced in the Savoie region, in the Alps. Its name originates from the French verb **racler** *(to scrape) because you scrape the cheese off the dish it is melted on. Traditionally,* **raclette** *was melted on a wood fire. Nowadays, one can use an electric device (**un appareil à raclette**) with individual pans, in which to melt the cheese. Boiled potatoes or slices of smoked meat are used to scrape the cheese off the pans.*

RACLETTE

pour 4 personnes

2 livres de raclette

1 livre de jambon de pays coupé en tranches (prosciutto, par exemple)

8 grosses pommes de terre

sel

poivre

Faire cuire les pommes de terre à l'eau.

Couper les pommes de terre en lamelles. Mettre un petit peu d'huile d'olive ou de pépin de raisin dans une poêle. Mettre les pommes de terre dans la poêle. Ajouter le jambon. Recouvrir avec le fromage qui aura été coupé en fines tranches préalablement. Laisser cuire jusqu'à ce que le fromage soit fondu.

Servir.

Technology

Video Program

Videocassette 1, Videocassette 5 (captioned version)
See Video Guide, pp. 15–20.

Camille et compagnie • Troisième épisode : *Max et l'écologie font bon ménage*

Today, Max must help his mother do household chores, but Camille and Sophie want him to help clean up a park. Max negotiates his chores with his mother and goes to meet Camille and Sophie at the park. Once there, he realizes he will have to work, and he is not sure that he made the right decision.

Quelles sont les problèmes écologiques les plus importants?

People from Côte d'Ivoire, Belgium, and Quebec talk about what they think are the most serious environmental problems. Two native speakers discuss the **Panorama Culturel** question and introduce the interviews.

Vidéoclips

- **Laden** ®: advertisement for washing machines
- **Pliz** ®: advertisement for furniture polish
- **Carolin** ®: advertisement for floor cleaner
- **News report:** Interview with single parents talking about their responsibilities.

Interactive CD-ROM Tutor

The **Interactive CD-ROM Tutor** contains videos, interactive games, and activities that provide students an opportunity to practice and review the material covered in Chapter 3.

Activity	Activity Type	Pupil's Edition Page
1. Vocabulaire	Jeu des paires	p. 67
2. Comment dit-on... ?	Chacun à sa place	p. 68
3. Comment dit-on... ?	Prenons note!	p. 68
4. Grammaire	Les mots qui manquent	p. 69
5. Grammaire	Méli-mélo	pp. 75, 77
6. Vocabulaire	Chasse au trésor Explorons! Vérifions!	p. 77
Panorama Culturel	Quels sont les problèmes écologiques les plus importants? Le bon choix	p. 76
A toi de parler	*Guided recording*	pp. 88–89
A toi d'écrire	*Guided writing*	pp. 88–89

Teacher Management System

Logging In

Logging in to the *Allez, viens!* TMS is easy. Upon launching the program, simply type "admin" in the password area of the log-in screen and press RETURN. Log on to **www.hrw.com/CDROMTUTOR** for a detailed explanation of the Teacher Management System.

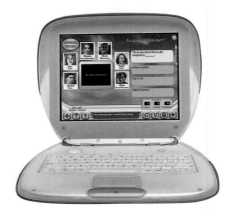

One-Stop Planner CD-ROM

To preview all resources available for this chapter, use the **One-Stop Planner CD-ROM**, Disc 1.

Internet Connection

ADRESSE: go.hrw.com
MOT-CLE: WA3 FRANCOPHONE EUROPE-3

*Have students explore the **go.hrw.com** Web site for many online resources covering all chapters. All Chapter 3 resources are available under the keyword **WA3 FRANCOPHONE EUROPE-3.** Interactive games help students practice the material and provide them with immediate feedback. You'll also find a printable worksheet that provides Internet activities that lead to a comprehensive online research project.*

Jeux interactifs

You can use the interactive activities in this chapter

- to practice grammar, vocabulary, and chapter functions
- as homework
- as an assessment option
- as a self-test
- to prepare for the Chapter Test

Activités Internet

Students look for information on line about organizations devoted to the protection of the environment. They list measures these organizations propose.

- In preparation for the **Activités Internet,** have students do the activities in the **Panorama Culturel** on page 76. In **Activité Internet** D, students are asked to pretend they are starting their own organization for the protection of the environment. Have groups of students work on that activity together. They exchange ideas on the name of their organization, what issues matter most to them, and what solutions their imaginary organization could propose.

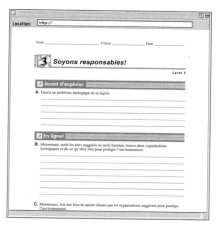

Projet

Have groups of students create a brochure describing various parks in francophone Europe. You might assign roles within each group. Some group members find sites on the Internet and gather the information; others write the text for each park in French; one person chooses pictures to illustrate the text; another prepares the lay-out; another assembles the brochure. Students should document their sources by noting the names and the URLs of all the sites they consulted.

Chapitre 3 : Soyons responsables!
Textbook Listening Activities Scripts

Mise en train

3   p. 66

Answers to Activity 3
1. Gilles
2. Karine
3. Mélanie
4. Charles

1. —Si je me souviens bien, tu n'as pas eu de très bonnes notes en français.

2. —Ecoute, tu es déjà fatiguée. Tu travailles beaucoup en semaine.

3. —Pas question. Tu ne vas pas faire tes devoirs à onze heures du soir.

4. —Oui, si tu ne rentres pas trop tard. Tes grands-parents viennent dîner et tu dois mettre la table.

Première étape

6   p. 67

1. —Tu veux aller voir un film?
—Euh, oui, bien sûr. Mais j'étais en train de faire la vaisselle. Tu peux attendre une demi-heure?
—Oui. Ça va. Ça ne commence pas avant vingt heures.

2. —C'est chouette, le camping, non?
—Oui, s'il ne pleut pas. Moi, j'ai peur qu'il... Ah, zut alors! J'ai oublié d'arroser le jardin.
—Ben, ça ne fait rien. Regarde, il commence à pleuvoir!

3. —Tu n'es pas encore prête?
—Euh, non. Il faut que je donne à manger au chat d'abord.
—Allez, dépêche-toi! On part!

4. —Ginette m'a dit de la retrouver au café à cinq heures. Tu viens?
—Je ne sais pas. Je voudrais bien, mais je dois d'abord rentrer pour sortir le chien.
—Bon, je viens avec toi. On peut la retrouver après, d'accord?
—D'accord.

5. —Tu viens avec nous à la plage samedi?
—Ce serait chouette! Mais j'ai un tas de choses à faire à la maison samedi. Je dois faire la lessive, passer l'aspirateur, nettoyer le parquet...
—Allez, bon week-end!!!

6. —C'est toujours comme ça avec les parents. Il faut, il faut, il faut!
—Oui, moi, c'est pareil. Et ce que je déteste plus que tout, c'est laver les vitres. Tu fais ça, toi?

Answers to Activity 6
1. Christiane
2. Christiane
3. Amina
4. Christiane
5. Amina
6. Christiane

9   p. 68

1. —Dis donc, tu veux bien que je sorte avec Roger après le dîner?
—Il faut d'abord que tu débarrasses la table et que tu fasses la vaisselle.
—Mais, ça va être trop tard après.
—Bon. Ça va pour cette fois.

2. —Papa, je peux dîner chez mes copains ce soir?
—Pas question. Tes grands-parents viennent dîner à la maison.
—Mais Papa...
—J'ai dit non.

3. —Dites, Michel m'a invité à sa boum ce soir. Je peux y aller?
—Oui, si tu as fini tes devoirs.
—Euh, je n'ai pas encore fini. Je pourrais les finir demain.
—Je regrette, mais si je dis oui, ça va être la même chose la prochaine fois.
—Mais c'est son anniversaire!
—Pas question!

4. —J'aimerais partir en vacances aux Etats-Unis.
—Tu as de l'argent pour y aller?
—Euh, non.
—Alors, je suis désolé, mais ce n'est pas possible.

5. —Papa, j'aimerais aller au concert de Vanessa Paradis avec mes copains.
—Et tu vas rentrer à quelle heure?
—Euh, ça dure jusqu'à minuit, et puis je dois revenir.
—Ah, non. Ça veut dire deux heures du matin, ça! Tu sais bien que tu n'as pas le droit de rentrer après minuit.

6. —Tu veux bien que je sorte ce soir?
—Où veux-tu aller?
—Au restaurant avec un copain.
—Oui, si tu rentres à onze heures au plus tard.
—D'accord.

7. —Maman, tu veux bien que j'invite Ali à dîner?
—Quand ça?
—Demain soir.
—Oui, bien sûr.

Answers to Activity 9
1. accordée
2. refusée
3. refusée
4. refusée
5. refusée
6. accordée
7. accordée

To preview all resources available for this chapter, use the **One-Stop Planner CD-ROM**, Disc 1.

Remise en train

19   p. 72

Answers to Activity 19
1. the fifth rule
2. the third rule
3. the second rule
4. the sixth rule
5. the first rule
6. the fourth rule

1. Tu dois constamment te tenir au courant du temps qu'il fait.

2. Tu ne dois jamais aller faire une randonnée tout seul.

3. Il faut que tu emportes un équipement approprié.

4. Si tu n'es pas sûr du chemin, il vaut mieux revenir sur tes pas.

5. Il faut que tu fasses un plan de ta randonnée avant de partir.

6. N'oublie pas de dire l'heure de ton départ et de ton arrivée à un adulte.

Deuxième étape

25   p. 75

Possible answers to Activity 25
1. Don't pick the flowers.
2. No hunting or fishing.
3. No smoking in the cafeterias or restrooms.
4. No littering.

Mesdames, messieurs, afin de préserver le parc, nous attirons votre attention sur certaines règles. Il est interdit de cueillir des fleurs, de chasser ou de pêcher dans le parc. Défense également de fumer dans les cafétérias et les toilettes du parc. De même, il est interdit de jeter des papiers ou des ordures par terre. Pour cela, nous avons des poubelles. Enfin, veuillez ne pas amener d'animaux domestiques dans le parc. Nous vous remercions et vous rappelons que respecter la nature, c'est respecter les autres.

27   p. 77

Answers to Activity 27
1. mauvaise
2. bonne
3. mauvaise
4. mauvaise
5. bonne

1. —Eh bien, ma mère, elle utilise des aérosols presque tous les jours, ou pour nettoyer la maison ou pour faire sa toilette.

2. —Mes cousins habitent loin de leur travail, mais ils prennent des transports en commun tout de même. Mes cousins François et Gilbert prennent le bus tous les jours, et ma cousine Alice partage sa voiture avec ses copains pour aller au travail.

3. —Mon frère Jean-Marc, il est pénible! Il n'arrête pas de déranger les autres en faisant du bruit. C'est la même chose tous les jours. Après l'école, il met sa musique tellement fort! Et puis, on lui a dit mille fois d'éteindre la télé et les lumières, mais il ne le fait jamais!

4. —Mon père continue à prendre des douches très longues, vingt minutes ou plus quelquefois! Je lui ai dit à quel point il gaspille l'eau, mais ça lui est égal, évidemment.

5. —Ma sœur Jeannine, c'est elle qui m'a appris à recycler l'aluminium et le papier. Et la semaine prochaine, nous allons planter des arbres avec notre groupe de scouts.

29   p. 78

Answers to Activity 29
1. reproche
2. excuse
3. reproche
4. reproche
5. excuse
6. reproche
7. reproche

1. —Tu sais bien que tu as tort de fumer, Etienne!

2. —Eh oui, je sais que c'est pas bien de gaspiller l'énergie, mais je suis pas le seul à le faire après tout, hein?

3. —Tu ferais mieux de marcher de temps en temps. Ce n'est pas bien de prendre ta voiture pour aller partout.

4. —Oui, bien sûr que tu n'es pas le seul, mais ce n'est pas une raison!

5. —Je n'ai pas le temps de recycler. Et puis, je ne suis pas obligé. Je suis quand même libre...

6. —Ce n'est pas parce que tout le monde gaspille l'eau que tu dois la gaspiller aussi.

7. —Et encore une fois, j'ai trouvé toutes les lumières allumées, et personne dans la pièce! Tu sais bien que tu ne dois pas oublier d'éteindre les lumières, Florence.

Mise en pratique

1   p. 88

—Maman, j'aimerais aller au Festival international du jazz. Mélanie m'a invitée à y aller avec elle. Tu veux bien que j'y aille?

—Tu penses passer la nuit à Montreux?

—Euh, oui.

—Tu as de l'argent pour ça?

—Mais, euh, non.

—Alors, je regrette, mais ce n'est pas possible.

—Bon. Et si je rentrais après le concert?

—Mais tu sais bien que tu n'as pas le droit de sortir après minuit, Sabine.

—Mais, Maman!

—N'insiste pas, Sabine, c'est non!

—Et si Mélanie peut me prêter de l'argent? Je peux y passer la nuit?

—Oui, si tu as fait tes devoirs. Et n'oublie pas que tu dois faire la vaisselle et la lessive avant de partir.

—D'accord, d'accord.

—Et je veux absolument que tu ranges ta chambre avant.

—Bon, bon.

Answers to Mise en pratique Activity 1
1. to the International Jazz Festival
2. Sabine doesn't have the money to spend the night in Montreux; She can go if Mélanie lends her the money.
3. She must do her homework, do the dishes, do the laundry, and pick up her room.

Chapitre 3 : Soyons Responsables!
Suggested Lesson Plans 50-Minute Schedule

Day 1

CHAPTER OPENER 5 min.
- Present Chapter Objectives, p. 63.
- Culture Note and Geography Link, ATE, pp. 62–63

MISE EN TRAIN 40 min.
- Presenting **Mise en train,** ATE, p. 64; using Video Program, Videocassette 1, see ATE, p. 65
- See Teaching Suggestions, Post-viewing Suggestions 1–2, Video Guide, p. 16.
- Teacher Notes, ATE, p. 65
- See Teaching Suggestions, Post-viewing Suggestions 3–4, Video Guide, p. 16
- Do Activities 1–4, p. 66, using Audio CD for Activity 3.
- Read and discuss **Note culturelle,** p. 66.

Wrap-Up 5 min.
- Do Activity 5, p. 66.

Homework Options
Cahier d'activités, Act. 1, p. 25

Day 2

MISE EN TRAIN
Quick Review 5 min.
- Check homework.
- Bell Work, ATE, p. 67

PREMIERE ETAPE
Vocabulaire, p. 67 20 min.
- Presenting **Vocabulaire,** ATE, p. 67
- Play Audio CD for Activity 6, p. 67.
- Travaux pratiques de grammaire, pp. 18–19, Activities 1–4
- Do Activity 7, p. 68.
- Have students do Activity 8, p. 68, in pairs.

Comment dit-on... ?, p. 68 20 min.
- Presenting **Comment dit-on... ?,** ATE, p. 68
- Play Audio CD for Activity 9, p. 68.
- Cahier d'activités, p. 27, Activity 5
- Travaux pratiques de grammaire, p. 20, Activities 5–6

Wrap-Up, 5 min.
- Tactile Learners, ATE, p. 68

Homework Options
Grammaire supplémentaire, Acts. 1–2, p. 84
Cahier d'activités, Acts. 2–3 and 6, pp. 26, 28

Day 3

PREMIERE ETAPE
Quick Review 5 min.
- Check homework.

Grammaire, p. 69 20 min.
- Presenting **Grammaire,** ATE, p. 69
- **Grammaire supplémentaire,** p. 85, Activities 3–5
- Do Activity 10, p. 69.
- Travaux pratiques de grammaire, pp. 21–23, Activities 7–10
- Have students do Activity 13, p. 70, in groups.

Vocabulaire, p. 70 20 min.
- Presenting **Vocabulaire,** ATE, p. 70
- Cahier d'activités, p. 29, Activity 9
- Travaux pratiques de grammaire, p. 26, Activities 16–17
- Do Activity 14, p. 71.
- Have students do Activities 15–16, p. 71.

Wrap-Up 5 min.
- Game: **Il faut que... ,** ATE, p. 69

Homework Options
Study for Quiz 3-1.
Cahier d'activités, Acts. 7–8, p. 28
Travaux pratiques de grammaire, Acts. 11–15, pp. 23–25

Day 4

PREMIERE ETAPE
Quick Review 3-1 20 min.
- Administer Quiz 3-1A or 3-1B.

REMISE EN TRAIN 25 min.
- Presenting **Remise en train,** ATE, pp. 72–73
- Do Activities 18–22, pp. 72–73, using Audio CD for Activity 19.
- Read and discuss **Note culturelle,** p. 73.
- Thinking Critically: Analyzing, ATE, p. 73

Wrap-Up 5 min.
- Do Activity 23, p. 73.

Homework Options
Cahier d'activités, Acts. 11–12, p. 30

Day 5

REMISE EN TRAIN
Quick Review 5 min.
- Check homework.

DEUXIEME ETAPE
RENCONTRE CULTURELLE 10 min.
- Presenting **Rencontre culturelle,** ATE, p. 74
- **Qu'en penses-tu?,** p. 74
- Language-to-Language, History Link, and Culture Note, ATE, p. 74
- Read and discuss **Savais-tu que... ?,** p. 74.

Comment dit-on... ? and **Note de grammaire, p. 75** 20 min.
- Presenting **Comment dit-on... ?,** ATE, p. 75
- Read and discuss **Note de grammaire,** p. 75.
- Do Activity 24, p. 75.
- Play Audio CD for Activity 25, p. 75.
- Travaux pratiques de grammaire, p. 27, Activities 18–19

PANORAMA CULTUREL 10 min.
- Presenting **Panorama Culturel,** ATE, p. 76
- Questions, ATE, p. 76

Wrap-Up 5 min.
- **Qu'en penses-tu?,** p. 76

Homework Options
Grammaire supplémentaire, Acts. 7–9, pp. 86–87

Day 6

DEUXIEME ETAPE
Quick Review 5 min.
- Check homework.

Vocabulaire, p. 77 20 min.
- Presenting **Vocabulaire,** ATE, p. 77
- Play Audio CD for Activity 27, p. 77.
- Travaux pratiques de grammaire, p. 28, Activities 20–22
- Do Activity 28, p. 77.
- Challenge, ATE, p. 77

Comment dit-on... ?, p. 78 20 min.
- Presenting **Comment dit-on... ?,** ATE, p. 78
- Play Audio CD for Activity 29, p. 78.
- Do Activity 30, p. 78.
- Cahier d'activités, pp. 32–33, Activities 16–18
- Have students do Activities 31–32, pp. 78–79, in pairs.

Wrap-Up 5 min.
- Group Work, ATE, p. 79

Homework Options
Study for Quiz 3-2.
Pupil's Edition, Activity 33, p. 79
Cahier d'activités, Act. 14, p. 31

One-Stop Planner CD-ROM

For alternative lesson plans by chapter section, to create your own customized plans, or to preview all resources available for this chapter, use the **One-Stop Planner CD-ROM**, Disc 1.

For additional homework suggestions, see activities accompanied by this symbol throughout the chapter.

Day 7

DEUXIEME ETAPE

Quiz 3-2 20 min.
- Administer Quiz 3-2A or 3-2B.

LISONS! 25 min.
- Using Prior Knowledge, ATE, p. 80
- Read and discuss **Stratégie pour lire,** p. 80.
- Do Prereading Activities A–B, p. 80.
- Have students read *Albert nez en l'air* and *Julie Boum,* pp. 80–82.
- Begin Reading Activities C–P, pp. 80–82.

Wrap-Up 5 min.
- Continue Reading Activities C–P, ATE, pp. 80–82.

Homework Options
Pupil's Edition, Activities C–P, pp. 80–82
Cahier d'activités, Act. 21, p. 35

Day 8

LISONS!

Quick Review 5 min.
- Go over homework.

LISONS! 15 min.
- Do Activity Q, p. 82.
- Reading/Writing Link, ATE, p. 82

ECRIVONS! 25 min.
- Discuss the strategy for **Ecrivons!,** p. 83, then have students work on their fables.

Wrap-Up 5 min.
- Allow time for peer and self-evaluation of fables.

Homework Options
Complete final drafts of fables for **Ecrivons!**

Day 9

ECRIVONS!

Quick Review 5 min.
- Have volunteers share their fables with the class.

MISE EN PRATIQUE

Chapter Review 40 min.
- Play Audio CD for Activity 1, p. 88.
- Have students do Activity 2, p. 88, in pairs.
- Do Activity 3, p. 88.
- Have students complete Activity 4, p. 89, in groups.
- **A toi de parler,** CD-ROM Tutor, Disc 1

Wrap-Up 5 min.
- Thinking Critically: Analyzing, ATE, p. 88

Homework Options
Cahier d'activités, Acts. 22–23, p. 36

Day 10

MISE EN PRATIQUE

Quick Review 5 min.
- Check homework.

Chapter Review 40 min.
- Have students do Activity 5, p. 89, in pairs.
- Have groups of students prepare demonstrations for **Jeu de rôle,** p. 89.
- Allow groups to perform **Jeu de rôle** demonstrations.
- Challenge, ATE, p. 89
- **A toi d'écrire,** CD-ROM Tutor

Wrap-Up 5 min.
- Begin **Que sais-je?,** p. 90.

Homework Options
Que sais-je?, p. 90

Day 11

MISE EN PRATIQUE

Quick Review 15 min.
- Go over **Que sais-je?,** p. 90.

Student Review 30 min.
- See Game: **Serpent!,** ATE, p. 90.
- Circumlocution, ATE, p. 91

Wrap-Up 5 min.
- Activities for Communication, p. 57, Realia 3-1 and Listening suggestion, p. 59

Homework Options
Activities for Communication, pp. 58–59, Realia 3-2: Writing suggestion

Day 12

MISE EN PRATIQUE

Quick Review 10 min.
- Have volunteers present their announcements or posters from Realia 3-2.

Chapter Review 40 min.
- Review Chapter 3. Choose from **Grammaire supplémentaire,** Grammar Tutor for Students of French, Activities for Communication, Listening Activities, Interactive CD-ROM Tutor, or **Jeux interactifs.**

Homework Options
Study for Chapter 3 Test.

Assessment

Test, Chapter 3 50 min.
- Administer Chapter 3 Test. Select from Testing Program, Alternative Assessment Guide, Test Generator, or Standardized Assessment Tutor.

Chapitre 3 : Soyons responsables!
Suggested Lesson Plans 90-Minute Block Schedule

Block 1

CHAPTER OPENER 10 min.
- Present Chapter Objectives, p. 63.
- Culture Note and Geography Link, ATE, pp. 62–63

MISE EN TRAIN 35 min.
- Presenting **Mise en train,** ATE, p. 64
- Do Activities 1–4, p. 66, using Audio CD for Activity 3.
- **Note culturelle,** p. 66

PREMIERE ETAPE
Vocabulaire, p. 67 40 min.
- Presenting **Vocabulaire,** ATE, p. 67
- Play Audio CD for Activity 6, p. 67.
- Building on Previous Skills, ATE, p. 67
- Do Activities 7–8, p. 68.

Wrap-Up 5 min.
- Teaching Transparency 3-1, using suggestion #1 from Vocabulary Practice Using Teaching Transparency 3-1

Homework Options
Cahier d'activités, pp. 25–26, Acts. 1–3
Travaux pratiques de grammaire, pp. 18–19, Acts. 1–4

Block 2

PREMIERE ETAPE
Quick Review 5 min.
- Kinesthetic Learners, ATE, p. 67

Comment dit-on... ?, p. 68 25 min.
- Presenting **Comment dit-on... ?,** ATE, p. 68
- Play Audio CD for Activity 9, p. 68.

Grammaire, p. 69 30 min.
- Presenting **Grammaire,** ATE, p. 69
- Do Activities 10–11, pp. 69–70.
- Game: Tic Tac Toe, ATE, p. 86

Vocabulaire, p. 71 25 min.
- Presenting **Vocabulaire,** ATE, p. 70
- Do Activities 14–15, p. 71.

Wrap-Up 5 min.
- Additional Practice, ATE, p. 69

Homework Options
Grammaire supplémentaire, pp. 84–85, Acts. 1–5
Cahier d'activités, pp. 27–29, Acts. 5–9
Travaux pratiques de grammaire, pp. 20–23, Acts. 5–11

Block 3

PREMIERE ETAPE
Quick Review 10 min.
- Listening Activities, p. 24, Additional Listening Activity 3-3

Grammaire, p. 69 15 min.
- Do Activity 12, p. 71.

Vocabulaire, p. 70 10 min.
- Presenting **Vocabulaire,** ATE, p. 70
- Do Activity 16, p. 72.

REMISE EN TRAIN 40 min.
- Presenting **Remise en train,** ATE, p. 72
- Do Activities 18–22, pp. 72–73, using Audio CD for Activity 19.
- **Note culturelle,** p. 73

RENCONTRE CULTURELLE 10 min.
- Have students look at the photos and read the captions, p. 74.
- Read and discuss **Qu'en penses-tu?** and **Savais-tu que...?,** p. 74.

Wrap-Up 5 min.
- Teaching Suggestion, ATE, p. 73

Homework Options
Have students study for Quiz 3-1.
Grammaire supplémentaire, p. 86, Act. 6
Cahier d'activités, pp. 29–30, Acts. 10–12
Travaux pratiques de grammaire, pp. 24–26, Acts. 12–17

For alternative lesson plans by chapter section, to create your own customized plans, or to preview all resources available for this chapter, use the **One-Stop Planner CD-ROM,** Disc 1.

For additional homework suggestions, see activities accompanied by this symbol throughout the chapter.

Block 4

PREMIERE ETAPE
Quick Review 10 min.
- Activities for Communication, pp. 9–10, Communicative Activity 3-1A and 3-1B

Quiz 3-1 20 min.
- Administer Quiz 3-1A or 3-1B.

DEUXIEME ETAPE
Comment dit-on... ?, p. 75 35 min.
- Presenting **Comment dit-on... ?,** ATE, p. 75
- Read and discuss **Note de grammaire,** p. 75.
- Do Activity 24, p. 75.
- Play Audio CD for Activity 25, p. 75.
- Do Activity 26, p. 75.

Vocabulaire, p. 77 15 min.
- Presenting **Vocabulaire,** ATE, p. 77
- Play Audio CD for Activity 27, p.77.

Wrap-Up 10 min.
- Visual Learners, ATE, p. 77

Homework Options
Grammaire supplémentaire, pp. 86–87, Acts. 7–8
Cahier d'activités, p. 31, Acts. 13–15
Travaux pratiques de grammaire, pp. 27–28, Acts. 18–20

Block 5

DEUXIEME ETAPE
Quick Review 10 min.
- Teaching Transparency 3-2, using suggestion #1 from Suggestions for Using Teaching Transparency 3-2

PANORAMA CULTUREL 20 min.
- Community Link, ATE, p. 76
- Presenting **Panorama Culturel,** ATE, p. 76
- Read and discuss **Qu'en penses-tu?,** p. 76.

Vocabulaire, p. 77 10 min.
- Presenting **Vocabulaire,** ATE, p. 77
- Do Activity 28, p. 77.

Comment dit-on... ?, p. 78 40 min.
- Presenting **Comment dit-on... ?,** ATE, p. 78
- **Note culturelle,** p. 78
- Play Audio CD for Activity 29, p. 78.
- Do Activity 30, p. 78.
- Do Activity 32, p. 79.

Wrap-Up 10 min.
- Group Work, ATE, p. 79

Homework Options
Have students study for Quiz 3-2.
Pupil's Edition, Activity 33, p. 79
Grammaire supplémentaire, p. 87, Act. 9
Cahier d'activités, pp. 32–34, Acts. 16–20
Travaux pratiques de grammaire, p. 28, Acts. 21–22

Block 6

DEUXIEME ETAPE
Quick Review 10 min.
- Activities for Communication, pp. 11–12, Communicative Activity 3-2A and 3-2B

Quiz 3-2 20 min.
- Administer Quiz 3-2A or 3-2B.

LISONS!, pp. 80–81 30 min.
- Do Prereading Activities A–B, using Prior Knowledge and Thinking Critically: Drawing Inferences, ATE, p. 80.
- Read *Albert le nez en l'air,* pp. 80–81.

MISE EN PRATIQUE 30 min.
- Play Audio CD for Activity 1, p. 88. See Slower Pace, ATE, p. 88.
- Do Activities 2–3, pp. 88–89.
- Thinking Critically: Analyzing, ATE, p. 88
- Activity 5, p. 89

Homework Options
Que sais-je?, p. 90
Interactive CD-ROM Tutor Games
Study for Chapter 3 Test

Block 7

MISE EN PRATIQUE
Quick Review 10 min.
- Game: **Jeu de société,** ATE, p. 61C

Chapter Review 35 min.
- Review Chapter 3. Choose from **Grammaire supplémentaire,** Grammar Tutor for Students of French, Activities for Communication, Listening Activities, Interactive CD-ROM Tutor, or **Jeux interactifs.**

Test, Chapter 3 45 min.
- Administer Chapter 3 Test. Select from Testing Program, Alternative Assessment Guide, Test Generator, or Standardized Assessment Tutor.

Chapter Opener

CHAPITRE 3

One-Stop Planner CD-ROM

For resource information, see the **One-Stop Planner,** Disc 1.

 Pacing Tips
The first and second **étapes** have more or less the same amount of material to cover. However, you might devote more time to the second **étape** if you want to make use of the cultural content presented in the **Rencontre culturelle** and the **Panorama Culturel.** For Lesson Plans and timing suggestions, see pages 61I–61L.

Meeting the Standards

Communication
- Asking for, granting, and refusing permission; expressing obligation, p. 68
- Forbidding, p. 75
- Reproaching; justifying your actions; rejecting other's excuses, p. 78

Cultures
- Culture Notes, pp. 62, 71, 73, 74
- Notes culturelles, pp. 66, 73, 78
- Panorama Culturel, p. 76
- Rencontre culturelle, p. 74

Connections
- Geography Link, p. 63
- History Link, p. 74
- Music Link, p. 71
- Multicultural Link, p. 76
- Reading/Writing Links, pp. 82, 83

Comparisons
- Language-to-Language, p. 74
- Thinking Critically, pp. 65, 73, 80, 82, 88

Communities
- Career Path, p. 88
- Community Links, pp. 73, 76
- De l'école au travail, p. 79

Cultures and Communities

Culture Note
Ecology is an important part of everyday life in Switzerland. Many laws have been passed to protect the country's forested areas, and strict controls on automobile emissions help to decrease air pollution. Explorations into the widespread use of alternative energy sources have been successful. About 500 hydroelectric plants supply energy to the country, without the negative effects of fossil fuels.

C H A P I T R E

3
Soyons responsables!

Objectives

In this chapter you will learn to

Première étape

- ask for, grant, and refuse permission
- express obligation

Deuxième étape

- forbid
- reproach
- justify your actions and reject others' excuses

 internet

go.hrw.com

ADRESSE: go.hrw.com
MOT-CLE: WA3 FRANCOPHONE EUROPE-3

◀ Un lac en Suisse

Focusing on Outcomes
Have students read the list of objectives and tell in what situations they might use each one. You might have them recall French words and expressions they already know that they can use to express the functions. (**Tu devrais... ; Tu ferais bien de... ; Désolé(e), j'ai des trucs à faire.**)

Teaching Suggestions
Ask students to name environmental groups they are familiar with and tell what these groups do to protect the environment. Ask students what they can do personally to protect the environment.

Have students find the answers to the following questions: **Combien de langues officielles est-ce qu'il y a en Suisse? (4) Lesquelles? (le français, l'allemand, l'italien, le romanche) Où se trouve la Suisse? (à l'est de la France, au nord de l'Italie) Quels sont certains produits qu'on trouve en Suisse? (le chocolat, les montres, le fromage)**

Connections and Comparisons

Geography Link
Have students research facts about Switzerland's geography. They might use the Internet or an encyclopedia to find their answers. Here are some possible questions: **Quelle chaîne de montagnes célèbre se trouve en Suisse? (Les Alpes) Dans quelle partie de la Suisse se trouvent ces montagnes? (dans le sud) Comment s'appelle le plus haut sommet de ces montagnes? (le Duffourspitze) Quelle est l'altitude de ce sommet en pieds? (15.000 pieds) Quel est le nom anglais du lac Léman?** *(Lake Geneva)* **Quels pays partagent des frontières avec la Suisse? (la France, l'Italie, l'Allemagne, l'Autriche, le Liechtenstein)**

STANDARDS: 3.1

Presenting
Mise en train

Have students look at the photos in the **Mise en train.** Ask what they think will happen in this episode. Then, play the recording as students read along. Stop the recording after each scene and make several true-false statements to check comprehension. **(Mélanie a déjà fait ses devoirs. faux)**

Additional Practice

Ask students the following questions about the report card at the top of page 65: **Quel est le nom de l'élève? (Foinereau) En quelle matière il est le plus fort? (en histoire-géo) Il a eu combien en français? (huit)**

Mise en train · *Je peux sortir?*

Cahier d'activités, p. 25, Act. 1

CD 3 Tr. 1

Stratégie pour comprendre
Look at the title of this story and at the photos on these two pages. Can you guess what this episode is about? What could be the connection between a grade report, a girl on the phone, and a movie poster?

1 Chez Mélanie...

Mélanie	Papa, est-ce que je peux aller au cinéma ce soir?
M. Bonvin	Ce soir? Est-ce que tu as fait tes devoirs?
Mélanie	Euh non, pas encore.
M. Bonvin	Alors, c'est non.
Mélanie	Mais Papa... Je peux les faire après le film!
M. Bonvin	Pas question. Tu ne vas pas faire tes devoirs à onze heures du soir.
Mélanie	Ecoute, Papa...
M. Bonvin	N'insiste pas, c'est comme ça.
Mélanie	J'en ai marre! C'est toujours la même chose!

2 Mélanie au téléphone...

Mélanie	Claire? Je suis désolée, je n'ai pas le droit de sortir. Il faut que je fasse mes devoirs.
Claire	Tant pis.
Mélanie	Ce sera pour la prochaine fois.
Claire	D'accord. Salut.

3 Chez Gilles...

Gilles	Dites, vous voulez bien que je parte faire une randonnée en montagne avec des copains?
Mme Fornereau	Quand ça?
Gilles	Pendant les vacances de Pâques.
M. Fornereau	Et ton examen d'entrée au lycée?
Gilles	C'est-à-dire que...
M. Fornereau	Si je me souviens bien, tu n'as pas eu de très bonnes notes en français.
Gilles	Non, c'est vrai, elles n'étaient pas terribles.
Mme Fornereau	Alors, pour ta randonnée, on est d'accord si tu as de bonnes notes en français. Sinon, tu restes ici pour réviser.
Gilles	D'accord.

Preteaching Vocabulary

Identifying Keywords

Have students skim the conversations for words they know. They should use their prior knowledge of French and try to recognize words that are used in English. Once students have identified such words, ask them to identify the ones that reveal the gist of the conversations taking place on these two pages. You might ask students to justify their choices. Make a list of the words on the board and ask students to guess what is happening in each dialogue, based on the words listed.

4 **Gilles au téléphone...**

Gilles Cyrille? J'ai parlé avec mes parents de notre projet de vacances.

Cyrille Ah oui? Qu'est-ce qu'ils ont dit?

Gilles Ils ne sont pas très chauds.

Cyrille Ah, dommage!

Gilles Attends, ils veulent bien. Mais il faut que je travaille mon français.

Cyrille C'est drôle! Mes parents m'ont dit la même chose!

BULLETIN TRIMESTR

NOM : *Fournereau*   PRENOM : *Gilles*
MATIERES   MOYENNE   COMMEN

Français	12	Peut f...
Français	8	Elève ...
Mathématiques	10	Trava...
Histoire	14	Bien

5 **Chez Karine...**

Karine Dites, je suis invitée à une soirée d'anniversaire. Est-ce que je peux y aller?

Mme Laborit Chez qui?

Karine Chez Jean-Michel. Samedi soir.

M. Laborit Hmm... d'accord, mais il faut que tu rentres à minuit au plus tard.

Karine Mais Papa, la soirée commence à neuf heures. C'est trop tôt, minuit.

M. Laborit J'ai dit minuit au plus tard.

Karine Mais je n'ai pas école le lendemain.

Mme Laborit Ecoute, tu es déjà fatiguée. Tu travailles beaucoup en semaine.

Karine Mais le week-end, c'est fait pour s'amuser!

6 **Karine au téléphone...**

Karine Jean-Michel? C'est d'accord pour samedi. Mais je dois rentrer à minuit.

Jean-Michel Dommage. Mais c'est pas grave. Tu auras quand même le temps de manger et de danser.

7 **Chez Charles...**

Charles Maman, ça te dérange si je vais chez Gabriel regarder une vidéo cet après-midi?

Mme Panetier Tu n'as pas de devoirs à faire?

Charles Non, j'ai tout fait.

Mme Panetier Tu as rangé ta chambre?

Charles Euh, non.

Mme Panetier Alors, il faut d'abord que tu ranges ta chambre.

Charles Je peux y aller après?

Mme Panetier Oui, si tu ne rentres pas trop tard. Tes grands-parents viennent dîner et tu dois mettre la table.

Charles D'accord. Je fonce ranger ma chambre.

8 **Charles au téléphone...**

Charles Gabriel, je ne peux pas venir tout de suite. Il faut d'abord que je fasse des trucs à la maison.

Gabriel O.K. A quelle heure est-ce que tu viens, alors?

Charles Vers trois heures.

Gabriel Bien. On t'attend pour regarder le film.

Teacher Notes

- Gilles wants to go hiking during Easter vacation (**les vacances de Pâques**). French students plan for this vacation just as American students plan for spring break.

- Remind students that a **bulletin trimestriel** is a notebook in which students' grades and teacher comments are recorded.

Teaching Suggestion

Have students try to guess the meaning of Gilles' statement about his parents, **Ils ne sont pas très chauds.** *(They aren't thrilled with the idea.)*

Thinking Critically

Analyzing Ask students to list all the reasons the parents give for granting or refusing permission. Do they think the reasons were valid? Why or why not? If students were parents, would they place the same restrictions on their children? Why or why not?

Camille et compagnie

You may choose to show students Episode 3: *Max et l'écologie font bon ménage* now or wait until later in the chapter. In the video, Max must help his mother do household chores, but Camille and Sophie want him to help clean up a park. Max negotiates his chores with his mother and goes to meet Camille and Sophie at the park. Once there, he realizes he will have to work, and he is not sure that he made the right decision.

Using the Captioned Video

As an alternative, you might want to show the captioned version of *Camille et compagnie : Max et l'écologie font bon ménage* on Videocassette 5. Some students may benefit from seeing the written words as they listen to the target language and watch the gestures and actions in context. This visual reinforcement of vocabulary and functions will facilitate students' comprehension and help reduce their anxiety before they are formally introduced to the new language in the chapter.

Teaching Suggestion

1 You might ask these questions during the presentation of *Je peux sortir?* to check comprehension.

Challenge

3 For additional listening practice, have students give other quotations from the **Mise en train** and have the class tell whether an adult or teenager is speaking.

4 Once students have listed the expressions, have them work with a partner. Student One reads aloud one of the expressions from his/her list and Student Two guesses the function of the expression. Have partners switch roles.

---

1 Tu as compris? These activities check for comprehension only. Students should not yet be expected to produce language modeled in **Mise en train**.

1. Qu'est-ce que ces jeunes demandent à leurs parents? for permission to go out/away
2. Qui obtient et qui n'obtient pas la permission? Gilles, Charles, and Karine do; Mélanie does not.
3. A quelles conditions les parents donnent leur permission?
Gilles must improve his French grades. Karine must return by midnight. Charles must clean his room.

2 Qui suis-je?

Complète les phrases et dis quel(le) jeune de *Je peux sortir?* parle.

 a.  b.  c.  d.
5 b

1. «Moi, je n'ai pas... 3 c
2. «Moi, je voudrais bien...
3. «Moi, il faut d'abord que...
4. «Moi, je dois...
5. «Moi, il faut que...

je fasse des trucs à la maison.»

je travaille mon français.»

le droit de sortir.» 1 d

faire une randonnée en montagne.» 2 b

rentrer à minuit.» 4 a

3 Qui parle? See scripts and answers on p. 61G.

Ecoutons C'est le parent de quel(le) jeune qui parle?

CD 3 Tr. 2

Mélanie		Karine	
	Charles		Gilles

4 Cherche les expressions See answers below.

What do the people in *Je peux sortir?* say to . . .

1. ask permission?
2. grant permission?
3. refuse permission?
4. protest?
5. end a conversation?
6. express disappointment?
7. express obligation?

5 Et maintenant, à toi

Est-ce que tes parents te permettent toujours de sortir? Sinon, leurs raisons sont-elles similaires à ou différentes de celles que donnent les parents dans *Je peux sortir?*

Note culturelle

On dit des Suisses qu'ils sont disciplinés, travailleurs et minutieux. Ils sont contents lorsqu'ils parviennent à faire quelque chose de constructif. Les enfants suisses doivent apprendre à travailler dur très jeunes. Même les plus jeunes doivent participer à quelques tâches ménagères et, plus ils grandissent, plus ils ont de responsabilités. Lorsque les adolescents sortent de l'école, ils savent que des heures de travail—devoirs pour l'école aussi bien que tâches ménagères—les attendent à la maison. Tout ce temps passé à travailler ensemble est peut-être l'une des raisons pour lesquelles les Suisses restent si proches de leur famille.

Answers

4
1. Est-ce que je peux... ? Vous voulez bien que je... ? Ça te dérange si je... ?
2. On est d'accord si... ; ... d'accord, mais il faut que... ; ... il faut d'abord que tu...
3. ... c'est non. Pas question.
4. Mais... ; Ecoute...
5. N'insiste pas, c'est comme ça.
6. Tant pis; ... dommage.
7. Il faut que je... ; Je dois...

Comprehension Check

Kinesthetic Learners

2 Write the sentence starters on a set of large cards and their completions on another set. Number the cards 1–10. Give the cards to ten students. Have the students stand at the front of the classroom and hold up their cards. Have students call out two numbers, read aloud the resulting sentence, and identify the speaker from the **Mise en train**. Continue until all the starters have been paired.

Slower Pace

3 As students listen, encourage them to note the most important details to help them answer. Stop the recording after each statement to allow students time to write. You might play each statement twice.

Vocabulaire

CD-ROM DISC 1

Chez toi, qui doit...

enlever la neige?

laver les vitres?

faire la lessive?

faire la poussière?

nettoyer le parquet?

faire le repassage?

arroser le jardin?

tondre la pelouse?

débarrasser la table
donner à manger
  au chat
faire la cuisine

faire la vaisselle
faire son lit
garder les enfants

mettre la table
nettoyer la salle de
  bains
passer l'aspirateur

ramasser les feuilles
to rake leaves
sortir le chien

Travaux pratiques de grammaire, pp. 18–19, Act. 1–4

Cahier d'activités, p. 26, Act. 2–3

See scripts and answers on p. 61G.

6 **C'est Christiane ou Amina?**

Lisons/Ecoutons Regarde les listes de tâches ménagères que Christiane et Amina doivent faire. Ecoute les conversations et dis si c'est Christiane ou Amina qui parle.

CD 3 Tr. 3

Christiane
débarrasser la table
faire la vaisselle
sortir le chien
faire la poussière
laver les vitres
arroser le jardin
faire le repassage

Amina
faire la lessive
faire la cuisine
mettre la table
passer l'aspirateur
nettoyer le parquet
donner à manger au chat
nettoyer les salles de bains

Communication for All Students

Kinesthetic Learners
Give commands (**Enlève la neige!**) and have students respond by miming the appropriate action.

Building on Previous Skills
Name rooms of a house (**la cuisine**) and have students suggest chores associated with them (**faire la vaisselle**).

Slower Pace
6 Have students copy the two lists and check off each chore they hear mentioned.

Première étape

CHAPITRE 3

Teaching Resources
pp. 67–71

PRINT
- Lesson Planner, p. 13
- Listening Activities, pp. 19–20, 23–24
- Activities for Communication, pp. 9–10, 57, 59, 93–94
- Travaux pratiques de grammaire, pp. 18–26
- Grammar Tutor for Students of French, Chapter 3
- Cahier d'activités, pp. 26–29
- Testing Program, pp. 45–48
- Alternative Assessment Guide, p. 32
- Student Make-Up Assignments, Chapter 3

MEDIA
- One-Stop Planner
- Audio Compact Discs, CD 3, Trs. 2–4, 15, 20–22
- Teaching Transparencies 3-1; **Grammaire supplémentaire** Answers; Travaux pratiques de grammaire Answers
- Interactive CD-ROM Tutor, Disc 1

Bell Work
Write the following lists on the board or on a transparency. Have students match them and then write sentence: **faire, tondre, sortir, laver; le chien, la voiture, la vaisselle, la pelouse**

Presenting Vocabulaire

Act out the new expressions as you tell students what you are doing. Write each chore on the board and have students who do that chore raise their hands. Write their names under each chore. Make true/false statements (**John fait la lessive.**) and ask students if they are true or false.

Teaching Resources
pp. 67–71

PRINT
▶ Lesson Planner, p. 13
▶ Listening Activities, pp. 19–20, 23–24
▶ Activities for Communication, pp. 9–10, 57, 59, 93–94
▶ Travaux pratiques de grammaire, pp. 18–26
▶ Grammar Tutor for Students of French, Chapter 3
▶ Cahier d'activités, pp. 26–29
▶ Testing Program, pp. 45–48
▶ Alternative Assessment Guide, p. 32
▶ Student Make-Up Assignments, Chapter 3

MEDIA
▶ One-Stop Planner
▶ Audio Compact Discs, CD 3, Trs. 2–4, 15, 20–22
▶ Teaching Transparencies 3-1; **Grammaire supplémentaire** Answers; Travaux pratiques de grammaire Answers
▶ Interactive CD-ROM Tutor, Disc 1

Answers
7 *Félicité:* tondre la pelouse; *Jean:* faire le repassage, faire la lessive; *Serge:* arroser le jardin, faire la vaisselle

---

7 **C'est à qui de le faire?**

Parlons Qu'est-ce que chacun des jeunes à droite doit faire? See answers below.

8 **C'est trop!**

Parlons Tu crois que tu fais trop de choses chez toi. Tu veux savoir ce que ton/ta camarade fait chez lui/elle. Demande-lui qui fait chaque tâche ménagère dans sa famille et dis-lui qui la fait chez toi. Dis si tu crois que c'est juste ou injuste et pourquoi.

Comment dit-on...?

Asking for, granting, and refusing permission; expressing obligation

To ask for permission:

J'aimerais aller au concert ce soir avec Jean-Luc.
Je peux inviter des amis?
Tu veux bien que je sorte?
 Is it OK with you if I go out?
Ça te dérange si je fais la vaisselle plus tard?
 Do you mind if . . .?

To grant permission:

Oui, bien sûr!
Ça va pour cette fois. *OK, just this once.*
Oui, si tu as fait tes devoirs.

To refuse permission:

Ce n'est pas possible.
Pas question.
Tu n'as pas le droit de sortir après minuit.
 You're not allowed to . . .

To express obligation:

Il faut que tu fasses tes devoirs d'abord.
 You have to do . . .
Tu dois garder ta petite sœur ce soir.

Cahier d'activités, p. 27, Act. 5

Tu te rappelles?

Devoir is an irregular verb.

devoir *(must, to have to)*

Je **dois**	
Tu **dois**	
Il/Elle/On **doit**	faire la
Nous **devons**	lessive.
Vous **devez**	
Ils/Elles **doivent**	

• The past participle of **devoir** is **dû.**
• **Tu devrais** *(You should)* is also a form of **devoir.**

Travaux pratiques de grammaire, p. 20, Act. 5–6 → Grammaire supplémentaire, p. 84, Act. 1–2

Cahier d'activités, p. 28, Act. 6

9 **Je peux... ?** See scripts and answers on p. 61G.

 Ecoutons Ecoute ces conversations et dis si les permissions sont accordées ou refusées.
CD 3 Tr. 4

Communication for All Students

Tactile Learners

7 Give props (a watering can, an iron) to various students, who tell what they must do with them. **(Je dois arroser le jardin.)** The class identifies the child in the illustration each student is portraying. **(C'est Serge.)**

Building on Previous Skills

8 Have students tell how often they do each chore, using **(deux) fois par semaine, le (lundi), souvent,** and so on.

Challenge

9 To extend this activity, ask students what the people are asking permission to do.

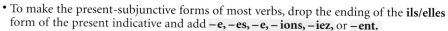

Grammaire

The subjunctive

All the verb forms you've already learned have been in the indicative mood. There's another mood used in French called the subjunctive. You have to use subjunctive verb forms in clauses after specific phrases that express *obligation* (**Il faut que...**) and *will* (**vouloir que...**). You'll learn more of these phrases later, along with some other uses of the subjunctive.

- To make the present-subjunctive forms of most verbs, drop the ending of the **ils/elles** form of the present indicative and add −**e**, −**es**, −**e**, −**ions**, −**iez**, or −**ent**.

rentr~~ent~~	Il faut qu'ils **rentrent** à dix heures.
finiss~~ent~~	Il faut que nous **finissions** avant de partir.
répond~~ent~~	Elle veut que je lui **réponde**.
sort~~ent~~	Tu veux bien que je **sorte** ce soir?

- Some irregular verbs, such as **prendre** and **venir,** have two stems to which you add the subjunctive endings. The stem for **nous** and **vous** comes from the **nous** form of the present tense. The other stem comes from the **ils/elles** form.

prendre: nous prenons- → **pren-** → que nous **prenions**
que vous **preniez**

ils/elles prennent → **prenn-** → que je **prenne**
que tu **prennes**
qu'il/elle **prenne**
qu'ils/elles **prennent**

venir: nous venons → **ven-** → que nous **venions**
que vous **veniez**

ils/elles viennent → **vienn-** → que je **vienne**
que tu **viennes**
qu'il/elle **vienne**
qu'ils/elles **viennent**

Grammaire supplémentaire,
pp. 85–86, Act. 3–6

Cahier d'activités,
p. 28, Act. 7–8

- Some irregular verbs have the same irregular stem for all the forms. The stem of the verb **faire** is **fass–.** You add the regular subjunctive endings to the irregular stem: Il faut que tu **fasses** ton lit!

Travaux pratiques
de grammaire,
pp. 21–25, Act. 7–15

10 **Grammaire en contexte**

Ecrivons Marc a trop de choses à faire! Qu'est-ce qu'il faut qu'il fasse? Regarde l'illustration à droite et complète ses phrases en utilisant les expressions ci-dessous. *See answers below.*

je sorte mon chien
je fasse mes devoirs
réparer mon vélo
ranger ma chambre
je trouve mon livre d'anglais
je garde ma petite sœur

Presenting
Grammaire

The subjunctive Explain the formation of the subjunctive. Then, write on the board two sentence starters: **Il faut que je...** and **Je veux qu'on...** Have students write down an activity they want to do (**faire des photos**) and an activity they must do (**mettre la table**). Then, have pairs of students form sentences that include the sentence starters and the activities they wrote. (**Il faut que je mette la table. Je veux qu'on fasse des photos.**)

Additional Practice
Have students suggest endings for these sentences: **Pour réussir en français, il faut que nous... ; Je voudrais que mes profs...**

Answers
10 Il faut que je sorte mon chien/fasse mes devoirs/trouve mon livre d'anglais/garde ma petite sœur. Je dois réparer mon vélo/ranger ma chambre.

Teaching Resources
pp. 67–71

PRINT
▸ Lesson Planner, p. 13
▸ Listening Activities, pp. 19–20, 23–24
▸ Activities for Communication, pp. 9–10, 57, 59, 93–94
▸ Travaux pratiques de grammaire, pp. 18–26
▸ Grammar Tutor for Students of French, Chapter 3
▸ Cahier d'activités, pp. 26–29
▸ Testing Program, pp. 45–48
▸ Alternative Assessment Guide, p. 32
▸ Student Make-Up Assignments, Chapter 3

MEDIA
▸ One-Stop Planner
▸ Audio Compact Discs, CD 3, Trs. 2–4, 15, 20–22
▸ Teaching Transparencies 3-1; **Grammaire supplémentaire** Answers; Travaux pratiques de grammaire Answers
▸ Interactive CD-ROM Tutor, Disc 1

Presenting
Vocabulaire

Using sock puppets, create and act out a conversation in which a parent reprimands a child, using the expressions in the **Vocabulaire**. Then, have the teenage puppet say or do something that will provoke one of these reprimands from students. (Be impolite, act disrespectful to someone, tell a fib, and so on.) Finally, ask students questions, such as **Tu partages toujours tes affaires?** to check comprehension.

Possible answers
11 Il faut qu'ils fassent la vaisselle, nettoient le parquet, fassent la lessive, lavent les vitres, sortent le chien.

---

11 **Quel désordre!**

Écrivons Regarde la maison de Marina après sa soirée! Qu'est-ce qu'il faut que Marina et son frère fassent? See answers below.

12 **Un drame!**

Écrivons/Parlons Avec ton/ta camarade, écris des dialogues pour illustrer les situations ci-dessous. Ensuite, jouez les scènes.

1. Michel veut aller au cinéma et demande la permission à son père. Son père veut bien, si Michel a fini ses devoirs.
2. Malika aimerait regarder un film à dix heures du soir. Sa mère refuse parce que c'est trop tard et parce que Malika a école demain. Malika insiste. Sa mère met un point final à la discussion.

13 **Je peux?**

a. **Parlons** Tu as reçu cette invitation pour une soirée. Demande à tes parents la permission d'y aller. Ils veulent en savoir plus : chez qui? avec qui? quand? à quelle heure? Ensuite, ils te donnent la permission à condition que tu fasses d'abord quelques tâches ménagères. Prépare et joue cette scène avec deux autres camarades.

b. **Parlons** Téléphone à Viviane pour accepter son invitation. Dis-lui que tu as des tâches à faire, mais que tu peux venir après ça.

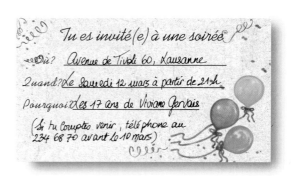

A la française

You can use words such as **dis donc** (*hey*), **dites** (*say*), **au fait** (*by the way*), and **alors** to start up a conversation or bring up a particular topic.

Tu es invité(e) à une soirée
Où? Avenue de Tivoli 60, Lausanne
Quand? Le samedi 12 mars à partir de 21h
Pourquoi? Les 17 ans de Viviane Gervais
(Si tu comptes venir, téléphone au 234 68 70 avant le 10 mars)

Vocabulaire

IL FAUT QUE TU...

Il faut que tu...

dises la vérité.	*tell the truth.*
manges mieux.	*eat better.*
respectes tes profs et tes parents.	*respect your teachers and your parents.*
aides les personnes âgées.	*help elderly people.*
partages tes affaires.	*share your things.*
prennes tes propres décisions.	*make up your own mind.*
conduises prudemment.	*drive safely.*
sois attentionné(e).	*be considerate.*
sois prudent(e).	*be careful/aware.*
sois plus responsable.	*be more responsible.*
sois tolérant(e).	*be tolerant.*
sois poli(e).	*be polite.*

Travaux pratiques de grammaire, p. 26, Act. 16–17

Cahier d'activités, p. 29, Act. 9

Communication for All Students

Visual Learners

11 Have one student come to the board and sketch one of the chores suggested by the illustration (**débarrasser la table**). He or she then calls on a classmate to write what Marina and her brother must do. (**Il faut qu'ils débarrassent la table.**)

Slower Pace

13 Before students begin, the student who will play the teenager writes down all of the necessary information about the party. Those who will play the parents make a list of the tasks they will require the teenager to do.

14 C'est pas bien, ça! *Possible answers:*

Parlons Ces gens n'ont pas une attitude très responsable. Dis-leur ce qu'il faut qu'ils fassent.

1. Il faut que tu partages tes affaires.

2. Il faut que vous mangiez mieux.

3. Il faut que vous soyez attentionnés.

4. Il faut que tu respectes ta mère.

15 Il faut que tu...

Ecrivons Parlons Quelles sont les choses que tes parents te rappellent souvent? Fais-en une liste et compare-la avec celle de ton/ta camarade.

LA VIE EST UN MYSTÈRE, CHARLIE BROWN... EN CONNAIS-TU L'EXPLICATION?

SOIS BONNE, NE FUME PAS, SOIS VIVE, SOURIS BEAUCOUP, MANGE INTELLIGEMMENT, ÉVITE LES CARIES ET, SURTOUT, RÉFLÉCHIS AVANT DE VOTER...

ÉVITE LES COUPS DE SOLEIL, AFFRANCHIS TES LETTRES CORRECTEMENT, AIME TOUTE CRÉATURE, ASSURE TES BIENS ET ENVOIE LA BALLE AVEC FORCE ET PRÉCISION...

NE BOUGE PAS! NE BOUGE SURTOUT PAS PARCE QUE JE TE PRÉPARE UN DE CES GNONS!..

16 Voilà ce qu'il faut faire

Parlons Ton ami(e) te téléphone pour discuter des problèmes suivants. Dis-lui ce qu'il/elle doit faire, à ton avis.

Il/Elle s'est foulé la cheville.

Il/Elle s'est fâché(e) parce que sa sœur a voulu emprunter son nouveau jean.

Il/Elle a eu une mauvaise note à une interro et l'a caché à ses parents.

Son grand-père ne peut plus conduire.

Il/Elle a grossi.

Il/Elle s'est disputé(e) avec ses parents.

Fumer, c'est pas ma nature!

17 Que c'est compliqué, tout ça!

Ecrivons/Parlons D'après toi, quelles sont les responsabilités et obligations d'un(e) adolescent(e)? Fais-en une liste et compare ta liste à celle de ton/ta camarade.

Première étape

CHAPITRE 3

Music Link
Play the song *Sur le pont de Nantes* (Level 2, Audio CD 5, Track 25). Have students listen carefully and tell what they think the song is about. You might copy the lyrics of the song on a transparency and have students read or sing along as you play the song. Ask students what the moral of the song is (you should not disobey your parents; otherwise, you'll probably get in trouble). For additional practice, have small groups create a conversation in which the mother gives the daughter unconditional or conditional approval.

Language Note
Affaires refers to a person's belongings in general. A parent might tell a child **Range tes affaires!** *(Put away your things!)* It can also mean *business* or *dealings.* Students might want to use the expressions **Ce n'est pas tes/mes affaires** *(It's none of your/my business)* or **Mêle-toi de tes affaires** *(Mind your own business).*

Assess
▶ Testing Program, pp. 45–48
  Quiz 3-1A, Quiz 3-1B,
  Audio CD 3, Tr. 15

▶ Student Make-Up Assignments
  Chapter 3, Alternative Quiz

▶ Alternative Assessment Guide,
  p. 32

Cultures and Communities

Culture Note
Point out to students that the phone number on the invitation consists of one group of three digits and two groups of two digits each. Phone numbers in Switzerland all have seven digits. Ask students to recall how French phone numbers are composed (five sets of two digits: 04.42.13.76.23, the first set being an area code) and what Canadian phone numbers look like (like American phone numbers, two sets of three digits and one set of four digits: 512–243–3982, the first set being an area code).

Presenting
Remise en train

Read aloud the advice in **Equipement adéquat.** Have students remind you what to pack for the trip as suggested by the advice (**Pense à prendre...**). Have students read the second brochure together. Then, play the recording and ask the questions in Activity 18.

Remise en train · *Laissez-les vivre!*

CD 3 Tr. 5

Finalement, les parents de Gilles lui ont donné la permission de partir avec ses copains. Ils sont allés faire une randonnée...

Equipement adéquat

En montagne, le temps peut changer soudainement et de manière inattendue (pluie, orage, grêle, neige jusqu'en basse altitude, même en été et en automne). Un équipement approprié est donc d'une importance vitale:

Chaussures de montagne à tige montante, avec semelles de caoutchouc profilées

Vêtements permettant de faire face à un changement de temps inattendu. Aujourd'hui, le principe de «couches super-posées» s'est imposé de manière générale; on préfère à une seule veste très chaude plusieurs vêtements légers portés les uns par-dessus les autres.

Protection contre le froid: pull-over, bonnet, gants, pantalons longs

Protection contre le soleil: chapeau, lunettes de soleil, crème solaire

Protection contre le vent et la pluie

Sac à dos avec bretelles larges et bien ajustées, et ceinture sur les hanches

Cartes pédestres et cartes nationales précises, à l'échelle 1:50 000 ou 1:25 000, guides d'excursions, éventuellement altimètre et boussole

Vivres et boissons: en particulier pour les enfants, prendre suffisamment à boire. Pas de boissons alcoolisées pendant les randonnées en montagne!

Pour les cas d'urgence: bande élastique et pansements rapides (sparadrap), éventuellement couverture de sauvetage, sif-flet à roulette, lampe de poche

Les bâtons de marche peuvent apporter une aide précieuse à la descente, car ils soulagent les articulations.

Faire des randonnées en montagne, sûrement!

18 **Tu as compris?** See answers below.
1. De quoi parlent les deux brochures?
2. Où sont Gilles et Isabelle?
3. Sur quoi est-ce qu'ils ne sont pas d'accord?
4. Comment est-ce que Gilles se justifie?
5. Quels sont les sentiments d'Isabelle?

19 **Ce qu'il faut faire** See scripts and answers on p. 61H.
🔊 **Ecoutons** Isabelle fait savoir à Gilles les six règles de la randonnée. De laquelle est-ce CD 3 Tr. 6 qu'elle parle?

These activities check for comprehension only. Students should not yet be expected to produce language modeled in **Remise en train.**

20 **Des reproches**
Dans la forêt, Isabelle fait des reproches à Gilles. Combine logiquement ses morceaux de phrases.

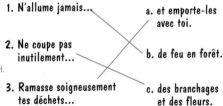

1. N'allume jamais...
2. Ne coupe pas inutilement...
3. Ramasse soigneusement tes déchets...

a. et emporte-les avec toi.
b. de feu en forêt.
c. des branchages et des fleurs.

Preteaching Vocabulary

Guessing Words from Context
Have students look at the images accompanying the texts on these pages and identify the context. Have them describe the image on page 72 first. What are the people doing? (They are hiking.) Draw students' attention to the title of the text. Do the words **équipement adéquat** remind them of English words? *(adequate equipment)* Based on the image and the title, have students guess what kind of recommendations they'll find in the text and have them identify keywords. Draw their attention to the document on page 73. Judging by the six images they see, ask them what they think the word **règles** means. *(rules)* Now that they know what the titles of both documents mean, they should be able to guess some of the rules and advice featured.

Answers
18 1. proper hiking equipment and safety rules for hiking in the mountains
2. in the mountains
3. whether it is all right to pick flowers
4. Everyone does it.
5. Isabelle thinks he shouldn't pick flowers, but she accepts them since they've already been picked.

Isabelle surprend Gilles en train de cueillir des fleurs.

Isabelle	Dis donc, tu n'as pas lu la brochure?
Gilles	Quoi?
Isabelle	Il est interdit de cueillir des fleurs!
Gilles	Mais c'est pour faire un tout petit bouquet.
Isabelle	Tu ne devrais pas. Regarde la brochure!
Gilles	Je ne suis pas le seul... tout le monde fait pareil!
Isabelle	Eh bien, ce n'est pas une raison.
Gilles	Tant pis. C'était pour toi, ces fleurs.
Isabelle	Pour moi? Euh... Eh bien, c'est gentil... Mais ce n'est pas une excuse!
Gilles	Tu ne les veux pas?
Isabelle	Euh... Maintenant qu'elles sont cueillies. C'est pas bien, mais... je te remercie quand même.
Gilles	Je te promets, c'est la dernière fois!

Les six règles des randonnées en montagne

1. Planifiez soigneusement chaque randonnée en montagne.
2. Ayez un équipement approprié et complet.
3. Ne vous lancez jamais seul(e) dans une randonnée en montagne.
4. Informez un parent, ou une connaissance, de votre randonnée.
5. Surveillez constamment l'évolution du temps.
6. Respectez le principe: «Dans le doute, faire demi-tour».

Note culturelle

La Suisse est connue pour sa neutralité. Mais ça ne veut pas dire qu'elle s'isole du reste du monde. Au contraire, elle collabore activement avec des organisations internationales comme la Croix-Rouge, l'OMS (l'Organisation mondiale de la santé) et l'UNESCO (l'Organisation des Nations Unies pour l'éducation, la science et la culture.) La Suisse fait un effort constant pour aider à résoudre les conflits internationaux et pour protéger les droits des prisonniers et réfugiés politiques. Elle apporte aussi son soutien aux pays en voie de développement dans les domaines éducatif, scientifique et technique.

 Cahier d'activités, p. 30, Act. 11–12

21 **Qu'est-ce qu'on emporte?**

Nomme au moins dix objets qu'il faut emporter quand on fait une randonnée en montagne. See answers below.

22 **Cherche les expressions**

What expressions do the teenagers in *Laissez-les vivre!* use to . . . See answers below.
1. say that something is not allowed?
2. make an excuse?
3. reproach someone?
4. reject an excuse?
5. make a promise?

23 **Et maintenant, à toi**

Est-ce que tu es déjà allé(e) dans un parc national? Quelles règles est-ce qu'il fallait respecter? Est-ce que tu as suivi ces règles? Pourquoi ou pourquoi pas?

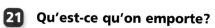

Comprehension Check

Thinking Critically

Comparing and Contrasting Ask students to compare the rules for the Swiss park with rules for local parks. Do they think the Swiss rules are more or less strict than those they're familiar with?

Analyzing Ask students if they think the park rules are fair and reasonable. Why or why not?

Teaching Suggestion

In English, ask students if they would pick the flowers if they were in Gilles' position. If they were in Isabelle's position, would they accept the flowers? Why or why not?

 Culture Note

The international organization known as the Red Cross, or Red Crescent in Muslim countries, was founded in 1863 as a humanitarian relief agency by Jean-Henri Dunant, a Swiss philanthropist.

Language Note

Students might want to know the following words from the **Remise en train**: **grêle** *(hail);* **caoutchouc** *(rubber);* **sifflet à roulette** *(whistle).*

Community Link

After students read the **Note culturelle,** have them find out if the organizations mentioned have branches in their city. They might also make a list of local organizations that have functions similar to those mentioned. You might even arrange for a representative from one of these groups to speak to the class.

 Camille et compagnie

As an alternative or in addition to the **Remise en train,** you may wish to show Episode 3 of *Camille et compagnie.* For suggestions and activities, see the *Video Guide.*

Answers

21 *Possible answers:*
chaussures de montagne, pull-over, bonnet, gants, pantalons longs, chapeau, lunettes de soleil, crème solaire, sac à dos, cartes pédestres, boissons, bande élastique

22 1. Il est interdit de...
2. Mais c'est pour... ; Tout le monde fait pareil!
3. Tu ne devrais pas.
4. ... ce n'est pas une raison; ... ce n'est pas une excuse!
5. Je te promets,...

Rencontre culturelle

Est-ce que tu connais la Suisse? Regarde les photos suivantes pour découvrir quelques caractéristiques de ce pays.

Les maisons qu'on appelle des chalets sont typiquement suisses.

Il y a beaucoup d'amateurs de ski en Suisse.

On parle plusieurs langues en Suisse.

La Suisse est aussi un centre financier important.

La Suisse est réputée pour ses belles montagnes.

On dit des montres suisses qu'elles sont d'excellente qualité.

Qu'en penses-tu?   See answers below.
1. Quelle impression ces photos te donnent de la Suisse?
2. Comment la géographie de la Suisse peut influencer son agriculture et son industrie?

Savais-tu que... ?

La Suisse est une confédération d'états semi-indépendants qu'on appelle cantons. Il y a quatre langues officielles en Suisse : l'allemand, le français, l'italien et le romanche. Les Alpes couvrent les trois cinquièmes du pays et le Jura, une autre chaîne de montagnes, en occupe une autre large portion. A partir d'un territoire aux ressources naturelles limitées, les Suisses ont créé une nation prospère. La Suisse est célèbre pour ses chocolats, ses fromages et ses autres produits laitiers. Mais la prospérité de ce pays vient surtout de son ingéniosité et de son savoir-faire. Par exemple, les banques suisses sont réputées dans le monde entier et les montres et horloges suisses sont célèbres pour leur exactitude et leur précision.

Connections and Comparisons

Comment dit-on...?

Forbidding

Veuillez ne pas marcher sur la pelouse.
Please do not . . .
Prière de ne pas fumer.
Please do not smoke.
Il est interdit de jeter des papiers.
It's forbidden to . . .
Interdiction de stationner.
Parking is not allowed.
Défense d'écrire sur les murs.
Do not . . .

Cahier d'activités, p. 31, Act. 13

Note de grammaire

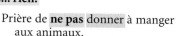

To use a negative form with a verb in the infinitive, place both the **ne** and the **pas** before the verb. Do the same with **ne... jamais** and **ne... rien.**

Prière de **ne pas** donner à manger aux animaux.
Il m'a promis de **ne jamais** le faire.
Je lui ai dit de **ne rien** manger.

Travaux pratiques de grammaire, p. 27, Act. 18–19

Grammaire supplémentaire, pp. 86–87, Act. 7–9

24 Les interdictions

Parlons Trouve l'interdiction que chaque symbole représente.

1. d   2. c   3. a   4. b

b. Il est interdit de manger.

d. Défense de pêcher.

a. Interdiction de stationner.

c. Défense de chasser.

25 Grammaire en contexte   See scripts and answers on p. 61H.

Ecoutons Pour préserver la nature, il faut respecter certaines règles. Le parc national de l'Engadine informe ses visiteurs. Ecoute le message et fais une liste de quatre interdictions.

CD 3 Tr. 7

26 C'est ma chambre!

 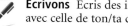

Ecrivons Ecris des interdictions à mettre sur la porte de ta chambre. Compare ta liste avec celle de ton/ta camarade.

Communication for All Students

Auditory Learners

24 Read aloud the rules given here and have students call out the numbers of the corresponding symbols.

Challenge

24 Have groups illustrate school rules or humorous rules they would like to see. Display the signs in the classroom.

Slower Pace

25 Play the recording four times. Have students listen for and note only one prohibited activity each time.

Teaching Resources
pp. 75, 77–79

Print 📖
▶ Lesson Planner, p. 15
▶ Listening Activities, pp. 20–21, 24–25
▶ Activities for Communication, pp. 11–12, 58–59, 93–94
▶ Travaux pratiques de grammaire, pp. 27–28
▶ Grammar Tutor for Students of French, Chapter 3
▶ Cahier d'activités, pp. 31–34
▶ Testing Program, pp. 49–52
▶ Alternative Assessment Guide, p. 32
▶ Student Make-Up Assignments, Chapter 3

Media
▶ One-Stop Planner
▶ Audio Compact Discs, CD 3, Trs. 7, 12–13, 16, 23–25
▶ Teaching Transparencies 3-2; **Grammaire supplémentaire** Answers; Travaux pratiques de grammaire Answers
▶ Interactive CD-ROM Tutor, Disc 1

Bell Work

Have students complete these sentences, using a different verb for each:

Chez moi, il faut que je...
Il ne faut pas que tu...
Le prof veut que nous...

Presenting
Comment dit-on... ?

Introduce the new expressions while acting out the forbidden activities. You might also use props (a toy car, a food wrapper, a crayon) to get the meaning across.

CHAPITRE 3

Teaching Resources
p. 76

PRINT 📖
▸ Video Guide, pp. 17, 19
▸ Cahier d'activités, p. 36

MEDIA 💿📹🖥
▸ One-Stop Planner
▸ Video Program
  Videocassette 1, 42:51–47:45
▸ Audio Compact Discs, CD 3,
  Trs. 8–11
▸ Interactive CD-ROM Tutor,
  Disc 1

Presenting
Panorama Culturel

Before you play the video, tell students to listen for keywords that they recognize. They should not be discouraged if they don't understand every word during the first viewing, since the issues are complex. Play the video and write on the board the keywords students suggest and their translations. Then play the video again and have students tell what they understood.

Questions

1. **Qu'est-ce qui gêne Alexandre?** (les saletés dans la rue)

2. **Qu'est-ce qu'Alexandre veut que le maire fasse?** (organise la population pour nettoyer la ville)

3. **Pour Micheline, quel problème est le plus important?** (les trous dans l'ozone)

4. **D'après Mathieu, qu'est-ce qu'il faut faire?** (consommer moins, recycler)

Quels sont les problèmes écologiques les plus importants?

We asked people what environmental issues they were most concerned about. Here's what they had to say.

Alexandre,
Côte d'Ivoire

«Les problèmes qui me gênent dans ma vie sont les saletés que l'on jette dans les rues... Quand on se promène dans la rue, on voit les saletés. Bon, si on est avec un étranger, il voit les saletés. Bon, ça ne lui fait pas plaisir. J'aimerais que le maire organise la population à nettoyer la ville.» Tr. 9

Micheline,
Belgique

«Il y a surtout le problème des trous dans l'ozone qui sont en train de réchauffer l'atmosphère. Si on ne fait pas quelque chose rapidement, il y aura de gros problèmes. On risque même de tous disparaître.» Tr. 10

Mathieu,
Québec

«Ce qu'on a détruit durant le siècle, on ne peut pas tout refaire... parce qu'on est dans un système où l'on consomme beaucoup. On consomme beaucoup trop. Et puis, c'est la consommation, c'est ça qui nous détruit. Il faut consommer moins, [ce] qui veut dire faire attention à ce qu'on prend et recycler. Je veux dire, quand on prend quelque chose, puis on le jette, mais on peut le reprendre et faire quelque chose d'autre.»

Tr. 11

Qu'en penses-tu?

1. Parmi les problèmes écologiques dont parlent les gens interviewés, lesquels te concernent le plus?

2. Est-ce qu'il y a des problèmes similaires dans ta région? Qu'est-ce qu'on propose pour résoudre ces problèmes?

3. Qu'est-ce que toi, tu peux faire pour protéger l'environnement?

Cultures and Communities

Community Link
Ask students which environmental issues they think are the most important and why.

 **Multicultural Link**
Have students research "green" political parties in different countries and international environmental organizations to find out what their goals are.

Teaching Suggestion
Write the interviewees' names on slips of paper. Have each student select a paper and write speech bubbles containing reprimands or interdictions that the interviewee might say. (**Il faut que tu penses à l'ozone! Défense de jeter des papiers par terre!**)

jeter des ordures...	to throw trash . . .	recycler...	to recycle . . .
par terre	on the ground	les boîtes (f.)	cans
dans l'eau		le verre	glass
gaspiller...	to waste . . .	le plastique	
l'énergie (f.)		le papier	
l'eau		éteindre...	to turn off/out . . .
utiliser des aérosols		la télé	
faire du bruit		les lumières (f.)	
fumer	to smoke	planter un arbre	to plant a tree
cueillir des fleurs	to pick flowers	partager son véhicule	to share a car
		prendre les transports en commun	to take public transportation

 CD-ROM DISC 1

Travaux pratiques de grammaire, p. 28, Act. 20–22

Cahier d'activités, p. 31, Act. 14

27 **C'est bien ou pas?** See scripts and answers on p. 61H.

CD 3 Tr. 12

Ecoutons Isabelle parle des habitudes de sa famille. Est-ce qu'elles sont bonnes ou mauvaises?

1. Sa mère
2. Ses cousins
3. Son frère
4. Son père
5. Sa sœur

28 **Protégeons notre planète!**

Lisons/Ecrivons Eric doit créer un poster publicitaire pour la semaine écologique organisée par son école. Aide-le à compléter le texte de son poster à l'aide des mots proposés ci-dessous.

6 utiliser des aérosols		fumer	5 prenez les transports en commun
plantez un arbre	1 par terre	7 éteignez la lumière	3 le papier
8 gaspiller	l'eau	2 recycler	4 partagez

Soyez responsables! Pour protéger notre planète, suivez ces quelques petits conseils. Pour commencer, ne jetez pas d'ordures ___1___ et pensez à ___2___ ce qui peut être réutilisé : les boîtes, le verre, le plastique et ___3___ sur lequel vous écrivez tous les jours. Pour réduire la pollution, ___4___ votre véhicule avec des amis ou ___5___. Vous réaliserez vite que le bus et le métro, c'est pas si mal. A la maison, évitez d'___6___; ils détruisent la couche d'ozone et mettent notre planète en danger. Quand vous sortez d'une pièce, ___7___ pour ne pas ___8___ l'énergie. C'est aussi simple que ça et vous serez fiers de contribuer à la protection de notre environnement.

Teaching Resources
pp. 75, 77–79

PRINT
▸ Lesson Planner, p. 15
▸ Listening Activities, pp. 20–21, 24–25
▸ Activities for Communication, pp. 11–12, 58–59, 93–94
▸ Travaux pratiques de grammaire, pp. 27–28
▸ Grammar Tutor for Students of French, Chapter 3
▸ Cahier d'activités, pp. 31–34
▸ Testing Program, pp. 49–52
▸ Alternative Assessment Guide, p. 32
▸ Student Make-Up Assignments, Chapter 3

MEDIA
▸ One-Stop Planner
▸ Audio Compact Discs, CD 3, Trs. 7, 12–13, 16, 23–25
▸ Teaching Transparencies 3-2; **Grammaire supplémentaire** Answers; Travaux pratiques de grammaire Answers
▸ Interactive CD-ROM Tutor, Disc 1

Presenting
Comment dit-on... ?

Show Transparency 3-2 and have volunteers tell what each person is doing. Pretending to be the park ranger, reproach each person on the transparency, using the new expressions. Using a different voice, make up an excuse to justify your action, as if you were the person in question. Pretend to be the park ranger again, and reject each person's excuse.

Comment dit-on...?

Reproaching; justifying your actions; rejecting others' excuses

To reproach someone:

Vous (ne) devriez (pas) gaspiller l'eau.
You should(n't) . . .
Tu as tort de fumer.
You're wrong to . . .
Ce n'est pas bien de cueillir des fleurs.
It's not good to . . .
Tu ferais bien de ne pas utiliser d'aérosols.
You'd do well not to . . .

To reject others' excuses:

Pense aux autres.
Think about other people.
Ce n'est pas une raison.
That's no reason.
Ce n'est pas parce que tout le monde le fait que tu dois le faire.

To justify your actions:
Je suis quand même libre, non?
I'm free, aren't I?
Tout le monde fait pareil.
Everybody does it.

 Cahier d'activités, pp. 32–33, Act. 16–18

Je ne suis pas le/la seul(e) à faire du bruit.
I'm not the only one who . . .

Note culturelle

Beaucoup d'immeubles européens ont un système électronique appelé minuterie. La minuterie aide à économiser l'électricité dans les couloirs et les autres endroits publics parce qu'elle éteint automatiquement les lumières après un certain temps.

See scripts and answers on p. 61H.

29 **Un reproche ou une excuse?**

Ecoutons Est-ce que ces personnes font des reproches ou trouvent des excuses?
CD 3 Tr. 13

30 **Pense aux autres!**

Parlons Quels reproches est-ce que tu peux faire à ces personnes?

Possible answers:

1. Tu ferais bien de ne pas jeter d'ordures par terre.
2. Tu devrais recycler.
3. Tu as tort de faire du bruit.
4. Vous devriez éteindre la télé et les lumières avant de partir.

31 **Mais non!**

 Parlons Ton/ta camarade ne respecte pas l'environnement et il/elle fait les choses suivantes. Tu vas lui faire des reproches pour qu'il/elle change ses habitudes. Il/Elle va trouver des excuses pour se justifier. Joue cette scène avec ton/ta camarade.

pêcher là où c'est interdit

fumer

cueillir des fleurs en montagne

faire de la moto dans la nature

jeter son chewing-gum par terre

avoir la télé et la chaîne stéréo allumées en même temps

mettre la musique très fort

Connections and Comparisons

Thinking Critically
Analyzing Ask students if they think the **minuterie**, described in the **Note culturelle**, is an effective way to save electricity. Ask for other suggestions on how to be energy efficient. Ask students if they have seen anything comparable to a **minuterie** in the United States, and have them describe the device.

Community Link
Ask students if, in their community or family, it is common practice to make recommendations concerning the environment. Ask them if they have ever been in a situation where they got reprimanded or have had to reproach someone about an action that could threaten the environment. Have a couple of volunteers give examples.

32 Un test

Lisons Parlons Fais ce test pour savoir si tu respectes l'environnement. Inscris le nombre de points que tu obtiens sur une feuille de papier. Ensuite, calcule ton score. Compare tes résultats avec ceux de ton/ta camarade.

En général, tu...
- ❏ jettes tes chewing-gums par terre. — 1 point
- ❏ les mets dans une poubelle. — 5 points
- ❏ ne manges pas de chewing-gums. — 6 points

Comme sport, tu fais...
- ❏ du vélo. — 6 points
- ❏ de la moto. — 2 points
- ❏ du ski. — 3 points

Quand tu écris, tu utilises...
- ❏ du papier recyclé. — 6 points
- ❏ du papier normal. — 4 points
- ❏ ce que tu as sous la main. — 4 points

Tu prends des douches de...
- ❏ deux minutes. — 6 points
- ❏ cinq minutes. — 3 points
- ❏ dix minutes. — 1 point

Chez toi, quand tu ne regardes pas la télé...
- ❏ tu l'éteins automatiquement. — 6 points
- ❏ tu la laisses allumée. — 1 point
- ❏ tu ne sais pas. — 1 point

Tu allumes ta chaîne stéréo...
- ❏ uniquement quand tu veux écouter de la musique. — 6 points
- ❏ dès que tu es dans ta chambre. — 4 points
- ❏ toute la journée. — 3 points

Tu circules à pied ou à vélo...
- ❏ le plus souvent possible. — 6 points
- ❏ rarement. — 3 points
- ❏ uniquement lorsque tu es obligé(e). — 1 point

Le total

RESULTATS

TU AS PLUS DE 30 POINTS :
Tu te sens très concerné(e) par les problèmes de l'environnement. Tu penses que, toi, tu peux faire quelque chose.

TU AS ENTRE 16 ET 30 POINTS :
L'environnement, ça t'intéresse. Mais ce n'est pas très important pour toi. Mais, individuellement, tu ne penses pas que tu peux améliorer les choses.

TU AS MOINS DE 16 POINTS :
L'environnement, ça ne t'intéresse pas. Pour toi, c'est abstrait.

(graph showing scale 0, 10, 20, 30, 40, 50)

33 Mon journal

Ecrivons Tu as pris des résolutions! Ecris quelques phrases dans ton journal pour décrire tes mauvaises habitudes, ou celles de tes amis, quant à l'environnement et ce qu'il faut que tu fasses, ou qu'ils fassent, pour les changer.

34

De l'école au travail

Ecrivons/Parlons You're working at an advertising agency. With a couple of classmates, write a script for a public service announcement, then act out the ad as it would appear on television. Your commercial should dramatize a scenario in which someone acts irresponsibly and makes excuses for his/her behavior when reproached by others. You'll need to show at the end of the ad why it's necessary to act responsibly.

Writing Assessment

34 You might use the following rubric when grading your students on this activity.

Writing Rubric	Points			
	4	3	2	1
Content (Complete– Incomplete)				
Comprehensibility (Comprehensible– Incomprehensible)				
Accuracy (Accurate– Seldom accurate)				
Organization (Well organized– Poorly organized)				
Effort (Excellent–Minimal)				

18–20: A   14–15: C   Under
16–17: B   12–13: D   12: F

Assess

▸ Testing Program, pp. 49–52
Quiz 3-2A, Quiz 3-2B
Audio CD 3, Tr. 16

▸ Student Make-Up Assignments, Chapter 3, Alternative Quiz

▸ Alternative Assessment Guide, p. 32

Communication for All Students

Visual Learners

32 Form seven groups and have each group illustrate one of the test items. Students may choose to show what one shouldn't do (littering) or what one should do (recycling). Have them write captions for their illustrations. You might display their illustrations around the room.

Group Work

Show *Teaching Transparency 3-2* again, and have small groups write and act out a dialogue based on the scene. One member acts as the park ranger and reproaches the visitors, who justify their actions.

Teaching Resources
pp. 80–82

PRINT
▸ Lesson Planner, p. 16
▸ Cahier d'activités, p. 35
▸ Reading Strategies and Skills Handbook, Chapter 3
▸ Joie de lire 3, Chapter 3
▸ Standardized Assessment Tutor, Chapter 3

MEDIA
▸ One-Stop Planner

Prereading
Activities A–B

Establishing a Purpose for Reading
Explain to students that establishing a reason for reading increases their efficiency and their understanding of the text. They can establish a purpose by looking at the title and the illustrations, as well as skimming the text. They may want to use these strategies to formulate questions that they can answer during and after a more thorough reading.

Reading
Activities C–D

Slower Pace
Remind students to scan the text and use the illustrations to locate the answers to these questions. For example, for Activity D, students should find the illustration of Albert's parents warning him and scan the text next to it for the specific answers.

Answers

A. Yes, the story will be about an absent-minded, accident-prone boy.

B. **Un nigaud** is a simpleton, and **un malin** is a crafty person; nouns; The two nouns are antonyms (opposites).

C. in a space station named Val-Fleuri; His absentmindedness gets him into trouble in space.

Lisons!

Stratégie pour lire
You probably encounter unfamiliar words every time you read French, but turning to the dictionary for every new word is time-consuming and can take all the fun out of reading. Instead, try figuring out the meaning of words from their context. What does the rest of the sentence say? How is the unfamiliar word related to the words around it? Is the word a noun? A verb? An objective? What clues do you get from illustrations or photos that accompany the text? Using contextual clues will make reading French quicker and more enjoyable.

For Activities A–C, see answers below.

A. Does the first picture give you any clue to what the reading will be about?

B. The introduction mentions people who are **nigauds** and **malins.** Can you figure out the meanings of these words from their context? What part of speech are they? How are they related to each other?

Albert Nez en l'air

C. Where does Albert live? Why is it a problem that he is **étourdi?**

D. Which of the following is *not* a warning that Albert's parents give him before the trip?
   1. **Attention à la circulation.**
   2. **Traverse seulement quand le feu est rouge.**
   3. <u>**Ne traverse pas sans regarder.**</u>
   4. **Prends les rues bleues.**

Dans la vie, il y a des malins, à qui il n'arrive jamais rien, et les nigauds, à qui il arrive plein d'accidents idiots. Comme les malins, il ne leur arrive jamais rien, c'est difficile de raconter leurs histoires. Les nigauds, c'est beaucoup plus rigolo. Voici donc quelques histoires de nigauds, pour tous les malins qui veulent rester malins, et les nigauds qui veulent devenir malins...

ALBERT NEZ EN L'AIR

Albert Nez en l'air vivait sur une petite base de l'espace nommée Val-Fleuri.

On y faisait pousser des plantes venues de toute la galaxie. Albert était très étourdi, ce qui est ennuyeux quand on habite dans l'espace.

Un jour, les parents d'Albert l'ont envoyé voir son tonton à Villeneuve-sur-Orbite, une grande ville de l'espace. Avant le départ, ils lui ont fait des recommandations : « Attention à la circulation. A Villeneuve-sur-Orbite, les rues bleues sont réservées aux piétons, les rues orange aux voitures et les rues jaunes aux vélos. Et on ne

peut traverser que si le feu est rouge. » Dans la fusée pour Villeneuve-sur-Orbite, Albert rêvassait un peu. A travers le hublot, il voyait la ville de l'espace se rapprocher...

Connections and Comparisons

Using Prior Knowledge
Ask students if they remember stories from their childhood and, if so, what messages they conveyed. Have them recall the themes of different fables and give the morals of popular children's stories. You might read a fable by Aesop or La Fontaine in English and have students tell what the moral is.

Thinking Critically
Drawing Inferences Tell students that *Albert Nez en l'air* is a fable and have them look at the illustrations and try to predict the moral. If they have difficulty, have them first tell as much as they can about each illustration in English.

STANDARDS: 1.2, 2.2, 3.1, 5.2

Il n'a pas entendu l'hôtesse qui lui demandait d'attacher sa ceinture. L'arrivée de la fusée sur la ville a été un peu brutale mais il faut dire qu'elle allait à 20 000 kilomètres à l'heure. Tout le monde est resté bien accroché à son siège, sauf Albert qui a été projeté à travers le hublot !

Albert s'est retrouvé au beau milieu d'un carrefour. Il a hésité : « Euh, la rue orange, c'est les piétons. La bleue...ça doit être les vélos. Et les voitures prennent la rue jaune ! A moins que ce ne soit la bleue ? » Albert a regardé le feu, qui était vert. Il s'est dit : « Bon, c'est vert, alors je peux passer ! » Albert est parti droit vers la rue orange. Manque de chance, un énorme camion à réaction arrivait à pleine vitesse...

Le camion a culbuté Albert à une telle vitesse que l'étourdi a traversé toute la ville, est passé à travers la bulle de verre et est parti comme une fusée dans l'espace...C'est pourquoi aujourd'hui, si vous demandez : « Où est Albert ? », tout le monde vous répond : «Dans la Lune !»

E. How can people travel on the following roads, according to Albert's parents?

c **1.** blue roads   **a.** by car

a **2.** orange roads   **b.** by bicycle

b **3.** yellow roads   **c.** on foot

F. Albert is hurled out of the spaceship because he forgets to . . .

   a. sit down when the spaceship lands.

   b. close the porthole.

   c. fasten his seatbelt.

G. Why didn't Albert hear what the flight attendant was saying?

   1. There was too much noise in the spaceship.

   2. He was looking out the window and didn't pay attention.

   3. He had fallen out of the spaceship.

H. Associe chaque mot de la colonne de gauche avec une définition de la colonne de droite.

c **1.** étourdi   **a.** une petite fenêtre ronde

a **2.** hublot

b **3.** s'accrocher à   **b.** se tenir à

d **4.** culbuter   **c.** qui oublie tout

   d. renverser

For Activities I–K, see answers below.

I. How does Albert end up on the moon?

J. Can you guess what the expression **être dans la lune** means? Why is it used at the end of the story?

K. Can you think of reasons why people might be **dans la lune?** Have you ever felt this way? Did anything unexpected happen to you? What might have happened?

Reading
Activities M–P

Slower Pace
Have students look at the illustrations and tell in English everything they think happened in the story. You might have students form small groups and share their impressions. Then, have them work together to answer the questions in Activities M through P.

Teaching Suggestion
P. Have students correct the false statements.

Challenge
P. Have partners write additional true-false statements and provide an answer key. Then, collect their papers and read the statements aloud to the class. You might make this activity a game, with players from two teams competing to respond to the statements.

Julie Boum
For Activities L and M, see answers below

L. Qui est Julie Boum? A quoi ressemble-t-elle?

M. What happens one day when Julie finds the door to her father's laboratory open?

N. Lequel de ces événements n'a pas eu lieu?
1. Julie est entrée dans le laboratoire de son père.
2. Une machine a coupé les tresses de Julie.
3. Julie a démonté la machine pour retrouver ses tresses.
4. Julie a mélangé des pilules vertes et des pilules bleues.
5. Le laboratoire a explosé en quelques centaines de morceaux.

O. The highlighted words in the following sentences are false cognates. Use context clues to figure out their true meanings.
1. Elle avait toujours envie de faire des **expériences** comme son papa.   experiments
2. Julie a appuyé sur le bouton mais rien ne s'est passé. Quelle **déception!**   disappointment
3. Elle a relevé la tête mais trop tard : sa tresse gauche avait été coupée **net.**   clear (off)

P. Vrai ou faux?
1. Julie Boum était une fille très maligne.   faux
2. Le père de Julie lui a permis de faire des expériences.   faux
3. Julie a joué avec une machine de son père.   vrai
4. Jim Boum avait inventé une pilule pour faire exploser sa fille.   faux
5. On n'a retrouvé que les tresses de Julie.   vrai

Q. Quelles sont les leçons que l'on peut tirer des fables que tu viens de lire?   See answers below.

Cahier d'activités, p. 35, Act. 21

JULIE BOUM

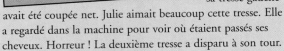

Julie Boum était la fille du célèbre savant, le professeur Jim Boum. C'était une fille très curieuse mais vraiment pas très maligne. Elle avait toujours envie de faire des expériences comme son papa... Un après-midi, Julie s'ennuyait un peu. Elle se promenait dans la maison quand elle a trouvé la porte du laboratoire ouverte.

Elle est entrée, bien décidée à explorer cet endroit mystérieux. Une drôle de machine, avec un bouton rouge, était accrochée au mur. On aurait dit une sorte de jouet... Julie a appuyé sur le bouton mais rien ne s'est passé. Quelle déception ! Julie s'est approchée un peu de la machine. Zouf ! elle a senti que ses cheveux étaient aspirés à l'intérieur. Elle a relevé la tête mais trop tard : sa tresse gauche avait été coupée net. Julie aimait beaucoup cette tresse. Elle a regardé dans la machine pour voir où étaient passés ses cheveux. Horreur ! La deuxième tresse a disparu à son tour.

Julie était bien embêtée. Elle a décidé de se faire repousser ses tresses grâce à la pilule pousse-minute, une invention de son papa. Il suffisait d'en avaler une pour que les cheveux poussent très vite !

Julie a ouvert le placard à pilules et a hésité un instant. Il y avait des pilules vertes et des bleues. « Le plus simple, c'est d'en prendre une de chaque ! » s'est dit Julie.

On n'a jamais bien su ce qui s'était passé. Les voisins ont entendu un grand « Bang » : le laboratoire a explosé en 726 morceaux. On a juste retrouvé les tresses de Julie, recrachées par la machine...

Connections and Comparisons

Postreading
Activity Q

Reading/Writing Link
Q. Have groups list other common morals for stories. (Don't put all your eggs in one basket. The grass is always greener on the other side of the fence.) You might have groups compete to see who can create the longest list. Have each member of the group keep a copy of the list to use in the **Ecrivons!** activities on page 83.

Thinking Critically
Comparing and Contrasting   Ask students to recall stories they know that have remarkable morals. You might have them recount some of those stories and explain what moral significance each story has.

Ecrivons!

Ta fable à toi

Comme tu peux voir, une fable est tout simplement une histoire avec une morale. Il y a beaucoup de fables traditionnelles, comme celles de l'écrivain grec Esope. Mais une fable peut aussi être moderne et amusante, comme celle que tu viens de lire. Maintenant, tu vas inventer une fable. Raconte une histoire qui a une morale.

Stratégie pour écrire

Sometimes writers know exactly how they want a story to end even before they start to write, and sometimes they allow the story to develop and create its own ending. When you know your ending beforehand, it's very important that you structure the story so that it leads steadily and logically to its conclusion. Making a brief outline of the events and details that you want to include in your story, in their proper order, will help you to do this.

A. Préparation

1. Choisis d'abord une morale dont tu veux parler. Pense à quelque chose qu'il ne faut pas faire ou à quelque chose qu'il est bon de faire. Voici quelques sujets possibles pour t'inspirer.

> ne pas être attentionné(e)
> ne penser qu'à soi
> ne rien vouloir partager
> ne pas protéger l'environnement
> faire des commérages
> ne pas être prudent(e)
> ne pas bien manger

2. Invente l'histoire d'une personne qui ne fait pas ce qu'elle devrait faire et raconte ce qui lui arrive.

3. Fais un plan.
   a. Ecris les événements principaux de ton histoire dans l'ordre où ils vont arriver.
   b. Pense aux détails de chaque événement et écris-les.

B. Rédaction

Fais un brouillon de ta fable en suivant ton plan.

C. Evaluation

1. Relis ton brouillon en essayant de répondre aux questions suivantes.
   a. Est-ce que tu as respecté l'ordre de ton plan?
   b. Est-ce que tu as oublié quelque chose?
   c. Est-ce qu'il y a des passages ou des détails qui ne sont pas importants pour comprendre l'histoire?
   d. Est-ce que les lecteurs vont comprendre la morale de ton histoire?

2. Fais les corrections nécessaires pour améliorer ton histoire. Ajoute plus de détails s'il le faut.

3. Rédige la version finale de ta fable. N'oublie pas de corriger les fautes d'orthographe, de grammaire et de vocabulaire.

Apply and Assess

Postwriting

Teaching Suggestion

C. Have students exchange papers. After the reviewer has read the story, he or she summarizes the story in English, listing the main events in order. If the reviewer's summary and the author's outline differ, they should examine the story together to suggest improvements.

Teacher Notes

- Encourage the process aspect of the **Ecrivons!** activities by making sure students always do each step of the writing assignment.

- You might use the portfolio evaluation forms (Evaluating Written Activities, Forms A and B) found in the *Alternative Assessment Guide* to help you evaluate students' final products.

Teaching Resources
p. 83

PRINT
▶ Lesson Planner, p. 16
▶ Cahier d'activités, p. 147
▶ Alternative Assessment Guide, p. 18
▶ Standardized Assessment Tutor, Chapter 3

MEDIA
▶ One-Stop Planner
▶ Test Generator, Chapter 3
▶ Interactive CD-ROM Tutor, Disc 1

Process Writing

Prewriting

Reading/Writing Link

A. 1. Have students refer to the lists they created for **Lisons!** (see Reading/Writing Link for Activity Q on page 82). Compile a class list on a transparency.

Teaching Suggestion

A. 3. Have students do a clustering (mapping) activity. They should write the main events in large circles, and then write relevant details in smaller circles connected to the large ones.

Writing

Teaching Suggestion

B. Encourage students to use sequencing words such as **d'abord, ensuite, et après,** and **enfin** to clarify the organization of their fable. You might give them the phrase **Il était une fois...** (*Once upon a time . . .*).

Grammaire supplémentaire

internet

go.hrw.com
.com

ADRESSE: go.hrw.com
MOT-CLE: WA3
FRANCOPHONE EUROPE-3

CHAPITRE 3

For **Grammaire supplémentaire** Answer Transparencies, see the *Teaching Transparencies* binder.

Première étape — **Objectives** Asking for, granting, and refusing permission; expressing obligation

1 Tu vas passer une semaine en Suisse avec la famille de Jérôme. Il t'explique que, chez lui, tout le monde a des tâches ménagères à faire. Prends des notes en utilisant le présent de **devoir** dans chaque phrase. (**p. 68**)

> **EXEMPLE** C'est à moi de sortir la poubelle.
> **Jérôme doit sortir la poubelle.**

1. C'est à mon père de faire la cuisine.
2. C'est à nous de ranger nos chambres.
3. C'est à toi de nettoyer la salle de bains.
4. C'est à mes frères de faire la vaisselle.
5. C'est à ma mère de passer l'aspirateur.
6. C'est à mes sœurs de ramasser les feuilles.
7. C'est à nous de faire la lessive.
8. C'est à mon père de débarrasser la table.
9. C'est à nous tous de faire nos lits.
10. C'est à toi de faire la poussière.

2 Ce week-end, tu gardes tes petits cousins Fabrice et Agathe. Dis-leur ce qu'ils doivent faire pour t'aider. Utilise le verbe **devoir** et les expressions données. (**p. 68**)

> **EXEMPLE** mettre la table (Fabrice et Agathe)
> **Vous devez mettre la table.**

1. donner à manger au chat (Agathe)
2. nettoyer la salle de bains (Fabrice)
3. passer l'aspirateur (Fabrice)
4. mettre la table (Fabrice et Agathe)
5. débarrasser la table (Agathe)
6. sortir le chien (Fabrice)
7. faire les lits (Fabrice et Agathe)
8. ne pas faire de bruit (Fabrice et Agathe)

Answers

1
1. Son père doit faire la cuisine.
2. Nous devons ranger nos chambres.
3. Je dois nettoyer la salle de bains.
4. Ses frères doivent faire la vaisselle.
5. Sa mère doit passer l'aspirateur.
6. Ses sœurs doivent ramasser les feuilles.
7. Nous devons faire la lessive.
8. Son père doit débarrasser la table.
9. Nous devons (tous) faire nos lits.
10. Je dois faire la poussière.

2
1. Tu dois donner à manger au chat.
2. Tu dois nettoyer la salle de bains.
3. Tu dois passer l'aspirateur.
4. Vous devez mettre la table.
5. Tu dois débarrasser la table.
6. Tu dois sortir le chien.
7. Vous devez faire les lits.
8. Vous ne devez pas faire de bruit.

Grammar Resources for Chapter 3

The **Grammaire supplémentaire** activities are designed as supplemental activities for the grammatical concepts presented in the chapter. You might use them as additional practice, for review, or for assessment.

For more grammar presentations, review, and practice, refer to the following:
• Travaux pratiques de grammaire
• Grammar Tutor for Students of French

• Grammar Summary on pp. R29–R54
• Cahier d'activités
• Grammar and Vocabulary quizzes (Testing Program)
• Test Generator
• Interactive CD-ROM Tutor
• **Jeux interactifs** at go.hrw.com

3 Tu poses les questions suivantes à tes amis pour apprendre ce qu'ils font comme tâches ménagères. Ecris leurs réponses. Utilise **il faut que** et le subjonctif de **faire** dans chaque réponse. (**p. 69**)

> **EXEMPLE**   Félix, est-ce que tu dois faire ton lit avant d'aller à l'école?
> **Oui, il faut que je le fasse avant d'y aller.**

1. Victor et Angèle, est-ce que vous devez faire la cuisine demain soir?
2. Est-ce que Sara et Adeline doivent faire le repassage une fois par semaine?
3. Est-ce que Daniel et moi devons faire la vaisselle après le dîner?
4. Est-ce que Jellel doit faire la lessive ce soir?
5. Est-ce que tu dois faire la poussière tout de suite?
6. Alain, est-ce que tu dois mettre la table?
7. Luc et Joëlle, est-ce que vous devez enlever la neige?

4 Nathalie doit faire certaines choses avant de sortir avec ses amis. Complète les phrases de sa mère avec les expressions suggérées par les images. N'oublie pas d'employer le subjonctif quand c'est nécessaire. (**p. 69**)

1. Tu veux sortir avec tes copains? C'est d'accord, mais il faut que tu _____ d'abord.

2. J'aimerais que tu avant de sortir, ma fille.

3. Tu dans ta chambre aussi, s'il te plaît.

4. Eh! N'oublie pas de/d' _____ en partant.

5 Nina demande à sa mère si elle peut faire certaines choses. Ecris les réponses de sa mère en utilisant **je veux bien que** et le subjonctif dans chaque réponse. (**p. 69**)

> **EXEMPLE**   —Ça te dérange si Rose vient me voir ce soir?
> —**Non, je veux bien qu'elle vienne.**

1. Ça te dérange si je lui téléphone tout de suite?
2. Nous pouvons regarder une vidéo?
3. Ça te dérange si on fait du pop-corn?
4. Je peux mettre ma chaîne stéréo?
5. On peut écouter MC Solaar?
6. Ça te dérange si elle passe la nuit ici?

Answers

3
1. Oui, il faut que nous la fassions.
2. Oui, il faut qu'elles le fassent une fois par semaine.
3. Oui, il faut que vous la fassiez.
4. Oui, il faut qu'il la fasse.
5. Oui, il faut que je la fasse tout de suite.
6. Oui, il faut que je la mette.
7. Oui, il faut que nous l'enlevions.

4
1. sortes/promènes le chien
2. passes l'aspirateur
3. fais la poussière
4. arroser le jardin

5 *Possible answers:*
1. Non, je veux bien que tu lui téléphones.
2. Oui, je veux bien que vous regardiez une vidéo.
3. Non, je veux bien que vous fassiez du pop-corn.
4. Oui, je veux bien que tu mettes ta chaîne stéréo.
5. Oui, je veux bien que vous écoutiez MC Solaar.
6. Non, je veux bien qu'elle passe la nuit ici.

Communication for All Students

 Game

Verb-Tense Race *In this game, students will practice various verb forms.*
This game can be played by two or more teams. Begin by giving the infinitive of a verb, a subject pronoun, and a tense or mood (**finir, tu, subjonctif**). Players should write a sentence, using the elements you gave. (**Il faut que tu finisses tes devoirs.**) Vary the subjects and tenses/mood. If two teams are playing, have one student from each team race to the board to write their sentence. If there are three or more teams, provide each team with sheets of construction paper and a thick marker. Team members work together to figure out and write down an answer. The first team to hold up a correct answer wins. If you need a tiebreaker, give two points for correct irregular verb forms or past participles.

For **Grammaire supplémentaire** Answer Transparencies, see the *Teaching Transparencies* binder.

Grammaire supplémentaire

WA3 FRANCOPHONE EUROPE-3

6 Lucien se comporte mal. Explique-lui ce qu'il doit faire pour changer son comportement. Utilise **Il faut que,** une des expressions dans la boîte et le subjonctif dans chaque phrase. (**p. 69**)

> partager ses affaires
> respecter ses profs
> faire ses devoirs
> conduire prudemment
> aider les personnes âgées
> prendre ses propres décisions
> laver les vitres
> garder son petit frère
> réparer son vélo

EXEMPLE   —J'aime bien conduire très vite.
—Il faut que tu conduises prudemment!

1. Je me moque de mes profs.
2. Je ne veux pas que ma sœur lise mes B.D.
3. Moi? Tondre la pelouse de Mémé? Jamais!
4. C'est à mes parents de décider où je vais en camp de vacances.

Deuxième étape   **Objectives** Forbidding; reproaching; justifying your actions and rejecting others' excuses

7 Perrine et Martin t'encouragent à respecter l'environnement. Martin te dit la même chose que Perrine, mais il utilise **tu ferais mieux de ne pas** et l'infinitif du verbe qui convient. Ecris les conseils de Martin. (**p. 75**)

EXEMPLE   PERRINE   Ce n'est pas bien d'utiliser des aérosols.
MARTIN   **Tu ferais mieux de ne pas utiliser d'aérosols.**

1. Ce n'est pas bien de laisser la télé allumée.
2. Ce n'est pas bien d'utiliser des pesticides sur ta pelouse.
3. Ce n'est pas bien de prendre des douches de vingt minutes.
4. Ce n'est pas bien de gaspiller l'eau.
5. Ce n'est pas bien de mutiler les arbres.
6. Ce n'est pas bien de jeter des ordures par terre.

Answers

6 1. Il faut que tu respectes tes profs.
2. Il faut que tu partages tes affaires.
3. Il faut que tu aides les personnes âgées.
4. Il faut que tu prennes tes propres décisions.

7 1. Tu ferais mieux de ne pas laisser la télé allumée.
2. Tu ferais mieux de ne pas utiliser de pesticides sur ta pelouse.
3. Tu ferais mieux de ne pas prendre de douches de vingt minutes.
4. Tu ferais mieux de ne pas gaspiller l'eau.
5. Tu ferais mieux de ne pas mutiler les arbres.
6. Tu ferais mieux de ne pas jeter d'ordures par terre.

Communication for All Students

Game
Tic Tac Toe   Make several tic tac toe grids. In each square, write an infinitive in parentheses followed by a sentence with the verb deleted: **(faire) Il faut que je _____ mes devoirs.** Distribute copies to groups of three. One student acts as judge. The other two students take turns filling in the blanks and putting an X or an O in the appropriate square, if the judge verifies that the verb form is correct. The first student to fill three vertically, horizontally, or diagonally adjoining squares wins.

8 Tu racontes à un/une ami(e) ce que ta mère t'a dit de ne pas faire. Complète les passages suivants en utilisant **ne pas** et l'infinitif du verbe qui convient. **(p. 75)**

EXEMPLE   MAMAN   Tu ne vas pas oublier de demander la permission à ton père!

TOI   **Ma mère m'a dit de ne pas oublier de demander la permission de mon père.**

1. Tu ne vas pas prendre la voiture!

2. Tu ne vas pas sortir avec Barthélémy!

3. Tu ne vas pas aller à la boum de Fernand!

4. Tu ne vas pas rentrer après minuit!

5. Tu ne vas pas donner à manger au chat!

6. Tu ne vas pas faire de bruit ce soir!

9 Pour chacune des situations suivantes, crée un panneau d'interdiction approprié. Choisis un symbole et écris une phrase pour l'accompagner. **(p. 75)**

EXEMPLE   Tu es dans un avion. **(b) Il est interdit de fumer dans l'avion.**

 a.   b.   c.   d.   e.

1. Tu es dans une réserve où l'on trouve des oiseaux rares.

2. Tu es au lac. C'est joli, mais l'eau n'est pas très propre.

3. Tu fais une visite en voiture d'un très vieux quartier qui a des rues étroites.

4. Tu es dans un restaurant.

5. Tu es dans un parc naturel où il y a des ours.

Answers

8 1. Ma mère m'a dit de ne pas prendre la voiture.

2. Ma mère m'a dit de ne pas sortir avec Barthélémy.

3. Ma mère m'a dit de ne pas aller à la boum de Fernand.

4. Ma mère m'a dit de ne pas rentrer après minuit.

5. Ma mère m'a dit de ne pas donner à manger au chat.

6. Ma mère m'a dit de ne pas faire de bruit ce soir.

9 *Possible answers:*

1. (e) Il est interdit de chasser dans la réserve.

2. (c) Défense de pêcher.

3. (d) Interdiction de stationner.

4. (b) Veuillez ne pas fumer.

5. (a) Il est interdit de manger dans le parc.

Review and Assess

You may wish to assign the **Grammaire supplémentaire** activities as additional practice or homework after presenting material throughout the chapter. Assign Activities 1–2 after **Tu te rappelles?** (p. 68), Activities 3–6 after **Grammaire** (p. 69), and Activities 7–9 after **Note de grammaire** (p. 75).

To prepare students for the **Etape** Quizzes and Chapter Test, we suggest doing the **Grammaire supplémentaire** activities in the following order. Have students complete Activities 1–6 before taking Quiz 3-1A or 3-1B; and Activities 7–9 before Quiz 3-2A or 3-2B.

Mise en pratique

internet

ADRESSE: go.hrw.com
MOT-CLE: WA3
FRANCOPHONE EUROPE-3

CD-ROM DISC 1

CHAPITRE 3

The **Mise en pratique** reviews and integrates all four skills and culture in preparation for the Chapter Test.

Teaching Resources
pp. 88–89

PRINT
▶ Lesson Planner, p. 16
▶ Listening Activities, p. 21
▶ Video Guide, pp. 17, 20
▶ Grammar Tutor for Students of French, Chapter 3
▶ Standardized Assessment Tutor, Chapter 3

MEDIA
▶ One-Stop Planner
▶ Video Program
  Videocassette 1, 47:47–52:22
▶ Audio Compact Discs, CD 3, Tr. 14
▶ Interactive CD-ROM Tutor, Disc 1

Teaching Suggestion

3 Ask students how much water they think the average person uses each day. Have them list the different ways we consume water (showers, laundry, drinking, watering the lawn, and so on). Then, have them try to guess which use consumes the most water. You might also ask them what percentage of the world population they think has running water (10%).

Career Path

Have students look at the brochure and think about the information that was needed to create it. Ask students what careers deal directly with the protection of our environment. How would their knowledge of a second language help them in these careers?

Language Note

Students might want to know the following words from the brochure: **robinet** *(faucet);* **s'écouler** *(to flow);* **reconnaissant** *(grateful);* **durée** *(level);* **courante** *(running);* **chasse d'eau** *(toilet flush);* **aboutir** *(to end up);* **cuisson** *(cooking).*

See scripts and answers on p. 61H.

1 Ecoute cette conversation entre Sabine et sa mère et réponds aux questions.

CD 3 Tr. 14

1. Où est-ce que Sabine veut aller?

2. Pourquoi est-ce que sa mère ne veut pas qu'elle y aille? A quelle condition est-ce qu'elle pourrait y aller?

3. Quelles sont trois choses que Sabine doit faire avant de partir?

2 Pense à quelque chose que tu voudrais faire et demande la permission à ton père/ta mère. Il/Elle te rappelle ce qu'il faut que tu fasses et il/elle refuse. Tu insistes. Enfin, tu obtiens la permission, à certaines conditions. Joue cette scène avec ton/ta camarade.

3 Lis cette brochure et réponds aux questions suivantes.   See answers at the bottom of p. 89.

AIDEZ-NOUS A...

Nous sommes parmi les 10% de privilégiés, sur cette planète, qui n'avons qu'à tourner un robinet pour obtenir de l'eau potable.

Si nous souhaitons conserver ce privilège, pensons aussi à tourner le robinet dans l'autre sens, afin que cette eau précieuse ne s'écoule pas inutilement.

Une des tâches du Département des travaux publics est de veiller sur la qualité de l'eau restituée à la nature. Pour y parvenir, il a besoin de votre aide sous deux formes:

**EVITER LE GASPILLAGE
LIMITER LA POLLUTION**

Votre récompense sera de bénéficier plus longtemps d'une eau de bonne qualité. Vos petits-enfants vous en seront reconnaissants. Les arbres, les fleurs et les oiseaux aussi.

Pour éviter le gaspillage

LE PETIT TRUC:
Remplissez entièrement la machine lorsque vous lavez le linge ou la vaisselle. Et n'ajoutez que le minimum de produit en fonction de la dureté de l'eau.

LE GESTE JUSTE:
Ne videz pas complètement votre chasse d'eau lorsque ce n'est pas nécessaire. Un petit geste économique à faire: rabattre le clapet ou remonter la manette!

LE BONS SENS:
Ne faites pas la vaisselle sous l'eau courante. Préférez la douche au bain!

TOUT CE QUE VOUS MELEZ A L'EAU DOIT ETRE TOT OU TARD RETIRE.

PROTEGER LES EAUX!

250 litres par personne et par jour

Savez-vous que chaque Genevois, pour son usage privé, utilise environ 250 litres d'eau par jour? Mais si on tient compte des besoins de l'industrie, de l'artisanat, du commerce et de l'agriculture, cette moyenne grimpe à 550 litres par personne.

Ces 550 litres disparaissent dans les canalisations et aboutissent aux stations d'épuration, où ils sont traités avant d'être rejetés dans le lac ou des rivières.

Le traitement de ces eaux est complexe et coûteux. Il nécessite une surveillance permanente. Pensez-y chaque fois que vous êtes tenté de laisser un robinet inutilement ouvert.

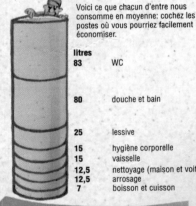

Voici ce que chacun d'entre nous consomme en moyenne: cochez les postes où vous pourriez facilement économiser.

litres	
83	WC
80	douche et bain
25	lessive
15	hygiène corporelle
15	vaisselle
12,5	nettoyage (maison et voiture)
12,5	arrosage
7	boisson et cuisson

Apply and Assess

Slower Pace

1 Have students read the questions before you play the recording. Ask them what they think the conversation will be about.

Thinking Critically

3 **Analyzing** Ask students for their reactions to the brochure. Were they surprised by the information? Have them evaluate the suggestions that are made for conserving water. Do they consider them reasonable? Do students do these things? Have students suggest additional ways to conserve water.

---

1. De quel type de brochure il s'agit? A ton avis, qui distribue cette brochure?

2. Quelles sont les deux actions principales que la brochure conseille de faire?

3. Qu'est-ce que tu peux faire pour économiser l'eau?

4. Quelle est la consommation moyenne d'eau à Genève? Qu'est-ce qu'on fait avec l'eau qui a déjà été utilisée?

5. Quelles activités font consommer le plus d'eau? Quelles activités font consommer le moins d'eau?

4 Tu veux préserver l'environnement. Avec deux autres élèves, pensez à un site naturel que vous voulez préserver. Ensuite, préparez une brochure pour attirer l'attention sur ce site et ce qu'il faut que tout le monde fasse pour le préserver.

5 Avec ton/ta camarade, crée quelques panneaux contenant les messages suivants.

No swimming.   No smoking.   Don't feed the animals.

No food or drink.   Don't pick the flowers.

No littering.   Don't walk on the grass.

6 **Jeu de rôle**

You and your friends are going to participate in a demonstration. Choose a good cause, such as forest conservation, animal protection, or water and air pollution. Make signs with slogans and plan what you're going to say to the crowd of onlookers. Act out this scene. The rest of the class will act as the onlookers who aren't very interested in the environment. Remind them of their obligations.

Apply and Assess

Visual Learners
5 Encourage students to illustrate their signs. They can either draw pictures, take photos, or find illustrations in magazines or on the Internet.

Challenge
6 As an extension of this activity, have students provide media coverage of the event. A student, who has experience with video cameras, films the demonstration, and additional volunteers act as reporters and interview the participants.

Teaching Suggestion
4 Have students find pictures, take photos, or draw illustrations of the site they will feature in their brochures. Remind them to make the brochure colorful and attention-getting. You might supply colored markers and old magazines and catalogues to students. This project is explained in more detail on page 61C.

📁 Portfolio
4 **Written** This activity is appropriate for students' written portfolios. For portfolio information, see *Alternative Assessment Guide*, pages iv–15.

Answers
3 1. brochure about water conservation; distributed by public utilities company
2. avoid waste and limit pollution
3. *Possible answers:* Run dishwasher and washing machine only when full. Don't wash dishes under running water. Take a shower instead of a bath.
4. 250 liters per day; It is channeled to a purification station, treated, and returned to the lakes or rivers.
5. WC; drinking and cooking

Answers

2 *Give:* Oui, bien sûr! Je veux bien. Ça va pour cette fois. Oui, si...
Refuse: Ce n'est pas possible. Pas question. Tu n'as pas le droit de...

4 *Possible answers:*
1. Tu dois faire la lessive.
2. Tu dois sortir le chien.
3. Il faut que tu tondes la pelouse.

8 *Possible answers:*
Je suis quand même libre, non? Tout le monde fait pareil. Je ne suis pas le/la seul(e) à...

Que sais-je?

 go.
hrw
.com
WA3 FRANCOPHONE EUROPE-3

Can you use what you've learned in this chapter?

Can you ask for, grant, and refuse permission?
p. 68

1 How would you ask permission to do something with a friend this weekend?
J'aimerais... ; Je peux... ? Tu veux bien que je... ? Ça te dérange si je... ?

2 If you were a parent, how would you give your teenager permission to do something? How would you refuse permission? *See answers below.*

3 What would you say to a friend who wanted to borrow your favorite cassette or CD? Oui, bien sûr! Ça va pour cette fois. Ce n'est pas possible. Pas question.

Can you express obligation?
p. 68

4 How would you tell your brother or sister that he or she has to . . .
1. do the laundry?   2. take out the dog?   3. mow the lawn?
See answers below.

Can you forbid someone to do something?
p. 75

5 How would you tell what these signs forbid? *Possible answers:*

1. Défense de fumer.   2. Interdiction de stationner.   3. Il est interdit de manger et de boire.

Can you reproach someone?
p. 78

6 What would you say to someone who . . . *Possible answers:*
1. throws trash out of the car window?   Tu ne devrais pas jeter d'ordures par terre.
2. uses aerosol sprays around the house?   Tu as tort d'utiliser des aérosols.
3. smokes?   Ce n'est pas bien de fumer. Tu ferais bien de ne pas fumer.

7 How would you reproach these people? *Possible answers:*

1.   Tu ne devrais pas faire de bruit.   2. Vous devriez éteindre la télé et les lumières avant de partir.

Can you justify your actions and reject others' excuses? p. 78

8 What would you say to justify an action of yours that angered someone?
See answers below.

9 What would you say to a child who makes excuses for doing something wrong?
Possible answers: Pense aux autres. Ce n'est pas une raison. Ce n'est pas parce que tout le monde le fait que tu dois le faire.

Review and Assess

Première étape

Asking for, granting, and refusing permission

J'aimerais...	I'd like . . .
Tu veux bien que... ?	Is it OK with you if . . . ?
Ça te dérange si... ?	Do you mind if . . . ?
Ça va pour cette fois.	OK, just this once.
Tu n'as pas le droit de...	You're not allowed to . . .

Expressing obligation

Il faut que tu... d'abord.	You have to . . . first.

Household chores

arroser le jardin	to water the garden/yard
donner à manger à	to feed
enlever la neige	to shovel snow
faire la cuisine	to cook
faire la lessive	to do the laundry
faire son lit	to make one's bed
faire la poussière	to dust
faire le repassage	to do the ironing
laver les vitres	to wash the windows
mettre la table	to set the table
nettoyer le parquet	to clean the floor
nettoyer la salle de bains	to clean the bathroom
passer l'aspirateur	to vacuum
ramasser les feuilles	to rake leaves
sortir le chien	to take out the dog
tondre la pelouse	to mow the lawn

Personal responsibilities

aider les personnes âgées	to help elderly people
conduire prudemment	to drive safely
dire la vérité	to tell the truth
manger mieux	to eat better
partager tes affaires	to share your things
prendre tes propres décisions	to make up your own mind
respecter tes profs et tes parents	to respect your teachers and parents
Il faut que tu sois . . .	You must be . . .
attentionné(e)	considerate
poli(e)	polite
prudent(e)	careful, aware
responsable	responsible
tolérant(e)	tolerant

Deuxième étape

Forbidding

Veuillez ne pas...	Please do not . . .
Prière de ne pas...	Please do not . . .
Il est interdit de...	It's forbidden to . . .
Interdiction de...	. . . is not allowed.
Défense de...	Do not . . .

Social responsibilities

cueillir des fleurs	to pick flowers
éteindre les lumières (f.)/ la télé	to turn off the lights/the TV
partager son véhicule	to share one's vehicle
planter un arbre	to plant a tree
prendre les transports en commun	to take public transportation
recycler les boîtes (f.)	to recycle cans
le papier	paper
le plastique	plastic
le verre	glass
faire du bruit	to make noise
fumer	to smoke
gaspiller	to waste
l'eau (f.)	water
l'énergie (f.)	energy
jeter des ordures par terre dans l'eau	to throw trash on the ground in the water
utiliser des aérosols	to use aerosol sprays

Reproaching

Vous (ne) devriez (pas)...	You should(n't) . . .
Tu as tort de...	You're wrong to . . .
Ce n'est pas bien de...	It's not good to . . .
Tu ferais bien de ne pas...	You'd do well not to . . .

Justifying your actions; rejecting others' excuses

Je suis quand même libre, non?	I'm free, aren't I?
Tout le monde fait pareil.	Everybody does it.
Je ne suis pas le/la seul(e) à...	I'm not the only one who . . .
Pense aux autres.	Think about other people.
Ce n'est pas une raison.	That's no reason.
Ce n'est pas parce que tout le monde le fait que tu dois le faire.	Just because everyone else does it doesn't mean you have to.

CHAPITRE 3

Teaching Suggestions

- Have students supply a completion for each expression under *Asking for, granting, and refusing permission, Forbidding,* and *Reproaching.*

- Have partners or small groups make lists of things they should do and things they shouldn't do.

- Have partners take turns calling out a verb from one of the expressions under *Household chores, Personal responsibilities,* or *Social responsibilities* (enlever) and completing the expression (enlever la neige).

Chapter 3 Assessment

▶ **Testing Program**
Chapter Test, pp. 53–58
Audio Compact Discs, CD 3, Trs. 17–19
Speaking Test, p. 296

▶ **Alternative Assessment Guide**
Portfolio Assessment, p. 18
Performance Assessment, p. 32
CD-ROM Assessment, p. 46

▶ **Interactive CD-ROM Tutor, Disc 1**
A toi de parler
A toi d'écrire

▶ **Standardized Assessment Tutor**
Chapter 3

▶ **One-Stop Planner, Disc 1**

Test Generator
Chapter 3

Review and Assess

② Circumlocution

Have students imagine that they are an exchange student living with a French family. The host parent asks what chores he or she does at home in the U.S. The student is trying to answer, but doesn't know some of the words in French and needs to use circumlocution skills to communicate.

Students will need to work with a partner, one playing the role of the student, the other the role of the parent. Have partners switch roles once the host parent has guessed two of the chores.

Chapitre 4 : Des goûts et des couleurs
Chapter Overview

Mise en train pp. 94–96	*Mon look, c'est mon affaire*

	FUNCTIONS	**GRAMMAR**	**VOCABULARY**	**RE-ENTRY**
Première étape pp. 97–103	• Asking for and giving opinions, p. 98 • Asking which one(s), p. 100 • Pointing out and identifying people and things, p. 100	• The interrogative and demonstrative pronouns, p. 101	• Clothing and styles, p. 97	• Clothing vocabulary (**Chapitre 10,** I) • Adjectives referring to clothing (**Chapitre 10,** I) • Asking for an opinion (**Chapitre 10,** I)

Remise en train pp. 104–105	*Chacun son style!*

Deuxième étape pp. 106–109	• Paying and responding to compliments, p. 108 • Reassuring someone, p. 108	• The causative **faire,** p. 107	• Hair and hair styles, p. 106	• Family vocabulary (**Chapitre 7,** I) • Paying a compliment (**Chapitre 10,** I)

Lisons! pp. 110–112	**Christian Lacroix Collection Automne/Hiver**	**Reading Strategy:** Building on what you know

Ecrivons! p. 113	**La Mode en l'an 2025**	**Writing Strategy:** Generating ideas by asking questions

Grammaire supplémentaire	**pp. 114–117**	**Première étape,** pp. 114–115	**Deuxième étape,** pp. 116–117

Review pp. 118–121	**Mise en pratique,** pp. 118–119	**Que sais-je?,** p. 120	**Vocabulaire,** p. 121

CULTURE

- **Note culturelle,** French clothing stores, p. 96
- **Panorama Culturel,** Fashion and personal style, p. 103
- **Note culturelle,** The French sense of fashion, p. 105
- Realia: *Mannequin d'un jour,* p. 108

Chapitre 4 : Des goûts et des couleurs
Chapter Resources

 **PRINT**

Lesson Planning

One-Stop Planner

**Lesson Planner with Substitute Teacher
Lesson Plans,** pp. 17–21, 67

Student Make-Up Assignments
- Make-Up Assignment Copying Masters, Chapter 4

Listening and Speaking

Listening Activities
- Student Response Forms for Listening Activities, pp. 27–29
- Additional Listening Activities 4-1 to 4-6, pp. 31–33
- Additional Listening Activities (song), p. 34
- Scripts and Answers, pp. 116–120

Video Guide
- Teaching Suggestions, pp. 22–23
- Activity Masters, pp. 24–26
- Script and Answers, pp. 87–90, 113

Activities for Communication
- Communicative Activities, pp. 13–16
- Realia and Teaching Suggestions, pp. 60–62
- Situation Cards, pp. 95–96

Reading and Writing

Reading Strategies and Skills Handbook, Chapter 4

Joie de lire 3, Chapter 4

Cahier d'activités, pp. 37–48

Grammar

Travaux pratiques de grammaire, pp. 29–40

Grammar Tutor for Students of French, Chapter 4

Assessment

Testing Program
- Grammar and Vocabulary Quizzes, **Etape** Quizzes, and Chapter Test, pp. 67–80
- Score Sheet, Scripts and Answers, pp. 81–87

Alternative Assessment Guide
- Portfolio Assessment, p. 19
- Performance Assessment, p. 33
- CD-ROM Assessment, p. 47

Student Make-Up Assignments
- Alternative Quizzes, Chapter 4

Standardized Assessment Tutor
- Reading, pp. 13–15
- Writing, p. 16
- Math, pp. 25–26

MEDIA

Online Activities

- Jeux interactifs
- Activités Internet

Video Program

- Videocassette 2
- Videocassette 5 (captioned version)

Audio Compact Discs

- Textbook Listening Activities, CD 4, Tracks 1–13
- Additional Listening Activities, CD 4, Tracks 19–25
- Assessment Items, CD 4, Tracks 14–18

Interactive CD-ROM Tutor, Disc 1

Teaching Transparencies
- Situation 4-1 to 4-2
- **Grammaire supplémentaire** Answers
- **Travaux pratiques de grammaire** Answers

  One-Stop Planner CD-ROM

Use the **One-Stop Planner CD-ROM with Test Generator** to aid in lesson planning and pacing.

For each chapter, the **One-Stop Planner** includes:

- Editable lesson plans with direct links to teaching resources
- Printable worksheets from resource books
- Direct launches to the HRW Internet activities
- Video and audio segments
- Test Generator
- Clip Art for vocabulary items

Chapitre 4 : Des goûts et des couleurs

Projects

Un magazine de mode

Students will create advertisements for a fashion magazine.

MATERIALS

✂ **Students may need**
- Construction paper or posterboard
- Colored markers or pens
- Fashion magazines
- French-English dictionaries

SUGGESTED SEQUENCE

1. Have students imagine a product or a line of products to advertise. They might choose articles of clothing, accessories, hair products, skin products, cologne, or other fashion-related items. You might have them look through several fashion magazines for ideas. Tell students they have the option of satirizing existing products instead of creating their own.

2. Have students name their products, design the packaging, and organize the scope of their advertising campaign. They should decide what claims they will make about their products (it makes your hair softer; it makes you look more chic); what audience they are appealing to (teenagers, working mothers, executives); and what the major selling point will be (the price, the "mystique," the effectiveness). Have them create a slogan for their products.

3. Have students write the text for their ads. They should look up any unfamiliar words in the dictionary. Have them hand in the text or exchange it with another group for editing.

4. Students should plan the layout of their ads. Have them sketch the products and decide on the placement of the text and the illustrations.

5. Have students finalize their ads on sheets of construction paper or posterboard.

GRADING THE PROJECT

Suggested Point Distribution (total = 100 points)

Content	20 points
Language use	20 points
Variety of vocabulary	20 points
Creativity/appearance	20 points
Effort/participation	20 points

Games

Qui a quoi?

In this game, students will practice recognizing vocabulary for clothing and clothing styles.

Procedure   For this game, you will need to prepare a stack of index cards with an article of clothing and a color (and style, if desired) written on them, such as **des gants à pois rouges.** In class, have students draw a grid of nine squares on a sheet of paper. Give each student several crayons or markers in the following colors: blue, green, red, black, and yellow. Then, have a volunteer call out an article of clothing (and a style, if desired), such as **un polo (à rayures).** Students draw the item in one of their squares and color it. Be sure students use each color at least once. Repeat with eight additional volunteers. Then, draw a card from your stack and ask who has that article of clothing in that color: **Qui a un foulard bleu?** If a student has drawn that article of clothing in the same color, he or she marks that square on the paper. After you call out ten or fifteen items, have students total the number of squares they've marked. The student with the most squares marked wins.

Chasse au trésor

In this game, students will practice vocabulary for clothing and clothing styles, as well as for hair and hair styles.

Procedure   To prepare for this game, make a list of twenty "scavenger hunt" items, such as **Trouve quelqu'un qui... (1) a un foulard à rayures; (2) s'est fait couper les cheveux la semaine dernière; (3) a une permanente.** Distribute copies to students. Then, have students circulate around the room to try to find someone who can answer each of their questions affirmatively. If a student answers **oui,** he or she signs next to the item on the list. Students may not sign their own lists, and they may use a classmate's name only once. Give students five minutes to try to complete the list. The student who has the most questions answered affirmatively when you call time is the winner. Have the winner read each item, along with the name of the person who answered **oui** to the question (**Gloria a un foulard à rayures. Bill s'est fait couper les cheveux la semaine dernière**). Then, you might ask the class which other students answered each question affirmatively. (**Qui a un foulard à rayures?**)

Storytelling

Mini-histoire

This story accompanies Teaching Transparency 4-2. The **mini-histoire** *can be told and retold in different formats, acted out, written as dictation, and read aloud to give students additional opportunities to practice all four skills. The following story is about two friends who are getting ready for a wedding ceremony.*

On est samedi. Il est 10 heures du matin. Virginie est chez le coiffeur. Elle veut avoir un beau chignon pour aller au mariage de son amie Saskia. Le mariage a lieu à 2 heures cet après-midi même. Pendant ce temps, son ami Paul est parti à la recherche d'une chemise et d'une cravate à porter avec son costume. Le vendeur lui propose deux possibilités : une chemise blanche avec une cravate classique ou une autre chemise blanche avec une cravate un peu plus à la mode. Paul est très classique mais aujourd'hui, il se sent une envie de folie. Il se décide donc pour la cravate bleue parsemée de cercles roses. Et il a très bien choisi. Pendant la réception de mariage, Gonzague, qui ne fait jamais de compliment en temps normal, le complimente sur sa cravate qu'il trouve très chic. Paul est très fier de son choix. De son côté, Virginie se fait complimenter sur sa coiffure et a déjà promis à quelques amies de leur téléphoner pour leur donner le nom de son coiffeur.

Traditions

Les Echarpes

Most French people consider wearing accessories, especially scarves, the key to looking chic. Although people have been wearing scarves since ancient times, the modern history of the scarf began in the late 1920's and early 1930's, when French **couturiers** began producing signature scarves to go with their collections. From that time on, even if one couldn't afford a designer dress or suit, one could afford a designer scarf. Scarves had multiple uses over the ensuing decades. They tied back hair, replaced hats and necklaces, and kept throats warm. Despite all their different incarnations, scarves continue today to be an essential part of a French woman's wardrobe. They are also considered the perfect gift, particularly those made by the designer Hermès®, whose flagship store is reputed to sell a scarf every 50 seconds during the holiday season. Have students experiment with different sizes of scarves to see how many different ways they can tie or wear them.

Recette

The **comté** *is a big, round cheese that is usually sold by the slice because of its massive size. It can weigh up to 50 kilos (approximately 110 pounds). To produce a cheese such as* **comté**, *one needs about 600 liters of milk, which is equivalent to the daily production of 20 cows.*

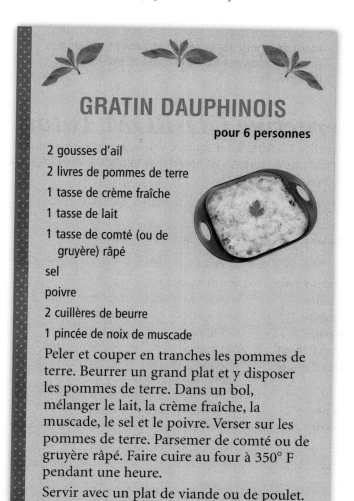

GRATIN DAUPHINOIS

pour 6 personnes

2 gousses d'ail

2 livres de pommes de terre

1 tasse de crème fraîche

1 tasse de lait

1 tasse de comté (ou de gruyère) râpé

sel

poivre

2 cuillères de beurre

1 pincée de noix de muscade

Peler et couper en tranches les pommes de terre. Beurrer un grand plat et y disposer les pommes de terre. Dans un bol, mélanger le lait, la crème fraîche, la muscade, le sel et le poivre. Verser sur les pommes de terre. Parsemer de comté ou de gruyère râpé. Faire cuire au four à 350° F pendant une heure.

Servir avec un plat de viande ou de poulet.

Technology

Video Program

Videocassette 2, Videocassette 5 (captioned version)
See Video Guide, pp. 21–28

Camille et compagnie • Quatrième épisode : *C'est tout à fait toi!*
Camille and Sophie are shopping for new clothes, but they have very different tastes. Sophie likes out-of-the-ordinary clothes, while Camille prefers conservative outfits. They separate to go to different stores. Max stays with Sophie to help her choose, but it turns out that they also have different opinions about clothes.

Quel est ton style de vêtements préféré?
Students from Quebec, Martinique, and Vietnam talk about what they like to wear. Two native speakers discuss the **Panorama Culturel** question and introduce the interviews.

Vidéoclips
- **Les Trois Suisses**®: advertisement for catalogue sales
- **Aguirre**®: advertisement for men's cologne
- **Mir couleurs**®: advertisement for laundry detergent

Interactive CD-ROM Tutor

The **Interactive CD-ROM Tutor** contains videos, interactive games, and activities that provide students an opportunity to practice and review the material covered in Chapter 4.

Activity	Activity Type	Pupil's Edition Page
1. Vocabulaire	Chasse au trésor Explorons! Vérifions!	p. 97
2. Comment dit-on… ?	Chacun à sa place	p. 98
3. Grammaire	Les mots qui manquent	p. 101
4. Vocabulaire	Jeu des paires	p. 106
5. Grammaire	Méli-mélo	p. 107
6. Comment dit-on… ?	Du tac au tac	pp. 98, 100, 108
Panorama Culturel	Quel est ton style de vêtements préféré? Le bon choix	p. 103
A toi de parler	*Guided recording*	pp. 118–119
A toi d'écrire	*Guided writing*	pp. 118–119

Teacher Management System

Logging In

Logging in to the *Allez, viens!* TMS is easy. Upon launching the program, simply type "admin" in the password area of the log-in screen and press RETURN. Log on to **www.hrw.com/CDROMTUTOR** for a detailed explanation of the Teacher Management System.

One-Stop Planner CD-ROM

To preview all resources available for this chapter, use the **One-Stop Planner CD-ROM,** Disc 1.

Internet Connection

internet

ADRESSE: go.hrw.com
MOT-CLE: WA3
FRANCOPHONE
EUROPE-4

*Have students explore the **go.hrw.com** Web site for many online resources covering all chapters. All Chapter 4 resources are available under the keyword **WA3 FRANCOPHONE EUROPE-4.** Interactive games help students practice the material and provide them with immediate feedback. You'll also find a printable worksheet that provides Internet activities that lead to a comprehensive online research project.*

Jeux interactifs

You can use the interactive activities in this chapter

- to practice grammar, vocabulary, and chapter functions
- as homework
- as an assessment option
- as a self-test
- to prepare for the Chapter Test

Activités Internet

Students look for sites on fashion and choose clothes. They also have to find a hairdresser's site and pick a hair style. Finally students have to describe the clothes and hair style they found on line, and give their opinion of them, using material from the chapter.

- In preparation for the **Activités Internet,** have students review the dramatic episode on Video-cassette 2, or do the activities in the **Panorama Culturel** on page 103. After completing the activity sheet, have students work with a partner and share the information they gathered in activities B and C on that sheet.

Projet

Have a group of students create virtual outfits for the young people in **Panorama Culturel.** First, students list what each interviewee says she likes to wear. Then they find sites that present the kind of clothes and fabrics described by the interviewees. Finally they write each interviewee a note telling her which sites to visit to find what she wants. You might organize students in groups of three, each person responsible for writing a note to one of the three interviewees. Students should document their sources by noting the names and the URLs of all the sites they consulted.

Chapitre 4 : Des goûts et des couleurs
Textbook Listening Activities Scripts

Première étape

7   **p. 97**

1. —Oui, elle était là.
   —Et qu'est-ce qu'elle portait?
   —Un pattes d'eph et un col roulé gris foncé. Elle aime bien la mode des années soixante-dix, tu sais.

2. —Oui, je lui ai parlé un peu.
   —Il va bien?
   —Oui, mais il a raté son examen d'anglais.
   —Oh, zut! Alors, il avait l'air de quoi?
   —Tu sais, il est toujours rigolo. Il portait un pantalon à pinces, une chemise à rayures, un gilet en laine et une cravate à pois. C'était trop drôle!

3. —Oui, elle est venue avec Ahmed.
   —Elle était en jean?
   —Non, elle avait sa jupe écossaise, un pull noir et ses bottes en cuir. Elle avait aussi un foulard imprimé. Ça faisait cloche, à mon avis.

4. —Si, je t'assure, elle est venue.
   —Alors là, vraiment, ça m'étonne. Je lui ai téléphoné mercredi, et elle m'a dit qu'elle s'était disputée avec Antoine, et qu'elle n'irait pas à la boum.
   —Ecoute, elle a dû changer d'avis parce que moi, je suis sûre que c'était elle. Elle portait son caleçon imprimé et le tee-shirt forme tunique que Corinne lui a offert pour son anniversaire.

5. —Tu sais, ça faisait longtemps que je ne l'avais pas vue, elle.
   —Tu trouves pas qu'elle a changé?
   —Si, beaucoup. Et puis, elle ne s'habille plus du tout comme avant.
   —Tu trouves? Qu'est-ce qu'elle portait? J'ai pas fait attention.
   —Elle avait une robe à col en V et des hauts talons.

Answers to Activity 7
1. Tatiana   3. Brigitte   5. Lian
2. Antoine   4. Nathalie

10   **p. 98**

1. —Comment tu trouves cette jupe?
   —Je la trouve pas mal. Surtout en bleu.

2. —Il te plaît, ce pantalon à pinces?
   —Non, pas du tout. Je préfère celui-là.

3. —Tu n'aimes pas cette cravate en soie?
   —Si, je l'aime bien. Elle est cool.

4. —Qu'est-ce que tu penses de ces hauts talons?
   —Je trouve qu'ils font vieux.

5. —Il est pas mal, ce gilet, non?
   —Ah, non. Il ne me plaît pas du tout.

6. —Regarde ces bottes. Qu'en penses-tu?
   —Je trouve qu'elles sont chic. J'aime bien ce genre de bottes.

Answers to Activity 10
1. aime   3. aime   5. n'aime pas
2. n'aime pas   4. n'aime pas   6. aime

16   **p. 100**

1. —Eh, comment tu trouves cette robe?
   —Laquelle?
   —Celle de la fille là-bas.
   —Mais quelle fille?
   —Là, la fille avec les lunettes.
   —Je la trouve jolie.

2. —Tiens, tu n'aimes pas le pantalon du garçon, là-bas?
   —Quel garçon?
   —Le garçon qui porte un chapeau.
   —Ah! Oui, il est pas mal, son pantalon.

3. —Il ne te plaît pas, le gilet?
   —Lequel?
   —Celui du garçon là-bas?
   —Quel garçon?
   —Eh bien, celui qui a un imperméable!
   —Oui, je l'aime bien.

4. —Tu n'aimes pas les bottes de cette fille?
   —Quelle fille?
   —Là, celle qui a une jupe à carreaux.
   —Bof, elles sont pas mal.

Answers to Activity 16
1. Michèle   3. Valentin
2. Sylvain   4. Annette

17   **p. 101**

1. —Comment tu le trouves?
   —Lequel?
   —Celui-là, à trente euros.
   —Il est pas mal. Mais je préfère celui-là.
   —Lequel?
   —Celui à trente-trois euros.

To preview all resources available for this chapter, use the **One-Stop Planner CD-ROM**, Disc 1.

2. —Elle est chouette, non?
—Laquelle?
—Celle-ci, là, dans la vitrine.
—Oui, tu as raison, elle est jolie.
—Celle-là aussi est pas mal.
—Bof, je ne l'aime pas tellement.

3. —Ceux-ci, ils ne te plaisent pas?
—Non, pas vraiment. Ils font trop vieux, je trouve.
—Et ceux-là?
—Ah oui, je préfère ceux-là. Ils sont cool.

4. —Elles sont géniales, celles-ci, tu ne trouves pas?
—Lesquelles?
—Là, les noires.
—Oh non, je ne les aime pas du tout. Tu ne préfères pas celles-là?
—Celles-là? Elles sont horribles!

Answers to Activity 17
1. un caleçon
2. une jupe écossaise
3. des hauts talons
4. des bottes

Deuxième étape

26   p. 106

1. Vous pourriez me couper les cheveux en brosse?

2. Pouvez-vous me couper les cheveux très court?

3. J'aimerais avoir les cheveux teints en bleu, s'il vous plaît.

4. Qu'est-ce je vous fais?

5. Vous voulez une permanente?

6. Je voudrais un nouveau look, des cheveux raides peut-être.

Answers to Activity 26
1. le client   3. le client   5. le coiffeur
2. le client   4. le coiffeur   6. la cliente

31   p. 108

1. —Elle est délirante, ta coupe à la Mohawk! Je te trouve très bien comme ça!
—Tu crois?

2. —Il ne fait pas trop vieux, ce gilet?
—Fais-moi confiance, il est très classe.

3. —Oh, je ne sais pas. Tu ne trouves pas que c'est un peu tape-à-l'œil?
—Crois-moi, c'est tout à fait toi!

4. —Elle est jolie, ta jupe. Elle va très bien avec tes yeux.
—Oh, c'est un vieux truc.

5. —Tu es sûr? C'est pas trop bizarre, cette couleur?
—Mais non! Et je ne dis pas ça pour te faire plaisir.

6. —Que tu es belle avec cette robe! Ça te va comme un gant!
—Oh, tu sais, je ne l'ai pas payée cher.

7. —Je ne sais pas si ça me va, cette coupe. Qu'en penses-tu?
—Je t'assure, elle est très réussie.

8. —Dis, qu'est-ce que tu penses de ce pull?
—Il est super.
—Vraiment?
—Oui, fais-moi confiance.

Answers to Activity 31
1. répond   3. rassure   5. rassure   7. rassure
2. rassure   4. répond   6. répond   8. rassure

Mise en pratique

1   p. 118

1. —Ce que je préfère, moi, c'est être la plus naturelle possible.

2. —Mon look, c'est dans le style des années soixante-dix!

3. —Je passe la plupart de mon temps à la campagne, donc je préfère porter des vêtements confortables.

4. —J'aime mettre mes yeux en valeur. J'utilise une ombre à paupières violette.

5. —Quand je ne travaille pas, je ne me maquille pas. Si je sors avec mes copains, je n'utilise pas beaucoup de maquillage.

6. —Mes vêtements préférés, c'est les chaussures à plate-forme, les pattes d'eph et les mini-jupes. C'est hyper cool!

Answers to Mise en pratique Activity 1
1. Elodie   3. Elodie   5. Elodie
2. Stéphanie   4. Stéphanie   6. Stéphanie

Chapitre 4 : Des goûts et des couleurs
Suggested Lesson Plans 50-Minute Schedule

Day 1

CHAPTER OPENER 5 min.
- Present Chapter Objectives, p. 93.
- Culture Notes and History Link, ATE, pp. 92–93

MISE EN TRAIN 40 min.
- Presenting **Mise en train**, ATE, p. 94; using Video Program, Videocassette 2, see ATE, p. 95.
- See Teaching Suggestions, Viewing Suggestions 1–2, Video Guide, p. 22.
- Language Note and Math Link, ATE, p. 95
- See Teaching Suggestions, Post-viewing Suggestions 1–2, Video Guide, p. 22.
- Do Activities 1–5, p. 96.
- Read and discuss **Note culturelle**, p. 96.

Wrap-Up 5 min.
- Do Activity 6, p. 96.

Homework Options
Cahier d'activités, Act. 1, p. 37

Day 2

MISE EN TRAIN
Quick Review 5 min.
- Check homework.
- Bell Work, ATE, p. 97

PREMIERE ETAPE
Vocabulaire, p. 97 20 min.
- Presenting **Vocabulaire**, ATE, p. 97
- Play Audio CD for Activity 7, p. 97.
- Travaux pratiques de grammaire, pp. 30–32, Activities 4–7
- Do Activities 8–9, p. 98, in pairs.
- **Vocabulaire à la carte**, p. 98

Comment dit-on... ?, p. 98 20 min.
- Presenting **Comment dit-on... ?**, ATE, p. 98
- Play Audio CD for Activity 10, p. 98.
- Building on Previous Skills, ATE, p. 99
- Cahier d'activités, p. 38, Activity 4
- Do Activity 11, p. 99.

Wrap-Up, 5 min.
- Additional Practice, ATE, p. 99

Homework Options
Cahier d'activités, Acts. 2–3, p. 38
Travaux pratiques de grammaire, Acts. 1–3, pp. 29–30

Day 3

PREMIERE ETAPE
Quick Review 5 min.
- Check homework.

Vocabulaire, p. 99 20 min.
- Travaux pratiques de grammaire, pp. 32–33, Activities 8–10
- Do Activity 12, p. 99.
- Cahier d'activités, p. 39, Activity 5
- Have students do Activities 13–14, pp. 99–100, in pairs.

Comment dit-on... ?, p. 100 20 min.
- Presenting **Comment dit-on... ?**, ATE, p. 100
- Play Audio CD for Activity 16, p. 100.
- Cahier d'activités, p. 40, Activity 7

Wrap-Up 5 min.
- Teaching Transparency 4-1, using suggestion #5 from Suggestions for using Teaching Transparency 4-1.

Homework Options
Travaux pratiques de grammaire, Acts. 11–12, p. 34

Day 4

PREMIERE ETAPE
Quick Review 5 min.
- Check homework.

Grammaire, p. 101 30 min.
- Presenting **Grammaire**, ATE, p. 101
- Play Audio CD for Activity 17, p. 101.
- Do Activity 18, p. 101.
- Travaux pratiques de grammaire, pp. 35–37, Activities 13–17
- Do part a of Activity 20, p. 102.
- Have students do part b of Activity 20, p. 102, in pairs.

Wrap-Up 15 min.
- Game: **J'en doute**, ATE, p. 102

Homework Options
Study for Quiz 4-1.
Grammaire supplémentaire, Acts. 1–3, pp. 114–115
Cahier d'activités, Acts. 8, p. 40

Day 5

PREMIERE ETAPE
Quiz 4-1 20 min.
- Administer Quiz 4-1A or 4-1B.

PANORAMA CULTUREL 25 min.
- See Teaching Suggestions, Pre-viewing Suggestion 1, Video Guide, p. 23
- Presenting **Panorama Culturel**, ATE, p. 103
- See Teaching Suggestions, Viewing Suggestions 1–2, Video Guide, p. 23.
- Questions, ATE, p. 103
- See Teaching Suggestions, Post-viewing Suggestions 1–2, Video Guide, p. 23.

Wrap-Up 5 min.
- **Qu'en penses-tu?**, p. 103

Homework Options
Cahier d'activités, Act. 22, p. 48

Day 6

PANORAMA CULTUREL
Quick Review 5 min.
- Check homework.

REMISE EN TRAIN 15 min.
- Presenting **Remise en train**, ATE, p. 104.
- Complete Activities 21–24, pp. 104–105.
- Read and discuss **Note culturelle**, p. 105.
- Do Activity 25, p. 105.

DEUXIEME ETAPE
Vocabulaire, p. 106 25 min.
- Presenting **Vocabulaire**, ATE, p. 106
- Play Audio CD for Activity 26, p. 106.
- Travaux pratiques de grammaire, pp. 38–39, Activities 18–21
- Review family vocabulary, pp. R17–R18.
- Have students do Activity 27, p. 106, in pairs.

Wrap-Up 5 min.
- Thinking Critically: Comparing and Contrasting, ATE, p. 105

Homework Options
Cahier d'activités, Acts. 12–15, pp. 43–44

One-Stop Planner CD-ROM

For alternative lesson plans by chapter section, to create your own customized plans, or to preview all resources available for this chapter, use the **One-Stop Planner CD-ROM**, Disc 1.

 For additional homework suggestions, see activities accompanied by this symbol throughout the chapter.

Day 7

DEUXIEME ETAPE
Quick Review 5 min.
- Check homework.

Grammaire, p. 107 20 min.
- Presenting **Grammaire**, ATE, p. 107
- Language Notes, ATE, p. 107
- Do Activity 28, p. 107.
- Travaux pratiques de grammaire, p. 40, Activities 22–23
- Cahier d'activités, p. 45, Activity 16
- Have students do Activity 29, p. 107, in pairs.

Comment dit-on... ?, p. 108 20 min.
- Presenting **Comment dit-on... ?**, ATE, p. 108.
- Play Audio CD for Activity 31, p. 108.
- Do Activity 32, p. 109.
- Cahier d'activités, pp. 45–46, Activities 17–19
- Have students do Activity 34, p. 109, in pairs.

Wrap-Up 5 min.
- Second Teaching Suggestion, ATE, p. 109

Homework Options
Study for Quiz 4-2.
Pupil's Edition, Activity 30, p. 108
Grammaire supplémentaire, Acts. 4–7, pp. 116–117
Cahier d'activités, Act. 20, p. 46

Day 8

DEUXIEME ETAPE
Quiz 4-2 20 min.
- Administer Quiz 4-2A or 4-2B.

LISONS! 25 min.
- Read and discuss **Stratégie pour lire**, p. 110.
- Do Prereading Activities A–C, p. 110.
- Have students read **Lisons!**, pp. 110–112.
- Do Reading Activities D–M, p. 111.

Wrap-Up 5 min.
- Language Notes, ATE, p. 111

Homework Options
Cahier d'activités, Act. 21, p. 47

Day 9

LISONS!
Quick Review 5 min.
- Check homework.

LISONS! 10 min.
- Do Activity N, p. 112.
- Thinking Critically: Analyzing, ATE, p. 112

ECRIVONS! 30 min.
- Read and discuss **Stratégie pour écrire**, p. 113, then have students work on their reports.

Wrap-Up 5 min.
- Allow time for peer and self-evaluation of student reports.

Homework Options
Complete final draft of fashion reports.

Day 10

ECRIVONS!
Quick Review 10 min.
- Allow volunteers to present their reports from **Ecrivons!** to the class.

MISE EN PRATIQUE
Chapter Review 35 min.
- Play Audio CD for Activity 1, p. 118.
- Have students do Activities 2–3, p. 118, in pairs.
- **A toi d'écrire,** CD-ROM Tutor, Disc 1

Wrap-Up 5 min.
- Have volunteers present their articles from Activity 2, p. 118, to the class.

Homework Options
Cahier d'activités, Acts. 10–11, p. 42

Day 11

MISE EN PRATIQUE
Quick Review 5 min.
- Check homework.

Chapter Review 40 min.
- Have students do Activity 4, p. 119, in pairs.
- Have groups work on fashion shows for **Jeu de rôle,** p. 119.
- Allow groups to present fashion shows.
- **A toi de parler,** CD-ROM Tutor, Disc 1

Wrap-Up 5 min.
- Begin **Que sais-je?,** p. 120.

Homework Options
Que sais-je?, p. 120

Day 12

MISE EN PRATIQUE
Quick Review 10 min.
- Go over **Que sais-je?,** p. 120.

Chapter Review 40 min.
- Review chapter functions, vocabulary, and grammar; choose from **Grammaire supplémentaire,** Grammar Tutor for Students of French, Activities for Communication, Listening Activities, Interactive CD-ROM Tutor, or **Jeux interactifs.**

Homework Options
Study for Chapter 4 Test.

Assessment

Test, Chapter 4 50 min.
- Administer Chapter 4 Test. Select from Testing Program, Alternative Assessment Guide, Test Generator, or Standardized Assessment Tutor.

Chapitre 4 : Des goûts et des couleurs
Suggested Lesson Plans 90-Minute Block Schedule

Block 1

CHAPTER OPENER 10 min.
- Present Chapter Objectives, p. 93.
- Cultural Notes and History Link, ATE, pp. 92–93

MISE EN TRAIN 30 min.
- Pre-viewing suggestions for *Camille et compagnie,* Video Guide, p. 22
- Show video for *Camille et companie,* Video Program, Videocassette 2.
- Viewing and post-viewing activities, Video Guide, p. 24
- **Note culturelle,** p. 96

PREMIERE ETAPE
Vocabulaire, p. 97 20 min.
- Presenting **Vocabulaire,** ATE, p. 97
- Play Audio CD for Activity 7, p. 97.
- Do Activity 8, p. 98.

Comment dit-on… ?, p. 98 25 min.
- Presenting **Comment dit-on… ?,** ATE, p. 98
- Play Audio CD for Activity 10, p. 98.
- Visual Learners, ATE, p. 98

Wrap-Up 5 min.
- Teaching Transparency 4-1, suggestion #1, from Vocabulary Practice using Teaching Transparency 4-1

Homework Options
Cahier d'activités, pp. 37–38, Acts. 1–3
Travaux pratiques de grammaire, pp. 29–32, Acts. 1–7

Block 2

PREMIERE ETAPE
Quick Review 5 min.
- Show students illustrations of various articles of clothing, using Teaching Transparency 4-1 or other illustrations. Have students name each item as you point to it.

Vocabulaire, p. 97 15 min.
- Do Activity 9, p. 98.

Comment dit-on… ?, p. 98 20 min.
- Building on Previous Skills, ATE, p. 99
- Do Activity 11, p. 99.

Vocabulaire, p. 99 40 min.
- Presenting **Vocabulaire,** ATE, p. 99
- Do Activities 12–13, p. 99.
- Do Activity 14, p. 100. See Visual Learners, ATE, p. 100.

Wrap-Up 10 min.
- Teaching Transparency 4-1, suggestion #3, from Suggestions for using Teaching Transparency 4-1

Homework Options
Cahier d'activités, pp. 38–39, Acts. 4–6
Travaux pratiques de grammaire, pp. 32–34, Acts. 8–12

Block 3

PREMIERE ETAPE
Quick Review 10 min.
- Listening Activities Book p. 31, Additional Listening Activity 4-2

Comment dit-on… ?, p. 100 20 min.
- Presenting **Comment dit-on… ?,** ATE, p. 100
- Kinesthetic Learners, ATE, p. 100
- Play Audio CD for Activity 16, p. 100.

Grammaire, p. 101 35 min.
- Presenting **Grammaire,** ATE, p. 101
- Play Audio CD for Activity 17, using Slower Pace suggestion, ATE, p. 101.
- Do Activity 18, p. 101.
- Teaching Transparency 4-1, using suggestion #2 from Vocabulary Practice using Teaching Transparency 4-1

PANORAMA CULTUREL 20 min.
- Presenting **Panorama Culturel,** ATE, p. 103
- Have students read and discuss the questions in **Qu'en penses-tu?,** p. 103.

Wrap-Up 5 min.
- Additional Practice, ATE, p. 101

Homework Options
Have students study for Quiz 4-1.
Grammaire supplémentaire, pp. 114–115, Acts. 1–3
Cahier d'activités, pp. 40–41, Acts. 7–9
Travaux pratiques de grammaire, pp. 35–37, Acts. 13–17

One-Stop Planner CD-ROM

For alternative lesson plans by chapter section, to create your own customized plans, or to preview all resources available for this chapter, use the **One-Stop Planner CD-ROM**, Disc 1.

 For additional homework suggestions, see activities accompanied by this symbol throughout the chapter.

Block 4

PREMIERE ETAPE
Quick Review 10 min.
- Activities for Communication, pp. 13–14, Communicative Activity 4-1A and 4-1B

Quiz 4-1 20 min.
- Administer Quiz 4-1A or 4-1B.

REMISE EN TRAIN 30 min.
- Presenting **Remise en train**, ATE, p. 104
- Do Activities 21–24, pp. 104–105.
- **Note culturelle**, p. 105

DEUXIEME ETAPE
Vocabulaire, p. 106 20 min.
- Presenting **Vocabulaire**, ATE, p. 106
- Play Audio CD for Activity 26, p. 106.
- Do Activity 27, p. 106.

Wrap-Up 10 min.
- Teaching Transparency 4-2, suggestion #2, from Suggestions for using Teaching Transparency 4-2

Homework Options
Cahier d'activités, pp. 42–44, Acts. 10–15
Travaux pratiques de grammaire, pp. 38–39, Acts. 18–19, 21

Block 5

DEUXIEME ETAPE
Quick Review 5 min.
- Bring in photos of various celebrities and have students describe each person's hairstyle.

Grammaire, p. 107 45 min.
- Presenting **Grammaire**, ATE, p. 107
- Do Activity 28, p. 107.
- **Grammaire supplémentaire,** Activity 6, p. 117
- Read and discuss **A la française**, p. 107.
- Language Notes, ATE, p. 107
- Do Activity 29, p. 107.

Comment dit-on... ?, p. 108 30 min.
- Presenting **Comment dit-on... ?**, ATE, p. 108
- Play Audio CD for Activity 31, ATE, p. 108.
- Do Activity 32, p. 109.

Wrap-Up 10 min.
- Teaching Transparency 4-2, suggestion #5, from Suggestions for using Teaching Transparency 4-2

Homework Options
Have students study for Quiz 4-2.
Grammaire supplémentaire, pp. 116–117, Acts. 4, 5, 7
Cahier d'activités, pp. 45–46, Acts. 16–20
Travaux pratiques de grammaire, pp. 39–40, Acts. 20, 22–23

Block 6

DEUXIEME ETAPE
Quick Review 10 min.
- Activities for Communication, pp. 15–16, Communicative Activity 4-2A and 4-2B

Quiz 4-2 20 min.
- Administer Quiz 4-2A or 4-2B.

LISONS! 40 min.
- Read **Lisons!**, p. 110–112.
- Do Prereading Activities A–C, p. 110.
- Read Culture Note, ATE, p. 110.
- Do Reading Activities D–M, Language Note, ATE, pp. 110–112.

MISE EN PRATIQUE 20 min.
- Play Audio CD for Activity 1, p. 118.
- Do Activities 2–3, p. 118.

Homework Options
Ecrivons!, p. 113, Acts. A–B
Que sais-je?, p. 120
Interactive CD-ROM Tutor
Study for Chapter 4 Test

Block 7

MISE EN PRATIQUE
Quick Review 15 min.
- **Jeu de rôle**, p. 119
- Collect homework.

Chapter Review 30 min.
- Review Chapter 4. Choose from **Grammaire supplémentaire,** Grammar Tutor for Students of French, Activities for Communication, Listening Activities, Interactive CD-ROM Tutor, or **Jeux interactifs.**

Test, Chapter 4 45 min.
- Administer Chapter 4 Test. Select from Testing Program, Alternative Assessment Guide, Test Generator, or Standardized Assessment Tutor.

CHAPITRE 4

One-Stop Planner CD-ROM

For resource information, see the **One-Stop Planner,** Disc 1.

Pacing Tips
The first **étape** has more content to cover than the second **étape.** You might keep that in mind when planning your lessons. For Lesson Plans and timing suggestions, see pages 91I–91L.

Meeting the Standards

Communication
- Asking for and giving opinions, p. 98
- Asking which one(s): pointing out and identifying people and things, p. 100
- Paying and responding to compliments; reassuring someone, p. 108

Cultures
- Culture Notes, p. 92
- Culture Note, p. 93
- Culture Note, p. 110
- Note culturelle, p. 96
- Note culturelle, p. 105
- Panorama Culturel, p. 103

Connections
- History Link, p. 93
- Math Link, p. 95

Comparisons
- Language-to-Language, p. 107
- Thinking Critically, pp. 103, 105, 109, 112

Communities
- Career Path, p. 110
- Community Links, pp. 97, 101
- De l'école au travail, p. 109

Cultures and Communities

Culture Notes
- Yves Saint-Laurent is known as one of the masters of **haute couture.** His designs have garnered numerous awards, such as the Neiman-Marcus Oscar and the Harper's Bazaar Oscar.
- Coco Chanel, born in 1883, is often considered one of the finest **couturières.** Her concept of fashion was casual and simple. She is famous for perfecting a design ideal for simple, understated evening wear.
- Pierre Cardin, an Italian-born Paris intellectual, is known for his avant-garde fashions that tend toward the extreme. For an idea of his style, see the costumes he designed for Jean Cocteau's 1946 film *Beauty and the Beast.*

CHAPITRE

4
Des goûts et des couleurs

Objectives

In this chapter you will learn to

Première étape

- ask for and give opinions
- ask which one(s)
- point out and identify people and things

Deuxième étape

- pay and respond to compliments
- reassure someone

internet

go. hrw .com	**ADRESSE:** go.hrw.com
	MOT-CLE: WA3 FRANCOPHONE EUROPE-4

◀ **Devant un grand magasin à Paris**

CHAPITRE 4

Focusing on Outcomes
Have students read the list of objectives. Then, have them list English expressions they might use to express the outcomes. You might also have them suggest French expressions they already know that accomplish the functions listed. Have a student compile a list of these expressions on a transparency.
NOTE: You may want to use the video to support the objectives. The self-check activities in **Que sais-je?** on page 120 help students assess their achievement of the objectives.

Culture Note
The photo on pages 92–93 features the awning alongside a **grand magasin** in Paris. The concept of **grands magasins** is practically an institution in France. These are usually three-to-four-story department stores that carry items of all kinds, except food. In a **grand magasin,** one can find clothing items (including designer clothes), perfume, and jewelry, as well as washing machines and furniture. Some of the most popular French **grand magasins** are Les Galeries Lafayette®, La Samaritaine®, Le Printemps®, and Le Bon Marché®.

Connections and Comparisons

History Link
Students might be interested to know that in eighteenth-century France, women wore huge **paniers** under their long skirts, which created a box-like frame on either side of the hips. **Mouches,** or artificial moles, were often applied to the face. In the nineteenth century, both men and women tossed aside the powdered wigs and make-up associated with court life in favor of simpler, more austere styles. Men's clothing was usually black and complemented by a silk top hat. In women's clothing, the tight waist was fashionable throughout the nineteenth century and was combined with a full skirt or even a bustle to create an hourglass effect. You might have students research other aspects of the history of fashion. They might choose a particular country or time period to research, and then report back to the class with their findings.

Presenting Mise en train

Have students look at the photos on pages 94–95. Then, have them make a chart with the outfits (**le pantalon noir, la jupe rose,** and so on) in a vertical column on the left, and **Axcelle** and **Jérôme** across the top. Play the audio recording and have students fill in the chart with a check mark if the person likes the item and an "X" if not. Finally, name each item and have volunteers tell who liked or disliked it.

Teaching Suggestion

Bring in magazine pictures of trendy styles. Have students give their opinions of each style.

Mise en train · *Mon look, c'est mon affaire*

Cahier d'activités, p. 37, Act. 1

CD 4 Tr. 1

Stratégie pour comprendre
Judging by the photos on these two pages, what do you think the theme of this episode is? Can you identify words in the text that refer to the items in the photos? Many words look like English words. Can you guess their meaning?

1
Jérôme	Ah, tu es allée chercher le courrier? Il y a quelque chose pour moi?
Axcelle	Non, rien pour toi, comme d'habitude.
Jérôme	Et ça, c'est quoi? Un magazine?
Axcelle	Non, c'est le catalogue printemps-été de Quelle®. J'espère qu'il y a des trucs bien.
Jérôme	Tu es vraiment obsédée par la mode, toi! De toute façon, il n'y a que ça qui vous intéresse, vous, les filles!

2 **Axcelle regarde le catalogue...**
Axcelle	Ouah! Génial, cet ensemble! Tu n'aimes pas?
Jérôme	Lequel?
Axcelle	Celui-là, le noir avec le pantalon à pattes d'eph.
Jérôme	Ah! Ne me dis pas que tu aimes vraiment ça! C'est affreux!
Axcelle	Tu comprends vraiment rien à la mode, toi! C'est super branché comme style et puis, si tu sortais un peu, tu verrais que tout le monde s'habille comme ça.
Jérôme	Ouais, ben, c'est peut-être à la mode, mais je trouve quand même ça ridicule!... Ça, par contre, je trouve que c'est très classe.
Axcelle	Le tailleur rose, là?
Jérôme	Oui, comment tu le trouves?

3
Axcelle	Pas mal, mais bon, je ne me vois pas aller à l'école comme ça. Ça fait un peu trop sérieux.

4
Jérôme	Peut-être, mais au moins, c'est élégant.
Axcelle	Tiens, regarde ce qu'elle porte, la fille, là.
Jérôme	Laquelle?
Axcelle	Celle avec le caleçon imprimé et le grand tee-shirt. J'aime bien ça. C'est sympa, ça peut se porter partout et c'est moins sérieux que ton tailleur. Qu'est-ce que tu en dis?
Jérôme	Ouais... J'aime bien ce genre de vêtements. C'est cool et puis... c'est moins bizarre que ton pattes d'eph. Bon, à mon tour de regarder un peu!
Axcelle	Ben, je croyais qu'il n'y avait que les filles qui s'intéressaient à la mode!
Jérôme	Oh, ça va, hein! Elle est où, la section «hommes»?
Axcelle	Après les enfants.

Preteaching Vocabulary

Recognizing Cognates
Have students look at the dialogue on these two pages and identify words that are used in English or words that look like those used in English (**magazine, style, ridicule, sérieux, élégant, tee-shirt, cool, bizarre, mariage, chic**). Remind students that just because French words and English words look alike, they don't necessarily mean the same thing. Some of the false cognates, or **faux amis,** found in the text are:

courrier	*mail*
mode	*fashion*
nul	*lame, uninteresting*
robe	*dress*
costume	*suit*

⑤ Jérôme   Ah, voilà... Oh là là, c'est nul! Il n'y a rien qui me plaît!

Axcelle   Du calme. Tu n'as pas tout vu. Tiens, il est chouette, ce gilet, non?

Jérôme   Ouah! Un gilet en cuir pour 50 € ! C'est hyper cool! Je crois que je vais le commander. En plus, j'ai vraiment plus rien à me mettre.

Axcelle   Tiens, au fait, tu as quelque chose pour le mariage de Joël et Virginie?

Jérôme   Tu fais bien d'en parler. Non, j'ai rien et je me demande ce que je pourrais bien mettre. A ton avis, un pantalon à pinces et une chemise, ça irait?

Axcelle   Euh... si j'étais toi, je mettrais plutôt un costume et une cravate.

Jérôme   Tu crois?

Axcelle   Ben, oui, c'est quand même un mariage! Et puis, je suis sûre que c'est ce que la plupart des hommes vont mettre.

Jérôme   Ce n'est pas trop habillé?

Axcelle   Ecoute! Au pire, tu seras le mieux habillé de tous, pour une fois!

Jérôme   Ah, très drôle. Va un peu à la page des costumes au lieu de dire n'importe quoi... Tiens, il te plaît, celui-là?

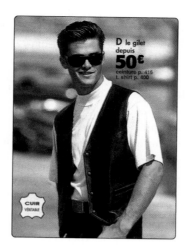

⑥ Axcelle   Ouais, je trouve qu'il est très chic. En tout cas, si tu l'achètes, prends aussi la cravate, elle va très bien avec.

Jérôme   Ouais, peut-être... Enfin, j'ai encore le temps d'y penser. Il reste deux mois avant le mariage.

Axcelle   Bon, retourne à la section «femmes» que je trouve quelque chose pour ce mariage, moi aussi... Tiens, voilà. Elle est parfaite, cette robe, non?

⑦ Jérôme   Tu rigoles ou quoi?

Axcelle   Non, pourquoi? Tu as quelque chose contre les robes à pois?

Jérôme   Ben, euh... T'étonne pas si je fais semblant de ne pas te connaître si tu mets ça au mariage!

Using the Captioned Video

 As an alternative, you might want to show the captioned version of *Camille et compagnie : C'est tout à fait toi!* on Videocassette 5. Some students may benefit from seeing the written words as they listen to the target language and watch the gestures and actions in context. This visual reinforcement of vocabulary and functions will facilitate students' comprehension and help reduce their anxiety before they are formally introduced to the new language in the chapter.

Language Note
Have students look at the photo of the woman in bell-bottoms next to the second scene and try to guess the literal meaning of **les pattes d'eph** *(elephant feet)*. Tell them that **eph** (pronounced "eff") is an abbreviated form of the word **éléphant**.

Visual/Tactile Learners
Have students bring in out-of-date clothing. Items from the 1960s, 1970s, and 1980s are especially good for this activity. Have students work in pairs. Students should create a tag for each item with the name of the item, a brief description, and a price in francs or euros. Then, collect all the tags, shuffle them, and have volunteers attach the tags to the appropriate items.

Math Link
Have students convert the clothing prices from euros to dollars. Current exchange rates should be available in local newspapers.

Camille et compagnie

You may choose to show students Episode 4: *C'est tout à fait toi!* now or wait until later in the chapter. In the video, Camille and Sophie are shopping for new clothes, but they have very different tastes. Sophie likes out-of-the-ordinary clothes, while Camille prefers conservative outfits. They separate to go to different stores. Max stays with Sophie to help her choose, but it turns out that they also have different opinions about clothes.

Teaching Suggestion

4 Remind students to scan for the information they need.

Language Note

Students might want to know the following words from the catalogue descriptions: **glissière** *(zipper);* **à pinces** *(pleated);* **épaulettes** *(shoulder pads);* **manche** *(sleeve);* **passepoilé** *(piped).*

Answers

2 1. Axcelle; le caleçon imprimé et le grand tee-shirt
2. Axcelle; le costume
3. Jérôme; l'ensemble noir avec le pantalon à pattes d'eph
4. Jérôme; la robe à pois
5. Axcelle; le tailleur rose

3 *Possible answers:*
décontractés : le gilet en cuir, le caleçon imprimé et le tee-shirt
très à la mode : le pantalon à pattes d'eph
branchés : le pantalon à pattes d'eph
chic : le tailleur rose, le costume et la cravate
sérieux : le tailleur rose
élégants : le tailleur rose

5 1. Tu n'aimes pas? Qu'est-ce que tu en dis? Il est chouette, ce... non? Il te plaît,... ? Elle est parfaite, cette... non? ... comment tu le trouves?
2. Lequel? Laquelle?
3. Celui-là,... ; Celle avec... ; ... celui-là
4. Génial, cet... ; C'est super branché... ; ... je trouve que c'est très classe... ; C'est élégant. J'aime bien, ça. C'est sympa,... ; J'aime bien... ; C'est cool... ; ... c'est moins bizarre que... ; C'est hyper cool! ... je trouve qu'il est très chic.
5. Ne me dis pas que tu aimes vraiment ça! C'est affreux! ... je trouve quand même ça ridicule! Ça fait un peu trop sérieux. T'étonne pas si je fais semblant de ne pas te connaître si tu mets ça.

---

1 **Tu as compris?** 2. trendy, latest styles; He prefers a more classic style. These activities check for comprehension only. Students should not yet be expected to produce language modeled in **Mise en train.**

1. Qu'est-ce qu'Axcelle reçoit au courrier? a clothing catalogue
2. Quel type de vêtements Axcelle aime porter? Qu'en pense Jérôme?
3. Pour quelle occasion ces jeunes cherchent des vêtements? a wedding
4. Qu'est-ce que Jérôme a envie de mettre? Et Axcelle? a suit and tie; a polka-dot dress

2 **Qui parle de quoi?** See answers below.

C'est l'opinion d'Axcelle ou de Jérôme? De quels vêtements est-ce qu'ils parlent?

1. «Ça peut se porter partout.»
2. «Si tu l'achètes, prends aussi la cravate, elle va très bien avec.»
3. «Ne me dis pas que tu aimes vraiment ça! C'est affreux!»
4. «T'étonne pas si je fais semblant de ne pas te connaître si tu mets ça au mariage!»
5. «Je ne me vois pas aller à l'école comme ça. Ça fait un peu trop sérieux.»

3 **Les styles**

Quels vêtements de ***Mon look, c'est mon affaire*** sont...
See answers below.

décontractés?		chic?
	très à la mode?	élégants?
branchés?		sérieux?

4 **Quels vêtements?**

Quel est le vêtement de ***Mon look, c'est mon affaire*** qui correspond à chacune des descriptions suivantes?

le costume   la robe à pois   le gilet en cuir   le pantalon à pattes d'eph

Une élégance raffinée pour ce costume réalisé dans un mélange de coton et polyester. Veste coupe classique avec fente dos, 1 poche poitrine et 2 poches intérieures. Pantalon à pinces, montage ville : fermeture par glissière.

Imprimé pastilles pour cette robe fluide. Entièrement boutonnée devant, taille appuyée par découpes devant et dos. Encolure en V, pinces sous poitrine. Manches courtes. Epaulettes. Base ample et dansante. Long. 90cm.

Une qualité de cuir superbe pour ce gilet sans manches. Empiècement avec double surpiqûre. 2 poches passepoilées. Fermeture par pressions. Dos 100% polyester rehaussé d'un lien et d'une boucle. 100% cuir (agneau).

Bien mode, le pantalon «pattes d'eph» avec base renforcée. Taille élastique. Entrejambes 72 cm env. 55% coton, 43% polyamide, 2% élasthanne.

5 **Cherche les expressions**

In ***Mon look, c'est mon affaire,*** what expressions do Axcelle and Jérôme use to . . .   See answers below.

1. ask an opinion?
2. ask which one(s)?
3. point out an item?
4. give a favorable opinion?
5. give an unfavorable opinion?

Note culturelle

La France est réputée pour sa haute couture. Mais bien sûr, tout le monde n'a pas les moyens de se payer des vêtements créés par des grands couturiers tels que Christian Dior® ou Nina Ricci®. Dans les grands magasins comme les Galeries Lafayette® ou le Printemps, on peut trouver des vêtements moins chers, mais de bonne qualité. Les jeunes peuvent également acheter des vêtements relativement bon marché dans des boutiques de mode telles que Kookaï®, NAF-NAF® et Ton sur ton®.

6 **Et maintenant, à toi**

Est-ce que tu t'es déjà habillé(e) pour une occasion spéciale? Laquelle? Quels vêtements est-ce que tu as choisis? Quel est ton look préféré?

Communication for All Students

Auditory Learners

2 Read the quotations aloud and call on students to identify the speaker.

Visual/Auditory Learners

2 Assign the letters a–f to the outfits on pages 94–95. Then, read each quotation aloud and have individuals give the letter of the related outfit.

Visual/Kinesthetic Learners

6 Instead of having students write out their responses, have them draw or find pictures of the type of outfit that they would wear for a special occasion and one that they would wear every day. Have them label their drawings or pictures in French, using vocabulary they already know.

Première étape

Objectives Asking for and giving opinions; asking which one(s); pointing out and identifying people and things

WA3 FRANCOPHONE EUROPE-4

Vocabulaire

La boîte à mode

- un costume
- une cravate en soie
- une robe à col en V
- un gilet en laine
- une chemise à rayures
- un pendentif
- un tee-shirt forme tunique
- une mini-jupe écossaise
- des gants (m.)
- un pantalon à pinces
- un caleçon à pois
- un col roulé
- un sac
- des hauts talons (m.)
- un collant
- des bottes (f.) en cuir

Si tu as oublié clothing vocabulary *va à la page R17.*

Travaux pratiques de grammaire, pp. 30–32, Act. 4–7

Cahier d'activités, p. 38, Act. 2–3

---

7 **A la fête** See scripts and answers on p. 91G.

CD 4 Tr. 2

Ecoutons Gabrielle et son amie Suzette parlent de ce que tout le monde portait à la fête hier soir. De qui est-ce qu'elles parlent?

Nathalie · Lian · Antoine · Brigitte · Tatiana · Ahmed · Etienne

---

Connections and Comparisons

Community Link

Form four or five groups. Give each group a card with the name of a celebrity and a location or event written on it (**Michael Jordan à un mariage** or **le président à Paris**). Then, have groups go to the board, draw their celebrity with what he or she might wear, and label at least four items of clothing. When the groups have finished, each member describes an article of clothing their celebrity is wearing. As an alternative, have groups draw on transparencies with colored markers.

STANDARDS: 1.2, 5.1

PREMIERE ETAPE   QUATRE-VINGT-DIX-SEPT   **97**

Première étape

CHAPITRE 4

Teaching Resources
pp. 97–102

PRINT
▸ Lesson Planner, p. 18
▸ Listening Activities, pp. 27–28, 31–32
▸ Activities for Communication, pp. 13–14, 60, 62, 95–96
▸ Travaux pratiques de grammaire, pp. 29–37
▸ Grammar Tutor for Students of French, Chapter 4
▸ Cahier d'activités, pp. 38–41
▸ Testing Program, pp. 67–70
▸ Alternative Assessment Guide, p. 33
▸ Student Make-Up Assignments, Chapter 4

MEDIA
▸ One-Stop Planner
▸ Audio Compact Discs, CD 4, Trs. 2–5, 14, 19–21
▸ Teaching Transparencies: 4-1; **Grammaire supplémentaire** Answers; Travaux pratiques de grammaire Answers
▸ Interactive CD-ROM Tutor, Disc 1

Bell Work
Have students describe their favorite outfit and tell why they like it. Have them write a second sentence describing a clothing style they dislike and telling why.

Presenting Vocabulaire

Bring in the real clothing items pictured here or magazine pictures of them. Hold up an item or picture and ask students questions about it. For example, you might hold up a polka-dot shirt and a striped shirt and say **C'est une chemise à pois. Et voici une chemise à rayures. Marie, tu préfères les chemises à pois ou à rayures?**

Presenting
Comment dit-on... ?

Bring to class magazine cutouts showing people wearing various types of clothes. Write the expressions for giving opinions on a transparency in two columns, labeled **Favorable** and **Unfavorable**. Show each picture as you ask a student his or her opinion of the outfit, using one of the new expressions. Have the student respond by giving a thumbs-up or a thumbs-down gesture. Depending on his or her gesture, make a **favorable** or **unfavorable** comment on the article of clothing in the picture. Have students repeat the new expressions after you.

---

8 **Je mets quoi, alors?**

Parlons Ton ami(e) ne sait pas quoi mettre. Donne-lui des conseils.

EXEMPLE

—Je ne sais pas quoi mettre avec...
—Tu devrais mettre...

> ma mini-jupe écossaise
> mon pattes d'eph
> mon pantalon à pinces
> ma robe à col en V
> mon costume
> mon caleçon imprimé

> ta chemise à rayures
> ta cravate en soie
> ton tee-shirt forme tunique
> ton col roulé
> ton foulard à pois
> ton pull bleu foncé

9 **Qu'est-ce qu'on met?**

Parlons Un(e) ami(e) français(e) te demande ce que les Américains mettent pour aller à ces endroits. Joue cette scène avec ton/ta camarade.

> au concert   à un mariage   à l'école
> au restaurant   à une interview pour un job
> à une boum

Vocabulaire à la carte

un pattes d'eph	*bell bottoms*
un débardeur	*a tank top*
un coupe-vent	*a windbreaker*
des bretelles (f.)	*suspenders, straps*
des bottines (f.)	*ankle boots*
des mocassins (m.)	*loafers*
à manches courtes/ longues	*short/long-sleeved*
en toile	*linen*
en daim	*suede*
à carreaux	*checked*
imprimé(e)	*printed*
bleu clair	*light blue*
bleu foncé	*dark blue*

Comment dit-on...?

Asking for and giving opinions

To ask for an opinion:

Comment tu trouves ce collant?
Tu n'aimes pas ce pendentif?
Elle te plaît, cette mini-jupe?
Qu'est-ce que tu penses de ces bottes?
Qu'en penses-tu?
What do you think of it?

To give a favorable opinion:

Je le trouve super.
Je l'aime bien.
Elle me plaît beaucoup.
J'aime bien ce genre de bottes.
I really like this type of . . .
C'est très bien, ça.

To give an unfavorable opinion:

Je le trouve moche.
Je ne l'aime pas tellement.
Elle ne me plaît pas du tout.
Je trouve qu'elles font vieux.
I think they look . . .
Ça fait vraiment cloche!
That looks really stupid!

Cahier d'activités, p. 38, Act. 4

10 **Chacun son opinion** See scripts and answers on p. 91G.

Ecoutons Ecoute ces jeunes qui parlent de vêtements. Ils les aiment ou pas?
CD 4 Tr. 3

Communication for All Students

Tactile Learners

8 Have partners draw each item in the word box on the left on separate pieces of paper and place them face-down in a pile. Have them do the same with the items in the word box on the right. Then, one partner selects a slip from the first pile and asks what to wear with that item. The other draws a slip from the second pile and suggests an item to wear.

Visual Learners

Distribute magazine pictures of various fashions to partners. Have them ask for and give their opinions of the outfit. Then, have pairs pass their picture to the pair on their right. Partners then ask for and give their opinions of the new outfit. Continue until all partners have seen each picture.

11 Qu'est-ce qu'ils se disent?

Parlons Ces jeunes sont en train de faire les magasins. Utilise les expressions de **Comment dit-on...?** pour recréer leurs conversations. *See answers below.*

1. 2. 3. 4.

Vocabulaire

affreux (-euse) *hideous*	**délirant(e)** *wild*	**hyper cool**	**sobre** *plain*
chic	**élégant(e)**	**ringard(e)** *corny*	**tape-à-l'œil** *gaudy*
classe *classy*	**génial(e)**	**sérieux (-euse)** *conservative*	**vulgaire** *tasteless*

Travaux pratiques de grammaire, pp. 32–34, Act. 8–12

Cahier d'activités, p. 39, Act. 5

Presenting
Vocabulaire

The day before you plan to present the vocabulary, assign each student one of the words. Have them find a magazine picture to illustrate their adjective, attach it to a piece of construction paper, and write the adjective on the reverse side. On the day of the presentation, collect the illustrations. Hold up each one, read aloud the adjective written on the back, and ask students if they agree with the opinion. **(C'est ringard, non? Comment tu trouves ça?)** Then, hold up magazine pictures of various outfits, asking **Comment tu trouves ça? C'est ringard ou hyper cool?**

12 Des vêtements pour tous les goûts

Parlons Tes amis portent les vêtements et accessoires suivants. Qu'est-ce que tu leur dis?

1. un tailleur bleu foncé et des hauts talons
2. des mocassins en daim noir
3. un pantalon à pinces, une chemise en coton et une cravate
4. un pattes d'eph à fleurs et un tee-shirt à rayures
5. un costume avec une chemise blanche à manches longues

> C'est...
> Je le/la/les trouve...
> Je trouve que ça fait...
> Je trouve ça...

13 Qu'en penses-tu?

 Lisons/Parlons Regarde ces vêtements. Tu penses acheter quelque chose, mais tu veux savoir ce qu'en pense ton/ta camarade. Demande-lui comment il/elle trouve ces vêtements.

D. Le gilet écossais sans manches. Très mode, il ajoute une petite note colorée à toute tenue. Réalisé en 50% acrylique, 45% laine et 5% autres fibres.
Rouge : 231.6946.
3 tailles : 34/36, 38/40, 42/44
42,50 €

G. La chemise à rayures. Col boutonné, poche poitrine à rabat boutonné, poignets à patte capucin, empiècement dos double avec pli creux et lichette. Entretien facile : elle est en 80% coton, 20% polyester.
Prune : 261.0111. Bleu : 271.0112.
Vert : 271.0115. Mousse : 271.0118.
4 encolures : 37/38 26 €
39/40, 41/42 28 € 43/44 29 €

I. Les bottes en cuir. Doublée en synthétique. Demi-semelle intérieure synthétique. Semelle extérieure en élastomère. Talon : 8 cm.
6 pointures : 36, 37, 38, 39, 40, 41
Noir : 521.2376. 73 €
Verni noir : 521.2379. 80 €

Additional Practice
Have students make a poster depicting their own personal sense of style by gathering magazine pictures or drawing illustrations. Have them include their favorite colors, patterns, and types of fabric on their posters. They might even glue bits of fabric or jewelry to their posters to add texture. Have them label each item and use the expressions of opinion from **Comment dit-on... ?** to describe their sense of style. **(Je les trouve super, ces cravates imprimées! J'aime bien ce genre de robe. J'aime bien les hauts talons.)** This activity might be done as a chapter project.

Communication for All Students

Slower Pace

13 Before students pair off, have them write down their impressions of each article of clothing. Have students use these notes to create their conversations.

Building on Previous Skills

Object pronouns Ask students how they decide whether to use the object pronoun **le, la,** or **les** when giving their opinion. Have them name articles of clothing that they would replace with **le, la,** and **les.** Then, show magazine pictures of various clothing items and ask individual students to give their opinions of them, using object pronouns. (**—Comment tu trouves cette cravate? —Je la trouve moche.**)

Possible Answers

11 1. —Qu'en penses-tu?
  —Je le trouve cool!
2. —Elle te plaît, cette robe?
  —Elle me plaît beaucoup.
3. —Qu'est-ce que tu penses de ces chaussures?
  —Je les trouve moches.
4. —Comment tu trouves ce sac?
  —Je trouve qu'il fait vieux.

Teaching Resources
pp. 97–102

PRINT
▸ Lesson Planner, p. 18
▸ Listening Activities, pp. 27–28, 31–32
▸ Activities for Communication, pp. 13–14, 60, 62, 95–96
▸ Travaux pratiques de grammaire, pp. 29–37
▸ Grammar Tutor for Students of French, Chapter 4
▸ Cahier d'activités, pp. 38–41
▸ Testing Program, pp. 67–70
▸ Alternative Assessment Guide, p. 33
▸ Student Make-Up Assignments, Chapter 4

MEDIA
▸ One-Stop Planner
▸ Audio Compact Discs, CD 4, Trs. 2–5, 14, 19–21
▸ Teaching Transparencies: 4-1; **Grammaire supplémentaire** Answers; Travaux pratiques de grammaire Answers
▸ Interactive CD-ROM Tutor, Disc 1

Presenting
Comment dit-on… ?

Place on two desks two items, identical except for the color. Tell students which item you prefer (**Ça, c'est la jupe que je préfère**). Then, ask a student **Quelle jupe tu préfères, la rouge ou la verte?** Have the student respond by saying either **la rouge** or **la verte**. Point to the item the student chose, and say **Tu préfères celle-ci?** if the student chose the item closest to him or her, or **Tu préfères celle-là?** for the other item. Then, ask another student **Et toi, tu aimes laquelle, celle-ci ou celle-là?** Repeat this process, using masculine articles of clothing.

14 Quel style!

Parlons Demande à ton/ta camarade ce qu'il/elle pense de ces différents styles. Est-ce que tu es d'accord?

15 Un style tout nouveau

a. Ecrivons Tu es styliste de mode. Avec tes camarades, crée une nouvelle ligne de vêtements. Dessine trois ensembles.

b. Ecrivons Avec tes camarades, faites votre publicité. Ecrivez une description de votre nouvelle ligne de vêtements. Créez un slogan pour attirer l'attention de vos clients potentiels.

grunge

baba

B.C.B.G.

punk

Comment dit-on...?

Asking which one(s); pointing out and identifying people and things

To ask which one(s):

> **Quelle** jupe est-ce que tu préfères?
> Tu aimes ces chemises? **Laquelle** est-ce que tu vas acheter?
> Tu essaies un jean? **Lequel?**

To point out and identify things:

> **Ça, c'est** la jupe que je préfère.
> Moi, j'aime bien **ces** chaussures-**là**.
> Je préfère **celles-là**. … *those.*
> **Celui du** garçon là-bas. *The one …*
> Tu n'aimes pas **le vert**?

To point out and identify people:

> Regarde **celui avec** les lunettes!
> … *the one (man/boy) with …*
> **Celle qui** parle à la vendeuse.
> *The one (woman/girl) who …*
> Tu vois **la fille au** pull bleu?
> … *the girl with/wearing the …*
> **Là-bas, le garçon qui** porte un pantalon rouge. *Over there, the boy who …*

Cahier d'activités, p. 40, Act. 7

16 La mode en ville See scripts on p. 91G.

CD 4 Tr. 4

Ecoutons Pendant que Julien et Marc attendent devant le cinéma, ils parlent des vêtements que portent les jeunes qui passent. De qui est-ce qu'ils parlent?

Sylvain 2

Michèle 1

Valentin 3

Annette 4

Communication for All Students

Visual Learners

14 After students have finished Activity 14, have them close their books. Hold up real clothes or pictures of them. Write the different styles (**punk, grunge, baba, B.C.B.G.**) on the board or on a transparency. Then name the article of clothing (**un blouson noir**) and have students tell which style(s) it represents (**punk**).

Kinesthetic Learners

Demonstrate the difference between the suffixes **-ci** and **-là** by pointing to a student near you and then to one in the back of the class, saying **Ce garçon-ci porte un tee-shirt, mais ce garçon-là porte un pull.** Then show students pairs of images showing people wearing different items of clothing and have them point at the pictures, using **-ci** and **-là**.

The interrogative and demonstrative pronouns

• When you want to ask *which one(s)*, use the appropriate interrogative pronoun to refer to the noun.

	masculine	*feminine*
singular	**lequel?**	**laquelle?**
plural	**lesquels?**	**lesquelles?**

—Je vais acheter ce pantalon.
—**Lequel?**
—Je trouve qu'ils sont moches, ces gants.
—**Lesquels?**

• When you want to say *this one, that one, these,* or *those,* use the appropriate demonstrative pronoun to refer to the noun.

	masculine	*feminine*
singular	**celui-là**	**celle-là**
plural	**ceux-là**	**celles-là**

Moi, je vais acheter **celui-là.** (ce sac-là)
Celle-là? Oui, je l'aime bien, mais elle coûte trop cher! (cette jupe-là)
Oh, je déteste **ceux-là!** Qu'est-ce qu'ils sont moches! (ces gilets-là)
Tu n'aimes pas **celles-là?** Moi je les adore! (ces bottes-là)

> Grammaire supplémentaire,
> pp. 114–115, Act. 1–3

> Cahier d'activités,
> p. 40, Act. 8

> Travaux pratiques
> de grammaire,
> pp. 35–37, Act. 13–17

17 **Grammaire en contexte**   See scripts and answers on pp. 91G–91H.

Ecoutons Ecoute ces conversations qui ont lieu dans une boutique de mode. De quoi est-ce qu'on parle?

CD 4 Tr. 5

> des bottes   un caleçon
> des hauts talons   une jupe écossaise

18 **Grammaire en contexte**

Lisons/Ecrivons Fabrice cherche un cadeau d'anniversaire pour sa sœur. Il ne sait pas quoi acheter. Djamila lui donne des conseils. Complète leur conversation avec un pronom interrogatif ou démonstratif.

DJAMILA   Pourquoi tu ne lui achètes pas des bottes? Qu'est-ce que tu penses de ces bottes-là?

FABRICE   ___1___ ?   Lesquelles

DJAMILA   Les blanches. Elles sont chic, non?

FABRICE   Moi, je préfère ___2___-là.   celles

DJAMILA   Bon, d'accord. Et ces gants-là? C'est une bonne idée, des gants, non?

FABRICE   ___3___ ?   Lesquels

DJAMILA   ___4___-là, les noirs.   Ceux

FABRICE   Oui, ils sont classe; mais, euh, je ne sais pas...

DJAMILA   Oh, regarde! J'adore ce col roulé. Qu'en penses-tu?   lequel

FABRICE   Je ne le vois pas. C'est ___5___ ?

DJAMILA   ___6___-là, à côté du pull bleu foncé. Tu vois, là-bas?   Celui

FABRICE   Oui, il est vachement bien! Je le prends!

Cultures and Communities

Community Link

As a class project, set up a flea market. Have students bring in some old ties, plastic sunglasses, and other small items. The object is for students to use the interrogative and demonstrative pronouns as often as possible, while acting as vendors or customers. The vendors offer suggestions and compliments, while the customers try to choose what to buy. You might model a sample conversation

with a student acting as the vendor.

—J'aime bien ces lunettes.
—Lesquelles? Celles-ci?
—Non, celles-là.
—Elles vous vont très bien, madame/ monsieur!
—Euh, j'hésite. Je peux voir celles-là?
—Lesquelles?
—...

Teaching Suggestions

20 a. Tell students that they must include in their conversation at least five clothing items, three favorable opinions, three unfavorable opinions, two interrogative pronouns, at least two demonstrative pronouns, one type of fabric, and one style of clothing.

20 b. Have students begin their collaboration by circling three of the best lines of their own dialogue. Have them underline one or two additional lines that they like. When partners get together, they should combine the best parts of both dialogues and compromise on the rest.

Assess

▶ Testing Program, pp. 67–70
Quiz 4-1A, Quiz 4-1B
Audio CD 4, Tr. 14

▶ Student Make-Up Assignments, Chapter 4, Alternative Quiz

▶ Alternative Assessment Guide, p. 33

Answers

19 *Possible answers:*
1. She likes plain clothes that are comfortable, like leggings, turtleneck sweaters, and tunic-style tee-shirts. Her classmates prefer miniskirts and bell-bottoms.
2. Stéphanie (agrees) **"Moi aussi, j'aime les vêtements simples"**; Florence (disagrees) **"J'aime les vêtements délirants"**; and Caroline (disagrees) **"C'est un moment où on peut porter ce qu'on veut."**
3. Florence talks about showing respect/tolerance for others; Caroline thinks it's cool to be fashionable.
4. *Answers will vary.*

---

19 **Le rôle de la mode** See answers below.

Lisons Lis la question de Sélima et les réponses de quelques jeunes. Ensuite, réponds aux questions.

> J'écris cette lettre pour savoir ce que vous pensez de la mode d'aujourd'hui. Je trouve qu'au lycée, beaucoup de filles portent des vêtements vraiment vulgaires, par exemple des pattes d'eph ou des mini-jupes trop courtes. A mon avis, c'est vraiment affreux! Moi, je préfère mettre des trucs plus sobres, comme par exemple un caleçon avec un tee-shirt forme tunique ou un col roulé. J'aime bien ce genre de vêtements parce que c'est confortable. Et vous, qu'est-ce que vous en pensez?
> Sélima

> Bonjour, Sélima. Personnellement, je pense que tu as raison. Moi aussi, j'aime les vêtements simples. Je trouve que les gens s'habillent souvent de façon vraiment ringarde ou vulgaire. Ils achètent leurs vêtements dans les boutiques à la dernière mode et c'est pour ça qu'ils pensent qu'ils sont hyper-cool. En fait, ils n'ont pas de personnalité et ils ne peuvent pas créer leur propre look. C'est dommage.
> Stéphanie

> Sélima, tu ne dois pas juger les gens d'après leurs vêtements. Nous avons tous des goûts différents, et c'est ça qui rend le monde intéressant. Moi, par exemple, j'aime les vêtements délirants, surtout les hauts talons. Je porte toujours des bijoux et je me maquille tous les jours. C'est mon style. Mais je respecte les filles qui préfèrent mettre des trucs plus sérieux. Toi aussi, tu dois apprendre à respecter les autres!
> Florence

> Salut, Sélima. Je voudrais répondre à ta question. A mon avis, la mode d'aujourd'hui est super et c'est très important de la suivre, surtout quand on est jeune. C'est un moment où on peut porter ce qu'on veut. Après, quand on travaille, c'est différent. Il faut mettre des vêtements sérieux tout le temps et c'est vraiment pas marrant. C'est pour ça que je pense qu'il faut profiter de notre jeunesse et s'amuser avec la mode.
> Caroline

1. Quelle est la différence entre les vêtements de Sélima et ceux de ses camarades?
2. Dans les trois réponses à Sélima, qui est d'accord et qui n'est pas d'accord avec elle?
3. Quelles raisons donnent les filles qui ne sont pas d'accord avec Sélima?
4. Avec qui est-ce que tu es d'accord? Pourquoi?

20 **Regarde les gens qui passent!**

a. Ecrivons Rémi et Céline sont à la terrasse d'un café. Ils regardent les passants et ils font des commentaires sur leurs vêtements. Imagine ce qu'ils disent et écris leur conversation.

b. Parlons Echange ton dialogue avec celui d'un(e) camarade. Travaillez ensemble pour faire un seul dialogue, puis jouez ce dialogue.

Communication for All Students

Game

J'en doute Form two teams. On the board, a player from one team writes a vocabulary expression **(en laine)** that an opposing player from the other team must use correctly in a sentence. **(En hiver, j'aime mettre des jupes en laine.)** If the opposing player doesn't know the meaning, he or she might try to bluff the other team by making up a sentence. The player at the board has the option of calling the opposing player's bluff by saying **J'en doute.** If the opposing player can't give the English definition of the word or expression, the challenger's team receives two points. If the opposing player can give the correct definition, however, they lose a point.

Quel est ton style de vêtements préféré?

We asked people for their ideas on fashion and personal style. Here's what they had to say.

Mélanie,
Québec

«Moi, c'est un bon gilet, puis un jean(s), c'est toujours ça que je porte. Des fois, je peux porter d'autres sortes de pantalons, pas de jeans, mais... un bon chandail et puis je suis bien là-dedans. Il faut que je sois confortable. Si je ne suis pas confortable, je ne le porterai pas.» Tr. 7

Sylviane,
Martinique

«J'aime surtout les vêtements... j'aime surtout les matières. J'aime beaucoup le coton, le lin, les matières naturelles, parce que, bon, on vit dans un pays où il fait très chaud et il faut pouvoir supporter la chaleur. Et j'aime beaucoup aussi les couleurs, parce que bon, je vis dans un pays ensoleillé, donc les couleurs sont des choses très importantes.»

Est-ce que c'est important d'être à la mode?

«Oui, c'est important d'être à la mode, parce que, bon, nous en Martinique, on a quand même ce côté un petit peu français et européen où on aime beaucoup les vêtements et on aime beaucoup se montrer.» Tr. 8

Céline,
Viêt-nam

«J'aime tout ce qui est hors du commun. Enfin... qui est pas tellement banal mais qui... qu'on peut pas voir tous les jours, quoi.»

Est-ce que c'est important d'être à la mode?

«Ça dépend. Je veux dire... Il y a certaines filles qui s'habillent mais qui n'ont rien à l'intérieur, qui n'ont pas un esprit très beau à l'intérieur. C'est pas très beau à l'intérieur. Donc, elles ont besoin de bien s'habiller. Mais enfin, ça dépend.» Tr. 9

Qu'en penses-tu?

1. Avec qui est-ce que tu es d'accord? Pourquoi?   2. See answers below.
2. Quelles raisons ces personnes donnent pour expliquer leur opinion de la mode?
3. Est-ce que tu penses que c'est important de suivre la dernière mode? Pourquoi ou pourquoi pas?

Teaching Resources
p. 103

PRINT
▶ Video Guide, pp. 23, 25
▶ Cahier d'activités, p. 48

MEDIA
▶ One-Stop Planner
▶ Video Program
  Videocassette 2, 06:40–11:30
▶ Audio Compact Discs, CD 4,
  Trs. 6–9
▶ Interactive CD-ROM Tutor, Disc 1

Presenting
Panorama Culturel

Before you play the video, have students suggest expressions they expect to hear. After each interview, ask **Quel est son style de vêtements préféré?** Ask the **Questions** below to check comprehension.

Questions

1. **Qu'est-ce que Mélanie aime mettre?** (un bon gilet et un jean, un bon chandail)
2. **Quelles matières est-ce que Sylviane aime?** (le coton, le lin, les matières naturelles)
3. **Pourquoi est-ce que Céline croit que certaines filles ont besoin de bien s'habiller?** (Elles n'ont pas un esprit très beau à l'intérieur.)

Answers
2. Mélanie likes to be comfortable. For Sylviane, natural materials and fabric color are important. In Martinique, they share a sense of fashion with Europeans. Céline likes to wear unusual clothing. She feels that some people dress well to make up for what they're lacking inside.

Connections and Comparisons

Thinking Critically
Analyzing Ask students **Est-ce que c'est important d'être à la mode?**

Teaching Suggestion
Ask students which interviewee they agree with most closely. Then, have them form small groups and discuss their answers to the questions in

Qu'en penses-tu? You might do a survey of the class before organizing the groups. Ask **Qui est d'accord avec Mélanie? Qui est d'accord avec Sylviane? Qui est d'accord avec Céline?** Then organize the groups so that each opinion is represented in each group.

Teaching Resources
pp. 104–105

PRINT
▸ Lesson Planner, p. 19
▸ Video Guide, pp. 22, 24
▸ Cahier d'activités, p. 42

MEDIA
▸ One-Stop Planner
▸ Video Program
   Camille et compagnie
   Videocassette 2, 00:50–06:36
   Videocassette 5 (captioned version), 20:50–26:36
▸ Audio Compact Discs, CD 4, Tr. 10

Presenting
Remise en train

Have students look at the photos on pages 104 and 105 and guess what the girls are talking about. Play the audio recording, pausing after each section to ask the related comprehension questions in Activity 21.

Remise en train ▪ *Chacun son style!*

CD 4 Tr. 10

Perrine	Oh, ça va être super ce soir!
Larissa	Je parie que Loïc va venir...
Perrine	Je crois pas! Il déteste le heavy metal.
Larissa	Ah oui, c'est vrai. Il est tellement B.C.B.G., tu trouves pas?
Perrine	Eh! Tu penses que je devrais mettre du mascara?
Larissa	Mmm... non. C'est trop tape-à-l'œil.
Perrine	Ah! Et mon rouge à lèvres orange, tu le trouves trop tape-à-l'œil aussi?
Larissa	Je ne sais pas, moi. Qu'est-ce que tu mets?
Perrine	Ben, soit ma mini-jupe noire avec un débardeur vert, soit ma robe violette.

21 **Tu as compris?**   See answers below.

1. De quoi parlent Perrine et Larissa?
2. Pour quelle occasion est-ce qu'elles se préparent?
3. Comment est-ce qu'elles se préparent?
4. Pourquoi est-ce que Perrine a changé de coiffure?
5. Est-ce que Larissa aime la nouvelle coiffure de Perrine?

22 **Vrai ou faux?**

1. Perrine et Larissa se préparent à sortir.   vrai
2. Larissa a déjà choisi ce qu'elle va mettre pour aller au concert.   faux
3. Les stylistes de Biguine ne font pas de coupes bizarres.   faux
4. Perrine s'est fait couper les cheveux comme d'habitude.   faux
5. Perrine va mettre sa mini-jupe noire avec son débardeur vert.   faux

23 **Choisis le bon mot**

Complète chaque phrase avec l'expression qui convient.   See answers below.

1. Larissa trouve le mascara de Perrine trop ▬▬▬ .
2. Perrine veut mettre du ▬▬▬ orange pour aller avec sa robe violette.
3. Larissa va emprunter ▬▬▬ de Perrine.
4. Les cheveux de Perrine sont ▬▬▬ et ▬▬▬ .
5. Chez Biguine, il y avait un garçon aux cheveux ▬▬▬ .

tape-à-l'œil	frisés
verts	l'ombre à paupières
rouge à lèvres	orange

These activities check for comprehension only. Students should not yet be expected to produce language modeled in **Remise en train.**

Answers

21 1. the evening to come, hair styles and make-up
2. heavy metal concert
3. putting on make-up, picking out clothes
4. She saw other clients getting wild haircuts.
5. yes

23 1. tape-à-l'œil
2. rouge à lèvres
3. l'ombre à paupières
4. frisés, orange
5. verts

Preteaching Vocabulary

Using Prior Knowledge
Tell students that, in this conversation, Perrine and Larissa are talking about what to wear to a concert. Have students skim through the text for words and expressions they already know. Have them give you the words they recognize as they read the text. Once they have identified the meaning of the words and phrases, have them guess how they're used in this scene. You might suggest that they look at the photos for context.

super	*great*
mini-jupe	*miniskirt*
robe	*dress*
violette	*purple*
orange	*orange*
vert	*green*

Larissa	Alors, je dirais le rouge à lèvres orange si tu mets ta robe violette. Et moi? Je me demande ce que je vais mettre... Oh, dis donc! Elle est géniale, ton ombre à paupières!
Perrine	Tu peux l'emprunter, si tu veux.
Larissa	Merci. Décidément, j'aime vraiment tes cheveux comme ça!
Perrine	Tu crois? Je suis allée chez Biguine hier. Je voulais juste me faire couper les cheveux comme d'habitude. Mais quand j'ai vu les autres clients! Ils avaient des coupes dingues!
Larissa	Ah oui?
Perrine	Ouais. Il y en avait une qui avait les cheveux tondus d'un côté, et longs et raides de l'autre. Un autre avait une coupe à la Mohawk.
Larissa	C'est pas vrai!
Perrine	Je te jure! Et il avait même les cheveux teints en vert.
Larissa	Et c'est pour ça que tu as décidé de te faire friser et teindre en orange?
Perrine	Ben oui. Tu es sûre que c'est pas trop bizarre?

Larissa	Mais non! L'orange te va très bien!
Perrine	Ouais! Justement, j'ai pensé que ça irait bien avec mon rouge à lèvres et avec ma robe violette.

Cahier d'activités, p. 42, Act. 10–11

24 Cherche les expressions

In *Chacun son style!*, what expressions do Perrine and Larissa use to . . . See answers below.

1. tell who they think will be at the concert?
2. ask for advice?
3. ask for an opinion?
4. give an opinion?
5. pay a compliment?
6. respond to a compliment?
7. express disbelief?
8. reassure a friend?

Note culturelle

En général, les Français ont tendance à s'habiller simplement et avec une touche personnelle. Les femmes et les jeunes filles ne se maquillent pas toujours et elles ont tendance à préférer les coiffures simples. Elles ne portent pas beaucoup de bijoux. Quand une femme porte de grosses boucles d'oreilles, elle porte rarement un bracelet ou un collier imposant. En général, les hommes ont aussi un style sobre et portent rarement de grosses bagues et des ceintures à grosses boucles.

25 Et maintenant, à toi

Quelle coupe de cheveux est-ce que tu préfères? Est-ce que tu as l'air plus ou moins sérieux(-euse) que les jeunes dans *Chacun son style!?*

Thinking Critically
25 Comparing and Contrasting Have students compare the hair styles shown with those they admire. Ask them to characterize the hair styles in the **Remise en train** as well as other styles they like.

Language Note
You might point out that the adjective **tondu** *(shaved)* comes from the verb **tondre** *(to shave, to mow).*

Camille et compagnie
As an alternative or in addition to the **Remise en train,** you may wish to show Episode 4 of *Camille et compagnie.* For suggestions and activities, see the *Video Guide.*

Answers
24
1. Je parie que... va venir.
2. Tu penses que je devrais... ?
3. Mon rouge à lèvres orange, tu le trouves trop tape-à-l'œil... ? Tu es sûre que c'est pas trop bizarre?
4. Ça va être super ce soir! C'est trop tape-à-l'œil.
5. Elle est géniale, ton ombre à paupières! Décidément, j'aime vraiment tes cheveux comme ça!
6. Tu crois?
7. C'est pas vrai!
8. Mais non! L'orange te va très bien!

Comprehension Check

Challenge
Give transparencies to small groups and have them write several multiple-choice test items about the **Remise en train,** such as **Perrine est allée... (a) au restaurant; (b) à un concert de heavy metal; (c) se faire couper les cheveux; (d) dans un grand magasin.** Collect the transparencies, project them, and have the class choose the appropriate answers.

Challenge
22 Have students find the phrases in the dialogue that contradict the **faux** statements. **(2. Je me demande ce que je vais mettre. 3. Ils avaient des coupes dingues! 4. ... tu as décidé de te faire friser et teindre en orange? 5. ... ça irait bien... avec ma robe violette.)**

Objectives Paying and responding to compliments; reassuring someone

WA3 FRANCOPHONE EUROPE-4

Teaching Resources
pp. 106–109

PRINT 📖
▸ Lesson Planner, p. 20
▸ Listening Activities, pp. 29, 32–33
▸ Activities for Communication, pp. 15–16, 61–62, 95–96
▸ Travaux pratiques de grammaire, pp. 38–40
▸ Grammar Tutor for Students of French, Chapter 4
▸ Cahier d'activités, pp. 43–46
▸ Testing Program, pp. 71–74
▸ Alternative Assessment Guide, p. 33
▸ Student Make-Up Assignments, Chapter 4

MEDIA 💿📹💻
▸ One-Stop Planner
▸ Audio Compact Discs, CD 4, Trs. 11–12, 15, 22–24
▸ Teaching Transparencies: 4-2; **Grammaire supplémentaire** Answers; Travaux pratiques de grammaire Answers
▸ Interactive CD-ROM Tutor, Disc 1

Bell Work

Display a picture of a person with an unusual haircut. Have students use vocabulary they just learned to give their opinion of the hairstyle. (**C'est ringard/délirant.**)

Presenting
Vocabulaire

Bring in pictures of different types of haircuts. Hold up each picture, name the style, and have students repeat. Next, have two volunteers come to the board. Give the name of a hairstyle. The first student to draw the hairstyle correctly takes the next turn naming a hairstyle for two new volunteers. Continue until all the vocabulary items have been drawn.

Vocabulaire

- la frange
- les cheveux frisés
- les cheveux courts
- les cheveux longs et raides
- une queue de cheval
- une moustache
- la coiffeuse (le coiffeur)
- une coupe
- un shampooing
- les cheveux en brosse

une barbe	*a beard*	**(se faire)**	*(to give yourself)*
les cheveux teints	*dyed/colored hair*	**une permanente**	*a perm*
un chignon	*a bun*	**se friser**	*to curl (hair)*
une coupe au carré	*a square cut*	**se maquiller**	*to put on make-up*
une natte	*a braid*	**se raser**	*to shave*
des pattes	*sideburns*	**se teindre**	*to dye (hair)*

Travaux pratiques de grammaire, pp. 38–39, Act. 18–21 | Cahier d'activités, pp. 43–44, Act. 12–15

26 **Chez le coiffeur** — See scripts and answers on p. 91H.

Ecoutons Qui dit chacune des phrases suivantes, le coiffeur ou le client/la cliente? CD 4 Tr. 11

27 **Voilà ma famille**

Parlons Dominique te montre une photo de sa famille. Demande-lui qui sont les gens sur la photo. Joue cette scène avec ton/ta camarade.

EXEMPLE —C'est qui, cette femme?
—Laquelle?
—Celle aux cheveux...
—C'est ma...

Si tu as oublié family vocabulary va à la page R17

Communication for All Students

Slower Pace

27 Before students begin, write **C'est qui, cette femme/cet homme?** on the board and have them give the interrogative and demonstrative pronouns they would use to respond.

Additional Practice

Bring magazine photos representing families. Organize students in groups of three or four. Give a photo to one student in each group. He or she will pretend that this is his or her family. Other students ask him or her questions on the model of Activity 27.

The causative *faire*

- If you want to say that you are *having something done*, use the verb **faire** with the *infinitive* of the verb that tells what you are having done.

Je **fais nettoyer** mon costume.
I'm having my suit cleaned.

Elle **a fait réparer** ses bottes.
She had her boots repaired.

- If the verb that tells what you are having done is reflexive, place the *reflexive pronoun* before the verb **faire**.

Je **me fais couper** les cheveux. (**se couper**)
I'm having my hair cut.

Il **s'est fait raser** la moustache. (**se raser**)
He had his mustache shaved.

Tu vas **te faire friser?** (**se friser**)
Are you going to get your hair curled?

> Travaux pratiques de grammaire, p. 40, Act. 22–23

> Grammaire supplémentaire, pp. 116–117, Act. 4–7

> Cahier d'activités, p. 45, Act. 16

28 **Grammaire en contexte**

Parlons Qu'est-ce que M. Mouchet fait faire aujourd'hui?

1.
Il se fait couper les cheveux.

2.
Il fait nettoyer ses vêtements.

3.
Il fait vérifier l'huile de sa voiture.

4.
Il fait tondre sa pelouse.

29 **Grammaire en contexte**

Parlons Ton ami(e) va chez le coiffeur mais ne sait pas comment il/elle veut se faire coiffer. Donne-lui des conseils. Ensuite, changez de rôle.

EXEMPLE
—Qu'est-ce que tu en penses, toi?
—Tu devrais te faire couper les cheveux en brosse.

se couper les cheveux
se friser
se raser la barbe
se teindre
se faire une permanente

A la française

You've already learned that French speakers drop certain words and letters when they speak informally.

C'est pas vrai! J'le trouve hyper-cool!
Je crois pas! T'as pas l'temps?

They also tend to run certain syllables and words together. Look at the pronunciation of these common phrases:

/shai pa/	(Je ne sais pas.)
/y'en a/	(Il y en a.)
/kes tu/	(Qu'est-ce que tu... ?)
/wes que tu/	(Où est-ce que tu... ?)
/ifait/	(Il fait...)

Remember, though, that it is not correct to write this way.

Connections and Comparisons

Language-to-Language

Ask students to think of idiomatic expressions in English that have to do with hair, such as *to split hairs* and *a hair-raising experience*. French and Spanish (**el pelo**) also have idioms involving hair. For example, in French, *to split hairs* is **couper les cheveux en quatre**. In Spanish, **tomarle el pelo a alguien** (literally, *to take someone's hair*)

translates in English as *to pull someone's leg*. Ask students if they can determine the meaning of these expressions: **tiré par les cheveux** *(farfetched)*, **se me pusieron los pelos de punta** *(hair-raising)*. You might also have students speculate about the origin of some of these expressions.

Presenting Grammaire

The causative faire Have students suggest in French services that can be done by a professional. Write their suggestions (**nettoyer ses vêtements**) on strips of transparency with a red pen. Then, call on six students to write the forms of the verb **faire** with a blue pen on strips of transparency. Write the subject pronouns in green on a third set of strips. Then, call on a student to use one strip of each color to form a sentence. (**Il fait nettoyer ses vêtements.**) Repeat the process until all the verbs have been used. (Note: If the verb is reflexive, students will have to place the reflexive pronoun before the form of **faire**.)

Using the Video Program

A la française Have students watch *C'est tout à fait toi!* from *Camille et compagnie* and raise their hands when they hear examples of informal speech.

Language Notes

- Tell students that when you say you've had something done, the past participle of **faire** will not show agreement. (**Elle s'est fait couper les cheveux.**)

- You might also explain that the person performing the service can be specified by using **par** followed by the person: **Je me suis fait couper les cheveux par ma sœur.**

Additional Practice

28 Have students rewrite the sentences as if they were having each service done. (**Je me fais couper les cheveux.**)

Teaching Resources
pp. 106–109

PRINT
▸ Lesson Planner, p. 20
▸ Listening Activities, pp. 29, 32–33
▸ Activities for Communication, pp. 15–16, 61–62, 95–96
▸ Travaux pratiques de grammaire, pp. 38–40
▸ Grammar Tutor for Students of French, Chapter 4
▸ Cahier d'activités, pp. 43–46
▸ Testing Program, pp. 71–74
▸ Alternative Assessment Guide, p. 33
▸ Student Make-Up Assignments, Chapter 4

MEDIA
▸ One-Stop Planner
▸ Audio Compact Discs, CD 4, Trs. 11–12, 15, 22–24
▸ Teaching Transparencies: 4-2; **Grammaire supplémentaire** Answers; Travaux pratiques de grammaire Answers
▸ Interactive CD-ROM Tutor, Disc 1

Presenting
Comment dit-on... ?

Write the expressions in random order on a transparency and use them to compliment students' clothing. After students respond to the compliments, reassure them, using the new expressions. Draw three columns on the board and label them with the **Comment dit-on...?** categories. Then, call on students to choose expressions from the transparency and to write them under the appropriate heading.

Answers

30 a. Avant : Elle a les cheveux longs et raides. Après : Elle a une coupe dégradée. Avant : Elle porte un chemisier blanc. Après : Elle porte un pull noir.

---

30 **Mannequin d'un jour**  See answers below.

Lis cet article et fais les activités suivantes.

a. **Lisons** Associe les mots AVANT et APRES à ces phrases.

Elle porte un chemisier blanc.

Elle a une coupe dégradée.

Elle porte un pull noir.

Elle a les cheveux longs et raides.

b. **Ecrivons** Maintenant, imagine que tu es un/une des stylistes de **Mannequin d'un jour.** Tu n'aimes pas le look qui a été conseillé à Liliane. Ecris un paragraphe dans lequel tu suggères une autre coupe de cheveux et d'autres vêtements pour Liliane.

AVANT

Les cheveux raides avec peu de volume, une peau fine et fragile.

PREMIERE ETAPE

LA COUPE DE CHEVEUX

Les cheveux de Liliane sont coupés sur une base de carré. Ils sont ensuite effilés tout autour de son visage. La frange est dégradée pour donner un effet déstructuré à l'ensemble de la coiffure (Coiffure réalisée par Arnaud pour Franck Provost)

DEUXIEME ETAPE

LE MAQUILLAGE

Application d'une poudre libre abricot pour faire ressortir son teint. Ses sourcils sont redessinés au crayon. Ensuite, pour agrandir son regard, pose d'un crayon noir sur les paupières supérieures et inférieures, avec une touche de mascara noir sur les cils supérieurs. Avec, pour la touche finale, un blush framboise coordonné au rouge à lèvres.

APRES

Un caleçon noir avec un petit pull chaussette très mode, et des bottines coordonnées (Vêtements et chaussures offerts par La Blanche Porte).

Comment dit-on...?

Paying and responding to compliments; reassuring someone

To pay a compliment:

> **Je te trouve très bien comme ça.**
> **Ça fait très bien.**
> **C'est tout à fait toi.**
> **Ça va avec tes yeux.**
> **Ça te va comme un gant.**
> *It fits you like a glove.*
> **Que tu es jolie avec ça!**
> *You really look . . . in that!*
> **C'est assorti à ton pull.**
> *That matches . . .*

To respond to a compliment:

> **Ça te plaît vraiment?**
> **Tu crois?**
> **C'est gentil.**
> **Oh, c'est un vieux truc.**
> *This old thing?*
> **Oh, tu sais, je ne l'ai pas payé(e) cher.**

To reassure someone:

> **Crois-moi,** c'est tout à fait toi.
> **Je t'assure,** c'est réussi. *Really, . . .*
> **Fais-moi confiance,** c'est très classe.
> *Trust me, . . .*

> **Je ne dis pas ça pour te faire plaisir.**
> *I'm not just saying that.*

Grammaire supplémentaire, p. 116, Act. 5

Cahier d'activités, pp. 45–46, Act. 17–20

---

31 **Tu crois?** See scripts and answers on p. 91H.

Ecoutons Ecoute ces conversations. Est-ce que ces gens répondent à un compliment ou est-ce qu'ils rassurent quelqu'un?

CD 4 Tr. 12

Communication for All Students

Building on Previous Skills

30 After students have answered **avant** or **après** for each item, have them write before-and-after sentences, using the **imparfait** and the present tense. (**Avant, elle avait les cheveux longs et raides. Maintenant, elle a une coupe dégradée.**)

Building on Previous Skills

Have students recall expressions for paying and responding to compliments in French. (**C'est tout à fait ton style. Il/Elle va très bien avec... ; Tu trouves?**)

32 On bavarde!

Lisons Mets en ordre les éléments de chacune des conversations que tu entends à cette boum.

a. Oui, elle te plaît? 2
Ah, tu t'es acheté une nouvelle jupe? 1
Je la trouve jolie. Elle va bien avec ton chemisier. 3
C'est gentil. Tu sais, je ne l'ai pas payée cher. 4

b. Euh, non. 2
En tout cas, c'est tout à fait toi! 3
Moi, je te trouve très bien comme ça. 5
Dis donc, il est nouveau, ton coupe-vent? 1
Oh, c'est un vieux truc. 4

c. Tu crois? 4
Oui, ça me va comment? 2
Dis-moi, tu t'es maquillée! 1
Je t'assure, ça va bien avec tes yeux. 5
Ça te va très bien. 3

d. Ah oui? 4
Tiens, tu es allée chez le coiffeur! 1
Ça te va très bien. 3
Comment tu trouves? 2
Je t'assure, c'est tout à fait toi. 5

e. Ça va avec ton style. 3
Oui. Qu'en penses-tu? 2
Vraiment? 4
Tu t'es fait couper les cheveux? 1
Fais-moi confiance, c'est très réussi. 5

33 Un nouveau look

a. **Parlons** Ton/ta camarade te téléphone pour te dire qu'il/elle s'est fait couper les cheveux. Il/Elle te raconte son rendez-vous chez le coiffeur.

b. **Parlons** Tu rencontres ton/ta camarade. Tu lui fais des compliments sur sa coupe de cheveux. Tu dois le/la rassurer parce qu'il/elle n'est pas certain(e) qu'il/elle aime ce nouveau style.

34 De l'école au travail

Parlons Imagine that you work as an intern on the set of a TV talk show. You are responsible for taking care of the guests and making sure they are comfortable before their appearance on the show. One of the guests is a famous French actress who is nervous about her appearance and asks for your opinion of what she's wearing. She shows you different outfits and asks which ones you prefer. Offer her reassurance and tell her which outfit you think she should wear and why. Act out this scene with your partner, then switch roles.

Connections and Comparisons

Thinking Critically

32 Comparing and Contrasting Ask students if the expressions they learned in this chapter reflect exchanges that would take place in their community. Do they see any difference between what the French and Americans say to compliment one another and to respond to compliments? Have them elaborate on their responses. Their answers might vary based on their social and ethnical backgrounds. Remind students that the French generally tend to downplay compliments. Expressions like **C'est un vieux truc** and **Je ne l'ai pas payé(e) cher** might not be as commonly used in the United States.

Teaching Suggestion

33 Have students write out these dialogues. They might exchange papers with a partner for editing and then turn in the final copy.

Speaking Assessment

34 You might use the following rubric when grading your students on this activity.

Speaking Rubric	Points			
	4	3	2	1
Content (Complete–Incomplete)				
Comprehension (Total–Little)				
Comprehensibility (Comprehensible–Incomprehensible)				
Accuracy (Accurate–Seldom accurate)				
Fluency (Fluent–Not fluent)				

18–20: A   14–15: C   Under
16–17: B   12–13: D   12: F

Teaching Suggestion
You might play the game **Chasse au trésor**, described on page 91C.

Assess

▶ Testing Program, pp. 71–74
Quiz 4-2A, Quiz 4-2B,
Audio CD 4, Tr. 15

▶ Student Make-Up Assignments, Chapter 4, Alternative Quiz

▶ Alternative Assessment Guide, p. 33

Lisons!

Teaching Resources
pp. 110–112

PRINT
▸ Lesson Planner, p. 21
▸ Cahier d'activités, p. 47
▸ Reading Strategies and Skills Handbook, Chapter 4
▸ Joie de lire 3, Chapter 4
▸ Standardized Assessment Tutor, Chapter 4

MEDIA
▸ One-Stop Planner

Prereading
Activities A–C

Using Prior Knowledge
Ask students for their opinion of high fashion (**haute couture**) and if they have ever been to a fashion show or seen one on TV. Ask them if they would like to wear fashions by famous designers. Have them list words and expressions that they associate with high fashion.

Teaching Suggestions
A–C. You might do these activities as a class and then have pairs or groups do the remaining activities.

Answers
A. fashion; a French designer
B. kinds of clothing, fabrics, colors, sizes, textures
C. **Haute couture** (high fashion, very expensive, high quality); **Prêt-à-porter** (ready-to-wear, high quality, off the rack, less expensive than **haute couture**); **Bazar** (a mixture of styles and influences)
D. general description of collection; specific designs

CHRISTIAN LACROIX
COLLECTION
HAUTE-COUTURE
AUTOMNE-HIVER

«Il y a incontestablement chez moi l'envie d'un vêtement net, épuré, structuré. Après les formes souples de ces dernières saisons, la mode se reconstruit. Les hanches sont dessinées, la taille étranglée avec des corselets. La jupe-cloche s'évase pour donner à la silhouette une forme sablier que souligne encore le retour de l'épaule. Bref, un structuré léger, qui ne verse jamais dans la roideur, et dont les matières très élaborées, les ornements, les détails de broderies servent encore à gommer tout ce qu'il pourrait avoir d'autoritaire. Tout en ayant le sentiment de demeurer fidèle à moi-même, cette collection me paraît à des années-lumière de l'an passé.»

HAUTE-COUTURE
AUTOMNE-HIVER

DIX
Trois-quart silhouetté en satin jade. Sweater en plumes rouges et roses. Jupe en velours incarnat.

ONZE
Veste cintrée en tweed artisanal bleu, bordeaux et argent à poignets de renard rouge. T-shirt en crêpe cyclamen brodé d'un collier trompe-l'œil. Jupe en velours pourpre.

DOUZE
Veste-corset en tissage artisanal pourpre et mordoré à poignets brodés. Pantalon masculin en lainage marine fileté de rouge.

PRET-A-PORTER
AUTOMNE-HIVER

QUARANTE-TROIS
Bustier en patches de maille et dentelle naturelle. Jupe longue en dentelle noire et or.

QUARANTE-QUATRE
Parka en cuir noir argenté à parements de Mongolie et brodé d'ex-votos. Mini-jupe de dentelle argent sur fuseau de velours noir à bandes dorées.

QUARANTE-CINQ
Parka en cuir «platine».

QUARANTE-SIX
Veste trapèze gansée à motifs de chenille «cœurs» noir et blanc. Liquette et pantalon large en crêpe imprimé «d'étoile» coordonné.

Stratégie pour lire
If a reading seems difficult at first, you can use your deductive reasoning skills to develop meaning. Start with a word you know and use it to figure out the words and phrases around it. How are they related to the familiar word? Do they modify it, like an adjective or adverb ? Do they show its action, like a verb? Once you understand whole phrases, link them together into longer passages. By building on what you know, you can turn a difficult reading into something coherent and understandable.

For Activities A–D, see answers below.

A. What is this reading selection about? Who is Christian Lacroix?

B. What kind of vocabulary do you expect to find in this type of reading?

C. What are the names of the three collections of clothing? What do the names suggest about the type of clothing you would find in each collection?

D. On pages 110 and 111, what information do you find in the paragraphs? In the short, numbered items?

Cultures and Communities

Culture Note
Christian Lacroix has never studied fashion. He is an art historian who, as a child, loved to sketch the traditional costumes of his hometown, Arles. Throughout his career, Lacroix has believed that fashion should be colorful and fun, even foolish, and should never be taken too seriously.

Career Path
French fashion shows vary from informal parades to grandiose runway events. A formal show might include original music scores, creative lighting, and specialized stage sets. Department stores have more intimate fashion shows. Ask students which languages they think would be useful to learn if they were to work in the fashion industry.

STANDARDS: 1.2, 2.2, 3.1

PRET-A-PORTER
AUTOMNE-HIVER

QUATRE-VINGT-TROIS
Caraco de taffetas «chaîne» fleuri bleu pastel brodé d'or et bordé de dentelle noire.

QUATRE-VINGT-QUATRE
Sweater de maille artisanale orné d'arabesques de gomme cuivrée et empierrée. Jupe de taffetas orange à fleurs chinoises sur jupon de taffetas à carreaux.

QUATRE-VINGT-CINQ
Bustier de maille artisanale orné d'arabesques de gomme cuivrée et empierrée à manches et basques de mousseline rousse. Jupe à trois étages en patches de taffetas bordé de dentelle.

BAZAR
AUTOMNE-HIVER

SEPT
Blouson en satin imper à col de peau lainée. Gilet XVIIIᵉ en peau lainée. Pull ras-du-cou en shetland. Jeans surteint.

HUIT
Coupe-vent en satin imper. Veste de gardian en velours gansé. Gilet de gardian en velours gansé. Chemise cintrée en jean. Jupon en madras de laine.

NEUF
Mini-blouson en satin imper et gilet de peau lainée. Gilet en shetland rayé. Col roulé en shetland rayé. Jupon en madras de laine contrasté.

BAZAR DE CHRISTIAN LACROIX
AUTOMNE-HIVER

«Cette collection «Bazar» n'a pas été pensée comme une ligne secondaire, «bis» ou «ter» mais comme une ligne complémentaire à la fois «autonome» et faite pour coexister avec le Prêt-à-Porter et même la Couture (une cliente de Haute-Couture vient souvent faire ses essayages en jeans et en T-shirt : autant qu'ils viennent de chez nous !) et pourquoi pas imaginer, ce n'est pas pour moi une utopie, une femme dont la tenue serait composée d'éléments des trois lignes confondues (Haute-Couture, Prêt-à-Porter et Bazar). Enfin, en tant que styliste, je ressentais le besoin de préparer le prochain millénaire en prouvant que la Maison Christian Lacroix, symbolique des années 80 qui l'ont vue naître, pouvait avoir sa propre version des années 90 et 2000, parler à la rue sans rien perdre de ses racines (le Sud, le métissage des cultures, l'histoire revisitée, toujours d'actualité).»

E. Lequel de ces adjectifs n'est pas utilisé par Christian Lacroix pour décrire sa collection de Haute Couture?

> net
> structuré
> souple
> léger
> élaboré
> autoritaire

F. How does Lacroix feel about clothing from his three lines being worn together?

They can be worn separately or combined.

G. Can you tell which descriptions match the outfits in the four sketches? *See answers below.*

H. How would you describe these clothes? *See answers below.*

> jupe en velours pourpre
> sweater de plumes
> parka en cuir noir
> mini-jupe de dentelle
> argent
> veste trapèze
> jupe à trois étages

I. What kind of information is given on page 112? *See answers below.*

J. Give examples of what elements make up the look of each of Lacroix's lines. *See answers below.*

Communication for All Students

Challenge
H. Form small groups. Type the French descriptions of the articles of clothing listed in this activity and distribute copies to students. Next to each item, have them list one additional article of clothing that is part of the same outfit. For example, next to **jupe en velours pourpre**, they might write **tee-shirt en crêpe cyclamen brodé.**

Language Notes
• **Haute couture,** or *high fashion,* refers to exclusive designs, usually very expensive and custom-tailored for patrons. **Prêt-à-porter,** or *ready-to-wear* clothing, is more affordable and available in stores.
• The term **bis,** used in the opening quotation for the **Bazar** line, means *twice.* It is also used in addresses to indicate two parts: **12** is *12A,* **12 bis** is *12B.* **12 ter** is *12C.*

Reading
Activities D–M

Teaching Suggestion
F. Have small groups read Lacroix's comments on the **Bazar** collection. Then, ask them the following questions: What does Lacroix think of this line? (It is complementary to his other lines.) What does he consider to be at the root of all his designs? (the South, multiculturalism, history revisited)

Terms in Lisons!
Students might want to know the following words from the reading: **taille** *(waist);* **épaule** *(shoulder);* **léger** *(light);* **mordoré** *(bronze);* **dentelle** *(lace);* **racines** *(roots).*

Answers
G. Sketch 1: onze
Sketch 2: quarante-quatre
Sketch 3: quatre-vingt-quatre
Sketch 4: neuf

H. purple velvet skirt, feathered sweater, black leather parka, silver lace mini-skirt, trapezoid jacket, three-tiered skirt

I. examples of the styles, fabrics, decorations, motifs, materials, and accessories that were used in the three lines of clothing and Lacroix's characterization of his average client

J. *Possible answers:*
Haute couture : *Formes* - vestes cintrées, épaulées et parfois corsetées; *Accessoires* - variations sur les chapeaux d'homme; *Ornements* - plumes, fourrures et dorures; *Matières* - cachemire, tweeds artisanaux et plumes
Prêt-à-porter : *Tissus* - mohair, rayures masculines; *Formes* - manteaux folkloriques trenches, parkas ethniques; *Accessoires* - chapeaux composites, bijoux ethniques; *Motifs* - Carreaux et rayures, tartans
Bazar : *Accessoires* - chapeaux de cuir et bérets jacquard, gants tricotés ou imprimés; *Matières* - du nylon matelassé ou non, du drap caban; *Chaussures* - bottes hautes lacées à bouts ronds en cuir frappé chocolat ou noir, Richelieux à semelle crantée et talon bobine en cuir frappé

CHAPITRE 4

Building on Previous Skills

L. Have students use their background knowledge to try to guess the meanings of the following words: **automnaux** *(fall);* **tressés** *(braided);* **fleuri** *(flowered);* **chinoises** *(Chinese);* **rayé** *(striped);* **vieilli** *(aged).*

Postreading

Activity N

Thinking Critically

N. Analyzing Ask students whether they agree with Christian Lacroix's definition of elegance. Ask them how they would define elegance. Have them name celebrities or other people they consider elegant.

COLLECTION HAUTE-COUTURE

FORMES
Vestes cintrées, épaulées et parfois corsetées, longues, silhouettées ou même étriquées. Jupes «trapèze», «cloche» ou ondulées. Quelques pantalons. Tuniques fluides, robes souples et corolles architecturées pour le cocktail, grandes jupes libres ou crinolines craquantes à minces hauts très précieux le soir, quelques fourreaux.

ORNEMENTS
Plumes, fourrures et dorures. Patches, pochoirs et peintures. Tubes, paillettes et sequins de music-hall, night-club et fête foraine dégradés, nacrés et irisés. Broderies orientalisantes.

ACCESSOIRES
Variations sur les chapeaux d'homme. Bijoux composites autour du cou. Sacs minuscules en bandoulière. Bottes, richelieux et sandales.

MATIERES
Cachemire, tweeds artisanaux et plumes, maille enrichie, jerseys enluminés et velours travaillés. Faille froissée, satin duchesse et brocarts métallisés. Dentelles toujours. Soies peintes, ombrées ou changeantes.

Q : Quelles sont les qualités que vous revendiquez chez les femmes qui sont fidèles au style Lacroix ?
C.L. : La liberté qu'elles prennent d'être différentes. Ma cliente n'est pas de celles qui cherchent à passer inaperçues. Elle étonne, elle détone, elle choque, au meilleur sens du terme. Parce qu'avant tout, elle est libre. Sans doute nous inscrivons-nous dans une évolution générale de la mode. Il me semble cependant qu'aujourd'hui les notions de passé, de présent, de futur sont dépourvues de signification. Le mot contemporain a bien vieilli en ce qui concerne le goût. Désormais, l'élégance la plus pointue mélange toutes les époques, tous les styles, toutes les catégories de vêtements, et même les catégories de prix.

PRET-A-PORTER

TISSUS
Mohair, tweeds artisanaux, rayures masculines, écossais, velours vieilli ou frappé d'or, crêpes, tulles de laine et georgette imprimés, satin damassé oriental, soies reliéfées, mousseline ombrée, taffetas «chaîne», cuirs platines ou pyrogravés, fausse fourrure et dentelles métalliques.

ACCESSOIRES
Chapeaux composites, bijoux ethniques, collants-dentelles, étoles patchworks, «guillies», boots et escarpins à talons aiguilles, ornements de cheveux, clous, ex-votos, passementeries, arabesques d'or et de sequins, motifs de gomme cuivrée empierrée.

FORMES
Manteaux folkloriques trenches, parkas ethniques, vestes étriquées, cardigans «historiques», smokings en patchworks de noirs, panoplies militaires, mini-kilts ou maxi-jupes «châlet», les robes sont des tuniques et parfois des maillots du soir.

MOTIFS
Carreaux et rayures, tartans, cachemires et fleurs géantes, peaux de bête et camouflage, bouquets chinois, tapis et tapisseries, pochoirs de dentelle.

BAZAR

ACCESSOIRES
Chapeaux de cuir et bérets jacquard, gants tricotés ou imprimés, gourmettes, bracelets, sautoirs, boucles d'oreilles, pendentifs et boutons de manchettes «Lettres, croix et clochettes», jambières et collants-dentelles, ceintures, «colliers-de-chien» et «poignets-de-force» en peau lainée, mouchoirs à breloques.

MATIERES
Du nylon matelassé ou non, du drap caban, des lainages à carreaux, des rayures masculines, du satin, du crêpe, de la peau, du jean, des tweeds, de la maille, du jersey et du tissu-cravate.

CHAUSSURES
Bottes hautes lacées à bouts ronds en cuir frappé chocolat ou noir. Richelieux à semelle crantée et talon bobine en cuir frappé ou en satin et vernis noir. Mocassins effilés à bouts carrés en satin et vernis noir ou en cuir frappé.

Christian Lacroix

K. Classe chaque objet dans la catégorie à laquelle il appartient.

chapeaux de cuir *Accessoires*	collants-dentelles *Accessoires*
lainages à carreaux *Matières*	fleurs géantes *Motifs*
bottes hautes lacées *Chaussures*	robes souples *Formes*
plumes, fourrures et dorures *Ornements*	

L. Recherche la racine de ces adjectifs pour en deviner le sens.

1. métallisé *metallic*
2. argenté *silvery*
3. doré *golden*
4. lainé *woolen*
5. épaulé *with shoulder pads*
6. bordé *edged*

M. How does Christian Lacroix characterize his average client? *free to be different*

N. D'après Lacroix, comment peut-on définir l'élégance? Et toi? Comment est-ce que tu la définis? *all periods, styles, categories, price ranges*

Cahier d'activités, p. 47, Act. 21

Communication for All Students

Tactile Learners

Bring in, or have students bring in, samples of the different types of fabric mentioned in the reading (leather, tweed, plaid wool, velour, satin, silk, taffeta, fake fur, feathers, lace, nylon, and denim). Have them feel the fabrics and ask them which ones they prefer.

Challenge

Have students draw one of the fashions described on pages 110–112 and exchange papers with a partner, who will try to identify the outfit the drawing was meant to convey.

STANDARDS: 1.2, 2.2, 3.1, 3.2

La Mode en l'an 2025

Tu viens de voir un exemple de mode créée par un grand couturier français. Dans l'activité suivante, tu vas pouvoir imaginer la mode du futur. On est en 2025. Tu es journaliste de mode pour l'émission **Paris branché** et tu dois faire un reportage sur la mode actuelle.

A. Préparation

1. Qu'est-ce qu'on porte en l'an 2025? Quel est le look à la mode? Pour t'en faire une idée, pose-toi les questions suivantes.

a. Comment est-ce que le monde a changé? Comment sont les gens en 2025? Comment est-ce que cela influence leurs goûts?

b. Est-ce qu'il y a de nouveaux tissus ou de nouvelles matières dont on peut faire des vêtements?

c. Est-ce qu'il y a des styles du passé qui reviennent à la mode?

2. Choisis un genre de vêtements particulier pour ton reportage, par exemple, les vêtements de soirée, les vêtements de sport ou les vêtements préférés des adolescents.

> **Stratégie pour écrire**
>
> Sometimes it's hard to come up with ideas for writing about an imaginary situation. One good way to jump-start your imagination is to ask yourself questions about the topic. For example, if you're asked to write about an imaginary place, you might ask yourself: How are the people there different from us? What's important to them? What do they do? Where do they live? How do they dress? Asking yourself these kinds of questions is a great way to generate ideas and help you get started. Don't be afraid to turn your imagination loose!

B. Rédaction

Fais un brouillon de ton reportage.

1. Décris le type de vêtements que tu as choisi. N'oublie pas d'ajouter quelques informations sur...

a. le style général des vêtements : décontracté, classique, habillé, sportif, etc.

b. les couleurs et les motifs

c. les tissus et les matières

d. les endroits où on porte ce genre de vêtements

e. le prix de ces vêtements

f. le genre de boutiques ou de magasins où on peut les acheter

2. A la fin du reportage, parle des catégories suivantes pour compléter le look.

a. accessoires

b. chaussures

3. Fais quelques dessins des vêtements que tu as décrits pour illustrer ton reportage.

C. Evaluation

1. Relis ton brouillon. Est-ce que tu peux ajouter quelques détails pour rendre ton reportage plus intéressant?

2. Corrige la grammaire, l'orthographe et le vocabulaire et rédige la version finale de ton reportage.

3. Devant la classe, joue le rôle du/de la journaliste et présente ton reportage à la télé.

Apply and Assess

Postwriting
Teaching Suggestions

C. 1. Have students write down the following questions and use them as a checklist: **Quel est le style des vêtements choisis? Où est-ce qu'on porte ces vêtements? Combien coûtent ces vêtements? Quels accessoires est-ce qu'on peut mettre avec ces vêtements?** Have them give their report and checklist to a partner, who will check their answers.

C. 3. For the oral report, have students write their notes on five to ten cards with one phrase on each card. Encourage them to practice their presentations with a friend and not to read directly from the cards. Remind them to use their summarizing skills when planning their oral reports.

> **Teaching Resources**
> **p. 113**
>
> **PRINT**
> ▶ Lesson Planner, p. 21
> ▶ Cahier d'activités, p. 148
> ▶ Alternative Assessment Guide, p. 19
> ▶ Standardized Assessment Tutor, Chapter 4
>
> **MEDIA**
> ▶ One-Stop Planner
> ▶ Test Generator, Chapter 4
> ▶ Interactive CD-ROM Tutor, Disc 1

Process Writing

Prewriting
Motivating Activity

Bring in fashion magazines from five, seven, and ten years ago. (They should be available at the local library.) As an alternative, have students describe the clothing styles of the sixties, seventies, and eighties and tell how they've changed over the years. You might also have them suggest societal factors that make specific fabrics and "looks" popular at certain times.

Teaching Suggestion

A. 1. Have students suggest trendy fabrics of the past (crushed velvet, mohair, polyester, lamé, crochet). You might also have them describe futuristic fabrics they imagine or have seen on television science-fiction shows.

Writing
Visual Learners

B. 1. Have students visualize the outfits that they will be describing. You might also have them sketch the outfits, including accessories and colors, before attempting to produce a written description of the fashions. If the resources are available, have students create their designs with computer-generated graphics.

Grammaire supplémentaire

CHAPITRE 4

For **Grammaire supplémentaire**
Answer Transparencies, see the
Teaching Transparencies binder.

Grammaire supplémentaire

Première étape **Objectives** Asking for and giving opinions; asking which one(s); pointing out and identifying people and things

1 Virginie demande l'avis de son ami(e) avant d'acheter certaines choses. Complète les conversations avec les pronoms interrogatifs et démonstratifs qui conviennent. **(p. 101)**

La boîte à mode

— Comment tu trouves ce col roulé violet?

— ___1___ ?

— ___2___ !

— Bof, je n'aime pas tellement.

— Qu'est-ce que tu penses de ces lunettes de soleil?

— ___3___ ?

— ___4___ !

— Elles sont hyper cool!

— J'aime bien ces hauts talons!

— ___5___ ?

— ___6___ !

— Ah oui, ils sont sensass!

— Tu aimes cette mini-jupe écossaise?

— ___7___ ?

— ___8___ !

— Mais non, elle est affreuse!

Grammar Resources for Chapter 4

The **Grammaire supplémentaire** activities are designed as supplemental activities for the grammatical concepts presented in the chapter. You might use them as additional practice, for review, or for assessment.

For more grammar presentations, review, and practice, refer to the following:
• Travaux pratiques de grammaire
• Grammar Tutor for Students of French

• Grammar Summary on pp. R29–R54
• Cahier d'activités
• Grammar and Vocabulary quizzes (Testing Program)
• Test Generator
• Interactive CD-ROM Tutor
• **Jeux interactifs** at <u>go.hrw.com</u>

Answers
1 1. Lequel
2. Celui-là
3. Lesquelles
4. Celles-là
5. Lesquels
6. Ceux-là
7. Laquelle
8. Celle-là

2 Valentin a été convoqué à un entretien d'embauche. Il demande à son ami Guy de lui donner des conseils sur quoi porter. Complète les phrases suivantes avec les pronoms interrogatifs et démonstratifs qui conviennent. (**p. 101**)

VALENTIN	Je ne sais pas quoi mettre. Qu'est-ce que tu en penses, toi?
GUY	Mets ton costume en laine!
VALENTIN	___1___ ? Le gris à rayures?
GUY	Oui, ___2___. Il fait très sérieux.
VALENTIN	Et comme chemise, qu'est-ce que je mets?
GUY	___3___. Elle te va très bien.
VALENTIN	Tu penses qu'il faut mettre une cravate?
GUY	Bien sûr!
VALENTIN	Ben, alors, ___4___ est-ce que je mets? La rouge à pois ou la bleue en soie?
GUY	Tu devrais mettre ___5___. L'autre est trop tape-à-l'œil.
VALENTIN	Bon, ben, qu'est-ce qu'il me faut encore? Ah, oui, des chaussures!
GUY	Tu n'as qu'à mettre ___6___.
VALENTIN	___7___ ? Les bleues ou les noires?
GUY	Les noires. Elles ont l'air très confortables.

3 Bella demande à sa mère si elle peut mettre certaines choses. Complète chaque réponse de sa mère avec un pronom interrogatif et un pronom démonstratif. (**p. 101**)

EXEMPLE	BELLA	Je peux mettre mon caleçon?
	MAMAN	**Lequel?** Le noir? Ah non, pas question! Je veux que tu mettes **celui-là.**

1. BELLA   Ça te dérange si je mets mes bottes?
   MAMAN   _____ ? Tes bottes lacées noires? Mais ça va pas! Je veux que tu mettes _____.

2. BELLA   Est-ce que je peux mettre une robe?
   MAMAN   _____ ? La robe à col en V? Absolument pas! Je veux que tu mettes _____.

3. BELLA   Je peux mettre mes boucles d'oreilles?
   MAMAN   _____ ? Celles que Mémé t'a données? Pas question! Je veux que tu mettes _____.

4. BELLA   Ça te dérange si je mets mon blouson?
   MAMAN   _____ ? Ton blouson en cuir? Mais non, c'est pas possible! Je veux que tu mettes _____.

5. BELLA   J'aimerais bien mettre mes hauts talons...
   MAMAN   _____ ? Tes hauts talons noirs? Pas question! Je veux que tu mettes _____.

6. BELLA   Est-ce que je peux mettre une jupe?
   MAMAN   _____ ? La mini-jupe orange? Absolument pas! Je veux que tu mettes _____.

Answers

2 1. Lequel
2. celui-là
3. Celle-là
4. laquelle
5. celle-là
6. celles-là
7. Lesquelles

3 1. Lesquelles; celles-là
2. Laquelle; celle-là
3. Lesquelles; celles-là
4. Lequel; celui-là
5. Lesquels; ceux-là
6. Laquelle; celle-là

CHAPITRE 4

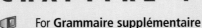 For **Grammaire supplémentaire** Answer Transparencies, see the *Teaching Transparencies* binder.

Deuxième étape   Objectives **Paying and responding to compliments; reassuring someone**

4 Tu rends visite à Lian qui habite dans un vieux manoir. Tu lui demandes qui s'occupe du bâtiment et du jardin. Donne les réponses de Lian en utilisant le **faire** causatif et l'infinitif du verbe qui convient. (**p. 107**)

> **EXEMPLE**   —Qui lave les vitres?
> —**On les fait laver.**

1. Qui enlève la neige?
2. Qui arrose la pelouse?
3. C'est ton père qui tond la pelouse, non?
4. Dis, c'est toi qui ramasses les feuilles?
5. Ton petit frère doit enlever les mauvaises herbes, non?

5 Tes amis te demandent ce que tu penses de leur nouveau look. Choisis la réponse appropriée. (**pp. 98, 107**)

1. Je me suis fait raser la moustache.
   a. Oh, c'est un vieux truc.
   b. Que tu es bien avec ça!
   c. C'est tout à fait ton style.

2. Regarde mes nouvelles bottes. Tu les aimes?
   a. Oh, je ne les ai pas payées cher.
   b. Je trouve qu'elles font très classe.
   c. Je ne te dis pas ça pour te faire plaisir.

3. Comment tu trouves ma coupe de cheveux?
   a. C'est assorti à tes yeux.
   b. C'est tout à fait toi.
   c. Ça te va comme un gant.

4. Qu'est-ce que tu penses de mon pull?
   a. Il te va comme un gant.
   b. Oh, c'est un vieux truc.
   c. Tu crois? C'est gentil.

Answers

4 1. On la fait enlever.
2. On la fait arroser.
3. Non, on la fait tondre.
4. Non, on les fait ramasser.
5. Non, on les fait enlever.

5 1. c
2. b
3. b
4. a

Communication for All Students

Slower Pace

4 You might want to have students do this activity in two phases. First they introduce the causative **faire** in their responses (**On fait laver les vitres**). Then they replace the object noun with an object pronoun (**On les fait laver**).

Challenge

5 As an extension to this activity, have students pair up and come up with statements or questions about their own appearance. The other student reacts to the statements and questions, giving his or her opinion. Make sure partners switch roles.

6 Qu'est-ce que les personnes suivantes vont se faire faire? Réponds en utilisant le **faire** causatif et une des expressions proposées. (**p. 107**)

la frange

les cheveux frisés

les cheveux courts

les cheveux longs et raides

la coiffeuse (le coiffeur)

une queue de cheval

une moustache

une coupe

un shampooing

les cheveux en brosse

se faire une permanente

se couper les cheveux

se laver les cheveux tous les jours

se raser

se teindre les cheveux

EXEMPLE   Claude aime avoir les cheveux très propres.
Il va se faire laver les cheveux tous les jours.

1. Fabienne voudrait avoir les cheveux violets.
2. Je n'aime pas avoir de moustache.
3. Liliane et Caroline aimeraient bien avoir les cheveux frisés.
4. Aziz et moi, nous préférons les cheveux courts.

7 Florence te conseille de faire faire certaines choses avant d'aller à un défilé de mode. Ecris ses conseils en utilisant **il faut que,** une forme du verbe **faire** et les expressions entre parenthèses. (**p. 107**)

EXEMPLE   (réparer ses bottines)   **Il faut que tu fasses réparer tes bottines.**

1. (nettoyer la jupe en velours pourpre)
2. (laver le débardeur imprimé)
3. (se maquiller)
4. (se couper la frange)
5. (se faire une queue de cheval)

Review and Assess

You may wish to assign the **Grammaire supplémentaire** activities as additional practice or homework after presenting material throughout the chapter. Assign Activities 1–3 after **Grammaire** (p. 101), Activities 4, 6, and 7 after **Grammaire** (p. 107), and Activity 5 after **Comment dit-on… ?** (p. 108).

To prepare students for the **Etape** Quizzes and Chapter Test, we suggest doing the **Grammaire supplémentaire** activities in the following order. Have students complete Activities 1–3 before taking Quiz 4-1A or 4-1B; and Activities 4–7 before Quiz 4-2A or 4-2B.

Answers

6 *Possible answers:*
  1. Elle va se faire teindre les cheveux.
  2. Je vais me faire raser.
  3. Elles vont se faire faire une permanente.
  4. Nous allons nous faire couper les cheveux.

7 1. Il faut que tu fasses nettoyer ta jupe en velours pourpre.
  2. Il faut que tu fasses laver ton débardeur imprimé.
  3. Il faut que tu te fasses maquiller.
  4. Il faut que tu te fasses couper la frange.
  5. Il faut que tu te fasses faire une queue de cheval.

CHAPITRE 4

The **Mise en pratique** reviews and integrates all four skills and culture in preparation for the Chapter Test.

Teaching Resources
pp. 118–119

PRINT
▶ Lesson Planner, p. 21
▶ Listening Activities, p. 29
▶ Video Guide, pp. 23, 26
▶ Grammar Tutor for Students of French, Chapter 4
▶ Standardized Assessment Tutor, Chapter 4

MEDIA
▶ One-Stop Planner
▶ Video Program
  Videocassette 2, 11:32–13:32
▶ Audio Compact Discs, CD 4, Tr. 13
▶ Interactive CD-ROM Tutor, Disc 1

Writing Assessment

2 You might use the following rubric when grading your students on this activity.

Writing Rubric	Points			
	4	3	2	1
Content (Complete– Incomplete)				
Comprehensibility (Comprehensible– Incomprehensible)				
Accuracy (Accurate– Seldom accurate)				
Organization (Well organized– Poorly organized)				
Effort (Excellent–Minimal)				

18–20: A   14–15: C   Under 12: F
16–17: B   12–13: D

Mise en pratique

internet
go.hrw.com
ADRESSE: go.hrw.com
MOT-CLE: WA3 FRANCOPHONE EUROPE-4

1 Lis ce que ces jeunes Françaises disent à propos de leur look. Ensuite, écoute bien. Est-ce que c'est Stéphanie ou Elodie qui parle? See scripts and answers on p. 91H.

CD 4
Tr. 13

look

Stéphanie

«Moi, je suis une fille de la campagne. Mon style est plutôt «nature». Je préfère les vêtements en laine, les jupes et les robes longues et les pochettes style péruvien, par exemple. Comme je passe la plupart de mon temps libre à la campagne, j'aime aussi porter de gros pulls et des jeans. Ces vêtements sont parfaits pour faire des balades avec mes chiens.»

Elodie

look

Beauté

«A mon avis, la beauté c'est la simplicité, alors je ne mets pas de make-up le jour. Le soir, si je sors avec des copains, je mets un peu de rouge à lèvres beige. C'est suffisant! Pour avoir les cheveux impec-cables, je les lave tous les matins avec un shampooing de Jean-Claude Biguine. Je ne mets jamais de parfum et les déodorants par-fumants, ce n'est pas mon truc.»

look

«J'aime tout ce qui est rétro et surtout les vêtements dans le style des années 70. J'adore mélanger tous les styles; des pattes d'eph avec un bustier en cuir ou une mini-jupe écossaise rouge avec une fausse fourrure violette, par exemple. Je mélange des fringues que je trouve aux puces avec des vêtements ultra-chic.»

2€   15€   40€   38€   25€   12€

Beauté

«Je change de make-up tous les jours selon mon humeur. En variant les couleurs, je deviens sage ou capricieuse, classique ou extravagante. Le soir, j'adore les tons violets et les faux cils pour faire ressortir mes yeux. Pour dessiner le contour de ma bouche, je mets un rouge à lèvres violet ou rouge. Le jour, je préfère ne pas mettre trop de make-up, juste un fond de teint clair et de la poudre transparente avec un rouge à lèvres mat.»

2 a. Tu travailles pour un magazine de mode français. Tu vas interviewer une célébrité sur son look. Joue cette scène avec ton/ta camarade. Puis, changez de rôle.

b. Ecris ton article pour le magazine. N'oublie pas de dire quels sont les vêtements préférés de la célébrité, comment il/elle préfère se coiffer et pourquoi.

3 a. Ton ami(e) a un entretien d'embauche. Il/Elle ne sait pas quoi mettre. Discute avec lui/elle d'un ensemble possible. Dis-lui ce que tu penses de ses idées et il/elle va aussi te donner son opinion.

b. Ton ami(e) a choisi quelque chose à mettre. Il/Elle l'essaie pour voir si ça lui va bien. Fais-lui des compliments et rassure-le/-la.

Apply and Assess

Challenge

1 You might ask students the following comprehension questions about the article:
Stéphanie aime utiliser quelle sorte de maquillage? Elle aime quel style de vêtements? Qu'est-ce qu'Elodie prend au petit déjeuner? Elle aime se maquiller? Pourquoi pas? Qu'est-ce qu'elle aime mettre comme vêtements?

Visual Learners

3 Have students use the photos on pages 94–95 as the basis for their dialogue.

4 Qu'est-ce que tu penses du look de ces mannequins français? Avec ton/ta camarade, parle de leurs vêtements et de leur look.

Brian porte un pantalon en coton blanc cassé extra large et une chemise rouge et blanche à carreaux. Comme chaussures, il porte des bottines en daim marron. Sur la tête, il a noué un bandana blanc et bleu qui apporte une note d'originalité à son style cool et confortable.

Patrice porte une veste et un gilet en lin gris clair, un pantalon en lin gris foncé, une chemise en coton, une cravate en soie rayée et un chapeau en paille. Le tout, création Hermès®

Jeu de rôle

5

With group members, create outfits to present in a fashion show. Make sketches of outfits and ask other group members their opinions. Then, decide together which outfits you're going to present and write descriptions of them. During the fashion show, take turns being models and the commentator who describes the clothing. As the audience, your classmates will point out the outfits that they find interesting and tell what they think of them. They'll also write down their opinions of each outfit. Which outfits are the most popular?

Teaching Suggestion

4 Encourage students to bring in pictures of additional looks to discuss.

Speaking Assessment

4 You might use the following rubric when grading your students on this activity.

Speaking Rubric	Points			
	4	3	2	1
Content (Complete–Incomplete)				
Comprehension (Total–Little)				
Comprehensibility (Comprehensible–Incomprehensible)				
Accuracy (Accurate–Seldom accurate)				
Fluency (Fluent–Not fluent)				

18–20: A   14–15: C   Under
16–17: B   12–13: D   12: F

Language Note

Students might want to know the following terms from the clothing advertisement: **en daim** *(suede);* **noué** *(knotted);* **en paille** *(straw).*

Apply and Assess

Cooperative Learning

5 Have students do this activity in small groups. Have them design a program for their fashion show. First, have them describe their style. They should list fabrics, patterns, and articles of clothing that they would like to feature. Have them draw several fashions and write a description of each article underneath the outfit. They should also write a paragraph explaining the philosophy behind their line of clothing. This activity could serve as an additional chapter project.

Teaching Resources
p. 120

PRINT
▶ Grammar Tutor for Students of French, Chapter 4

MEDIA
▶ Interactive CD-ROM Tutor, Disc 1
▶ Online self-test

go.hrw.com
WA3 FRANCOPHONE EUROPE-4

Additional Practice

3 For more practice, have students ask "which one(s)?" referring to the photos on pages 94–95 of the **Mise en train.**

Answers

1 *Possible answers:*
1. Elle te plaît, cette chemise? Qu'en penses-tu?
2. Tu n'aimes pas ce pantalon? Qu'est-ce que tu penses de ce pantalon?
3. Comment tu trouves ce pendentif?

2 1. *Like:* Elle me plaît beaucoup. Je la trouve super.
Dislike: Elle ne me plaît pas du tout. Je la trouve moche.
2. *Like:* J'aime bien. J'aime bien ce genre de pantalon.
Dislike: Je n'aime pas tellement. Je trouve qu'il fait vieux.
3. *Like:* Il est super.
Dislike: Il fait vraiment ringard!

6 Je te trouve très bien comme ça. Ça fait très bien. C'est tout à fait toi. Ça te va comme un gant. Que tu es... avec ça! C'est assorti à...

Que sais-je?

Can you use what you've learned in this chapter?

1 How would you ask your friend's opinion of these items? *See answers below.*

1.   2.   3.

Can you ask for and give opinions? p. 98

2 How would you give your opinion of the items in number 1 if you liked them? If you disliked them? *See answers below.*

Can you ask which one(s)? p. 100

3 Your friend is pointing out some things she likes, but you can't tell which one(s) she's talking about. How do you ask? *Possible answers:*

1.   Lequel?   2.   Laquelle?   3.   Lesquels?

4 How would your friend answer your questions in number 3?
Possible answers: **1.** Celui-là.   **2.** Celle-là.   **3.** Ceux-là, les noirs.

Can you point out and identify people and things? p. 100

5 How would you identify the following people if you didn't know their names? *Possible answers:* **1.** Là-bas, le garçon qui porte un chapeau. Celui avec un chapeau. **2.** Celle avec les lunettes. La fille aux lunettes.

1.   2.

Can you pay and respond to compliments? p. 108

6 How would you compliment a friend on an article of clothing? *See answers below.*

7 How would you respond if someone complimented you on your clothing? *Possible answers:* Ça te plaît vraiment? Tu crois? C'est gentil. Oh, c'est un vieux truc. Oh, tu sais, je ne l'ai pas payé(e) cher.

Can you reassure someone? p. 108

8 What would you say to reassure a friend who is uncertain about a new haircut or article of clothing? *Possible answers:* Crois-moi, c'est tout à fait toi. Je t'assure, c'est réussi. Fais-moi confiance, c'est très classe. Je ne dis pas ça pour te faire plaisir.

Review and Assess

Group Work

Have students answer all the questions in **Que sais-je?** Then, have small groups write and act out skits in which they use as many of their answers as possible. You might even have a competition to see which group can use the most expressions in their skit. As students perform their skits, assign a scorekeeper and give him or her a list of the answers. The scorekeeper checks off each answer that is used. After all the groups have performed their skits, the scorekeeper announces which group used the most expressions.

STANDARDS: 1.2

Première étape

Asking for and giving opinions

Qu'est-ce que tu penses de... ?	What do you think of . . .?
Qu'en penses-tu?	What do you think of it?
J'aime bien ce genre de...	I like this type of . . .
Je trouve qu'ils/ elles font...	I think they look . . .
Ça fait vraiment cloche!	That looks really stupid!

Clothing and styles

un caleçon	leggings
un collant	panty hose, tights
un col roulé	a turtleneck sweater
un costume	a man's suit
des gants (m.)	gloves
un gilet	a vest
des hauts talons (m.)	high heels
une mini-jupe	a miniskirt

un pendentif	a pendant
un sac	a purse
à col en V	V-necked
à pinces	pleated
à pois	polka-dot
à rayures	striped
écossais(e)	plaid
en laine	wool
en soie	silk
forme tunique	tunic style

Describing clothing or hairstyles

affreux(-euse)	hideous
classe	classy
délirant(e)	wild
élégant(e)	elegant, sophisticated
hyper cool	super cool
ringard(e)	corny
sérieux(-euse)	conservative
sobre	plain
tape-à-l'œil	gaudy
vulgaire	tasteless

Asking which one(s)

Quel(s)/ Quelle(s)... ?	Which . . .?
Lequel/Laquelle?	Which one?
Lesquels/ Lesquelles?	Which ones?

Pointing out and identifying people and things

Celui-là/Celle-là.	That one.
Ceux-là/Celles-là.	Those.
Celui du...	The one . . .
Celui avec...	The one (man/boy) with . . .
Celle qui...	The one (woman/ girl) who . . .
La fille au...	The girl in the/ with the . . .
Là-bas, le garçon qui...	Over there, the boy who . . .

Deuxième étape

Paying and responding to compliments

Que tu es... avec ça!	You really look . . . in that!
Ça te va comme un gant.	That fits you like a glove.
C'est assorti à...	That matches . . .
Oh, c'est un vieux truc.	This old thing?
Oh, tu sais, je ne l'ai pas payé(e) cher.	Oh, it wasn't expensive.

Reassuring someone

Crois-moi, ...	Believe me, . . .
Je t'assure, ...	Really, . . .
Fais-moi confiance, ...	Trust me, . . .
Je ne dis pas ça pour te faire plaisir.	I'm not just saying that.

Hair and hair styles

une barbe	a beard
les cheveux	hair
courts	short
frisés	curly
longs	long
raides	straight
teints	dyed
en brosse	a crew cut
un chignon	a bun
un coiffeur/une coiffeuse	a hair stylist/barber
une coupe	a haircut
une coupe au carré	a square cut
la frange	bangs
une moustache	a mustache
une natte	a braid
des pattes (f.)	sideburns
une permanente	a perm

une queue de cheval	a pony tail
un shampooing	a shampoo
faire + inf.	to have (something) done
se friser	to curl one's hair
se maquiller	to put on make-up
se raser	to shave
se faire une permanente	(to give oneself) a perm

Vocabulaire

CHAPITRE 4

Circumlocution

Have students think of an interesting outfit using the vocabulary for clothing items they learned in this chapter. They want to purchase the items to create a similar look for themselves. Have students imagine that they are purchasing these items from a salesperson who speaks only French. Students must describe the outfit in detail, without using the actual names for the clothes and accessories. The salesperson should make a sketch of the outfit to confirm what his or her customer would like.

Review and Assess

Game

Trouvez les cinq! Begin by writing on a transparency five words or expressions from one of the vocabulary categories. Then, have students form rows of five or six. The first student in each row has a sheet of paper and a pen, and the others have pens. Call out the category. Beginning with the first student in each row, each student writes a word or expression from that category on the paper and then passes it to the student behind him or her. Call time after one minute and show the transparency with the five words or expressions you've written. One student from each row counts the number of expressions that match yours and are correctly written and gives the results. The team with the most matches wins.

Teaching Resources
pp. 122–125

PRINT
▶ Lesson Planner, p. 22
▶ Video Guide, pp. 27–28

MEDIA
▶ One-Stop Planner
▶ Video Program
   Videocassette 2, 13:57–18:52
▶ Interactive CD-ROM Tutor, Disc 2
▶ Map Transparency 4

go.hrw.com
WA3 FRANCOPHONE
AFRICA

Teaching Suggestion
Ask students to identify the countries that make up francophone Africa and give any information that is unique to this region. Have students recall what they already know about the history, food, animals, climate, famous people, and other aspects of Africa.

Background Information
There is no single francophone culture in Africa. The territory is too vast and the diversity of ethnic groups too great. **L'Afrique francophone** can be divided into North, West, and Central Africa. The francophone region can be further divided by religion (Islam, Christianity, animism, and others), and by ethnic composition.

CHAPITRES 5, 6, 7, 8

Allez, viens en Afrique francophone!

	Le Maroc	La Tunisie	Le Sénégal	La République centrafricaine
Population	30.122.000	9.593.000	9.987.000	3.512.000
Superficie (km²)	459.000	154.000	197.000	622.000
Capitale	Rabat	Tunis	Dakar	Bangui
Spécialités	pastilla, thé à la menthe	couscous, tajine	maffé, chawarma	dengbé

Autres états et régions francophones : l'Algérie, le Bénin, le Burkina Faso, le Burundi, le Cameroun, les Comores, le Congo, la Côte d'Ivoire, Djibouti, le Gabon, la Guinée, l'île Maurice, le Mali, la Mauritanie, Madagascar, Mayotte, le Niger, la République démocratique du Congo, la Réunion, le Ruanda, les Seychelles, le Tchad, le Togo

WA3 FRANCOPHONE
AFRICA

VIDEO   CD-ROM DISC 2

Une mosquée en Afrique ▶

Cultures and Communities

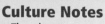

Culture Notes
• The photo on pages 122–123 shows a mosque, a Muslim place of worship. Mosques are generally large, elaborate buildings that not only serve as places of prayer, but also as tombs and as places of religious instruction. The word *mosque* comes from the Arabic **masjid**, which means *a place of adoration*. Mosques generally have a **mihrab** *(prayer niche)* that faces the holy city of Mecca and between one and six **minarets** *(towers)*, from which the faithful are called to prayer by the **muezzins** *(criers)*.

• A Muslim's chief responsibilities are summarized in the Five Pillars of Faith: the profession of faith **(shahadah)**, prayer **(salat)** five times a day, almsgiving, fasting during the holy month of Ramadan, and a pilgrimage, or **hajj**, to Mecca once during his or her lifetime.

 Using the Almanac and Map

Terms in the Almanac

- **Le Maroc** is located in North Africa on the southern side of the Strait of Gibraltar. The country has primarily an agricultural economy, although it is one of the top producers of phosphates in the world. Oranges and sheep are also important exports.

- **Rabat,** the capital of Morocco, is the center of an important textile industry and is known for its carpets, blankets, and leather goods.

- **thé à la menthe:** tea made with a special variety of mint

- **La Tunisie** is located on the Mediterranean coast halfway between Gibraltar and the Suez Canal. Tourism is an important industry, and Tunisia's main exports are oil, phosphates, and olive oil.

- **couscous:** kernels of cracked wheat or semolina, boiled or steamed, and eaten with chicken or meat and vegetables

- **tajine:** a stew made with various meats and vegetables

- **Le Sénégal,** which forms a flat plain barely above sea level on the westernmost point of Africa, is one of the world's largest producers of peanuts.

- **maffé:** beef, chicken, or lamb cooked in peanut sauce and served with rice

- **chawarma:** grilled meat in pita bread, originally Lebanese

- **La République centrafricaine,** one of the world's leading diamond producers, is a tropical, landlocked country located nearly in the center of Africa.

- **dengbé:** wild game eaten with a sauce made with peanut butter or okra

Connections and Comparisons

Using the Map
Have students use a map of Africa to determine which countries in the almanac are in the desert, which are islands, which are located in North Africa, which in Central Africa, and which in West Africa. Have them identify the countries bordered by the Mediterranean Sea and those bordered by the Atlantic and Indian Oceans. Ask students to consider how being landlocked might affect some countries' economy.

Geography Link
The Arabic word **maghreb,** a region of which Morocco, Algeria, and Tunisia are part, means *time or place of sunset* or *island of the west.* The term is used to distinguish the region from the **mashriq,** the eastern Islamic world.

Using the Photo Essay

① **Le désert du Sahara,** the largest desert in the world, stretches west to east 5,000 kilometers from the Atlantic Ocean to the Red Sea and north to south for 2,000 kilometers. The Sahara, which means *desert* in Arabic, covers parts of Morocco, Algeria, Tunisia, Libya, Egypt, the Sudan, Chad, Niger, Mali, Mauritania, and Western Sahara. Inhabited by nomads and camel herders, the area receives very little rainfall. Over the years, the Sahara has been expanding, sometimes naturally and sometimes because of man's assault on the fragile ecology of the region.

② **Le baobab,** a tropical tree with a large trunk up to nine meters (30 feet) in diameter, is known for its pulpy, yellow fruit called monkey bread. This tree has a number of practical uses. Its immense trunk can store water, and its leaves can be eaten either fresh or dried. The monkey bread fruit can be made into a sherbet-like, refreshing drink, and its shell, which resembles a gourd, can be used as a container. The bark serves as material for musical instruments, packing paper, rope, and even cloth.

③ While the **costumes traditionnels** vary throughout the continent of Africa, there is some similarity in the way the people in sub-Saharan francophone countries dress. For important occasions, it is common for both men and women to wear long, embroidered robes **(boubous).** For daily wear, women often wear a colorful **pagne** *(a length of cloth)* wrapped around their waist as a skirt, a matching scarf, and a loose top. The same cloth is used to make men's casual clothes, which consist of loose-fitting shirts and pants.

L'Afrique francophone

En Afrique, la francophonie ne représente pas tout à fait la culture traditionnelle française telle qu'on la trouve en Europe. La langue française a été introduite par les colons français. Dans certains de ces pays, le mélange des cultures a été très bien accepté par les populations. Beaucoup de jeunes parlent français et continuent leurs études en France avec l'aide de bourses du gouvernement français; ils rentrent alors dans leur pays avec un diplôme qui leur donne accès à des postes importants. Par contre, dans d'autres pays comme l'Algérie, l'union des cultures ne s'est pas faite aussi parfaitement parce qu'il y a un mouvement très puissant qui cherche à préserver les traditions religieuses et culturelles.

📶 internet

go.hrw.com
ADRESSE: go.hrw.com
MOT-CLE: WA3
FRANCOPHONE AFRICA

① **Le Sahara**
Ce désert recouvre une grande partie de l'Afrique du Nord.

② **Le baobab**
C'est un arbre typiquement africain. Souvent, les villages sont construits près d'un baobab.

③ **Les Africains**
Malgré l'influence de la culture française, les peuples africains sont restés très proches de leurs traditions. Partout en Afrique, les gens portent encore des costumes traditionnels.

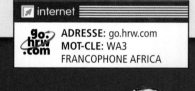

Cultures and Communities

Culture Notes
• Camels are truly animals of the desert. Their stomachs are especially adapted to conserve water, and they can live off water, fat, and nutrients stored in their hump for several days, if necessary. Their wide feet and long eyelashes protect them from the heat and sand.
• Three francophone African countries have changed their names in the last 20 years: la

République Démocratique du Congo (formerly Zaire), **le Bénin** (formerly Dahomey), and le **Burkina Faso** (formerly Upper Volta).
• **Griots** are praise singers, entertainers, and oral historians found primarily in West Africa. Often wanderers, they form a social caste of their own in many places. Many play a five-stringed, leather-covered, wooden instrument.

Aux chapitres 5, 6, 7 et 8, tu vas découvrir l'Afrique francophone avec Omar, Moktar, Lucie et Zhora. Omar habite à Dakar, capitale du Sénégal. Avec Moktar, tu vas visiter un souk du Maroc. Puis, tu vas aller en République centrafricaine pour un safari-photo avec Lucie. A la fin de ton voyage, tu vas faire la connaissance de Zhora qui habite en Tunisie, destination touristique très recherchée des Français.

Culture Notes

 Souks (*outdoor markets*) are commonplace throughout Morocco. Smaller villages and towns generally have a particular market day (**Souk el Tnine** – *Monday market,* **Souk el Arba** – *Wednesday market*). They also have their own special **souk** quarter, whereas larger cities have several individual **souks,** each of which is devoted to a particular craft. Village markets are not open on Fridays, when the main prayers are held in the mosques.

4 Les souks
C'est comme ça qu'on appelle les marchés marocains. On y trouve des épices, des légumes et une grande variété de produits artisanaux.

6 Abidjan is the economic capital and largest city of Côte d'Ivoire.

7 Casablanca, the largest city and main port of Morocco, is also a commercial and industrial center. The city, familiarly called **Casa,** was modeled after the French city of Marseilles and is the site of the **Grande Mosquée Hassan II,** named after the late king of Morocco.

5 La République centrafricaine
Dans ce pays couvert en partie de savanes, on peut voir de nombreux animaux sauvages.

Teaching Suggestion
Have each student choose a francophone African country to research.

Thinking Critically
Observing Have students examine the photos for examples of arid, desert climates as opposed to more moderate climates. They might notice sand as opposed to grass, the scarcity of trees, and the whitewashed buildings.

6 Abidjan
Cette métropole de gratte-ciel et de larges avenues est la ville principale de la Côte d'Ivoire.

7 Casablanca
Cette ville marocaine est un grand port artificiel.

Connections and Comparisons

Geography Link
5 There are two types of savannah, one caused by fire and the other by climate. In parts of Africa, where there are marked wet and dry seasons, the savannah is generally formed as a result of the climate. During the dry season, there is not enough water to support the growth of trees and overgrazing causes desertification.

Language-to-Language
A **lingua franca** is a third language used between two speakers of different languages. For example, in the Central African Republic, Sango, originally a trading language spoken along the Ubangi River (**Oubangui** in French), is the national language and is spoken by nearly everyone.

Chapitre 5 : C'est notre avenir
Chapter Overview

Mise en train pp. 128–130	*L'avenir, c'est demain*			

	FUNCTIONS	**GRAMMAR**	**VOCABULARY**	**RE-ENTRY**
Première étape pp. 131–135	• Asking about and expressing intentions, p. 133 • Expressing conditions and possibilities, p. 133	• The future, p. 134	• Future choices and plans, p. 132	• The subjunctive (**Chapitre 3**, III) • The **passé composé** (**Chapitre 1**, III)

Remise en train pp. 136–137	*Passe ton bac d'abord!*			

Deuxième étape pp. 138–143	• Asking about future plans, p. 140 • Expressing wishes, p. 140 • Expressing indecision, p. 140 • Giving advice, p. 140 • Requesting information, p. 142 • Writing a formal letter, p. 142	• The conditional, p. 141 • Inversion, p. 143	• Careers, p. 139	• Giving advice (**Chapitre 12**, II) • The imperfect (**Chapitre 1**, III) • Making a telephone call (**Chapitre 9**, I)

Lisons! pp. 144–146	**L'Enfant noir**	**Reading Strategy:** Recognizing the **passé simple**
Ecrivons! p. 147	**Une lettre de candidature**	**Writing Strategy:** Using details and structure in persuasive writing
Grammaire supplémentaire	**pp. 148–151**	**Première étape,** pp. 148–149 **Deuxième étape,** pp. 150–151
Review pp. 152–155	**Mise en pratique,** pp. 152–153 **Que sais-je?,** p. 154	**Vocabulaire,** p. 155

CULTURE

• **Note culturelle,** Careers and education in Senegal, p. 130
• **Rencontre culturelle,** Overview of Senegal, p. 131
• **Panorama Culturel,** Planning for a career, p. 138
• **Note culturelle,** Types of job training, p. 139

Chapitre 5 : C'est notre avenir
Chapter Resources

Lesson Planning

 One-Stop Planner

Lesson Planner with Substitute Teacher Lesson Plans, pp. 22–26, 68

Student Make-Up Assignments
- Make-Up Assignment Copying Masters, Chapter 5

Listening and Speaking

Listening Activities
- Student Response Forms for Listening Activities, pp. 35–37
- Additional Listening Activities 5-1 to 5-6, pp. 39–41
- Additional Listening Activities (song), p. 42
- Scripts and Answers, pp. 121–125

Video Guide
- Teaching Suggestions, pp. 30–31
- Activity Masters, pp. 32–34
- Scripts and Answers, pp. 90–92, 113

Activities for Communication
- Communicative Activities, pp. 17–20
- Realia and Teaching Suggestions, pp. 63–65
- Situation Cards, pp. 97–98

Reading and Writing

Reading Strategies and Skills Handbook, Chapter 5

Joie de lire 3, Chapter 5

Cahier d'activités, pp. 49–60

Grammar

Travaux pratiques de grammaire, pp. 41–53

Grammar Tutor for Students of French, Chapter 5

Assessment

Testing Program
- Grammar and Vocabulary Quizzes, **Etape** Quizzes, and Chapter Test, pp. 89–102
- Score Sheet, Scripts and Answers, pp. 103–109

Alternative Assessment Guide
- Portfolio Assessment, p. 20
- Performance Assessment, p. 34
- CD-ROM Assessment, p. 48

Student Make-Up Assignments
- Alternative Quizzes, Chapter 5

Standardized Assessment Tutor
- Reading, pp. 17–19
- Writing, p. 20
- Math, pp. 25–26

Online Activities
- Jeux interactifs
- Activités Internet

Video Program
- Videocassette 2
- Videocassette 5 (captioned version)

Audio Compact Discs
- Textbook Listening Activities, CD 5, Tracks 1–13
- Additional Listening Activities, CD 5, Tracks 19–25
- Assessment Items, CD 5, Tracks 14–18

Interactive CD-ROM Tutor, Disc 2

Teaching Transparencies
- Situation 5-1 to 5-2
- **Grammaire supplémentaire** Answers
- **Travaux pratiques de grammaire** Answers

  One-Stop Planner CD-ROM

Use the **One-Stop Planner CD-ROM with Test Generator** to aid in lesson planning and pacing.

For each chapter, the **One-Stop Planner** includes:
- Editable lesson plans with direct links to teaching resources
- Printable worksheets from resource books
- Direct launches to the HRW Internet activities
- Video and audio segments
- Test Generator
- Clip Art for vocabulary items

Chapitre 5 : C'est notre avenir
Projects ··

Les Carrières

Students will create a poster to advertise a particular career of their choice. They will also give an oral presentation in which they act as a representative of that field, encouraging other students to consider it as a profession.

MATERIALS
✂ **Students may need**
- French-English dictionaries
- Posterboard
- Colored markers or pens
- Encyclopedias
- Current magazines
- College catalogues

SUGGESTED SEQUENCE

Before students begin their projects, invite bilingual members of the community to the class (travel agents, bank representatives, business consultants). Have them talk about their training, what they do, and how they use a second language in their work. Encourage students to ask them questions, either spontaneous or prepared in advance.

1. Have students choose a career from the **Vocabulaire** on page 139. They might refer to the **Vocabulaire à la carte** on page 140, the Additional Vocabulary at the back of the book, or French-English dictionaries to find additional careers.

2. Once students have chosen a career, have them do a mapping or clustering activity. They should write their chosen profession (**médecin**) in the center of a sheet of paper and circle it. Then, they should write several major characteristics they associate with that profession in separate circles around the central circle (helps people, medical school, money). Then, they should continue by surrounding each of these circles with additional circles containing related ideas.

3. Have students research their profession. They might interview a friend, relative, or community member in that field, check the encyclopedia for a definition and history of the profession, and find information in magazines or college catalogues about the necessary training, employment opportunities, average salary, and so on.

4. Have students organize their oral presentation and plan the layout of their posters. Remind them that they are acting as a representative of their profession during a "career day" at school. If they choose to be a doctor, they should be prepared to tell the class why they chose to be a doctor, what training is necessary, what it is like to be a doctor, and what their everyday duties and responsibilities are.

5. Have students give their oral presentations to the class, using their posters to encourage their classmates to choose their profession. Class members should ask questions, just as they would if a guest were visiting the class. The class members will receive grades for their participation in other students' presentations.

GRADING THE PROJECT

You might grade students' projects on thoroughness and accuracy of content, creativity of visuals, oral presentation, accuracy of language use, and participation in other students' presentations.

Suggested Point Distribution (total = 100 points)
Content...20 points
Creativity of visuals ....20 points
Oral presentation ....20 points
Language use ....20 points
Participation...20 points

Games ··

Qu'est-ce que tu ferais?

In this game, students will practice the conditional by telling what they would do in certain situations.

Procedure   To prepare for this game, describe different situations on index cards. (**La voiture tombe en panne.**) Suggestions for situations are given below. Put the cards in a box or a bag. Then, form three to five teams. A player from the first team selects a card and shows it to the other team members. The team members each write one sentence telling what they would do in that situation. For example, if the situation were **La voiture tombe en panne,** an appropriate sentence might be **Je trouverais une station-service.** Players from the first team take turns reading their sentences aloud to the other teams until a member of another team correctly names the situation. The team gets one point for each sentence that its members read before the situation is guessed. The team with the most points at the end of three rounds wins. You might appoint a scorekeeper/judge to tabulate the points for each round and to verify the correct answers.

possible situations:

1. **Tu as oublié tes clés.**

2. **Tu es au chômage.**

3. **Tu dois passer ton bac.**

4. **Tu n'as pas d'argent pour le déjeuner.**

Storytelling

Mini-histoire

This story accompanies Teaching Transparency 5-2. The ***mini-histoire*** *can be told and retold in different formats, acted out, written as dictation, and read aloud to give students additional opportunities to practice all four skills. The following story concerns Valentine who is trying to decide what she should do after high school.*

«Voyons voir! Par où commencer avec tous ces catalogues? Ce qui me plairait, c'est d'avoir un travail où je gagne bien ma vie et où je sois indépendante».

Valentine commence à feuilleter les catalogues.

«Je pourrais être pilote de ligne. Je m'imagine très bien au commande d'un avion de ligne. Je pourrais beaucoup voyager. Je crois que j'aimerais bien voyager aux quatre coins du monde. Ouh, il faut être bon en maths…

Docteur? Je pourrais être médecin… Non, je ne supporte pas la vue du sang. O.K., je ne serai pas médecin.

Et, pourquoi pas architecte? J'aime dessiner, j'ai beaucoup d'imagination… «Etre bon en maths…» Je crois que ce métier n'est pas pour moi, non plus. Je ne serai pas architecte.

Quoi d'autre? … avocat? Ce serait bien. Pas de maths, pas de physique. Il faut être bon en français, en histoire… si je connais d'autres langues je peux faire du droit international… et voyager. C'est décidé, je serai avocate.»

Traditions

La Musique au Sénégal

Music is perhaps Senegal's richest artistic tradition. For centuries the **griots,** praise singers or minstrels of the artisan class, have used song and oral narrative to pass down the history, traditions, and myths of Senegal's native peoples. Not only does traditional music create a strong sense of cultural identity and history, but it also serves a social purpose. Each social occasion or event, and each social group (warriors, women, hunters, etc.) has its own distinct type of music. All of the music is polyrhythmic and played only on instruments made from local materials, such as gourds, leather, cow horns, and shells. In recent years, this traditional music of the country's rural areas has given birth to a distinctive world beat popular in Senegal's cities and throughout the globe. Find a recording of Senegalese music like that of international star Youssou N'dour and play it for students.

Recette

*The **Yassa au poulet** is a dish from the Casamance region, in Senegal. If you'd like to follow the Senegalese tradition, you'll have to rinse your hands in cold water before sitting at the table. A jug of water and a bucket are usually provided for that purpose at the entrance to the dining room.*

YASSA AU POULET

pour 6 personnes

1 gros poulet coupé en morceaux

3 gros oignons coupés

1 piment

1 tasse d'huile d'arachide

8 citrons verts

sel

poivre

thym, laurier

Faire mariner le poulet dans le jus des 8 citrons verts avec un oignon coupé en lamelles. Assaisonner de sel, poivre, thym et laurier. Laisser mariner pendant 10 heures.

Retirer le poulet de la marinade et le faire griller, soit sur un gril, soit au four pendant 50 minutes.

Pendant que le poulet cuit, préparer la sauce. Passer la marinade. Faire chauffer l'huile dans une casserole, ajouter les deux autres oignons coupés et la marinade. Porter à ébullition. Ajouter le poulet cuit. Laisser mijoter pendant 10 à 15 minutes.

Servir avec du riz.

Video Program

Videocassette 2, Videocassette 5 (captioned version)
See Video Guide, pp. 29–33.

Camille et compagnie • Cinquième épisode : *L'avenir est à nous*

Max, Laurent, and Camille are talking about their dream professions. Max would like to be a reporter-photographer. At the beginning of the episode, he is writing a letter to a school of journalism. Laurent would like to continue working on cars. He plans to attend a vocational school to become a technician. Camille would like to study business in an American university and become a business woman. As for Sophie, her dream is to become an actress.

Quel métier aimerais-tu faire?

Students from around the francophone world talk about their plans for the future. Two native speakers discuss the question and introduce the interviews.

Vidéoclips

- **AGF**®: advertisement for insurance
- **Crédit foncier**®: advertisement for a bank
- **Peugeot Gentry**®: advertisement for a car
- **Musical interlude:** Le Sénégal
- **News report:** Employees evaluate their boss.

Interactive CD-ROM Tutor

The **Interactive CD-ROM Tutor** contains videos, interactive games, and activities that provide students an opportunity to practice and review the material covered in Chapter 5.

Activity	Activity Type	Pupil's Edition Page
1. Vocabulaire	Jeu des paires	p. 132
2. Grammaire	Les mots qui manquent	p. 134
3. Vocabulaire	Chasse au trésor Explorons! Vérifions!	p. 139
4. Comment dit-on... ?	Du tac au tac	pp. 133, 140
5. Grammaire	Chacun à sa place	pp. 133, 134, 141
6. Comment dit-on... ?	Méli-mélo	p. 142
Panorama Culturel	Quel métier aimerais-tu faire? Le bon choix	p. 138
A toi de parler	*Guided recording*	pp. 152–153
A toi d'écrire	*Guided writing*	pp. 152–153

Teacher Management System

Logging In

Logging in to the *Allez, viens!* TMS is easy. Upon launching the program, simply type "admin" in the password area of the log-in screen and press RETURN. Log on to **www.hrw.com/CDROMTUTOR** for a detailed explanation of the Teacher Management System.

One-Stop Planner CD-ROM

To preview all resources available for this chapter, use the **One-Stop Planner CD-ROM,** Disc 2.

Internet Connection

ADRESSE: go.hrw.com
MOT-CLE: WA3 FRANCOPHONE AFRICA-5

*Have students explore the **go.hrw.com** Web site for many online resources covering all chapters. All Chapter 5 resources are available under the keyword **WA3 FRANCOPHONE AFRICA-5.** Interactive games help students practice the material and provide them with immediate feedback. You'll also find a printable worksheet that provides Internet activities that lead to a comprehensive online research project.*

Jeux interactifs

You can use the interactive activities in this chapter

- to practice grammar, vocabulary, and chapter functions
- as homework
- as an assessment option
- as a self-test
- to prepare for the Chapter Test

Activités Internet

Students look for information about the Senegalese education system, using the vocabulary and phrases from the chapter.

- In preparation for the **Activités Internet,** have students review the dramatic episode on Video-cassette 2, or do the activities in the **Panorama Culturel** on page 138. After completing the activity sheet, have students work with a partner and share the information they gathered in activities B and C on that sheet. Then ask each pair of students to share what they learned with the class.

Projet

Have groups of students find out about the educational system of another francophone country. Assign a different country to each group, then have them compile their findings for a composite of francophone educational systems. Students can research information about the programs available, admission requirements, costs, and so on. Remind students to document their sources by noting the names and the URLs of all the sites they consulted. You may want to have each group present their findings to the rest of the class.

Première étape

6 p. 132

Answers to Activity 6
1. non	4. non	7. oui
2. oui	5. oui	8. non
3. non	6. non	9. oui

1. —Tu te souviens de nos années au lycée? C'était pas facile quand même à notre époque, hein?
   —Ah, c'est sûr! Moi, j'ai passé mon bac deux fois avant de l'avoir. J'avais vingt ans quand je l'ai eu.

2. —Ah bon? Je ne m'en souviens pas. Remarque, j'étais sûrement déjà au service militaire, je l'ai fait juste après le bac.

3. —C'était quand même moins difficile de trouver du travail dans notre jeunesse. J'ai arrêté mes études après le lycée et j'ai trouvé un emploi tout de suite.

4. —Moi, j'ai fait le bon choix quand j'ai décidé de faire une école technique. Je n'ai jamais eu de problèmes pour trouver un emploi.

5. —Moi, si. Après l'université, je suis resté au chômage pendant deux mois.

6. —Ne te plains pas. Moi, ça a duré un an et demi. Tiens, c'est aussi à cette époque-là que je me suis marié.

7. —Et toi, à quel âge est-ce que tu t'es marié déjà? Vingt-trois ans?
   —Mais, non. Moi, je me suis marié à vingt-sept ans. Dis-moi, c'était quoi déjà, ton premier travail?

8. —Souviens-toi, chauffeur. J'ai passé mon permis à vingt-deux ans et juste après, j'ai commencé à travailler pour l'entreprise de Khalid. Ça, c'est vraiment un bon souvenir pour moi.

9. —En tout cas, moi, mon meilleur souvenir, c'est la naissance de ma fille. J'avais vingt-neuf ans.

7 p. 133

1. —Dis donc, Prosper, qu'est-ce que tu comptes faire après le lycée?
   —Eh bien, travailler. Si je ne trouve pas de travail, je commencerai un apprentissage en août, à l'hôtel de mon oncle. Mais ce que je veux vraiment faire, c'est travailler comme chauffeur. J'adore conduire. J'ai passé mon permis en mai, tu sais.

2. —Félicitations pour ton bac, Prisca!
   —Merci.
   —Et qu'est-ce que tu penses faire maintenant?
   —Je compte entrer à l'université en septembre.
   —C'est bien, ça.
   —Ouais, mais je dois quitter ma famille si je vais à Dakar. Je pense habiter avec mon oncle et ma tante, mais ils ont beaucoup d'enfants. S'ils sont bruyants, je ne pourrai pas étudier.
   —Ben, qu'est-ce que tu peux faire, alors?
   —Il est possible que je prenne un appartement avec une copine.
   —Bonne idée!

3. —Tiens, Séka. On m'a dit que tu as réussi ton bac.
   —Oui.
   —Félicitations! Alors, qu'est-ce que tu comptes faire?
   —J'ai l'intention de ne faire absolument rien cet été. C'était tellement dur, le bac, tu sais. Je vais me reposer cet été. Je pense partir en vacances en juillet et, en août, je compte rendre visite à mon frère à Thiès. Il se peut que je travaille un peu avec lui. Il a une épicerie.

4. —Alors, Angèle, ça s'est bien passé, ton bac?
   —Oui, j'ai réussi.
   —Formidable! Qu'est-ce que tu comptes faire maintenant?
   —Ben, je vais me marier cet été.
   —Vraiment?
   —Oui, et peut-être que je travaillerai après.
   —Qu'est-ce que tu veux faire?
   —Oh, je ne sais pas. Il se peut que j'aie un enfant avant de travailler.
   —Alors, bonne chance!

Answers to Activity 7
1. Angèle	5. Prisca
2. Prosper, Angèle	6. *no one*
3. Prosper	7. Séka
4. Prisca	8. Prisca

Deuxième étape

Answers to Activity 18
1. mécanicien	5. secrétaire
2. médecin ou	6. professeur
infirmier/infirmière	ou institutrice
3. plombier	7. architecte
4. écrivain	

18 p. 139

1. —La voiture de Mme Bonfils? Je l'ai réparée. Quelle voiture est-ce que je répare maintenant?
   —La voiture de M. Koré. C'est la bleue, là-bas, à côté de la Mercedes.
   —Bon, d'accord.

2. —J'ai mal à la gorge, à la tête et au ventre. J'ai aussi de la fièvre.
   —C'est la grippe, sans doute. Je vais prendre votre température. Ouvrez la bouche, s'il vous plaît.

3. —Que je suis heureuse que vous soyez arrivé! Vous voyez, il y a de l'eau partout!
   —Ça vient d'où, madame?
   —Du lavabo. C'est par ici, la salle de bains.

4. —Salut, Fabrice. Ça avance, le roman?
   —Oh, pas trop bien. J'ai commencé à écrire, mais je me suis aperçu que j'avais encore des recherches à faire.
   —Donc, tu ne finiras pas à la date prévue?
   —Euh, probablement pas.

5. —Vous pourriez taper cette lettre, Bernard?
   —Bien sûr, madame.
   —Et après ça, n'oubliez pas de téléphoner à M. Raynaud pour arranger un rendez-vous.
   —Oui, madame.

6. —Bonjour.
   —Bonjour, Mlle Kanon.
   —Vous avez des questions avant de commencer l'interro?

7. —On fait construire un nouveau bâtiment ici, alors?
   —Oui, c'est moi qui fais les plans.
   —Ah bon?
   —Oui, il y aura quarante étages. Ce sera très moderne.

One-Stop Planner CD-ROM

To preview all resources available for this chapter, use the **One-Stop Planner CD-ROM**, Disc 2.

22   p. 141

1. —Alors, Yasmine, tu sais ce que tu vas faire?
—Bien sûr! J'ai l'intention d'entrer à l'université et d'étudier l'histoire.

2. —Eh, Mamadou, tu as des projets pour l'année prochaine?
—Pas vraiment. Je ne sais pas encore ce que je vais faire.

3. —Dis, Fatou, qu'est-ce que tu veux faire plus tard?
—Je n'en ai aucune idée. Je me demande si je vais continuer mes études.

4. —Omar, tu as des projets pour plus tard?
—Oui, oui. J'ai plein de projets. Mais mon rêve, c'est de faire du théâtre.

5. —Dis donc, Fatima, tu sais ce que tu vas faire plus tard?
—Euh, j'ai du mal à me décider. Il y a la boutique de ma famille, mais il y a aussi l'université. Je n'arrive pas à prendre une décision.

6. —Eh Habib, tu sais ce que tu vas faire après le lycée?
—Ce qui me plairait, c'est de voyager un peu avant de commencer l'université. J'aimerais bien passer du temps en France chez mon oncle.

7. —Alors, Thérèse, qu'est-ce que tu vas faire plus tard?
—Oh, je ne sais pas trop. Je voudrais trouver un travail, mais je ne sais pas quelle sorte de travail. Je n'en ai vraiment aucune idée.

Answers to Activity 22

1. sait	3. hésite	5. hésite	7. hésite
2. hésite	4. sait	6. sait	

26   p. 142

—Institut de promotion industrielle.
—Oui, bonjour, monsieur.
—Bonjour, mademoiselle.
—J'aimerais avoir des renseignements sur votre école.
—Oui, mademoiselle.
—Je voudrais savoir ce qu'il y a comme cours.
—Nous offrons des cours de gestion, informatique et techniques de commercialisation.
—Est-ce que les cours sont le jour ou le soir?
—Les deux.
—Et, euh, quand est-ce que les cours commencent?
—Vous pouvez commencer tous les trois mois.
—Il y a des conditions d'inscription?
—Oui, mademoiselle. Il faut que vous ayez au moins vingt et un ans, et que vous ayez votre bac.
—Bien. Pourriez-vous me dire quels sont les frais d'inscription?
—Ça dépend des cours que vous prenez. Ça pourrait faire de trois mille francs à quatre mille francs.
—Mmm... Est-ce que vous pourriez m'envoyer une brochure?
—Bien sûr. Quelle est votre adresse?

Answers to Activity 26

g, b, d, f, a, e, c

Mise en pratique

1   p. 152

—Tiens, Karim! Ça va?
—Oui, ça va bien maintenant que c'est fini, le bac.
—Moi aussi. Quel cauchemar, hein?
—Ouais. Mais, je ne sais pas ce que je veux faire maintenant. J'ai du mal à me décider. Et toi, qu'est-ce que tu penses faire?
—Moi, je compte entrer à l'université en automne. J'habiterai avec la famille de mon oncle. Il se peut que je passe l'été chez eux aussi, pour travailler dans leur boutique. Mais ce que je veux faire, c'est voyager et me reposer un peu avant de commencer l'université.
—C'est bien, ça. Alors, tout est décidé pour toi.
—Et toi, tu n'as pas de projets, alors?
—Mon rêve, c'est de voyager, tu sais. Mais sans argent, ce n'est pas possible.
—Alors, il faudrait que tu travailles.
—Eh oui, mais qu'est-ce que je peux faire? Je n'en ai aucune idée. Je ne sais plus ce que je veux.
—Tu ne veux pas continuer tes études, alors?
—Jamais de la vie! C'est fini, les études!
—Mais si tu ne te prépares pas, tu ne trouveras jamais de travail.
—Ouais.
—Tu ferais bien de t'inscrire dans une école technique.
—Mais je me demande laquelle. Ce qui me plairait, c'est de rencontrer beaucoup de gens.
—Bon, tu veux rencontrer des gens et tu aimes voyager, n'est-ce pas?
—Oui.
—J'ai une idée, moi. Pourquoi pas travailler dans un hôtel? Tu n'as pas vu l'article dans le journal d'hier à propos de l'Ecole de Formation Hôtelière et Touristique?
—Ben, non.
—Tu devrais le lire. Ça semble très intéressant. Si j'étais toi, je demanderais des renseignements sur cette école.
—Tu me passes l'article?
—Bien sûr!

Answers to Mise en pratique Activity 1

1. vrai	3. faux	5. faux	7. vrai
2. vrai	4. faux	6. faux	8. vrai

3   p. 152

Bonjour, j'aimerais avoir des renseignements sur votre village-hôtel. Pourriez-vous me dire ce qu'on peut y faire comme sports? Je voudrais également savoir si on peut pêcher. Pourriez-vous me dire si les bungalows sont climatisés? Est-ce que vous pourriez m'envoyer une brochure? Mon nom est Ousmane Loukour. Mon adresse est 6, avenue Georges Pompidou, à Dakar. Je vous remercie.

Answers to Mise en pratique Activity 3

M. Loukour wants to know what sports activities are available at the hotel, if there is fishing, if the bungalows are air-conditioned, and if the hotel could send him a brochure; Karim will send the second, more formal letter.

Chapitre 5: C'est notre avenir
Suggested Lesson Plans *50-Minute Schedule*

Day 1

CHAPTER OPENER 5 min.
- Present Chapter Objectives, p. 127.
- Community Link and Language Note, ATE, pp. 126–127

MISE EN TRAIN 40 min.
- Present **Mise en train**, pp. 128–129, using Video Program, Videocassette 2.
- See Teaching Suggestions, Viewing Suggestions 1–2, Video Guide, p. 30.
- Language Note and Culture Notes, ATE, pp. 128–129.
- See Teaching Suggestions, Post-viewing Suggestions 1–3, Video Guide, p. 30.
- Do Activities 1–4, p. 130.
- Read and discuss **Note culturelle**, p. 130.

Wrap-Up 5 min.
- Do Activity 6, p. 130.

Homework Options
Cahier d'activités, Acts. 1–2, p. 49

Day 2

MISE EN TRAIN
Quick Review 5 min.
- Check homework.

RENCONTRE CULTURELLE 15 min.
- Presenting **Rencontre culturelle**, ATE, p. 131
- **Qu'en penses-tu?**, p. 131
- Culture Notes, ATE, p. 131
- Read and discuss **Savais-tu que…?**, p. 131.
- Thinking Critically: Synthesizing, ATE, p. 131

PREMIERE ETAPE
Vocabulaire, p. 132 20 min.
- Presenting **Vocabulaire**, ATE, p. 132
- Play Audio CD for Activity 6, p. 132.
- Teaching Transparency 5-1, Vocabulary Practice, Listening Activity 1
- Cahier d'activités, p. 50, Activity 3
- Travaux pratiques de grammaire, p. 41, Activities 1–2
- Teaching Transparency 5-1, Vocabulary Practice, Speaking Activity 3

Wrap-Up, 10 min.
- Tactile/Auditory Learners, ATE, p. 132

Homework Options
Travaux pratiques de grammaire, Acts. 3–4, p. 42

Day 3

PREMIERE ETAPE
Quick Review 5 min.
- Check homework.

Comment dit-on… ?, p. 133 20 min.
- Presenting **Comment dit-on… ?**, ATE, p. 133
- Play Audio CD for Activity 7, p. 133.
- Cahier d'activités, pp. 50–51, Activities 4–6
- Travaux pratiques de grammaire, pp. 43–44, Acitivities 5–7
- Do Activity 8, p. 133.

Grammaire, p. 134 20 min.
- Presenting **Grammaire**, ATE, p. 134
- Do Activity 9, p. 134.
- Travaux pratiques de grammaire, pp. 45–48 Activities 8–13
- Do Activities 11–12, p. 135.

Wrap-Up 5 min.
- Additional Practice, ATE, p. 135

Homework Options
Study for Quiz 5-1
Grammaire supplémentaire, Acts. 1–4, pp. 148–149
Cahier d'activités, Acts. 8–9, p. 52

Day 4

PREMIERE ETAPE
Quiz 5-1 20 min.
- Administer Quiz 5-1A or 5-1B.

REMISE EN TRAIN 20 min.
- Presenting **Remise en train**, ATE, p. 136
- Do Activities 14–16, pp. 136–137.
- Thinking Critically: Synthesizing, ATE, p. 137

Wrap-Up 10 min.
- Do Activity 17, p. 137. See Teaching Suggestion, Activity 17, ATE, p. 137.

Homework Options
Cahier d'activités, Act. 12, p. 54

Day 5

REMISE EN TRAIN
Quick Review 5 min.
- Check homework.

PANORAMA CULTUREL 20 min.
- Video Guide, p. 30, Pre-viewing Suggestions 1–2
- Presenting **Panorama Culturel**, ATE, p. 138
- Video Guide, p. 30, Viewing Suggestions 1–2
- Questions, ATE, p. 138
- **Qu'en penses-tu?**, p. 138

DEUXIEME ETAPE
Vocabulaire, p. 139 20 min.
- Presenting **Vocabulaire**, ATE, p. 139
- Play Audio CD for Activity 18, p. 139.
- Do Activity 19, p. 140.
- **Stratégie pour lire** and **Note culturelle**, p. 139.
- Cahier d'activités, p. 55, Activities 13–14
- Have students do Activity 20, p. 140, in pairs.

Wrap-Up 5 min.
- Kinesthetic Learners, ATE, p. 140

Homework Options
Pupil's Edition, Activity 21, p. 140
Travaux pratiques de grammaire, Acts. 14–17, pp. 49–50

Day 6

DEUXIEME ETAPE
Quick Review 5 min.
- Check homework.

Comment dit-on… ?, p. 140 20 min.
- Presenting **Comment dit-on…?**, ATE, p. 140
- Play Audio CD for Activity 22, p. 141.
- Cahier d'activités, pp. 55–56, Activities 15–16
- Additional Practice, ATE, top of p. 141
- Have students do Activity 23, p. 141, in pairs.

Grammaire, p. 141 20 min.
- Presenting **Grammaire**, ATE, p. 141
- Do Activity 24, p. 142.
- Travaux pratiques de grammaire, pp. 51–52, Activities 18–20
- **Grammaire supplémentaire**, pp. 150–151, Activities 5–7
- Do Activity 25, p. 142.

Wrap-Up 5 min.
- Additional Practice, ATE, bottom of p. 141

Homework Options
Cahier d'activités, Acts. 17–19, pp. 56–57

One-Stop Planner CD-ROM

For alternative lesson plans by chapter section, to create your own customized plans, or to preview all resources available for this chapter, use the **One-Stop Planner CD-ROM,** Disc 2.

 For additional homework suggestions, see activities accompanied by this symbol throughout the chapter.

Day 7

DEUXIEME ETAPE

Quick Review 5 min.
- Check homework.

Comment dit-on... ?, p. 142 20 min.
- Presenting **Comment dit-on... ?,** ATE, p. 142
- Career Path, ATE, p. 142
- Play Audio CD for Activity 26, p. 142.
- Cahier d'activités, p. 58, Activity 21
- Teaching Transparency 5-2, Writing Suggestion 5

Note de grammaire, p. 143 15 min.
- Read and discuss **Note de grammaire,** p. 143.
- Do Activity 27, p. 143.
- Do Activity 28, p. 143.
- Have students do Activity 29, p. 143, in pairs.

Wrap-Up 10 min.
- See Game: **Catégories,** ATE, p. 143

Homework Options
Study for Quiz 5-2
Pupil's Edition, Activity 30, p. 143
Grammaire supplémentaire, Acts. 8–9, p. 151

Day 8

DEUXIEME ETAPE

Quiz 5-2 20 min.
- Administer Quiz 5-2A or 5-2B.

LISONS! 25 min.
- Read and discuss **Stratégie pour lire,** p. 144.
- Do Prereading Activities A–B, p. 144 and Family Link, ATE, p. 144.
- Have students read **Lisons!,** pp. 144–146.
- Do Reading Activities C–K, pp. 144–146.

Wrap-Up 5 min
- Teacher Note, ATE, p. 145

Homework Options
Cahier d'activités, Act. 22, p. 59

Day 9

LISONS!

Quick Review 15 min.
- Check homework.
- Do Activities L–M, p. 146.

ECRIVONS! 30 min.
- Read and discuss **Stratégie pour écrire,** p. 147, then have students work on their letters.

Wrap-Up 5 min.
- Allow time for peer and self-evaluation of student letters.

Homework Options
Complete final draft of letters.

Day 10

ECRIVONS!

Quick Review 10 min.
- Have students do the third step of Activity C, p. 147.

MISE EN PRATIQUE 35 min.
- Play Audio CD for Activity 1, p. 152.
- Do Activity 2, p. 152.
- Building on Previous Skills, ATE, p. 152
- Play Audio CD for Activity 3, p. 152.
- **A toi de parler,** CD-ROM Tutor Disc 2

Wrap-Up 5 min.
- Activities for Communication, p. 97, Situation (global): Interview

Homework Options
Cahier d'activités, Act. 23, p. 60

Day 11

MISE EN PRATIQUE

Quick Review 5 min.
- Check homework.

Student Review 40 min.
- Do Activity 4, p. 153.
- Game: **Je regrette!,** ATE, p. 153
- Activities for Communication, p. 97, Situation 5-2: Interview
- **A toi d'écrire,** CD-ROM Tutor, Disc 2

Wrap-Up 5 min.
- Begin **Que sais-je?,** p. 154.

Homework Options
Que sais-je?, p. 154

Day 12

MISE EN PRATIQUE

Quick Review 20 min.
- Go over **Que sais-je?,** p. 154.
- Have pairs of students do **Jeu de rôle,** p. 153.

Chapter Review 30 min.
- Teaching Transparency 5-1, Vocabulary Practice, Listening Activity 1
- Review Chapter 5. Choose from **Grammaire supplémentaire,** Grammar Tutor for Students of French, Activities for Communication, Listening Activities, Interactive CD-ROM Tutor, or **Jeux interactifs.**

Homework Options
Study for Chapter 5 Test.

Assessment

Test, Chapter 5 50 min.
- Administer Chapter 5 Test. Select from Testing Program, Alternative Assessment Guide, Test Generator, or Standardized Assessment Tutor.

Chapitre 5 : C'est notre avenir
Suggested Lesson Plans   *90-Minute Block Schedule*

Block 1

CHAPTER OPENER   5 min.
- Present Chapter Objectives, p. 127
- Language Note, ATE, p. 127

MISE EN TRAIN   40 min.
- Note culturelle, p. 130
- Presenting **Mise en train**, ATE, p. 128
- Do Activities 1–4, p. 130.

PREMIERE ETAPE
Vocabulaire, p. 132   20 min.
- Presenting **Vocabulaire**, ATE, p. 132
- Culture Note, ATE, p. 133
- Play Audio CD for Activity 6, p. 132. See Tactile/Auditory Learner, ATE, p. 132

RENCONTRE CULTURELLE   20 min.
- Presenting **Rencontre culturelle**, ATE, p. 131
- Read and discuss **Qu'en penses-tu?** and **Savais-tu que... ?**, p. 131.

Wrap-Up   5 min.
- Listening Activities, Additional Listening Activity 5-1, p. 39

Homework Options
Thinking Critically: Synthesizing, ATE, p. 131
Cahier d'activités, pp. 49–50, Acts. 1–3
Travaux pratiques de grammaire, p. 41, Acts. 1–2

Block 2

PREMIERE ETAPE
Quick Review   5 min.
- Name an event from **Vocabulaire**, p. 132, and have students identify the associated prop. See Presenting **Vocabulaire**, ATE, p. 132.

Comment dit-on...?, p. 133   40 min.
- Presenting **Comment dit-on...?**, ATE, p. 133
- Play Audio CD for Activity 7, p. 133.
- **Tu te rappelles?**, p. 133, with Reteaching: The subjunctive, ATE, p. 133
- Do Activity 8, p. 133.

Grammaire, p. 134   40 min.
- Presenting **Grammaire**, ATE, p. 134
- Challenge, ATE, p. 134
- Do Activities 9–10, pp. 134–135.

Wrap-Up   5 min.
- Visual Learners, ATE, p. 134

Homework Options
Grammaire supplémentaire, pp. 148–149, Acts. 1–3
Cahier d'activités, pp. 50–52, Acts. 4–8
Travaux pratiques de grammaire, pp. 42–46, Acts. 3–9

Block 3

PREMIERE ETAPE
Quick Review   10 min.
- Teaching Transparency 5-1, using suggestion #6 from Suggestions for Using Teaching Transparency 5-1

Grammaire, p. 134   35 min.
- Do Activities 11–13, p. 135.

REMISE EN TRAIN   35 min.
- Presenting **Remise en train**, ATE, p. 136
- Do Activities 14–16, pp. 136–137.
- First Teaching Suggestion, ATE, p. 137

Wrap-Up   10 min.
- Additional Practice, ATE, p. 135

Homework Options
Have students study for Quiz 5-1.
Grammaire supplémentaire, p. 149, Act. 4
Cahier d'activités, pp. 52–54, Acts. 9–12
Travaux pratiques de grammaire, pp. 46–48, Acts. 10–13

One-Stop Planner CD-ROM

For alternative lesson plans by chapter section, to create your own customized plans, or to preview all resources available for this chapter, use the **One-Stop Planner CD-ROM,** Disc 2.

 For additional homework suggestions, see activities accompanied by this symbol throughout the chapter.

Block 4

PREMIERE ETAPE

Quick Review 10 min.
- Activities for Communication, pp. 17–18, Communicative Activity 5-1A and 5-1B

Quiz 5-1 20 min.
- Administer Quiz 5-1A or 5-1B.

DEUXIEME ETAPE

Vocabulaire, p. 139 25 min.
- Presenting **Vocabulaire,** ATE, p. 139
- **Note culturelle** and **De bons conseils,** p. 139
- Play Audio CD for Activity 18, p. 139.
- Do Activity 19, p. 139.

Comment dit-on...?, p. 140 30 min.
- Presenting **Comment dit-on...?,** ATE, p. 140
- Tactile Learners, ATE, p. 140
- Play Audio CD for Activity 22, p. 141.
- Do Activity 23, p. 141.

Wrap-Up 5 min.
- Kinesthetic Learners, ATE, p. 140

Homework Options
Pupil's Edition, Activity 21, p. 140
Cahier d'activités, pp. 55–56, Acts. 13–16
Travaux pratiques de grammaire, pp. 49–50, Acts. 14–17

Block 5

DEUXIEME ETAPE

Quick Review 10 min.
- Activities for Communication, pp. 19–20, Communicative Activity 5-2A and 5-2B

Grammaire, p. 141 25 min.
- Presenting **Grammaire,** ATE, p. 141
- Game: Verb Toss, ATE, p. 141
- Do Activity 24, p. 142.

Comment dit-on...?, p. 142 45 min.
- Presenting **Comment dit-on...?,** ATE, p. 142
- Play Audio CD for Activity 26, p. 142.
- Read and discuss **Note de grammaire,** p. 143.
- Do Activities 27–29, p. 143.

Wrap-Up 10 min.
- Listening Activities, p. 41, Additional Listening Activity 5-6

Homework Options
Have students study for Quiz 5-2.
Pupil's Edition, Activity 30, p. 143
Grammaire supplémentaire, pp. 150–151, Acts. 5–9
Cahier d'activités, pp. 56–58, Acts. 17–21
Travaux pratiques de grammaire, pp. 51–53, Acts. 18–21

Block 6

DEUXIEME ETAPE

Quick Review 10 min.
- Game: **Qu'est-ce que tu ferais?,** ATE, 125C

Quiz 5-2 20 min.
- Administer Quiz 5-2A or 5-2B.

LISONS! 30 min.
- Read and discuss **Stratégie pour lire,** p. 144
- Do Prereading Activities A–B, p. 144.
- Have students read the first section of the excerpt from **L'Enfant noir,** pp. 144–145.
- Do Reading Activities C–D, p. 144; Teacher Note, ATE, p. 145.
- Have students read the second section of the excerpt from **L'Enfant noir,** pp. 145–146.
- Do Activities E–F, p. 145.

MISE EN PRATIQUE 30 min.
- Play Audio CD for Activity 1, p. 152.
- Have students read and compare the letters in Activity 3, p. 152, using Audio CD 5.
- Have students read letters of Activity 5, p. 153.

Homework Options
Que sais-je?, p. 154
Finish Activity 4, Pupil's Edition, p. 153.
Study for Chapter 5 Test

Block 7

MISE EN PRATIQUE

Quick Review 10 min.
- Go over answers to **Que sais-je?,** p. 154.
- **Jeu de rôle,** p. 153

Chapter Review 30 min.
- Review Chapter 5. Choose from **Grammaire supplémentaire,** Grammar Tutor for Students of French, Activities for Communication, Listening Activities, Interactive CD-ROM Tutor, or **Jeux interactifs.**

Test, Chapter 5 50 min.
- Administer Chapter 5 Test. Select from Testing Program, Alternative Assessment Guide, Test Generator, or Standardized Assessment Tutor.

Chapter Opener

One-Stop Planner CD-ROM

For resource information, see the **One-Stop Planner,** Disc 2.

 Pacing Tips
The first **étape** has slightly less material to cover than the second **étape**. In the first **étape**, you might make use of the cultural content in the **Rencontre culturelle**, on page 131. For Lesson Plans and timing suggestions, see pages 125I–125L.

Meeting the Standards

Communication
- Asking about and expressing intentions; expressing conditions and possibilities, p. 133
- Asking about future plans; expressing wishes; expressing indecision; giving advice, p. 140
- Requesting information; writing a formal letter, p. 142

Cultures
- Culture Notes, pp. 129, 130, 131, 133
- Notes culturelles, pp. 130, 139
- Panorama Culturel, p. 138
- Rencontre culturelle, p. 131

Connections
- Family Link, p. 144
- Music Link, p. 144
- Geography Links, pp. 131, 135, 146

Comparisons
- Language-to-Language, p. 141
- Thinking Critically, pp. 131, 135, 137, 138

Communities
- Career Path, p.142
- Community Links p. 126, 138
- De l'école au travail, p. 143

Cultures and Communities

Community Link
Ask students for their definitions of success. Ask them to name people they think are successful or those they admire, and to give reasons for their choices. Have students visualize their own lives in five years. What will they be doing? Where will they be living?

Will they go to college or will they want to find a job right after high school? Why? Will they want to get married? What kind of careers would they like to have and why? Go back to the role models students named earlier and have them guess what professional paths those people took to become what they are.

5
C'est notre avenir

Objectives

In this chapter you will learn to

Première étape

- ask about and express intentions
- express conditions and possibilities

Deuxième étape

- ask about future plans
- express wishes
- express indecision
- give advice
- request information
- write a formal letter

 internet

 ADRESSE: go.hrw.com
MOT-CLE: WA3 FRANCOPHONE
AFRICA-5

◄ La sortie d'une école à Dakar

Focusing on Outcomes
Have students list expressions in English they associate with the objectives.
NOTE: You may want to use the video to support the objectives. The self-check activities in **Que sais-je?** on page 154 help students assess their achievement of those objectives.

Language Note
Have students look at the chapter title, **C'est notre avenir.** Ask what words they recognize in **avenir** (à and **venir**). Then, have them try to guess what the title means.

Connections and Comparisons

Group Work
Collect reference materials about Senegal from your local library or travel agencies. Bring them to class and distribute them to small groups. Give students ten minutes to write down as many facts about Senegal as they can find. You might have groups elect one member to report their findings to the class.

If time allows, have students search the Internet for more information on Senegal. Assign each group a different topic to research. **(la géographie, l'histoire, l'économie, etc...)** You might have one person in each group search the Internet, have another student summarize the information, and another member of the group present their findings to the class.

PRINT
- Lesson Planner, p. 22
- Video Guide, pp. 30, 32
- Cahier d'activités, p. 49

MEDIA
- One-Stop Planner
- Video Program
  Camille et compagnie
  Videocassette 2, 18:56–23:32
  Videocassette 5 (captioned version), 26:47–31:23
- Audio Compact Discs, CD 5, Tr. 1

Language Note
Explain that **chômage** means *unemployment*. **Au chômage** means *unemployed*.

Presenting
Mise en train

Play the audio recording, pausing after each interview to ask students what they understood. Then, play the recording again, asking about each person's plans after high school.

Mise en train · *L'avenir, c'est demain*

Stratégie pour comprendre
L'avenir, c'est dans un ou deux ans. C'est le bac, l'université, le travail, le mariage... Comment est-ce que ces jeunes Sénégalais voient leur avenir après le lycée?

CD 5 Tr. 1

Cahier d'activités, p. 49, Act. 1 – 2

L'année prochaine, j'aurai dix-huit ans et je passerai mon bac. Ensuite, si je le réussis, j'entrerai à l'université. Je voudrais faire des études de médecine. Dans sept ou huit ans, si tout va bien, il se peut que je sois médecin. Bien sûr, si je rencontre une fille que j'aime, il est possible que je me marie et que j'aie des enfants. Mais ça, c'est pour plus tard. Pour l'instant, le principal, c'est de réussir mon bac.

1 Lamine, 17 ans, Dakar

J'ai du mal à imaginer mon avenir. Je ne sais pas ce que je ferai après le bac. Peut-être que j'arrêterai mes études et que je travaillerai avec mes parents. Ils ont une boutique de vêtements et ils voudraient que je travaille avec eux. Ça ne m'intéresse pas tellement, mais il faut bien que je gagne de l'argent. Et ici, à Dakar, il y a beaucoup de chômage. Enfin, j'ai encore un an pour réfléchir.

2 Fatima, 17 ans, Dakar

Plus tard, j'ai l'intention d'être musicien. J'espère que je serai célèbre, mais bon, je ne rêve pas trop. En tout cas, après mon bac, j'arrêterai mes études et je me consacrerai entièrement à la musique. Je joue déjà du saxophone dans un petit groupe de World Music. C'est mon rêve et je pense que je réussirai. Le seul problème, c'est convaincre mes parents. Je ne sais pas s'ils seront d'accord. Il faut que j'en parle avec eux. Mais j'attendrai le bon moment!

3 Omar, 16 ans, Dakar

Preteaching Vocabulary

Recognizing Cognates
Have students skim the paragraphs for words they recognize from English. Ask them to list the words and then have them explain how these words contribute to an overall understanding of each person's hopes for the future. For example, how does the word **médecine** help them understand Lamine's goals? Students might wish to work in pairs to consolidate their lists before sharing them with the whole class.

université	**saxophone**
médecine	**import-export**
principal	**chauffeur**
boutique	**banque**
musique	

Après le bac, je pense voyager. Mon frère habite en France et j'irai peut-être le rejoindre. Il m'écrit qu'il aime beaucoup la vie là-bas. Au début, c'était difficile, mais il s'est bien intégré. Il travaille dans une entreprise d'import-export. Il fait venir des vêtements sénégalais. Moi, ça me plairait bien comme travail. J'aime beaucoup la mode. Ici, c'est difficile pour une fille de trouver du travail. Mais ce ne sera pas facile d'obtenir un permis de travail pour la France. Et puis, mes parents ne sont pas d'accord. Ils pensent qu'il vaut mieux rester dans son pays que d'aller vivre dans un autre pays. Alors, il faudra que j'attende d'être majeure. Quand j'aurai dix-huit ans, je prendrai une décision.

4 Safiétou, 16 ans, Dakar

Moi, quand j'aurai vingt et un ans, je passerai immédiatement mon permis de conduire pour être chauffeur de taxi, comme mon père. J'aime beaucoup conduire. Et puis, dans un taxi, on rencontre des tas de gens, des touristes, surtout. Je discute beaucoup avec mon père, il aime son métier. Je crois que ça me plaira aussi. Je ne sais pas si je ferai ça toute ma vie, mais, pour l'instant, ça m'intéresse.

5 Ousmane, 18 ans, Saint-Louis

Après le bac, moi, j'ai décidé de partir en vacances un mois pour me reposer du lycée! J'ai l'intention d'aller à la plage et de jouer au volley avec les copains. Après, je ferai une école de commerce à Dakar. Là-bas, j'habiterai chez mon oncle. Quand je serai à Dakar, je tiens à aller au cinéma et au concert parce qu'ici, quand on veut sortir, il n'y a pas grand-chose. C'est une petite ville, avec un seul lycée et assez peu de distractions. Une fois en ville, je compte travailler, bien sûr, mais aussi m'amuser! Après, quand j'aurai mon diplôme de l'école de commerce, je chercherai du travail dans une banque. C'est ça qui m'intéresse.

6 Penda, 17 ans, Joal-Fadiout

Using the Captioned Video

As an alternative, you might want to show the captioned version of *Camille et compagnie : L'avenir est à nous* on Videocassette 5. Some students may benefit from seeing the written words as they listen to the target language and watch the gestures and actions in context. This visual reinforcement of vocabulary and functions will facilitate students' comprehension and help reduce their anxiety before they are formally introduced to the new language in the chapter.

Culture Notes

• **Saint-Louis**, named after Louis XIV of France, is Senegal's fourth largest city. It was built on an island at the mouth of the Senegal River in 1659 as the administrative capital of the French West African territories. Famous for its beautiful colonial architecture with wooden or wrought iron balconies, Saint-Louis is sometimes called "the New Orleans of West Africa."

• **Joal-Fadiout** is comprised of two separate villages: Joal on the mainland and Fadiout, a small island linked to Joal by a footbridge. Joal is the birthplace of Senegal's former president and world-renowned writer and poet, Léopold Senghor. The island of Fadiout was formed from seashells that piled up over the years. Inhabitants of this island pound shells to make cement, which they use to build their houses.

 Camille et compagnie

You may choose to show students Episode 5: *L'avenir est à nous* now or wait until later in the chapter. In the video Max is writing a letter to a school of journalism because his dream is to become a journalist. Later, Laurent, Camille, and Sophie join Max and they all discuss their plans for the future. Camille would like to study business in the United States, Sophie dreams of being an actress, and Laurent would like to become a car technician.

Mise en train

Challenge

3 Have students react to each of the statements according to their own plans. For example, to react to the statement **Lamine n'a pas l'intention de se marier**, students might say **Moi non plus! Je préfère rester célibataire.** or **Moi, si. Je voudrais bien me marier.**

Teaching Suggestions

5 You might have students write their responses in their journal.

5 Have students interview a classmate about his or her future plans. Then, compile a list of students' plans on the board.

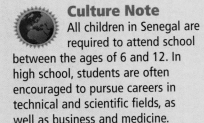

Culture Note
All children in Senegal are required to attend school between the ages of 6 and 12. In high school, students are often encouraged to pursue careers in technical and scientific fields, as well as business and medicine.

Answers

4 1. ... si je le réussis... ; ... si tout va bien... ; si je rencontre une fille que j'aime...
2. ... il se peut que... ; ... il est possible que... ; ... peut-être que...
3. Je ne sais pas ce que je ferai...
4. ... j'ai l'intention de... ; je pense... ; .... j'ai décidé de... ; ... je tiens à ... ; ... je compte...
5. ... il faut bien que... ; ... il faudra que...
6. C'est mon rêve... ; ... ça me plairait bien... ; ... ça m'intéresse.

---

1 **Tu as compris?** 1. near the end of secondary school

These activities check for comprehension only. Students should not yet be expected to produce language modeled in Mise en train.

1. A quel moment de leur vie ces personnes écrivent leur lettre?
2. Ces lettres répondent à quelles questions? What are your plans for the future?
3. Qu'est-ce que ces jeunes veulent faire?
   3. go to a university, work in parents' store, become a musician, travel, become a taxi driver, go on vacation

2 **C'est qui?**
Associe les jeunes de *L'avenir, c'est demain* aux projets qu'ils ont pour l'avenir.

Lamine

Penda

Safiétou   Ousmane

Penda — **partir en vacances**

Penda — **travailler dans une banque**

Ousmane — **passer son permis de conduire**

Safiétou — **aller en France**

Penda — **faire une école de commerce**

Ousmane — **être chauffeur de taxi**

Lamine — **faire des études de médecine**

travailler avec son frère — Safiétou

3 **Vrai ou faux?**

1. Fatima est contente à l'idée de travailler dans la boutique de ses parents. faux
2. Omar veut arrêter ses études et se consacrer à sa musique. vrai
3. Le frère de Safiétou vend des vêtements sénégalais en France. vrai
4. Les parents de Safiétou veulent bien qu'elle habite chez son frère. faux
5. Ousmane serait content de pouvoir rencontrer des touristes. vrai
6. Penda pense chercher du travail dans une entreprise d'import-export. faux

4 **Cherche les expressions**

What expressions do the teenagers in *L'avenir, c'est demain* use to . . . See answers below.

1. express a condition?
2. express a possibility?
3. express indecision?
4. express an intention?
5. express an obligation?
6. express interest in something?

5 **Et maintenant, à toi**

Qu'est-ce que tu penses faire après le lycée? Est-ce que tu vas faire comme un des jeunes de *L'avenir, c'est demain?*

Note culturelle

L'emploi est très limité pour les jeunes Sénégalais, et surtout pour ceux qui n'habitent pas dans les villes. La plupart des gens travaillent dans l'agriculture et, en général, les jeunes sont tenus de travailler aux champs, comme leurs parents. Même si légalement, les enfants doivent faire six ans d'école au minimum, en réalité environ 55% des enfants sénégalais vont à l'école primaire et 10% à l'école secondaire. Très peu de jeunes Sénégalais vont à l'université.

Comprehension Check

Game

4 Play this activity as a game. Before class, prepare a list of functional expressions from the **Mise en train**, such as **Il est possible que je me marie.** In class, form two or more teams. Place a bell on a desk at the front of the room. Have one player from each team come to the front. Call out the first expression. The first student to ring the bell has the chance to answer by telling which function the expression serves *(expressing a possibility)*. If a player responds correctly, his or her team wins a point. If he or she answers incorrectly, his or her team loses a point. Then, the next players come to the front. Continue until all the expressions have been used.

STANDARDS: 1.2, 2.1, 3.2, 4.2

Rencontre culturelle

Qu'est-ce que tu sais du Sénégal? Pour t'en faire une meilleure idée, regarde ces photos.

Un marché en plein air

Dakar, la capitale du Sénégal

L'arachide est le produit agricole principal.

La musique traditionnelle est toujours populaire.

La pêche est une activité très importante.

On peut acheter des masques dans les marchés d'artisans.

Possible answers: **1.** mix of urban and rural, modern and traditional
2. shopping at outdoor markets, listening to music, fishing, shopping at artisans' markets

Qu'en penses-tu?

1. Quelle impression est-ce que ces photos donnent du Sénégal?
2. D'après ces photos, quelles sont certaines activités sénégalaises? Est-ce que tu penses que d'autres pays francophones participent à ces activités? Et les gens de ta région?

Savais-tu que... ?

Le Sénégal est un pays d'Afrique occidentale qui comprend beaucoup de groupes ethniques, comme les Wolofs, les Serers, les Dialos et les Toucouleurs. Beaucoup de Sénégalais vivent à Dakar, la capitale et le centre économique et commercial du Sénégal. Mais plus de la moitié de la population vit à la campagne et pratique des coutumes vieilles de centaines d'années. Un chef ou un groupe de doyens gouverne chaque village et prend des décisions pour toute la communauté. L'agriculture est la ressource économique principale du Sénégal. Les Sénégalais, jeunes et vieux, participent aux récoltes, à l'élevage et à la pêche. A la ville comme à la campagne, les traditions séné-galaises se retrouvent dans l'art, l'artisanat, la musique et la danse. Il y a même des sports de tradition purement sénégalaise, comme par exemple, la lutte sans frappe, qu'on pratique dans les villages depuis le dix-septième siècle.

Objectives Asking about and expressing intentions; expressing conditions and possibilities

WA3 FRANCOPHONE
AFRICA-5

 Bell Work
Have students write three sentences in response to the question **Qu'est-ce que tu vas faire cet été?**

Presenting
Vocabulaire

Write the new sentences on a transparency and cover it with a sheet of paper. Show props (a diploma, a driver's license, a college T-shirt, the want ads, a plastic wedding ring, a baby doll) as you tell the story, pretending to be Adja's father. Uncover each expression on the transparency as you say it. Then, name several events and have students identify the correct prop.

Vocabulaire

Regarde ce que le père d'Adja a fait dans sa jeunesse.

A dix-huit ans, il **a réussi son bac.**

Ensuite, il **a fait son service militaire.**

Puis, à vingt et un ans, il **a passé son permis de conduire.**

Après, il **est entré à l'université.**

Il **a fini ses études.**

Il **a été** deux mois **au chômage.**
He was unemployed. . .

Ensuite, il **a trouvé un travail.**

A vingt-sept ans, il **s'est marié.**

Et, à vingt-neuf ans, il **a eu une fille,** Adja.

arrêter ses études	**faire une école technique**
choisir un métier *to choose a career*	**obtenir son diplôme**
faire un apprentissage *to do an apprenticeship*	**quitter sa famille** *to leave home*

Cahier d'activités, p. 50, Act. 3   Travaux pratiques de grammaire, pp. 41–42, Act. 1–4

6 **Qui parle?** See scripts and answers on p. 125G.

 Ecoutons Ecoute le père d'Adja et ses amis parler de leurs souvenirs de jeunesse et décide si la personne qui parle est le père d'Adja ou non.
CD 5 Tr. 2

Communication for All Students

Challenge
Write on a transparency the various stages of Adja's father's life in random order and have students number the stages in a logical order. You might choose vocabulary not illustrated on page 132 (**arrêter ses études, choisir un métier, faire un apprentissage, etc.**) as substitutes for Adja's father's experience.

Tactile/Auditory Learners
6 Have students write the vocabulary expressions at random on a sheet of paper. As they listen to the recording, have them number the vocabulary expressions on their paper in sequence according to what they hear.

Comment dit-on...?

Asking about and expressing intentions; expressing conditions and possibilities

To ask about intentions:

Qu'est-ce que tu as l'intention de faire
en juillet?
Qu'est-ce que tu comptes faire cet été?
What do you plan to do . . . ?
Qu'est-ce que tu penses faire après le bac?
Qu'est-ce que tu vas faire l'année prochaine?

To express intentions:

J'ai l'intention de partir en vacances.
Je compte passer mon permis cet été.
I'm planning on . . .
Après le bac, **je pense** travailler.
Je tiens à continuer mes études.
I really want to . . .

To express conditions:

Si je réussis mon bac, j'entrerai à
l'université. *If . . . ,*
Si j'habite à Dakar, je chercherai
un travail.

To express possibilities:

Peut-être que je travaillerai. *Maybe . . .*
Il se peut que je fasse un apprentissage.
It might be that . . .
Il est possible que je fasse des études
de médecine. *It's possible that . . .*

*Note that you use the subjunctive with the expressions **Il se peut que** and **Il est possible que**.

Cahier d'activités, pp. 50–51, Act. 4–6

Grammaire supplémentaire,
p.148, Act. 1

---

7 **Projets d'avenir**   See scripts and answers on p. 125G.

Ecoutons Ecoute ces jeunes qui parlent de leurs projets pour après le lycée. Qui a l'intention de...

CD 5 Tr. 3   1. se marier?
2. trouver un travail?
3. faire un apprentissage?
4. entrer à l'université?
5. prendre un appartement?
6. faire son service militaire?
7. partir en vacances?
8. quitter sa famille?

Séka   Prosper
Prisca
Angèle

Tu te rappelles?

Do you remember the forms of the subjunctive that you learned in Chapter 3? Take the **-ent** off of the present tense **ils/elles** form of the verb and add the endings **-e, -es, -e, -ions, -iez, -ent**. Remember that some verbs have irregular stems, but use the regular endings. Have you noticed some new uses of the subjunctive?

Travaux pratiques de grammaire,
pp. 43–44, Act. 5–7

8 **Il se peut que je...**   See answers below.

Parlons Qu'est-ce que Bertille pense faire après le lycée? Complète ses phrases.

1.
Il se peut que je...
2.
3.
4.

Cultures and Communities

Culture Note

Most francophone countries require 10 months of military service for young men 16 or older. Until recently, the French military service was required of all males aged 18. The service could sometimes be substituted for **coopération,** a community service fulfilled in other countries. From now on, the French army will be made up of professional soldiers. In Switzerland, all men between 20 and 50 must serve in a reserve militia. However, after an initial training period, this usually involves only an occasional week or so of service per year.

Presenting
Comment dit-on... ?

Make two sets of transparency strips. On the first set, write the questions for asking about intentions (**Qu'est-ce que tu penses faire...?**) and sentence starters for expressing conditions (**Si je me marie,...**). On the second set, write logical responses for the phrases in the first set. (**Après le bac, je pense entrer à l'université; ... il est possible que j'aie des enfants.**) As you read aloud each strip in the first set and the second set, place the strips on the overhead projector. Have students repeat the new expressions after you. Once you have read aloud all the strips, remove them from the projector. Place the strips from the first set in a shoe box and scatter the completions set on your desk in random order. Have volunteers come to the projector, pick a strip from the shoe box, and try to find the appropriate completion among the strips on your desk.

Reteaching
The subjunctive   Write **Il se peut que je _____ mes devoirs** on the board. Have a volunteer fill in the blank (**fasse**) and explain how to form the subjunctive. Then, have students express their intentions (**Je tiens à finir mes études**) as you write their sentences on the board. Have the class change each sentence, using **Il se peut que...** to express possibility.

Answers
8 1. (j')entre à l'université.
2. voyage.
3. me marie.
4. fasse un apprentissage.

Presenting
Grammaire

The future Write **parler, choisir,** and **vendre** on the board. Make one set of index cards with the future endings on them and another set with the subject pronouns. Tape a subject pronoun card in front of each verb and the appropriate ending card at the end. Erase the final **-e** of **vendre** when you add the endings. Have students repeat the forms after you.

The future

You've learned to use **aller** with an infinitive to say that you are *going to do* something. Now you will learn how to say that you *will do* something.

Je **prendrai** une décision.	Il **retrouvera** des amis.
I will make . . .	*He'll meet . . .*

- To form the future tense of most verbs, add the endings **-ai, -as, -a, -ons, -ez, -ont** to the infinitive. If the infinitive ends in **-re**, drop the final **e** before you add the endings.

Je **parlerai** français.	Nous **voyagerons** au Sénégal.
Tu **choisiras** un métier.	Vous **sortirez** après minuit.
Il/Elle/On **vendra** des fruits.	Ils/Elles **prendront** une décision.

- Verbs that have a spelling change in the present tense have the same change in their future stem.

j' **achète** → j' **achèterai**   elle **appelle** → elle **appellera**

- Some irregular verbs have a special stem to which you add the regular endings. Here are some of the most common ones:

Grammaire supplémentaire, pp.148–149, Act. 2–4

aur- (avoir)	**fer-** (faire)	**ser-** (être)
deviendr- (devenir)	**ir-** (aller)	**verr-** (voir)
devr- (devoir)	**pourr-** (pouvoir)	**viendr-** (venir)
enverr- (envoyer)	**saur-** (savoir)	**voudr-** (vouloir)

Je **ferai** mes devoirs.   On **viendra** à neuf heures.

Cahier d'activités, p. 52, Act. 8–9

Travaux pratiques de grammaire, pp. 45–48, Act. 8–13

9 **Grammaire en contexte**

Ecrivons Christine adore deviner l'avenir des autres! Complète sa conversation avec son cousin Gérard.

GERARD Dis, Christine, à ton avis, qu'est-ce que je ___1___ (devenir)?   *deviendrai*

CHRISTINE D'abord, tu ___2___ (réussir) ton bac.   *réussiras*

GERARD Et après?

CHRISTINE Après ça, tu ___3___ (entrer) à l'université.   *entreras*

GERARD Ah non! J'en ai marre des études! Je ___4___ (chercher) un travail.   *chercherai*

CHRISTINE Non, tu ___5___ (finir) tes études à l'université.   *finiras*

GERARD Et pourquoi? Qu'est-ce que je ___6___ (faire) après?   *ferai*

CHRISTINE Si tu finis, tu ___7___ (être) peut-être diplomate.   *seras*

GERARD Mais je ne veux pas être diplomate.

CHRISTINE Et pourquoi pas? Comme, ça, tu ___8___ (pouvoir) voyager partout.   *pourras*

GERARD Euh...

CHRISTINE Tu ___9___ (aller) dans beaucoup de pays étrangers. Tu ___10___ (voir) le monde entier, quoi. Tu ___11___ (apprendre) beaucoup de langues...   *iras, verras, apprendras*

GERARD Oui, ça pourrait être intéressant, mais j'ai l'intention de me marier. Est-ce que j'___12___ (avoir) des enfants?   *aurai*

CHRISTINE Oui. Et ta famille ___13___ (vivre) avec toi.   *vivra*

GERARD Et on ___14___ (acheter) une grande maison?   *achètera*

CHRISTINE Oui! Ce ___15___ (être) nécessaire à cause de tes sept enfants!   *sera*

Communication for All Students

Visual Learners
Have partners write down three things they plan to do in the future. Then, have partners draw illustrations of their activities and take turns trying to guess each activity. (**Tu te marieras!**)

Challenge
After presenting the grammar, have partners write down something about their present feelings and activities that would lead their partner to make a prediction as to what they will do in the future. (prompt: **J'aime les voitures.**/ response: **Tu achèteras une voiture.**) Students should take turns reading and responding to their prompts.

10 Grammaire en contexte

Parlons Safiétou et Penda se marieront cet été. Imagine leur vie pendant les vingt années à venir. *See answers below.*

Elle . . .

> quitter sa famille
> travailler comme
> professeur
> écrire un livre
> aller en France

Il . . .

> finir ses études
> chercher un travail
> devenir banquier
> avoir une barbe
> faire un apprentissage

Ils . . .

> avoir des enfants
> acheter une maison
> prendre des vacances
> chaque année
> faire un voyage en
> Amérique

11 Grammaire en contexte

Parlons Qu'est-ce qu'Adjoua fera si elle rend visite à son frère à Paris? *Possible answers:*

1.
Elle visitera le Louvre.

2.
Elle mangera des pâtisseries.

3.
Elle ira voir l'Arc de triomphe.

4.
Elle fera les magasins.

12 Tes phrases à toi

Parlons/Écrivons Fais des phrases pour décrire ce que tes amis et toi ferez peut-être après le lycée.

> Moi, je
> Mes amis
> Un(e) de mes ami(e)s
> Mes amis et moi, nous

> choisir un métier
> se marier
> prendre un appartement
> entrer à l'université
> chercher du travail

> dormir jusqu'à midi
> entrer dans une école technique
> gagner de l'argent
> voyager beaucoup

13 Leurs projets d'avenir

Écrivons/Parlons Avant le bac, ces jeunes disent à leurs parents ce qu'ils veulent faire plus tard. Avec ton/ta camarade, écris les dialogues entre ces jeunes et un de leurs parents. Puis, jouez ces scènes.

> Chakib rêve de devenir footballeur professionnel.

> Aïcha hésite entre aller à l'université et travailler comme vendeuse.

> Marina veut trouver un travail et habiter à Dakar.

> Farouk ne sait pas ce qu'il veut faire.

Connections and Comparisons

Thinking Critically

Comparing and Contrasting Have students turn to the **Vocabulaire** on page 132 and compare their future plans to what Adja's father did. Then, have them discuss how and why their plans might be different than those of an African student. (They don't have mandatory military service.)

Geography Link

As an extension of Activity 11, have students substitute other cities (in the United States or in the rest of the world) for Paris, and come up with four things that Adjoua could do and see in those places. You might have them work on this activity in different stages. First students choose a city and think of four things to do and see there. Then they write four things Adjoua will do in that city.

Additional Practice

12 Students write five activities on a sheet of paper. Collect and redistribute the papers at random. Students should write a paragraph about their plans, using expressions, such as **ensuite**, and the list of activities they were given.

Speaking Assessment

13 You might use the following rubric when grading your students on this activity.

Speaking Rubric	Points			
	4	**3**	**2**	**1**
Content (Complete–Incomplete)				
Comprehension (Total–Little)				
Comprehensibility Comprehensible–Incomprehensible				
Accuracy Accurate–Seldom accurate)				
Fluency (Fluent–Not fluent)				

18–20: A	14–15: C	Under
16–17: B	12–13: D	12: F

Assess

▶ Testing Program, pp. 89–92
Quiz 5-1A, Quiz 5-1B,
Audio CD 5, Tr. 14
▶ Student Make-Up Assignments
Chapter 5, Alternative Quiz
▶ Alternative Assessment Guide,
p. 34

10 Answers
(Elle) quittera sa famille/travaillera comme professeur/écrira un livre/ira en France. (Il) finira ses études/cherchera un travail/deviendra banquier/aura une barbe/fera un apprentissage. (Ils) auront des enfants/achèteront une maison/prendront des vacances chaque année/feront un voyage en Amérique.

Presenting
Remise en train

Play the audio recording and have students listen with their books closed. Stop the recording after the first scene. Ask who is having the discussion, what it is about, what the boy wants to do, and how his parents react. Then, play the recording again and have students note the parents' objections and how Omar counters them. Ask students whether they agree with Omar or his parents. Then, play the second scene and have students listen for the advice Dana gives Omar.

Answers

14
1. his future
2. become a musician
3. limited prospects, poor pay, difficult profession
4. Omar should get information from the music school to convince his parents.
5. He is a prospective student; he has played saxophone for five years.
6. what courses are offered, the price, how long the training lasts, when classes begin

Remise en train · *Passe ton bac d'abord!*

CD 5 Tr. 4

Omar Zidane habite à Dakar, au Sénégal. Pour lui, c'est bientôt la fin du lycée. Qu'est-ce qu'il va faire après? Il a une discussion à ce sujet avec ses parents.

Mme Zidane Alors, Omar? Tu as réfléchi? Tu sais ce que tu veux faire après ton bac?

Omar Euh, oui. J'aimerais faire de la musique.

Mme Zidane De la musique!

Omar Oui, du saxophone. Je voudrais faire une école de musique.

M. Zidane Tu ferais mieux d'entrer à l'université pour faire des études sérieuses.

Omar Pourquoi? C'est pas sérieux, la musique?

Mme Zidane Tu sais bien, il n'y a pas beaucoup de débouchés. Il y a tellement de groupes. Tu ferais mieux de devenir médecin ou ingénieur, ou...

Omar Mais, maman, si je ne réussis pas à percer, je pourrai toujours devenir professeur de musique.

M. Zidane Tu sais, ce n'est pas très bien payé, professeur.

Omar Et alors? Ce n'est pas l'argent qui m'intéresse, c'est la musique!

Mme Zidane Ecoute, il faut d'abord que tu penses à ton bac. Après, on verra. Mais il faut que tu réfléchisses sérieusement. Musicien, c'est une profession difficile.

Omar Un jour, je serai célèbre. Et quand on me demandera comment je suis devenu musicien, je dirai : «Ça a été très dur. Mes parents ne voulaient pas que je fasse de la musique!»

14 **Tu as compris?** See answers below.

1. De quoi parlent Omar et ses parents?
2. Qu'est-ce qu'Omar voudrait faire?
3. Pourquoi ses parents sont inquiets?
4. Qu'est-ce que Dana conseille à Omar?
5. Quels types d'informations Omar donne dans sa lettre?
6. Quels types d'informations est-ce qu'il demande?

a. Un jour, je serai célèbre.

b. La musique, c'est un métier difficile.

c. Tu ferais mieux de devenir médecin ou ingénieur.

d. C'est pas sérieux, la musique?

e. Si je ne réussis pas, je pourrai toujours devenir professeur de musique.

f. Professeur de musique, ce n'est pas bien payé.

g. Il faudrait que tu fasses des études sérieuses.

h. Il n'y a pas de débouchés. Il y a trop de groupes.

i. Ce n'est pas l'argent qui m'intéresse.

15 **Mais moi, je veux!** See answers on p. 137.

Décide si c'est Omar ou ses parents qui diraient les phrases suivantes, puis récris leur conversation.

These activities check for comprehension only. Students should not yet be expected to produce language modeled in **Remise en train**.

Preteaching Vocabulary

Using Prior Knowledge

Have students look at the word **débouchés** on page 136. Ask them to try to guess the meaning from the context and from the word that is contained within it **(bouche)**. Have them guess at the connection between the literal meaning *(waterway)* and the figurative meaning *(opening)* and their connection to the anatomical term *(mouth)*. Have them think of equivalent geographical terms in English (i.e., the mouth of the river). Ask them what other words they can find that have a literal and figurative meaning.

percer
réfléchir
dur

Quelques jours plus tard, Omar parle à son amie Dana de sa conversation avec ses parents.

Omar Tu sais, j'ai parlé avec mes parents.

Dana Ah oui? Et qu'est-ce qu'ils ont dit?

Omar Eh bien, ils ne veulent pas que je fasse de la musique.

Dana Pourquoi?

Omar Ils disent qu'il n'y a pas de débouchés.

Dana Tu leur as expliqué que tu pouvais devenir professeur de musique?

Omar Oui. Mais ils veulent que je réfléchisse. Bref, ils ne sont pas d'accord.

Dana Tu sais, tu devrais te renseigner auprès d'une école de musique. Peut-être qu'avec plus d'informations, tu pourrais convaincre tes parents.

Omar Tu as raison, je vais me renseigner un peu mieux.

Omar a finalement écrit une lettre à une école de musique pour avoir plus de renseignements.

Omar Zidane
28, rue Vincent
Dakar

Dakar, le 12 mai

Monsieur le Directeur,
Je me permets de vous écrire parce que j'ai entendu parler de votre école. J'aimerais beaucoup faire des études de musique après mon baccalauréat. Je joue du saxophone depuis cinq ans. Actuellement, je fais partie d'un groupe de World Music, mais j'aimerais me perfectionner. Auriez-vous l'amabilité de m'envoyer des renseignements sur votre école? Je voudrais savoir quels cours sont offerts, le prix, la durée de la formation et quand les cours commencent. Vous serait-il possible de m'envoyer une brochure?

Avec mes remerciements anticipés, veuillez accepter, Monsieur le directeur, l'expression de mes salutations respectueuses.

Omar Zidane

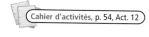
Cahier d'activités, p. 54, Act. 12

See answers below.

16 Cherche les expressions

According to **Passe ton bac d'abord!,** what expressions would you use to . . .

1. ask about someone's plans?
2. express a wish?
3. give advice?
4. express an obligation?
5. begin a letter?
6. request information?
7. end a letter?

17 Et maintenant, à toi

Et toi? Est-ce que tu as déjà parlé de ton avenir avec tes parents? Est-ce que vous êtes d'accord?

Comprehension Check

Thinking Critically

- **Comparing and Contrasting** Have students read the letter on this page. Ask them how the language is different than what they're used to hearing and have them suggest why. (It is a business letter and therefore, more formal.) Ask them what formulaic expressions we use in English in formal business letters (*Dear Madam or Sir:, I* would greatly appreciate it if . . . , Thank you for your time and attention to this matter, Sincerely, and so on).

- **Synthesizing** Have students suggest informal expressions they use every day and then restate them in more formal English. *(Hey, man. S'up?; Good afternoon, sir. How are you?)*

Teaching Suggestions

Have students reread Omar's letter on this page and suggest problems he may have pursuing a career in music and convincing his parents.

17 You might have students write a brief entry in their journals about discussions they've had with their parents concerning their future.

 VIDEO **Camille et compagnie**

As an alternative or in addition to the **Remise en train,** you may wish to show Episode 5 of **Camille et compagnie.** For suggestions and activities, see the *Video Guide.*

Answers

15
a. Omar	f. ses parents
b. ses parents	g. ses parents
c. ses parents	h. ses parents
d. Omar	i. Omar
e. Omar	

Answers may vary:
g, d, h, c, e, f, i, b, a

16
1. Tu sais ce que tu veux faire... ?
2. J'aimerais... ; Je voudrais...
3. Tu ferais mieux de... ; ...tu devrais...
4. Il faut d'abord que tu...
5. Monsieur (le Directeur),
6. Auriez-vous l'amabilité de m'envoyer des renseignements sur... ?
   Vous serait-il possible de m'envoyer une brochure?
7. Avec mes remerciements anticipés, veuillez accepter, Monsieur... l'expression de mes salutations respectueuses.

Teaching Resources
p. 138

PRINT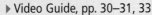
▸ Video Guide, pp. 30–31, 33
▸ Cahier d'activités, p. 60

MEDIA
▸ One-Stop Planner
▸ Video Program
  Videocassette 2, 23:35–26:58
▸ Audio Compact Discs, CD 5,
  Trs. 5–8
▸ Interactive CD-ROM Tutor, Disc 2

Presenting
Panorama Culturel

On the board, write statements about the interviewees without naming them. **(Cette personne voudrait être vétérinaire. Cette personne aime les langues. Cette personne aime analyser).** Then, play the video and have students raise their hands when they can identify the people described on the board. Finally, play the video again and ask the **Questions** below.

Questions

1. **Qui voudrait être journaliste?** (Marieke, Mélanie)

2. **Quel métier est-ce que Rodolphe aimerait faire?** (avocat international)

3. **Comment est-ce que Rodolphe imagine sa vie dans dix ans?** (Il aura une situation fixe, une bonne situation.)

4. **Mélanie hésite entre quels métiers?** (reporter et vétérinaire)

5. **Pourquoi est-ce qu'elle hésite à étudier la médecine vétérinaire?** (Il faut avoir de très bonnes notes.)

Quel métier aimerais-tu faire?
We asked some young people about their plans for the future. Here's what they had to say.

Marieke,
France

«Plus tard, j'aimerais beaucoup faire du journalisme parce que j'aime bien enfin... écrire. Beaucoup. J'adore écrire, donc ça serait plutôt dans la presse. Et parce que... le contact, j'aime beaucoup. Je m'intéresse beaucoup à l'actualité. Enfin, c'est quelque chose que... Analyser, critiquer, j'aime beaucoup ça.» Tr. 6

Rodolphe,
Martinique

«J'aurais aimé être avocat international. Parce que, à mon avis, c'est un métier qui est intéressant. Et puis, bon, comme je m'intéresse aux langues, donc, je pense que ça peut me permettre de pratiquer. Dans dix ans, j'imagine ma vie avec optimisme, assez bien. Je me vois vivre d'une manière assez bien, avec une situation fixe et une bonne situation.» Tr. 7

Mélanie,
Québec

«J'aimerais être reporter pour un journal, ou encore être vétérinaire; c'est très différent, mais c'est deux choses que j'aime beaucoup. J'aimerais être chroniqueuse sportive. Chroniqueur sportif, j'aimerais beaucoup ça. Et puis, le problème, c'est qu'en médecine vétérinaire, il faut avoir des très bonnes notes. C'est ce qui m'empêche un peu d'aller là-dedans. C'est trop exigeant.» Tr. 8

Qu'en penses-tu?

1. Quels sont les projets que font ces jeunes?
2. Est-ce que les professions qu'ils mentionnent t'intéressent?
3. Quelles professions t'intéressent? Pourquoi?

1. become a journalist, international attorney, newspaper reporter, veterinarian, sports columnist

---

Connections and Comparisons

Community Link
Have students list professions that they are interested in pursuing. Compile a list on the board and have them name advantages and disadvantages of each one.

Thinking Critically
Analyzing Ask students which interviewee they most easily relate to. If none of the interviewees share their aspirations, have students write a sentence or two about what they would have said in the interview.

Deuxième étape

Objectives Asking about future plans; expressing wishes; expressing indecision; giving advice; requesting information; writing a formal letter

go.hrw.com

WA3 FRANCOPHONE AFRICA-5

Deuxième étape

Vocabulaire

Quel métier est-ce que tu choisiras?

un ingénieur

un médecin

un plombier

un tailleur

un acteur/une actrice

un agent de police/ *a police officer*
un policier

un(e) architecte

un(e) avocat(e) *a lawyer*

un chauffeur

un(e) comptable *an accountant*

un(e) dentiste

un écrivain *a writer*

un homme/ *a businessman/woman*
une femme d'affaires

un(e) infirmier(-ière) *a nurse*

un instituteur/ *an elementary*
une institutrice *school teacher*

un(e) journaliste

un(e) mécanicien(ne)

un(e) ouvrier(-ière) *a worker*

un(e) pharmacien(ne)

un pilote

un professeur

un(e) secrétaire

un(e) serveur(-euse)

un(e) technicien(ne)

Cahier d'activités, p. 55, Act. 13–14

Travaux pratiques de grammaire, pp. 49–50, Act. 14–17

DE BONS CONSEILS

The names of some careers in French have traditionally had only a masculine form. You can use the masculine form to refer to both women and men: **C'est un médecin** (He or *she is a doctor*). If you want to make it clear that you're talking about a woman, you can add the word **femme** to the masculine form: **C'est une femme médecin.**

Note culturelle

Les pays francophones offrent des formations formelles et informelles aux jeunes qui ne vont pas à l'université. Au Sénégal, les adultes ont la responsabilité d'enseigner leur métier aux jeunes membres de leur famille. Souvent, les jeunes ne gagnent pas d'argent pendant leur apprentissage. Ce transfert de connaissances professionnelles d'une génération à l'autre est très important dans un pays comme le Sénégal où il y a beaucoup de chômeurs.

 18 **C'est quel métier?**

See scripts and answers on p. 125G.

 Écoutons Écoute ces conversations et identifie les métiers des personnes qui parlent. C'est un(e)...

CD 5 Tr. 9 Il est/Elle est...

Communication for All Students

Game

To prepare to play, you will need a card with a profession written on it for each member of the class, and a stopwatch. Form two teams. Then, divide the cards into two sets and put each set in a bag. On your command, the first player from the first team selects a card from the team's bag and mimes that profession. The second player on the team tries to guess the profession. If the second player calls out the correct French word, he or she then selects a card from the box and mimes the word for the third player. Teammates are not allowed to help the player who is guessing. When the last player guesses correctly, stop the stopwatch and write the team's time on the board. Then, the second team draws cards and mimes the professions in the same manner, racing to beat the first team's time.

Teaching Resources
pp. 139–143

PRINT
▸ Lesson Planner, p. 25
▸ Listening Activities, pp. 36–37, 40–41
▸ Activities for Communication, pp. 19–20, 64–65, 97–98
▸ Travaux pratiques de grammaire, pp. 49–53
▸ Grammar Tutor for Students of French, Chapter 5
▸ Cahier d'activités, pp. 55–58
▸ Testing Program, pp. 93–96
▸ Alternative Assessment Guide, p. 34
▸ Student Make-Up Assignments, Chapter 5

MEDIA
▸ One-Stop Planner
▸ Audio Compact Discs, CD 5, Trs. 9–11, 15, 22–24
▸ Teaching Transparencies: 5-2; **Grammaire supplémentaire** Answers; Travaux pratiques de grammaire Answers
▸ Interactive CD-ROM Tutor, Disc 2

Bell Work

Have students write a story about an imaginary friend's plans for the future. Tell them to use a variety of verbs.

Presenting
Vocabulaire

Have each student illustrate one profession from the **Vocabulaire** and label their drawing, or have magazines available which they can cut pictures from to label. Hold each one up and identify the profession. (**Il est journaliste.**) Ask **Qu'est-ce qu'il/elle fait?** The response should be something like: **Il écrit pour un journal.**

Teaching Resources
pp. 139–143

PRINT
- Lesson Planner, p. 25
- Listening Activities, pp. 36–37, 40–41
- Activities for Communication, pp. 19–20, 64–65, 97–98
- Travaux pratiques de grammaire, pp. 49–53
- Grammar Tutor for Students of French, Chapter 5
- Cahier d'activités, pp. 55–58
- Testing Program, pp. 93–96
- Alternative Assessment Guide, p. 34
- Student Make-Up Assignments, Chapter 5

MEDIA
- One-Stop Planner
- Audio Compact Discs, CD 5, Trs. 9–11, 15, 22–24
- Teaching Transparencies: 5-2; **Grammaire supplémentaire** Answers; Travaux pratiques de grammaire Answers
- Interactive CD-ROM Tutor, Disc 2

Presenting
Comment dit-on... ?

Write the new expressions on a transparency. Use a different color for each function (blue for asking about future plans, red for expressing wishes, and so on). Then, act out both roles of a conversation in which a parent and a student are discussing the student's future plans. Use as many of the new expressions as possible. As you use each expression, point to it on the transparency. Ask students which function each color represents.

---

19 Devinettes

Parlons Réfère-toi au vocabulaire de la page 139 pour deviner le métier des personnes suivantes.

1. M. Laval vend des médicaments. *pharmacien*
2. Pierrick conduit la voiture d'une star de cinéma. *chauffeur*
3. Mme Martel dessine des plans de maison pour ses clients. *architecte*
4. Paul porte un uniforme bleu et il fait respecter la loi. *policier*
5. Les élèves de Maryline ont sept ans. *institutrice*

20 Qui suis-je?

Parlons Choisis une profession et décris-la. Ton/ta camarade devinera quel métier tu décris.

EXEMPLE — Je m'occupe des malades.
— Tu es médecin?
— Oui.

21 Mon journal

Écrivons Quels sont les métiers qui t'intéressent? Pourquoi? Est-ce que tu as déjà décidé de ce que tu feras plus tard?

Vocabulaire à la carte

un(e) **assistant(e) social(e)** *a social worker*

un(e) **banquier(-ière)**

un(e) **dessinateur(-trice)** *a commercial artist*

un(e) **diplomate**

un(e) **électricien(ne)**

un(e) **fonctionnaire** *a government employee*

un **juge**

un **mannequin** *a model*

un(e) **menuisier(-ière)** *a carpenter*

un(e) **programmeur(-euse)**

un(e) **psychiatre** *a psychiatrist*

un(e) **scientifique**

un **soldat** *a soldier*

un(e) **vétérinaire**

Comment dit-on...?

Asking about future plans; expressing wishes; expressing indecision; giving advice

To ask about future plans:

Tu sais ce que tu veux faire?
Do you know what you want to do?
Tu as des projets? *Do you have plans?*
Qu'est-ce que tu veux faire plus tard?
What do you want to do . . . ?

To express wishes:

Je voudrais aller à l'université.
J'aimerais bien commencer à travailler.
Ce qui me plairait, c'est de voyager.
Mon rêve, c'est d'être dentiste.
My dream is to . . .

To express indecision:

Pas vraiment.
Je ne sais pas trop.
Non, je me demande.
Je n'en ai aucune idée. *I have no idea.*
J'ai du mal à me décider.
I'm having trouble deciding.
Je ne sais plus ce que je veux.
I don't know what I want anymore.

To give advice:

Tu n'as qu'à trouver un travail.
All you have to do is . . .
Tu devrais te renseigner.
Tu ferais mieux/bien de penser à ton bac.
Il faudrait que tu écrives à l'école de musique. *You ought to . . .*
Il vaudrait mieux que tu travailles.
It would be better if . . .

Cahier d'activités, pp. 55–56, Act. 15–16

Communication for All Students

Kinesthetic Learners

20 As a variation, have students work in small groups and take turns miming a profession. The first group member to correctly guess the profession (**Tu es médecin!**) takes the next turn. Continue until each student has had at least two turns.

Tactile Learners

On a sheet of paper, write wishes (**Je voudrais aller à l'université**) and corresponding advice in random order. (**Il faudrait que tu étudies.**) Distribute copies to partners. Have them cut apart the statements and advice, match them, and take turns stating the wishes and giving the advice.

22 **Tu sais ce que tu vas faire?** See scripts and answers on p. 125H.

 Ecoutons Est-ce que ces gens savent ce qu'ils vont faire ou est-ce qu'ils hésitent?

CD 5 Tr. 10

23 **Tu ferais bien de...**

Parlons Ton/ta camarade te parle de ce qu'il/elle voudrait faire. Donne-lui des conseils. Changez de rôle.

EXEMPLE
—Ce qui me plairait, c'est de parler russe.
—Tu n'as qu'à trouver un travail en Russie.

DESIR
aller à l'université
acheter une voiture
être acteur/actrice
arrêter ses études
passer son permis de conduire
quitter sa famille
apprendre à jouer du piano
se marier
devenir musicien(ne)
écrire un roman
???

CONSEILS
attendre un peu
étudier
choisir un métier pratique
chercher un emploi
prendre des leçons de conduite
y réfléchir
aller à l'université
obtenir un diplôme
???

Grammaire

The conditional

Generally, you use the conditional in French when you want to tell what you *would* do under certain conditions. You might also use the conditional to be polite. Look at these examples:

Il **gagnerait** beaucoup d'argent comme médecin. *He would earn . . .*
Si j'avais plus de temps, j'**étudierais** avec Marthe.
   If I had more time, I would study . . .
Je **voudrais** des renseignements, s'il vous plaît. *I would like . . .*

- To make the forms of the conditional, start with the same stem you use to make the future tense, but add the endings of the imperfect: **-ais, -ais, -ait, -ions, -iez, -aient.** Remember to drop the **-e** from infinitives ending in **-re.**

Je **choisirais**
Tu **choisirais** } le bleu.
Il/Elle/On **choisirait**

Nous **dirions**
Vous **diriez** } la vérité.
Ils/Elles **diraient**

Grammaire supplémentaire, pp. 150–151, Act. 5–7

Cahier d'activités, pp. 56–57, Act. 17–19

- The future and the conditional have the same irregular stems. (See page 134.)

Je **serais** content de continuer mes études.
Tu **ferais** bien d'étudier.

Travaux pratiques de grammaire, pp. 51–52, Act. 18–20

Connections and Comparisons

Language Note
Point out to students that they should use the conditional in French when they want to say *would* + verb in English. However, tell them that this applies when the action might or could happen *in the future.* To say what would often happen in the past, such as: *When I was young, I would often go to the park,* the **imparfait** should be used.

Language-to-Language
You might tell students that, even though the French and the English conditionals look very different from each other, one can draw parallels between the formation of those two modes in both languages. As much as the French future tense and the conditional have common stems, the English future form *will* and conditional form *would* also share the same stem.

Additional Practice
Have students refer to the transparency from the Presentation page 140 as you ask various individuals about their future plans. If a student expresses indecision, call on a classmate to give advice. (**Jessica, tu peux lui donner des conseils?**)

Presenting
Grammaire

The conditional   Begin by asking students what they would do in certain situations (if they went to college or inherited a million dollars). Have them give their answers as infinitive phrases (**acheter une voiture**), which you write on a transparency. Write the future stem next to each infinitive. Then, write the conditional endings next to the stems. Tell what you would do, using the activities on the board (**J'achèterais une voiture**), and ask students if they would do the same. (**Et toi, tu achèterais une voiture?**)

Game
Verb Toss   Write an infinitive on the board. Then, toss a beach ball to a student as you call out a subject pronoun. The student calls out the appropriate conditional form and tosses the ball to another student, while saying a different subject pronoun. After several turns, write a different infinitive and continue.

Teacher Note
The use of the conditional with **si** clauses will be presented in Chapter 8.

Additional Practice
For more practice with the conditional, you might have students play the game "**Qu'est-ce que tu ferais?**" described on page 125C.

Presenting
Comment dit-on... ?

Write a formal business letter on a transparency, using the new expressions. Read it aloud, underlining the new expressions as you read, and have students repeat.

Answers
24
1. voudrions
2. aimerait
3. intéresserait
4. aimeraient
5. trouverais
6. gagnerais
7. pourrais
8. rencontrerais
9. serais
10. ferais

---

24 **Grammaire en contexte**   See answers below.

Lisons Antoine, le correspondant français de ta classe, te demande des conseils au sujet de ses études. Complète son message avec le conditionnel des verbes entre parenthèses.

> Bientôt le bac! Après le bac, ma sœur et moi, nous _____**1**_____ (vouloir) aller à l'université. Ma sœur _____**2**_____ (aimer) faire des études de médecine. Moi, je crois que l'archéologie m' _____**3**_____ (intéresser), mais mes parents ne sont pas d'accord. Ils _____**4**_____ (aimer) que j'étudie le droit. Ils disent que je _____**5**_____ (trouver) un travail plus facilement et que je _____**6**_____ (gagner) plus d'argent. Ils ont peut-être raison, mais moi, je veux voyager. Si j'étais archéologue, je _____**7**_____ (pouvoir) aller en Egypte et en Grèce. Je _____**8**_____ (rencontrer) aussi beaucoup de gens. Je pense que je _____**9**_____ (être) plus heureux. Et toi, qu'est-ce que tu _____**10**_____ (faire) à ma place?

25 **Grammaire en contexte**

Ecrivons Réponds au message d'Antoine de l'activité 24. Dis-lui ce que tu ferais, si tu étais à sa place. Tu peux aussi lui donner d'autres conseils et suggérer plusieurs métiers qui pourraient aussi l'intéresser. Utilise le conditionnel dans ta réponse.

Comment dit-on...?

Requesting information; writing a formal letter

To request information:

> **Pourriez-vous m'envoyer des renseignements sur** votre école?
> *Would you send me some information about . . . ?*
> **Je voudrais savoir** quels cours sont offerts.
> **Vous serait-il possible de** m'envoyer une brochure sur votre école?
> *Would it be possible for you to . . . ?*

To begin a formal letter:

> **Monsieur/Madame,**
> **En réponse à votre lettre du...**
> *In response to your letter of . . .*
> **Suite à notre conversation téléphonique,...**
> *Following our phone conversation, . . .*

To end a formal letter:

> **Je vous prie d'agréer, Monsieur/Madame, l'expression de mes sentiments distingués.**
> *Very truly yours, . . .*

Cahier d'activités, p. 58, Act. 21

26 **Au téléphone**   See scripts and answers on p. 125H.

CD 5 Tr. 11

Ecoutons Ecoute Armenan qui téléphone à une école technique. Mets les phrases suivantes dans l'ordre d'après la conversation.

a. Elle demande quels sont les frais d'inscription.
b. Armenan veut savoir quels cours elle pourrait suivre.
c. L'employé demande l'adresse d'Armenan.
d. Elle demande à quelle heure les cours sont offerts.
e. Elle demande à l'employé de lui envoyer une brochure.
f. Elle demande quand les cours commencent.
g. L'employé répond à l'appel d'Armenan.

Cultures and Communities

Career Path

Being able to write a formal letter in another language is important for anyone planning to study or work abroad. French employers, just as their American counterparts, will often require job applicants to submit a cover letter explaining why they are interested in the position for which they're applying. In addition to a résumé, it is not unusual for French employers to request a handwritten letter. Graphology, or the analysis of personality through handwriting, is often used in France as a means of screening job applicants. Thus, a **lettre manuscrite** is often requested of applicants. Hand-writing samples can reveal general aspects of the applicant's personality that can help the employer decide how well the prospective employee would be suited to the workplace.

Note de grammaire

You've already learned several ways to form questions. A formal way to form questions is to reverse the order of the subject and the verb. Notice that you place a hyphen between the verb and the subject pronoun and that you insert a **-t-** between a verb that ends with a vowel and **il/elle**.

Comment **allez-vous,** monsieur?
Pourriez-vous me dire où se trouve la gare?
Va-t-il à Paris?

Inversion occurs in literature, in formal letters or speeches, and in very polite conversations, but it is not used often in conversational speech.

Grammaire supplémentaire, p. 151, Act. 8–9

Travaux pratiques de grammaire, p. 53, Act. 21

27 Grammaire en contexte

Ecrivons Récris ces phrases d'une façon plus polie en utilisant l'inversion. *See answers below.*

1. Est-ce que tu peux me donner des conseils?
2. Vous pourriez me rapporter des timbres?
3. Elles ont combien de sœurs?
4. Il veut du café?
5. Est-ce qu'elle joue du piano?
6. Vous avez reçu ma lettre?
7. Il va à la bibliothèque?
8. Tu peux me téléphoner plus tard?

28 Une lettre officielle *See answers below.*

Lisons/Ecrivons Un de tes camarades veut passer une année dans un lycée français. Il te demande de l'aider à écrire une lettre à M. Durand, le directeur des échanges franco-américains. Remplace les parties soulignées par des mots ou expressions plus polis.

(1) Bonjour,

Je vous écris parce que (2) je veux obtenir des renseignements sur les échanges franco-américains. (3) Vous pourriez me donner des informations sur les lycées français? Quand (4) est-ce que je dois m'inscrire? (5) Vous avez des brochures? (6) Est-ce que vous pouvez m'en envoyer une?

Merci d'avance.
(7) Au revoir.

29 Pourriez-vous me renseigner?

Parlons Tu voudrais passer ton permis de conduire. Téléphone à une auto-école pour demander combien ça coûte, à quelles heures et quels jours les cours sont offerts et comment s'inscrire. Joue cette scène avec ton/ta camarade.

30

 De l'école au travail

 Ecrivons Ecris une lettre à une université ou à une école technique. Avant de l'écrire, réfléchis à ce que tu voudrais faire plus tard comme métier. Dans ta lettre, présente-toi, parle du métier qui t'intéresse et demande des renseignements. N'oublie pas d'utiliser les formules de politesse.

Communication for All Students

Challenge
To have students practice recognizing inversion in questions, play *Frère Jacques* (Level 1, Audio CD 1, Track 43) and *Le Carillonneur* (Level 1, Audio CD 3, Track 33). Ask students to listen for examples of inversion in the songs. Distribute copies of the lyrics (*Listening Activities*, Level 1, pages 10, 26) to students and ask them to underline the questions that use inversion.

Visual Learners
To practice inversion, have students write short questions on strips of paper. They should start with the informal style. **(Tu aimes la pizza? Il veut aller au cinéma?)** Have them cut the strips in pieces and reorganize the words to form formal questions. Remind students to make additional strips with **-t-** to be added when necessary.

♟ **Game**

Catégories Form two teams. Name a topic or function from the chapter, such as *careers* or *expressing indecision*. Have the teams take turns giving related words or expressions until one team can no longer continue. The last team to suggest an appropriate word or expression wins a point.

Assess
▶ Testing Program, pp. 93–96
  Quiz 5-2A, Quiz 5-2B
  Audio CD 5, Tr. 15

▶ Student Make-Up Assignments, Chapter 5, Alternative Quiz

▶ Alternative Assessment Guide, p. 34

Answers

27 1. Peux-tu me donner des conseils?
  2. Pourriez-vous me rapporter des timbres?
  3. Combien de sœurs ont-elles?
  4. Veut-il du café?
  5. Joue-t-elle du piano?
  6. Avez-vous reçu ma lettre?
  7. Va-t-il à la bibliothèque?
  8. Peux-tu me téléphoner plus tard?

28 *Possible answers:*
  1. Monsieur
  2. je voudrais
  3. Pourriez-vous
  4. dois-je
  5. Avez-vous
  6. Vous serait-il possible de
  7. Je vous prie d'agréer, Monsieur, l'expression de mes sentiments distingués.

Lisons!

Teaching Resources
pp. 144–146

PRINT
▸ Lesson Planner, p. 26
▸ Cahier d'activités, p. 59
▸ Reading Strategies and Skills Handbook, Chapter 5
▸ Joie de lire 3, Chapter 5
▸ Standardized Assessment Tutor, Chapter 5

MEDIA
▸ One-Stop Planner

Prereading
Activities A–B

Family Link
Ask students how they would feel if they had to leave home for an extended period of time, perhaps to go to school or to find work. Would they be sad? Scared? Excited? Then, ask them how they would feel if, when they arrived where they were going, they were completely disappointed by what they found there. Tell them to keep these things in mind as they read this excerpt from *L'Enfant noir.*

Possible answers
A. The narrator is a man telling about his experience as a young boy in Africa.

B. a young boy's experience growing up in Africa

C. This is a very important event for Laye, because he describes in detail his emotions, especially how sad he feels. He also describes in detail how sad his family and village are about his leaving.

D. Laye's father tells him to be brave and to work hard. He expects him to do well since they made sacrifices for him.

L'Enfant noir

Stratégie pour lire
You've learned two past tenses in French, **le passé composé** and **l'imparfait.** A third past tense, **le passé simple,** refers to specific, isolated, completed actions in the past, much like the **passé composé.** However, whereas the **passé composé** is used in spoken and written French, the **passé simple** is only a written tense, used primarily in French literature. The **passé simple** of regular verbs is formed by adding specific endings to the stem of the verb, which is formed by removing the **-er, -ir,** or **-re.** When you see an unfamiliar verb form in a text, try to identify the stem. Use strategies you've learned, such as context clues, to figure out the meaning of any unfamiliar words.

For Activities A–D, see answers below.

A. Scan the first paragraph. Who is the narrator? What information have you learned in Chapter 5 that might be important to understanding the narrator's point of view?

B. Knowing who the narrator is, what do you think you'll read about in the story?

C. How important an occasion is this for Laye, his family, and his village? How do you know?

D. What advice does Laye's father give him? What does he expect from him?

L'Enfant noir

J'avais quinze ans, quand je partis pour Conakry. J'allais y suivre l'enseignement technique à l'école Georges Poiret, devenue depuis le Collège technique.

Je quittais mes parents pour la deuxième fois. Je les avais quittés une première fois aussitôt après mon certificat d'études, pour servir d'interprète à un officier qui était venu faire des relevés de terrain dans notre région et en direction du Soudan. Cette fois, je prenais un congé beaucoup plus sérieux.

Depuis une semaine, ma mère accumulait les provisions. Conakry est à quelque 600 kilomètres de Kouroussa et, pour ma mère, c'était une terre inconnue, sinon inexplorée, où Dieu seul savait si l'on mange à sa faim.

La veille de mon départ, un magnifique festin réunit dans notre concession marabouts et féticheurs, notables et amis et, à dire vrai, quiconque se donnait la peine de franchir le seuil, car il ne fallait, dans l'esprit de ma mère, éloigner personne : il fallait tout au contraire que des représentants de toutes les classes de la société assistassent au festin, afin que la bénédiction qui m'accompagnerait fût complète.

— Que la chance te favorise ! Que tes études soient bonnes ! Et que Dieu te protège !

Je passai une triste nuit. J'étais très énervé, un peu angoissé aussi, et je me réveillai plusieurs fois.

Ma mère me réveilla à l'aube, et je me levai sans qu'elle dût insister. Je vis qu'elle avait les traits tirés, mais elle prenait sur elle, et je ne dis rien : je fis comme si son calme apparent me donnait réellement le change sur sa peine. Mes bagages étaient en tas dans la case.

—Cours vite faire tes adieux maintenant ! dit ma mère.

J'allai dire au revoir aux vieilles gens de notre concession et des concessions voisines, et j'avais le cœur gros. Ces hommes, ces femmes, je les connaissais depuis ma plus tendre enfance, depuis toujours je les avais vus à la place même où je les voyais, et aussi, j'en avais vu disparaître : ma grand-mère paternelle avait disparu ! Et reverrais-je tous ceux auxquels je disais à présent adieu ?

Quand je revins près de ma mère et que je l'aperçus en larmes devant mes bagages, je me mis à pleurer à mon tour. Je me jetais dans ses bras et je l'étreignis.

—Mère ! criai-je.

Je l'entendais sangloter, je sentais sa poitrine douloureusement se soulever.

—Mère, ne pleure pas ! dis-je. Ne pleure pas !

Connections and Comparisons

Music Link
To have students practice recognizing the **passé simple** before they begin the reading, write the following infinitives in random order on the board: **entreprendre, venir, tirer, tomber, être, sauter, prendre,** and **mettre.** Distribute copies of the lyrics of the song *Il était un petit navire* (*Listening Activities,* page 82) to small groups and play the song as students read along. Then, have them read the song again and circle eight unfamiliar verb forms they find (**entreprit, vinrent, tira, tomba, fût, sautèrent, prit,** and **mit**). To avoid confusing students, tell them to exclude the last three lines in the sixth and eighth stanzas, as these contain verb forms in the **passé antérieur.** Finally, ask students to use context clues and familiar roots in the verb forms they circled to try to match them with their infinitives on the board.

STANDARDS: 1.2, 2.1, 2.2, 3.1, 3.2, 4.2

Mais je n'arrivais pas moi-même à refréner mes larmes et je la suppliai de ne pas m'accompagner à la gare, car il me semblait qu'alors je ne pourrais jamais m'arracher à ses bras. Elle me fit signe qu'elle y consentait.

Mon père m'avait rapidement rejoint et il m'avait pris la main, comme du temps où j'étais encore enfant. Je ralentis le pas : j'étais sans courage, je sanglotais éperdument.

—Allons ! allons ! mon petit, dit-il. N'es-tu pas un grand garçon ?

Mais sa présence même, sa tendresse même — et davantage encore maintenant qu'il me tenait la main — m'enlevaient le peu de courage qui me restait, et il le comprit.

—Je n'irai pas plus loin, dit-il. Nous allons nous dire adieu ici : il ne convient pas que nous fondions en larmes à la gare, en présence de tes amis; et puis je ne veux pas laisser ta mère seule en ce moment : ta mère a beaucoup de peine ! J'en ai beaucoup aussi. Nous avons tous beaucoup de peine, mais nous devons nous montrer courageux. Sois courageux ! Mes frères, là-bas, s'occuperont de toi. Mais travaille bien ! Travaille comme tu travaillais ici. Nous avons consenti pour toi des sacrifices; il ne faut point qu'ils demeurent sans résultat.

Dans la cour, où l'on me donna les premières indications, au dortoir, où j'allai ranger mes vêtements, je trouvai des élèves venus comme moi de Haute-Guinée, et nous fîmes connaissance; je ne me sentis pas seul. Un peu plus tard, nous entrâmes en classe. Nous étions, anciens et nouveaux, réunis dans une même grande salle. Je me préparai à mettre les bouchées doubles, songeant à tirer déjà quelque parti de l'enseignement qu'on donnerait aux anciens, tout en m'en tenant évidemment au mien propre; mais presque aussitôt je m'aperçus qu'on ne faisait pas grande différence entre anciens et nouveaux : il semblait plutôt qu'on s'apprêtait à répéter aux anciens, pour la deuxième, voire pour la troisième fois, le cours qu'on leur avait seriné dès la première année. « Enfin, on verra bien ! » pensai-je; mais j'étais néanmoins troublé : le procédé ne me paraissait pas de bon augure.

Pour commencer, on nous dicta un texte très simple. Quand le maître corrigea les copies, j'eus peine à comprendre qu'elles pussent fourmiller de tant de fautes. C'était, je l'ai dit, un texte très simple, sans surprises, où pas un de mes compagnons de Kouroussa n'eût trouvé occasion de trébucher. Après, on nous donna un problème à résoudre; nous fûmes très exactement deux à trouver la solution ! J'en demeurai atterré : était-ce là l'école où j'accéderais à un niveau supérieur ? Il me sembla que je retournais plusieurs

E. Mets ces événements dans le bon ordre. 6 2 7 4 3 1 5
1. Laye se plaint à son oncle de sa nouvelle école.
2. La mère de Laye lui dit au revoir.
3. Laye commence à penser que les cours sont trop faciles.
4. Laye quitte son village pour aller à Conakry.
5. L'oncle de Laye lui conseille de rester à Conakry.
6. Il y a une grande fête pour souhaiter bonne chance à Laye.
7. Laye dit au revoir à son père.

F. Vrai ou faux?
1. La nouvelle école de Laye est si proche du village qu'il peut rendre visite à ses parents pendant les week-ends. faux
2. Dès la fin de la première semaine, Laye est déçu par sa nouvelle école. vrai
3. Laye trouve que les cours sont trop difficiles. faux
4. L'oncle de Laye lui dit qu'il devrait être fier d'apprendre à travailler de ses mains. vrai
5. La famille de Laye considère que les études sont très importantes. vrai
6. Laye est très content de quitter sa famille. faux

G. Associe les mots de la colonne de gauche à ceux de la colonne de droite qui y sont apparentés.

refréner — frein
je ralentis — lent
fourmiller — fourmi
zébrées d'éraflures — zèbre
travailleur — travailler
éperdument — perdre

Reading
Activities C–K

Teacher Note
Camara Laye (1928-1979) was born in Kouroussa, Guinea. He spent the first fifteen years of his life in this small **malinké** village on the banks of the Niger River. He then left his family and moved to Conakry, the capital of Guinea, to attend a technical trade school. Upon completing his studies in Guinea, Laye continued his education in France, and it was there that he wrote *L'Enfant noir*. A semi-auto-biographical work, *L'Enfant noir* was an effort to recapture the magic and memories of childhood in the homeland that Laye missed. Upon his return in 1956, however, he found that the values and lifestyle he had cherished had been replaced by political upheaval and violence, which prompted a sequel to *L'Enfant noir*, entitled *Dramouss*. Laye was greatly influenced by the **Négritude** movement, a literary and social movement which affirmed a separate black identity and personality. *L'Enfant noir*, reflects this influence by painting a tableau of idyllic life in a traditional African village before the influences and technology of the Western world produced inevitable changes.

Terms in Lisons!
Students might want to know the following words as they read *L'Enfant noir*: **congé** *(vacation)*, **festin** *(feast)*, **sangloter** *(to sob)*, **dortoir** *(dormitory)*.

Communication for All Students

Challenge
F. For each statement, have a volunteer read the sentence(s) in the text that supports whether the statement is true or false. You might have students modify the false statements to make them true. (**La nouvelle école de Laye est très loin du village. Il ne peut pas rendre visite à ses parents pendant le week-end. / Laye trouve que les cours sont très/trop faciles. / Laye est triste de quitter sa famille.**)

Lisons!

Group Work

I. Divide the class into two groups. Have one group create a list of arguments Laye's uncle could use to convince his nephew that technical training would be beneficial to him. Ask the other group to come up with reasons why formal education is more important than technical training. Have the two groups hold a debate in which they present their positions on the issue.

Postreading

Activities L–M

Challenge

Have students write a paragraph telling what career they would like to pursue and what preparation they think is necessary to work in the field that interests them. Have students consider the obstacles they will face and how they will deal with them.

Possible answers

I. Laye views education as a means of bettering himself and developing his intellect. His uncle views education as a means of finding a well-paying job.

J. When his uncle says "une carrière de gratte-papier," he means a career as a pencil-pusher. Civil service and administrative positions might fall into this category.

K. Laye's uncle tells him that a technician is not necessarily a manual worker and that he wishes he had followed a track towards a technical position. He recommends that Laye stay at his school.

H. En te référant au contexte et à la racine des mots, associe chaque mot de la colonne de gauche à son équivalent de la colonne de droite. **1.** i **2.** d **3.** f **4.** a **5.** h **6.** g **7.** e **8.** b **9.** c

1. franchir le seuil
2. éloigner
3. larmes
4. refréner
5. ralentis le pas
6. éperdument
7. fourmiller
8. zébrées
9. travailleur

a. arrêter
b. à rayures
c. quelqu'un qui travaille
d. ne pas permettre d'entrer
e. être plein de
f. ce qui sort des yeux quand on pleure
g. tristement
h. marche moins vite
i. entrer

For Activities I–K, see answers below.

I. How does Laye's view of education differ from his uncle's?

J. Que veut dire l'oncle de Laye par "une carrière de gratte-papier"? Quelles professions appartiennent à cette catégorie?

K. Quel conseil l'oncle de Laye lui donne-t-il? Pourquoi lui donne-t-il ce conseil?

L. If you found yourself in a similar situation, would your reaction be similar to or differ from Laye's?

M. Does your community place the same importance on education as Laye's family and community? Why or why not?

Cahier d'activités, p. 59, Act. 22

---

années en arrière, que j'étais assis encore dans une des petites classes de Kouroussa. Mais c'était bien cela : la semaine s'écoula sans que j'eusse rien appris. Le dimanche, je m'en plaignis vivement à mon oncle :

—Rien ! je n'ai rien appris, mon oncle ! Tout ce qu'on nous a enseigné, je le savais depuis longtemps. Est-ce la peine vraiment d'aller à cette école ? Autant regagner Kouroussa tout de suite !

—Non, dit mon oncle; non ! Attends un peu !

—Il n'y a rien à attendre ! J'ai bien vu qu'il n'y avait rien à attendre !

—Allons ! Ne sois pas si impatient ! Es-tu toujours si impatient ! Cette école où tu es, peut-être bien est-elle à un niveau trop bas pour ce qui regarde l'enseignement général, mais elle peut te donner une formation pratique que tu ne trouveras pas ailleurs. N'as-tu pas travaillé dans les ateliers ?

Je lui montrai mes mains : elles étaient zébrées d'éraflures, et les pointes des doigts me brûlaient.

—Mais je ne veux pas devenir un ouvrier ! dis-je.

—Pourquoi le deviendrais-tu ?

—Je ne veux pas qu'on me méprise !

—Écoute-moi attentivement, dit mon oncle. Tous les élèves venant de Kouroussa ont toujours dédaigné l'école technique, toujours ils ont rêvé d'une carrière de gratte-papier. Est-ce une telle carrière que tu ambitionnes ? Une carrière où vous serez perpétuellement treize à la douzaine ? Si réellement ton choix s'est fixé sur une telle carrière, change d'école. Mais dis-toi bien ceci, retiens bien ceci : si j'avais vingt ans de moins, si j'avais mes études à refaire, je n'eusse point été à l'École normale; non ! j'aurais appris un bon métier dans une école professionnelle : un bon métier m'eût conduit autrement loin !

—Mais alors, dis-je, j'aurais aussi bien pu ne pas quitter la forge paternelle !

—Tu aurais pu ne pas la quitter. Mais, dis-moi, n'as-tu jamais eu l'ambition de la dépasser ?

Or j'avais cette ambition; mais ce n'était pas en devenant un travailleur manuel que je la réaliserais; pas plus que l'opinion commune, je n'avais de considération pour de tels travailleurs.

—Mais qui te parle de travailleur manuel ? dit mon oncle. Un technicien n'est pas nécessairement un manuel et, en tout cas, il n'est pas que cela : c'est un homme qui dirige et qui sait, le cas échéant, mettre la main à la pâte. Or les hommes qui dirigent des entreprises, ne savent pas tous mettre la main à la pâte, et ta supériorité sera là justement. Crois-moi : demeure où tu es !

From *L'Enfant noir* by Camara Laye. Copyright © **Librairie Plon**. Reprinted by permission of the publisher.

Connections and Comparisons

Geography Link

Ask students to recall what they learned about educational opportunities in Africa in Levels 1 and 2. Students should remember that in Côte d'Ivoire, few students go on to high school; instead, many learn a trade or work in the agricultural sector. Divide the class into small groups and have them research information related to education, the labor market, and the economy of Guinea. Have them find out if Guinea's economy depends primarily on agriculture, industry, or services. Ask them to use the information they find to deduce what type of education or training a young person from Guinea might benefit from.

Ecrivons!

Une lettre de candidature

Tu as vu une annonce dans le journal pour un emploi qui t'intéresse. Comment poser ta candidature? En général, les employeurs demandent un **curriculum vitae (C.V.)** et une **lettre de motivation.** Maintenant, tu vas écrire une lettre de candidature pour un emploi. Dans cette lettre, il faut convaincre l'employeur que tu es le meilleur candidat/la meilleure candidate pour le poste.

> **Stratégie pour écrire**
> Details and structure are two of the most important elements in persuasive writing. To be as convincing as possible, you must choose facts and examples that will have the greatest impact on your audience. Try to predict your readers' concerns and address them. The structure of your argument also influences the effectiveness of your writing. Begin with your second-best points, followed by the weakest ones, and then put your strongest arguments last. Your most convincing argument will have a bigger impact if it is the last thing your audience reads.

A. Préparation

1. Parmi ces emplois, choisis celui qui t'intéresserait le plus :

   a. apprenti cuisinier dans un restaurant français

   b. photographe stagiaire *(trainee)* dans une agence de mannequins

   c. employé saisonnier *(seasonal)* aux Nations-Unies

   d. serveur dans le café d'un grand hôtel

   e. apprenti journaliste pour le journal *Le Monde*

   f. secrétaire stagiaire bilingue dans un cabinet d'avocats

2. Fais une liste de tes qualifications et qualités (tu peux les imaginer) pour persuader l'employeur de ton expérience et de ton intérêt.

3. Pense à ce dont l'employeur a besoin. Est-ce qu'il y a d'autres détails que tu pourrais ajouter pour donner une image positive de toi à l'employeur?

4. Mets en ordre les détails que tu as écrits et termine avec les points les plus forts de ton argumentation pour avoir le maximum d'effet.

B. Rédaction

Fais le brouillon de ta lettre. N'oublie pas les formules de politesse nécessaires.

En réponse à votre annonce parue dans ...	*In reply to your advertisement in . . .*
poser sa candidature pour un emploi	*to apply for a position*
une entrevue	*an interview*
Veuillez trouver ci-joint mon curriculum vitae.	*Please find enclosed my résumé.*
Dans l'attente de votre réponse, ...	*I look forward to hearing from you.*

C. Evaluation

1. Compare ta lettre à celles que tu as vues dans le chapitre:

   a. Est-ce que tu montres que tu possèdes toutes les qualifications nécessaires pour l'emploi?

   b. Est-ce que ses détails et sa structure rendent ta lettre convaincante?

   c. Est-ce que ton style est adéquat?

2. Rédige la version finale de ta lettre. N'oublie pas de corriger les fautes d'orthographe, de grammaire et de vocabulaire.

3. Donne ta lettre à un petit groupe de camarades qui jouent le rôle des employeurs. Ils vont la lire et dire si tu les as persuadés de t'accorder une entrevue.

> **Teaching Resources**
> **p. 147**
>
> **PRINT**
> ▶ Lesson Planner, p. 26
> ▶ Cahier d'activités, p. 149
> ▶ Alternative Assessment Guide, p. 20
> ▶ Standardized Assessment Tutor, Chapter 5
>
> **MEDIA**
> ▶ One-Stop Planner
> ▶ Test Generator, Chapter 5
> ▶ Interactive CD-ROM Tutor, Disc 2

Process Writing

Prewriting

Teaching Suggestion

A. 3. Have students answer the following questions an employer might ask: How does your background prepare you for this position? Why are you applying for *this* job in particular? Why should I hire *you* instead of someone else? What makes *you* the best candidate for the job?

Challenge

A. As students list their qualifications, have them also consider why an employer might object to hiring them (too young, not enough experience, won't stay long enough to complete the job). Have them jot down arguments that would pre-empt these objections (I'm consistent, reliable, enthusiastic about the field) and include them in their letters.

Writing

Slower Pace

B. Encourage students to borrow appropriate phrases from Omar's letter on page 137. Suggest they also use phrases such as **J'ai l'intention de...** or **Je compte...** from **Comment dit-on... ?** on page 133 to relate their future plans to the position.

Apply and Assess

Postwriting

Teaching Suggestions

C. Once students have written their rough drafts, have them underline each of their points. Then, have them evaluate the structure of their argument. Are their second-best points first? Is their strongest point last?

Pair Work

Before students write their final drafts, have them pair off. Partners exchange their letters and comment on both content and form. While reviewing their partner's letter, students should ask themselves the questions listed in Paragraph 1 and correct the spelling, grammar, and vocabulary.

Grammaire supplémentaire

CHAPITRE 5

For **Grammaire supplémentaire**
Answer Transparencies, see the
Teaching Transparencies binder.

Première étape   **Objectives** Asking about and expressing intentions; expressing conditions and possibilities

1 La mère de Mamadou lui dit ce qu'elle veut qu'il fasse de sa vie. Finis ses phrases avec l'expression suggérée par l'image. Attention! Tu vas devoir employer le subjonctif dans certaines phrases. (**p. 133**)

1. Mon fils, je veux que tu _____.

2. C'est essentiel si tu veux _____ comme prof.

3. Après, je voudrais que tu _____.

4. Puis, tu peux _____. Le rêve de tous les parents, c'est de devenir des grands-parents.

2 Une conseillère d'orientation demande à des étudiants ce qu'ils vont faire après le bac. Utilise les expressions entre parenthèses pour écrire leurs réponses. N'oublie pas de mettre les verbes au futur. (**p. 134**)

> **EXEMPLE**   —Ousmane, qu'est-ce que vous comptez faire si vous réussissez au bac?
> (aller dans une école technique)
> **—J'irai dans une école technique.**

1. Omar et Adja, qu'est-ce que vous avez l'intention de faire en septembre? (passer son permis de conduire)

2. Et Penda, qu'est-ce qu'il va devenir s'il n'obtient pas de permis de travail pour la France? (être chauffeur de taxi, comme son père)

3. Et Lamina et Chakib, qu'est-ce qu'ils ont l'intention de faire après le lycée? (faire du journalisme)

4. Et Bertille, qu'est-ce qu'elle pense faire? (chercher du travail dans une entreprise d'import-export)

5. Qu'est-ce que tu veux faire quand tu prendras ta retraite? (se consacrer à la musique)

Possible answers

1 1. obtiennes ton diplôme/finisses tes études
2. trouver un travail/travailler
3. te maries/trouves une femme
4. avoir des enfants

2 1. Nous passerons notre permis de conduire.
2. Il sera chauffeur de taxi...
3. Ils feront du journalisme.
4. Elle cherchera du travail...
5. Je me consacrerai à la musique.

Grammar Resources for Chapter 5

The **Grammaire supplémentaire** activities are designed as supplemental activities for the grammatical concepts presented in the chapter. You might use them as additional practice, for review, or for assessment.

   For more grammar presentations, review, and practice, refer to the following:
• Travaux pratiques de grammaire
• Grammar Tutor for Students of French

• Grammar Summary on pp. R29–R54
• Cahier d'activités
• Grammar and Vocabulary quizzes (Testing Program)
• Test Generator
• Interactive CD-ROM Tutor
• **Jeux interactifs** at <u>go.hrw.com</u>

3 Karine imagine l'avenir de Marisa. Qu'est-ce qu'elle lui raconte? Complète ses phrases en utilisant une des expressions de la boîte et le futur du verbe qui convient. (**p. 134**)

> entrer dans une école de commerce
>
> rejoindre son frère à Dakar
>
> trouver un travail dans une banque
>
> obtenir son diplôme
>
> réussir au bac
>
> devenir ministre des finances
>
> avoir un enfant
>
> se marier
>
> faire un voyage aux Etats-Unis
>
> gagner beaucoup d'argent

1. **A dix-huit ans, <u>tu réussiras au bac.</u>**
2. Après, _____
3. Tu _____
4. Et _____
5. Ensuite, _____
6. Et _____
7. A trente ans, _____
8. Et _____

4 Tes amis ne savent pas trop quoi faire après le bac. Dis-leur ce qui va se passer s'ils décident de faire certaines choses plutôt que d'autres. (**p. 134**)

EXEMPLE
—J'hésite entre quitter ma famille et travailler dans la boutique de mes parents.
—**Si tu quittes ta famille, tu ne travailleras pas dans la boutique de tes parents.**

1. Nous hésitons entre prendre un appartement et faire construire une maison.
2. J'hésite entre écrire un roman et créer une B.D.
3. Karim hésite entre faire un apprentissage et entrer à l'université.
4. J'hésite entre me consacrer à la médecine et devenir chroniqueur sportif.
5. Nous hésitons entre avoir un enfant et voyager.
6. Malika et sa sœur hésitent entre partir en vacances et prendre des leçons de conduite.
7. Jocelyne hésite entre aller à l'université et travailler dans le café de ses parents.

Grammaire supplémentaire

CHAPITRE 5

Possible answers

3
1. tu réussiras au bac.
2. tu rejoindras ton frère à Dakar.
3. entreras dans une école de commerce.
4. tu obtiendras ton diplôme.
5. tu trouveras un travail dans une banque.
6. tu gagneras beaucoup d'argent.
7. tu deviendras ministre des finances.
8. tu te marieras

4
1. Si vous prenez un appartement, vous ne ferez pas construire de maison.
2. Si tu écris un roman, tu ne créeras pas de B.D.
3. S'il fait un apprentissage, il n'entrera pas à l'université.
4. Si tu te consacres à la médecine, tu ne deviendras pas chroniqueur sportif.
5. Si vous avez un enfant, vous ne voyagerez pas.
6. Si elles partent en vacances, elles ne prendront pas de leçons de conduite.
7. Si elle entre à l'université, elle ne travaillera pas dans le café de ses parents.

Communication for All Students

Challenge
2 Have students give alternative options in their responses, using different verbs in the future. They could also ask each other the questions, taking turns playing the roles of the counselor and the student, giving a negative answer, and then adding the alternative.

Visual Learners
4 Have students make a cartoon strip in which characters consider the outcomes of each set of future possibilities. Have students illustrate the characters' futures in thought bubbles. They might add possibilities and practice role-playing with a partner.

WA3 FRANCOPHONE
AFRICA-5

CHAPITRE 5

For **Grammaire supplémentaire**
Answer Transparencies, see the
Teaching Transparencies binder.

Deuxième étape   **Objectives** Asking about future plans; expressing wishes; expressing indecision; giving advice; requesting information; writing a formal letter

5 Tes amis te racontent ce qu'ils aiment faire. Dis-leur ce que tu ferais après le bac si tu étais eux. Utilise **si j'étais toi** et une des expressions de la boîte. (**p. 141**)

> faire des études de médecine vétérinaire
> aller en Angleterre
> aller voir la conseillère d'orientation
> travailler son saxophone
> devenir pilote
> commencer par faire des films vidéo
> devenir mécanicien

EXEMPLE   —J'aime réparer les vieilles voitures.
    —**Si j'étais toi, je deviendrais mécanicien.**

1. Je voudrais faire partie d'un groupe de World Music.
2. Comme j'aimerais faire du cinéma!
3. Ce qui me plairait, c'est de soigner les animaux.
4. Ce qui m'intéresse, c'est d'avoir un bon travail.
5. Ce qui me plaît, c'est de voyager.
6. J'aimerais bien parler anglais.

6 Tu viens de recevoir une lettre de Prune. Remplis les blancs avec le conditionnel des verbes entre parenthèses. (**p. 141**)

> Mon rêve, c'est d'aller en Afrique! Si je pouvais, j' __1__ (aller) voir Penda, mon meilleur ami. Il habite Dakar, la capitale du Sénégal. On __2__ (se promener) partout dans la ville. S'il faisait trop chaud, on __3__ (pouvoir) se baigner dans la mer. Penda me __4__ (présenter) sa famille. Sa mère et ses sœurs m' __5__ (apprendre) à faire des plats sénégalais. Peut-être que nous __6__ (faire) les courses dans un marché en plein air; j' __7__ (aimer) bien faire ça. L'ambiance des marchés doit être fantastique, à mon avis! Le week-end, les cousins de Penda nous __8__ (emmener) écouter de la musique traditionnelle dans leur village. Qu'est-ce qu'on __9__ (s'amuser)! Avant de rentrer en France, j' __10__ (acheter) un balafon à Penda pour le remercier. Penda, c'est un vrai musicien! Il __11__ (adorer) ça, c'est sûr.

Answers

5
1. Si j'étais toi, je travaillerais mon saxophone.
2. Si j'étais toi, je commencerais par faire des films vidéo.
3. Si j'étais toi, je ferais des études de médecine vétérinaire.
4. Si j'étais toi, j'irais voir la conseillère d'orientation.
5. Si j'étais toi, je deviendrais pilote.
6. Si j'étais toi, j'irais en Angleterre.

6
1. irais
2. se promènerait
3. pourrait
4. présenterait
5. apprendraient
6. ferions
7. aimerais
8. emmèneraient
9. s'amuserait
10. achèterais
11. adorerait

Communication for All Students

Challenge

6 Have students write their own letters, using the conditional, after they have completed Prune's. Have them use hers as a model, but they should supply information about themselves as much as possible.

Slower Pace/ Auditory Learners

8 Review the formation of questions with inversion with students before beginning the exercise. Have students call out informal questions that can be changed to inversion and write them on the board or on an overhead transparency. Go over several of the questions in Activity 8 orally before students write their answers.

7 Complète chaque phrase avec une des expressions de la boîte. N'oublie pas de mettre le verbe au conditionnel. (**p. 141**)

> devenir dentiste chercher un emploi
>
> quitter sa famille se marier
>
> être riche l'adorer passer son permis de conduire

1. Si je trouvais un appartement à Thiès, …
2. Si nous avions un enfant, …
3. Si tu tombais amoureux, …
4. Si vous vous spécialisiez dans les dents, …
5. Si mes parents gagnaient à la loterie, …
6. Si Mounia prenait des leçons de conduite, …
7. Si j'étais au chômage, …

8 Récris les questions suivantes. Utilise l'inversion dans chacune. (**p. 143**)

1. Est-ce qu'elles sont femmes d'affaires?
2. Il sait ce qu'il veut faire après le bac?
3. Est-ce que vous voulez venir avec nous chez le conseiller d'orientation?
4. Tu veux devenir diplomate, Eric?
5. Est-ce que je pourrais aller à l'université, à ton avis?
6. Nous passons le bac le 28 juin?
7. Est-ce qu'il joue du saxophone?

9 Utilise les fragments suivants pour créer des questions en utilisant l'inversion. (**p. 143**)

1. pouvoir / tu / des conseils / donner / me
2. vous / des renseignements / envoyer / je / que / vous / vouloir
3. nous / quand / partir / pour Dakar
4. préférer / ils / policiers / devenir / avocats / ou
5. passer / permis / il / été / son / cet / de conduire
6. se trouver / l'école de commerce / savoir / où / elles
7. elle / être / architecte
8. compter / faire / vous / après le bac / un apprentissage

Review and Assess

You may wish to assign the **Grammaire supplémentaire** activities as additional practice or homework after presenting material throughout the chapter. Assign Activity 1 after **Tu te rappelles?** (p. 133), Activities 2–4 after **Grammaire** (p. 134), Activities 5–7 after **Grammaire** (p. 141), and Activities 8–9 after **Grammaire** (p. 143).

To prepare students for the **Etape** Quizzes and Chapter Test, we suggest doing the **Grammaire supplémentaire** activities in the following order. Have students complete Activities 1–4 before taking Quiz 5-1A or 5-1B; and Activities 5–9 before Quiz 5-2A or 5-2B.

Answers

7
1. je quitterais ma famille.
2. nous l'adorerions.
3. tu te marierais.
4. vous deviendriez dentiste.
5. ils seraient riches.
6. elle passerait son permis de conduire.
7. je chercherais un emploi.

8
1. Sont-elles femmes d'affaires?
2. Sait-il ce qu'il veut faire après le bac?
3. Voulez-vous venir avec nous chez le conseiller d'orientation?
4. Veux-tu devenir diplomate, Eric?
5. Pourrais-je aller à l'université, à ton avis?
6. Passons-nous le bac le 28 juin?
7. Joue-t-il du saxophone?

Possible Answers:

9
1. Peux-tu me donner des conseils?
2. Voulez-vous que je vous envoie des renseignements?
3. Quand partons-nous pour Dakar?
4. Préfèrent-ils devenir policiers ou avocats?
5. Passe-t-il son permis de conduire cet été?
6. Savent-elles où l'école de commerce se trouve?
7. Est-elle architecte?
8. Comptez-vous faire un apprentissage après le bac?

Mise en pratique

The **Mise en pratique** reviews and integrates all four skills and culture in preparation for the Chapter Test.

Teaching Resources
pp. 152–153

PRINT 📖
▸ Lesson Planner, p. 26
▸ Listening Activities, p. 37
▸ Video Guide, pp. 31, 33–34
▸ Grammar Tutor for Students of French, Chapter 5
▸ Standardized Assessment Tutor, Chapter 5

MEDIA 💿 📼
▸ One-Stop Planner
▸ Video Program
  Videocassette 2, 27:00–33:52
▸ Audio Compact Discs, CD 5, Trs. 12–13
▸ Interactive CD-ROM Tutor, Disc 2

Slower Pace

1 Before playing the recording, form groups of three and assign either Karim or Sandrine to each one. As they listen to the recording, group members concentrate specifically on their assigned person. Then, have them respond to the true-false statements about their person. Finally, have the groups share their information about Karim and Sandrine.

Answers

2 1. training in cooking, restaurant and hotel management
2. to make available to the hotel and tourist industries competent and efficient staff
3. to practice the best profession in the world with enthusiasm and pleasure
4. students from various African countries

Mise en pratique

internet
ADRESSE: go.hrw.com
MOT-CLE: WA3
FRANCOPHONE AFRICA-5

1 Ecoute la conversation de Karim et Sandrine et dis si les phrases suivantes sont vraies ou fausses. *See scripts and answers on p. 125H.*

CD 5
Tr. 12

1. Karim a réussi son bac.
2. Sandrine compte entrer à l'université.
3. Sandrine ne va pas quitter sa famille.
4. Karim sait ce qu'il veut faire plus tard.
5. Karim a l'intention de continuer ses études.
6. Sandrine conseille à Karim de s'inscrire dans une école technique.
7. Karim voudrait un travail où il puisse rencontrer des gens.
8. Sandrine conseille à Karim de lire un article dans le journal.

2 Lis l'article que Sandrine a donné à Karim. Puis, réponds aux questions. *See answers below.*
1. What sort of preparation did these young people receive?
2. According to the school's director, what is the purpose of this program?
3. What does the director expect of the graduates?
4. Who attends this school?

3 C'est le premier jour d'apprentissage de Karim à l'hôtel. Son supérieur lui a dit de prendre les messages et de répondre aux questions par écrit. Ecoute le message de M. Loukour et fais une liste de ses demandes. Puis, choisis la lettre que Karim lui enverra. *See scripts and answers on p. 125H.*

CD 5
Tr. 13

HOTELLERIE -P.B. SAMB
De nouveaux professionnels sur le marché

Une trentaine d'élèves de diverses nationalités de l'Ecole de Formation Hôtelière et Touristique ont reçu vendredi soir leur diplôme.

Tous les candidats ayant réussi cette année, le ministre du Tourisme a félicité la direction et les professeurs de l'école, ainsi que les responsables d'entreprises qui ont contribué à leur formation en les encadrant au niveau des stages pratiques.

Les candidats de cuisine et pâtisserie, restaurant et gestion hôtelière reçoivent une formation de deux ou trois ans axée sur des disciplines relatives à un enseignement pratique doublée de techniques professionnelles, scientifiques, d'expression française ou de langues étrangères.

Il s'agit de «mettre à la disposition des industries hôtelières et touristiques des agents compétents et efficaces», selon le directeur de l'école. En leur souhaitant bonne chance dans leur vie professionnelle, le directeur les a invités à exercer «le plus beau métier du monde avec passion et un plaisir quotidien».

L'EFHT reçoit, en effet, chaque année, outre les élèves sénégalais, des ressortissants d'autres pays africains.

En réponse à votre demande, veuillez trouver ci-joint les renseignements que vous nous avez demandés. Notre village-hôtel se trouve au centre de la ville, proche des musées et des meilleurs restaurants. Le climat de la région est très doux et permet beaucoup d'activités de plein air dont la liste se trouve dans la brochure ci-jointe. En vous remerciant d'avance de votre attention, veuillez agréer, Monsieur, l'expression de nos salutations distinguées.

Suite à votre appel téléphonique du 20 juin, nous vous envoyons les renseignements que vous nous avez demandés. Notre établissement offre les sports suivants : tennis, planche à voile, pirogue et pêche. Sachez également que tous nos bungalows sont climatisés, comme vous pourrez le constater dans la brochure que vous trouverez ci-jointe. En vous remerciant d'avance de votre attention, nous vous prions d'agréer, Monsieur, l'expression de nos sentiments respectueux.

Apply and Assess

Building on Previous Skills

2 Have students use their reading strategies to answer these questions. Have them scan the text for the specific answers to the questions. You might even have a contest to see who can write correct answers to the questions in the shortest amount of time.

Additional Practice

3 Have students note the differences between the two letters. Then, using the letters as models, have students respond to the following situation: M. Loukour calls the restaurant. He wants to know if they can serve **couscous** and **tajine** for a business lunch he is planning during his stay in Morocco. Have students write a formal reply letter to M. Loukour, confirming the plans.

---

4 Lis ces lettres que quelques jeunes Sénégalais ont envoyées à un magazine de jeunes francophones. Ecris des réponses que tu enverras au magazine. Compare tes réponses à celles de ton/ta camarade.

Je vous écris parce que j'ai un petit problème. Je ne sais vraiment pas quoi faire. Je vais bientôt passer le bac et je n'ai aucune idée pour mon avenir. Mes parents me proposent de travailler dans leur boutique de disques, mais ça ne m'intéresse pas beaucoup. Je préférerais continuer mes études. Mais pour quoi faire? Je suis bonne en langues et je suis nulle en maths. Est-ce que vous avez des conseils à me donner?

Marisa

J'ai 17 ans. Je vais passer le bac à la fin de l'année. J'aimerais bien continuer mes études, mais j'hésite. Mes parents n'ont pas beaucoup d'argent. Quand je serai à l'université, il faudra qu'ils continuent à m'aider financièrement. Je ne sais pas quoi faire. Peut-être que je devrais commencer à travailler? Est-ce que quelqu'un a le même genre de problème? Répondez-moi.

Yasser

J'aimerais faire du cinéma, mais mes parents ne veulent pas. Ils sont tous les deux médecins. Ils préféreraient que j'entre à l'université et que je fasse des études de médecine. Ils disent qu'il n'y a pas d'avenir dans le cinéma. Pourtant j'ai déjà fait plusieurs films vidéo. Mais je ne sais pas à qui les montrer. Je ne sais même pas s'ils sont bons ou mauvais. Si j'avais l'avis de quelqu'un, je pourrais prendre une décision.

Mamadou

5 ## Jeu de rôle

Talk to a parent about what you're thinking of doing after high school. Explain what you want to do with your future and why. Your parent is not very happy with your choice and tries to discourage you from it. Try to convince him or her. Change roles.

Apply and Assess

♟ Game

Je regrette! Have partners create a set of 20–25 cards with either **Marisa, Yasser**, or **Mamadou** written on them. Have them shuffle the deck, deal three cards to each player, and place the rest of the deck face down. The goal is to have the greatest number of matched cards. The first player asks a question about one of the people on his or her cards. If the player has a **Marisa** card,

he or she might ask **Tu es nulle en maths?** If the other player has a card for the person who would answer yes, he or she gives the card to the first player, who sets the two matching cards aside. If the other player does not have the card, he or she says **Je regrette,** and the first player draws a card from the deck. The game ends when one player's hand is empty.

Mise en pratique

CHAPITRE 5

Teaching Suggestion

4 Have students write a letter to the magazine in which they describe their own options and ask the readers for advice.

📁 Portfolio

4 **Written** This activity is appropriate for students' written portfolios. For portfolio information, see *Alternative Assessment Guide,* pages iv–15.

Que sais-je?

Can you use what you've learned in this chapter?

Can you ask about and express intentions? p. 133

1 How would you ask a friend what he or she plans to do after graduation? *Qu'est-ce que tu penses/vas/comptes faire? Qu'est-ce que tu as l'intention de faire?*

2 How would you tell what you plan to do? *Je pense/compte/tiens à... ; j'ai l'intention de...*

Can you express conditions and possibilities? p. 133

3 How would you tell someone what you will do, given these conditions? *Possible answers:*
1. Si je me marie,... *j'aurai des enfants.*
2. Si j'entre à l'université,... *je ferai des études de médecine.*
3. Si je gagne de l'argent,... *je pourrai prendre un appartement.*
4. Si je trouve un travail,... *je quitterai ma famille.*

4 How would you tell someone that you might do these things? *See answers below.*

1. 2. 3.

Can you ask about future plans? p. 140

5 How would you ask someone about his or her future plans? *Tu sais ce que tu veux faire? Tu as des projets? Qu'est-ce que tu veux faire plus tard?*

Can you express wishes? p. 140

6 How would you tell what you would like to do in the future? *Je voudrais... ; J'aimerais bien... ; Ce qui me plairait, c'est de... ; Mon rêve, c'est de ...*

Can you express indecision? p. 140

7 How would you express indecision about your future plans? *Pas vraiment. Je ne sais pas trop. Non, je me demande. Je n'en ai aucune idée. J'ai du mal à me décider. Je ne sais plus ce que je veux.*

Can you give advice? p. 140

8 How would you advise a friend who . . . *See answers below.*

> failed an exam?
> doesn't have any pocket money?
> would like to go to college?
> wants to be a teacher?
> is uncertain about his or her choice of profession?

Can you request information and write a formal letter? p. 142

9 How would you request information about courses, costs, and so forth from a school or university? *Pourriez-vous m'envoyer des renseignements sur votre école? Je voudrais savoir... ; Vous serait-il possible de m'envoyer une brochure sur votre école?*

10 How would you write the closing of the letter in number 9? *Je vous prie d'agréer, Monsieur/Madame, l'expression de mes sentiments distingués.*

Possible answers

4
1. Peut-être que je ferai un apprentissage.
2. Il est possible que je voyage.
3. Il se peut que je cherche un travail.

8 *failed an exam:* Tu n'as qu'à étudier plus.

doesn't have any pocket money: Tu devrais travailler.

would like to go to college: Tu ferais bien d'étudier.

wants to be a teacher: Tu devrais travailler avec les enfants.

is uncertain about his or her choice of profession: Il faudrait que tu te renseignes.

Review and Assess

Game
Que sais-je? Form two teams. Have a player from each team come to the board. Ask a question at random from the **Que sais-je?** The first player to write a correct response on the board wins a point for his or her team. You might offer the winning player the chance to win a bonus point by giving a second possible answer to the question. The team with the most points at the end of the game wins.

Additional Practice

4 Have students also write about one or two things that they plan to do.

8 You might have students work with a partner to create a two-line dialogue for each situation.

Première étape

Asking about and expressing intentions

Qu'est-ce que tu penses faire?	What do you think you'll do?
Qu'est-ce que tu as l'intention de faire?	What do you intend to do?
Qu'est-ce que tu comptes faire?	What do you plan to do?
Je pense...	I think I'll . . .
Je compte...	I'm planning on . . .
Je tiens à...	I really want to . . .

Expressing conditions and possibilities

Si ... ,	If . . . ,
Peut-être que...	Maybe . . .
Il se peut que...	It might be that . . .
Il est possible que...	It's possible that . . .

Future choices and plans

arrêter/finir ses études	to stop/finish one's studies
avoir un enfant	to have a child
choisir un métier	to choose a career
entrer à l'université	to start college
être au chômage	to be unemployed

faire un apprentissage	to do an apprenticeship
faire une école technique	to go to a technical school
faire son service militaire	to do one's military service
obtenir son diplôme	to get one's diploma
se marier	to get married
passer son permis de conduire	to get one's driver's license
quitter sa famille	to leave home
réussir son bac	to pass one's baccalaureat exam
trouver un travail	to find a job

Deuxième étape

Asking about future plans

Tu sais ce que tu veux faire?	Do you know what you want to do?
Tu as des projets?	Do you have plans?
Qu'est-ce que tu veux faire...?	What do you want to do . . . ?

Expressing wishes

J'aimerais bien...	I'd really like . . .
Ce qui me plairait, c'est de...	What I would like is to . . .
Mon rêve, c'est de...	My dream is to . . .

Expressing indecision

Je ne sais pas trop.	I really don't know.
Non, je me demande.	No, I wonder.
Je n'en ai aucune idée.	I have no idea.
J'ai du mal à me décider.	I'm having trouble deciding.
Je ne sais plus ce que je veux.	I don't know what I want anymore.

Giving advice

Tu n'as qu'à...	All you have to do is . . .
Tu ferais mieux/bien de...	You would do better/well to . . .
Il faudrait que tu...	You ought to . . .

Il vaudrait mieux que...	It would be better if . . .

Careers

un acteur/une actrice	an actor/an actress
un agent de police/un policier	a police officer
un(e) architecte	an architect
un(e) avocat(e)	a lawyer
un chauffeur	a driver
un(e) comptable	an accountant
un(e) dentiste	a dentist
un écrivain	a writer
un homme/une femme d'affaires	a businessman/woman
un(e) infirmier(-ière)	a nurse
un ingénieur	an engineer
un(e) instituteur (-trice)	an elementary school teacher
un(e) journaliste	a journalist
un(e) mécanicien(ne)	a mechanic
un médecin	a doctor
un(e) ouvrier(-ière)	a worker
un(e) pharmacien(ne)	a pharmacist
un pilote	a pilot
un plombier	a plumber
un(e) secrétaire	a secretary
un(e) serveur (-euse)	a server
un tailleur	a tailor
un(e) technicien(ne)	a technician

Requesting information

Pourriez-vous m'envoyer des renseignements sur...?	Could you send me information on . . . ?
Je voudrais savoir...	I would like to know . . .
Vous serait-il possible de...?	Would it be possible for you to . . . ?

Writing a formal letter

Monsieur/Madame,	Sir/Madam,
En réponse à votre lettre du...	In response to your letter of . . .
Suite à notre conversation téléphonique,...	Following our telephone conversation, . . .
Je vous prie d'agréer, Monsieur/Madame, l'expression de mes sentiments distingués.	Very truly yours, . . .

Vocabulaire

? Circumlocution

Have students work in pairs. One partner will play the role of an American who has just moved to a city in a francophone country, the other partner the role of a French-speaking resident of that city. The newcomer is trying to establish contacts with various professional people in the community (doctors, lawyers), but, unable to remember the correct terms for the different professions, has to describe what a person in a particular profession does. The resident tries to guess the profession and offers advice on how to contact someone in that profession. Students should take turns playing each role.

Chapter 5 Assessment

▸ **Testing Program**
Chapter Test, pp. 97–102
Audio Compact Discs, CD 5, Trs. 16–18

Speaking Test, p. 297

▸ **Alternative Assessment Guide**
Portfolio Assessment, p. 20
Performance Assessment, p. 34
CD-ROM Assessment, p. 48

▸ **Interactive CD-ROM Tutor, Disc 2**

CD-ROM
DISC 2

A toi de parler
A toi d'écrire

▸ **Standardized Assessment Tutor**
Chapter 5

▸ **One-Stop Planner, Disc 2**
Test Generator
Chapter 5

Review and Assess

♟ Game

Dis-moi! Write 20 vocabulary words or expressions on a grid of 20 squares. Make and distribute two copies for every three students. Have two students cut the squares apart and take ten squares each. The third student, who is the judge and timekeeper for the partners, receives a copy of all the words. Students take turns giving clues to get their partner to say all the words or expressions on the squares within 20 seconds. Students may use French words or gestures to try to get the meaning across. The squares containing the words that were not correctly guessed should be put into a pile. At the end of the game, all three students should write a sentence containing each of the words or expressions from this pile.

Chapitre 6 : Ma famille, mes copains et moi
Chapter Overview

Mise en train pp. 158–160	*Naissance d'une amitié*

	FUNCTIONS	**GRAMMAR**	**VOCABULARY**	**RE-ENTRY**
Première étape pp. 161–165	• Making, accepting, and refusing suggestions, p. 161 • Making arrangements, p. 162 • Making and accepting apologies, p. 164	• Reciprocal verbs, p. 162 • The past infinitive, p. 164		• Reflexive verbs (**Chapitres 4, 5, 7,** II) • Making and responding to suggestions (**Chapitre 8,** II) • Making plans (**Chapitre 6,** I) • Apologizing and accepting an apology (**Chapitre 10,** II)

Remise en train pp. 166–167	*Ahlên, merhabîn*

Deuxième étape pp. 168–173	• Showing and responding to hospitality, p. 169 • Expressing and responding to thanks, p. 169 • Quarreling, p. 173		• Family relationships, p. 171	• Family vocabulary (**Chapitre 7,** I) • The imperative (**Chapitre 1,** II)

Lisons! pp. 174–176	**Les Trois Femmes du roi** **La Petite Maison**	**Reading Strategy:** Taking cultural context into account

Ecrivons! p. 177	**Une histoire d'attitude**	**Writing Strategy:** Using graphic devices

Grammaire supplémentaire	**pp. 178–181**	**Première étape,** pp. 178–179	**Deuxième étape,** pp. 179–181

Review pp. 182–185	**Mise en pratique,** pp. 182–183	**Que sais-je?,** p. 184	**Vocabulaire,** p. 185

CULTURE

• **Note culturelle,** Bargaining in North Africa, p. 160
• **Panorama Culturel,** Values of francophone teenagers, p. 165
• **Rencontre culturelle,** Overview of Morocco, p. 168
• **Note culturelle,** Hospitality in Morocco, p. 170

Chapitre 6 : Ma famille, mes copains et moi
Chapter Resources

PRINT

Lesson Planning
 One-Stop Planner

Lesson Planner with Substitute Teacher Lesson Plans, pp. 27–31, 69

Student Make-Up Assignments
- Make-Up Assignment Copying Masters, Chapter 6

Listening and Speaking
Listening Activities
- Student Response Forms for Listening Activities, pp. 43–45
- Additional Listening Activities 6-1 to 6-6, pp. 47–49
- Additional Listening Activities (song), p. 50
- Scripts and Answers, pp. 126–131

Video Guide
- Teaching Suggestions, pp. 36–37
- Activity Masters, pp. 38–40
- Scripts and Answers, pp. 93–95, 113–114

Activities for Communication
- Communicative Activities, pp. 21–24
- Realia and Teaching Suggestions, pp. 66–68
- Situation Cards, pp. 99–100

Reading and Writing
Reading Strategies and Skills Handbook, Chapter 6

Joie de lire 3, Chapter 6

Cahier d'activités, pp. 61–72

Grammar
Travaux pratiques de grammaire, pp. 54–62

Grammar Tutor for Students of French, Chapter 6

Assessment
Testing Program
- Grammar and Vocabulary Quizzes, **Etape** Quizzes, and Chapter Test, pp. 111–124
- Score Sheet, Scripts and Answers, pp. 125–131
- Midterm Exam, pp. 133–140
- Score Sheet, Scripts, and Answers, pp. 141–146

Alternative Assessment Guide
- Portfolio Assessment, p. 21
- Performance Assessment, p. 35
- CD-ROM Assessment, p. 49

Student Make-Up Assignments
- Alternative Quizzes, Chapter 6

Standardized Assessment Tutor
- Reading, pp. 21–23
- Writing, p. 24
- Math, pp. 25–26

MEDIA

 Online Activities
- Jeux interactifs
- Activités Internet

 Video Program
- Videocassette 2
- Videocassette 5 (captioned version)

 Audio Compact Discs
- Textbook Listening Activities, CD 6, Tracks 1–13
- Additional Listening Activities, CD 6, Tracks 24–30
- Assessment Items, CD 6, Tracks 14–18
- Midterm Exam, CD 6, Tracks 19–23

Interactive CD-ROM Tutor, Disc 2

Teaching Transparencies
- Situation 6-1 to 6-2
- **Grammaire supplémentaire** Answers
- **Travaux pratiques de grammaire** Answers

  One-Stop Planner CD-ROM

Use the **One-Stop Planner CD-ROM with Test Generator** to aid in lesson planning and pacing.

For each chapter, the **One-Stop Planner** includes:
- Editable lesson plans with direct links to teaching resources
- Printable worksheets from resource books
- Direct launches to the HRW Internet activities
- Video and audio segments
- Test Generator
- Clip Art for vocabulary items

Chapitre 6 : Ma famille, mes copains et moi

Projects ······················

Une publicité pour le Maroc

*Students will create and perform a television commercial for the **Office de tourisme du Maroc** to encourage visitors to come to Morocco.*

MATERIALS

✂ **Students may need**
- Posterboard
- Construction paper
- Markers
- Scissors
- Glue
- Camcorder
- Videocassette

SUGGESTED SEQUENCE

1. Have students suggest elements of a successful commercial. You might find travel videos from various states or countries (from Morocco, if possible) and have students analyze them and tell why they are effective.

2. Have groups choose their approach and decide what they will feature in their ad. They should refer to the **Mise en train** on pages 158–159, the **Remise en train** on pages 166–167, and the **Rencontre culturelle** on page 168 for information on Moroccan culture.

3. Students should write a script for their commercial. They should suggest at least three interesting things to do and see in Morocco.

4. After the script is written, each group member should proofread it to check for variety of vocabulary and accuracy of language.

5. Have students write the final script and make copies for the group. They should plan the staging of the commercial, incorporating props or posters. Have them rehearse their commercial in front of another group.

6. Have groups perform their commercials for the class. You might videotape their commercials and use them to introduce this chapter next year.

GRADING THE PROJECT

Suggested Point Distribution (total = 100 points)
```
Completion of requirements.................20 points
Language use...........................20 points
Creativity/presentation...........................20 points
Pronunciation ...........................20 points
Effort/participation..............................20 points
```

Games ······················

Le Football américain

In this game, students will practice the functions and vocabulary presented in the chapter

Procedure   To prepare for the game, make one set of cards with the functions written on them (*making suggestions, accepting suggestions,* and so on). Make another set of thirteen cards: eight with *rush,* three with *pass,* one with *interception,* and one with *penalty* written on them. Draw a football field on the board. Write an "X" on one twenty-yard line and an "O" on the other twenty-yard line to represent the teams. Divide the class into two teams. To play the game, a player from the first team draws a card from the pile and follows the appropriate instruction:

- *Pass:* The teacher draws a function card, and the player uses an appropriate word or expression that serves that function in a logical sentence. If the sentence is correct, the player rolls a die, multiplies the number by ten, and moves his or her team the corresponding number of yards on the field.

- *Rush:* Instructions are the same as those for *Pass,* but the number on the die is doubled.

- *Penalty:* The teacher draws a function card and has a player from the opposing team use a related word or expression in a logical sentence. If the opposing player is correct, he or she rolls the die and moves the advancing team back the corresponding number of yards.

- *Interception:* The teacher draws a function card and has a player from the opposing team use an appropriate word or expression in a logical sentence. If the sentence is correct, the opposing player's team may take the next turn.

Teams should alternate turns. Teams receive six points for crossing the goal line. When a team crosses the goal line, they may take another turn to try for an extra point. The team with the most points at the end of play wins.

Teacher Note   In this game, you might also use functions from preceding chapters to review previously learned expressions for the Midterm Exam.

Storytelling

Mini-histoire

This story accompanies Teaching Transparency 6-2. The **mini-histoire** can be told and retold in different formats, acted out, written down, and read aloud to give students additional opportunities to practice all four skills. The story is about Sophie and Séverine, two friends who meet up after class.

Depuis que Sophie et Séverine ne sont plus dans le même lycée, elles passent tout leur temps libre au téléphone. Sophie demande à Séverine : «On se voit aujourd'hui?» «Oui, on se donne rendez-vous à quelle heure et où?» répond Séverine. Elles décident de se retrouver devant le marchand de glaces à cinq heures. Sophie est la première à arriver, un peu en avance. Séverine est souvent en retard de cinq ou dix minutes. Mais, à cinq heures vingt, elle n'est toujours pas arrivée et Sophie commence à s'impatienter. Quand Séverine arrive, à cinq heures vingt-cinq, Sophie lui demande : «Tu le fais exprès de toujours être en retard?» Séverine lui explique qu'elle est en retard parce que son ami Guillaume l'a invitée à aller boire un café après les cours. Elle doit le retrouver au cinéma un peu plus tard.

Traditions

La Cérémonie du thé

In Morocco, hot mint tea is often served before or after a meal and during most business and social exchanges. A tall teapot, called a **barrahd,** small decorative glasses, and octagonal boxes of mint, sugar, and tea are brought out on a tray called a **siniyya.** After the tea has brewed, the host or hostess stirs it one or two times, holds the teapot high, and pours a stream of steaming tea into a glass held far below. The tea is then returned to the pot. Finally, he or she pours tea with the same flourish into all the glasses.

Recette

The traditional preparation of **couscous** is rather long and involved, but pre-cooked **couscous** is now available in many supermarkets. The word **couscous** can be used to describe either the semolina alone or the entire dish comprised of the semolina and stew.

COUSCOUS

pour 6 à 8 personnes

1 poulet
1/2 tasse de raisins secs
3 tasses de couscous instantané
3 tasses d'eau
3 carottes
1 tasse de pois chiches
2 courgettes

1 navet	1 tasse de beurre
3 tomates	1 pincée de safran
2 oignons	1 cuillère à café de coriandre
3 cuillères d'huile d'olive	1 cuillère à café de cannelle
	poivre, sel

Couper les légumes. Dans une marmite, faire cuire à feu doux les tomates, les carottes, les courgettes, le navet et les oignons dans un litre d'eau au moins. Ajouter l'huile d'olive et un peu de beurre. Ajouter les épices : safran, coriandre, cannelle, poivre et sel.

Faire cuire le poulet dans une marmite pendant une demi-heure, accompagné d'un oignon, de safran, de sel et de poivre. L'ajouter aux légumes et laisser cuire le tout encore une heure.

Faire bouillir 4 1/2 tasses d'eau. Quand l'eau bout, verser le couscous et le retirer du feu. Laisser le couscous absorber l'eau. Faire fondre le beurre dans une grande poêle et y ajouter le couscous. L'égrainer avec une fourchette. Ajouter les raisins secs.

Pour servir, placer le couscous dans un grand plat rond et y verser les légumes et le poulet.

Videocassette 2, Videocassette 5 (captioned version)
See Video Guide, pp. 35–39.

Video Program

Camille et compagnie • Sixième épisode : *Une étoile est née*

Sophie is auditioning for a play. The producer of the play explains to her and her male counterpart, Julien, what their roles are. Then Sophie and Julien perform their audition. Sophie leaves the theater dissatisfied with her performance, and the producer decides that she is too old for the part. But at the last minute, he thinks of another role for her.

Qu'est-ce qui est important dans la vie?
Students from around the francophone world tell what's important to them. Two native speakers discuss the **Panorama Culturel** question and introduce the interviews.

 Vidéoclips
- **Petit Gervais®**: advertisement for cheese
- **Pouss'Mousse®**: advertisement for soap
- **Renault®**: advertisement for a car
- **News report**: Grandparents' role in the family

Interactive CD-ROM Tutor

The **Interactive CD-ROM Tutor** contains videos, interactive games, and activities that provide students an opportunity to practice and review the material covered in Chapter 6.

Activity	Activity Type	Pupil's Edition Page
1. Grammaire	Les mots qui manquent	p. 162
2. Comment dit-on... ?	Le bon choix	pp. 162, 164
3. Grammaire	Les mots qui manquent	p. 164
4. Comment dit-on... ?	Chacun à sa place	p. 169
5. Vocabulaire	Chacun à sa place Explorons! Vérifions!	p. 171
6. Comment dit-on... ?	Prenons note!	p. 173
Panorama Culturel	Qu'est-ce qui est important dans la vie? Le bon choix	p. 165
A toi de parler	*Guided recording*	pp. 182–183
A toi d'écrire	*Guided writing*	pp. 182–183

Teacher Management System

Logging In
Logging in to the *Allez, viens!* TMS is easy. Upon launching the program, simply type "admin" in the password area of the log-in screen and press RETURN. Log on to **www.hrw.com/CDROMTUTOR** for a detailed explanation of the Teacher Management System.

One-Stop Planner CD-ROM

To preview all resources available for this chapter, use the **One-Stop Planner CD-ROM**, Disc 2.

Internet Connection

internet

go.hrw.com

ADRESSE: go.hrw.com
MOT-CLE: WA3 FRANCOPHONE AFRICA-6

*Have students explore the **go.hrw.com** Web site for many online resources covering all chapters. All Chapter 6 resources are available under the keyword **WA3 FRANCOPHONE AFRICA-6**. Interactive games help students practice the material and provide them with immediate feedback. You'll also find a printable worksheet that provides Internet activities that lead to a comprehensive online research project.*

Jeux interactifs

You can use the interactive activities in this chapter

- to practice grammar, vocabulary, and chapter functions
- as homework
- as an assessment option
- as a self-test
- to prepare for the Chapter Test

Activités Internet

Students look for information about Moroccan culture and cuisine, using the vocabulary and phrases from the chapter.

- In preparation for the **Activités Internet,** have students review the dramatic episode on Video-cassette 2, or do the activities in the **Panorama Culturel** on page 165. In Activity D, students are asked to write a letter to one of the institutions they researched to find out more information about their programs of study. Have partners exchange their paragraphs and edit each other's work.

Projet

Have students research etiquette and customs of Morocco and other francophone countries of North Africa. You might want to assign groups of students specific areas of research, such as table manners, greeting and leave-taking customs, and gender roles. Remind students to document their sources by noting the names and the URLs of all the sites they consulted. You may have the groups compile their findings into a cultural guide for students visiting North Africa.

Première étape

Answers to Activity 7
1. refuse   3. accepte   5. refuse
2. refuse   4. refuse   6. accepte

7   p. 161

1. —Ça t'intéresse d'aller à la piscine avec nous?
   —Impossible, je suis pris. J'ai un cours de piano.

2. —Dis, ça te plairait de faire du camping avec nous pendant les vacances?
   —J'aimerais bien, mais je vais chez mes grands-parents.

3. —Ça t'intéresse d'aller au cinéma ce soir?
   —Bonne idée, ce serait sympa.

4. —Tu ne voudrais pas aller te promener dans le parc cet après-midi?
   —C'est gentil, mais il faut que je rentre. Mes parents m'attendent.

5. —J'ai une idée. Ça te plairait de faire un pique-nique ce week-end?
   —J'aimerais bien, mais je n'ai pas le temps. Il faut que j'étudie mes maths.

6. —Ça vous intéresse d'aller voir Cheb Khaled en concert demain?
   —Moi, j'aimerais bien.
   —Moi aussi, ça me plairait beaucoup.

10   p. 162

Answers to Activity 10
samedi vers deux heures; à la porte Boujeloud; du shopping

MALIKA   Dis, Rachida, ça t'intéresse d'aller faire du shopping dans la médina cet après-midi ?

RACHIDA   Impossible, je suis prise. Je dois aller voir ma tante. Tu as des projets pour samedi?

MALIKA   Non, je n'ai rien de prévu.

RACHIDA   Alors, ça te plairait d'y aller samedi?

MALIKA   Oui, ça me plairait bien. Comment on fait?

RACHIDA   Si tu veux, on se téléphone demain.

MALIKA   Oui... Ou alors, on pourrait se donner rendez-vous à la porte Boujeloud.

RACHIDA   D'accord. A quelle heure est-ce qu'on se retrouve?

MALIKA   On peut se retrouver après le déjeuner. Vers deux heures.

RACHIDA   Ça marche.

MALIKA   Alors, à samedi. Deux heures. Porte Boujeloud.

15   p. 164

1. Oh, ça ne fait rien. C'était une vieille cassette. Je ne l'écoutais plus.

2. Ne t'inquiète pas. Il n'y a pas de mal. Tu n'oublieras pas la prochaine fois, j'en suis sûr.

3. Pardonnez-moi. Je ne savais pas qu'il fallait faire ça.

4. Ne t'en fais pas. Il n'y a pas de mal. J'avais l'intention de la faire nettoyer de toute façon.

5. Désolé d'avoir oublié notre rendez-vous. J'étais tellement occupé, ça m'est complètement sorti de la tête.

6. Je m'excuse d'être en retard. C'est la dernière fois. Je te le promets.

7. Oh, c'est pas grave! Mais n'oublie pas de me téléphoner la prochaine fois que tu rentres tard. Je m'inquiète, tu sais.

8. Je m'en veux de ne pas lui avoir écrit. Je vais lui envoyer une lettre tout de suite.

Answers to Activity 15
1. répond à une excuse   5. s'excuse
2. répond à une excuse   6. s'excuse
3. s'excuse   7. répond à une excuse
4. répond à une excuse   8. s'excuse

Deuxième étape

24   p. 169

Answers to Activity 24
1. c   2. b   3. d   4. a

1. —Ça me fait plaisir de vous voir.
   —Moi aussi.

2. —Asseyez-vous, je vous en prie.
   —Merci bien.

3. —Qu'est-ce que je vous sers?
   —Je prendrais bien un verre de thé, s'il vous plaît.

4. —Donnez-moi votre manteau.
   —Merci. Vous êtes bien aimable.

28   p. 171

Answer to Activity 28
a

ERIC   Salut, Ahmed! Ça va?

AHMED   Oui, ça va bien, allez, entre! Eric, je te présente mon père.

M. HABEK   Bonjour, Eric.

ERIC   Bonjour, monsieur.

AHMED   Et ma mère.

MME HABEK   Bonjour.

ERIC   Bonjour, madame. Je suis content de faire votre connaissance.

MME HABEK   Donnez-moi votre veste.

ERIC   Merci.

MME HABEK   Asseyez-vous, mettez-vous à l'aise.

ERIC   Merci, c'est gentil.

AHMED   Eric, viens. Je te présente mon arrière-grand-père. Grand-Papa, c'est Eric.

GRAND-PAPA   Bonjour.

ERIC   Bonjour, monsieur.

One-Stop Planner CD-ROM

To preview all resources available for this chapter, use the **One-Stop Planner CD-ROM**, Disc 2.

AHMED   Allons dans la cuisine. Je vais te présenter ma sœur. C'est l'aînée. Elle s'est mariée l'année dernière. Tu vas rencontrer son mari plus tard.

ERIC   Dis, ton arrière-grand-père, il va bien?

AHMED   Oui. Mais tu sais, il est souvent triste depuis que sa femme est morte. Voilà ma sœur Soumia.

SOUMIA   Bonjour, Eric.

ERIC   Bonjour.

SOUMIA   Qu'est-ce que je peux t'offrir?

ERIC   Je voudrais bien du thé, s'il te plaît.

SOUMIA   Bien sûr.

AHMED   Allal, mon cousin, va arriver dans une minute.

ERIC   Il est jeune?

AHMED   Pas tellement. Il a trente-cinq ans.

ERIC   Il est marié?

AHMED   Non, il est encore célibataire.

M. HABEK   Salut, Allal. Voilà le copain d'Ahmed, Eric. Eric, c'est mon neveu, Allal.

ERIC   Bonjour.

ALLAL   Bonjour.

AHMED   Ah, voilà mon petit frère, Aziz. C'est le benjamin. Viens ici, Aziz. Je te présente Eric.

32   **p. 173**   Answers to Activity 32
1. Moktar   2. Moktar   3. Amina   4. Amina   5. Moktar

1. —Pleurnicheuse!
—Mais tu n'as pas le droit d'entrer dans ma chambre!
—Tant pis pour toi!
—Je vais le dire à Maman!
—Rapporteuse!

2. —Tu pourrais baisser la musique? C'est tellement fort. J'essaie de faire mes devoirs, tu sais.
—Tu es casse-pieds!
—Si tu ne baisses pas, je vais te prendre ton CD.
—Oh, tu me fais peur.
—Et voilà.
—Arrête! Ça suffit! Je baisse. D'accord?

3. —Et voilà, encore une fois j'ai gagné.
—Tricheur!
—Mauvaise joueuse! C'est pas de ma faute si tu es nulle.
—Oh, ça va, hein?
—Mais c'est toi qui as commencé.
—Mais t'as triché.
—Arrête! Y en a marre!

4. —Eh! Arrête de faire ce bruit! Tu le fais exprès?
—Euh, non.
—Ben, tu m'énerves, à la fin.
—Bon, désolé. J'arrête.
—Eh, tu peux arrêter d'agiter le pied comme ça?
—Oh, fiche-moi la paix!

5. —Bas les pattes! C'est mon bureau!
—Mais je cherchais juste un stylo.
—Va trouver ton stylo ailleurs. T'as pas le droit de fouiller dans mes affaires.
—Tu me prends la tête! Tu as peur que je lise ton journal? Tiens, justement! Voyons...
—Eh! Donne-moi ça! Mêle-toi de tes oignons!

Mise en pratique

1   **p. 182**

MARTIN   Alors, qu'est-ce qu'il y a à voir à Marrakech?

ALI   Oh, il y a plein de choses à voir et à faire. Il y a des musées, des palais, des souks. Et aussi les gens. Il faut rencontrer des Marocains, si tu veux connaître le Maroc.

MARTIN   Et la place Jemaa el Fna? On m'a dit que c'est intéressant. Qu'est-ce que tu en penses?

ALI   Oh, c'est dingue! Il y a des conteurs, des musiciens, des vendeurs d'eau...

MARTIN   Il y a des charmeurs de serpents?

ALI   Bien sûr. Ça t'intéresse d'en voir?

MARTIN   Oui.

ALI   Alors, on peut y aller demain matin, si tu veux.

MARTIN   D'accord. A quelle heure est-ce qu'on se donne rendez-vous?

ALI   Vers huit heures, ça va?

MARTIN   Oui. Et où est-ce qu'on se retrouve?

ALI   Place de Bâb Fteuh.

MARTIN   D'accord.

ALI   Tu ne voudrais pas déjeuner chez moi après ça?

MARTIN   Si, ce serait sympa.

ALI   Bon. Après, je t'emmène à la maison pour rencontrer ma famille. Comme ça, tu pourras goûter des plats marocains.

MARTIN   Oh, ce serait chouette!

ALI   Dis donc, ça te plairait de voir le palais de la Bahia?

MARTIN   J'aimerais bien, mais je n'aurai pas le temps. J'ai rendez-vous avec mes parents.

ALI   Bon. D'accord.

Answers to Mise en pratique Activity 1
1. b, d, e   3. vers huit heures
2. b, e   4. c

Chapitre 6: Ma famille, mes copains et moi
Suggested Lesson Plans *50-Minute Schedule*

Day 1

CHAPTER OPENER 5 min.
- Present Chapter Objectives, p. 157.
- Photo flash!, Culture Note, ATE, p. 156

MISE EN TRAIN 40 min.
- Presenting **Mise en train**, p. 158, using Video Program, Videocassette 2.
- See Teaching Suggestions, Viewing Suggestions 1–2, Video Guide, p. 36.
- Culture Note, ATE, p. 159
- See Teaching Suggestions, Post-viewing Suggestions 1–2, Video Guide, p. 36.
- Do Activities 1–5, p. 160.
- Read and discuss **Note culturelle**, p. 160.

Wrap-Up 5 min.
- Do Activity 6, p. 160.

Homework Options
Cahier d'activités, Acts. 1–2, p. 61

Day 2

MISE EN TRAIN
Quick Review 5 min.
- Check homework.

PREMIERE ETAPE
Comment dit-on... ?, p. 161 20 min.
- Presenting **Comment dit-on... ?**, ATE, p. 161
- Play Audio CD for Activity 7, p. 161.
- Cahier d'activités, p. 62, Activity 2
- Do Activities 8–9, pp. 161–162.

Comment dit-on... ?, p. 162 20 min.
- Presenting **Comment dit-on... ?**, ATE, p. 162
- Play Audio CD for Activity 10, p. 162.
- See Vocabulary Practice Using Teaching Transparency 6-1, Speaking Activity 2, Teaching Transparencies.
- Building on Previous Skills, ATE, p. 162.
- Travaux pratiques de grammaire, p. 54, Activity 1

Wrap-Up 5 min.
- Teaching Transparency 6-1, Culture Suggestions 6–7

Homework Options
Cahier d'activités, Act. 4, p. 62
Travaux pratiques de grammaire, Act. 2, p. 55

Day 3

PREMIERE ETAPE
Quick Review 5 min.
- Check homework.

Grammaire, p. 162 20 min.
- Presenting **Grammaire**, ATE, p. 162
- Do Activity 11, p. 162.
- Travaux pratiques de grammaire, pp. 55–57, Acts. 3–7
- Do Activities 12–13, p. 163.
- Do Activities 14, p. 163, in pairs.
- Read and discuss **A la française**, p. 163.

Comment dit-on... ?, p. 164 15 min.
- Presenting **Comment dit-on... ?**, ATE, p. 164
- Play Audio CD for Activity 15, p. 164.
- Cahier d'activités, p. 64, Activity 8
- Teaching Transparency 6-1, Suggestions for Using Teaching Transparencies, Suggestion 5

Wrap-Up 10 min.
- Building on Previous Skills, ATE, p. 163

Homework Options
Grammaire supplementaire, Acts. 1–2, p. 178
Cahier d'activités, Acts. 5–6, p. 63

Day 4

PREMIERE ETAPE
Quick Review 5 min.
- Check homework.

Grammaire, p. 164 20 min.
- Presenting **Grammaire**, ATE, p. 164
- Travaux pratiques de grammaire, pp. 58–59, Activity 8–11
- Cahier d'activités, p. 65, Activity 9
- Do Activity 16, p. 164.

PANORAMA CULTUREL 15 min.
- See Teaching Suggestions, Pre-viewing Suggestions 1–2, Video Guide, p. 36.
- Presenting **Panorama Culturel**, ATE, p. 165
- See Teaching Suggestions, Viewing Suggestion, Video Guide, p. 37.
- Questions, ATE, p. 165
- **Qu'en penses-tu?**, p. 165

Wrap-Up 10 min.
- Game: **Désolé(e)!**, ATE, p. 164

Homework Options
Study for Quiz 6-1
Activity 17, p. 164

Day 5

PREMIERE ETAPE
Quiz 6-1 20 min.
- Administer Quiz 6-1A or 6-1B.

REMISE EN TRAIN 25 min.
- Presenting **Remise en train**, ATE, p. 166
- Do Activities 18–22, pp. 166–167.
- Thinking Critically: Comparing and Contrasting, ATE, p. 167

Wrap-Up 5 min.
- Thinking Critically: Analyzing, ATE, p. 167

Homework Options
Cahier d'activités, Acts. 10–11, p. 66

Day 6

REMISE EN TRAIN
Quick Review 5 min.
- Check homework.

RENCONTRE CULTURELLE 10 min.
- Presenting **Rencontre culturelle**, ATE, p. 168
- **Qu'en penses-tu?**, p. 168
- Read and discuss **Savais-tu que… ?**, p. 168.
- Culture Note, ATE, p. 168

DEUXIEME ETAPE
Comment dit-on... ?, p. 169 25 min.
- Presenting **Comment dit-on... ?**, ATE, p. 169
- Play Audio CD for Activity 24, p. 169.
- Cahier d'activités, p. 67, Activity 12
- Read and discuss **Note culturelle**, p. 170.
- Do Activities 25–26, p. 170.
- Challenge, ATE, p. 170

Wrap-Up 10 min.
- Culture Note, ATE, p. 170
- Thinking Critically: Comparing and Contrasting, ATE, p. 171

Homework Options
Pupil's Edition, Activity 27, p. 170

⌀ **One-Stop** Planner CD-ROM

For alternative lesson plans by chapter section, to create your own customized plans, or to preview all resources available for this chapter, use the **One-Stop Planner CD-ROM**, Disc 2.

 For additional homework suggestions, see activities accompanied by this symbol throughout the chapter.

Day 7

DEUXIEME ETAPE

Quick Review 5 min.
- Check homework.

Vocabulaire, p. 171 20 min.
- Presenting **Vocabulaire**, ATE, p. 171
- Play Audio CD for Activity 28, p. 171.
- Travaux pratiques de grammaire, pp. 60–61, Acts. 12–15
- Cahier d'activités, pp. 68–69, Acts. 13–14,
- Have students do Activity 30, p. 172, in groups.

Comment dit-on... ?, p. 173 20 min.
- Presenting **Comment dit-on... ?**, ATE, p. 173
- Read and discuss **A la française**, p. 173.
- Play Audio CD for Activity 32, p. 173.
- Cahier d'activités, p. 70, Activities 15–17
- Have students do Activity 33, p. 173, in pairs.

Wrap-Up 5 min.
- Do Activity 34, p. 173

Homework Options
Study for Quiz 6-2
Pupil's Edition, Activities 29 and 31, p. 172
Travaux pratiques de grammaire, Acts. 16–17, p. 62

Day 8

DEUXIEME ETAPE

Quiz 6-2 20 min.
- Administer Quiz 6-2A or 6-2B.

LISONS! 25 min.
- Read and discuss **Stratégie pour lire**, p. 174.
- Do Prereading Activities A–B, p. 174.
- Culture Note, ATE, p. 174
- Have students read **Lisons!**, pp. 174–176.
- Do Reading Activities C–P, pp. 174–176.

Wrap-Up 5 min
- Thinking Critically: Analyzing, ATE, p. 175
- Thinking Critically: Analyzing, ATE, p. 176

Homework Options
Complete Activities C–P, pp. 174–176.
Cahier d'activités, Act. 18, p. 71

Day 9

LISONS!

Quick Review 5 min.
- Check homework.

LISONS! 10 min.
- Do Activity Q, p. 176.
- Thinking Critically: Q. Synthesizing, ATE, p. 176

ECRIVONS! 30 min.
- Read and discuss **Stratégie pour écrire**, p. 177, then have students work on their stories.

Wrap-Up 5 min.
- Allow time for peer and self-evaluation of student stories.

Homework Options
Complete final draft of stories.

Day 10

ECRIVONS!

Quick Review 10 min.
- Have volunteers share their stories with the class.

MISE EN PRATIQUE 35 min.
- Play Audio CD for Activity 1, p. 182.
- Do Activity 2, p. 183.
- Language Note and Culture Note, ATE, p. 182
- Have students do Activities 3–4, p. 183, in pairs.
- **A toi de parler**, CD-ROM Tutor

Wrap-Up 5 min.
- Activities for Communication, p. 99, Situation (global): Interview.

Homework Options
Cahier d'activités, Act. 19, p. 72

Day 11

MISE EN PRATIQUE

Quick Review 5 min.
- Check homework.

Student Review 40 min.
- Do Activity 5, p. 183.
- Have students prepare conversations for **Jeu de rôle**, p. 183.
- Have groups present conversations for **Jeu de rôle**, p. 183.
- **A toi d'écrire**, CD-ROM Tutor, Disc 2

Wrap-Up 5 min.
- Begin **Que sais-je?**, p. 184.

Homework Options
Que sais-je?, p. 184
Pupil's Edition, p. 183, Activity 5

Day 12

MISE EN PRATIQUE

Quick Review 20 min.
- Go over **Que sais-je?**, p. 184.
- Collect written assignment, Activity 5, p. 183.

Chapter Review 30 min.
- Review Chapter 6. Choose from **Grammaire supplémentaire**, Grammar Tutor for Students of French, Activities for Communication, Listening Activities, Interactive CD-ROM Tutor, or **Jeux interactifs**.

Assessment

Test, Chapter 6 50 min.
- Administer Chapter 6 Test. Select from Testing Program, Alternative Assessment Guide, Test Generator, or Standardized Assessment Tutor.

Chapitre 6 : Ma famille, mes copains et moi
Suggested Lesson Plans 90-Minute Block Schedule

Block 1

CHAPTER OPENER 10 min.
- Present Chapter Objectives, p. 157
- Culture Note and Photo Flash!, ATE, pp. 156–157

MISE EN TRAIN 40 min.
- Presenting **Mise en train**, ATE, p. 158
- Culture Note, ATE, p. 159
- **Note culturelle**, p. 160
- Do Activities 1–4, p. 160.
- Thinking Critically: Comparing and Contrasting, ATE, p. 160
- Do Activity 5, p. 160.

PREMIERE ETAPE
Comment dit-on...?, p. 161 20 min.
- Presenting **Comment dit-on...?**, ATE, p. 161
- Play Audio CD for Activity 1, p. 161.
- Do Activity 8, p. 161.

Comment dit-on...?, p. 162 15 min.
- Presenting **Comment dit-on...?**, ATE, p. 162
- Play Audio CD for Activity 10, p. 162.
- Building on Previous Skills, ATE, p. 162

Wrap-Up 5 min.
- Randomly read aloud expressions from **Comment dit-on...?**, p. 161. Have students tell you whether each expression is making a suggestion, accepting a suggestion, or refusing a suggestion.

Homework Options
Pupil's Edition, Activity 9, p. 162
Cahier d'activités, pp. 61–62, Acts. 1–4
Travaux pratiques de grammaire, pp. 54–55, Acts. 1–2

Block 2

PREMIERE ETAPE
Quick Review 10 min.
- Activities for Communication, pp. 21–22, Communicative Activity 6-1A and 6-1B

Grammaire, p. 162 35 min.
- Presenting **Grammaire**, ATE, p. 162
- Language Note, ATE, p. 163
- Do Activities 11–12, pp. 162–163.

Comment dit-on...?, p. 164 10 min.
- Presenting **Comment dit-on...?**, ATE, p. 164
- Play Audio CD for Activity 15, p. 164.

Grammaire, p. 164 20 min.
- Presenting **Grammaire**, ATE, p. 164
- Do Activity 16, p. 164.

Wrap-Up 15 min.
- Game: **Désolé(e)!**, ATE, p. 164

Homework Options
Pupil's Edition, Activity 17, p. 164
Grammaire supplémentaire, pp. 178–179, Acts. 1–3
Cahier d'activités, p. 63, Act. 5
Travaux pratiques de grammaire, pp. 55–59, Acts. 3–11

Block 3

PREMIERE ETAPE
Quick Review 5 min.
- Teaching Transparency 6-1, using suggestion #1 on Suggestions for Using Teaching Transparency 6-1

Grammaire, p. 162 30 min.
- A la française, p. 163
- Do Activities 13–14, p. 163.

RENCONTRE CULTURELLE 15 min.
- Presenting **Rencontre culturelle**, ATE, p. 168

REMISE EN TRAIN 30 min.
- Presenting **Remise en train**, ATE, p. 166, using Audio CD
- Do Activities 18–20, pp. 166–167.
- Culture Notes, ATE, p. 167

Wrap-Up 10 min.
- Game: **Vrai ou faux?**, ATE, p. 168

Homework Options
Have students study for Quiz 6-1.
Cahier d'activités, pp. 63–64, Acts. 6–9

One-Stop Planner CD-ROM

For alternative lesson plans by chapter section, to create your own customized plans, or to preview all resources available for this chapter, use the **One-Stop Planner CD-ROM**, Disc 2.

For additional homework suggestions, see activities accompanied by this symbol throughout the chapter.

Block 4

PREMIERE ETAPE
Quick Review 10 min.
- Listening Activities, p. 47, Additional Listening Activity 6-2

Quiz 6-1 20 min.
- Administer Quiz 6-1A or 6-1B.

DEUXIEME ETAPE
Comment dit-on...?, p. 169 35 min.
- Presenting **Comment dit-on...?**, ATE, p. 169
- **Note culturelle**, p. 170
- Play Audio CD for Activity 24, p. 169. See Slower Pace suggestion, ATE, p. 169.
- Do Activities 25–26, p. 170.

Vocabulaire, p. 171 20 min.
- Presenting **Vocabulaire**, ATE, p. 171
- Language Notes, ATE, p. 171
- Play Audio CD for Activity 28, p. 171.

Wrap-Up 5 min.
- Additional Practice, ATE, p. 171

Homework Options
Grammaire supplémentaire, p. 179, Act. 4
Cahier d'activités, pp. 67–70, Acts. 12–15
Travaux pratiques de grammaire, pp. 60–61, Acts. 12–15

Block 5

DEUXIEME ETAPE
Quick Review 5 min.
- Teaching Transparency 6-2, using suggestion #1 from Vocabulary Practice Using Teaching Transparency 6-2

Vocabulaire, p. 171 25 min.
- Teaching Transparency 6-2, Suggestions for Using Teaching Transparency 6-2, Suggestion 2
- Do Activities 30–31, p. 172.

PANORAMA CULTUREL 20 min.
- Presenting **Panorama Culturel**, ATE, p. 165
- Questions, ATE, p. 165
- Read and discuss **Qu'en penses-tu?**, p. 165.

Comment dit-on... ?, p. 173 35 min.
- Presenting **Comment dit-on... ?**, ATE, p. 173
- **A la française**, p. 173
- Play Audio CD for Activity 32, p. 173.
- Do Activity 33, p. 173.

Wrap-Up 5 min.
- Activities for Communication, p. 100, Situation 6-2: Role-play

Homework Options
Have students study for Quiz 6-2.
Pupil's Edition, Activity 29, p. 172
Grammaire supplémentaire, pp. 180–181, Acts. 5–7
Cahier d'activités, p. 70, Acts. 15–17
Travaux pratiques de grammaire, p. 62, Acts. 16–17

Block 6

DEUXIEME ETAPE
Quick Review 10 min.
- Activities for Communication, pp. 23–24, Communicative Activity 6-2A and 6-2B

Quiz 6-2 20 min.
- Administer Quiz 6-2A or 6-2B.

MISE EN PRATIQUE 25 min.
- Play Audio CD for Activity 1, p. 182.
- Do Activities 3–4, p. 183.

LISONS! 35 min.
- Read and discuss **Stratégie pour lire**, p. 174.
- Prereading Activities A–B, p. 174
- Read part of *Les Trois Femmes du roi*, pp. 174–175 out loud. Have students follow along in their books.
- Activities C–F, pp. 174–175

Homework Options
Que sais-je?, p. 184
Finish reading *Les Trois Femmes du roi*, pp. 175–176
Interactive CD-ROM Tutor: Games
Study for Chapter 6 Test

Block 7

MISE EN PRATIQUE
Quick Review 10 min.
- Check homework.
- **Que sais-je?**, p. 183

Chapter Review 35 min.
- Review Chapter 6. Choose from **Grammaire supplémentaire**, Grammar Tutor for Students of French, Activities for Communication, Listening Activities, Interactive CD-ROM Tutor, or **Jeux interactifs**.

Test, Chapter 6 45 min.
- Administer Chapter 6 Test. Select from Testing Program, Alternative Assessment Guide, Test Generator, or Standardized Assessment Tutor.

CHAPITRE 6

For resource information, see the **One-Stop Planner,** Disc 2.

Pacing Tips
The first **étape** has slightly less material to cover than the second **étape.** You might keep that in mind when planning your lessons, and make use of the cultural content in the **Panorama Culturel** on page 165. For Lesson Plans and timing suggestions, see pages 155I–155L.

Meeting the Standards

Communication
- Making, accepting, and refusing suggestions, p. 161
- Making arrangements, p. 162
- Making and accepting apologies, p. 164
- Showing and responding to hospitality; expressing and responding to thanks, p. 169
- Quarreling, p. 173

Cultures
- Culture Notes, pp. 156, 159, 167, 168, 170, 171, 174, 182
- Notes culturelles, pp. 160, 170
- Panorama Culturel, p. 165
- Rencontre culturelle, p. 168

Connections
- Community Links, pp. 165, 173
- Reading/Writing Link, p. 176

Comparisons
- Language-to-Language, p. 156
- Thinking Critically, pp. 160, 165, 167, 171, 173, 175, 176

Communities
- De l'école au travail, p. 173

Cultures and Communities

Language-to-Language
Arabic is the official language of Morocco, although French is widely spoken. Students might want to learn a few Arabic phrases and use them in the chapter activities: **Salam Walaykoom** (sah LAM wuh LAY kum—*Hello*); **Minfadlik** (min FAHD lik—*Please*); **Shokran** (SHOK run—*Thank you*).

Culture Note

The Moroccan concept of family generally extends beyond the nuclear family. In a traditional Moroccan household, the parents, all unmarried children, and any married sons and their families live together under the same roof. When daughters marry, they leave home to live with their husband's family.

CHAPITRE

6
Ma famille, mes copains et moi

Objectives

In this chapter you will learn to

Première étape

- make, accept, and refuse suggestions
- make arrangements
- make and accept apologies

Deuxième étape

- show and respond to hospitality
- express and respond to thanks
- quarrel

 internet

ADRESSE: go.hrw.com
MOT-CLE: WA3 FRANCOPHONE AFRICA-6

◀ **Le thé à la menthe dans une famille marocaine**

Focusing on Outcomes
Have students read the objectives listed on this page. Have them recall French expressions they've learned that serve these functions.

NOTE: You may want to use the video to support the objectives. The self-check activities in **Que sais-je?** on page 184 help students assess their achievement of the objectives.

Photo Flash!
The man in this photo is preparing to serve mint tea (**thé à la menthe**), the national drink of Morocco.

Communication for All Students

Challenge

Write the following expressions on butcher paper and have students try to guess which function they fulfill. **Ça te plairait d'aller au souk?** *(making suggestions);* **Tu es bête comme tes pieds!** *(quarreling);* **Donnez-moi votre manteau.** *(showing hospitality);* **A quelle heure est-ce qu'on se donne rendez-vous?** *(making arrangements);* **Je vous remercie.** *(expressing thanks);* **Pardonne-**

moi d'avoir manqué notre rendez-vous. *(making apologies).*

If students have trouble guessing the function, read the expressions with the proper intonation to help them. You might even overact each phrase to make it easier for students to guess.

Teaching Resources
pp. 158–160

PRINT
▸ Lesson Planner, p. 27
▸ Video Guide, pp. 36, 38
▸ Cahier d'activités, p. 61

MEDIA
▸ One-Stop Planner
▸ Video Program
Camille et compagnie
Videocassette 2, 34:07–40:38
Videocassette 5 (captioned version), 31:31–38:02
▸ Audio Compact Discs, CD 6, Tr. 1

Teaching Suggestion
Before students read *Naissance d'une amitié,* have them describe their impressions of Morocco, based on the photos. Ask them what they would want to know about Morocco before visiting there.

Presenting
Mise en train

On a transparency, write brief summaries of the scenes in random order. To summarize the first scene, you might write **Raphaël et ses parents se séparent.** Then, play the recording. Pause after each scene and have students choose the correct summary.

Mise en train ▪ *Naissance d'une amitié*

Cahier d'activités, p. 61, Act. 1

CD 6 Tr. 1

Stratégie pour comprendre
The Simenot family is visiting the city of Fès, in Morocco. Look at the photos to find out what they're doing there. Where does the scene take place? Then look at the characters' names. Is Moktar a typical French name? Can you guess what the situation is before reading the dialogue?

1

M. Simenot	Qu'est-ce que vous voulez voir?
Mme Simenot	Moi, j'aimerais bien voir les magasins de poteries et de tapis.
M. Simenot	Bonne idée.
Raphaël	Moi, je préférerais me promener. Ça vous embête si on se sépare?
Mme Simenot	Pas du tout. Mais comment on fait pour se retrouver?
M. Simenot	On peut se donner rendez-vous devant la Porte Boujeloud.
Raphaël	D'accord. A quatre heures, ça va?
M. Simenot	Bon, ça va.

2

Moktar	Bonjour. Tu es français?
Raphaël	Oui.
Moktar	Je m'appelle Moktar. Et toi?
Raphaël	Raphaël.
Moktar	Tu as vu mes beaux tapis? Ils sont pas chers.
Raphaël	Je te remercie, mais je n'ai pas d'argent. Je viens juste ici pour visiter.
Moktar	Tu es en vacances?
Raphaël	Oui.
Moktar	Ça te dit de prendre un thé?
Raphaël	Je te remercie, mais...
Moktar	Tu sais, au Maroc, il ne faut jamais refuser un thé.
Raphaël	Alors, j'accepte.

3

Moktar	Tiens.
Raphaël	Merci... Aïe! C'est brûlant!
Moktar	Excuse-moi, j'aurais dû te prévenir. C'est comme ça qu'on boit le thé au Maroc. Très chaud.
Raphaël	C'est délicieux. Qu'est-ce que tu mets dedans?
Moktar	De la menthe.
Raphaël	Tu travailles ici?
Moktar	Oui, je tiens la boutique quand mes parents sont absents. Ils sont allés acheter des tapis dans le sud.

Preteaching Vocabulary

Using Prior Knowledge
Tell students that in the story, Moktar and Raphaël are just getting to know each other. Various invitations are extended and accepted or refused. Ask them if they can recognize these based on some expressions they already know. Then have students go through the text and identify the invitations (**Ça te dit de prendre un thé?**) and the acceptances and/or refusals (**Je te remercie mais. . ., Alors j'accepte**). Ask them to identify who is doing most of the inviting. Why do they think this is?

Raphaël	Tu ne vas plus au lycée?
Moktar	Non, j'ai arrêté à seize ans. J'ai l'intention de continuer l'affaire de mes parents… Alors, comment tu trouves le Maroc?
Raphaël	Tu sais, nous sommes arrivés hier seulement. Mais pour l'instant, je trouve les gens très accueillants.
Moktar	Vous allez rester à Fès?
Raphaël	Quelques jours seulement. Après, on compte aller à Marrakech.
Moktar	C'est chouette, Marrakech. C'est un peu bruyant, mais c'est très animé. Tu aimeras beaucoup.
Raphaël	Qu'est-ce qu'il y a à voir à Fès?
Moktar	Oh, des tas de choses. C'est d'une richesse! Vous devriez aller voir le Dar el Makhzen. C'est un immense palais où le roi réside quand il vient à Fès. Les portes sont magnifiques.
Raphaël	Ah oui?
Moktar	Oui. Et surtout, je vous conseille d'aller vous promener sur la place du Vieux Méchouar. C'est très sympa. Il y a des danseurs, des conteurs, des musiciens…

4
Raphaël	Je ne sais pas si on aura le temps.
Moktar	Encore du thé?
Raphaël	Volontiers… Dis-moi, quelle heure il est?
Moktar	Quatre heures.
Raphaël	Oh là là! Excuse-moi, j'ai rendez-vous avec mes parents. Je suis déjà en retard…

5
Moktar	Qu'est-ce que tu fais demain? Tu as des projets?
Raphaël	Non, je suis libre. Je n'ai rien de prévu.
Moktar	Si tu veux, on peut se revoir.
Raphaël	Je veux bien.
Moktar	Ça t'intéresse d'aller écouter de la musique marocaine?
Raphaël	Oui, ça me plairait bien.
Moktar	Si ça te dit, on peut aller à un concert demain soir.
Raphaël	Moi, j'aimerais bien. Mais il faut que je demande la permission à mes parents. Comment on fait?

Moktar	On peut se téléphoner. Vous êtes à l'hôtel?
Raphaël	Oui, on est à l'hôtel Moussafir.
Moktar	Bon. Je te téléphone demain matin. Et si tes parents sont d'accord, on peut se retrouver à l'hôtel en fin d'après-midi.
Raphaël	Génial. Allez, il faut que j'y aille. Comment on dit «au revoir» en arabe?
Moktar	Bes-slama.
Raphaël	Bes-slama.

Using the Captioned Video

 As an alternative, you might want to show the captioned version of *Camille et compagnie : Une étoile est née* on Videocassette 5. Some students may benefit from seeing the written words as they listen to the target language and watch the gestures and actions in context. This visual reinforcement of vocabulary and functions will facilitate students' comprehension and help reduce their anxiety before they are formally introduced to the new language in the chapter.

Teaching Suggestion
Find a map of Fez in a travel guide or encyclopedia. Distribute copies and have students locate the places mentioned in the **Mise en train**. Have them locate one or two other attractions and find out about them. You might write to the Moroccan tourist board (**ONMT**) at the following address for maps and additional information: 20 E. 46th St., New York, NY, 10017.

 ### Culture Note
• The **Porte Boujeloud**, **Bab Boujeloud** in Arabic, is the brightly-colored western gate of the district of **Fès El Bali** (*Old Fez*). This older district of the city is an intricate web of small lanes and alleys. **Fès El Djedid** (*New Fez*) dates from the thirteenth century and consists of royal palaces and gardens.

 ### Camille et compagnie

You may choose to show students Episode 6: *Une étoile est née* now or wait until later in the chapter. In the video Sophie is auditioning for a play. The producer of the play explains the characters' relationship, and Sophie and her male counterpart, Julien, perform for their audition. At the end of the episode, Sophie expresses her disappointment, but the producer is impressed with her and thinks of another potential role for Sophie.

Mise en train

Language Note

3 **Médina** refers to the original Arab part of a Moroccan city. The **kasbah,** or *fortress-palace,* is usually located in this area.

Thinking Critically

4 **Comparing and Contrasting** After students have done the activity, have them do it again, this time imagining that the clues refer to the United States rather than Morocco. For example, in response to the second clue, they would list a typical American drink, perhaps iced tea or cola. Then, have partners compare the Moroccan list to the American one.

Synthesizing

Ask students to name other places or situations in which bargaining is expected (car dealerships, flea markets, garage sales, real estate purchases).

Answers

4 1. le Dar el Makhzen
2. le thé à la menthe
3. un tapis
4. la place du Vieux Méchouar à Fès
5. **Bes-slama** (au revoir)

5 1. Ça te dit de prendre un thé? Encore du thé?
2. ... j'accepte. Volontiers...
3. Excuse-moi...
4. Vous devriez... ; Je vous conseille de...
5. Qu'est-ce que tu fais demain? Tu as des projets?
6. Si tu veux, on peut... ; Si ça te dit, on peut... ; Ça t'intéresse de...?
7. Je veux bien. Oui, ça me plairait bien. Moi, j'aimerais bien.
8. On peut se donner rendez-vous... On peut se téléphoner. ... on peut se retrouver à...

---

1 **Tu as compris?**   These activities check for comprehension only. Students should not yet be expected to produce language modeled in **Mise en train.**

1. Que fait la famille Simenot à Fès?   vacationing
2. Pourquoi Raphaël se sépare de ses parents?   to go for a walk
3. Où est-ce qu'il rencontre Moktar? Pourquoi est-ce que Moktar parle à Raphaël?   carpet store; He hopes to sell a carpet.
4. Qu'est-ce que les deux garçons décident de faire?   to go listen to Moroccan music the next evening.

2 **Mets dans le bon ordre**

Mets ces phrases dans le bon ordre d'après *Naissance d'une amitié.*   1, 4, 6, 2, 5, 3

1. Moktar propose un thé à Raphaël.
2. Raphaël demande l'heure à Moktar.
3. Moktar apprend à Raphaël un mot en arabe.
4. Moktar dit à Raphaël ce qu'il devrait voir à Fès.
5. Moktar dit qu'il va téléphoner à Raphaël à l'hôtel Moussafir.
6. Moktar propose un autre verre de thé à Raphaël.

3 **Alors, raconte!**

Les parents de Raphaël lui posent des questions sur Moktar. Complète leur conversation.

MME SIMENOT	Qu'est-ce qu'il fait dans la médina?		MME SIMENOT	Qu'est-ce qu'il veut faire plus tard?
RAPHAEL	Il...	travaille dans la boutique de tapis de ses parents.	RAPHAEL	Il... veut continuer l'affaire de ses parents.
M. SIMENOT	Il ne va pas au lycée?		M. SIMENOT	Qu'est-ce qu'il t'a conseillé de voir à Fès?
RAPHAEL	Non, il...	a arrêté à seize ans.	RAPHAEL	Il... m'a conseillé de voir le Dar el Makhzen et la place du Vieux Méchouar.

4 **Ça, c'est le Maroc!**   See answers below.

Trouve les choses suivantes dans *Naissance d'une amitié.*

1. quelque chose à voir à Fès
2. une boisson typiquement marocaine
3. un objet artisanal marocain typique
4. un endroit où on trouve des danseurs
5. une expression en arabe

5 **Cherche les expressions**   See answers below.

What does Moktar or Raphaël say to . . .

1. offer tea?
2. accept an offer?
3. apologize?
4. give advice?
5. ask about someone's plans?
6. make a suggestion?
7. accept a suggestion?
8. arrange to meet someone?

6 **Et maintenant, à toi**

Raconte comment tu as rencontré un(e) de tes ami(e)s. Tu étais où? Dans quelle situation?

Note culturelle

Au Maroc, comme dans d'autres pays d'Afrique du Nord, le marchandage fait partie du rituel commercial. Les Occidentaux sont habitués à des prix fixes, mais les marchands arabes fixent leurs prix avec l'idée que les clients vont marchander. Ils prévoient que les clients vont offrir la moitié du prix annoncé, ou même moins!

Comprehension Check

Tactile Learners

2 Have students copy each of these sentences onto a separate slip of paper, and then arrange them in order on their desks.

Challenge

2 Once students have arranged the sentences in the correct order, have them rewrite the sentences as a brief narrative, adding connecting words and, if they desire, personal commentaries on the events.

Challenge

3 Have students imagine they are Raphaël's parents and write down one or two additional questions they might ask him. Then, have them ask their questions of a partner, who responds as Raphaël.

Comment dit-on...?

Making, accepting, and refusing suggestions

To make a suggestion:

> **Ça t'intéresse d'**aller écouter de la musique?
> *Would you be interested in . . . ?*
> **Ça te plairait de** visiter le musée?
> *Would you like to . . . ?*
> **Tu ne voudrais pas** aller te promener dans la médina?

To accept a suggestion:

> **Ce serait sympa.** *That would be nice.*
> Oui, **ça me plairait beaucoup.**
> *I'd like that a lot.*
> **Si, j'aimerais bien.**

To refuse a suggestion:

> **Impossible, je suis pris(e).** *I'm busy.*
> **J'aimerais bien, mais** je n'ai pas le temps.
> *I'd like to, but . . .*
> **C'est gentil, mais j'ai un rendez-vous.**
> *That's nice of you, but I've got an appointment.*

 Cahier d'activités, p. 62, Act. 2

7 **Invitation refusée ou acceptée?** See scripts and answers on p. 155G.

 Ecoutons Ecoute ces conversations. Est-ce que ces personnes refusent ou acceptent les suggestions qu'on leur fait?

CD 6 Tr. 2

Possible answers: Ça te plairait de (d')... ?/Ça t'intéresse de... ?/Tu ne voudrais pas... ?
a. aller à la piscine;   **b.** aller au café;   **c.** aller au musée;   **d.** faire de l'équitation;
e. jouer au football;   **f.** aller au cinéma

8 **Qu'est-ce qu'il propose?**

Parlons Fahmi voudrait sortir ce week-end. Qu'est-ce qu'il propose à son ami Youssef? Utilise différentes expressions.

a.

b.

c.

d.

e.

f.

Communication for All Students

Challenge

8 After doing this activity, have students pair off and act out Fahmi's and Youssef's conversation. One student plays the part of Fahmi and suggests things to do and places to go. The other student plays the part of Youssef and alternately accepts and refuses the suggestions. Make sure

that students include the negative expression **Tu ne voudrais pas... ?** when they make suggestions and that their partners respond to it with **si** instead of **oui**. Students should switch roles after a while.

Teaching Resources
pp. 161–164

PRINT
- Lesson Planner, p. 28
- Listening Activities, pp. 43, 47–48
- Activities for Communication, pp. 21–22, 66, 68, 99–100
- Travaux pratiques de grammaire, pp. 54–59
- Grammar Tutor for Students of French, Chapter 6
- Cahier d'activités, pp. 62–65
- Testing Program, pp. 111–114
- Alternative Assessment Guide, p. 35
- Student Make-Up Assignments, Chapter 6

MEDIA
- One-Stop Planner
- Audio Compact Discs, CD 6, Trs. 2–4, 14, 24–26
- Teaching Transparencies: 6-1; **Grammaire supplémentaire** Answers; Travaux pratiques de grammaire Answers
- Interactive CD-ROM Tutor, Disc 2

Bell Work
Have students write a note to a friend to suggest activities: **aller au marché, voir un film, se baigner, faire une promenade dans la médina.** Then, have them accept or reject each suggestion.

Presenting
Comment dit-on... ?

Write expressions for accepting and refusing suggestions on large index cards. Draw two columns on the board labeled **oui** and **non.** Suggest doing an activity, using one of the new expressions. Have students respond with **oui** or **non.** Select a card reflecting each student's response, read it aloud, and tape it under the appropriate heading.

Teaching Resources
pp. 161–164

PRINT
- Lesson Planner, p. 28
- Listening Activities, pp. 43, 47–48
- Activities for Communication, pp. 21–22, 66, 68, 99–100
- Travaux pratiques de grammaire, pp. 54–59
- Grammar Tutor for Students of French, Chapter 6
- Cahier d'activités, pp. 62–65
- Testing Program, pp. 111–114
- Alternative Assessment Guide, p. 35
- Student Make-Up Assignments, Chapter 6

MEDIA
- One-Stop Planner
- Audio Compact Discs, CD 6, Trs. 2–4, 14, 24–26
- Teaching Transparencies: 6-1; **Grammaire supplémentaire** Answers; Travaux pratiques de grammaire Answers
- Interactive CD-ROM Tutor, Disc 2

Presenting
Comment dit-on... ?

Write the new phrases and **Je ne sais pas, lundi après-midi, devant le cinéma,** and **à cinq heures** on strips. Call on individuals to match all questions with an answer.

Grammaire

Reciprocal Verbs Engage a student in a conversation. Say to the others **Nous nous parlons**. Have partners act out other actions, such as **téléphoner,** as you ask the class what they're doing.

Answers
11 1. s'est rencontrés 2. nous sommes regardés 3. s'est parlé 4. se revoir
5. nous sommes donné
6. vous retrouvez

---

9 ### Tu es libre ce week-end?

Ecrivons Tu es en classe. Tu veux proposer à ton/ta camarade de faire quelque chose ce week-end. Ecris-lui un petit mot et passe-lui le bout de papier. Il/Elle te répond sur la même feuille.

Comment dit-on...?

Making arrangements

To make arrangements:

Comment est-ce qu'on fait?
How should we work this out?
Quand est-ce qu'on se revoit?
When are we getting together?

Où est-ce qu'on se retrouve?
A quelle heure est-ce qu'on se donne rendez-vous?
What time are we meeting?

> Cahier d'activités, p. 62, Act. 4

10 ### Le rendez-vous de Malika   See scripts and answers on p. 155G.

Ecoutons Malika et Rachida se donnent rendez-vous. Quand est-ce qu'elles vont se retrouver? Où? Qu'est-ce qu'elles vont faire?

CD 6 Tr. 3

> Travaux pratiques de grammaire, pp. 54–55, Act. 1–2

Si tu as oublié **reflexive verbs** va à la page R47.

Grammaire

Reciprocal verbs

In addition to their reflexive meanings, the pronouns **se, nous,** and **vous** also have a reciprocal meaning. They mean (*to/for/at*) *each other* when added to a verb.

On **se** revoit l'année prochaine?
Will we see each other next year?

Vous **vous** êtes rencontrés sur la place?
Did you meet each other on the square?

- Make the past participle agree with the reciprocal pronoun when the pronoun is the direct object of the verb.

  Nous **nous** sommes rencontrés hier.
  We met (each other) yesterday.

- You don't change the past participle if the reciprocal pronoun is the <u>indirect object</u> of the verb. Some verbs that take an indirect object are **dire, parler, téléphoner, demander, écrire, offrir,** and **conseiller.**

  Ils **se** sont parlé. (*to each other*)
  Nous **nous** sommes écrit. (*to each other*)

> Grammaire supplémentaire, p. 178, Act. 1–2 →

> Cahier d'activités, p. 63, Act. 5–6

> Travaux pratiques de grammaire, pp. 55–57, Act. 3–7

11 ### Grammaire en contexte

Ecrivons Complète le petit mot que ton ami Ivan t'a envoyé avec les formes des verbes entre parenthèses.   See answers below.

> Hier, j'ai fait la connaissance d'une fille super. On ___1___ (se rencontrer) à la piscine. Nous ___2___ (se regarder) pendant un moment et puis on ___3___ (se parler). Comme on voulait vraiment ___4___ (se revoir), je lui ai demandé si ça lui plairait d'aller au café avec moi. Malheureusement, elle était prise. Alors, nous ___5___ (se donner) rendez-vous samedi prochain. Sophie, Marc et toi, vous allez bien au ciné samedi? On peut venir avec vous? À quelle heure vous ___6___ (se retrouver) là-bas?

Communication for All Students

Building on Previous Skills
Have students recall their daily morning routine. Write their suggestions on a transparency, underlining the reflexive verbs. Then, ask students **Tu t'es levé(e) à quelle heure? Tu t'es brossé les dents à quelle heure?** Have a student explain how to conjugate reflexive verbs in the present and the **passé composé.**

Kinesthetic Learners
After presenting the **Grammaire,** write the following verbs on the board: **regarder, sourire à, parler à, téléphoner à,** and **écrire à.** Pair off students and have them use the verbs on the board to make statements directed at their partners, while they act out their statements. Then, have them use reciprocal pronouns to say what they are doing to each other.

12 Grammaire en contexte

Parlons Raconte l'histoire d'amour de Laure et Vincent d'après les images suivantes.

1. **se voir**
Laure et Vincent se sont vus.

2. **se téléphoner**
Ils se sont téléphoné.

3. **se donner rendez-vous**
Ils se sont donné rendez-vous.

4. **se disputer**
Ils se sont disputés.

5. **se quitter**
Ils se sont quittés.

6. **se réconcilier**
Ils se sont réconciliés

13 Grammaire en contexte

Ecrivons Ecris quelques phrases pour décrire tes rapports avec trois ou quatre des personnes suivantes.

1. ton/ta meilleur(e) ami(e)
2. tes parents
3. ton/ta petit(e) ami(e)
4. tes grands-parents
5. tes profs
6. ton frère/ta sœur

se dire tout   se voir souvent   s'entendre bien

se comprendre   s'aimer   se disputer

se téléphoner tous les jours   se parler

14 On se téléphone?

Parlons Tu as rencontré un garçon/une fille intéressant(e) et tu voudrais le/la revoir. Pose-lui des questions pour fixer un rendez-vous. Joue cette scène avec un(e) camarade.

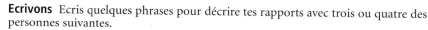

A la française

French speakers use the subject pronoun **on** more often than **nous**, especially in informal speech. Try using **on** when you mean *we*: **On s'aime.** *(We love each other.)*. If you need to emphasize *we*, you can say **Nous, on...**

Nous, on aime les escargots. Pas toi? *We like escargots. Don't you?*

Communication for All Students

Challenge

12 Before students open their books, write the verbs from this activity on a transparency and have students tell you in what order they think the actions occurred. Number the verbs according to their directions. Then, have partners create their own version of Laure and Vincent's romance, using connecting words and adding places, times, and even additional characters and events.

Building on Previous Skills

13 Have students compare their relationships with these people in the past with their relationships now. (**Avant, mes parents et moi, on se disputait souvent, mais maintenant, on s'entend bien.**)

Language Note

Point out that **parler, donner, écrire,** and **téléphoner** take indirect objects and therefore, their past participles do <u>not</u> agree with the reciprocal pronouns in the **passé composé. (Ils se sont téléphoné.) Chercher** and **regarder,** however, take direct objects, so their past participles may show agreement. **(Ils se sont regardés.)** You might have students list in two columns the verbs that take a direct object and those that take an indirect object. You might also refer them to the appropriate section of the Grammar Summary at the back of the book.

Additional Practice

12 Have students retell the story as if they were Laure or Vincent, using **on**.

Speaking Assessment

14 You might use the following rubric when grading your students on this activity.

Speaking Rubric	Points			
	4	3	2	1
Content (Complete– Incomplete)				
Comprehension (Total–Little)				
Comprehensibility (Comprehensible– Incomprehensible)				
Accuracy (Accurate– Seldom accurate)				
Fluency (Fluent–Not fluent)				

18–20: A   14–15: C   Under
16–17: B   12–13: D   12: F

Rush into the classroom and make apologies to several students for being late, using the new expressions. As you apologize to a student, give him or her a card with one of the expressions for accepting an apology. The student responds with the expression on the card.

Grammaire

The past infinitive Write these sentence starters on the board: **Je m'excuse de... , Je suis désolé(e) de... ,** and **Pardonne-moi de...** Then, draw two columns labeled **action** and **excuse.** Ask a student to suggest in French an action someone might apologize for **(arriver en retard).** In the **action** column, write a statement in the **passé composé,** using the student's suggestion. **(Je suis arrivé(e) en retard.).** Then, in the **excuse** column, write the sentence with the starter and the past infinitive, **(Je m'excuse d'être arrivé(e) en retard).** Repeat this process several times. Then ask students to deduce how past infinitives are formed.

Assess

▸ Testing Program, pp. 111–114
Quiz 6-1A, Quiz 6-1B,
Audio CD 6, Tr. 14

▸ Student Make-Up Assignments,
Chapter 6, Alternative Quiz

▸ Alternative Assessment Guide,
p. 35

Answers

16 Je suis désolée d'(e)/Je m'en veux d'(e)/Je m'excuse d'(e)/Pardonne-moi d'(e)
1. avoir perdu ton livre de français.
2. avoir oublié notre rendez-vous.
3. m'être disputée avec toi.
4. être arrivée en classe en retard.
5. ne pas t'avoir téléphoné.
6. avoir répété ton secret.

Comment dit-on...?

Making and accepting apologies

To make an apology:

Je m'excuse d'être en retard.
I'm sorry for . . .
Je suis vraiment désolé(e) d'avoir oublié de te téléphoner.
Pardonne-moi de ne pas avoir répondu.
Pardon me for . . .
Je m'en veux d'avoir dit ça.
I feel bad that . . .

To accept an apology:

Ce n'est pas grave.
Ça ne fait rien.
Il n'y a pas de mal.
Ne t'inquiète pas. *Don't worry about it.*
Ça arrive à tout le monde. *It happens to everybody.*

> Cahier d'activités, p. 64, Act. 8

15 **Ce n'est pas grave.** See scripts and answers on p. 155G.

 Ecoutons Ecoute ces dialogues. Est-ce qu'on s'excuse ou est-ce qu'on répond à une excuse?
CD 6 Tr. 4

Grammaire

The past infinitive

A verb following a conjugated verb other than **avoir** or **être** must be an infinitive. The infinitives you've used so far are present infinitives. Infinitives may also express past time: Je suis désolé **d'avoir oublié** (to have forgotten). To make the past infinitive, use **avoir** or **être** in the infinitive and the past participle of the verb. Use **être** with the verbs that require **être** in the **passé composé.**

Je m'excuse d'**être arrivé(e)** trop tard. *I'm sorry I arrived too late.*
Je suis vraiment désolée de m'**être réveillée** si tard. *I'm really sorry I woke up so late.*
Je m'en veux de ne pas **avoir dit** au revoir. *I feel bad that I didn't say goodbye.*

Grammaire supplémentaire, p. 179, Act. 3

> Cahier d'activités, p. 65, Act. 9

> Travaux pratiques de grammaire, pp. 58–59, Act. 8–11

16 **Grammaire en contexte**

Parlons Aïcha ne s'est pas très bien comportée *(didn't behave well)* la semaine dernière. Comment est-ce qu'elle s'excusera auprès de tout le monde? See answers below.
1. Elle a perdu le livre de français de son amie.
2. Elle a oublié son rendez-vous avec Jean-Marc.
3. Elle s'est disputée avec sa mère.
4. Elle est arrivée en classe en retard.
5. Elle n'a pas téléphoné à son amie.
6. Elle a répété le secret de sa meilleure amie.

17 **Mon journal**

Ecrivons Décris tes rapports avec ton/ta meilleur(e) ami(e). Comment est-il/-elle? Comment es-tu? Pourquoi est-ce que vous vous entendez bien? Est-ce qu'il y a quelque chose que tu n'aimes pas chez lui/elle et qu'il/elle n'aime pas chez toi?

Communication for All Students

Game
Désolé(e)! This game is to practice the past infinitive. Form two teams. Within each team, have students find a partner, choose an activity for which they might apologize, and create a short skit in which one apologizes and the other accepts the apology. In their skits, students should not specifically state what they are apologizing for, but give clues about it. For example, if students were acting out an apology for being late, they might say **Je m'excuse. Je n'ai pas entendu mon réveil, et j'ai raté le bus pour aller à l'école.** The other team then must identify the situation **(Tu t'excuses d'être arrivé(e) en retard)** in order to win a point. Have teams take turns performing their skits.

Qu'est-ce qui est important dans la vie?

We asked some people what's important to them. Here's what they told us.

Viviane,
Côte d'Ivoire

«Dans la vie, pour moi, ce qui compte, ce sont les parents. D'abord, il faut leur obéir, être à leur service, faire ce qui est mieux, ce qu'ils aiment.» Tr. 6

Stanislas,
France

«Ce qui est important, c'est des... A mon avis, ce qui est important, c'est des relations avec des gens, l'argent, parce qu'il en faut et bien vivre, la qualité de vie.» Tr. 7

Micheline,
Belgique

«Trouver justement un métier qu'on aime. Il faut réussir. Pour réussir, il faut être heureux. Et pour être heureux, il faut trouver un métier qu'on aime. Il faut être heureux dans sa famille, d'une façon ou d'une autre. Ça peut être être marié, ne pas être marié. Ça n'a pas d'importance... Et vivre aussi dans un pays qu'on aime.»

Qu'est-ce qui est important dans le choix d'une profession?

«Il faut l'aimer. Il faut aimer le métier que l'on choisit, et si on l'aime pas, il faut avoir le courage de changer rapidement.» Tr. 8

1. *Viviane:* parents
   Stanislas: interpersonal relationships, money, quality of life
   Micheline: finding a career one likes, having a happy family life, living in a country one likes, having the courage to find the right career

Qu'en penses-tu?

1. D'après chacune de ces personnes, qu'est-ce qui est important?
2. Avec qui est-ce que tu es d'accord? Pourquoi?
3. Est-ce que tu n'es pas d'accord avec quelqu'un? Pourquoi?
4. D'après toi, quelles autres choses sont importantes dans la vie?

Connections and Comparisons

Community Link
Have students ask the interview question, "What is most important in life?" to people in the community and compare the answers with their own. You might have students share their findings with the class, being sure to respect the privacy of the people they interviewed.

Thinking Critically
Analyzing   Have students make a list of what they think is important when choosing a career. Then, have them compare their lists to what Micheline says. Ask them to expand on what Micheline says. Why is she using the word **courage** in this context?

Teaching Resources
p. 165

PRINT
▸ Video Guide, pp. 36–37, 39
▸ Cahier d'activités, p. 72

MEDIA
▸ One-Stop Planner
▸ Video Program
  Videocassette 2, 40:41–44:37
▸ Audio Compact Discs, CD 6, Trs. 5–8
▸ Interactive CD-ROM Tutor, Disc 2

Presenting
Panorama Culturel

Have students list the things they find important in life. Then, play the video. Have students check each item on their list they hear mentioned. Play the video again. This time, ask students to note additional things the interviewees mention. Compile this list on a transparency and have students rate each item on a scale of 1–10, with 10 being the most important and 1 the least important. Have students use these lists as they discuss the questions in **Qu'en penses-tu?** with a partner.

Questions

1. Qui pense qu'il est très important de trouver un métier qu'on aime? (Micheline)
2. Qu'est-ce qui est le plus important pour Viviane? (les parents) Et pour Stanislas? (les relations avec les gens et l'argent)
3. Est-ce que Micheline croit qu'il faut se marier pour être heureux? (non)

Presenting
Remise en train

Have students look at the photos on pages 166–167 and anticipate what will happen in the story. Then, play the audio recording, pausing after each scene. After the first scene, ask **Qu'est-ce que M. Simenot a oublié de faire?** (retirer ses chaussures) After they drink the tea, ask **Combien d'enfants ont les Moussa? (huit) Qu'est-ce que les Moussa proposent de faire le lendemain** *(the next day)***? (aller au mariage d'une cousine)** After the wedding scene, ask **Qu'est-ce qu'on mange au mariage? (de la pastilla) Qu'est-ce que la mariée porte? (une coiffe)** Then, ask students for their reactions to Moroccan food and weddings.

Answers
18 1. at Moktar's home
   2. Mme Moussa greets them in Arabic. They have to take off their shoes.
   3. Moroccan customs, their families
   4. to a cousin's wedding
   5. It's a family occasion.
   6. The groom's family asks for the woman's hand, the couple signs a contract, the groom gives the bride presents.

Remise en train · *Ahlên, merhabîn*

CD 6 Tr. 9

Moktar et Raphaël sont allés au concert. Le lendemain, la famille Moussa accueille la famille Simenot chez elle.

Moktar	Ça me fait plaisir de te voir.
Raphaël	Moi aussi.
Moktar	Je vous présente mes parents.
M. Simenot	Madame.
Mme Moussa	Ahlên, merhabîn.
Moktar	Ma mère vous souhaite la bienvenue.
Mme Moussa	Bonjour. Entrez, s'il vous plaît.
M. Simenot	Vous êtes bien aimable.
Moktar	Mettez-vous à l'aise.
Raphaël	Papa, il faut retirer tes chaussures.
M. Simenot	Ah, excusez-moi. Je suis navré.
Mme Moussa	Ça ne fait rien. Vous savez, c'est la coutume ici, mais si ça vous gêne, ce n'est pas important.
M. Simenot	Non, non, pas du tout.
Mme Moussa	Qu'est-ce que je vous sers? Vous savez, ici, nous ne servons pas d'alcool. Mais nous avons des jus de fruit et, bien sûr, du thé à la menthe.
M. Simenot	Je prendrais bien du thé.

M. Simenot	Oui, ça ira très bien.
Raphaël	Pour moi aussi, s'il vous plaît.
Mme Moussa	Asseyez-vous, je vous en prie.
M. Simenot	Merci.

Amina apporte le thé.

Amina	Bonjour.
M. Moussa	Ma fille, Amina...
Moktar	Fais gaffe. Amina a le chic pour renverser le thé.
Amina	Oh, ça va, hein! C'est pas moi qui ai renversé la cafetière hier.

---

18 **Tu as compris?** See answers below.

1. Où est la famille Simenot?
2. Qu'est-ce qui se passe quand les Simenot arrivent?
3. De quoi parlent les deux familles?
4. Où est-ce que les Moussa invitent les Simenot?
5. Pourquoi les Simenot hésitent à accepter l'invitation des Moussa?
6. Quelles sont les principales phases d'un mariage marocain?

19 **Vrai ou faux?**

1. On sert du thé à la menthe.   vrai
2. Amina renverse souvent le thé.   vrai
3. C'est Amina qui a commencé la dispute. faux
4. Les Simenot ont deux enfants.   faux
5. Amina va se marier demain.   faux
6. La mariée porte une coiffe très élaborée.   vrai

These activities check for comprehension only. Students should not yet be expected to produce language modeled in **Remise en train.**

20 **Qu'est-ce qu'ils font?**

Trouve dans le dialogue des phrases pour décrire les situations suivantes.

1. Il faut retirer tes chaussures.   2. Asseyez-vous, je vous en prie.

3. C'est lui qui a commencé.   4. Qu'est-ce que c'est?

Preteaching Vocabulary

Guessing Words from Context

Ask students what is going on in the opening scene of the story. Have them identify the context to help them figure out the meanings of unfamiliar words. What other word besides **navré** could be used in the situation when M. Simenot uses it?(**désolé**) Have them choose alternative expressions for the unfamiliar words in the text and then have them explain how the context helped them to figure out the meaning.

navré- *deeply sorry*
retirer- *take off*
gêne- *bother*
fais gaffe- *watch out*
ravis- *delighted*

Moktar	Rapporteuse!
M. Moussa	Ça suffit, les enfants!
Amina	C'est lui qui a commencé.
M. Simenot	Euh... et vous avez d'autres enfants?
M. Moussa	Nous avons huit enfants. Tous sont mariés sauf Moktar et Amina. Et vous?
M. Simenot	Nous avons un autre fils, Jean. Il va se marier en août.
M. Moussa	Félicitations. Au fait, nous allons au mariage de ma cousine demain. Vous voulez venir avec nous?
Mme Simenot	Oh, non. C'est pour la famille.
M. Moussa	Mais non! Pas du tout. Ils seront ravis de vous avoir!
Mme Simenot	Bon, si vous pensez vraiment qu'on ne dérange pas.

A la fête de mariage...

Raphaël	Oh, c'est bon, ça! Qu'est-ce que c'est?
Moktar	Ça, c'est de la pastilla.
Raphaël	C'est fait avec du poulet?
Moktar	Non, c'est du pigeon. Il y a aussi des amandes.
Raphaël	Mmm... J'adore! Dis donc, c'est quand, la cérémonie?

Moktar	Il n'y a pas vraiment de cérémonie comme chez toi. D'abord, la famille de l'homme demande la main de la femme..., puis, les fiancés signent un contrat. Ensuite, le fiancé donne des cadeaux à sa future femme.
Raphaël	Et après?
Moktar	Et puis, on fait la fête.
Raphaël	Oh, dis donc, ta cousine, qu'est-ce qu'elle a sur la tête?
Moktar	Les mariées marocaines ont toujours des coiffes très élaborées.
Raphaël	Cool. Je parie que le mariage de mon frère ne sera pas aussi chouette.

Cahier d'activités, p. 66, Act. 10–11

21 C'est le Maroc?

Après avoir lu **Ahlên, merhabîn,** est-ce que ces traditions te semblent marocaines ou non?

1. En général, les gens sont très accueillants. *oui*
2. On préfère boire du thé glacé. *non*
3. On offre des boissons alcoolisées aux invités. *non*
4. On retire ses chaussures en entrant dans une maison. *oui*
5. Les mariées s'habillent de façon très simple. *non*
6. La cérémonie de mariage a lieu dans une église. *non*
7. On mange du pigeon. *oui*

22 Cherche les expressions

What do the Moussa and Simenot families say to . . . See answers below.

1. welcome someone?
2. introduce someone?
3. offer something to drink?
4. ask someone to sit down?
5. tell someone to be careful?
6. accuse someone of being a tattletale?
7. express congratulations?
8. ask what something is?

23 Et maintenant, à toi

Comment est-ce qu'on accueille des invités dans ton pays? Est-ce que ça se fait comme au Maroc, ou est-ce que c'est différent?

Comprehension Check

Thinking Critically

23 Comparing and Contrasting Ask students the following questions: What might a host do instead of asking a guest to remove his or her shoes? (take his or her coat) What might a host offer a guest? (soft drink, iced tea) Would a host invite a guest to a wedding? (no) What invitation might a host make? (to come by for coffee later)

Analyzing Have students compare Moroccan wedding customs with those of the United States. Ask them what could account for the differences.

Answers

22 1. **Ahlên, merhabîn.** (Bonjour. Entrez, s'il vous plaît.)
2. Je vous présente...
3. Qu'est-ce que je vous sers?
4. Asseyez-vous, je vous en prie.
5. Fais gaffe.
6. Rapporteuse!
7. Félicitations.
8. Qu'est-ce que c'est?

Rencontre culturelle

CHAPITRE 6

Building on Previous Skills

Have students complete the following sentences, based on their impressions of Morocco from the Location Opener, the **Mise en train**, and the **Remise en train. Le Maroc, c'est...** ; **Les Marocains sont...** ; **Au Maroc, on...** Have volunteers share what they wrote.

Presenting
Rencontre culturelle

Have students look at the photos and answer the questions in **Qu'en penses-tu?** with a partner. Have small groups read the **Savais-tu que... ?** paragraph together. Then, have students close their books. Pretend you're going to visit Morocco, but you don't know anything about it. Have students tell you what they've learned about Morocco.

Culture Note

The leather tanneries in Fez, located in the **Souk Dabbaghin,** are a striking sight. Huge vats of brightly-colored dyes are arranged in honeycomb patterns. Vegetable-based dyes, including saffron, indigo, and mint, have replaced the more dangerous chemical dyes used in the past. Once the leather is dyed, it is spread out on the rooftops in colorful sheets to dry in the sun.

Challenge

Play the game **Vrai ou faux?**, using information questions rather than true-false statements. (Qu'est-ce que c'est qu'un souk? Quelle ville est le centre artistique et intellectuel du Maroc?)

Est-ce que tu connais le Maroc? Regarde les photos suivantes pour découvrir quelques caractéristiques de ce pays.

Casablanca, la plus grande ville du Maroc

Fès, centre spirituel, intellectuel et artistique du Maroc

Les artisans marocains sont renommés.

Les belles plages des côtes méditerranéenne et atlantique

Le quartier des tanneurs de cuir

Qu'en penses-tu?

1. Quelle impression ces photos donnent du Maroc?
2. Quelles sont les différences et les similarités entre le Maroc et les Etats-Unis?

Possible answers: **1.** mix of modern and traditional, many crafts, natural beauty
2. *Similarities:* modern cities, natural attractions
Differences: marketplace instead of mall

Savais-tu que... ?

Le Maroc est un pays montagneux situé sur la côte nord-ouest de l'Afrique. Ce pays a de magnifiques plages sur la côte atlantique et sur la côte méditerranéenne. L'arabe est la langue officielle du Maroc, mais beaucoup de Marocains parlent aussi français. La plupart des Marocains sont d'origine arabe ou berbère. Les Berbères sont au Maroc depuis très longtemps et les Arabes s'y sont installés au 17ème siècle avant Jésus-Christ. Ils ont introduit l'islam dans la culture marocaine. Maintenant, le Maroc est un pays presque entièrement musulman; dans tous les villages marocains, il y a une mosquée. Les Marocains sont célèbres dans toute l'Afrique du Nord et en Europe pour la qualité de leur artisanat. Dans les marchés arabes, appelés souks, on peut acheter des tapis, des poteries, des produits en cuir et des objets en cuivre. Dans les villages, il y a souvent un seul marché, mais dans les grandes villes comme Fès ou Marrakech, il y a des marchés spécialisés, comme, par exemple, les souks de tapis et de poterie.

Cultures and Communities

Game

Vrai ou faux? Compose about twenty true–false statements about Morocco, based on the **Savais-tu que... ?**, the **Mise en train,** and the **Remise en train. (Un souk est un plat marocain. Fès est un centre artistique du Maroc.)** Form two teams. Each team selects a spokesperson. Read aloud a statement to the members of one team, who discuss it and have their spokesperson give their response. If the response is correct, the team wins a point. If not, the other team has a chance to take the point, either by correcting the statement if it is false or by providing an additional fact about the subject if the statement is true.

Comment dit-on...?

Showing and responding to hospitality; expressing and responding to thanks

CD-ROM DISC 2

To welcome someone:

Ça me fait plaisir de vous voir.
I'm happy to see you.
Entrez, je vous en prie. *Come in, please.*
Donnez-moi votre manteau. *Give me . . .*
Mettez-vous à l'aise. *Make yourself comfortable.*
Asseyez-vous. *Sit down.*

To respond:

Moi aussi.

Merci.
Vous êtes bien aimable.
C'est gentil.

To offer food or drink:

Je vous sers quelque chose?
Can I offer you something?
Qu'est-ce que je peux vous offrir?
What can I offer you?

To respond:

Je prendrais bien un verre de thé.
I'd like some . . .
Vous auriez des biscuits? *Would you have . . . ?*

To express thanks:

Merci bien/mille fois.
Je vous remercie. *Thank you.*
C'est vraiment très gentil de votre part.

To respond to thanks:

De rien.
Je vous en prie.
(Il n'y a) pas de quoi.
C'est tout à fait normal. *You don't have to thank me.*

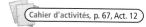
Cahier d'activités, p. 67, Act. 12

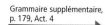
Grammaire supplémentaire, p. 179, Act. 4

---

24 **Chez M. Ben Assouan**   See scripts and answers on p. 155G.

Ecoutons Ecoute M. Ben Assouan qui accueille ses invités. Choisis l'image qui correspond à ce qu'il dit.
CD 6 Tr. 10

a.

b.

c.

d.

Communication for All Students

Slower Pace

24 Have students tell in English what is happening in each illustration and what the people might be saying. Then, play the recording, pausing after each dialogue to have students respond.

Challenge

24 After doing Activity 24, replay the recording, stopping after each one of M. Ben Assouan's lines. Ask students to imagine that they are M. Ben Assouan's guests. Have them look at the **Comment dit-on... ?** expressions and come up with appropriate answers to their host's statements and questions.

Teaching Resources
pp. 169–173

PRINT
- Lesson Planner, p. 30
- Listening Activities, pp. 44–45, 48–49
- Activities for Communication, pp. 23–24, 67–68, 99–100
- Travaux pratiques de grammaire, pp. 60–62
- Grammar Tutor for Students of French, Chapter 6
- Cahier d'activités, pp. 67–70
- Testing Program, pp. 115–118
- Alternative Assessment Guide, p. 35
- Student Make-Up Assignments, Chapter 6

MEDIA
- One-Stop Planner
- Audio Compact Discs, CD 6, Trs. 10–12, 15, 27–29
- Teaching Transparencies: 6-2; **Grammaire supplémentaire** Answers; Travaux pratiques de grammaire Answers
- Interactive CD-ROM Tutor, Disc 2

Bell Work
Write the following sentences on the board and have students write responses: **Ça t'intéresse d'aller au souk? Où est-ce qu'on se retrouve? Pardonne-moi d'avoir oublié notre rendez-vous.**

Presenting
Comment dit-on... ?

Prepare a skit in which you welcome a guest into your home. Act out both sides of the conversation, using props and gestures. Have students repeat the new expressions after you. Then, say aloud the new expressions, and have students tell you which function each one serves.

Teaching Resources
pp. 169–173

PRINT
▸ Lesson Planner, p. 30
▸ Listening Activities, pp. 44–45, 48–49
▸ Activities for Communication, pp. 23–24, 67–68, 99–100
▸ Travaux pratiques de grammaire, pp. 60–62
▸ Grammar Tutor for Students of French, Chapter 6
▸ Cahier d'activités, pp. 67–70
▸ Testing Program, pp. 115–118
▸ Alternative Assessment Guide, p. 35
▸ Student Make-Up Assignments, Chapter 6

MEDIA
▸ One-Stop Planner
▸ Audio Compact Discs, CD 6, Trs. 10–12, 15, 27–29
▸ Teaching Transparencies: 6-2; **Grammaire supplémentaire** Answers; Travaux pratiques de grammaire Answers
▸ Interactive CD-ROM Tutor, Disc 2

Additional Practice

25 Once students have completed this activity, have partners create and act out a two- or three-line conversation in which one person is expressing thanks to another.

Culture Note

If you are invited to a Moroccan family's home, it is considered polite to bring a small gift for the hosts, just as in other francophone countries. Sweet pastries or tea and sugar are acceptable gifts.

Note culturelle

L'hospitalité est un concept très important dans les cultures nord-africaines. C'est un honneur de recevoir des invités, et même une famille qui n'a pas beaucoup d'argent prend grand soin de ses invités. La tradition est de servir du thé à la menthe. C'est mal élevé de refuser le thé et on peut en accepter plusieurs verres.

25 Merci infiniment!

Lisons On te remercie. Choisis la réponse appropriée.

1. Merci bien de m'avoir prêté ton cardigan. J'avais tellement froid!
   - a. Vous êtes bien aimable!
   - b. De rien.
   - c. Tu as toujours froid!

2. Je vous remercie de m'avoir répondu si vite.
   - a. Ne vous inquiétez pas.
   - b. Mettez-vous à l'aise.
   - c. Je vous en prie.

3. Si tu ne m'avais pas aidé, j'aurais raté l'examen. Je ne sais pas comment te remercier!
   - a. Fais tes devoirs tous les jours!
   - b. C'est tout à fait normal!
   - c. Ils sont difficiles, ces examens.

4. Dis donc, on m'a donné le job. Merci mille fois. C'était vraiment gentil de ta part!
   - a. Ne sois pas en retard!
   - b. Tu aimeras ce travail.
   - c. Il n'y a pas de quoi.

26 Méli-mélo!

Lisons M. Fikri rend visite à son collègue. Mets leur conversation dans le bon ordre. *Possible answers:*

«Donnez-moi votre manteau.» 5
«Mettez-vous à l'aise.» 7
«Ça me fait plaisir de vous voir.» 3
«Qu'est-ce que je peux vous offrir?» 9
«Entrez, je vous en prie.» 1
«Bien sûr.» 11

«Vous auriez du thé?» 10
«Moi aussi.» 4
«Vous êtes bien aimable.» 6
«Merci.» 2
«C'est gentil.» 8

27 Merci mille fois!

Ecrivons Ecris un petit mot de remerciement à ton/ta camarade qui...

t'a invité(e) à sa boum.   t'a conseillé(e).   t'a envoyé une carte postale.   t'a donné un C.D.

Communication for All Students

Kinesthetic Learners

26 Write each of M. Fikri's lines on a large card of one color and distribute them to six students. Do the same with his colleague's lines, using cards of a different color. Have these twelve students stand at the front of the room, holding their cards. Then, have their classmates rearrange them in the logical order of the conversation.

Challenge

26 Once students have completed the activity, have them write their own conversations in which they welcome a friend to their home. Have partners perform their conversation for the class.

l'aîné(e) *the oldest child*

l'arrière-grand-mère
great-grandmother

l'arrière-grand-père
great-grandfather

le/la benjamin(e) *the youngest child*

le/la cadet(te) *the younger child*

les jumeaux/jumelles *twins*

le neveu *nephew*

la nièce *niece*

la petite-fille *granddaughter*

le petit-fils *grandson*

célibataire *single*

divorcé(e)

marié(e)

mort(e)

veuf/veuve *widowed*

*Voilà la photo de ma famille que tu m'as demandée. Je t'explique qui est tout le monde. La vieille dame, ce n'est pas ma grand-mère, c'est mon **arrière-grand-mère**, Teta. Elle est **veuve**. A côté d'elle, il y a mon père et ma mère. Leurs parents sont morts. Mon père est **le petit-fils** de Teta. Tu te rends compte comme elle est vieille? Bon, il y a aussi ma sœur, Souad. Elle est **mariée**. Là, à côté de moi, c'est son mari Karim. De l'autre côté, c'est mon frère, Hassan. C'est **l'aîné**. Il a 25 ans. Il est **célibataire**. Il ne veut pas se marier! Et moi, tu vois, je suis le **benjamin**. Alors, tout le monde attend ton arrivée avec impatience. Tu seras reçu comme un roi.*

Cahier d'activités,
pp. 68–69, Act. 13–14

Travaux pratiques de
grammaire,
pp. 60–62, Act. 12–17

28 **La famille d'Ahmed**   See scripts on p. 155H.

Ecoutons Ahmed a invité Eric chez lui. Ecoute leur conversation et décide quelle photo représente la famille d'Ahmed.

CD 6
Tr. 11

a.

b.

Connections and Comparisons

Thinking Critically
Comparing and Contrasting Have students compare Moroccan and American gestures of hospitality. Have them consider the following questions: In America, is it common to invite acquaintances you've just met to dinner? Is it acceptable to refuse a beverage that is offered?

Culture Note
Explain to students that when someone offers them something in English and they reply with *Thank you*, people might assume that they are accepting the offer. However, when French-speaking people respond with **Merci**, it might mean that they're refusing. So, if students want some of what is offered, they should say **Oui, merci.**

Presenting
Vocabulaire

On a transparency, sketch a family tree that illustrates the relationships described in the letter. Label the relationships. You might indicate the ages of three children to explain **l'aîné(e)**, **le/la cadet(te)**, and **le/la benjamin(e)**. Read the letter aloud and point to each family member on the tree as you mention the person. Then, ask students to explain the vocabulary. (**Qu'est-ce que c'est qu'un arrière-grand-père? C'est le père d'un de vos grands-parents.**) You might also ask the class about their own family relationships (**Qui est l'aîné(e)?**), being sure to respect students' privacy.

Building on Previous Skills
Have students identify the family members in the illustration in the **Vocabulaire**, using **Voici...** , **A sa droite...** , and so on. Have them add details about each person. (**Il est pénible. Elle aime jouer au tennis.**)

Additional Practice
Ask students either–or questions about the marital status of various celebrities.

Slower Pace
28 Before you play the recording, have students point out the differences between the photos.

Language Notes
• Students might want to use the phrase **fils/fille unique** for *only child*.

• The word **benjamin** originates from the Biblical story of Joseph. Benjamin was the youngest son of Jacob and the brother of Joseph.

• **Les jumelles** also means *binoculars*, referring to the "twin" lenses.

Teaching Resources
pp. 169–173

PRINT
- Lesson Planner, p. 30
- Listening Activities, pp. 44–45, 48–49
- Activities for Communication, pp. 23–24, 67–68, 99–100
- Travaux pratiques de grammaire, pp. 60–62
- Grammar Tutor for Students of French, Chapter 6
- Cahier d'activités, pp. 67–70
- Testing Program, pp. 115–118
- Alternative Assessment Guide, p. 35
- Student Make-Up Assignments, Chapter 6

MEDIA
- One-Stop Planner
- Audio Compact Discs, CD 6, Trs. 10–12, 15, 27–29
- Teaching Transparencies: 6-2; **Grammaire supplémentaire** Answers; Travaux pratiques de grammaire Answers
- Interactive CD-ROM Tutor, Disc 2

Portfolio

 30 Oral This activity is appropriate for students' oral portfolios. For portfolio information, see *Alternative Assessment Guide,* pages iv–15.

Teaching Suggestion

31 Have students rewrite and complete these sentences in reference to their own families. Students might prefer to use an imaginary family.

---

29 Les relations frères-sœurs

Lisons/Ecrivons Lis ces remarques de quelques jeunes francophones et complète les phrases ci-dessous.

Saïd
Je peux parler de mes ennuis à ma grande sœur et je peux aussi lui emprunter de l'argent. On se fait confiance. Après la mort de mon père, je ne pouvais pas m'arrêter de pleurer et ma sœur venait toujours essayer de me réconforter dans ma chambre.

Gilles
Mon grand frère m'interdit d'aller dans sa chambre mais lui, il vient toujours fouiller dans la mienne. Il s'imagine qu'il peut me donner des ordres parce qu'il est l'aîné!

Hélène
Mes frères et sœurs doivent aller au lit plus tôt que moi parce qu'ils sont plus jeunes. Mais si je rentre plus tard que prévu quand je sors, mes parents ne sont pas contents parce qu'ils disent que je donne le mauvais exemple aux petits.

Djamila
Pour énerver ma sœur quand on regarde la télé ensemble, je change de chaîne sans lui demander son avis.

Sylvie
Mes deux frères me font tout le temps des blagues et m'embêtent quand je parle au téléphone avec mes copains. Et quand je fais mes devoirs, ils font beaucoup de bruit juste pour m'embêter.

1. _____ ne peut pas faire ses devoirs parce que ses frères font du bruit.   Sylvie
2. La sœur de _____ est compréhensive et elle l'aide à résoudre ses problèmes.   Saïd
3. Quand _____ veut embêter sa sœur, elle change de chaîne sans lui demander.   Djamila
4. Le frère de _____ entre souvent dans sa chambre pour fouiller dans ses affaires.   Gilles
5. _____ n'aime pas avoir à donner l'exemple à ses petits frères et sœurs.   Hélène

30 Mettez-vous à l'aise!

 Parlons Ta famille a organisé une soirée. Tu accueilles les invités. Ils te remercient. N'oublie pas de présenter tes amis à chaque membre de ta famille. Joue cette scène avec tes camarades. Changez de rôle.

31 Ma famille

Ecrivons Complète les phrases suivantes avec le mot qui convient.

1. Mon arrière-grand-père est mort en mille neuf cent quatre-vingt-cinq. Alors, mon arrière-grand-mère est _____.   veuve
2. Mes grands-parents ont dix petits-fils et douze _____.   petites-filles
3. Michèle a dix-huit ans. Sa sœur Sophie a seize ans et son frère Joseph a quatorze ans. Elle est _____ et Joseph est _____.   l'aînée; le benjamin
4. Mon oncle Ali n'est pas marié. Il préfère rester _____.   célibataire
5. La grand-mère de ma mère, c'est mon _____.   arrière-grand-mère
6. Mes cousines Yamilé et Rachida ont toutes les deux dix-sept ans. Elles sont _____.   jumelles

jumelles	arrière-grand-père
marié	célibataire
petites-filles	veuve veuf
l'aînée	arrière-grand-mère
la benjamine	le benjamin

Communication for All Students

Cooperative Learning

29 Have students stage a talk show to discuss the letters in this activity. Ask for five volunteers to act as the guests. Assign one letter to each guest. The guests assume the identities of the writers. Ask another student to be the host of the show. The host prepares questions to ask the guests, based on their letters. The remaining students comprise the studio audience. They should each prepare one or two questions to ask each guest during the show. You might want to videotape the show.

Comment dit-on...?

Quarreling

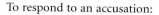

To accuse someone:

Rapporteur(-euse)! *Tattletale!*
Pleurnicheur(-euse)! *Crybaby!*
Tricheur(-euse)! *Cheater!*
Tu m'énerves, à la fin! *You're really bugging me!*
Tu es vraiment casse-pieds! *You're such a pain!*
Tu me prends la tête! *You're driving me crazy!*

To respond to an accusation:

Oh, ça va, hein? *Oh, cut it out!*
Arrête!
Ça suffit!
Tu le fais exprès? *Are you doing that on purpose?*
Mêle-toi de tes oignons! *Mind your own business!*
Fiche-moi la paix! *Leave me alone!*
Casse-toi! *Get out of here!*
Tant pis pour toi! *Tough!*

To justify a quarrel:

C'est toujours la même chose!
C'est lui/elle qui a commencé!
Il/Elle m'a traité(e) d'imbécile!
   He/She called me a . . . !
C'est toujours moi qui prends!
   I'm always the one who gets blamed!

Cahier d'activités, p. 70, Act. 15–17

Grammaire supplémentaire, pp. 180–181, Act. 5–7

A la française

You might hear some of these expressions exchanged between siblings or close friends, and they might even be used in a joking manner. However, as a non-native French speaker, you should be very careful with these expressions. Using these expressions with or around people you don't know very well could be considered rude, inappropriate, or even hostile.

---

32 **Les enfants terribles**   See scripts and answers on p. 155H.

 Ecoutons Ecoute ces disputes. Comment est-ce qu'elles ont commencé? A ton avis, est-ce que c'est la faute de Moktar ou d'Amina?
CD 6 Tr. 12

33 **Arrête!**

 **Parlons** Ton frère/ta sœur t'énerve quand il/elle fait les choses ci-dessous. Tu le lui dis, et ça provoque une dispute. Joue ces scènes avec ton/ta camarade.

- emprunter tes CD sans te le demander
- se moquer de toi devant tes amis
- changer de chaîne alors que tu regardes quelque chose à la télé
- monopoliser le téléphone
- entrer dans ta chambre et fouiller dans tes affaires
- abîmer tes affaires

34 **De l'école au travail**

 Parlons Une famille française t'a engagé(e) comme baby-sitter et tu trouves que les enfants que tu gardes sont insupportables. Tes camarades, qui jouent le rôle des enfants, se disputent tout le temps. Tu dois les empêcher de se disputer mais ils se justifient chaque fois.

Connections and Comparisons

Lisons!

Teaching Resources
pp. 174–176

PRINT
▶ Lesson Planner, p. 31
▶ Cahier d'activités, p. 71
▶ Reading Strategies and Skills Handbook, Chapter 6
▶ Joie de lire 3, Chapter 6
▶ Standardized Assessment Tutor, Chapter 6

MEDIA
▶ One-Stop Planner

Prereading
Activities A–B

Using Prior Knowledge
Begin a discussion about fairy tales. Ask students to describe the characters in their favorite fairy tales and to tell how the stories end. Have students suggest lessons and values that might be taught through a story.

Teaching Suggestion
Call students' attention to the title of the first story, *Les Trois Femmes du roi*. Ask them to find one element in the title common to fairy tales and one culturally different (it's about a king; polygamy).

Answers
A., B. *Answers will vary.*

C. outside a house; three sisters telling what they would do if the king married them

D. He is frightened. There is great respect and fear for the king among his subjects.

E. In their culture, young women are not supposed to leave the house or speak to outsiders; They fear punishment if suspected of breaking this restriction; *Answers will vary.*

Les Trois Femmes du roi

Une nuit, le roi dit à son vizir :
- Allons faire le tour de la ville pour voir si tout est tranquille.

Ils se promènent. Les gens dorment ; il n'y a personne dans les rues. Tout à coup, ils voient de la lumière qui passe sous la porte d'une maison.
- Qui a encore sa lampe allumée à cette heure-ci ? dit le roi.

Ils s'arrêtent, mettent l'oreille contre la porte et écoutent ce que l'on dit derrière. Une jeune fille parle et dit à ses sœurs :
- Si le roi m'épousait, je pourrais faire manger tous les gens du pays avec un seul plat de couscous.

Une autre dit :
- S'il m'épousait, je pourrais habiller tous les gens du pays avec un seul morceau de tissu.
- Moi, dit la voix la plus jeune, je lui donnerais un garçon et une fille et ils auraient des cheveux d'argent.

Le lendemain, le roi envoie des gens à la maison où il a entendu du bruit.

Le père des jeunes filles est un homme vieux et pauvre. En entendant frapper à la porte, il demande :
- Qui frappe ?
- Viens ! Le roi veut te parler. Le père a très peur. Il se demande pourquoi le roi veut le voir. Il demande à ses filles :

- Est-ce que vous avez parlé à des gens ? Est-ce que vous vous êtes disputées avec quelqu'un ?
- Non, père, n'aie pas peur ! disent-elles. Nous ne connaissons personne. Nous ne nous sommes disputées avec personne. Jamais nous ne sommes sorties de la maison.

Le vieillard sort et, tremblant de peur, suit les gens qui l'emmènent chez le roi.
- Bon vieillard, lui dit le roi. As-tu des filles ?
- Oui, Seigneur.
- Combien ?
- Trois.
- Veux-tu me les donner en mariage ? Je veux me marier avec toutes les trois, comme cela est permis par Dieu et son Prophète.
- Avec plaisir, ô Roi ! répond le père. Je n'ai pas trouvé de bergers pour devenir leurs maris et toi, Roi, tu les veux toutes les trois !

Le roi fait faire les fêtes du mariage et fait amener ses trois femmes à son palais.

Un jour, le roi dit à l'une de ses trois femmes :
- Tu as dit un jour que, si le roi t'épousait, tu pourrais faire manger tous les gens du pays avec un seul plat de couscous. Fais ce plat de couscous, je veux voir si tu as dit vrai.
- Je ferai ce couscous, ô Roi. Donne-moi seulement un demi-sac de farine.

Le lendemain, quand la femme a reçu du roi un demi-sac de farine, elle envoie quelqu'un acheter un sac de sel. Puis elle fait le couscous en mettant pour chaque part de farine deux parts de sel. Après elle le fait cuire. Alors le roi dit à tous les

---

Stratégie pour lire

Stories set in your own culture are easy to understand because you can relate to them. When you read a story set in another country, however, you may be misled if you assume that the society and customs there are exactly the same as where you live. In order to best understand a story, think about the culture that it represents. What do you know that can help you? If you're not familiar with the country in the story, you may want to find out more about it. Taking the cultural context of a story into account will enable you to understand it better and will make it more enjoyable, too.

Les Trois Femmes du roi
For activities A-E, see answers below.

A. What fairy tales do you remember from your childhood? What characters or themes are usually found in children's stories?

B. Do you imagine that stories from other cultures are the same as or different than those told in the United States? Why?

C. Où sont le roi et son vizir ? Qu'est-ce qu'ils entendent ?

D. What is the father's reaction to being called in to see the king? What does this tell you about the relationship between the king and his subjects?

E. When questioned by their father, why do the daughters insist that they have not even left the house? Why would that be important? Is that something important in your culture?

Connections and Comparisons

Language Notes
• A **vizir** *(vizier)* is a high official in a Muslim government. An English equivalent might be *prime minister.*

• When the king mentions **son Prophète**, he is referring to Mohammed.

• You might tell students that **épouser** means *to marry someone.*

Culture Note
In Islam, polygamy is permitted by the Koran. Traditionally, men may take up to four wives simultaneously, but they are encouraged to take only as many as their financial means will allow. In recent times, however, most Muslim countries have enacted laws to tighten up marital relationships.

gens de venir et toute la grande maison est pleine. Il apporte le plat, le pose au milieu de la grande salle et invite tout le monde à manger. Mais chaque fois que quelqu'un prend une boulette de couscous, il la crache aussitôt parce qu'elle est trop salée. Les serviteurs disent :

- Mangez, messieurs !

Mais ils ont peur que le roi se mette en colère et ils répondent :

- Non, merci, nous en avons mangé beaucoup, c'est très bon, mais nous n'avons plus faim.

Et ils repartent tous chez eux sans dire que le couscous est trop salé. Quand ils sont partis, le roi voit que le plat est encore plein. Il est très heureux et dit :

- Dieu est avec moi ! Ma femme a dit vrai.

Il veut manger un peu de couscous et le crache lui aussi. Il se met en colère et va trouver sa femme :

- Tu as menti! Personne n'a mangé de ce couscous. Il était trop salé.

- Oui, mais tous les invités ont dit qu'ils en avaient mangé et qu'ils n'avaient plus faim !

- C'est vrai, tu n'as pas menti, répond le roi.

Un autre soir, il dit à son autre femme :

- Tu as dit un jour que, si le roi t'épousait, tu pourrais habiller tous les gens du pays avec un seul morceau de tissu. Fais cela, je le veux !

- Donne-moi un morceau de tissu, ô Roi, et tu verras que j'ai dit vrai.

Le lendemain matin, pendant que le roi appelle tous les gens, la femme coupe le tissu en petits bouts très fins. Puis elle se met au-dessus de la porte de la ville et dit au roi de faire passer tous les gens l'un derrière l'autre. Alors, elle laisse tomber sur chacun d'eux un petit bout de tissu que chacun attrape à la main. Quand ils sont passés, les gens disent au revoir au roi et rentrent chez eux sans rien dire. Ils n'osent pas dire qu'on s'est moqué d'eux parce qu'ils ont peur d'avoir la tête coupée. Le roi dit à sa femme :

- Tu n'as pas habillé tous les gens du pays !

- Si ! Chacun a eu sa part et ils sont tous partis contents.

- C'est vrai ; tu n'as pas menti !

La troisième femme, la plus jeune, avait dit :

- Si le roi m'épousait, je lui donnerais un garçon et une fille et ils auraient des cheveux d'argent.

Elle a peur que le roi se rappelle ce qu'elle a dit. Elle prie Dieu chaque jour et enfin, un enfant grandit dans son ventre. Ses sœurs pensent :

- Le roi va préférer notre sœur à cause de cet enfant. Que faire ?

Elles demandent conseil à une vieille qui leur dit :

- Attendez ! Je vous aiderai.

Quand l'enfant va naître, les deux sœurs appellent la vieille. Elle arrive avec une grande boîte dans laquelle elle a caché deux petits chiens. Elle dit qu'elle va soigner la maman et entre dans la chambre. Deux enfants naissent, un garçon et une fille, et ils ont tous les deux des cheveux d'argent. Alors la vieille prend les deux enfants ; elle les met dans la boîte et, à leur place, elle met les deux petits chiens. Puis elle va dire au roi :

Teacher Note
F. Before they do this activity, you might tell students that **couscous** is the national dish of Morocco. For more information, see the Location Opener on pages 106–109 and the recipe on page 155D.

Additional Practice
J. For listening practice, read aloud additional true–false statements about the story and have students raise their left hand if the statement you read is true and their right hand if it is false.

F. Quelles sont les remarques qui n'ont pas été faites par les trois filles? b,d

«Si le roi m'épousait...

a. je pourrais habiller tous les gens du pays avec un seul morceau de tissu.»

b. je pourrais construire des logements pour tous les gens du pays avec un seul bout de bois.»

c. je lui donnerais des enfants avec des cheveux d'argent.»

d. je pourrais changer la paille en or.»

e. je pourrais faire manger tous les gens avec un seul plat de couscous.»

For activities G-I, see answers below.

G. Look over the first story and find some examples of cultural differences. How does this information affect your understanding of the story?

H. What did the first and second wives do when asked to fulfill their vows? Why didn't the people of the kingdom complain? What was the king's reaction?

I. Pourquoi est-ce que les deux premières épouses sont jalouses de la troisième? Que font-elles?

J. Vrai ou faux?
1. Les enfants ont des cheveux d'argent. vrai
2. Le roi fait enfermer sa femme dans un donjon. faux
3. Les deux enfants vont en bateau au pays du pêcheur et de sa femme. faux
4. Le pêcheur est très heureux de trouver les enfants. vrai
5. Les enfants savent depuis leur naissance qu'ils sont les enfants du roi. faux

Connections and Comparisons

Thinking Critically
G. Analyzing For each of the cultural differences students found in Activity G, have students explain how the mores of the society affect the characters' behavior or the plot of the story.

Ask students if they can think of tales in their own culture(s) that derive from specific mores and rules of society. Have them point out common traits between some Western tales and *Les Trois Femmes du roi.* (An example would be *Cinderella* where the honest sister is ultimately rewarded and the evil sisters punished.)

Possible answers

G. form of government (monarchy vs. democracy), expectations for young women (restrictions against leaving the house or speaking to outsiders vs. relative freedom), and marriage practices (arranged marriages and polygamy vs. choice of mate and monogamy); It explains the sisters' and the king's actions.

H. The first wife cooked a dish of couscous so heavily salted no one would eat it, and the second distributed scraps of cloth too tiny to wear; The people did not complain in either case, for fear of angering the king; The king agreed that his wives didn't lie.

I. They think the king will prefer the third wife if she fulfills her vow to produce two silver-haired children; They ask an old woman for advice and replace the babies with two dogs.

Thinking Critically

K. Analyzing Have students compare the means of punishment described in the story with those they are familiar with. Have them give examples of punishments in the past that were intended to humiliate (the public stocks, the dunce cap). Ask students to suggest possible purposes of punishment (to separate from society, to reform, to humiliate).

Reading/Writing Link

Assign partners one paragraph of the story to summarize. Have them write a one- or two-sentence summary on a slip of paper. Then, gather all the papers and put them in a box. Have a student draw the papers from the box one at a time, read them aloud, and tape them on the board in the order of the story, according to the instructions of the class.

Answers

K. She was put in a dog cage and treated like an animal because she supposedly gave birth to dogs, making her a failure as a woman in the eyes of society; *Answers will vary.*

L. When they travel to his country, the king hears about them and sends for them.

M. They are reunited and live happily with the king; *Answers will vary.*

N. It emphasizes how difficult it is to find true friends. Moroccan culture places a high value on friendship.

P. *Les Trois Femmes du roi:* You should be careful what you promise to others.
La Petite Maison: True friends are hard to find.

- Votre femme a eu deux enfants, mais ils ressemblent à des chiens !

Alors le roi se met en colère et donne l'ordre d'enfermer sa femme dans la cage où vivent tous les chiens de la maison. Les sœurs et la vieille la conduisent à la cage et là, elle mange et vit avec les bêtes. La vieille va jeter à la mer la grosse boîte où sont les deux enfants. La mer emporte la boîte très loin, vers un pays où vivent un pêcheur et sa femme. Un jour le pêcheur, qui est dans son bateau, voit la boîte. Il s'approche, ouvre la boîte et voit deux petits enfants, avec des cheveux qui brillent comme le soleil. Il rentre chez lui très heureux, montre les enfants à sa femme et tous deux décident de les garder et de les élever. Les enfants grandissent heureux. Ils étudient le Coran et aident le pêcheur et sa femme dans leur travail.

Mes amis, vous voulez connaître la fin de l'histoire. Eh bien, écoutez !

Un jour, les deux enfants se disputent avec d'autres enfants. Ceux-ci leur disent :
- Vous êtes des étrangers ! Le pêcheur et sa femme ne sont pas vos parents. Ils vous ont trouvés dans une boîte sur la mer.

Alors les deux enfants, très tristes, disent au revoir en pleurant au pêcheur et à sa femme et s'en vont en bateau, très loin, sur la mer. Ils arrivent dans le pays du roi ; et là, ils ont beaucoup d'aventures et beaucoup de malheurs.

Un jour, le roi entend dire qu'il y a dans son pays deux jeunes gens qui ont des cheveux d'argent. Il se rappelle ce que lui a dit sa troisième femme autrefois et il les fait chercher. Quand les deux jeunes gens arrivent devant lui, il leur demande :
- Qui sont vos parents ?
- Nous ne les connaissons pas. Nous avons été trouvés un jour, il y a quinze ans, dans une grande boîte très loin d'ici sur la mer.

Alors le roi leur tend les bras et s'écrie :
- C'est vous ! Vous êtes mes enfants ! Il y a quinze ans, quand vous êtes nés, on m'a dit que vous ressembliez à des chiens, et j'ai fait jeter votre mère dans une cage !

Et aussitôt il donne l'ordre qu'on aille chercher leur mère et qu'on jette les deux sœurs à sa place dans la cage aux chiens.

Les deux jeunes gens vivent alors heureux auprès du roi et de leur mère. Mais ils n'oublient pas le pêcheur et sa femme et leur envoient souvent de riches cadeaux.

La Petite Maison

Un homme construit une petite maison dans un endroit très étroit. Des gens passent et lui disent :
- Ta maison est trop petite !
Il leur répond :
- Vous dites que ma maison est trop petite, mais je serais content si je pouvais un jour la remplir de vrais amis.

For activities K-P, see answers below.

K. Why do you think the third wife was treated so harshly? How do you think her punishment was chosen? What punishments would be the most humiliating to people in your culture?

L. How are the children finally reunited with their real father?

M. Qu'arrive-t-il aux deux enfants et à leur mère à la fin de l'histoire? Est-ce que le dénouement de cette histoire te semble juste?

La Petite Maison

N. What is the message of this little story? How does your knowledge of Moroccan culture help you better understand its point?

O. Quelle histoire as-tu préférée? Pourquoi? Est-ce que tu connais des histoires semblables à celles-ci?

P. Quelle est la morale de ces deux histoires?

Q. Thinking back to stories you remember from your childhood, do they reflect American culture? Why or why not?

Cahier d'activités, p. 71, Act. 18

Communication for All Students

Postreading
Thinking Critically

N. Synthesizing After students have read *La Petite Maison,* have them pair off. One partner is a friend who doesn't understand Moroccan culture very well and asks questions about the story. The other partner retells the story and explains the message according to Moroccan culture.

Q. Synthesizing Have students rewrite either the first or the second story as they think it would happen today in the United States. For example, the three wives might become three job applicants for a political position. Students might illustrate their stories and include them in their portfolios.

STANDARDS: 1.2, 2.1, 2.2, 3.1, 3.2, 4.2

Ecrivons!

Une histoire d'attitude

Les histoires que tu viens de lire parlent des relations entre les gens. Maintenant, c'est à toi d'écrire une histoire où tu expliques comment, à ton avis, les gens devraient se comporter les uns envers les autres.

A. Préparation

D'abord, pense à la façon dont les gens agissent les uns envers les autres.

1. Fais un tableau pour organiser tes idées clairement.

   a. Divise ton tableau en deux colonnes : *Positive* et *Negative*.

> **Stratégie pour écrire**
> No matter what the topic or purpose for writing, a writer must organize his or her ideas in a logical way. Many writers find graphic devices to be useful tools for organizing ideas. Time lines, charts, and diagrams are all examples of graphic devices that can help writers to visualize their ideas and clarify their thinking. The type of graphic device you choose will depend on what you're writing about. For example, a time line depicts a chronological progression of events, a comparison-and-contrast chart shows how two things are similar and different, and a flow chart shows the different steps involved in a process. When starting out on a writing task, try using a graphic device appropriate to your topic to help you organize your thoughts.

   b. Remplis chaque colonne avec des choses que les gens font souvent, comme, par exemple, *Lying* ou *Being honest*.

   c. Examine ton tableau. Choisis quelque chose que tu voudrais mettre en valeur dans ton histoire.

2. Imagine le scénario de ton histoire.

   a. Qui est ton personnage principal? Quelle est son attitude?

   b. Quelles vont être les conséquences des actions du personnage principal sur les autres personnages?

   c. Est-ce que le personnage principal va être récompensé pour ses bonnes actions ou bien est-ce qu'il sera puni pour ses mauvaises actions?

3. Esquisse *(Outline)* les événements principaux de ton histoire.

B. Rédaction

Maintenant, fais un brouillon de ton histoire. N'oublie pas...

1. de décrire en détails le comportement de ton personnage principal.

2. d'expliquer les conséquences que ses actions ont sur les autres.

3. de bien montrer le rapport entre l'attitude du personnage principal et la fin de ton histoire.

C. Evaluation

1. Lis ton histoire à ton/ta camarade. Réfléchissez aux questions suivantes.

   a. Est-ce que l'histoire est claire? Est-ce qu'elle suit un ordre logique?

   b. Est-ce que c'est une histoire intéressante? Est-ce que tu pourrais ajouter des détails pour la rendre plus vivante?

2. Corrige les fautes d'orthographe, de grammaire et de vocabulaire.

3. Ecris la version finale de ton histoire.

Apply and Assess

Postwriting
Teaching Suggestion

C. After students read their stories to a partner, have them ask the partner the questions listed under the Teaching Suggestion for Activity B. If the partner has difficulty describing the main character or finding the moral of the story, the pair should look at the timeline or outline from Part A together and discuss ways to make the message clearer.

Visual Learners
C. Have the writer's partner draw a timeline or chart of the events as he or she listens to the story. Then, the partners should compare this timeline to the one the writer made in Part A.

Teaching Resources
p. 177

PRINT
▶ Lesson Planner, p. 31
▶ Cahier d'activités, p. 150
▶ Alternative Assessment Guide, p. 21
▶ Standardized Assessment Tutor, Chapter 6

MEDIA
▶ One-Stop Planner
▶ Test Generator, Chapter 6
▶ Interactive CD-ROM Tutor, Disc 2

Process Writing

Prewriting
Teaching Suggestion

A. 1. Do this activity as a class so students will have a broad range of behaviors from which to choose their topics. Have students include "pet peeve" behaviors and "I like it when . . . " behaviors.

A. 2. You might refer students to some fables or fairy tales *(The Fox and the Crow, Cinderella)* to help them decide how they want their own story to end. Have them discuss how the characters in each story behaved and why.

Visual Learners
A. 3. Have students draw their outline as a timeline. Have them write a description of the main character at one end and how he or she is going to end up at the opposite end. Then, have them write in the main events that will effect this change.

Writing
Teaching Suggestion

B. To help students focus, suggest they keep these three questions in mind as they write: **Comment est le personnage principal? Quelles sont les conséquences de ses actions? Quelle est la morale de l'histoire?**

Grammaire supplémentaire

internet

ADRESSE: go.hrw.com
MOT-CLE: WA3
FRANCOPHONE AFRICA-6

Première étape

Objectives Making, accepting, and refusing suggestions; making arrangements; making and accepting apologies

1 Mets les verbes entre parenthèses au passé composé. N'oublie pas de faire l'accord du participe passé, s'il y a lieu. (**p. 162**)

> Pendant leurs vacances à Fès, Béatrice et Christian ___1___ (se promener) dans la médina. Ils ___2___ (se disputer) et ils ___3___ (se quitter). Quelques heures plus tard, ils ___4___ (se retrouver) par hasard sur la place du Vieux Méchouar. Ils ont décidé de se réconcilier. Puis, ils ___5___ (se dire) des mots d'amour et ils ___6___ (s'embrasser). A minuit, ils ___7___ (s'offrir) des bagues de fiançailles. Le lendemain matin, ils ___8___ (se marier) et le soir même, on a fait la fête à l'hôtel Moussafir.

2 Réponds aux questions de Rachid selon l'exemple. N'oublie pas de mettre les verbes au futur. (**p. 162**)

> **EXEMPLE** —Tu vas me téléphoner demain?
> —**Oui, on se téléphonera.** or **Oui, nous nous téléphonerons.**

1. Tu me parleras plus tard?
2. Je te verrai ce soir?
3. Tu penses que Babette va écrire à Marie?
4. A ton avis, est-ce que Théo va quitter Laure?
5. Tu es sûr que tu vas te réconcilier avec Clarisse?
6. Tu crois que je vais m'entendre avec ton père?
7. Tu penses que Georges et Claire vont se marier?
8. A ton avis, est-ce que Karine va donner un cadeau à Manon?

Answers

1
1. se sont promenés
2. se sont disputés
3. se sont quittés
4. se sont retrouvés
5. se sont dit
6. se sont embrassés
7. se sont offert
8. se sont mariés

2
1. Oui, on se parlera **or** Oui, nous nous parlerons.
2. Oui, on se verra **or** Oui, nous nous verrons.
3. Oui, je pense qu'elles s'écriront.
4. Oui, ils se quitteront.
5. Oui, je suis sûr(e) que nous nous réconcilierons.
6. Oui, je crois que vous vous entendrez.
7. Oui, je pense qu'ils se marieront.
8. Oui, elles se donneront des cadeaux.

Grammar Resources for Chapter 6

The **Grammaire supplémentaire** activities are designed as supplemental activities for the grammatical concepts presented in the chapter. You might use them as additional practice, for review, or for assessment.

For more grammar presentations, review, and practice, refer to the following:
• Travaux pratiques de grammaire
• Grammar Tutor for Students of French

• Grammar Summary on pp. R29–R54
• Cahier d'activités
• Grammar and Vocabulary quizzes (Testing Program)
• Test Generator
• Interactive CD-ROM Tutor
• **Jeux interactifs** at go.hrw.com

3 Hier, Ismaïl a rendu visite aux parents de Selwa. Il s'est très mal comporté. Maintenant, il s'excuse auprès de son amie. Ecris ses excuses en utilisant **Je m'excuse** et l'infinitif passé du verbe qui convient. (**p. 164**)

> EXEMPLE —Tu n'as même pas dit bonjour à ma mère!
> —**Je m'excuse de ne pas avoir dit bonjour à ta mère.**

1. Tu n'as pas retiré tes chaussures!
2. Tu n'as pas enlevé ton chapeau!
3. Tu n'as pas bu ton thé à la menthe!
4. Tu as renversé la théière!
5. Tu as parlé tout le temps!
6. Tu as embêté le bébé!
7. Tu n'es pas arrivé à l'heure!

Deuxième étape   **Objectives** Showing and responding to hospitality; expressing and responding to thanks; quarreling

4 Moktar a invité Raphaël chez ses parents qui habitent à Fès. Raphaël remercie Moktar de son hospitalité en utilisant **Merci de** et l'infinitif passé dans chaque phrase. (**pp. 164, 169**)

> EXEMPLE Moktar a présenté sa famille à Raphaël.
> **Merci de m'avoir présenté ta famille.**

1. Moktar a offert un jus de fruit à Raphaël.
2. Moktar lui a montré la boutique de tapis de ses parents.
3. Moktar lui a fait goûter des cornes de gazelle.
4. Moktar lui a appris à dire «au revoir» en arabe.
5. Moktar a invité Raphaël au mariage de sa cousine.
6. Moktar lui a conseillé d'aller voir le Dar el Makhzen.
7. Moktar lui a donné un souvenir.

Answers

3 1. Je m'excuse de ne pas avoir retiré mes chaussures.
2. Je m'excuse de ne pas avoir enlevé mon chapeau.
3. Je m'excuse de ne pas avoir bu mon thé à la menthe.
4. Je m'excuse d'avoir renversé la théière.
5. Je m'excuse d'avoir parlé tout le temps.
6. Je m'excuse d'avoir embêté le bébé.
7. Je m'excuse de ne pas être arrivé à l'heure.

4 1. Merci de m'avoir offert un jus de fruit.
2. Merci de m'avoir montré la boutique de tapis de tes parents.
3. Merci de m'avoir fait goûter des cornes de gazelle.
4. Merci de m'avoir appris à dire «au revoir» en arabe.
5. Merci de m'avoir invité au mariage de ta cousine.
6. Merci de m'avoir conseillé d'aller voir le Dar el Makhzen.
7. Merci de m'avoir donné un souvenir.

Communication for All Students

Slower Pace

1 Read the paragraph out loud and have students supply the missing verbs orally. Then, ask them which past participles require agreement and why. Have students work in pairs to check each other's written work and then go over the paragraph on the board or on an overhead transparency.

Kinesthetic Learners

3 Have students work in pairs and take turns acting out each faux pas as one partner reads it out. Then the student playing the role of Ismaïl should contritely offer his or her excuses. Students should then write their answers, checking each other's work for accuracy. Students could also think of situations in which they have had to apologize to friends, and write those out.

Grammaire supplémentaire

WA3 FRANCOPHONE
AFRICA-6

CHAPITRE 6

For **Grammaire supplémentaire**
Answer Transparencies, see the
Teaching Transparencies binder.

5 Pauline raconte à Cécile comment la mère de son amie Soumia l'a reçue chez elle. Lis les descriptions de Pauline et imagine sa conversation avec la mère de Soumia. (**p. 169**)

> **EXEMPLE** PAULINE Je lui ai demandé si elle avait du jus de fruit.
> PAULINE **Vous auriez du jus de fruit?**

1. PAULINE Elle m'a dit d'entrer.
   LA MÈRE _____

2. PAULINE Elle était contente de me voir.
   LA MÈRE _____

3. PAULINE Elle m'a offert à boire.
   LA MÈRE _____

4. PAULINE Je l'ai remerciée.
   PAULINE _____

5. PAULINE Elle a répondu à mes remerciements.
   LA MÈRE _____

6 Saïd et Sélima sont frère et sœur. Ecris les réponses de Sélima aux questions de Saïd. Utilise les expressions entre parenthèses. N'oublie pas de mettre le verbe au conditionnel. (**pp. 141, 173**)

> **EXEMPLE** —Qu'est-ce que tu ferais si je me moquais de toi devant tes amies?
> (te tirer les cheveux)
> **—Je te tirerais les cheveux!**

1. Qu'est-ce que tu ferais si je venais fouiller dans ta chambre?
   (te demander de partir)

2. Qu'est-ce que tu ferais si je t'ennuyais pendant que tu parlais au téléphone?
   (te dire de me ficher la paix)

3. Qu'est-ce que tu ferais si je lisais tes lettres?
   (te conseiller de te mêler de tes oignons)

4. Qu'est-ce que tu ferais si je bavardais pendant que tu regardais la télé?
   (te dire de la fermer)

5. Qu'est-ce que tu ferais si je racontais ce que tu as fait à Maman?
   (te traiter de rapporteur)

6. Qu'est-ce que tu ferais si je te prenais le C.D. que tu viens d'acheter?
   (te demander de me le rendre immédiatement)

Answers

5 *Answers may vary:*
1. Entrez, je vous en prie.
2. Ça me fait plaisir de vous voir.
3. Je vous sers quelque chose?
4. Je vous remercie.
5. Je vous en prie.

6
1. Je te demanderais de partir!
2. Je te dirais de me ficher la paix!
3. Je te conseillerais de te mêler de tes oignons!
4. Je te dirais de la fermer!
5. Je te traiterais de rapporteur!
6. Je te demanderais de me le rendre immédiatement!

Communication for All Students

Slower Pace

5 Have students practice the subjunctive with **Il faut que** and appropriate behaviors before they use the conditional of **falloir.** Ask them **Qu'est-ce qu'il faut faire?** in order to elicit responses. Then have them complete the sentences with the conditional forms. Have partners do the last three sentences and check each other's work.

Challenge

7 After students have completed the dialogue between Fatima and Parvine, have them write a dialogue based on Activity 7, but between another pair of siblings. The dialogue can be based on a dispute with their own siblings or characters from a book or movie. Students can then work in pairs to act out the dialogues and present them to the class.

7 Fatima et sa sœur Parvine se disputent tout le temps. Complète leurs conversations avec l'expression appropriée. (**p. 173**)

1. **FATIMA** Je vais dire à Maman que tu as cassé son beau vase.
   PARVINE _____!

2. **PARVINE** Quand on joue aux cartes, c'est toujours moi qui gagne!
   FATIMA _____!

3. **LA MÈRE** Fatima, sois gentille avec ta petite sœur.
   FATIMA _____!

4. **PARVINE** Tiens, tu as reçu une carte de Mansour. Qu'est-ce qu'il t'écrit?
   FATIMA _____!

5. **PARVINE** Aïe! Arrête! Tu me tires les cheveux! J'ai mal!
   FATIMA _____!

6. **PARVINE** Je ne trouve plus le tee-shirt que tu m'as prêté...
   FATIMA Tu perds toujours ce que je te prête!
   _____?

7. **FATIMA** Maman est fâchée parce que j'ai eu 5 à mon interro de maths.
   PARVINE _____! Tu n'avais qu'à étudier!

8. **PARVINE** Je peux t'accompagner chez Aziz?
   FATIMA Non! _____!

Possible answers
1. Rapporteuse
2. Tricheuse
3. C'est toujours moi qui prends
4. Mêle-toi de tes oignons
5. Pleurnicheuse
6. Tu le fais exprès
7. Tant pis pour toi
8. Casse-toi

The **Mise en pratique** reviews and integrates all four skills and culture in preparation for the Chapter Test.

Language Note

Students might want to know the following terms from the brochure: **fripes** *(used clothing)*; **couronné** *(crowned, topped)*; **lanternon** *(lantern, decorative ornament)*; **nef** *(nave)*; **coupole** *(dome)*; **cèdre doré** *(gilded cedar).*

Culture Note

The **Djemaa-el-Fna** is a centrally located square in Marrakesh. In the evening, snake charmers, acrobats, trained monkeys, boy dancers, musicians, and story-tellers fill the square. The acrobats, who are primarily from Tazeroualt, often perform in European circuses. Among the music groups are the **Aïssaoua,** who play instruments that resemble oboes **(ghaitahs),** and the Andalusian-sounding string groups, who play fiddles and lute-like instruments, called **ouds.**

Mise en pratique

See scripts and answers on p. 155H.

1 Martin vient de trouver un nouvel ami, Ali, à Marrakech. Ecoute leur conversation et réponds aux questions suivantes.

CD 6
Tr. 13

1. Lesquelles des activités suivantes est-ce qu'Ali propose à Martin?
   a. d'aller au souk el-Kebir
   b. de déjeuner chez lui
   c. de prendre un jus d'orange
   d. d'aller voir le palais de la Bahia
   e. d'aller à la place Jemaa-el-Fna

2. Lesquelles des suggestions d'Ali est-ce que Martin accepte?

3. A quelle heure est-ce qu'ils se donnent rendez-vous?

4. Où est-ce qu'ils se retrouvent?
   a. sur la place Jemaa-el-Fna   b. au palais de la Bahia   c. sur la place de Bâb Fteuh

Le guide du ROUTARD MAROC

La place Jemaa-el-Fna : Le matin, Jemaa-el-Fna est un immense marché. Cela va des délicieux jus d'orange pressés, aux épices et aux herbes médicinales, en passant par les écrivains publics à l'ombre de leur parapluie noir, et les diseuses de bonne aventure. Puis, peu à peu les vendeurs d'eau font leur apparition. Quand la chaleur se fait moins forte, les principaux acteurs entrent en scène : charmeurs de serpents au son de leur flûte, danseurs gnaouas tournant comme des derviches au son des tambourins, vendeurs de fripes étalant leurs frusques sur le sol, restaurants ambulants avec roulante et brasero. Les pickpockets sont à la fête, principalement autour des conteurs qui attirent grand nombre de badauds.

Les souks : Pénétrer seul dans les souks relève de l'exploit, car rares sont ceux qui parviennent à échapper aux guides insistants. Voici quelques conseils :
• Suivre un groupe de touristes et faire semblant d'être avec eux, du moins pour les premiers mètres du parcours, les plus difficiles.
• Ne pas porter de tee-shirts ou de sacs évoquant des marques connues de voyagistes. Sinon, vous êtes sûr d'être repéré immédiatement.

Le minaret de la Koutoubia : la Tour Eiffel locale. Tout le monde le connaît et il sert de point de repère. Son décor est différent sur chaque face. Sa tour, aussi haute que celles de Notre-Dame de Paris, est couronnée d'un lanternon surmonté de quatre boules dorées. La légende voudrait nous faire croire qu'elles sont d'or pur et que l'influence des planètes leur permet de tenir en équilibre !

La mosquée de la kasbah :se repère aisément grâce à son minaret aux entrelacs de couleur turquoise qui se détachent du ciel. Vous ne pourrez rien voir d'autre puisque la mosquée, dont la salle de prière ne comprend pas moins de onze nefs, est réservée aux musulmans.

Les tombeaux saadiens :Ouvert de 8h30 à 12h et de 14h30 à 17h30 ou 18h. Fermé le mardi. Joli mausolée de Moulay Ahmed el-Mansour, mort de la peste à Fès en 1603, et qui repose, entouré de ses fils, sous une coupole de cèdre doré que supportent douze colonnes de marbre de Carrare. Le jardin est un havre de paix.

Le palais de la Bahia : Visite, obligatoirement accompagnée d'un guide, de 8h30 à 12h et de 14h30 à 18h. Ces horaires peuvent toutefois varier selon la saison. Construite vers 1880, cette riche demeure princière est un chef-d'œuvre de l'art marocain. Sur plus de 8 ha, des appartements superbement décorés débouchent sur des patios fleuris.

A voir aussi:
Le souk des Teinturiers, le souk Chouars (bois), le souk du Cuivre, le souk Smata (cuir), le souk des Bijoutiers, le souk-el-Kebir (cuir), le souk Zrabia (caftans, tapis), les kissarias (vêtements, étoffes).

Apply and Assess

Slower Pace

1 Have students copy the choices onto a separate sheet of paper. Then, play the recording and have students check off each suggestion they hear. Play the recording a second time and have students mark a + next to the suggestions that Martin accepts. Play the recording a third time and have students answer questions 3 and 4.

Challenge

1 Have students close their books. Tell them to listen for and write down the activities Ali suggests and the one he and Martin decide on. Then, play the recording. You might offer a point for each correct activity that students wrote down and two points for correctly identifying the activity the boys decide to do. The student(s) with the most points win(s).

2 Lis ces extraits d'un guide français sur ce qu'on peut voir à Marrakech et réponds aux questions suivantes. See answers below.

1. What are some things you might see if you visit the **place Jemaa-el-Fna?** What should you be aware of?

2. What kind of souks could you visit? What problem might you run into when going into this area? What does the guidebook suggest you do?

3. With what monument could you compare the **minaret de la Koutoubia?** Why?

4. What can you see at the **tombeaux saadiens?**

5. Which of the sites is a masterpiece of Moroccan art? Do you need a guide?

3 A Marrakech, tu as rencontré quelqu'un avec qui tu voudrais faire un tour de la ville. Propose-lui de visiter des endroits qui sont mentionnés dans le guide. Il/Elle va aussi faire des suggestions. Décidez ensemble de ce que vous allez faire pendant votre séjour. N'oubliez pas de fixer les jours, les heures et les endroits où vous allez vous retrouver.

4 Avec un partenaire, imagine une situation où ton/ta meilleur(e) ami(e) a fait quelque chose qui t'a rendu(e) furieux/furieuse. Vous vous disputez et il/elle s'excuse. Comme il/elle est vraiment désolé(e), tu acceptes ses excuses. Créez un dialogue, puis jouez cette situation.

5 Ton correspondant marocain vient bientôt passer une année aux Etats-Unis. Il voudrait savoir si les Américains sont aussi accueillants que les Marocains. Ecris-lui une lettre où tu lui expliques comment on accueille les gens dans la région où tu habites.

6 **Jeu de rôle**

You're going to a cousin's wedding. Act out the following scenes with classmates.

- When you arrive at your cousin's house, his family greets you and tries to make you feel at home.

- The night before the wedding, your cousin's fiancée shows up looking angry. They have a quarrel. They make up, however, and apologize to each other and to you.

- On the day of the wedding, there are some family members attending whom you don't know. Your cousin tells you who they are and introduces you.

Félicitations pour votre mariage

Apply and Assess

Additional Practice

2 You might also ask students the following questions: **Qu'est-ce qu'on peut acheter sur la place Jemaa el Fna le matin? (du jus d'orange, des épices et des herbes médicinales) Comment est le minaret de la Koutoubia? (son décor est différent sur** chaque face) **Est-ce que les touristes peuvent entrer dans la mosquée de la kasbah? (non) Quand est-ce que les tombeaux saadiens sont ouverts? (de 8h30 à 12h et de 14h30 à 17h30 ou 18h) Le palais de la Bahia a été construit en quelle année? (vers 1880)**

Mise en pratique

CHAPITRE 6

Additional Practice

2 Type a list of the descriptions of the various sites without naming them. Have students work in pairs to identify each one. For example, you might write:

1. **Son minaret est de couleur turquoise.**

2. **On peut y acheter des épices.**

3. **Son lanternon est surmonté de quatre boules dorées.**

4. **On joue du tambourin là-bas.**

As an alternative, read a description aloud and call on the first student to raise his or her hand to identify the site.

Answers

2 1. *Possible answers:* public scribes, water vendors, snake charmers, dancers, storytellers; pickpockets

2. *Souks:* dyed goods, wood, copper, leather, jewelry, caftans, carpets, clothes, fabric; self-appointed guides; attach yourself to a group of tourists, avoid dressing like a tourist.

3. the Eiffel Tower; The minaret is a landmark recognized by all.

4. the tomb of Moulay Ahmed el-Mansour and his sons

5. the Bahia Palace; yes

Que sais-je?

Teaching Resources
p. 184

PRINT
▸ Grammar Tutor for Students of French, Chapter 6

MEDIA
▸ Interactive CD-ROM Tutor, Disc 2
▸ Online self-test

 go.hrw.com
WA3 FRANCOPHONE
AFRICA-6

Possible answers

1 1. Ça t'intéresse d'aller danser?
2. Ça te plairait de jouer au tennis?
3. Tu ne voudrais pas regarder la télé?

4 Comment est-ce qu'on fait? Quand/Où est-ce qu'on se retrouve? A quelle heure est-ce qu'on se donne rendez-vous?

6 Ce n'est pas grave. Ça ne fait rien. Il n'y a pas de mal. Ne t'inquiète pas. Ça arrive à tout le monde.

7 a. Entrez, je vous en prie. Ça me fait plaisir de vous voir. Donnez-moi votre manteau.
b. Mettez-vous à l'aise. Asseyez-vous.
c. Je vous sers quelque chose? Qu'est-ce que je peux vous offrir?

8 a. Merci. Moi aussi. Vous êtes bien aimable.
b. C'est gentil.
c. Je prendrais bien... ; Vous auriez...?

11 a. Tu m'énerves, à la fin! Tu es vraiment casse-pieds! Tu me prends la tête!
b. C'est toujours moi qui prends!
c. Casse-toi!

Que sais-je?

Can you use what you've learned in this chapter?

Can you make, accept, and refuse suggestions?
p. 161

1 How would you suggest the following activities to a friend? *See answers below.*

1.   2.   3.

2 How would you accept the suggestions in number 1?
Possible answers: Ce serait sympa. Oui, ça me plairait beaucoup. Si, j'aimerais bien.

3 How would you refuse the suggestions in number 1? *Possible answers:* Impossible, je suis pris(e). J'aimerais bien, mais je n'ai pas le temps. C'est gentil, mais j'ai un rendez-vous.

Can you make arrangements?
p. 162

4 You and your friend have decided to do one of the activities pictured above. What would you say to make the necessary arrangements? *See answers below.*

Can you make and accept apologies?
p. 164

5 You've just broken your best friend's CD player. How do you apologize? *Possible answers:* Je m'excuse. Je suis vraiment désolé(e). Pardonne-moi. Je m'en veux d'avoir fait ça.

6 How would you accept the apology in number 5? *See answers below.*

Can you show and respond to hospitality?
p. 169

7 What would you say to your guests when . . . *See answers below.*
a. they've just arrived at your home?
b. you've taken their coats and they're standing inside the doorway?
c. you'd like to offer them something to eat or drink?

8 How would you respond as a guest in each of the situations in number 7? *See answers below.*

Can you express and respond to thanks?
p. 169

9 How would you thank these people? *Possible answers:*
a. A good friend lends you a new CD. Je te remercie. C'est vraiment très gentil de ta part.
b. A stranger stops to help pick up some things you've dropped. Merci bien/mille fois.

10 How would you respond if you were the people in number 9? *Possible answers:* **a.** De rien. Je t'en prie. **b.** (Il n'y a) pas de quoi. C'est tout à fait normal.

Can you quarrel?
p. 173

11 What would you say in the following situations? *See answers below.*
a. Your sister is annoying you while you try to do your homework.
b. You get in trouble for something your classmate did.
c. Your little brother enters your room and starts looking through your things.

Review and Assess

♟ Game

Réponse-question Create a 5 X 5 grid on a transparency. Across the top, label the columns A through E. Label the horizontal rows 100 through 500. In each square, write the answer to one of the questions in **Que sais-je?** Cover each of the squares. Form two teams. The first player calls out a letter and a point value (A, 100). Uncover that square. The player asks a question for the response written in the square. For example, a question for **C'est gentil, mais j'ai un rendez-vous.** would be *How would you refuse a suggestion?* If the player's question is correct, his team earns the appropriate point value, and the next player from the same team takes a turn. If the player responds incorrectly, the opposing team has a chance to suggest a correct question.

Première étape

Making, accepting, and refusing suggestions

Ça t'intéresse de... ?	Would you be interested in . . .?
Ça te plairait de... ?	Would you like to . . .?
Tu ne voudrais pas... ?	Wouldn't you like to . . .?
Ce serait sympa.	That would be nice.
Ça me plairait beaucoup.	I'd like that a lot.
Je suis pris(e).	I'm busy.

J'aimerais bien, mais...	I'd like to, but . . .
C'est gentil, mais j'ai un rendez-vous.	That's nice of you, but I've got an appointment.

Making arrangements

Comment est-ce qu'on fait?	How should we work this out?
Quand est-ce qu'on se revoit?	When are we getting together?

A quelle heure est-ce qu'on se donne rendez-vous?	What time are we meeting?

Making and accepting apologies

Je m'excuse de...	I'm sorry for . . .
Pardonne-moi de...	Pardon me for . . .
Je m'en veux de...	I feel bad that . . .
Ça arrive à tout le monde.	It happens to everybody.
Ne t'inquiète pas.	Don't worry about it.

Deuxième étape

Showing and responding to hospitality

Entrez, je vous en prie.	Come in, please.
Ça me fait plaisir de vous voir.	I'm happy to see you.
Donnez-moi...	Give me . . .
Mettez-vous à l'aise.	Make yourself comfortable.
Asseyez-vous.	Sit down.
Vous êtes bien aimable.	That's kind of you.
Je vous sers quelque chose?	Can I offer you something?
Qu'est-ce que je peux vous offrir?	What can I offer you?
Je prendrais bien...	I'd like some . . .
Vous auriez... ?	Would you have . . . ?

Expressing and responding to thanks

Merci bien/mille fois.	Thank you very much.
Je vous remercie.	Thank you.
C'est vraiment très gentil de votre part.	That's very nice of you.
De rien.	You're welcome.

Je vous en prie.	You're very welcome.
(Il n'y a) pas de quoi.	It's nothing.
C'est tout à fait normal.	You don't have to thank me.

Family relationships

l'aîné(e)	the oldest child
l'arrière-grand-mère	great-grandmother
l'arrière-grand-père	great-grandfather
le/la benjamin(e)	the youngest child
le/la cadet(te)	the younger child
les jumeaux/jumelles	twins
le neveu	nephew
la nièce	niece
la petite-fille	granddaughter
le petit-fils	grandson
célibataire	single
divorcé(e)	divorced
marié(e)	married
mort(e)	dead
veuf/veuve	widowed

Quarreling

Rapporteur(-euse)!	Tattletale!
Pleurnicheur(-euse)!	Crybaby!
Tricheur(-euse)!	Cheater!
Tu m'énerves, à la fin!	You're really bugging me!
Tu es vraiment casse-pieds!	You're such a pain!
Tu me prends la tête!	You're driving me crazy!
Oh, ça va, hein?	Oh, cut it out!
Arrête!	Stop!
Ça suffit!	That's enough!
Tu le fais exprès?	Are you doing that on purpose?
Mêle-toi de tes oignons!	Mind your own business!
Fiche-moi la paix!	Leave me alone!
Casse-toi!	Get out of here!
Tant pis pour toi!	Tough!
C'est toujours la même chose!	It's always the same!
C'est lui/elle qui a commencé!	He/She started it!
Il/Elle m'a traité(e) de... !	He/She called me a . . .!
C'est toujours moi qui prends!	I'm always the one who gets blamed!

Review and Assess

Circumlocution

Have partners cut out several magazine pictures (or bring photos from home) that represent families and different family members. One partner plays the role of an exchange student from a francophone country, while the other plays a member of the American host family. Using their pictures, they pretend to be looking at the host family's photo album. The exchange student points to a member of the family in a picture and asks who it is. The host cannot remember the exact French words for the names of family members, so he or she must give clues while the exchange student tries to guess the relationship. (—C'est qui, cette femme?/—Euh, c'est la mère de mon grand-père./—C'est ton arrière-grand-mère?/—Oui.)

CHAPITRE 6

Teaching Suggestions

- Have students make flash cards for the vocabulary expressions. Encourage them to review by showing the French or English side of the card to a partner, who gives the equivalent word or expression and uses it in a logical sentence.

- Have students write the words for family relationships in two columns, those that refer to males in one and those that refer to females in the other. They might also add other family vocabulary they've learned to these lists.

Chapter 6 Assessment

▸ **Testing Program**
Chapter Test, pp. 119–124
 Audio Compact Discs, CD 6, Trs. 16–18
Speaking Test, p. 297

Midterm Exam, pp. 133–140
Score Sheet, pp. 141–143
Listening Scripts, pp. 144–145
Answers, p. 146
 Audio Compact Discs, CD 6, Trs. 19–23

▸ **Alternative Assessment Guide**
Portfolio Assessment, p. 21
Performance Assessment, p. 35
CD-ROM Assessment, p. 49

▸ **Interactive CD-ROM Tutor, Disc 2**
A toi de parler
A toi d'écrire

▸ **Standardized Assessment Tutor**
Chapter 6

▸ **One-Stop Planner, Disc 2**
Test Generator
Chapter 6

Chapitre 7 : Un safari-photo
Chapter Overview

Mise en train pp. 188–190	*Un safari, ça se prépare!*

	FUNCTIONS	**GRAMMAR**	**VOCABULARY**	**RE-ENTRY**
Première étape pp. 191–197	• Making suppositions, p. 193 • Expressing doubt and certainty, p. 193 • Asking for and giving advice, p. 195	• Indicative versus subjunctive, p. 193 • Using the subjunctive, p. 196	• Rain forest and savannah, p. 192 • Packing for a safari, p. 194	• The subjunctive (**Chapitre 3**, III) • Travel items and camping equipment (**Chapitres 1, 12**, II) • Asking for and giving advice (**Chapitre 12**, II)

Remise en train pp. 198–199	*Le safari, c'est l'aventure!*

Deuxième étape pp. 200–203	• Expressing astonishment, p. 201 • Cautioning someone, p. 202 • Expressing fear, p. 202 • Reassuring someone, p. 202 • Expressing relief, p. 202	• Irregular subjunctive forms, p. 203	• African animals, p. 200	• The conditional (**Chapitre 5**, III) • The subjunctive (**Chapitre 3**, II)

Lisons! pp. 204–206	**Le Cimetière des éléphants; La Tortue et le léopard**	**Reading Strategy:** Understanding linking words

Ecrivons! p. 207	**Une histoire d'animaux**	**Writing Strategy:** Using sequencing words

Grammaire supplémentaire	**pp. 208–211**	**Première étape,** pp. 208–209	**Deuxième étape,** pp. 210–211

Review pp. 212–215	**Mise en pratique,** pp. 212–213	**Que sais-je?,** p. 214	**Vocabulaire,** p. 215

CULTURE

- **Note culturelle,** Wildlife in the Central African Republic, p. 190
- **Rencontre culturelle,** Overview of the Central African Republic, p. 191
- **Panorama Culturel,** Stereotypical impressions of francophone regions, p. 197

Chapitre 7 : Un safari-photo
Chapter Resources

PRINT

Lesson Planning

One-Stop Planner

Lesson Planner with Substitute Teacher Lesson Plans, pp. 32–36, 70

Student Make-Up Assignments
- Make-Up Assignment Copying Masters, Chapter 7

Listening and Speaking

Listening Activities
- Student Response Forms for Listening Activities, pp. 51–53
- Additional Listening Activities 7-1 to 7-6, pp. 55–57
- Additional Listening Activities (song), p. 58
- Scripts and Answers, pp. 132–136

Video Guide
- Teaching Suggestions, pp. 42–43
- Activity Masters, pp. 44–46
- Scripts and Answers, pp. 95–98, 114

Activities for Communication
- Communicative Activities, pp. 25–28
- Realia and Teaching Suggestions, pp. 69–71
- Situation Cards, pp. 101–102

Reading and Writing

Reading Strategies and Skills Handbook, Chapter 7

Joie de lire 3, Chapter 7

Cahier d'activités, pp. 73–84

Grammar

Travaux pratiques de grammaire, pp. 63–72

Grammar Tutor for Students of French, Chapter 7

Assessment

Testing Program
- Grammar and Vocabulary Quizzes, **Etape** Quizzes, and Chapter Test, pp. 147–160
- Score Sheet, Scripts and Answers, pp. 161–167

Alternative Assessment Guide
- Portfolio Assessment, p. 22
- Performance Assessment, p. 36
- CD-ROM Assessment, p. 50

Student Make-Up Assignments
- Alternative Quizzes, Chapter 7

Standardized Assessment Tutor
- Reading, pp. 27–29
- Writing, p. 30
- Math, pp. 51–52

MEDIA

Online Activities
- Jeux interactifs
- Activités Internet

Video Program
- Videocassette 3
- Videocassette 5 (captioned version)

Audio Compact Discs
- Textbook Listening Activities, CD 7, Tracks 1–13
- Additional Listening Activities, CD 7, Tracks 19–25
- Assessment Items, CD 7, Tracks 14–18

Interactive CD-ROM Tutor, Disc 2

Teaching Transparencies
- Situation 7-1 to 7-2
- **Grammaire supplémentaire** Answers
- **Travaux pratiques de grammaire** Answers

One-Stop Planner CD-ROM

Use the **One-Stop Planner CD-ROM with Test Generator** to aid in lesson planning and pacing.

For each chapter, the **One-Stop Planner** includes:
- Editable lesson plans with direct links to teaching resources
- Printable worksheets from resource books
- Direct launches to the HRW Internet activities
- Video and audio segments
- Test Generator
- Clip Art for vocabulary items

Chapitre 7 : Un safari-photo

Projects

Mon safari-photo

Students will prepare a slide show of their photo safari in the Central African Republic, with a commentary on each slide. The "slides" will actually be transparencies that students draw and project.

MATERIALS
✂ **Students may need**
- Travel guides
- Transparencies
- Encyclopedias
- Colored pens for transparencies

SUGGESTED SEQUENCE

1. Have students use travel guides and encyclopedias to find out more about what they might see on a photo safari in the Central African Republic. They might also find out more about the animals they are "photographing." Encourage them to use the information in the Chapter Opener on pages 186–187, the **Mise en train** on pages 188–190, the **Rencontre Culturelle** on page 191, and the **Remise en train** on pages 198–199. They should also invent interesting incidents that will happen during the imaginary trip (a narrow escape from a lion, losing one's camera to the jaws of a crocodile, and so on).

2. Have groups decide what they will "photograph." They should give an account of the entire trip, including the preliminary packing and vaccinations, the plane or train ride there, the animals they see, and any exciting incidents or narrow escapes that occur during the trip.

3. Next, groups should draw their "slides" on transparencies.

4. Once students have created the slides, they should write a brief commentary about each one, using the functions from the chapter. If students have difficulty drawing, you might have them trace illustrations from their book onto a transparency. Students might assign two or three slides to each group member. The entire group should edit the commentaries.

5. Groups present their slide shows and tell the class the story of their trip. Each group member should read part of the commentary. One member should be responsible for changing the slides during the presentation.

GRADING THE PROJECT
You might base students' grades on thoroughness of content, creativity of visuals, oral presentation, and accuracy of language use. You might also assign individual students a grade based on their individual effort and participation in the project.

Suggested Point Distribution (total = 100 points)
Content...30 points
Creativity of visuals ....20 points
Oral presentation..................................15 points
Language use...15 points
Effort/participation..............................20 points

Games

Mots enchaînés

In this game, students will practice chapter vocabulary.

Procedure   This game may be played by the whole class or small groups. Assign one vocabulary word to each student. Tell students to write down their word and practice saying it. Then, have each student say his or her word aloud. Next, have students form a circle. If they are playing the game in small groups, have each group form a circle. Appoint a timekeeper within each group. Begin the game by having a student say a sentence that includes both his or her vocabulary word and a second vocabulary word. For example, if a student's word were **un serpent,** he or she might say **Tu as vu le serpent et le rhinocéros là-bas?** The student whose word is **le rhinocéros** continues the game by saying an original sentence that includes his or her word and the word of another student. If no student has the word **rhinocéros,** the student making the sentence comes up with another vocabulary word. Students must say a logical sentence within five or ten seconds. The goal is to keep the game going as long as possible.

Storytelling

Mini-histoire

*This story accompanies Teaching Transparency 7-1. The **mini-histoire** can be told and retold in different formats, acted out, written as dictation, and read aloud to give students additional opportunities to practice all four skills. The following story tells about Hubert and Lucie, two safari guides.*

Hubert et Lucie sont guides dans le parc national de Bamingui Bangoran. Ils se préparent à emmener des touristes voir les animaux de la réserve. Avant chaque expédition, ils distribuent à chaque touriste une liste d'affaires qu'ils doivent emporter. Cependant, il y a toujours des gens qui oublient quelque chose. Alors, depuis plusieurs mois, Hubert et Lucie ont décidé de se préparer comme s'ils étaient eux-mêmes des touristes. Ils emmènent des jumelles, un appareil-photo, des lunettes de soleil, de la crème solaire, etc... qu'ils prêtent aux touristes quand ces derniers ont oublié leurs affaires. Ce que les touristes apprécient le plus : l'appareil-photo. Ils pensent même en acheter un second. Il n'est pas rare que des touristes se battent pour avoir l'appareil ou plus tard pour la pellicule!

Traditions

La Forêt tropicale

Like their ancestors before them, the indigenous people of the Dzanga-Sangha Reserve in the Central African Republic turn to the rain forest to meet many of their daily needs. Plants are gathered for food, medicine, building materials, jewelry, toys, and even make-up. For example, the bark of the **Malanga** tree provides medicine, while its wood and trunk are used to build boats and oars. The sap from rubber trees is used to make balls and tops, while twigs from the **Ngemba** make handy toothbrushes and are added to sauces to enrich their flavor. Although women traditionally do most of the plant gathering, the knowledge of which plants to use for different purposes is known by all, having been passed on from one generation to the next. Have students research five plants from the rain forest to find out how they are used by local peoples and if they are used in products they themselves consume.

Recette

There are two words for peanut *in French: the scientific term **arachide** and the more commonly used term **cacahouète**. Peanuts originated in South America. The Aztec name for peanut is **tlacacahuatl**, from which **cacahouète** is derived. Peanuts were introduced to Africa by the Spanish and Portuguese during the colonial era. Senegal is one of the top producers of peanuts.*

POTAGE A L'ARACHIDE

pour 6 personnes

1 tasse d'arachides

2 blancs de poulet

1/2 tasse de beurre

1 cuillère à soupe de farine

4 tasses de bouillon de volaille

1 tasse de crème fraîche

Faire fondre le beurre dans une casserole. Ajouter la farine. Mélanger. Ajouter un petit peu de bouillon et porter le tout à ébullition. Faire cuire les blancs de poulet, les hacher et mélanger avec la crème fraîche. Passer le poulet au tamis avec le bouillon. Faire griller les cacahouètes et les piler. Ajouter au bouillon et laisser mijoter.

Technology

Video Program

Videocassette 3, Videocassette 5 (captioned version)
See Video Guide, pp. 41–45.

Camille et compagnie • Septième épisode : *Nos amies les bêtes*

Max and Laurent share the same passion for animals and photography, but their approach to wildlife is very different. Laurent takes Max on a tour of a zoo with all the equipment necessary to survive in the wilderness. Max prefers to see animals in their natural habitat. He takes Laurent to the Camargue where animals live in the wild. However, Max is not as organized as Laurent, and the two friends find only insects and a few birds.

Quelle est l'image de ta région?

Students from around the francophone world tell what their region is known for. Two native speakers discuss the **Panorama Culturel** question and introduce the interviews.

Vidéoclips

- **Commercial for Grundig®**: electronic equipment
- **Music video: Alors regarde** performed by Patrick Bruel
- **News report:** active vacations

Interactive CD-ROM Tutor

The **Interactive CD-ROM Tutor** contains videos, interactive games, and activities that provide students an opportunity to practice and review the material covered in Chapter 7.

Activity	Activity Type	Pupil's Edition Page
1. Vocabulaire	Jeu des paires	p. 192
2. Vocabulaire	Chasse au trésor Explorons! Vérifions!	p. 194
3. Comment dit-on... ?	Le bon choix	pp. 193, 195
4. Grammaire	Les mots qui manquent	p. 196
5. Vocabulaire	Chasse au trésor Explorons! Vérifions!	p. 200
6. Grammaire	Les mots qui manquent	p. 203
Panorama Culturel	Quelle est l'image de ta région? Le bon choix	p. 197
A toi de parler	*Guided recording*	pp. 212–213
A toi d'écrire	*Guided writing*	pp. 212–213

Teacher Management System

Logging In

Logging in to the *Allez, viens!* TMS is easy. Upon launching the program, simply type "admin" in the password area of the log-in screen and press RETURN. Log on to **www.hrw.com/CDROMTUTOR** for a detailed explanation of the Teacher Management System.

One-Stop Planner CD-ROM

To preview all resources available for this chapter, use the **One-Stop Planner CD-ROM**, Disc 2.

Internet Connection

internet

| ADRESSE: go.hrw.com |
| MOT-CLE: WA3 FRANCOPHONE AFRICA-7 |

*Have students explore the **go.hrw.com** Web site for many online resources covering all chapters. All Chapter 7 resources are available under the keyword **WA3 FRANCOPHONE AFRICA-7.** Interactive games help students practice the material and provide them with immediate feedback. You'll also find a printable worksheet that provides Internet activities that lead to a comprehensive online research project.*

Jeux interactifs

You can use the interactive activities in this chapter

- to practice grammar, vocabulary, and chapter functions
- as homework
- as an assessment option
- as a self-test
- to prepare for the Chapter Test

Activités Internet

Students look for information on line about a French region and record activities and dishes from the area, using the vocabulary and phrases from the chapter.

- After completing the activity sheet, have students share with a partner the information they gathered in Activities B, C and D on that sheet. Then partners share what they learned with the class. In Activity D, students are asked to create a brochure for tourists. Have partners exchange their brochures and edit each other's work.

Projet

Have groups of students select a wild animal they might see on a safari in Central Africa. Students can research information about the animal's habitat. They can also find out if the animal is raised or hunted for commercial reasons and if it is a threatened or endangered species. If so, they can find out what organizations are involved with the protection of the animal and what they are doing. Remind students to document their sources by noting the names and the URLs of all the sites they consulted. You may want to have each group present its findings to the rest of the class.

Chapitre 7 : Un safari-photo
Textbook Listening Activities Scripts

Première étape

7 p. 192

1. —Chut! Les gazelles viennent boire au point d'eau. Ne fais pas de bruit. Tu vas leur faire peur.

2. —Attention! Tu vas tomber dans l'eau. On ne peut pas se baigner dans la rivière.

3. —Il faut rester dans la voiture. Même si tu ne vois pas d'animaux, il se peut qu'il en arrive un très vite. Et il y a aussi des serpents qu'on ne voit pas dans la brousse.

4. —Regarde les oiseaux! Et ces fleurs tropicales, elles sont vraiment belles, non? Comment elle s'appelle, celle-là?

Answers to Activity 7
1. savane
2. forêt
3. savane
4. forêt

9 p. 193

1. Je suis sûr qu'il y a de beaux animaux là-bas.

2. Mais je ne suis pas certain qu'on puisse voir les forêts.

3. Je ne suis pas certain que la cuisine soit bonne.

4. Je ne pense pas qu'on puisse se promener dans la savane.

5. Mais je suis sûr qu'on verra des Pygmées.

6. Ça m'étonnerait qu'il y ait de bonnes routes.

7. Je ne suis pas sûr qu'on puisse boire l'eau.

Answers to Activity 9
1. certitude   5. certitude
2. doute   6. doute
3. doute   7. doute
4. doute

11 p. 194

Salut, c'est Mathieu. Bientôt le grand départ! J'espère que tu n'as rien oublié. Pense à prendre ton caméscope. Emporte aussi trois cassettes. A mon avis, on n'en trouvera pas facilement là-bas. Moi, je prends mon appareil-photo et des pellicules. Au fait, est-ce que tu as pensé à prendre un chapeau? Emporte aussi de la crème solaire. Il va faire très chaud là-bas. Et n'oublie surtout pas ta gourde et ta trousse de premiers soins avec des pansements et un désinfectant. Au fait, est-ce que tu as acheté des jumelles? Bon! A jeudi à l'aéroport. Salut!

Answers to Activity 11
un caméscope, des cassettes, un chapeau, de la crème solaire, une gourde, une trousse de premiers soins, des pansements, un désinfectant, des jumelles

13 p. 195

—Ça me plairait de faire un safari en République centrafricaine. Mais je voulais savoir... est-ce qu'il y a des préparatifs à faire avant de partir?

—Oui, un peu, mais ce n'est pas bien difficile. D'abord, il est très important que vous vous fassiez vacciner contre la fièvre jaune et le choléra. Ensuite, il faut que vous consultiez un médecin car il est essentiel que vous suiviez un traitement contre le paludisme.

—Est-ce qu'il est nécessaire que j'obtienne un visa?

—Euh, non, mais il faut que vous ayez un passeport, bien sûr.

—Bon, ben, qu'est-ce qu'il faut que j'emporte?

—Eh bien, des vêtements légers, en coton de préférence.

—Est-ce qu'il est nécessaire d'emporter un manteau?

—Euh, non. Mais prenez un pull pour la nuit.

—Et quoi d'autre?

—Euh... , voyons, il faut que vous emportiez de la lotion anti-moustique et que vous preniez une trousse de premiers soins avec pansements, désinfectant et comprimés pour purifier l'eau.

—Eh bien! Je vais plutôt aller faire du camping dans le sud de la France!

Answers to Activity 13
se faire vacciner, consulter un médecin, prendre son passeport, emporter de la lotion anti-moustique, emporter une trousse de premiers soins

One-Stop Planner CD-ROM

To preview all resources available for this chapter, use the **One-Stop Planner CD-ROM**, Disc 2.

Deuxième étape

25 p. 201

1. Oh dis donc! Regarde un peu! Qu'est-ce qu'elle est rapide, cette gazelle!

2. Oh là là! Il fait chaud et j'ai soif. Quand est-ce qu'on retourne à l'hôtel?

3. Est-ce qu'il y a des serpents? J'ai peur des serpents, tu sais.

4. Qu'est-ce qu'elle est drôle, cette autruche!

5. Ah non! Je n'en peux plus, moi! Ça fait trois heures qu'on les attend, les éléphants!

6. Ouah! C'est fou comme elle est grande, cette girafe!

7. Oh, tu as vu? Le lion est en train de tuer le gnou. Je ne peux pas regarder ça.

8. Tu as vu comme il court vite, ce guépard?

Answers to Activity 25

1. oui	4. oui	7. non
2. non	5. non	8. oui
3. non	6. oui	

28 p. 202

a. 1. Je vous signale qu'il ne faut pas sortir de la voiture.

2. Faites gaffe! Il y a des scorpions. N'oubliez pas de regarder où vous marchez.

3. Calmez-vous! Les éléphants sont gros, mais ils ont peur de vous.

4. N'ayez pas peur. Les singes vont crier s'il y a un danger.

5. Attention aux rhinocéros! Ils sont méchants!

6. Méfiez-vous! Les hyènes ne sont pas grandes, mais elles sont vraiment méchantes!

b. 1. J'ai très peur des animaux sauvages. Ils sont imprévisibles!

2. Ouf! On a eu chaud! Tu as vu comme il était furieux, le rhinocéros?

3. Oh! Il fait tellement noir! J'ai la frousse! Tu entends ces bruits? C'est un animal, tu crois?

4. On a eu de la chance! Ça arrive souvent que les jeeps tombent en panne?

5. J'ai peur que ce soit un scorpion. On peut mourir d'une piqûre de scorpion, non?

6. Ouf! On l'a échappé belle! N'arrête pas la voiture la prochaine fois, d'accord?

Answers to Activity 28

a. 1. avertit	3. rassure	5. avertit
2. avertit	4. rassure	6. avertit
b. 1. peur	3. peur	5. peur
2. soulagement	4. soulagement	6. soulagement

Mise en pratique

3 p. 213

1. —Et voilà les chutes de Boali. Qu'est-ce qu'elles sont belles! On y a fait un pique-nique. Je n'avais jamais vu d'aussi grandes chutes d'eau. C'était merveilleux!

2. —Et là, c'est notre premier jour dans la brousse. Vous voyez les lions qui dorment? On y est restés deux heures. Ils n'ont pas bougé d'un pouce. C'était mortel.

3. —Là, c'est le jour où on est allés dans la forêt tropicale. On se promenait et tout d'un coup, juste devant nous, on a vu des Pygmées! Ouah! Imaginez un peu! On a même parlé avec eux. Qu'est-ce qu'ils étaient gentils!

4. —Oh ça, c'était le deuxième jour dans la savane. Vous voyez, il n'y avait pas d'animaux! On a attendu pendant des heures. Il faisait chaud. C'était pas amusant!

5. —Ça, c'est ma photo préférée de la forêt. Qu'est-ce qu'elle est belle, cette forêt! Il y avait des papillons partout! Ils étaient super grands! Je n'avais jamais vu de papillons aussi grands!

6. —Et là, c'est l'endroit où nous avons dormi. C'était vraiment horrible! Il y avait des fourmis, des araignées et beaucoup de moustiques. J'avais oublié ma lotion anti-moustique! Et en plus, il y avait des babouins qui arrêtaient pas de s'approcher de notre tente!

Answers to Mise en pratique Activity 3

a, c, e

Chapitre 7 : Un safari-photo
Suggested Lesson Plans 50-Minute Schedule

Day 1

CHAPTER OPENER 5 min.
- Present Chapter Objectives, p. 187.
- Geography Link, ATE, p. 186
- Thinking Critically: Drawing Inferences, ATE, p. 187

MISE EN TRAIN 40 min.
- Presenting **Mise en train**, ATE, p. 188, using Video Program, Videocassette 3. See Using Prior Knowledge, ATE, p. 188.
- See Teaching Suggestions, Viewing Suggestions 1–2, Video Guide, p. 42.
- Culture Note and Language Notes, ATE, p. 189
- See Teaching Suggestions, Post-viewing Suggestions 1–3, Video Guide, p. 42.
- Do Activities 1–5, p. 190.
- Read and discuss **Note culturelle**, p. 190.

Wrap-Up 5 min.
- Do Activity 6, p. 190.

Homework Options
Cahier d'activités, Act. 1, p. 73

Day 2

MISE EN TRAIN
Quick Review 5 min.
- Check homework.

RENCONTRE CULTURELLE 20 min.
- Presenting **Rencontre culturelle**, ATE, p. 191
- **Qu'en penses-tu?**, p. 191
- Read and discuss **Savais-tu que...?**, p. 191
- Culture Notes and Language Note, ATE, p. 191
- History Link, ATE, p. 191

PREMIERE ETAPE
Vocabulaire, p. 192 20 min.
- Presenting **Vocabulaire**, ATE, p. 192
- Play Audio CD for Activity 7, p. 192.
- Travaux pratiques de grammaire, pp. 63–64, Activities 1–3
- Do Activity 8, p. 192.

Wrap-Up, 5 min.
- See Suggestions for Using Teaching Transparency 7-1, Listening Activity 2, Teaching Transparencies.

Homework Options
Cahier d'activités, Act. 2, p. 74

Day 3

PREMIERE ETAPE
Quick Review 5 min.
- Check homework.

Comment dit-on... ? and **Note de grammaire, p. 193** 25 min.
- Presenting **Comment dit-on... ?**, ATE, p. 193
- Play Audio CD for Activity 9, p. 193.
- Read and discuss **Note de grammaire,** p. 193.
- Travaux pratiques de grammaire, pp. 64–65, Activity 4
- Have students do Activity 10, p. 193, in pairs.

Vocabulaire, p. 194 15 min.
- Presenting **Vocabulaire**, ATE, p. 194
- Play Audio CD for Activity 11, p. 194.
- Cahier d'activités, p. 75, Activity 4
- Do Activity 12, p. 194.

Wrap-Up 5 min.
- Game: **Laissez tomber!**, ATE, p. 194

Homework Options
Cahier d'activités, Act. 3, pp. 74–75
Travaux pratiques de grammaire, Acts. 5–6, pp. 65–66

Day 4

PREMIERE ETAPE
Quick Review 5 min.
- Check homework.

Comment dit-on... ?, p. 195 15 min
- Presenting **Comment dit-on... ?**, ATE, p. 195
- Play Audio CD for Activity 13, p. 195.
- Cahier d'activités, p. 76, Activity 5
- Do Activity 14, p. 195.

Grammaire, p. 196 20 min.
- Presenting **Grammaire**, ATE, p. 196
- Do Activity 15, p. 196.
- Travaux pratiques de grammaire, pp. 67–68, Activities 8–9
- Cahier d'activités, p. 76, Activity 6
- Have students do Activity 16, p. 196, in pairs.

Wrap-Up 10 min.
- Game: **Il faudrait que vous...**, ATE, p. 196

Homework Options
Study for Quiz 7-1
Grammaire supplémentaire, Acts. 1–4, pp. 208–209
Travaux pratiques de grammaire, Act. 7, pp. 66–67

Day 5

PREMIERE ETAPE
Quiz 7-1 20 min.
- Administer Quiz 7-1A or 7-1B.

PANORAMA CULTUREL 25 min.
- See Teaching Suggestions, Pre-viewing Suggestions 1–2, Video Guide, pp. 42–43.
- Presenting **Panorama Culturel**, ATE, p. 197
- See Teaching Suggestions, Viewing Suggestions 1–2, Video Guide, p. 43
- Questions, ATE, p. 197
- **Qu'en penses-tu?**, p. 197

Wrap-Up 5 min.
- Post-viewing Suggestion 1, Video Guide, p. 43

Homework Options
Cahier d'activités, Act. 17, p. 84

Day 6

PREMIERE ETAPE
Quick Review 5 min.
- Check homework.

REMISE EN TRAIN 20 min.
- Presenting **Remise en train**, ATE, p. 198
- Culture Note, ATE, p. 199
- Do Activities 17–20, pp. 198–199.
- Biology Link, ATE, p. 199
- Do Activity 21, p. 199.

DEUXIEME ETAPE
Vocabulaire, p. 200 20 min.
- Presenting **Vocabulaire**, ATE, p. 200
- Do Activities 22–23, pp. 200–201.
- Cahier d'activités, pp. 79–80, Activities 10–11
- Have students do Activity 24, p. 201, in pairs.

Wrap-Up 5 min.
- Poetry Link, ATE, p. 200

Homework Options
Travaux pratiques de grammaire, Acts. 10–11, p. 69

 **One-Stop** Planner CD-ROM

For alternative lesson plans by chapter section, to create your own customized plans, or to preview all resources available for this chapter, use the **One-Stop Planner CD-ROM, Disc 2.**

 For additional homework suggestions, see activities accompanied by this symbol throughout the chapter.

Day 7

DEUXIEME ETAPE
Quick Review 5 min.
• Check homework.

Comment dit-on... ?, p. 201 20 min.
• Presenting **Comment dit-on... ?,** ATE, p. 201
• Read and discuss **A la française,** p. 201.
• Play Audio CD for Activity 25, p. 201.
• Cahier d'activités, p. 81, Activity 12
• Do Activities 26–27, p. 201.

Comment dit-on... ?, p. 202 20 min.
• Presenting **Comment dit-on... ?,** ATE, p. 202
• Play Audio CD for Activity 28, p. 202.
• Cahier d'activités, p. 81, Activity 13
• Do Activities 29–30, p. 202.

Wrap-Up 5 min.
• Challenge, ATE, p. 202

Homework Options
Travaux pratiques de grammaire, Acts. 12–13, p. 70

Day 8

DEUXIEME ETAPE
Quick Review 5 min.
• Check homework.

Grammaire, p. 203 30 min.
• Presenting **Grammaire,** ATE, p. 203
• Do Activity 31, p. 203.
• Travaux pratiques de grammaire, pp. 71–72, Activities 14–16
• Cahier d'activités, p. 82, Activity 14
• Have students do Activity 32, p. 203, in pairs.

Wrap-Up 15 min
• Game: **Catégories,** ATE, p. 203

Homework Options
Study for Quiz 7-2
Grammaire supplémentaire, Acts. 5–8, pp. 210–211.

Day 9

DEUXIEME ETAPE
Quiz 7-2 20 min.
• Administer Quiz 7-2A or 7-2B.

LISONS! 25 min.
• Read and discuss **Stratégie pour lire,** p. 204.
• Do Prereading Activity A, p. 204.
• Culture Note, ATE, p. 204
• Have students read **Lisons!,** pp. 204–206.
• Do Reading Activities B–Q, pp. 204–206.

Wrap-Up 5 min.
• Additional Practice, ATE, p. 205

Homework Options
Cahier d'activités, Act. 16, p. 83

Day 10

DEUXIEME ETAPE
Quick Review 5 min.
• Check homework.

LISONS! 20 min.
• Do Activity R, p. 206.
• Thinking Critically: Comparing and Contrasting, ATE, p. 206

ECRIVONS! 20 min.
• Read and discuss the **Stratégie pour écrire,** p. 207, then have students work on their stories.

Wrap-Up 5 min.
• Allow time for peer and self-evaluation of student stories.

Homework Options
Complete final draft of stories.

Day 11

ECRIVONS!
Quick Review 5 min.
• Have volunteers share their stories with the class.

MISE EN PRATIQUE 40 min.
• Do Activities 1–2, p. 212.
• Ecology Link, ATE, p. 212
• Play Audio CD for Activity 3, p. 213.
• Have students do Activity 4, p. 213, in pairs.

Wrap-Up 5 min.
• Begin Activity 5, p. 213.

Homework Options
Complete Activity 5, p. 213
Que sais-je?, p. 214

Day 12

MISE EN PRATIQUE
Quick Review 20 min.
• Collect homework and go over **Que sais-je?,** p. 214.
• Have students do **Jeu de rôle,** p. 213 in small groups.

Chapter Review 30 min.
• Review Chapter 7. Choose from **Grammaire supplémentaire,** Grammar Tutor for Students of French, Activities for Communication, Listening Activities, Interactive CD-ROM Tutor, or **Jeux interactifs.**

Homework Options
Study for Chapter 7 Test.

Assessment

Test, Chapter 7 50 min.
• Administer Chapter 7 Test. Select from Testing Program, Alternative Assessment Guide, Test Generator, or Standardized Assessment Tutor.

Chapitre 7 : Un safari-photo
Suggested Lesson Plans *90-Minute Block Schedule*

Block 1

CHAPTER OPENER   10 min.
- Present Chapter Objectives, p. 187
- Geography Link and Thinking Critically: Drawing Inferences, ATE, pp. 186–187

MISE EN TRAIN   40 min.
- Presenting **Mise en train,** ATE, p. 188
- Language Notes and Culture Note, ATE, p. 189
- Do Activities 1–5, p. 190.

PREMIERE ETAPE
Vocabulaire, p. 192   20 min.
- Presenting **Vocabulaire,** ATE, p. 192
- Play Audio CD for Activity 7, p. 192.
- Do Activity 8, p. 192.

RENCONTRE CULTURELLE   15 min.
- Presenting **Rencontre culturelle,** ATE, p. 191

Wrap-Up   5 min.
- See Suggestions for Using Teaching Transparency 7-1, Listening Activity 2, Teaching Transparencies.

Homework Options
Cahier d'activités, pp. 73–74, Acts. 1–2
Travaux pratiques de grammaire, pp. 63–64, Acts. 1–3

Block 2

PREMIERE ETAPE
Quick Review   5 min.
- Have students identify each item as you hold up illustrations of the vocabulary items from **Vocabulaire,** p. 192.

Comment dit-on... ?, p. 193   30 min.
- Presenting **Comment dit-on... ?,** ATE, p. 193
- Play Audio CD for Activity 9, p. 193.
- Read and discuss **Note de grammaire,** p. 193.
- Do Activity 10, p. 193.

Vocabulaire, p. 194   30 min.
- Presenting **Vocabulaire,** ATE, p. 194
- Play Audio CD for Activity 11, p. 194.
- Do Activity 12, p. 194.

Comment dit-on... ?, p. 195   20 min.
- Presenting **Comment dit-on... ?,** ATE, p. 195
- Slower Pace, ATE, p. 195
- Play Audio CD for Activity 13, p. 195.
- Do Activity 14, p. 195

Wrap-Up   5 min.
- Challenge, ATE, p. 195

Homework Options
Pupil's Edition, Activity 14, p. 195
Cahier d'activités, pp. 74–76, Acts. 3–5
Travaux pratiques de grammaire, pp. 65–67, Acts. 4–7

Block 3

PREMIERE ETAPE
Quick Review   10 min.
- Activities for Communication, pp. 25–26, Communicative Activity 7-1A and 7-1B

Grammaire, p. 196   25 min.
- Presenting **Grammaire,** ATE, p. 196
- Do Activities 15–16, p. 196.

PANORAMA CULTUREL   15 min.
- Presenting **Panorama Culturel,** ATE, p. 197
- Read and discuss **Qu'en penses-tu?,** p. 197.

REMISE EN TRAIN   35 min.
- Presenting **Remise en train,** ATE, p. 198
- Culture Note and Biology Link, ATE, p. 199
- Do Activities 17–20, pp. 198–199.

Wrap-Up   5 min.
- Game: **Il faudrait que vous...,** ATE, p. 196

Homework Options
Have students study for Quiz 7-1.
Grammaire supplémentaire, pp. 208–209, Acts. 2–4
Cahier d'activités, pp. 76–78, Acts. 6–9
Travaux pratiques de grammaire, p. 68, Acts. 8–9

One-Stop Planner CD-ROM

For alternative lesson plans by chapter section, to create your own customized plans, or to preview all resources available for this chapter, use the **One-Stop Planner CD-ROM**, Disc 2.

For additional homework suggestions, see activities accompanied by this symbol throughout the chapter.

Block 4

PREMIERE ETAPE
Quick Review 10 min.
- Listening Activities, p. 56, Additional Listening Activity 7-3

Quiz 7-1 20 min.
- Administer Quiz 7-1A or 7-1B.

DEUXIEME ETAPE
Vocabulaire, p. 200 30 min.
- Presenting **Vocabulaire**, ATE, p. 200
- Poetry Link, ATE, p. 200
- Do Activities 22–23, pp. 200–201.

Comment dit-on... ?, p. 201 25 min.
- Presenting **Comment dit-on... ?,** ATE, p. 201
- Language-to-Language, ATE, p. 201
- Play Audio CD for Activity 25, p. 201.
- Additional Practice, ATE, p. 201

Wrap-Up 5 min.
- Teaching Transparency 7-2, using suggestion #2 on Suggestions for Using Teaching Transparency 7-2

Homework Options
Grammaire supplèmentaire, p. 208, Act. 1
Cahier d'activités, pp. 79–81, Acts. 10–12
Travaux pratiques de grammaire, pp. 69–70, Acts. 10–13

Block 5

DEUXIEME ETAPE
Quick Review 10 min.
- Activities for Communication, pp. 27–28, Communicative Activity 7-2A and 7-2B

Comment dit-on... ?, p. 201 15 min.
- Do Activity 26, p. 201.

Comment dit-on... ?, p. 202 25 min.
- Presenting **Comment dit-on... ?,** ATE, p. 202
- Play Audio CD for Activity 28, p. 202
- Do Activities 29–30, p. 202.

Grammaire, p. 203 35 min.
- Presenting **Grammaire**, ATE, p. 203
- Do Activities 31–32, p. 203.

Wrap-Up 5 min.
- Listening Activities, p. 57, Additional Listening Activity 7-6

Homework Options
Pupil's Edition, Activity 27, p. 201
Have students study for Quiz 7-2.
Grammaire supplémentaire, pp. 210–211, Acts. 5–8
Cahier d'activités, p. 82, Acts. 14–15
Travaux pratiques de grammaire, pp. 71–72, Acts. 14–16

Block 6

DEUXIEME ETAPE
Quick Review 10 min.
- Game: **Catégories**, ATE, p. 203

Quiz 7-2 20 min.
- Administer Quiz 7-2A or 7-2B.

LISONS! 25 min.
- Have students read and discuss **Stratégie pour lire**, p. 204.
- Do Prereading Activities A and B, p. 204.
- Have students read **Lisons!**, pp. 204–205.
- Do Reading Activities C, E, and I, pp. 204–205.

MISE EN PRATIQUE 35 min.
- Play Audio CD for Activity 3, p. 213.
- Do Activities 4–5, p. 213.

Homework Options
Pupil's Edition, Acts. 1–2, p. 212
Que sais-je?, p. 214
Study for Chapter 7 Test.

Block 7

MISE EN PRATIQUE
Quick Review 10 min.
- Have students continue to work on Activity 2, p. 212.

Chapter Review 35 min.
- Review Chapter 7. Choose from **Grammaire supplémentaire**, Grammar Tutor for Students of French, Activities for Communication, Listening Activities, Interactive CD-ROM Tutor, or **Jeux interactifs.**

Test, Chapter 7 45 min.
- Administer Chapter 7 Test. Select from Testing Program, Alternative Assessment Guide, Test Generator, or Standardized Assessment Tutor.

Chapter Opener

 One-Stop Planner CD-ROM

For resource information, see the **One-Stop Planner**, Disc 2.

Pacing Tips

In this chapter, the first **étape** has more material than the second **étape**. You might keep that in mind when planning your lessons. For Lesson Plans and timing suggestions, see pages 185I–185L.

Meeting the Standards

Communication
- Making suppositions; expressing doubt and certainty, p. 193
- Asking for and giving advice, p. 195
- Expressing astonishment, p. 201
- Cautioning someone; expressing fear; reassuring someone; expressing relief, p. 202

Cultures
- Culture Notes, pp. 189, 191, 199, 204, 213
- Note culturelle, p. 190
- Panorama Culturel, p. 197
- Rencontre culturelle, p. 191

Connections
- History Link, p. 191
- Literature Link, p. 207
- Geography Link, p. 186
- Biology Link, p. 199
- Ecology Link, p. 212
- Multicultural Link, p. 200
- Science Link, p. 192
- Poetry Link, p. 200

Comparisons
- Language-to-Language, pp. 201, 203
- Thinking Critically, pp. 187, 197, 206

Communities
- Career Path, p. 190
- Community Links, pp. 197, 203
- De l'école au travail, p. 203
- Family Link, p. 207

Connections and Comparisons

Geography Link
- Have students locate **la République centrafricaine** on the map of Africa on page xxv in their book, or *Map Transparency 4* (**L'Afrique francophone**). Re-enter *asking for information* and *describing a place* by asking questions, such as **Où se trouve la République centrafricaine? C'est au nord ou au sud de la République démocratique du Congo?**

- Have students recall what they already know about Africa. You might ask them to recall what they learned about Côte d'Ivoire in Levels 1 and 2, and what they learned about Senegal and Morocco in Level 3. Ask them what there is to see and do in these countries. (**Qu'est-ce qu'il y a à voir et à faire là-bas?**)

CHAPITRE

7

Un safari-photo

Objectives

In this chapter you will learn to

Première étape

- make suppositions
- express doubt and certainty
- ask for and give advice

Deuxième étape

- express astonishment
- caution someone
- express fear
- reassure someone
- express relief

ADRESSE: go.hrw.com
MOT-CLE: WA3 FRANCOPHONE AFRICA-7

◀ **Un safari-photo en Afrique**

Focusing on Outcomes
Have students list expressions they've already learned that serve the functions listed on this page. (*making suppositions:* **Je crois que... ; Je parie que...** ; *expressing doubt and certainty:* **C'est possible. Je ne crois pas;** *asking for and giving advice:* **Qu'est-ce que tu me conseilles? Tu devrais...** ; *expressing astonishment:* **C'est pas vrai;** *cautioning:* **Tu ne devrais pas...** ; *expressing fear:* **J'ai peur de...** ; *reassuring someone:* **Tu vas t'y faire. Ne t'en fais pas.**)

NOTE: You may want to use the video to support the objectives. The self-check activities in **Que sais-je?** on page 214 help students assess their achievement of the objectives.

Communication for All Students

Thinking Critically
Drawing Inferences Have students tell what they would expect to see in the Central African Republic, based on the photo on pages 186–187.

Challenge
Have students search the Internet or an encyclopedia to find out what kind of wildlife and vegetation can be seen in the Central African Republic. You might suggest that they search French-speaking sites and write down the names of various animals and trees in French. Have them present their lists to the class.

Cahier d'activités, p. 73, Act. 1

CD 7 Tr. 1

Stratégie pour comprendre
Look at the title of this episode and at the photos. Can you guess the gist of this story? What are the characters planning? Why is the adult character on the phone? Why is the boy thinking of a doctor?

1

Lucie	Oh, dis donc! Regarde les éléphants!
Joseph	Oh, oui! Ils sont super! Ça serait chouette d'aller en Afrique. On verrait des tas d'animaux sauvages.
Lucie	Je parie qu'il y a des lions et des tigres partout!
Joseph	Tu sais, je ne crois pas qu'il y ait de tigres en Afrique.
Lucie	Ah, bon... Alors, Papa, on va en Afrique pour les vacances? On pourrait faire un safari.

Pour se cacher dans la savane, la girafe a des taches brunes.

2 **M. Zokoue** Ah! Bravo! Ma fille veut tuer des éléphants maintenant!

Lucie Mais non, Papa! Un safari-photo, bien sûr! Les safaris, c'est illégal! Et puis, tu sais bien que je déteste qu'on tue les animaux!

L'éléphant va boire. Avec sa trompe, il pompe 100 litres d'eau par jour.

3

Joseph	Du calme, du calme. On a compris.
M. Zokoue	De toute façon, ça coûte très cher, les safaris.
Lucie	Oh, allez, quoi!
M. Zokoue	Et puis, ça doit être très dangereux...
Joseph	Mais non, tout le monde va en Afrique maintenant. Et puis, ça serait chouette d'aller en République centrafricaine puisque c'est là où Pépé est né.
Lucie	Tu imagines si on pouvait aller dans son village pour voir comment c'est...
Joseph	Je me demande si on a encore de la famille là-bas... Tu crois qu'ils mangent des araignées?
Lucie	Ça doit être cool!
M. Zokoue	Bon, bon... on verra.

Preteaching Vocabulary

Identifying Keywords
Ask students what is going on in the story. Have them identify keywords to help them figure out the situation. Which words reveal the gist of the conversation in the opening scene? **(vacances, Afrique, safari-photo, animaux sauvages)** Which familiar words help students figure out the meanings of unfamiliar words around them? **(vaccinations, moustiques)**

vacances *vacation*
Afrique *Africa*
animaux sauvages *wild animals*
un safari-photo *photo safari*
vaccinations *vaccinations*
des moustiques *mosquitoes*
la fièvre jaune *yellow fever*
le paludisme *malaria*
une piqûre *a shot*

4 Lucie et Joseph ont persuadé leur père d'aller en République centrafricaine. Il est maintenant nécessaire qu'ils organisent leur voyage.

M. Zokoue	Bon. Si on veut faire un safari cette année, il faut que je prenne les billets maintenant. Ça vous dit toujours?
Lucie	Bien sûr que ça me dit!
M. Zokoue	Et toi, Joseph?
Joseph	Moi aussi... mais...
M. Zokoue	Qu'est-ce qu'il y a?
Joseph	Euh, je me demande s'il y aura des moustiques.
Lucie	Oh, ils ne vont pas te manger, hein?
M. Zokoue	Joseph a raison. Les moustiques sont féroces en Afrique. Ils peuvent transmettre des maladies. Il faudra bien se protéger.
Joseph	Tu vois!
M. Zokoue	Ah! Au fait, je dois appeler l'ambassade pour savoir ce qu'on doit faire avant de partir.

5

M. Zokoue	Bonjour, Madame, je pars en République centrafricaine pour les vacances.
L'employée	Oui?
M. Zokoue	Quelles sont les vaccinations obligatoires?
L'employée	Eh bien, il faut que vous vous fassiez vacciner contre la fièvre jaune.
M. Zokoue	Est-ce qu'il faut un traitement particulier pour le paludisme?
L'employée	Oui, pour ça vous devriez consulter un médecin.
M. Zokoue	Merci beaucoup. Au revoir.
Lucie	Alors, qu'est-ce qu'elle a dit? On doit se faire vacciner?
M. Zokoue	Oui, c'est obligatoire.
Joseph	Quoi! Une piqûre!
M. Zokoue	J'ai bien peur que ce soit nécessaire.

6

Joseph	Ah non, alors!
Lucie	Quel trouillard, je t'assure!
M. Zokoue	Ecoutez, c'est simple, les enfants. Pas de piqûre, pas de safari!

7 Enfin, avant de partir, il faut que M. Zokoue et ses enfants fassent leurs valises.

Joseph	Tu crois que je devrais prendre des cassettes?
M. Zokoue	Je ne crois pas que ce soit la peine. Tu n'auras pas le temps de les écouter. Mais n'oublie pas ton appareil-photo.
Lucie	Tu seras trop occupé à tuer les moustiques pour écouter de la musique.
Joseph	Oh, arrête! On ne te demande rien! Papa, tu penses que je prends un pull?
M. Zokoue	Oui, il vaut mieux. Tu en auras peut-être besoin. Il peut faire froid la nuit.
Lucie	Est-ce qu'on emporte de la crème solaire?
M. Zokoue	Bien sûr. Il va faire très chaud. Il faut aussi qu'on achète de la lotion anti-moustique. Surtout, c'est très important qu'on emporte une trousse de premiers soins avec des pansements, un désinfectant et des comprimés pour purifier l'eau.
Lucie	Eh ben! C'est vraiment l'aventure!

Language Notes

- Tell students that **Pépé,** used in the third scene, is a familiar term for *grandfather.*
- **Le paludisme,** which M. Zoukoue mentions to the employee, is *malaria,* a common disease in tropical African countries characterized by severe chills and high fever. Female mosquitos carry the disease and transmit it through their bites.

Culture Note
Although yellow fever is easily prevented by vaccination, it is still common in many African countries. Most countries in Central Africa require vaccination against the disease as a condition for entry. Visitors are also advised to take pre-travel, preventive measures against cholera, typhoid, and hepatitis.

Camille et compagnie
You may choose to show students Episode 7: *Nos amies les bêtes* now or wait until later in the chapter. In the video Laurent takes Max on a tour of a zoo, but Max says he'd rather see animals in their natural habitat. He proposes that they go to the natural reserve of Camargue. Laurent proves to be very organized and well prepared to survive in wilderness.

Using the Captioned Video

 As an alternative, you might want to show the captioned version of *Camille et compagnie : Nos amies les bêtes* on Videocassette 5. Some students may benefit from seeing the written words as they listen to the target language and watch the gestures and actions in context. This visual reinforcement of vocabulary and functions will facilitate students' comprehension and help reduce their anxiety before they are formally introduced to the new language in the chapter.

Teaching Suggestion

2 As an alternative, rewrite these sentences on a transparency, omitting key words, such as **tigres, dangereux, moustiques, trouillard, piqûre**. List the omitted words below the sentences and have students complete the sentences with the appropriate words.

Auditory Learners

2 Read the quotations aloud and have students identify the speakers.

Career Path

Ask students if they would like to work in countries whose cultures are very different from their own. Ask them if they have heard of programs where students can work abroad as volunteers. If so, have them tell what they know about the work of these organizations, the requirements of such work, and the benefits.

Answers

3 *Un pull :* Il peut faire froid la nuit. *De la lotion anti-moustique :* Les moustiques sont féroces et ils peuvent transmettre des maladies. *De la crème solaire :* Il va faire très chaud. *Des pansements :* C'est très important qu'on emporte une trousse de premiers soins. *Des comprimés :* pour purifier l'eau. *Un appareil-photo :* C'est un safari-photo.

5 1. Regarde...
2. Je parie que... ; Ça doit être...
3. ... je ne crois pas que...
4. Mais non... ; Ah non, alors! Je déteste que...
5. Du calme, du calme.
6. ... il faut que... ; Il faudra bien... ; ... je dois... ; ... vous devriez... ; J'ai bien peur que ça soit nécessaire. C'est très important que...
7. Est-ce qu'il faut... ? Tu crois que je devrais... ? ... tu penses que je prends... ? Est-ce qu'on emporte... ?
8. ... il faut que vous... ; Je ne crois pas que ce soit la peine. ... il vaut mieux. Il faut qu'on... ; ... c'est important qu'on...

---

1 **Tu as compris?** These activities check for comprehension only. Students should not yet be expected to produce language modeled in **Mise en train.**
1. Où va la famille Zokoue pour les vacances? Central African Republic
2. Qu'est-ce que les Zokoue vont faire pendant les vacances? go on a photo safari
3. Pourquoi M. Zokoue hésite à partir? It's expensive and dangerous.
4. Qu'est-ce que Lucie et Joseph disent à leur père pour le persuader de partir en vacances?
5. Qu'est-ce qu'ils doivent faire avant de partir en vacances?
buy the tickets, get vaccinations, pack

4. A lot of people go to Africa. Their grandfather was born there.

2 **Qui dit quoi?**
Est-ce que c'est Lucie, Joseph ou M. Zokoue qui parle?
1. «Je parie qu'il y a des lions et des tigres partout!» Lucie
2. «De toute façon, ça coûte très cher, les safaris. Et puis, ça doit être très dangereux.» M. Zokoue
3. «Euh, je me demande s'il y aura des moustiques.» Joseph
4. «Quel trouillard, je t'assure!» Lucie
5. «Ecoutez, c'est simple. Pas de piqûre, pas de safari!» M. Zokoue

3 **Qu'est-ce qu'on emporte?**
D'après *Un safari, ça se prépare!*, lesquels de ces objets est-ce que les Zokoue vont emporter en Afrique? Pourquoi? See answers below.

> une robe   un pull   des cassettes
> de la lotion anti-moustique   des bottes
> de la crème solaire   des pansements
> des comprimés
> de l'aspirine   un appareil-photo

4 **Mets dans le bon ordre**
Mets ces phrases dans le bon ordre d'après *Un safari, ça se prépare!* 3, 1, 4, 5, 2
1. Lucie et Joseph proposent de passer les vacances en République centrafricaine.
2. Les Zokoue font leurs valises.
3. Lucie et Joseph lisent un article sur l'Afrique.
4. Joseph se demande s'il y aura des moustiques.
5. M. Zokoue téléphone à l'ambassade.

5 **Cherche les expressions**
What do Lucie, Joseph, and M. Zokoue say to . . . See answers below.
1. point out something?
2. make a supposition?
3. express doubt?
4. make a strong objection?
5. reassure someone?
6. express necessity?
7. ask for advice?
8. give advice?

6 **Et maintenant, à toi**
Est-ce que tu aimerais faire un safari-photo? Pourquoi ou pourquoi pas? Quels animaux est-ce que tu aimerais voir?

Note culturelle

Il y a beaucoup d'animaux sauvages en République centrafricaine. Dans le nord du pays, il y a la savane où on peut voir des lions, des léopards, des buffles, des éléphants, des hyènes et des antilopes. Dans le sud, la forêt tropicale abrite une des dernières colonies de gorilles d'Afrique. Dans la forêt, on trouve aussi beaucoup de chimpanzés, d'autres types de singes et des écureuils géants. Au bord des rivières, il y a des hippopotames, des crocodiles et des rhinocéros. Dans tout le pays, on peut voir de nombreuses espèces d'oiseaux, de serpents, de chauves-souris et de papillons. La République centrafricaine est un vrai paradis zoologique.

Comprehension Check

Slower Pace

3 On a transparency, list the reasons why the Zokoues are taking the various items with them and have students match the reasons with the items listed in the word box.

Auditory Learners

5 Play the recording of *Un safari, ça se prépare.* Pausing it each time one of the functional expressions is used, ask students which function is represented by that expression.

Rencontre culturelle

Qu'est-ce que tu sais sur la République centrafricaine? Pour t'en faire une meilleure idée, regarde ces photos.

Bangui est une grande ville moderne.

Les ouvriers agricoles récoltent des grains de café, l'un des produits d'exportation essentiels.

Les traditions africaines sont observées lors de nombreuses cérémonies.

L'Oubangui, source de vie

Qu'en penses-tu?

1. Quelles impressions ces photos te donnent de la République centrafricaine?
2. D'après ces photos, quelles sont les activités des habitants de la République centrafricaine? Quels sont leurs moyens de subsistance?

> 1. *Possible answers:* The Central African Republic has modern cities as well as traditional villages. The Oubangui river is an important geographic feature. Agriculture is important economically. 2. shopping, ceremonies; business, agriculture, fishing

Savais-tu que... ?

La République centrafricaine est située à l'intérieur de l'Afrique. Elle partage ses frontières avec le Cameroun, le Congo, la République démocratique du Congo, le Soudan et le Tchad. La rivière Oubangui joue un rôle important dans l'économie de la République centrafricaine. Elle fournit l'eau douce et permet la pêche et le transport de produits d'exportation comme les diamants, le café, le bois et le coton. La République centrafricaine est composée de nombreux groupes ethniques comme les Mbakas, les Bandas et les Mandjas. Il y a aussi les Pygmées, un des plus anciens groupes ethniques d'Afrique. C'est un peuple de petite taille qui habite dans la forêt tropicale. Le français est la langue officielle du gouvernement centrafricain et du système éducatif, mais le sangho est la langue nationale. C'est la langue la plus parlée en République centrafricaine.

Using Prior Knowledge

The day before the presentation, ask students to find out one fact about the Central African Republic. The day of the presentation, have students share their findings. You might ask students for their reactions to the information.

Presenting
Rencontre culturelle

Have students read the photo captions and write down the cognates they find. Explain any words students don't understand. Then, have groups write an additional sentence for each caption. Have them read their captions aloud. Finally, have partners read the paragraph under **Savais-tu que... ?**

Teaching Suggestion

Create a categorizing activity based on **Savais-tu que... ?** Write the categories *National language, Official language, Exports,* and *Ethnic groups* on the board and have students list the appropriate items under each one. *(French; Sango; diamonds, coffee, wood, cotton; Baya, Banda, Mandja, Ubangi)*

Language Note

Although French is the official language of the Central African Republic, **Sango** is the national language. The country is one of the few African countries whose diverse ethnic groups get along well, primarily because of the existence of this common language.

Cultures and Communities

History Link

The Central African Republic was granted its independence in 1960, after being a French colony for almost fifty years. Until that time, it was part of French Equatorial Africa and was known as **Oubangui-Chari.** The variety of ethnic groups in the country, as in other countries in Africa, is due to the migration of people from the coasts of Africa who fled the slave trade.

Culture Notes

• Bangui, the capital of the Central African Republic, is a major commercial and industrial center. It also has the **musée de Boganda,** which displays African musical instruments and Pygmy utensils.

• The Banda society is primarily agrarian. They grow corn, cassava, peanuts, and sweet potatoes.

Première étape

Objectives Making suppositions; expressing doubt and certainty; asking for and giving advice

WA3 FRANCOPHONE AFRICA-7

Teaching Resources
pp. 192–196

PRINT
▸ Lesson Planner, p. 33
▸ Listening Activities, pp. 51–52, 55–56
▸ Activities for Communication, pp. 25–26, 69, 71, 101–102
▸ Travaux pratiques de grammaire, pp. 63–68
▸ Grammar Tutor for Students of French, Chapter 7
▸ Cahier d'activités, pp. 74–77
▸ Testing Program, pp. 147–150
▸ Alternative Assessment Guide, p. 36
▸ Student Make-Up Assignments, Chapter 7

MEDIA
▸ One-Stop Planner
▸ Audio Compact Discs, CD 7, Trs. 2–5, 14, 19–21
▸ Teaching Transparencies: 7-1; **Grammaire supplémentaire** Answers; Travaux pratiques de grammaire Answers
▸ Interactive CD-ROM Tutor, Disc 2

Bell Work

Have students write a five-sentence letter to a friend who is planning a trip to Africa. They should tell what clothing to bring and what sites to see in African countries.

Presenting
Vocabulaire

Find pictures of the vocabulary items. As you show them, ask questions, such as **Un papillon, c'est beau ou dangereux?** Next, give examples of the vocabulary items, such as Woody Woodpecker, the Seine, or maple, and have students categorize each one.

Vocabulaire

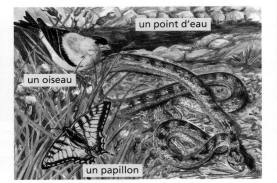

une araignée — une mouche — un point d'eau — un oiseau — l'herbe (f.) — des fourmis (f.) — un papillon

la forêt tropicale | **la savane**

un arbre **la brousse** **un moustique** **une rivière** **un serpent** **la végétation tropicale**

Travaux pratiques de grammaire, pp. 63–64, Act. 1–3 | Cahier d'activités, p. 74, Act. 2

---

7 **Forêt ou savane?** See scripts and answers on p. 185G.

Ecoutons Ecoute ces touristes qui visitent la République centrafricaine. Est-ce qu'ils se trouvent dans la forêt tropicale ou dans la savane?

CD 7 Tr. 2

8 **Mais il y a plein de bêtes!**

Parlons Complète la conversation entre Joseph et Lucie en employant les images données.

JOSEPH Un safari, c'est une bonne idée, mais il y a tellement d'insectes! Ecoute! Il y a des centaines de . On peut attraper le paludisme, tu sais.
moustiques

LUCIE Bon. On peut se faire vacciner.

fourmis   araignées
JOSEPH Et puis, il y a des et des . Je parie qu'il y a même des scorpions!

LUCIE Il faut que tu fasses attention, c'est tout.

serpents   mouches
JOSEPH Tu sais bien que j'ai peur des . Et n'oublie pas les tsé-tsé. On pourrait mourir, quoi.

LUCIE Ecoute! Si tu veux, tu peux toujours rester à la maison!

Connections and Comparisons

Science Link

The tse-tse fly, mentioned in Joseph's last line of the dialogue in Activity 8, is a carrier of the sleeping sickness virus.

You might have students look for information on the Internet or in an encyclopedia about the tse-tse fly and/or other insects found in that region of Africa. Ask them what they know about the rain forest and what animals they would expect to see there. Ask them what animals can be found both in the rain forest and in their own region.

STANDARDS: 1.2, 3.1

Comment dit-on...?

Making suppositions; expressing doubt and certainty

To make a supposition:

> **On pourrait sûrement** faire une balade
> s'il fait beau.
> **Je parie qu'**il y a des serpents.
> **Ça doit être** magnifique.
> *It must be . . .*
> **Il doit y avoir** des lions.
> *There must be . . .*

To express doubt:

> **Ça m'étonnerait qu'**il y ait des ours.
> *I'd be surprised if . . .*
> **Je ne suis pas sûr(e) que** ce soit une bonne
> idée. *I'm not sure that . . .*
> **Je ne suis pas certain(e) qu'**il y fasse chaud la
> nuit. *I'm not certain that . . .*
> **Je ne pense pas qu'**on puisse sortir de la jeep.
> *I don't think that . . .*

To express certainty:

> **Je suis certain(e) qu'**il y aura des lions.
> *I'm certain that . . .*
> **Je suis sûr(e) qu'**il y pleut beaucoup.
> *I'm sure that . . .*
> **Je sais qu'**il y a des moustiques.
> **Je suis convaincu(e) que** c'est dangereux.
> *I'm convinced that . . .*

Cahier d'activités,
pp. 74–75, Act. 3

Note de grammaire

How do you know which verb form to use
after new expressions you learn?

* If there's only one subject, the second verb
  is in the infinitive: Je sais **prendre** des
  photos.
* If there are two clauses, with a different
  subject in each clause, you'll have to
  decide whether the second verb should be
  in the subjunctive or indicative mood.

  > Je sais qu'il y **a** des moustiques.
  > Ça m'étonnerait qu'il y **ait** des ours.

* Look for patterns to help you decide
  which verb form to use. For example,
  expressions used to express doubt usually
  take the subjunctive. Expressions that convey certainty usually take the indicative.

Travaux pratiques de
grammaire, pp. 64–65, Act. 4

Grammaire supplémentaire,
p. 208, Act. 1

9 **Doute ou certitude?** See scripts and answers on p. 185G.

Ecoutons Ecoute les remarques de ces gens.
Est-ce qu'ils expriment une certitude ou un
doute?

CD 7 Tr. 3

10 **Grammaire en contexte**

Parlons Ton ami(e) te propose de faire un
safari, mais ça ne te dit pas trop. Vous discutez de votre voyage éventuel en imaginant
comment ça serait.

EXEMPLE
> —Je parie que(qu')...
> —On pourrait sûrement...
> —Ça doit être...
> —Il doit y avoir...

formidable.

goûter des plats africains.

il y a des
serpents venimeux.

voir des chutes
d'eau impressionnantes.

photographier
de beaux animaux.

il y a des moustiques.

rencontrer des
gens intéressants.

intéressant.

des forêts magnifiques.

il y a des araignées.

il fait trop chaud.

Communication for All Students

Group Work

Make two posters of cartoon characters, one featuring **Dominique Doute**, the other **Cécile Sûre**.
Dominique Doute should look doubtful, and
Cécile Sûre should have an air of certainty. Have
students find pictures that inspire doubt (a picture
of Santa Claus) or certainty (a snowy landscape).

Have them write speech bubbles next to them containing expressions of **Dominique's** or **Cécile's**
reaction. (**Je ne suis pas sûr(e) que le Père Noël
existe** or **Je sais qu'il a neigé.**) Then, they should
affix the pictures to the appropriate posters.

Teaching Resources
pp. 192–196

PRINT 📖
▶ Lesson Planner, p. 33
▶ Listening Activities, pp. 51–52, 55–56
▶ Activities for Communication, pp. 25–26, 69, 71, 101–102
▶ Travaux pratiques de grammaire, pp. 63–68
▶ Grammar Tutor for Students of French, Chapter 7
▶ Cahier d'activités, pp. 74–77
▶ Testing Program, pp. 147–150
▶ Alternative Assessment Guide, p. 36
▶ Student Make-Up Assignments, Chapter 7

MEDIA 💿📼
▶ One-Stop Planner
▶ Audio Compact Discs, CD 7, Trs. 2–5, 14, 19–21
▶ Teaching Transparencies: 7-1; **Grammaire supplémentaire** Answers; Travaux pratiques de grammaire Answers
▶ Interactive CD-ROM Tutor, Disc 2

Presenting
Vocabulaire

Bring to class the vocabulary items or pictures of them. Hold each item or picture up, tell students that you need this item for your trip **(Il me faut une torche.)** and have them repeat the new words after you. Then, spread the items or pictures on your desk, divide the class into two teams, and have a player from each one come to the front. Using vocabulary students know, describe one of the items on your desk without naming it. **(J'en ai besoin pour voir le soir.)** The first player to grab the correct item wins a point.

En partant pour un safari, il ne faut pas oublier d'emporter...

Travaux pratiques de grammaire, pp. 65–66, Act. 5–6

Cahier d'activités, p. 75, Act. 4

- un appareil-photo
- un imperméable
- des pansements (m.)
- de la lotion anti-moustique
- un désinfectant
- une gourde
- un caméscope et des cassettes (f.)
- une trousse de premiers soins
- des pellicules (f.)
- des lunettes (f.) de soleil
- de la crème solaire
- une torche
- des jumelles (f.)
- une carte de crédit
- un passeport
- des chèques (m.) de voyage

11 **Le message de Mathieu** See scripts and answers on p. 185G.

Ecoutons Mathieu laisse un message sur le répondeur de Frédéric pour lui rappeler ce qu'il doit emporter pour le safari. Fais une liste de six choses qu'il ne doit pas oublier. CD 7 Tr. 4

12 **N'oublie pas!**

Parlons Sabine se prépare pour partir faire un safari. Elle te demande de regarder sa liste et de lui dire ce qu'elle a oublié.

> caméscope, cassettes
> appareil-photo, pellicules
> jumelles
> chaussures de marche
> torche
> lotion anti-moustique
> chapeau
> crème solaire
> lunettes de soleil
> trousse de premiers soins
> gourde
> passeport
> chèques de voyage

Communication for All Students

♟ Game
Laissez tomber! Form two teams. Give each student a vocabulary item or a picture of one. You might also include additional articles of clothing that students can name in French. Have two students hold up a sheet of butcher paper between the two teams so that the members of each team can't see each other. Have the first player from each team approach the sheet and hold up his or her picture or item. When you say **Laissez tomber!**, the students holding the sheet of butcher paper lower it. The two players look at the picture the opposing player is holding and try to name the item in French. The first player to name the item correctly wins a point for his or her team. Team members are not allowed to give help. Then, the students hold up the sheet again, and the next two players take their turn.

Comment dit-on...?

Asking for and giving advice

To ask for advice:

> **Tu crois que je devrais** emporter des jumelles?
> *Do you think I should . . . ?*

> **Tu penses qu'il vaudrait mieux** se faire vacciner?
> *Do you think it'd be better to . . . ?*

To respond:

> **Je crois que ça vaut mieux.**
> *I think that's better.*
> **A mon avis, c'est plus sûr.**
> *In my opinion, it's safer.*
> **Ce n'est pas la peine.** *It's not worth it.*
> **Je ne crois pas que ce soit utile.**
> *I don't think it's worthwhile.*

To give advice:

> **Il faudrait que** tu prennes de la lotion anti-moustique. *You ought to . . .*
> **Il est très important que** tu emportes une trousse de premiers soins.
> **Il est essentiel que** tu te fasses vacciner.
> **Il est nécessaire que** tu prennes un imperméable et des bottes.

Cahier d'activités, p. 76, Act. 5

13 **Préparatifs pour l'Afrique** See scripts and answers on p. 185G.

 Ecoutons Dans une agence de voyages, tu entends cette conversation entre un client et l'employée. D'après l'employée, lesquels de CD 7 Tr. 5 ces préparatifs sont nécessaires pour aller en République centrafricaine?

14 **Cher Justin**

Ecrivons Ton correspondant, Justin, qui habite en République centrafricaine, va venir passer un mois chez toi. Il t'a envoyé cette lettre pour te demander ce qu'il doit faire comme préparatifs avant son départ. Ecris-lui une lettre et réponds à ses questions en utilisant les expressions de **Comment dit-on... ?**

See answer below.

se faire vacciner

acheter des bottes

obtenir un visa

prendre son passeport

emporter une trousse de premiers soins

prendre un manteau

consulter un médecin

emporter de la lotion anti-moustique

acheter une valise

acheter des jumelles

Bonjour de Bangui!

Hier, j'ai appris la bonne nouvelle. Je pars pour les Etats-Unis le mois prochain. Je ne sais pas trop quoi prendre. Est-ce que tu peux me donner des conseils pour les préparatifs? Est-ce que je dois demander un visa à l'ambassade américaine? Je n'ai pas encore mon passeport non plus. Tes amis parlent français? A ton avis, est-ce que je dois prendre un dictionnaire? Et comme vêtements, tu penses qu'il vaudrait mieux que je prenne des pulls et des manteaux ou des shorts et des tee-shirts? Est-ce que je dois aller voir un docteur avant de partir? Il y a beaucoup d'insectes chez toi? Tu crois que je devrais prendre de la lotion anti-moustique? Réponds-moi vite!

A bientôt,
Justin

Presenting
Comment dit-on... ?

Write **oui** and **non** on two large index cards and place them on your desk. Then, tell the students you're going on a trip to the Central African Republic. Show one of the items or pictures you used for the Presentation on page 194 and ask if you should take it along. (**Tu crois que je devrais emporter mon passeport?**) Respond using one of the new expressions (**Oui, il est essentiel que tu l'emportes.**) and place the item or picture next to the appropriate index card on your desk. Once you have used all the items and new expressions, repeat this process, using a different vacation destination. (**Je vais en Floride. Tu penses que je devrais prendre mon passeport?**) This time, write possible responses on index cards (**Non, ce n'est pas la peine/ Oui, il faudrait que tu le/la/les prennes...**) and have volunteers select an appropriate card to respond, based on your destination.

Possible answers

14 Il est essentiel que tu demandes un visa. Il est très important que tu prennes ton passeport. Prends un dictionnaire. A mon avis, c'est plus sûr. Comme vêtements, il faudrait que tu emportes des tee-shirts et des shorts. Ne va pas chez le docteur. Ce n'est pas la peine. N'emporte pas de lotion anti-moustique. Je ne crois pas que ce soit utile.

Presenting
Grammaire

Using the subjunctive Hang four posterboards around the room. Label them **Norbert Nécessité, Emile Emotion, Dominique Doute,** and **Paul Possibilité.** Write the new expressions on large cards and read them aloud, one at a time. Call on students to tape the cards to the appropriate posters. When the cards are in place, form four groups and assign a poster to each one. Groups should write several completions for each expression, according to their "characters." For **Emile Emotion,** the group might complete **J'ai peur que (qu')...** with **... un lion nous mange!**

Assess

▶ Testing Program, pp. 147–150
Quiz 7-1A, Quiz 7-1B
Audio CD 7, Tr. 14

▶ Student Make-Up Assignments, Chapter 7, Alternative Quiz

▶ Alternative Assessment Guide, p. 36

Grammaire

Using the subjunctive

You've already learned to use the subjunctive after expressions of *wishing* and *obligation*. You also use the subjunctive after many expressions of . . .

necessity:
Il est nécessaire qu'on se fasse vacciner.
Il est essentiel que...
Il est important que...
Il faudrait que...
Il vaudrait mieux que...

doubt:
Je ne crois pas qu'il y **ait** des tigres.
Je ne pense pas que...
Ça m'étonnerait que...
Je ne suis pas sûr(e) que...
Je ne suis pas certain(e) que...

possibility:
Il est possible que ce **soit** dangereux.
Il se peut que...

emotion:
Je suis désolé(e) que tu ne puisses pas venir.
Je suis heureux(-euse) que...
J'ai peur que...

Travaux pratiques de grammaire, pp. 66–67, Act. 7

Si tu as oublié the subjunctive va à la page 69.

Cahier d'activités, pp. 76–77, Act. 6–8

Grammaire supplémentaire, pp. 208–209, Act. 2–4

Travaux pratiques de grammaire, pp. 67–68, Act. 8–9

15 Grammaire en contexte

Parlons Lucie et Joseph parlent de leur voyage en Afrique. Choisis une proposition qui pourrait compléter chaque phrase ci-dessous. See answers below.

1. «Il faudrait que(qu')...
2. «Je suis sûr(e) que(qu')...
3. «Je suis désolé(e) que(qu')...
4. «J'ai peur que(qu')...
5. «Il se peut que(qu')...
6. «Je crois bien que(qu')...

il y a de beaux animaux.»

tu restes dans la jeep.»

on se fasse vacciner.»

tu ne puisses pas venir.»

on partira en safari.»

il fasse trop chaud.»

on va goûter des plats africains.»

16 On part en Afrique!

a. Parlons Tu veux faire un safari, mais tu dois convaincre ton ami(e) qui n'a pas très envie de t'accompagner. Dis-lui ce que tu crois que vous pourrez y faire et y voir.

b. Parlons Vous avez décidé de faire le safari! Maintenant, discutez de ce qu'il faut que vous fassiez avant de partir. Demande à ton ami(e) ce que tu devrais emporter.

Communication for All Students

Game
Il faudrait que vous... Begin the game by saying **Je vais en République centrafricaine. Qu'est-ce que je dois faire?** The first student gives advice, such as **Il faudrait que vous vous fassiez vacciner.** The second student repeats the first piece of advice and adds another. (**Il faudrait que vous vous fassiez vacciner et il est essentiel que vous emportiez un appareil-photo.**) A player is out when he or she makes a mistake.

Possible answers

15 1. *Il faudrait qu(e)* : tu restes dans la jeep/on se fasse vacciner.

2. *Je suis sûr(e) qu(e)* : il y a de beaux animaux/on partira en safari.

3. *Je suis désolé(e) qu(e)* : tu ne puisses pas venir.

4. *J'ai peur qu(e)* : tu ne puisses pas venir/il fasse trop chaud.

5. *Il se peut qu(e)* : il fasse trop chaud.

6. *Je crois bien qu(e)* : on va goûter des plats africains.

PANORAMA CULTUREL

Quelle est l'image de ta région?

Cities, regions, and even countries can have a reputation. We wanted to know what people thought of specific places. Here's what they told us.

Emmanuel,
France

«La réputation de la Provence, c'est d'être un peu, surtout à Marseille, d'être un peu bagarreur, d'être un peu «m'as-tu-vu». C'est-à-dire, de se montrer un peu. C'est vrai que c'est souvent le cas à Marseille, hein. Parce que c'est souvent des jeunes qui font ça... Mais les vrais Marseillais sont pas comme ça, quoi.» Tr. 7

Betty,
Martinique

«Bon alors, les étrangers pensent que la Martinique est une île merveilleuse où il fait toujours très beau, où on peut pratiquer des sports nautiques comme le surf, le ski nautique, où le sable est fin et chaud et où on peut vivre des expériences nouvelles avec un compagnon quelquefois. Ils pensent que la Martinique est une île très accueillante ou très chaleureuse aussi, où il est bon de vivre.» Tr. 8

Christian,
France

«Ben, en fait, nous [les Français] sommes un peuple assez libre et nous avons inventé la démocratie. Et je crois que beaucoup de pays nous envient notre système politique, d'autre part, bien que ce soit pas un système parfait.» Tr. 9

Qu'en penses-tu?

1. Quelle est la réputation de ta région? Est-ce que tu penses que cette réputation est justifiée? Pourquoi ou pourquoi pas?

2. Quel pays étranger est-ce que tu voudrais visiter? Comment est-ce que tu imagines ce pays?

3. Est-ce que tu es d'accord avec ce que disent les gens interviewés? Pourquoi ou pourquoi pas?

Cultures and Communities

Community Link

Ask students what a stereotype is (an oversimplified generalization). Ask them for examples of stereotypes of people from different regions (California, New York, Texas).

Thinking Critically

Analyzing Have students reconsider the stereotypes they listed for the Community Link. Do they think these impressions are accurate? Have them discuss how such generalizations about groups of people are formed.

STANDARDS: 1.2, 2.1, 2.2, 3.2, 4.2   **PANORAMA CULTUREL   CENT QUATRE-VINGT-DIX-SEPT   197**

Teaching Resources
p. 197

PRINT
▶ Video Guide, pp. 42–43, 45
▶ Cahier d'activités, p. 84

MEDIA
▶ One-Stop Planner
▶ Video Program
  Videocassette 3, 8:58–12:20
▶ Audio Compact Discs, CD 7,
  Trs. 6–9
▶ Interactive CD-ROM Tutor, Disc 2

Presenting
Panorama Culturel

Ask students what they think people from metropolitan France and from Martinique are like. Then, play the video. Ask students if these people agree with the image others have of their region. Play the video again and ask the **Questions** below.

Questions

1. D'après Emmanuel, quelle est la réputation des Provençaux? (d'être bagarreurs, m'as-tu-vu)

2. Est-ce qu'Emmanuel croit que les vrais Marseillais sont comme ça? (non)

3. D'après Betty, que pensent les étrangers de la Martinique? (C'est une île merveilleuse où il fait toujours beau.)

4. Qu'est-ce que les Français ont inventé, d'après Christian? (la démocratie)

Teaching Resources
pp. 198–199

PRINT
▶ Lesson Planner, p. 34
▶ Video Guide, pp. 42, 44
▶ Cahier d'activités, p. 78

MEDIA
▶ One-Stop Planner
▶ Video Program
Camille et compagnie
Videocassette 3, 00:51–08:55
Videocassette 5 (captioned version), 38:11–46:15
▶ Audio Compact Discs, CD 7, Tr. 10

Presenting
Remise en train

Draw or find pictures of a gazelle, monkeys, lions, elephants, and a rhinoceros and tape them to the board. Then, play the audio recording. Pause after each scene and have students identify the animal being discussed and the context of the discussion. Then, have volunteers arrange the pictures in the order in which they are mentioned in the recording.

Remise en train • *Le safari, c'est l'aventure!*

CD 7 Tr. 10

Les Zokoue sont maintenant en République centrafricaine dans le parc national Bamingui-Bangoran, accompagnés par un guide.

1
M. Zokoue Oh! Regardez comme c'est beau, les enfants!
Lucie Est-ce que les animaux sont protégés ici?
Le guide Oui, la chasse est illégale. Malheureusement, il y a des braconniers. C'est pour ça qu'on doit surveiller la réserve en permanence.
Joseph Des braconniers? Qu'est-ce qu'ils tuent comme animaux?
Le guide Eh bien, les éléphants pour leur ivoire, les singes et les guépards pour leur fourrure et les rhinocéros pour leur corne.
Lucie C'est dégoûtant! Ça me rend malade!

2
Lucie Eh, tu as vu?
Joseph Non, qu'est-ce que c'était?
Lucie Une gazelle... Vous pourriez arrêter la voiture, s'il vous plaît? J'aimerais prendre une photo.
Joseph Tu es folle! Reste ici, c'est dangereux!
M. Zokoue Méfie-toi, Lucie, j'ai peur qu'il y ait des lions.
Le guide N'ayez pas peur. S'il y avait un lion, la gazelle le sentirait et elle s'enfuirait.

3
Lucie Vous avez entendu?
Joseph Quoi?
Lucie Ces bruits horribles! Ces cris! Je me demande ce que c'est.
Le guide Ne vous en faites pas, ce sont des singes. On ne les voit pas facilement. Ils se cachent dans les arbres... Tenez, vous les voyez, là?
Lucie Ah oui! Oh, super!

17 **Tu as compris?** See answers below.
1. Où est la famille Zokoue? Qu'est-ce qu'elle fait?
2. Qu'est-ce qui inquiète Lucie?
3. Qu'est-ce que Lucie veut prendre en photo?
4. Est-ce que le guide pense que c'est dangereux de sortir de voiture?
5. Qu'est-ce qui inquiète Joseph?
6. Qu'est-ce qui se passe quand Lucie essaie de photographier le rhinocéros?

These activities check for comprehension only. Students should not yet be expected to produce language modeled in **Remise en train**.

18 **Vrai ou faux?**
1. La chasse est illégale dans les réserves. vrai
2. Les singes chantent de belles chansons. faux
3. Le lion laisse les meilleurs morceaux à ses petits. faux
4. On chasse les rhinocéros pour leur corne. vrai
5. Les gnous sont les animaux les plus forts de la brousse. faux
6. Les rhinocéros vont plus vite que les voitures. faux

Answers
17 1. in the Bamingui-Bangoran National Park; taking a guided tour
2. poachers' killing of animals
3. a gazelle
4. yes
5. He worries about the vehicle breaking down in the middle of the elephant herd.
6. It charges.

Preteaching Vocabulary

Guessing Words from Context

Ask students what is going on in the story. Have them make predictions about what some of the unfamiliar words might mean based on the surrounding phrases and words around them. For example, Joseph's question **Qu'est-ce qu'ils tuent comme animaux?** after he says **Des braconniers?** can help them figure out the meaning of **bracon-** niers *(poachers)*. Have them find other phrases and words that can help them figure out the context of the story.

braconniers	**la loi de la nature**
surveiller	**un gnou**
la réserve	**le troupeau**
en permanence	

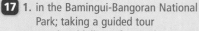

4   **M. Zokoue**   Regardez là-bas! Une famille de lions!

    Lucie   Qu'est-ce qu'ils mangent?

   Le guide   Un gnou, sûrement.

    Lucie   Mais, c'est horrible!

   Joseph   Mais non, c'est la loi de la nature. Les plus forts mangent les plus faibles.

  M. Zokoue   Vous avez vu comme le lion se garde les meilleurs morceaux? C'est vraiment le roi des animaux!

5   **Joseph**   Oh, dis donc! C'est dingue! Qu'est-ce qu'ils sont gros, ces éléphants! Euh, qu'est-ce qu'on ferait si on tombait en panne au milieu du troupeau?

   Le guide   On ne ferait rien. J'appellerais la base et on attendrait. Mais j'espère que ça ne nous arrivera pas parce que les éléphants sont imprévisibles. Ils pourraient nous attaquer s'ils avaient peur.

    Joseph   Euh... Vous êtes sûr que vous avez fait le plein d'essence avant de partir?

6   **M. Zokoue**   Regardez, il y a un rhinocéros là-bas.

    Lucie   Vous pourriez vous arrêter, s'il vous plaît?

   Le guide   Faites attention, les rhinocéros peuvent charger.

  M. Zokoue   Tu ferais peut-être mieux de rester dans la jeep pour prendre ta photo.

   Le guide   Ne vous inquiétez pas, je le surveille... Mais restez près de nous.

    Lucie   D'accord.

Lucie se prépare à prendre une photo du rhinocéros.

    Lucie   Souris, petit rhino... Souris.

   Le guide   Attention, remontez vite!

    Lucie   Mais quoi?

  M. Zokoue   Remonte, Lucie, dépêche-toi! Le rhinocéros charge!

    Lucie   Aïe! Aïe! Aïe!

   Le guide   Ne paniquez pas, mais remontez vite.

Elle remonte dans la voiture.

   Le guide   Accrochez-vous! On va aller très vite!

   Joseph   Ben, dis donc! On l'a échappé belle!

    Lucie   Chouette alors! Comme dans les films!

Cahier d'activités, p. 78, Act. 9

19   **Ils sont comment, les animaux?**

Associe chaque animal à sa description.

Le singe...		
L'éléphant...	est le roi des animaux.	Le lion
La gazelle...	est imprévisible.	L'éléphant
Le rhinocéros...	peut charger.	Le rhinocéros
Le lion...	vit dans les arbres.	Le singe
	sent le lion quand il arrive.	La gazelle

20   **Cherche les expressions**

How do the people in *Le safari, c'est l'aventure!* . . . See answers below.

1. express disgust?
2. give a warning?
3. reassure someone?
4. express astonishment?
5. express relief?

21   **Et maintenant, à toi**

Quels animaux est-ce que tu voudrais voir si tu faisais un safari-photo en Afrique?

Comprehension Check

Challenge

20   Once students have located the expressions, have them also answer *Who?* and *Why?* for each one. For example, for #1 **(C'est dégoûtant! Ça me rend malade!)**, students would tell who said it (Lucie) and why. (People who kill animals for their fur or their horns disgust her.)

Group Work

20   Form five groups and assign a question to each one. Have them find all the expressions in the **Remise en train** that express the given function.

Culture Note

The Bamingui-Bangoran national park, a woodland savannah, is home to the animals known as the "big four" (elephants, lions, leopards, and rhinos), among others. New measures have been taken to prevent poaching, which has been a serious problem. Between 1970 and 1990, the rhinoceros population dropped from about 60,000 to 4,000, and the elephant population from 80,000 to 3,000.

Biology Link

There are five different species of rhinoceros, all of which live in Africa and tropical Asia. Tell students that the rhinoceros' horn is actually made of keratin, which is a protein found in hair. You might have students guess how much the average rhinoceros weighs (three to five tons).

 Camille et compagnie

As an alternative or in addition to the **Remise en train,** you may wish to show Episode 7 of *Camille et compagnie.* For suggestions and activities, see the *Video Guide.*

Answers

20
1. C'est dégoûtant! Ça me rend malade!
2. Méfie-toi! Faites attention... ; Attention...
3. N'ayez pas peur. Ne vous en faites pas... ; Ne vous inquiétez pas... ; Ne paniquez pas...
4. Oh! Regardez comme c'est beau... ! Oh, super! Oh, dis donc! C'est dingue! Qu'est-ce qu'ils sont gros, ces éléphants!
5. Ben, dis donc! On l'a échappé belle!

Bell Work
Write a supposition on the board, such as **Il doit y avoir des lions**. Have students write two sentences, one in which they doubt the statement, and another in which they express their certainty of it.

Presenting
Vocabulaire

Hold up drawings or pictures of the animals and ask students either-or questions about them, such as **Quel animal est gris, la girafe ou l'éléphant?** Then, ask **Quel animal a une corne? Quels animaux sont féroces?**, using appropriate gestures to get the meaning across.

Deuxième étape

Objectives Expressing astonishment; cautioning someone; expressing fear; reassuring someone; expressing relief

WA3 FRANCOPHONE AFRICA-7

Vocabulaire

Le guépard est l'animal le plus rapide : quand il poursuit sa proie, il peut courir à une vitesse de 110 km/h.

L'éléphant (m.), l'animal le plus **lourd** de la terre, a de grandes oreilles plates, des défenses en ivoire et une longue trompe dont il se sert pour boire et pour se laver. L'éléphant utilise aussi sa trompe pour ramasser ou attraper ce qu'il veut manger.

La girafe est un grand mammifère roux et beige. Grâce à son très long cou, elle réussit à attraper les feuilles tout en haut des arbres.

Le rhinocéros est un gros herbivore qui possède une ou deux **cornes** qu'il utilise pour donner des coups aux autres rhinocéros avec qui il se bat. Les rhinocéros sont chassés par les braconniers pour leurs cornes.

L'hippopotame (m.) est un énorme animal dont le nom veut dire "cheval du fleuve". Il est très à l'aise dans l'eau où il se baigne dans la journée. Puis le soir, il sort de l'eau pour chercher sa nourriture.

Le singe passe la plupart de son temps dans les arbres. Il est très agile et il peut se balancer ou sauter d'un arbre à l'autre rapidement et très facilement.

Le zèbre ressemble beaucoup au cheval, mais il a des rayures noires et blanches grâce auxquelles il peut se cacher dans la brousse.

Le lion est souvent appelé le roi des animaux. Il passe la plupart de son temps à dormir. Quand la lionne a attrapé **une proie**, le lion vient manger les meilleurs morceaux, puis c'est le tour des lionnes et enfin, celui des lionceaux.

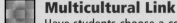

Travaux pratiques de grammaire, p. 69, Act. 10–11 — Cahier d'activités, pp. 79–80, Act. 10–11

22 Quel animal?

1. L'éléphant 2. le guépard 3. rhinocéros 4. L'hippopotame 5. les singes 6. Le zèbre 7. la girafe 8. le lion

Ecrivons Complète ces phrases avec le nom de l'animal approprié.

1. _____ utilise sa trompe pour boire.
2. L'animal qui court le plus vite est _____.
3. Quand deux _____ se battent, ils utilisent leurs cornes.
4. _____ est un très gros animal qui adore se baigner dans l'eau.
5. C'est dans les arbres que _____ passent la plupart de leurs journées.
6. _____ a une belle robe blanche et noire à rayures.
7. Le cou de _____ est presque aussi long que son corps.
8. On appelle souvent _____ le roi des animaux.

Vocabulaire à la carte

une antilope	
une autruche	*an ostrich*
un babouin	*a baboon*
un flamant	*a flamingo*
une gazelle	
un gorille	
une hyène	*a hyena*
un vautour	*a vulture*

Connections and Comparisons

Poetry Link
For additional practice with the vocabulary, read aloud the poem *Le Zèbre* (*Listening Activities*, page 58). Ask students to make a list of African animals they recognize. Then, copy the poem on a transparency and circle all the animal names. Have students check their work against the transparency and ask for volunteers to look up the other animals in the dictionary.

Multicultural Link
Have students choose a country and find out what animals are native to it. They might also find out about any unique or endangered species that live there and what efforts have been made to protect them. Have students report their findings.

23 **Qu'il est féroce, le lion!**

Parlons D'après toi, quel est l'animal le plus... ?

féroce	méchant	laid	courageux	fort
agile	mignon	lourd		rapide
dangereux		timide	intelligent	

24 **Devine!**

 Parlons Décris un animal sans le nommer. Ton/ta camarade va deviner de quel animal tu parles.

Comment dit-on...?

Expressing astonishment

Oh, dis donc! *Wow!*
Ça alors! *How about that!*
C'est pas vrai!
Ouah! *Wow!*
C'est le pied! *Cool! Neat!*
Tiens! Regarde un peu! *Hey! Check it out!*
Qu'est-ce qu'elle est grande, cette girafe!
 How . . . he/she/it is!

C'est fou comme elle va vite, cette gazelle!
 I can't believe how . . . !
Quel paysage incroyable!
Tu as vu comme il est gros, l'hippopotame?
 Did you see how . . . ?
Je n'ai jamais vu un aussi gros éléphant.

 Cahier d'activités, p. 81, Act. 12

---

25 **Quelle est leur réaction?**

See scripts and answers on p. 185H.

 Ecoutons Ecoute les remarques de ces gens qui visitent la savane. Est-ce qu'ils expriment leur étonnement ou non?

CD 7 Tr. 11

A la française

French speakers often begin a sentence with a subject pronoun, like **il, elle,** or **ça,** and then repeat the noun subject at the end of the sentence for emphasis. Look at these examples: **C'est fou comme il est grand, cet éléphant!** or **Ça doit être magnifique, la savane.**

26 **Ouah!**

 Ecrivons Voici des photos de ton safari que tu vas envoyer à ta famille et à tes amis. Décris chaque scène et exprime ton étonnement à propos de chaque scène. *Possible answers:*

1.
C'est fou comme il va vite, ce guépard!

2.
Je n'ai jamais vu une aussi grande bouche!

3.
Quels beaux papillons!

4.
Qu'est-ce qu'ils sont gros, ces éléphants!

27 **Mon journal**

 **Ecrivons** Imagine un voyage plein d'aventures. Où est-ce que tu irais? Qu'est-ce que tu y ferais? Quels animaux tu verrais? Comment est-ce que ça serait?

Si tu as oublié **the conditional** va à la page 141.

Travaux pratiques de grammaire, p. 70, Act. 12–13

Deuxième étape

CHAPITRE 7

Presenting
Comment dit-on... ?

As homework, have students find large pictures of people or things they find impressive. As volunteers show their pictures to the class, comment on them, using the new phrases for expressing astonishment. Each time, write the expression you use on the board. Have students repeat the new expressions. Then, collect all the pictures and shuffle them. Have students take turns picking a picture and taping it to the board next to the related expression.

Language-to-Language
Call attention to the expression **C'est le pied!** and ask students to guess its literal meaning *(It's the foot!)*. Then, ask volunteers to explain what idiomatic expressions are and to recall other such expressions they've learned. **(Ça coûte les yeux de la tête./C'est un navet...**). If you have native speakers of other languages in your class, have them give examples of idiomatic expressions in their language and ask them to explain their meaning.

Additional Practice
Read statements or show pictures from the *Guinness Book of World Records* and prompt students to react to each one with astonishment.

Communication for All Students

Kinesthetic Learners

25 If students hear an expression of astonishment, have them respond by dropping their jaws and cupping both hands over their cheeks. If the speaker does not express astonishment, they should shrug their shoulders.

Visual Learners

26 Have students create a photo album of their trip to the Central African Republic. They should find or draw pictures of unusual animals and sights that they saw there and tape or glue them to sheets of construction paper. Then, have them write captions underneath each picture, using the new expressions. Have them design and make an attractive cover for their albums and then fasten all the pages together. This activity could be a chapter project.

Teaching Resources
pp. 200–203

PRINT 📖

▶ Lesson Planner, p. 35
▶ Listening Activities, pp. 52–53, 56–57
▶ Activities for Communication, pp. 27–28, 70–71, 101–102
▶ Travaux pratiques de grammaire, pp. 69–72
▶ Grammar Tutor for Students of French, Chapter 7
▶ Cahier d'activités, pp. 79–82
▶ Testing Program, pp. 151–154
▶ Alternative Assessment Guide, p. 36
▶ Student Make-Up Assignments, Chapter 7

MEDIA 💿📹💻

▶ One-Stop Planner
▶ Audio Compact Discs, CD 7, Trs. 11–12, 15, 22–24
▶ Teaching Transparencies: 7-2; **Grammaire supplémentaire** Answers; Travaux pratiques de grammaire Answers
▶ Interactive CD-ROM Tutor, Disc 2

Presenting
Comment dit-on... ?

Create a humorous dialogue between a cowardly lion and his reassuring friend, the mouse, using the expressions from **Comment dit-on... ?** Using sock puppets, act out the dialogue for the class. Then, write the new expressions on a transparency. Read them aloud and have students repeat after you.

Possible answers

30 1. Ne bougez pas!
2. Méfiez-vous! Je vous signale que les animaux peuvent charger.
3. Attention aux fourmis!
4. Fais gaffe! Il serait plus prudent de rester dans la voiture.

Comment dit-on...?

Cautioning someone; expressing fear; reassuring someone; expressing relief

To caution someone:

> **Je vous signale que** les animaux peuvent charger. *I'm warning you that . . .*
> **Il serait plus prudent de** rester dans la voiture. *It would be wiser to . . .*
> **Faites attention/gaffe!** *Look out!*
> **Attention aux** araignées! *Watch out for . . .!*
> **Méfiez-vous!** *Be careful!*
> **Ne bougez pas.** *Don't move.*

To express fear:

> **J'ai très peur des** lions.
> **J'ai peur que** ce soit un serpent.
> **J'ai la frousse!** *I'm scared to death!*

To reassure someone:

> **Ne vous en faites pas.**
> **N'ayez pas peur.** *Don't be afraid.*
> **Calmez-vous!**
> **Pas de panique!**

To express relief:

> **On a eu de la chance!** *We were lucky!*
> **Ouf! On a eu chaud!**
> *Whew! That was a real scare!*
> **On l'a échappé belle!** *That was close!*

 Cahier d'activités, p. 81, Act. 13

28 **Dans la savane**   See scripts and answers on p. 185H.

a. Ecoutons Ecoute les remarques de ces gens qui explorent la savane. Est-ce qu'ils avertissent ou rassurent quelqu'un?

CD 7 Tr. 12

b. Ecoutons Maintenant, écoute ces gens et dis s'ils expriment leur peur ou leur soulagement.

29 **Du calme!**

Lisons Choisis la réponse appropriée pour rassurer la personne qui a fait les remarques suivantes.

1. «Oh! Il y a des araignées! J'ai très peur des araignées.»
   a. Les araignées sont méchantes. **b.** Regarde un peu! **c.** N'ayez pas peur.
2. «Voilà, on s'est perdus et il fait déjà nuit. J'ai la frousse!»
   a. Rapporteur! **b.** Ne t'en fais pas! **c.** On a eu chaud!
3. «Tu as entendu? J'ai peur que ce soit un lion.»
   a. Quel lion énorme! **b.** On l'a échappé belle. **c.** Pas de panique!

30 **Attention!**

Parlons Qu'est-ce que tu dirais pour avertir ces gens?   See answers below.

1.   2.   3.   4.

Communication for All Students

Challenge

29 Once students have completed the activity, have them write additional statements that would elicit the remaining responses. For example, for the two remaining responses in #1, **Les araignées sont méchantes** and **Regarde un peu!**, students might write **Comment sont les araignées?** and **Tiens, il y a un guépard!** You might have students exchange papers with a partner, who writes the appropriate response next to each statement.

30 For writing practice, tell students to imagine they are on a photo safari and to write a diary entry telling what happened to them in each of the instances pictured here.

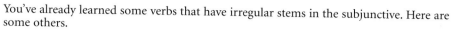

Grammaire

Irregular subjunctive forms

You've already learned some verbs that have irregular stems in the subjunctive. Here are some others.

- To form the subjunctive of the verb **pouvoir,** add the regular subjunctive endings to the stem **puiss-.**

  Je ne pense pas qu'on **puisse** toucher les animaux.

- To form the subjunctive of the verb **aller,** add the regular endings to the stems **all-** (for the **nous** and **vous** forms) and **aill-** (for all other forms).

que j'**aille**	que nous **allions**
que tu **ailles**	que vous **alliez**
qu'il/elle/on **aille**	qu'ils/elles **aillent**

  Je ne veux pas que tu **ailles** en Afrique.
  J'ai peur que vous **alliez** trop vite.

- All the subjunctive forms of the verbs **être** and **avoir** are irregular.

que je **sois**	que nous **soyons**	que j'**aie**	que nous **ayons**
que tu **sois**	que vous **soyez**	que tu **aies**	que vous **ayez**
qu'il/elle/on **soit**	qu'ils/elles **soient**	qu'il/elle/on **ait**	qu'ils/elles **aient**

  Il a peur que ce **soit** trop dangereux.
  Je ne pense pas qu'il y **ait** d'orignaux.

  > Cahier d'activités,
  > p. 82, Act. 14

  > Grammaire supplémentaire,
  > pp. 210–211, Act. 5–8

  > Travaux pratiques de grammaire, pp. 71–72, Act. 14–16

31 **Grammaire en contexte**

Ecrivons Fabien et Suzanne parlent d'un voyage qu'ils pourraient faire avec leurs amis. Complète leur conversation en mettant les verbes au subjonctif.

FABIEN   Ben moi, j'ai peur que ce ___1___ (être) dangereux!   soit

SUZANNE   Moi aussi. Il se peut qu'il y ___2___ (avoir) des serpents!   ait

FABIEN   Oui. Et il est fort possible que les animaux ___3___ (être) féroces.   soient

SUZANNE   Bien sûr. Je ne crois pas qu'on ___4___ (pouvoir) sortir de la voiture.   puisse

FABIEN   Sans doute pas. Il faudra que tu ___5___ (prendre) tes photos de l'intérieur de la voiture.   prennes

SUZANNE   En plus, mes parents ne voudront pas que j'y ___6___ (aller). Ils auraient trop peur.   aille

FABIEN   Et n'oublie pas qu'il est nécessaire qu'on se ___7___ (faire) vacciner.   fasse

SUZANNE   Bon, ben, finalement, je ne crois pas que ce ___8___ (être) une bonne idée!   soit

32   De l'école au travail

Ecrivons Imagine que tu travailles dans un zoo et qu'on t'a demandé de créer une nouvelle brochure pour la visite du zoo. Dessine une carte du zoo qui montre l'endroit où les animaux vivent. Pour chaque animal, décris son style de vie.

Connections and Comparisons

Community Link
If possible, organize a field trip to a local zoo and have students observe some of the animals mentioned in the chapter. You might have students take notes on what they learn during the visit, and then write a brief report of their impressions and observations.

Language-to-Language
31 Have students explain why the subjunctive is used in each sentence. Hang the posters illustrating the use of the subjunctive (see Presentation on page 196) and have students point to the appropriate one. Ask students if they are aware of instances where mood determines the tense or mode used in English. (An example would be *He demanded that the criminal be punished.*)

STANDARDS: 1.2, 1.3, 4.1, 5.1, 5.2

Deuxième étape

CHAPITRE 7

Presenting
Grammaire

Irregular subjective forms
Write the subject pronouns and the subjunctive stems of each irregular verb on the board and have volunteers add the endings. Then, write on a transparency sentence starters that require the subjunctive. Write subject pronouns and infinitives (**tu/être**) on cards and put them in a bag. Have students select a card and use the subject pronoun and verb to complete one of the sentence starters.

Game
Catégories Write the five functions from this **étape** on the board. Form two or more teams. Name a function (*expressing astonishment*) and have the teams take turns giving sentences that demonstrate it. (**C'est fou comme le guépard va vite!**) Teams win a point for each sentence. You might use *African animals* as an additional category.

Assess
▶ Testing Program, pp. 151–154
   Quiz 7-2A, Quiz 7-2B
   Audio CD 7, Tr. 15

▶ Student Make-Up Assignments, Chapter 7, Alternative Quiz

▶ Alternative Assessment Guide, p. 36

Lisons!

Teaching Resources
pp. 204–206

PRINT
▶ Lesson Planner, p. 36
▶ Cahier d'activités, p. 83
▶ Reading Strategies and Skills, Chapter 7
▶ Joie de lire 3, Chapter 7
▶ Standardized Assessment Tutor, Chapter 7

MEDIA
▶ One-Stop Planner

Prereading
Activity A
Teaching Suggestion
Have students recall stories that have animals as the main characters (*The Tortoise and the Hare, Goldilocks and the Three Bears, Little Red Riding Hood, The Three Little Pigs*). Have them name the animals in each story. Then, ask them how they would characterize these stories. What do they expect an animal story to be like?

Reading
Activity B–Q
Teaching Suggestion
Have students make two columns, one labeled **Les éléphants** and the other, **Les hommes.** Have them list the characteristics of each. For example, under **Les éléphants**, students might write **gros, forts, peau épaisse.**

LE CIMETIERE DES ELEPHANTS

Autrefois, le peuple des éléphants vivait au bord de la rivière Sankourou. Il avait pour roi le puissant et sage Khoro. Un jour, le petit tisserin s'est posé sur la défense de Khoro et lui a raconté, tout effrayé :

«Hélas, puissant Khoro ! C'est terrible ! Une foule d'êtres noirs à deux pattes est arrivée dans notre pays. Ils possèdent de drôles d'objets qui tuent. Ils s'étendent partout et dévastent tout sur leur passage.»

Khoro a souri : « Je connais ces êtres. Ce sont les hommes. Ils sont petits et ne sont pas très forts. Leurs armes ne peuvent pas transpercer l'épaisse peau des éléphants.»

Cependant, peu de temps après, Khoro a cessé de sourire. Les hommes noirs n'étaient ni très grands, ni très forts, mais ils étaient nombreux. Certes, leurs armes ne pouvaient transpercer l'épaisse peau des éléphants.

Toutefois, une flèche bien lancée pouvait tuer un éléphant, si elle le frappait à l'œil. Les hommes brûlaient les forêts pour en faire des champs. En outre, une terrible sécheresse éprouvait le pays. Les éléphants étaient aux abois. Ils mouraient de faim et par les armes des hommes noirs. C'est alors que le puissant Roi des Eléphants a rassemblé ses sujets et leur a dit :

«Cette terre n'est plus bénie des dieux. La famine et les hommes noirs nous font souffrir. Nous devons partir d'ici. Nous irons vers le soleil couchant. Notre route sera droite, comme l'était jusqu'à présent notre vie. Nous passerons sur tout ce qui se trouvera sur notre chemin, que ce soient les marécages ou les hommes noirs. Nous sommes peut-être un petit peuple, mais chacun de nous est plus fort que dix fois dix singes. Nous atteindrons notre but. Il n'en reste pas moins que ce pays a toujours été notre terre. Aussi, nous y reviendrons quelques jours chaque année, le premier mois qui suit la saison des pluies. Ainsi, nos enfants le connaîtront, les vieux et

Stratégie pour lire
Understanding linking words can help you see the connection between ideas. Some common French linking words are **pourtant** *(yet)*, **cependant** *(however)*, **néanmoins** *(nevertheless)*, **alors** *(so, therefore)*, and **ainsi** *(thus, in this way)*. Linking words can connect ideas in several different ways. They can continue or expand on an idea, show a cause-and-effect relationship, or express a contradiction. Notice how the linking word functions in this example: **Ce travail est dangereux. Il faut cependant le faire.** As you begin to read more sophisticated texts in French, paying attention to the linking words will help you to understand not only the events of the story, but also the more subtle relationship of ideas.

LE CIMETIERE DES ELEPHANTS

A. Who are the «**peuple**» that this story is about? Who is Khoro? *elephants; their king*

B. Who are «**les êtres noirs à deux pattes**»? What problem do they present? Why isn't Khoro worried about them at first? *See answers below.*

C. Lequel de ses événements n'a rien à voir avec l'arrivée des humains?

Les hommes brûlaient les forêts.

Il y avait une terrible sécheresse.

Une tornade a détruit leur terre.

Les hommes noirs tuaient les éléphants.

Cultures and Communities

Culture Note
The African elephant is the largest living land animal. It weighs up to eight tons (7,500 kilograms) and stands ten to thirteen feet tall. These elephants may live in either the jungle or in the savannah. They migrate with the seasons, depending on the availability of food and water. Because they are becoming increasingly rare, regulations against poaching have been established, and conservation parks have been created to protect them.

Answers
B. humans; They're taking over and destroying everything in their way; They are small and weak, and their weapons can't pierce an elephant's thick hide.

STANDARDS: 1.2, 2.2, 3.1

les malades pourront y vivre leurs derniers instants.»

Ainsi a parlé le puissant Khoro, et il en a été comme il a dit. Le passage des éléphants ressemblait à celui d'une tornade : les arbres ont été arrachés, les champs piétinés, les villages détruits. Beaucoup d'hommes ont péri. La force des éléphants était effrayante.

Cela s'est passé il y a longtemps, très longtemps, mais chaque année, les éléphants continuent à emprunter le même chemin pour montrer leur ancienne patrie à leurs petits et pour que les vieux puissent y mourir. Depuis ce temps, on ne trouve plus de cadavres d'éléphants dans la forêt car ceux-ci vont mourir sur les bords de la rivière Sankourou. Là se trouve leur cimetière bien que personne ne sache l'endroit exact.

LA TORTUE ET LE LEOPARD

Les enfants étaient agités à cause du formidable chasseur qui était passé par leur village ce matin-là. Ce qui les avait impressionnés le plus, c'était la quantité de gris-gris qu'il portait sur lui.

«Quand je serai grand, moi aussi je serai chasseur !» a dit l'un des enfants.

Son oncle, qui l'avait entendu, lui a dit : «Si tu veux vraiment devenir un grand chasseur, il te faudra apprendre beaucoup de choses. Tu devras savoir construire des pièges efficaces pour duper les animaux que tu voudras attraper ; ils sont intelligents,

tu sais, et ce n'est pas aussi facile que tu crois de les capturer.»

«Oh, raconte-nous une histoire de pièges !» dit le petit garçon. Les autres enfants voulaient aussi que l'oncle leur raconte une histoire. «Oui, raconte-nous une histoire! Raconte-nous une histoire !»

Voici ce que l'oncle leur a raconté :

Un jour, Dame Tortue, perdue dans ses pensées, rentrait joyeusement chez elle. En d'autres mots, elle traînait sa carapace un peu plus vite que d'habitude. Mais, elle n'avançait pas très vite car elle s'arrêtait constamment pour sentir une fleur sauvage par ici, ou pour manger un bouton de fleur par là. Elle aurait dû faire attention à des choses plus importantes. Ainsi, sur son chemin, il y avait comme un grand tapis de feuilles de palmier qu'un serpent svelte traversait. Sans réfléchir, la tortue le suivait quand, tout à coup, les feuilles ont cédé sous elle. Boum! Elle est tombée dans le piège que les chasseurs d'un village alentour avaient creusé au milieu du chemin.

Grâce à sa carapace très dure, elle ne s'est pas blessée. Mais comment allait-elle sortir de ce piège ? Elle savait bien qu'elle devait s'échapper avant le lendemain matin si elle ne voulait pas finir dans la soupe du village.

Alors, Dame Tortue a commencé à réfléchir sérieusement. Elle réfléchissait toujours quand elle a

Additional Practice
D. For more practice with linking words, have students look for linking words in *Les Trois Femmes du roi* and *La Petite Maison* on pages 174–176.

Terms in Lisons!
Students might want to know the following words from *Le Cimetière des éléphants*: **défense** *(tusk);* **pattes** *(paws);* **épais(se)** *(thick);* **champs** *(fields);* **marécage** *(swamp);* **but** *(goal);* from *La Tortue et le léopard:* **creuser** *(to dig);* **tacheté** *(spotted).*

D. Find three examples of linking words in *Le Cimetière des éléphants.* What purpose does each of these words serve? How does it connect one idea with another?   See answers below.

E. Quelle décision Khoro prend-il pour sauver ses sujets?   quitter leur pays

F. Find the sentence that begins «**Aussi, nous y reviendrons...** » near the end of the last paragraph on page 204. In this sentence, **aussi** doesn't mean *also*. Figure out what it means from the way it connects that sentence to the ones before.   *therefore*

G. Quelles raisons donne Khoro pour retourner chaque année au pays des éléphants?

H. Cite les effets du passage des éléphants.
For activities G and H, see answers below.

I. Mets ces événements dans le bon ordre.

4   Les éléphants partent du bord de la rivière.

5   Les éléphants reviennent à la rivière pour mourir.

2   Les hommes font souffrir les éléphants.

1   Les hommes arrivent à la rivière.

3   Le roi Khoro parle à ses sujets.

J. What phenomenon is explained in the last paragraph?
See answers below.

Cahier d'activités, p. 83, Act. 16

Communication for All Students

Slower Pace
G., H. You might make a list of the answers to each of these activities, along with some incorrect answers. Have students choose the correct answers from the lists.

Challenge
I. Once students have completed this activity, have them draw or find pictures to illustrate each event. Then, students should write a caption for each picture and paraphrase the story. You might have volunteers present their stories to the class, holding up their illustrations as they retell the story in their own words.

Teaching Suggestions

Ask students who is speaking at the beginning of *La Tortue et le léopard* (some children, an uncle of one of the children). What has happened? (A great hunter has entered the village.) What is the effect of the visitor's presence? (The children all want to become hunters.) Who tells the story and why? (the uncle; He is advising the children that a great hunter needs to be able to set good traps.) From this introduction, have students predict the content of the story that the uncle tells.

M. Have students give the contextual clues they used to figure out the meaning of the words.

Q. Have students work in groups to discuss what they think the moral of the story might be and report their results to the class.

Answers

K. She is daydreaming, stopping to smell wildflowers, and eating buds. Not paying attention, she doesn't notice a trap in her path.

N. She treats the leopard like an unwanted guest in "her" hole. Angered, he throws her out.

O. to save his strength for the hunters; She escaped both the hunters and the leopard.

Q. *Possible answer:* Cleverness can triumph over adversity and can be more important than physical strength.

R. Common elements include animals with human characteristics, physical danger, and escape. The hunters in the first story are killing masses of elephants out of greed. The hunters in the second story are trapping individual animals for food. *Answers will vary.*

---

entendu un grand boum... C'était un magnifique léopard, grand, languissant, souple et féroce qui venait de tomber dans le piège, lui aussi. Son grognement montrait bien qu'il n'appréciait pas le stratagème que les chasseurs avaient utilisé pour le capturer.

Dame Tortue pensait plus vite qu'elle ne marchait. Avant que le léopard ne la remarque, elle s'est mise à crier d'une voix hautaine : «Mais qu'est-ce que tu fais ici, et qui t'a enseigné de pareilles manières ? Tu n'as donc jamais appris qu'on ne s'invite pas chez une dame, comme ça ?»

Le léopard s'est retourné et a regardé Dame Tortue d'un air stupéfait.

«Tu ne sais donc pas que je ne reçois jamais après la tombée de la nuit ?» a continué la tortue. «Sors d'ici, espèce de voyou tacheté !»

C'était plus que le léopard ne pouvait supporter d'une vieille dame aussi laide. Avec un grognement féroce, il a saisi la tortue et l'a lancée en l'air d'un grand coup de patte. «Sors de ce trou toi-même, espèce de vieille gourde osseuse au cou ridé !» il lui a crié. «Je fais ce que je veux !»

«Merci beaucoup, grand léopard» a doucement répondu la tortue de là où elle avait atterri. «Je te conseille d'économiser tes forces pour demain, quand les chasseurs viendront te chercher. Bonne nuit !»

Dame Tortue est alors partie, soulagée et reconnaissante d'avoir eu autant de chance. Elle était aussi très fière d'avoir si bien su échapper à la fois aux chasseurs et au léopard.

LA TORTUE ET LE LEOPARD

K. Name three things Dame Tortue is doing at the beginning of the story. How do her actions lead her to fall into the trap? See answers below.

L. Who falls into the trap next? a leopard

M. Réfère-toi au contexte et aux illustrations pour deviner le sens de ces mots.

carapace   shell

un piège   a trap

gave way

trou   hole

cédé

threw

lancée

N. Comment fait Dame Tortue pour se libérer? See answers below.

O. What advice does Dame Tortue give the leopard? Why does she feel clever at the end of the story? See answers below.

P. Vrai ou faux?
1. Dame Tortue faisait attention à son chemin en rentrant chez elle. faux
2. Le léopard est tombé dans le piège avant la tombée de la nuit. faux
3. Dame Tortue a imaginé un stratagème pour sortir du piège. vrai
4. Le léopard a gentiment aidé Dame Tortue à sortir du piège. faux
5. Le léopard était obligé d'attendre les chasseurs pour sortir du piège. vrai
6. Dame Tortue n'est pas très maligne. faux

Q. What lessons does the story suggest? See answers below.

R. Name three elements that are common to both tales. How is the subject of hunting treated differently in the two stories? Why? How do you feel about hunting? See answers below.

Communication for All Students

Postreading
Thinking Critically

R. Comparing and Contrasting Have students compare and contrast the two stories. Have groups draw two columns on a sheet of paper, one labeled *Similarities* and the other *Differences*. They should list as many as they can in each column. They might consider the characters involved in each story and their personality traits, the setting, the basic problem, and how the problem was resolved.

Analyzing Have students suggest adjectives to describe the turtle and the leopard in this story. (*turtle:* resourceful; *leopard:* impatient)

Une histoire d'animaux

Tu viens de lire deux histoires d'animaux. Dans ces histoires, les animaux ont des person-nalités distinctes, avec des qualités et des défauts propres aux humains. Maintenant toi aussi, tu vas écrire une histoire avec des animaux qui ont des caractéristiques humaines. Tu vas utiliser tes personnages pour raconter ton histoire.

A. Préparation

1. Quel type d'histoire est-ce que tu préfères raconter?

   a. Tu peux écrire un mythe. Comme *Le Cimetière des éléphants*, ton mythe devra expli-quer le comportement particulier d'un groupe d'animaux.

   b. Tu peux choisir d'écrire une fable comme *La Tortue et le léopard*. Il doit y avoir, dans ta fable, une morale que tu veux enseigner aux autres.

   c. Si tu préfères, tu peux créer l'histoire de ton choix, à condition qu'elle ait des animaux pour personnages.

2. Imagine l'intrigue de ton histoire. Qu'est-ce qui se passera?

3. Qui vont être les personnages de ton his-toire? Fais une courte description de chacun des personnages principaux et explique son rôle dans l'histoire.

4. Fais une liste où tu notes les événements dans l'ordre où ils arriveront. Assure-toi que tu n'as pas oublié d'événements importants.

> **Stratégie pour écrire**
>
> Sequencing, the way you put the events of a story in order, is an important part of storytelling. The action in a story should proceed logically, with no gaps or jumps to break the reader's atten-tion. Sequencing words such as **d'abord, ensuite, puis,** and **enfin** are useful in relat-ing the order of events in a story. Linking words such as those you learned on page 204 can help you relate one sentence to another. Proper sequencing of your sen-tences and ideas will create a smooth narra-tive flow in a story.

B. Rédaction

1. Fais un brouillon de ton histoire en suivant ton plan. Vérifie que tu as suivi un ordre logique dans l'action de l'histoire.

2. Utilise quelques-uns des mots suivants pour montrer l'ordre des événements.

au début	puis	cependant	néanmoins
d'abord	ensuite	mais	en fait
pendant que	après	alors	parce que
quand	à la fin	et	

3. Pour lier les différentes idées et rendre ton histoire plus agréable à lire, utilise certains des mots ci-dessus.

C. Evaluation

1. Relis ton brouillon.

   a. Est-ce que tu as raconté les événements principaux de l'histoire dans un ordre logique?

   b. Est-ce que tu as utilisé des mots de liaison entre les différents événements?

2. Vérifie la grammaire et l'orthographe de ton histoire et fais les corrections nécessaires.

3. Donne ton histoire à un(e) camarade de classe. Est-ce que le but de l'histoire est clair?

> **Teaching Resources**
> **p. 207**
>
> PRINT
> ▶ Lesson Planner, p. 36
> ▶ Cahier d'activités, p. 151
> ▶ Alternative Assessment Guide, p. 22
> ▶ Standardized Assessment Tutor, Chapter 7
>
> MEDIA
> ▶ One-Stop Planner
> ▶ Test Generator, Chapter 7
> ▶ Interactive CD-ROM Tutor, Disc 2

Process Writing

Prewriting

Literature Link

A. Ask students to explain the difference between a myth and a fable. (A myth serves to explain a practice, belief, or natural phenome-non. A fable usually has animals as its main characters and teaches a moral lesson.)

Writing

Slower Pace

B. 2. Before students try to use these words in their stories, have them write a sentence using each one.

📁 Portfolio

Written This activity is appropriate for students' written portfolios. For portfolio information, see *Alternative Assessment Guide*, pages iv–15.

Apply and Assess

Postwriting

Teaching Suggestion

C. 1. Have students number the events on their papers in red, and mark the linking words they used with a highlighter. Have students set their drafts aside for a day or two. When they pick them up again, they'll evaluate them better.

Visual Learners

Students might also illustrate their story. They should choose several key events, draw pictures for them, and copy the corresponding text underneath.

Family Link

Have students share their stories with their families.

Grammaire supplémentaire

CHAPITRE 7

For **Grammaire supplémentaire** Answer Transparencies, see the *Teaching Transparencies* binder.

Grammaire supplémentaire

CD-ROM DISC 2

internet

go.hrw.com
ADRESSE: go.hrw.com
MOT-CLE: WA3
FRANCOPHONE AFRICA-7

Première étape **Objectives** Making suppositions; expressing doubt and certainty; asking for and giving advice

1 Pour chacune des phrases suivantes, choisis le verbe approprié et dis si l'animal décrit est l'éléphant ou le léopard. (**p. 193**)

EXEMPLE Cet animal peut (grimpe/<u>grimper</u>) dans un arbre. **le léopard**

1. Je trouve qu'il (a/avoir) une belle fourrure, cet animal.
2. Je crois que cet animal (est/être) végétarien. Il ne mange que des plantes.
3. Cet animal aime (passe/passer) la nuit à chasser. Il dort pendant la journée.
4. On dit que cet animal aime (mange/manger) des cacahouètes.
5. Je pense que cet animal (est/être) le plus lourd de la terre.
6. Cet animal aime (mange/manger) de la viande.
7. On dit que cet animal (a/avoir) une peau très épaisse.
8. Je pense que cet animal (est/être) moins gros qu'un lion, mais aussi féroce.

2 Ta petite sœur Marie essaie de te décourager d'aller en République centrafricaine avec un(e) ami(e). Tu lui réponds en utilisant **ça m'étonnerait que** et le subjonctif du verbe qui convient. (**p. 196**)

EXEMPLE —Je suis sûre que vous aurez la fièvre jaune!
—**Ça m'étonnerait que nous ayons la fièvre jaune.**

1. Je suis sûre qu'il fera très froid la nuit!
2. Je suis certaine que vous ne verrez pas de papillons!
3. Je parie que vous ne rencontrerez pas de gens intéressants!
4. A mon avis, vous ne trouverez pas d'éléphants dans la savane!
5. Je suis convaincue que vous n'apprendrez pas le sangho!
6. Je suis sûre qu'on ne se reverra plus!
7. Je suis sûre que des bêtes féroces vous attaqueront.
8. Je parie que vous tomberez en panne au milieu de la savane.

Answers

1 1. a; le léopard
2. est; l'éléphant
3. passer; le léopard
4. manger; l'éléphant
5. est; l'éléphant
6. manger; le léopard
7. a; l'éléphant
8. est; le léopard

2 Ça m'étonnerait...
1. qu'il fasse très froid la nuit.
2. que nous ne voyions pas de papillons.
3. que nous ne rencontrions pas de gens intéressants.
4. que nous ne trouvions pas d'éléphants dans la savane.
5. que nous n'apprenions pas le sangho.
6. qu'on ne se revoie plus.
7. que des bêtes féroces nous attaquent.
8. que nous tombions en panne au milieu de la savane.

Grammar Resources for Chapter 7

The **Grammaire supplémentaire** activities are designed as supplemental activities for the grammatical concepts presented in the chapter. You might use them as additional practice, for review, or for assessment.

For more grammar presentations, review, and practice, refer to the following:
• Travaux pratiques de grammaire
• Grammar Tutor for Students of French

• Grammar Summary on pp. R29–R54
• Cahier d'activités
• Grammar and Vocabulary quizzes (Testing Program)
• Test Generator
• Interactive CD-ROM Tutor
• **Jeux interactifs** at <u>go.hrw.com</u>

3 Mme Jacob est au téléphone avec sa fille Agnès qui va bientôt aller à Bangui. Mets les verbes entre parenthèses au présent de l'indicatif ou au subjonctif. (p. 196)

—Agnès, chérie, il faudrait que tu ___1___ (faire) ta valise, quand même!......

—Qu'est-ce que tu dis? Tu ne sais pas quoi prendre! Bon, ben, il doit faire très chaud là-bas, non? Alors, il est essentiel que tu ___2___ (prendre) des vêtements légers......

—Comment? Ah oui, tu as raison. Il est fort possible que la chaleur ___3___ (être) intense! Il est donc nécessaire que tu ___4___ (emporter) de la crème solaire et un chapeau.....

—Qu'est-ce que tu dis, chérie? Mais, je n'en sais rien, moi! Il vaudrait mieux que tu ___5___ (appeler) l'ambassade. Je suis certaine qu'il ___6___ (falloir) prendre son passeport, mais pour le visa... Ah, Agnès, chérie, j'avais presque oublié! Je suis sûre que tu ___7___ (pouvoir) attraper des tas de maladies là-bas. Il est important que tu te ___8___ (protéger). En fait, il vaudrait mieux que tu te ___9___ (faire) vacciner...

—Tu dis? Tu as déjà consulté un médecin. Ah bon, Dieu merci!

4 Inès et Milo font un safari au parc national Bamingui-Bangoran. Complète leurs conversations avec le subjonctif des verbes entre parenthèses. (p. 196)

Le GUIDE Comme il y a beaucoup de braconniers, il est nécessaire que nous ___1___ (garder) la réserve.

INES Est-ce qu'il se peut que les braconniers ___2___ (tuer) les éléphants, si vous ne les surveillez pas?

INES Je voudrais que tu ___3___ (faire) une photo des lions, mais il faudrait d'abord que tu ___4___ (arrêter) la voiture.

MILO Tu veux que j'___5___ (arrêter) la voiture? Pas question! J'ai peur que les lions nous ___6___ (manger).

MILO Fais gaffe! J'entends des singes! Il se peut qu'ils nous ___7___ (attaquer)!

INES Je ne pense pas, mais il vaudrait mieux qu'on ___8___ (rester) dans la voiture.

INES Regarde là-bas! Des gazelles! Qu'est-ce qu'elles sont belles!

MILO Mais tais-toi! J'ai peur qu'elles nous ___9___ (entendre)!

MILO Tu as vu? Un rhinocéros! Si on allait lui dire bonjour?

INES Mais ça va pas, toi! Il faut que nous ___10___ (rester) assez loin. Il est fort possible qu'il ___11___ (charger)!

Answers

3
1. fasses
2. prennes
3. soit
4. emportes
5. appelles
6. faut
7. peux
8. protèges
9. fasses

4
1. gardions
2. tuent
3. fasses
4. arrêtes
5. arrête
6. mangent
7. attaquent
8. reste
9. entendent
10. restions
11. charge

Communication for All Students

Slower Pace

4 Review the situations in which the subjunctive is used before beginning the activity. Then go over the formation of the subjunctive and fill in the first three blanks with students on the board or on an overhead transparency. Allow students to work in pairs and check each other's work for the remaining sentences. When students are finished, have them explain their answers. Ask them about the subjunctive of **-er** verbs. Why are they easy to remember? (because the forms are the same as the indicative except for the **nous** and **vous** forms)

Grammaire supplémentaire

CHAPITRE 7

For **Grammaire supplémentaire** Answer Transparencies, see the *Teaching Transparencies* binder.

Deuxième étape

Objectives Expressing astonishment; cautioning someone; expressing fear; reassuring someone; expressing relief

5 Qu'est-ce qui se passe dans *Le Cimetière des éléphants?* Safiétou et Ababacar ne sont pas d'accord. Complète les passages suivants en utilisant **Je ne pense pas que** et le sub-jonctif du verbe qui convient. (**p. 203**)

> **EXEMPLE** —Khoro, c'est le roi des hommes!
> **—Je ne pense pas qu'il soit le roi des hommes.**

1. Le petit tisserin a très envie d'accueillir les hommes.
2. Khoro fait confiance aux hommes.
3. Les hommes sont gentils avec les éléphants.
4. Les éléphants peuvent rester dans leur pays.
5. Les éléphants vont vers le soleil levant.
6. Les éléphants font attention à tout sur leur chemin.
7. Les éléphants sont heureux de voir arriver les hommes.
8. Les armes des hommes ne présentent aucun danger pour les éléphants.
9. Cela s'est passé l'année dernière.
10. On sait exactement où se trouve le cimetière des éléphants.

6 Complète les phrases suivantes avec le subjonctif d'**être** ou de **pouvoir,** selon le cas. (**p. 203**)

1. Il est essentiel que nous _____ conscients de la surexploitation de la nature.
2. Je ne pense pas qu'il _____ inutile de lutter contre la chasse illégale des rhinocéros.
3. Il est important que tu _____ membre du WWF.
4. Ça m'étonnerait qu'on _____ arrêter le transport illicite de perroquets.
5. Il faudrait que vous _____ plus concernés par ces problèmes.
6. Je ne pense pas que nous _____ sauver toutes les espèces végétales qui sont en voie de disparition.
7. Il est important qu'on _____ éviter le massacre des éléphants.
8. Il est essentiel que les lois de protection de l'environnement _____ plus strictes.
9. Je ne suis pas certain que les Chinois _____ sauver le panda.
10. Ça m'étonnerait qu'on _____ sauver le tigre en Inde.

Answers

5 Je ne pense pas...
1. que le petit tisserin ait très envie d'accueillir les hommes.
2. que Khoro fasse confiance aux hommes.
3. que les hommes soient gentils avec les éléphants.
4. que les éléphants puissent rester dans leur pays.
5. que les éléphants aillent vers le soleil levant.
6. que les éléphants fassent attention à tout sur leur chemin.
7. que les éléphants soient heureux de voir arriver les hommes.
8. que les armes des hommes ne présentent aucun danger pour les éléphants.
9. que cela se soit passé l'année dernière.
10. qu'on sache exactement où se trouve le cimetière des éléphants.

6
1. soyons
2. soit
3. sois
4. puisse
5. soyez
6. puissions
7. puisse
8. soient
9. puissent
10. puisse

Communication for All Students

Challenge

6 Have students complete the sentences and check their work at the board or on an overhead transparency. Then have them compose original sentences similar to those in Activity 6, about wildlife preservation in their region or state. They could then illustrate their work with drawings or magazine cut-outs for display in the classroom.

Kinesthetic Learners

8 Have partners take turns acting out each animal as one partner reads the sentence. Students should then write their answers, checking each other's work for accuracy. Students could also create a skit in which they use the subjunctive to describe different animals in the style of a popular, wildlife, reality-based television show.

7 Fais des phrases avec les mots suivants. Mets le verbe au subjonctif, s'il le faut. **(p. 203)**

1. Il est important que / les enfants / avoir des responsabilités
2. Camille / avoir peur que / vous / avoir des soucis
3. Ses parents / avoir peur que / elle avoir un accident
4. Je sais que / il y faire / très chaud
5. Ça m'étonnerait que / tu / avoir 18 ans
6. Il se peut que / je / aller te voir à Bangui
7. Je ne pense pas que / nous / avoir faim après ce dîner
8. Il est possible que / nous / aller nous promener en bateau sur l'Oubangui
9. Je veux bien que / tu / aller me chercher un café
10. Je suis convaincu que / ce / être trop dangereux
11. Il est fort possible que / ils / aller en Afrique cet été

8 Complète chacune des devinettes suivantes avec le verbe qui convient. Ensuite, regarde les images et donne le nom de l'animal décrit en français. Attention! Certaines phrases contiennent un verbe au subjonctif. **(p. 203)**

EXEMPLE   Je ne pense pas que cet animal **soit** (être) végétarien.   **Le guépard**

1. Cet animal aime _____ (passer) toute la journée dans l'eau.
2. Je ne pense pas que ces animaux _____ (pouvoir) voler.
3. Je crois que ces animaux _____ (aimer) beaucoup les fleurs.
4. Je ne crois pas que tu _____ (pouvoir) courir aussi vite que cet animal.
5. Ça m'étonnerait que ces animaux _____ (manger) de la viande.
6. Je sais que ces animaux _____ (pouvoir) voler.

Possible answers

7
1. Il est important que les enfants aient des responsabilités.
2. Camille a peur que vous ayez des soucis.
3. Ses parents ont peur qu'elle ait un accident.
4. Je sais qu'il y fait très chaud.
5. Ça m'étonnerait que tu aies 18 ans.
6. Il se peut que j'aille te voir à Bangui.
7. Je ne pense pas que nous ayons faim après ce dîner.
8. Il est possible que nous allions nous promener en bateau sur l'Oubangui.
9. Je veux bien que tu ailles me chercher un café.
10. Je suis convaincu que c'est trop dangereux.
11. Il est fort possible qu'ils aillent en Afrique cet été.

8
1. passer; l'hippopotame
2. puissent; le guépard, l'hippopotame, les éléphants
3. aiment; les papillons
4. puisses; le guépard
5. mangent; les éléphants, les papillons, l'hippopotame
6. peuvent; les papillons

Review and Assess

You may wish to assign the **Grammaire supplémentaire** activities as additional practice or homework after presenting material throughout the chapter. Assign Activity 1 **Note de grammaire** (p. 193), Activities 2–4 after **Grammaire** (p. 196), and Activities 5–8 after **Grammaire** (p. 203).

To prepare students for the **Etape** Quizzes and Chapter Test, we suggest doing the **Grammaire supplémentaire** activities in the following order. Have students complete Activities 1–4 before taking Quiz 7-1A or 7-1B; and Activities 5–8 before Quiz 7-2A or 7-2B.

Mise en pratique

CHAPITRE 7

The **Mise en pratique** reviews and integrates all four skills and culture in preparation for the Chapter Test.

Teaching Resources
pp. 212–213

PRINT
▶ Lesson Planner, p. 36
▶ Listening Activities, p. 53
▶ Video Guide, pp. 43, 45–46
▶ Grammar Tutor for Students of French, Chapter 7
▶ Standardized Assessment Tutor, Chapter 7

MEDIA
▶ One-Stop Planner
▶ Video Program
  Videocassette 3, 12:24–19:41
▶ Audio Compact Discs, CD 7, Tr. 13
▶ Interactive CD-ROM Tutor, Disc 2

Ecology Link

Before an international ban on ivory was instituted in 1990, the elephant population of some African countries had dropped by as much as 89%. Once the ban was in effect, almost one hundred countries honored it, and the price of ivory fell dramatically. Craft items and jewelry that were once made of ivory are now available in a plastic imitation, which is virtually indistinguishable from authentic ivory.

Answers

1 1. preventing the poaching of endangered species
2. to sell their skins, horns, feathers, fur, or ivory for profit
3. Collectors and tourists contribute by buying animals and products made from them.
4. Wild animals risk extinction. People and domestic animals risk contracting diseases.
5. Refuse to buy products such as ivory and furs that are taken from wild animals.

Mise en pratique

1 En Afrique, un gardien d'une réserve que tu visites te donne ce dépliant. Lis-le et réponds aux questions suivantes. *See answers below.*

PLUS JAMAIS ÇA!

Savez-vous que 3 200 espèces animales et 40 000 espèces végétales sont menacées d'extinction? Le commerce international de la vie sauvage est la deuxième cause de disparition de celles-ci. Malgré la réglementation existante, un négoce illégal important persiste. Pour lutter contre celui-ci, un bureau TRAFFIC vient d'être créé en France. Agissez avec lui, aidez-le...

WWF France

LES FAITS
Dans le monde entier, singes, éléphants, rhinocéros, félins, crocodiles, perroquets, tortues... sont tués pour leur peau, leurs plumes, leur ivoire, ou capturés vivants : Pour 1 animal vendu jusqu'à 20 meurent durant la capture et les transports. Le bénéfice tiré du trafic illicite de la vie sauvage représente 1/3 du commerce total et profite à une «mafia» internationale. Les collectionneurs, les touristes contribuent à la sur-exploitation de la faune et de la flore sauvages qui participe à l'appauvrissement des pays en développement.

LES RISQUES
Pour la vie sauvage : Dans le monde 3 200 espèces animales sont menacées d'extinction et 40 000 espèces végétales sont en voie de disparition.
Pour l'homme : Le trafic d'animaux véhicule des maladies trans-missibles à l'homme ou aux animaux domestiques et d'élevage. Certains animaux sont porteurs de la rage, de la fièvre jaune...

LES SOLUTIONS
Prise de conscience : Vous êtes concernés! Vous êtes la meilleure arme contre la surexploitation de la vie sauvage et de son trafic. Evitez d'acheter : ivoire, corail, écailles de tortue, peaux et fourrures, insectes, objets en plume, animaux sauvages, vivants ou empaillés. Réfléchissez, renseignez-vous!

AIDEZ-NOUS A PROTEGER LA VIE

1. What is this brochure about?
2. According to the brochure, why are these animals hunted?
3. Who contributes to the problem besides poachers? How?
4. What risks to people and to animals are mentioned?
5. What does the brochure recommend that each person do to help solve the problem?

2 Après avoir lu le dépliant, tu veux faire quelque chose pour la protection des animaux. Ecris une lettre à tes camarades où tu leur expliques ce qu'il faut faire pour sauver les animaux.

☐ Je désire participer à la lutte contre le commerce illégal de la vie sauvage et verse un don de :
  ☐ 100 F   ☐ 200 F   ☐ 500 F et +
☐ Je désire devenir membre du WWF
En étant membre, je reçois la Revue PANDA (au moins 4 fois l'an) et le PANDA Nouvelles (4 à 6 fois l'an)
☐ Mlle ☐ Mme ☐ M. ☐ Famille ☐ Firme

Nom

Prénom

Rue, No

No postal   Localité

Année de naissance   Signature
  (au-dessous de 16 ans, celle du répondant)

☐ Je m'intéresse aux activités de la section WWF de ma région et désire une information à ce sujet.
☐ J'aimerais également devenir membre de la section WWF de ma région qui agit (par des travaux pratiques) pour la protection de la nature locale. Cotisation annuelle supplémentaire à celle du WWF Suisse: max. Fr.5.- (pour les jeunes membres de moins de 20 ans pas de supplément).

Apply and Assess

Additional Practice

1 Ask students the following questions about the brochure: **Combien d'espèces d'animaux sont en voie de disparition? (3.200) Comment s'appelle le bureau qui lutte contre le négoce illégal d'animaux? (TRAFFIC) De quels animaux s'agit-il? (les singes, les éléphants, les rhinocéros, les félins, les crocodiles, les perroquets, les tortues)**

Building on Previous Skills

2 Encourage students to use expressions they've already learned for persuading and reproaching: **Tu (ne) devrais (pas)... ; Tu ferais bien de... ; Tu as tort de... ; Ce n'est pas bien de...**

STANDARDS: 1.2, 1.3, 3.1

3 Ecoute Roger qui montre à sa classe les diapositives de son voyage en Afrique. Quels endroits l'ont vraiment impressionné? *See scripts and answers on p. 185H.*

CD 7
Tr. 13

a.

b.

c.

d.

e.

f.

4 Tu vas faire un safari avec ton ami(e). Tu lui décris comment sera le paysage et quels animaux vous pourrez y voir, d'après toi. Il/Elle s'est renseigné(e) et te dit s'il/si elle croit que tu as raison. Faites aussi une liste de ce qu'il faut faire avant de partir et de ce qu'il faut emporter. Si ton ami(e) oublie quelque chose, fais-lui des suggestions.

5 Imagine que tu es dans la brousse africaine. Ecris tes aventures des trois premiers jours. Ensuite, raconte-les à ton/ta camarade.

6 **Jeu de rôle**

You and your friends are camping in a reserve. Suddenly, you hear noises that sound like gunshots. Wondering what the noises could be, you decide to go see what's happening. As you come over a hill, you see poachers. Knowing that you could be in danger, you leave immediately. When you reach a village, you look for a phone to call the reserve patrol. Act out this scene with your classmates. At the appropriate times remember to:

- express fear
- warn your friends
- make suppositions
- reassure one another
- express your relief

Apply and Assess

Visual Learners

3 Type brief descriptions of each slide featured in this activity. For example, for the first slide, you might write **Les chutes de Boali sont magnifiques!** Make copies of the descriptions, distribute them, and have students match the slides with the descriptions.

Challenge

3 Have students write captions for the slides. They might write captions that Roger would have written, or captions based on their own impressions of Africa. If students write about their own impressions, you might have volunteers read a caption aloud and have the class try to guess which photo it describes.

Mise en pratique

Speaking Assessment

4 You might use the following rubric when grading your students on this activity.

Speaking Rubric	Points			
	4	3	2	1
Content (Complete–Incomplete)				
Comprehension (Total–Little)				
Comprehensibility (Comprehensible–Incomprehensible)				
Accuracy (Accurate–Seldom accurate)				
Fluency (Fluent–Not fluent)				

18–20: A 14–15: C Under
16–17: B 12–13: D 12: F

Culture Notes

- The **chutes de Boali,** shown in Photo **a** in Activity 3, are located about one hundred kilometers northwest of Bangui in the southern part of the Central African Republic. The falls are controlled by a dam, which was built by the Chinese.

- Point out the Pygmies in Photo **c** in Activity 3. The people of this ethnic group are famous for their height, which averages about four feet. Their lifestyle includes hunting and gathering nuts and roots available in the rain forest. A nomadic people, they are constantly moving to areas where food is more plentiful.

Que sais-je?

WA3 FRANCOPHONE
AFRICA-7

Teaching Resources
p. 214

PRINT
▸ Grammar Tutor for Students of French, Chapter 7

MEDIA
▸ Interactive CD-ROM Tutor, Disc 2
▸ Online self-test

go.hrw.com
WA3 FRANCOPHONE
AFRICA-7

Possible answers

2 1. Ça m'étonnerait qu'il y ait des chiens.
2. Je suis sûr(e) qu'il y aura des zèbres.
3. Je ne suis pas certain(e) qu'il y ait des ours.
4. Je suis convaincu(e) qu'il y aura des girafes.

3 Tu crois que je devrais prendre... ; Tu penses qu'il vaudrait mieux emporter...
1. de la lotion anti-moustique?
2. des jumelles?
3. des chèques de voyage?

4 1. Il faudrait que... / Il est important que... / Il est essentiel que tu prennes de la lotion anti-moustique/des jumelles/des chèques de voyage.
2. Ce n'est pas la peine de... ; Je ne crois pas que ce soit utile d'emporter de la lotion anti-moustique. Il est nécessaire que tu prennes des jumelles et des chèques de voyage.

5 Oh, dis donc! Ça alors! C'est pas vrai! Oh là là! Ouah! C'est le pied! Tiens! Regarde un peu! Qu'est-ce qu'(e)... ! C'est fou comme... ; Quel(le)... ! Tu as vu comme... ? Je n'ai jamais vu un(e) aussi...

7 1. J'ai très peur des serpents et des araignées.
2. J'ai la frousse!

Can you use what you've learned in this chapter?

Can you make suppositions? p. 193

1 How would you make suppositions about what you would see on a safari?
On pourrait sûrement voir... ; Je parie qu'il y a... ; Ça doit être... ; Il doit y avoir...

Can you express doubt and certainty? p. 193

2 How would you express your doubt or certainty about seeing the following animals on safari in Africa?   See answers below.

1.   2.   3.   4.

Can you ask for and give advice? p. 195

3 How would you ask if these items are necessary for a trip?   See answers below.

1.   2.   3.

4 How would you tell a friend whether or not the items in number 3 are necessary for . . .   See answers below.
1. a trip to Africa?   2. a trip to the North Pole?

Can you express astonishment? p. 201

5 How would you express your feelings about something really impressive?
See answers below.

Can you caution someone? p. 202

6 How would you warn people in these situations?   *Possible answers:*
1. A friend is about to step out into a busy street without looking.   Méfie-toi!
2. A relative is traveling to a country where the mosquitoes carry malaria.   Attention aux moustiques!
3. A friend is approached by a mean dog.   Fais gaffe!

Can you express fear? p. 202

7 How would you express fear of . . .   See answers below.
1. snakes and spiders?   2. a horror movie you're watching?

Can you reassure someone? p. 202

8 How would you reassure someone who is afraid of the things in number 7?
Ne vous en faites pas. Ne t'en fais pas. N'ayez pas peur. N'aie pas peur. Calmez-vous! Calme-toi! Pas de panique!

Can you express relief? p. 202

9 How would you express your relief at . . .   *Possible answers:*
1. not getting bitten by a mean dog?   Je l'ai échappé belle! J'ai eu chaud!
2. not getting a bad grade at school?   Ouf! J'ai eu de la chance!

Review and Assess

Additional Practice

2 Bring in, or have students bring in, additional pictures of animals that would or would not be seen on a photo safari in the Central African Republic. Have students express doubt or certainty about seeing them.

4 Have students suggest additional items one might need to bring on trips to these places.

Challenge

7 8 Have students combine their answers for Activities 7 and 8 to create a two-line dialogue in which one person reassures a frightened friend.

Première étape

Making suppositions

On pourrait sûrement...	We'd be able to . . . for sure.
Ça doit être...	It must be . . .
Il doit y avoir...	There must be . . .

Expressing doubt and certainty

Ça m'étonnerait que...	I'd be surprised if . . .
Je (ne) suis (pas) sûr(e) que...	I'm (not) sure that . . .
Je (ne) suis (pas) certain(e) que...	I'm (not) certain that . . .
Je ne pense pas que...	I don't think that . . .
Je sais que...	I know that . . .
Je suis convain-cu(e) que...	I'm convinced that . . .

Rain forest and savannah

une araignée	a spider
un arbre	a tree
la brousse	the brush
une fourmi	an ant

l'herbe (f.)	grass
une mouche	a fly
un oiseau	a bird
un papillon	a butterfly
le paysage	scenery
un point d'eau	a watering hole
une rivière	a river
la savane	the savannah
un serpent	a snake
la végétation tropicale	tropical vegetation

Asking for and giving advice

Tu crois que je devrais... ?	Do you think I should . . .?
Tu penses qu'il vaudrait mieux... ?	Do you think it'd be better to . . .?
Je crois que ça vaut mieux.	I think that's better.
A mon avis, c'est plus sûr.	In my opinion, it's safer.
Ce n'est pas la peine.	It's not worth it.

Je ne crois pas que ce soit utile.	I don't think it's worthwhile.
Il faudrait que...	You ought to . . .
Il est très important que...	It's very important that . . .
Il est essentiel que...	It's essential that . . .
Il est nécessaire que...	It's necessary that . . .

Packing for a safari

un caméscope	a camcorder
une carte de crédit	a credit card
de la crème solaire	sunscreen
un désinfectant	disinfectant
une gourde	a canteen
des jumelles (f.)	binoculars
des pansements (m.)	bandages
une pellicule	a roll of film
une torche	a flashlight

CHAPITRE 7

Circumlocution
Have students work with a partner. One will pretend to be a tourist on safari, the other an absent-minded safari guide. The guide points out an animal that they encounter, but can't remember the name. He or she must describe the animal's appearance, eating habits, and so on until the tourist guesses the name of the animal. (**—Et là, vous voyez, c'est un gros animal qui habite dans l'eau./ —C'est un hippo-potame, monsieur/madame./ — Oui, c'est ça, un hippopotame.**) After the tourist guesses the name of the animal, have partners switch roles.

Deuxième étape

Expressing astonishment

Oh, dis donc!	Wow!
Ça alors!	How about that!
Ouah!	Wow!
C'est le pied!	Cool! Neat!
Tiens! Regarde un peu!	Hey! Check it out!
C'est fou comme... !	I can't believe how . . . !
Tu as vu comme... ?	Did you see how . . . ?
Je n'ai jamais vu un(e) aussi...	I've never seen such a . . .
Qu'est-ce qu'il/ elle est... !	How . . . he/she/ it is!

African animals

une corne	a horn
un éléphant	an elephant

une girafe	a giraffe
un guépard	a cheetah
un hippopotame	a hippopotamus
un lion	a lion
lourd(e)	heavy
la proie	the prey
un rhinocéros	a rhinoceros
un singe	a monkey
une trompe	a trunk
un zèbre	a zebra

Cautioning and reassuring someone

Je vous signale que...	I'm warning you that . . .
Il serait plus prudent de...	It would be wiser to . . .
Faites attention/ gaffe!	Look out!
Attention à... !	Watch out for . . . !

Méfiez-vous!	Be careful!
Ne bougez pas.	Don't move.
N'ayez pas peur.	Don't be afraid.
Calmez-vous!	Calm down!
Pas de panique!	Don't panic!

Expressing fear and relief

J'ai très peur de (que)...	I'm very afraid of (that) . . .
J'ai la frousse!	I'm scared to death!
On a eu de la chance!	We were lucky!
Ouf! On a eu chaud!	Whew! That was a real scare!
On l'a échappé belle!	That was close!

Chapter 7 Assessment

▶ **Testing Program**
Chapter Test, pp. 155–160
 Audio Compact Discs, CD 7, Trs. 16–18
Speaking Test, p. 298

▶ **Alternative Assessment Guide**
Portfolio Assessment, p. 22
Performance Assessment, p. 36
CD-ROM Assessment, p. 50

▶ **Interactive CD-ROM Tutor, Disc 2**
A toi de parler
A toi d'écrire

▶ **Standardized Assessment Tutor**
Chapter 7

▶ **One-Stop Planner, Disc 2**
Test Generator
 Chapter 7

Review and Assess

Game
Loto! Have students make a 5 X 5 grid on a sheet of paper and write in each square one of the words or expressions from the **Vocabulaire**. While students are making their grids, write the vocabulary expressions on slips of paper and place them in a box. When students have completed their grid, begin the Bingo game by drawing slips and calling out the expressions. Students who have written that expression on their grid should mark it with a scrap of paper or a coin. When a student has marked five squares in a row, he or she calls out **Loto!**, shows you the grid, and reads aloud the French expressions he or she has marked. Then, the entire class writes sentences, using the expressions marked.

Chapitre 8 : La Tunisie, pays de contrastes
Chapter Overview

Mise en train pp. 218–220	*Bisous de Nefta*

	FUNCTIONS	GRAMMAR	VOCABULARY	RE-ENTRY
Première étape pp. 221–227	• Asking someone to convey good wishes, p. 222 • Closing a letter, p. 222 • Expressing hopes or wishes, p. 225 • Giving advice, p. 225	• **Si** clauses, p. 225	• Traditional Life, p. 223	• The imperfect (**Chapitre 1**, III) • The conditional (**Chapitre 5**, III) • The imperative (**Chapitre 1**, II)

Remise en train pp. 228–229	*Salut de Tunis*

Deuxième étape pp. 230–233	• Complaining, p. 231 • Expressing annoyance, p. 231 • Making comparisons, p. 232	• The comparative, p. 232	• City life, p. 230	• Intonation (**Chapitre 1**, I) • Adjective agreement (**Chapitre 1**, II) • Describing what a place was like (**Chapitre 1**, III)

Lisons! pp. 234–236	**Enfance d'une fille**	**Reading Strategy:** Relating parts of the story to the main idea

Ecrivons! p. 237	**Un récit familial**	**Writing Strategy:** Brainstorming

Grammaire supplémentaire	**pp. 238–241**	**Première étape,** pp. 238–240	**Deuxième étape,** pp. 240–241

Review pp. 242–245	**Mise en pratique,** pp. 242–243	**Que sais-je?,** p. 244	**Vocabulaire,** p. 245

CULTURE

• **Rencontre culturelle,** Overview of Tunisia, p. 221

• **Note culturelle,** Traditional and modern life in Tunisia, p. 224

• **Panorama Culturel,** Modernization in francophone countries, p. 227

• **Note culturelle,** Traditional and modern styles of dress in Tunisia, p. 233

Chapitre 8 : La Tunisie, pays de contrastes
Chapter Resources

PRINT

Lesson Planning

 One-Stop Planner

Lesson Planner with Substitute Teacher Lesson Plans, pp. 37–41, 71

Student Make-Up Assignments
- Make-Up Assignment Copying Masters, Chapter 8

Listening and Speaking

Listening Activities
- Student Response Forms for Listening Activities, pp. 59–61
- Additional Listening Activities 8-1 to 8-6, pp. 63–65
- Additional Listening Activities (song), p. 66
- Scripts and Answers, pp. 137–141

Video Guide
- Teaching Suggestions, pp. 48–49
- Activity Masters, pp. 50–52
- Scripts and Answers, pp. 98–101, 114–115

Activities for Communication
- Communicative Activities, pp. 29–32
- Realia and Teaching Suggestions, pp. 72–74
- Situation Cards, pp. 103–104

Reading and Writing

Reading Strategies and Skills Handbook, Chapter 8

Joie de lire 3, Chapter 8

Cahier d'activités, pp. 85–96

Grammar

Travaux pratiques de grammaire, pp. 73–81

Grammar Tutor for Students of French, Chapter 8

Assessment

Testing Program
- Grammar and Vocabulary Quizzes, **Etape** Quizzes, and Chapter Test, pp. 169–182
- Score Sheet, Scripts and Answers, pp. 183–189

Alternative Assessment Guide
- Portfolio Assessment, p. 23
- Performance Assessment, p. 37
- CD-ROM Assessment, p. 51

Student Make-Up Assignments
- Alternative Quizzes, Chapter 8

Standardized Assessment Tutor
- Reading, pp. 31–33
- Writing, p. 34
- Math, pp. 51–52

MEDIA

 Online Activities
- Jeux interactifs
- Activités Internet

 Video Program
- Videocassette 3
- Videocassette 5 (captioned version)

 Audio Compact Discs
- Textbook Listening Activities, CD 8, Tracks 1–13
- Additional Listening Activities, CD 8, Tracks 19–25
- Assessment Items, CD 8, Tracks 14–18

 Interactive CD-ROM Tutor, Disc 2

Teaching Transparencies
- Situation 8-1 to 8-2
- **Grammaire supplémentaire** Answers
- **Travaux pratiques de grammaire** Answers

 One-Stop Planner CD-ROM

Use the **One-Stop Planner CD-ROM with Test Generator** to aid in lesson planning and pacing.

For each chapter, the **One-Stop Planner** includes:

- Editable lesson plans with direct links to teaching resources
- Printable worksheets from resource books
- Direct launches to the HRW Internet activities
- Video and audio segments
- Test Generator
- Clip Art for vocabulary items

Chapitre 8 : La Tunisie, pays de contrastes

Projects

Ma ville, hier et aujourd'hui

Students will prepare and videotape a documentary program for French television in which they describe how their city or town has changed in the last fifty years. Students will conduct research in the library or media center and interview some of their city's older residents. Their program should also include visual aids, such as old newspapers and maps, posters they create, or computer-generated graphics.

MATERIALS

✂ Students may need

- Reference materials, such as old newspapers, magazines, and maps
- Cassette recorder
- Audiocassette
- Camcorder

- Videocassette
- Posterboard
- Colored markers
- Computer (for graphics, if available)

SUGGESTED SEQUENCE

1. Have students begin by researching their city's history in the library or media center. You might allow class time for students to do their preliminary research. They should find out how and when the town was founded and what people or businesses were important at that time.

2. Have students prepare a list of interview questions they would like to ask their interviewees. They should also translate the questions into French, since their documentary will be for a French TV station.

3. Then, students should interview at least five people who have lived in the city for the last twenty to fifty years. They might choose to record the interviews on audio- or videocassette so they can play clips of the interviews during their program.

4. Have students organize the information they intend to present in their documentary and write their scripts. Remind them that they need to pique their audience's interest in the first thirty seconds of the program, so they should lead in with their most interesting facts. Then, they should summarize their research and interviews.

5. If students recorded their interviews, they might choose to play five- or ten-second clips during their presentation.

In this case, they should prepare a voice-over French translation, which they may record at this time or simply read aloud over the recording during the presentation. You might offer help with the translations.

6. Students should create and/or organize any charts, graphs, or photos for their presentation.

7. Have students record their documentaries on videocassette, using all the audiovisual materials they have organized.

GRADING THE PROJECT

You might base students' grades on thoroughness of content, organization, use and creativity of audiovisual aids, oral presentation, and language use.

Suggested Point Distribution (total = 100 points)
Content..25 points
Organization ....25 points
Audiovisual aids....................................15 points
Oral presentation..................................20 points
Language use...15 points

Games

Arrêtez!

In this game, students will practice chapter vocabulary.

Procedure   Choose several words from the **Vocabulaire** on page 245. Write the words on a transparency and cover it with a sheet of paper. To begin the game, uncover the first word on the list. Students must write new words that begin with the letters of that word. For example, if the word you uncover is **poterie**, students might write **poule** for **p, olive** for **o, tapis** for **t,** and so on. The student who finishes first calls out **Arrêtez!,** and the other students put down their pens. The student who called out **Arrêtez!** reads his or her words aloud. If the words are all appropriate, that student wins ten points. Then, uncover another word and continue the game.

Variation   Give students thirty seconds to write as many words as possible that begin with each letter. Call time and award points for each word that is correctly spelled.

Storytelling

Mini-histoire

This story accompanies Teaching Transparency 8-2. The mini-histoire can be told and retold in different formats, acted out, written down, and read aloud to give students additional opportunities to practice all four skills. In the following story, Yasmina sends a letter to her best friend in France. In her letter, she describes the city of Tunis.

Chère Isabelle,

Dans ta dernière lettre tu m'as demandé de te décrire Tunis. Ça ressemble à n'importe quelle autre grande ville. Il y a de grands immeubles modernes qui se construisent à côté de bâtiments plus traditionnels. Il y a un centre-ville très animé et il y a une banlieue comme à Paris, le soleil en plus. Dans un sens, ce n'est pas très différent. Comme dans toutes les grandes villes, il y a des embouteillages. Il y a aussi beaucoup de monde dans les rues; certaines de ces personnes se promènent tranquillement, d'autres sont pressées. Il y a beaucoup de pollution comme à Paris. Voilà.
Yasmina.

Traditions

Les Tapis tunisiens

Carpet weaving is one of the oldest and most important home industries in Tunisia. Children are trained from an early age to assist their family members in the weaving process. The carpets, made on ancient looms, often feature traditional patterns of bright blue and red, or copy the patterns of Persian carpets. Although they take several years to weave, they last forever. The carpets of Kairouan and Gafsa are the most famous. Many of them are considered to be fine works of art. In fact, they are often bought as a cash investment, protected in bank vaults, and used as collateral for loans. Have students investigate the weaving process and the motifs and patterns used in Tunisian carpets and report their findings to the class.

Recette

*The Tunisians have dinner as late as 10 P.M. They sometimes have meat or fish with couscous, and they try not to drink while eating couscous to avoid feeling bloated. Another very popular dinner served in Tunisia is **tajine**.*

TAJINE DE BOULETTES DE POISSON

pour 6 personnes

1 1/2 livre de poisson (sole, cabillaud, bar...)

4 cuillères à soupe de persil

2 gousses d'ail

2 oignons finement coupés

1/2 tasse de miettes de pain

1/2 cuillère à café de harissa

1 œuf

de l'huile d'olive

Sauce

2 gousses d'ail

3 cuillères à soupe d'huile d'olive

2 tasses de purée de tomates

2 tasses de bouillon de poisson

Boulettes de poisson:
Hacher finement le poisson. Ajouter tous les ingrédients sauf l'œuf et l'huile d'olive. Mélanger. Une fois que tout est bien mélangé, ajouter l'œuf. Quand l'œuf est bien incorporé à la pâte, faire les boulettes. Mettre suffisamment d'huile dans une poêle pour faire frire les boulettes.

Sauce:
Faire chauffer l'huile dans une casserole. Ajouter le reste des ingrédients. Lorsque la sauce commence à bouillir réduire le feu. Ajouter les boulettes de poisson et laisser mijoter pendant 20 minutes. Servir dans un plat chaud et parsemer de persil.

Technology

Video Program

Videocassette 3, Videocassette 5 (captioned version)
See Video Guide, pp. 47–51.

Camille et compagnie • Huitième épisode : *La Nouvelle Vie d'Azzedine*

Azzedine, a young Tunisian, is writing a letter to his friend Sébastien about his new life in Aix-en-Provence. He describes his favorite café, where Camille works as a waitress. This is where Camille and Azzedine meet for the first time. Azzedine shows Camille photographs of his hometown, Nefta, and the two friends compare lifestyles in Aix and in Tunisia. Then Sophie arrives, complaining that she has been splashed by a motorbike.

Cette ville a beaucoup évolué?

Students from around the francophone world talk about progress and change. Two native speakers discuss the **Panorama Culturel** question and introduce the interviews.

Vidéoclips

- **Music Video: C'est le dernier qui a parlé** performed by Amina
- **News report:** Students talk about differences between the sexes.

Interactive CD-ROM Tutor

The **Interactive CD-ROM Tutor** contains videos, interactive games, and activities that provide students an opportunity to practice and review the material covered in Chapter 8.

Activity	Activity Type	Pupil's Edition Page
1. Comment dit-on… ?	Prenons note!	p. 222
2. Vocabulaire	Jeu des paires	p. 223
3. Grammaire	Les mots qui manquent	p. 225
4. Vocabulaire	Chasse au trésor Explorons! Vérifions!	p. 230
5. Comment dit-on… ?	Méli-mélo	p. 232
6. Grammaire	Le bon choix	p. 232
Panorama Culturel	Cette ville a beaucoup évolué? Le bon choix	p. 227
A toi de parler	*Guided recording*	pp. 242–243
A toi d'écrire	*Guided writing*	pp. 242–243

Teacher Management System

Logging In

Logging in to the *Allez, viens!* TMS is easy. Upon launching the program, simply type "admin" in the password area of the log-in screen and press RETURN. Log on to **www.hrw.com/CDROMTUTOR** for a detailed explanation of the Teacher Management System.

Internet Connection

One-Stop Planner CD-ROM

To preview all resources available for this chapter, use the **One-Stop Planner CD-ROM**, Disc 2.

ADRESSE: go.hrw.com
MOT-CLE: WA3 FRANCOPHONE AFRICA-8

*Have students explore the **go.hrw.com** Web site for many online resources covering all chapters. All Chapter 8 resources are available under the keyword **WA3 FRANCOPHONE AFRICA-8.** Interactive games help students practice the material and provide them with immediate feedback. You'll also find a printable worksheet that provides Internet activities that lead to a comprehensive online research project.*

Jeux interactifs

You can use the interactive activities in this chapter

- to practice grammar, vocabulary, and chapter functions
- as homework
- as an assessment option
- as a self-test
- to prepare for the Chapter Test

Activités Internet

Students look for information about Tunisian cities and regions, using the vocabulary and phrases from the chapter.

- After completing the activity sheet, have students work with a partner and share the information they gathered in Activity B on that sheet. Then ask each pair of students to share what they learned with the class. In Activity C, students are asked to write a letter to a friend describing their life as they imagine it would be in Tunisia. Have partners exchange their letters and edit each other's work.

Projet

Have groups of students research and plan a tour of Tunisia. Students can research information about transportation available, lodging possibilities, tourist attractions, and other activities. Have them plan their itinerary and map their route for visiting at least three cities or villages in Tunisia. Remind students to document their sources by noting the names and the URLs of all the sites they consulted. You may want to have each group present its findings and itinerary to the class.

Première étape

7 **p. 222**   Answers to Activity 7
1, 3, 5

1. —Tu sais ce que je vais faire pendant les vacances? De la plongée avec Ahmed.
—Ah oui? Ça fait longtemps que je ne l'ai pas vu, Ahmed. Salue-le pour moi.
—D'accord!

2. —Je vais au cinéma avec des copains. Tu veux venir avec nous?
—Je voudrais bien, mais je ne peux pas. Je dois faire mes devoirs.
—Dommage. Peut-être la prochaine fois.
—Oui, j'espère.

3. —Tu as entendu? Malika s'est cassé la jambe.
—Comment c'est arrivé?
—Elle est tombée de vélo. Je vais la voir à l'hôpital. Tu veux venir avec moi?
—Je ne peux pas aujourd'hui. Mais embrasse-la pour moi et dis-lui que je pense à elle.
—D'accord. Compte sur moi.

4. —Alors, tu reviens en août?
—Oui, fin août.
—Bon. Je te téléphonerai. Allez, je parie que ça va être chouette, la Tunisie.
—Oui, sans doute.
—Tu nous manqueras. Allez, dépêche-toi. Tu vas rater l'avion.
—Bon, d'accord. Au revoir.
—Au revoir.

5. —Alors, bon voyage! Surtout, sois sage. Fais mes amitiés à ton oncle et à ta tante. Et dis-leur que je vais leur écrire.
—Tu peux compter sur moi.
—Allez, dépêche-toi, le train va partir!

12 **p. 224**   Answers to Activity 12
1. f   2. a   3. d   4. e   5. g   6. b   7. c

1. AMIRA   Tu vois comment il trait la vache?
   KARIM   C'est cool. Je peux le faire, moi aussi? Tu m'apprends?
   AMIRA   Oui, si tu veux, mais je t'assure, c'est pas si cool que ça.

2. KARIM   Qu'est-ce qu'elle fait, la femme là-bas?
   AMIRA   Oh, elle va donner à manger aux poules. Regarde comme elles sont agitées.

3. AMIRA   Attention à la chèvre! Elle mange tout, tu sais. Tu ferais bien de mettre tes mains dans tes poches.

4. KARIM   Il est où, ton frère?
   AMIRA   Il garde les moutons. Ils sont en train de brouter.
   KARIM   Est-ce que vous les tondez?
   AMIRA   Oui, c'est mon frère et mon père qui les tondent. On utilise leur laine pour faire des tapis.

5. AMIRA   Tu vois? Ce sont nos champs de blé.
   KARIM   Alors, quand est-ce qu'on récolte le blé?
   AMIRA   Bientôt. Nos cousins vont nous aider.

6. KARIM   C'est cool, l'artisanat tunisien.
   AMIRA   Oui. Regarde cet homme là-bas. Tu vois ce qu'il fait?
   KARIM   Oui, il fait de la poterie.
   AMIRA   Oui, ici, on est très connus pour notre poterie.

7. KARIM   Il est très beau, ce paysage, avec tous ces palmiers et ces dattiers.
   AMIRA   Il y en a chez toi?
   KARIM   Oh, pas vraiment.
   AMIRA   Les dattiers, c'est très important chez nous. Si tu veux, tu peux faire la cueillette des dattes avec nous.
   KARIM   Chouette!

14 **p. 225**

1. —Mes parents veulent que j'habite à la ferme avec mon oncle cet été. Bah! Quel cauchemar! Je n'aime pas la campagne, moi.
—A ta place, je leur en parlerais. Il faut qu'ils sachent ce que tu veux.

2. —Moi, je n'ai aucune idée de ce que je voudrais faire. Et toi?
—Moi, si j'avais le choix, je partirais en Afrique. Il y a tellement de choses à faire et à voir là-bas!

3. —Je ne pourrai pas y aller si je ne trouve pas de travail, mais il n'y a rien en ce moment.
—Si j'étais toi, je demanderais au supermarché. J'ai un cousin qui y travaille. Il dit que c'est pas mal.

4. —Si c'était possible, j'habiterais chez mes cousins à la campagne.
—Mais pourquoi?
—Parce que c'est tellement tranquille. J'aimerais tellement vivre dans le calme!

5. —Dis, Saïd, où est-ce que tu habiterais si tu avais le choix?
—Oh, ça serait chouette si je pouvais habiter au bord de la mer.

6. —Cet été, j'ai le choix entre aller à la campagne chez mes grands-parents ou aller en ville, chez mon frère. Qu'est-ce que tu en penses?
—Si j'étais toi, j'irais à la campagne. Tu pourrais découvrir quelque chose de nouveau. Ça te changerait un peu.

7. —Si seulement je pouvais faire un voyage en Tunisie.
—Ah, oui? Pourquoi?

The following scripts are for the Listening Activities found in the *Pupil's Edition*. For Student Response Forms, see *Listening Activities*, pages 59–61. To provide students with additional listening practice, see *Listening Activities*, pages 63–66.

One-Stop Planner CD-ROM

To preview all resources available for this chapter, use the **One-Stop Planner CD-ROM**, Disc 2.

—Ben, tu sais que j'adore l'archéologie. J'aimerais visiter les ruines de Carthage. Ce serait super, non?

—Oui... peut-être.

Answers to Activity 14

1. donne des conseils
2. aimerait faire
3. donne des conseils
4. aimerait faire
5. aimerait faire
6. donne des conseils
7. aimerait faire

Deuxième étape

Answers to Activity 25

1. ville
2. campagne
3. ville
4. campagne
5. ville
6. ville
7. campagne
8. ville

25   p. 230

1. Comment? Je ne t'entends pas. La rue est si bruyante à cette heure-ci. Il va falloir qu'on aille à l'intérieur pour parler.

2. N'oublie pas de donner à manger aux poules, Fatima.

3. Pardon, madame. Il y a un arrêt de bus près d'ici?

4. C'est vraiment agréable ici, n'est-ce pas? Les palmiers, les dattiers, les couchers de soleil, qu'est-ce que c'est tranquille!

5. Zut alors! On va être en retard! C'est toujours la même chose, ces embouteillages!

6. Eh! Dites donc!! Vous ne pouvez pas regarder où vous allez? Qu'est-ce qu'ils sont mal élevés, ces gens!

7. Oh, je suis crevé! Ce n'est pas facile de s'occuper des chameaux. Ils sont méchants, tu sais!

8. Voilà l'immeuble où j'habite. Qu'est-ce tu en penses? Il est vraiment moderne, non?

27   p. 231

Answers to Activity 27

1. non
2. oui
3. non
4. oui
5. non
6. oui
7. oui
8. non

1. Ah non! On va manquer le film! J'en ai ras le bol de ces embouteillages!

2. Tu as entendu, il y a un nouveau cinéma tout près d'ici. Cinq minutes à pied. Cool, non?

3. Oh, c'est l'horreur, cette pollution, tu sais. Je n'arrive plus à respirer.

4. Oh, dis donc, il est géant, ce magasin de vidéos. Je parie qu'ils ont absolument tout ce qu'on veut.

5. Tu sais ce qui m'est arrivé? Quelqu'un m'est rentré dedans et mes lunettes sont tombées. Je commence à en avoir marre de ces gens mal élevés!

6. C'est tellement animé, la ville. Comme c'est bien d'avoir beaucoup de choses à faire et à voir!

7. On va essayer le restaurant marocain, ce soir. On m'a dit que c'était très bon. Tu viens avec nous?

8. On construit un immeuble derrière chez nous. C'est insupportable, à la fin, tout ce bruit.

28   p. 231

1. C'est l'horreur!
2. C'est insupportable, à la fin!
3. J'en ai ras le bol!
4. Je commence à en avoir marre!
5. Vous vous prenez pour qui?
6. Non mais, surtout, ne vous gênez pas!
7. Ça va pas, non?!
8. Ça commence à bien faire, hein?
9. Dites donc, ça vous gênerait de baisser votre musique?

Mise en pratique

3   p. 243

LEÏLA   Dis, Hoda, qu'est-ce que tu penses faire cet été?

HODA   Ben, ça serait chouette si je pouvais aller à la mer, mais je ne pense pas que ce soit possible.

LEÏLA   Pourquoi pas?

HODA   Ma famille n'y va pas cette année.

LEÏLA   Si j'étais toi, je demanderais à mes parents la permission d'y aller avec des copines.

HODA   Mais ils ne seront pas d'accord. Ça, je le sais déjà.

LEÏLA   Dommage. Qu'est-ce que tu pourrais faire d'autre?

HODA   Ben, il y a mon oncle et ma tante qui m'ont invitée à passer l'été chez eux en Tunisie.

LEÏLA   Cool!

HODA   Si seulement je pouvais y aller, je me baladerais un peu dans le pays.

LEÏLA   Ça serait vachement bien!

HODA   Oui, mais, je n'ai pas l'argent pour le billet.

LEÏLA   A ta place, je chercherais du travail. Avec un mois de salaire, tu pourrais te payer le voyage.

HODA   Si c'était possible, je m'occuperais des enfants des Marzouk. Ils partent en vacances pendant le mois de juin.

LEÏLA   Pourquoi tu ne le fais pas?

HODA   Ils m'ont déjà demandé, mais j'ai refusé parce que je ne savais pas que j'aurais besoin de travailler.

LEÏLA   Si j'étais toi, je leur téléphonerais tout de suite. Il se peut qu'ils n'aient pas encore trouvé quelqu'un.

HODA   Oui, c'est peut-être une bonne idée.

Answers to Mise en pratique Activity 3

Souhaits: aller à la mer; passer l'été chez son oncle et sa tante en Tunisie; s'occuper des enfants des Marzouk

Conseils: demander à tes parents la permission d'y aller avec des copines; chercher un travail; téléphoner aux Marzouk

Chapitre 8: La Tunisie, pays de contrastes
Suggested Lesson Plans *50-Minute Schedule*

Day 1

CHAPTER OPENER 5 min.
- Present Chapter Objectives, p. 217.
- Thinking Critically: Observing, Culture Note, and Language Note, ATE, pp. 216–217

MISE EN TRAIN 40 min.
- Presenting **Mise en train**, p. 218, using Video Program, Videocassette 3.
- See Teaching Suggestions, Viewing Suggestions 1–2, Video Guide, p. 48.
- Culture Notes and Language Note, ATE, p. 219
- See Teaching Suggestions, Post-viewing Suggestions 1–2, Video Guide, p. 48.
- Do Activities 1–5, p. 220.

Wrap-Up 5 min.
- Do Activity 6, p. 220.

Homework Options
Cahier d'activités, Act. 1, p. 85

Day 2

MISE EN TRAIN
Quick Review 5 min.
- Check homework.

RENCONTRE CULTURELLE 20 min.
- Presenting **Rencontre culturelle**, ATE, p. 221
- **Qu'en penses-tu?**, p. 221
- Read and discuss **Savais-tu que… ?**, p. 221.
- Culture Note and Language-to-Language, ATE, p. 221
- History Link, ATE, p. 221

PREMIERE ETAPE
Comment dit-on… ?, p. 222 20 min.
- Presenting **Comment dit-on… ?**, ATE, p. 222
- Play Audio CD for Activity 7, p. 222.
- Cahier d'activités, p. 86, Activity 2.
- Do Activity 8, p. 222.
- Have students do Activity 9, p. 222, in pairs.

Wrap-Up, 5 min.
- Begin Activity 10, p. 222.

Homework Options
Pupil's Edition, Act. 10, p. 222

Day 3

PREMIERE ETAPE
Quick Review 5 min.
- Have volunteers share letters from Activity 10, p. 222.

Vocabulaire, p. 213 25 min.
- Presenting **Vocabulaire**, ATE, p. 223
- Do Activity 11, p. 223.
- Play Audio CD for Activity 12, p. 224.
- Read and discuss **Note culturelle**, p. 224.
- Travaux pratiques de grammaire, pp. 73–74, Activities 1–3.
- Do Activity 13, p. 224.

Comment dit-on… ?, p. 215 15 min.
- Presenting **Comment dit-on… ?**, ATE, p. 225
- Play Audio CD for Activity 14, p. 225.
- See Suggestions for Using Teaching Transparency 8-1, Speaking Suggestion 4, Teaching Transparencies.

Wrap-Up 5 min.
- Literature Link and History Link, ATE, p. 224.

Homework Options
Cahier d'activités, Acts. 3–5, pp. 86–87

Day 4

PREMIERE ETAPE
Quick Review 5 min.
- Check homework.

Grammaire, p. 225 25 min.
- Presenting **Grammaire**, ATE, p. 225
- Travaux pratiques de grammaire, pp. 74–75, Acts. 4–6.
- Do Activities 15–16, p. 225–226.
- **Grammaire supplémentaire**, pp. 238–240, Acts. 2–5.
- Do Activities 17 and 19, p. 226, in pairs.

PANORAMA CULTUREL 15 min.
- Presenting **Panorama Culturel**, ATE, p. 227
- See Viewing Suggestion 1, Video Guide, p. 49.
- Questions, ATE, p. 227
- **Qu'en penses-tu?**, p. 227

Wrap-Up 5 min.
- Cahier d'activités, Activity 21, p. 96

Homework Options
Study for Quiz 8-1
Pupil's Edition, Activity 18, p. 226
Travaux pratiques de grammaire, Acts. 7–9, pp. 76–77

Day 5

PREMIERE ETAPE
Quiz 8-1 20 min.
- Administer Quiz 8-1A or 8-1B.

REMISE EN TRAIN 25 min.
- Presenting **Remise en train**, p. 228
- Do Activities 20–23, pp. 228–229.
- Culture Note, ATE, p. 229
- Do Activity 24, p. 229.

Wrap-Up 5 min.
- Challenge, ATE, p. 229

Homework Options
Cahier d'activités, Acts. 6–7, 11–12, pp. 88, 90

Day 6

REMISE EN TRAIN
Quick Review 5 min.
- Check homework.

DEUXIEME ETAPE
Vocabulaire, p. 230 20 min.
- Presenting **Vocabulaire**, ATE, p. 230
- Play Audio CD for Activity 25, p. 230.
- Do Activity 26, p. 230.
- Travaux pratiques de grammaire, pp. 78–79, Acts. 10–13.
- Game: **Mots associés**, ATE, p. 230

Comment dit-on… ?, p. 231 20 min.
- Presenting **Comment dit-on… ?**, ATE, p. 231
- Read and discuss **A la française**, p. 231.
- Play Audio CD for Activities 27–28, p. 231.
- Do Activity 29, p. 231.
- Have students do Activity 30, p. 231, in groups.

Wrap-Up 5 min.
- Architecture Link, ATE, p. 231

Homework Options
Cahier d'activités, Acts. 14–15, p. 92

One-Stop Planner CD-ROM

For alternative lesson plans by chapter section, to create your own customized plans, or to preview all resources available for this chapter, use the **One-Stop Planner CD-ROM**, Disc 2.

For additional homework suggestions, see activities accompanied by this symbol throughout the chapter.

Day 7

DEUXIEME ETAPE

Quick Review 5 min.
- Check homework.

Comment dit-on... ?, p. 232 15 min.
- Presenting **Comment dit-on... ?,** ATE, p. 232
- Do Activity 31, p. 232.
- Cahier d'activités, p. 93, Activity 16.

Grammaire, p. 232 25 min.
- Presenting **Grammaire,** ATE, p. 232
- Do Activity 32, p. 233.
- Travaux pratiques de grammaire, pp. 80–81, Activities 14–16.
- Do Activity 34, p. 233.
- Read and discuss **Note culturelle,** p. 233.
- Have students do Activity 35, p. 233, in pairs.

Wrap-Up 5 min.
- Using Prior Knowledge, ATE, p. 232

Homework Options
Study for Quiz 8–2
Pupil's Edition, Activity 34, p. 233
Cahier d'activités, Acts. 17–18, pp. 93–94

Day 8

DEUXIEME ETAPE

Quiz 8-2 20 min.
- Administer Quiz 8-2A or 8-2B.

LISONS! 25 min.
- Read and discuss **Stratégie pour lire,** p. 234.
- Do Prereading Activity A, p. 234.
- Culture Note, ATE, p. 234
- Have students read **Lisons!,** pp. 234–236.
- Do Reading Activities B–M, pp. 234–236.

Wrap-Up 5 min.
- Culture Note, ATE, p. 235

Homework Options
Cahier d'activités, Act. 20, p. 95

Day 9

DEUXIEME ETAPE

Quick Review 5 min.
- Check homework.

LISONS! 10 min.
- Do Activity R, p. 236.
- History Link and Community Link, ATE, p. 236

ECRIVONS! 30 min.
- Read and discuss the **Stratégie pour écrire,** p. 237, then have students work on their compositions.

Wrap-Up 5 min.
- Allow time for peer and self-evaluation of compositions.

Homework Options
Complete final draft of compositions.

Day 10

ECRIVONS!

Quick Review 10 min.
- Have volunteers share their stories with the class.

MISE EN PRATIQUE 35 min.
- Do Activity 1, p. 242.
- Career Path, ATE, p. 242
- Have students do Activity 2, p. 243, in pairs.
- Play Audio CD for Activity 3, p. 243.
- **A toi d'écrire,** CD-ROM Tutor

Wrap-Up 5 min.
- Activities for Communication, p. 103, Situation (global): Interview

Homework Options
Cahier d'activités, Act. 22, p. 96

Day 11

MISE EN PRATIQUE

Quick Review 5 min.
- Check homework.

Student Review 40 min.
- Do Activities 4–5, p. 243.
- Have students prepare conversations for **Jeu de rôle,** p. 243.
- Have groups present conversations for **Jeu de rôle.**
- **A toi de parler,** CD-ROM Tutor, Disc 2

Wrap-Up 5 min.
- Begin **Que sais-je?,** p. 244.

Homework Options
Que sais-je?, p. 244

Day 12

MISE EN PRATIQUE

Quick Review 20 min.
- Go over **Que sais-je?,** p. 244.
- Additional Practice, ATE, p. 242.

Chapter Review 30 min.
- Review Chapter 8. Choose from **Grammaire supplémentaire,** Grammar Tutor for Students of French, Activities for Communication, Listening Activities, Interactive CD-ROM Tutor, or **Jeux interactifs.**

Homework Options
Study for Chapter 8 Test.

Assessment

Test, Chapter 8 50 min.
- Administer Chapter 8 Test. Select from Testing Program, Alternative Assessment Guide, Test Generator, or Standardized Assessment Tutor.

Chapitre 8 : La Tunisie, pays de contrastes
Suggested Lesson Plans *90-Minute Block Schedule*

Block 1

CHAPTER OPENER 5 min.
- Present Chapter Objectives, p. 217
- Culture Note and Focusing on Outcomes, ATE, pp. 216–217

MISE EN TRAIN 40 min.
- Presenting **Mise en train,** ATE, p. 218
- Culture Notes, ATE, p. 219
- Do Activities 1–5, p. 220.

RENCONTRE CULTURELLE 20 min.
- Presenting **Rencontre culturelle,** ATE, p. 221
- Teaching Suggestion #1, ATE, p. 221

PREMIERE ETAPE 20 min.
- **Comment dit-on... ?,** p. 222
- Presenting **Comment dit-on... ?,** ATE, p. 222
- Play Audio CD for Activity 7, p. 222.
- Do Activity 8, p. 222.

Wrap-Up 5 min.
- Thinking Critically: Comparing and Contrasting, ATE, p. 220

Homework Options
Grammaire supplémentaire, p. 238, Act. 1
Cahier d'activités, pp. 85–86, Acts. 1–2

Block 2

PREMIERE ETAPE
Quick Review 10 min.
- Listening Activities, p. 63, Additional Listening Activity 8-1.

Comment dit-on... ?, p. 222 10 min.
- Do Activity 9, p. 222.

Vocabulaire, p. 223 30 min.
- Presenting **Vocabulaire,** ATE, p. 223
- Additional Practice, ATE, p. 223
- **Note culturelle,** p. 224
- Do Activity 11, p. 223.
- Play Audio CD for Activity 12, p. 224.
- Do Activity 13, p. 224.

Comment dit-on... ?, p. 225 15 min.
- Presenting **Comment dit-on... ?,** ATE, p. 225
- Play Audio CD for Activity 14, p. 225.

Grammaire, p. 225 20 min.
- Presenting **Grammaire,** ATE, p. 225
- Additional Practice, ATE, p. 225
- Do Activity 15, p. 225.

Wrap-Up 5 min.
- Teaching Transparency 8-1, using suggestion #2 on Suggestions for Using Teaching Transparency

Homework Options
Pupil's Edition, Activity 10, p. 222
Grammaire supplémentaire, pp. 238–239, Acts. 2–4
Cahier d'activités, pp. 86–88, Acts. 3–7
Travaux pratiques de grammaire, pp. 73–75, Acts. 1–6

Block 3

PREMIERE ETAPE
Quick Review 10 min.
- Activities for Communication, Communicative Activity 8-1A and 8-1B, pp. 29–30

Grammaire, p. 225 20 min.
- Do Activities 16–17, p. 226.

REMISE EN TRAIN 30 min.
- Presenting **Remise en train,** ATE, p. 228
- Do Activities 21–23, pp. 228–229.

DEUXIEME ETAPE
Vocabulaire, p. 230 20 min.
- Presenting **Vocabulaire,** ATE, p. 230
- Play Audio CD for Activity 25, p. 230.
- Do Activity 26, p. 230.

Wrap-Up 10 min.
- Game: **Mots associés,** ATE, p. 230

Homework Options
Have students study for Quiz 8-1.
Grammaire supplémentaire, p. 240, Act. 5
Cahier d'activités, pp. 88–92, Acts. 8–14
Travaux pratiques de grammaire, pp. 76–79, Acts. 7–13

One-Stop Planner CD-ROM

For alternative lesson plans by chapter section, to create your own customized plans, or to preview all resources available for this chapter, use the **One-Stop Planner CD-ROM**, Disc 2.

For additional homework suggestions, see activities accompanied by this symbol throughout the chapter.

Block 4

PREMIERE ETAPE
Quick Review 10 min.
- Teaching Transparency 8-1, using suggestion #4 on Suggestions for Using Teaching Transparency 8-1

Quiz 8-1 20 min.
- Administer Quiz 8-1A or 8-1B.

Comment dit-on... ?, p. 231 40 min.
- Presenting **Comment dit-on... ?,** ATE, p. 231
- Play Audio CD for Activities 27–28, p. 231.
- Do Activity 30, p. 231.

PANORAMA CULTUREL 15 min.
- Presenting **Panorama Culturel,** ATE, p. 227
- Read and discuss **Qu'en penses-tu?,** p. 227.
- Questions, ATE, p. 227

Wrap-Up 5 min.
- Listening Activities, p. 64, Additional Listening Activity 8-4

Homework Options
Cahier d'activités, p. 92, Act. 15

Block 5

DEUXIEME ETAPE
Quick Review 10 min.
- Teaching Transparency 8-2, using suggestion #3 on Suggestions for Using Teaching Transparency 8-2

Comment dit-on... ?, p. 232 20 min.
- Presenting **Comment dit-on... ?,** ATE, p. 232
- Do Activity 31, p. 232.
- **Note culturelle,** p. 233

Grammaire, p. 232 35 min.
- Presenting **Grammaire,** ATE, p. 232
- Do Activities 32–33, p. 233.

LISONS! 15 min.
- Have students imagine what it would be like to grow up in a family in Tunisia, according to what they've learned in the chapter.
- Read and discuss **Stratégie pour lire,** p. 234.
- Read aloud through the paragraph that begins "**J'étais toute gosse...,**" as students read along in their books.
- Do Prereading and Reading Activities A–B, p. 234.

Wrap-Up 10 min.
- Activities for Communication, p. 104, Situation 8-2: Role-play

Homework Options
Have students study for Quiz 8-2.
Have students continue reading **Enfance d'une fille,** pp. 234–236.
Grammaire supplémentaire, pp. 240–241, Acts. 6–9
Cahier d'activités, pp. 93–94, Acts. 16–19
Travaux pratiques de grammaire, pp. 80–81, Acts. 14–16

Block 6

DEUXIEME ETAPE
Quick Review 10 min.
- Activities for Communication, pp. 31–32, Communicative Activity 8-2A and 8-2B

Quiz 8-2 20 min.
- Administer Quiz 8-2A or 8-2B.

LISONS! 30 min.
- Finish **Lisons!,** pp. 234–236.
- Culture Note, ATE, p. 235
- Do Reading Activities E–J, p. 235.

MISE EN PRATIQUE 30 min.
- Do Activities 1–2, 4, pp. 242–243.
- Play Audio CD for Activity 3, p. 243.

Homework Options
Que sais-je?, p. 244
Study for Chapter 8 Test.

Block 7

MISE EN PRATIQUE
Quick Review 15 min.
- **Jeu de rôle,** p. 243
- Go over answers to **Que sais-je?,** p. 244.

Chapter Review 30 min.
- Review Chapter 8. Choose from **Grammaire supplémentaire,** Grammar Tutor for Students of French, Activities for Communication, Listening Activities, Interactive CD-ROM Tutor, or **Jeux interactifs.**

Test, Chapter 8 45 min.
- Administer Chapter 8 Test. Select from Testing Program, Alternative Assessment Guide, Test Generator, or Standardized Assessment Tutor.

Chapter Opener

One-Stop Planner CD-ROM

For resource information, see the **One-Stop Planner**, Disc 2.

Pacing Tips
The first and second **étapes** have approximately the same amount of material to cover. In the first **étape**, you might make use of the cultural content in the **Panorama Culturel**, on page 227, which is closely related to the theme of the **étape** (changes in cities). For Lesson Plans and timing suggestions, see pages 215I–215L.

Meeting the Standards

Communication
- Asking someone to convey good wishes; closing a letter, p. 222
- Expressing hopes or wishes; giving advice, p. 225
- Complaining; expressing annoyance, p. 231
- Making comparisons, p. 232

Cultures
- Culture Notes, pp. 216, 219, 221, 229, 234, 235
- Notes culturelles, pp. 224, 233
- Panorama Culturel, p. 227
- Rencontre culturelle, p. 221

Connections
- History Links, pp. 221, 224, 236
- Literature Link, p. 224
- Architecture Link, p. 231
- Music Link, p. 232

Comparisons
- Language-to-Language, pp. 221, 223
- Thinking Critically, pp. 217, 218, 220, 227

Communities
- Career Path, p. 242
- Community Links, pp. 216, 227, 236
- De l'école au travail, p. 233
- Family Link, p. 234

Cultures and Communities

Community Link
Have students list things they associate with life a hundred years ago, and things they associate with modern life. Ask them to compare the advantages and disadvantages of living in the past with living today. Ask if they would prefer to have lived in the past rather than the present, and why.

Culture Note
Since traffic jams are common and buses aren't air-conditioned, people often choose to walk around Tunis. Bus travel is relatively inexpensive, however, as is the light train metro system.

Focusing on Outcomes
Have students list French expressions they've already learned that accomplish these functions.

NOTE: You may want to use the video to support the objectives. The self-check activities in **Que sais-je?** on page 244 help students assess their achievement of the objectives.

Language Note
Ask students if they can see a familiar word in **embouteillages (bouteille)**. Ask them if they know of an expression for traffic jams that uses the corresponding English word *bottle (bottlenecks)*.

Objectives

In this chapter you will learn to

Première étape

- ask someone to convey good wishes
- close a letter
- express hopes or wishes
- give advice

Deuxième étape

- complain
- express annoyance
- make comparisons

internet

ADRESSE: go.hrw.com
MOT-CLE: WA3 FRANCOPHONE AFRICA-8

◀ La médina de Sousse en Tunisie

Communication for All Students

Thinking Critically
Observing Have students tell what they would expect to see in a typical Tunisian city, based on the photo on pages 216–217 (modern office buildings, older traditional buildings, traffic jams, people in traditional dress, people in modern dress).

Challenge
Ask students these questions: **Qu'est-ce que vous voyez sur cette photo? (des voitures, des gens, etc...) Est-ce que c'est en France? (non) Comment savez-vous que ce n'est pas en France? (L'architecture n'est pas française.) Est-ce que les maisons vous rappellent les maisons d'un autre pays? (le Maroc)**

Teaching Resources
pp. 218–220

PRINT
▸ Lesson Planner, p. 37
▸ Video Guide, pp. 48, 50
▸ Cahier d'activités, p. 85

MEDIA
▸ One-Stop Planner
▸ Video Program
Camille et compagnie
Videocassette 3, 19:58–24:26
Videocassette 5 (captioned version), 46:24–50:52
▸ Audio Compact Discs, CD 8, Tr. 1

Thinking Critically
Observing Have students look at the photos on pages 218–219 and tell whether they reflect a traditional or a modern lifestyle. Ask them if the lifestyle depicted in the photos appeals to them, and why or why not.

Presenting
Mise en train

Tell students they are going to hear a letter that Zohra wrote to her cousin Aïcha in Tunis. Have them listen for Zohra's complaint and a description of her mother's life. Play the recording. Then, create true-false statements about the letter. (**Zohra va rendre visite à Aïcha.**) Play the recording again, pause it at the appropriate moments, read the statements, and have students respond.

Mise en train · *Bisous de Nefta*

Cahier d'activités, p. 85, Act. 1

CD 8 Tr. 1

Stratégie pour comprendre
Before reading the letter, notice the photos and their captions. What do you think Zohra is telling Aïcha about her life in Nefta? Skim the letter and find positive and negative aspects of Zohra's life there that she mentions.

Ils récoltent des dattes.

Regarde ce beau coucher de soleil!

Voilà nos moutons!

Chère Aïcha,
Ce soir, il y a un coucher de soleil génial. La lumière se reflète dans les branches des palmiers. Tout est super calme. Je pense à toi, dans ta grande ville. Est-ce qu'il y a des couchers de soleil comme ça à Tunis? J'aimerais tellement que tu sois là. Tu es ma confidente et c'est avec toi que je m'amuse le mieux. Ça serait sympa si tu pouvais venir pendant les vacances. Moi, c'est sûr, je ne pourrai pas aller te voir à Tunis. Quelle barbe! C'est la saison des dattes. Si tu venais, on pourrait les cueillir ensemble. Et puis, le soir, on se baladerait sur l'avenue Bourguiba ou dans la palmeraie. On irait discuter sous les arbres de la Corbeille. On se lèverait tôt le matin pour aller voir le soleil se lever! Et puis, toutes les deux, on s'occuperait des moutons et on aiderait maman aussi. Tu sais, elle est super fatiguée en ce moment. Ça serait vraiment chouette.

Qu'est-ce qu'elle est fatiguée, maman!

Preteaching Vocabulary

Recognizing Cognates
Ask students to find words in Zohra's letter that look similar to words they know in English. Read the letter out loud and have them look at the photos and the words they already know to help them figure out the overall meaning. Ask them which cognates help them to know that Zohra is talking about specific future plans at the beginning of the second page of the letter. (**l'archéologie, l'université**)

se reflète *reflect*
branches *branches*
confidente *confidante*
discuter *discuss*
secret *secret*
l'archéologie *archeology*
l'université *university*
architraditionnels *extremely traditional*
prince charmant *prince charming*

STANDARDS: 1.2, 2.1, 3.2, 4.1

C'est très tranquille, Nefta.

Mais, bon, peut-être que tu as d'autres projets. Je vais te dire un secret : dans deux ans, après mon bac, j'aimerais bien étudier l'archéologie à l'université de Tunis. Enfin, il faut d'abord que j'en parle à Papa et Maman. J'ai peur qu'ils disent non. Il faudrait que j'arrive à les convaincre. Tu les connais, ils sont architraditionnels. Pour eux, une fille n'a pas besoin de faire d'études. A la place, ils voudraient que je me marie et que je m'occupe de ma maison et de mes enfants. Maman m'a même trouvé un mari! Elle voudrait que j'épouse Mustafa, le fils des voisins. Il est gentil, mais il est loin d'être mon prince charmant! Et puis je n'ai que dix-sept ans et j'aimerais quand même bien avoir le droit de choisir mon mari moi-même! Ça, tu vois, c'est un truc que maman ne comprend pas. Elle, elle s'est mariée à quatorze ans. Ce sont ses parents qui lui ont choisi son mari. Et, toute sa vie, elle s'est occupée de nous et de la maison. Encore maintenant, c'est elle qui fait tout à la maison. Elle va chercher l'eau au puits, elle porte le bois sur sa tête, elle fait la cuisine. Elle veut que je fasse comme elle. Tu as de la chance d'avoir des parents modernes, toi! Bon, il faut que je te laisse. Bisous à oncle Khaled et tante Brigitte, et à Rachid aussi. Dis-leur que je pense à eux et que je vais leur écrire. Maman et Papa vous embrassent tous très fort. A bientôt.

Zohra

P.S. Au fait, merci pour ta carte. La vue de Tunis était super. C'est quand même beau, la Tunisie! Ecris-moi vite! Grosses bises.

Les femmes travaillent tout le temps.

Me voilà avec Ahmed et Hassan.

Culture Note
The family unit is central to the traditional Tunisian social structure. It includes not just parents and children, but the entire extended family, sometimes even married sons. It used to be common to marry within the extended family. In recent years, however, with more Tunisians moving to the big cities, social networks are widening beyond the family unit.

Language Note
Many Arabic first names have lexical meanings: **Aïcha** means *fortunate;* **Zohra,** *glowing* or *flower;* **Aziz,** *darling* or *beloved;* **Hassan,** *doer of good* and *pious;* **Ali,** *of high morals;* **Imed,** *pillar;* **Rachid,** *wise man;* **Samir,** *storyteller;* **Mona,** *wish.* **Aïcha** is a popular Arab name because it was the name of one of the prophet Mohammed's wives.

Camille et compagnie
You may choose to show students Episode 8: *La Nouvelle Vie d'Azzedine* now or wait until later in the chapter. In the video Camille meets Azzedine, a young student from Tunisia. Azzedine tells Camille about life in his country. They talk about the differences between his home town, Nefta, and Aix-en-Provence. Finally, Sophie shows up angry because she was splashed by a motorcycle.

Using the Captioned Video

As an alternative, you might want to show the captioned version of *Camille et compagnie : La Nouvelle Vie d'Azzedine* on Videocassette 5. Some students may benefit from seeing the written words as they listen to the target language and watch the gestures and actions in context. This visual reinforcement of vocabulary and functions will facilitate students' comprehension and help reduce their anxiety before they are formally introduced to the new language in the chapter.

Additional Practice

3 Have students suggest additional things that Zohra or her parents might say, based on *Bisous de Nefta,* and read them aloud to their classmates, who will try to identify the speakers.

Thinking Critically

6 **Comparing and Contrasting** You might have students compare and contrast life in a traditional and a non-traditional family. In this discussion, be careful to respect students' privacy and personal views.

1 **Tu as compris?** These activities check for comprehension only. Students should not yet be expected to produce language modeled in **Mise en train**.

1. A qui est-ce que Zohra écrit? her cousin Aïcha
2. A quel moment de la journée elle écrit?
3. Qu'est-ce que Zohra aime là où elle habite? **2.** sunset **3.** quiet, natural beauty
4. Qu'est-ce qu'elle n'aime pas dans sa vie en famille? traditional gender roles
5. Quel secret Zohra confie à Aïcha?
6. Qu'est-ce qu'elle demande à Aïcha de faire?

5. She wants to study archaeology at the University of Tunis. **6.** greet her family, write back

2 **Vrai ou faux?**

1. Aïcha est la sœur de Zohra. faux
2. Nefta est au nord de la Tunisie. faux
3. Il y a de beaux couchers de soleil à Nefta. vrai
4. Aïcha habite un petit village calme. faux
5. Tunis est plus grand que Nefta. vrai
6. A Tunis, il y a une université. vrai
7. Zohra veut faire des études de médecine. faux

3 **C'est qui?**

A ton avis, qui pourrait dire les phrases suivantes? Zohra ou ses parents?

1. «Ce qui est important, c'est de faire des études.» Zohra
2. «Les femmes doivent s'occuper de la maison.» ses parents
3. «Une fille devrait se marier très jeune.» ses parents
4. «Pour une femme, c'est inutile de faire des études.» ses parents
5. «Il faut qu'une femme puisse choisir son mari.» Zohra
6. «Mustafa serait un bon mari.» ses parents

4 **Qu'est-ce qu'elle a dit?**

Aïcha dit à sa mère qu'elle a reçu une lettre de Zohra. Complète leur dialogue avec des mots de la lettre.

AÏCHA J'ai reçu une lettre de Zohra. Elle vous _____ bien fort. embrasse
SA MERE C'est gentil. Comment va sa mère?
AÏCHA Elle est _____ . super fatiguée
SA MERE Est-ce que Zohra va venir nous voir?
AÏCHA Elle ne pourra pas. C'est la saison des _____ . dattes
SA MERE Est-ce qu'elle sait ce qu'elle veut faire après son bac? étudier l'archéologie, archi traditionnels
AÏCHA Elle veut _____ . Mais elle a peur que ses parents disent non. Tu sais, ils sont _____ .
SA MERE Je vais leur en parler. Si elle venait à Tunis, elle pourrait habiter avec nous.
AÏCHA Super, je le lui dirai. A propos, elle m'invite chez elle pour les vacances. Elle dit qu'on pourrait _____ . Je peux y aller? cueillir des dattes ensemble
SA MERE Si tu as de bonnes notes.

5 **Cherche les expressions**

What expressions does Zohra use in her letter to . . . See answers below.

1. express a wish?
2. express an obligation?
3. express a concern?
4. convey good wishes to someone?
5. thank someone?
6. end her letter?

6 **Et maintenant, à toi**

Est-ce que tu préfères que tes parents soient plutôt traditionnels, comme ceux de Zohra, ou plutôt modernes, comme ceux d'Aïcha? Pourquoi?

Comprehension Check

Slower Pace

4 Provide the missing words on a transparency for students to refer to as they complete the dialogue with a partner.

Game

5 Have students form small groups. Give them one minute to supply as many expressions as possible for numbers 1–6. Students may list previously learned expressions, as well as new expressions from Zohra's letter. After one minute, call time. Groups win one point for each previously learned expression and two points for each new expression on their lists. Tally the points and declare a winner. Have a member of the winning group read their list aloud.

Answers

5 1. J'aimerais... ; Ça serait sympa/chouette si...
2. Il faut/faudrait que...
3. J'ai peur que...
4. Bisous à... ; Dis-leur que je pense à eux. Maman et Papa vous embrassent tous très fort.
5. Merci pour...
6. A bientôt. Grosses bises.

Rencontre culturelle

Qu'est-ce que tu sais sur la Tunisie? Pour t'en faire une meilleure idée, regarde ces photos.

Le Tunis moderne : une ville pleine d'activité

Les chameaux sont utilisés pour le labour des terres.

Le Tunis ancien : la médina avec ses marchés traditionnels

On voit encore l'influence française en Tunisie.

Dans le sud, les oasis accueillent nomades et touristes.

Qu'en penses-tu?

1. Quelles impressions ces photos te donnent de la Tunisie?
2. Sur ces photos, quels différents types de Tunisiens est-ce que tu peux identifier?

Possible answers: **1.** desert climate, mix of modern and traditional, Arab and French. **2.** city dwellers, farmers, nomads (animal herders)

Savais-tu que... ?

La Tunisie est un petit pays d'Afrique du Nord constitué de montagnes, de prairies et de désert. Beaucoup de Tunisiens vivent en ville, sur la côte et dans le nord du pays, où le climat est propice à l'agriculture. La majorité de la population tunisienne est arabe, mais la population la plus ancienne est berbère. Tunis, la capitale, est à la fois une cité ancienne et le centre industriel, politique et culturel du pays. La partie ancienne de Tunis, appelée médina, est constituée de petites rues étroites, de boutiques et de marchés en plein air. Le quartier moderne de la ville a de grands immeubles et des boulevards bordés d'arbres. La Tunisie a été un protectorat français pendant soixante-quinze ans. L'influence française est présente dans l'architecture des bâtiments gouvernementaux et dans le style des parcs, des restaurants et des cafés. L'arabe est la langue officielle de la Tunisie, mais le français est toujours présent dans les écoles, l'administration et le commerce.

Communication for All Students

Première étape

Objectives Asking someone to convey good wishes; closing a letter; expressing hopes or wishes; giving advice

WA3 FRANCOPHONE AFRICA-8

Teaching Resources
pp. 222–226

PRINT
▸ Lesson Planner, p. 38
▸ Listening Activities, pp. 59–60, 63–64
▸ Activities for Communication, pp. 29–30, 72, 74, 103–104
▸ Travaux pratiques de grammaire, pp. 73–77
▸ Grammar Tutor for Students of French, Chapter 8
▸ Cahier d'activités, pp. 86–89
▸ Testing Program, pp. 169–172
▸ Alternative Assessment Guide, p. 37
▸ Student Make-Up Assignments, Chapter 8

MEDIA
▸ One-Stop Planner
▸ Audio Compact Discs, CD 8, Trs. 2–4, 14, 19–21
▸ Teaching Transparencies: 8-1; **Grammaire supplémentaire** Answers; Travaux pratiques de grammaire Answers
▸ Interactive CD-ROM Tutor, Disc 2

Bell Work
Have students list three French expressions each to open and close a formal business letter (see Chapter 5) and a letter to a French pen pal.

Presenting
Comment dit-on... ?

Remind students that there are several ways of closing a letter in French. Prepare one or two short letters on a transparency with the new expressions in a different color ink. Read the letters aloud. Show students a letter with blank lines for the closing and have them supply the appropriate closings.

Comment dit-on...?

Asking someone to convey good wishes; closing a letter

To ask someone to convey good wishes:

Embrasse ta tante **pour moi.**
Give . . . a kiss for me.
Fais-lui/-leur **mes amitiés.**
Give . . . my regards.
Salue-le/-la/-les **de ma part.**
Tell . . . hi for me.
Dis-lui **que je vais** lui **écrire.**
Dis-lui **que je pense à** elle/lui.

To close a letter:

Bien des choses à tes parents.
All the best to . . .
Je t'embrasse bien fort.
Hugs and kisses.
Grosses bises. *Hugs and kisses.*
Bisous à tes cousins. *Kisses to . . .*

 Cahier d'activités, p. 86, Act. 2 | Grammaire supplémentaire, p. 238, Act. 1 →

7 **Salue-le de ma part** See scripts on p. 215G.

Ecoutons Indique les dialogues où quelqu'un transmet ses amitiés. 1, 3, 5

CD 8 Tr. 2

8 **Fais nos amitiés à la famille!**

Ecrivons Djamil va rendre visite à plusieurs membres de sa famille cet été. Ses parents veulent leur faire leurs amitiés. Complète chacune de leurs recommandations avec des mots ou expressions du **Comment dit-on... ?**
1. Quand tu arrives, _____ tes grands-parents pour moi. *embrasse*
2. N'oublie pas de dire à Karim que je vais _____ écrire. *lui*
3. Quand tu verras tes cousins, _____ de notre part. *salue-les*
4. Tu vas rendre visite à Habib et Salima? _____ nos amitiés. *Fais-leur*
5. Et quand tu verras oncle Aziz, salue-_____ de ma part. *le*
6. Et n'oublie pas de dire à tante Zohra que je _____ à elle. *pense*

9 **Embrasse tout le monde pour nous!**

 Parlons Habib va passer ses vacances chez ses cousins. Imagine la conversation qu'il a avec sa famille avant de partir. Joue cette scène avec ton/ta camarade.

10 **On pense à toi**

 Ecrivons Ecris une lettre à un(e) camarade qui passe six mois chez ses grands-parents en Tunisie. Raconte-lui les dernières nouvelles et n'oublie pas de transmettre les amitiés de tes camarades de classe.

Communication for All Students

Auditory Learners
After presenting **Comment dit-on...?** Have students close their books. Read Zohra's letter, on page 219, out loud. Have students raise their hands as soon as they hear an expression from the **Comment dit-on... ?** box. Write the expressions on the board and have students recall their meaning.

Slower Pace
7 Before they do this activity, have students close their books. Read the expressions from **Comment dit-on... ?** at random and have students tell you if the phrases you're reading would be used to convey good wishes or to close a letter.

STANDARDS: 1.1, 1.2, 1.3, 5.1

En Tunisie, on pratique encore des activités traditionnelles.

On fait de l'artisanat (m.), de la poterie,

des tapis (m.),

des objets (m.) en cuivre

et des bijoux (m.).

On fait la cueillette (*harvest*) des dattes (f.),

des figues (f.)

et des olives (f.).

On cultive le blé.

On élève (*raise*) des chameaux (m.),

des moutons (m.)

et des chèvres (f.).

On donne à manger aux poules (f.).

On trait les vaches (f.).

Cahier d'activités, pp. 86–87, Act. 3–5

Travaux pratiques de grammaire, pp. 73–74, Act. 1–3

11 Comme chez nous *Answers will vary.*

Lisons Lesquelles des activités du **Vocabulaire** sont aussi bien américaines que tunisiennes?

Connections and Comparisons

Language-to-Language
Compile on the board a list of English words for live animals and the meat from those animals (cow/beef). Have students copy the list on a sheet of paper. Then, tell them that in French different words are used as well. Ask students to find an example in the **Vocabulaire**. Students should remember that **poule** refers to live chickens, whereas **poulet** refers to chicken meat. As homework, have small groups choose another language and find in the appropriate dictionary the equivalents of the various English words on their lists to see if the language they selected also uses different words.

Teaching Resources
pp. 222–226

PRINT
▶ Lesson Planner, p. 38
▶ Listening Activities, pp. 59–60, 63–64
▶ Activities for Communication, pp. 29–30, 72, 74, 103–104
▶ Travaux pratiques de grammaire, pp. 73–77
▶ Grammar Tutor for Students of French, Chapter 8
▶ Cahier d'activités, pp. 86–89
▶ Testing Program, pp. 169–172
▶ Alternative Assessment Guide, p. 37
▶ Student Make-Up Assignments, Chapter 8

MEDIA
▶ One-Stop Planner
▶ Audio Compact Discs, CD 8, Trs. 2–4, 14, 19–21
▶ Teaching Transparencies: 8-1; **Grammaire supplémentaire** Answers; Travaux pratiques de grammaire Answers
▶ Interactive CD-ROM Tutor, Disc 2

Teaching Suggestion

12 Before students listen to the recording, have them write one sentence to accompany each illustration. For example, for **a**, they might write **On élève des poules.**

Additional Practice

12 Make a statement referring to the animal or object in an illustration, using an object pronoun. (**On le cultive.**) Have students try to guess the animal or object the pronoun refers to (**le blé**).

Answers

13 *Kairouan:* les objets en cuivre et les tapis; *Nabeul*: les chameaux; *Tozeur:* les dattes; *Dougga:* le blé; *Sfax:* les olives; *Monastir:* les bijoux; *Douz:* les moutons et les chèvres; *Bizerte:* la pêche; *Tabarka:* la plongée; *Carthage:* les ruines romaines; *Sousse:* la plage

---

12 **Notre vie en Tunisie** See scripts and answers on p. 215G.

Ecoutons Karim rend visite à ses cousins en Tunisie. Amira lui montre où ils habitent. Quelles images est-ce que tu associes à leurs conversations?

CD 8 Tr. 3

a.   b.   c.

d.   e.

f.   g.

Note culturelle

La Tunisie est un mélange remarquable d'ancien et de moderne. D'un côté, dans les villes tunisiennes, on peut voir de grands immeubles, des aéroports et des transports en commun. Les gens conduisent des voitures de sport, utilisent des ordinateurs et s'habillent à la dernière mode parisienne. D'un autre côté, dans la campagne tunisienne, le style de vie n'a pas beaucoup changé au cours des siècles. La population rurale vit en partie de l'élevage de chèvres et de moutons. Les nomades se déplacent à travers le pays avec leurs troupeaux de chameaux. Ils s'arrêtent pour boire aux mêmes oasis où s'arrêtaient leurs ancêtres il y a mille ans.

13 **Qu'est-ce qu'on y fait?** See answers below.

Parlons Regarde cette carte. Dis ce qu'on voit et ce qu'on fait en Tunisie selon les régions.

Connections and Comparisons

Literature Link

Have students locate Carthage on the map in Activity 13. Ask students if they have read about Carthage, and if so, where. Some may have read Virgil's *Aeneid,* in which the mythical hero Aeneas arrives in Carthage while the queen of Phoenicia, Dido, is having the city built. Their subsequent romance comes to a tragic end when Aeneas leaves her to pursue his destiny.

History Link

After the Romans destroyed Carthage in 146 B.C., Julius Caesar reestablished it in 46 B.C. The city grew, and its population flourished, but it was later ransacked by Vandal and Arab invaders. You might have students find out more about the history of Carthage and other Tunisian cities.

Comment dit-on...?

Expressing hopes or wishes; giving advice

To express a hope or wish:

> **Si seulement je pouvais,** j'habiterais à la campagne.
> *If only I could, . . .*
> **Si j'avais le choix,** j'irais à l'université.
> *If I had the choice, . . .*
> **Si c'était possible,** j'habiterais à Tunis. *If it were possible, . . .*
> **Ça serait chouette si** je pouvais danser.
> *It would be great if . . .*
> **Qu'est-ce que j'aimerais** partir en vacances!
> *I'd really like to . . .*

Ça serait chouette si je pouvais aller en Tunisie!

To give advice:

> **Si c'était moi,** je chercherais du travail.
> *If it were me, . . .*
> **Si j'étais toi,** j'en parlerais avec mes parents.
> *If I were you, . . .*
> **A ta place,** j'irais à la campagne.
> *If I were in your place, . . .*

14 Qu'est-ce qu'ils disent? See scripts and answers on p. 215G.

 Ecoutons Ecoute ces dialogues. Est-ce que les gens parlent de ce qu'ils aimeraient faire ou est-ce qu'ils donnent des conseils?
CD 8 Tr. 4

Grammaire

Si clauses

To say that *if* something *were* so, something else *would* happen, begin one part, or clause, of your sentence with **si** *(if)* and put the verb in the imperfect; in the other clause, put the verb in the conditional.

> **Si** elle **habitait** dans une grande ville, elle **serait** plus stressée.
> *If she lived in a big city, she would be more stressed.*

- You don't always have to begin your sentence with the **si** clause.
> Ça **serait** chouette **si** j'**habitais** à la campagne.

Grammaire supplémentaire, pp. 238–240, Act. 2–5

Cahier d'activités, p. 88, Act. 6–7

Travaux pratiques de grammaire, pp. 76–77, Act. 7–9

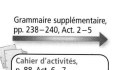

Travaux pratiques de grammaire, pp. 74–75, Act. 4–6

 Si tu as oublié the imperfect va à la page R49.

15 Grammaire en contexte See answers below.

 Parlons Fais des phrases avec les éléments suivants. **Si j'allais... je...**

> photographier des animaux sauvages au Maroc acheter de la dentelle en France
> manger du couscous acheter une montre au Sénégal manger du chocolat
> visiter le Louvre boire du thé en Tunisie en Suisse visiter des ruines romaines
> en Belgique emporter des vêtements légers en République centrafricaine acheter un tapis

Communication for All Students

Challenge

Form two teams. A player from one team assumes the identity of a celebrity, an historical figure, or even a cartoon character. Members of the opposing team may then ask up to 20 questions to try to discover the player's identity. Questions should include a **si** clause, for example: **Si tu étais des chaussures, quelle sorte de chaussures est-ce que tu serais?** The player answers according to

the identity he or she has chosen. For example, if the player chose to be Shaquille O'Neal (an NBA basketball player), the response to the question above might be **Je serais des baskets.** You might suggest the following sample questions: **Si tu étais une chanson, laquelle est-ce que tu serais? Si tu suivais un cours au lycée, lequel est-ce que tu suivrais? Si tu étais un plat, quel plat est-ce que tu serais?**

19 You might use the following rubric when grading your students on this activity.

Speaking Rubric	Points			
	4	3	2	1
Content (Complete–Incomplete)				
Comprehension (Total–Little)				
Comprehensibility (Comprehensible–Incomprehensible)				
Accuracy (Accurate–Seldom accurate)				
Fluency (Fluent–Not fluent)				

18–20: A	14–15: C	Under
16–17: B	12–13: D	12: F

Assess

▸ Testing Program, pp. 169–172
  Quiz 8-1A, Quiz 8-1B,
  Audio CD 8, Tr. 14

▸ Student Make-Up Assignments
  Chapter 8, Alternative Quiz

▸ Alternative Assessment Guide,
  p. 37

---

16 ### Grammaire en contexte

Parlons Qu'est-ce qu'ils rêvent de faire?

Si je pouvais, je(j')... *Possible answers:*

1. étudierais l'archéologie.   2. aurais une belle voiture.   3. vivrais à la montagne.   4. irais à la plage.

17 ### Grammaire en contexte

 Parlons Parle d'un problème avec ton/ta camarade. Il/Elle te conseillera.

EXEMPLE   —J'ai besoin d'argent.

              —Si j'étais toi, je chercherais du travail.

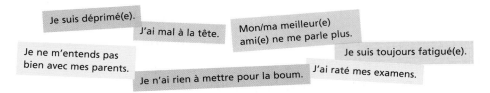

Je suis déprimé(e).

J'ai mal à la tête.

Mon/ma meilleur(e) ami(e) ne me parle plus.

Je ne m'entends pas bien avec mes parents.

Je suis toujours fatigué(e).

Je n'ai rien à mettre pour la boum.

J'ai raté mes examens.

18 ### Je pense à toi

Ecrivons Ecris une lettre à ton/ta correspondant(e) tunisien(ne) pour lui dire ce que vous feriez s'il/si elle venait chez toi.

> Chère Aïcha,
> Je serais tellement contente si tu venais me voir. Je pourrais te montrer ma ville.
> D'abord, on irait...

19 ### Te voilà de retour!

Parlons Ton ami(e) et sa famille reviennent d'un voyage en Tunisie. Il/Elle te parle de ce qu'ils y ont fait. Pose-lui des questions sur le pays et dis-lui ce que tu voudrais faire si tu y allais. Avant de le/la quitter, transmets tes amitiés à sa famille.

Communication for All Students

Auditory Learners

17 Once students have completed the activity as directed, have volunteers repeat aloud some of the advice they gave. (**Si j'étais toi, je lui téléphonerais.**) Have their classmates try to guess which problem the advice applies to. (**Mon/ma meilleur(e) ami(e) ne me parle plus.**)

Challenge

Have students write several sentence starters and their completions on individual strips of paper. (**Si j'étais le/la président(e) des Etats-Unis,... / ... j'inviterais le professeur à dîner à la Maison Blanche.**) Have them exchange all of their strips with a partner, who will match the sentence starters with their completions.

PANORAMA CULTUREL

Cette ville a beaucoup évolué?

We asked some people how their cities have changed since they've been living there. Here's what they told us.

Gilles,
France

«Ouais, énormément, elle [Paris] change tous les jours, et je m'intéresse énormément à la ville. Je fais des choses particulières. Je prends des photos, justement. Chaque fois qu'un immeuble est détruit, je viens le prendre en photo avant qu'il n'existe plus et que soit reconstruit un truc qui ne soit pas beau, quoi. Donc, j'essaie de, justement, garder des traces de la vie de Paris, et je suis assez nostalgique du vieux Paris des années 1900 jusqu'à 1940.»
Tr. 6

Sylviane,
Martinique

«La Martinique a énormément changé. Je dois dire que je suis née en Martinique. J'ai passé la plupart de mon enfance en Martinique. J'ai beaucoup voyagé, mais justement, lors de mes voyages, de mes différents voyages, on voit quand même des évolutions complètement différentes. L'art de vivre martiniquais est en train de s'européaniser et c'est dommage quelque part.»
Tr. 7

Qu'en penses-tu?

1. De quelles sortes de changements est-ce que ces gens parlent? Est-ce que ta région connaît les mêmes types de changements? Comment est-ce que ces changements ont influencé le style de vie des gens? See answers below

2. Choisis une ville du monde francophone qui t'intéresse. Recherche l'histoire de cette ville pour savoir comment elle était il y a 50 ou 100 ans.

Pierre,
Québec

«Dû à l'automation, l'informatique, aujourd'hui, les gens sont obligés d'aller dans des grands centres pour continuer à gagner leur vie. Parce que l'évolution, comme vous savez, a tout transformé au niveau de tous les pays.» Tr. 8

Cultures and Communities

Community Link
The day before the presentation, give students a homework assignment. Have them ask an adult friend or family member how their city, or a city where he or she previously lived, has changed over the years. In class, have students share their findings. They might also include their impressions of how things have changed in the time they've lived in the area.

Thinking Critically
Drawing conclusions Have students reread Sylviane's interview and think about why Martinique is said to have changed so much since she was born. She says **"L'art de vivre martiniquais est en train de s'européaniser..."** Ask students why they think that would be.

CD 8 Tr. 9

Aïcha répond vite à la lettre de Zohra.

Quelle chaleur!
Et quelle pollution!

Que c'est bruyant, les
grandes villes!

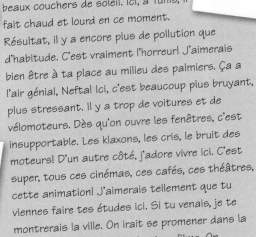

Chère Zohra,
Merci pour ta lettre. Elle m'a fait super plaisir. Qu'est-ce que tu as de la chance! Moi aussi, j'aimerais voir de beaux couchers de soleil. Ici, à Tunis, il fait chaud et lourd en ce moment. Résultat, il y a encore plus de pollution que d'habitude. C'est vraiment l'horreur! J'aimerais bien être à ta place au milieu des palmiers. Ça a l'air génial, Nefta! Ici, c'est beaucoup plus bruyant, plus stressant. Il y a trop de voitures et de vélomoteurs. Dès qu'on ouvre les fenêtres, c'est insupportable. Les klaxons, les cris, le bruit des moteurs! D'un autre côté, j'adore vivre ici. C'est super, tous ces cinémas, ces cafés, ces théâtres, cette animation! J'aimerais tellement que tu viennes faire tes études ici. Si tu venais, je te montrerais la ville. On irait se promener dans la médina. On irait voir les derniers films. On

20 Tu as compris? See answers below.
1. De quoi est-ce qu'Aïcha se plaint?
2. Quelles sont les différences entre l'endroit où Aïcha habite et l'endroit où Zohra habite?
3. Qu'est-ce qu'Aïcha veut faire pour aider sa cousine?
4. Quelle nouvelle Aïcha apprend à Zohra?

21 Comment est-elle?
Choisis parmi les phrases à droite celles qui décrivent le mieux Aïcha.

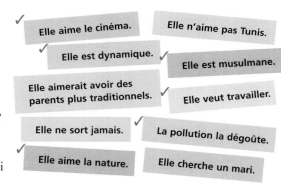

✓ Elle aime le cinéma.   Elle n'aime pas Tunis.
✓ Elle est dynamique.   Elle est musulmane.
Elle aimerait avoir des parents plus traditionnels.   Elle veut travailler.
Elle ne sort jamais.   ✓ La pollution la dégoûte.
✓ Elle aime la nature.   Elle cherche un mari.

These activities check for comprehension only. Students should not yet be expected to produce language modeled in **Remise en train.**

Teaching Resources
pp. 228–229

PRINT
▶ Lesson Planner, p. 39
▶ Video Guide, pp. 48, 50
▶ Cahier d'activités, p. 90

MEDIA
▶ One-Stop Planner
▶ Video Program
   Camille et compagnie
   Videocassette 3, 19:58–24:26
   Videocassette 5 (captioned version), 46:24–50:52
▶ Audio Compact Discs, CD 8, Tr. 9

Presenting
Remise en train

Read aloud the photo captions. Have students make the thumbs-up gesture if Aïcha is describing a positive aspect of the city, and a thumbs-down gesture if she is complaining about Tunis. Then, play the recording. Tell students to listen carefully for differences between Aïcha's lifestyle and Zohra's. Finally, ask the comprehension questions in Activity 20.

Answers
20 1. the heat, pollution, noise, stress, traffic
2. Tunis is a big, noisy, crowded, lively city. Nefta is a small, quiet, slow-paced village.
3. She'll ask her parents to convince Zohra's parents to let Zohra continue her studies.
4. She has a boyfriend.

Preteaching Vocabulary

Guessing Words from Context
Have students look at the photos on pages 228 and 229. Where does Aïcha live? How do they know? Ask students to find words and phrases in the first page of the letter that show the contrast between Nefta and Tunis. (**ça a l'air génial, bruyant**) What other words and phrases in the letter offer clues as to the meanings of certain words?

il fait chaud et lourd *the weather is hot and heavy*
pollution *pollution*
au milieu des palmiers *among the palm trees*
ça a l'air génial *it seems nice*
bruyant *noisy*
stressant *stressful*
c'est insupportable *it's unbearable*
animation *liveliness*

s'amuserait bien, tu sais. Essaie de convaincre tes parents. Remarque, je les comprends. Pour eux, c'est pas normal qu'une fille veuille travailler. C'est contre la tradition. Tu sais ce que je vais faire? Je vais demander à Papa et Maman s'ils peuvent parler à tes parents. Je suis sûre qu'ils pourront les convaincre. Heureusement que je n'ai pas ces problèmes avec eux. S'ils voulaient choisir mon mari à ma place, ils m'entendraient! Tout ce qu'ils demandent, c'est que je me marie avec un musulman. Ben, ça, on verra! Pour l'instant, ce qui m'intéresse, moi, c'est de gagner ma vie! Au fait, je ne t'ai pas dit? Figure-toi que j'ai un petit ami. Il s'appelle Chakib. Je crois que tu l'aimerais beaucoup. C'est un poète. Il écrit des poésies géniales. Je pourrais te parler de lui pendant des heures. Bon, je te laisse. Tu sais, je voudrais bien venir te voir pendant les vacances, mais c'est impossible. J'ai trouvé un job pour l'été. Je vais travailler au festival de Tunis. Ça me plaît bien et ça me fera un peu d'argent. C'est vraiment bête, mais j'espère qu'on se verra quand même bientôt. Bien des choses à tes parents et à tes frères. Grosses bises.

Aïcha

Tunis, c'est super animé!

C'est génial de se promener dans la médina.

Voilà Chakib, c'est un vrai poète!

22 Cherche les expressions

What does Aïcha say in her letter to . . .   See answers below.
1. express envy?
2. express a wish?
3. complain?
4. compare Tunis and Nefta?
5. express certainty?
6. break some news?
7. express an impossibility?
8. excuse herself?
9. end her letter?

Cahier d'activités, p. 90, Act. 11–12

23 La vie à Tunis

D'après Aïcha, quels sont les avantages de Tunis? Quels en sont les inconvénients?   See answers below.

24 Et maintenant, à toi

Où est-ce que tu habites? En ville comme Aïcha ou à la campagne comme Zohra? D'après toi, quels sont les avantages et les inconvénients des deux?

Comprehension Check

Teaching Suggestions
• Have students write their answers to Activity 22 on separate, small pieces of paper. Collect them and put them in a box. Select one at a time, read it aloud (**Je suis sûre que...**), and have students tell which function the expression serves (*expressing certainty*).

• Have students imagine what will happen to Aïcha and Zohra in the future.

Challenge
24 You might have students expand their answers by telling why they prefer the city or the country and writing their reasons in their journals.

 Culture Note
Students might be interested in the different types of traditional clothing worn in Tunisia. A **burnous** is a heavy, wool cloak with a hood, usually draped around the shoulder and worn during the winter. A **djellaba** is a robe of fine cotton or wool with sleeves and a hood, which is worn in Tunisia only by men. A **jebba** is a dressy, hoodless, lounging robe with sleeves, worn by either men or women.

 Camille et compagnie

As an alternative or in addition to the **Remise en train,** you may wish to show Episode 8 of *Camille et compagnie.* For suggestions and activities, see the *Video Guide.*

Answers
22 1. Qu'est-ce que tu as de la chance! J'aimerais bien être à ta place.
2. J'aimerais bien/tellement... ; Je voudrais bien... ; J'espère que...
3. C'est vraiment l'horreur! Il y a trop de... ; ... c'est insupportable.
4. Ici, c'est beaucoup plus... ; D'un autre côté,...
5. Je suis sûr(e) que...
6. Au fait, je ne t'ai pas dit?
7. ... c'est impossible.
8. C'est vraiment bête, mais...
9. Grosses bises.

23 *Avantages:* cinémas, cafés, théâtres, animation
Inconvénients: pollution, bruit, stress

Objectives Complaining; expressing annoyance; making comparisons

WA3 FRANCOPHONE AFRICA-8

Teaching Resources
pp. 230–233

PRINT
- Lesson Planner, p. 40
- Listening Activities, pp. 60–61, 64–65
- Activities for Communication, pp. 31–32, 73–74, 103–104
- Travaux pratiques de grammaire, pp. 78–81
- Grammar Tutor for Students of French, Chapter 8
- Cahier d'activités, pp. 91–94
- Testing Program, pp. 173–176
- Alternative Assessment Guide, p. 37
- Student Make-Up Assignments, Chapter 8

MEDIA
- One-Stop Planner
- Audio Compact Discs, CD 8, Trs. 10–12, 15, 22–24
- Teaching Transparencies: 8-2; **Grammaire supplémentaire** Answers; Travaux pratiques de grammaire Answers
- Interactive CD-ROM Tutor, Disc 2

Bell Work
Have students write three or more sentences contrasting life in the city and life in the country, using words they know.

Presenting
Vocabulaire

Bring in magazine pictures of the vocabulary items. Show the pictures and ask questions about them, such as **Est-ce que les chauffeurs s'arrêtent toujours aux passages pour piétons?**

Answers
26 1. ces gratte-ciel 2. les immeubles 3. le vélomoteur 4. des gens mal élevés 5. un embouteillage 6. une place de stationnement 7. un passage pour piétons

Vocabulaire

Labels: un immeuble · un arrêt de bus · une place de stationnement · un embouteillage · une foule · un vélomoteur · un passage pour piétons · un trottoir

le bruit *noise*	**la circulation** *traffic*	**des gens mal élevés** *impolite people*	
des gens pressés *people in a hurry*	**un gratte-ciel** *a skyscraper*	**la pollution** *pollution*	

Cahier d'activités, p. 91, Act. 13 · Travaux pratiques de grammaire, pp. 78–79, Act. 10–13

25 **Où sont-ils?** See scripts and answers on p. 215H.

 Ecoutons Ecoute ces remarques. Est-ce que les gens sont à la campagne ou à la ville?
CD 8 Tr. 10

26 **C'est pas vrai!** See answers below.

Ecrivons Zohra rend visite à Aïcha. Complète leur conversation avec les mots du **Vocabulaire.**

ZOHRA Oh dis donc, qu'est-ce qu'ils sont grands, ___1___!

AICHA Oui, un peu plus et on se croirait à New York, non?

ZOHRA Oui, tu as raison. Ailleurs, ___2___ sont beaucoup moins grands. Eh, regarde un peu cet homme, là-bas, sur ___3___! Tu as vu comme il crie!

AICHA Tu sais, il y a ___4___ partout, mais j'ai l'impression qu'il y en a encore plus dans les grandes villes qu'ailleurs! Oh là là! Cette circulation, c'est vraiment l'horreur! Oh non! Encore ___5___! On ne va jamais arriver à l'heure!

ZOHRA Ben, j'espère qu'en arrivant là-bas, on va trouver ___6___ facilement.

AICHA Ça m'étonnerait! Le parking n'est pas très grand.

ZOHRA Attention! Cette femme est en plein milieu de la route!

AICHA Incroyable! Il y a ___7___ là, à dix mètres, mais non, elle traverse à côté!

ZOHRA Bon, restons calmes! On est presque au musée.

Communication for All Students

 Game

Mots associés On index cards, make lists of several words grouped by category. For example, **un trottoir, une rue,** and **un tapis** would be categorized as *Things you walk on;* **à un arrêt de bus, chez le médecin,** and **à l'aéroport** would be categorized as *Places where you wait.* Form two or more teams and have a player from each team stand up. Read a list aloud. The first player to identify the category wins a point for his or her team.

Comment dit-on...?

Complaining; expressing annoyance

To complain:

C'est l'horreur!
This is just horrible!
C'est insupportable, à la fin!
I won't put up with this!
J'en ai ras le bol!
I've really had it!
Je commence à en avoir marre!
I've just about had it!

To express annoyance at someone:

Non mais, vous vous prenez pour qui?
Who do you think you are?
Surtout ne vous gênez pas! *Well just go right ahead!*
Ça va pas, non?!
Are you out of your mind?!
Ça commence à bien faire, hein?
Enough is enough!
Dites donc, ça vous gênerait de bouger?
Hey, do you think you can . . .?

Cahier d'activités, p. 92, Act. 14–15

 27 **La vie en ville** See scripts and answers on p. 215H.

 Écoutons Écoute ces remarques. Est-ce que ces gens sont contents d'habiter en ville? CD 8 Tr. 11

28 **Ne t'énerve pas!** See scripts on p. 215H.

 Écoutons Écoute l'intonation des phrases suivantes et répète-les.
CD 8 Tr. 12

À la française

You've learned that changing the pitch of your voice when you speak is called *intonation.* French speakers use different intonations to express emotions such as excitement or annoyance, just as English speakers do. The same words can mean something completely different when spoken with a different intonation. Remember to pay attention to intonation when you learn new expressions.

 29 **Ras le bol!**

Écrivons Nabil et Farid achètent leurs billets de train pour aller chez leurs cousins à la campagne. Imagine et écris leur dialogue d'après les images. *Possible answers:*

1. Je commence à en avoir marre!
2. Non, mais, vous vous prenez pour qui?
3. Ça commence à bien faire, hein!

 30 **Ça va pas, non?!**

Parlons Il y a des gens qui t'embêtent en faisant les choses indiquées à droite. Tu leur demandes poliment d'arrêter, mais ils refusent. Qu'est-ce que tu leur dis? Joue cette scène avec tes camarades.

monopolise un téléphone public.

te pousse dans le métro.

met la radio très fort.

fume là où c'est interdit.

te marche sur les pieds.

parle très fort au cinéma.

Deuxième étape

Language Note
Tell students that **gratte-ciel** is invariable, so it does not change form: **les gratte-ciel.**

Presenting
Comment dit-on... ?

Storm into the classroom, complaining about a meeting or a phone call that you just had, using the new expressions. Use gestures and intonation to convey your exasperation. Then, act out one of your pet peeves. Express your annoyance at the situation, using appropriate intonation. Have students repeat the expressions, imitating your intonation.

Additional Practice

Project on a transparency a list of annoying situations. Tell a student that he or she is in one of these situations (John, you're in the lunch line, and it's not moving) and have the student react with one of the new expressions. (**J'en ai ras le bol!**) Then, call on a second student to reassure the first one, using an expression he or she has already learned. (**Il n'y a pas le feu!**)

Slower Pace

29 Before students write their dialogues, have them describe each situation in English.

Connections and Comparisons

Architecture Link

Call students' attention to the architecture in the background of the illustrations in Activity 29. Tunisian architecture reflects both Byzantine and Roman influences. The Romanesque arch in illustration 1 and the painted tiles in all the illustrations are common decorative features. The hand-painted tiles in particular have been popular since the seventeenth century, adorning the interiors of both private homes and public buildings. These tiles, painted by hand with elaborate geometrical motifs, were originally made in the Tunisian town of Nabeul. Today, less expensive, factory-made versions from Italy have replaced the hand-painted tiles.

Teaching Resources
pp. 230–233

PRINT
▶ Lesson Planner, p. 40
▶ Listening Activities, pp. 60–61, 64–65
▶ Activities for Communication, pp. 31–32, 73–74, 103–104
▶ Travaux pratiques de grammaire, pp. 78–81
▶ Grammar Tutor for Students of French, Chapter 8
▶ Cahier d'activités, pp. 91–94
▶ Testing Program, pp. 173–176
▶ Alternative Assessment Guide, p. 37
▶ Student Make-Up Assignments, Chapter 8

MEDIA
▶ One-Stop Planner
▶ Audio Compact Discs, CD 8, Trs. 10–12, 15, 22–24
▶ Teaching Transparencies: 8-2; **Grammaire supplémentaire** Answers; Travaux pratiques de grammaire Answers
▶ Interactive CD-ROM Tutor, Disc 2

Presenting
Comment dit-on... ?

Have students find sentences in Zohra's and in Aïcha's letters that describe their respective cities. (**Ici, c'est beaucoup plus bruyant, plus stressant.**) As students mention words such as **embouteillage,** hold up pictures to illustrate them.

Grammaire

The comparative List in one column adjectives that describe the city and the country. In a second column, write nouns associated with each place, such as **bruit** or **arbres.** Compare city and country life, using the adjectives.

Comment dit-on...?

Making comparisons

Dans mon village, **ce n'était pas comme ça.** . . . *it wasn't like this.*
Ici, c'est stressant, **tandis que** chez moi, c'est tranquille. *Here . . . , whereas . . .*
A la campagne, il y a **moins d'**embouteillages. . . . *less/fewer . . .*
A Tunis, il y a **plus de** bruit. . . . *more . . .*
Tunis est **plus** grand **que** Nefta.
Nefta est une ville **moins** bruyante **que** Tunis.

> Cahier d'activités, p. 93, Act. 16

31 On se dispute

Lisons/Parlons Latifa et Mona vont passer leurs vacances ensemble. Latifa veut aller dans une grande ville mais Mona préfère aller à la campagne. Elles se disputent. Qui fait les remarques suivantes, Latifa ou Mona?

Latifa
«Il y a plus de choses à voir.»

Mona
«Et puis, c'est plus tranquille!»

Latifa
«En tout cas, c'est plus animé.»

Mona
«Peut-être, mais c'est moins stressant.»

Mona   Mona
«Mais il y a moins de pollution.»

Mona
«Oui, mais il y a moins de monde.»

«D'accord, mais c'est moins ennuyeux!»

Latifa

Grammaire

The comparative

- To compare nouns, use **plus de, moins de,** and **autant de** *(as many/much)* before the noun. Use **que** or **qu'** *(than)* to continue the comparison.

    Il fait **plus de** bruit **que** l'autre voisin.
    Elle a **moins d'**argent **que** son frère.
    Tu achètes **autant de** livres **que** moi.

- To compare adjectives and adverbs, use **plus, moins,** or **aussi** *(as).* Remember to make the adjectives agree with the nouns they refer to.

    Les gens sont **plus** pressés en ville **qu'**à la campagne.
    Mon village est **moins** pollué **que** la ville.
    La campagne est **aussi** intéressante **que** la ville.

- English uses only one word, *better,* as the comparative of both the adjective *good* and the adverb *well.* There are two words for *better* in French.

    You use **meilleur(e)(s)** to say that something *is better* than something else.
    Les fruits sont **meilleurs** à la campagne **qu'**en ville.
    You use **mieux** to say that something is *done better.*
    On mange **mieux** à la campagne **qu'**en ville.

> Grammaire supplémentaire, pp. 240–241, Act. 6–9

> Cahier d'activités, pp. 93–94, Act. 17–18

> Travaux pratiques de grammaire, pp. 80–81, Act. 14–16

Connections and Comparisons

Using Prior Knowledge
Have students think of a place where they used to live or an imaginary one. Ask them questions about it. (**C'est plus ou moins tranquille ici? Il y a plus d'embouteillages là-bas?**)

Music Link
After presenting the **Grammaire,** play the song *Vive la rose* (Level 2, CD 10, Track 25) and ask students to listen for comparisons. Then, copy the lyrics (*Listening Activities,* Level 2, page 82) on a transparency and have volunteers come to the projector and circle the comparative forms in the song.

32 Grammaire en contexte

Parlons Utilise les mots suivants pour créer des phrases qui comparent la ville et la campagne. *See answers below.*

EXEMPLE moins / chèvre / vache
A la ville, il y a moins de chèvres et de vaches qu'à la campagne.

1. plus / embouteillage
2. avoir / autant / ami
3. moins / gens mal élevés / gens pressés
4. bon / fruit / légume

5. moins / air pollué / bruit
6. plus / musée / cinéma
7. moins / intéressant / magasin
8. gens / être / moins / stressé

33 Grammaire en contexte

Lisons/Parlons M. Fouad habite Tunis, mais il a passé sa jeunesse à la campagne et celle-ci lui manque. Continue son monologue.

EXEMPLE  —Oh, les gens étaient plus polis. Il y avait moins de stress. Et en plus...

vie	nourriture
problèmes	voisins
pollution	bruit
voitures	emploi
gens	stress
campagne	temps libre

pressé	travailleur
simple	bon
difficile	amusant
cher	compliqué
grand	pollué
sympa	énervant
tranquille	bruyant

Note culturelle

Dans les grandes villes tunisiennes, on porte des vêtements traditionnels et contemporains. Quelquefois, on porte même les deux styles ensemble. Les hommes s'habillent souvent à l'occidentale mais portent un chapeau typiquement arabe appelé **chéchia**. Les femmes tunisiennes combinent souvent leurs vêtements modernes avec un grand voile traditionnel qu'elles utilisent quelquefois pour porter des provisions et même leurs bébés.

34 Mon journal

Ecrivons Est-ce que tu habites en ville ou à la campagne? Compare l'endroit où tu vis avec un autre endroit, plus grand ou plus petit.

35 De l'école au travail

 Parlons You're working at the information desk of an international government agency for the summer. A French-speaking person has arrived late for an appointment due to traffic and parking problems. He or she will have to wait another two hours for a later appointment and is very frustrated. Act out this scene with a partner, then change roles.

Communication for All Students

Group Work

Have students organize a formal debate on the topic "City life is better than country life." Divide the class into pros and cons. Have each side prepare their arguments. For larger classes, you might have each side break into small groups.

The teacher begins the discussion by posing the question. You might videotape this debate and keep the recording to use as introductory material for the chapter next year.

📁 **Portfolio**

35 **Oral** This activity is appropriate for students' oral portfolios. For portfolio information, see *Alternative Assessment Guide,* pages iv–15.

Assess

▸ Testing Program, pp. 173–176
Quiz 8-2A, Quiz 8-2B
Audio CD 8, Tr. 15

▸ Student Make-Up Assignments, Chapter 8, Alternative Quiz

▸ Alternative Assessment Guide, p. 37

Possible answers

32 1. Il y a plus d'embouteillages à la ville qu'à la campagne.
2. On peut avoir autant d'amis à la campagne qu'à la ville.
3. Il y a moins de gens mal élevés et moins de gens pressés à la campagne.
4. Les fruits et les légumes sont meilleurs à la campagne qu'à la ville.
5. L'air est moins pollué et il y a moins de bruit à la campagne.
6. A la ville, il y a plus de musées et de cinémas.
7. On trouve moins de magasins intéressants à la campagne.
8. Les gens sont moins stressés à la campagne qu'à la ville.

CHAPITRE 8

Teaching Resources
pp. 234–236

PRINT

▶ Lesson Planner, p. 41
▶ Cahier d'activités, p. 95
▶ Reading Strategies and Skills Handbook, Chapter 8
▶ Joie de lire 3, Chapter 8
▶ Standardized Assessment Tutor, Chapter 8

MEDIA

▶ One-Stop Planner

Prereading
Activity A

Using Prior Knowledge
In order to help students to find the key sentence in this paragraph, you might suggest that they scan the text preceding that paragraph for a word they are familiar with and that appears several times in the text. (**fille**) Suggest that another familiar word in the text is the opposite of **fille**. (**fils**) Students can now infer that this passage is about genders and should be able to locate the key sentence in the given paragraph.

Reading
Activities B–M

Teaching Suggestion
C. Once students have listed the family's expectations for Gisèle, have them give their own reactions. You might have them list what they think today's parents expect from their children.

Answers
B. The anecdote reveals the secondary status of women in traditional Tunisian culture and shows the root of the author's rebellion.

Lisons!

ENFANCE D'UNE FILLE

Edouard décroche le téléphone :
- Une petite fille, crie le correspondant... Tu as une petite fille !
- Merci, dit Edouard.
- Une très mignonne petite fille ! précise le correspondant. *Mabrouk* !
- Merci, répète Edouard.

Il raccroche. Pendant une quinzaine de jours, chaque fois qu'on lui demandera si sa femme a accouché, Edouard, mon père, répondra sans sourciller :

« Pas encore... C'est pour bientôt... Mais pas encore... »

Quinze jours pour se faire à l'idée qu'il a cette malchance : une fille...

Puis il finira par se persuader qu'après tout, il a sauvé l'honneur, puisqu'il a déjà un fils aîné. Alors, il avouera enfin :

« Eh bien oui ! Elle a accouché : c'est une fille... »

La fille, c'est moi.

Ainsi commence l'aventure...

J'étais toute gosse quand on m'a raconté l'histoire de ma naissance. Ce déclic du téléphone raccroché, ce « mabrouk » crispé, je me souviens les avoir entendus résonner comme un glas. Ils m'ont poursuivie longtemps et continuent de me poursuivre. Ils me disaient la malédiction d'être née femme. Comme un glas, et en même temps, comme un appel, un départ. Je crois que la révolte s'est levée très tôt en moi. Très dure, très violente. Sans aucun doute indispensable pour faire face à ce clivage que j'ai retrouvé dans toute ma vie : j'étais une femme dans un monde pour hommes.

Aussi loin que remontent mes souvenirs, tout, dans mon enfance, dans mon éducation, dans mes études, dans ce qui était permis ou défendu, devait me rappeler que je n'étais née que femme. Ma sœur et moi, nous n'avons absolument pas été élevées comme nos frères.

Notre éducation procédait de ce découpage saignant : « Toi, tu es une fille. Il faut que tu apprennes la cuisine, le ménage. Et tu te marieras, le plus vite possible. Lui, c'est un garçon. Il faut, - on en trouvera les moyens, à tout prix - qu'il fasse des études, qu'il gagne bien sa vie. » Le mariage d'un garçon, c'est affaire personnelle. Le mariage d'une fille, c'est l'affaire des parents : cela ne la regarde pas. D'ailleurs, nos parents nous l'expliquaient : la naissance d'une fille représente une responsabilité épouvantable. Il faut bien sûr l'assumer. Il faut surtout s'en décharger sur un mari, le plus rapidement possible.

Je crois que ma mère a mis un certain acharnement, peut-être inconscient, à maintenir ce clivage. Comme si, au fond, elle voulait reproduire ce qu'elle avait subi. Mon père aussi. Mais d'une certaine manière, il était plus neutre, il avait plus de recul, il était *l'homme*.

Stratégie pour lire
When you read in French, do you sometimes concentrate so much on understanding vocabulary and grammar that you lose track of what the reading itself is about? To solve this problem, first find the main idea, usually located near the beginning of the reading. Then think about how the different parts of the reading relate to the main idea. Do the subtopics act as definitions, summaries, paraphrases, or illustrations of the main topic? Are they results or consequences of the main idea, or even causes of it?

A. ... j'étais une femme dans un monde pour hommes.

A. In the paragraph that begins **J'étais toute gosse...,** find the sentence that gives the main idea of the reading.

B. How does the first passage relate to the main idea? Why does the author relate the story of her birth?   See answers below.

C. What are three things Gisèle was told that a girl is supposed to do?   cook, clean house, marry

D. According to the author, which of the following does NOT describe how women were treated or how they felt?

asphyxiées   blessées   sacrifiées
privilégiées   opprimées

Cultures and Communities

Family Link
Ask students to list stories about growing up in a family (*The Diary of Anne Frank, Little House on the Prairie*). Have students imagine what it would be like to grow up in a Tunisian family, according to what they've read in the **Mise en train** and the **Remise en train.**

Culture Note
After a restrictive childhood in a traditional Tunisian home, Gisèle Halimi became a persistent advocate of women's rights. In 1971, she co-founded a women's rights group in France, along with the writer Simone de Beauvoir and several others. In 1981, she was elected to the **Assemblée nationale,** where she served as an active proponent of women's rights until 1984.

Victime de son éducation, ma mère a été mariée à moins de quinze ans. A seize ans, elle avait son premier enfant. Blessée, donc, mais fière, fière de sa maternité et fière de ses blessures, comme certains martyrs. Opprimée dans son plus jeune âge, niée dès son existence, passant sans transition, de la terrible autorité de mon grand-père, authentique *paterfamilias* de tribu, à celle de mon père, son mari, tout naturellement, elle opprimait à son tour.

Quand je refusais de me marier, à seize ans, elle me disait : « A ton âge, moi j'avais des enfants. » A travers moi, elle voulait revivre sa vie. Comme pour la justifier. Je comprends très bien cette démarche. Perpétuer les choses provoque toujours moins de heurts que vouloir les changer.

C'est quand nos études ont pris une certaine importance que j'ai ressenti la discrimination. Après le certificat d'études, il a été question que mon frère continue. Dans la famille, on était décidé à se priver de tout pour qu'il ait un diplôme. Pendant ce temps, j'avais progressé toute seule. Mais ça n'avait jamais intéressé personne. Mon frère n'était pas très bon élève, en cinquième. Il avait des colles. Il truquait. Il imitait, sur les bulletins scolaires, la signature paternelle. Et moi, je continuais mon chemin. Je réussissais. Mais personne ne me demandait quoi que ce soit. Au fond, personne ne s'en apercevait.

A dix ans, je savais déjà qu'il ne fallait pas compter sur un effort financier de mes parents pour m'aider à aller au lycée qui était payant. Et même assez cher. Je m'étais renseignée. J'avais appris qu'il existait un concours des bourses, uniquement ouvert à une certaine catégorie sociale d'élèves. Celle à laquelle j'appartenais : les élèves pauvres. Pour réussir, il fallait faire un très bon score. J'ai donc passé cet examen. J'ai même été reçue en tête, autant que je me souvienne. J'obtenais de très bonnes notes, mais elles passaient toujours inaperçues. J'arrivais pour dire : « Je suis première en français. » C'était le moment même où se déclenchait un drame parce que mon frère était dernier en mathématiques. Il était homme et son avenir d'homme occupait toute la place. A en être asphyxiée. Toute l'attention était tournée vers lui. Je ne suis même pas sûre qu'on m'entendait quand je parlais de mes professeurs et de mes cours. Il m'a fallu accumuler beaucoup de succès, réussir mes examens de licence à la faculté pour que mes parents commencent à dire : « C'est pas mal, ce qu'elle fait. Après tout, peut-être est-elle un cas un peu particulier? » Mais à l'époque, ça ne les intéressait pas, c'était secondaire.

Vint le moment où il fallut me décider au mariage. En clair, me marier, c'était arrêter mes études. A l'époque, ma mère aurait beaucoup souhaité me faire épouser un marchand d'huiles, fort riche et sympathique au demeurant. Il avait trente-cinq ans. Moi, j'en avais seize. C'était tout à fait dans les normes du mariage, en Tunisie.

Je ne voulais pas me marier. Je voulais étudier.

E. What kind of life had Gisèle's mother known? How are her experiences reflected in the way she raised her daughter? See answers below.

F. Qui dirait les choses suivantes, Gisèle ou son frère?

« Je devais ranger, faire la vaisselle. » Gisèle

« Tout le monde se prive pour que j'aie une éducation. » brother

« Mon mariage, c'est l'affaire de mes parents. » Gisèle

« Personne ne s'intéresse à mon éducation. » Gisèle

For Activities G–J, see answers below.

G. Pourquoi est-ce que l'auteur nous parle du genre d'étudiant qu'était son frère? En quoi cela a-t-il rapport avec le sujet?

H. Que pense Gisèle du mariage traditionnel, arrangé par les parents? Comment sa mère réagit-elle?

I. How did Gisèle save money for her education? Why is this significant, in relation to the main idea?

J. How does the author feel about her family today? Does she blame them for the way she was raised?

Communication for All Students

Slower Pace

F. Before students do this activity, have them give a general description in English of both Gisèle and her brother. You might even have them compare these people to characters in a TV program or a book that they are familiar with.

Challenge

F. Have students suggest additional things that Gisèle or her brother might say, read them to the class, and have their classmates indicate who might say each statement.

Teaching Suggestion

H. Ask students for their reactions to the traditional marriage arrangement in Tunisia. Do they think they would react as Gisèle did, or would they have a different reaction?

Culture Note

It was a great accomplishment that Gisèle Halimi saved money for her own education because, in traditional Tunisian society, women were rarely allowed to own property. Instead, their dowry or inheritance would be paid to their guardian, either their father or their husband. Since in the past most women did not have jobs and worked in the home, they generally had no way to earn independent incomes.

Possible answers

E. She married quite young; she was dominated first by her father, then by her husband. She oppressed her own daughters in order to justify her own life.

G. As a student, he was far inferior to his sister, but the parents spent money on his education, not hers, because he was a boy. This is more evidence that the author was "a woman in a man's world."

H. Gisèle rejected a traditional marriage in favor of further education; Her mother didn't understand her.

I. She tutored a male student in mathematics and Latin. She knew that her parents would not help her pay for her education because she was a girl. It is ironic that she financed her education by tutoring a male student and that her parents had to pay extra for her less gifted brother to be educated, while Gisèle, a bright student, had to earn her own money to finance her education.

J. She still cares about them; She doesn't blame them. She considers them all victims.

Lisons!

Teaching Suggestions

K. As an extension of this activity, you might ask students if they think male and female children in the U.S. are treated differently, based on their experience. If they do, ask them to give examples.

Group Work

L. Have students work in groups to find the answers to the following questions about the news article: How does this article relate to the story? (It begins by mentioning the story and how difficult it was for Gisèle's father to accept her.) What proof is given that, in 1994, female babies are no longer considered a curse? (Examples of birth announcements of female babies are given.) Who modernized the laws? (the president, Habib Bourguiba)

Answers

K. *Answers will vary.*

L. about 60 years; She went to France and became a lawyer and a militant. She became her father's favorite child.

M. Tunisia gained its independence from France, and President Bourguiba modernized the laws; Tunisian women were given legal rights, women's consciousness seemed to be raised, and they began to form some powerful groups.

N. By 1927, women had the right to vote, but they did not yet have equal opportunities in many areas; Now they have additional legal protection, more political power, and better access to education and professional careers.

Je revois toujours ma mère mettre son doigt sur sa tempe et dire : « Gisèle, elle ne veut pas se marier, elle veut étudier... », comme pour expliquer par ce geste : « Elle ne tourne pas rond cette fille! Elle est vraiment bizarre! » On a pensé que cela me passerait.

Mon frère avait redoublé deux fois. Je l'ai donc très vite rattrapé. On s'est finalement retrouvés dans la même classe. C'est à ce moment-là qu'il a quitté le lycée. Renvoyé je crois.

Mes parents ont enregistré cet échec toujours sans commentaire à mon égard. Je me demande cependant si mes succès n'ont pas été considérés, à ce moment-là, comme quelque chose de néfaste. Je bouleversais une règle établie, un ordre. Alors que personne ne s'occupait de moi, que je continue de progresser mais discrètement, comme dans une routine quotidienne, passe encore. Mais que je me fasse remarquer en coiffant au poteau l'homme, l'aîné de la famille, celui à qui on devait passer le flambeau de l'honneur, c'était trop!

L'offensive pour me marier s'est alors faite plus dure, car il fallait rétablir le processus : je me mariais, j'arrêtais mes études et mes parents continuaient à faire des sacrifices pour mon frère. Je me souviens même d'un fait important, compte tenu de notre niveau de vie : on est allé jusqu'à payer au garçon des leçons particulières de mathématiques. Cela représentait pour nous un luxe inouï.

Quelques années plus tard, c'est moi qui donnais des leçons particulières, au fils d'un avocat chez lequel mon père faisait des remplacements de secrétaire. J'étais en seconde, au lycée. Avec ces leçons de mathématiques et de latin, je voulais mettre

de l'argent de côté : j'avais décidé que j'irais à l'université en France et je savais que personne ne m'aiderait. C'était assez symbolique : mon frère avait besoin de leçons particulières ; moi, j'en donnais et je gagnais déjà le pouvoir d'apprendre.

Ce que je dis ici peut paraître dur à l'égard d'êtres auxquels je reste *affectivement* très liée, mais j'essaie d'être objective, de dire comment les choses se sont passées. Cela ne change rien à ce que j'éprouve pour ma mère, ma sœur, mon père, ces *victimes*. Je ne veux pas les accabler. Je voudrais les éclairer, de l'*intérieur*. J'explique pour eux et pour moi, l'aliénation qui fut la *nôtre*, qui reste, en grande partie, la leur. Je dénonce. D'une certaine manière, je les réhabilite aussi. De toutes manières, je viens d'eux, de ce milieu, et je ne l'oublie pas. Moi, j'étais déterminée à aller mon chemin, que ça plaise ou non. Et mon chemin passait d'abord par cette envie démesurée que j'avais de lire, d'apprendre, de connaître.

LES TUNISIENNES EN MARCHE

L'avocate et militante Gisèle Halimi a déjà relaté une anecdote significative entourant sa naissance. Son père, dont elle deviendra l'enfant préféré, mit quinze jours à accepter que son deuxième enfant fut une fille. C'était en 1927. En Tunisie. Aujourd'hui, il est fréquent de lire dans le carnet mondain des trois quotidiens de Tunis des faire-part de naissance ainsi rédigés : La famille est comblée par la nouveau-née... Inès a donné plus de joie à sa famille... Une jolie poupée prénommée Khaoula est venue égayer le foyer de... En 1994, en Tunisie, les petites filles ne sont plus une malédiction.

C'est le Président Habib Bourguiba qui, dans la foulée de l'indépendance, a entrepris de moderniser les lois. Le 13 août 1956, il promulgue le Code du statut personnel, véritable révolution qui fait de la femme une adulte en lui donnant un statut et des droits juridiques... A partir de là, les femmes, conscientes de leur existence, commencent à se regrouper en associations avec lesquelles il faudra désormais compter.

La Tunisienne, comparée à ses sœurs marocaines et algériennes, avance d'un pas allégé et rapide. « La Tunisie s'est toujours distinguée par une ouverture et un appel — aussi bien des hommes que des femmes — vers une législation plus favorable à ces dernières. »

Cahier d'activités, p. 95, Act. 20

For Activities K–N, see answers below.

K. A ton avis, doit-on traiter différemment les garçons et les filles?

L. The excerpt on the right is from a magazine article. How much time has passed since the events related by Gisèle Halimi in **Enfance d'une fille?** What changed during her lifetime?

M. Quel changement a eu lieu en Tunisie en 1956? Fais une liste de trois conséquences que ce changement a apporté dans la vie des femmes tunisiennes.

N. Quel était la situation des femmes aux Etats-Unis dans les années vingt? Comment cette situation a-t-elle changé?

Connections and Comparisons

Postreading

History Link

N. Significant events for women in American history include the Seneca Falls Convention of 1848, which launched the women's suffrage movement, and the passing of the Nineteenth Amendment in 1920, which granted women the right to vote.

Community Link

Habib Bourguiba once said "When still a young child, I told myself that if one day I had the power to do so, I would make haste to redress the wrong done to women." In 1956, he had the power. He abolished the **sharia,** a civil code based on the Koran, and established reform. Polygamy was outlawed, women obtained the right to vote, and legislation on equal pay was instituted.

Ecrivons!

Un récit familial

Dans ce passage de *La Cause des femmes,* l'auteur Gisèle Halimi décrit les difficultés qu'elle a eu à grandir dans une famille tunisienne traditionnelle. Maintenant, tu vas écrire un récit familial. Parle de ta propre famille, d'une famille imaginaire ou d'une famille de la télé.

> ### Stratégie pour écrire
> Brainstorming is a useful technique for generating ideas for your writing. In brainstorming, you quickly write down all the ideas that pop into your head when you think about your topic. Write single words or short phrases instead of complete sentences, and don't worry about whether the ideas are good or bad, relevant, or too far-fetched. It may even help to give yourself a time limit of thirty seconds or a minute to jot down all your thoughts. Once you've finished, evaluate your ideas: keep the best ones and add information, examples, and details where needed.

A. Préparation

1. Avant de commencer à écrire, réponds aux questions suivantes pour déterminer si la famille de ton choix est traditionnelle ou moderne.

   a. Est-ce que les deux parents travaillent?

   b. Est-ce qu'ils s'occupent tous les deux des enfants?

   c. Est-ce que les enfants bénéficient d'une certaine indépendance?

   d. Comment est-ce que les parents partagent les tâches ménagères?

   e. S'il y a des enfants des deux sexes, est-ce que les corvées domestiques sont partagées de façon équitable entre les filles et les garçons?

   f. Est-ce que les garçons et les filles ont les mêmes droits et les mêmes responsabilités?

   g. Qu'est-ce que les parents espèrent pour l'avenir de leurs enfants? L'université? Une carrière professionnelle? Le mariage? Est-ce qu'ils espèrent les mêmes choses pour les garçons et pour les filles?

2. Maintenant, décide si cette famille est traditionnelle, moderne ou un mélange des deux. Ecris tes idées sur ce sujet pendant à peu près dix minutes. Trouve des exemples qui montrent si cette famille est plutôt traditionnelle ou plutôt moderne.

3. Relis ce que tu as écrit pour en garder l'essentiel. Fais un plan pour organiser tes idées principales. Si possible, ajoute des détails et d'autres informations appropriées.

B. Rédaction

Fais un brouillon de ton récit familial en suivant ton plan.

C. Evaluation

1. Fais une évaluation de ton récit. Est-ce que tu as bien suivi ton plan?

2. Est-ce que ton argumentation est logique? Est-ce que tu as clairement expliqué pourquoi tu trouves que cette famille est moderne ou traditionnelle? As-tu choisi de bons exemples?

3. Relis ton récit. Fais attention...

   a. à l'accord des sujets avec les verbes.   c. à l'orthographe.

   b. aux accents.   d. à la position et à l'accord des adjectifs.

4. Fais les changements nécessaires.

Apply and Assess

Postwriting
Auditory Learners
C. 2. Have students summarize the main points of their story for a partner, as if they were giving a speech. If the listener is confused, or if the writer is unable to describe the points clearly, the writer might reevaluate the structure of the essay.

Teaching Suggestion
C. 3. Have students exchange papers with a partner. The partner should check for the four items listed and underline or circle anything that is questionable, writing the letter of the criterion next to it. For example, if the partner thinks that a word may be spelled incorrectly, he or she should circle it and write **c** next to it.

Teaching Resources
p. 237

PRINT
- Lesson Planner, p. 41
- Cahier d'activités, p. 152
- Alternative Assessment Guide, p. 23
- Standardized Assessment Tutor, Chapter 8

MEDIA
- One-Stop Planner
- Test Generator, Chapter 8
- Interactive CD-ROM Tutor

Process Writing

Prewriting
Teaching Suggestions
A. Have students take out several sheets of paper. Read over the questions in A. 1. with students. Then, pull out a stopwatch. Tell students they have exactly five minutes to brainstorm. Tell them to label one column **Une famille traditionnelle** and the other one **Une famille moderne** and to write down everything they can think of to go in each column. At this stage, tell them not to worry about sentence structure, spelling, or punctuation.

A. 3. Once students have brainstormed about their families, have them evaluate their ideas. With a different-colored pen, they should circle the ideas they might want to use, cross out those that they don't, and put a star by the ones they want to feature in their stories.

Writing
Teaching Suggestion
B. Remind students that they might add to or delete from their original plan.

CHAPITRE 8

 For **Grammaire supplémentaire** Answer Transparencies, see the *Teaching Transparencies* binder.

Grammaire supplémentaire

 CD-ROM DISC 2

Première étape **Objectives** Asking someone to convey good wishes; closing a letter; expressing hopes or wishes; giving advice

1 Remplace les mots en caractères gras avec le pronom d'objet direct ou indirect, selon le cas. (**pp. 46, 222**)

1. Dis bonjour **à ton père** de ma part.
2. Embrasse **ta tante** pour moi.
3. Donne des bisous **à tes cousins** pour moi.
4. Salue **ton père** pour moi.
5. Dis **à ta grand-mère** que je vais écrire bientôt.
6. Fais mes amitiés **à tes parents.**
7. Dis **à Mamie** que je pense à elle.

2 D'abord, lis ce que dit Zohra. Ensuite, complète ce que Didier dit. N'oublie pas de mettre le verbe à l'imparfait. (**p. 225**)

| EXEMPLE | DIDIER | **Ça serait chouette si j'avais des parents architraditionnels!** |
| | ZOHRA | C'est pas si chouette que ça d'avoir des parents archi-traditionnels! |

1. DIDIER Ça serait chouette si ma mère…
   ZOHRA C'est pas si chouette que ça d'aller chercher l'eau au puits.
2. DIDIER Ça serait chouette si ma sœur…
   ZOHRA C'est pas si chouette que ça de porter le bois sur sa tête.
3. DIDIER Ça serait chouette si mon père…
   ZOHRA C'est pas si chouette que ça d'élever des moutons.
4. DIDIER Ça serait chouette si Leïla et toi, vous…
   ZOHRA C'est pas si chouette que ça de faire des tapis.
5. DIDIER Ça serait chouette si mes oncles…
   ZOHRA C'est pas si chouette que ça de cultiver des dattes.
6. DIDIER Ça serait chouette si moi, je…
   ZOHRA C'est pas si chouette que ça de devoir traire les vaches.
7. DIDIER Ça serait chouette si ma sœur et moi, nous...
   ZOHRA C'est pas si chouette que ça de faire la cueillette des figues.
8. DIDIER Ça serait chouette si mes parents...
   ZOHRA C'est pas si chouette que ça de donner à manger aux chameaux.

Answers

1
1. Dis-lui bonjour de ma part.
2. Embrasse-la pour moi.
3. Donne-leur des bisous pour moi.
4. Salue-le pour moi.
5. Dis-lui que je vais lui écrire une lettre bientôt.
6. Fais-leur mes amitiés.
7. Dis-lui que je pense à elle.

2
1. allait chercher l'eau au puits.
2. portait le bois sur sa tête.
3. élevait des moutons.
4. faisiez des tapis.
5. cultivaient des dattes.
6. devais traire les vaches.
7. faisions la cueillette des figues.
8. donnaient à manger aux chameaux.

Grammar Resources for Chapter 8

The **Grammaire supplémentaire** activities are designed as supplemental activities for the grammatical concepts presented in the chapter. You might use them as additional practice, for review, or for assessment.

For more grammar presentations, review, and practice, refer to the following:
• Travaux pratiques de grammaire
• Grammar Tutor for Students of French

• Grammar Summary on pp. R29–R54
• Cahier d'activités
• Grammar and Vocabulary quizzes (Testing Program)
• Test Generator
• Interactive CD-ROM Tutor
• **Jeux interactifs** at <u>go.hrw.com</u>

3 Qu'est-ce que ces personnes feraient si elles habitaient dans les villes tunisiennes suivantes? Réponds en utilisant **si** et l'imparfait d'**habiter** dans la première partie de chaque réponse et le conditionnel du verbe qui convient dans la deuxième. (**p. 225**)

EXEMPLE   Je / Sfax / cultiver des olives
Si j'habitais à Sfax, je cultiverais des olives.

1. Nous / Bizerte / aller à la pêche avec notre oncle Rachid
2. Selwa / Carthage / se promener souvent parmi les ruines romaines
3. Vous / Tozeur / manger des dattes à tous les repas
4. Tu / Kairouan / faire de la poterie
5. Je / Douz / garder les moutons de mon frère aîné
6. Moussa et Yasmine / Sousse / voir de très beaux couchers de soleil

4 Complète ces phrases avec l'imparfait ou le conditionnel, selon le cas. (**pp. 13, 141, 225**)

EXEMPLE   Si je _____ (visiter) la médina, je _____ (acheter) des objets en cuivre.
Si je visitais la médina, j'achèterais des objets en cuivre.

1. Si je/j' _____ (aller) en Tunisie, je/j' _____ (acheter) des tapis.

2. Si je/j' _____ (habiter) dans une ferme, je/j' _____ (donner) à manger aux poules.

3. Si je/j' _____ (aller) dans un restaurant à Sfax, je/j' _____ (manger) des olives.

4. Si je/j' _____ (être) dans le désert, je/j' _____ (regarder) un beau coucher de soleil.

5. Si je/j' _____ (visiter) la Tunisie, je/j' _____ (faire) beaucoup de photos.

Answers

3 1. Si nous habitions à Bizerte, nous irions à la pêche avec notre oncle Rachid.
2. Si Selwa habitait à Carthage, elle se promènerait souvent parmi les ruines romaines.
3. Si vous habitiez à Tozeur, vous mangeriez des dattes à tous les repas.
4. Si tu habitais à Kairouan, tu ferais de la poterie.
5. Si j'habitais à Douz, je garderais les moutons de mon frère aîné.
6. Si Moussa et Yasmine habitaient à Sousse, ils verraient de très beaux couchers de soleil.

4 1. allais, achèterais
2. habitais, donnerais
3. allais, mangerais
4. étais, regarderais
5. visitais, ferais

Communication for All Students

Slower Pace

4 Review the situations in which the imperfect and conditional are used before students complete the sentences. Then go over the formation of the imperfect and conditional and complete the first two blanks with students on the board or on an overhead transparency. Allow students to work in pairs and check each other's work for the remaining sentences. When students are finished have them explain their answers. As a class, come up with additional sentences to make sure the students can apply what they have just practiced. You might suggest that students write about what they would do if they could go anywhere in the world for their next vacation.

Grammaire supplémentaire

CHAPITRE 8

For **Grammaire supplémentaire** Answer Transparencies, see the *Teaching Transparencies* binder.

Grammaire supplémentaire

WA3 FRANCOPHONE AFRICA-8

5 Samir te raconte ce qui lui plaît et ce qu'il aimerait faire. Dis-lui ce que tu ferais si tu étais lui. Dans chaque phrase, utilise **à ta place** et une des expressions de la boîte. N'oublie pas de mettre les verbes au conditionnel. (**p. 225**)

emprunter une djellaba à son père	essayer le couscous
trouver un travail	chercher une petite amie
partir en vacances	visiter les ruines de Carthage
acheter un caméscope	parler à mes parents
aller dans la médina	

EXEMPLE —Ce qui me plaît, c'est le Tunis ancien.
—**A ta place, j'irais dans la médina.**

1. Qu'est-ce que j'aimerais me marier!
2. Je m'intéresse à l'histoire romaine.
3. Ce qui m'intéresse, c'est de gagner ma vie.
4. Je trouve ça très cool, les vêtements traditionnels!
5. Si seulement je pouvais faire une vidéo sur Tunis!
6. Ce qui me plaît, c'est de goûter la cuisine locale.
7. Ce que je voudrais, c'est me reposer.
8. Ce qui serait cool, c'est d'avoir mon propre appartement.

Deuxième étape   Objectives Complaining; expressing annoyance; making comparisons

6 Fais des comparaisons dans les phrases suivantes. Remarque qu'il y a des phrases avec des noms et des expressions contenant des adverbes et des adjectifs. (**p. 232**)

EXEMPLE Il y a ... habitants à Tunis ... à Nefta.
Il y a plus d'habitants à Tunis qu'à Nefta.

1. En , c'est ... pollué ... au .

2. En Tunisie, il y a ...  ... aux Etats-Unis.

3. Les  sont ... animées ... les .

4. Dans ma famille, il y a ... ... filles.

Communication for All Students

Visual Learners/Challenge

6 Have students complete the activity and then allow them to work in pairs to come up with four additional sentences in which they use drawings or pictures to elicit comparisons among different people, places, and animals. When the pairs have finished, have them present and explain their answers.

Challenge

7 After students have finished the activity, have them write additional sentences, using the imperfect based on the model given in the **exemple.** Students should try to use actual facts that they might have learned in history or social studies class to write about how things used to be.

7 Gisèle te parle de son enfance. Utilise les fragments donnés et **plus de... que** ou **moins de... que**, selon le cas. N'oublie pas de mettre les verbes à l'imparfait. (**p. 232**)

EXEMPLE   les hommes / avoir (+) droits / les femmes
            Les hommes avaient plus de droits que les femmes.

1. les filles / avoir (+) choses à faire / les garçons
2. ma sœur et moi, nous / avoir (−) liberté / notre frère
3. je / avoir (+) succès à l'école / mon frère
4. je / réussir à (+) examens / lui
5. A 16 ans, ma mère / avoir (+) enfants / moi
6. Mes parents / avoir (−) argent / les parents de mes camarades

8 Fais des phrases selon l'exemple. Pour chaque phrase, utilise **plus... que, moins... que, ou aussi... que** et un des adjectifs de la boîte. (**p. 232**)

> intéressant
> bruyant
> beau
> loin
> pressé
> bête
> chaud

EXEMPLE   vêtements en laine (+) vêtements en coton
            Les vêtements en laine sont plus chauds que les vêtements en coton.

1. moutons (+) chèvres
2. gens à la campagne (−) gens en ville
3. films tunisiens (=) films français
4. la campagne (−) la ville
5. poteries bleues (+) poteries blanches

9 Remplis les blancs avec **mieux** ou la forme correcte de **meilleur.** (**p. 232**)

AICHA   J'en ai marre de Tunis! La pollution et les embouteillages, c'est l'horreur!

ALI   Ne t'en fais pas trop! C'est bientôt les vacances! Ça te fera du bien! Tu iras ____1____, je t'assure!

AICHA   Si on allait à Nefta! Ça te dirait? L'air (m.) y est ____2____ qu'à Tunis. On dormirait chez mon cousin!

ALI   Ça serait chouette! Là-bas, on dort ____3____. On y mange ____4____. Bref, on va ____5____.

Review and Assess

You may wish to assign the **Grammaire supplémentaire** activities as additional practice or homework after presenting material throughout the chapter. Assign Activity 1 after **Comment dit-on... ?** (p. 222), Activities 2–5 after **Grammaire** (p. 225), and Activities 6–9 after **Grammaire** (p. 232).

To prepare students for the **Etape** Quizzes and Chapter Test, we suggest doing the **Grammaire supplémentaire** activities in the following order. Have students complete Activities 1–5 before taking Quiz 8-1A or 8-1B; and Activities 6–9 before Quiz 8-2A or 8-2B.

Possible answers

7 1. Les filles avaient plus de choses à faire que les garçons.
2. Ma sœur et moi, nous avions moins de liberté que notre frère.
3. J'avais plus de succès à l'école que mon frère.
4. Je réussissais à plus d'examens que lui.
5. A 16 ans, ma mère avait plus d'enfants que moi.
6. Mes parents avaient moins d'argent que les parents de mes camarades.

8 1. Les moutons sont plus bêtes que les chèvres.
2. Les gens à la campagne sont moins pressés que les gens en ville.
3. Les films tunisiens sont aussi intéressants que les films français.
4. La campagne est moins bruyante que la ville.
5. Les poteries bleues sont plus belles que les poteries blanches.

9 1. mieux
2. meilleur
3. mieux
4. mieux
5. mieux

Mise en pratique

internet

go.hrw.com
ADRESSE: go.hrw.com
MOT-CLE: WA3
FRANCOPHONE AFRICA-8

The **Mise en pratique** reviews and integrates all four skills and culture in preparation for the Chapter Test.

Teaching Resources
pp. 242–243

PRINT
▸ Lesson Planner, p. 41
▸ Listening Activities, p. 61
▸ Video Guide, pp. 49, 51–52
▸ Grammar Tutor for Students of French, Chapter 8
▸ Standardized Assessment Tutor, Chapter 8

MEDIA
▸ One-Stop Planner
▸ Video Program
  Videocassette 3, 28:28–34:08
▸ Audio Compact Discs, CD 8, Tr. 13
▸ Interactive CD-ROM Tutor, Disc 2

Career Path

Because of the number of visitors certain areas attract, many tourist offices or Chambers of Commerce across the United States have brochures in several languages and sometimes hire guides who are proficient enough in another language to conduct tours of various monuments and attractions for foreign visitors. Often, summer jobs are available for young people interested in such work. Ask your students if they think they would like to be a guide and how they think such an experience might be beneficial.

1 Lis cette brochure et réponds aux questions suivantes.

*T*unis s'affirme Capitale. Non seulement aux yeux des touristes qui y trouvent shopping et distractions sportives et culturelles, mais en tant que centre politique, administratif, économique moderne. Siège d'organisations internationales, Tunis accueille également de nombreux congrès tout au long de l'année. Le festival de Carthage et les Journées cinématographiques et théâtrales, qui prennent également pour cadre les vestiges de la prestigieuse cité antique, sont l'occasion de rencontres internationales réputées. Tunis est une ville de caractère. Tunis a une âme. L'âme de Tunis, c'est à travers le contact, la discussion, le travail des habitants que le visiteur peut la deviner.

P·O·I·N·T·S F·O·R·T·S

En Ville
...Perspective Avenue Bourguiba, depuis la Place de l'Afrique. Centre National de l'Artisanat.
...Parc du Belvédère : panorama, zoo, piscine
...Dans la Médina : la Grande Mosquée, les souks couverts, terrasses de marchands de tapis ; mosquée Sidi Youssef ; musée lapidaire.
...Sidi Bou Khrissan ; musée des Arts et des Traditions populaires

En Banlieue
...Carthage : colline de Byrsa : panorama ; musée national ; quartier de l'Odéon. Les thermes d'Antonin et le musée de plein air ; le tophet ; les ports et le musée de la mer de Salammbô.
...La Marsa-Gammarth et le «Café Saf-Saf» ; les plages, les installations hôtelières et touristiques. Musée du Bardo. Chelles antiques.

See answers below.

1. According to the brochure, what might you do or see in Tunis?
2. Other than tourism, what are some possible reasons for visiting Tunis?
3. What does the brochure recommend as a way to discover the "soul of Tunis"?
4. How is Tunis important to Tunisian politics?
5. What places of interest near Tunis are mentioned in the brochure?

Apply and Assess

Additional Practice

1 After completing this activity, have partners create short skits in which one student plays the role of an employee at the tourist office in Tunis and the other the role of a visitor from France. The visitor should ask for information about Tunis, including what there is to see and do there. The employee should respond to the visitor's questions and encourage him or her to visit the various places and attractions mentioned in the brochure.

Possible answers
1 1. shopping, sports and cultural attractions, festivals
2. business, political activity, the Festival of Carthage, cinema and theater festivals
3. getting to know its inhabitants
4. It's the capital. It hosts many international conferences throughout the year.
5. Carthage, beaches, museums

STANDARDS: 1.1, 1.2, 3.2

2 Tu vas passer six mois avec une famille tunisienne. Tu dois décider où tu voudrais habiter. On t'a donné le choix entre une grande ville et un petit village à la campagne. Avec ton/ta camarade, parle de ce qu'il y a à faire et à voir là-bas. Compare les deux endroits. Ton/Ta camarade te donnera des conseils.

3 Hoda parle de ce qu'elle désire faire cet été, mais elle a des problèmes. Leïla lui propose des solutions. Fais une liste de trois des souhaits de Hoda et des conseils que Leïla lui donne. See scripts and answers on p. 215H.

CD 8 Tr. 13

4 Relis la **Rencontre culturelle** et les **Notes culturelles** du chapitre et puis, trouve les mots qui décrivent...

1. un peuple qui vivait en Tunisie avant l'arrivée des Arabes.   les Berbères
2. une sorte de chapeau que les hommes portent en Tunisie.   une chéchia
3. un vêtement porté par les femmes tunisiennes.   un sifsari
4. le vieux quartier d'une ville où il y a beaucoup de souks.   la médina

5 a. Tu es parti(e) en Tunisie il y a deux semaines. Ecris une carte postale à tes camarades de la classe de français. N'oublie pas de transmettre tes amitiés à tes autres copains.

b. Après trois mois en Tunisie, un magazine tunisien te demande d'écrire un article sur tes impressions du pays. Ecris un récit de ce que tu as fait et décris ce que tu as vu. N'oublie pas de comparer les diverses régions que tu as visitées.

6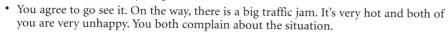

Jeu de rôle

You're visiting a friend who lives in a very big city. Your friend wants to show you one of the city's famous attractions. Act out the following situations with your partner.

- You agree to go see it. On the way, there is a big traffic jam. It's very hot and both of you are very unhappy. You both complain about the situation.
- You finally arrive at your destination, but someone zooms in front of you into the last parking space. You express your annoyance.
- You and your friend stand in line to get tickets and someone cuts in front of you. You're both furious!
- Finally you get to go in, but a few minutes later, someone announces that the attraction is about to close. Now you've really had it!

Apply and Assess

Teaching Suggestions

4 Refer students to the **Notes culturelles** in the chapter. You might have several students volunteer to become "experts" on a particular cultural topic. Assign a **Note culturelle** or part of the **Rencontre culturelle** to each volunteer. Have them read over the information carefully, and then prepare a creative presentation of their cultural topic. They might bring in visual aids, such as guide books, or make their own drawings to accompany their presentation.

6 Encourage students to have one partner try to reassure and calm the other, using expressions they've already learned from Chapter 2. (**Du calme, du calme. Sois patient(e)! On a largement le temps.**)

STANDARDS: 1.1, 1.2, 1.3, 3.1, 5.1

Challenge

3 Have students tell in French what advice they would give Hoda, including what they would do if they were in Hoda's position.

Writing Assessment

5 You might use the following rubric when grading your students on this activity.

Writing Rubric	Points			
	4	3	2	1
Content (Complete–Incomplete)				
Comprehensibility (Comprehensible–Incomprehensible)				
Accuracy (Accurate–Seldom accurate)				
Organization (Well organized–Poorly organized)				
Effort (Excellent–Minimal)				

18–20: A   14–15: C   Under 12: F
16–17: B   12–13: D

Teaching Resources
p. 244

PRINT 📖
▶ Grammar Tutor for Students of French, Chapter 8

MEDIA 📀📼📚
▶ Interactive CD-ROM Tutor, Disc 2
▶ Online self-test

go.hrw.com
WA3 FRANCOPHONE
AFRICA-8

Possible answers

3 1. Ça serait chouette si je pouvais aller en Afrique. Qu'est-ce que j'aimerais aller en Afrique! Si j'avais le choix, j'irais en Afrique.
2. Si c'était possible, j'achèterais une nouvelle voiture.
3. Si seulement je pouvais aller à l'université.

4 1. Si j'étais toi, j'étudierais beaucoup plus.
2. Si c'était moi, j'en parlerais avec eux.
3. A ta place, j'irais en Tunisie.

6 *Answers will vary.*
1. Non mais, vous vous prenez pour qui? Non mais, surtout ne vous gênez pas!
2. Ça va pas, non?!
3. Ça commence à bien faire, hein? Dites donc, ça vous gênerait de ne pas parler?

7 1. Le français est plus intéressant que la géométrie.
2. *Aladdin* est moins violent que *Henry V.*
3. New York City, c'est stressant, tandis que Boise, c'est tranquille.

Que sais-je?

WA3 FRANCOPHONE
AFRICA-8

Can you use what you've learned in this chapter?

Can you ask someone to convey good wishes? **p. 222**

1 A friend who has been visiting you is about to go back home to her family. What would you say to send your best wishes?
Embrasse... pour moi. Fais-lui/leur mes amitiés. Salue-le/la/les de ma part. Dis-lui que je vais lui écrire. Dis-lui que je pense à elle/lui.

Can you close a letter? **p. 222**

2 How would you end a letter to a friend?
Bien des choses à... ; Je t'embrasse bien fort. Grosses bises. Bisous à...

Can you express hopes or wishes? **p. 225**

3 How would you express a wish to . . . See answers below.
1. travel in Africa?   2. buy a new car?   3. go to college?

Can you give advice? **p. 225**

4 What advice would you give to a friend . . . See answers below.
1. who's having trouble with a school subject?
2. whose parents are very strict?
3. who wants to live in another country?

Can you complain? **p. 231**

5 What would you say to complain if you were in these situations? *Possible answers:*

1.
J'en ai ras le bol!

2.
C'est l'horreur!

3.
Je commence à en avoir marre!
C'est insupportable, à la fin!

Can you express annoyance? **p. 231**

6 How would you express your annoyance if . . . See answers below.
1. someone shoved in front of you as you were boarding the bus?
2. someone grabbed an item from you that you wanted to buy?
3. the people behind you at the movies were talking loudly during the film?

Can you make comparisons? **p. 232**

7 How would you compare the following? See answers below.
1. your favorite and least favorite school subjects
2. the last two movies you saw
3. two places where you've lived or have visited

Review and Assess

Teaching Suggestions

• You might have teams compete to write down the answers to all of the questions in the shortest amount of time.

• Once students have written all of their responses, challenge them to write a letter like the ones in the **Mise en train** and **Remise en train** in which they use as many of the answers as possible. Have students exchange papers with a partner, who acts as a scorekeeper by counting the number of responses used and declaring the total. You might declare a winner for the class.

STANDARDS: 1.2

Première étape

Asking someone to convey good wishes

Embrasse... pour moi.	Give . . . a kiss for me.
Fais mes amitiés à...	Give . . . my regards.
Salue... de ma part.	Tell . . . hi for me.
Dis à... que je vais lui écrire.	Tell . . . that I'm going to write.
Dis à... que je pense à elle/lui.	Tell . . . that I'm thinking about her/him.

Closing a letter

Bien des choses à...	All the best to . . .
Je t'embrasse bien fort.	Hugs and kisses.
Grosses bises.	Hugs and kisses.
Bisous à...	Kisses to . . .

Traditional life

le(s) bijou(x) (m.)	jewelry
un chameau	a camel
une chèvre	a goat
le cuivre	brass, copper
cultiver le blé	to grow wheat
une datte	a date
élever	to raise
faire de l'artisanat (m.)	to make crafts
faire la cueillette	to harvest
une figue	a fig
un mouton	a sheep
une olive	an olive
la poterie	pottery
une poule	a chicken
un tapis	a rug
traire les vaches (f.)	to milk the cows

Expressing hopes or wishes

Si seulement je pouvais,...	If only I could, . . .
Si j'avais le choix,...	If I had a choice, . . .
Si c'était possible,...	If it were possible, . . .
Ça serait chouette si...	It would be great if . . .
Qu'est-ce que j'aimerais... !	I'd really like to . . . !

Giving advice

Si c'était moi, ...	If it were me, . . .
Si j'étais toi, ...	If I were you, . . .
A ta place, ...	If I were in your place, . . .

Deuxième étape

City life

un arrêt de bus	a bus stop
le bruit	noise
la circulation	traffic
un embouteillage	a traffic jam
une foule	a crowd
les gens mal élevés	impolite people
les gens pressés	people in a hurry
un gratte-ciel	a skyscraper
un immeuble	a building
un passage pour piétons	a pedestrian crossing
une place de stationnement	a parking place
la pollution	pollution
un trottoir	a sidewalk
un vélomoteur	a moped

Complaining

C'est l'horreur!	This is just horrible!
C'est insupportable, à la fin!	I won't put up with this!
J'en ai ras le bol!	I've really had it!
Je commence à en avoir marre!	I've just about had it!

Expressing annoyance

Non mais, vous vous prenez pour qui?	Who do you think you are?
Non mais, surtout, ne vous gênez pas!	Well just go right ahead!
Ça va pas, non?!	Are you out of your mind?!

Ça commence à bien faire, hein?	Enough is enough!
Dites donc, ça vous gênerait de... ?	Hey, do you think you can . . .?

Making comparisons

Ce n'était pas comme ça.	It wasn't like this.
Ici, ... tandis que...	Here . . ., whereas . . .
moins de... que	fewer . . . than . . .
plus de... que	more . . . than . . .
autant de... que...	as many/as much . . . as . . .
plus... que...	more . . . than . . .
moins... que...	less . . . than . . .
aussi... que...	as . . . as . . .

Circumlocution Have students work in pairs. One partner will be an American who lives in a large city, the other a Tunisian who lives in the country. Both are in an Internet chatroom for francophone students. The American is describing aspects of life in the city, but can't remember the exact terms for everything. He or she should write a sentence describing something about city life without naming it directly. **(Ici, il y a beaucoup de grands immeubles.)** Then, the American passes the sentence to the Tunisian, who writes his or her guess as to what is being described. **(Ah oui? Il y a beaucoup de gratte-ciel là où tu habites?)**

Chapter 8 Assessment

▸ **Testing Program**
Chapter Test, pp. 177–182
Audio Compact Discs, CD 8, Trs. 16–18
Speaking Test, p. 298

▸ **Alternative Assessment Guide**
Portfolio Assessment, p. 23
Performance Assessment, p. 37
CD-ROM Assessment, p. 51

▸ **Interactive CD-ROM Tutor, Disc 2**
A toi de parler
A toi d'écrire

▸ **Standardized Assessment Tutor**
Chapter 8

▸ **One-Stop Planner, Disc 2**
Test Generator
Chapter 8

Review and Assess

Game

Dialogues logiques Have students form small groups. Give a transparency to each group. Then, call out two words or expressions from the **Vocabulaire (J'en ai ras le bol! A ta place,...).** Give groups one minute to write a logical dialogue that includes the words or expressions. Call time and collect the transparencies. Project them, read them aloud to the class, and then award two points to the team that wrote the best dialogue. You might choose to have teams vote on the best dialogue, with the restriction that they cannot vote for their own. You might also have two members of the winning group act out their dialogue. Continue the game by calling out two more expressions. You might play for five rounds or to ten points.

Teaching Resources
pp. 246–249

PRINT
▸ Lesson Planner, p. 42
▸ Video Guide, pp. 53–54

MEDIA
▸ One-Stop Planner
▸ Video Program
  Videocassette 3, 34:21–39:15
▸ Interactive CD-ROM Tutor, Disc 3
▸ Map Transparency 5

go.hrw.com
WA3 FRANCOPHONE AMERICA

Background Information
France once owned much of Canada and the United States west of the Mississippi River. Today, the only vestiges of **La Nouvelle-France**, explored by Jacques Cartier in 1534, are the francophone province of Quebec, scattered francophone areas in other Canadian provinces, and the islands of Saint-Pierre and Miquelon, which are French possessions. In the United States, French is spoken in Louisiana. In South America, French Guiana is the sole remaining French enclave. In the Caribbean, French is spoken in Martinique, Guadeloupe, and Haiti.

CHAPITRES 9,10,11,12

Allez, viens en Amérique francophone!

	Le Québec	La Louisiane	La Guadeloupe
Population	7.138.000	4.372.000	426.493
Superficie (km²)	1.667.926	125.625	1.709
Villes importantes	Montréal Québec	La Nouvelle-Orléans Baton Rouge Lafayette	Pointe-à-Pitre
Spécialités	ragoût de boulettes, tourtière, tarte à la ferlouche	jambalaya, soupe au gombo, écrevisses à l'étouffée	crabes farcis, boudin créole, acras de morue

Autres états et régions francophones :
la Nouvelle-Angleterre (région des Etats-Unis), Haïti, la Martinique, Saint-Pierre-et-Miquelon, la Guyane française

WA3 FRANCOPHONE AMERICA

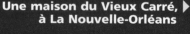

▸ **Une maison du Vieux Carré, à La Nouvelle-Orléans**

Cultures and Communities

Architecture Link
New Orleans' historic French Quarter is full of picturesque Spanish-style houses like the one shown on pages 246–247. These houses are indicative of the city's colorful and culturally rich architecture. French and Spanish traditions are combined with the subtropical climate to give New Orleans a Mediterranean flavor.

Culture Note
La Nouvelle-Orléans was named for Philippe d'Orléans, Duke of Orleans and brother of Louis XIV. The city of Orléans, is located on the Loire river. Its proximity to Paris (about 100 km, or 63 miles) allows many Orléans inhabitants to work in the capital and live in their city, especially since Orléans is connected to Paris by the T.G.V. (**Le Train à Grande Vitesse**).

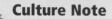

 Using the Almanac and Map

Terms in the Almanac

- **Le Québec** has always played an important role in Canadian politics because of its size, population, and the prominence of its leaders.
- **Montréal,** the largest French-speaking city outside of France, was founded in 1642 on the site of an Indian village called Hochelaga.
- **Québec,** the capital of Quebec province, was founded as a fur-trading post by Samuel de Champlain in 1608.
- **tourtière:** a meat pie eaten especially at Christmas
- **tarte à la ferlouche:** a pie made with molasses or maple syrup and raisins
- **La Louisiane** was named by Robert Cavelier de La Salle in honor of King Louis XIV of France. It became a French crown colony in 1731, and was later transferred to the United States as part of the Louisiana Purchase in 1803.
- **Baton Rouge** is the capital of Louisiana.
- **Lafayette** is located in the heart of Cajun country along the Vermilion River.
- **La Guadeloupe** has been a French **département d'outre-mer** since 1946. Christopher Columbus landed on the islands in 1493 and named them after a monastery (Santa María de Guadeloupe) in Spain.
- **Pointe-à-Pitre** is Guadeloupe's largest city, main port, and capital.
- **crabes farcis:** stuffed land crab
- **boudin créole:** a spicy sausage
- **acras de morue:** cod fritters

Connections and Comparisons

Using the Map
Using the map on this page or *Map Transparency 5,* have students locate the areas listed under **Autres états et régions francophones** in the almanac. You might have small groups do research on these areas and report their findings to the class.

History Link
New Orleans is renowned for its tradition of Mardi Gras festivities. The "Fat Tuesday" carnival has been celebrated by the French since the Middle Ages. It takes place just before Lent and represents a last opportunity for Catholics to eat to their heart's content before this forty-six-day fast. Lent finishes on Easter Sunday.

Using the Photo Essay

❶ **L'Acadie** was a francophone region in what is now Nova Scotia and New Brunswick, Canada. When the area was ceded to the British in 1755, the **Acadiens** who chose not to swear allegiance to the English were deported during a period called **le Grand Dérangement.** Families were separated and set adrift in different ships with few provisions and few trained sailors. This period is the setting of Henry Wadsworth Longfellow's poem *Evangeline,* about a woman who is separated from her love during **le Grand Dérangement.** Many Acadians perished during this time, but some were reunited in Louisiana, where they became known as **Cajuns** or **Cadiens.** (See Teacher Note on page 249.)

❶ **Vermilionville** is a 23-acre historical theme park dedicated to preserving traditional Cajun life. It houses replicas of a Creole plantation home, an overseer's cottage, a cotton gin, a chapel, a blacksmith shop, and a schoolhouse. Cajun storytellers, artisans, and even cooks add to the park's authentic ambiance. The Acadian Village is a similar park that features a model of a nineteenth-century Cajun village.

❷ The French quarter, with its famous wrought-iron balconies, has long attracted tourists to New Orleans. The plans for this 180-block district were drawn by the architect Adrien de Pauger in 1722 for the Sieur de Bienville. Many of the district's streets still bear their original names (**rue St Louis, rue Bourbon, rue Ste Anne**).

L'Amérique francophone

Il y a 11 millions de francophones sur le continent américain. Dans les régions francophones, l'influence de la culture française est très évidente. Mais, en raison de l'éloignement de la France, chaque région a développé sa propre identité culturelle et linguistique. Par exemple, les Québécois ont une interprétation différente de certains mots et ils ont inventé d'autres mots et expressions pour les choses qui n'existaient pas en France. Les langues créoles des Antilles combinent des éléments du français, de l'anglais, de l'espagnol et des langues africaines. Le «cajun» de Louisiane est un mélange de français et d'anglais, mais aussi d'espagnol, d'allemand, de langues africaines et de langues indiennes d'Amérique.

📄 internet

ADRESSE: go.hrw.com
MOT-CLE: WA3 FRANCOPHONE AMERICA

❶ Vermilionville
C'est un village acadien de Louisiane qui a été reconstitué pour les touristes.

❷ Le Vieux Carré
Ce quartier de La Nouvelle-Orléans, avec ses balcons en fer forgé et ses bougainvilliers, attire beaucoup de touristes, en particulier pendant la saison de mardi gras.

❸ Les Cajuns
Dans la région des bayous, au sud de Baton Rouge et de Lafayette, la musique, la cuisine et la langue sont «cajuns».

Connections and Comparisons

History Links

❶ The Cajun city of Lafayette is named after **le marquis de Lafayette** (1757–1834), a French nobleman and military officer who sympathized with the American cause during the American Revolution. He offered his assistance and became a close associate of George Washington. Later, he returned to France and secured aid for the Americans from the French government.

❹ The first inhabitants of the island of Montreal were the St. Lawrence **Hurons.** When the Sieur de Maisonneuve founded the missionary colony of Ville-Marie there in 1642, many conflicts with the Native Americans ensued.

4 Montréal
C'est une grande métropole à l'américaine qui a préservé ses racines françaises.

5 Le marché de Pointe-à-Pitre
Comme dans les autres villes des Antilles, ce marché de Guadeloupe est très coloré.

Aux chapitres 9, 10, 11, et 12
tu vas aller sur le continent américain. D'abord, tu vas visiter Montréal, une ville du Québec qui est la deuxième ville francophone du monde. Ensuite, avec Pascal, tu vas découvrir la plongée sous-marine à la Guadeloupe, une île des Antilles françaises. Pour finir, tu vas accompagner Simon à Lafayette, en Louisiane, pour y découvrir les écrevisses et le jazz.

6 La Soufrière
C'est un volcan actif de la Guadeloupe.

7 Les chutes de Carbet
Elles sont au milieu de la forêt tropicale de la Guadeloupe.

4 Only two-thirds of Montreal's population is of French descent. Because of the campaigns of the **Front de Libération du Québec** in the 1960s, nearly 100,000 English-speakers left Montreal for Toronto, which benefited greatly from the migration.

Culture Notes
6 La Soufrière, which peaks at 4,813 feet, is the highest point in the Lesser Antilles. It erupted in 1590, in 1797–1798, in 1836, and in 1956. Although it is popular among hikers, the 200-foot climb to the top over steep and rocky terrain can be dangerous.

7 The **chutes du Carbet,** a series of three magnificent waterfalls, impressed Columbus when he first arrived on the island. The three falls measure 65 feet, 360 feet, and 410 feet. The river that feeds the falls begins in the Soufrière volcano.

Teacher Note
You might tell students that **Cadien,** or **Cadjun,** is often preferred to **Cajun** by speakers of French in Louisiana.

Cultures and Communities

Community Link
5 The markets of Guadeloupe, like those of Martinique, are filled with a variety of colorful fruits. Ask students if they remember what kind of fruits are found in Martinique. Typical fruits and vegetables of the West Indies are lime, pineapple, guava, sapodilla, star fruit or carambola, sugar cane, cherimoya, mango, papaya, banana, prickly pear, capsicum, bottle gourd, ginger, yam, okra, pumpkin, coconut, maize, chayote or christophene, orange, and chili. Sugar was introduced to the West Indies in the fifteenth century, and Friar Tomás de Berlanga introduced the banana. The cherimoya, lime, melon, and grapefruit were all brought by the Incas.

Chapitre 9 : C'est l'fun!
Chapter Overview

Mise en train pp. 252–254	*La télé, ça se partage*

CULTURE

- **Note culturelle,** Multilingual broadcasting in Canada, p. 254
- **Rencontre culturelle,** Overview of Montreal, p. 255
- **Panorama Culturel,** Favorite types of movies, p. 261
- **Note culturelle,** The film industry of Canada, p. 264
- **Realia:** Movie listing, p. 264

Chapitre 9 : C'est l'fun!
Chapter Resources

PRINT

Lesson Planning

 One-Stop Planner

 Lesson Planner with Substitute Teacher Lesson Plans, pp. 42–46, 72

Student Make-Up Assignments
- Make-Up Assignment Copying Masters, Chapter 9

Listening and Speaking

Listening Activities
- Student Response Forms for Listening Activities, pp. 67–69
- Additional Listening Activities 9-1 to 9-6, pp. 71–73
- Additional Listening Activities (song), p. 74
- Scripts and Answers, pp. 142–146

Video Guide
- Teaching Suggestions, pp. 56–57
- Activity Masters, pp. 58–60
- Scripts and Answers, pp. 102–104, 115

Activities for Communication
- Communicative Activities, pp. 33–36
- Realia and Teaching Suggestions, pp. 75–77
- Situation Cards, pp. 105–106

Reading and Writing

Reading Strategies and Skills Handbook, Chapter 9

Joie de lire 3, Chapter 9

Cahier d'activités, pp. 97–108

Grammar

Travaux pratiques de grammaire, pp. 82–88

Grammar Tutor for Students of French, Chapter 9

Assessment

Testing Program
- Grammar and Vocabulary Quizzes, **Etape** Quizzes, and Chapter Test, pp. 191–204
- Score Sheet, Scripts and Answers, pp. 205–211

Alternative Assessment Guide
- Portfolio Assessment, p. 24
- Performance Assessment, p. 38
- CD-ROM Assessment, p. 52

Student Make-Up Assignments
- Alternative Quizzes, Chapter 9

Standardized Assessment Tutor
- Reading, pp. 35–37
- Writing, p. 38
- Math, pp. 51–52

MEDIA

 Online Activities
- Jeux interactifs
- Activités Internet

Video Program
- Videocassette 3
- Videocassette 5 (captioned version)

Audio Compact Discs
- Textbook Listening Activities, CD 9, Tracks 1–12
- Additional Listening Activities, CD 9, Tracks 18–24
- Assessment Items, CD 9, Tracks 13–17

 Interactive CD-ROM Tutor, Disc 3

Teaching Transparencies
- Situation 9-1 to 9-2
- **Grammaire supplémentaire** Answers
- **Travaux pratiques de grammaire** Answers

One-Stop Planner CD-ROM

Use the **One-Stop Planner CD-ROM with Test Generator** to aid in lesson planning and pacing.

For each chapter, the **One-Stop Planner** includes:
- Editable lesson plans with direct links to teaching resources
- Printable worksheets from resource books
- Direct launches to the HRW Internet activities
- Video and audio segments
- Test Generator
- Clip Art for vocabulary items

Chapitre 9 : C'est l'fun!
Projects

Une bande-annonce

Students will create a movie plot and write and act out two short clips from their movie to be shown at a class awards ceremony in which the class will act as judges. Students will videotape or perform their clips for the class, preceded by an introduction that includes a brief plot summary and an explanation of how the clips relate to the overall plot of the movie.

MATERIALS

✄ **Students may need**
- Videocassette
- Video camera
- Props appropriate to their scripts

SUGGESTED SEQUENCE

1. Have students form small groups. You might assign a specific type of movie to each group (**une comédie musicale, un film d'espionnage**). Then, have groups create the plot and characters of their film. They should write a one-page summary of the movie, including a brief description of the major characters, the locations, and the plot. Group members should edit the summary.

2. Have students choose two scenes they want to feature in their movie clips. Then, have them write short dialogues for these scenes. Remind them that these scenes should not only be representative of the movie, but should also get the judges' attention.

3. Groups should assign members to be the actors and actresses in each of the scenes. One or two students should be directors for the scenes. The actors and actresses should memorize their lines and rehearse the scenes according to the director's instructions.

4. Students should write a brief introduction for their clips. They should include the film title and genre, the names of the actors, actresses, and director(s), a brief plot summary, and an explanation of how the clips to be shown relate to the movie's plot.

5. Have students videotape their clips. They might include background music or props to establish the mood.

6. Stage the awards ceremony in class. One student from each group introduces their movie and then shows the clips. If video resources aren't available, have students perform their clips "live" for the class. After all the movie clips have been presented, have the class vote on the best movie. Tally their votes and announce the winner.

GRADING THE PROJECT

You might give an overall grade to the group, based on appropriate content, creativity, use of visual aids, and language use. You might also assign individual grades for effort and participation in the project.

Suggested Point Distribution (total = 100 points)
Content..20 points
Creativity...20 points
Visual aids ....20 points
Language use...20 points
Effort/participation..............................20 points

Games

Mémoire

In this game, students will practice the vocabulary for television programs and types of movies.

Procedure   To prepare for this game, write the French vocabulary words for television programs and types of movies on index cards. On another set of cards, write the titles of movies or television programs that exemplify the categories in the first set. Number each card on the reverse side. Then, tape the cards to the board so that only the numbers are visible. To play the game, form two teams. The first player calls out two numbers. Turn over the two cards that bear those numbers. If both a category (**une comédie musicale**) and an example of that category *(West Side Story)* are revealed, the player keeps the cards, and may win a point for his or her team. In order to win the point, the player must express his or her opinion of the program or movie on the cards. If no match is uncovered, the opposing team takes a turn. The team with the most points wins.

Storytelling

Mini-histoire

*This story accompanies Teaching Transparency 9-2. The **mini-histoire** can be told and retold in different formats, acted out, written as dictation, and read aloud to give students additional opportunities to practice all four skills. The following story concerns four friends who just saw a movie and are discussing what they think of it.*

Olivier, Gaëlle, Marie-Jo et Natasha viennent de sortir du cinéma. Ils ont vu *Le Monstre qui a mangé Montréal*. Natasha a beaucoup aimé le film. Elle a trouvé ça génial. Elle a surtout beaucoup aimé la scène du monstre qui mange tous les gratte-ciel du centre-ville. Elle trouve aussi que le monstre était mignon. Par contre, Gaëlle a détesté le film. Elle a trouvé ça nul et elle ne veut plus jamais retourner voir un film de ce genre. Marie-Jo et Olivier sont plus modérés. Ils n'ont pas trouvé le film génial, mais ils n'ont pas détesté non plus. Ils pensent qu'il y avait des scènes intéressantes et que les effets spéciaux étaient excellents.

Traditions

La Ville souterraine

Ever since the pioneers settled the area in the 16th and 17th centuries, the people of Quebec have used their ingenuity to find ever more efficient ways to deal with the region's cold weather. One such effort is Montreal's Underground City, begun in the 1960s as a refuge from the city's bitter winters and humid summers. Today the underground network consists of 22 kilometers of passages lined with shops, movie theaters, concert halls, restaurants, offices, hotels, and apartments. The passages connect people to everything from the city's subway and train system to the stock exchange. It is said that soon Montrealers will have no need ever to go outside due to the Underground City's continuing expansion. Have students discuss the advantages and disadvantages of living, working, and engaging in leisure activities in an underground city.

Recette

*Since the fifties, Canada has dramatically increased the number of its festivals honoring the maple tree and maple syrup. It's a way to pay tribute to spring, from mid-March to the end of April. Perhaps the most famous of those festivals takes place in Plessiville. This is where the **Grands Maîtres Sucriers** competition takes place each year.*

TARTE A L'ERABLE
pour 6 personnes

Pâte brisée

2 tasses de farine

1/2 tasse de sucre

1/2 tasse de beurre

1 œuf

Garniture

1 tasse de crème fraîche   2 c. à soupe de beurre

1 tasse de sirop d'érable   3/4 tasse de farine

Pâte brisée

Faire fondre le beurre. Placer la farine dans un grand bol. Faire un puits. Y mettre le sucre et l'œuf. Commencer à mélanger doucement. Ajouter le beurre petit à petit. Faire une boule du mélange. Si la boule est trop beurrée, ajouter un peu de farine.

Cuire au four pendant 20 minutes.

Garniture

Faire bouillir ensemble le sirop d'érable et la crème fraîche. Faire fondre le beurre et ajouter la farine pour faire un «roux». Ajouter le mélange de sirop d'érable/crème fraîche. Cuire pendant 5 minutes. Verser sur la pâte à tarte. Laisser refroidir.

Servir avec de la crème chantilly ou de la crème anglaise.

Chapitre 9 : C'est l'fun!
Technology

Video Program
Videocassette 3, Videocassette 5 (captioned version)
See Video Guide, pp. 55–60.

Camille et compagnie • Neuvième épisode : *Le Rêve de Sophie*
While talking about movies on the phone, Camille and Sophie realize that they have very different tastes. Sophie likes comedies, but Camille prefers dramas and spy movies. Camille invites Sophie to go to the aquarium with her, Max, and Azzedine the next day, but Sophie has an audition for a commercial and cannot go. Just after their phone conversation, Sophie falls asleep and dreams that she is a movie star being interviewed on a television talk show. When she wakes up, her photo is on the cover of the TV guide!

Quel genre de film préfères-tu?
People from around the francophone world talk about the kinds of films they like. Two native speakers discuss the **Panorama Culturel** question and introduce the interviews.

Vidéoclips
- **Music video: J'ai peur de t'aimer** performed by Alexandre Sterling
- **News report:** careers in communication

Interactive CD-ROM Tutor

The **Interactive CD-ROM Tutor** contains videos, interactive games, and activities that provide students an opportunity to practice and review the material covered in Chapter 9.

Activity	Activity Type	Pupil's Edition Page
1. Vocabulaire	Jeu des paires	p. 256
2. Grammaire	Méli-mélo	p. 258
3. Comment dit-on... ?	Chacun à sa place	pp. 257, 259
4. Vocabulaire	Chasse au trésor Explorons! Vérifions!	p. 264
5. Grammaire	Les mots qui manquent	p. 266
6. Comment dit-on... ?	Du tac au tac	pp. 265, 266
Panorama Culturel	Quel genre de film préfères-tu? Le bon choix	p. 261
A toi de parler	*Guided recording*	pp. 276–277
A toi d'écrire	*Guided writing*	pp. 276–277

Teacher Management System
Logging In
Logging in to the *Allez, viens!* TMS is easy. Upon launching the program, simply type "admin" in the password area of the log-in screen and press RETURN. Log on to **www.hrw.com/CDROMTUTOR** for a detailed explanation of the Teacher Management System.

One-Stop Planner CD-ROM

To preview all resources available for this chapter, use the **One-Stop Planner CD-ROM**, Disc 3.

Internet Connection

ADRESSE: go.hrw.com
MOT-CLE: WA3 FRANCOPHONE AMERICA-9

*Have students explore the **go.hrw.com** Web site for many online resources covering all chapters. All Chapter 9 resources are available under the keyword **WA3 FRANCOPHONE AMERICA-9.** Interactive games help students practice the material and provide them with immediate feedback. You'll also find a printable worksheet that provides Internet activities that lead to a comprehensive online research project.*

Jeux interactifs

You can use the interactive activities in this chapter

- to practice grammar, vocabulary, and chapter functions
- as homework
- as an assessment option
- as a self-test
- to prepare for the Chapter Test

Activités Internet

Students look for information about French-language television programming and movies, using the vocabulary and phrases from the chapter.

- In preparation for the **Activités Internet,** have students review the dramatic episode on Video-cassette 3, or do the activities in the **Panorama Culturel** on page 261.
- After students have completed the activity sheet, you might group them according to the movie genres they chose for Activity C. Have them compare notes and compile their findings to present to the rest of the class.

Projet

Have groups of students research the French-language films that are available in your area or through the Internet. If French-language television is available in your school, students can research the programming for the upcoming week through cable or satellite. Remind students to document their sources by noting the names and the URLs of all the sites they consulted. Have students nominate movies or television programs suitable to be shown in class. You will probably want to make the final selection yourself and preview the program before showing it in class. Once you have decided what you want to show, you might involve students in acquiring and showing the program.

Première étape

6 p. 256

Ce soir sur TV Cinq : à dix-huit heures, vous pourrez voir *Le Canada en guerre*, qui, comme son titre l'indique, vous fera découvrir le Canada pendant la Deuxième Guerre mondiale. Filmé de dix-neuf cent quarante et un à dix-neuf cent quarante-cinq par Yves Boisseau, ce programme en noir et blanc présente, entre autres, des interviews de nombreuses personnes qui ont vécu pendant la guerre. Puis à dix-neuf heures trente, vous retrouverez tous nos amis de *Zap* dans un nouvel épisode intitulé *Vive la rentrée*. Eh oui, pour ces jeunes gens aussi, c'est la rentrée des classes. A vingt heures, vous pourrez voir la deuxième partie d'*Emilie, la passion d'une vie*. Pour ceux d'entre vous qui n'ont pas pu voir la première partie, c'est l'histoire d'une jeune institutrice au début du siècle. Puis, à vingt et une heures, *Pour tout dire* : Anne-Marie Dussault présente un reportage sur l'écologie au Canada, le hit-parade des tubes de la semaine et des interviews avec quelques stars qu'on peut voir en ce moment au Festival des Films du monde. Enfin, à vingt et une heures trente, Annick Maurin présentera la dernière édition du journal télévisé.

Au programme de SRC, tout d'abord, les informations avec *Ce soir* à dix-huit heures. Puis, à dix-neuf heures, Pierre Morel reçoit deux nouveaux candidats qui s'affronteront dans notre émission *Des chiffres et des lettres*. A dix-neuf heures trente, vous pourrez voir un classique d'après l'œuvre d'Hergé. C'est *Tintin et le lac aux requins*, un programme qui ravira les grands comme les petits. Puis, à vingt heures, place à la musique et au cinéma avec *Ad lib*. Ce soir, l'animatrice Corinne Laroche reçoit notamment Roch Voisine, Céline Dion, le groupe Maracas et de nombreux autres invités. Enfin, à vingt et une heures, Patrice Norton vous fera découvrir le monde d'une des plus grandes stars, Joséphine Baker, dans *J'ai deux amours, la vie de Joséphine Baker*.

Answers to Activity 6
1. un documentaire 2. une série 3. un magazine télévisé
4. les informations 5. un jeu télévisé 6. un dessin animé
7. une émission de variétés

10 p. 257

1. —Tu te souviens de la pub pour le parfum où les femmes hurlaient et fermaient les fenêtres?
   —Oui. Elle était bizarre, cette pub.
   —Tu l'as dit!
2. —Les pubs pour les parfums, elles sont toujours trop dramatiques, tu trouves pas?

   —Non, pas du tout. Elles sont quelquefois assez impressionnantes.
3. —Moi, je déteste les pubs pour les lessives. Elles sont d'un stupide. Elles ne sont pas réalistes, et puis, ces lessives, elles sont toutes pareilles, de toute façon.
   —Tu as raison. Moi aussi, ça m'énerve.
4. —Tu regardes les pubs politiques? Elles sont tellement hypocrites, tu trouves pas?
   —A vrai dire, je m'en fiche.
5. —La pub pour la pizza où le grand chien blanc danse la conga, elle est marrante comme tout, non?
   —Tu rigoles? Elle est nulle!
6. —Elle est drôle, la pub où le réparateur attend parce qu'il n'y a pas de machines à laver à réparer, tu ne trouves pas?
   —Tu te fiches de moi? Elle est mortelle.
7. —Elle est sympa, la pub où il y a le petit lapin mécanique. Tu trouves pas?
   —Bof, je ne fais jamais attention aux pubs. Je m'en fiche.
8. —Moi, je trouve que les pubs pour les voitures sont vraiment sexistes!
   —Là, tu as raison! Je ne les aime pas du tout, moi non plus!
   —C'est scandaleux, comme elles exploitent les femmes.

Answers to Activity 10
1. d'accord   3. d'accord   5. pas d'accord   7. indifférent
2. pas d'accord 4. indifférent 6. pas d'accord   8. d'accord

16 p. 259

1. —Il est où, le programme?
   —Chut! Tu ne vois pas que je regarde ce film?
2. —Oh, il est mortel, ce film. Tu as la télécommande? Ça t'embête si je change de chaîne?
   —Ça m'est égal. Je ne regarde pas.
3. —C'est pas vrai! Qu'est-ce qu'il a...
   —Ne parle pas si fort, s'il te plaît.
4. —Eh, Benoît, baisse le son! Ça me casse les oreilles, ton truc.
5. —On peut tout voir comme ça.
   —Ah non! Ça vous gênerait de vous asseoir? On ne voit rien!
6. —Oh! Je commence vraiment à en avoir marre!
7. —Ça vient juste de commencer. On n'en a pas manqué beaucoup. Euh, pardon, je m'excuse...
   —Vous pourriez vous taire, s'il vous plaît? On aimerait bien entendre quelque chose!
8. —Eh, les enfants, vous pourriez faire un peu moins de bruit?

The following scripts are for the Listening Activities found in the *Pupil's Edition*. For Student Response Forms, see *Listening Activities,* pages 67–69. To provide students with additional listening practice, see *Listening Activities,* pages 71–74.

One-Stop Planner CD-ROM

To preview all resources available for this chapter, use the **One-Stop Planner CD-ROM**, Disc 3.

9. —Je suis désolé, Maxime. Je crois que j'ai cassé ton magnétoscope.
—Oh, c'est pas vrai! Tu ne pourrais pas faire attention?

10. —Tais-toi, Emilie. Le prof va t'entendre.

Answers to Activity 16
1, 3, 4, 7, 8, 10

Deuxième étape

27 **p. 265**

Answers to Activity 27
1. oui	3. non	5. non
2. oui	4. oui	6. oui

1. —Qu'est-ce que tu as vu comme film?
—J'ai vu *Casablanca.*
—Ah oui? C'était comment?
—Ça m'a beaucoup plu. C'est super, c'est un classique avec Ingrid Bergman et Humphrey Bogart. Si tu veux voir un bon film, je te le recommande.

2. —Comment tu as trouvé *Danse avec les loups?* Il paraît que c'est pas mal.
—C'est très bien fait. Il y a de beaux paysages et l'histoire est intéressante. Kevin Costner joue très bien.
—Tu me le conseilles?
—Sans hésiter. C'est à ne pas manquer!

3. —Qu'est-ce que tu as vu au cinéma dernièrement?
—J'ai vu *Grosse Fatigue,* avec Michel Blanc et Carole Bouquet.
—Ça t'a plu?
—Ça ne m'a pas emballé. Carole Bouquet joue pas mal, mais je n'aime pas le jeu de Michel Blanc. Et puis, l'histoire n'a aucun intérêt.

4. —Au fait, c'était comment, *Maman, j'ai encore raté l'avion?*
—C'est moins bien que le premier, mais c'est pas mal. Macaulay Culkin joue bien et c'est drôle. Je ne me suis pas ennuyé une seconde. Va le voir, c'est génial.

5. —Tu sais ce que j'ai vu ce week-end? *La Reine Margot.*
—Alors? Comment tu as trouvé ça?
—Je me suis ennuyée à mourir.
—Ah oui? Pourtant, on m'a dit que c'était pas mal.
—Les acteurs sont mauvais. C'est vraiment nul! N'y va pas!

6. —Si tu veux voir un bon film, je te recommande *La Fille de d'Artagnan.*
—C'est vraiment bien?
—Ça m'a beaucoup plu. C'est assez spécial, mais c'est drôle. Et puis, il y a de l'action. Tu verras, si tu vas le voir. Il y a aussi de magnifiques décors.

30 **p. 266**

Answers to Activity 30
1. vrai   2. vrai   3. faux   4. faux   5. faux

FABRICE   J'ai vu un bon film hier. Ça se passe à côté de Montréal.

ALINE   De quoi ça parle?

FABRICE   C'est l'histoire de Chomi, un jeune homme qui étudie le cinéma et qui joue au hockey. Il a une amie qui s'appelle Olive. Ils passent tout leur temps ensemble. Et puis, Chomi rencontre une fille qui s'appelle Coyote. Il tombe amoureux d'elle. Olive et Chomi ne se voient plus. C'est très bien fait. Et puis, il y a Mitsou qui joue le rôle de Coyote.

ALINE   Mitsou, la chanteuse?

FABRICE   Oui. Elle joue très bien dans ce film.

ALINE   Et comment est-ce que ça se termine?

FABRICE   Finalement, Olive accepte la relation entre Coyote et Chomi. Je te le recommande. Ça m'a beaucoup plu.

Mise en pratique

1 **p. 276**

Answers to Mise en pratique Activity 1
e, b, c, d, f, a

DIDIER   Oh, c'est vraiment nul, ces feuilletons, tu trouves pas?

SIMONE   Tu l'as dit!

DIDIER   Alors, il y a autre chose?

SIMONE   Attends, je regarde dans le programme. Hmm..., voilà. Il y a un film.

DIDIER   C'est quoi?

SIMONE   Ça s'appelle *Vestiges du jour.*

DIDIER   C'est une histoire d'amour? Bof, les histoires d'amour, ça ne me branche pas trop.

SIMONE   On m'a dit que c'était très bien, en fait, que c'était à ne pas manquer.

DIDIER   Il n'y a pas autre chose?

SIMONE   Evidemment, toi, tu préfères les films d'horreur.

DIDIER   Et alors?

SIMONE   Tu sais bien que je déteste les films d'horreur. Ça a une mauvaise influence sur le public, ça encourage la violence, et puis, c'est révoltant.

DIDIER   Oh, regarde! Il y a *Dracula* à neuf heures moins dix. Passe-moi la télécommande!

SIMONE   Mais, écoute...

DIDIER   Tais-toi. Ça a déjà commencé!

Chapitre 9 : C'est l'fun!
Suggested Lesson Plans 50-Minute Schedule

Day 1

CHAPTER OPENER 10 min.
- Present Chapter Objectives, p. 251.
- Culture Note, ATE, p. 250

MISE EN TRAIN 35 min.
- Presenting **Mise en train**, ATE, p. 252
- Culture Note and Language Note, ATE, p. 253
- Do Activities 1–4, p. 254.
- Read and discuss **Note culturelle**, p. 254.

Wrap-Up 5 min.
- Do Activity 5, p. 254.

Homework Options
Cahier d'activités, Act. 1, p. 97

Day 2

MISE EN TRAIN
Quick Review 5 min.
- Check homework.

RENCONTRE CULTURELLE 15 min.
- Presenting **Rencontre culturelle**, ATE, p. 255
- **Qu'en penses-tu?**, p. 255
- Read and discuss **Savais-tu que…?**, p. 255.
- Culture Note and Language-to-Language, ATE, p. 255
- Thinking Critically: Comparing and Contrasting, ATE, p. 255

PREMIERE ETAPE
Vocabulaire, p. 256 25 min.
- Presenting **Vocabulaire**, ATE, p. 256
- Play Audio CD for Activity 6, p. 256.
- Cahier d'activités, p. 98, Activity 2
- Do Activity 7, p. 256.
- Have students do Activity 8, p. 257, in groups.

Wrap-Up 5 min.
- Do Activity 9, p. 257.

Homework Options
Travaux pratiques de grammaire, Acts. 1–4, pp. 82–83

Day 3

PREMIERE ETAPE
Quick Review 5 min.
- Check homework.

Comment dit-on… ?, p. 257 25 min.
- Presenting **Comment dit-on… ?**, ATE, p. 257
- Play Audio CD for Activity 10, p. 257.
- Cahier d'activités, p. 99, Activity 4
- Have students do Activities 11–12, p. 257, in pairs.

Vocabulaire, p. 258 15 min.
- Presenting **Vocabulaire**, ATE, p. 258
- Do Activity 13, p. 258.
- Cahier d'activités, pp. 99–100, Activities 5–6
- See Vocabulary Practice Using Teaching Transparency 9-1, Speaking Suggestion 3, Teaching Transparencies.

Wrap-Up 5 min.
- Game: **Vingt questions**, ATE, p. 257

Homework Options
Travaux pratiques de grammaire, Acts. 5–6, p. 84

Day 4

PREMIERE ETAPE
Quick Review 5 min.
- Check homework.

Grammaire and **Note de grammaire, pp. 258–259** 25 min.
- Presenting **Grammaire**, ATE, p. 258
- Travaux pratiques de grammaire, pp. 85–86, Acts. 7–9
- Do Activity 14, p. 259.
- Discuss **Note de grammaire**, p. 259.
- **Grammaire supplémentaire**, p. 273, Act. 4
- Do Activity 15, p. 259.

Comment dit-on… ?, p. 259 15 min.
- Presenting **Comment dit-on… ?**, ATE, p. 259
- Play Audio CD for Activity 16, p. 259.
- Do Activity 17, p. 260.
- Have students do Activity 19, p. 260, in pairs.

Wrap-Up 5 min.
- Challenge, ATE, p. 260

Homework Options
Study for Quiz 9-1
Travaux pratiques de grammaire, Act. 10, p. 86
Cahier d'activités, Acts. 7–9, pp. 100–101
Grammaire supplémentaire, Acts. 1–3, pp. 272–273

Day 5

PREMIERE ETAPE
Quiz 9-1 20 min.
- Administer Quiz 9-1A or 9-1B.

PANORAMA CULTUREL 10 min.
- Presenting **Panorama Culturel**, ATE, p. 261
- Questions, ATE, p. 261
- Discuss **Qu'en penses-tu?**, p. 261.
- Culture Note, ATE, p. 261

REMISE EN TRAIN 15 min.
- Presenting **Remise en train**, ATE, p. 262
- Do Activities 20–22, pp. 262–263.
- Culture Note, ATE, p. 263

Wrap-Up 5 min.
- Do Activity 24, p. 263.

Homework Options
Cahier d'activités, Act. 11, p. 102

Day 6

REMISE EN TRAIN
Quick Review 5 min.
- Check homework.

DEUXIEME ETAPE
Vocabulaire, p. 264 20 min.
- Presenting **Vocabulaire**, ATE, p. 264
- Do Activity 25, p. 264.
- Read and discuss **Note culturelle**, p. 264.
- Cahier d'activités, p. 103, Activities 12–13
- Do Activity 26, p. 264.

Comment dit-on… ?, p. 265 20 min.
- Presenting **Comment dit-on… ?**, ATE, p. 265
- Play Audio CD for Activity 27, p. 265.
- Cahier d'activités, p. 104, Activity 14
- Do Activity 28, p. 265.
- Have students do Activity 29, p. 265, in groups.

Wrap-Up 5 min.
- Game: **Pas d'accord**, ATE, p. 265

Homework Options
Travaux pratiques de grammaire, Act. 11, p. 87

One-Stop Planner CD-ROM

For alternative lesson plans by chapter section, to create your own customized plans, or to preview all resources available for this chapter, use the **One-Stop Planner CD-ROM**, Disc 3.

 For additional homework suggestions, see activities accompanied by this symbol throughout the chapter.

Day 7

DEUXIEME ETAPE
Quick Review 5 min.
- Check homework.

Comment dit-on... ?, p. 266 15 min.
- Presenting **Comment dit-on... ?**, ATE, p. 266
- Play Audio CD for Activity 30, p. 266.
- Cahier d'activités, p. 105, Activity 15

Grammaire, p. 266 25 min.
- Presenting **Grammaire**, ATE, p. 266
- Do Activity 31, p. 267.
- Travaux pratiques de grammaire, p. 88, Acts. 12–13
- Do Activity 32, p. 267.
- Read and discuss **A la française**, p. 267.
- Have students do Activity 34, p. 267, in pairs.

Wrap-Up 5 min.
- Teaching Suggestions, ATE, p. 267

Homework Options
Study for Quiz 9-2
Pupil's Edition, Activity 33, p. 267
Grammaire supplémentaire, Acts. 5–9, pp. 273–275
Cahier d'activités, Acts. 16–17, pp. 105–106

Day 8

DEUXIEME ETAPE
Quiz 9-2 20 min.
- Administer Quiz 9-2A or 9-2B.

LISONS! 25 min.
- Read and discuss **Stratégie pour lire**, p. 268.
- Do Prereading Activity A, p. 268.
- Have students read **Lisons!**, pp. 268–270.
- Do Reading Activities B–M, pp. 268–270.

Wrap-Up 5 min.
- Additional Practice, ATE, p. 270

Homework Options
Cahier d'activités, Act. 19, p. 107

Day 9

LISONS!
Quick Review 5 min.
- Check homework.

LISONS! 10 min.
- Do Postreading Activities N–O, p. 270.

ECRIVONS! 30 min.
- Read and discuss the **Stratégie pour écrire**, p. 271, then have students work on their scenes.

Wrap-Up 5 min.
- Allow time for peer and self-evaluation of scenes.

Homework Options
Complete final draft of scenes.

Day 10

ECRIVONS!
Quick Review 10 min.
- Have volunteers share their scenes with the class.

MISE EN PRATIQUE 35 min.
- Play Audio CD for Activity 1, p. 276.
- Have students do Activity 2, p. 276, in pairs.
- Career Path, ATE, p. 276
- Do Activity 3, p. 276–277.
- **A toi d'écrire**, CD-ROM Tutor, Disc 3

Wrap-Up 5 min.
- Activities for Communication, p. 105, Situation (global): Interview

Homework Options
Cahier d'activités, Acts. 20–21, p. 108

Day 11

MISE EN PRATIQUE
Quick Review 5 min.
- Check homework.
Student Review 40 min.
- Do Activity 5, p. 277.
- Have students prepare interviews for **Jeu de rôle**, p. 277.
- Have pairs present interviews for **Jeu de rôle**.
- **A toi de parler**, CD-ROM Tutor or DVD Tutor

Wrap-Up 5 min.
- Begin **Que sais-je?**, p. 278.

Homework Options
Que sais-je?, p. 278

Day 12

MISE EN PRATIQUE
Quick Review 15 min.
- Do Activity 4, p. 277.
- Go over **Que sais-je?**, p. 278.

Chapter Review 35 min.
- Review Chapter 9. Choose from **Grammaire supplémentaire**, Grammar Tutor for Students of French, Activities for Communication, Listening Activities, Interactive CD-ROM Tutor, or **Jeux interactifs.**

Homework Options
Study for Chapter 9 Test.

Assessment

Test, Chapter 9 50 min.
- Administer **Chapter 9 Test.** Select from Testing Program, Alternative Assessment Guide, Test Generator, or Standardized Assessment Tutor.

Chapitre 9 : C'est l'fun!
Suggested Lesson Plans 90-Minute Block Schedule

Block 1

CHAPTER OPENER 5 min.
- Present Chapter Objectives, p. 251
- Culture Note, ATE, p. 250

MISE EN TRAIN 20 min.
- Pre-viewing suggestions, Video Guide, p. 56
- Show *Camille et compagnie: Le Rêve de Sophie*, Video Program (Videocassette 3)
- Viewing and Post-viewing activities, Video Guide, p. 58
- **Note culturelle**, p. 254

RENCONTRE CULTURELLE 25 min.
- Presenting **Rencontre culturelle**, ATE, p. 255
- Read and discuss **Qu'en penses-tu?**, p. 255
- Language-to-Language, ATE, p. 255

PREMIERE ETAPE
Vocabulaire, p. 256 20 min.
- Have students suggest a list of their favorite TV programs.
- Presenting **Vocabulaire**, ATE, p. 256
- Play Audio CD for Activity 6, p. 256.
- Do Activity 7, p. 256.

Comment dit-on... ?, p. 257 15 min.
- Presenting **Comment dit-on... ?**, ATE, p. 257
- Play Audio CD for Activity 10, p. 257.

Wrap-Up 5 min.
- Game: **Vingt questions**, ATE, p. 257

Homework Options
Pupil's Edition, Activity 9, p. 257
Cahier d'activités, pp. 98–99, Acts. 2–4
Travaux pratiques de grammaire, pp. 82–83, Acts. 1–4

Block 2

PREMIERE ETAPE
Quick Review 5 min.
- Bell Work, ATE, p. 256

Comment dit-on... ?, p. 257 25 min.
- Briefly review the expressions in **Comment dit-on... ?**, p. 257.
- Do Activities 11–12, p. 257.

Vocabulaire, p. 258 15 min.
- Presenting **Vocabulaire**, ATE, p. 258
- Do Activity 13, p. 258.

Grammaire, p. 258 40 min.
- Presenting **Grammaire**, ATE, p. 258
- Language Note, ATE, p. 258
- Do Activity 14, p. 259.
- Read and discuss **Note de grammaire**, p. 259.
- Do Activity 15, p. 259.

Wrap-Up 5 min.
- Auditory Learners, ATE, p. 259

Homework Options
Grammaire supplémentaire, pp. 272–273, Acts. 1–4
Cahier d'activités, p. 99, Act. 5
Travaux pratiques de grammaire, pp. 84–86, Acts. 5–10

Block 3

PREMIERE ETAPE
Quick Review 5 min.
- Listening Activities, p.72, Additional Listening Activity 9-3

Comment dit-on... ?, p. 259 30 min.
- Presenting **Comment dit-on... ?**, ATE, p. 259
- Play Audio CD for Activity 16, p. 259.
- Do Activity 17, p. 260.
- Do Activity 19, p. 260.

REMISE EN TRAIN 30 min.
- Presenting **Remise en train**, ATE, p. 262
- Do Activities 20–23, pp. 262–263.

DEUXIEME ETAPE
Vocabulaire, p. 264 15 min.
- Read and discuss **Note culturelle**, p. 264.
- Presenting **Vocabulaire**, ATE, p. 264
- Do Activity 25, p. 264.

Wrap-Up 10 min.
- Teaching Transparency 9-1, using suggestion #3 from Suggestions for Using Teaching Transparency 9-1

Homework Options
Have students study for Quiz 9-1.
Pupil's Edition, Activity 18, p. 260
Cahier d'activités, pp. 100–103, Acts. 6–13

One-Stop Planner CD-ROM

For alternative lesson plans by chapter section, to create your own customized plans, or to preview all resources available for this chapter, use the **One-Stop Planner CD-ROM**, Disc 3.

For additional homework suggestions, see activities accompanied by this symbol throughout the chapter.

Block 4

DEUXIEME ETAPE

Quick Review 10 min.
- Activities for Communication, pp. 33–34, Communicative Activity 9-1A and 9-1B

Quiz 9-1 20 min.
- Administer Quiz 9-1A or 9-1B.

Vocabulaire, p. 264 15 min.
- Language-to-Language, ATE, p. 264
- Do Activity 26, p. 264.

PANORAMA CULTUREL 20 min.
- Presenting **Panorama Culturel**, ATE, p. 261
- Questions, ATE, p. 261
- Discuss **Qu'en penses-tu?**, p. 261.

Comment dit-on... ?, p. 265 20 min.
- Presenting **Comment dit-on... ?**, ATE, p. 265
- Play Audio CD for Activity 27, ATE, p. 265.
- Do Activity 28, p. 265.

Wrap-Up 5 min.
- Teaching Transparency 9-2, using suggestion #1 from Vocabulary Practice Using Teaching Transparency 9-2

Homework Options
Cahier d'activités, pp. 104–105, Acts. 14–15
Travaux pratiques de grammaire, p. 87, Act. 11

Block 5

DEUXIEME ETAPE

Quick Review 5 min.
- Listening Activities, p. 72, Additional Listening Activity 9-4

Comment dit-on... ?, p. 265 20 min.
- Teaching Suggestion, ATE, p. 265
- Do Activity 29, p. 265.

Comment dit-on... ?, p. 266 15 min.
- Presenting **Comment dit-on... ?**, ATE, p. 266
- Play Audio CD for Activity 30, p. 266.

Grammaire, p. 266 40 min.
- Presenting **Grammaire**, ATE, p. 266
- Do Activity 31, p. 267.
- Read and discuss **A la française**, p. 267.
- Do Activities 32–33, p. 267.

Wrap-Up 10 min.
- Auditory Learners, ATE, p. 266

Homework Options
Have students study for Quiz 9-2.
Grammaire supplémentaire, pp. 273–275, Acts. 5–7
Cahier d'activités, pp. 105–106, Acts. 16–18
Travaux pratiques de grammaire, p. 88, Acts. 12–13

Block 6

DEUXIEME ETAPE

Quick Review 15 min.
- Have students do **Grammaire supplémentaire**, p. 275, Activities 8–9, then go over the activities as a class.

Quiz 9-2 20 min.
- Administer Quiz 9-2A or 9-2B.

LISONS! 25 min.
- Do Prereading Activity A, p. 268 and Teaching Suggestion, ATE, p. 268.
- Read **Lisons!**, pp. 268–270.
- Do Reading Activities C–M, pp. 268–270.
- Do Postreading Activity N, p. 270.

MISE EN PRATIQUE 15 min.
- Play Audio CD for Activity 1, p. 276.
- Do Activities 2–3, pp. 276–277.

ECRIVONS! 15 min.
- Begin Activity A, p. 271.

Homework Options
Pupil's Edition, Activity 5, p. 277
Finish Pupil's Edition, Activity A, p. 271.
Que sais-je?, p. 278
Study for Chapter 9 Test.

Block 7

MISE EN PRATIQUE

Quick Review 15 min.
- Check and collect homework.
- **Jeu de rôle**, p. 277

Chapter Review 30 min.
- Review Chapter 9. Choose from **Grammaire supplémentaire**, Grammar Tutor for Students of French, Activities for Communication, Listening Activities, Interactive CD-ROM Tutor, or **Jeux interactifs.**

Test, Chapter 9 45 min.
- Administer Chapter 9 Test. Select from Testing Program, Alternative Assessment Guide, Test Generator, or Standardized Assessment Tutor.

Chapter Opener

One-Stop Planner CD-ROM

For resource information, see the **One-Stop Planner**, Disc 3.

Pacing Tips
The first **étape** has more material to cover than the second **étape,** including cultural content found in the **Rencontre culturelle** and the **Panorama Culturel.** You might keep this in mind when planning your lessons. For Lesson Plans and timing suggestions, see pages 249I–249L.

Meeting the Standards
Communication
• Agreeing and disagreeing; expressing indifference, p. 257
• Making requests, p. 259
• Asking for and making judgments; asking for and making recommendations, p. 265
• Asking about and summarizing a story, p. 266

Cultures
• Culture Notes, pp. 250, 253, 255, 257, 261, 263
• Note culturelle, p. 254
• Note culturelle, p. 264
• Panorama Culturel, p. 261
• Rencontre culturelle, p. 255

Connections
• Multicultural Link, p. 254
• Music Link, p. 259
• Reading/Writing Link, p. 271

Comparisons
• Language-to-Language, pp. 255, 264
• Thinking Critically, pp. 254, 255, 268

Communities
• Career Path, p. 276
• Community Links, pp. 257, 261
• De l'école au travail, p. 267

Cultures and Communities

Culture Note
Set between the St. Lawrence River and the downtown skyscrapers, the historic district of **Vieux-Montréal** was once surrounded by walls. Its countless, narrow streets are never far from the spot where French settlers founded the city in 1642. An exceptional historic center, the city still bustles with life today and attracts tourists and natives alike. The street in the photo on pages 250–251, with its eighteenth- and nineteenth-century greystone buildings, is representative of the small town atmosphere that **Vieux-Montréal** has preserved to this day.

CHAPITRE

9
C'est l'fun!

Objectives

In this chapter you will learn to

Première étape

- agree and disagree
- express indifference
- make requests

Deuxième étape

- ask for and make judgments
- ask for and make recommendations
- ask about and summarize a story

 internet

ADRESSE: go.hrw.com
MOT-CLE: WA3 FRANCOPHONE
AMERICA-9

◀ **La place Jacques-Cartier, à Montréal**

CHAPITRE 9

Focusing on Outcomes

Have students read the list of objectives. Form six groups and assign a function to each one. Have them list French words and expressions they already know to accomplish their function. Then, gather the papers, read each group's list aloud, and have the class try to guess the function the group was assigned. You may want to use the video to support the objectives. The self-check activities in **Que sais-je?** on page 278 help students assess their achievement of the objectives.

Connections and Comparisons

History Link

The place **Jacques-Cartier** in **Vieux-Montréal,** once the city's main marketplace, is now crowded with cafés that serve as popular meeting places for the city's inhabitants. At the center of the place stands the monument to Lord Nelson. This column, similar to the one in London's Trafalgar Square, was actually constructed a few years before its English counterpart to commemorate Nelson's naval victory at Trafalgar in 1805.

Presenting
Mise en train

Tell students they are going to hear a brother and sister disagree about what to watch on TV. Ask students to listen for what each person wants to watch. Play the recording, pausing after each scene to ask comprehension questions. Then, have students listen for Danielle's and Fabien's opinions of commercials as you play the last scene.

Mise en train ▪ *La télé, ça se partage*

Cahier d'activités, p. 97, Act. 1

CD 9 Tr. 1

Stratégie **pour comprendre**
Take a quick look at the photos on these two pages to decide what this episode is all about. The title will also help you to figure it out. Judging by the expressions on the characters' faces, how do you think they feel? Can you guess why? Scan through the dialogue for familiar words to help you guess the context.

1 **Fabien** Qu'est-ce qu'il y a ce soir à la télé?
Danielle C'est le troisième épisode d'*Emilie, la passion d'une vie.*

19 h 30	20 h 00	20 h 30	21 h 00
Ma maison	Sous un ciel variable		Enjeux
Zap	Emilie, la passion d'une vie		Pour tout dire...
Le Grand Journal		Détecteurs de mensonges	Visa santé
Piment fort	Cinéma : La Chèvre		
			Columbo : Jeux d'ombre

2 **Fabien** Qu'est-ce que c'est, ça?
Danielle C'est un feuilleton super. C'est l'histoire d'une jeune fille, Emilie, qui vit au Québec au début du siècle...
Fabien Tu te fiches de moi? Ça a l'air mortel, ton truc! Tu me passes le programme, s'il te plaît... ? Eh! Il y a *La Chèvre*, avec Gérard Depardieu!
Danielle Pas question! Moi, je veux regarder *Emilie*.
Fabien Toi, tu ferais mieux de faire tes devoirs. C'est plus important.
Danielle Tu parles! J'ai une idée, on n'a qu'à tirer à pile ou face.
Fabien Euh, tu crois? Je n'ai jamais de chance, moi.
Danielle C'est la seule solution... Alors, pile ou face?

LA CHÈVRE
PIERRE RICHARD GÉRARD DEPARDIEU
un film de FRANCIS VEBER

3 **Fabien** Si je dis pile, ça va être face, et si je dis face, ça va être pile, alors je dis... face!
Danielle Pile! T'as perdu!
Fabien C'est pas vrai! C'est toujours la même chose!
Danielle T'inquiète pas, tu pourras le voir, ton film. Tu n'as qu'à l'enregistrer.

Preteaching Vocabulary

Identifying Keywords
Have students skim Fabien and Danielle's conversation for words they know. Ask them to list those words and to explain how they help with their overall understanding of the story. Then have them identify words that they might not know yet, but seem to be important to the story. Then have volunteers give their versions of the story, based on their comprehension of the keywords.

la télé *TV*
un feuilleton *series*
tirer à pile ou face *flip a coin*
enregistrer *to record*
le magnétoscope *VCR*
la pub *commercial*
Ça m'énerve. *It bugs me.*
Ça ne me dérange pas. *It doesn't bother me.*

Ce soir-là, devant la télévision...

4

Fabien	Ça y est, j'ai mis le magnétoscope en route!
Danielle	Chut, le feuilleton commence!
Fabien	J'espère que je n'ai pas raté le début.
Danielle	Mais tais-toi, enfin!
Fabien	C'est Emilie, celle-là?
Danielle	Non, c'est une villageoise. Emilie est plus jeune... Tiens, c'est elle.
Fabien	Elle est pas terrible.
Danielle	Ça te dérangerait de me laisser regarder tranquillement?
Fabien	Et lui, qui c'est?
Danielle	C'est Ovida.
Fabien	Pourquoi est-ce qu'ils se disputent?
Danielle	Parce qu'ils s'aiment.
Fabien	C'est vraiment nul, ton feuilleton.
Danielle	Bon, si tu ne peux pas te taire, va réviser tes maths et fiche-moi la paix!
Fabien	Oh! Ça va! La télé est à tout le monde.

Un quart d'heure plus tard...

5

Fabien	Zut, la pub! C'est vraiment barbant, à la fin. Ils coupent toujours les films au meilleur moment.
Danielle	Au contraire, c'est pour créer du suspense.
Fabien	Moi, ces pubs pour des lessives ou des céréales, ça m'énerve!
Danielle	Moi, pas du tout. Ça ne me dérange pas. Ça permet de faire une petite pause. Et puis il y a de bonnes pubs. Tiens, regarde celle-là. Elle est chouette, tu trouves pas?
Fabien	Tu rigoles! Tu es vraiment une esclave de la pub, toi!
Danielle	Mais non! Je m'informe, c'est tout. C'est toi qui as tort de tout critiquer comme ça!

6

Fabien	Bon, ça recommence? J'en ai marre, moi.
Danielle	Quoi?
Fabien	Eh bien, ton feuilleton, là, *Emilie.*
Danielle	Ah! Parce que ça t'intéresse maintenant?
Fabien	Pas du tout, mais je trouve ça tellement bête que ça me fait rire.
Danielle	Quel hypocrite!
Fabien	Pense ce que tu veux, je m'en fiche!
Danielle	Ben...
Fabien	Tais-toi, ça reprend! Monte un peu le son, on n'entend rien.

Using the Captioned Video

 As an alternative, you might want to show the captioned version of *Camille et compagnie : Le Rêve de Sophie* on Videocassette 5. Some students may benefit from seeing the written words as they listen to the target language and watch the gestures and actions in con- text. This visual reinforcement of vocabulary and functions will facilitate students' comprehension and help reduce their anxiety before they are formally introduced to the new language in the chapter.

 Culture Note
In the 1981 film, *La Chèvre,* Gérard Depardieu plays a detective who teams up with a clumsy partner to try to find another man's daughter, reported missing in Mexico.

Language Note
Students might want to know that **pile** is used in several colloquial expressions to mean *just right:* **Ça tombe pile.** *(That's just what I needed.);* **à deux heures pile** *(two o'clock on the dot);* **arriver pile** *(to arrive at the right moment).*

Building on Previous Skills
Have students use their reading strategies and their background knowledge to try to guess the meaning of the following words: **feuilleton, enregistrer, magnéto-scope, pub, monte** *(soap opera, to record, VCR, commercial, turn up).*

Camille et compagnie
You may choose to show students Episode 9: **Le Rêve de Sophie** now or wait until later in the chapter. In the video, Camille and Sophie talk about movies on the phone and realize that they don't have the same tastes. Sophie likes comedies, while Camille prefers dramas. Camille proposes that they go to the aquarium with Max and Azzedine the next day, but Sophie can't go because she has an audition for a commercial. After their phone conversation, Sophie falls asleep and has a dream that she is a star.

Mise en train

Teaching Suggestion

Note culturelle Have groups read the **Note culturelle**. Then, have them write one or two true-false statements about the note. Collect the statements, read them aloud, and have the class respond.

Multicultural Link

Have students compare the programming available in their area with Canadian programming. In the United States, are foreign-language channels or stations available on TV or radio? In what language? On what channel or station?

Answers

1
1. discussing what to watch on TV
2. *Emilie; La Chèvre*
3. coin toss
4. Fabien can record his film on the VCR.
5. Commercials irritate Fabien, but Danielle likes them.
6. He grows interested in it.

4
1. C'est l'histoire de...
2. Tu te fiches de moi? Pas question! Tu parles! Au contraire. ... pas du tout. Tu rigoles! Mais non! C'est toi qui as tort...
3. Tu ferais mieux de... ; Tu n'as qu'à...
4. Chut! Tais-toi! Ça te dérangerait de me laisser regarder tranquillement? Si tu ne peux pas te taire, va réviser tes maths et fiche-moi la paix!
5. C'est pas vrai! C'est toujours la même chose! Fiche-moi la paix! Zut... ! C'est vraiment barbant... ; ... ça m'énerve! J'en ai marre...
6. Ça ne me dérange pas. ... je m'en fiche!

These activities check for comprehension only. Students should not yet be expected to produce language modeled in **Mise en train**.

1 **Tu as compris?** See answers below.
1. Qu'est-ce que Fabien et Danielle font?
2. Qu'est-ce que Danielle veut regarder à la télévision? Et Fabien?
3. Comment est-ce qu'ils décident du programme qu'ils vont regarder?
4. Quel compromis est-ce que Danielle suggère?
5. Que pensent Danielle et Fabien des publicités à la télévision?
6. Est-ce que Fabien change d'opinion? Comment?

2 **Qui dit quoi?**

Est-ce que c'est Fabien ou Danielle qui parle?

Danielle
«Tu peux enregistrer ton film.»

Danielle
«Ah! Parce que ça t'intéresse maintenant?»

«Ton feuilleton, il a l'air mortel!»

Fabien

«C'est bien, la pub. Ça permet de faire une petite pause.»

Danielle

«Ça m'énerve, la pub!»

Fabien

3 **Fais ton choix**
1. *Emilie, la passion d'une vie* est...
   a. une publicité.
   b. un feuilleton.
   c. un film avec Gérard Depardieu.
2. Danielle suggère à Fabien...
   a. d'aller voir *La Chèvre* au cinéma.
   b. d'aller réviser ses maths.
   c. de regarder *Emilie* avec elle.
3. Quand Danielle et Fabien tirent à pile ou face,...
   a. Danielle gagne.
   b. Fabien gagne.
   c. ils perdent la pièce.
4. Selon Danielle, Emilie et Ovida se disputent parce qu'ils...
   a. ne veulent pas regarder la même émission à la télé.
   b. se détestent.
   c. s'aiment.
5. Pour Fabien, la publicité, c'est...
   a. bon pour permettre une petite pause.
   b. bien pour créer du suspense.
   c. nul.

Note culturelle

La radio et la télévision canadiennes reflètent la diversité des cultures que l'on trouve dans le pays. Il y a deux chaînes nationales de télévision, une en français et une en anglais. Il y a également des chaînes de télévision privées comme CTV (en anglais) et TVA (en français). Les stations de radio, elles aussi, offrent des programmes dans les deux langues. Parfois, certains programmes sont même diffusés en dialecte inuit ainsi qu'en de nombreuses autres langues parlées par des Canadiens venus de différentes régions du monde.

4 **Cherche les expressions**

What expressions do Fabien and Danielle use to . . . See answers below.
1. summarize a plot?
2. disagree?
3. give advice?
4. ask someone to be quiet?
5. express annoyance?
6. express indifference?

5 **Et maintenant, à toi**

Est-ce que ça t'arrive souvent de te disputer avec quelqu'un pour la télé?

Comprehension Check

Auditory Learners

2 Read these sentences aloud and have students identify the speakers.

Slower Pace

3 Have students close their books. Read the sentences and two of the choices aloud as either-or questions. (***Emilie, la passion d'une vie* est une publicité ou un feuilleton?**)

Thinking Critically

5 **Analyzing** Have students tell how they resolve disputes over minor issues, such as what to watch on television. You might have students share their ideas in small groups and then discuss the merits and disadvantages of each method.

STANDARDS: 1.2, 2.2, 3.2, 4.2

Rencontre culturelle

Qu'est-ce que tu sais sur Montréal? Pour t'en faire une meilleure idée, regarde ces photos.

Les petites rues du Vieux-Montréal sont pleines de charme.

Montréal est aussi un grand port.

Montréal est une ville ultra-moderne et dynamique.

Montréal est un centre artistique et culturel.

Les habitants de Montréal apprécient les activités de plein air.

Qu'en penses-tu?

1. Quelle impression ces photos te donnent de Montréal?
2. Qu'est-ce que tu pourrais faire si tu habitais à Montréal?

Possible answers:
1. busy, modern port city with many fun things to do
2. shop, dine at cafés, sight-see, do business, go to parks, visit the port

Savais-tu que... ?

Montréal est la seconde ville francophone du monde, mais la plupart de ses habitants parlent aussi anglais. C'est le centre des affaires de la province de Québec. Montréal est aussi un grand port, bien qu'elle se trouve à 450 kilomètres de l'océan Atlantique! En plus d'être un des centres économiques du Canada, Montréal est une ville qui bouge grâce à une vie culturelle riche en activités. Chaque année, Montréal accueille le Festival international de jazz. Son industrie cinématographique et musicale se développe un peu plus chaque jour. Montréal propose aussi beaucoup d'activités sportives et de plein air. Le quartier le plus populaire de Montréal est sans doute le Vieux-Montréal avec ses boutiques, ses cafés et ses ruelles pavées. Dans ces ruelles, les artistes exposent leurs toiles et les musiciens, danseurs et jongleurs partagent leurs talents avec les passants.

Connections and Comparisons

Language-to-Language
Ask students to recall French-Canadian expressions or words they know that are different than standard French (**bienvenue** for **de rien**, **patate** for **pomme de terre...**). Ask them what language has influenced the evolution of the French language in Canada (English), and why (proximity to the U.S.). Ask students how English might influence Spanish in Mexico and the southern part of the U.S. Ask any native speakers of Spanish in your class to think of words they use that reflect the influence of English. (Near Mexico, people might hear **troca** for *truck,* for example.) Finally, have students guess the meaning of the French-Canadian term **un sous-marin** (a submarine sandwich).

CHAPITRE 9

Activating Prior Knowledge
Write the following categories on the board: *Cities/Places, Things to do, Things to see, Animals, Things to bring,* and *Language.* Then, for each category, have students write French words and expressions they already know referring to French-speaking Canada.

Teacher Note
Students learned about Quebec City in Chapter 4 of Level 1 and about the province of Quebec in Chapter 12 of Level 2.

Presenting
Rencontre culturelle

Have small groups look at the photos and read the captions. Ask them for their impressions of Montreal. Read aloud true-false statements about the captions, such as **Montréal est une ville traditionnelle et ennuyeuse,** and have students respond **(faux).** Finally, have groups read **Savais-tu que... ?**

Culture Note
As in the United States, the monetary unit of Canada is the dollar. Coins are available in denominations of 5, 10, and 25 cents, one dollar, and two dollars. The dollar coin is sometimes referred to as a "loonie" because of the bird depicted on its face.

Thinking Critically
Comparing and Contrasting
Have students compare Montreal to their own city or town. They might consider whether their town is more traditional or modern, whether more indoor or outdoor activities are popular, and what special events take place.

Rencontre culturelle

Teaching Resources
pp. 256–260

PRINT
▸ Lesson Planner, p. 43
▸ Listening Activities, pp. 67–68, 71–72
▸ Activities for Communication, pp. 33–34, 75, 77, 105–106
▸ Travaux pratiques de grammaire, pp. 82–86
▸ Grammar Tutor for Students of French, Chapter 9
▸ Cahier d'activités, pp. 98–101
▸ Testing Program, pp. 191–194
▸ Alternative Assessment Guide, p. 38
▸ Student Make-Up Assignments, Chapter 9

MEDIA
▸ One-Stop Planner
▸ Audio Compact Discs, CD 9, Trs. 2–4, 13, 18–20
▸ Teaching Transparencies: 9-1; **Grammaire supplémentaire** Answers; Travaux pratiques de grammaire Answers
▸ Interactive CD-ROM Tutor, Disc 3

Bell Work
Have students write a brief description of their favorite TV program for a French pen pal (**C'est l'histoire de...**)

Presenting
Vocabulaire

Write students' favorite TV programs on a transparency and project it. Then, ask students to regroup the programs by genre. Write the groupings on the board as students make suggestions. Next, point to and identify one of the programs in French by genre (*Animaniacs®* **est un dessin animé**) and ask questions about others.

Première étape

Objectives Agreeing and disagreeing; expressing indifference; making requests

WA3 FRANCOPHONE AMERICA-9

Vocabulaire

Qu'est-ce qu'il y a à la télé ce soir?

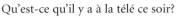

un feuilleton   une série   un vidéoclip   les informations (f.)

la météo   une publicité   un dessin animé   un jeu télévisé

un documentaire   un magazine télévisé   une émission de variétés   un reportage sportif

Cahier d'activités, p. 98, Act. 2   Travaux pratiques de grammaire, pp. 82–83, Act. 1–4

6 **Le programme ce soir**   See scripts and answers on p. 249G.

Ecoutons Ecoute le programme de la soirée. De quel genre d'émissions est-ce que l'annonceur parle?

CD 9 Tr. 2
1. *Le Canada en guerre*
2. *Vive la rentrée*
3. *Pour tout dire*
4. *Ce soir*
5. *Des chiffres et des lettres*
6. *Tintin et le lac aux requins*
7. *Ad lib*

7 **Devine!**

Parlons Choisis l'émission ou le programme qui correspond à chacune des descriptions suivantes.

1. Les candidats choisissent des lettres et essaient de deviner des mots.   un jeu télévisé
2. C'est pour essayer de vendre quelque chose.   une publicité
3. On y décrit le temps qu'il va faire dans la région où on habite.   la météo/les informations
4. Ça peut parler de la vie des animaux en Afrique, par exemple.   un documentaire
5. On sait ce qui se passe dans le monde en regardant ce programme.   les informations
6. Les groupes y chantent leurs dernières chansons.   des vidéoclips
7. Ça peut raconter l'histoire de deux jeunes qui s'aiment.   un feuilleton

Communication for All Students

Slower Pace

6 Make a chart with three columns on the board and write the following headers in the columns: **Titre / Mots-clés / Genre**. List the programs' titles in the first column. Play the audio, stopping at the end of the first segment, and ask students to suggest keywords from the segment that help to determine the type of program. (**noir et blanc, interview**, etc.) Write the suggestions in the second column. Then ask students to guess the program, based on the keywords. Place students in groups of two or three and have them proceed the same way for the other segments. Make sure to stop the recording between each segment to give students time to discuss and write their answers.

8 Sondage

Parlons/Ecrivons Ton/ta correspondant(e) canadien(ne) t'a demandé quelles émissions les jeunes Américains regardent. Demande à tes camarades ce qu'ils regardent le plus souvent. Note les deux émissions les plus populaires pour trois catégories du **Vocabulaire.** Compare tes notes avec celles de ton/ta camarade.

9 Mon journal

Ecrivons Quels genres d'émissions est-ce que tu préfères regarder? Pourquoi?

Comment dit-on...?

Agreeing and disagreeing; expressing indifference

To express agreement:

> **Je suis d'accord avec toi.**
> **Moi aussi,** j'aime bien les feuilletons.
> **Moi non plus,** je n'aime pas la pub.
> **Tu as raison.**
> **Tu l'as dit!** *You said it!*
> **Tout à fait!** *Absolutely!*

To express disagreement:

> **Pas du tout.**
> **Tu parles!** *No way!*
> **Tu te fiches de moi?** *Are you kidding me?*
> **Tu rigoles!** *You're joking!*
> **Tu as tort.**

To express indifference:

> **Je m'en fiche.** *I don't give a darn.*
> **Ça m'est vraiment égal.**
> *It's really all the same to me.*
> **Peu importe.** *It doesn't matter much.*

Si tu as oublié *expressing opinions* va à la page R14.

Cahier d'activités, p. 99, Act. 4

10 La publicité   See scripts and answers on p. 249G.

Ecoutons Ecoute ces gens qui parlent de la publicité. Est-ce que la personne qui répond est d'accord, pas d'accord ou indifférente?
CD 9 Tr. 3

11 C'est cool, les vidéoclips!

Parlons Est-ce que tu as vu le dernier vidéoclip de ces stars? Qu'est-ce que tu en penses? Parles-en avec ton/ta camarade qui te dira s'il/si elle est d'accord avec toi.

Jewel	Garth Brooks	Wallflowers	U2
Shania Twain	Ricky Martin		Céline Dion
Gipsy Kings	R.E.M.	Paula Cole	MC Solaar

12 Tu rigoles!

Ecrivons/Parlons Fais une liste de quatre émissions que tu aimes et de quatre autres que tu n'aimes pas. Montre ta liste à ton/ta camarade et donne-lui ton opinion sur chaque émission. Il/Elle va te dire s'il/si elle est d'accord et pourquoi.

Cultures and Communities

Culture Notes
• Originally from Senegal, MC Solaar is a popular French rap musician whose songs promote peace and communication as alternatives to violence.

• Roch Voisine is a popular Canadian singer.

Community Link
Have students call or visit a local radio or TV station to find out about the different types of programs available. They might also find out which programs are the most and least popular.

Game
Vingt questions Have one student think of a TV program. His or her classmates then ask up to twenty yes-no questions to try to determine the show he or she is thinking of. **(C'est un dessin animé? Est-ce que le personnage principal est un chat?)**

Presenting
Comment dit-on... ?

Before class, have one student practice acting as the dummy for your ventriloquist's act. Tell the student to move his or her lips when you place your hand on his or her shoulder and to stop when you remove your hand. In class, have the "dummy" sit at the front. Stand behind him or her. Introduce the dummy as **Christophe/Christine Poupée.** Ask him or her about a controversial topic, such as commercials. **(Eh bien, Christophe/Christine, tu trouves les pubs marrantes, n'est-ce pas?)** Then, place your hand on the dummy's shoulder. As he or she moves his or her lips, give a response out of the side of your mouth. **(Mais tu rigoles! Je déteste les pubs!)** Include all of the new expressions in your conversation with the dummy.

Visual/Auditory Learners
11 If the resources are available, have students bring in music videos or songs by the artists listed. Show a short segment of a video or play an excerpt from a song. Then call for volunteers to exchange opinions about the video or song and express their agreement or disagreement with each other.

Teaching Resources
pp. 256–260

PRINT
- Lesson Planner, p. 43
- Listening Activities, pp. 67–68, 71–72
- Activities for Communication, pp. 33–34, 75, 77, 105–106
- Travaux pratiques de grammaire, pp. 82–86
- Grammar Tutor for Students of French, Chapter 9
- Cahier d'activités, pp. 98–101
- Testing Program, pp. 191–194
- Alternative Assessment Guide, p. 38
- Student Make-Up Assignments, Chapter 9

MEDIA
- One-Stop Planner
- Audio Compact Discs, CD 9, Trs. 2–4, 13, 18–20
- Teaching Transparencies: 9-1; **Grammaire supplémentaire** Answers; Travaux pratiques de grammaire Answers
- Interactive CD-ROM Tutor, Disc 3

Presenting
Vocabulaire

Bring in the real items or pictures of them. Talk about each item while pointing to it or grabbing it. **(Je veux changer de chaîne. Où est la télécommande? Ah! La voilà!)**

Grammaire

Negative expressions Write the following sentence on the board: **Je ne regarde pas la télévision.** Have a volunteer circle the negative expression **ne... pas** and explain its placement. Repeat this process with other sentences.

Vocabulaire

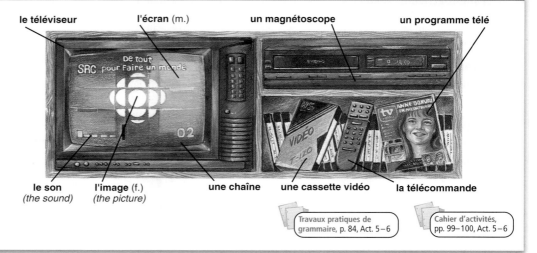

le téléviseur — l'écran (m.) — un magnétoscope — un programme télé

le son (the sound) — l'image (f.) (the picture) — une chaîne — une cassette vidéo — la télécommande

> Travaux pratiques de grammaire, p. 84, Act. 5–6

> Cahier d'activités, pp. 99–100, Act. 5–6

13 **Voilà comment on fait**

Parlons Explique comment enregistrer une émission. Complète le texte en t'inspirant des images.

Alors, d'abord, il faut que tu vérifies l'heure de l'émission dans le (programme télé). Ensuite, allume ton (téléviseur). Puis, choisis la (chaîne) qui t'intéresse. Mets une  (cassette vidéo) dans ton  (magnétoscope). Quand tu as l' (image) sur l' (écran), prends ta (télécommande) et appuie sur le bouton «enregistrement».

Grammaire

Negative expressions

Ne... rien (*nothing*) and **ne... pas encore** (*not yet*) are placed around the conjugated verb, just like **ne... pas, ne... plus,** and **ne... jamais.**

> Je **ne** peux **rien** entendre. Ça **n**'a **pas encore** commencé.

When you use **ne... personne** in the **passé composé, personne** immediately follows the past participle:

> Elle **n**'a rencontré **personne** au cinéma.

Notice the placement of **rien** and **personne** when they are used as subjects:

> **Personne ne** regardait la télé. **Rien n**'est tombé.

> Grammaire supplémentaire, pp. 272–273, Act. 1–3

Notice the placement of **ne... aucun(e)** (*no, not any*), **ne... ni... ni...** (*neither . . . nor . . .*), and **ne... nulle part** (*nowhere*):

> Je **n**'ai **aucune** chance. Il **n**'aime **ni** les feuilletons **ni** les drames.
> **Ni** mon frère **ni** ma sœur n'aime la télé.
> Je **ne** vois la télécommande **nulle part.**

> Cahier d'activités, p. 100, Act. 7

> Travaux pratiques de grammaire, pp. 85–86, Act. 7–9

Communication for All Students

Challenge

13 Type the paragraph with blanks where the illustrations appear. Distribute copies and have students fill in the blanks.

Challenge

Write the following question words on the board and have students tell which negative expressions could logically be used in answer to them: **où, qui, quand, qu'est-ce que.** (*Answers:* **ne... nulle part; ne... personne; ne... jamais, ne... plus, ne... pas encore; ne... rien, ne... aucun(e)**)

Language Note

Make sure students understand that **ne... aucun(e)** (*not a single, not a one, no kind of*) is more emphatic than **ne... pas.**

14 Grammaire en contexte

1. e 2. a 3. d
4. b 5. c

Lisons Quelles sont les réponses appropriées aux questions suivantes?

1. Qu'est-ce qu'il y a après le film?
2. Est-ce que le film est fini?
3. Tu veux voir un film ou un feuilleton?
4. Tu as trouvé quelque chose à voir?
5. Où est la télécommande?

a. Non, il n'a pas encore commencé.
b. Non, il n'y a aucun programme intéressant en ce moment!
c. Je ne sais pas. Je ne la vois nulle part.
d. Ni l'un ni l'autre. Je préfère voir un reportage.
e. Il n'y a plus rien. C'est la fin des programmes.

Note de grammaire

Although the expression **ne... que** may look similar to the negative expressions you've learned, it has the positive meaning of *only*. When you use **ne... que,** you place **ne** before the conjugated verb and **que** immediately before the word or phrase it refers to.

Il **ne** regarde **que** le sport.
He watches only sports.

Il **ne** regarde la télé **qu'**avec ses amis.
He watches TV only with his friends.

Travaux pratiques de grammaire, p. 86, Act. 10

Grammaire supplémentaire, p. 273, Act. 4

---

15 Grammaire en contexte

Parlons Lisette et Gisèle parlent au téléphone. Choisis une des expressions négatives ou **ne... que** pour compléter leur conversation.

LISETTE Hier soir, j'ai regardé *Les Meilleures Intentions*. Tu l'as vu, toi?

GISELE Non, je __n'__ ai __rien__ regardé hier. Je __ne__ regarde la télé __que__ le samedi soir parce que je __n'__ ai __plus__ le temps depuis que je travaille.

LISETTE Moi non plus. J'ai trop de devoirs à faire en ce moment.

GISELE Je __n'__ ai __pas encore__ vu le nouveau vidéoclip de Céline Dion. Tu l'as vu, toi?

LISETTE Euh, non. Je __n'__ ai vu __ni__ celui de Céline __ni__ celui de Roch Voisine.

GISELE Dis donc, Lisette, tu veux aller au cinéma?

LISETTE Je voudrais bien, mais je __ne__ peux aller __nulle part__ cet après-midi. Je dois étudier.

Comment dit-on...?

Making requests

To ask someone to be quiet:

Chut! *Shhh!*
Tais-toi! *Be quiet!*
Ne parle pas si fort. *Don't speak so loudly.*
Tu pourrais faire moins de bruit?
Could you make less noise?
Vous pourriez vous taire, s'il vous plaît?
Could you please be quiet?

To ask someone to adjust the volume:

Baisse le son. *Turn down the volume.*
Monte le son, on n'entend rien.
Turn up the volume.

Cahier d'activités, p. 101, Act. 9

---

16 Qu'est-ce qu'on demande?

Scripts and answers on pp. 249G–249H

Ecoutons Ecoute ces conversations. Dans lesquelles est-ce qu'on demande à quelqu'un de se taire?

CD 9 Tr. 4

Connections and Comparisons

Music Link

For additional practice with negative expressions, prepare copies of the lyrics of the song *Il n'y en a pas comme nous* (*Listening Activities,* Level 1, page 66) and distribute them to students. Play the song (Level 1, Audio CD 8, Track 32) as students read or sing along. Ask them to underline all the negative expressions as they hear them (**ne... pas, ne... guère,** and **ne... pas beaucoup).** Then, have students use the negative expressions they found in the song to create three sentences. You might have students look up the meaning of **guère** in the dictionary before they begin writing their sentences.

Auditory Learners

14 Have students close their books. Read each question aloud and have students tell which negative expression they would use in the answer. Then, have them open their books and do the activity as directed. When students have matched the questions and answers, have partners take turns reading and answering the questions.

Teaching Suggestion

Before the **Comment dit-on... ?** presentation, ask students to describe situations in which their talking might disturb others (during a test, at the movies, in a library). Then, ask them what they might do or say to others who were doing the same in these situations.

Presenting
Comment dit-on... ?

On the board draw a TV with a volume control knob and bring in a radio. After turning on the radio to represent the sound of the TV, have two volunteers sit facing the TV and talk quietly. Pull up a chair next to them and ask them to be quiet, using the new expressions. (**Chut!**) Ask them to adjust the volume as well (**Baisse le son!),** having them respond appropriately, while you adjust the volume of the radio accordingly.

---

19 You might use the following rubric when grading your students on this activity.

Speaking Rubric	Points			
	4	3	2	1
Content (Complete–Incomplete)				
Comprehension (Total–Little)				
Comprehensibility (Comprehensible–Incomprehensible)				
Accuracy (Accurate–Seldom accurate)				
Fluency (Fluent–Not fluent)				

18–20: A	14–15: C	Under
16–17: B	12–13: D	12: F

Teaching Suggestion

19 Before students begin this activity, you might ask them several comprehension questions about the TV program guide. (*Dr. Quinn* **passe à quelle heure?**)

Assess

▸ Testing Program, pp. 191–194
Quiz 9-1A, Quiz 9-1B
Audio CD 9, Tr. 13

▸ Student Make-Up Assignments, Chapter 9, Alternative Quiz

▸ Alternative Assessment Guide, p. 38

---

17 **Qu'est-ce qu'ils disent?**   *Possible answers:*

Parlons Qu'est-ce que ces personnes peuvent dire pour faire taire ces gens qui font du bruit?

1. Baisse le son!

2. Tu pourrais faire moins de bruit?

3. Vous pourriez vous taire, s'il vous plaît?

4. Chut!

18 **Alors, là!**

Ecrivons Danielle et Fabien essaient de choisir quelle émission regarder à la télé. Malheureusement, ils n'aiment pas les mêmes genres de programmes. Après plusieurs suggestions, ils tombent enfin d'accord sur une émission et commencent à la regarder, mais Fabien fait trop de bruit et Danielle n'entend rien. Imagine et écris leur conversation. Utilise au moins deux expressions négatives dans ta conversation.

Si tu as oublié **quarreling** *va à la page R9.*

19 **Jeu de rôle**

Parlons You want to watch something on TV with a Canadian friend. You try to pick a program from the TV listing that you both want to watch. Unfortunately, you have different preferences and can't agree on anything. You finally make a choice together, but you're not happy with it and you get bored. Act out this conversation with a partner.

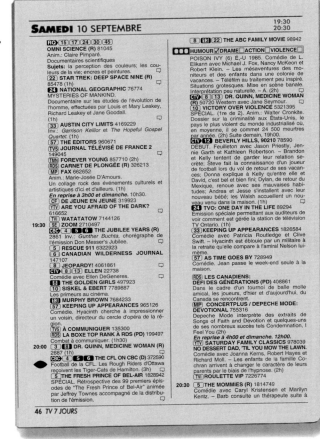

Communication for All Students

Challenge

Game Write the vocabulary from this **étape** on index cards and put them in a bag. Form two teams and have the first player come to the front. Select a card from the bag. Depending on the card you draw, you might hold up an item (**la télécommande**), give the name of a TV program *(Bugs Bunny),* mime an expression (**Chut!**), or give an English equivalent. *(You said it!)* If the player correctly identifies what is written on the card, his or her team wins a point, and the turn passes to the next team. Continue until all players have had a turn.

PANORAMA CULTUREL

Quel genre de film préfères-tu?

We asked people about the kinds of movies they
like. Here's what they told us.

Teaching Resources
p. 261

PRINT
▸ Video Guide, pp. 56–57, 59
▸ Cahier d'activités, p. 108

MEDIA
▸ One-Stop Planner
▸ Video Program
  Videocassette 3, 44:10–47:10
▸ Audio Compact Discs, CD 9,
  Trs. 5–8
▸ Interactive CD-ROM Tutor, Disc 3

Catherine,
Québec

«J'aime beaucoup les
comédies. J'aime aussi les
choses historiques, mais
je regarde souvent les
films pour leurs acteurs.
Quand il y a des acteurs
qui m'intéressent, je
regarde les films. Et puis
j'aime, en tout cas... Je
suis une des rares qui
aiment vraiment les
films français. J'aime
beaucoup.»   Tr. 6

Sébastien,
France

«Les films que je préfère,
ce sont les films de
science-fiction, Steven
Spielberg, parce que
j'adore les effets spéciaux,
tout ce qui touche au
grandiose. Sinon, j'aime
bien aussi les comédies,
comédies françaises. Je
trouve ça assez drôle, et
voilà.»
Tr. 7

Jennifer,
France

«J'aime bien tous les
films, de préférence les
films d'action, les films
sur les problèmes de
tous les jours, sur les problèmes plus importants.»
Tr. 8

Qu'en penses-tu?

1. Qui aime les mêmes films que toi?
2. Quels films francophones est-ce que tu as vus? Est-ce qu'ils sont différents des films
   américains? Si oui, de quelle manière?
3. Où est-ce que tu peux aller pour voir des films étrangers près de chez toi?

Presenting
Panorama Culturel

Before playing the video, write
on the board clues about the
interviewees, such as **Cette personne aime les films de
science-fiction.** Then, play the
video and have students use the
clues to try to guess the identity
of the interviewees. Ask the
Questions below to check comprehension. Finally, have
partners read the interviews
together and tell whether they
like the same types of films as
the interviewees.

Cultures and Communities

Culture Note
The Canadian film industry is known for
its diversity, the high quality of its films,
and a lack of commercialization. Several well-
known directors are Arthur Lamothe, Pierre
Perrault, and Denys Arcand, who has earned
numerous film awards.

Community Link
Have students list all the different types of films
they can think of (comedy, drama, science-
fiction). Write their suggestions on a transparency.
You might also have students call out the names
of well-known actors and actresses and have the
class associate the names with the genres. Poll the
class to find out which type of film is the most
popular.

Questions

1. **Quel genre de film est-ce que
   Catherine préfère?** (les comédies,
   les choses historiques)
2. **Est-ce que Catherine aime les
   films français?** (oui)
3. **Pourquoi est-ce que Sébastien
   aime les films de science-
   fiction?** (Il aime les effets
   spéciaux.) **Est-ce qu'il aime les
   comédies?** (oui)
4. **Quel genre de film est-ce que
   Jennifer préfère?** (les films
   d'action)

Presenting
Remise en train

Play the recording, pausing after each scene to ask questions about the film being discussed. (*L'Union sacrée* **est un film policier ou un drame?**) Ask who recommends the film and why.

Teaching Suggestion
Have students look at the movie advertisements on pages 262–263 and infer the genres of the movies from the ads.

Answers

21 C'est un drame: *Le Grand Bleu;* C'est avec Patrick Bruel: *L'Union sacrée;* C'est réalisé par Luc Besson: *Le Grand Bleu;* C'est un film policier: *L'Union sacrée;* C'est avec Chuck Norris: *Sidekicks;* C'est une comédie: *Mon père, ce héros;* C'est avec Gérard Depardieu: *Mon Père, ce héros;* C'est un film de karaté: *Sidekicks*

Remise en train ▪ *D'accord, pas d'accord*

CD 9 Tr. 9

Vendredi, à Montréal, à la sortie du lycée...

1
Fabien Qu'est-ce que tu vas faire, ce week-end?
Dina Ma cousine vient à Montréal. J'aimerais bien l'emmener au cinéma, mais je ne sais pas trop quoi aller voir. Qu'est-ce que tu as vu comme bons films récemment?
Fabien De bien, j'ai vu *L'Union sacrée.*
Dina Ah, oui? J'en ai beaucoup entendu parler. C'était comment?
Fabien C'était super. Tu devrais aller le voir, je suis sûr que ça te plairait. C'est un film policier avec Patrick Bruel et Richard Berry. C'est plein d'action et de suspense; et en plus, c'est drôlement bien fait. Et puis, les acteurs sont super et on ne s'ennuie pas une seconde.
Dina Ça a l'air pas mal. C'est quoi exactement, l'histoire?
Fabien Alors, tu vois, Berry fait partie des services secrets. Bruel, lui, il est flic. Au début, ils ne s'aiment pas du tout, mais ils sont obligés de travailler ensemble pour arrêter des terroristes. Voilà, je ne t'en dis pas plus. Je t'assure, il faut vraiment que tu ailles voir ce film.

2
Marie De quel film est-ce que tu parles?
Fabien De *L'Union sacrée.*
Marie Bof... c'est pas terrible!
Fabien Ah non, je ne suis pas d'accord. J'ai trouvé ça très bien, moi.
Marie Toi, de toute façon, tu aimes tous les films avec Patrick Bruel.
Fabien Et alors? Il est génial comme acteur!

20 Tu as compris?
1. De quoi est-ce que ces adolescents parlent? *movies*
2. Est-ce qu'ils sont d'accord? *No*
3. Quels conseils est-ce que Dina décide de suivre? *No one's.*

21 C'est quel film?
Indique le film dont on parle. *See answers below.*

«C'est un film policier.»
«C'est avec Patrick Bruel.»
«C'est avec Gérard Depardieu.»
«C'est une comédie.»
«C'est un drame.»
«C'est réalisé par Luc Besson.»
«C'est avec Chuck Norris.»
«C'est un film de karaté.»

These activities check for comprehension only. Students should not yet be expected to produce language modeled in **Remise en train.**

Preteaching Vocabulary

Recognizing Cognates
Have students skim the conversations for words that look similar to English words. Ask them to explain how those words help understand the story. Have them look especially at the film titles. Have them work in pairs to come up with explanations of what the films might be about and the opinions of the people discussing them, based in part on their use of cognates to help comprehension.

l'union *union*
l'action *action*
le suspense *suspense*
les terroristes *terrorists*
un héros *hero*
une adolescente *a teenage girl*
le karaté *karate*
un drame *a drama*

3 **Marie** Bof. En tout cas, moi, je te conseille plutôt d'aller voir *Mon père, ce héros* avec Gérard Depardieu.

Fabien Alors ça, c'est vraiment nul!

Marie N'importe quoi. C'est très drôle.

Dina De quoi ça parle?

Marie Ça parle d'une adolescente qui est en vacances avec son père dans une île. Elle rencontre un garçon super mignon et elle lui fait croire que son père est son petit ami.

Fabien En tout cas, moi, j'ai trouvé ça plutôt lourd et je n'ai pas ri une seule fois.

Marie Ne l'écoute pas. C'est vraiment marrant.

4 **Adrien** Tu devrais plutôt aller voir *Sidekicks*.

Dina Qu'est-ce que c'est?

Adrien C'est l'histoire d'un garçon qui a des problèmes avec les autres enfants du quartier. Dans ses rêves, il vit toutes sortes d'aventures avec son idole, Chuck Norris. A la fin, il décide de prendre des leçons de karaté.

Marie Ça m'étonnerait que Dina veuille voir un film de karaté!

Adrien Et pourquoi pas? Il y a beaucoup d'action et c'est très bien fait.

5 **Marie** Moi, je lui conseille plutôt *Le Grand Bleu.* C'est un film de Luc Besson, un drame.

Adrien Il paraît que c'est très mauvais. C'est long, c'est ennuyeux, c'est...

Dina Bon, euh, écoutez, merci pour vos conseils. Finalement, je crois que je ferais mieux de réfléchir et de choisir moi-même!

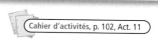
Cahier d'activités, p. 102, Act. 11

22 **Vrai ou faux?**

1. Dans *L'Union sacrée*, Bruel et Berry travaillent ensemble pour arrêter des terroristes.   vrai

2. Dans *Mon père, ce héros*, le père croit que sa fille va se marier avec un garçon super mignon.   faux

3. Dans *Sidekicks*, Chuck Norris est prof de karaté.   faux

4. *Le Grand Bleu* est un film court mais plein d'action et de suspense.   faux

5. Dina décide d'aller voir *Le Grand Bleu.*   faux

23 **Cherche les expressions**

What expressions do the teenagers use in ***D'accord, pas d'accord*** to . . .   See answers below.

1. ask someone to recommend a film?

2. make a recommendation?

3. make a positive judgment?

4. make a negative judgment?

5. ask what a movie is about?

6. summarize a movie?

24 **Et maintenant, à toi**

Quels genres de films est-ce que tu aimes? Quel est ton film préféré?

Culture Note
Gérard Depardieu, a prolific actor who has played different roles in over 50 films since his debut in 1965, has also directed and coproduced several films. In the 1990s, he made his American film debut, starring in the English-language films *Green Card* and *My Father the Hero.*

VIDEO **Camille et compagnie**
As an alternative or in addition to the **Remise en train,** you may wish to show Episode 9 of ***Camille et compagnie.*** For suggestions and activities, see the *Video Guide.*

Answers
23 1. Qu'est-ce que tu as vu comme bons films récemment?

2. Tu devrais aller le voir, je suis sûr que ça te plairait. Je t'assure, il faut vraiment que tu ailles voir ce film. Je te conseille plutôt d'aller voir... ; Tu devrais plutôt aller voir... ; Moi, je lui conseille plutôt... ;

3. C'était super. C'est drôlement bien fait/très drôle/vraiment marrant. J'ai trouvé ça très bien, moi. Il est génial comme acteur.

4. ... c'est pas terrible! C'est long/ennuyeux/vraiment nul. J'ai trouvé ça plutôt lourd et je n'ai pas ri une seule fois. Il paraît que c'est très mauvais.

5. C'est quoi exactement, l'histoire? De quoi ça parle? Qu'est-ce que c'est?

6. C'est un film... ; C'est avec... ; C'est... ; Au début... ; Ça parle de... ; C'est l'histoire de... ; A la fin, ...

Comprehension Check

Auditory Learners

21 Read these quotations aloud and have students tell which films they refer to.

Challenge

21 As an alternative to this activity, have students scan the conversation on pages 262–263 to find one detail about each film: the main actor, the genre, or the director. Ask for volunteers to read their findings aloud and have the class try to identify the movie.

Challenge
Have students scan the conversation and write down all the judgments that the friends make about the films. Then have students tell whether each remark is positive or negative, who made it, and which film it refers to.

Objectives Asking for and making judgments; asking for and making recommendations; asking about and summarizing a story

WA3 FRANCOPHONE AMERICA-9

Vocabulaire

un film d'action
    d'aventures
    d'espionnage *(spy)*
    de guerre *(war)*
    d'horreur
    de science-fiction

un film classique
    étranger *(foreign)*
    historique
    policier

une comédie
une comédie musicale
un drame
une histoire d'amour
un western

Cahier d'activités, p. 103, Act. 12–13

Travaux pratiques de grammaire, p. 87, Act. 11

25 **Il y en a pour tous les goûts**

Lisons/Parlons Devine de quel genre de film il s'agit.

1. C'est drôle.   1. une comédie   2. un film historique
2. Il y a de beaux costumes du XVIe siècle.
3. Ça se passe dans l'espace.   un film de science-fiction
4. Un détective cherche l'auteur d'un crime.   un film policier
5. Le personnage principal est un monstre.   un film d'horreur
6. Il y a des sous-titres en anglais.   un film étranger

26 **Qu'est-ce qu'on joue?**

Lisons Lis ces résumés de films. A quel genre appartient chaque film?   See answers below.

Note culturelle

Pendant très longtemps, l'industrie cinématographique canadienne a souffert de la compétition du cinéma hollywoodien. Maintenant, le Canada est un des plus gros producteurs de films documentaires et non-commerciaux. L'Office national du film du Canada a déjà produit près de 20 000 films de fiction, documentaires et dessins animés. Leurs qualités artistiques et techniques sont reconnues grâce à des films comme *Mon Oncle Antoine* et *Le Château de sable* qui ont été récompensés par différents festivals dans le monde entier. Le Festival des films du monde de Montréal est un des plus importants festivals internationaux.

PONT DE LA RIVIERE KWAI (LE) — Amér.,coul. (57). De David Lean : Pendant la deuxième guerre mondiale, les Japonais capturent des soldats anglais et les forcent à travailler à la construction d'un pont de chemin de fer. Le Colonel Nicholson, qui au départ refuse de coopérer, finit par voir ce pont comme une source de fierté et un symbole de réussite personnelle. Mais un commando envoyé par l'état-major anglais s'apprête à détruire le pont. Avec Alec Guinness, William Holden.

VIEILLE DAME ET LES PIGEONS (LA) — Can., Dessin animé, coul. (94). De Alison Snowden et David Fine : Paris, années 60. Un policier affamé découvre dans un square une vieille dame qui nourrit les pigeons de mets succulents. Un film d'une grande originalité qui mêle humour et cruauté. Au même programme : 'L'Anniversaire de Bob'.

AMI AFRICAIN (L') — Amér.— coul. (94). De Stewart Raffill : Au nord du Kenya, des touristes sont pris en otages par des braconniers, tueurs d'éléphants. La protection inattendue du chef des troupeaux parviendra-t-elle à sauver deux jeunes gens en fuite? Avec Jennifer McComb, Ashley Hamilton, Timothy Ackroyd, Mohamed Nangurai.

SITCOM — Franç., coul. (98). De François Ozon : Dans une famille bourgeoise ultra-classique, le père a ramené un soir un rat de laboratoire à la maison. Depuis cet événement anodin, le fils, un étudiant introverti, et sa sœur aînée se comportent de manière fort étrange... Conçue comme un sitcom (unité de lieu), cette farce rare preuve d'un mauvais goût absolu et d'un humour noir dérangeant. Une bombe indispensable du cinéma français. Avec Evelyne Dandry, François Marthouret, Marina De Van, et Adrian De Van.

PATRIOTES (LES) — Franç., coul. (93). De Eric Rochant : A 18 ans, Ariel Brenner, d'origine juive, quitte Paris et sa famille pour entrer dans les rangs du Mossad où il va être initié à l'art de la manipulation. Avec Yvan Attal, Richard Masur, Allen Garfield, Yossaï Banai, Nancy Allen, Maurice Bénichou, Hippolyte Girardot, Jean-François Stévenin, Christine Pascal, Bernard Le Coq, Roger Mirmont, Myriem Roussel, Sandrine Kiberlain.

LA POMME — Iran., coul. (98). De Samira Makhmalbaf : Dans un quartier pauvre de Téhéran, des familles dénoncent aux services sociaux un homme qui séquestre ses fillettes depuis leur naissance...Le réalisateur iranien Mohsen Makhmalbaf au scénario et au montage laisse sa place derrière la caméra à sa fille de 18 ans, qui s'inspire d'un fait divers pour son premier film. Avec Massoumeh Naderi, Zahra Naderi, Ghorbanali Naderi, Azizeh Mohamadi, et Zahra Saghrisaz.

Connections and Comparisons

Language-to-Language

On the Internet or in a French-speaking magazine, find a listing of movies currently shown in a French-speaking region of the world. Draw three columns on a transparency. List the original titles of English-speaking movies in the first column and their French translations at random in the second column. Have students match the titles. Then ask them for each movie's genre and write it in the third column. As a challenge, suggest other film titles and have students create French translations. Remind students that translations are not always literal. To guide them, you might share some typical French films' titles.

Comment dit-on...?

**Asking for and making judgments;
asking for and making recommendations**

To ask for judgments:

C'était comment?
Comment tu as trouvé ça?

To make a positive judgment:

Ça m'a beaucoup plu. *I liked it.*
J'ai trouvé ça amusant/pas mal.
Il y avait de bonnes scènes d'action.
Je ne me suis pas ennuyé(e) une seconde.
Ça m'a bien fait rire.
   It really made me laugh.

To make a negative judgment:

C'est nul/lourd. *It's no good/dull.*
C'est un navet.
Ça n'a aucun intérêt.
   It's not interesting at all.
Je n'ai pas du tout aimé.
Ça ne m'a pas emballé(e).
   It didn't do anything for me.
Je me suis ennuyé(e) à mourir.
   I was bored to death.

To ask someone to recommend a movie:

Qu'est-ce que tu as vu comme bon film?
**Qu'est-ce qu'il y a comme bons films
   en ce moment?**

To recommend a movie:

Tu devrais aller voir *La Chèvre.*
Je te recommande *Au revoir les enfants.*
Va voir *Les Visiteurs,* **c'est génial
   comme film.**
C'est à ne pas manquer! *Don't miss it!*

To advise against a movie:

Ne va surtout pas voir *Ça reste entre nous.*
Evite d'aller voir *La Famille Pierrafeu®.*
   Avoid seeing . . .
N'y va pas!
Ça ne vaut pas le coup! *It's not worth it!*

Cahier d'activités, p. 104, Act. 14

27 **C'était comment?** See scripts and answers on p. 249H.

Ecoutons Ecoute ces conversations. Est-ce que ces gens recommandent les films qu'ils ont vus ou pas?

CD 9 Tr. 10

28 **De bons conseils**

Lisons/Parlons Quelques personnes ont fait des recommandations à propos des films qu'elles ont vus. Choisis une phrase dans la boîte de droite pour compléter chaque phrase à gauche.

See answers below.

«Oh, ça m'a beaucoup plu.
«Ça m'a bien fait rire.
«Oh! C'est nul.
«Il y a de beaux costumes.
«Ça n'a aucun intérêt.
«Ça ne m'a pas emballé.

Ça ne vaut pas le coup!»
Je te le recommande.»
C'est à ne pas manquer!»
Evite d'aller le voir.»
N'y va pas!»
Tu devrais aller le voir.»

29 **Qu'est-ce qu'il y a comme bons films?**

Parlons Quelqu'un dans ton groupe a envie d'aller voir un film. Chaque élève lui en recommande un. Pour chaque film, les autres disent s'ils sont du même avis ou non. S'ils ne sont pas d'accord, ils lui disent d'éviter ce film et en recommandent un autre.

Communication for All Students

Game

Pas d'accord Have students form groups of three, one judge and two players. One player makes a judgment about a movie. (**Ça m'a beaucoup plu,** *Henry V.*) The other agrees or disagrees (**Tu rigoles! C'est lourd!**) and makes a judgment about a different movie, using a different expres-sion. (**Mais** *Aladdin,* **j'ai trouvé ça amusant.**) The first player reacts to the judgment, and so on. Players may use previously learned expressions. No repetitions are allowed. The goal is to keep the game going as long as possible.

Presenting
Comment dit-on... ?

Write the titles of several movies on large index cards. Then, draw two columns on the board. At the top of one column, draw a thumbs-up gesture, and at the top of the other, draw a thumbs-down gesture. Show one of the cards and ask students what they think about the movie on the card. Have students respond by making a thumbs-up or thumbs-down gesture. If the majority of your students think the movie was good, tape the card in the thumbs-up column on the board. As you comment on the movie and recommend it to students, use the new phrases and facial expressions and ges-tures to convey meaning. (**Ça m'a bien fait rire. C'est à ne pas manquer!**) Repeat with other movies until all the new expressions have been used, writing each one on the board.

Teaching Suggestion

Have students rewrite the expressions for recommending and advising against a movie, substituting the titles of various movies they've seen. You might have them read their recommendations aloud and have the class express agreement or disagreement by a show of hands.

Possible answers
28 Oh, ça m'a beaucoup plu; Je te le recommande.
Ça m'a bien fait rire; C'est à ne pas manquer!
Oh! C'est nul; Evite d'aller le voir.
Il y a de beaux costumes; Tu devrais aller le voir!
Ça n'a aucun intérêt; N'y va pas!
Ça ne m'a pas emballé; Ça ne vaut pas le coup!

Teaching Resources
pp. 264–267

PRINT

▸ Lesson Planner, p. 45
▸ Listening Activities, pp. 68–69, 72–73
▸ Activities for Communication, pp. 35–36, 76–77, 105–106
▸ Travaux pratiques de grammaire, pp. 87–88
▸ Grammar Tutor for Students of French, Chapter 9
▸ Cahier d'activités, pp. 103–106
▸ Testing Program, pp. 195–198
▸ Alternative Assessment Guide, p. 38
▸ Student Make-Up Assignments, Chapter 9

MEDIA

▸ One-Stop Planner
▸ Audio Compact Discs, CD 9, Trs. 10–11, 14, 21–23
▸ Teaching Transparencies: 9-2; **Grammaire supplémentaire** Answers; Travaux pratiques de grammaire Answers
▸ Interactive CD-ROM Tutor, Disc 3

Presenting
Comment dit-on... ?

Draw three columns labeled **De quoi ça parle?**, **Comment ça commence?**, and **Comment ça se termine?** Write a movie title above the table and fill out each column, using the new expressions (**Ça parle de... ; Au début,... ; A la fin,...**).

Grammaire

Relative pronouns Tell students that **qui** is usually followed by a verb, and that **que** and **dont** are always followed by subjects. Then, write sentence starters on the board and have students complete each one: **C'est l'histoire d'un chat qui...**

Comment dit-on...?

Asking about and summarizing a story

To ask what a story is about:

De quoi ça parle?
Comment est-ce que ça commence?
How does it begin?
Comment ça se termine? *How does it end?*

To summarize a story:

Ça parle d'un pays où il y a une guerre civile.
C'est l'histoire d'une femme qui joue du piano.
Il s'agit d'un homme au chômage.
It's about . . .
Ça se passe en France. *It takes place . . .*
Au début, ils ne s'aiment pas.
At the beginning, . . .
A ce moment-là, il tombe malade.
At that point, . . .
A la fin, sa femme revient. *At the end, . . .*

Cahier d'activités, p. 105, Act. 15

---

30 **De quoi ça parle?** See scripts and answers on p. 249H.

Ecoutons Ecoute Fabrice, un jeune Canadien, qui parle d'un film qu'il a vu. Ensuite, dis si les phrases suivantes sont vraies ou fausses.

CD 9 Tr. 11

1. Ça se passe près de Montréal.
2. C'est l'histoire d'un jeune homme qui s'appelle Chomi.
3. Ça parle d'un jeune homme qui est malade.
4. Au début de l'histoire, Chomi passe tout son temps avec Coyote.
5. A la fin de l'histoire, Olive est très fâchée.

Grammaire

Relative pronouns

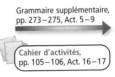

To make longer, more sophisticated sentences, you can join two or more clauses by using the relative pronouns **qui** (*who, that*) and **que** (*whom, that, which*). Use **qui** as the <u>subject</u> of a clause and **que** as the <u>object</u> of a clause.

• Since **qui** acts as a subject, it is usually followed by a verb. Since **que** acts as an object, it is normally followed by a subject.

   C'est l'histoire d'une femme **qui** est très grande. *(who)*
   Ça, c'est la femme **que** tu as rencontrée au café. *(whom)*

• English speakers often leave out the pronoun *that*, but French speakers must use its equivalent, **que**.

   Il n'a pas aimé le film **que** nous avons vu.
   He didn't like the movie (that) we saw.

• Drop the **e** from **que** before a vowel sound. Never drop the **i** from **qui**.

   Elle a aimé le poème **qu'**elle a lu. C'est elle **qui** écrit les poèmes.

• Use the word **dont** if you mean *whose* or *about/of/from whom* or *which*.

   Tu connais l'actrice **dont** il parle? *(about whom)*
   Ça, c'est le garçon **dont** la sœur est une actrice célèbre. *(whose)*

Grammaire supplémentaire, pp. 273–275, Act. 5–9

Cahier d'activités, pp. 105–106, Act. 16–17

Travaux pratiques de grammaire, pp. 87–88, Act. 12–13

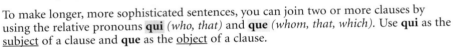

Communication for All Students

Auditory Learners

Grammaire For additional practice with relative pronouns, divide the class into several teams. Play the song *Le Pommier à Jean Renaud* (Level 2, Audio CD 6, Track 30), asking teams to count the number of times they hear the relative pronoun **qui** (35 times). The first team to give the correct number in French wins the game.

Game

Quel film? Have students think of a film or TV show and write three clues about it. Form two teams. A player from one team gives the first clue about his or her film. (**C'est l'histoire d'une femme qui...**) If the opposing team does not guess the movie, the player's team wins a point, and the player gives a second clue. Continue until the opposing team guesses the movie title.

31 Grammaire en contexte 1. e 2. d 3. a 4. b 5. f 6. c

Lisons/Parlons Complète chacune des phrases suivantes.

1. Le film...
2. C'est l'histoire de deux hommes...
3. La dame...
4. La comédie musicale...
5. Ça parle d'un petit garçon....
6. Je n'ai pas encore vu le drame...

a. dont tu parles est actrice.
b. qui passe au Trianon est nulle.
c. que Sophie recommande.
d. qui partent vivre en Afrique.
e. que j'ai vu hier est amusant.
f. dont le chien a disparu.

32 C'est l'histoire de...

Ecrivons/Parlons Fabien raconte l'intrigue d'un film qu'il recommande à Dina. Complète son récit avec **qui, que** ou **dont**.

C'est l'histoire d'un médecin ___qui___ fuit. Un soir, il arrive chez lui et découvre ___que___ sa femme a été tuée par un homme ___dont___ il ne connaît pas l'identité et ___qui___ n'a qu'un bras. Personne ne veut croire ___que___ cet homme existe vraiment. C'est le médecin ___qui___ est accusé du meurtre. Il est arrêté. Dans le bus ___qui___ conduit les prisonniers à la prison, il y a une bagarre ___qui___ cause un accident. Le bus est sur le point d'exploser et tout le monde s'échappe. Mais le médecin essaie de sauver quelqu'un ___dont___ les mains sont attachées au siège par des menottes. Après, il s'enfuit et il devient «le fugitif» ___que___ la police recherche pendant le reste du film. Bon, je ne t'en dis pas plus. Va le voir. C'est génial comme film!

33 C'est à ne pas manquer!

Ecrivons Un de tes camarades écrit à son correspondant pour lui expliquer l'intrigue d'un film qu'il a vu. Récris sa lettre en liant les phrases avec des pronoms relatifs quand c'est possible.

See answers below.

A la française

In French, as in English, you can use the present tense to tell what happened in the past. This makes stories more vivid. For example, if you're telling a story about someone who broke his arm, you might say: "So, he *falls* off the bike and *breaks* his arm!"

C'est l'histoire d'un savant. Ce savant s'appelle Frankenstein. Pendant ses études de médecine, Frankenstein rencontre un homme. Cet homme lui parle de ses expériences secrètes pour créer un être humain. Mais, avant de mourir, l'homme dit à Frankenstein de ne pas poursuivre les expériences. L'homme lui avait parlé de ces expériences. Le jeune savant refuse de prendre ces conseils au sérieux. Frankenstein se sert de ces secrets pour créer un être humain. Cet être humain est un monstre. Le monstre est furieux. Le corps et le visage sont horribles. D'abord, il ne comprend pas d'où il vient. Puis, il trouve le journal du savant. Frankenstein avait laissé le journal dans la poche de son manteau. Le monstre est très laid. Il le sait. Et personne ne l'aime. Il demande à Frankenstein de lui créer une compagne. Cette compagne lui ressemble. Je ne te raconte pas la fin... Tu verras. C'est assez terrifiant, mais c'est génial!

34 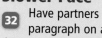 De l'école au travail

Parlons You work for a Canadian TV station and you're responsible for proposing the new fall prime-time programs. Pick programs you think the public will like. Make a timetable of programs that you'll present to your supervisors. For each program, be prepared to give the type of show, a title, a summary, and the names of the actors who'll be in it.

Communication for All Students

Slower Pace

32 Have partners do this activity. Then, write the paragraph on a transparency and have a student act as the teacher, asking the class to fill in the blanks and justify their answers. The student should praise correct answers. (**Bravo! Très bien!**)

Visual Learners

As an extra challenge, have students draw a story board as their partners tell their film plot.

CHAPITRE 9

Teaching Suggestion
To close this **étape**, tell students that they are on the selection committee for the Academy Awards. Have them form groups to discuss and nominate films for awards in the following categories: **Meilleure comédie, Meilleure comédie musicale, Meilleur drame, Meilleur film d'espionnage, Meilleur film de guerre,** and **Meilleur film historique.** Collect their nominations and announce the winners (**Et le gagnant est...**).

Assess

▸ Testing Program, pp. 195–198
Quiz 9-2A, Quiz 9-2B
Audio CD 9, Tr. 14

▸ Student Make-Up Assignments, Chapter 9, Alternative Quiz

▸ Alternative Assessment Guide, p. 38

Answers

33 C'est l'histoire d'un savant qui s'appelle Frankenstein. Pendant ses études de médecine, Frankenstein rencontre un homme qui lui parle de ses expériences secrètes pour créer un être humain. Mais, avant de mourir, l'homme dit à Frankenstein de ne pas poursuivre les expériences dont il avait parlé. Le jeune savant refuse de prendre ces conseils au sérieux. Frankenstein se sert de ces secrets pour créer un être humain qui est un monstre. Le monstre, qui ne comprend d'abord pas d'où il vient et dont le corps et le visage sont horribles, est furieux. Puis, il trouve le journal que le savant avait laissé dans la poche de son manteau. Le monstre sait qu'il est très laid et que personne ne l'aime. Il demande à Frankenstein de lui créer une compagne qui lui ressemble. Je ne te raconte pas la fin... Tu verras que c'est assez terrifiant, mais c'est génial!

Lisons!

Teaching Resources
pp. 268–270

PRINT
▶ Lesson Planner, p. 46
▶ Cahier d'activités, p. 107
▶ Reading Strategies and Skills Handbook, Chapter 9
▶ Joie de lire 3, Chapter 9
▶ Standardized Assessment Tutor, Chapter 9

MEDIA
▶ One-Stop Planner

Prereading
Activity A

Teaching Suggestion
Have students look at the photos on pages 268–270 and try to guess what the movie scene will be about.

Reading
Activities C–M

Teaching Suggestion
C.–E. Have students do these activities in groups. They should give the line of the script on which they based their answer to each question.

Answers
A. 1. Argentinian pampas; summer
   2. siblings Felipe, Daniel, and Laura and their grandfather Federico
   3. Daniel must prove his manhood by breaking a wild horse. Laura must find her place as a woman in a macho culture.
   4. **grandir:** *grow up;* **vieillir:** *to grow older;* **grandir** applies to the children, and **vieillir** applies to the grandfather.
B. 1. The stage directions are in italics in paragraph form; They describe the actors' movements.
   2. emotions, tone of voice

FIERRO...L'ETE DES SECRETS
SYNOPSIS
Les trois enfants d'une famille de Buenos Aires passent leurs vacances d'été à la ferme de leur grand-père dans la Pampa argentine. Pour le petit Felipe, neuf ans, c'est le bonheur parfait : un nouveau petit chiot et les gâteries de son grand-père. Pour Daniel, 12 ans, c'est l'occasion de prouver qu'il est un homme, en réussissant à dompter un cheval sauvage. Quant à Laura, 13 ans, elle n'est plus une fillette, mais pas encore une femme. Comment va-t-elle aborder l'adolescence dans ce monde traditionnellement macho? Le grand-père Federico, un homme fier et buté, devra exorciser ses vieux principes pour conserver l'amour de ses petits-enfants qui grandissent et surtout celui de Laura. *FIERRO... l'été des secrets* raconte la fin de l'enfance, ses joies, ses passions, les difficultés de grandir et de vieillir.

Film intelligent qui ne sous-estime pas les jeunes, *Fierro... l'été des secrets* confirme une fois de plus la qualité et l'originalité des CONTES POUR TOUS.
— Paul Toutant
RADIO-CANADA

Des paysages superbes, des images très belles et une histoire qui retient l'attention non seulement des jeunes, mais aussi des grands.
— Claude Bergeron
LE NOUVELLISTE

Tous les aspects de ce film sont d'une qualité exceptionnelle: la photographie superbe de Thomas Vamos, la musique admirable de Osvaldo Montes, la réalisation parfaitement maîtrisée de André Melançon, le scénario tout en finesse de Geneviève Lefèbvre, le jeu parfait des comédiens.
—Prat
VARIETY

Stratégie pour lire
Actively picture in your mind what you are reading—the setting, the way the characters look and are dressed, their actions and speech. Visualization enables you to create a context for what you are reading. If you come across a word you don't know, you can use this context to figure out the meaning of the word.

A. Read the synopsis of the story and answer the following questions.   See answers below.
   1. Where does the story take place? At what time of year?

   2. Who are the main characters in the story and how are they related to one another?
   3. What will be significant for Daniel and for Laura this summer?
   4. What is the difference between **grandir** and **vieillir?** To which characters do these words apply?
B. Look over the first dozen lines of the scene and answer these questions.   See answers below.
   1. Which parts of the scene are the stage directions? What added information do they give?
   2. What information is given by the words in parentheses next to each speaker's name?
C. Why did Federico have the colt Ruano brought to the ranch?   so Daniel could break him

Connections and Comparisons

Activating Prior Knowledge
Before students begin to read the script, you might ask them to name American movies about childhood experiences.

Thinking Critically
Comparing and Contrasting   Have students read the synopsis of *Fierro... L'été des secrets* to determine if the character's relationships in the story and in their own culture are similar. If they think not, have them point out elements that, in their opinion, depart from the way children are raised in their own region, culture, or family. You might have them point out other details that differ from their own experience, besides family relationships.

83. INT. JOUR. SALLE A MANGER

Federico termine son café. Il s'apprête à sortir. Daniel entre.

DANIEL : Ils viennent d'amener Ruano.

Federico se lève en souriant. Il se dirige vers le vestibule.

FEDERICO : J'ai pensé que ça serait plus facile pour toi de le dompter ici.

Daniel s'assoit.

FEDERICO (se méprenant) : Repose-toi un peu aujourd'hui ; tu continueras demain.

Il monte quelques marches d'escalier.

DANIEL : Je ne le monterai pas demain.

FEDERICO : Prends le temps qu'il te faut.

DANIEL : Je ne veux plus le dompter.

Federico s'arrête au milieu de l'escalier.

FEDERICO (surpris) : Qu'est-ce que tu veux dire ?

DANIEL (ferme) : Je ne veux plus le dompter.

Federico le dévisage un moment en silence. Arrivée de Felipe qui vient de la cuisine, suivi d'Anna. Ils se tiennent dans l'encadrement de la porte.

FEDERICO : C'est à cause de l'accident ?

DANIEL : Non, pas du tout.

FEDERICO : Explique-toi.

DANIEL : Ce cheval-là n'est pas pour moi.

FEDERICO : C'est toi qui l'as choisi.

Daniel garde le silence, les yeux dans le vague. Federico poursuit.

FEDERICO : C'est pas possible. Tu ne vas pas te laisser dominer par un cheval... Pas toi...

Laura sort de sa chambre et s'approche de la rembarde de l'escalier. Elle assiste à la conversation.

Daniel ne répond toujours pas.

FEDERICO : Il te fait peur ? C'est ça ?

Daniel lève les yeux et soutient le regard de son grand-père.

DANIEL (ferme) : J'ai pas peur !

FEDERICO : Je ne comprends pas, Daniel... (Un temps.) Je ne comprends pas... Si ce n'est pas de la peur, c'est quoi ? ... de la lâcheté ?

ANNA : Federico !

Daniel s'est durci sous l'accusation.

DANIEL : Tu ne peux pas comprendre. J'ai essayé...

FEDERICO (le coupant) : Puis, au premier obstacle, tu démissionnes !

DANIEL (ferme) : On n'est pas fait pour aller ensemble, c'est tout.

FEDERICO : C'est trop facile !

DANIEL (il hausse le ton) : Non, c'est pas facile !

Terms in Lisons!
Students might want to know the following words from the script: **encadrement de la porte** (*doorway*); **se durcir** (*to harden*); **les dents serrées** (*with gritted teeth*).

Teaching Suggestion
J. If students made lists of the characters' personalities as suggested on page 268, have them refer to them now.

D. Which of the following is NOT a synonym for **dompter**?

> dominer   ~~se soumettre~~   imposer sa volonté

E. What reason does Daniel give for not wanting to continue trying to break Ruano?

  a. He's afraid of the horse because of an accident.

  b. He's found another horse he prefers.

  c. He and the horse just aren't meant for each other.

F. How does Federico react when Daniel refuses to break the horse?   with anger

G. How does Laura intervene? Why? Does Federico pay any attention to her?   See answers below.

H. How does Federico treat the people he loves, according to Laura?   He dominates them.

I. Name two things Federico does as a result of Laura's outburst.   See answers below.

J. To whom does each of these statements refer?

Federico «Ça ne te regarde pas.»

«Tu me déçois beaucoup.» Federico

«Je ne veux plus le dompter.» Daniel

«Tu nous aimes comme tu aimes ton cheval.» Laura

«Tu veux dompter les gens que tu aimes aussi?» Laura

«On n'est pas fait pour aller ensemble.» Daniel

Communication for All Students

Auditory Learners
To help students visualize the scene, you might have five students take the parts of Daniel, Federico, Anna, Laura, and Felipe and read the scene aloud.

Slower Pace
C., F., G., H. Write the questions in these activities on a transparency, together with several multiple-choice answers for each one. For example, for C., you might give the following choices: (a) because it was sick; (b) so the family could ride together; (c) so Daniel could break him; (d) as a companion for Laura. Have students choose the correct answer from the choices given. You might go over the answers orally, asking students to quote the line from the script that supports their choice.

Answers
G. She tells her grandfather he has no right to speak to her brother that way; She's angry; No, he tells her it's none of her business.

I. He tells her to take the next train home to Buenos Aires, and until then, to stay in her room.

Lisons!

Additional Practice

Have students name the characters for whom the following stage directions were written: **ferme** *(Daniel)*; **indignée** *(Laura)*; **les dents serrées** *(Federico)*; **voix basse** *(Felipe)*; **voix sourde** *(Federico)*; **furieuse** *(Laura)*. Have volunteers read the corresponding lines aloud, following the directions.

Postreading

Activities N–O

Teaching Suggestion

N. Have students describe specific conflicts that they've seen depicted on TV or in a movie and tell how they were resolved. You might have them take notes on the situations described to use for the **Ecrivons!** activities.

Teaching Suggestion

Have students assume the identity of one of the characters from *Fierro... l'été des secrets* and tell what they would have done in this scene. Have volunteers read the corresponding lines aloud, following the directions.

FEDERICO : Tu me déçois, Daniel... Tu me déçois beaucoup.

Il ne bouge pas. Laura intervient.

LAURA (indignée mais pas agressive) : T'as pas le droit de lui dire ça.

FEDERICO : Ça, ça ne te regarde pas. Tais-toi !

ANNA : Federico, calme-toi. Tu vas pas faire une scène pour un cheval ?

FEDERICO (voix sourde) : Ne vous mêlez pas de ça. C'est à Daniel que je parle.

Il descend l'escalier.

FEDERICO (à Daniel) : Si tu n'es pas capable d'imposer ta volonté, tu ne seras pas capable de mener ta vie ! Comprends-tu ? Tu n'as pas le choix ; ou tu t'imposes, ou tu te soumets.

Laura descend l'escalier à son tour. Sa voix tremble un peu.

LAURA : Et les gens que tu aimes ? Tu veux les dompter aussi ? C'est ça ?

Federico l'ignore, il continue à s'adresser à Daniel.

FEDERICO : Comprends-tu ?

Laura a atteint le bas de l'escalier. D'un geste impulsif, elle pousse la potiche qui se trouve sur la colonne de l'escalier. La lourde potiche s'effondre avec fracas. Tout le monde sursaute.

LAURA (furieuse) : Ecoute-moi !

Federico se retourne. Felipe et Daniel

regardent Laura, stupéfaits. Elle a l'air d'une furie.

LAURA : Pourquoi ? Pourquoi tu fais ça ? Tu dis que tu veux qu'on soit heureux, mais tu décides toujours pour nous... Tu nous aimes comme tu aimes ton cheval ; va à droite, va à gauche, arrête... Puis quand on fait pas comme tu veux, ça ne fait pas ton affaire ! Pourquoi tu fais ça ? J'en ai assez, moi.

Federico la regarde un moment ; il est blême.

FEDERICO (les dents serrées) : Moi aussi j'en ai assez. Je ne veux plus rien entendre de toi. T'es pas bien ici ? Alors, tu fais tes bagages et tu pars par le prochain train. Et je t'interdis de sortir de ta chambre jusqu'à ton départ. Tu retournes à Buenos Aires !

FELIPE (à voix basse) : Comme grand-maman...

Seul Federico l'a entendu. Il lui jette un regard étrange. Il se tourne alors vers Daniel :

FEDERICO : Toi, on se reparlera ce soir.

Il se dirige vers la porte extérieure et la claque.

K. Réfère-toi au contexte pour deviner le sens de ces mots de vocabulaire.

to tame **apprivoiser**	stubborn **buté**	to approach **aborder**
to quit, give up **démissionner**	pale, livid **blême**	railing **la rembarde**
to stare at **dévisager**		cowardice **la lâcheté**

L. According to Federico, why must a person be able to impose his will on others? What does this reveal about his character? See answers below.

M. Why do you think Federico finds it more difficult to deal with his grandchildren as they grow up? See answers below.

N. Nomme quelques conflits typiques auxquels sont confrontés les adultes et les adolescents lorsque les adolescents grandissent et deviennent plus indépendants. See answers below.

O. Formez des groupes de quatre étudiants. Chaque groupe choisit un conflit décrit dans l'activité N. Deux étudiants jouent le rôle de l'adolescent et doivent faire une liste d'arguments défendant leur point de vue. Les deux autres prennent le parti des parents. Chaque personne présente son point de vue et ensemble ils essaient de trouver différentes solutions au(x) conflit(s).

Cahier d'activités, p. 107, Act. 19

Communication for All Students

Auditory Learners

K. Locate the sentence from the scene in which each of these words is used and read it aloud, using appropriate intonation. Then, have students do the activity as directed.

Slower Pace

K. Write the definitions of these words on a transparency and have students match the French words with their English equivalents.

STANDARDS: 1.2, 1.3, 3.1, 3.2

Ecrivons!

Un scénario de télévision

Maintenant que tu as lu une scène de *Fierro... l'été des secrets,* tu vas pouvoir devenir scénariste à ton tour. Avec un/une camarade, écrivez une petite scène pour une série télévisée dans laquelle deux personnages essaient de résoudre un désaccord.

 Stratégie pour écrire

A good writer will be careful to maintain consistency in all aspects of writing: mood, point of view, characterization, tone, and so on. For example, a menacing character in a horror story probably wouldn't say something humorous right in the middle of a scary scene. Likewise, a current slang expression would sound out of place in the script of a historical movie. To keep your work consistent, keep to the plan you made before you began to write; when you've finished your writing, read it over and check for things that seem illogical, out of place, or out of character.

A. Préparation

1. Choisissez le genre de série que vous voulez créer : une comédie, un drame, une série policière. Est-ce que vous voulez que votre série soit sérieuse ou drôle?

   a. Qu'est-ce qui se passe dans votre série?

   > un mari et sa femme
   > une famille
   > un enfant et ses parents
   > deux jeunes qui sont dans la même équipe de sport
   > deux personnes qui travaillent au même endroit
   > un garçon et une fille qui sortent ensemble
   > deux bons/bonnes ami(e)s

   b. Qui sont les personnages principaux? Ci-dessus, tu trouveras quelques exemples possibles.

   • Faites une liste d'adjectifs pour décrire les personnalités de vos personnages.
   • Rédigez ensuite une brève description de chaque personnage.

   c. Quel genre de relation ont les personnages? Est-ce qu'ils s'entendent bien ou pas? Quel problème ont-ils? Choisissez ce qui va se passer dans la scène que vous allez écrire.

2. Jouez votre scène. Improvisez un dialogue adapté à votre scène. Prenez des notes.

B. Rédaction

1. En utilisant vos notes, faites un plan de votre script. Puis, vérifiez que...

   a. le problème des personnages est présenté de façon claire.
   b. les réactions et les commentaires des personnages sont appropriés à la fois au contexte et à leur personnalité.

2. Rédigez votre dialogue en suivant le plan que vous avez fait.

3. Après avoir écrit le dialogue, ajoutez-y des instructions de mise en scène.

C. Evaluation

1. Quand vous avez terminé, relisez votre scène et répondez aux questions suivantes.

   a. Est-ce que le dialogue est réaliste?
   b. Est-ce que les réactions des personnages sont appropriées à leur personnalité et au contexte de l'histoire?

2. Vérifiez la grammaire et l'orthographe de votre histoire et faites les corrections nécessaires.

Apply and Assess

Postwriting

Cooperative Learning

Once students have written and edited their "pilot episodes," they might produce and videotape them. Have students form small groups, read each member's script, and decide which one to produce. Then, the writer acts as director and the others are the actors and actresses. Students might even compose and record an introductory theme song for the episode. This activity is appropriate for students' oral portfolios.

Teaching Resources
p. 271

PRINT
▸ Lesson Planner, p. 46
▸ Cahier d'activités, p. 153
▸ Alternative Assessment Guide, p. 24
▸ Standardized Assessment Tutor, Chapter 9

MEDIA
▸ One-Stop Planner
▸ Test Generator, Chapter 9
▸ Interactive CD-ROM Tutor, Disc 3

Process Writing

Prewriting

Reading/Writing Link
A. 2. You might have students visualize the setting, action, and mood of their scene before they start writing the dialogue.

Kinesthetic Learners
A. These students might need to walk through the actions in their scene with a partner.

Writing

Teaching Suggestion
B. Encourage students to keep a visual image of their characters in mind as they write their scenes to avoid inconsistency.

Portfolio

Written You might have students include all their work for Sections A–C in their written portfolios. For portfolio information, see *Alternative Assessment Guide,* pages iv–15.

Grammaire supplémentaire

CHAPITRE 9

For **Grammaire supplémentaire** Answer Transparencies, see the *Teaching Transparencies* binder.

Grammaire supplémentaire

Première étape

Objectives Agreeing and disagreeing; expressing indifference; making requests

1 Crée une question pour chacune des réponses de Nora. (**p. 258**)

EXEMPLE   Je ne vais nulle part ce week-end.
        Où est-ce que tu vas ce week-end?

1. Non, il ne m'a rien montré.
2. Non, je n'en ai jamais vu.
3. Je ne parle à personne.
4. Non, je n'en ai aucune idée.
5. Non, je n'aime ni les pubs ni les vidéoclips.
6. Non, je ne suis jamais allé(e) à Paris.
7. Ils ne vont nulle part ce week-end.
8. Non, Marie ne connaît personne ici.
9. Anne n'a ni frère ni sœur.
10. Non, je ne vois le programme télé nulle part.

2 Choisis la photo qui correspond à chaque phrase. (**p. 258**)

a.   b.   c.    d.

1. Tu sais ce qui est arrivé à Caro? C'est parce qu'elle ne fait jamais ses devoirs.
2. Ce sont les jours où personne ne va à l'école.
3. Ni l'eau couleur turquoise ni les fruits exotiques de cet endroit ne l'intéressaient. Il voulait aller en Russie pendant les vacances d'hiver.
4. Tu ne verras ça nulle part.

Answers

1
1. Est-ce qu'Olivier t'a montré son téléviseur?
2. Est-ce que tu as déjà vu des documentaires canadiens?
3. A qui est-ce que tu parles?
4. Est-ce que tu as une idée de ce que tu vas faire demain?
5. Est-ce que tu aimes les pubs et les vidéoclips?
6. Est-ce que tu es déjà allé(e) à Paris?
7. Où est-ce que Jean at Gilles vont ce week-end?
8. Est-ce que Marie connaît des gens ici?
9. Est-ce qu'Anne a des frères et des sœurs?
10. Tu vois le programme télé?

2
1. d
2. b
3. a
4. c

Grammar Resources for Chapter 9

The **Grammaire supplémentaire** activities are designed as supplemental activities for the grammatical concepts presented in the chapter. You might use them as additional practice, for review, or for assessment.

For more grammar presentations, review, and practice, refer to the following:
- Travaux pratiques de grammaire
- Grammar Tutor for Students of French

- Grammar Summary on pp. R29–R54
- Cahier d'activités
- Grammar and Vocabulary quizzes (Testing Program)
- Test Generator
- Interactive CD-ROM Tutor
- **Jeux interactifs** at <u>go.hrw.com</u>

3 Ça fait trois jours que Sophie est à Montréal. Elle n'y a pas fait grand-chose. Ecris ses réponses aux questions de Cora en utilisant une des expressions de la boîte dans chaque réponse. (**p. 258**)

> ne... nulle part   ne... pas encore
> ne... ni... ni...
> ne... personne   ne... rien

1. Tu es déjà allée te promener dans le Vieux-Montréal?
2. Tu as rencontré des gens intéressants au Festival des films du monde?
3. Tu as vu *L'Union sacrée* et *Le Grand Bleu*?
4. Tu as regardé le feuilleton à la télé ce matin?
5. Tu es allée au cinéma hier soir?

4 Amélie, la petite sœur de ton copain Xavier, te parle des habitudes de son frère. Complète ses remarques en utilisant **ne... que,** le verbe qui convient et l'expression entre parenthèses. (**p. 259**)

EXEMPLE   Ça m'étonnerait qu'il regarde un documentaire à la télé. (des films d'action)
D'habitude, il ne regarde que des films d'action à la télé.

1. Ça m'étonnerait qu'il regarde les informations avec toi. (des dessins animés)
2. Ça m'étonnerait qu'il lise des romans. (des B.D.)
3. Ça m'étonnerait qu'il écoute Céline Dion. (MC Solaar)
4. Ça m'étonnerait qu'il choisisse la chaîne qui t'intéresse. (les chaînes qui l'intéressent)
5. Ça m'étonnerait qu'il te parle de ses problèmes. (à son poisson rouge!)

Deuxième étape   **Objectives** Asking for and making judgments; asking for and making recommendations; asking about and summarizing a story

5 Complète les phrases suivantes avec les mots proposés. Choisis la réponse la plus logique pour chaque phrase. (**p. 266**)

> les enfants sont devenus médecins
> il est amoureux   le fils était en prison
> le fils était pirate

1. La femme dont _____ pleurait tous les jours. Elle était si seule!
2. La femme dont _____ avait plein de bijoux cachés dans son jardin.
3. La femme dont _____ était fière de sa famille.
4. Ça, c'est la femme dont _____ . Il ne parle que d'elle!

Communication for All Students

Auditory Learners

2 Have students cover up the sentences as you read each one out loud. Then have them identify the photos by letter (either in writing or they can volunteer answers). As an extension of this activity, have students work in pairs and draw pictures or use available magazine cutouts to create an activity similar to this one. Different sets of pairs can then exchange illustrations and answers. Volunteers can present their activity to the class. You might also have the pairs sketch their illustrations on blank overhead transparencies so that the whole class can see them.

Answers

3 1. Non, je n'y suis pas encore allée.
   2. Non, je n'y ai rencontré personne d'intéressant.
   3. Non, je n'ai vu ni *L'Union sacrée* ni *Le Grand Bleu.*
   4. Non, je n'ai rien regardé à la télé ce matin.
   5. Non, je ne suis allée nulle part hier soir.

4 1. D'habitude, il ne regarde que des dessins animés.
   2. D'habitude, il ne lit que des B.D.
   3. D'habitude, il n'écoute que MC Solaar.
   4. D'habitude, il ne choisit que les chaînes qui l'intéressent.
   5. D'habitude, il n'en parle qu'à son poisson rouge.

5 1. le fils était en prison
   2. le fils était pirate
   3. les enfants sont devenus médecins
   4. il est amoureux

For **Grammaire supplémentaire** Answer Transparencies, see the *Teaching Transparencies* binder.

Grammaire supplémentaire

6 Pour chacune des phrases suivantes, choisis le pronom relatif qui convient (**qui, que** ou **dont**). Ensuite, relis les phrases et donne le nom du film dont il s'agit d'après l'illustration. (**p. 266**)

1. Dans ce film, il s'agit d'un Texan _____ s'énerve quand les gens du village ne sont pas gentils avec son cheval.
2. Dans ce film, les personnages _____ il s'agit sont un couple de danseurs de New York.
3. C'est l'histoire d'un type _____ on cherche parce qu'il a volé des documents secrets à l'ambassade de Russie.
4. L'animal _____ ce film parle est une sorte de dinosaure gigantesque et furieux.
5. A la fin, on voit sur une chaise le masque _____ le criminel a porté pendant tout le film.
6. Le meurtrier est un personnage _____ on ne connaît l'identité qu'à la fin du film.
7. Ça parle d'un lézard géant _____ attaque une ville du Québec.
8. La femme _____ la mission est racontée dans ce film est capitaine d'un vaisseau spatial.

Answers

6 1. qui, *Un Cowboy, un bandit, un cheval*
2. dont, *On danse à Broadway*
3. qu', *L'Agent 99 a disparu*
4. dont, *Le Monstre qui a mangé Montréal*
5. que, *Le Meurtrier est parmi nous*
6. dont, *Le Meurtrier est parmi nous*
7. qui, *Le Monstre qui a mangé Montréal*
8. dont, *La Conquête de la planète inconnue*

Communication for All Students

Auditory Learners

8 Ask students the questions out loud and have volunteers respond with a sentence using **qui** or **que**. After you have gone over the activity as a whole class, have students work individually to write more questions like the ones modeled here. Then have them work in pairs to ask each other their questions orally for more practice.

Slower Pace

9 Complete the first three activities with the class and ask volunteers to explain their choices. Then have students work in groups to complete Activity 9. Have each group record their strategies for selecting the correct relative pronoun. When all the groups have finished, have them present their answers and strategies to the class.

7 Pour savoir ce qu'Eliane te dit, fais des phrases logiques avec les éléments des deux colonnes. (**p. 266**)

1. Il est sympa, le restaurant
2. Il était rigolo, le garçon
3. Il m'a fait penser à un acteur
4. J'ai bien aimé la boisson
5. Il est où, le livre
6. Ça te dirait d'aller voir le film

a. qu'il t'a donné?
b. qu'il nous a offerte.
c. dont il nous a parlé?
d. qui est venu nous retrouver.
e. qu'on a trouvé au centre-ville.
f. dont j'oublie le nom.

8 Pierre et Axcelle sont allés au Festival des films du monde. Axcelle pose beaucoup de questions et Pierre lui répond. Utilise **qui** ou **que** selon le cas. (**p. 266**)

EXEMPLE　AXCELLE　Ce festival attire des gens du monde entier, non?
PIERRE　**Oui, c'est un festival qui attire des gens du monde entier.**

1. Dis! Tu aimes bien cette actrice-là?
2. C'est pas vrai! Ce film a été réalisé par des jeunes?
3. Mais dis donc! Cet étudiant-là vient de débuter sa carrière dans le cinéma?
4. Tu préfères ce genre de film, non?
5. Ce réalisateur-là t'a beaucoup marqué?
6. Tu rigoles! Tu aimerais bien interviewer cette star-là?

9 Complète les phrases suivantes avec **qui, que** ou **dont**. (**p. 266**)

1. *L'Ami africain* raconte l'histoire de touristes _____ sont pris en otage par des braconniers.
2. *Le Pont de la rivière Kwaï,* c'est le film _____ je t'ai parlé l'autre jour.
3. *Les Patriotes?* Tu ne t'en souviens pas? Mais c'est le film français _____ nous avons vu l'année dernière à Montréal!
4. *Mon père, ce héros* parle d'une fille _____ fait croire à un garçon que son père est son petit ami. Bizarre, non?
5. *La Reine Margot,* c'est le film _____ j'ai conseillé à Jacques.
6. *Henry V* parle de la conquête de la France par les Anglais. C'est un film _____ te plairait!
7. *Roméo et Juliette,* c'est le film de Zeffirelli _____ je préfère.
8. L'acteur _____ j'ai oublié le nom joue dans *Madame Doubtfire.*

Review and Assess

You may wish to assign the **Grammaire supplémentaire** activities as additional practice or homework after presenting material throughout the chapter. Assign Activities 1–3 after **Grammaire** (p. 258), Activity 4 after **Note de grammaire** (p. 259), and Activities 5–9 after **Grammaire** (p. 266).

To prepare students for the **Etape** Quizzes and Chapter Test, we suggest doing the **Grammaire supplémentaire** activities in the following order. Have students complete Activities 1–4 before taking Quiz 9-1A or 9-1B; and Activities 5–9 before Quiz 9-2A or 9-2B.

Mise en pratique

internet

go.
hrw
.com

ADRESSE: go.hrw.com
MOT-CLE: WA3
FRANCOPHONE AMERICA-9

CD-ROM
DISC 3

CHAPITRE 9

The **Mise en pratique** reviews and integrates all four skills and culture in preparation for the Chapter Test.

Teaching Resources
pp. 276–277

PRINT
▶ Lesson Planner, p. 46
▶ Listening Activities, p. 69
▶ Video Guide, pp. 57, 59–60
▶ Grammar Tutor for Students of French, Chapter 9
▶ Standardized Assessment Tutor, Chapter 9

MEDIA
▶ One-Stop Planner
▶ Video Program
  Videocassette 3, 47:12–53:37
▶ Audio Compact Discs, CD 9, Tr. 12
▶ Interactive CD-ROM Tutor, Disc 3

Career Path

Tell students that film critics and journalists sometimes get to travel all over the world to cover various film festivals and interview actors, actresses, and directors. Ask them to think of reasons why knowledge of a foreign language would be beneficial to people choosing such a career.

See scripts and answers on p. 249H

1 Ecoute la conversation entre Didier et Simone. Ensuite, mets le résumé de leur conversation dans le bon ordre.

CD 9 Tr. 12

a. Didier demande à Simone de se taire.

b. Didier n'aime pas les histoires d'amour.

c. Simone recommande un film à Didier.

d. Simone n'aime pas les films d'horreur.

e. Simone et Didier sont d'accord.

f. Didier veut la télécommande.

2 **Parlons** Ton/ta camarade va te raconter l'intrigue d'un film. Essaie de deviner de quel film il s'agit. Changez de rôle. N'oubliez pas d'utiliser **qui, que** et **dont**.

3 Lis le texte et réponds aux questions à la page suivante. See answers below.

LE FESTIVAL DES FILMS DU MONDE DE MONTREAL

Le Festival des films du monde de Montréal a lieu tous les ans du 22 août au 2 septembre. Cette année, c'est la dix-huitième édition. Au programme, présentations des films, rencontres avec les stars et attribution des prix. Nous avons voulu partager cet événement haut en couleurs avec vous. Pour cela, Pierre Arnaud est allé interviewer Emma Halvick du magazine *Canada Cinéma*.

▶ Quand a lieu le Festival des films du monde de Montréal?
- Le festival se déroule du 22 août au 2 septembre.

▶ Quel genre de films est-ce qu'on peut voir au festival et combien y a t-il de présentations?
- C'est un festival où l'on peut voir plus de deux cents films du monde entier, avec chaque année, un hommage rendu à un pays en particulier. Cette année, par exemple, c'est la Turquie.

▶ Combien de catégories différentes de films est-ce qu'il y a?
- Il y a neuf catégories de films. On peut voir toutes sortes de films : des comédies, des drames, des films d'espionnage, des films de guerre. Bref, il y en a pour tous les goûts.

▶ C'est la première fois que vous êtes chargée de couvrir ce festival?
- Non, c'est la deuxième année que je viens. Avec autant de plaisir que la première année, d'ailleurs. Vous savez, j'adore le cinéma, alors pour moi, c'est formidable d'avoir l'occasion de faire un reportage sur un festival du cinéma.

▶ Qu'est-ce qui vous plaît tant dans un festival du cinéma?
- Tout me plaît. J'ai l'occasion de voir des films étrangers que je ne pourrais pas voir ailleurs. Et puis, c'est merveilleux de pouvoir rencontrer et interviewer toutes ces stars.

▶ Combien de films voyez-vous en moyenne chaque année? Et quel est votre genre de films préféré?

- En général, je vois une trentaine de films. Personnellement, je préfère les films historiques. Cette année, j'ai vu un très bon film martiniquais. Ça se passe au début du siècle et ça parle de la vie d'une famille qui possède une plantation de canne à sucre. C'est à ne pas manquer, à mon avis.

▶ Quelle est la star qui vous a le plus marquée cette année?
- Carole Bouquet, je crois. Elle est très impressionnante, surtout dans son dernier film. C'est un drame qui raconte l'histoire d'une femme qui a beaucoup de problèmes.

▶ Comment fonctionne le jury? Qui en sont les membres?
- Le jury est composé de six personnes plus le président. D'ailleurs, cette année, c'est Carole Bouquet qui est présidente. Les membres sont soit des acteurs, soit des producteurs, soit des réalisateurs, soit des critiques de cinéma. Après avoir vu les films en compétition, ils délibèrent jusqu'à ce qu'ils aient attribué les prix.

Answers

3
1. movies from around the world
2. seeing foreign movies and meeting and interviewing movie stars
3. a drama: a woman with a lot of problems
4. historical films: it's about the life of a family that owns a sugar cane plantation; yes

---

Apply and Assess

Challenge

1 Once students have completed the activity, type the statements in the correct order and distribute copies to partners. Have them reconstruct the conversation, based on the statements. For the first event (**Didier veut la télécommande**), students might write **Tu pourrais me passer la télécommande?**

Slower Pace

3 Before students read the interview, have them scan the introductory paragraph to find out when the festival is held, what is on the program, and who is being interviewed.

---

1. What kinds of movies are shown at the Montreal film festival?

2. What does Emma Halvick particularly like about being at the festival?

3. What type of movie was Carole Bouquet in? What is it about?

4. What type of movies does Emma Halvick say she likes best? What was the story of the movie from Martinique that Emma Halvick says she saw? Does she recommend it?

4 Ton ami(e) et toi, vous vous trouvez à Montréal au moment du Festival des films du monde. Vous regardez passer toutes les stars et vous discutez des films dans lesquels elles jouent. Dites ce que vous en pensez et si vous les recommandez.

5 Tu es critique de cinéma et tu es au Festival des films du monde avec un/une collègue qui travaille pour la même revue que toi. Choisissez un film à critiquer. Toi, tu écris une critique positive et ton/ta camarade en écrit une négative. Présentez vos critiques à la classe.

6 ## Jeu de rôle

You're a journalist at the **Festival des films du monde** in Montreal. Interview a star. He/She will tell you about a new movie he/she has just made: what kind of movie it is, what it's about, what other actors/actresses are in it, and what he/she thinks about it. Remember to ask his/her opinion of other movies at the festival. Act out this scene with a classmate. Change roles.

Mise en pratique

CHAPITRE 9

Teaching Suggestion

4 Before students begin the activity, have the class name movies in which each actor or actress pictured here has starred. You might also name, or bring in magazine pictures of, additional popular movie stars for students to discuss.

Writing Assessment

5 You might use the following rubric when grading your students on this activity.

Writing Rubric	Points			
	4	3	2	1
Content (Complete– Incomplete)				
Comprehensibility (Comprehensible– Incomprehensible)				
Accuracy (Accurate– Seldom accurate)				
Organization (Well organized– Poorly Organized)				
Effort (Excellent–Minimal)				

18–20: A   14–15: C   Under
16–17: B   12–13: D   12: F

Apply and Assess

Additional Practice

5 Have students organize and design a program for a film festival in their own town. They should decide where the films will be shown and which films will be featured. They should include a map of the locations involved and listings and critiques of all the films featured. This activity could be used as an additional chapter project.

Que sais-je?

Teaching Resources
p. 278

PRINT
▸ Grammar Tutor for Students of French, Chapter 9

MEDIA
▸ Interactive CD-ROM Tutor, Disc 3
▸ Online self-test

go.hrw.com
WA3 FRANCOPHONE
AMERICA-9

Teaching Suggestions

4 • Ask students how these situations differ. (The first involves strangers; the others, family members.)

• You might have students get together with a partner and combine related items, such as questions 11 and 12, to create a dialogue.

Can you use what you've learned in this chapter?

Can you agree and disagree?
p. 257

1 You and a friend have just seen a movie together. Your friend thought the movie was great. How would you express your agreement with your friend? Je suis d'accord avec toi. Moi aussi, j'ai beaucoup aimé ce film. Tu as raison. Tu l'as dit! Tout à fait!

2 How would you say that you disagree with your friend's opinion of the movie? Pas du tout. Tu parles! Tu te fiches de moi? Tu rigoles! Tu as tort.

Can you express indifference?
p. 257

3 Your friend wants to know which TV show you want to watch next. What do you say if you really have no preference? Je m'en fiche. Ça m'est vraiment égal. Peu importe.

Can you make requests?
p. 259

4 How would you ask the people in these situations to be quiet?

Chut! Vous pourriez vous taire, s'il vous plaît?
You're at a movie, and the people behind you are talking loudly.

Baisse le son!
You're talking on the telephone, and your brother has the TV turned up too loud.

You're trying to watch a TV show, and your little sister is making noise.
Tu pourrais faire moins de bruit?

Can you ask for and make judgments?
p. 265

5 What would you say to ask a friend her opinion of a TV program you've just seen together? Comment tu as trouvé ça?

6 How would you answer the question in number 5 if you liked the program? See answers below.

7 How would you answer the question in number 5 if you disliked the program? C'était nul/lourd. Ça n'avait aucun intérêt. Je n'ai pas du tout aimé. Ça ne m'a pas emballé(e). Je me suis ennuyé(e) à mourir.

Can you ask for and make recommendations?
p. 265

8 How would you ask a friend to recommend a movie? Qu'est-ce que tu as vu comme bon film? Qu'est-ce qu'il y a comme bons films en ce moment?

9 How would you recommend a movie you've just seen to a friend? Tu devrais aller voir... ; Je te recommande... ; Va voir... , c'est génial comme film. C'est à ne pas manquer!

10 What would you say if your friend wanted to go see a movie you thought was terrible? Ne va surtout pas voir... ; Evite d'aller voir... ; N'y va pas! Ça ne vaut pas le coup!

Can you ask about and summarize a story?
p. 266

11 How do you ask a friend what a movie is about? De quoi ça parle?

12 How would you tell someone about the last movie you saw? Ça parle de... ; C'est l'histoire de... ; Il s'agit de... ; Ça se passe... ; Au début,... ; À ce moment-là,... ; A la fin,...

Review and Assess

♞ Game

Allez-y! Form four teams and give a transparency and a pen to each one. Make four sets of index cards, each set bearing the numbers 1–12 (48 cards total), and put each set of cards in a bag. Give one bag to each team. Have one member from each team select four cards from the bag and place them face-down on his or her desk. Then, call out **Allez-y!** Teams turn their cards over and write on their transparency the answers to the questions from **Que sais-je?** that correspond to the numbers their teammate drew. After two minutes, tell students to put down their pens. Have one member from each team bring their cards and transparency to the front. Show the cards and the transparency and have the class verify that the questions were answered correctly. Award one point for each correct answer.

Answers

6 Ça m'a beaucoup plu. J'ai trouvé ça amusant/pas mal. Il y avait de bonnes scènes d'action. Je ne me suis pas ennuyé(e) une seconde. Ça m'a bien fait rire.

STANDARDS: 1.2

Première étape

Agreeing and disagreeing

Tu as raison.	You're right.
Tu l'as dit!	You said it!
Tout à fait!	Absolutely!
Tu parles!	No way!
Tu te fiches de moi?	Are you kidding me?
Tu rigoles!	You're joking!
Tu as tort.	You're wrong.

Expressing indifference

Je m'en fiche.	I don't give a darn.
Peu importe.	It doesn't matter.
ne... aucun(e)	no . . .
ne... ni... ni...	neither . . . nor . . .
ne... nulle part	nowhere
ne... que	only
ne... personne	no one
ne... rien	nothing

Television programming

un dessin animé	a cartoon
un documentaire	a documentary
une émission de variétés	a variety show
un feuilleton	a soap opera
les informations (f.)	the news
un jeu télévisé	a game show
un magazine télévisé	a magazine show
la météo	the weather report
une publicité	a commercial
un reportage sportif	a sportscast
une série	a series
un vidéoclip	a music video

The television

une cassette vidéo	a videocassette
une chaîne	a channel
l'écran (m.)	the screen
l'image (f.)	the picture
un magnétoscope	a videocassette recorder
un programme télé	a TV guide/listing
le son	the sound
la télécommande	the remote
le téléviseur	the television set

Making requests

Chut!	Shhh!
Tais-toi!	Be quiet!
Ne parle pas si fort.	Don't speak so loudly.
Tu pourrais faire moins de bruit?	Could you make less noise?
Vous pourriez vous taire, s'il vous plaît?	Could you please be quiet?
Baisse/Monte le son.	Turn down/ up the volume.

Deuxième étape

Asking for and making judgments

C'était comment?	How was it?
Comment tu as trouvé ça?	How did you like it?
Ça m'a beaucoup plu.	I liked it a lot.
J'ai trouvé ça amusant/pas mal.	It was funny/not bad.
Il y avait de...	There were . . .
Je ne me suis pas ennuyé(e) une seconde.	I wasn't bored a second.
Ça m'a bien fait rire.	It really made me laugh.
C'est nul/lourd.	It's no good/dull.
C'est un navet.	It's trash.
Ça n'a aucun intérêt.	It's not interesting at all.
Je n'ai pas du tout aimé.	I didn't like it at all.
Ça ne m'a pas emballé(e).	It didn't do anything for me.
Je me suis ennuyé(e) à mourir.	I was bored to death.

Asking for and making recommendations

Qu'est-ce que tu as vu comme bon film?	What good movies have you seen?
Qu'est-ce qu'il y a comme bons films en ce moment?	What good movies are out now?
Tu devrais aller voir...	You should go see . . .
Je te recommande...	I recommend . . .
Va voir... , c'est génial comme film.	Go see . . . , it's a great movie.
C'est à ne pas manquer!	Don't miss it!
N'y va pas!	Don't go!
Ne va surtout pas voir...	Really, don't go see . . .
Evite d'aller voir...	Avoid seeing . . .
Ça ne vaut pas le coup!	It's not worth it!

Types of movies

une comédie	a comedy
une comédie musicale	a musical
un drame	a drama
un film d'espionnage	a spy film
de guerre	a war movie
étranger	a foreign film
historique	a historical movie

Asking about and summarizing a story

De quoi ça parle?	What's it about?
Comment est-ce que ça commence?	How does it start?
Comment ça se termine?	How does it end?
Ça parle de...	It's about . . .
C'est l'histoire de...	It's the story of . . .
Il s'agit de...	It's about . . .
Ça se passe...	It takes place . . .
Au début,...	At the beginning, . . .
A ce moment-là,	At that point, . . .
A la fin, ...	At the end, . . .

Review and Assess

♞ Game

Vedettes! To practice vocabulary for TV programs and movie genres, write the names of popular television and movie stars on large cards and tape one on each student's back so that he or she cannot see it. Have students circulate, asking other students yes-no questions to try to determine their identity. **(Je suis une femme? Je suis actrice de télévision? J'ai fait de la publicité? Est-ce que je joue dans des drames?)** When students have correctly guessed their identity, they should write their celebrity's name on the board.

CHAPITRE 9

 Circumlocution
Have students work in pairs. One student is an exchange student in France, and the other is a member of the host family. The two of them are discussing the types of television programs they like and dislike. The host asks what types of programs the guest likes. The guest can't remember the exact terms for the types of programs, so he or she must describe them, while the host tries to guess what they are. (—**Quel genre d'émissions tu préfères? —Euh, j'aime les émissions avec des personnes qui essaient de gagner de l'argent. —Ah bon, tu aimes les jeux télévisés?**) Have students switch roles.

Chapter 9 Assessment

▸ **Testing Program**
Chapter Test, pp. 199–204
🔊 Audio Compact Discs, CD 9, Trs. 15–17
Speaking Test, p. 299

▸ **Alternative Assessment Guide**
Portfolio Assessment, p. 24
Performance Assessment, p. 38
CD-ROM Assessment, p. 52

▸ **Interactive CD-ROM Tutor, Disc 3**
 A toi de parler
A toi d'écrire

▸ **Standardized Assessment Tutor**
Chapter 9

▸ **One-Stop Planner, Disc 3**
🖱 Test Generator
Chapter 9

Chapitre 10 : Rencontres au soleil
Chapter Overview

Mise en train pp. 282–284	*La plongée, quelle aventure!*			

	FUNCTIONS	**GRAMMAR**	**VOCABULARY**	**RE-ENTRY**
Première étape pp. 285–291	• Bragging, p. 287 • Flattering, p. 287 • Teasing, p. 290	• The superlative, p. 288	• Sea life, p. 286	• Forms of the comparative (**Chapitre 8**, III) • Adjective agreement (**Chapitre 1**, II)

Remise en train pp. 292–293	*Des nouvelles de Guadeloupe*			

Deuxième étape pp. 294–297	• Breaking some news, p. 295 • Showing interest, p. 295 • Expressing disbelief, p. 295 • Telling a joke, p. 297	• The past perfect, p. 295	• Everyday life, p. 294	• Reciprocal verbs (**Chapitre 6**, III) • Breaking some news (**Chapitre 9**, II)

Lisons! pp. 298–300	**O'gaya**	**Reading Strategy** Understanding literary devices

Ecrivons! p. 301	**Une transformation incroyable!**	**Writing Strategy** Using an appropriate style

Grammaire supplémentaire	**pp. 302–305**	**Première étape,** pp. 302–303	**Deuxième étape,** pp. 304–305

Review pp. 306–309	**Mise en pratique,** pp. 306–307	**Que sais-je?,** p. 308	**Vocabulaire,** p. 309

CULTURE

- **Note culturelle,** Climate and natural assets of Guadeloupe, p. 284
- **Rencontre culturelle,** Overview of Guadeloupe, p. 285
- **Panorama Culturel,** Typical school days, p. 291
- **Note culturelle,** Greetings in Guadeloupe, p. 293

Chapitre 10 : Rencontres au soleil
Chapter Resources

 **PRINT**

Lesson Planning

 One-Stop Planner

Lesson Planner with Substitute Teacher Lesson Plans, pp. 47–51, 73

Student Make-Up Assignments
- Make-Up Assignment Copying Masters, Chapter 10

Listening and Speaking

Listening Activities
- Student Response Forms for Listening Activities, pp. 75–77
- Additional Listening Activities 10-1 to 10-6, pp. 79–81
- Additional Listening Activities (song), p. 82
- Scripts and Answers, pp. 147–152

Video Guide
- Teaching Suggestions, pp. 62–63
- Activity Masters, pp. 64–66
- Scripts and Answers, pp. 104–107, 115–116

Activities for Communication
- Communicative Activities, pp. 37–40
- Realia and Teaching Suggestions, pp. 78–80
- Situation Cards, pp. 107–108

Reading and Writing

Reading Strategies and Skills Handbook, Chapter 10

Joie de lire 3, Chapter 10

Cahier d'activités, pp. 109–120

Grammar

Travaux pratiques de grammaire, pp. 89–95

Grammar Tutor for Students of French, Chapter 10

Assessment

Testing Program
- Grammar and Vocabulary Quizzes, **Etape** Quizzes, and Chapter Test, pp. 213–226
- Score Sheet, Scripts and Answers, pp. 227–233

Alternative Assessment Guide
- Portfolio Assessment, p. 25
- Performance Assessment, p. 39
- CD-ROM Assessment, p. 53

Student Make-Up Assignments
- Alternative Quizzes, Chapter 10

Standardized Assessment Tutor
- Reading, pp. 39–41
- Writing, p. 42
- Math, pp. 51–52

 **MEDIA**

 Online Activities
- Jeux interactifs
- Activités Internet

Video Program
- Videocassette 4
- Videocassette 5 (captioned version)

 Audio Compact Discs
- Textbook Listening Activities, CD 10, Tracks 1–13
- Additional Listening Activities, CD 10, Tracks 19–25
- Assessment Items, CD 10, Tracks 14–18

 Interactive CD-ROM Tutor, Disc 3

 Teaching Transparencies
- Situation 10-1 to 10-2
- **Grammaire supplémentaire** Answers
- **Travaux pratiques de grammaire** Answers

  One-Stop Planner CD-ROM

Use the **One-Stop Planner CD-ROM with Test Generator** to aid in lesson planning and pacing.

For each chapter, the **One-Stop Planner** includes:
- Editable lesson plans with direct links to teaching resources
- Printable worksheets from resource books
- Direct launches to the HRW Internet activities
- Video and audio segments
- Test Generator
- Clip Art for vocabulary items

Chapitre 10 : Rencontres au soleil

Projects

Venez à l'aquarium

Students will create a brochure for a new aquarium that will be opening in Pointe-à-Pitre. The brochure should include illustrations of and information about the marine life on display.

> **MATERIALS**
>
> ✂ **Students may need**
> - Construction paper
> - Scissors
> - Colored markers
> - Old magazines and catalogues
> - Tape or glue
> - Stapler and staples
> - Encyclopedias
> - French-English dictionaries

SUGGESTED SEQUENCE

1. Students should list the types of marine life they will feature in their brochure. They might look up additional marine life in the dictionary. Then, have them look up the marine life they've chosen in an encyclopedia and take notes.

2. Have students draw or cut out pictures of some of the marine life they will include in their aquarium.

3. Students should create the slogans they want to use to promote their aquarium. Remind them that they should make sensational claims. They might use the superlative to brag about the size of the aquarium, the variety of marine life on display, the low cost, or the location.

4. Have students plan the layout of their brochures. They should design an attractive cover to catch tourists' attention and make sure that the pages that follow are colorful and interesting.

5. Have students copy the text of their brochures onto construction paper, tape or glue the illustrations in the appropriate places, and staple the pages of the brochures together.

> **GRADING THE PROJECT**
>
> Suggested Point Distribution (total = 100 points)
> - Content...30 points
> - Language use...30 points
> - Creativity..20 points
> - Design..20 points

Games

On a fini!

In this fast-paced game, students will practice the chapter vocabulary.

Procedure To prepare for the game, write expressions from the chapter vocabulary list on separate index cards, omitting one word from the expression. (**Tu es ____ ou quoi?**) You will need one card for each student in the class. Then, form three teams and have them sit in rows. Put a card for each team member in a team bag. Give each team's bag to the first team member. Then, call out **Allez-y!** to begin the game. The first player on each team selects a card, writes the missing word on a sheet of paper, keeps the card, and passes the bag to the player behind him or her, who does the same. Players may not pass the bag until they have finished writing their word and have put their pen down. When the last player in the row has finished, he or she calls out **On a fini!** Then, have the players on the team that finished first read aloud their completed expressions. If all are correct, that team wins. You might shuffle and redistribute the cards and play a second round.

Jeu de rythme

In this game, students will practice the chapter functions.

Procedure To play the game, have students sit in a circle. All players should slap both thighs twice, clap their hands twice, and snap their fingers twice. They must keep up this rhythm during the game. Questions and answers must be given when players snap their fingers. To begin the game, players start the rhythm. During the finger snaps, ask a question or make a statement that requires a response. (**Je ne t'ai pas dit?**) During the next finger snaps, call out a student's name (Bob). That student must give an appropriate response during the following snaps. (**Non, raconte!**) Then, during the next snaps, that student names another student (Julie), who must ask a question or make a statement during the following snaps. A student who fails to give a correct question, statement, or response during the snaps is out.

Sample questions/statements and responses:

1. Réveille-toi un peu!/Lâche-moi, tu veux?

2. Alors, là, tu m'épates!/Oh, j'en ai vu d'autres.

3. Marie a embouti sa voiture./Qui t'a dit ça?

4. Je me suis fiancé(e)./Je n'en reviens pas!

5. Arrête de délirer!/Qu'est-ce que tu en sais?

Storytelling

Mini-histoire

This story accompanies Teaching Transparency 10-1. The **mini-histoire** *can be told and retold in different formats, acted out, written as dictation, and read aloud to give students additional opportunities to practice all four skills. In the following story, Valérie talks about her vacation in Guadeloupe.*

Cet été, je suis allée en vacances à la Guadeloupe. Pendant mes vacances, j'ai fait plein de trucs géniaux. D'abord, à la Guadeloupe, il fait toujours beau et chaud. Un jour, je suis allée faire de la plongée sous-marine. C'était génial! J'ai vu plein de poissons de toutes les couleurs. J'ai même vu une tortue de mer. Elle était très gentille. J'ai pu la caresser. Il y avait aussi des requins dans la mer. J'ai même vu une énorme méduse et une pieuvre. J'ai aussi participé à un concours de châteaux de sable. Mon château était aussi grand que moi. Et devinez quoi? J'ai gagné le premier prix.

Traditions

La Pêche à la Guadeloupe

Fishing is one of Guadaloupe's most time-honored industries. Although coast fishing in modern boats exists, the majority of fishermen continue to use traditional methods, catching several kinds of fish, crustaceans, and mollusks from small, colorful boats called **saintoises.** All year round they bring their catch to market, providing a mainstay to the island's port economies. Several towns regularly hold **fêtes des marins** and **fêtes du poisson et de la mer** to celebrate their fishermen and the bounty of the sea. The festivals include parades, processions, and dances; however, the most important events are the Mass for the fishermen and the blessing of the sea. Have students research the fishing industry in a region of the United States, such as southern Louisiana, and compare its methods and customs to those of Guadaloupe.

Recette

Creole cuisine is a blend of traditional French, African, and Indian cooking styles. In addition to this rich heritage, creole dishes utilize ingredients native to the Caribbean region.

GATEAU CREOLE

pour 6 à 8 personnes

Garniture

5–6 bananes

1/2 tasse de sucre roux

1/2 tasse de noix de coco râpée

1 cuillère à café de cannelle

1 pincée de sel

1 cuillère à café d'extrait de vanille

le jus d'un citron

1/2 tasse de compote de pomme

Pâte brisée

2 tasses de farine

1/2 tasse de sucre

1/2 tasse de beurre

1 œuf

Pâte brisée

Faire fondre le beurre. Placer la farine dans un grand bol. Faire un puits. Y mettre le sucre et l'œuf. Commencer à mélanger doucement. Ajouter le beurre petit à petit. Faire une boule. Si la boule est trop beurrée, ajouter un peu de farine. Etaler la pâte dans un moule.

Cuire au four pendant 20 minutes.

Garniture

Mélanger tous les ingrédients sauf les bananes. Etaler la pâte obtenue dans le moule sur la pâte brisée. Eplucher les bananes et les couper en rondelles. Disposer celles-ci dans le moule. Faire cuire au four à 400° F pendant 30 minutes.

Technology

Video Program

Videocassette 4, Videocassette 5 (captioned version)
See Video Guide, pp. 61–66.

Camille et compagnie • Dixième épisode : *C'est pas la mer à boire!*

Camille and Max are meeting their new friend, Azzedine, at the aquarium in Marseilles to look at the animal life there. While waiting for Azzedine, Max tells Camille about an old friend, but Camille is distracted. She tells Max that she will be going to Louisiana soon on an exchange program. Max keeps telling corny jokes and Azzedine proudly recounts his diving experience.

Tu peux décrire une de tes journées typiques?

People from around the francophone world talk about their daily routines. Two native speakers discuss the **Panorama Culturel** question and introduce the interviews.

Vidéoclips

- **Sirop Sport**®: advertisement for fruit syrup
- **Music video: Quand le jour se lève** performed by Daniel Bélanger
- **News report:** average time spent in cars

Interactive CD-ROM Tutor

The **Interactive CD-ROM Tutor** contains videos, interactive games, and activities that provide students an opportunity to practice and review the material covered in Chapter 10.

Activity	Activity Type	Pupil's Edition Page
1. Vocabulaire	Chasse au trésor Explorons! Vérifions!	p. 286
2. Grammaire	Méli-mélo	p. 288
3. Comment dit-on… ?	Le bon choix	pp. 287, 290
4. Vocabulaire	Jeu des paires	p. 294
5. Comment dit-on… ?	Prenons note!	p. 295
6. Grammaire	Les mots qui manquent	p. 295
Panorama Culturel	Tu peux décrire une de tes journées typiques? Le bon choix	p. 291
A toi de parler	*Guided recording*	pp. 306–307
A toi d'écrire	*Guided writing*	pp. 306–307

Teacher Management System

Logging In

Logging in to the *Allez, viens!* TMS is easy. Upon launching the program, simply type "admin" in the password area of the log-in screen and press RETURN. Log on to **www.hrw.com/CDROMTUTOR** for a detailed explanation of the Teacher Management System.

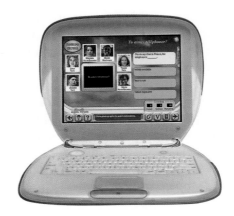

One-Stop Planner CD-ROM

To preview all resources available for this chapter, use the **One-Stop Planner CD-ROM**, Disc 3.

Internet Connection

internet

ADRESSE: go.hrw.com
MOT-CLE: WA3
FRANCOPHONE
AMERICA-10

*Have students explore the **go.hrw.com** Web site for many online resources covering all chapters. All Chapter 10 resources are available under the keyword **WA3 FRANCOPHONE AMERICA-10.** Interactive games help students practice the material and provide them with immediate feedback. You'll also find Internet activities that lead to a printable worksheet that provides a comprehensive online research project.*

Jeux interactifs

You can use the interactive activities in this chapter

- to practice grammar, vocabulary, and chapter functions
- as homework
- as an assessment option
- as a self-test
- to prepare for the Chapter Test

Activités Internet

Students look for information about scuba diving and aquatic life, using the vocabulary and phrases from the chapter.

- In preparation for the **Activités Internet**, have students review the dramatic episode on Video-cassette 4, or do the activities in the **Panorama Culturel** on page 291. After completing the activity sheet, have students work with a partner and share the information they gathered in Activities B and C. Then ask each pair of students to share what they learned with the class.

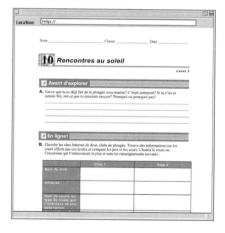

Projet

Have each group of students further research one of the aquatic creatures they learned about in Activity C. Students can create a brief presentation about the creature, including its habitat, what it eats, and other information about it. Encourage them to include pictures in their presentations. Remind students to document their sources by noting the names and the URLs of all the sites they consulted.

Chapitre 10 : Rencontres au soleil
Textbook Listening Activities Scripts

Première étape

8 **p. 286**
Answers to Activity 8
1. h   2. d   3. a   4. c   5. e   6. b   7. f   8. g

1. Eh bien, vous voyez, ça, c'est le requin qu'on a vu. J'avais vraiment peur, moi!

2. Voilà mon château de sable. Vous voyez, il est entouré de crabes!

3. Ça, c'est la pieuvre qu'on a vue. Mais elle est partie très vite parce qu'on lui a fait peur.

4. Ça, c'est un récif de corail. C'est vraiment quelque chose d'extraordinaire!

5. Ici, ce sont tout simplement des rochers. Vous voyez le nombre d'algues qu'il y a dessus?

6. Regardez comme elles sont mignonnes, les tortues!

7. Regardez le nombre de coquillages qu'on peut trouver sur la plage. Mais il faut faire attention : vous voyez, il y a aussi des méduses.

8. Et là, je cherchais des étoiles de mer et j'ai vu des hippocampes.

11 **p. 288**
Answers to Activity 11
1. garçon   2. fille   3. fille   4. garçon   5. garçon   6. fille

1. GARÇON C'est pas pour me vanter, mais moi, j'ai escaladé un volcan.
FILLE Ah ouais? C'était dangereux?
GARÇON Oh, j'en ai vu d'autres.
FILLE Tu en as, du courage.

2. GARÇON Oh, ça m'énerve, l'algèbre. C'est trop difficile.
FILLE Mais non, c'est fastoche!
GARÇON Vraiment, tu trouves pas ça difficile?
FILLE Non, pas du tout.
GARÇON Ouah! Tu es calée.

3. GARÇON Alors, tu as gagné?
FILLE Bien sûr! Oh, tu sais bien que c'est moi qui nage le mieux. Les autres pouvaient aller se rhabiller.
GARÇON Oui, c'est vrai. Tu es vraiment la meilleure.

4. FILLE C'est pas vrai! Tu n'as pas piloté l'avion toi-même!
GARÇON Mais si. C'était la première fois. Et, c'est pas pour me vanter, mais on m'a dit que je me suis très bien débrouillé.
FILLE Tu es vraiment le garçon le plus doué que je connaisse.

5. FILLE Pas possible! Tu as gagné le concours?
GARÇON Ben oui. C'est moi le meilleur, tu sais bien.
FILLE Tu es fortiche quand même.

6. GARÇON Tu es descendue jusqu'à quelle profondeur?
FILLE Jusqu'à vingt mètres.
GARÇON Tu n'as pas eu peur des requins?
FILLE Ben non. J'en ai vu d'autres, tu sais.
GARÇON Alors là, tu m'épates!

17 **p. 290**
Answers to Activity 17
1, 3, 4, 7, 8

1. ANGÈLE Il est super sympa, non?
BRIGITTE Il essaie de t'impressionner, c'est tout.
ANGÈLE Moi, je crois qu'il est sincère.

BRIGITTE Réveille-toi un peu!
ANGÈLE Oh, ça va, hein?

2. BRIGITTE Il y a un nouveau film que je voudrais voir. Ça te dit d'aller le voir avec moi?
ANGÈLE Quand ça?
BRIGITTE Samedi soir.
ANGÈLE Bon. Où est-ce qu'on se retrouve?

3. BRIGITTE Oh! Attention! Tu vas tomber...
ANGÈLE Oh!!! Ah, zut alors! Je suis toute mouillée maintenant!
BRIGITTE Ben, t'en rates pas une, toi!
ANGÈLE Ecoute, ça peut arriver à tout le monde.

4. BRIGITTE Tu as vu? Je suis arrivée la première. C'est moi, la meilleure!
ANGÈLE C'est ça, tu es la meilleure.
BRIGITTE Ben quoi, c'est vrai!
ANGÈLE Non mais, tu t'es pas regardée!

5. ANGÈLE Brigitte, dépêche-toi!
BRIGITTE Mais on a largement le temps.
ANGÈLE Oui, mais moi, je veux arriver en avance. Comme ça, on pourra trouver de bonnes places.
BRIGITTE D'accord.

6. BRIGITTE Ça t'a plu, ce film?
ANGÈLE Bof, ça ne m'a pas emballée. C'était un peu bizarre, à mon avis.
BRIGITTE Oui, je suis tout à fait de ton avis. Je n'ai pas très bien compris, et puis, c'était ennuyeux à mourir!

7. BRIGITTE Dis, Angèle! On va être en retard! Mais qu'est-ce que tu fabriquais?
ANGÈLE Euh, je voulais juste lui parler une minute.
BRIGITTE Et l'interro dans tout ça?
ANGÈLE Mais il était mignon.
BRIGITTE Non mais, t'es amoureuse ou quoi?
ANGÈLE Lâche-moi, tu veux?

8. ANGÈLE Dis donc, Brigitte, qu'est-ce que tu regardes?
BRIGITTE Rien.
ANGÈLE Hmm. C'est pas Vincent par hasard?
BRIGITTE Euh... peut-être. Il est mignon, non?
ANGÈLE Oui, mais il a vingt-deux ans.
BRIGITTE Oui, je sais, mais...
ANGÈLE Oh, arrête de délirer!
BRIGITTE Et toi, arrête de m'embêter!

Deuxième étape

26 **p. 294**
Answer to Activity 26
1. Lucien   2. Mireille   3. Luc   4. Julien et Bruno   5. Thérèse

1. —Oh là là. Ça a été une vraie catastrophe.
—Qu'est-ce qui s'est passé?
—Le jour où il a eu son permis, il a emmené des copains à la plage dans la voiture de son père. Et devine ce qui est arrivé.
—Je ne sais pas, moi. Raconte!
—Eh ben, il a embouti la voiture de son père en revenant.
—Oh, quelle angoisse!

The following scripts are for the Listening Activities found in the *Pupil's Edition*. For Student Response Forms, see *Listening Activities*, pages 75–77. To provide students with additional listening practice, see *Listening Activities*, pages 79–82.

One-Stop Planner CD-ROM

To preview all resources available for this chapter, use the **One-Stop Planner CD-ROM**, Disc 3.

2. —Et elle? Qu'est-ce qu'elle devient? Toujours aussi sportive?
—Ben, tu es pas au courant?
—Non, au courant de quoi?
—Elle a fait une mauvaise chute de cheval.
—Ah bon? C'est grave?
—Ben, elle s'est fait mal au dos et le médecin lui a dit de ne pas faire de sport pendant au moins deux mois.
—Oh, c'est bête, ça!

3. —Alors, là, tu vas pas me croire.
—Raconte.
—Eh ben, l'autre jour, j'ai rencontré sa sœur et tu sais ce qu'elle m'a dit?
—Non, quoi?
—Il a rencontré une fille, il est tombé amoureux d'elle et il s'est fiancé avec elle.
—Pas possible!

4. —C'est arrivé à la boum de Frédéric. Je ne sais pas exactement comment ça a commencé, mais ils se sont bagarrés.
—Oh, ces deux-là, vraiment ils exagèrent! Toujours prêts à se faire remarquer.
—Ouais. Et puis, c'était pas très sympa pour Frédéric. Le pauvre, ça a complètement cassé l'ambiance à sa fête.

5. —Elle est super contente. Figure-toi qu'à sa dernière visite chez l'orthodontiste, il lui a dit qu'elle n'avait plus besoin de ses bagues et il les lui a enlevées.
—Génial! Remarque, ça faisait longtemps qu'elle les avait.
—Oui, au moins deux ans.

28 **p. 295**

Answers to Activity 28
1, 3, 6, 7

1. —Dis donc, Emilie, tu savais que M. Souchet allait déménager?
—Ah oui? Qui t'a dit ça?
—Michel. Il a entendu dire qu'il avait accepté un poste à Paris.
—Alors, qui va être notre professeur de maths?
—Aucune idée.

2. —Oh, Sylvie, je suis vraiment désolée de ne pas t'avoir téléphoné.
—Tu sais, je me demandais où tu étais passée.
—Ben, j'ai été privée de sortie et de téléphone. Je ne pouvais pas t'appeler.
—Bon, il n'y a pas de mal.

3. —Dis, Julien, tu connais la dernière?
—Non, quoi?
—J'ai entendu dire que Lisette allait rompre avec son petit ami.
—Oh là là!
—Ce n'est pas tout. Figure-toi qu'elle a dit à Sophie qu'elle voulait sortir avec toi.
—Qui t'a dit ça?
—Leïla.

4. —Oh! J'en ai marre de ce cours!
—Qu'est-ce qui est arrivé? Pourquoi?
—J'ai raté un autre examen. Ma moyenne va être nulle.
—Ne t'en fais pas trop, mais tu sais bien qu'il faut que tu passes plus de temps à étudier.
—Oui, mais...
—Tu devrais parler au prof. Peut-être qu'il te permettra de repasser l'examen.

5. —Dis, Than, je vais voir Céline Dion en concert vendredi soir. Ça t'intéresse d'y aller?
—Peut-être. Je dois demander la permission à mes parents. Je te téléphonerai pour te dire si c'est d'accord ou pas.
—O.K.

6. —Regarde! Voilà Daniel. C'est génial ce qui lui est arrivé!
—Euh, quoi?
—Je ne t'ai pas dit?
—Non. Raconte!
—Ben, l'équipe de l'université l'a accepté.
—Je n'en reviens pas.
—C'est pas tout.
—Quoi?
—Comme il va jouer pour l'université, il va avoir une bourse.

7. —Tu connais la dernière?
—Non.
—Ben, Isabelle est allée au concert de Patrick Bruel.
—Et alors?
—J'ai entendu dire qu'elle l'a rencontré.
—Ça m'étonnerait.
—Si! Et il paraît même qu'il veut sortir avec elle.
—N'importe quoi!

34 **p. 297**

Answers to Activity 34
1. début   3. milieu   5. début   7. début
2. fin   4. fin   6. milieu

1. —Est-ce que tu connais l'histoire de l'homme qui a acheté un poisson pour l'anniversaire de sa femme?
—Non, raconte!

2. —Pour arriver de l'autre côté!
—Elle est nulle, ta blague!

3. —... et alors il dit au policier qu'il n'en sait rien.
—Et puis?

4. —Et le fils dit qu'il ne peut plus mettre sa chaussure.
—Elle est bien bonne! Tu en as une autre?

5. —Quel est le point commun entre un éléphant et une fourmi?
—Je ne sais pas. C'est quoi?

6. —... et l'autre lui répond «J'en ai marre de tes bêtises!»
—Et alors?

7. —Quelle est la différence entre un prof de français et un prof d'espagnol?
—Euh, je ne sais pas. Dis-moi.

For the listening scripts of the **Mise en pratique**, see *Listening Activities*, page 149.

Chapitre 10 : Rencontres au soleil
Suggested Lesson Plans 50-Minute Schedule

Day 1

CHAPTER OPENER 10 min.
- Present Chapter Objectives, p. 281.
- Career Path, ATE, p. 281
- Marine Biology Link, Geography Link, and Culture Note, ATE, pp. 280–281

MISE EN TRAIN 35 min.
- Presenting **Mise en train**, ATE, p. 282
- Physics Link and Culture Note, ATE, p. 283
- Do Activities 1–5, p. 284.
- Read and discuss **Note culturelle**, p. 284

Wrap-Up 5 min.
- Do Activity 6, p. 284.

Homework Options
Cahier d'activités, Act. 1, p. 109

Day 2

MISE EN TRAIN
Quick Review 5 min.
- Check homework.

RENCONTRE CULTURELLE 15 min.
- Presenting **Rencontre culturelle**, ATE, p. 285
- **Qu'en penses-tu?**, p. 285
- Read and discuss **Savais-tu que… ?**, p. 285.
- Culture Notes and Literature Link, ATE, p. 285
- Thinking Critically: Comparing and Contrasting, ATE, p. 285

PREMIERE ETAPE
Vocabulaire, p. 286 25 min.
- Presenting **Vocabulaire**, ATE, p. 286
- Do Activity 7, p. 286.
- Play Audio CD for Activity 8, p. 286.
- Cahier d'activités, p. 110, Acts. 2–3
- Do Activity 9, p. 287.

Wrap-Up, 5 min.
- Do Activity 10, p. 287.

Homework Options
Travaux pratiques de grammaire, Acts. 1–2, p. 89

Day 3

PREMIERE ETAPE
Quick Review 5 min.
- Check homework.

Comment dit-on… ?, p. 287 15 min.
- Presenting **Comment dit-on… ?**, ATE, p. 287
- Play Audio CD for Activity 11, p. 288.
- Cahier d'activités, p. 111, Acts. 4–5
- Do Activity 12, p. 288.

Grammaire, p. 288 25 min.
- Presenting **Grammaire**, ATE, p. 288
- Do Activity 13, p. 289.
- Travaux pratiques de grammaire, pp. 91–92, Acts. 5–7
- **Grammaire supplémentaire**, pp. 302–303, Acts. 1–4
- Do Activity 14, p. 289.
- Have students do Activity 16, p. 289, in pairs.

Wrap-Up 5 min.
- Game: **C'est nous, les meilleurs!**, ATE, p. 288

Homework Options
Cahier d'activités, Acts. 6–7, pp. 111–112

Day 4

PREMIERE ETAPE
Quick Review 5 min.
- Check homework.

Comment dit-on… ?, p. 290 20 min.
- Presenting **Comment dit-on… ?**, ATE, p. 290
- Play Audio CD for Activity 17, p. 290.
- Do Activity 18, p. 290.
- Cahier d'activités, p. 113, Acts. 9–10
- Challenge, ATE, p. 290

PANORAMA CULTUREL 20 min.
- Presenting **Panorama Culturel**, ATE, p. 291
- See Teaching Suggestions, Viewing Suggestion 1, Video Guide, p. 63.
- Questions, ATE, p. 291
- Discuss **Qu'en penses-tu?**, p. 291.

Wrap-Up 5 min.
- Thinking Critically: Analyzing, ATE, p. 291

Homework Options
Study for Quiz 10-1
Pupil's Edition, Activity 19, p. 290

Day 5

PREMIERE ETAPE
Quiz 10-1 20 min.
- Administer Quiz 10-1A or 10-1B.

REMISE EN TRAIN 25 min.
- Presenting **Remise en train**, ATE, p. 292
- Do Activities 20–22, p. 292.
- Read and discuss **Note culturelle**, p. 293.
- Do Activities 23–24, p. 293.
- Language-to-Language, ATE, p. 293

Wrap-Up 5 min.
- Do Activity 25, p. 293.

Homework Options
Cahier d'activités, Act. 11, p. 114

Day 6

REMISE EN TRAIN
Quick Review 5 min.
- Check homework.

DEUXIEME ETAPE
Vocabulaire, p. 294 20 min.
- Presenting **Vocabulaire**, ATE, p. 294
- Play Audio CD for Activity 26, p. 294.
- Cahier d'activités, p. 115, Acts. 12–13
- Do Activity 27, p. 294.
- See Vocabulary Practice Using Teaching Transparency 10-2, Speaking Suggestion #2, Teaching Transparencies.

Comment dit-on… ?, p. 295 20 min.
- Presenting **Comment dit-on… ?**, p. 295
- Play Audio CD for Activity 28, p. 295.
- Cahier d'activités, p. 116, Act. 14
- Do Activity 29, p. 295.

Wrap-Up 5 min.
- Additional Practice, ATE, p. 295

Homework Options
Travaux pratiques de grammaire, Acts. 8–9, p. 93

One-Stop Planner CD-ROM

For alternative lesson plans by chapter section, to create your own customized plans, or to preview all resources available for this chapter, use the **One-Stop Planner CD-ROM**, Disc 3.

 For additional homework suggestions, see activities accompanied by this symbol throughout the chapter.

Day 7

DEUXIEME ETAPE
Quick Review 5 min.
- Check homework.

Grammaire, p. 295 25 min.
- Presenting **Grammaire**, ATE, p. 295
- **Grammaire supplémentaire**, pp. 304–305, Acts. 5–6
- Do Activities 30–31, p. 296.
- Cahier d'activités, p. 117, Acts. 16–17
- Have students do Activity 33, p. 296, in pairs.

Comment dit-on... ?, p. 297 15 min.
- Presenting **Comment dit-on... ?**, p. 297
- Play Audio CD for Activity 34, p. 297.
- Read and discuss **A la française**, p. 297.
- Cahier d'activités, p. 118, Act. 19
- Do Activity 35, p. 297.
- Do Activity 36, p. 297, in groups.

Wrap-Up 5 min.
- Teacher Note, ATE, p. 297

Homework Options
Study for Quiz 10-2.
Pupil's Edition, Activity 32, p. 296
Travaux pratiques de grammaire, Acts. 10–12, pp. 94–95

Day 8

DEUXIEME ETAPE
Quiz 10-2 20 min.
- Administer Quiz 10-2A or 10-2B.

LISONS! 25 min.
- Read and discuss **Stratégie pour lire**, p. 298.
- Do Prereading Activity A, p. 298 and Teaching Suggestion, ATE, p. 298.
- Language Arts Link, ATE, p. 298
- Have students read **Lisons!**, pp. 298–300.
- Do Reading Activities B–R, pp. 298–300.

Wrap-Up 5 min.
- Challenge, ATE, p. 299

Homework Options
Cahier d'activités, Act. 20, p. 119

Day 9

LISONS!
Quick Review 5 min.
- Check homework.

LISONS! 10 min.
- Do Postreading Activities S–T, p. 300.

ECRIVONS! 30 min.
- Read and discuss the **Stratégie pour écrire**, p. 301, then have students work on their articles.

Wrap-Up 5 min.
- Allow time for peer and self-evaluation of articles.

Homework Options
Complete final draft of articles.

Day 10

ECRIVONS!
Quick Review 10 min.
- Have volunteers share their articles with the class.

MISE EN PRATIQUE 35 min.
- Play Audio CD for Activity 1, p. 306.
- Do Activity 2, p. 306.
- Slower Pace and Language Note, ATE, p. 306
- Have students do Activity 4, p. 307, in pairs.
- **A toi de parler**, CD-ROM Tutor

Wrap-Up 5 min.
- Activities for Communication, p. 108, Situation (global): Role-Play

Homework Options
Cahier d'activités, Acts. 21–22, p. 120

Day 11

MISE EN PRATIQUE
Quick Review 5 min.
- Check homework.

Student Review 40 min.
- Have students prepare scripts for **Jeu de rôle**, p. 307.
- Have pairs present scenes for **Jeu de rôle.**
- Game: Tic Tac Toe, ATE, p. 308
- **A toi d'écrire**, CD-ROM Tutor, Disc 3

Wrap-Up 5 min.
- Begin **Que sais-je?**, p. 308.

Homework Options
Que sais-je?, p. 308
Pupil's Edition, Activity 3, p. 307

Day 12

MISE EN PRATIQUE
Quick Review 15 min.
- Go over **Que sais-je?**, p. 308.
- Collect homework.

Chapter Review 35 min.
- Review Chapter 10. Choose from **Grammaire supplémentaire**, Grammar Tutor for Students of French, Activities for Communication, Listening Activities, Interactive CD-ROM Tutor, or **Jeux interactifs.**

Homework Options
Study for Chapter 10 Test.

Assessment

Test, Chapter 10 50 min.
- Administer **Chapter 10 Test.** Select from Testing Program, Alternative Assessment Guide, Test Generator, or Standardized Assessment Tutor.

Chapitre 10 : Rencontres au soleil!
Suggested Lesson Plans 90-Minute Block Schedule

Block 1

CHAPTER OPENER 10 min.
- Present Chapter Objectives, p. 281.
- Geography Link, ATE, p. 280

MISE EN TRAIN 25 min.
- Pre-viewing suggestions, Video Guide, p. 62
- Show *Camille et compagnie: C'est pas la mer à boire!*, Video Program (Videocassette 3)
- Viewing suggestions, Video Guide, p. 62
- Viewing and Post-viewing activities, Video Guide, p. 64
- **Note culturelle**, p. 284

PREMIERE ETAPE
Vocabulaire, p. 286 25 min.
- Presenting **Vocabulaire**, ATE, p. 286
- Do Activity 7, p. 286.
- Play Audio CD for Activity 8, p. 286.
- Do Activity 9, p. 287.

Comment dit-on... ?, p. 287 25 min.
- Presenting **Comment dit-on... ?**, ATE, p. 287
- Play Audio CD for Activity 11, p. 288.
- Language Note and Additional Practice, ATE, p. 287

Wrap-Up 5 min.
- Teaching Transparency 10-1, using suggestion #1 from Vocabulary Practice Using Teaching Transparency 10-1

Homework Options
Pupil's Edition, Activity 10, p. 287
Cahier d'activités, pp. 110–111, Acts. 2–4
Travaux pratiques de grammaire, pp. 89–90, Acts. 1–4

Block 2

PREMIERE ETAPE
Quick Review 5 min.
- Listening Activities, p. 79, Additional Listening Activity 10-2

Comment dit-on... ?, p. 287 20 min.
- Do Activity 12, p. 288.

Grammaire, p. 288 30 min.
- Building on Previous Skills, ATE, p. 287
- Presenting **Grammaire**, ATE, p. 288
- Do Activities 13–15, p. 289.

RENCONTRE CULTURELLE 20 min.
- Presenting **Rencontre culturelle**, ATE, p. 285
- Discuss **Qu'en penses-tu?**, p. 285.
- Culture Notes, ATE, p. 285

Wrap-Up 15 min.
- Thinking Critically: Comparing and Contrasting, ATE, p. 285

Homework Options
Grammaire supplémentaire, pp. 302–303, Acts. 1–4
Cahier d'activités, pp. 11–112, Acts. 5–8
Travaux pratiques de grammaire, pp. 91–92, Acts. 5–7

Block 3

PREMIERE ETAPE
Quick Review 5 min.
- Listening Activities, p. 79, Additional Listening Activity 10-1

Grammaire, p. 288 30 min.
- Do Activity 16, p. 289.

Comment dit-on... ?, p. 290 25 min.
- Presenting **Comment dit-on... ?**, ATE, p. 290
- Play Audio CD for Activity 17, p. 290.
- Do Activity 18, p. 290.

REMISE EN TRAIN 20 min.
- Presenting **Remise en train**, ATE, p. 292
- Do Activities 20–24, pp. 292–293.
- **Note culturelle**, p. 293

Wrap-Up 10 min.
- Teaching Transparency 10-1, using suggestion #1 from Suggestions for Using Teaching Transparency 10-1

Homework Options
Have students study for Quiz 10-1.
Pupil's Edition, Activity 19, p. 290
Cahier d'activités, pp. 113–114, Acts. 9–11

One-Stop Planner CD-ROM

For alternative lesson plans by chapter section, to create your own customized plans, or to preview all resources available for this chapter, use the **One-Stop Planner CD-ROM**, Disc 3.

 For additional homework suggestions, see activities accompanied by this symbol throughout the chapter.

Block 4

PREMIERE ETAPE
Quick Review 10 min.
- Activities for Communication, pp. 37–38, Communicative Activity 10-1A and 10-2B

Quiz 10-1 20 min.
- Administer Quiz 10-1A or 10-1B.

DEUXIEME ETAPE
Vocabulaire, p. 294 25 min.
- Presenting **Vocabulaire**, ATE, p. 294
- Play Audio CD for Activity 26, p. 294.
- Do Activity 27, p. 294.

Comment dit-on... ?, p. 295 30 min.
- Presenting **Comment dit-on... ?**, ATE, p. 295
- Play Audio CD for Activity 28, p. 295.
- Do Activity 29, p. 295.

Wrap-Up 5 min.
- Challenge, ATE, p. 295

Homework Options
Cahier d'activités, pp. 115–116, Acts. 12–14
Travaux pratiques de grammaire, p. 93, Acts. 8–9

Block 5

DEUXIEME ETAPE
Quick Review 10 min.
- Activities for Communication, pp. 39–40, Communicative Activity 10-2A and 10-2B

Grammaire, p. 295 30 min.
- Presenting **Grammaire**, ATE, p. 295
- Additional Practice, ATE, p. 295
- Do Activities 30–31, p. 296.

Comment dit-on... ?, p. 297 20 min.
- Presenting **Comment dit-on... ?**, ATE, p. 297
- Play Audio CD for Activity 34, p. 297.
- Do Activity 35, p. 297.

LISONS! 25 min.
- Read **Stratégie pour lire**, p. 298.
- Prereading Activity A, p. 298 and Teaching Suggestion, ATE, p. 298
- Read the first page of *O'gaya*, as students read along in their books.
- Reading Activities B–D, p. 298

Wrap-Up 5 min.
- Teaching Suggestions, second suggestion, ATE, p. 298

Homework Options
Have students study for Quiz 10-2.
Grammaire supplémentaire, pp. 304–305, Acts. 5–7
Cahier d'activités, pp. 116–118, Acts. 15–19
Travaux pratiques de grammaire, pp. 94–95, Acts. 10–12

Block 6

DEUXIEME ETAPE
Quick Review 10 min.
- Listening Activities, p. 81, Additional Listening Activity 10-6

Quiz 10-2 20 min.
- Administer Quiz 10-2A or 10-2B.

LISONS! 30 min.
- Have students summarize what has happened so far in *O'gaya.*
- Read the second page of *O'gaya* aloud, as students read along in their books.
- Do Activities E–J, p. 299.
- Have students finish reading *O'gaya*, pp. 299–300.
- Do Activities N–P, pp. 299–300.

MISE EN PRATIQUE 30 min.
- Play Audio CD for Activity 1, p. 306.
- Do Activity 2, p. 306.
- Do Activity 4, p. 307.

Homework Options
Pupil's Edition, Activity 3, p. 307
Que sais-je?, p. 308
Study for Chapter 10 Test

Block 7

MISE EN PRATIQUE
Quick Review 10 min.
- **Jeu de rôle,** p. 307

Chapter Review 35 min.
- Review Chapter 10. Choose from **Grammaire supplémentaire,** Grammar Tutor for Students of French, Activities for Communication, Listening Activities, Interactive CD-ROM Tutor, or **Jeux interactifs.**

Test, Chapter 10 45 min.
- Administer Chapter 10 Test. Select from Testing Program, Alternative Assessment Guide, Test Generator or Standardized Assessment Tutor.

Chapter Opener

 One-Stop Planner CD-ROM

For resource information, see the **One-Stop Planner**, Disc 3.

 Pacing Tips
Chapter 10 presents rather complex grammar points to students. You may wish to practice these points, using all the resources provided in the *Cahier d'activités* and the *Travaux pratiques de grammaire*. For suggested Lesson Plans and timing suggestions, see pages 279I–279L.

Meeting the Standards

Communication
- Bragging; flattering, p. 287
- Teasing, p. 290
- Breaking some news; showing interest; expressing disbelief, p. 295
- Telling a joke, p. 297

Cultures
- Culture Notes, pp. 281, 283, 285
- Note culturelle, p. 284
- Note culturelle, p. 293
- Panorama Culturel, p. 291
- Rencontre culturelle, p. 285

Connections
- Marine Biology Links, pp. 280, 286
- Physics Link, p. 283
- Music Link, p. 285
- Literature Link, p. 285
- Community Link, p. 286
- Geology Link, p. 289
- Language Arts Link, p. 298

Comparisons
- Language-to-Language, p. 293
- Thinking Critically, pp. 285, 291, 297

Communities
- Career Path, p. 281
- Community Link, p. 300
- De l'école au travail, p. 297

Connections and Comparisons

Geography Link
Guadeloupe has over 150 miles of coastline, which is home to a variety of marine life. Lobsters, crabs, and shrimp are abundant, as well as murex, conch, triton, abalone, oysters, mussels, and sea urchins. Parrotfish, French angelfish, queen triggerfish, cardinals, and peacockfish are among the more unusual species that inhabit the archipelago's numerous coral reefs.

Marine Biology Link
You might ask students what they know about coral reefs and how they are formed. Coral reefs are partially made of living structures formed by the skeletons of various coral polyps. Their shells, made of calcium carbonate, form a rigid limestone structure. Mud, sediment, and even living algae fall into the holes in the formation and become part of the living structure.

10
Rencontres au soleil

Objectives

In this chapter you will learn to

Première étape

- brag
- flatter
- tease

Deuxième étape

- break some news
- show interest
- express disbelief
- tell a joke

 internet

| ADRESSE: go.hrw.com |
| MOT-CLE: WA3 FRANCOPHONE AMERICA-10 |

◄ **Le monde aquatique est riche à la Guadeloupe.**

Focusing on Outcomes

Have students read the list of objectives and tell in what situations they might use each one. Then, have them suggest expressions they might use in English to serve each function. You may want to use the video to support the objectives. The self-check activities in **Que sais-je?** on page 308 help students assess their achievement of the objectives.

Career Path

Many French children and teenagers attend summer camps (**les colonies de vacances**) during their vacations. Some of these programs include trips abroad. The young people who supervise students (**les animateurs**) are usually required to know the language of the country they visit. Ask students if they would be interested in accompanying a group of young students to France or any other francophone country and why.

Chapter Sequence

Cultures and Communities

Building on Previous Skills

Point out the **madras** fabric on this page and ask students what they remember about it. (It is a plaid cotton fabric, usually in bright primary colors, that is used for traditional headdresses as well as everyday clothing in Martinique and Guadeloupe.)

 ### Culture Note

Seafood is the basis of many culinary specialties in Guadeloupe. **Chatrou** is a dish made with a small octopus cooked in a red bean stew. **Blaff,** or creole-poached fish or shellfish, is another specialty. **Calalou** is a thick soup made with crabs, tomatoes, and okra base. **Crabes farcis** are stuffed crabs.

Cahier d'activités, p. 109, Act. 1

Teaching Resources
pp. 282–284

PRINT
▶ Lesson Planner, p. 47
▶ Video Guide, pp. 62, 64
▶ Cahier d'activités, p. 109

MEDIA
▶ One-Stop Planner
▶ Video Program
Camille et compagnie
Videocassette 4, 00:50–06:59
Videocassette 5 (captioned version), 55:58–1:02:07
▶ Audio Compact Discs, CD 10, Tr. 1

Presenting
Mise en train

Have students make suppositions about what might happen in *La plongée, quelle aventure!*, based on the photos on pages 282–283. Then, play the recording, pausing after each scene to ask what happened. You might also ask the related questions from Activity 1 on page 284.

CD 10 Tr. 1

Stratégie pour comprendre
Have you ever gone scuba diving or snorkling? Can you guess what kind of conversation goes on between people who have watched sea life in its natural environment and those who haven't? In this episode, Pascal has a chance to brag about his first experience under water.

1 **Pascal** Salut, Maxime! Ça va?
Maxime Très bien. Et toi? Tu as passé un bon week-end?
Pascal Excellent. Devine ce que j'ai fait.
Maxime Je ne sais pas.
Pascal De la plongée.
Maxime Ah oui? De la plongée sous-marine?
Pascal Oui. C'était la première fois.
Maxime Alors, comment tu as trouvé ça?
Pascal Génial. Au début, j'avais un peu peur, mais une fois dans l'eau... Ouah! Regarde un peu les deux filles là-bas. Si on allait leur parler? Je les ai déjà vues hier. Elles ont l'air sympas.
Maxime Ouais, pourquoi pas?
Pascal Excusez-moi, mesdemoiselles, on s'est pas déjà rencontrés quelque part?

2 **Brigitte** Euh... non, je crois pas.
Pascal Ah bon, pourtant... je dois sûrement confondre avec quelqu'un d'autre. Au fait, moi, c'est Pascal. Et lui, c'est Maxime.
Brigitte Bonjour. Moi, c'est Brigitte et ma copine, c'est Angèle.
Maxime Vous êtes d'ici?
Brigitte Non, on habite à Paris. On est là pour les vacances.
Maxime Il fait beau aujourd'hui.
Brigitte Oui, un peu chaud, mais bon.
Pascal Je disais juste à Maxime que ce week-end, j'avais fait de la plongée.

3 **Angèle** Ah oui? Mais c'est dangereux ça, non?
Pascal Oh non. C'est fastoche, ça.
Angèle Tu es descendu à quelle profondeur?
Pascal Oh, à une quinzaine de mètres. Au fond de la mer, j'ai vu des poissons magnifiques, de toutes les couleurs, des étoiles de mer, d'énormes crabes. Et puis, vous ne devinerez jamais ce que j'ai vu.

Preteaching Vocabulary

Guessing Words from Context
Have students look at the pictures on both pages. Then have them make guesses about what might be going on in the story. Ask them what activity Pascal is bragging about. **(la plongée sous-marine).** Have them come up with a list of words they don't know and guesses about their meaning, based on contextual information. Have volunteers share their lists with the class and then have them tell how they arrived at their guesses. Finally, have students give a synopsis of the story, based on context.

la plongée sous-marine *scuba diving*
fastoche *easy*
profondeur *depth*
un requin *a shark*
se vanter *to brag*
épater *to amaze*
délirer *to be delirious*

4

Angèle	Raconte!
Pascal	Un requin!
Angèle	C'est pas vrai!
Pascal	Si, je t'assure. Il est même passé à moins de deux mètres de moi.
Angèle	Pas possible! Dis donc, tu as dû avoir peur, non?
Pascal	Oh, tu sais, j'en ai vu d'autres.
Angèle	Tu en as, du courage!
Pascal	C'est pas pour me vanter, mais moi, j'adore l'aventure.
Brigitte	Oh, je t'en prie!
Pascal	Enfin, bref, je me suis approché du requin et j'ai essayé de lui faire peur. D'ailleurs, ça a marché. Il m'a regardé et il est parti.

5

Angèle	Alors là, tu m'épates!
Pascal	Si ça vous intéresse, on peut faire de la plongée ensemble.
Angèle	Oh ça serait chouette! Tu pourrais m'apprendre...
Brigitte	Euh, je ne crois pas qu'on ait le temps.
Angèle	Mais, Brigitte...
Brigitte	Au fait, tu as vu quelle heure il est? Il faut qu'on rentre à l'hôtel. Bon. Ben, à plus tard, hein?
Pascal	Vous savez, on vient souvent par ici. Comme ça, si vous nous cherchez...

Brigitte et Angèle s'en vont.

Brigitte	Non, mais tu es amoureuse ou quoi?
Angèle	Lâche-moi, tu veux? Il a l'air sympa, c'est tout. Et vachement courageux en plus.

6

Brigitte	Réveille-toi un peu! Il essayait de nous impressionner, c'est tout. Il n'arrêtait pas de se vanter.
Angèle	Qu'est-ce que tu en sais? Moi, en tout cas, je crois qu'il était sincère.
Brigitte	Oh! Arrête de délirer!

Pendant ce temps-là...

Pascal	C'est dommage. Je crois que j'avais mes chances avec Angèle.
Maxime	Non mais, tu t'es pas regardé?

7

Pascal	Ben quoi? Elle est folle de moi, cette fille. Je crois que je vais essayer de la revoir.
Maxime	Oh, ça va. Je parie que tu n'en es même pas capable.
Pascal	Tu me crois pas? Eh ben, on va voir!

Using the Captioned Video

 As an alternative, you might want to show the captioned version of *Camille et compagnie : C'est pas la mer à boire!* on Video-cassette 5. Some students may benefit from seeing the written words as they listen to the target language and watch the gestures and actions in context. This visual reinforcement of vocabulary and functions will facilitate students' comprehension and help reduce their anxiety before they are formally introduced to the new language in the chapter.

Mise en train

CHAPITRE 10

Physics Link

Ask students if they have ever heard of "the bends" in reference to scuba diving, and if they know why scuba divers must strictly respect time and depth limits. (Below 30 feet, the pressure of the water on the diver's body causes various physiological reactions. For example, nitrogen bubbles may be released in the bloodstream. If a diver exceeds the time limits at a given depth, nitrogen builds up in the body, and *decompression sickness* (**un accident de décompression**) can occur, causing convulsions, nausea, paralysis, or even death.)

Culture Note

SCUBA (Self-Contained Underwater Breathing Apparatus) diving is a popular pastime in Guadeloupe. Many divers explore its coastal waters each year, and over twenty diving clubs on the islands offer classes to tourists interested in trying the sport.

Camille et compagnie

You may choose to show students Episode 10: *C'est pas la mer à boire!* now or wait until later in the chapter. In this episode Camille, Max, and Azzedine meet at the aquarium in Marseilles. While waiting for Azzedine, Max tells Camille some new jokes, but he notices that Camille is distracted. She tells Max that she has been accepted in an exchange program in Louisiana. Azzedine joins them and they start exploring the aquarium.

Challenge

3 Form seven groups and assign a scene from the **Mise en train** to each one. Have them compose a one-sentence summary of their scene and write it on the board or on a transparency. Once all the summaries have been written, have the class arrange them in order according to the **Mise en train**.

Answers

1 1. at a beach in Guadeloupe
2. Pascal went scuba diving during the weekend.
3. Angèle and Brigitte
4. Pascal's dive
5. He brags about his courage.
6. Angèle is impressed. Brigitte is not.
7. The girls return to their hotel without committing to seeing the boys again.
8. Brigitte thinks Angèle is naive to be impressed by Pascal. Maxime doesn't think Pascal has a chance with Angèle.

5 1. Excusez-moi,... on s'est pas déjà rencontrés quelque part?
2. C'est fastoche, ça. Oh, tu sais, j'en ai vu d'autres. C'est pas pour me vanter, mais moi...
3. Ah oui? Raconte!
4. Oh, je t'en prie!
5. Tu en as, du courage! Alors là, tu m'épates!
6. Non, mais tu es amoureuse ou quoi? Réveille-toi un peu! Arrête de délirer! Non mais, tu t'es pas regardé? Oh, ça va. Je parie que tu n'en es même pas capable.
7. Lâche-moi, tu veux? Qu'est-ce que tu en sais? Eh ben, on va voir!

1 **Tu as compris?** See answers below.

These activities check for comprehension only. Students should not yet be expected to produce language modeled in **Mise en train**.

1. Où sont Maxime et Pascal?
2. De quoi est-ce qu'ils parlent?
3. Qui est-ce qu'ils rencontrent?
4. De quoi est-ce qu'ils parlent avec les filles?
5. Quelle est l'attitude de Pascal?
6. Comment est-ce que les filles réagissent?
7. Comment finit la conversation?
8. Qu'est-ce que Brigitte pense de l'attitude d'Angèle? Qu'est-ce que Maxime pense de l'attitude de Pascal?

2 **Qui dit quoi?**

Qui fait les remarques suivantes, Brigitte, Pascal, Angèle ou Maxime?

1. «Elle est folle de moi, cette fille.» Pascal
2. «Non, mais tu es amoureuse ou quoi?» Brigitte
3. «Je crois qu'il était sincère.» Angèle
4. «Réveille-toi un peu!» Brigitte
5. «Non mais, tu t'es pas regardé!» Maxime
6. «C'est pas pour me vanter, mais moi, j'adore l'aventure.» Pascal
7. «Alors là, tu m'épates!» Angèle

3 **Mets dans le bon ordre**

Mets ces phrases dans le bon ordre d'après *La plongée, quelle aventure!* 8, 2, 4, 6, 7, 5, 1, 3

1. Brigitte et Angèle s'en vont.
2. Maxime et Pascal engagent la conversation avec les filles.
3. Brigitte se moque *(teases)* d'Angèle.
4. Pascal se vante devant Angèle et Brigitte.
5. Brigitte coupe la conversation.
6. Angèle est très impressionnée.
7. Pascal propose aux filles de faire de la plongée avec eux.
8. Pascal est allé faire de la plongée.

4 **Vrai ou faux?**

1. C'est la première fois que Pascal voit Angèle et Brigitte. faux
2. Maxime demande à Angèle de sortir avec lui. faux
3. Pascal dit qu'il a vu un requin. vrai
4. Angèle voudrait faire de la plongée. vrai
5. Brigitte est très impressionnée par l'histoire de Pascal. faux

5 **Cherche les expressions** See answers below.

What do the teenagers in *La plongée, quelle aventure!* say to . . .

1. strike up a conversation?
2. brag?
3. show interest?
4. show disbelief?
5. flatter someone?
6. tease someone?
7. respond to teasing?

6 **Et maintenant, à toi**

Qu'est-ce que tu penses de la façon dont Pascal et Maxime ont abordé les filles? Comment est-ce que tu abordes quelqu'un que tu aimerais rencontrer?

Note culturelle

La Guadeloupe est formée de plusieurs îles. Il y fait doux toute l'année et la température moyenne est de 80 degrés Fahrenheit sur la côte. Le seul endroit où la température peut descendre jusqu'à 40 degrés est le sommet du volcan la Soufrière. Le climat tropical de la Guadeloupe et sa longue saison des pluies produisent une végétation abondante, avec des mangroves et des forêts denses. La côte est dotée de baies et de plages qui sont particulièrement belles à Basse-Terre, une des îles principales de la Guadeloupe. La température de l'eau autour des îles est propice à une faune aquatique abondante et surtout à beaucoup d'espèces de poissons comme les tarpons et les raies.

Comprehension Check

Visual/Auditory Learners

2 Write the quotations on large strips of posterboard. Write the characters' names across the chalkboard. Then, show each quotation, read it aloud, and have a volunteer tape it to the board under the appropriate name.

Auditory Learners

5 You might read aloud the expressions that serve the functions listed in this activity, using appropriate intonation. (**Alors, là, tu m'épates!**) Have students call out the related functions in English *(to flatter someone)*.

Rencontre culturelle

Est-ce que tu connais la Guadeloupe? Regarde les photos suivantes pour découvrir quelques caractéristiques de cette île.

On peut voir des fleurs magnifiques dans la forêt tropicale.

Pointe-à-Pitre, chef-lieu de la Guadeloupe

L'agriculture est un secteur important de l'économie de la Guadeloupe.

La fête des Cuisinières, un événement gastronomique haut en couleurs

La musique fait partie de la vie quotidienne.

Qu'en penses-tu?

1. Quelle impression ces photos te donnent de la Guadeloupe?
2. D'après ces photos, quelles sont certaines activités des Guadeloupéens?

Possible answers:
1. tropical country with urban and natural areas, agriculture and business-based economy, music and cuisine are important
2. visiting a tropical forest, attending festivals, playing and listening to music

Savais-tu que... ?

La Guadeloupe est un groupe d'îles situées dans les Caraïbes, à environ 120 kilomètres au nord de la Martinique. Après sa découverte par Christophe Colomb en 1493, la Guadeloupe est devenue une colonie française. En 1946, elle est devenue un département d'outre-mer (DOM), c'est-à-dire une partie de la France, et ses habitants ont les mêmes droits et avantages que les autres citoyens français. L'agriculture est une ressource importante de la Guadeloupe et les bananes et le sucre représentent la majorité de ses produits d'exportation. La musique et la danse jouent un rôle très important dans la culture guadeloupéenne. La fête des Cuisinières est un événement annuel où les cuisinières locales défilent dans les rues en costumes colorés avec des plats délicieux qu'elles ont préparés.

Presenting
Rencontre culturelle

Have students look at the photos, read the captions, and tell all they can about Guadeloupe. Then, have volunteers read the paragraph under **Savais-tu que... ?** aloud, as students listen with their books closed. Ask questions about the information they heard. (Where is Guadeloupe located? Who discovered it? What is its association with France? What are the island's major exports? Who are the participants in the **fête des Cuisinières?**)

Music Link
Softly play some **zouk** music by Kassav' or another artist, as you read aloud a selection from a Caribbean author (see Literature Link below). Tell students that the Carib word for Guadeloupe was **Karukera,** which means *Island of beautiful waters,* and ask them to visualize the island.

Literature Link
Guadeloupe is the birthplace of the poet Saint-John Perse and the novelist Maryse Condé, among others. Some of Condé's short novels, including *Segu* and *Crossing the Mangrove,* describe creole life in Guadeloupe and are available in English translation.

Thinking Critically
Comparing and Contrasting
Have students compare the **fête des Cuisinières** with a local event that has similar festivities.

Cultures and Communities

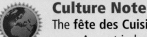

Culture Note
The **fête des Cuisinières** takes place every August in honor of the patron saint of cooks, **Saint Laurent.** The women chefs of the island dress up in the traditional **madras.** In lieu of the traditional headdress, the women wear elaborate baskets filled with native fruits, such as mangoes, papayas, breadfruit, and christophenes, and decorated with miniature kitchen utensils. This colorful parade winds its way through the streets of Pointe-à-Pitre to the **cathédrales Saint-Pierre et Saint-Paul,** where High Mass is held. Then, the festivities continue with a five-hour feast, followed by music and dancing.

Première étape

Objectives Bragging; flattering; teasing

go.
hrw
.com
WA3 FRANCOPHONE
AMERICA-10

Teaching Resources
pp. 286–290

PRINT
▶ Lesson Planner, p. 48
▶ Listening Activities, pp. 75–76, 79–80
▶ Activities for Communication, pp. 37–38, 78, 80, 107–108
▶ Travaux pratiques de grammaire, pp. 89–92
▶ Grammar Tutor for Students of French, Chapter 10
▶ Cahier d'activités, pp. 110–113
▶ Testing Program, pp. 213–216
▶ Alternative Assessment Guide, p. 39
▶ Student Make-Up Assignments, Chapter 10

MEDIA
▶ One-Stop Planner
▶ Audio Compact Discs, CD 10, Trs. 2–4, 14, 19–21
▶ Teaching Transparencies: 10-1; **Grammaire supplémentaire** Answers; Travaux pratiques de grammaire Answers
▶ Interactive CD-ROM Tutor, Disc 3

Bell Work
Have students think of a beach they've been to or have seen pictures of. Have them list words they associate with the beach.

Presenting
Vocabulaire

On a large sheet of paper have students draw the scene in **Vocabulaire.** Tell them what you saw on a "snorkeling adventure," and have them point to the items.

Possible answers

7 *à manger:* un crabe, un espadon
vivant: du corail, des hippocampes
animaux dont on peut avoir peur: un requin, un crabe, une pieuvre

Vocabulaire

L'île de la Guadeloupe est réputée pour la beauté de ses fonds marins.

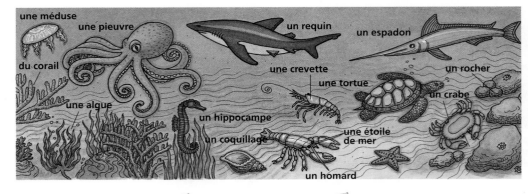

une méduse · une pieuvre · un requin · un espadon · du corail · une crevette · une tortue · un rocher · une algue · un crabe · un hippocampe · une étoile de mer · un coquillage · un homard

(Cahier d'activités, p. 110, Act. 2–3) (Travaux pratiques de grammaire, p. 89, Act. 1–2)

7 Les fonds marins

Parlons Parmi ce que tu vois dans le **Vocabulaire,** qu'est-ce qu'on peut manger? Qu'est-ce qui est vivant? De quoi est-ce qu'on peut avoir peur? See answers below.

8 Les vacances de Dianne See scripts and answers on p. 279G.

Ecoutons Dianne montre des diapos de ses vacances à la Guadeloupe à ses camarades de classe. De quelle diapo est-ce qu'elle parle?

CD 10 Tr. 2

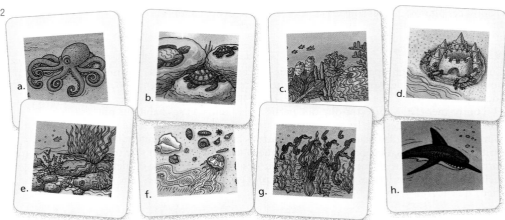

a. · b. · c. · d. · e. · f. · g. · h.

Connections and Comparisons

Marine Biology Link
Have students find out more about the habits of sharks and report their findings to the class. Although sharks do live in the Caribbean, the majority of shark attacks reported each year take place off the coasts of Florida and California. Sharks are not often spotted in the coastal waters of Guadeloupe, because dolphins, natural enemies of sharks, are often nearby.

Community Link
Ask students if they know of organizations for the protection of the marine environment. Ask them if they have heard of incidents that endangered the marine environment and of measures taken to counteract the effects of such incidents.

9 Raconte

Ecrivons Pascal raconte à Maxime ce qu'il a vu quand il a plongé. Complète leur conversation d'après les images.

MAXIME Ça s'est bien passé, la plongée?

PASCAL C'était super.

MAXIME Qu'est-ce que tu as vu?

PASCAL Ben, d'abord, j'ai vu des tortues qui mangeaient. Sur les rochers, il y avait beaucoup

coquillages de et d'  étoiles de mer.

MAXIME Et quoi d'autre?

PASCAL Ensuite, on est passés par un endroit où il y avait beaucoup d' 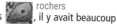 algues.

On m'a dit que c'est là qu'il y a des  crevettes, mais je n'en ai pas vu.

Après quelques mètres, on est arrivés à un récif de corail. C'était beau.

MAXIME Tu as vu de gros poissons?

PASCAL Bien sûr. De loin, on a vu un  espadon, et puis il y avait une

 pieuvre qui est passée tout près de moi.

MAXIME Cool!

PASCAL Et juste avant de partir, on a vu un 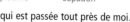 requin.

MAXIME C'est pas vrai!

PASCAL Si. C'était hyper cool. On m'a dit qu'il n'était pas dangereux.

Par contre, une m'a piqué! Ça m'a fait

vraiment mal. méduse

10 C'est cool, la plongée

Ecrivons Tu as fait de la plongée pendant tes vacances à la Guadeloupe. Ecris une carte postale à tes camarades pour leur raconter ce que tu as vu.

Comment dit-on...?

Bragging; flattering

To brag:

C'est fastoche, ça! *That's so easy!*
C'est pas pour me vanter, mais...
  I'm not trying to brag, but . . .
Oh, j'en ai vu d'autres. *I've done/seen bigger and better things.*
C'est moi, le/la meilleur(e).
  I'm the best.
C'est moi qui nage le mieux.
  I. . . the best.

To flatter someone:

Tu es fortiche/calé(e). *You're really strong/good at that.*
Alors là, tu m'épates! *I'm really impressed!*
Tu en as, du courage. *You've really got courage.*
Tu es vraiment le/la meilleur(e).
Tu es le garçon le plus cool que je connaisse.
  You're the . . . -est . . . I know.

 Cahier d'activités, p. 111, Act. 4–5

Première étape

CHAPITRE 10

Presenting
Comment dit-on... ?

Bring in several pictures of different sports, activities, or incredible achievements. Show one of the pictures and act out both sides of a conversation (or use puppets) in which you brag about the achievements (**C'est pas pour me vanter, mais moi, j'ai fait une randonnée sur le mont Everest** or **Le ski nautique? C'est fastoche, ça!**) and another person flatters you. **(Alors là, tu m'épates!)** Have students repeat the new expressions after you. Finally, write sentences that use the new expressions on separate index cards and place them in a box. Have volunteers pick a card and read the sentence aloud, using appropriate gestures and facial expressions. The other students try to guess which function the sentence models.

Language Note
Point out that in the expression **C'est moi qui... le mieux,** the verb that follows **qui** will be in the first person singular form: **C'est moi qui fais le mieux de la plongée.**

Additional Practice
Have students write a sentence, bragging about a real or imaginary accomplishment. **(C'est pas pour me vanter, mais j'ai eu cent à l'interro de maths.)** Have students exchange papers and write a response.

Communication for All Students

Game
Pictionnaire Write the vocabulary words from page 286 on separate index cards. Form two teams. Have one player from the first team select a card and draw a picture depicting the word. If his or her team calls out the correct French word within 30 seconds, the team wins a point.

Building on Previous Skills
Have partners tell about an activity in which they excel, using expressions they already know (**C'est en... que je suis le/la meilleur(e); ..., c'est mon fort**).

Teaching Resources
pp. 286–290

PRINT
▶ Lesson Planner, p. 48
▶ Listening Activities, pp. 75–76, 79–80
▶ Activities for Communication, pp. 37–38, 78, 80, 107–108
▶ Travaux pratiques de grammaire, pp. 89–92
▶ Grammar Tutor for Students of French, Chapter 10
▶ Cahier d'activités, pp. 110–113
▶ Testing Program, pp. 213–216
▶ Alternative Assessment Guide, p. 39
▶ Student Make-Up Assignments, Chapter 10

MEDIA
▶ One-Stop Planner
▶ Audio Compact Discs, CD 10, Trs. 2–4, 14, 19–21
▶ Teaching Transparencies: 10-1; **Grammaire supplémentaire** Answers; Travaux pratiques de grammaire Answers
▶ Interactive CD-ROM Tutor, Disc 3

Presenting
Grammaire

The superlative Bring to class three books of various sizes. Ask students to point to the largest and the smallest one. (**Quel livre est le plus grand? Le moins grand?**) Then, demonstrate the superlative by describing one of the books. (**Ça, c'est le meilleur livre des trois. C'est le livre le plus intéressant des trois.**) Next, ask students about their favorites. (**Quel est le meilleur livre/film du monde?**) Write these sentences on the board. Have students comment on the structure of the sentences and the various placements of the adjectives.

---

11 **Qui se vante?** See scripts and answers on p. 279G.

Ecoutons Ecoute ces conversations. Est-ce que c'est le garçon ou la fille qui se vante?

 CD 10 Tr. 3

12 **C'est pas pour me vanter, mais...**

Ecrivons Bernard est très fier de lui. Il parle avec son cousin de ce qu'il a fait ou sait faire. Imagine et écris ce que Bernard dit. Utilise les mots et expressions proposés. Puis, écris ce que son cousin pourrait répondre pour flatter Bernard.

C'est pas pour me vanter, mais...	...., c'est fastoche, ça!	danser
	faire de la plongée et voir une pieuvre énorme	C'est moi, le meilleur...
avoir 18 à l'interro de français	faire du deltaplane	C'est moi qui... le mieux...

Grammaire

The superlative

To make the superlative forms in French, you just use the comparative forms along with the appropriate definite articles.

Si tu as oublié **the forms of the comparative** *va à la page 232.*

Adjectives:

Ce coquillage est **le plus grand.** Celui-ci est **le moins grand.**
  This shell is the biggest.   *This one is the smallest.*
Ce sont **les meilleures** régions pour la plongée.
  These are the best regions for diving.

- If the adjective usually precedes the noun, put the superlative construction and the adjective before the noun.

  Gilles est **le plus grand** garçon de l'équipe.
    Gilles is the tallest boy on the team.

- If the adjective usually follows the noun, put the article in front of the noun and repeat it in front of the superlative construction.

  Le requin est **le** poisson **le plus** dangereux du monde.
    The shark is the most dangerous fish in the world.

- Notice that you use **de** to say *in/of* after the superlative.

  Tu es **la fille la plus** courageuse **de** notre classe.
    You're the most courageous girl in our class.

- Don't forget to make the articles and adjectives agree with the nouns.

Adverbs:

- In a superlative construction with an adverb, always use the article **le.**

  C'est Brigitte qui court **le plus vite.** *Brigitte runs the fastest.*
  C'est Pascal qui court **le moins vite.** *Pascal runs the slowest.*
  C'est moi qui chante **le mieux.** *I sing the best.*

Travaux pratiques de grammaire, p. 90, Act. 3–4

Grammaire supplémentaire, pp. 302–303, Act. 1–4

Cahier d'activités, pp. 111–112, Act. 6–7

Travaux pratiques de grammaire, pp. 91–92, Act. 5–7

Communication for All Students

Game
C'est nous, les meilleurs! Compose a sentence using the superlative. Write each sentence section on two index cards. (**C'est elle qui/danse/le mieux**) Form two teams and distribute a set of cards to members of each team. To play the game, read one of your sentences aloud. (**C'est elle qui danse le mieux.**) The students from each team who hold the cards bearing the words of your sentence race to the front and arrange themselves in order to form the sentence, holding their cards in front of them. The first team to form the correct sentence wins.

13 Grammaire en contexte

Ecrivons Complète les phrases suivantes avec le superlatif des adjectifs et des adverbes entre parenthèses.

EXEMPLE Ces algues sont sûrement _____ (−/long) de toutes.
Ces algues sont sûrement les moins longues de toutes.

1. C'est Elodie qui nage _____ (−/vite).   le moins vite
2. Le requin est l'animal marin _____ (+/dangereux).   le plus dangereux
3. De nous tous, c'est Martin qui parle français _____ (+/bien).   le mieux
4. A mon avis, c'est cette étoile de mer qui est _____ (+/mignon).   la plus mignonne
5. Les hippocampes sont vraiment les animaux _____ (+/bizarre).   les plus bizarres
6. _____ (+/beau) plages sont à l'ouest de l'île.   Les plus belles
7. Regarde un peu cette tortue! Ça doit être _____ (+/gros) de toutes.   la plus grosse
8. Je n'aime pas trop ces coquillages-là. Ce sont _____ (−/joli).   les moins jolis

14 Grammaire en contexte

Parlons Fais des phrases pour dire comment ces animaux sont, à ton avis.

EXEMPLE La tortue est l'animal marin le moins rapide.   See answers below.

mignon
gros
bizarre
dangereux
moche
rapide
beau

15 Grammaire en contexte

Parlons Pascal croit qu'il fait tout mieux que les autres. Qu'est-ce qu'il pourrait dire à propos des activités suivantes pour impressionner une fille?   See answers below.

EXEMPLE De tous les garçons, c'est moi qui chante le mieux.

parler anglais	conduire	danser
sauter	chanter nager	s'habiller

bien	haut
prudemment	vite

16 L'endroit le plus beau du monde

Parlons Pendant tes vacances à la Guadeloupe, tu téléphones à ton ami(e) pour lui dire ce que tu as fait et vu. Tu es impressionné(e), donc tu exagères. Tu es fier/fière de toi et tu te vantes un peu. Joue cette scène avec ton/ta camarade. Changez de rôle.

Connections and Comparisons

Geology Link

The islands of Grande-Terre and Basse-Terre have surprisingly different topographies. Grande-Terre is composed mostly of limestone outcroppings, called **mornes.** Its coasts consist of rocky, jagged cliffs, notably the **Pointe des châteaux,** against which the water crashes dramatically. Basse-Terre, in contrast, is mountainous, with several peaks, deep gorges, cascading waterfalls, mountain streams, and lush tropical rain forests.

Additional Practice

14 You might expand this activity by having students describe other animals they've studied in Chapter 12 of Level 2 and Chapter 7 of this book (**orignal, ours, loup, écureuil, renard, raton laveur, mouffette, canard, éléphant, girafe, guépard, hippopotame, lion, rhinocéros, singe, zèbre**).

Teaching Suggestion

16 As an alternative, you might have students write their friend a letter in which they tell about their experiences in Guadeloupe. This activity is appropriate for students' written portfolios.

Possible answers

14 Le requin est l'animal marin le plus dangereux. La crevette est l'animal marin le plus mignon. L'hippocampe est l'animal marin le plus mignon. La tortue est le plus gros animal marin. La méduse est l'animal marin le plus moche. La pieuvre est l'animal marin le plus bizarre. L'étoile de mer est l'animal marin le plus bizarre.

15 C'est moi qui parle anglais le mieux/qui conduis le plus prudemment/qui danse le mieux/qui saute le plus haut/qui chante le mieux/qui nage le plus vite/qui m'habille le mieux.

Comment dit-on...?

Teasing

To tease someone:

Tu es amoureux/amoureuse ou quoi? *Are you . . . or what?*
Non mais, tu t'es pas regardé(e)! *If you could see how you look!*
Réveille-toi un peu! *Get with it!*
Tu en rates pas une, toi! *You don't miss a thing, do you? (sarcastic)*
Arrête de délirer! *Stop being so silly!*

To respond to teasing:

Lâche-moi, tu veux? *Will you give me a break?*
Je t'ai pas demandé ton avis. *I didn't ask your opinion.*
Oh, ça va, hein! *Oh, give me a break!*
Qu'est-ce que tu en sais? *What do you know about it?*
Ça peut arriver à tout le monde. *It could happen to anyone.*
Et toi, arrête de m'embêter! *Stop bothering me!*

Cahier d'activités, p. 113, Act. 9–10

17 **Lâche-moi, tu veux?** See scripts and answers on p. 279G.

Ecoutons Ecoute ces dialogues entre Brigitte et Angèle. Dans quelles conversations est-ce qu'elles se taquinent?
CD 10 Tr. 4

18 **Qu'est-ce que tu en sais?**

Lisons Ton/Ta meilleur(e) ami(e) se moque de toi. Choisis la bonne réponse pour te défendre.

1. Tu en rates pas une, toi!
   a. Mais le bus n'est pas arrivé à l'heure.
   b. Ben, ça peut arriver à tout le monde!
   c. Oui, c'est vrai. J'ai raté un autre examen.

2. Tu es amoureux/amoureuse ou quoi?
   a. J'en ai vu d'autres.
   b. Je ne suis jamais tombé(e) amoureux/amoureuse.
   c. Lâche-moi, tu veux?

3. Arrête de délirer!
   a. Mais c'est amusant de délirer!
   b. Et toi, arrête de m'embêter!
   c. Oh, c'est fastoche, ça!

4. Non, mais tu t'es pas regardé(e)!
   a. Je t'ai pas demandé ton avis.
   b. Je n'ai pas de miroir.
   c. Si, je suis très beau/belle.

5. Réveille-toi un peu!
   a. Je n'ai pas de réveil.
   b. Oh, j'ai sommeil.
   c. Oh, ça va, hein!

19 **C'est fastoche, la plongée**

Ecrivons Ces jeunes viennent de faire de la plongée. Ils parlent de ce qu'ils ont vu. Pendant la conversation, ils se vantent, se flattent et se taquinent. Ecris leur conversation.

Communication for All Students

Challenge

18 Once students have completed the activity, have them write a dialogue in which they use one of the expressions and the appropriate response.

Group Work

Organize students in groups of three or four. One student boasts about something he or she did or can do. (**C'est moi qui danse le mieux. Je suis le/la meilleur(e) en sport. C'est fastoche de...**) The other students respond by teasing or disbelieving him or her. (**Non mais, tu t'es pas regardé(e)! Réveille-toi un peu! Arrête de délirer!**) Students should take turns boasting and responding.

PANORAMA CULTUREL

Tu peux décrire une de tes journées typiques?

We asked some students to describe a typical school day. Here's what they told us.

Evelyne, France

«En semaine, ben, je me lève vers six heures et demie. Je fais ma toilette. Je m'habille et je vais déjeuner. Je prends le bus et j'arrive ici à huit heures, enfin, un peu avant huit heures. Je vais en cours de huit heures à midi. Je mange en vitesse de midi à une heure. Après, de une heure à six heures j'ai cours. A six heures, je prends le bus et j'arrive à sept heures à la maison. Et après, je mange, je travaille ou je regarde la télé et puis, je vais me coucher.»
Tr. 6

Epie, Côte d'Ivoire

«Je me réveille à cinq heures. Je me lave. Je fais ma toilette. Je m'habille. Je prends mon petit dé-jeuner, puis je prends la route de l'école. Arrivée à l'école, je vais en classe. Nous faisons les cours et, à midi, je repars à la mai-son. Puis, je regarde la télévision et puis, je mange. Dans l'après-midi, je vais me coucher. Si on a cours le soir, je repars à l'école, et puis je reviens. Le soir, j'étudie et puis, je vais dormir.»
Tr. 7

Marie, France

«Je me lève vers six heures et demie. Je vais dans la salle de bains. Je me lave un petit peu. Je m'habille. Après, je vais donner à manger à mes chevaux. Après, je déjeune, puis ma mère, elle m'emmène avec mes petites sœurs à l'école. Après, la matinée, on travaille. A midi, je mange en ville avec des copines ou des copains, et l'après-midi, je retourne à l'école, et ma mère vient me chercher le soir à six heures. Et après, je me baigne ou je regarde la télé et après, je vais tra-vailler. Et le soir, je mange et après, je donne à manger à mes chevaux et à mon chien, et je vais me coucher.»
Tr. 8

Qu'en penses-tu?

1. Est-ce que les habitudes de ces élèves diffèrent de celles des élèves américains? Comment? *Classes last until 6:00 P.M.*
2. Laquelle de ces élèves a des habitudes comparables aux tiennes?

Connections and Comparisons

Thinking Critically

- **Analyzing** Have students read Epie's inter-view. Ask them what is unusual about her school routine. (She takes a nap in the early afternoon and has classes later in the afternoon.) Have stu-dents use their knowledge of Côte d'Ivoire to try to explain her schedule. (most schools and busi-nesses close down during the hottest hours of the day and reopen later in the afternoon.)

- **Comparing and Contrasting** Ask students to list activities they do every day. Have them pick the interviewee whose schedule differs most from their own. Have them point out the differ-ences in French. You might ask them to try to explain why the interviewee's schedule is differ-ent from theirs.

Teaching Resources
p. 291

PRINT
▸ Video Guide, pp. 62–63, 65
▸ Cahier d'activités, p. 120

MEDIA
▸ One-Stop Planner
▸ Video Program
  Videocassette 4, 07:02–11:02
▸ Audio Compact Discs, CD 10,
  Trs. 5–8
▸ Interactive CD-ROM Tutor, Disc 3

Presenting
Panorama Culturel

Before you play the video, have students list French words or expressions they expect to hear, given the interview question. List in random order on three separate transparencies the activities that each interviewee describes. Play the video of the first interview. Then, project the transparency on which you wrote the interviewee's activities and have students number them in the correct order.

Questions

1. **A quelle heure est-ce qu'Evelyne arrive chez elle le soir?** (à sept heures) **Qu'est-ce qu'elle fait le soir?** (Elle travaille ou elle regarde la télévision.)

2. **Qui se lève le plus tôt?** (Epie)

3. **Qu'est-ce qu'Epie fait l'après-midi?** (Elle se couche.)

4. **Qu'est-ce que Marie fait que les autres ne font pas?** (Elle donne à manger à ses chevaux et à son chien.)

Teaching Resources
pp. 292–293

PRINT 📖
▶ Lesson Planner, p. 49
▶ Video Guide, pp. 62, 64
▶ Cahier d'activités, p. 114

MEDIA 💿 📼 🗄
▶ One-Stop Planner
▶ Video Program
   Camille et compagnie
   Videocassette 4, 00:50–06:59
   Videocassette 5 (captioned version), 55:58–1:02:07
▶ Audio Compact Discs, CD 10, Tr. 9

Presenting
Remise en train

Have students read the introduction on page 292. Then, assign to small groups the names of the people Joëlle mentions. Tell them to listen for and note any news pertaining to their assigned person. Play the audio recording and have groups report back to the class what they think happened to their assigned person.

Teaching Suggestion

Ask students what they would write about to a pen pal or friend who had moved away. Then, have students look at the photos on this page and imagine what Joëlle is writing about.

Answers
20 1. She misses her friend and she wants to share some news.
2. what has happened since Marie-France left Guadeloupe
3. Lyon

Remise en train · *Des nouvelles de Guadeloupe*

CD 10 Tr. 9

Joëlle écrit à une amie, Marie-France, qui a quitté la Guadeloupe il y a quelques mois. Elle lui raconte tout ce qui s'est passé depuis son départ. Et il s'en est passé des choses!

20 Tu as compris? See answers below.
1. Pourquoi est-ce que Joëlle écrit sa lettre?
2. Quelles nouvelles est-ce qu'elle annonce à Marie-France?
3. Où est-ce qu'elle va envoyer sa lettre?

21 C'est qui?
Dans la lettre de Joëlle, trouve le nom d'une personne qui...
1. a raté son bac. Michel
2. s'est mariée. Julie
3. s'est disputée avec son petit ami. Viviane
4. a participé à un relais. Joëlle
5. s'est cassé la jambe. Prosper

22 Trouve la suite!
Complète les phrases suivantes avec les mots dans la boîte.

à la Martinique	dans le vieux centre
dans la boutique	à un concert de salsa

1. Hier, Joëlle est allée _____ avec Viviane.
2. Le mari de Julie habite _____.
3. Pour le moment, Michel travaille _____ de son père.
4. Joëlle aimerait pouvoir aller se promener _____ avec Marie-France.

1. à un concert de salsa   2. à la Martinique
3. dans la boutique   4. dans le vieux centre

These activities check for comprehension only. Students should not yet be expected to produce language modeled in Remise en train.

Preteaching Vocabulary

Identifying Keywords
Have students look at the letter from Joëlle. Ask them to skim through the letter for words that they know. Have them find as many key verbs as possible and have them indicate the meanings of those they know. Have partners compile a list of unfamiliar verbs and their likely meanings. Have each pair present their lists to the class and brainstorm as a whole class about the meanings of key verbs.

se promener *to go for a walk*
se fâcher *to get angry*
se casser la jambe *to break a leg*
rater le bac *to fail the bac (exam)*
repasser *to take again*

Ma chère Marie-France,

Si tu savais comme tu me manques. Quand je sors de l'école, je me dis, «Tiens, si Marie-France était là, on irait se promener dans le vieux centre ou sur la place des Victoires.» Hier, j'ai pensé à toi. Je suis allée écouter un concert de salsa. Tu aurais adoré ça. Tout le monde était debout et dansait! J'y suis allée avec Viviane. Je ne t'ai pas dit? Elle et Paul se sont fâchés. Ils ne se parlent plus depuis trois mois. Paul me téléphone et me parle de Viviane, et Viviane ne me parle que de Paul. Au fait, tu savais que Prosper s'était cassé la jambe? Il est tombé en faisant une randonnée à la Soufrière. Je suis allée le voir à l'hôpital. Il a le moral, mais il a eu peur. Tu connais la dernière? Figure-toi que Julie, la sœur de Raoul, s'est mariée. Non, mais, tu te rends compte! Elle n'a que vingt ans. Je n'ai jamais vu son mari mais j'ai entendu dire qu'il est sympa. Il est martiniquais et je crois qu'elle va aller habiter avec lui à Fort-de-France. Ah, et puis tu connais la meilleure? Tiens-toi bien. Michel a raté son bac. Je me demande vraiment comment il a fait. Il avait toujours de super notes. Il a dû paniquer le jour de l'examen. Il va le repasser cette année. Mais en attendant, il travaille dans la boutique de son père. Le pauvre! Lui qui voulait se lancer dans l'informatique! Comme tu vois, depuis que tu es partie, beaucoup de choses ont changé. Pour ma part, je n'arrête pas. Je suis vachement occupée. En plus, j'essaie de continuer mon entraînement. Je cours au moins une heure par jour. Je ne t'ai pas dit? On a gagné un relais où il y avait les meilleures athlètes des Antilles. C'est génial, non? Ecris-moi vite pour me raconter ce que tu fais à Lyon. J'espère qu'il ne fait pas trop froid. Ici, comme tu peux l'imaginer, il fait un temps super. On va à la plage tous les week-ends. Je te laisse. Gros bisous.

Joëlle

Cahier d'activités, p. 114, Act. 11

Note culturelle

En Guadeloupe, les gens prennent plaisir à se parler. Par exemple, quand ils se rencontrent dans la rue, ils n'hésitent pas à avoir de longues conversations au sujet de leur vie, des dernières nouvelles ou de la famille. Un échange rapide du genre «Salut! Comment ça va? A bientôt!» peut être considéré mal élevé.

23 Vrai ou faux?

1. Viviane et Paul se sont réconciliés.   faux
2. Joëlle trouve que Julie était trop jeune pour se marier.   vrai
3. Michel veut étudier l'informatique.   vrai
4. Joëlle va à la plage tous les jours.   faux
5. Beaucoup de choses ont changé.   vrai

24 Cherche les expressions See answers below.

What expressions does Joëlle use to . . .

1. say she misses someone?
2. describe a hypothetical situation?
3. break some news?
4. make a supposition?
5. express pity?
6. end her letter?

25 Et maintenant, à toi

Est-ce que tu as des amis qui ont déménagé?
Est-ce que tu leur écris quelquefois?
Qu'est-ce que tu leur dis dans tes lettres?

VIDEO

Camille et compagnie

As an alternative or in addition to the **Remise en train,** you may wish to show Episode 10 of *Camille et compagnie.* For suggestions and activities, see the *Video Guide.*

Language-to-Language

Ask students what language, besides French, is spoken in the French Antilles (Creole), what languages they think it is a mixture of (French, Spanish, African languages, English, and Portuguese), and why they think these particular languages have influenced Creole (influence of the French, proximity to English-speaking islands and countries, early influence of the Portuguese and Spaniards, use of various African languages and dialects). Try to obtain something written in Creole and bring copies to class. Have students work together to highlight the words whose origins they are able to deduce.

Comprehension Check

Visual Learners

21 On a transparency, draw visual cues to represent each event described in the letter (a wedding ring, a trophy, crutches). If possible, you might bring in these items. Then, point to the pictures or items and call on students to name the person associated with them.

Language Note

25 Ask students if they recognize a word within **déménager (ménage).** Tell them that **déménager** means *to move* and ask them to explain the literal meaning of the word *(to uproot the household).*

Answers

24 1. Si tu savais comme tu me manques.
2. Si Marie-France était là,...
3. Je ne t'ai pas dit? Au fait, tu savais que... ? Tu connais la dernière? Figure-toi que... ; Ah, et puis tu connais la meilleure?
4. Il a dû paniquer le jour de l'examen.
5. Le pauvre!
6. Je te laisse. Gros bisous.

WA3 FRANCOPHONE AMERICA-10

Bell Work

Presenting
Vocabulaire

Vocabulaire

Depuis que Marie-France a quitté la Guadeloupe, il s'en est passé des choses!

Luc **s'est fiancé.**

Etienne **s'est acheté un vélomoteur.**

Mireille **s'est fait mal au dos en faisant du cheval.**

Lucien **a embouti la voiture** de son père.

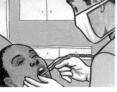

Thérèse **s'est fait enlever les bagues.**

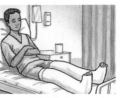

Michel **s'est cassé les jambes.**

Julien et Bruno **se sont bagarrés.**

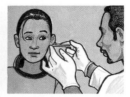

Ophélia **s'est fait percer les oreilles.**

avoir des boutons *to have acne*
déménager *to move*

perdre du poids *to lose weight*
prendre des leçons de conduite *to take driving lessons*

Travaux pratiques de grammaire, p. 93, Act. 8–9

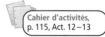
Cahier d'activités, p. 115, Act. 12–13

26 **Depuis ton départ...** See scripts and answers on p. 279H.

Ecoutons Sabine téléphone à son amie qui a déménagé pour lui donner des nouvelles. Regarde les jeunes dans le **Vocabulaire.** De qui est-ce qu'elle parle?

CD 10 Tr. 10

27 **Qu'est qui s'est passé?** 1. c 2. e 3. a 4. b 5. d

Lisons/Ecrivons Lis les phrases suivantes et décide ce qui est arrivé à chaque fille.

1. Paula n'habite plus à Lyon.
2. Julie a de très belles dents.
3. Iman est allée chez le docteur.
4. Dina ne prend plus le bus.
5. Chloé porte une très jolie bague.

a. Elle s'est fait mal au bras.
b. Elle s'est acheté un vélomoteur.
c. Elle a déménagé.
d. Elle s'est fiancée.
e. Elle s'est fait enlever les bagues.

Si tu as oublié **reciprocal verbs** va à la page 162.

Communication for All Students

Kinesthetic Learners

Challenge

Comment dit-on...?

Breaking some news; showing interest; expressing disbelief

To break some news:

Tu savais que... ?
Tu connais la dernière? *Have you heard the latest?*
J'ai entendu dire que... *I've heard that . . .*
Figure-toi que... *Can you imagine that . . .*
Si tu avais vu ce qu'elle portait! *If you could have seen . . .*

To show interest:

Raconte! *Tell me!*
Oh là là!
Qui t'a dit ça? *Who told you that?*
Et alors?

To express disbelief:

Mon œil! *No way!*
Je n'en reviens pas. *I don't believe it.*
N'importe quoi! *Yeah, right!*

> Cahier d'activités, p. 116, Act. 14

---

28 **Les dernières nouvelles** See scripts and answers on p. 279H.

 Ecoutons Tu entends les conversations suivantes à la cantine. Dans quelles conversations est-ce qu'on donne des nouvelles?
CD 10 Tr. 11

29 **Je n'en reviens pas**

 Parlons Invente trois nouvelles incroyables en t'aidant des expressions proposées. Ensuite, annonce ces nouvelles à ton/ta camarade en utilisant les phrases dans le **Comment dit-on... ?** Il/Elle va exprimer des doutes.

> s'acheter une voiture de sport
> rencontrer une fille super
> gagner à la loterie
> se disputer à une boum
> prendre des leçons de conduite
> tomber amoureux
> se bagarrer
> se fiancer
> se faire mal à la main

Grammaire

The past perfect

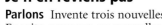

In English you use the past perfect tense to say that something happened even farther in the past than some other event. This tense is called the **plus-que-parfait** in French and you use it the same way in French as in English.

Elle m'a dit ce qu'il **avait fait.** *She told me what he had done.*

• To form the **plus-que-parfait,** you use the **imparfait** of **avoir** or **être** and add the past participle.

j' **avais dit**	j' **étais allé(e)**
tu **avais dit**	tu **étais allé(e)**
il/elle/on **avait dit**	il/elle/on **était allé(e)(s)**
nous **avions dit**	nous **étions allé(e)s**
vous **aviez dit**	vous **étiez allé(e)(s)**
ils/elles **avaient dit**	ils/elles **étaient allé(e)s**

> Grammaire supplémentaire, pp. 304–305, Act. 5–6

> Cahier d'activités, p. 117, Act. 16–17

> Travaux pratiques de grammaire, pp. 94–95, Act. 10–12

• The rules for agreement of past participles are the same as for the **passé composé.**

Communication for All Students

Challenge

After presenting **Comment dit-on...?,** create a four-line dialogue in which the first speaker breaks some news, the second speaker shows interest, the first speaker tells the news, and the second speaker expresses disbelief. Write the lines in scrambled order on a transparency. Have partners number them in the correct order and read the dialogue aloud. Then have each student in a pair write another four-line dialogue on a piece of paper, cut it in strips, scramble the strips, and pass them to their partner. Partners should put the strips of paper in the correct order and read the dialogues to each other.

Presenting
Comment dit-on... ?

The day before the presentation, have students write a statement describing an incredible event. In class, call on several students to read their statements aloud. React with interest or disbelief. Then, make up an incredible story (the principal being abducted by space aliens) and break the news to the class. Prompt students to respond with the new expressions.

Grammaire

The past perfect Before class, write **samedi** on the board and have several students write what they did on Saturday underneath it. (**J'ai embouti ma voiture.**) Then, in a second column, write **lundi** on the board. Underneath it, write several different expressions, such as **Pierre m'a dit que...** Write and say a sentence, using one clause from each column. (**Pierre m'a dit qu'il avait embouti sa voiture samedi.**) Use a clause from each column to construct similar sentences. Have students give the English equivalents.

Additional Practice

Grammaire On a sheet of paper, write several sentence starters (**On m'a dit que... ; J'ai entendu dire que...**) and several possible endings for each (**... tu étais allé(e) à la fête. ... ils avaient perdu leur chien**). Make one copy for every two students, cut the starters and endings apart, and distribute the pieces to partners. Have them assemble several logical sentences and take turns reading them aloud and responding to the news.

Answers

30 avait vu; avait téléphoné; avait demandé; s'était trouvé; avait invité; était venue; avait fini; avait rencontré; avais parlé; n'avait pas menti; est arrivé

31 Elle m'a dit qu'elle était tombée malade, avait été opérée, était allée à l'hôpital, avait obtenu une bourse, était entrée à l'université, avait perdu du poids, était partie en vacances, s'était trouvé un petit ami, s'était acheté une voiture, avait travaillé pendant l'été.

32 Eric n'avait pas assez étudié et avait raté son interro de géo; avait embouti la voiture de ses parents; s'était disputé avec Martin et s'était bagarré à la récréation; s'était fait mal à la jambe pendant le cours de gym; était rentré très tard à la maison et avait été privé de sortie

---

30 **Grammaire en contexte**

Ecrivons Juliette raconte à Lucie ce qui est arrivé à leurs amis. Complète leur conversation en utilisant le passé composé ou le plus-que-parfait. See answers below.

JULIETTE Tu connais la dernière? Benoît et Delphine ont cassé.

LUCIE C'est pas vrai! Qui t'a dit ça? Raconte!

JULIETTE Delphine. Elle m'a dit qu'elle (voir) Benoît au café avec une autre fille. Alors, elle lui (téléphoner) et elle lui (demander) s'il (se trouver) une nouvelle petite amie. Il a répondu qu'il (inviter) cette fille au café parce qu'elle (venir) de Martinique pour voir son frère. Mais Delphine ne l'a pas cru, alors elle lui a dit qu'elle en (finir) avec lui et qu'elle aussi (rencontrer) quelqu'un d'autre. Mais, tu vois, je lui ai dit que j'(parler) avec le frère de Benoît et qu'il (ne pas mentir).

LUCIE Qu'est-ce qui (arriver)?

JULIETTE Elle était fâchée. Elle a refusé de m'écouter.

31 **Grammaire en contexte**

Parlons Ta correspondante guadeloupéenne t'a envoyé une lettre. Elle te raconte tout ce qui s'est passé cette année. Tes camarades sont curieux. Raconte-leur ce qu'elle a écrit dans sa lettre. Utilise le plus-que-parfait. See answers below.

Elle m'a dit que...

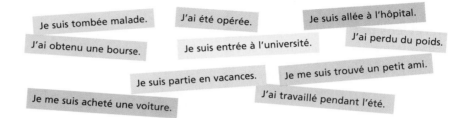

Je suis tombée malade. J'ai été opérée. Je suis allée à l'hôpital.
J'ai obtenu une bourse. Je suis entrée à l'université. J'ai perdu du poids.
Je suis partie en vacances. Je me suis trouvé un petit ami.
Je me suis acheté une voiture. J'ai travaillé pendant l'été.

32 **Grammaire en contexte**

Ecrivons Ton ami Eric a passé une très mauvaise journée hier. Ecris un petit mot à un(e) ami(e) pour lui raconter ce qui est arrivé à Eric. Utilise les expressions proposées et le plus-que-parfait. See answers below.

Eric a passé une journée horrible hier. Il m'a dit qu'il était arrivé à l'école en retard et...

> ne pas étudier assez et rater son interro de géo   emboutir la voiture de ses parents
>
> se disputer avec Martin et se bagarrer à la récréation
>
> se faire mal à la jambe pendant le cours de gym
>
> rentrer très tard à la maison et être privé de sortie

33 **N'importe quoi!**

 Parlons Parle à ton/ta camarade des dernières aventures des personnages d'un feuilleton ou d'une série télévisée que tu connais.

Communication for All Students

Game
Sentence Scrambler To prepare for this game, write the individual words of various sentences on strips of transparency. (**J'ai entendu dire que Monique était tombée amoureuse de Philippe. Julie m'a dit qu'elle s'était cassé la jambe.**) Put the transparency strips for each sentence in a separate envelope. To play the game, form two teams. Scatter the transparency strips for the first sentence on the overhead. Have two players from one team come to the overhead and try to rearrange the words in a logical order within a designated time limit. If they form the sentence within the allotted time, they win a point for their team. Then, the opposing team takes a turn. You might play until one team has earned a specified number of points.

Comment dit-on...?

Telling a joke

To bring up a joke:

J'en connais une bonne.
I've got a good one.
Est-ce que tu connais l'histoire de... ?
Do you know the one about . . .?

To relate a joke:

Quelle est la différence entre... et... ?
Quel est le point commun entre... et... ?
What do . . . and . . . have in common?
C'est l'histoire d'un mec qui...
It's about a guy who . . .

To continue a story:

... et alors, il dit que... *. . . so he says . . .*
... et l'autre lui répond... *. . . and the other one answers . . .*

To respond to a joke:

Elle est bien bonne! *That's a good one!*
Elle est nulle, ta blague! *What a bad joke!*

Grammaire supplémentaire, p. 305, Act. 7

Cahier d'activités, p. 118, Act. 19

34 **Elle est bien bonne!**

See scripts and answers on p. 279H.

Ecoutons Ecoute ces conversations et dis si c'est le début, le milieu ou la fin d'une blague.

CD 10
Tr. 12

A la française

Can you guess which of the phrases in the **Comment dit-on... ?** on page 295 this gesture expresses?*

35 **Méli-mélo!**

Lisons Joëlle raconte une blague à Viviane. Mets leur conversation dans le bon ordre.

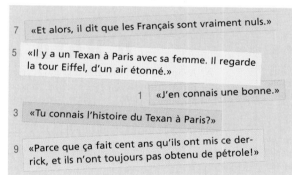

7 «Et alors, il dit que les Français sont vraiment nuls.»

5 «Il y a un Texan à Paris avec sa femme. Il regarde la tour Eiffel, d'un air étonné.»

1 «J'en connais une bonne.»

3 «Tu connais l'histoire du Texan à Paris?»

9 «Parce que ça fait cent ans qu'ils ont mis ce derrick, et ils n'ont toujours pas obtenu de pétrole!»

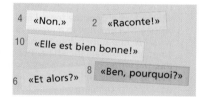

4 «Non.» 2 «Raconte!»

10 «Elle est bien bonne!»

6 «Et alors?» 8 «Ben, pourquoi?»

36 De l'école au travail

Parlons Tu es animateur/animatrice de l'émission de radio *Les Bruits qui courent* et tu interviewes des vedettes sur les derniers événements extravagants de leur vie. Tes camarades vont jouer le rôle des personnalités interviewées. Questionne-les sur les derniers cancans qui courent à leur sujet dans les journaux à sensation.

१९ ११ ५O*

Connections and Comparisons

Thinking Critically

Analyzing After students have done Activity 35, have them tell why this joke is funny. You might prompt their answers by asking questions, such as **Est-ce que la tour Eiffel est vraiment un derrick? Qu'est-ce que c'est en réalité?**

Pourquoi le Texan pense que c'est un derrick? You might expand this activity by asking similar questions about the other joke suggested in the Teacher Note on this page.

Presenting
Comment dit-on... ?

Using a toy telephone, pretend to call a friend and tell the person a joke. **(Tu connais l'histoire de la petite fille paresseuse qui a eu une mauvaise note en histoire? Elle dit à son père : «Papa, tu connais la dernière?» Et il lui répond «Euh, non. Raconte.» Et sa fille lui répond «Eh bien, c'est moi!»)** Then, pretend to listen as the other person tells a joke and react to it. **(Elle est nulle, ta blague!)** Finally, write a summary of a joke on the board (see Teacher Note below) and have partners practice telling it.

Teacher Note

Here is a joke you might want to share with your students:

Un volontaire de la marine parle au médecin. Le médecin lui demande : «Vous savez nager?» Et le garçon lui répond : «Pourquoi? Vous n'avez pas de bateaux?»

Assess

▸ Testing Program, pp. 217–220
Quiz 10-2A, Quiz 10-2B
Audio CD 10, Tr. 15

▸ Student Make-Up Assignments, Chapter 10, Alternative Quiz

▸ Alternative Assessment Guide, p. 39

Teaching Resources
pp. 298–300

PRINT
▸ Lesson Planner, p. 51
▸ Cahier d'activités, p. 119
▸ Reading Strategies and Skills Handbook, Chapter 10
▸ Joie de lire 3, Chapter 10
▸ Standardized Assessment Tutor, Chapter 10

MEDIA
▸ One-Stop Planner

Prereading
Activity A

Teaching Suggestion
Ask students to name stories in which the main characters are animals *(The Three Little Pigs)* and stories that are related to the sea *(The Little Mermaid)*. If students are familiar with *The Little Mermaid,* have them summarize the story and describe the main characters.

Reading
Activities B–R

Teaching Suggestion
B., C. Have students read the questions in Activities B and C before they read the first two paragraphs of the story.

Teaching Suggestions
• Have students guess from context the meanings of the following words that appear on this page: **horloge, sanguine, sursautent** *(clock; veranda, porch; give a start, jump).*

• Once students have done Activities A–D, ask them for their first impressions of O'gaya (a dreamer, wistful). Have them predict the rest of the story from what they've read so far and what they know of O'gaya.

Lisons!

Tout au fond de la mer chaude des Caraïbes, dans une maison entourée d'une véranda, vit une famille d'étoiles de mer : la famille Micabwa.

O'gaya, la fille aînée, n'est toujours pas rentrée; pourtant là-haut, à l'horizon, le soleil a déjà mis sa robe de chambre sanguine.

Toute la famille est à table : papa Micabwa mange de bon appétit et Fia, sa fille cadette, se ressert de la salade d'algues.

L'horloge siffle neuf coups. Maman Micabwa aime bien cette horloge qu'ils ont rapportée de leur dernier voyage aux îles Galapagos. L'horloge? C'est un énorme coquillage bleuté, un coquillage-temps. Comment sait-il l'heure? Nul ne le sait. Au neuvième coup, les coraux de la porte tintinnabulent : O'gaya, gracieuse étoile de mer, passe sous la pierre de lumière.

Papa Micabwa s'installe sous la véranda, dans son fauteuil à bascule pour boire une tisane d'anémones sauvages. La petite sœur s'éclipse dans sa chambre et revient, pailletée d'argent.

- Maman, je vais danser avec...

La fin de sa phrase est couverte par le vrombissement d'une superbe coquille Saint-Jacques pilotée par un jeune poulpe :

- Bonsoir, papa Micabwa, je vous enlève Fia pour la soirée.

- Ne l'enlace pas trop avec tous tes bras, lui répond malicieusement papa Micabwa.

Fia envoie un baiser à son père, la Saint-Jacques démarre dans un tourbillon de sable. Papa Micabwa reste songeur, il pense à O'gaya : «Il faudra que je lui parle : elle a l'air triste ces temps-ci.»

Maman Micabwa et O'gaya sortent toutes les deux sous la véranda. O'gaya s'installe sur les marches et maman Micabwa dans sa berceuse. Les étoiles luisent doucement dans l'eau de la nuit. O'gaya soupire :

- Je voudrais tant être une *étoile de ciel.*

Papa et maman Micabwa sursautent :

- Que dis-tu?

O'gaya se tourne vers eux et répète :

- Je voudrais tant être une *étoile de ciel.*

Stratégie pour lire
Literature, such as a poem, story, or novel, is very different from the formal and objective writing that you find in a report or essay. The writer of literature is free to use imagination, emotion, and dramatic effect. To accomplish this, the writer can use literary techniques such as analogy and figurative language. An *analogy* is a comparison made between two things to show how they are alike. Figurative language, such as simile, metaphor, and personification, describes something by comparing it to something else. A *simile* compares two things by saying that one is like the other; this is usually expressed in French by the word **comme** or sometimes **tel.** A *metaphor* states that one thing is another: **Cet homme est un monstre d'égoïsme.** *Personification* gives human characteristics to an animal or object. Learning to recognize and understand these literary techniques when you read French will enable you to better understand and enjoy what you read.

O'GAYA

A. Avant de lire l'histoire d'O'gaya, regarde les illustrations. Où cette histoire se passe-t-elle? Quelles créatures en sont les caractères principaux? *dans la mer; les étoiles de mer*

B. Dans le fond de quelle mer vit la famille Micabwa?
   a. la mer Méditerranée
   b. la mer des Caraïbes
   c. la mer Egée

C. Que fait la famille Micabwa au début de l'histoire? Qui n'est pas là? *ils dînent; O'gaya*

D. Vrai ou faux?
   1. O'gaya mange avec sa famille. *faux*
   2. Fia est la fille aînée de la famille. *faux*
   3. L'ami de Fia est un poulpe. *vrai*
   4. Le père d'O'gaya s'inquiète pour elle. *vrai*

Connections and Comparisons

Language Arts Link
Before students begin to read, ask them for English examples of the literary devices mentioned in **De bons conseils.** You might have students write down one example of a *simile* (She shone like the sun), one of a *metaphor* (He was a raging bull of a man), and one of *personification* (the tree waved at the family). Then collect the papers, read the examples aloud, and have students tell which literary device is exemplified by each sentence. As an alternative, you might write the types of devices on a large sheet of butcher paper and have volunteers write examples below each one.

- Hélas! Nous ne pouvons pas t'aider ma petite fille, répond maman Micabwa.

- Mais, ajoute papa Micabwa, je connais la tortue millénaire Man Dou, elle pourrait te conseiller.

Déjà, O'gaya saute de joie :

- Pourrais-je partir dès demain?

Papa et maman Micabwa sourient tendrement :

- Mais, bien sûr ma chérie, tu pourras partir demain.

Le lendemain matin, O'gaya est si excitée qu'elle n'arrive pas à boire son lait d'éponge. Elle embrasse ses parents et part. Papa et maman Micabwa ne sont pas trop inquiets; l'heure est venue pour O'gaya de grandir et de vivre ses rêves. La voilà partie! Elle avance vite, quand, tout à coup, une rangée de dents lui barre la route.

- Hé ! Où va-t-on ainsi, sans plus se gêner? Vous prenez mon domaine pour un jardin public peut-être? demande Morfyo le requin. O'gaya frissonne, rassemble son courage et répond :

- M. Morfyo, je rêvais, et je suis entrée par hasard sur vos terres.

- Et à quoi rêves-tu, petite impudente?

- Je rêve d'être une *étoile de ciel*. Et je vais

voir si la tortue Man Dou peut m'aider!

Morfyo éclate de rire et des milliers de bulles se forment autour de lui.

- Ecoute, petite, des «comme toi», je n'en ai jamais vu. Vouloir vivre dans le ciel ! Je n'en crois pas mes ouïes!

O'gaya n'essaie pas de fuir et fait face au requin :

- Allez-vous me manger M. Morfyo ? demande-t-elle.

- Et en plus, tu as de l'audace ! Décidément, petite, tu m'es bien sympathique. Allez, je t'emmène, grimpe sur mon dos !

Le redoutable requin, son habit noir décoré d'une étrange fleur, O'gaya, se dirige sans hésitation vers la demeure de la tortue Man Dou.

Sur le chemin, ils croisent des poissons-pipelettes en pleine conversation qui, de stupeur, restent bouche-bée.

Morfyo dépose O'gaya à la porte de Man Dou. La petite étoile de mer descend quelques marches et dans un bassin de sable, elle voit une énorme tortue à la carapace brune et jaune comme les gorgones-éventail.

- Man Dou ! Man Dou ! appelle-t-elle timidement.

Une tête apparaît hors de la carapace, deux yeux d'or fondu la fixent.

Teaching Suggestion

You might ask students the following additional questions about the story: How does O'gaya feel about the trip? (excited) How does she show this? (She can't finish her sponge milk.) How do her parents feel about her leaving? (They aren't worried because they know it's time for their daughter to fulfill her own dreams.) How does she feel when she encounters the shark? (frightened) What offer does the shark make to O'gaya? (to carry her on his back) How did the other fish react to the sight of the shark and O'gaya? (They stood in open-mouthed astonishment.)

Additional Practice

K., L. Have students find a metaphor used to describe Man Dou **(deux yeux d'or fondu).**

Teaching Suggestion

Have students write a brief description in English of the characters they've encountered in the story so far, as if they were giving actors and actresses descriptions of their roles in a play.

E. Find five details that the author uses to draw an analogy between the Micabwa family and a human family.   *See answers below.*

F. Qu'est-ce qu'O'gaya rêve de devenir?   *une étoile de ciel*

G. The turtle Man Dou is a thousand years old. Why do O'gaya's parents send her to speak to the turtle? What does this tell you about this culture's attitude toward its elders?   *See answers below.*

H. Quelle est la première créature qu'elle rencontre?   *un requin*

I. What do you think **Je n'en crois pas mes ouïes !** means? If **ouïe** means *hearing* and **ouïes** means *gills*, what pun has the shark made?   *See answers below.*

J. Quelles sont les qualités d'O'gaya que le requin admire?   *son ambition et son audace*

K. What metaphor is found in the sentence that begins **Le redoutable requin...** ?   *See answers below.*

L. What simile do you find in the paragraph that begins **Morfyo dépose O'gaya...** ?   *See answers below.*

M. Recherche ces mots de vocabulaire et réfère-toi au contexte pour deviner leur sens.

tintinnabulent tinkle	**frissonne** tremble
vrombissement humming	**se pelotonne** curl up
tourbillon swirl	**frémit** shiver
luisent shine	**tisse** weave
grimpe climb	

N. What kind of creature is Man Kya? What deal does O'gaya make with Man Kya to realize her dream?   *See answers below.*

O. What metaphor is used to describe Man Kya's strange collection?   *See answers below.*

Answers

E. *Possible answers:* house with a porch, dinner table, clock brought back from trip, papa Micabwa having tea on the porch, sister's date

G. She can give advice; The culture values the wisdom of its elders.

I. *I can't believe my ears.* The shark is making a pun by transforming the usual expression (referring to ears) to suit his own physiology (gills).

K. *habit noir* (shark skin compared to black clothing), *étrange fleur* (O'gaya's star shape compared to a flower)

L. *à la carapace brune et jaune comme les gorgones-éventail* (with a brown and yellow shell like fan coral)

N. Man Kya is a spider crab; O'gaya must give Man Kya her eyes.

O. *fruits étranges et colorés* (eyes compared to strange, colored fruit)

Communication for All Students

Challenge

Have students write French captions for each of the illustrations on pages 298–299, telling what is happening in the story at that point.

Slower Pace

M. If some students have difficulty guessing some of the words listed, encourage other students who know the meaning of those words to mime them for those who don't.

Kinesthetic Learners

P. Have five volunteers mime the actions described here and have their classmates tell them in what order to stand.

Postreading

Activities S–T

Teaching Suggestion

T. You might have students discuss their answers to these questions in small groups or write their answers in their journals.

Visual Learners

Have students draw their own illustrations for the story, based on their interpretation of the events and the descriptions of the characters.

Terms in Lisons!

Students might want to know the following words from the story: **berceuse** *(cradle);* **bulle** *(bubble);* **emmener** *(to take with);* **demeure** *(home);* **cligne** *(blink);* **goémon** *(seaweed).*

Community Link

If students do the cooperative learning activity described on this page, you might have them perform their play at a local elementary school to promote interest in foreign languages.

Answers

R. Because the story is really about human dreams and what it takes to attain them. The characters must seem real in order for the story to have its full impact.

- Il faut que cela soit bien important pour que tu oses me réveiller !

- Oh! Oui, Man Dou, je voudrais être une *étoile de ciel.*

Man Dou cligne des yeux :

- Une *étoile de ciel!* Je ne peux rien faire pour toi, mais va voir l'araignée d'eau, Man Kya, elle n'habite pas loin d'ici. Bonne chance!

Man Dou se pelotonne à nouveau dans sa carapace.

O'gaya s'en va. Elle n'est pas longue à trouver la demeure de Man Kya, un antre de fougères marines.

- Man Kya, êtes-vous là?

- Oui, oui, entrez donc, j'arrive.

O'gaya soulève un rideau de longues et lourdes algues de goémon : elle se retrouve face à l'araignée d'eau.

- Que désires-tu petite? demande-t-elle d'une voix aigrelette.

- Etre une *étoile de ciel.*

- Une *étoile de ciel !* Drôle d'idée; enfin, si tu le désires ! Connais-tu le prix de mes services ?

- Non, répond O'gaya, étonnée.

- Pour ce que tu me demandes, le tarif est de deux yeux.

- Mes yeux ? dit d'une voix angoissée O'gaya.

- Oui, viens voir mon jardin!

Elle sort, O'gaya la suit. Dans l'enclos, poussent des coraux ; pendus aux branches, des yeux les regardent, fruits étranges et colorés.

- Que penses-tu de ma belle collection ? Alors, que décides-tu?

O'gaya frémit, mais son rêve est trop profondément gravé en elle pour être effacé par le temps. Elle accepte le marché et donne ses yeux. Alors, l'araignée d'eau Man Kya tisse une échelle avec le fil magique qu'elle sécrète.

L'ouvrage terminé, elle souffle trois notes dans une énorme conque. A la troisième note, un grand oiseau, une frégate noire, plonge. Elle lui met les deux boucles de l'échelle dans le bec et lui ordonne de les accrocher à un croissant de lune. La frégate remonte donc à la surface; l'échelle se déroule dans toute sa splendeur argentée.

Man Kya guide O'gaya et lui souhaite bon voyage.

La petite étoile de mer se hisse sur l'échelle, fil à fil, jusqu'au ciel.

Alors le soir, doux comme un baiser, se pose sur la mer chaude des Caraïbes; dans la maison du fond de l'eau, papa et maman Micabwa, assis sous la véranda, pensent tendrement à O'gaya.

Soudain, un reflet inattendu attire leur attention, ils se lèvent et regardent : tout là-haut, une petite étoile luit dans l'eau de la nuit.

P. Mets ces événements dans le bon ordre.

> **3** Man Kya souffle trois notes dans une énorme conque.

> **5** O'gaya se hisse sur l'échelle jusqu'au ciel.

> **4** Un oiseau accroche l'échelle à un croissant de lune.

> **1** O'gaya donne ses yeux à l'araignée d'eau.

> **2** Man Kya tisse une échelle.

Q. What simile do you find in the paragraph that begins **Alors le soir,... ?**
doux comme un baiser (soft as a kiss)

R. Why is personification an essential part of this story?   See answers below.

S. What need do you think O'gaya's dream expresses? What qualities are necessary for her to attain her dream?
Self-actualization; ambition, courage, self-sacrifice

T. Qu'est-ce que tu rêves de devenir quand tu seras adulte? Qu'est-ce que tu penses devoir faire pour réaliser ce rêve? Serais-tu prêt(e) à faire un grand sacrifice pour réaliser ce rêve, si nécessaire?

Cahier d'activités, p. 119, Act. 20

Connections and Comparisons

Cooperative Learning

Tell students that they are going to present the story of O'gaya as a play or puppet show for French elementary-school students. Have them work in groups to write a script in French for the play, based on the story they have just read. Remind them to include stage directions for the actors and actresses. Group members assume the roles of director, stage hand, set designer, and actors and actresses. The actors and actresses must memorize their lines. The director plans the staging and directs the production. The stage hand helps with costumes, gathers the props, and keeps them in order. The designer creates the set. Have students perform their play for the class and record it on videotape.

Ecrivons!

Une transformation incroyable!

Il y a beaucoup de façons de raconter une histoire. La même suite d'événements peut paraître très différente selon le format et le style de la présentation. Dans cette activité, tu vas raconter l'histoire d'Ogaya à la manière des journaux à sensation. Décris les événements en les exagérant et essaie de rendre ton histoire aussi dramatique et intéressante que possible.

> **Stratégie pour écrire**
> Style is a general term for the characteristics of a piece of writing. The style in which you write will usually be determined by what you are writing. For example, an academic paper requires a formal and objective tone, a high level of language, and a strict organization. A letter to a friend is informal, usually with slang expressions and a very loose organization. Advertising style often produces short, crisp sentences with words that appeal to the emotions. It's important that you use the accepted style for a type of writing, since violating that style might be considered unacceptable or ineffective.

A. Préparation

1. Avec ton/ta camarade, essayez de répondre aux questions suivantes.

   a. À quoi ressemble un journal à sensation? Est-ce que tu en connais? Qu'est-ce qui le rend différent d'un journal normal?

   b. Quels genres d'événements et de citations est-ce qu'on trouve dans les articles des journaux à sensation? Quelle sorte de photos est-ce qu'on peut y voir?

   c. Cherche la définition du mot *sensationalism* dans un dictionnaire anglais. En quoi est-ce que ces journaux font appel au sensationnalisme?

2. Fais un plan des événements principaux de l'histoire d'O'gaya.

B. Rédaction

1. Rédige le brouillon de ton histoire dans le style qu'utilisent les journaux à sensation.

   a. Regarde ton plan. Mets l'accent sur les parties de l'histoire qui sont les plus intéressantes.

   b. Choisis des mots que tu peux utiliser pour que l'histoire soit plus dramatique et plus sensationnelle.

   c. Change un peu les faits et exagère les détails pour rendre ton histoire plus dramatique.

   d. Illustre ton récit avec des citations réelles ou imaginaires.

C. Evaluation

1. Après avoir fini ton brouillon, relis ce que tu as écrit.

   a. Est-ce que tu as bien raconté ton histoire dans un style journalistique au lieu de simplement répéter les faits?

   b. Est-ce que ton récit est réellement intéressant et dramatique?

2. Rédige la version finale de ton article en prenant soin de corriger l'orthographe, la grammaire et le vocabulaire.

3. Illustre ton histoire avec des photos bizarres et peu crédibles telles que celles qu'on peut trouver dans un journal à sensation. Tu peux soit faire des dessins, soit découper des photos dans un vrai magazine.

Apply and Assess

Postwriting
Teaching Suggestions

• Ask the class for words and phrases they used in their papers to exaggerate the story and write them on a transparency. Then, have students reread and edit their stories, perhaps adding some of the words and expressions suggested by their classmates.

• Have students reread their rough draft with these questions in mind. Would their introduction inspire a reader to read further? Is the information distributed evenly throughout the article or is it given in its entirety at the beginning? If so, students should make sure that they develop that information in the middle of their article to hold the reader's attention all the way to the end.

Teaching Resources
p. 301

PRINT
▶ Lesson Planner, p. 51
▶ Cahier d'activités, p. 154
▶ Alternative Assessment Guide, p. 25
▶ Standardized Assessment Tutor, Chapter 10

MEDIA
▶ One-Stop Planner
▶ Test Generator, Chapter 10
▶ Interactive CD-ROM Tutor, Disc 3

Process Writing

Prewriting

Teaching Suggestion
You might suggest that students ask themselves the following questions to make their stories more sensationalistic: Were the parents devastated by the tragedy? Was O'gaya an exceptional child with extraordinary powers? Did Man Kya have a hidden agenda, perhaps linked to the jealous sister?

Writing

Auditory Learners
To give students an idea of how to sensationalize the story, read aloud a short factual story you have written or an interesting news article from the paper. Ask students what the facts of the story are. List them on the board. Then, ask students to suggest a sensationalistic headline for the story. Tell them to exaggerate the story by adding dramatic details.

Portfolio
Written This activity is appropriate for students' written portfolios. For portfolio information, see *Alternative Assessment Guide*, pages iv–15.

Grammaire supplémentaire

Première étape   Objectives Bragging; flattering; teasing

1 Fais des phrases avec les mots suivants. Utilise le superlatif de l'adjectif qui convient dans chaque phrase. (**p. 288**)

EXEMPLE   La Guadeloupe / île paradisiaque / la mer des Caraïbes
La Guadeloupe est l'île la plus paradisiaque de la mer des Caraïbes!

1. Ses habitants / les gens / accueillant / le monde
2. Sa végétation / la végétation / luxuriant / la région
3. Son climat / le climat / agréable / les tropiques
4. Ses hôtels / les hôtels / luxueux / que j'aie jamais vus
5. Ses plages / les plages / beau / les Antilles
6. Ses animaux marins / créature / bizarre / le monde
7. Ses restaurants / les restaurants / bon / la région
8. Son corail / le corail / coloré / les Antilles
9. Son carnaval / le carnaval / connu / les Antilles
10. L'île de Basse-Terre / l'île / grand / la Guadeloupe
11. La fête des Cuisinières / la fête / important / l'île
12. Ses coquillages / les coquillages / beau / que j'aie vus

Answers

1
1. Ses habitants sont les gens les plus accueillants du monde.
2. Sa végétation est la végétation la plus luxuriante de la région.
3. Son climat est le climat le plus agréable des tropiques.
4. Ses hôtels sont les hôtels les plus luxueux que j'aie jamais vus.
5. Ses plages sont les plages les plus belles des Antilles.
6. Ses animaux marins sont les créatures les plus bizarres du monde.
7. Ses restaurants sont les meilleurs restaurants de la région.
8. Son corail est le corail le plus coloré des Antilles.
9. Son carnaval est le carnaval le plus connu des Antilles.
10. L'île de Basse-Terre est la plus grande île de la Guadeloupe.
11. La fête des Cuisinières est la fête la plus importante de l'île.
12. Ses coquillages sont les plus beaux coquillages que j'aie vus.

Grammar Resources for Chapter 10

The **Grammaire supplémentaire** activities are designed as supplemental activities for the grammatical concepts presented in the chapter. You might use them as additional practice, for review, or for assessment.

For more grammar presentations, review, and practice, refer to the following:
• Travaux pratiques de grammaire
• Grammar Tutor for Students of French

• Grammar Summary on pp. R29–R54
• Cahier d'activités
• Grammar and Vocabulary quizzes (Testing Program)
• Test Generator
• Interactive CD-ROM Tutor
• **Jeux interactifs** at <u>go.hrw.com</u>

2 Maurice, ton ami guadeloupéen, te parle de sa famille. Complète ses remarques en utilisant le superlatif de l'adjectif qui convient et ... **que je connaisse.** (p. 288)

EXEMPLE   Ma sœur Martine est une fille très courageuse.
            En fait, c'est la fille la plus courageuse que je connaisse!

1. Mon frère Prosper est un plongeur très prudent. En fait, …
2. Mes cousins Rose et Pierre sont des enfants très timides. En fait, …
3. Mon père est un homme très sérieux. En fait, …
4. Ma mère est une femme très intelligente. En fait, …
5. Mon cousin Yves est un joueur de football très doué. En fait, …

3 Tes amis sont les meilleurs et ils le savent bien! Complète les dialogues suivants en utilisant le superlatif de l'adjectif qui convient. (**p. 288**)

EXEMPLE   —Vraiment, Fabien! C'est toi qui danse le mieux!
            —**Oui, c'est moi, le meilleur!**

1. Janine, c'est toi qui nages le plus vite!
2. Lisette et Laure, c'est vous qui conduisez le plus prudemment!
3. C'est moi qui cours le plus lentement, je sais bien!
4. C'est Viviane qui finit le plus vite!
5. C'est Gilles et Monique qui lisent le plus vite.
6. C'est Noël qui étudie le plus sérieusement.

4 Complète les dialogues suivants en utilisant le superlatif de l'adverbe qui convient. (**p. 288**)

EXEMPLE   BRIGITTE   Maxime conduit très prudemment!
            PASCAL   Oui, mais c'est moi qui **conduis le plus prudemment!**

1. BRIGITTE   Qu'est-ce qu'il saute haut, Eric!
   PASCAL   Oui, mais c'est moi qui…

2. BRIGITTE   C'est fou ce que Maryse nage vite!
   PASCAL   Oui, mais c'est moi qui…

3. BRIGITTE   A mon avis, Suzanne s'habille très bien.
   PASCAL   Oui, mais c'est moi qui…

4. BRIGITTE   Comme il court vite, ce garçon!
   PASCAL   Oui, mais c'est moi qui…

5. BRIGITTE   C'est fou comme Isabelle parle bien anglais.
   PASCAL   Oui, mais c'est moi qui…

Communication for All Students

Challenge

1 After students have completed this activity, have them use drawings or magazine cutouts to illustrate either your own community or town or an imaginary place. Then have them write a new activity modeled on this one. Redistribute the students' work and have them work individually on the activities created by their classmates.

Auditory Learners

3 Read the sentences out loud and have volunteers answer with the targeted forms of the superlatives. Then have students work in pairs. Tell them to take turns reading the sentences to each other and responding out loud with the appropriate superlatives. Have students write their responses once they have practiced them orally.

Answers

2 1. c'est le plongeur le plus prudent que je connaisse.
   2. ce sont les enfants les plus timides que je connaisse.
   3. c'est l'homme le plus sérieux que je connaisse.
   4. c'est la femme la plus intelligente que je connaisse.
   5. c'est le joueur de football le plus doué que je connaisse.

3 1. Oui, c'est moi, la plus rapide!
   2. Oui, c'est nous, les plus prudentes!
   3. Oui, c'est toi, le plus lent, or Oui, c'est toi, la plus lente!
   4. Oui, c'est elle, la plus rapide!
   5. Oui, c'est eux, les plus rapides.
   6. Oui, c'est lui, le plus sérieux.

4 1. saute le plus haut!
   2. nage le plus vite!
   3. m'habille le mieux!
   4. cours le plus vite!
   5. parle le mieux anglais.

Grammaire supplémentaire

CHAPITRE 10

 For **Grammaire supplémentaire** Answer Transparencies, see the *Teaching Transparencies* binder.

Grammaire supplémentaire

  WA3 FRANCOPHONE AMERICA-10

Deuxième étape Objectives Breaking some news; showing interest; expressing disbelief; telling a joke

5 La grand-mère guadeloupéenne d'Ophélia vient de te raconter l'histoire d'O'gaya, l'étoile de mer qui voudrait être une étoile de ciel. Ophélia veut savoir si tu as compris. Complète la conversation suivante avec le plus-que-parfait des verbes entre parenthèses. (**p. 295**)

OPHELIA   Dis! Tu as bien compris qu'O'gaya ___1___ (aller) voir Man Dou la tortue parce qu'elle voulait être une étoile de ciel?

TOI   Ah oui. Et j'ai compris qu'elle ___2___ (rencontrer) Morfyo le requin.

OPHELIA   Très bien! Mais est-ce que tu savais qu'O'gaya ___3___ (demander) au requin s'il allait la manger?

TOI   Non.

OPHELIA   Et tu ne savais pas non plus que le requin lui ___4___ (dire) qu'il la trouvait sympathique?

TOI   Je n'en avais aucune idée.

OPHELIA   Mais tu as dû quand même comprendre que le requin l'___5___ (emmener) sur son dos?

TOI   Ah, oui. Et que la tortue ___6___ (proposer) à O'gaya d'aller voir l'araignée d'eau.

OPHELIA   Pas mal.... Hmm... Voyons... Est-ce que tu as compris qu'O'gaya ___7___ (devoir) donner ses yeux à l'araignée d'eau?

TOI   Oui, ça j'ai bien compris. Et je crois avoir compris que l'araignée ___8___ (tisser) une échelle et l'___9___ (accrocher) à la lune.

OPHELIA   C'est ça! Et à la fin de l'histoire? Tu sais ce qui s'est passé?

TOI   Si je ne me trompe pas, ta grand-mère a dit qu'O'gaya___10___ (monter) jusqu'au ciel sur l'échelle?

OPHELIA   Oui, c'est ça!

Communication for All Students

Challenge

5 After students have completed this activity have them think of a legend or fairy tale they know well, and retell it the same way that Ophélia does here. Have them take turns retelling the story to a partner and checking comprehension, and then have them write the activity, using the correct plus-que-parfait forms.

Kinesthetic Learners

7 Copy the sentences in the box onto large strips of construction paper. Ask for five volunteers and give each of them one of the sentence strips. Ask the volunteers to line up with their sentences in the order that they appear in the box. Then have the remaining class members tell the volunteers where to stand, so that the joke appears in the correct order.

Answers

5
1. était allée
2. avait rencontré
3. avait demandé
4. avait dit
5. avait emmenée
6. avait proposé
7. avait dû
8. avait tissé
9. avait accrochée
10. était montée

6 Crée des questions avec les mots suivants. Commence chaque question par **Vous saviez que...** N'oublie pas de mettre le verbe au plus-que-parfait. (**p. 295**)

    EXEMPLE   Chantal et Frédéric / se quitter
                      Vous saviez que Chantal et Frédéric s'étaient quittés?

    1. Serge / aller à la boum de Bénédicte déguisé en Batman
    2. Ousmane et Milo / écrire une nouvelle chanson
    3. Blanche et Jonathan / se marier
    4. Michael Jordan / faire une pub pour des pizzas
    5. Agnès / se casser le bras
    6. Harrison et Margot / se fiancer
    7. Chloé / emboutir la voiture de ses parents
    8. Adamou et moi / se bagarrer

7 Ton copain Raphaël te raconte une blague, mais il mélange tout et tu ne comprends rien. Remets sa blague dans le bon ordre. (**p. 297**)

«Un petit Marseillais dit à sa mère : »

«Et sa mère lui répond : »

« Une souris grosse comme un éléphant! »

« Maman! Je viens de voir une souris énorme! »

« Ecoute, ça fait trente-six mille fois que je te dis de ne pas exagérer! »

    1. _____
    2. _____
    3. _____
    4. _____
    5. _____

Possible answers

6 1. ... Serge était allé à la boum de Bénédicte déguisé en Batman?
    2. ... Ousmane et Milo avaient écrit une nouvelle chanson?
    3. ... Blanche et Jonathan s'étaient mariés?
    4. ... Michael Jordan avait fait une pub pour des pizzas?
    5. ... Agnès s'était cassé le bras?
    6. ... Harrison et Margot s'étaient fiancés?
    7. ... Chloé avait embouti la voiture de ses parents?
    8. ... Amadou et moi, nous nous étions bagarrés?

7 1. Un petit Marseillais dit à sa mère:
    2. Maman! Je viens de voir une souris énorme!
    3. Une souris grosse comme un éléphant!
    4. Et sa mère lui répond:
    5. Ecoute, ça fait trente six mille fois que je te dis de ne pas exagérer!

Review and Assess

You may wish to assign the **Grammaire supplémentaire** activities as additional practice or homework after presenting material throughout the chapter. Assign Activities 1–4 after **Grammaire** (p. 288), Activities 5–6 after **Grammaire** (p. 295), and Activity 7 after **Comment dit-on... ?** (p. 297).

To prepare students for the **Etape** Quizzes and Chapter Test, we suggest doing the **Grammaire supplémentaire** activities in the following order. Have students complete Activities 1–4 before taking Quiz 10-1A or 10-1B; and Activities 5–7 before Quiz 10-2A or 10-2B.

The **Mise en pratique** reviews and integrates all four skills and culture in preparation for the Chapter Test.

Teaching Resources
pp. 306–307

PRINT
▶ Lesson Planner, p. 51
▶ Listening Activities, p. 77
▶ Video Guide, pp. 63, 65–66
▶ Grammar Tutor for Students of French, Chapter 10
▶ Standardized Assessment Tutor, Chapter 10

MEDIA
▶ One-Stop Planner
▶ Video Program
   Videocassette 4, 11:05–16:58
▶ Audio Compact Discs, CD 10, Tr. 13
▶ Interactive CD-ROM Tutor, Disc 3

Teaching Suggestion

Ask students the following questions about the article on Guadeloupe: **Où est-ce qu'on peut voir du corail?** (sur presque toutes les plages) **Qu'est-ce qu'il y a autour des coraux?** (des poissons de toutes les couleurs) **De quelle couleur sont les oursins qu'on peut manger?** (blancs) **Quels animaux est-ce qu'il est interdit de chasser quand on fait de la plongée?** (les langoustes et les tortues)

Mise en pratique

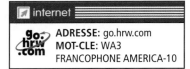

1 Ecoute ces conversations entre Nathalie et son frère Nicolas. Qui est-ce qui se moque de l'autre, Nathalie ou Nicolas? For scripts and answers, See Listening Activities, page 149.
CD 10 Tr. 13

2 Lis cet article du site "La Faune sous-marine de la Guadeloupe." Ensuite, réponds aux questions à la page 307.

La Guadeloupe

La Faune sous-marine de la Guadeloupe

Avec la mer Rouge et les lagons du Pacifique, les Antilles possèdent les fonds sous-marins les plus spectaculaires du monde.
Un site protégé a été créé autour des Ilets Pigeon en face de Malendure sur la Basse-Terre, où même les non-sportifs peuvent admirer les beautés sous-marines à bord de bateaux à fonds de verre.
Mais en Guadeloupe, nul besoin d'être un plongeur émérite pour pouvoir admirer le spectacle des poissons multi-colores, un simple masque et un tuba vous permettent d'explorer les récifs coralliens présents sur pratiquement toutes les plages et souvent même dans une eau peu profonde, mais toujours chaude et limpide.

Les coraux aux noms souvent poétiques comme Gorgones en forme d'éventails jaunes, bruns ou violets, Cornes d'Elans, Pâte à Chaux, Cerveaux de Vénus méritent la visite à eux seuls. Mais autour d'eux zigzague une foule de poissons de toutes les couleurs: les Sergents-majors jaunes et bleus, les Poissons-Papillons avec un deuxième œil fictif, les Poissons-perroquets, les Poissons-coffres, les Soleils écarlates, les Poissons-lunes, les Poissons-scorpions, les Balistes ...

Sur le sable vous pourrez voir des oursins blancs, les seuls comestibles ici, des étoiles de mer ou un des nombreux coquillages dont les Lambis, les Casques ou les Tritons sont les plus grandes espèces.

Les eaux de la Guadeloupe n'ont pratiquement pas d'habitants dangereux, il faut toutefois éviter les épines des oursins noirs non-comestibles, le Corail de Feu orange qui provoque des brûlures, les rares Méduses, la Murène et le Barracuda.

En haute mer, lors d'une sortie de pêche au gros, les Frégates vous indiquent des Dorades, des Thazards, des Thons, des Espadons, des Raies Manta et de temps en temps un Requin-marteau ou une famille de Cachalots et vous pourrez admirer le spectacle magnifique des poissons volants, les Exocets.

Respectez la mer !
La tentation est grande de cueillir des fragments de corail. Sachez que la récolte de coraux vivants est interdite - un récif met des dizaines d'années à se reconstituer ! Respectez les réglementations de capture de tortues et de langoustes, il n'y a que de cette façon que ce paradis aquatique le restera encore pour de nombreuses années.

Apply and Assess

Slower Pace

2 Before beginning the activity, have partners read the article together and make a list of the various sea creatures that are mentioned. Then, ask them to write what type of creature each one is, based on the information in the article, or have them categorize the creatures as fish, shells, protected animals, edible animals, dangerous marine life, and so on.

Language Note

2 Students might want to know the following terms from the article: **le plongeur émérite** *(very proficient diver);* **les récifs coralliens** *(coral reefs);* **mériter** *(to deserve);* **profond** *(deep);* **limpide** *(clear);* **les oursins** *(sea urchins);* **les épines** *(spines);* **non-comestibles** *(non-edible);* **les brûlures** *(burns);* **la langouste** *(lobster);* **les poissons volants** *(flying fish).*

STANDARDS: 1.2, 3.1

1. If you don't like to scuba dive, how can you see the under-sea beauty of the Antilles?

2. What are **Cerveaux de Vénus** and **Gorgones?**

3. According to this article, what edible delicacies are found on the beaches of Guadeloupe?

4. What are two kinds of fish the article mentions? Two kinds of shells?

5. What dangerous marine life does the article mention?

6. Are you allowed to take pieces of live coral? Why or why not?

3 Ton/ta correspondant(e) guadeloupéen(ne) voudrait avoir des nouvelles des Etats-Unis. Ecris-lui une lettre dans laquelle tu lui racontes les dernières nouvelles sur quelques célébrités.

4 Choisis une des situations suivantes. Tu te vantes. Si ton/ta camarade est impressionné(e), il/elle va te flatter. S'il/Si elle ne l'est pas, il/elle va te taquiner. Changez de rôle.

> Tu as une nouvelle voiture.
>
> Tu es le/la meilleur(e) dans un sport.
>
> Tu as piloté un avion.
>
> Tu as fait de la plongée.
>
> Tu as fait du deltaplane.
>
> Tu as les meilleures notes de la classe.

5 **Jeu de rôle**

Your French class is having a party in honor of your pen pal from Guadeloupe, who is visiting. At the party, you'll break some news, tell jokes, brag, flatter, and tease each other. With a group of your classmates, write out a script for this scene and act it out. Remember to include the following situations.

• Each of you makes up two bits of news to tell the others.

• The pen pal talks about what it's like in Guadeloupe. He/She makes up an event to brag about. The others flatter him/her.

• Each of you teases one of your friends.

Apply and Assess

Slower Pace

3 Have volunteers write each bit of news in Activity 3 as if they were relating it to a friend. (**Tu connais la nouvelle? On m'a dit que Jennie Garth avait joué dans un téléfilm.**) Then, have students write their letters as described in the activity.

Group Work

5 You might have students elect a director to help them stage their scene. Since all of the conversations cannot happen simultaneously, the director might decide to have two or three different scenes, each focusing on a different character. Students might videotape their scenes and use them later as a review for the test.

Mise en pratique

CHAPITRE 10

Speaking Assessment

4 You might use the following rubric when grading your students on this activity.

Speaking Rubric	Points			
	4	3	2	1
Content (Complete– Incomplete)				
Comprehension (Total–Little)				
Comprehensibility Comprehensible– Incomprehensible				
Accuracy (Accurate– Seldom accurate)				
Fluency (Fluent–Not fluent)				

18–20: A	14–15: C	Under
16–17: B	12–13: D	12: F

Teaching Suggestion

4 You might have partners act out the scenes for their classmates, who try to guess the situation.

Answers

2 1. snorkeling
2. types of coral
3. white sea urchins, starfish, and sea shells
4. *fish:* butterfly fish, parakeet fish *shells:* Lambis shells and Casques shells
5. sharks, sea urchins, jellyfish, orange coral, moray eel, and barracuda
6. No, because it takes years to grow back.

Que sais-je?

Teaching Resources
p. 308

PRINT
▸ Grammar Tutor for Students of French, Chapter 10

MEDIA
▸ Interactive CD-ROM Tutor, Disc 3
▸ Online self-test

go.hrw.com
WA3 FRANCOPHONE
AMERICA-10

Teaching Suggestion

8 9 10 You might have students use their answers to these activities to write and act out a brief skit about one friend telling a joke to another.

♞ Game

Tic Tac Toe Write the questions from **Que sais-je?** on index cards and put them in a bag. If a question has sub-questions, write each one on a separate card. Then, draw a tic tac toe grid on the board. In each of the squares, write a number to represent the number of questions that must be answered in order to put a marker in that square. In the top row, write the following numbers: **2** in the first square, **1** in the second, and **2** in the third. In the middle row, write **1**, **3**, and **1**. In the bottom row, write **2**, **1**, and **2**. Then, form two teams and have the first team select a square. Draw the appropriate number of cards from the bag and ask the team the questions. Team members may confer with one another, but only one member may answer. If the team answers the question(s) correctly, place an X or an O in the square. Put the cards back in the bag. Then, have the next team take a turn. If the same question is drawn a second time, players must use a different expression to answer it.

Que sais-je?

Can you use what you've learned in this chapter?

Can you brag?
p. 287

1 What would you say to brag in the following situations? *Possible answers:*
1. You finish an assignment before everyone else.   C'était fastoche, ça!
2. You win a race.   C'est moi qui cours le plus vite.
3. You get the highest grade on a test.
   C'est pas pour me vanter, mais c'est moi, le/la meilleur(e).

Can you flatter?
p. 287

2 What would you say to flatter a person if he/she were . . .   *Possible answers:*
1. really athletic?   Tu es fortiche. Tu es vraiment le/la meilleur(e).
2. a good student?   Tu es calé(e).
3. very artistic?   Alors, là, tu m'épates! Tu es l'artiste le/la plus doué(e) que je connaisse.

Can you tease?
p. 290

3 What would you say to tease the people in these situations?
1. Your friend seems to have a crush on someone.   Tu es amoureux(-euse) ou quoi?
2. Your brother gets dressed to go out on a date and none of his clothes match.   Non mais, tu t'es pas regardé!
3. You're playing tennis with a friend who keeps missing the ball.
   Réveille-toi un peu!

4 How would you respond to the teasing in number 3?
1. Oh, ça va, hein!   2. Lâche-moi, tu veux?   3. Ça peut arriver à tout le monde.

Can you break some news?
p. 295

5 What would you say to tell a friend what happened to these people?
Possible answers:

  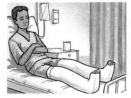

Ils se sont fiancés.   Elle s'est fait mal au dos.   Il s'est cassé les (deux) jambes.

Can you show interest?   p. 295

6 How would you show interest in something a friend was saying?
Ah oui? Qui t'a dit ça? Raconte! Et alors?

Can you express disbelief?   p. 295

7 What would you say if you didn't believe what your friend was telling you?
Mon œil! Ça m'étonnerait. N'importe quoi!

Can you tell a joke?
p. 297

8 How would you introduce a joke?
J'en connais une bonne. Est-ce que tu connais l'histoire de... ?

9 What would you say if you heard a joke you liked?   Elle est bien bonne!

10 What would you say if the joke were bad?   Elle est nulle, ta blague!

Review and Assess

♞ Game

Des blancs To prepare for the game, form five teams and give a transparency to each one. Assign each team five expressions from the chapter. Teams work together to write a logical paragraph or dialogue, using the expressions. Then, they copy it onto a transparency, leaving blank spaces where the assigned vocabulary should be. Collect the transparencies. To play the game, project the transparencies one at a time for thirty seconds each. Teams will write down the words they would use to fill in the blanks. They should sit out the round involving the transparency they created, so that each team will have four sets of answers. After you have shown the last transparency, have teams read their answers aloud and either verify or correct them. The team that filled in the most blanks correctly wins.

Bragging

C'est fastoche, ça!	That's so easy!
C'est pas pour me vanter, mais...	I'm not trying to brag, but . . .
Oh, j'en ai vu d'autres.	I've done/seen bigger and better things.
C'est moi, le/la meilleur(e).	*I'm* the best.
C'est moi qui... le mieux.	*I . . . the best.*

Flattering

Tu es fortiche/ calé(e).	You're really strong/good at that.
Alors là, tu m'épates!	I'm really impressed!
Tu en as, du courage.	You've really got courage.
Tu es vraiment le/la meilleur(e).	You're really the best.

Tu es le/la... le/la plus... que je connaisse.	You're the . . . -est . . . I know.

Sea life

une algue	seaweed
un coquillage	a shell
du corail	coral
un crabe	a crab
une crevette	a shrimp
un espadon	a swordfish
une étoile de mer	a starfish
un hippocampe	a seahorse
un homard	a lobster
une méduse	a jellyfish
une pieuvre	an octopus
un requin	a shark
un rocher	a rock
une tortue	a turtle

Teasing

Tu es amoureux/ amoureuse ou quoi?	Are you in love or what?

Non mais, tu t'es pas regardé(e)!	If you could see how you look!
Réveille-toi un peu!	Get with it!
Tu en rates pas une, toi!	You don't miss a thing, do you? (sarcastic)
Arrête de délirer!	Stop being so silly!
Lâche-moi, tu veux?	Will you give me a break?
Je t'ai pas demandé ton avis.	I didn't ask your opinion.
Oh, ça va, hein!	Oh, give me a break!
Qu'est-ce que tu en sais?	What do you know about it?
Ça peut arriver à tout le monde.	It could happen to anyone.
Et toi, arrête de m'embêter!	Stop bothering me!

 Circumlocution
Have students work with a partner. One partner has recently returned from a visit to an aquarium. On this trip, he or she took several pictures and is showing the pictures to the French exchange student. Since he or she doesn't know the terms for the sea creatures, the student gives a description to the French friend, who guesses what his or her friend is describing. (**—C'est un animal qui ne peut pas marcher vite! —C'est une tortue? —Oui, c'est ça.**)

Deuxième étape

Everyday life

s'acheter quelque chose	to buy oneself something
avoir des boutons	to have acne
se bagarrer	to fight
se casser le/la...	to break one's . . .
déménager	to move
emboutir la voiture	to wreck the car
se faire enlever les bagues	to get one's braces off
se faire mal à...	to hurt one's . . .
se faire percer les oreilles	to get one's ears pierced
se fiancer	to get engaged
perdre du poids	to lose weight
prendre des leçons de conduite	to take driving lessons

Breaking some news

Tu savais que... ?	Did you know that . . . ?

Tu connais la dernière?	Have you heard the latest?
J'ai entendu dire que...	I've heard that . . .
Figure-toi que...	Can you imagine that . . .
Si tu avais vu... !	If you could have seen . . . !

Showing interest

Oh là là!	Oh, wow!
Qui t'a dit ça?	Who told you that?
Raconte!	Tell me!
Et alors?	And then?

Expressing disbelief

Mon œil!	No way!
Je n'en reviens pas.	I don't believe it.
N'importe quoi!	Yeah, right!

Telling a joke

J'en connais une bonne.	I've got a good one.

Est-ce que tu connais l'histoire de... ?	Do you know the one about . . . ?
Quelle est la différence entre... et... ?	What's the difference between . . . and . . . ?
Quel est le point commun entre... et... ?	What do . . . and . . . have in common?
C'est l'histoire d'un mec qui...	It's about a guy who . . .
... et alors, il dit que...	. . . so he says . . .
... et l'autre lui répond...	. . . and then the other one answers . . .
Elle est bien bonne!	That's a good one!
Elle est nulle, ta blague!	What a bad joke!

Chapter 10 Assessment

▶ **Testing Program**
Chapter Test, pp. 221–226
Audio Compact Discs, CD 10, Trs. 16–18
Speaking Test, p. 299

▶ **Alternative Assessment Guide**
Portfolio Assessment, p. 25
Performance Assessment, p. 39
CD-ROM Assessment, p. 53

▶ **Interactive CD-ROM Tutor, Disc 3**
A toi de parler
A toi d'écrire

▶ **Standardized Assessment Tutor**
Chapter 10

▶ **One-Stop Planner, Disc 3**
Test Generator
Chapter 10

Review and Assess

♘ Game

Cercle de mots Make two identical sets of flash cards with French words or expressions on one side and their English equivalents on the other. Form two teams and have each one sit in a circle. Designate one student on each team to be the captain and one to be the judge. Then, distribute one card to each member of both teams. The captain begins by showing the English equivalent on his or her card to the teammate on his or her left. That student responds by giving the French expression. When the judge has verified the response, that student shows the English side of his or her own card to the student on his or her left. When all team members have had a turn, the captain stands up. The team whose captain stands up first wins.

Chapitre 11 : Laissez les bons temps rouler!
Chapter Overview

Mise en train pp. 312–314	*L'Arrivée à Lafayette*			

	FUNCTIONS	**GRAMMAR**	**VOCABULARY**	**RE-ENTRY**
Première étape pp. 315–319	• Asking for confirmation, p. 316 • Asking for and giving opinions, p. 318 • Agreeing and disagreeing, p. 318		• Musical instruments, p. 317 • Kinds of music, p. 317	• Renewing old acquaintances (**Chapitre 1**, III) • Types of music (**Chapitre 11**, II) • Agreeing and disagreeing (**Chapitre 9**, III) • Asking for and giving opinions (**Chapitre 4**, III)

Remise en train pp. 320–321	*Un festival cajun*			

Deuxième étape pp. 322–327	• Asking for explanations, p. 323 • Making observations, p. 326 • Giving impressions, p. 326		• Cajun food, p. 324	• Food vocabulary (**Chapitre 3**, II) • Emphasizing likes (**Chapitre 4**, II) • Relative pronouns **ce qui** and **ce que** (**Chapitre 4**, II)

Lisons! pp. 328–330	**Froumi et Grasshopper** **La Cigale et la fourmi**	**Reading Strategy** Understanding a dialect

Ecrivons! p. 331	**Un poète en herbe**	**Writing Strategy** Using poetic devices

Grammaire supplémentaire	**pp. 332–335**	**Première étape,** p. 332	**Deuxième étape,** pp. 333–335

Review pp. 336–339	**Mise en pratique,** pp. 336–337	**Que sais-je?,** p. 338	**Vocabulaire,** p. 339

CULTURE

- **Note culturelle,** Festivals in Louisiana, p. 314
- **Rencontre culturelle,** Overview of Louisiana, p. 315
- **Note culturelle,** Music in Louisiana, p. 317
- **Realia:** Letters from teenagers about music, p. 319
- **Panorama Culturel,** Parties and celebrations, p. 322

Chapitre 11 : Laissez les bons temps rouler!
Chapter Resources

 **PRINT**

Lesson Planning

 One-Stop Planner

Lesson Planner with Substitute Teacher Lesson Plans, pp. 52–56, 74

Student Make-Up Assignments
- Make-Up Assignment Copying Masters, Chapter 11

Listening and Speaking

Listening Activities
- Student Response Forms for Listening Activities, pp. 83–85
- Additional Listening Activities 11-1 to 11-6, pp. 87–89
- Additional Listening Activities (song), p. 90
- Scripts and Answers, pp. 153–158

Video Guide
- Teaching Suggestions, pp. 68–69
- Activity Masters, pp. 70–72
- Scripts and Answers, pp. 107–109, 116

Activities for Communication
- Communicative Activities, pp. 41–44
- Realia and Teaching Suggestions, pp. 81–83
- Situation Cards, pp. 109–110

Reading and Writing

Reading Strategies and Skills Handbook, Chapter 11

Joie de lire 3, Chapter 11

Cahier d'activités, pp. 121–132

Grammar

Travaux pratiques de grammaire, pp. 96–101

Grammar Tutor for Students of French, Chapter 11

Assessment

Testing Program
- Grammar and Vocabulary Quizzes, **Etape** Quizzes, and Chapter Test, pp. 235–248
- Score Sheet, Scripts and Answers, pp. 249–255

Alternative Assessment Guide
- Portfolio Assessment, p. 26
- Performance Assessment, p. 40
- CD-ROM Assessment, p. 54

Student Make-Up Assignments
- Alternative Quizzes, Chapter 11

Standardized Assessment Tutor
- Reading, pp. 43–45
- Writing, p. 46
- Math, pp. 51–52

 **MEDIA**

 Online Activities
- Jeux interactifs
- Activités Internet

Video Program
- Videocassette 4
- Videocassette 5 (captioned version)

 Audio Compact Discs
- Textbook Listening Activities, CD 11, Tracks 1–13
- Additional Listening Activities, CD 11, Tracks 19–25
- Assessment Items, CD 11, Tracks 14–18

 Interactive CD-ROM Tutor, Disc 3

Teaching Transparencies
- Situation 11-1 to 11-2
- **Grammaire supplémentaire** Answers
- **Travaux pratiques de grammaire** Answers

  One-Stop Planner CD-ROM

Use the **One-Stop Planner CD-ROM with Test Generator** to aid in lesson planning and pacing.

For each chapter, the **One-Stop Planner** includes:
- Editable lesson plans with direct links to teaching resources
- Printable worksheets from resource books
- Direct launches to the HRW Internet activities
- Video and audio segments
- Test Generator
- Clip Art for vocabulary items

Chapitre 11 : Laissez les bons temps rouler!

Projects

La Cuisine cajun

Students will stage a Cajun cooking show.

> **MATERIALS**
> ✂ **Students may need**
> - Cajun cookbooks
> - French-English dictionaries
> - Food items
> - Cooking utensils
> - Camcorder
> - Videocassette

SUGGESTED SEQUENCE

1. All students should bring to class cookbooks with Cajun or creole recipes to share. Partners will look through the cookbooks and select a recipe to feature on their show.

2. Next, students write a list of the necessary ingredients in French. They should also write out simple, step-by-step instructions on how to prepare the dish they've selected.

3. Have students write the script for their cooking show. This script should include simplified instructions for preparing the recipe, as well as interesting dialogue about Cajun cuisine. For example, when the "chef" is demonstrating the instruction **Ensuite, il faut ajouter du piment**, the helper might comment **Du piment?! Ça va être épicé!** The chef might respond **Dans la cuisine cajun, tu sais, on utilise toujours beaucoup d'épices.** You might show excerpts of television cooking shows to give students ideas about what to say in their dialogue.

4. Partners then plan the staging of their show. They should collect the necessary ingredients and utensils. They might also hold several "dress rehearsals" to practice timing and coordination.

5. Although this project does not require it, students might prepare the recipe at home and distribute samples to the class after their demonstration.

6. Have students perform their shows for the class. Have volunteers videotape their classmates' performances.

> **GRADING THE PROJECT**
> Suggested Point Distribution (total = 100 points)
> Content..25 points
> Language/vocabulary use ....25 points
> Creativity..25 points
> Presentation ....25 points

Games

Dialogues spontanés

In this game, students will create dialogues, using vocabulary from this and preceding chapters. This game can be used to review vocabulary and functions in preparation for the final exam.

Procedure Tell partners to write a dialogue, each line of which must begin with a different letter of the alphabet in alphabetical order. That is, the first letter of the first speaker's line must be A, the first letter of the second speaker's line must be B, and so on. A sample dialogue is given below. Players take turns writing lines and may refer to the alphabetical glossary at the back of the book. You might give prizes for the dialogue that uses the entire alphabet, for the most interesting yet logical dialogue, and for the dialogue that includes the most chapter vocabulary.

Sample dialogue:

—Alain, c'était comment, tes vacances en Louisiane?
—Ben, super!
—C'était intéressant, la musique zydeco?
—D'habitude, je n'aime pas trop la musique, mais le zydeco, j'adore!
—Et tu as vu des alligators?
—...

Vingt questions

In this guessing game, students will practice vocabulary for Cajun food.

Procedure This game can be played by the entire class or by small groups. Write the names of Cajun dishes and ingredients typically used in Cajun cuisine on separate index cards and put them in a bag. If several small groups are playing, each group will need a set of cards and a bag. One player draws a card from the bag. Then, the class tries to determine the dish or ingredient by asking up to twenty yes-no questions. (**C'est un légume? C'est un plat? C'est épicé?**) If you play this game with small groups, you might set a time limit and see which group can guess the most items in that time.

Variation This game could also focus on different kinds of music and musical instruments. Instead of selecting a vocabulary card, the player assumes the identity of a famous musician or singer. (Harry Connick, Jr.) The player's teammates then ask yes-no questions to determine the type of music and instrument the artist plays. (**Tu fais du rap? Tu joues de la flûte?**)

Storytelling

Mini-histoire

This story accompanies Teaching Transparency 11-2. The **mini-histoire** *can be told and retold in different formats, acted out, written as dictation, and read aloud to give students additional opportunities to practice all four skills. In the following story, the Martins, who are spending their vacation in New Orleans, are having lunch and trying to decide what to do next.*

La famille Martin est en vacances à La Nouvelle-Orléans. Alors qu'elle est en train de déguster un repas typiquement cajun, elle discute de ce qu'elle va faire une fois le repas fini. Madame Martin voudrait visiter une plantation mais son mari, lui, préférerait aller écouter un concert de jazz dans le vieux carré. Les enfants ne sont pas d'accord. Guillaume, leur fils, a un sens de l'aventure un peu plus developpé et il aimerait aller donner à manger aux crocodiles dans les bayous. Sa sœur, Stéphanie, voudrait voir la parade du carnaval. Après une longue discussion, ils tombent d'accord. Ils vont aller visiter la plantation. Sur la plantation, il y a une réserve de crocodiles et les touristes peuvent les nourrir. Ils dîneront ensuite dans un restaurant où il y a un concert de jazz, et après dîner, ils iront à la parade du carnaval.

Traditions

Le Courir de mardi gras

The **Courir de mardi gras,** the rural Mardi Gras celebration of southern Louisiana, dates back to when the Acadians first settled the area. Although altered by frontier influences, it stems from the medieval **fête de la Quémande,** a ceremonial begging ritual. Bands of masked and costumed riders on horseback visit farmhouses throughout the countryside "begging" for contributions to a communal gumbo. Once granted permission to enter a property, the riders charge toward the house where they dance and sing for donations of chickens, onions, and other ingredients for the gumbo. At the end of the day, a **fais do-do,** or dance, is held in town, where the entire community celebrates and eats the communal gumbo. Ask students if they know of other traditions that may also have their roots in the **fête de la Quémande.** Have them compare those traditions to the **Courir de mardi gras.**

Recette

Bell peppers originate from the Americas. They actually belong to the fruit category. Green, yellow, and red bell peppers are the same species at different stages of maturity. Red peppers are the sweetest, yellow peppers the juiciest, and green peppers the fruitiest, but most bitter. The best time to eat bell peppers is between May and October.

SALADE CREOLE

pour 6 personnes

Salade

2 poivrons rouges

2 poivrons verts

1 oignon

3 branches de céleri

2 tomates

1/2 tasse d'olives vertes

Vinaigrette

8 cuillères à soupe d'huile d'olive

2 cuillères à soupe de vinaigre blanc

1 gousse d'ail hachée

basilic

sel

poivre

Salade

Couper les légumes. Les mélanger dans un saladier. Mettre au frigidaire jusqu'au moment de servir.

Vinaigrette

Mélanger l'huile d'olive, le vinaigre, l'ail, le sel, le poivre et le basilic.

Verser la vinaigrette sur la salade au moment de servir.

Technology

Videocassette 4, Videocassette 5 (captioned version)
See Video Guide, pp. 67–72.

Video Program

Camille et compagnie • Onzième épisode : *Il faut de tout pour faire un gombo*

Max, Laurent, Azzedine, and Sophie are organizing a Cajun dinner party for Camille before she leaves for Louisiana. Sophie and Azzedine go to the market to buy the necessary ingredients to make a chicken gumbo and spinach-stuffed mushrooms, while Max and Laurent go to the library to check out a few CDs of Cajun music. But there are a few problems. Sophie and Azzedine cannot find okra and decide to use green beans instead. Azzedine loves the music Max has selected, but Laurent doesn't. Unfortunately for Camille, the dinner is ruined, because the mushrooms are burned and the gumbo is too spicy. So, the five friends decide to get a pizza.

Comment est-ce qu'on fait la fête ici?

People from around the francophone world talk about parties and celebrations. Two native speakers discuss the **Panorama Culturel** question and introduce the interviews.

Vidéoclips

- **Lactel®**: Advertisement for milk with a long shelf life
- **News report:** La rue des Beaux arts

Interactive CD-ROM Tutor

The **Interactive CD-ROM Tutor** contains videos, interactive games, and activities that provide students an opportunity to practice and review the material covered in Chapter 11.

Activity	Activity Type	Pupil's Edition Page
1. **Vocabulaire**	Jeu des paires	p. 317
2. **Comment dit-on... ?**	Chacun à sa place	p. 318
3. **Vocabulaire**	Chacun à sa place	p. 324
4. **Vocabulaire**	Prenons note!	p. 324
5. **Grammaire**	Les mots qui manquent	p. 326
6. **Comment dit-on... ?**	Du tac au tac	pp. 316, 318, 323, 326
Panorama Culturel	Comment est-ce qu'on fait la fête ici? Le bon choix	p. 322
A toi de parler	*Guided recording*	pp. 336–337
A toi d'écrire	*Guided writing*	pp. 336–337

Teacher Management System

Logging In

Logging in to the *Allez, viens!* TMS is easy. Upon launching the program, simply type "admin" in the password area of the log-in screen and press RETURN. Log on to **www.hrw.com/CDROMTUTOR** for a detailed explanation of the Teacher Management System.

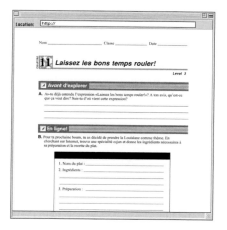

One-Stop Planner CD-ROM

To preview all resources available for this chapter, use the **One-Stop Planner CD-ROM**, Disc 3.

Internet Connection

📶 internet

go. hrw .com **ADRESSE:** go.hrw.com
MOT-CLE: WA3
FRANCOPHONE
AMERICA-11

*Have students explore the __go.hrw.com__ Web site for many online resources covering all chapters. All Chapter 11 resources are available under the keyword **WA3 FRANCO-PHONE AMERICA-11.** Interactive games help students practice the material and provide them with immediate feedback. You'll also find a printable worksheet that provides Internet activities that lead to a comprehensive online research project.*

Jeux interactifs

You can use the interactive activities in this chapter

- to practice grammar, vocabulary, and chapter functions
- as homework
- as an assessment option
- as a self-test
- to prepare for the Chapter Test

Activités Internet

Students look for information about Cajun food and music, using the vocabulary and phrases from the chapter.

- After completing the activity sheet, have students work with a partner and share the information they gathered in Activities B and C on that sheet. Then ask each pair of students to share what they learned with the class. In Activity D, students are asked to write about their impressions of Cajun culture in their journals. Have partners exchange their journal entries and edit each other's work.

Projet

Have groups of students select a Cajun song they discovered in Activity C and find out more about it. They might research the song's origin, the musical instruments with which it is traditionally played, and any recordings that might be available. Have them find and distribute the lyrics, then play or sing it for the class. Remind students to document their sources by noting the names and the URLs of all the sites they consulted.

Textbook Listening Activities Scripts

Première étape

6   p. 316
Answers to Activity 6
2, 3, 5, 6, 7

1. —Tiens, Robert! Dis donc, tu n'as pas changé, toi!
—Toi non plus! C'est dommage qu'on ne se voie pas plus souvent.
—Oui, c'est vrai. Pourquoi tu ne me donnes pas ton numéro de téléphone? On pourrait peut-être sortir un de ces soirs.
—Bonne idée.

2. —Emilie? C'est bien toi? Je ne pensais pas que tu pourrais venir, tu habites si loin. Tu vis toujours à Denver, non?
—Oui, mais je suis en vacances dans la région en ce moment.

3. —Carole? Non, elle n'est pas venue.
—Pourquoi?
—Ben, tu sais, avec son travail, elle est toujours à l'étranger. Je crois qu'elle est en Europe en ce moment d'ailleurs.
—Ah oui, c'est vrai. Elle est bien journaliste.

4. —Je n'ai jamais revu Simon. Et toi?
—Moi non plus. Tu sais, on n'était pas très amis tous les deux.

5. —Et qu'est-ce qu'il devient, le frère de Michelle?
—Si je me souviens bien, il est dans l'armée. Je crois qu'il habite à Austin.

6. —Dis, Laure, tu as vu... zut, comment elle s'appelle, cette fille, déjà?
—Quelle fille?
—Tu sais bien, celle qui sortait avec David.
—Ah! Tu veux dire Jeanne.

7. —Michel, quelle bonne surprise! Je ne m'attendais pas à te voir ici.
—Je suis venu accompagner ma sœur. Tu sais à quel point elle est timide, elle ne voulait pas venir toute seule.
—Ta sœur, elle s'appelle Marianne, c'est ça?
—Oui.

9   p. 317

a. 1. [Jazz music]
   2. [Rock music]
   3. [Country music]
   4. [Rap music]
   5. [Cajun music]
   6. [Classical music]
   7. [Blues music]
   8. [Dance music]

b. 1. [A piano]
   2. [A saxophone]
   3. [A flute]
   4. [A bass guitar]
   5. [Drums]
   6. [A violin]
   7. [An accordion]
   8. [A synthesizer]
   9. [A trumpet]
   10. [A drum machine]

Answers to Activity 9

a. 1. jazz	3. country	5. musique cajun	7. blues
2. rock	4. rap	6. musique classique	8. dance
b. 1. un piano	5. une batterie	9. une trompette	
2. un saxophone	6. un violon	10. une boîte à rythmes	
3. une flûte	7. un accordéon		
4. une basse	8. un synthé(tiseur)		

13   p. 318

ANNE   Qu'est-ce que tu penses de ce C.D. de Miles Davis?
SIMON   Je le trouve hyper cool, moi. Tu sais bien que j'adore le jazz.
ANNE   Moi aussi, j'adore. Et le blues, ça te branche?
SIMON   Oui, ça m'éclate.
ANNE   Quel artiste de blues est-ce que tu préfères?
SIMON   Ben moi, j'aime bien Patricia Kaas. Qu'est-ce que tu en penses, toi?
ANNE   Ben, moi, je préfère Billie Holiday.
SIMON   Tu as entendu parler des Pixies?
ANNE   Euh, c'est un groupe de rock, non?
SIMON   Oui, c'est ça.
ANNE   Ça te branche, le rock?
SIMON   Oui, beaucoup. Et toi, ça te plaît?
ANNE   Euh, pas tellement. Moi, je préfère la dance.
SIMON   Oh. C'est nul, ça.
ANNE   Mais non, pas du tout. Moi, j'aime bien ce genre de rythmes.
SIMON   Chacun ses goûts.
ANNE   Oui, c'est vrai. Il y a des gens qui adorent le rap, par exemple.
SIMON   Ben moi, j'aime beaucoup. C'est vachement branché.
ANNE   Hmm. Moi, je trouve que c'est pas mal, mais...
SIMON   Je suppose que tu préfères le country?
ANNE   Ben oui. C'est très bien, le country.
SIMON   Tu délires ou quoi? C'est nul comme musique!
ANNE   Mais non, tu as tort! C'est très chouette!
SIMON   N'importe quoi!

Answers to Activity 13

Simon aime :	Anne est d'accord?
le jazz	oui
le blues	oui
le rock	non
le rap	oui, mais elle préfère le country

Deuxième étape

22   p. 323
Answers to Activity 22
2, 3, 6, 7, 8

1. —Tu vois le tee-shirt là-bas?
—Lequel?
—Celui avec «J'aime La Nouvelle-Orléans» écrit dessus.
—Oui.
—Il est chouette, non?

2. —Hmm. C'est très bon. Comment est-ce qu'on appelle ça?
—Ça, c'est du boudin. Tu aimes ça, vraiment?
—Oui, c'est délicieux.

3. —Qu'est-ce que ça veut dire, Atchafalaya?
—Oh, c'est le nom d'un marais très connu ici.

4. —Bon. Ben, à quelle heure est-ce qu'on se donne rendez-vous?
—A huit heures? Ça te va?
—Oui, ça me va.

5. —Tu ne sais pas où on vend des pâtisseries?
—Si. Je connais une excellente pâtisserie qui s'appelle Poupart.

6. —Qu'est-ce que c'est, ça, là-bas?
—Oh, ça, c'est le musée du jazz. Tu veux le visiter?
—Oui, bonne idée!

7. —Comment est-ce qu'on fait les bananes Foster?
—On fait sauter les bananes dans du beurre et puis on les flambe.

8. —D'où vient le nom Louisiane?
—Ça vient du roi Louis XIV. C'était le roi de France au moment où les Français sont arrivés ici.

9. —Où est-ce que tu as dormi?
—Dans un bed & breakfast installé sur une ancienne plantation.
—C'était cher?
—Oui, assez cher.

25 **p. 325**
Answers to Activity 25
1. f 2. e 3. a 4. b 5. c 6. d

1. SIMON Qu'est-ce que tu vas prendre, toi?
ANNE Oh, je ne sais pas. J'hésite. Et toi?
SIMON Ben, moi, je vais essayer les crevettes frites. C'est mon plat préféré et on m'a dit qu'elles sont excellentes ici.

2. SIMON Dis, c'est bien un sandwich, ça?
ANNE Oui.
SIMON Ben, qu'est-ce qu'il y a dedans?
ANNE Il peut y avoir des écrevisses, des huîtres ou de la viande. Là, tu vois? Celui-là est aux huîtres.
SIMON Ça a l'air bon.
ANNE Oui, tu devrais en goûter un.

3. SIMON Qu'est-ce que c'est, les huîtres Rockefeller, déjà?
ANNE C'est un hors-d'œuvre aux huîtres et aux épinards.
SIMON Tu as bien dit que c'était assez salé, non?
ANNE Ah non. Pas du tout. C'est pas très salé.

4. SIMON Comment est-ce qu'on fait le gombo?
ANNE Tu veux en faire chez toi?
SIMON Oui, j'adore.
ANNE Bon. C'est pas trop compliqué. Il faut des okras, du riz, des crevettes, du crabe et quelques épices. Je te donnerai la recette, si tu veux.

5. SIMON C'est bien un dessert, ça?
ANNE Oui.
SIMON Qu'est-ce qu'il y a dedans?
ANNE Il y a du pain, du lait, de la crème et des raisins secs.
SIMON Je vais en prendre.

6. SIMON Comment on appelle ça, déjà?
ANNE Quoi?
SIMON Ce plat-là, avec du riz.
ANNE Lequel? Celui avec du poulet, du porc et des saucisses?
SIMON Oui, celui-là.
ANNE On appelle ça du «jambalaya».

29 **p. 326**
Answers to Activity 29
1, 3, 4, 7

1. ELISE Je suis contente d'être venue faire un tour dans ce marché.
PAUL Tu vois, je t'avais bien dit que ça te plairait.
ELISE Oui. Ce qui est vraiment intéressant, c'est de voir toutes ces épices qu'on n'a pas en France.

2. PAUL Dis, Elise, tu voudrais faire un pique-nique demain?
ELISE Bien sûr. Où ça?
PAUL Au parc Audubon. Voyons, qu'est-ce que tu voudrais manger?
ELISE Pourquoi pas des po-boys?
PAUL Bonne idée.

3. ELISE Ce que j'adore ici, c'est l'ambiance. Les gens sont vraiment très accueillants et ils adorent faire la fête.
PAUL Tu vois, je t'avais bien dit que la Louisiane était l'endroit idéal pour passer tes vacances.

4. ELISE Tiens! Regarde un peu. Elle a l'air d'être vraiment vieille, cette maison-là.
PAUL Mais bien sûr! C'est une maison ante-bellum. Tu veux en faire la visite?
ELISE Oui, pourquoi pas.

5. PAUL Allez, dépêche-toi! On risque d'être en retard et de rater le début du concert.
ELISE Mais on a largement le temps.
PAUL Non. Il est déjà huit heures.
ELISE Oh, c'est pas vrai! Zut alors!

6. ELISE Qu'est-ce que c'est, ces bonbons-là?
PAUL Ce sont des pralines. Tu veux goûter? C'est très bon. Tiens.
ELISE Mmm, j'adore.
PAUL Oui. Moi aussi.

7. ELISE Comment est-ce qu'il s'appelle, ce musée, déjà?
PAUL Le musée Conti.
ELISE C'est la première fois que je visite un musée de cire.
PAUL Qu'est-ce que tu en dis?
ELISE Ben, les visages sont vraiment bien faits. On dirait que les personnages sont vivants!

For the listening scripts of the **Mise en pratique**, see *Listening Activities*, page 155.

Chapitre 11 : Laissez les bons temps rouler!
Suggested Lesson Plans *50-Minute Schedule*

Day 1

CHAPTER OPENER 10 min.
- Present Chapter Objectives, p. 311.
- Culture Note and Language Note, ATE, pp. 310–311

MISE EN TRAIN 35 min.
- Presenting **Mise en train**, ATE, p. 312
- Community Link and Culture Notes, ATE, pp. 312–314
- Do Activities 1–4, p. 314.
- Read and discuss **Note culturelle**, p. 314

Wrap-Up 5 min.
- Do Activity 5, p. 314.

Homework Options
Cahier d'activités, Act. 1, p. 121

Day 2

MISE EN TRAIN
Quick Review 5 min.
- Check homework.

RENCONTRE CULTURELLE 20 min.
- Presenting **Rencontre culturelle**, ATE, p. 315
- **Qu'en penses-tu?**, p. 315
- Read and discuss **Savais-tu que… ?**, p. 315.
- Culture Note, History Link, and Language Notes, ATE, p. 315

PREMIERE ETAPE
Comment dit-on… ?, p. 316 20 min.
- Presenting **Comment dit-on… ?**, ATE, p. 316
- Play Audio CD for Activity 6, p. 316.
- Cahier d'activités, p. 122, Acts. 2–3

Wrap-Up 5 min.
- Have students do Activity 8, p. 316, in pairs.

Homework Options
Pupil's Edition, Activity 7, p. 316

Day 3

PREMIERE ETAPE
Quick Review 5 min.
- Check homework.

Vocabulaire, p. 317 20 min.
- Presenting **Vocabulaire**, ATE, p. 317
- Play Audio CD for Activity 9, p. 317.
- Cahier d'activités, p. 123, Acts. 4–5
- Do Activities 10–11, pp. 317–318.
- Read and discuss **Note culturelle**, p. 317.
- Have students do Activity 12, p. 318, in pairs.

Comment dit-on… ?, p. 318 20 min.
- Presenting **Comment dit-on… ?**, ATE, p. 318
- Play Audio CD for Activity 13, p. 318.
- Cahier d'activités, pp. 124–125, Acts. 6–8
- Do Activity 14, p. 319.
- Have students do Activity 15, p. 319, in pairs.
- Read and discuss **A la française**, p. 319.

Wrap-Up 5 min.
- Activity 16, p. 319

Homework Options
Study for Quiz 11-1
Pupil's Edition, Activity 17, p. 319
Grammaire supplémentaire, Act. 1, p. 332
Travaux pratiques de grammaire, Acts. 1–4, pp. 96–97

Day 4

PREMIERE ETAPE
Quiz 11-1 20 min.
- Administer Quiz 11-1A or 11-1B.

REMISE EN TRAIN 25 min.
- Presenting **Remise en train**, ATE, p. 320
- Do Activities 18–20, pp. 320–321.
- Culture Notes, ATE, p. 321

Wrap-Up 5 min.
- Do Activity 21, p. 321.

Homework Options
Cahier d'activités, Act. 9, p. 126

Day 5

REMISE EN TRAIN
Quick Review 5 min.
- Check homework

PANORAMA CULTUREL 20 min.
- Presenting **Panorama Culturel**, ATE, p. 322
- See Viewing Suggestion 1, Video Guide, p. 69. Do Viewing Activity, Video Guide, p. 71.
- Questions, ATE, p. 322
- Discuss **Qu'en penses-tu?**, p. 322.
- Thinking Critically: Comparing and Contrasting, ATE, p. 322

DEUXIEME ETAPE
Comment dit-on… ?, p. 323 20 min.
- Presenting **Comment dit-on… ?**, ATE, p. 323
- Play Audio CD for Activity 22, p. 323.
- Read and discuss **A la française**, p. 323.
- Do Activity 23, p. 323.
- Have students do Activity 24, p. 324, in pairs.

Wrap-Up 5 min.
- Culture Notes, ATE, p. 324

Homework Options
Cahier d'activités, Act. 10, p. 127

Day 6

DEUXIEME ETAPE
Quick Review 5 min.
- Check homework.

Vocabulaire, p. 324 20 min.
- Presenting **Vocabulaire**, ATE, p. 324
- Play Audio CD for Activity 25, p. 325.
- Travaux pratiques de grammaire, pp. 99–100, Acts. 7–9
- Do Activity 26, p. 325.
- Do Activity 28, p. 325, in groups.

Comment dit-on… ?, p. 326 20 min.
- Presenting **Comment dit-on… ?**, ATE, p. 326
- Do Activity 29, p. 326.
- Read and discuss **Tu te rappelles?**, p. 326.
- Cahier d'activités, p. 130, Acts. 16–17
- **Grammaire supplémentaire**, pp. 334–335, Acts. 8–10
- Do Activities 31–32, p. 327.

Wrap-Up 5 min.
- Do Activity 33, p. 327, in groups.

Homework Options
Study for Quiz 11-2
Cahier d'activités, Acts. 11–15, pp. 127–129
Travaux pratiques de grammaire, Acts. 10–12, pp. 100–101

One-Stop Planner CD-ROM

For alternative lesson plans by chapter section, to create your own customized plans, or to preview all resources available for this chapter, use the **One-Stop Planner CD-ROM**, Disc 3.

 For additional homework suggestions, see activities accompanied by this symbol throughout the chapter.

Day 7

DEUXIEME ETAPE

Quiz 11-2 20 min.
- Administer Quiz 11-2A or 11-2B.

LISONS! 25 min.
- Read and discuss **Stratégie pour lire**, p. 328.
- Do Prereading Activity A, p. 328 and Teaching Suggestion, ATE, p. 328.
- Culture Note, ATE, p. 328
- Have students read **Lisons!**, pp. 328–330.
- Do Reading Activities B–J, pp. 328–330.

Wrap-Up 5 min.
- Building on Previous Skills, ATE, p. 329

Homework Options
Cahier d'activités, Act. 18, p. 131

Day 8

LISONS! 20 min.
- Do Activity K, p. 330
- Challenge, ATE, p. 330

ECRIVONS! 25 min.
- Read and discuss the **Stratégie pour écrire** p. 331, then have students work on their poems.

Wrap-Up 5 min.
- Allow time for peer and self-evaluation of poems.

Homework Options
Complete final draft of poems.

Day 9

ECRIVONS!

Quick Review 10 min.
- Have volunteers share their poems with the class.

MISE EN PRATIQUE 35 min.
- Play Audio CD for Activity 1, p. 336.
- Language Note, ATE, p. 336
- Play Audio CD for Activity 2, p. 337. See Tactile Learners, ATE, p. 337.
- **A toi d'écrire,** CD-ROM Tutor, Disc 3

Wrap-Up 5 min.
- Activities for Communication, p. 110, Situation (global): Role-Play

Homework Options
Cahier d'activités, Act. 19, p. 132

Day 10

MISE EN PRATIQUE

Quick Review 5 min.
- Check homework.

Student Review 45 min.
- Have students do Activity 4, p. 337, in pairs.
- Do Activity 5, p. 337.
- **A toi de parler,** CD-ROM Tutor or DVD Tutor
- Show **Vidéoclips,** Video Program, Videocassette 4.
- See Pre-viewing, Viewing, and Post-viewing Suggestions, Video Guide, p. 69.

Homework Options
Complete articles for Act. 5, p. 337.

Day 11

MISE EN PRATIQUE

Quick Review 10 min.
- Have volunteers share articles from Activity 5, p. 337.

Student Review 30 min.
- Have groups of students prepare scenes for **Jeu de rôle,** p. 337.
- Have groups present scenes from **Jeu de rôle.**
- Activities for Communication, p. 109, Situation (global): Interview

Wrap-Up 10 min.
- Begin **Que sais-je?,** p. 338.

Homework Options
Que sais-je?, p. 338

Day 12

MISE EN TRAIN

Quick Review 15 min.
- Go over **Que sais-je?,** p. 338.
- Do Activity 3, p. 337.

Chapter Review 35 min.
- Review Chapter 11. Choose from **Grammaire supplémentaire,** Grammar Tutor for Students of French, Activities for Communication, Listening Activities, Interactive CD-ROM Tutor, or **Jeux interactifs.**

Homework Options
Study for Chapter 11 Test.

Assessment

Test, Chapter 11 50 min.
- Administer **Chapter 11 Test.** Select from Testing Program, Alternative Assessment Guide, Test Generator, or Standardized Assessment Tutor.

Chapitre 11 : Laissez les bons temps rouler!
Suggested Lesson Plans 90-Minute Block Schedule

Block 1

CHAPTER OPENER 10 min.
- Present Chapter Objectives, p. 311.
- Language Note and Culture Note, ATE, pp. 310–311

MISE EN TRAIN 35 min.
- Presenting **Mise en train,** ATE, p. 312
- Do Activities 1–4, p. 314.
- **Note culturelle,** p. 314
- Culture Notes and Community Link, ATE, pp. 312–314

RENCONTRE CULTURELLE 15 min.
- Presenting **Rencontre culturelle,** ATE, p. 315
- Language Notes and Culture Note, ATE, p. 315

PREMIERE ETAPE
Comment dit-on... ?, p. 316 25 min.
- Presenting **Comment dit-on... ?,** ATE, p. 316
- Play Audio CD for Activity 6, p. 316.
- Do Activity 7, p. 316.

Wrap-Up 5 min.
- Listening Activities, p. 87, Additional Listening Activity 11-1

Homework Options
Cahier d'activités, pp. 121–122, Acts. 1–3

Block 2

PREMIERE ETAPE
Quick Review 5 min.
- Assign students an identity and then ask them questions using the expressions from **Comment dit-on... ?,** p. 316.

Comment dit-on... ?, p. 316 10 min.
- Do Activity 8, p. 316.

Vocabulaire, p. 317 35 min.
- Presenting **Vocabulaire,** ATE, p. 317
- Play Audio CD for Activity 9, p. 317.
- Do Activities 10–11, pp. 317–318.
- **Note culturelle,** p. 317

Comment dit-on... ?, p. 318 30 min.
- Presenting **Comment dit-on... ?,** ATE, p. 318
- Play Audio CD for Activity 13, p. 318.
- Do Activity 14, p. 319.

Wrap-Up 10 min.
- Activities for Communication, pp. 41–42, Communicative Activity 11-1A and 11-1B

Homework Options
Grammaire supplémentaire, p. 332, Acts. 1–3
Cahier d'activités, pp. 123–124, Acts. 4–7
Travaux pratiques de grammaire, pp. 96–97, Acts. 1–4

Block 3

PREMIERE ETAPE
Quick Review 5 min.
- Teaching Transparency 11-1, using suggestion #2 from Vocabulary Practice Using Teaching Transparency 11-1

Vocabulaire, p. 317 10 min.
- Do Activity 12, p. 318.

Comment dit-on... ?, p. 318 15 min.
- Listening Activities, p. 87, Additional Listening Activity 11-2
- Do Activity 15, p. 319.

REMISE EN TRAIN 30 min.
- Presenting **Remise en train,** ATE, p. 320
- Culture Notes, ATE, p. 321
- Do Activities 18–20, pp. 320–321.

DEUXIEME ETAPE
Comment dit-on... ?, p. 323 25 min.
- Presenting **Comment dit-on... ?,** ATE, p. 323
- **A la française,** p. 323
- Play Audio CD for Activity 22, p. 323.
- Do Activity 23, p. 323.

Wrap-Up 5 min.
- Ask students questions using the expressions in **Comment dit-on... ?,** p. 323.

Homework Options
Have students study for Quiz 11-1.
Pupil's Edition, Activities 16–17, p. 319
Cahier d'activités, pp. 125–127, Acts. 8–11

One-Stop Planner CD-ROM

For alternative lesson plans by chapter section, to create your own customized plans, or to preview all resources available for this chapter, use the **One-Stop Planner CD-ROM,** Disc 3.

For additional homework suggestions, see activities accompanied by this symbol throughout the chapter.

Block 4

DEUXIEME ETAPE

Quick Review 5 min.
- Teaching Transparency 11-1, using suggestion #1 from Vocabulary Practice Using Teaching Transparency 11-1

Quiz 11-1 20 min.
- Administer Quiz 11-1A or 11-1B.

Comment dit-on... ?, p. 323 15 min.
- Do Activity 24, using Slower Pace/Visual Learners suggestion, ATE, p. 324.

Vocabulaire, p. 324 25 min.
- Presenting **Vocabulaire,** ATE, p. 324
- Play Audio CD for Activity 25, p. 325.
- Do Activities 26–27, p. 325.

PANORAMA CULTUREL 20 min.
- Presenting **Panorama Culturel,** ATE, p. 322
- **Qu'en penses-tu?,** p. 322
- Thinking Critically: Comparing and Contrasting, ATE, p. 322

Wrap-Up 5 min.
- Teaching Transparency 11-2, using suggestion #1 from Vocabulary Practice Using Teaching Transparency 11-2

Homework Options
Grammaire supplémentaire, pp. 333–334, Acts. 4–7
Cahier d'activités, pp. 128–129, Acts. 12–15
Travaux pratiques de grammaire, pp. 98–100, Acts. 5–9

Block 5

DEUXIEME ETAPE

Quick Review 10 min.
- Activities for Communication, pp. 43–44, Communicative Activity 11-2A and 11-2B

Comment dit-on... ?, p. 326 45 min.
- Presenting **Comment dit-on... ?,** ATE, p. 326
- Play Audio CD for Activity 29, p. 326.
- Challenge: **Tu te rappelles?,** ATE, p. 326:
- Do Activities 30–31, pp. 326–327.

LISONS! 30 min.
- **Stratégie pour lire,** p. 328
- Prereading and Reading Activities A–B, p. 328
- Teaching Suggestion, ATE, p. 328
- Culture Note and Language Note, ATE, p. 328
- Read *Froumi et Grasshopper* aloud as students read along silently.
- Do Reading Activities C–D, p. 329.

Wrap-Up 5 min.
- Do Activity E, p. 329.

Homework Options
Have students study for Quiz 11-2.
Grammaire supplémentaire, pp. 334–335, Acts. 8–10
Cahier d'activités, p. 130, Acts. 16–17
Travaux pratiques de grammaire, pp. 100–101, Acts. 10–12

Block 6

DEUXIEME ETAPE

Quick Review 15 min.
- Listening Activities, p. 89, Additional Listening Activity 11-6

Quiz 11-2 20 min.
- Administer Quiz 11-2A or 11-2B.

LISONS! 25 min.
- Do Activity F, p. 329.
- Read aloud *La Cigale et la fourmi,* p. 330, as students read along silently.
- Do Activities G–H, p. 330.
- Do Activity I, p. 330.

MISE EN PRATIQUE 30 min.
- Do Activity 1, p. 336.
- Play Audio CD for Activity 2, p. 337.
- Do Activity 4, p. 337.

Homework Options
Que sais-je?, p. 338
Pupil's Edition, Activity K, p. 330
Study for Chapter 11 Test.

Block 7

MISE EN PRATIQUE

Quick Review 15 min.
- Collect homework.
- **Jeu de rôle,** p. 337

Chapter Review 30 min.
- Review Chapter 11. Choose from **Grammaire supplémentaire,** Grammar Tutor for Students of French, Activities for Communication, Listening Activities, Interactive CD-ROM Tutor, or **Jeux interactifs.**

Test, Chapter 11 45 min.
- Administer Chapter 11 Test. Select from Testing Program, Alternative Assessment Guide, Test Generator, or Standardized Assessment Tutor.

CHAPITRE 11

One-Stop Planner CD-ROM

For resource information, see the **One-Stop Planner,** Disc 3.

Pacing Tips
In this chapter, students will mainly learn vocabulary and functional expressions already covered in Levels 1 and 2. This chapter offers an excellent opportunity to review material in a new context. For suggested Lesson Plans and timing suggestions, see pages 309I–309L.

Meeting the Standards

Communication
- Asking for confirmation, p. 316
- Asking for and giving opinions; agreeing and disagreeing, p. 318
- Asking for explanations, p. 323
- Making observations; giving impressions, p. 326

Cultures
- Culture Notes, pp. 311, 313, 314, 315, 321, 324, 328
- Note culturelle, p. 314
- Note culturelle, p. 317
- Panorama Culturel, p. 322
- Rencontre culturelle, p. 315

Connections
- History Links, pp. 315, 317
- Community Links, pp. 312, 322
- Literature Link, p. 330
- Music Link, p. 329
- Language Arts Link, p. 331

Comparisons
- Language-to-Language, p. 316
- Thinking Critically, p. 322

Communities
- Career Path, p. 318
- Community Links, pp. 310, 318
- De l'école au travail, p. 327

Connections and Comparisons

Community Link
Name or bring in pictures of crawfish, gumbo, jambalaya, the French Quarter in New Orleans, red beans and rice, Dixieland jazz, po-boys, and Mardi Gras masks or beads. Ask students what region of the United States they associate with these items. Then, ask them if they've ever been to Louisiana. If so, have volunteers share their experiences. For more tourist information about Louisiana, consult the list of professional resources on page T46.

Language Note
Call students' attention to the title, **Laissez les bons temps rouler!,** and ask them what the equivalent English expression is. *(Let the good times roll!)*

C H A P I T R E

11
Laissez les bons temps rouler!

Objectives

In this chapter you will review and practice how to

Première étape

- ask for confirmation
- ask for and give opinions
- agree and disagree

Deuxième étape

- ask for explanations
- make observations
- give impressions

📶 internet

go.hrw.com

ADRESSE: go.hrw.com
MOT-CLE: WA3 FRANCOPHONE
AMERICA-11

◀ **La Nouvelle-Orléans pendant le carnaval**

C H A P I T R E 1 1

Focusing on Outcomes
Have students read the list of objectives. Form groups and assign two functions to each one. Have students in each group make a list of expressions they already know to accomplish their functions. Gather the lists and read the expressions at random. Have the class guess the function accomplished by each expression.

Teacher Note
You might tell students that **cadien** is often preferred to **cajun** by speakers of French in Louisiana.

Cultures and Communities

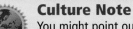

Culture Note
You might point out the costumes featured on pages 310–311. For the Mardi Gras celebrations in New Orleans, costumes are often elaborate and always colorful, with beadwork and feathers. During the festivities, masked participants often ride colorful floats and toss trinkets, such as beads and plastic doubloons, to onlookers.

Using Prior Knowledge
Name various foods typical of Louisiana (gumbo, po-boys, crawfish), as well as others that aren't (**crêpes, pastilla, pâté**). Have students tell which ones are typical dishes from Louisiana and what countries or regions the other dishes are typical of. (Morocco, France)

Mise en train · *L'Arrivée à Lafayette*

Cahier d'activités,
p. 121, Act. 1

Teaching Resources
pp. 312–314

PRINT
▶ Lesson Planner, p. 52
▶ Video Guide, pp. 68–70
▶ Cahier d'activités, p. 121

MEDIA
▶ One-Stop Planner
▶ Video Program
  Camille et compagnie
  Videocassette 4, 17:12–24:30
  Videocassette 5 (captioned version), 1:02:16–1:09:34
▶ Audio Compact Discs, CD 11, Tr. 1

Presenting
Mise en train

Read the introductory paragraph aloud. Then, have students look at the photos on pages 312–313 and tell what they think Simon and his relatives are going to talk about. Write several key words from the **Mise en train** on the board (Paris, Montpellier, **grand-mère,** alligator, 1982, 1980, Félicie). Tell the students to listen carefully to try to identify each word and its significance. Play the audio recording, pausing after each scene to have students identify the words.
(Paris, c'est la ville où Simon est né.)

Community Link
Ask students if their town or state has a museum or organization with programs similar to those at the Acadian Village that promote traditional dances and history.

CD 11 Tr. 1

> **Stratégie pour comprendre**
> Simon Laforest is French. He's just arrived in Lafayette, Louisiana, to spend Easter with his American cousins. Judging by the photos, what is Simon discovering in Lafayette?

① M. Laforest Si je me souviens bien, tu es né à Paris.
Simon Oui, c'est ça.
M. Laforest Et tu habites toujours à Montpellier?
Simon Oui, oui...
M. Laforest Et comment va ta famille?
Simon Oh, ça va...
M. Laforest Et ta grand-mère? Elle est toujours aussi marrante?
Simon Oh, vous savez, elle, rien ne l'arrête.
M. Laforest Je me souviens d'elle, quand elle est venue ici. J'avais onze ans. Je garde un très bon souvenir d'elle. Elle dansait rudement bien sur la musique cajun! Et puis, je l'ai revue quand nous sommes venus chez vous, à Montpellier.

Simon Vous savez, j'ai toujours le petit alligator en peluche que vous m'aviez offert.
M. Laforest Ah, oui?
Simon C'était en quelle année, déjà?
M. Laforest Si je me souviens bien, c'était en 1982. Tu devais avoir deux ou trois ans. Tu es bien né en 1980?
Simon Oui, c'est ça.
M. Laforest Ta sœur, elle, elle n'était pas encore née. Comment elle s'appelle, déjà?
Simon Félicie.
M. Laforest Est-ce que tu connais l'histoire de notre famille?

② Simon Euh, non. Papa me l'a racontée, mais j'ai oublié.
M. Laforest Tu vois, au XVIIIème siècle, nos ancêtres ont dû quitter l'Acadie. Un des frères Laforest, Clément, est venu habiter en Louisiane; l'autre, Hubert, est parti en France. Nous, nous sommes les descendants de Clément. Et ta famille descend d'Hubert.

③ Anne Oh, Papa! On peut parler d'autre chose? Du présent, par exemple? Tu sais, Simon, ici, il y a plein de choses à faire. Il y a des tas de festivals. Tiens, rien que ce mois-ci, il y a le Festival International de Louisiane, ici, à Lafayette, le Festival de l'Ecrevisse à Breaux Bridge et le Jazz and Heritage Festival à La Nouvelle-Orléans.

Preteaching Vocabulary

Guessing Words from Context
Have students look at the pictures on both pages. Ask them what kind of person Simon's grandmother is, based on Monsieur Laforest's description. **(marrante)** Have them guess the meaning of some keywords based on contextual information. Have volunteers share their words with the class and have them explain how they arrived at their guesses.

Finally, have students give a synopsis of the conversation, based on what they figured out from context.
marrante *funny*
rudement bien *very well*
l'écrevisse *crawfish*
la trompette *trumpet*
la batterie *the drums*
bruyant *noisy*

4 **Anne** Tu aimes le jazz, toi?

Simon Oui, c'est super!

Anne Génial! Moi aussi! Je vis pour le jazz. Mon rêve, c'est de devenir musicienne professionnelle de jazz.

Simon Tu joues de quoi?

Anne De la trompette.

Simon Chouette! Moi, je joue de la batterie. Tu aimes le rock aussi?

Anne Euh, pas tellement. Je trouve que c'est trop bruyant, trop violent...

Simon Tu rigoles! Tu as seize ans et tu n'aimes pas le rock?

Anne Ben non. J'aime mieux la dance. Qu'est-ce que tu en penses, toi?

Simon Oh, c'est nul!

Anne Tu trouves? Bon, on peut toujours écouter du jazz ensemble, puisque tu aimes ça.

Simon D'accord.

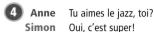

5 **M. Laforest** Tu sais, Simon, on a tout un programme pour toi. Pour commencer, on pourrait aller au Village Acadien.

Simon Qu'est-ce que c'est?

M. Laforest C'est un musée en plein air qui présente les traditions acadiennes, la manière dont vivaient nos ancêtres, leur histoire...

Anne Oui, c'est pas mal. Mais surtout la semaine prochaine, on va aller au Festival international de Louisiane. Tu vas voir, c'est vraiment cool! Il y aura...

M. Laforest Voilà. On est arrivés. Bienvenue chez nous.

Using the Captioned Video

Culture Note

The Acadian Village in Lafayette is a replica of a nineteenth-century Cajun town. It is so realistic that it has been used in several movies as an authentic historical set. The home and paraphernalia of a local hero, Dudly LeBlanc, a senator and spokesperson for the Cajun people, are on display there.

Teaching Suggestion

Assign a number to each photo on this page. Then, have partners choose lines from the conversation to serve as captions for the photos. For example, for the photo at the top right, students might choose **Tu aimes le jazz, toi?** Say the number of a photo and call on two students, who will read their caption aloud.

Camille et compagnie

You may choose to show students Episode 11: *Il faut de tout pour faire un gombo* now or wait until later in the chapter. In the video Sophie, Azzedine, Laurent, and Max decide to prepare a special Cajun dinner party for Camille, who is soon going to Louisiana. Sophie and Azzedine go to the market, while Laurent and Max choose some music. Sophie and Azzedine cannot find okra and decide to use green beans instead. Later, Azzedine puts too much cayenne pepper in the gumbo and Sophie forgets the mushrooms in the oven. The dinner is spoiled, so the five friends decide to get pizza.

Teaching Suggestion

2 Have students find passages from the **Mise en train** to support their choices.

Teaching Suggestion

Note culturelle Have students read the calendar of events under the **Note culturelle** and tell what the festivals celebrate (zydeco, duck, shrimp, oil, Cajun heritage, sugar cane, frogs, cattle, cotton, folklore, rice, sweet potato). You might have them use a dictionary to look up any unfamiliar words.

Culture Note

In Louisiana, festivals occur almost every weekend of the year. They vary from ethnic celebrations, such as the **Festival international de Louisiane** and the **Festivals acadiens** in Lafayette, to harvest and food-oriented festivities, such as the Rice Festival in Crowley, the Breaux Bridge Crawfish Festival, and the World Championship Crawfish Etouffée Cook-off in Eunice.

Answers

4 1. Si je me souviens bien... ; Et tu habites toujours à... ? Elle est toujours... ? Tu es bien né en... ?
2. ... c'est super! Génial! Chouette! ... c'est pas mal.
3. Oui, c'est ça.
4. Je trouve que c'est trop bruyant, trop violent. C'est nul!
5. Tu rigoles! Ben non.
6. Qu'est-ce que c'est?
7. Bienvenue chez nous.

---

1 **Tu as compris?**   These activities check for comprehension only. Students should not yet be expected to produce language modeled in **Mise en train**.

1. Quelle relation est-ce qu'il y a entre Simon, Anne et Mr. Laforest?   distant cousins
2. Où est-ce que leur conversation se passe?   in the car
3. De quoi parle M. Laforest?   their families, family history
4. De quoi parle Anne?   music, festivals
5. Quels intérêts est-ce que Simon et Anne ont en commun?   jazz
6. Qu'est-ce que M. Laforest et Anne veulent faire visiter à Simon?   Village Acadien, Festival international de Louisiane

2 **Qui suis-je?**

Qui dirait les phrases suivantes, M. Laforest, Anne ou Simon?

Simon
> Je joue de la batterie parce que j'adore le rock.

Anne
> Je voudrais que Simon s'amuse bien pendant son séjour.

M. Laforest
> Je voudrais raconter à Simon l'histoire de notre famille.

Anne
> Le rock? Ça ne me branche pas tellement. C'est trop bruyant.

Anne
> Je rêve d'aller à La Nouvelle-Orléans et de devenir musicienne de jazz.

Simon
> Qu'est-ce que c'est, le Village Acadien?

3 **Vrai ou faux?**

1. M. Laforest a visité Montpellier en 1982.   vrai
2. La grand-mère de Simon ne sort plus.   faux
3. M. Laforest a oublié le nom de la sœur de Simon.   vrai
4. La famille de Simon descend de Clément.   faux
5. Anne et Simon vont écouter du rock ensemble.   faux
6. Le Village Acadien est l'endroit où les musiciens cajuns habitent.   faux
7. Il n'y a que deux grands festivals en Louisiane chaque année.   faux

4 **Cherche les expressions**

What expressions do the people in *L'Arrivée à Lafayette* use to . . .   See answers below.

1. ask for confirmation?
2. give a positive opinion?
3. agree?
4. give a negative opinion?
5. disagree?
6. ask for an explanation?
7. welcome someone?

5 **Et maintenant, à toi**

Est-ce que tu as déjà voyagé dans un endroit que tu ne connaissais pas? Pourquoi est-ce que tu y es allé(e)? Qu'est-ce que tu y as fait et vu?

Note culturelle

«Laissez les bons temps rouler!» est une expression populaire en Louisiane et il y a une bonne raison pour ça. Les Louisianais semblent être nés pour faire la fête et toutes les excuses sont bonnes pour célébrer la nourriture, la musique et la danse. Il y a des danses hebdomadaires appelées « fais do-do » et des festivals qui célèbrent le riz, les écrevisses ou les patates douces. Mardi Gras est sans aucun doute la plus grande de ces fêtes et la plus fastueuse de toutes. Il commence par une succession de bals et de soirées. Le dernier mardi avant le carême marque la fin de la fête qui se termine avec des parades très colorées et le carnaval.

Septembre

Festival du Zydeco du Sud-Ouest de la Louisiane à Plaisance • *Festival du Canard à Gueydan, Festival de la Crevette et du Pétrole Louisianais à Morgan City* • *Festivals Acadiens à Lafayette* • *Festival et Foire de la Canne à Sucre à New Iberia* • *Festival de la "Grenouille" à Rayne*

Octobre

Festival du Bétail à Abbeville • *Festival de l'Héritage et de la Musique Cajun à Lafayette* • *Festival du Coton et "Tournoi de la Ville Platte"* • *Festival du Folklore Louisianais à Eunice* • *Festival International du Riz à Crowley* • *Festival de la "Patate Douce" à Opelousas*

Comprehension Check

Auditory Learners

2 Read these statements aloud and have students tell who might have said them. For further listening practice, create additional statements that Anne, Monsieur Laforest, and Simon might say, read them aloud, and have students identify the speakers.

Challenge

2 Have students write additional statements or questions that Anne, Simon, and Monsieur Laforest might say. Have them exchange papers with a partner, identify the speakers, and then return their papers to the writer for correction.

Rencontre culturelle

Qu'est-ce que tu sais sur la Louisiane? Pour t'en faire une meilleure idée, regarde les photos.

Les écrevisses sont un plat typique de Louisiane.

Il y a de nombreux bayous en Louisiane.

C'est à La Nouvelle-Orléans que le jazz est né.

Le Café du Monde à la Nouvelle-Orléans

On peut visiter de magnifiques plantations.

Qu'en penses-tu?

1. Quelle impression ces photos te donnent de la Louisiane?
2. Quelles différences culturelles sont illustrées sur ces photos?

Possible answers: **1.** It's a state known for its Cajun cuisine, bayous, jazz music, French influences, and beautiful Southern plantations. **2.** Cajun - cuisine, French - cafés

Savais-tu que... ?

L'héritage français de la Louisiane remonte à 1682. A cette époque, l'explorateur Cavelier de la Salle a annexé des millions d'hectares de terre en Amérique du Nord, y compris la Louisiane actuelle, au nom de la France. Au début des années 1700, la Louisiane était une colonie prospère. Sa capitale, La Nouvelle-Orléans, était un centre culturel et politique important. En 1803, la France a vendu le territoire maintenant appelé Louisiane aux Etats-Unis. L'influence française y est restée très forte et a été renforcée par la présence et la culture des colons venus d'Acadie, au Canada. Les Acadiens se sont installés dans le sud de la Louisiane quand les Anglais les ont chassés du Canada dans les années 1750. On appelle leurs descendants les «Cajuns», du mot «Acadien». La langue cajun est un mélange de formes françaises, d'idiomes anglais, espagnols et allemands et de langues africaines et indiennes.

Objectives Asking for confirmation; asking for and giving opinions; agreeing and disagreeing

WA3 FRANCOPHONE AMERICA-11

Teaching Resources
pp. 316–319

PRINT
▸ Lesson Planner, p. 53
▸ Listening Activities, pp. 83–84, 87–88
▸ Activities for Communication, pp. 41–42, 81, 83, 109–110
▸ Travaux pratiques de grammaire, pp. 96–97
▸ Grammar Tutor for Students of French, Chapter 11
▸ Cahier d'activités, pp. 122–125
▸ Testing Program, pp. 235–238
▸ Alternative Assessment Guide, p. 40
▸ Student Make-Up Assignments, Chapter 11

MEDIA
▸ One-Stop Planner
▸ Audio Compact Discs, CD 11, Trs. 2–4, 14, 19–21
▸ Teaching Transparencies: 11-1; **Grammaire supplémentaire** Answers; Travaux pratiques de grammaire Answers
▸ Interactive CD-ROM Tutor, Disc 3

Bell Work

Have students write answers to the following questions: **Comment tu trouves le jazz? Tu aimes mieux le rock ou le country? Ça te plaît, le rap?**

Presenting
Comment dit-on... ?

On the board or on a transparency, write information about an imaginary person. Include the person's name, address, profession, marital status, number of brothers and sisters or children, and their names. Then, using the new expressions, ask for confirmation about the facts presented in the information.

Comment dit-on...?

Asking for confirmation

To ask for confirmation:

Vous habitez toujours à Bordeaux?
Do you still live . . . ?
Il y a **bien** trois garçons dans ta famille? *. . . , right?*
Comment elle s'appelle, **déjà?** *. . . again?*
Ta mère a cinquante ans, **c'est ça?** *. . . , right?*

Si je me souviens bien, tu es né en 1984.
If I remember correctly, . . .
Si je ne me trompe pas, tu as 16 ans.
If I'm not mistaken, . . .

Cahier d'activités, p. 122, Act. 2–3

Grammaire supplémentaire, p. 332, Act. 1–2

---

6 **Réunion des anciens élèves** See scripts and answers on p. 309G.

Ecoutons Tu es à la réunion des anciens élèves de ton lycée. Tu entends les conversations suivantes. Dans quelles conversations est-ce que ces gens vérifient des informations?

CD 11 Tr. 2

---

7 **Méli-mélo!**

Ecrivons Agnès et Julie ne se sont pas vues depuis longtemps. Récris leur conversation dans le bon ordre.

«Vous êtes bien trois sœurs?» 3

«Si je me souviens bien, elle va à l'université, c'est ça?» 9

«Tu habites toujours Abbeville?» 1

«Et l'aînée, comment elle s'appelle, déjà?» 7

«Oui, avec ma famille.» 2

«Si je ne me trompe pas, la benjamine s'appelle Jacqueline.» 5

«Non. Elle s'appelle Audrey.» 6

«Mais non. Elle est toujours chez nous. Elle travaille.» 10

«Edith.» 8

«Oui, c'est ça.» 4

---

8 **Ça fait longtemps!**

Parlons A une soirée de ton club de français, tu vois un(e) camarade de classe de l'année dernière. Pose-lui des questions pour vérifier ce que tu te rappelles à son sujet. Changez de rôle.

Si tu as oublié renewing old acquaintances va à la page 9.

Connections and Comparisons

Language-to-Language

Ask students what type of confirming expressions they would use in English in the course of a normal conversation. Remind them that in French there is no such thing as stress, or voice inflection, to emphasize the most important part of a sentence. So, while in English one stresses a specific word to give it more weight, in French one tends to add small words, such as **bien**, as in **Il y a bien trois garçons dans ta famille?** or **c'est ça**, as in **Ta mère a cinquante ans, c'est ça?** A similar case is found in the use of the personal pronouns **moi, toi, lui, elle, nous, vous, eux, elles.** To say *I have three brothers* (as opposed to *you*), one would say **Moi, j'ai trois frères.**

STANDARDS: 1.1, 1.2, 1.3, 4.1, 5.1

  la batterie le piano le chant

la guitare l'accordéon (m.) la flûte le violon

le rock la musique cajun la musique classique le blues

 la basse le micro le saxophone la boîte à rythmes la trompette le synthé

le jazz le country le rap la dance

Cahier d'activités, p. 123, Act. 4-5   Travaux pratiques de grammaire, pp. 96-97, Act. 1-4

9 **Une oreille musicale**   See scripts and answers on p. 309G.

a. **Ecoutons** Identifie le genre des extraits de musique suivants.

b. **Ecoutons** Identifie l'instrument que tu entends.

CD 11 Tr. 3

10 **De quoi est-ce qu'on joue?**

Parlons/Ecrivons Regarde ce studio de musique. Qu'est-ce qu'il y a comme instruments? Quels genres de musique est-ce qu'on pourrait produire ici?   See answers below.

Note culturelle

Il y a trois types de musique associée à la Louisiane : la musique cajun, la musique zydeco et le jazz. Les Acadiens ont apporté la musique folklorique française. Cette musique est devenue la musique cajun qui utilise l'accordéon, le violon et le triangle. Les musiciens noirs américains ont créé une variante de la musique cajun avec le son du frottoir et des cuillères. Le jazz est sans doute la plus grande contribution musicale que les Etats-Unis ont apportée au monde de la musique. Né à la Nouvelle-Orléans, le jazz est une combinaison de musiques africaines, religieuses et de fanfares.

Answers
10 *Instruments:* une guitare, une basse, un piano, une batterie, un saxophone, une trompette
Genres de musique: du rock, de la musique classique, du jazz, du country, du blues

Teaching Resources
pp. 316–319

PRINT
▶ Lesson Planner, p. 53
▶ Listening Activities, pp. 83–84, 87–88
▶ Activities for Communication, pp. 41–42, 81, 83, 109–110
▶ Travaux pratiques de grammaire, pp. 96–97
▶ Grammar Tutor for Students of French, Chapter 11
▶ Cahier d'activités, pp. 122–125
▶ Testing Program, pp. 235–238
▶ Alternative Assessment Guide, p. 40
▶ Student Make-Up Assignments, Chapter 11

MEDIA
▶ One-Stop Planner
▶ Audio Compact Discs, CD 11, Trs. 2–4, 14, 19–21
▶ Teaching Transparencies: 11-1; **Grammaire supplémentaire** Answers; Travaux pratiques de grammaire Answers
▶ Interactive CD-ROM Tutor, Disc 3

Presenting
Comment dit-on... ?

Bring in several CDs and pictures of artists who represent different types of music. Hold up a CD and a picture and pretend to ask the artists their opinion of the type of music represented by the CDs. Then give your opinion of the type of music, as if you were the artist. **(Non, je trouve ça nul.)**

Possible answers

 11 à une soirée, au bal du lycée: du rock; à un mariage: de la musique classique; dans un restaurant: du jazz; au coin de la rue: du rap; à la mi-temps d'un match, dans une discothèque: de la dance; à un rodéo: du country

---

11 Qu'est-ce qu'on y entend?

Parlons A ton avis, quels genres de musique seraient appropriés dans les situations à droite? See answers below.

> à une soirée   à la mi-temps d'un match
> au coin de la rue   dans un restaurant
> à un mariage   à un rodéo
> dans une discothèque   au bal annuel du lycée

12 Devine!

 Parlons Pense à un musicien/une musicienne célèbre. Ensuite, dis aux autres élèves le genre de musique auquel il/elle est associé(e). Les autres élèves te posent des questions pour essayer de deviner qui c'est. Changez de rôle.

Comment dit-on...?

Asking for and giving opinions; agreeing and disagreeing

To ask for an opinion:

> **Comment tu trouves ça,** le jazz?
> **Tu n'aimes pas** la dance?
> **Ça te plaît,** le rap?
> **Qu'est-ce que tu penses du** blues?
> **Ça te branche,** le country?
> *Are you into . . . ?*

To give a positive opinion:

> **Je trouve ça** hyper cool.
> **Si, j'aime beaucoup.**
> **Ça me plaît beaucoup.**
> **Ça m'éclate.** *I'm wild about it.*
> **Je n'écoute que ça.**
> *That's all I . . .*

To give a negative opinion:

> **Je trouve ça nul.**
> **Je n'aime pas du tout.**
> **Ça ne me plaît pas du tout.**
> **Je n'aime pas tellement ça.**
> **Ça ne me branche pas trop.**
> *I'm not into that.*

To agree:

> **Je suis d'accord avec toi.**
> **Moi aussi,** j'aime bien le jazz.
> **Moi non plus,** je n'aime pas la dance.
> **Ça, c'est sûr.**
> *That's for sure.*
> **Tu as raison.**

To disagree:

> **Pas du tout.**
> **Tu parles!**
> **Tu rigoles!**
> **Tu délires ou quoi?**
> *Are you crazy or what?*
> **N'importe quoi!**

Grammaire supplémentaire, p. 332, Act. 3

 Cahier d'activités, pp. 124–125, Act. 6–8

13 J'aime, je n'aime pas See scripts and answers on p. 309G.

Ecoutons Ecoute Anne et Simon parler de musique. Quels genres de musique est-ce que Simon aime? Est-ce qu'Anne est d'accord ou pas?
CD 11 Tr. 4

Cultures and Communities

Career Path
Ask students if they would be interested in a career in the music industry. Many professions in the music industry involve traveling abroad or working with people from all over the world. Ask students how they think knowledge of one or more foreign languages might help a journalist for a music magazine or someone who organizes concerts or coordinates music festivals.

Community Link
You might invite musicians from a community band or orchestra to speak to the class about their personal experiences with music and the musical opportunities that are available in the community.

14 Quelle musique écoutez-vous?

Lisons Lis ces lettres que quelques francophones ont envoyées à un magazine de jeunes et réponds aux questions suivantes. *See answers below.*

1. What kinds of music do these teenagers like? What are their favorite groups?
2. Give five reasons why music is important to these teenagers.
3. What words do they use to describe the music they like?
4. List some places where French teenagers can listen to music.
5. Which teenager plays an instrument? Which one likes to dance?

"La musique m'accompagne dans la vie" «La musique me détend quand je suis stressée, me tonifie quand je suis déprimée, me repose quand je suis à bout... Bref, elle m'accompagne dans tous les moments de ma vie. Mon chanteur préféré, c'est Bob Marley, même s'il est mort quand j'étais très jeune. Il nous a laissé un souvenir impérissable, indémodable : sa voix, magique, planante, pleine de messages et d'émotions. J'adore le reggae et je dirais presque que je n'écoute que ça : UB 40, Tonton David... et d'autres.»
Marie-Laure, Challans

"La musique est un langage universel" «Salut Hervé. La musique tient une très grande place dans ma vie. Ce que j'écoute principalement c'est le hard rock, le funk et le rock tout simplement, qu'il soit américain, anglais, irlandais et bien sûr français. Car la musique est un langage universel. Je joue de la guitare, et la musique est mon passe-temps, que ce soit en l'écoutant ou en la produisant de mes propres mains. Avec elle, on peut danser, se relaxer ou se défouler. On peut aussi y trouver un moyen de découvrir sa personnalité. Moi, par exemple, j'adore les groupes comme Pearl Jam et les Smashing Pumpkins. Ce sont tous des groupes grunges et ils représentent ma génération. J'aime partager cette musique avec mes amis.»
Raphaëlle, Pointe-à-Pitre (Guadeloupe)

"Tous aiment me voir danser" «Cher Hervé. J'adore la musique et j'ai un CD de Queen, mais je préfère la techno-dance! J'écoute East 17 et Ace of Base. Au collège, pendant la cantine, il y a plusieurs foyers ouverts : le foyer vidéo, le CDI, la permanence et... le foyer musique! Je suis un bon danseur alors après le repas, je fonce au foyer musique pour danser... Tout le monde aime me voir danser. Je me suis fait beaucoup d'amis comme ça... »
Yoann, Quimper

---

15 Ça te branche?

Parlons Demande à ton/ta camarade ce qu'il/elle aime comme genre de musique. Quels sont ses compositeurs, chanteurs, musiciens ou groupes préférés?

16 Tu connais?

a. **Ecrivons** Imagine que tu es français(e). Tu as entendu parler de quelques nouveaux groupes américains. Tu voudrais les connaître. Ecris une lettre à ton/ta correspondant(e) américain(e) pour lui demander qui ils sont et s'il/si elle les aime.

b. **Parlons** Echange ta lettre avec celle de ton/ta camarade. Il/Elle jouera le rôle de ton/ta correspondant(e). Il/Elle va lire ta lettre et y répondre.

17 Mon journal

Ecrivons Est-ce que la musique est importante pour toi? Quels genres de musique préfères-tu? Quand est-ce que tu en écoutes? Avec qui? Pourquoi?

A la française

English speakers must use a direct object pronoun with verbs such as *like* or *love*: *Jazz? I love it!* When speaking informally to peers, French speakers often do not use an object pronoun, especially if what they're referring to is not a physical object: **Tu aimes le jazz, toi? Moi, j'adore!** or **Le rock? Moi, je n'aime pas trop.**

Communication for All Students

Group Work

To close this **étape**, have students stand in two lines facing one another. The students in one line should have cards on which a type of music or the name of a musician is written. The students holding the cards ask the students standing opposite them for their opinion of the music or person written on the card. The students facing them respond accordingly. At your signal, one line moves down one student, and the students repeat the process.

Language Note

Students might want to know the following words from the letters: **se détendre** *(to relax)*; **se défouler** *(to unwind)*; **planante** *(groovy)*.

Teaching Suggestions

14 Form small groups and assign a letter to each one. Have them write several true-false statements about their letter, exchange papers with another group, write their responses, and return them for correction.

15 You might have students stage this activity as an interview, with one student playing the role of the host and the other acting as a guest on a talk show. They might videotape their skits.

Assess

▶ Testing Program, pp. 235–238
Quiz 11-1A, Quiz 11-1B
Audio CD 11, Tr. 14

▶ Student Make-Up Assignments, Chapter 11, Alternative Quiz

▶ Alternative Assessment Guide, p. 40

Answers

14 1. rock, reggae, technopop, hard rock, funk, grunge
Marie-Laure: Bob Marley, UB40, Tonton David
Raphaëlle: Pearl Jam, Smashing Pumpkins
Yoann: East 17, Ace of Base
2. *Possible answers:* It's relaxing. You can dance to it. You can discover yourself through it. Music is with us at all moments of our life. Music is a universal language.
3. magique, planante, pleine de messages et d'émotions, langage universel
4. home, school foyer
5. Raphaëlle; Yoann

CD 11 Tr. 5

Teaching Resources
pp. 320–321

PRINT
▸ Lesson Planner, p. 54
▸ Video Guide, pp. 68–70
▸ Cahier d'activités, p. 126

MEDIA
▸ One-Stop Planner
▸ Video Program
Camille et compagnie
Videocassette 4, 17:12–24:30
Videocassette 5 (captioned version), 1:02:16–1:09:34
▸ Audio Compact Discs, CD 11, Tr. 5

Teaching Suggestion
Read the following list of activities aloud and have students tell which ones are typical of Louisiana: **écouter du jazz, manger un po-boy, écouter du rap, manger un croissant, manger du jambalaya, danser sur de la musique zydeco.**

Presenting
Remise en train

Have students look at the photos on pages 320–321 and try to guess what the Laforest family and Simon did last weekend. Then, tell students to listen for three things that the Laforests do at the festival (**écouter du jazz/du zydeco, manger au restaurant, danser**). Play the recording and ask the questions in Activity 18.

Les Laforest ont emmené Simon au Festival international de Louisiane. Dans la rue, ils s'arrêtent devant un groupe de musique cajun.

1
Anne Dis, Simon, ça te branche vraiment, cette musique?
Simon Oh, c'est pas mal. Pourquoi? Qu'est-ce que tu proposes d'autre?
Anne Ben, on pourrait aller écouter du jazz.
Simon Oui, si tu veux.
Anne Papa, Maman, ça vous embête si Simon et moi, on va se balader de notre côté?
M. Laforest Non, pas du tout. On peut se retrouver plus tard au restaurant.

Anne et Simon sont maintenant dans un petit café où un groupe de jazz est en train de jouer.

2
Anne Alors, qu'est-ce que tu en penses?
Simon C'est vraiment le pied. Ce qui est intéressant, c'est que ce genre de jazz est vraiment différent de ce qu'on entend en France. Comment est-ce qu'on appelle ça, déjà?
Anne Dixieland.
Simon Ah, oui. C'est ça.
Anne Tu sais, si ça te plaît vraiment, on pourrait peut-être aller au festival de jazz à La Nouvelle-Orléans. C'est la semaine prochaine.
Simon Ça serait super!

3
Anne On pourrait se promener dans le Vieux Carré et aller manger des beignets au café du Monde. Tu en as entendu parler?
Simon Oui, bien sûr.
Anne Et je pourrais te montrer un de mes endroits préférés, le musée du jazz... Oh là là! Tu as vu l'heure?
Simon Ah, oui. On devait retrouver tes parents à huit heures, non?
Anne Oui, au Randol's. On y va?

---

18 **Tu as compris?**

1. A quel événement assiste la famille Laforest? Festival international de Louisiane
2. Pourquoi est-ce que Anne et Simon partent de leur côté? They want to listen to some jazz.
3. Qu'est-ce que Anne veut montrer à Simon à la Nouvelle-Orléans? the jazz museum
4. Où est-ce qu'ils retrouvent M. et Mme. Laforest pour dîner? Quel genre d'endroit est-ce que c'est? Randol's; a Cajun restaurant
5. Pourquoi est-ce que Anne est embarrassée? Her parents get up to dance.

These activities check for comprehension only. Students should not yet be expected to produce language modeled in Remise en train.

19 **Mets dans le bon ordre**

Mets ces phrases dans le bon ordre d'après *Un festival cajun.* 2, 4, 5, 3, 1, 6

1. Les Laforest dansent.
2. Simon et Anne écoutent du jazz.
3. Simon hésite entre le gombo et le jambalaya.
4. Anne propose à Simon d'aller visiter La Nouvelle-Orléans.
5. Anne et Simon arrivent au restaurant.
6. Anne a honte.

Preteaching Vocabulary

Identifying Keywords
Have students look at the conversations and identify important words and phrases throughout. Ask them what words and phrases move the story along. What situations are they used in? Ask students to describe the situations that the characters are in for each conversation. As volunteers provide keywords and expressions, write them on the board or on an overhead transparency.

Ça te branche vraiment? *Do you really like that?*
se balader *to walk around*
C'est vraiment le pied! *It's really great!*
Tout me tente. *Everything looks good.*
gombo *gumbo (okra-based soup)*
C'est assez épicé. *It's spicy.*
Oh, la honte! *I'm so embarrassed!*
C'est pas vrai! *I don't believe this!*

Au restaurant Randol's, Simon et les Laforest sont en train de regarder la carte.

Bienvenue chez Randol's où nous servons les meilleurs fruits de mer du pays cadjin. Restaurant favori des habitants de la région, Randol's, c'est le bon temps à la mode cadjine!

Une abondance de mets cadjins vous attendent chez Randol's, réputé pour ses crabes cuits à la vapeur. La cuisson à la vapeur conserve toute la saveur et nos épices-maison apportent une touche bien cadjine.

4 M. Laforest Qu'est-ce que tu veux, Simon?

Simon Je ne sais vraiment pas quoi prendre. Tout me tente.

M. Laforest Pourquoi tu ne prends pas une spécialité d'ici? Du gombo, par exemple?

Simon Qu'est-ce que c'est?

Mme Laforest C'est une soupe.

Simon Qu'est-ce qu'il y a dedans?

Mme Laforest C'est à base d'okras et de riz avec des crevettes et du crabe. C'est assez épicé.

M. Laforest Simon, pourquoi tu n'essaies pas le jambalaya? C'est du riz avec du jambon, des saucisses, des crevettes et du crabe. C'est délicieux.

Simon Euh, je vous laisse choisir pour moi.

Un peu plus tard, toujours au restaurant...

5 Mme Laforest Ça y est, le groupe de zydeco commence à jouer! Comment tu trouves ça, Simon?

Simon J'aime bien, mais je préfère quand même le jazz.

Mme Laforest Tiens, Boudreaux, si on montrait un peu à Simon comment on danse chez nous?

M. et Mme Laforest se lèvent et vont danser.

6 Anne Oh, la honte! C'est pas vrai!

Simon Ben quoi? Au moins, ils s'amusent! Et puis, ils dansent pas si mal que ça!

Anne Oh, tu sais, il paraît que c'est de famille.

Simon Tiens, on dirait que tu as entendu parler de ma grand-mère, toi aussi!

---

20 Cherche les expressions

What do Simon, Anne, or her parents say to . . . See answers below.

1. ask for an opinion?
2. make a suggestion?
3. ask for permission?
4. make an observation?
5. ask for an explanation?
6. express indecision?
7. give an impression?
8. express embarrassment?

Cahier d'activités, p. 126, Act. 9

21 Et maintenant, à toi

Est-ce que tu es déjà allé(e) à un festival? C'était comment? Est-ce qu'il y a un festival là où tu habites? C'est un festival de quoi? Qu'est-ce qu'on peut y faire et y manger?

Cultures and Communities

Culture Notes

• The **Festival international de Louisiane** in April features music, food, crafts, and other cultural aspects of French-speaking areas, such as Africa, Canada, and the Caribbean.

• The French Quarter (**le Vieux Carré**) is where francophone residents of the city used to live.

The area has been declared a national historic landmark. The former English-speaking area, known as the Garden District, is located a few miles from the center of town. This residential district's stately old homes feature elaborate wrought-iron work.

Teaching Suggestions

• Have volunteers read a quotation from the text (**Oh, la honte! C'est pas vrai!**) and have their classmates try to identify the speaker (**Anne**).

• You might ask students the following questions about the **Remise en train: Quelle sorte de jazz est-ce qu'on écoute en Louisiane?** (Dixieland) **Qu'est-ce que c'est, le gombo?** (une soupe à base d'okras et de riz avec des crevettes et du crabe) **Et le jambalaya?** (du riz avec du jambon, des saucisses, des crevettes et du crabe) **Quelle sorte de musique est-ce que les Laforest écoutent au restaurant?** (zydeco)

Camille et compagnie

As an alternative or in addition to the **Remise en train,** you may wish to show Episode 11 of *Camille et compagnie.* For suggestions and activities, see the *Video Guide.*

Answers

20 1. ... ça te branche vraiment, cette musique? Alors, qu'est-ce que tu en penses? Comment tu trouves ça?

2. On pourrait... ; ... je pourrais te montrer... ; On y va? Pourquoi tu ne prends pas... ? ... pourquoi tu n'essaies pas... ? ... si on... ?

3. Ça vous embête si... ?

4. ... on dirait que...

5. Comment est-ce qu'on appelle ça, déjà? Qu'est-ce que c'est? Qu'est-ce qu'il y a dedans?

6. Je ne sais vraiment pas quoi prendre. Tout me tente.

7. Ce qui est intéressant, c'est que...

8. Oh, la honte!

Teaching Resources
p. 322

PRINT 📖
▸ Video Guide, pp. 69, 71
▸ Cahier d'activités, p. 132

MEDIA
▸ One-Stop Planner
▸ Video Program
  Videocassette 4, 24:33–28:54
▸ Audio Compact Discs, CD 11,
  Trs. 6–9
▸ Interactive CD-ROM Tutor, Disc 3

Presenting
Panorama Culturel

Read the interview question aloud and have students suggest keywords and phrases they might hear in the interviews. Play the video and have students tell what they understood. Next, write the **Questions** below on the board, play the video again, and have students answer the questions.

Questions

1. **A la Martinique, comment s'appelle la fête qui a lieu en février?** (le Carnaval)

2. **Comment est-ce qu'on fête le Carnaval à la Martinique?** (Des gens dansent dans la rue; il y a des soirées extraordinaires.)

3. **Où est-ce que Clémentine va quand elle sort avec des copains?** (dans des discothèques ou au restaurant)

4. **Qu'est-ce qu'on fait aux fêtes de Jennifer?** (On mange, on discute, on s'amuse, on danse.)

Comment est-ce qu'on fait la fête ici?

We asked people to talk to us about parties and celebrations. Here's what they had to say.

Sandra,
Martinique

«En Martinique, on fait la fête tout le temps, tous les week-ends déjà, c'est la fête. Par contre, on a de très grandes fêtes qui sont d'une part le Carnaval, qui est une très grande fête nationale ici en Martinique et dans la Caraïbe, et c'est au mois de février. On a trois jours de Carnaval pleins, avec des vidés, des gens dans la rue qui dansent, et le soir, avec des soirées extraordinaires, etc. Nous avons aussi la fête de Noël, qui est aussi une fête qui marche bien ici, où il y a pas mal de festivités et d'activités.»
Tr. 7

Clémentine,
France

«Alors, la fête... On fait la fête. On trouve toujours quelque chose à fêter, même s'il n'y en a pas vraiment. Donc, on sort le soir ou des fois les week-ends. On est souvent entre copains, nombreux. Soit on fait des soirées chez d'autres copains, soit on sort dans des discothèques ou bien au restaurant.» Tr. 8

Jennifer,
France

«Quand je fais la fête, premièrement, j'invite mes amis. Je les appelle par téléphone. On se retrouve chez moi ou chez quelqu'un d'autre. Puis, on achète à manger, des boissons, et on discute toute la soirée. On s'amuse. On danse.»
Tr. 9

Qu'en penses-tu?

1. Quels événements est-ce que ces personnes célèbrent?   **Carnaval**, Christmas, anything at all

2. Quand tu fais la fête avec tes amis ou ta famille, qu'est-ce que tu fais? Qu'est-ce qui est différent de ou similaire à ce que les personnes interviewées font?

Connections and Comparisons

Community Link
Ask students to name local festivals and celebrations and to explain how they are celebrated (parades, concerts, dances, parties, fireworks).

Thinking Critically
Comparing and Contrasting Have small groups discuss how they celebrate national holidays, such as the Fourth of July, Valentine's Day, and so on. Then, have them compare what they do with what the interviewees do.

Deuxième étape

Objectives Asking for explanations; making observations; giving impressions

WA3 FRANCOPHONE
AMERICA-11

Deuxième étape

CHAPITRE 11

Comment dit-on...?

Asking for explanations

To ask for an explanation:

Qu'est-ce que c'est?
Comment est-ce qu'on appelle ça?
Qu'est-ce que ça veut dire, «zydeco»?
What does . . . mean?
Qu'est-ce qu'il y a dans le po-boy?
Comment est-ce qu'on fait le gombo?
D'où vient le mot «cajun»?
Where does the word . . . come from?
Comment on dit «dix» en anglais?

EUH, QU'EST-CE QUE C'EST?

Cahier d'activités, p. 127, Act. 10

Grammaire supplémentaire,
p. 333, Act. 4–5

See scripts and answers on pp. 309G–309H

22 CD 11 Tr. 10

Qu'est-ce que tu veux dire?

Ecoutons Ecoute ces personnes parler de leurs séjours en Louisiane. Dans quelles conversations est-ce qu'on demande à quelqu'un d'expliquer quelque chose?

23

Qu'est-ce que c'est?

Lisons Trouve les bonnes réponses aux questions de Simon.

1. Qu'est-ce que c'est, le zydeco?   b

2. Comment est-ce qu'on appelle ce sandwich?   a

3. D'où vient le mot «cajun»?   e

4. Qu'est-ce qu'il y a dans le jambalaya?   c

5. Qu'est-ce que ça veut dire, «cocodrie»?   f

6. Comment on dit «La Nouvelle-Orléans» en anglais?   d

A la française

French-speaking people rarely use the passive voice (a sentence construction in which the subject <u>receives</u> the action instead of <u>doing</u> it). For expressions such as *French is spoken here, What is that called?* or *How is gumbo made?* use **on** and a verb in the active voice: **On parle français ici, Comment est-ce qu'on appelle ça? Comment est-ce qu'on fait le gombo?**

a. On appelle ça un «po-boy.»

b. C'est un genre de musique.

c. Il y a du riz et du jambon.

d. New Orleans.

e. Ça vient du mot «acadien».

f. Ça veut dire «alligator».

go.hrw.com

Teaching Resources
pp. 323–327

PRINT
▶ Lesson Planner, p. 55
▶ Listening Activities, pp. 84–85, 88–89
▶ Activities for Communication, pp. 43–44, 82–83, 109–110
▶ Travaux pratiques de grammaire, pp. 98–101
▶ Grammar Tutor for Students of French, Chapter 11
▶ Cahier d'activités, pp. 127–130
▶ Testing Program, pp. 239–242
▶ Alternative Assessment Guide, p. 40
▶ Student Make-Up Assignments, Chapter 11

MEDIA
▶ One-Stop Planner
▶ Audio Compact Discs, CD 11, Trs. 10–12, 15, 22–24
▶ Teaching Transparencies: 11-2; **Grammaire supplémentaire** Answers; Travaux pratiques de grammaire Answers
▶ Interactive CD-ROM Tutor, Disc 3

Bell Work
Have students write whether they agree or disagree with each of the following statements: **Je trouve le jazz hyper cool. A mon avis, le rock, c'est nul. Le country, c'est pas terrible.**

Presenting
Comment dit-on... ?

Write the following answers in random order on the board (**Qu'est-ce que c'est? On appelle ça un stylo, un genre de musique de Louisiane, des huîtres frites, on y met des okras et du riz et on le fait cuire, du mot «Acadien,»** "ten") and have students match the questions and responses.

Teaching Resources
pp. 323–327

PRINT
▶ Lesson Planner, p. 55
▶ Listening Activities, pp. 84–85, 88–89
▶ Activities for Communication, pp. 43–44, 82–83, 109–110
▶ Travaux pratiques de grammaire, pp. 98–101
▶ Grammar Tutor for Students of French, Chapter 11
▶ Cahier d'activités, pp. 127–130
▶ Testing Program, pp. 239–242
▶ Alternative Assessment Guide, p. 40
▶ Student Make-Up Assignments, Chapter 11

MEDIA
▶ One-Stop Planner
▶ Audio Compact Discs, CD 11, Trs. 10–12, 15, 22–24
▶ Teaching Transparencies: 11-2; **Grammaire supplémentaire** Answers; Travaux pratiques de grammaire Answers
▶ Interactive CD-ROM Tutor, Disc 3

Presenting
Vocabulaire

Find or draw pictures of the food items. If possible, bring in some of the ingredients as well (spinach, salt, okra, rice, spices, raisins, oysters). Then, put on a chef's hat and apron and stage a Cajun cooking show. Hold up each ingredient or its picture as you mention it. (**D'abord, vous mettez des okras et du riz dans une casserole.**) Then, repeat the cooking instructions, having students point to the items as you go.

---

24 Qu'est-ce que ça veut dire?

Lisons/Parlons Tu ne sais pas ce que sont les choses suivantes sur ces publicités. Demande à ton/ta camarade de te donner des explications. Varie les expressions que tu utilises.

le two-step
le zydeco
l'origine du mot «cajun»
le Festival international de Louisiane
le jambalaya

Possible answers:

Qu'est-ce que ça veut dire, «two-step»?

1.

Qu'est-ce que c'est?

2.

3. Qu'est-ce qu'il y a dans le jambalaya?

Qu'est-ce que ça veut dire, «zydeco»?

4.

5. D'où vient le mot «cajun»?

Travaux pratiques de grammaire, p. 98, Act. 5–6

Vocabulaire

La Cuisine Cajun

Le po-boy : la spécialité de la Louisiane la plus connue et la moins chère. C'est en fait un sandwich qui peut contenir du poisson, **des écrevisses** (f.), des huîtres, de la viande... Il constitue un repas à lui tout seul.

Des huîtres cuites Bienville (au jambon et aux champignons) ou Rockefeller (**aux épinards**) (m.): Elles sont plus grosses qu'en France et presque pas **salées**.

Le gombo : la grande spécialité régionale. C'est une soupe faite à base **d'okras** (m.) avec du riz, **des crevettes** (f.), **du crabe** et **des épices** (f.). En hiver, **l'andouille** (f.) et le poulet remplacent souvent les crabes et les crevettes.

Le jambalaya : une autre des grandes spécialités louisianaises, est préparée à partir d'une énorme quantité de riz à laquelle on ajoute du jambon, du poulet, **des saucisses** (f.), du porc frais, des crevettes et du crabe.

Les crustacés : la véritable attraction de la Louisiane. Les Cajuns connaissent plusieurs recettes pour préparer les crabes, crevettes et écrevisses qui abondent dans les eaux du delta : **en bisque** (f.), **à la vapeur**, le plus souvent **frits**. La meilleure préparation : **au court-bouillon**. On vous apporte généralement un plateau d'un kilo de ces braves bêtes, épicées à souhait.

Des poissons : les eaux des bayous et celles du golfe du Mexique fournissent de nombreuses espèces, dont l'omniprésent catfish que les Louisianais savent préparer de nombreuses façons, **farci au** crabe, par exemple.

Des desserts : les Cajuns sont très amateurs de **pouding au pain** (m.), genre de pain perdu truffé aux **raisins secs** (m.).

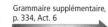

Cahier d'activités, pp. 127–129, Act. 11–15

Travaux pratiques de grammaire, pp. 99–100, Act. 7–9

Grammaire supplémentaire, p. 334, Act. 6

Cultures and Communities

Culture Notes

• Cajun and creole cuisine are both popular in Louisiana. Cajun food is typically hearty and prepared with locally available ingredients, such as bay leaves, filé powder (a thickening agent made from sassafras leaves), and cayenne pepper. It tends to be spicier than creole cuisine, which features complex recipes that draw on a broad array of spices.

• Additional Cajun dishes are **andouille,** a spicy, smoked sausage stuffed with lean pork or chitterlings; **boudin,** a seasoned rice and pork sausage; **boulette,** a seasoned, round meat fritter, similar to a hush puppy; **crawfish étouffée,** peeled **crawfish tails** smothered in a sauce of pepper, garlic, and onions and thickened with a roux (flour browned in butter or oil) or with butter; and **maque choux,** corn stew.

25 **La cuisine cajun** See scripts and answers on p. 309H.

 Ecoutons Ecoute Simon et Anne parler de la cuisine cajun. De quel plat est-ce qu'ils parlent?

CD 11
Tr. 11

a.   b.   c.

d.   e.   f.

26 **Comment on appelle ce plat, déjà?**

 Lisons Ton ami(e) ne sait pas quoi choisir au restaurant où vous dînez à La Nouvelle-Orléans. Il/Elle ne se souvient plus du nom des plats qu'il/elle aime. Lis ses descriptions et choisis la spécialité que chacune décrit.

c **1.** C'est un sandwich aux écrevisses.

e **2.** C'est une soupe dans laquelle il y a du riz, des okras et du crabe.

f **3.** C'est délicieux. Il y a du riz, du jambon et du porc dedans.

b **4.** Ce sont des crustacés très épicés cuits au court-bouillon.

a **5.** C'est un dessert excellent plein de raisins secs.

d **6.** C'est un hors-d'œuvre avec des épinards dedans.

a. du pouding au pain
b. des écrevisses
c. un po-boy
d. des huîtres Rockefeller
e. du gombo
f. du jambalaya

27 **Ça a l'air bon**

 Parlons Choisis quelques plats du **Vocabulaire** à la page 324. Demande à ton/ta camarade s'il/si elle les a déjà goûtés ou voudrait les goûter. Il/Elle va te donner son opinion. Dis-lui si tu es d'accord et si tu voudrais les goûter.

28 **Qu'est-ce qu'il y a dedans?**

Parlons Ton club de français a décidé de faire une fête cajun. Tu vas préparer des plats cajuns avec tes amis. Discutez de ce que vous voudriez cuisiner et de ce que vous devez acheter. Faites une liste des plats et des ingrédients. Joue cette scène avec tes camarades.

Teaching Suggestions

27 Students might also talk about their own favorite dishes. They should ask their partner if he or she is familiar with the dish and explain it, if necessary.

28 If the resources are available, have students organize a Cajun and creole food day in class. Some students might investigate the origins of Cajun and creole specialties, while others might find recipes for them in cookbooks and make them for the class to sample. The po-boy sandwich, jambalaya, red beans and rice, and bread pudding are fairly easy to prepare.

Communication for All Students

Slower Pace

25 Before you play the recording, have students identify each dish in French. Then, play the recording and have students do the activity as directed.

Cooperative Learning

28 Have groups plan and hold their Cajun festival. They should decide on the food, the entertainment, a date, a time, and a location. One student, the chef, makes the grocery list. Another student designs the menu and the program. Finally, all group members prepare a brief skit that will take place at the festival. At the festival, one student acts as the host and greets the guests, who sit down, taste the food and ask questions about it, compliment the food and the music, and thank the host for the evening.

Presenting
Comment dit-on... ?

Bring in copies of several works of art by artists with different styles. Make observations about them, using expressions from **Comment dit-on... ?**

Possible answers

30 Ce que... j'ai trouvé super, c'était la musique; c'était de manger au Café du Monde/je ne comprends pas, c'est pourquoi on porte des masques pendant mardi gras/mon frère a adoré, c'était la cuisine. Ce qui... était incroyable, c'était les alligators; c'était l'histoire des Acadiens/m'a plu, c'était de me promener dans le Vieux Carré/m'a ennuyé, c'était le musée/est génial, c'est le marché français.

Comment dit-on...?

Making observations; giving impressions

To make an observation:

Ce qui est incroyable, **c'est** les épices.
Ce qui saute aux yeux, c'est les couleurs des costumes. *What catches your eye is . . .*
Ce qui me branche vraiment, c'est le jazz.
Ce que je trouve super, c'est mardi gras.
Ce que j'adore/j'aime, c'est voir les gens danser.

To give an impression:

On dirait que les Cajuns aiment bien s'amuser. *It looks like . . .*
Il me semble que les bâtiments sont vieux. *It seems to me that . . .*
J'ai l'impression que le blues est populaire ici.
Ils ont l'air d'aimer danser. *They seem to . . .*

29 **Impression ou observation?**   See scripts and answers on p. 309H.

 Ecoutons Ecoute Elise parler de son séjour en Louisiane. Dans quelles conversations est-ce qu'elle donne une impression ou fait une observation?
CD 11 Tr. 12

Tu te rappelles?

Do you remember the pronouns **ce qui** and **ce que**?

Grammaire supplémentaire, pp. 334–335, Act. 7–10

- **Ce qui** is a subject, and it is usually followed directly by a verb.
  Ce qui est incroyable, c'est leurs masques.
  Tu ne comprends pas **ce qui** est important.

- **Ce que** is an object, and it is usually followed directly by a subject.
  Ce que j'adore, c'est le jazz.
  Je ne sais pas **ce qu'**elle fait.

Cahier d'activités, p. 130, Act. 16–17

Travaux pratiques de grammaire, pp. 100–101, Act. 10–12

30 **Ce qui m'a plu...**

Lisons/Parlons Michelle parle du voyage de sa famille en Louisiane. Fais six ou sept phrases en employant les mots suivants.   See answers below.

| Ce que Ce qui | était incroyable, m'a plu, j'ai trouvé super, m'a ennuyée, je ne comprends pas, mon frère a adoré, est génial, | c'était les alligators. c'était les beignets. c'était la cuisine. c'était l'histoire des Acadiens. c'était la musique. c'était le musée. c'est pourquoi on porte des masques pendant mardi gras. c'était de se promener dans le Vieux Carré. c'est le marché français. c'était de manger au Café du Monde. |

Communication for All Students

Auditory Learners
29 Play the recording a second time and have students tell what Elise is commenting on.

Challenge
Tu te rappelles?   Write several sentence endings on the board or on a transparency. (... j'aime bien, c'est le gombo; ... m'intéresse, c'est l'his-toire des Acadiens.) Have students complete them with either **ce qui** or **ce que**.

Challenge
30 Once students have combined the elements to make complete sentences, have them write a letter that Michelle might have sent to a friend back home.

31 Grosses bises de Louisiane

Ecrivons Marianne est allée en Louisiane pour rendre visite à ses cousins. Elle a écrit cette lettre à sa meilleure amie en France. Complète sa lettre avec **ce qui** ou **ce que.**

Salut Hélène,

Ça va? Moi, ça va très bien. C'est super, la Louisiane! Tu avais raison. Voilà ___ce que___ j'ai fait pendant les trois premiers jours. Le premier jour, on m'a emmenée à un festival. On a écouté du jazz. C'était super. Tu sais ___ce que___ j'ai mangé? Une tarte aux écrevisses. ___Ce qui___ m'étonne, c'est que j'ai trouvé ça très bon. Puis, le deuxième jour, on a loué un canoë pour faire un tour du Bassin de l'Atchafalaya. Tu ne devineras jamais ___ce qui___ s'est passé. Un alligator s'est approché de nous. ___Ce que___ je ne comprends pas, c'est pourquoi le guide l'a encouragé à venir plus près. Il avait l'air d'avoir faim! ___Ce qui___ m'a fait peur, c'est qu'il est venu tout près de moi. Mais, évidemment, le guide savait ___ce qu'___ il faisait, et l'alligator ne nous a pas attaqués. Puis, le troisième jour, on est allés visiter une planta-tion. ___Ce qui___ était vraiment super, c'était les meubles d'époque, et puis, tu sais ___ce qu'___ on a vu dehors? Des champs de cannes à sucre. Demain, on va voir le chêne d'Evangéline. C'est l'arbre du célèbre poème de Longfellow. ___Ce qui___ est encore plus intéressant, c'est que c'est un des plus vieux arbres des Etats-Unis. Bon, je t'écrirai à nouveau la semaine prochaine.

32 Ce qui saute aux yeux,...

Ecrivons Pendant tes vacances en Louisiane, tu as pris beaucoup de photos. Avant de les envoyer à des amis, écris tes impressions et tes observations au verso. Utilise **ce qui, ce que** et les expressions de **Comment dit-on... ?** dans tes phrases. See answers below.

a.

b.

c.

d.

33

 De l'école au travail

Ecrivons Tu es journaliste pour un magazine de tourisme. Tu viens de rentrer d'un voyage en Louisiane. Ecris un article où tu donnes tes impressions et où tu fais des observations sur la Louisiane. N'oublie pas de parler des endroits que tu as visités, de la musique que tu as écoutée et de la cuisine que tu as goûtée.

Cultures and Communities

Additional Practice

To close this **étape,** have students imagine you're on a class trip to Louisiana. Start a conversation about the visit. Have students make observations about the music, food, and attractions. (**Ce qui me branche vraiment, c'est le zydeco.**) Occa-sionally, call on students to ask for an explanation of something a student mentions. (**Je ne comprends pas. Charles, demande à Marc d'expliquer ce que c'est que «le zydeco».**)

STANDARDS: 1.1, 1.3, 5.1, 5.2

Deuxième étape

CHAPITRE 11

Challenge

31 Once students have completed the activity, have them write their own letter in which they give their impressions of what they saw during an imagined trip to Louisiana.

Portfolio

32 **Written** This activity is appro-priate for students' written portfolios. You might also have students bring in real photos they took on a recent vacation, or maga-zine pictures to represent an imagi-nary vacation. Have them give their impressions and observations. For portfolio information, see *Alternative Assessment Guide,* pages iv–15.

Auditory Learners

32 After students write their cap-tions, have volunteers read one of their captions aloud. Have their classmates try to guess which photo it refers to.

Assess

▸ Testing Program, pp. 239–242
 Quiz 11-2A, Quiz 11-2B
 Audio CD 11, Tr. 15

▸ Student Make-Up Assignments, Chapter 11, Alternative Quiz

▸ Alternative Assessment Guide, p. 40

Possible answers

32 a. Ce qui est incroyable, c'est les alligators.
 b. Ils ont l'air de bien s'amuser pendant mardi gras!
 c. Ce qui est intéressant, c'est les bâtiments.
 d. On dirait que les Cajuns aiment bien manger.

Lisons!

Teaching Resources
pp. 328–330

PRINT
▸ Lesson Planner, p. 56
▸ Cahier d'activités, p. 131
▸ Reading Strategies and Skills Handbook, Chapter 11
▸ Joie de lire 3, Chapter 11
▸ Standardized Assessment Tutor, Chapter 11

MEDIA
▸ One-Stop Planner

Prereading
Activity A

Teaching Suggestion
Before reading the fables, ask students what a fable is. Have volunteers give examples of fables they've read and briefly summarize them for the class. Then, ask students what the purpose of a fable is and how it differs from a short story or a novel. Ask them to list elements that are usually present in fables. You might have students use the story of O'gaya from Chapter 10 as an example.

Possible answers
A. 1. They are two different versions of the same fable; poems
   2. an ant and a grasshopper in the first fable, and an ant and a cicada in the second one
B. 1. vous comprends (vous comprenez); mo pourras (je pourrai); vous peux passer (vous pouvez passer)
   2. to viens pas aider moi (tu ne viens pas m'aider); mo pourras donne toi quelque chose (je pourrai te donner quelque chose); to pas connais comment mo (tu ne me connais pas)
   3. rivé (arrivé); mandé (demandé)

Froumi et Grasshopper
Wilson "Ben Guiné" Mitchell
(from *Cajun and Creole Folktales*)

Ah, *well*, et ça semble vrai, tout ça, vous comprends? Une froumi travaille tout l'été. Il t'apé ramasser des quoi et pi il emplit une maison. Il mandé Grasshopper, comme ça, li dit, "Comment ça se fait to viens pas aider moi? Mo pourras donne toi quelque chose."

"O!" Grasshopper dit, "O non!" Li dit, "Moi, mo pas gain le temps pour embêter avec toi!" Li dit, "Mo joue l'accordéon pour mon *living*."

Froumi dit, "*All right, go ahead,* mais," li dit, "mo va, quand li parti, sauterelle, commencer mettre du manger à côté." Li met.

Et là, *well*, quand ça rivé dans l'hiver, il y avait la glace. Tout quelque chose té glacé! Vous comprends ça? Tout quelque chose té glacé! Froumi li, té dans sa maison.

Grasshopper cogné, "Tac, tac, tac."
Li dit, "Hé, hé, hé, *who's there?*"
Li dit, "C'est moi, Grasshopper, *let me in!*"
Froumi dit, "To pas connais comment mo dis toi dans l'été-là? Mo travaille avec vous

Stratégie pour lire
A dialect is a form of a language used in a certain area or by a certain group of people. It may differ from the standard language in grammar, vocabulary, spelling, and pronunciation. If you are reading a text written in a dialect and you come across a word you don't recognize, ignore the grammatical ending and focus on understanding the root of the word. Look for recurring patterns in grammar and vocabulary and figure them out, using contextual clues. Dialects are often influenced by other languages. Look for words and expressions that are borrowed or translated directly. Familiar French words may be used with different meanings in a dialect. Remember that your goal is to understand the main message.

A. Preview the illustrations, titles, and organization of the readings.   See answers below.
   1. What kinds of texts are these?
   2. Who are the main characters?

Froumi et Grasshopper

B. Creole languages often originate when the speakers of two or more different languages try to communicate with each other. The creole spoken in Louisiana is obviously influenced by standard French, but it follows its own unique rules. Before you read *Froumi et Grasshopper*, skim the text and see if you can find examples of . . .   See answers below.
   1. how subject-verb agreement in Creole is different from standard French.

Cultures and Communities

Culture Note
The fables of Jean de la Fontaine (1621–1695) are considered masterpieces of French literature. His *Fables* contain twelve books presented in three collections dating from 1668, 1678, and 1694. They convey a moral by mirroring the human experience in the animal world. La Fontaine was influenced by Aesop, among others.

Language Note
You might point out to students that **fourmi** is feminine in standard French, although it is referred to with **il** in *Froumi et Grasshopper*.

autres. T'étais apé jouer la musique. *O poor Grasshopper, go and play for your living!*" Li frémé sa petite porte, "Cabô!" Li té couché dans sa maison et Grasshopper té gelé. Yé trouvé li en haut les cannes maïs. C'est pas vrai, ça? Hein? Li travaille tout le temps l'été, mais quand ça fait froid, vous p'alé oir li. Vous peux passer en haut où li gain nique-là. Li dans sa maison, li. Mais Grasshopper, li dans l'été, c'est là li n-homme. C'est là li n-homme. Ça apé jouer, mais quand ça fait frette-là, li gelé, li voulait rentrer, mais Froumi dit li, "O non! Peux pas vini. O non!" Et ça semble vrai, hein? Il n'y a rien qu'est plus malin qu'une froumi, mais ça qu'est plus bête qu'un *grasshopper?*"

Reading
Activities B–I

Teaching Suggestion
You might complete Activities B and C as a class, and then have students complete Activities D and E in pairs.

Building on Previous Skills
Have students recall what they learned about the **passé simple**. Then, have them tell which verb tenses the authors of the two fables use. (*Froumi et Grasshopper:* the present tense (**semble, travaille, connais**) and the **passé composé** (**rivé, mandé**); *La Cigale et la Fourmi:* the **passé simple** (**se trouva, alla**) and the **imparfait** (**faisiez, chantais**)) Ask them how the **passé composé** is formed in Creole French (without the helping verbs: **té couché, yé trouvé**).

2. grammatical forms or sentence structures used in Creole that are not used in standard French.

3. Creole words or phrases that have been formed by dropping a syllable from a word or phrase in standard French.

C. Est-ce que tu peux trouver l'équivalent français des expressions créoles que tu as rencontrées dans le texte?

1. vini   g
2. mandé   e
3. mo   f
4. li   c
5. frémé   b
6. ça fait frette   d
7. to   a

a. tu/toi
b. fermer
c. il
d. il fait froid
e. demander
f. je/moi
g. venir

D. Vrai ou faux?
1. La sauterelle a aidé la fourmi tout l'été.   faux
2. La fourmi joue de l'accordéon.   faux
3. On a retrouvé la sauterelle gelée sur un épi de maïs.   vrai
4. La fourmi ne laisse pas la sauterelle entrer dans sa maison.   vrai

E. D'après ce que tu as appris dans ce chapitre, en quoi est-ce que Froumi et Grasshopper sont-ils le reflet de la culture de la Louisiane?   See answers below.

La Cigale et la fourmi

F. Now you're going to read a version of the same fable written by La Fontaine in the seventeenth century. What do you think will be different in this version?
See answers below.

Connections and Comparisons

Music Link
After students have completed Activity C, play the song *Travailler, c'est trop dur* (Audio CD 11, Track 25) to have students practice identifying differences between standard French and Cajun French. Ask them to listen for grammatical forms or sentence structures that are different than standard French and for instances where letters or syllables are dropped. Then, distribute copies of the lyrics (*Listening Activities,* page 90) and have partners circle the differences they find. Finally, have students use what they learned in this chapter to find reflections of Cajun culture in the song (importance of music and dancing, of playing the violin, of dancing the waltz).

Possible answers
E. The grasshopper plays the accordion. The grasshopper is found frozen on an ear of corn. The language used is a mixture of French and English.
F. The language used will be standard French. The story will reflect French culture instead of Louisiana culture.

Postreading
Activities J–K

Teaching Suggestion

J. Divide the class into two groups and hold a debate to discuss the pros and cons of the ant's behavior. Have one group agree with the ant and offer reasons for its behavior. The other group should disagree and tell what they think the ant should have done and why.

Literature Link

After students have completed the reading activities, have them work in small groups and do research in the library or on the Internet to find another fable representative of a particular culture in the French-speaking world. They might consult other fables by Jean de la Fontaine. Ask them to summarize the fable in English and tell what the moral is.

La Cigale et la fourmi
(La Fontaine)

La cigale, ayant chanté
     Tout l'été,
Se trouva fort dépourvue
Quand la bise fut venue :
Pas un seul petit morceau
De mouche ou de vermisseau.
Elle alla crier famine
Chez la fourmi sa voisine,
La priant de lui prêter
Quelque grain pour subsister
Jusqu'à la saison nouvelle.
« Je vous paierai, lui dit-elle,
Avant l'Oût, foi d'animal,
Intérêt et principal. »
La fourmi n'est pas prêteuse;
C'est là son moindre défaut.
« Que faisiez-vous au temps chaud? »
Dit-elle à cette emprunteuse.
—Nuit et jour à tout venant
Je chantais, ne vous déplaise.
—Vous chantiez? j'en suis fort aise :
Eh bien! dansez maintenant. »

G. Ordonne ces événements dans l'ordre dans lequel ils apparaissent dans la fable.

> La fourmi refuse d'aider la cigale. **5**
>
> La cigale chante. **1**
>
> La cigale n'a plus rien à manger. **2**
>
> La fourmi demande à la cigale ce qu'elle faisait tout l'été. **4**
>
> La cigale vient frapper à la porte de la fourmi pour lui demander à manger. **3**

H. Qui, de la fourmi ou de la cigale, ferait les commentaires suivants?

1. Il faut travailler dur pendant l'été. la fourmi

2. J'aime m'amuser et je ne pense pas au lendemain. la cigale

3. Je vous donnerai de l'argent plus tard si vous me donnez à manger. la cigale

4. Vous n'auriez pas dû chanter tout l'été. la fourmi

5. Maintenant que l'hiver est là, j'ai faim et froid. la cigale

I. Relis les deux fables. En quoi sont-elles semblables? En quoi diffèrent-elles? See answers below.

J. What is the moral of these fables? What do you think of the ant's behavior? What would do you have done in her place? Why?

K. Now rewrite the story from the ant's or the cicada/grasshopper's point of view. You may retell the events in the form of an interview, a short story, a poem, or a letter to a friend.

Cahier d'activités, p. 131, Act. 18

Communication for All Students

Challenge

K. Have small groups use their knowledge of other francophone cultures to rewrite the story or create a different, short version of it that represents another francophone culture (Canadian, African, Provençal . . .). To help students get started, have them suggest objects, food, animals, language, and so on that they associate with each area (African drums in Africa, different animals found in Africa, the Caribbean, and Canada, French-Canadian expressions such as **C'est l'fun,** food specialties or ingredients typically used in particular regions). Have each group create a short skit and perform it for the class as other students try to guess which culture, country, or area is being portrayed.

Possible answers

I. The characters in both fables are insects, the stories are similar in content and they end the same way. The first fable is written in Cajun French, while the language in the second fable is standard literary French.

STANDARDS: 1.2, 2.2, 3.1, 3.2, 4.2, 5.2

Ecrivons!

Un poète en herbe

Réfléchis aux poèmes que tu viens de lire. Qu'est-ce qui différencie un poème d'une nouvelle ou d'un essai? Les poèmes mettent souvent l'accent sur une expérience, une émotion, un objet ou une personne en particulier. Ils utilisent des techniques poétiques et montrent le sens caché des choses. Dans cette activité, tu vas pouvoir créer ton propre poème ou ta propre chanson.

> **Stratégie pour écrire**
> Writers of poetry use a variety of techniques to communicate emotion and meaning, and to create interesting effects with the sounds of language. They use figurative language and **imagery**, words or phrases that appeal to the senses, to create vivid or startling descriptions of a subject. **Rhyme** is often associated with poetry, but there are other effective means of using sounds to convey feeling and mood, such as **repetition** and **rhythm**. Try experimenting with these poetic techniques and see how they add to the depth and intensity of your poetry or song lyrics.

A. Préparation

1. D'abord, choisis le sujet de ton poème. Tu peux parler d'...
   a. une personne qui joue un rôle important dans ta vie.
   b. un objet que tu aimes beaucoup ou que tu trouves original.
   c. un moment particulier de ta vie, important ou non.
   d. une expérience intéressante que tu as vécue.
2. Pour faire la description de ce que tu as choisi comme sujet, fais une liste d'adjectifs et de verbes pour décrire les caractéristiques particulières de ton sujet.
3. Pour parler de tes sentiments ou de tes émotions, fais une liste de mots ou d'images pour exprimer la joie, la solitude, l'appartenance...

B. Rédaction

1. Fais un brouillon de ton poème/ta chanson. Souviens-toi que ton but principal est de décrire ton sujet de façon vivante et intéressante.
2. Pendant que tu écris ton brouillon, essaie de créer des effets de son intéressants.
   a. Peux-tu utiliser une série de mots qui commencent par le même son?
   b. Peux-tu terminer tes phrases par des mots qui riment?
   c. Peux-tu combiner tes mots de façon à créer un certain rythme?
3. Essaie de faire ressortir les idées principales en répétant certaines phrases importantes.

C. Evaluation

1. Relis ton brouillon. Est-ce que tu as réussi à décrire ton sujet de façon intéressante ou à bien exprimer une émotion? Essaie de remplacer certains mots par des mots plus forts ou par des mots qui décrivent mieux ton sujet.
2. Maintenant, lis ton poème/ta chanson tout haut. Les sonorités sont-elles agréables? Cherche des endroits où tu peux répéter une phrase importante ou ajouter une nouvelle rime. Fais les changements nécessaires.
3. Corrige les fautes d'orthographe et de grammaire, puis rédige la version finale de ton poème/ta chanson. Fais-le/la lire à ton/ta camarade. Si tu as écrit une chanson et que tu as une idée du genre de musique que tu voudrais, chante ta chanson.

> **Teaching Resources**
> **p. 331**
>
> **PRINT**
> ▶ Lesson Planner, p. 56
> ▶ Cahier d'activités, p. 155
> ▶ Alternative Assessment Guide, p. 26
> ▶ Standardized Assessment Tutor, Chapter 11
>
> **MEDIA**
> ▶ One-Stop Planner, Disc 3
> ▶ Test Generator, Chapter 11
> ▶ Interactive CD-ROM Tutor

Process Writing

Prewriting

Language Arts Link
You might have students bring in poems and copy one of them onto a transparency. Have students list poetic devices they find (simile, metaphor, repetition, alliteration, irony) and have them define and give additional examples of these devices.

Building on Previous Skills
A. 2. Before students start writing, have them visualize the subject of their poem. Then, have them list adjectives to describe what they see and the feelings that the image conveys.

Writing

Auditory/Kinesthetic Learners
B. Auditory learners may need to hear the words and rhythm of their poem in order to write. Encourage them to say the words aloud and to experiment with different combinations of words. Kinesthetic learners might need to hum, clap, or sing to get a feel for the rhythm of their verse.

Apply and Assess

Postwriting

Teaching Suggestion
C. Encourage self-correction. Have students look for words or phrases in their poems that "aren't quite right."

When students have finished writing their poems, ask for volunteers to read their work out loud.

After each reading, have the class tell what each poem is about. You might prompt their answers with questions such as **De quoi parle le poème de... ? Est-ce que ce poème est triste ou gai?**

Grammaire supplémentaire

internet

ADRESSE: go.hrw.com
MOT-CLE: WA3
FRANCOPHONE AMERICA-11

Première étape — Objectives Asking for confirmation; asking for and giving opinions; agreeing and disagreeing

1 Complète les phrases suivantes avec les formes correctes des verbes entre parenthèses. Ensuite, relis l'histoire et trouve la phrase qui n'est pas logique dans le contexte de l'histoire. (**p. 316**)

Si je/j' ___1___ (se souvenir) bien, c'était l'automne 76. J'étais ce qu'on appelait à l'époque un «hippie», un baba-cool. D'habitude, je/j' ___2___ (se lever) vers 11 heures du matin, je/j' ___3___ (s'habiller)—je/j' ___4___ (mettre) mon pattes d'eph préféré, bien sûr!—puis je/j' ___5___ (se promener) dans le quartier avec l'espoir de trouver une manif. Mais ce matin-là, j'avais pris rendez-vous chez le coiffeur. Je voulais ___6___ (se faire) faire une permanente. Je/J' ___7___ (se lever) tôt et puis je suis allé au parc, où j'ai passé toute la journée à dormir sur l'herbe. C'était cool. Qu'est-ce que j'étais beau avec les cheveux frisés!

2 Récris les phrases suivantes sur une feuille de papier en mettant les adverbes à la bonne place. (**p. 316**)

1. Tu habites à Baton Rouge? (toujours)
2. Des po-boys, du jambalaya, du pouding au pain. On a mangé pendant les vacances! (bien)
3. Vous êtes à l'adresse indiquée sur la feuille, 12 rue Toulouse? (bien)
4. Si je me souviens, tu avais cinq ans quand tu es venu en Louisiane pour la première fois. (bien)
5. Comment elle s'appelle? (déjà)
6. Tu l'as traversé, le pont sur le lac Pontchartrain? (déjà)

3 Marie-Line demande à ses amis quels genres de musique ils aiment. Ecris leurs réponses à l'aide des informations données entre parenthèses. Rappelle-toi qu'avec **aimer, adorer,** etc., tu n'as pas besoin d'un pronom d'objet quand tu parles d'une abstraction. (**p. 318**)

EXEMPLE — Paul, tu aimes le jazz, toi? (+)
— Oui, j'adore!

1. Anne et Marc, vous aimez la musique cajun? (+)
2. Ça te plaît, la musique classique? (−)
3. Est-ce que tu aimes le blues? (+)
4. Emile et Jeanne, ça vous plaît, le country? (−)

Answers

1
1. me souviens
2. me levais
3. m'habillais
4. mettais
5. me promenais
6. me faire
7. me suis levé

sentence that is out-of-place: Je me suis levé tôt et puis je suis allé au parc, où j'ai passé toute la journée à dormir sur l'herbe.

2
1. Tu habites toujours à Baton Rouge?
2. Des po-boys, du jambalaya, du pouding au pain, on a bien mangé pendant les vacances!
3. Vous êtes bien à l'adresse indiquée sur la feuille, 12 rue Toulouse?
4. Si je me souviens bien, tu avais cinq ans quand tu es venu en Louisiane pour la première fois.
5. Comment elle s'appelle, déjà?
6. Tu l'a déjà traversé, le pont sur le lac Pontchartrain?

3 *Possible answers:*
1. Oui, nous aimons bien.
2. Non, je n'aime pas trop.
3. Oui, j'aime bien.
4. Non, nous n'aimons pas trop.

Grammar Resources for Chapter 11

The **Grammaire supplémentaire** activities are designed as supplemental activities for the grammatical concepts presented in the chapter. You might use them as additional practice, for review, or for assessment.

For more grammar presentations, review, and practice, refer to the following:
• Travaux pratiques de grammaire
• Grammar Tutor for Students of French

• Grammar Summary on pp. R29–R54
• Cahier d'activités
• Grammar and Vocabulary quizzes (Testing Program)
• Test Generator
• Interactive CD-ROM Tutor
• **Jeux interactifs** at go.hrw.com

4 Trouve la question qui correspond à chaque réponse, puis relis les phrases et trouve la solution de l'énigme parmi les animaux et objets représentés. (**p. 323**)

le chat

le poisson rouge

le canari

la pomme

— Qu'est-ce qu'il mange?

— Il est de quelle taille?

— Où est-ce qu'il habite?

— Qu'est-ce que c'est?

1. _____

— Oh, c'est un animal.

2. _____

— Chez les gens. Il y en a qui sont sauvages, aussi.

3. _____

— Il est tout petit.

4. _____

— Ah, des graines et des insectes!

Ce dont on parle, c'est du/de la _____ .

5 Maintenant, à toi de poser les questions! Ecris une question pour chaque réponse ci-dessous. (**p. 323**)

EXEMPLE   Je l'ai traité d'imbécile parce qu'il m'énervait.
           Pourquoi tu as traité ton frère d'imbécile?

1. Tu sais bien qu'on a cours à une heure!
2. C'est en octobre.
3. Mon actrice préférée, c'est Sandrine Bonnaire. Elle est géniale.
4. C'est un nom qui vient de l'anglais. Ça veut dire «amusement».
5. Mais je n'ai rien fait, moi!
6. Il y a de la farine, du sucre, du beurre et des œufs dedans.
7. En français, on appelle cet animal un «guépard».

Answers

4 1. —Qu'est-ce que c'est?
2. —Où est-ce qu'il habite?
3. —Il est de quelle taille?
4. —Qu'est-ce qu'il mange?
answer to riddle: le canari

5 Possible answers:
1. A quelle heure est-ce qu'on a cours?
2. C'est quand, la rentrée des classes?
3. Qui est ton actrice préférée?
4. D'où vient le mot «fun»?
5. Qu'est-ce que tu as fait?
6. Qu'est-ce qu'il y a dans un gâteau?
7. Comment est-ce qu'on dit «chee-tah» en français?

Communication for All Students

Slower Pace

1 Read the paragraph out loud without the missing verbs and have students think about which form of the verb to put in each blank. Then have volunteers provide answers and explain why they made the choices that they did. When all of the verbs have been provided in their correct forms, have volunteers write their final answers on the board or on an overhead transparency.

Kinesthetic Learners

3 Have students work in groups. Distribute large index cards and black and red markers to each group. Students should then write out each word of the sentences on an index card in black ink and the adverb in red ink. Next have groups put their sentences in order. Finally, have each group explain why they placed their adjective where they did.

Grammaire supplémentaire

CHAPITRE 11

For **Grammaire supplémentaire** Answer Transparencies, see the *Teaching Transparencies* binder.

Grammaire supplémentaire

WA3 FRANCOPHONE AMERICA-11

6 Mets les lettres suivantes dans le bon ordre pour trouver ce qui est sur la liste de commissions de Cédric. Ecris chaque mot avec son article partitif. Pour trouver ce que Cédric va préparer, arrange les lettres soulignées. **(pp. 19, 324)**

EXEMPLE SNABANE **des bananes**

1. N̲ARFIE̲
2. FŒ̲SU
3. T̲ILA
4. CUR̲E̲S
5. ELI̲HU
   et un BOL A MELAN̲GER...
6. Cédric will be making: des __ __ __ __ __ __ __ __

7 Complète les phrases suivantes avec les mots proposés pour faire des phrases logiques. Ensuite, donne ton opinion sur chaque phrase (**d'accord** ou **pas d'accord**). **(p. 266, 326)**

> a. me dégoûte. J'aime les autres ingrédients de la pizza.
>
> b. je préfère! Ils sont trop beaux!
>
> c. on fait à l'école est toujours intéressant.
>
> d. aiment regarder des matches de tennis à la télé.

1. Dans ma famille, il n'y a que mes frères qui...
2. Il n'y a que le fromage qui...
3. De tous les chiens, c'est les colleys que/qu'
4. Le travail que/qu'...

8 Récris les phrases suivantes en utilisant **ce qui** or **ce que,** selon le cas. **(p. 326)**

EXEMPLE Ça me branche, la musique cajun!
Ce qui me branche, c'est la musique cajun!

1. J'adore les crustacés!
2. Le jazz me plaît vraiment!
3. La cuisine créole, je trouve ça incroyable!
4. J'aime les vieux meubles!
5. Les champs de canne à sucre sautent aux yeux!

Answers

6 1. de la farine
2. des œufs
3. du lait
4. du sucre
5. de l'huile
6. beignets

7 1. d
2. a
3. b
4. c

8 *Possible answers:*
1. Ce que j'adore, c'est les crustacés.
2. Ce qui me plaît, c'est le jazz.
3. Ce que je trouve incroyable, c'est la cuisine créole.
4. Ce que j'aime, c'est les vieux meubles.
5. Ce qui saute aux yeux, c'est les champs de canne à sucre.

Communication for All Students

Challenge
6 After students have completed the activity individually, have them work with a partner to create another shopping list based on a different recipe. Once they have selected the recipe and scrambled the words, collect the lists and give them to different pairs. Next have students unscramble the new lists and provide the correct partitive article for each item listed.

Visual/Auditory Learners
10 Have students cover the sentences as you read each one aloud. Have them choose the drawing that best matches the sentence. Have them complete the activity, using the correct forms of the verbs. As an extension of this activity have students create their own drawings and write an activity, using this one as a model. Then have them pair off to complete each other's work.

9 Hier soir, Maya est sortie avec Zinedine. Maintenant, elle te raconte leur rendez-vous. Remplis les blancs avec **ce qui** ou **ce que** selon le cas. (**p. 326**)

1. Devine _____ s'est passé!
2. Tu sais _____ il m'a dit?
3. _____ je trouve charmant, c'est son sourire!
4. _____ me plaît, c'est sa façon de s'habiller!
5. _____ saute aux yeux, c'est ses beaux cheveux!
6. Tu ne devineras jamais _____ il m'a offert!

10 Pour chaque phrase, donne la forme appropriée du verbe entre parenthèses. Ensuite, identifie une illustration pour l'accompagner. (**p. 326**)

a.

b.

c.

d.

1. On _____ (dire) que ces Louisianais savent bien s'amuser!
2. Il me semble que je/j' _____ (entendre) quelque part la légende d'un bayou plein de bêtes féroces.
3. Ils ont l'air de bien _____ (connaître) leurs instruments.
4. Quand on la regarde de loin, on a l'impression qu'elle _____ (être) hantée.

Review and Assess

You may wish to assign the **Grammaire supplémentaire** activities as additional practice or homework after presenting material throughout the chapter. Assign Activities 1–2 after **Comment dit-on... ?** (p. 316), Activity 3 after **Comment dit-on... ?** (p. 318), Activities 4–5 after **Comment dit-on... ?** (p. 323), Activity 6 after **Vocabulaire** (p. 324), and Activities 8–10 after **Tu te rappelles?** (p. 326). Activity 7 is a review of the relative pronouns presented in Chapter 9.

To prepare students for the **Etape** Quizzes and Chapter Test, we suggest doing the **Grammaire supplémentaire** activities in the following order. Have students complete Activities 1–3 before taking Quiz 11-1A or 11-1B; and Activities 4–10 before Quiz 11-2A or 11-2B.

Answers

9 *Possible answers:*
1. ce qui
2. ce qu'
3. Ce que
4. Ce qui
5. Ce qui
6. ce qu'

10 1. dirait, c
2. ai entendu, d
3. connaître, a
4. est, b

Mise en pratique

CHAPITRE 11

The **Mise en pratique** reviews and integrates all four skills and culture in preparation for the Chapter Test.

Teaching Resources
pp. 336–337

PRINT

▶ Lesson Planner, p. 56
▶ Listening Activities, p. 85
▶ Video Guide, pp. 69, 71–72
▶ Grammar Tutor for Students of French, Chapter 11
▶ Standardized Assessment Tutor, Chapter 11

MEDIA

▶ One-Stop Planner
▶ Video Program
  Videocassette 4, 28:58–31:47
▶ Audio Compact Discs, CD 11, Tr. 13
▶ Interactive CD-ROM Tutor, Disc 3

Language Note
Students might want to know the following terms from the recipes: **un pouce** *(thumb);* **une poêle** *(frying pan);* **égoutter** *(to drain, to drip);* **du laurier** *(bay leaf);* **brasser** *(to stir, to mix);* **mijoter** *(to simmer).*

Mise en pratique

internet

go.hrw.com
ADRESSE: go.hrw.com
MOT-CLE: WA3
FRANCOPHONE AMERICA-11

1 Lis ces recettes et réponds aux questions suivantes.

BEIGNETS DE BANANE

2 grosses bananes bien mûres, écrasées
1 tasse (250 ml.) de farine tamisée
2 cuillères à thé (10 ml.) de poudre à pâte
1 gros œuf

¼ tasse (60 ml.) de lait
1 cuillère à thé (5 ml.) de sucre
1 cuillère à thé (5 ml.) d'essence de vanille
Pincée de sel
Huile

Dans un bol à mélanger, mettre la farine, le sucre, la poudre à pâte et le sel. Battre l'œuf avec le lait et la vanille. Incorporer à la farine et bien mélanger. Ajouter les bananes et bien mélanger à nouveau. Mettre 1 pouce (2.5 cm) de pâte dans une poêle épaisse et chauffer à environ 375°F (190°C). Laisser tomber la pâte par cuillerées dans l'huile chaude et frire jusqu'à ce que les beignets soient bruns et dorés, en les tournant pour les frire également. Retirer et égoutter sur du papier absorbant. Saupoudrer de sucre en poudre.

CREVETTES ET JAMBON JAMBALAYA

2 livres (1 kg.) de crevettes, décortiquées et déveinées
1 tasse (250 ml.) de jambon, haché gros
1 piment vert, haché fin
½ tasse (125 ml.) de céleri, haché fin
2 tasses (500 ml.) de tomates, hachées
1 gros oignon, haché fin

1 gousse d'ail, émincée
2 cuillères à table (30 ml.) de persil, émincé
6 cuillères à thé (28 g.) de beurre
1 feuille de laurier (retirer avant de servir)
3 tasses (750 ml.) de riz bouilli chaud
1 cuillère à thé (5 ml.) de sel
6 gouttes de Tabasco®

Dans une poêle épaisse, faire fondre 4 cuillères à thé (20 g.) de beurre à feu doux et sauter le piment, le céleri, l'oignon et le persil pour qu'ils soient transparents et légèrement brunis. Ajouter les tomates, l'ail et la feuille de laurier. Brasser constamment. Ajouter le sel et le Tabasco et cuire jusqu'à ce que le mélange commence à bouillir. Baisser le feu et mijoter 20 minutes, pour que le mélange épaississe. Dans une autre poêle, sauter les crevettes et le jambon dans 2 cuillères à thé (10 g.) de beurre. Quand les crevettes sont fermes et rosées, ajouter au mélange de tomates et cuire 5 minutes de plus. Ajouter le riz. Brasser pour bien mélanger jusqu'à ce que le riz soit bien enrobé et qu'il ait absorbé la sauce. Servir immédiatement.

1. Est-ce que ces phrases sont vraies ou fausses?
   1. Les beignets de bananes sont frits.   vrai
   2. On a besoin de beurre pour faire les deux recettes.   faux
   3. Pour faire les beignets, il faut d'abord mélanger les bananes avec le lait.   faux
   4. Il n'y a pas de légumes dans le jambalaya.   faux
   5. Pour faire le jambalaya, il faut de la viande et du riz.   vrai

2. Quelle recette on choisit si on...
   1. veut manger un bon dessert?   beignets de banane
   2. aime les crustacés?   crevettes et jambon jambalaya
   3. a envie de manger quelque chose qui est épicé?   crevettes et jambon jambalaya

Apply and Assess

Visual Learners

1 Bring in some of the ingredients for the recipes on this page (banana, green pepper, egg, rice, celery). Hold up each ingredient and have students tell which recipe calls for it.

Teaching Suggestion
Give students the following instructions and have them match each one to the correct recipe.

1. Baisser le feu et mijoter 20 minutes. *(Crevettes et jambon jambalaya)*
2. Brasser constamment. *(Crevettes et jambon jambalaya)*
3. Incorporer à la farine et bien mélanger. *(Beignets de banane)*
4. Saupoudrer de sucre en poudre. *(Beignets de banane)*
5. Ajouter les tomates, l'ail et la feuille de laurier. *(Crevettes et jambon jambalaya)*

2 Mathieu et Nadine décident ce qu'ils vont faire pendant leur visite en Louisiane. Ecoute leur conversation et mets les événements dans le bon ordre. For scripts, see *Listening Activities*, page 155.

CD 11
Tr. 13

5 Mathieu demande à Nadine son opinion sur ce qu'elle mange.

Nadine propose d'aller au Village Acadien. 1

3 Mathieu en donne une opinion négative.

Nadine fait une observation. 4

Mathieu donne son impression sur la cuisine cajun. 7

2 Mathieu demande une explication au sujet du Village Acadien.

Mathieu demande une explication au sujet du gombo. 6

3 Tu vas faire un voyage de cinq jours en Louisiane avec tes camarades. Où est-ce que tu veux aller? Qu'est-ce que tu veux faire? Fais des suggestions. Tes camarades vont te donner leur opinion. S'ils ne sont pas d'accord, ils vont proposer quelque chose d'autre. Quand vous aurez décidé, faites un programme de ce que vous allez faire chaque jour.

4 Tu es en Louisiane et tu as quelques questions à poser à l'employé(e) de l'office de tourisme. Tu lui demandes de t'expliquer les mots suivants. Si tu crois les connaître, vérifie que tu as raison.

«jambalaya»   «zydeco»
«Atchafalaya»
«cajun»   «gombo»
«po-boy»
«fais do-do»   «mardi gras»

5 Jeu de rôle

You're visiting friends in southern Louisiana. They take you to a Cajun restaurant and dance hall. Act out the following scenes with your partners.

a. You don't know what to order, so your friends make suggestions. Because you're not familiar with the foods they suggest, you ask for some explanation. After you taste what you've ordered, your friends want to know what you think. Give your opinion and add an observation about Cajun food.

b. At the dance hall, you and your friends discuss your music preferences. When the live band starts to play, you don't know what kind of music it is. You ask your friends. They tell you and then ask you what you think of the music and dancing. Give them your impressions.

Apply and Assess

Tactile Learners

2 Type the sentences on a sheet of paper and distribute copies to students. Have them cut apart the sentences, listen to the recording, and rearrange the slips of paper according to what they hear.

Challenge

2 Once students have arranged the sentences in the proper order (see Tactile Learners) have them recreate an approximation of the actual conversation.

STANDARDS: 1.1, 1.2, 1.3, 5.1

Teacher Note

4 If students have questions about the words in the box next to Activity 4, have them refer to the **Notes culturelles** in the chapter.

Speaking Assessment

4 You might use the following rubric when grading your students on this activity.

Speaking Rubric	Points			
	4	3	2	1
Content (Complete–Incomplete)				
Comprehension (Total–Little)				
Comprehensibility (Comprehensible–Incomprehensible)				
Accuracy (Accurate–Seldom accurate)				
Fluency (Fluent–Not fluent)				

18–20: A   14–15: C   Under
16–17: B   12–13: D   12: F

Teaching Suggestion

5 For Part **b**, encourage students to bring in music to use in the skit. They might also have group members act as the band members and dancers mentioned in the discussion.

Que sais-je?

WA3 FRANCOPHONE
AMERICA-11

Teaching Resources
p. 338

PRINT
▸ Grammar Tutor for Students of French, Chapter 11

MEDIA
▸ Interactive CD-ROM Tutor, Disc 3
▸ Online self-test

go.hrw.com
WA3 FRANCOPHONE
AMERICA-11

Can you use what you've learned in this chapter?

Can you ask for confirmation?
p. 316

1 You run into someone you haven't seen in a long time. How would you ask for confirmation about . . .   *Possible answers:*
1. his or her brother's name?   Ton frère s'appelle... , c'est ça?
2. where he or she lives?   Tu habites toujours à... ?
3. his or her age?   Tu as bien... ans, c'est ça?
4. where he or she goes to school?   Si je ne me trompe pas, tu vas à... ?

Can you ask for and give an opinion?
p. 318

2 How would you ask a friend's opinion of your favorite music?
Possible answers: Qu'est-ce que tu penses de... ?   Ça te branche,... ?

3 How would you express your opinions about the following types of music?
Possible answers:

> le rock   la musique classique   le rap
>   le jazz   le country

Positive opinion: Je trouve ça hyper cool. J'aime beaucoup. Ça me plaît beaucoup. Ça m'éclate. Je n'écoute que ça.
Negative opinion: Je trouve ça nul. Je n'aime pas du tout. Ça ne me plaît pas du tout. Je n'aime pas tellement ça. Ça ne me branche pas trop.

Can you agree and disagree?
p. 318

4 A friend gives an opinion about a CD you've just bought. How would you express your agreement?   Je suis d'accord avec toi. Moi aussi, j'aime bien... ; Moi non plus, je n'aime pas... ; Ça, c'est sûr. Tu as raison.

5 What do you say if you don't agree with your friend?
Pas du tout. Tu parles! Tu rigoles! Tu délires ou quoi? N'importe quoi!

Can you ask for explanations?
p. 323

6 What do you say to ask . . .   See answers below.
1. what something is?   4. what ingredients are in a dish?
2. what something is called?   5. how to say something in French?
3. what something means?

Can you make observations?
p. 326

7 What observations would you make about . . .   See answers below.
1. your town?   3. a place you visited?
2. your school?   4. learning French?

Can you give impressions?
p. 326

8 How would you give your impressions of these situations?   *Possible answers:*

1. On dirait qu'ils s'amusent bien.   2. Ils ont l'air de s'ennuyer.   3. Il me semble que ce garçon a peur.

Answers

6 1. Qu'est-ce que c'est?
2. Comment est-ce qu'on appelle ça?
3. Qu'est-ce que ça veut dire,... ?
4. Qu'est-ce qu'il y a dans... ?
5. Comment on dit... en français?

7 *Possible answers:*
1. Ce que j'aime, c'est les musées.
2. Ce que je trouve super, c'est les professeurs.
3. Ce qui est incroyable, c'est la cuisine locale.
4. Ce qui est intéressant, c'est la culture dans les pays francophones.

Review and Assess

♞ **Game**
Catégories   This game is played like Scattergories®. In small groups, students take turns calling out a category of functions or vocabulary from the chapter, while the rest of the group writes one word or expression in that category. Students should be allowed a few seconds to write the answer down. After all categories have been called and responses written, the group members call out their answers. If two or more players have the same answer, they must cross it off their lists, and they receive no points for it. Students receive one point for each word or phrase remaining on their lists that was not duplicated by another group member.

Vocabulaire

Asking for confirmation

toujours... ?	still ... ?
bien... ?	really ... ?
..., déjà?	... again?
Si je me souviens bien,...	If I remember correctly, . . .
Si je ne me trompe pas,...	If I'm not mistaken, . . .

Musical instruments

l'accordéon (m.)	the accordion
la basse	the bass (guitar)
la batterie	the drums
la boîte à rythmes	the drum machine
le chant	singing
la flûte	the flute
la guitare	the guitar

le micro (le microphone)	the mike (the microphone)
le piano	the piano
le saxophone	the saxophone
le synthé (le synthétiseur)	the synthesizer
la trompette	the trumpet
le violon	the violin

Kinds of music

le blues	blues
le country	country music
la dance	dance music
le jazz	jazz
la musique cajun	Cajun music
la musique classique	classical music
le rap	rap
le rock	rock

Asking for and giving opinions

Qu'est-ce que tu penses de... ?	What do you think of . . . ?
Ça te branche,... ?	Are you into . . . ?
Ça m'éclate.	I'm wild about it.
Je n'écoute que ça.	That's all I listen to.
Ça ne me branche pas trop.	I'm not into that.

Agreeing and disagreeing

Ça, c'est sûr.	That's for sure.
Tu délires ou quoi?	Are you crazy or what?

Vocabulaire

Teaching Suggestions

- Have students write a skit, using one word or expression from each category in the **Vocabulaire**.
- Have partners ask each other for explanations of the vocabulary words: **Comment on dit** *drums* **en français? Comment on dit «écrevisses» en anglais?**

Deuxième étape

Asking for explanations

Qu'est-ce que c'est?	What's that?
Comment est-ce qu'on appelle ça?	What is that called?
Qu'est-ce que ça veut dire,... ?	What does . . . mean?
Qu'est-ce qu'il y a dans... ?	What's in . . . ?
Comment est-ce qu'on fait... ?	How do you make . . . ?
D'où vient le mot... ?	Where does the word . . . come from?
Comment on dit... ?	How do you say . . . ?

Cajun food

à la vapeur	steamed
l'andouille (f.)	andouille sausage
au court-bouillon	boiled

les crustacés (m.)	shellfish
les écrevisses (f.)	crawfish
en bisque	bisque
les épices (f.)	spices
les épinards (m.)	spinach
farci(e) (à)	stuffed (with)
frit(e)	fried
le gombo	gumbo
le jambalaya	jambalaya
des okras (m.)	okra
le po-boy	po-boy sandwich
le pouding au pain	bread pudding
les raisins secs	raisins
salé(e)	salty
les saucisses (f.)	sausages

Making observations

Ce qui est intéressant/ incroyable, c'est...	What's interesting/ incredible is . . .

Ce qui saute aux yeux, c'est...	What catches your eye is . . .
Ce qui me branche vraiment, c'est...	What I'm really crazy about is . . .
Ce que je trouve super, c'est...	What I think is super is . . .
Ce que j'adore/ j'aime, c'est...	What I love/like is . . .

Giving impressions

On dirait que...	It looks like . . .
Il me semble que...	It seems to me that . . .
J'ai l'impression que...	I have the impression that . . .
Ils ont l'air de...	They seem to . . .

Chapter 11 Assessment

▶ **Testing Program**
Chapter Test, pp. 243–248
Audio Compact Discs, CD 11, Trs. 16–18
Speaking Test, p. 300

▶ **Alternative Assessment Guide**
Portfolio Assessment, p. 26
Performance Assessment, p. 40
CD-ROM Assessment, p. 54

▶ **Interactive CD-ROM Tutor, Disc 3**
A toi de parler
A toi d'écrire

▶ **Standardized Assessment Tutor**
Chapter 11

▶ **One-Stop Planner, Disc 3**
Test Generator
Chapter 11

Review and Assess

Circumlocution

Have students work in pairs. One student is a French exchange student in Louisiana, and the other is a member of the American host family. They are at a Cajun food festival, and the exchange student is asking the host about different foods being served. He or she will ask about a certain food by describing the ingredients and the host will give the correct name for the dish. (—**Comment est-ce qu'on appelle ça, cette soupe avec des crevettes, des okras et du crabe? / —Ça, c'est du gombo.**) Then, have partners switch roles.

Chapitre 12 : Echanges sportifs et culturels

Chapter Overview

Mise en train pp. 342–344	*A nous les Jeux olympiques!*			

	FUNCTIONS	**GRAMMAR**	**VOCABULARY**	**RE-ENTRY**
Première étape pp. 345–349	• Expressing anticipation, p. 348 • Making suppositions, p. 348 • Expressing certainty and doubt, p. 348	• The future after **quand** and **dès que,** p. 348	• Sports and equipment, p. 345	• Sports vocabulary (**Chapitre 4,** I) • The future (**Chapitre 5,** III)

Remise en train pp. 350–351	*Un rendez-vous sportif et culturel*			

Deuxième étape pp. 352–355	• Inquiring, p. 353 • Expressing excitement and disappointment, p. 355		• Places of origin, p. 352	• Prepositions with countries (**Chapitre 11,** I) • Introducing people (**Chapitre 7,** I) • Asking someone's name and age and giving yours (**Chapitre 1,** I) • Offering encouragement (**Chapitre 12,** II)

Lisons! pp. 356–358	**Articles about francophone athletes**	**Reading Strategy** Combining strategies
Ecrivons! p. 359	**Un article de magazine**	**Writing Strategy** Doing research
Grammaire supplémentaire	**pp. 360–363**	**Première étape,** pp. 360–361 **Deuxième étape,** pp. 362–363
Review pp. 364–367	**Mise en pratique,** pp. 364–365 **Que sais-je?,** p. 366	**Vocabulaire,** p. 367

CULTURE

• **Note culturelle,** Sporting events in the francophone world, p. 344   • **Panorama Culturel,** Regional stereotypes, p. 354

Chapitre 12 : Echanges sportifs et culturels   *Review Chapter*
Chapter Resources

PRINT

Lesson Planning

 **One-Stop Planner**

Lesson Planner with Substitute Teacher Lesson Plans, pp. 57–61, 75

Student Make-Up Assignments
- Make-Up Assignment Copying Masters, Chapter 12

Listening and Speaking

Listening Activities
- Student Response Forms for Listening Activities, pp. 91–93
- Additional Listening Activities 12-1 to 12-6, pp. 95–97
- Additional Listening Activities (song), p. 98
- Scripts and Answers, pp. 159–163

Video Guide
- Teaching Suggestions, pp. 74–75
- Activity Masters, pp. 76–78
- Scripts and Answers, pp. 109–111, 116

Activities for Communication
- Communicative Activities, pp. 45–48
- Realia and Teaching Suggestions, pp. 84–86
- Situation Cards, pp. 111–112

Reading and Writing

Reading Strategies and Skills Handbook, Chapter 12

Joie de lire 3, Chapter 12

Cahier d'activités, pp. 133–144

Grammar

Travaux pratiques de grammaire, pp. 102–107

Grammar Tutor for Students of French, Chapter 12

Assessment

Testing Program
- Grammar and Vocabulary Quizzes, **Etape** Quizzes, and Chapter Test, pp. 257–270
- Score Sheet, Scripts and Answers, pp. 271–277, 287–292
- Final Exam, pp. 279–286
- Score Sheet, Scripts and Answers, pp. 287–292

Alternative Assessment Guide
- Portfolio Assessment, p. 27
- Performance Assessment, p. 41
- CD-ROM Assessment, p. 55

Student Make-Up Assignments
- Alternative Quizzes, Chapter 12

Standardized Assessment Tutor
- Reading, pp. 47–49
- Writing, p. 50
- Math, pp. 51–52

MEDIA

 Online Activities
- Jeux interactifs
- Activités Internet

 Video Program
- Videocassette 4
- Videocassette 5 (captioned version)

 Audio Compact Discs
- Textbook Listening Activities, CD 12, Tracks 1–11
- Additional Listening Activities, CD 12, Tracks 22–28
- Assessment Items, CD 12, Tracks 12–16
- Final Exam, CD 12, Tracks 17–21

 Interactive CD-ROM Tutor, Disc 3

Teaching Transparencies
- Situation 12-1 to 12-2
- **Grammaire supplémentaire** Answers
- **Travaux pratiques de grammaire** Answers

  One-Stop Planner CD-ROM

Use the **One-Stop Planner CD-ROM with Test Generator** to aid in lesson planning and pacing.

For each chapter, the **One-Stop Planner** includes:
- Editable lesson plans with direct links to teaching resources
- Printable worksheets from resource books
- Direct launches to the HRW Internet activities
- Video and audio segments
- Test Generator
- Clip Art for vocabulary items

Projects ·····················

Cette année-là aux Jeux

Students will write and produce a booklet that features the host city and champion athletes from the Olympic Games of any given year. The cover of the booklet, illustrated with drawings, cutouts, or computer-generated graphics, will feature the Games for that year. The first page of the booklet will give background and tourist information about the host city. Five additional pages will give information on five champion athletes who competed in the Games and information about the events they participated in. Encourage students to incorporate the vocabulary and functions of the chapter in their text.

MATERIALS

✂ **Students may need**
- Encyclopedias
- Construction paper
- Stapler
- Colored pencils or markers
- Magazines or catalogues
- Almanacs
- Typewriter or word processor
- Computer-generated graphics

SUGGESTED SEQUENCE

1. Students research the Olympic Games of a particular year and decide which events to feature.

2. Students research the host city of the Olympic Games they have chosen. They should gather historical information as well as information on local sights that would be of interest to tourists.

3. Students then research the five sporting events they have chosen. They should look up historical information about the sport as well as the basic rules and necessary equipment.

4. Next, students should find out who won the events they've selected in the year they've chosen, where the winning athletes were from, and any pertinent information about them.

5. Students then imagine an interview between one of the athletes and a sports reporter. They might create the interview in three stages: before the athlete leaves his or her home country to attend the Games, at the Games before his or her event takes place, and after the event (or after he or she has received a medal).

6. Students write a rough draft of the information they will include in their booklets, using the notes they have taken during their research, and looking up in the dictionary any French terms they need. Students should edit their papers, and then exchange papers with a partner for additional corrections and comments.

7. Students type or write the text neatly on the pages they will include in the booklet: the cover, the host city information page, and the five pages featuring the champion athletes and their events.

8. Students illustrate the booklet where appropriate.

9. Have students exchange their booklets in class, share them with other French classes, or display them in the school library.

GRADING THE PROJECT

You might base students' grades on content, language use, visual presentation, and creativity.

Suggested Point Distribution (total = 100 points)
Content..25 points
Language use...25 points
Visual presentation ....25 points
Creativity..25 points

Games ··································

Mots associés

In this game, students will review all the functional expressions and vocabulary they've learned in Chapters 1–12.

Procedure   Distribute several index cards to each student in the class. On one side of the cards, students should write lists of several words and/or expressions grouped by category (**l'escrime, le judo, la gymnastique**). On the reverse side, they should write the category *(Olympic sports)*. Examples of additional categories are given below. You might assign each student one chapter in the book from which to choose his or her categories. Collect the cards and edit them. Then, form two teams and have the first player from each team stand up. Read aloud the list from one of the cards. The first player to identify the category wins a point for his or her team.

Sample categories:
- Places where you wait
- Things to do in Tunisia
- Things your parent might say to you
- Things you might write to an advice columnist
- Things you might write in a business letter

Storytelling

Mini-histoire

This story accompanies Teaching Transparency 12-1. The mini-histoire can be told and retold in different formats, acted out, written as dictation, and read aloud to give students additional opportunities to practice all four skills. In the following story, Yamilé wants to watch the Olympic Games on television, but she can't decide on a channel.

«Deux heures… Il y a les J.O. à la télé. Je vais regarder ça pendant quelques minutes avant d'aller chez Khaled».

Yamilé allume la télévision.

«Natation, bof! Ce n'est pas très passionnant. Base-ball, c'est encore pire. Je ne comprends rien à ce jeux. Boxe, quelle horreur! Ah, de la gynastique. Ça, c'est bien. Je vais regarder ce qu'il y a sur les autres chaînes et s'il n'y a rien de mieux, je reviens sur la gym. Haltérophilie, pas génial. Athlétisme… bof. Je préfère la gym. Basket, c'est comme le base-ball, je n'aime pas. Equitation… on ne voit pas souvent ça à la télé. Et puis les chevaux, ils sont tellement beaux. Dernière chaîne, tir à l'arc. Bon. Je vais regarder la gym et l'équitation. Je vais zapper de l'un à l'autre».

Traditions

Le Tour de France

One of the most popular sporting traditions in France is cycling. France ranks number one in the world in track cycling competition and has an impressive record in mountain biking, but it is best known for the road cycling of the famous **Tour de France.** Each July, the French and tourists alike put everything on hold to watch **le Tour,** the world's most prestigious bicycle race covering over 3,000 miles of varied terrain. Everyone wants to know who will wear the coveted jerseys awarded to the cyclist who leads the race (**maillot jaune**), has the most points (**maillot vert**), and rules the mountains (**maillot à pois rouge**). Although long dominated by the French, two Americans won the tour in the last century: Greg LeMond and Lance Armstrong.

Recette

*The **charlotte** was named after Queen Charlotte, wife of king George III of England. The **charlotte au chocolat** is filled with chocolate mousse and served cold, unlike other types of **char-lottes.** It can be decorated with strawberries and raspberries, whipped cream, or chocolate shavings.*

CHARLOTTE AU CHOCOLAT

pour 6 personnes

Le gâteau

24 à 30 boudoirs

1 tasse de lait

La mousse

8 oz de chocolat noir pâtissier en morceaux

3 cuillères à soupe de café

5 œufs

La mousse

La préparer au moins 4 heures à l'avance. Faire fondre le chocolat dans une casserole avec le café.

Séparer le blanc et le jaune des œufs. Ajouter les jaunes au chocolat fondu. Bien mélanger.

Battre les blancs en neige très ferme. Ajouter le chocolat fondu petit à petit.

Le gâteau

Verser le lait dans un bol. Tremper un à un les boudoirs dans le lait. Disposer les boudoirs au fond du moule et sur les côtés. Ajouter la moitié de la mousse au chocolat. Placer une couche de boudoirs dessus. Ajouter le reste de la mousse au chocolat. Placer une dernière couche de boudoirs.

Mettre au frigidaire pendant au moins 12 heures. Décorer au moment de servir.

Technology

Video Program

Videocassette 4, Videocassette 5 (captioned version)
See Video Guide, pp. 73–78.

Camille et compagnie • Douzième épisode : *Une sauterelle pleine d'avenir*

Sophie invites her friends to attend the filming of her first role in a commercial for the sports equipment store *La Sauterelle sportive*. When Camille, Azzedine, Max, and Laurent arrive at the store, they can't find Sophie. While waiting for her, the boys take a tour of the store and run into archery champion, Jean-Jacques Vandamme. Sophie's friends ask an actor dressed as a grasshopper where Sophie is, only to find out that the grasshopper is Sophie! Sophie is ashamed of her role and costume, but her friends comfort her and applaud her acting debut.

Quelle est l'image d'une personne typique de cette région?

People from around the francophone world talk about stereotypical images. Two native speakers discuss the **Panorama Culturel** question and introduce the interviews.

Vidéoclips

- **Pentel**®: advertisement for pens
- **Le Trèfle**®: advertisement for toilet tissue
- **Banania**®: advertisement for cocoa
- **News report:** the variety of cultures that co-exist in an H.L.M.

Interactive CD-ROM Tutor

The **Interactive CD-ROM Tutor** contains videos, interactive games, and activities that provide students an opportunity to practice and review the material covered in Chapter 12.

Activity	Activity Type	Pupil's Edition Page
1. Vocabulaire	Jeu des paires	p. 345
2. Comment dit-on… ?	Chacun à sa place	p. 348
3. Grammaire	Les mots qui manquent	p. 348
4. Vocabulaire	Chasse au trésor Explorons! Vérifions!	p. 352
5. Comment dit-on… ?	Chacun à sa place	p. 353
6. Comment dit-on… ?	Chacun à sa place	p. 355
Panorama Culturel	Quelle est l'image d'une personne typique de cette région? Le bon choix	p. 354
A toi de parler	*Guided recording*	pp. 364–365
A toi d'écrire	*Guided writing*	pp. 364–365

Teacher Management System

Logging in

Logging in to the *Allez, viens!* TMS is easy. Upon launching the program, simply type "admin" in the password area of the log-in screen and press RETURN. Log on to **www.hrw.com/CDROMTUTOR** for a detailed explanation of the Teacher Management System.

One-Stop Planner CD-ROM

To preview all resources available for this chapter, use the **One-Stop Planner CD-ROM**, Disc 3.

Internet Connection

internet

ADRESSE: go.hrw.com
MOT-CLE: WA3
FRANCOPHONE
AMERICA-12

*Have students explore the **go.hrw.com** Web site for many online resources covering all chapters. All Chapter 12 resources are available under the keyword **WA3 FRANCOPHONE AMERICA-12**. Interactive games help students practice the material and provide them with immediate feedback. You'll also find a printable worksheet that provides Internet activities that lead to a comprehensive online research project.*

Jeux interactifs

You can use the interactive activities in this chapter

- to practice grammar, vocabulary, and chapter functions
- as homework
- as an assessment option
- as a self-test
- to prepare for the Chapter Test

Activités Internet

Students look for information about events in the Olympic Games, using the vocabulary and phrases from the chapter.

- After completing the activity sheet, have students work with a partner and share the information they gathered in Activities B and C on that sheet. In Activity D, students are asked to write a letter in which they share their plans for an imaginary trip to the Olympic Games. Have partners exchange their letters and edit each other's work.

Projet

Have groups of students select an event in the upcoming Olympic Games. Students can research the major teams or individual athletes expected to compete in the event and find out about the rules of the sport. Have them prepare a brief presentation to share their findings with the class. Encourage them to include photos or videos in their presentations. Remind students to document their sources by noting the names and the URLs of all the sites they consulted.

Textbook Listening Activities Scripts 🔊

Première étape

6 p. 345

1. —Tiens! Regarde un peu! Il est en train de soulever deux cent cinquante-cinq kilos. Il en a les yeux qui lui sortent de la tête!
   —Ah, ouais. Il est vraiment fort, ce Russe. Je crois qu'il va gagner.

2. —Ils sont vraiment étroits, ces bateaux.
   —Oui. Je ne vois pas comment huit personnes peuvent s'asseoir dedans.
   —Et puis, comment est-ce qu'ils font pour ne pas s'emmêler les rames?
   —Je n'en ai aucune idée, moi.

3. —Tu as vu ça, toi?
   —Euh, qu'est-ce qui est arrivé?
   —Le tireur, là, il a manqué son tir.
   —Et alors?
   —Ben, la flèche est arrivée dans le chapeau d'un homme là-bas.
   —Il ferait bien de choisir un autre sport, non?

4. —Dis donc, il y a une faute à chaque fois que le cheval touche un obstacle?
   —Bien sûr.
   —Oh, zut alors!
   —Tu sais, la même chose lui est arrivée l'année passée. Le cheval a eu peur et elle est tombée.
   —Donc, c'est fini, pour elle, la compétition?
   —Ça, c'est sûr.

5. —Ben, dis donc. Regarde le plongeur. Il va partir de cette position, tu crois?
   —Evidemment. Ça a l'air dangereux, tu trouves pas?
   —Oui. J'ai peur qu'il se cogne la tête contre le plongeoir.
   —Moi aussi.

6. —C'est bien pour les filles qu'elles n'aient pas besoin de faire les anneaux.
   —Oui, mais, à la place, il faut qu'elles passent à la poutre.
   —Oui, c'est vraiment dur, ça. Surtout quand on a le trac.
   —Oui, c'est très facile de tomber. Et après ça, bien sûr, c'est fini.

7. —Qu'est-ce qu'elle est grande, cette piscine!
   —Bien sûr, c'est une piscine olympique.
   —Est-ce que c'est le crawl ou le papillon, la prochaine épreuve?
   —C'est le papillon.
   —C'est le Chinois, le plus rapide, non?
   —Oui, je crois.

8. —C'est vachement bien de pouvoir regarder d'ici.
   —Oui.

—Quand je regarde à la télé, ça m'embête parce que tout est mélangé.
—Moi aussi, ça m'énerve. Ils ne montrent jamais une épreuve en entier. Le lancer du disque, puis le saut à la perche, puis le saut en longueur...
—Oui. Moi, j'aime bien pouvoir voir tous les concurrents.

9. —Ils sont vraiment bons!
   —Tiens! Tu as vu comme il a lancé le ballon à son équipier qui a marqué les deux points?
   —Non. Ça s'est passé trop vite.

10. —Tu veux bien m'expliquer ce qui se passe?
    —Bien sûr.
    —Tu sais que je ne comprends rien aux règles. Tout ce que je sais, c'est qu'on porte un kimono blanc avec une ceinture. Je ne verrais pas la différence entre ça et du karaté.
    —Bon. Je t'explique.

Answers to Activity 6

1. l'haltérophilie	6. la gymnastique
2. l'aviron	7. la natation
3. le tir à l'arc	8. l'athlétisme
4. l'équitation	9. le basket-ball
5. le plongeon acrobatique	10. le judo

12 p. 348

1. SÉVERINE Tu crois que je devrais emporter un parapluie? Je parie qu'il pleut beaucoup là-bas.

   FRÈRE C'est pas la peine. Je suis sûr que tu pourras en acheter un sur place, si tu en as besoin.

2. SÉVERINE Oh! J'ai failli oublier mon appareil-photo. Tu veux bien me l'amener?

   FRÈRE Il est où, dans ton placard? Voyons... Je ne pense pas qu'il soit là.

3. SÉVERINE Il doit y avoir des stars, tu crois pas? Quand je verrai Keanu Reeves, je vais lui demander son autographe.

   FRÈRE Tu sais, Séverine, ça m'étonnerait que tu le voies.

4. SÉVERINE Il me tarde de voir les épreuves de natation. Tu crois que ça va être bien?

   FRÈRE Ça, c'est sûr.

5. SÉVERINE Vivement que j'arrive aux Etats-Unis. Ça doit être vachement intéressant, tu crois pas?

   FRÈRE Oui, mais je ne suis pas certain que tu puisses voir beaucoup de choses. C'est grand, tu sais. Et tu seras tout le temps au village olympique.

Answers to Activity 12
Supposition: 1, 3   *Impatience:* 4, 5   *Neither:* 2

One-Stop Planner CD-ROM

To preview all resources available for this chapter, use the **One-Stop Planner CD-ROM**, Disc 3.

Deuxième étape

24 **p. 353**

Answers to Activity 24
1. pays
2. autre chose
3. pays
4. pays
5. autre chose
6. pays

1. —Salut. Je m'appelle Odile. Et toi?
—Saïd.
—Tu es d'où?
—De Marrakech, au Maroc.
—C'est bien comme ville?
—Oui. C'est super. C'est très animé. Il y a des tas de choses à faire.

2. —Moi, je suis vraiment impatient de voir la natation.
—Moi aussi.
—Tu vas voir le deux cents mètres crawl ce soir?
—Non, malheureusement, je n'ai pas pu avoir de place.
—Dommage. Je parie que ça va être super!

3. —Tu es africaine?
—Oui.
—Cool! C'est comment, la vie là-bas?
—C'est bien. Il fait toujours beau chez moi, en République centrafricaine.
—Il ne fait pas trop chaud?
—Non. Grâce à la forêt tropicale, il fait moins chaud qu'ailleurs.

4. —Et, qu'est-ce qu'on y mange? C'est pareil qu'ici?
—Euh, je crois qu'on a plus ou moins les mêmes choses, mais on ne mange pas autant de viande que chez toi et puis, il y a quelques plats qu'on ne mange pas chez toi...
—Par exemple?
—Eh bien, le singe.
—On mange ça chez toi? Ouah!

5. —Zut alors! On s'est encore perdus. Je crois qu'on est déjà passés devant ce bâtiment il y a dix minutes.
—Ah non! C'est pas vrai! On va rater le début du match.
—Bon. Je vais demander à cette jeune fille-là. Pardon, vous savez où se trouve le gymnase?

6. —Dis-moi, est-ce que tout le monde porte ces robes, euh, je ne sais pas comment ça s'appelle, chez toi?
—Tu veux dire des sifsaris et des djellabas?
—Oui, c'est ça.
—C'est un habit assez traditionnel. La plupart des jeunes portent les mêmes vêtements que toi. Mais on peut choisir selon l'occasion.
—Ah oui?

28 **p. 355**

Answers to Activity 28
1. gagné
2. perdu
3. perdu
4. perdu
5. gagné
6. gagné
7. perdu
8. perdu

1. La médaille d'argent! Et moi qui pensais que ça serait déjà bien si j'arrivais en finale. J'arrive pas à y croire!

2. Tout allait bien, jusqu'à ce que le coureur qui était à ma gauche coupe en face de moi. C'est à ce moment-là que je suis tombé. J'ai vraiment pas de chance!

3. Les Russes nous ont battus. Ils nous ont mis une raclée. Ils ont marqué quatre-vingt-quatre points, et nous seulement trente-huit. Quelle angoisse!

4. On avait arrêté la compétition parce que le Canadien s'était fait mal. Quand on a recommencé, je voulais m'échauffer à nouveau mais on ne me l'a pas permis. C'est pas juste!

5. Tu ne devineras jamais ce qui m'est arrivé. C'est trop cool. J'ai eu un dix à l'épreuve de barres asymétriques!

6. Ecoute! J'ai battu le record de saut à la perche et c'est moi qui détiens le nouveau record! C'est vraiment le pied, non?

7. Oh, j'en ai vraiment marre! Tu sais, je ne rate jamais mon tir. Je ne comprends vraiment pas ce qui s'est passé.

8. Si seulement j'avais pu rester sur le cheval. C'est vraiment embarrassant de tomber comme ça! Qu'est-ce que je peux être nul!

Mise en pratique

2 **p. 365**

Answers to Mise en pratique Activity 2
1. c
2. g
3. d
4. a
5. h
6. e
7. b
8. f

1. Elle n'a vraiment pas eu de chance, la pauvre. D'abord, elle est tombée des barres asymétriques, et puis le jour suivant, elle est tombée de la poutre.

2. Les Russes étaient vraiment très bons. On ne pouvait pas les arrêter. Là, vous voyez, c'est le moment où ils ont fait le panier qui les a fait gagner.

3. Ça, c'est mon athlète préférée, Marie-José Pérec. Je l'admire tellement. Là, c'est elle pendant la course de fond. Elle est vraiment bonne!

4. Vous savez, depuis quelque temps, j'ai envie de faire du judo. C'est vachement intéressant. Cette fille-là, c'est une Française. Elle s'appelle Cathy Fleury. C'est elle qui a gagné.

5. Et ça, c'est le Chinois qui a gagné la plupart des épreuves de natation. Il est formidable.

6. Regardez ce pauvre type-là. Je ne sais pas qui c'est, mais je l'ai vu tomber de son cheval. Il ne s'est pas fait mal, heureusement, mais quelle angoisse, hein?

7. C'est vraiment curieux, cette tenue et ces masques qu'ils portent. Je ne comprends pas très bien les règles de l'escrime, mais c'est fascinant à observer.

8. Ça, c'était vraiment génial. Vous voyez? Là, c'est le moment où l'Américain a battu le record de saut à la perche. La foule était en délire!

Chapitre 12 : Echanges sportifs et culturels *Review Chapter*

Suggested Lesson Plans *50-Minute Schedule*

Day 1

CHAPTER OPENER 10 min.
- Present Chapter Objectives, p. 341.
- History Link, ATE, p. 340

MISE EN TRAIN 35 min.
- Presenting **Mise en train**, ATE, p. 342
- Geography Link, ATE, p. 343
- Do Activities 1–4, p. 344.
- Read and discuss **Note culturelle**, p. 344.
- Culture Notes, ATE, p. 344

Wrap-Up 5 min.
- Do Activity 5, p. 344.

Homework Options
Cahier d'activités, Act. 1, p. 133

Day 2

PREMIERE ETAPE
Quick Review 10 min.
- Check homework.
- Bell Work, ATE, p. 345

Vocabulaire, p. 345 30 min.
- Presenting **Vocabulaire**, ATE, p. 345
- Play Audio CD for Activity 6, p. 345.
- Cahier d'activités, pp. 134–135, Acts. 2–4
- Travaux pratiques de grammaire, p. 102, Acts. 1–2
- Do Activities 7–8, p. 346.
- Have students do Activity 9, p. 347, in pairs.
- Read and discuss **Tu te rappelles?**, p. 347.
- Have students do Activity 10, p. 347, in groups.

Wrap-Up, 10 min.
- Language-to-Language, ATE, p. 347
- Visual Learners, ATE, p. 345

Homework Options
Travaux pratiques de grammaire, Acts. 3–5, p. 103

Day 3

PREMIERE ETAPE
Quick Review 5 min.
- Check homework.

Comment dit-on... ?, p. 348 20 min.
- Presenting **Comment dit-on... ?**, ATE, p. 348
- Play Audio CD for Activity 12, p. 348.
- Cahier d'activités, p. 136, Acts. 6–7
- Read and discuss **De bons conseils**, p. 348.

Grammaire, p. 348 20 min.
- Presenting **Grammaire**, ATE, p. 348
- Do Activity 13, p. 349
- **Grammaire supplémentaire**, pp. 360–361, Acts. 2–5
- Do Activity 14, p. 349.
- Have students do Activity 15, p. 349, in pairs.
- Culture Note, ATE, p. 349

Wrap-Up 5 min.
- Do Activity 16, p. 349.

Homework Options
Study for Quiz 12-1
Travaux pratiques de grammaire, Acts. 6–7, p. 104
Cahier d'activités, Act. 8, p. 137

Day 4

PREMIERE ETAPE
Quiz 12-1 20 min.
- Administer Quiz 12-1A or 12-1B.

REMISE EN TRAIN 25 min.
- Presenting **Remise en train**, ATE, p. 350
- Do Activities 17–20, pp. 350–351.
- Visual/Auditory Learners, ATE, p. 351

Wrap-Up 5 min.
- Do Activity 21, p. 351.

Homework Options
Cahier d'activités, Act. 10, p. 138

Day 5

REMISE EN TRAIN
Quick Review 5 min.
- Check homework.

DEUXIEME ETAPE
Vocabulaire, p. 352 20 min.
- Presenting **Vocabulaire**, ATE, p. 352
- Do Activity 22, p. 352.
- Read and discuss **Tu te rappelles?**, p. 352.
- Travaux pratiques de grammaire, pp. 106–107, Acts. 11–13
- **Grammaire supplémentaire**, pp. 362–363, Acts. 6–8
- Have students do Activity 23, p. 353, in pairs.

Comment dit-on... ?, p. 353 20 min.
- Presenting **Comment dit-on... ?**, ATE, p. 353
- Play Audio CD for Activity 24, p. 353.
- Cahier d'activités, pp. 140–141, Acts. 12–13
- Do Activity 25, p. 353.

Wrap-Up 5 min.
- Do Activity 26, p. 353.

Homework Options
Cahier d'activités, Act. 11, p. 139
Travaux pratiques de grammaire, Acts. 8–10, pp. 105–106

Day 6

DEUXIEME ETAPE
Quick Review 5 min.
- Check homework.

Comment dit-on... ?, p. 355 20 min.
- Presenting **Comment dit-on... ?**, ATE, p. 355
- Do Activity 28, p. 355.
- Cahier d'activités, pp. 141–142, Acts. 14–15
- Do Activity 29, p. 355.
- Have students do Activity 31, p. 355, in groups.

PANORAMA CULTUREL 20 min.
- Presenting **Panorama Culturel**, ATE, p. 354
- See Teaching Suggestions, Viewing Suggestion 1, Video Guide, p. 75.
- Questions, ATE, p. 354
- Discuss **Qu'en penses-tu?**, p. 354.

Wrap-Up 5 min.
- Thinking Critically: Analyzing, ATE, p. 354

Homework Options
Study for Quiz 12-2.
Pupil's Edition, Activity 30, p. 355

One-Stop Planner CD-ROM

For alternative lesson plans by chapter section, to create your own customized plans, or to preview all resources available for this chapter, use the **One-Stop Planner CD-ROM**, Disc 3.

 For additional homework suggestions, see activities accompanied by this symbol throughout the chapter.

Day 7

DEUXIEME ETAPE

Quiz 12-2 20 min.
- Administer Quiz 12-2A or 12-2B.

LISONS! 25 min.
- Read and discuss **Stratégie pour lire**, p. 356.
- Do Prereading Activities A–B, p. 356 and Motivating Activity, ATE, p. 356.
- Language Note and Culture Notes, ATE, p. 356
- Have students read **Lisons!**, pp. 356–358.
- Do Reading Activities C–J, ATE, pp. 357–358.

Wrap-Up 5 min.
- Building on Previous Skills, ATE, p. 358

Homework Options
Cahier d'activités, Act. 17, p. 143

Day 8

LISONS! 10 min.
- Do Activity K, p. 358.
- Check homework.

ECRIVONS! 25 min.
- Read and discuss the **Stratégie pour écrire**, p. 359, then have students work on their articles.

Wrap-Up 15 min.
- Allow time for peer and self-evaluation of articles.

Homework Options
Complete final draft of articles.

Day 9

ECRIVONS!

Quick Review 10 min.
- Have volunteers share their articles with the class.

MISE EN PRATIQUE 35 min.
- Do Activity 1, p. 364.
- Career Path, ATE, p. 364
- Play Audio CD for Activity 2, p. 365. See Tactile/Auditory Learners, ATE, p. 365.
- **A toi d'écrire,** CD-ROM Tutor, Disc 3

Wrap-Up 5 min.
- Activities for Communication, p. 112, Situation (global): Role-Play

Homework Options
Cahier d'activitès, Act. 18, p. 144

Day 10

MISE EN PRATIQUE

Quick Review 5 min.
- Check homework.

Student Review 45 min.
- Do Activity 4, p. 365.
- **A toi de parler,** CD-ROM Tutor or DVD Tutor
- Show **Vidéoclips**, Video Program, Videocassette 4.
- See Pre-viewing, Viewing, and Post-viewing Suggestions, Video Guide, p. 75.

Homework Options
Complete essays for Activity 4, p. 365.

Day 11

MISE EN PRATIQUE

Quick Review 10 min.
- Have volunteers share essays from Activity 4, p. 365.

Student Review 30 min.
- Have groups of students prepare situations for **Jeu de rôle**, p. 365.
- Have groups present situations from **Jeu de rôle.**
- Activities for Communication, p. 111, Situation (global): Interview

Wrap-Up 10 min.
- Begin **Que sais-je?**, p. 366.

Homework Options
Que sais-je?, p. 366

Day 12

MISE EN PRATIQUE

Quick Review 15 min.
- Go over **Que sais-je?**, p. 366.
- Have students do Activity 3, p. 365, in groups.

Chapter Review 35 min.
- Review Chapter 12. Choose from **Grammaire supplémentaire**, Grammar Tutor for Students of French, Activities for Communication, Listening Activities, Interactive CD-ROM Tutor, or **Jeux interactifs.**

Homework Options
Study for Chapter 12 Test.

Assessment

Test, Chapter 12 50 min.
- Administer **Chapter 12 Test.** Select from Testing Program, Alternative Assessment Guide, Test Generator, or Standardized Assessment Tutor.

Chapitre 12 : Echanges sportifs et culturels *Review Chapter*

Suggested Lesson Plans *90-Minute Block Schedule*

Block 1

CHAPTER OPENER   5 min.
- Present Chapter Objectives, p. 341.
- History Link, ATE, p. 340

MISE EN TRAIN   35 min.
- Presenting **Mise en train**, ATE, p. 342
- Do Activities 1–4, p. 344.
- **Note culturelle**, p. 344
- Teacher Suggestion and Geography Link, ATE, p. 343

PREMIERE ETAPE
Vocabulaire, p. 345   40 min.
- Presenting **Vocabulaire**, ATE, p. 345
- Play Audio CD for Activity 6, p. 345.
- Do Activity 7, p. 346.
- Review **Tu te rappelles?**, p. 347.
- Do Activity 9, p. 347.

Wrap-Up   10 min.
- Activities for Communication, pp. 45–46, Communicative Activity 12-1A and 12-1B

Homework Options
Pupil's Edition, Activity 8, p. 346
Grammaire supplémentaire, p. 360, Act. 1
Cahier d'activités, pp. 133–135, Acts. 1–5
Travaux pratiques de grammaire, pp. 102–103, Acts. 1–5

Block 2

PREMIERE ETAPE
Quick Review   5 min.
- Visual Learners, ATE, p. 345

Vocabulaire, p. 345   15 min.
- Do Activity 10, p. 347.

Comment dit-on... ?, p. 348   20 min.
- Presenting **Comment dit-on... ?**, ATE, p. 348
- Play Audio CD for Activity 12, p. 348.
- Read and discuss **De bons conseils**, p. 348.

Grammaire, p. 348   40 min.
- Presenting **Grammaire**, ATE, p. 348
- Do Activities 13–15, p. 349.

Wrap-Up   10 min.
- Game: **Quand je...**, ATE, p. 349

Homework Options
Have students study for Quiz 12-1.
Pupil's Edition, Activity 11, p. 347
Grammaire supplémentaire, pp. 360–361, Acts. 2–5
Cahier d'activités, pp. 136–137, Acts. 6–9
Travaux pratiques de grammaire, p. 104, Acts. 6–7

Block 3

PREMIERE ETAPE
Quick Review   10 min.
- Teaching Transparency 12-1, using suggestion #4 on Suggestions for Using Teaching Transparency 12-1

Quiz 12-1   20 min.
- Administer Quiz 12-1A or 12-1B.

REMISE EN TRAIN   25 min.
- Presenting **Remise en train**, ATE, p. 350
- Do Activities 17–20, pp. 350–351.

DEUXIEME ETAPE
Vocabulaire, p. 352   30 min.
- Presenting **Vocabulaire**, ATE, p. 352
- Geography Link, ATE, p. 352
- Read and discuss **Tu te rappelles?**, p. 352.
- Do Activities 22–23, pp. 352–353.

Wrap-Up   5 min.
- On separate pieces of paper, write the names of various countries and draw the corresponding colored flag. Distribute the illustrations to students. Have each student hold up the illustration of the flag and say where he or she is from, according to the flag he or she is holding.

Homework Options
Grammaire supplémentaire, pp. 362–363, Acts. 6–8
Cahier d'activités, pp. 138–139, Acts. 10–11
Travaux pratiques de grammaire, pp. 105–107, Acts. 8–12

 **One-Stop** Planner CD-ROM

For alternative lesson plans by chapter section, to create your own customized plans, or to preview all resources available for this chapter, use the **One-Stop Planner CD-ROM**, Disc 3.

 For additional homework suggestions, see activities accompanied by this symbol throughout the chapter.

Block 4

DEUXIEME ETAPE
Quick Review 10 min.
- Teaching Transparency 12-2, using suggestion #3 on Vocabulary Practice Using Teaching Transparency 12-2

Comment dit-on... ?, p. 353 20 min.
- Presenting **Comment dit-on... ?,** ATE, p. 353
- Play Audio CD for Activity 24, p. 353.
- Do Activity 25, p. 353.

Comment dit-on... ?, p. 355 35 min.
- Presenting **Comment dit-on... ?,** ATE, p. 355
- Play Audio CD for Activity 28, p. 355.
- Do Activity 29, using Slower Pace, ATE, p. 355.
- Do Activity 31, p. 355.

PANORAMA CULTUREL 15 min.
- Presenting **Panorama Culturel,** ATE, p. 354
- Read and discuss as a class **Qu'en penses-tu?,** p. 354.

Wrap-Up 10 min.
- Teaching Suggestion, ATE, p. 353

Homework Options
Have students study for Quiz 12-2.
Pupil's Edition, Activity 30, p. 355
Cahier d'activités, pp. 140–142, Acts. 12–16
Travaux pratiques de grammaire, p. 107, Act. 13

Block 5

DEUXIEME ETAPE
Quick Review 10 min.
- Activities for Communication, pp. 47–48, Communicative Activity 12-2A and 12-2B

Quiz 12-2 20 min.
- Administer Quiz 12-2A or 12-2B.

LISONS! 35 min.
- Motivating Activity, ATE, p. 356
- Do Activities A–C, p. 357.
- Have students read **Le Sport et le monde francophone,** pp. 356–357.
- Teaching Suggestion #1, ATE, p. 357
- Do Activities D–F, p. 357.

MISE EN PRATIQUE 20 min.
- Play Audio CD for Activity 2, p. 365.
- Do Activity 3, p. 365.

Wrap-Up 5 min.
- Listening Activities, p. 97, Additional Listening Activity 12-6

Homework Options
Que sais-je?, p. 366

Block 6

LISONS!
Quick Review 10 min.
- Game: **Quel sport?,** ATE, p. 366

LISONS! 30 min.
- Do Activity G, p. 358.
- Have students read **Allez, les bleus! La Coupe du monde** and **Handball, le Mondiale,** p. 358
- Activities H–K, p. 358

MISE EN PRATIQUE 50 min.
- Do Activity 1, p. 364.
- Do Activity 4, p. 365.
- Circumlocution, ATE, p. 367
- Game: **Dis-le!,** ATE, p. 367

Homework Options
Study for Chapter 12 Test.

Block 7

MISE EN PRATIQUE
Quick Review 10 min.
- **Jeu de rôle,** p. 365

Chapter Review 35 min.
- Review Chapter 12. Choose from **Grammaire supplémentaire,** Grammar Tutor for Students of French, Activities for Communication, Listening Activities, Interactive CD-ROM Tutor, or **Jeux interactifs.**

Test, Chapter 12 45 min.
- Administer Chapter 12 Test. Select from Testing Program, Alternative Assessment Guide, Test Generator, or Standardized Assessment Tutor

One-Stop Planner CD-ROM

For resource information, see the **One-Stop Planner,** Disc 3.

Pacing Tips
Chapter 12 is a review chapter set within a new cultural context. While students will recognize most of the functions and grammatical structures, there is some new vocabulary as well as new cultural information for them to master for the chapter quizzes and test. For suggested Lesson Plans and timing suggestions, see pages 339I–339L.

Meeting the Standards

Communication
- Expressing anticipation; making suppositions; expressing certainty and doubt, p. 348
- Inquiring, p. 353
- Expressing excitement and disappointment, p. 355

Cultures
- Culture Notes, pp. 344, 349
- Note culturelle, p. 344
- Panorama Culturel, p. 354

Connections
- History Link, p. 340
- Geography Links, pp. 343, 352
- Reading/Writing Link, p. 357
- Poetry Link, p. 364

Comparisons
- Community Link, p. 354
- Language-to-Language, p. 347
- Thinking Critically, p. 354

Communities
- Career Path, p. 364
- De l'école au travail, p. 355

Connections and Comparisons

History Link
Have students research the history of the ancient and modern Olympic Games. The Olympic Games date from 8 B.C., when Iphitos, king of Pisa, and Lycurgus, the Spartan law giver, organized sporting competitions in Olympia, Greece. A statue of Zeus was erected there, and the site was declared sacred. The winners of the events would attend a banquet and be crowned with an olive wreath. The ancient Games were held for the last time in 393 A.D. Richard Chandler, an Englishman, discovered the site of the sanctuary in 1766, and German archaeologists excavated the site from 1875 to 1881. A French scholar and educator, Baron Pierre de Coubertin, proposed the establishment of the modern Olympic Games and became president of the International Olympic Committee. The first modern Games were held in Athens, Greece, in 1896.

C H A P I T R E

12
Echanges sportifs et culturels

Objectives

In this chapter you will review and practice how to

Première étape

- express anticipation
- make suppositions
- express certainty and doubt

Deuxième étape

- inquire
- express excitement and disappointment

 internet

go.
hrw
.com
ADRESSE: go.hrw.com
MOT-CLE: WA3 FRANCOPHONE
AMERICA-12

◀ **Un stade pendant les Jeux olympiques**

Focusing on Outcomes
After students read the chapter objectives, ask them to recall the expressions they learned in Chapter 1 for inquiring. (**C'était comment, tes vacances? Ça s'est bien passé? Tu t'es bien amusé(e)?**) Ask them to recall the expressions they learned in Chapter 7 for making suppositions (**On pourrait sûrement... , Je parie que... , Ça doit être... , Il doit y avoir...**), for expressing doubt (**Ça m'étonnerait que... , Je ne suis pas sûr(e)...**), and for expressing certainty (**Je suis certain(e) que... , Je suis sûr(e) que... , Je sais que... , Je suis convaincu(e) que...**).

Communication for All Students

Challenge
Write the following statements and questions on the board or on a transparency and have students try to match them to the functional objectives listed on this page: **Je ne crois pas. Qu'est-ce qui est typique de chez toi? J'ai vraiment pas de** chance. Ça doit être cool! C'est trop cool! Je suis vraiment impatient(e) de partir. *(expressing doubt, inquiring, expressing disappointment, making suppositions, expressing excitement, expressing anticipation)*

Teaching Resources
pp. 342–344

PRINT
▶ Lesson Planner, p. 57
▶ Video Guide, pp. 74, 76
▶ Cahier d'activités, p. 133

MEDIA
▶ One-Stop Planner
▶ Video Program
Camille et compagnie
Videocassette 4, 32:02–37:44
Videocassette 5 (captioned version), 1:09:42–1:15:24
▶ Audio Compact Discs, CD 12, Tr. 1

Presenting
Mise en train

Before you play the recording, have students look at the photos and predict what sporting events will be discussed in each dialogue. Then, play the recording. Pause it after each scene to ask what sport the athlete will participate in and how he or she is feeling.

Mise en train ▪ *A nous les Jeux olympiques!*

 Cahier d'activités, p. 133, Act. 1

CD 12 Tr. 1

Stratégie pour comprendre
Have you ever encouraged someone who was participating in a competition? What do people say when they're not sure about winning? What can you say to reassure them? Before reading these four exchanges, look at the photos and flags. Can you guess where each athlete comes from and what sport he or she practices?

1 Lisette téléphone à Julie pour lui souhaiter bonne chance aux Jeux olympiques.

Lisette Allô, Julie? Alors, tu es prête pour le grand départ?
Julie Ne m'en parle pas! J'ai un trac fou!
Lisette T'en fais pas. Ça va aller.
Julie Je suis vraiment impatiente de partir. Tu sais, c'est ma première compétition olympique. Je me demande comment ça sera. En tout cas, je suis sûre que ça va être impressionnant.
Lisette Moi, je parie que tu vas gagner la médaille d'or!

Julie Tu parles! Ça m'étonnerait. Il doit y avoir des tas d'escrimeuses beaucoup plus fortes que moi, des championnes qui ont plus d'expérience. Surtout les Allemandes! Je suis certaine que c'est elles qui vont gagner. Si je suis au meilleur de ma forme, je pourrai peut-être arriver en demi-finale. Ça serait déjà très bien.
Lisette Oh, arrête. Si tu penses comme ça, tu ne gagneras rien du tout. Un conseil : répète trois fois «C'est moi la meilleure!»
Julie C'est moi la meilleure, c'est moi la meilleure, c'est moi la meilleure!
Lisette Voilà. Très bien.
Julie En tout cas, il me tarde d'assister aux épreuves d'athlétisme. Tu imagines un peu! Tous les meilleurs athlètes du monde réunis! Vivement que j'arrive! Au moins, j'aurai cette consolation si je ne gagne pas...
Lisette Oh non! Tu ne vas pas recommencer! Je parie que tout va très bien se passer. Allez. Je t'embrasse et bonne chance!

2 Ali entre dans la chambre de son frère Youssef qui est en train de faire ses valises.

Ali Salut. Alors, tu as tout ce qu'il te faut?
Youssef Oui, je crois.
Ali Pense à prendre ton maillot.
Youssef Très drôle! Je serai le seul plongeur olympique sans maillot!
Ali Alors, tu as le trac?
Youssef Oh, tu sais, c'est pas pour me vanter, mais je crois que j'ai mes chances.
Ali Oh, arrête de délirer! Tu as vu qui est en compétition? L'Américain, là, il a beaucoup plus d'expérience que toi. C'est la troisième fois qu'il participe aux Jeux olympiques. Ça m'étonnerait que tu le battes.
Youssef Tu es vraiment encourageant, toi. Ça arrive souvent que les plus jeunes concurrents gagnent, tu sais.
Ali Ouais. Bon, ben... bonne chance, hein.

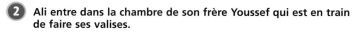

Preteaching Vocabulary

Guessing Words from Context
Have students look at the pictures on both pages. Then, have them make guesses about what is going on in the conversations. Ask them what the main concern of each competitor is. How did they know? Tell students to read each conversation in order to find words that help contextualize the situation of each athlete.

le trac *stage fright*
les escrimeuses *female fencers*
le plongeur *diver*
les épreuves d'athlétisme *track and field trials*
les concurrents *competitors*
l'entraînement *training*
un champion de lutte *wrestling champion*

STANDARDS: 1.2, 3.1

3 A sa dernière séance d'entraînement avant de partir, Ophélia discute avec son entraîneur.

M. Duval	Eh bien, Ophélia? Tu n'as pas l'air en forme.
Ophélia	Oh, je ne sais pas. Ça fait tellement longtemps que je m'entraîne. Ça doit être le stress, sûrement.
M. Duval	Allez! Encore un effort! C'est pas la mer à boire. Tu y es presque! Tu imagines si Marie-José Pérec parlait comme ça? Tu ferais mieux de te concentrer sur ton entraînement. Tu sais ce que je dis toujours...
Ophélia	Oui, je sais : «On n'arrive à rien sans rien.»
M. Duval	C'est ça. Et n'oublie pas que, même si c'est beaucoup de travail maintenant, tu seras vraiment heureuse quand tu seras sur le podium.
Ophélia	Oui, je sais. Ça va sûrement être génial. Il y aura des champions de tous les pays... Ça sera chouette de parler à des Africains... Je n'ai jamais rencontré d'Africains. Et puis, il me tarde d'aller aux Etats-Unis... Je me demande s'il y a beaucoup d'Américains qui parlent français, parce que mon anglais n'est pas terrible...
M. Duval	Oui. Enfin, n'oublie quand même pas l'entraînement.
Ophélia	Ça, je sais que je peux compter sur vous pour me le rappeler!

4 Mademba est à l'aéroport avec sa famille qui lui dit au revoir avant son départ pour les Etats-Unis.

Mme Kaussi	Tu es sûr que tu as tout ce qu'il te faut?
Mademba	Mais oui, Maman. T'en fais pas.
Mme Kaussi	Fais attention. Tu sais ce qu'on dit. Ça peut être dangereux de se promener aux Etats-Unis...

Mademba	N'aie pas peur. Tu sais, je suis champion de lutte! Je sais me défendre!
Mme Kaussi	Bon. Mais quand même, méfie-toi. Et laisse ton argent dans ta chambre.
Mademba	Mais Maman, les Etats-Unis, c'est civilisé! Je parie que je vais me faire des tas de copains tout de suite. Il doit y avoir plein de francophones en compétition.
Adjouba	Et n'oublie pas que tu m'as promis de demander un autographe à Lu Li.
Mademba	Oui, oui. Je sais. Je ferai de mon mieux mais je ne suis pas certain de pouvoir la voir.
Adjouba	Pourquoi? Tu ne vas pas aller voir les épreuves de gymnastique?
Mademba	Tu sais, ça m'étonnerait que j'aie le temps. J'ai mon entraînement et puis je veux voir autant de matches de basket que possible. Bon. Je dois y aller. Dès que je serai installé, je vous appellerai.
Mme Kaussi	Allez! Au revoir, mon petit, et bonne chance! On est fiers de toi.
Adjouba	Envoie-nous une carte postale dès que tu pourras... Et n'oublie pas de me rapporter quelque chose.
Mademba	Oui, oui! Allez, à bientôt!

Using the Captioned Video

As an alternative, you might want to show the captioned version of *Camille et compagnie : Une sauterelle pleine d'avenir* on Videocassette 5. Some students may benefit from seeing the written words as they listen to the target language and watch the gestures and actions in context. This visual reinforcement of vocabulary and functions will facilitate students' comprehension and help reduce their anxiety before they are formally introduced to the new language in the chapter.

Mise en train

CHAPITRE 12

Teaching Suggestion
Play the first two segments of the recording and ask who is more confident, Julie or Youssef (Youssef). Do the same for the third and fourth segments. (Mademba is more confident than Ophélia.)

Geography Link
Ask students to explain or research the significance of the five rings on the Olympic flag. (They represent the five Olympic continents of the world.) Have them name the continents (Africa, America, Asia, Australia, Europe).

Camille et compagnie
You may choose to show students Episode 12: *Une sauterelle pleine d'avenir* now or wait until later in the chapter. In this episode Sophie invites her friends to attend the filming of a commercial in which she is acting. When Camille, Max, Laurent, and Azzedine arrive at the sports equipment store where the commercial is being shot, they don't see Sophie anywhere. It turns out that Sophie is disguised as a grasshopper, because the name of the store is **La Sauterelle sportive.** Sophie is ashamed of her costume, but cheers up when her friends comfort and applaud her.

CHAPITRE 12

Teaching Suggestion

1 Have students create additional comprehension questions about the **Mise en train** to ask the class.

Culture Notes

• The **Tour de France** was established in 1903 by Henri Desgrange, a French journalist and cyclist. The annual race covers about 4,000 kilometers over varied terrain throughout France and parts of neighboring countries. The race is divided into 21 day-long segments, or **étapes.** The rider with the lowest overall time wins. For more detail on the **Tour de France,** see the **Traditions** section on page 339D.

• The French Open, or the Roland Garros tennis tournament, is one of four major world tennis championships. It is held at the **Stade Roland-Garros** on the outskirts of Paris. It has the only hard (clay) court in world competition.

Answers

1 1. Olympic Games in U.S.
2. as they prepare to leave their home countries
3. Julie is nervous; Youssef is confident of his chances.
4. her training
5. His mother is proud, but concerned for his safety. Adjouba, Mademba's sister, sees a chance to get a gymnast's autograph.

4 1. T'en fais pas. Ça va aller. N'aie pas peur.
2. Je suis vraiment impatiente de... ; Il me tarde de... ; Vivement que... ! Dès que...
3. Je parie que... ; Il doit y avoir... ; Ça doit être...
4. Ça m'étonnerait. ... je ne suis pas certain de... ; Je me demande...
5. C'est moi, la meilleure! C'est pas pour me vanter, mais...
6. Oh, arrête de délirer!
7. Allez! Encore un effort! C'est pas la mer à boire. Tu y es presque!
8. Un conseil : ... ; Tu ferais mieux de... ; ... n'oublie pas...
9. Fais attention. ... méfie-toi.

---

1 **Tu as compris?** See answers below.

These activities check for comprehension only. Students should not yet be expected to produce language modeled in Mise en train.

1. Où est-ce que ces jeunes vont?
2. Quand et où est-ce que chaque conversation se passe?
3. Quels sont les sentiments de Julie à propos de sa compétition? Et ceux de Youssef?
4. De quoi parle l'entraîneur avec Ophélia?
5. Que pense la famille de Mademba de son voyage aux Etats-Unis?

2 **Qui dit quoi?**

Quel(le) jeune fait ces remarques dans *A nous les Jeux olympiques?*

Mademba
Tu sais, je suis champion de lutte! Je sais me défendre.

Ophélia
Ça sera chouette de parler à des Africains.

Julie
Si je suis au meilleur de ma forme, je pourrai peut-être arriver en demi-finale.

Julie
Il doit y avoir des tas d'escrimeuses beaucoup plus fortes que moi.

Ophélia
Je me demande s'il y a beaucoup d'Américains qui parlent français, parce que mon anglais n'est pas terrible.

Youssef
Oh, tu sais, c'est pas pour me vanter, mais je crois que j'ai mes chances.

3 **Vrai ou faux?**

1. Julie compte gagner la médaille d'or. faux
2. Elle n'a pas envie de voir d'autres sports. faux
3. Youssef a oublié son maillot de bain. faux
4. Il a un trac fou. faux
5. Youssef pense que le plongeur américain va gagner. faux
6. M. Duval dit à Ophélia d'arrêter de s'entraîner et de se reposer. faux
7. Ophélia voudrait rencontrer beaucoup de gens aux Jeux olympiques. vrai
8. Mademba compte assister à beaucoup d'épreuves de gymnastique. faux

4 **Cherche les expressions**

What do the people in *A nous les Jeux olympiques!* say to . . . See answers below.
1. reassure someone?
2. express anticipation?
3. make a supposition?
4. express doubt?
5. brag?
6. tease?
7. encourage someone?
8. give advice?
9. caution someone?

5 **Et maintenant, à toi**

Est-ce que tu as déjà participé à une compétition ou à un événement sportif? Comment est-ce que tu t'es préparé(e)? Est-ce que tu étais inquiet/inquiète, impatient(e), sûr(e) de toi?

Note culturelle

Les événements sportifs internationaux, comme les Jeux olympiques ou les coupes du monde, sont l'occasion de réunir des sportifs de tous les pays dans un cadre amical. De tels événements permettent de promouvoir la compréhension et l'acceptation des différences entre les peuples. Parmi les événements sportifs liés au monde francophone, il y a le Tour de France qui est sans doute la compétition cycliste la plus renommée; il y a aussi le rallye Paris-Dakar, course automobile et moto qui relie les capitales de la France et du Sénégal. Le tournoi de tennis de Roland-Garros, connu aux Etats-Unis sous le nom de *French Open,* est aussi célèbre.

Comprehension Check

Challenge

3 As students do this activity, have them correct the false statements with complete sentences. Encourage them to use as many expressions, verbs tenses, and structures studied throughout the year as possible. Ask for volunteers to read the statements out loud. Possible answers: 1. **Julie pense qu'elle ne va pas gagner la médaille** d'or. 2. Elle veut assister aux épreuves d'athlétisme. 3. Youssef imagine ce qui arriverait s'il oubliait son maillot. 4. Il n'a pas le trac. 5. Youssef pense qu'il a des chances de gagner. 6. M. Duval encourage Ophélia à s'entraîner. 8. Mademba pense qu'il n'aura pas le temps d'assister aux épreuves de gymnastique.

go.hrw.com

WA3 FRANCOPHONE AMERICA-12

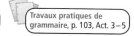

Vocabulaire

Cahier d'activités, pp. 134–135, Act. 2–5

Travaux pratiques de grammaire, p. 103, Act. 3–5

CD-ROM DISC 3

le ballon
le panier

le basket-ball

l'escrimeur (euse)
l'épée (f.)
le masque
la tenue

l'escrime (f.)

le bâton
le casque
le lanceur
la balle
le frappeur

le base-ball

les barres (f.) asymétriques
les anneaux (m.)
la poutre
l'entraîneur (m.)

la gymnastique

le saut à la perche
le lancer du disque
la course de fond
le saut en longueur

l'athlétisme (m.)

le plongeoir

le plongeon acrobatique (plonger)

les rames (f.)

l'aviron (m.)

l'arc (m.)
la flèche

le tir à l'arc (tirer)

les haltères (m.)

l'haltérophilie (f.)

la boxe
le cyclisme

l'équitation (f.)
le judo

la lutte
la natation

Si tu as oublié
sports
va à la page R18.

Travaux pratiques de grammaire, p. 102, Act. 1-2

6 **Aux Jeux olympiques** See scripts and answers on p. 339G.

 Ecoutons Ecoute les conversations de ces spectateurs aux Jeux olympiques. A quelles épreuves est-ce qu'ils assistent?
CD 12 Tr. 2

Communication for All Students

Visual Learners

Bring in and have students bring in pictures of athletes performing the various sports. Tape them to the board. Then, call on a student to be "it." Have volunteers tell the student to show them or give them various pictures. (**Montre-moi la photo de la personne qui fait du judo. Donne-moi la photo de la personne qui fait du tir à l'arc.**)

Kinesthetic Learners

Divide the class into two groups. Have volunteers come to the front of the class and mime various sports presented on this page. Students in each group guess the sport and earn ten points for each correct guess. Students who volunteer to mime earn five extra points for their team.

Teaching Resources
pp. 345–349

PRINT
▸ Lesson Planner, p. 58
▸ Listening Activities, pp. 91, 95–96
▸ Activities for Communication, pp. 45–46, 84, 86, 111–112
▸ Travaux pratiques de grammaire, pp. 102–104
▸ Grammar Tutor for Students of French, Chapter 12
▸ Cahier d'activités, pp. 134–137
▸ Testing Program, pp. 257–260
▸ Alternative Assessment Guide, p. 41
▸ Student Make-Up Assignments, Chapter 12

MEDIA
▸ One-Stop Planner
▸ Audio Compact Discs, CD 12, Trs. 2–3, 12, 22–24
▸ Teaching Transparencies: 12-1; **Grammaire supplémentaire** Answers; Travaux pratiques de grammaire Answers
▸ Interactive CD-ROM Tutor, Disc 3

Bell Work

Have students write two or three sentences about sports or activities they participate in, would like to participate in, or enjoy watching.

Presenting Vocabulaire

Act out each sport, describing your activities. (**Je fais du basket-ball. Voilà mon ballon et le panier est là-haut.**) If possible, bring in sports equipment as props. Finally, have volunteers mime the activities and ask the class **Qu'est-ce qu'il/elle fait?** and prompt students to answer **Il/Elle fait de la natation.**

Answers

7 1. une épée - d, l'escrime
2. une rame - g, l'aviron
3. un bâton - h, le base-ball
4. une flèche - i, le tir à l'arc
5. une poutre - e, la gymnastique
6. un panier - b, le basket-ball
7. des anneaux - a, la gymnastique
8. un masque - f, l'escrime
9. des haltères - j, l'haltérophilie
10. un casque - c, le base-ball

8 2. *de la gymnastique* : barres, anneaux, agrès, ballon, musique, ou rien du tout
de l'escrime : des chaussures de sport, un vieux gant, une salle où l'on te prêtera fleuret, masque et veste
du basket : un ballon, des paniers, un terrain
du tir à l'arc : un arc, des flèches, des cibles

---

7 ## Quel sport?

Lisons Associe ces objets à leurs images. Pour quel sport est-ce qu'ils sont nécessaires?

1. une épée   3. un bâton   5. une poutre   7. des anneaux   9. des haltères
2. une rame   4. une flèche   6. un panier   8. un masque   10. un casque

See answers below.

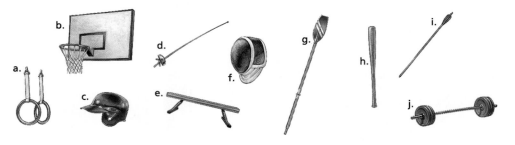

8 ## Sportez-vous bien!

Lisons Regarde ce tableau et réponds aux questions suivantes.

BASKETBALL	GYMNASTIQUE	TIR A L'ARC	ESCRIME
QUI	**QUI**	**QUI**	**QUI**
Les plus grands sont favorisés. Les «pivots» américains (joueur central autour de qui pivote le jeu) mesurent au moins 2,10 m (1,90 m pour les femmes).	Sport en soi, la gym est aussi la préparation à tous les sports (vélo, tennis, ski...). Bien courir, bien lacer ses chaussures, bien respirer, c'est de la gym !	Ceux qui sont précis dans leurs gestes ou veulent le devenir.	Ceux qui ont le sens de l'observation, de la volonté, qui aiment prendre des décisions rapides.
QUOI	**QUOI**	**QUOI**	**QUOI**
Un ballon (600 g environ), des paniers, un terrain de 24 m sur 13 m où s'affrontent deux équipes de cinq joueurs.	Avec ou sans accessoires (barres, anneaux, agrès, ballon...), avec ou sans musique, seul ou à plusieurs.	Un arc, droit ou démontable, assorti à votre taille et à votre force. Des flèches proportionnelles à la longueur de vos bras. Des cibles.	Des chaussures de sport, un vieux gant, une salle où l'on vous prêtera, la première année, fleuret, masque et veste.
POURQUOI	**POURQUOI**	**POURQUOI**	**POURQUOI**
Un jeu plein de vivacité, qui peut s'interpréter décontracté, comme les chaussures qui portent son nom.	Pour se décontracter, bouger avec aisance, lutter contre le mal de dos ou le ras-le-bol scolaire, mieux vivre dans sa tête, grâce à un corps flexible comme un élastique.	Un sport qui monte : olympique depuis 1972. Se pratique en salle et au grand air.	Pour apprendre à se défendre dans la vie, avec adresse et politesse.

1. Trouve un sport...

a. qui est une bonne préparation pour tous les sports.   la gynastique

b. qui est bien pour ceux qui sont précis dans leurs gestes.   le tir à l'arc

c. où les plus grands sont favorisés.

d. pour ceux qui aiment prendre des décisions rapides.   c. le basket-ball
d. l'escrime

2. Qu'est-ce qu'il te faut pour faire...See answers below.

de la gymnastique?
de l'escrime?   du basket?
du tir à l'arc?

Communication for All Students

Slower Pace
7 You might give students a model on which to base their answers. (**C'est une épée. On en a besoin pour faire de l'escrime.**)

Auditory Learners
7 Name a piece of equipment (**une flèche**) and have students tell what sport it's associated with (**le tir à l'arc**).

Language Note
Students might want to know the following words from the sports poster: **lutter** (*to battle, fight*); **cible** (*target*); **fleuret** (*foil*).

Tu te rappelles

Do you remember what verb tenses to use in **si** clauses? If the verb in the **si** clause is in the imperfect, then the verb in the other clause is in the conditional.

Si j'**étais** toi, je **verrais** les épreuves de gymnastique.

Il **réussirait** s'il **faisait** un effort.

Grammaire supplémentaire, p. 360, Act. 1

9 Qu'est-ce que tu en dis?

Parlons Ton ami(e) pense essayer un nouveau sport. Il/Elle te demande ton opinion. Tu lui donnes des conseils.

EXEMPLE —Je pense faire du plongeon acrobatique. Qu'est-ce que tu en dis?
—Si j'étais toi, je ferais plutôt de la natation. C'est moins dangereux.

a.

b.

dangereux	fatigant
cool	
ennuyeux	intéressant
dur	
facile	génial
amusant	
cher	bon pour la santé

c.

d.

e.

10 Sondage

Parlons Ton correspondant français voudrait savoir quels sports sont les plus populaires chez toi. Fais un sondage dans ta classe. Demande à tes camarades de nommer par ordre de préférence cinq sports qu'ils aiment faire et cinq sports qu'ils aiment regarder à la télé. Compare tes résultats à ceux de tes camarades.

11 Mon journal

Ecrivons Est-ce que le sport est important pour toi? Pourquoi ou pourquoi pas? Qu'est-ce que tu fais comme sport? Pourquoi est-ce que tu aimes ce sport?

Teaching Suggestions

9 Before they begin this activity, have students list the sports pictured here. Then, have them write down the adjectives they associate with the various sports. Have students use the lists they made to create their conversations.

10 Have several volunteers list on the board ten sports and activities their classmates suggest. Then, have the entire class decide on a way to take the poll. They might use a yes-no vote, a graded scale (**pas du tout, un peu, beaucoup**), or a numerical scale (1–10). Next, have the volunteers ask students to raise their hands in response to their questions about the various sports. (**Qui aime la natation? Qui aime un peu la natation? Qui croit que la natation mérite un «dix»?**) Have the pollsters record the totals on the board.

Connections and Comparisons

Language-to-Language

Bring a French dictionary to class. Have students look up the following words to find their origins: **gymnastique** (from the Latin *gymnasticus*), **asymétrique** (from the Greek *asummetria*), **athlète** (from the Greek *athlon* for "combat" and the Latin *athleta*), **lutte** (from the Latin *lutca*), **disque** (from the Latin *discus*), **équitation** (from the Latin *equitatio*), and **haltère** (from the Greek *haltêre* and the Latin *halteres*). Ask students why they think many of the terms for athletic activities have Greek or Latin origins. You might refer to the History Link on page 340 of the *Annotated Teacher's Edition*. Then, have them list other French terms for sports and physical activities to see if they can find additional words with Greek or Latin origins.

Teaching Resources
pp. 345–349

PRINT
▸ Lesson Planner, p. 58
▸ Listening Activities, pp. 91, 95–96
▸ Activities for Communication, pp. 45–46, 84, 86, 111–112
▸ Travaux pratiques de grammaire, pp. 102–104
▸ Grammar Tutor for Students of French, Chapter 12
▸ Cahier d'activités, pp. 134–137
▸ Testing Program, pp. 257–260
▸ Alternative Assessment Guide, p. 41
▸ Student Make-Up Assignments, Chapter 12

MEDIA
▸ One-Stop Planner
▸ Audio Compact Discs, CD 12, Trs. 2–3, 12, 22–24
▸ Teaching Transparencies: 12-1; **Grammaire supplémentaire** Answers; Travaux pratiques de grammaire Answers
▸ Interactive CD-ROM Tutor, Disc 3

Presenting
Comment dit-on... ?

Tell students that you're going to the Olympics, and make logical or illogical suppositions about your trip, using the new expressions. Have students tell whether your suppositions are logical or not, and then correct the illogical ones.

Grammaire

Quand and **dès que** Write several sentences that include **quand** and **dès que** on the board with their English equivalents next to them. Ask students how French and English differ with regard to the tense used after these conjunctions.

Comment dit-on...?

Expressing anticipation; making suppositions; expressing certainty and doubt

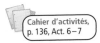

To express anticipation:

Il me tarde de voir les épreuves de judo.
I can't wait to . . .
Je suis vraiment impatient(e) de partir!
Vivement que je reçoive ma première médaille d'or! *I just can't wait to . . .*
Dès que je serai là-bas, je mangerai un hot-dog.
As soon as I get there, . . .
Quand je verrai mes athlètes préférés, je leur demanderai un autographe.

To express certainty:

Je suis sûr(e)/certain(e) que le basket-ball va être super.
Ça, c'est sûr.
Je n'en ai aucun doute. *I have no doubt (of it).*

To make a supposition:

Ça doit être cool!
Il doit y avoir beaucoup de francophones.
Je parie que les Russes vont gagner.
On pourra sûrement rencontrer des gens intéressants.

To express doubt:

Je ne suis pas sûr(e)/certain(e) que les escrimeurs français puissent gagner.
Je ne pense/crois pas qu'on puisse obtenir de places pour la gymnastique.
Ça m'étonnerait qu'il gagne la médaille d'or.

Cahier d'activités, p. 136, Act. 6–7

Grammaire supplémentaire, p. 360, Act. 2

See scripts and answers on p. 339G.

12 **Vivement les Jeux!**

Ecoutons Séverine part aux Etats-Unis. Elle discute avec son frère en faisant ses valises. Indique les conversations où elle fait une supposition et celles où elle exprime son impatience.

CD 12 Tr. 3

DE BONS CONSEILS

The suffix **-eur/-euse** generally indicates a person who does the action a verb expresses. If **plonger** means *to dive,* who is a **plongeur**? You know the verb **jouer** means *to play.* How would you say *a player*? What are the words for the people who do these activities: **nager, sauter, courir, tirer, recevoir**?

Grammaire supplémentaire, p. 361, Act. 5

Grammaire

The future after *quand* and *dès que*

You've learned that you generally use the future tense in French in the same way as you do in English. However, when talking about a future event in French, you use the future tense following the conjunctions **quand** and **dès que,** whereas in English, you use the present tense. Look at these examples:

Je serai heureuse **quand** je **serai** sur le podium.
I'll be happy when I am on the podium.

Je vais lui demander son autographe **dès que** je le **verrai.**
I'm going to ask for his autograph as soon as I see him.

Grammaire supplémentaire, p. 360–361, Act. 3–4

Cahier d'activités, p. 137, Act. 8

Travaux pratiques de grammaire, p. 104, Act. 6–7

Communication for All Students

♞ Game
Quand je... Write various infinitives on transparency strips and put them in a bag. On additional transparency strips, have students write sentence starters, using the expressions in **Comment dit-on... ?** Collect their sentence starters, edit them, and put them in a separate bag. Then, form two teams. The first player from the first team comes to the front, draws a strip from each bag, and places the strips on the overhead for the teams to see. Then, the player has twenty or thirty seconds to compose a meaningful sentence, using the starter and the appropriate verb tense. Players win a point for each correct sentence, and teams alternate turns.

13 Grammaire en contexte

Lisons/Écrivons Un ami t'a envoyé ce message électronique. Complète le message avec les verbes entre parenthèses. *See answers below.*

> Bientôt les Jeux! Je suis vraiment impatient de partir. Dès que je ___1___ (trouver) le temps, je te ___2___ (téléphoner) pour te raconter comment c'est. Je veux voir plein de choses là-bas. Mon équipe va devoir beaucoup s'entraîner, mais quand on ___3___ (pouvoir), nous ___4___ (aller) voir les épreuves d'escrime. On adore tous ça dans l'équipe! Marc et Sophie sont sûrs de rencontrer ton athlète préféré. Sophie m'a dit que quand ils le ___5___ (voir), ils lui ___6___ (demander) un autographe pour toi. Et dès que je l'___7___ (avoir), je te l'___8___ (envoyer). Alors, envoie-moi ton adresse dès que tu ___9___ (pouvoir). Bon, je dois te laisser. A bientôt.
>
> Pierrick

14 Grammaire en contexte

Lisons/Parlons Nadine essaie d'imaginer comment ça sera aux Jeux olympiques. Qu'est-ce qu'elle dit? Utilise les mots et expressions pour faire des phrases complètes. *See answers below.*

1. quand/athlète préféré/je/demander/voir/lui/autographe/je

3. parier/je/la médaille d'or de judo/gagner/je

2. impatient/voir/vraiment/aller/épreuves de natation/être/je

4. je/dès que/sympa/je/beaucoup/arriver/francophones/rencontrer

15 C'est trop cool!

 Parlons Tu as gagné un voyage pour aller voir un de ces événements sportifs et tu te demandes comment ça sera. Ton/ta camarade te donnera son avis. Tu lui diras si tu crois qu'il/elle a raison. Changez de rôle.

le Superbowl	le Tour de France
Wimbledon	la Coupe du monde
le rallye Paris-Dakar	Roland-Garros

16 Que faire aux Jeux olympiques?

 Écrivons Imagine que tu es un(e) athlète et que tu vas participer aux Jeux olympiques pour la première fois. Écris une lettre à ton/ta meilleur(e) ami(e) pour lui dire ce que tu veux faire et voir là-bas et comment tu penses que ça sera.

Cultures and Communities

Culture Note

15 The Paris-Dakar Rally is a car and motorcycle race that takes place every year. In late January, participants set off from Paris, France, to cross the Sahara Desert in the world's most treacherous, off-road rally. The course usually takes about twenty days to complete. In 1993, the French swept the awards at the rally, with Bruno Saby taking the grand prize.

This rally was founded by Frenchman Thierry Sabine in 1980, after he got lost in the Sahara Desert and became fascinated with its overpowering beauty and harshness. In 2001, for the first time in the history of the rally, a woman won the race. Her name is Jutta Kleischmidt and she is from Germany.

♞ Game

Prepare a set of index cards. On one side of each card, write the French words for a sport or a piece of equipment. On the reverse side of each card, write the word(s) students are not allowed to use to define the sport or equipment. For example, you might write **l'escrime** on one side of a card, and **à ne pas dire: l'épée** on the reverse side. Then, form two teams. The first player from one team selects a card and, without saying any form of the word written on the reverse side, tries to get his or her teammates to say the word written on the front. For example, if the player drew the card described above, he or she might say **Je porte une tenue blanche et un masque.**

Assess

▸ Testing Program, pp. 257–260 Quiz 12-1A, Quiz 12-1B, Audio CD 12, Tr. 12

▸ Student Make-Up Assignments Chapter 12, Alternative Quiz

▸ Alternative Assessment Guide, p. 41

Answers

13 1. trouverai
2. téléphonerai
3. pourra
4. irons
5. verront
6. demanderont
7. aurai
8. enverrai
9. pourras

14 *Possible answers:*
1. Quand je verrai mon athlète préféré, je lui demanderai un autographe.
2. Je suis vraiment impatiente d'aller voir les épreuves de natation.
3. Je parie que je vais gagner la médaille d'or de judo.
4. Dès que j'arriverai, je rencontrerai beaucoup de francophones sympas.

Teaching Resources
pp. 350–351

PRINT
▸ Lesson Planner, p. 59
▸ Video Guide, pp. 74, 76
▸ Cahier d'activités, p. 138

MEDIA
▸ One-Stop Planner
▸ Video Program
  Camille et compagnie
  Videocassette 4, 32:02–37:44
  Videocassette 5 (captioned version), 1:09:42–1:15:24
▸ Audio Compact Discs, CD 12, Tr. 4

Presenting
Remise en train

Ask students questions about the photos on pages 350–351, such as the following: **Mademba et Yvonne assistent à quelle sorte de match? (un match de basket) Sur la deuxième photo, Yvonne a l'air triste ou plutôt gênée? (gênée) A la page 351, c'est une photo de la Suisse ou de la Guadeloupe? (de la Guadeloupe) Regardez la photo de Julie. Elle a l'air d'avoir perdu ou d'avoir gagné? (d'avoir gagné)** Then, play the audio recording and ask students the comprehension questions in Activity 17.

Teaching Suggestion

Ask students if they have ever had the opportunity to meet people from different cultures. If so, ask them to share their experiences. If not, ask them to imagine what questions they might like to ask them, and what they would like these people to know about their own culture.

Remise en train ▪ *Un rendez-vous sportif et culturel*

CD 12 Tr. 4

Quelques-uns des athlètes participant aux Jeux olympiques sont allés voir la finale de basket-ball.

① Mademba You beg my pardon, madame, is it lane euh, vingt-deux?

Yvonne Yes. Tu peux me parler en français, si tu veux. Je suis du Canada.

Mademba Super! Je m'appelle Mademba. Je suis du Sénégal. Je suis ici pour la lutte. Et toi?

Yvonne Moi, c'est Yvonne. Je joue au volley.

Mademba Au fait, c'est quoi, le score?

Yvonne Trente à vingt-sept pour les Etats-Unis.

Mademba Oh, zut alors! Allez, les Russes!

Yvonne Ah, non! Je suis pour les Américains, moi. Ils sont vraiment bons. Dis, tu as vu leur match contre les Brésiliens?

Mademba Oui, je l'ai vu à la télé avant de venir.

Yvonne Vous avez la télé au Sénégal?

Mademba Bien sûr. Et on a aussi des téléphones, des ordinateurs, des voitures, des avions... Il n'y a pas que des petits villages au Sénégal, il y a aussi des grandes villes modernes comme Dakar, par exemple.

Yvonne Oh, pardon. Tu dois penser que je suis vraiment stupide.

② Mademba Non, pas du tout. Beaucoup de gens pensent comme toi. Je trouve ça dommage que les gens ne s'intéressent pas à la culture des autres.

Yvonne Oui, c'est vraiment bête. On a vraiment de la chance d'être ici. Tu sais, j'aimerais bien que tu me racontes comment c'est dans ton pays. Dis donc, après le match, on peut aller manger quelque chose et discuter?

Mademba Ça serait super. Et comme ça, tu pourras me parler du Canada.

Yvonne D'accord.

---

17 ## Tu as compris?   See answers on page 351.

1. Quel est le sujet de ces conversations?
2. Quelles sont les choses qu'Hélène veut faire à la Guadeloupe?
3. Pourquoi est-ce qu'Yvonne est embarrassée?
4. Qu'est-ce que Julie et Jean-Paul ont particulièrement aimé de leur expérience des Jeux olympiques.

18 ## Mets dans le bon ordre

Mets dans le bon ordre les événements d'*Un rendez-vous sportif et culturel.*

3 Yvonne donne le score à Mademba.

6 Mademba parle de son pays.

2 Mademba rencontre Yvonne.

1 Mademba cherche son siège.

5 Yvonne fait une gaffe.

4 Mademba encourage les Russes.

These activities check for comprehension only. Students should not yet be expected to produce language modeled in Remise en train.

Preteaching Vocabulary

Recognizing Cognates

Have students skim the conversations for words they know, and particularly words they recognize from English. Ask them to list the words and have them explain how these words contribute to an overall understanding of each conversation. For example, how does the word **score** help contextualize the setting of Mademba and Yvonne's conversation?

le score *the score*
des téléphones *telephones*
la culture *culture*
super *super*
discuter *to discuss*
les forêts tropicales *tropical forests*
la médaille *medal*
impressionnante *impressive*

Ophélia et Hélène passent leur dernière soirée aux Jeux à la finale de basket.

3
Hélène Dis donc, il est super, ce match. A ton avis, qui va gagner?

Ophélia Je ne sais pas.

Hélène Qu'est-ce qu'il y a? Tu as l'air triste.

Ophélia Un peu, oui. Demain tu vas rentrer chez toi et moi aussi. On ne se verra plus.

Hélène C'est vrai. Mais je vais t'écrire et t'envoyer plein de photos.

Ophélia Moi aussi. Tu sais, je ne t'oublierai pas. Et puis, tu dois absolument venir passer un mois chez moi cet été. D'accord?

4
Hélène Pas de problème. Il me tarde de voir la Guadeloupe. Ça sera super de voir les belles plages et les forêts tropicales. Et puis, je veux aussi me balader dans les marchés, rencontrer plein de gens et danser le zouk.

Ophélia Et moi, je suis vraiment impatiente de voir toutes les montagnes couvertes de neige qu'il y a chez toi, en Suisse. N'oublie pas que tu dois m'apprendre à skier.

A la mi-temps, Julie et Jean-Paul échangent leurs impressions des Jeux.

5
Jean-Paul Alors, Julie, ça fait comment d'avoir eu la médaille d'or?

Julie C'est trop cool! Mais j'arrive toujours pas à y croire.

Jean-Paul Félicitations. Tu étais vraiment impressionnante.

Julie Arrête, tu vas me faire rougir. J'ai eu de la chance, c'est tout.

Jean-Paul Moi, par contre, qu'est-ce que j'ai pu être nul! On va se moquer de moi en Belgique. Quelle angoisse!

Julie Ne t'en fais pas! Ça peut arriver à tout le monde!

Jean-Paul C'est vrai. Et puis, tu sais, en venant ici, j'ai rencontré des gens super et j'ai pu apprendre toutes sortes de choses sur leurs pays.

Julie Oui, moi aussi. Et je pense que ça sera le meilleur souvenir que je garderai de ces Jeux olympiques.

19 **Vrai ou faux?**

1. Yvonne est pour les Russes. _faux_
2. Il y a de grandes villes modernes au Sénégal. _vrai_
3. Mademba voudrait connaître le Canada. _vrai_
4. Ophélia est impatiente de faire du ski. _vrai_
5. Hélène ne s'intéresse pas du tout à la culture des autres. _faux_
6. Julie n'est même pas arrivée en finale. _faux_
7. Jean-Paul n'a pas aimé les Jeux olympiques. _faux_

Cahier d'activités, p. 138, Act. 10

20 **Cherche les expressions**

What do the people in *Un rendez-vous sportif et culturel* say to . . . See answers below.

1. give their name and nationality?
2. inquire about someone's country?
3. root for a team?
4. express embarrassment?
5. express excitement?
6. congratulate someone?
7. express disappointment?

21 **Et maintenant, à toi**

Est-ce que tu as déjà rencontré des gens d'un autre pays? Qu'est-ce que tu as appris sur leur pays?

Visual/Auditory Learners

20 Read aloud each of the French expressions that accomplish these functions, using appropriate gestures and facial expressions to convey meaning. **(Quelle angoisse!)** Have students tell in English which function you are demonstrating *(expressing disappointment)*.

 Camille et compagnie

As an alternative or in addition to the **Remise en train,** you may wish to show Episode 12 of *Camille et compagnie.* For suggestions and activities, see the *Video Guide.*

Answers

17 1. Mademba/Yvonne: the basketball finals they're watching, Senegal Ophélia/Hélène: keeping in touch with and visiting each other, Guadeloupe, Switzerland Jean-Paul/Julie: Julie's gold medal and Jean-Paul's defeat, the experience of attending the Olympics
2. see beaches and tropical forests, walk through markets, meet people, dance the zouk
3. She asks Mademba if they have TV in Senegal.
4. meeting people, learning about their cultures

20 1. Je m'appelle... ; Moi, c'est... Je suis du...
2. Vous avez... au... ? J'aimerais bien que tu me racontes comment c'est dans ton pays.
3. Allez, les Russes!
4. Oh, pardon. Tu dois penser que je suis vraiment stupide.
5. Ça serait super. C'est trop cool!
6. Félicitations. Tu étais vraiment impressionnante.
7. Quelle angoisse!

Deuxième étape

Objectives Inquiring; expressing excitement and disappointment

go.
hrw
.com

WA3 FRANCOPHONE AMERICA-12

Teaching Resources
pp. 352–353, 355

PRINT
▸ Lesson Planner, p. 60
▸ Listening Activities, pp. 92, 96–97
▸ Activities for Communication, pp. 47–48, 85–86, 111–112
▸ Travaux pratiques de grammaire, pp. 105–107
▸ Grammar Tutor for Students of French, Chapter 12
▸ Cahier d'activités, pp. 139–142
▸ Testing Program, pp. 261–264
▸ Alternative Assessment Guide, p. 41
▸ Student Make-Up Assignments, Chapter 12

MEDIA
▸ One-Stop Planner
▸ Audio Compact Discs, CD 12, Trs. 5, 10, 13, 25–27
▸ Teaching Transparencies: 12-2; **Grammaire supplémentaire** Answers; Travaux pratiques de grammaire Answers
▸ Interactive CD-ROM Tutor, Disc 3

 Bell Work
On the board, tape four pictures of athletes engaged in Olympic sports. Have students write a caption for each photo, incorporating one of the following functions for each one: expressing anticipation, expressing certainty, expressing doubt, and making suppositions.

Presenting
Vocabulaire

Assume the identity of one of the teen-agers in the **Vocabulaire** and give clues to your nationality (**Chez moi, je fais la cueillette des dattes**) until students guess the country correctly. (**Vous venez de Tunisie!**)

Vocabulaire

Regarde les gens que Julie a rencontrés aux Jeux olympiques.

Je viens d'**Algérie**.

Je viens de **Côte d'Ivoire**.

Je viens de **Belgique**.

Je viens de **Guadeloupe**.

Je viens de **Tunisie**.

Je viens du **Niger**.

Je viens du **Maroc**.

Je viens de **Suisse**.

Je viens du **Sénégal**.

Je viens d'**Haïti**.

Je viens du **Canada**.

Je viens de **République centrafricaine**.

l'Afrique (f.) **du Sud**   le Brésil   les Etats-Unis (m.)   le Mexique
l'Allemagne (f.)   la Chine   l'Italie (f.)   la République démocratique du Congo
l'Angleterre (f.)   l'Espagne (f.)   le Japon   la Russie

> Cahier d'activités, p. 139, Act. 11

> Travaux pratiques de grammaire, pp. 105–106, Act. 8–10

> Grammaire supplémentaire, p. 362, Act. 6

22 **C'est typique de chez nous!**
Parlons Dans quel pays est-ce qu'on peut voir les choses suivantes?

a.
en Belgique

b.
En Côte d'Ivoire

c.
en Tunisie

d.
en République centrafricaine

e.
au Maroc

f.
à la Guadeloupe

g.
en Suisse

Tu te rappelles?
Do you remember how to say *in* or *to* a country? Use **au** before masculine countries and **en** before feminine countries. Use **en** before any country starting with a vowel and **aux** before all plural countries.

> Grammaire supplémentaire, p. 363, Act. 7–8

> Travaux pratiques de grammaire, pp. 106–107, Act. 11–13

Connections and Comparisons

Geography Link
Display a large world map. Tell volunteers where they are from (**Tu es de Chine**) and have them mark the appropriate country with a tag.

A variation on this theme is to hide the country names on a world map, or to use a map with no country names. Point out countries on the map and say **Je viens d'ici.** Students should respond by saying **Vous venez d'Allemagne, Vous venez du Niger, Vous venez des Etats-Unis,** etc. You might choose to review the various French-speaking locations presented throughout the book.

23 Si tu allais...

Parlons Après le lycée, ton/ta camarade voudrait voyager. Tu lui proposes des endroits où aller. Il/Elle te dira comment il/elle pense que ça sera là-bas. Dis si tu es d'accord.

EXEMPLE
—Si tu allais au Brésil, tu pourrais voir l'Amazone.
—Je parie que c'est sauvage, là-bas.
—Oui, c'est sûr.

visiter le Kremlin   voir des éléphants
voir la tour Eiffel   visiter la Tour de Londres
aller à Berlin   voir des temples
voir des pyramides mayas   visiter le Vatican
voir la Grande Muraille de Chine

Comment dit-on...?

Inquiring

To inquire about someone's country:

Tu viens d'où?
C'est comment, la vie là-bas?
Qu'est-ce qu'on y mange?
On porte des pagnes **chez toi**?
Vous avez/Il y a des téléviseurs **chez vous**?
Qu'est-ce qui est typique de chez toi?

CD-ROM DISC 3

Cahier d'activités, pp. 140–141, Act. 12–13

24 Au village olympique   See scripts and answers on p. 339H.

Ecoutons Ecoute ces conversations qui ont lieu au village olympique. Est-ce que ces gens posent des questions sur le pays de quelqu'un ou sur autre chose?
CD 12 Tr. 5

25 Méli-mélo!

Lisons/Parlons Crée un dialogue entre deux athlètes qui se rencontrent aux Jeux olympiques.

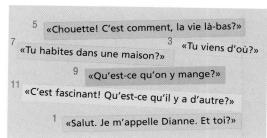

5 «Chouette! C'est comment, la vie là-bas?»
7 «Tu habites dans une maison?»
3 «Tu viens d'où?»
9 «Qu'est-ce qu'on y mange?»
11 «C'est fascinant! Qu'est-ce qu'il y a d'autre?»
1 «Salut. Je m'appelle Dianne. Et toi?»

8 «Oui, moi, j'habite dans une maison en ville, mais mes parents habitent dans une case au village.»
10 «Ce qui est typique de chez nous, c'est les cassaves.»
6 «C'est super.»
2 «Moi, c'est Koli.»
4 «De République centrafricaine.»

26 C'est comment, la vie là-bas?

Ecrivons Pendant leur séjour au village des Jeux olympiques, ces jeunes francophones se rencontrent à la cantine. Ils voudraient connaître d'autres pays. Ils vont se poser des questions et faire des suppositions. Imagine et écris leurs dialogues.

Communication for All Students

Challenge
24 Play the recording again and have students tell what each person is being asked about.

Challenge
26 You might have students memorize, rehearse, and act out their dialogues for the class.

Tactile/Visual Learners
25 Have students write each question or statement on a separate strip of paper and arrange the strips to form a logical conversation.

Presenting
Comment dit-on... ?

Write a dialogue in which a reporter interviews a visiting space alien, using the expressions for inquiring. In class, act out the dialogue, using a sock puppet or a stuffed animal as your interviewee. Then, ask the class about your interviewee. **(Il/Elle est d'où? Qu'est-ce qui est typique de chez lui/elle?)** Next, write the questions in **Comment dit-on... ?** in one column on a transparency. In a second column, write the answers your interviewee gave in random order. Have partners match the questions with the answers and read the dialogue aloud.

Teaching Suggestion
Have students choose to represent one of the countries they've studied this year. You might give them a few minutes to look over the cultural information in the appropriate chapter. Then, have them write answers to the questions in **Comment dit-on... ?** as if they were from that country. Have volunteers read their answers aloud. For each response, have the class give the question that the student is answering. Then, have the class name the country the student comes from.

CHAPITRE 12

Teaching Resources
p. 354

PRINT
▸ Video Guide, pp. 75, 77
▸ Cahier d'activités, p. 144

MEDIA
▸ One-Stop Planner
▸ Video Program
  Videocassette 4, 37:48–41:38
▸ Audio Compact Discs, CD 12,
  Trs. 6–9
▸ Interactive CD-ROM Tutor, Disc 3

Presenting
Panorama Culturel

Write statements on the board about various stereotypes from the interviews, such as **Il aime les frites. Il a un accent bizarre.** Play the video and have students tell which interviewee mentioned the stereotype. Then, describe the interviewees aloud **(Il ne veut pas ressembler aux autres.)** and have students identify the speaker.

Questions

1. **Pourquoi est-ce que Christian dit que les Français sont individualistes?** (parce qu'ils ont du mal à se ressembler, à être comme les autres)

2. **Qu'est-ce qui est important pour un Ivoirien typique?** (l'idée de la paix)

3. **D'après Micheline, qu'est-ce que les Belges aiment?** (les moules, les frites)

4. **Pourquoi est-ce que les Français se moquent des Belges?** (parce qu'ils ont un accent bizarre)

Quelle est l'image d'une personne typique de cette région?

We talked to people about the image others have of a typical person from their region or country. Here's what they told us.

Christian,
France

«Ah! Un Français typique, c'est un Français atypique. Il n'y a pas de Français typique. Peut-être, ce qui fait la particularité des Français, c'est que... ils ont du mal à être... à se ressembler, comme les autres. Nous sommes individualistes.»
Tr. 7

Taki,
Côte d'Ivoire

«L'Ivoirien typique, c'est celui-là qui aime la paix, parce que... Ici, la paix, on le dit souvent, est une seconde religion. Donc, l'Ivoirien typique pour moi, c'est celui-là qui est imprégné de l'idée de paix. C'est celui-là qui aime son prochain et qui est tolérant, donc, envers son prochain.» Tr. 8

Micheline,
Belgique

«Le Belge typique est un... [Il] aime les moules et [les] frites. Il est rigolo. Il aime la vie. Et par contre, c'est pas toujours très vrai parce qu'en fait, il y en a de sinistres qui n'aiment pas rire du tout. Il a aussi un accent bizarre, disent les Français, qui se moquent beaucoup d'eux.» Tr. 9

Qu'en penses-tu?

1. Quelle image as-tu des Français en général? des Suisses? des Belges? des habitants d'Afrique francophone? et des Antillais? Sur quoi bases-tu ton opinion?

2. A ton avis, quelle image est-ce que les étrangers ont des Américains? D'où viennent ces idées?

Connections and Comparisons

Thinking Critically
Analyzing Have students tell why stereotyping is not a fair way of evaluating people. (It does not account for individuality and limits one's cultural perceptions.)

Community Link
You might discuss question 2 of **Qu'en penses-tu?** with the entire class. Tell students that in France and other French speaking countries people watch many television programs and movies produced in the United States. They also listen a lot to American music. Ask students what effect they think this has on the impression foreigners have of Americans.

27 C'est pareil qu'ici?

Parlons Choisis un pays d'un des chapitres du livre. Imagine que tu es un(e) athlète de ce pays qui participe aux Jeux olympiques. Tu y rencontres un(e) Américain(e) qui va te poser des questions sur ton pays. Tu vas aussi lui poser des questions sur les Etats-Unis. Joue cette scène avec ton/ta camarade, puis changez de rôles.

Comment dit-on...?

Expressing excitement and disappointment

To express excitement:

Génial!
C'est trop cool!
J'arrive pas à y croire! *I can't believe it!*
C'est pas possible!
C'est vraiment le pied!
Youpi! *Yippee!*

To express disappointment:

Les boules! *Darn!*
J'en ai vraiment marre!
J'ai vraiment pas de chance.
C'est pas juste. *It's not fair.*
Quelle angoisse! *This is the worst!*
Qu'est-ce que je peux être nul(le)! *I can't do anything right!*

Cahier d'activités, pp. 141–142, Act. 14–15

28 Figure-toi que... *See scripts and answers on p. 339H.*

Ecoutons Ecoute ces jeunes qui téléphonent chez eux pour raconter à leurs parents ce qui leur est arrivé aux Jeux olympiques. Est-ce qu'ils ont gagné ou perdu?
CD 12 Tr. 10

29 Qu'est-ce qu'ils disent?

Parlons Qu'est-ce que ces jeunes athlètes disent à propos de ce qui leur est arrivé aux Jeux olympiques? *Possible answers:*

1. C'est trop cool!

2. Les boules!

3. J'arrive pas à y croire!

4. Quelle angoisse!

30 C'est pas possible!

Ecrivons Imagine que tu as participé aux Jeux olympiques. Ecris une carte postale à un(e) ami(e). Dis-lui comment la compétition s'est passée pour toi et qui tu as rencontré d'intéressant.

31  De l'école au travail

Parlons You're working as an intern for a local TV news station, and you're helping a reporter interview some of the francophone athletes. Remember to ask them questions about where they are from and how they did in the competition.

Communication for All Students

Slower Pace

29 Before students begin this activity, have them tell what is happening in each illustration and whether the athletes are excited or disappointed.

Pair Work

Have students pair up and choose a country to research before class. One student plays the role of a sports journalist and the other, the role of an athlete from the country he or she has chosen. The "athlete" should not reveal the country name and the journalist must ask questions to guess the country.

Teaching Suggestion

27 Have students reread the **Notes culturelles** and the **Rencontre culturelle** for the country they chose before they begin the activity.

Presenting
Comment dit-on... ?

Tell students about several happy events and express your excitement. You might show pictures to enhance your presentation. For example, show a picture of a sports car and say **Je viens d'acheter cette voiture! Géniale, non? C'est vraiment le pied d'avoir une voiture comme ça!** Then, act out regrettable events and express your disappointment. For example, drop and break a toy camera, saying **Les boules! Oh là là, quelle angoisse!** Next, project a transparency on which you have written the expressions in **Comment dit-on... ?** Describe situations to students, showing pictures or objects when possible, and prompt them to respond with appropriate expressions. **(Valérie, tu as gagné un voyage en France! Qu'est-ce que tu en dis? Pascal, je suis désolé(e), tu as eu 5 à ton interro de maths.)**

Assess

▶ Testing Program, pp. 261–264
Quiz 12-2A, Quiz 12-2B
Audio CD 12, Tr. 13

▶ Student Make-Up Assignments, Chapter 12, Alternative Quiz

▶ Alternative Assessment Guide, p. 41

Lisons!

Teaching Resources
pp. 356–358

PRINT 📖
▸ Lesson Planner, p. 61
▸ Cahier d'activités, p. 143
▸ Reading Strategies and Skills
  Handbook, Chapter 12
▸ Joie de lire 3, Chapter 12
▸ Standardized Assessment Tutor,
  Chapter 12

MEDIA 💿📼🖥️
▸ One-Stop Planner

Prereading
Activities A–B

Motivating Activity
Ask students what their favorite
Olympic events are. Ask them if certain countries usually seem to excel
in particular sports. Have students
name a favorite athlete and tell
in what event(s) the athlete
participates.

Reading
Activities C–J

Language Note
Ask students if they can define **fauteuil roulant** from the section about
Philippe Couprie. Other **fauteuils** are
the **fauteuil à bascule** *(rocking
chair)*, and the **fauteuil pliant**
(folding chair).

Lisons!

LE SPORT ET LE MONDE FRANCOPHONE

La naissance de l'Olympisme moderne a eu lieu
en 1894, avec la création du Comité Olympique,
consécration des efforts de Pierre de Coubertin.
Le développement des activités physiques était
alors très encouragé par le gouvernement
républicain français qui voulait créer une élite
forte. Mais, même si depuis le début des Jeux
olympiques modernes, les francophones ont
contribué à leur succès, l'influence de la France
et des francophones n'est pas assez reconnue
dans le monde du sport. Voici le portrait de
plusieurs athlètes francophones qui méritent
bien nos applaudissements pour leurs
accomplissements hors du commun.

Les Jeux olympiques en chiffres

Le nombre de sports présents aux Jeux olympiques est
en constante augmentation. En 1896, à Athènes, il y
avait seulement 9 sports en compétition. En 1948, à
Londres, il y avait 17 sports et à Atlanta en 1996, 26. En
l'an 2000, à Sydney, il y avait 28 sports. Comme le nombre de sports augmente, le nombre de médailles dis-
tribuées augmente aussi. A Sydney, on a distribué 300
médailles d'or, soit 29 de plus qu'à Atlanta et 43 de plus
qu'à Barcelone.

**Nombre de médailles que les Français ont gagnées pen-
dant les derniers Jeux olympiques d'été :**

Atlanta 1996 :   15 médailles d'or
                   7 médailles d'argent
                   15 médailles de bronze

Sydney 2000 :   13 médailles d'or
                   14 médailles d'argent
                   11 médailles de bronze

Brigitte Guidal

La France possède depuis
quelques années une
bonne équipe de canoë-
kayak. Dans l'équipe, on
peut citer Brigitte Guidal
qui a gagné sa première
médaille olympique à
Sydney après huit années
de compétition de haut niveau. Cependant, cette
médaille d'argent n'est pas sa première bonne performance au niveau mondial en canoë-kayak. Elle a été
sacrée championne du monde en 1997 et championne
d'Europe en l'an 2000.

Stratégie pour lire
While each chapter of this book has presented a single reading strategy, in reality you'll
usually use a combination of strategies to help you understand and get more out of what
you read. For example, if you're reading an autobiographical story written by a person from a
different country, it will be important to identify the narrator's point of view and to take the
cultural context of the story into account. In addition, you may need to use some of the
comprehension strategies you've learned, such as using linking words, contextual clues, and
deductive reasoning, in order to understand new words and the relationship of ideas in the
reading. The style of the reading may require you to use strategies for understanding literary
techniques or dialect, or for relating the subtopics to the main idea. Whatever type of
reading you're faced with, remember that you have a variety of strategies available for
meeting the challenges it presents.

Cultures and Communities

Additional Practice
C. Slower Pace On a transparency, write the
names of the athletes in one column and the
sports in which they participate in random order
in a second column. Have students match the athletes with their sports.

Culture Notes
• Students might be interested to know
  that the five colors of the Olympic
rings (blue, yellow, black, green, and red) represent at least one color from the flag of every
country that participates in the Games.
• The 1996 Atlanta Olympics were the 100th
anniversary of the Olympic Games.

Hicham El Guerrouj

Hicham El Guerrouj est né au Maroc en 1974. Depuis le milieu des années 1990, il domine la course de fond du 1500 mètres sur les pistes d'athlétisme du monde. Il a été sacré champion du monde du 1500 mètres en 1997 et 1998. Malgré sa domination, Hicham El Guerrouj n'a pas encore réussi à conquérir le titre olympique. A Atlanta, il a échoué au dernier tour de piste lorsqu'il est tombé. En l'an 2000, à Sydney, le Kenyan Noah Ngeny l'a battu d'un quart de seconde. Malgré ça, Hicham El Guerrouj reste sans doute l'un des meilleurs coureurs de fond de tous les temps.

Laura Flessel

On la surnomme la «guêpe». Née à la Guadeloupe en 1971, Laura Flessel n'a pas volé son surnom. Elle a commencé l'escrime lorsqu'elle n'avait que six ans. En 1990, elle a passé son baccalauréat et est partie pour la France métropolitaine où elle est entrée à l'INSEP. En 1996, elle a remporté la médaille d'or à l'épée aux Jeux olympiques d'Atlanta. En 1998 et 1999, elle a remporté deux titres de championne du monde. Cependant, aux Jeux olympiques de Sydney, elle a dû se contenter de la médaille d'argent. En plus d'être une sportive de haut niveau, Laura Flessel doit aussi concilier sa carrière professionnelle dans le tourisme d'affaires avec son rôle de maman.

Christine Arron

En 1998, la performance de Christine Arron aux 17èmes Championnats d'Europe d'athlétisme a fait oublier l'absence de Marie-José Pérec. Arron a battu le record d'Europe en remportant le titre continental à l'épreuve du 100 mètres à Budapest, en 10 secondes 73. Cette victoire constitue la troisième meilleure performance mondiale de tous les temps.

Philippe Couprie

Il est l'un des meilleurs spécialistes mondiaux de course en fauteuil roulant. Il fait partie du Pontoise Olympique Club, un club dédié à la course en fauteuil qui est célèbre pour les excellents athlètes qu'il regroupe (Moustapha Badid fait aussi partie de ce club). Philippe Couprie a été sept fois champion de France de semi-marathon, une fois deuxième, et il a obtenu le record de France du 1500 mètres en juin 1996, à Paris, puis à nouveau, aux Jeux olympiques d'Atlanta. Parmi ses autres exploits, on peut noter un titre de vice-champion olympique de marathon à Séoul, en 1988, et le record du monde de marathon à Boston, en 1989. Pour ce qui est de distances plus courtes, Philippe Couprie a été vice-champion du monde du 1500 mètres à Göteborg en 1995, champion olympique du 4 x 400 mètres à Atlanta en 1996 et il a obtenu la médaille de bronze du 1500 mètres aux Jeux olympiques d'Atlanta. En l'an 2000, à Sydney, il a encore obtenu une médaille pour le 4 fois 400 mètres, mais cette fois, une médaille d'argent.

* Create several true-false statements about the athletes featured in the article. Read the statements aloud and have students respond.

* Ask students which of the featured athletes they would most like to interview, and what they would like to know about them. You might also ask what other athletes they would like to interview about their sport.

Le Sport et le monde francophone

A. Preview the articles on the first two pages of the reading. What are they about? How is the information organized?

B. Now, make predictions about the articles based on your preview. What kind of information and vocabulary do you expect to find?

C. According to the introduction and the photographs, what are some of the sports and sporting events that French-speakers have played important roles in?

D. Qui était Pierre de Coubertin? Que lui doit-on?

For Activities A–F, see answers below.

E. Quel(le) athlète…
   1. a gagné une médaille d'or olympique?
   2. a gagné sa première médaille olympique à Sydney?
   3. a été champion du monde du 1500 mètres?
   4. a été sept fois champion de France de semi-marathon?
   5. a commencé à pratiquer son sport à l'âge de six ans?
   6. a battu le record du monde de marathon à Boston?

F. Dans quel sport est-ce que Laura Flessel excelle? Pourquoi l'appelle-t-on «la guêpe», à ton avis?

Possible answers

A. The article tells how the Olympics began and discusses some successful francophone athletes. The information is organized into profiles of the different athletes.

B. *Answers will vary.*

C. track, fencing, wheelchair racing, kayak racing

D. Pierre de Coubertin created the first Olympic committee, which was the beginning of the modern-day Olympics.

E. 1. Laura Flessel
   2. Brigitte Guidal
   3. Hicham El Guerrouj
   4. Philippe Couprie
   5. Laura Flessel
   6. Philippe Couprie

F. Laura Flessel; l'escrime; *answers will vary.*

Connections and Comparisons

Reading/Writing Link

Assign one of the athletes featured on pages 356–357 to students. Have them use their paraphrasing skills to summarize the athlete's interview. Remind them that they don't need to understand every word to summarize, just the general idea. Then, have volunteers read their summaries aloud to the class and have the class guess the name of the athlete being described.

CHAPITRE 12

Challenge

Have students write a one-page journal entry from the point of view of Zinedine Zidane. They should reflect on their part in the victorious soccer game and what it means to them. After they finish, have them share what they wrote in small groups and come up with one journal entry per group. Then, have each group read their entry aloud.

Postreading

Activity K

Teaching Suggestion

At this time, have students recall their predictions from Activity B on page 357 and verify whether they were accurate or not. As students look over the reading, have them tell what helped them most in making these predictions.

Possible answers

G. These articles are about the World Cup for soccer and handball. One expects to find information about which teams were involved, some of the key players, and the final scores.

H. Millions of fans wearing make-up celebrated in the streets. Americans usually celebrate this way, too, and often have parades for the winning team as well.

J. *Answers will vary.*

K. *Answers will vary.*

ALLEZ, LES BLEUS!

La période de grâce des «Bleus» a commencé en 1998 lorsqu'ils ont gagné la Coupe du monde. Elle a continué en l'an 2000 avec leur victoire pendant la Coupe d'Europe. Si la France a largement dominé le Brésil pendant la Coupe du monde en gagnant par trois buts à zéro, elle a eu beaucoup de mal à battre l'Italie lors de la finale de la Coupe d'Europe. Ce n'est que pendant les prolongations que la France a réussi à gagner grâce au but en or de Trézéguet.

Après la victoire de la France face au Brésil, plusieurs millions de supporters ont manifesté leur joie et leur enthousiasme dans les rues de Paris et de la France entière. On n'avait pas vu cela depuis la Libération (1945). La même manifestation de joie et d'enthousiasme a éclaté de nouveau après la victoire finale des "Bleus" contre l'Italie pendant la Coupe d'Europe.

Deux personnalités du monde du football

Zinedine Zidane

Zinedine Zidane, surnommé «Zizou», est peut-être le footballeur français le plus connu depuis Michel Platini. Pendant la finale de la Coupe du monde, il a marqué de la tête 2 des 3 buts. Malgré sa popularité, Zizou est très modeste et préfère parler de ses coéquipiers plutôt que de ses propres exploits.

Fabien Barthez

L'équipe de France de football doit aussi beaucoup de ses succès à son gardien de but, Fabien Barthez. Il aime dire que certains jours, il se sent invincible. Il est aussi le porte-bonheur de l'équipe. Plusieurs joueurs de l'équipe de France vont toucher le crâne rasé de Barthez avant chaque match pour se porter chance.

LE HANDBALL

Qu'est-ce qu'on appelle «handball» en France? C'est un sport d'équipe qui se pratique en salle avec un ballon à la main. Chaque équipe est composée de sept joueurs, dont un gardien de but. C'est un sport rapide et physique qui se pratique dans de nombreux pays européens et d'Afrique du Nord.

Le handball est de plus en plus populaire en France grâce à l'équipe nationale qui a gagné deux titres de champion du monde sur trois finales disputées depuis 1990. Ainsi, l'équipe de France de handball, surnommée les «Barjots», a remporté le titre de champion du monde en 1995. Les «Costauds» de 2001 ont remporté le titre mondial (28-25) face à la Suède qui domine la compétition depuis plusieurs années. Le joueur le plus connu de l'équipe de handball française est le capitaine de l'équipe, Jackson Richardson. Richardson vient de la Réunion et a participé aux différentes Coupes du monde depuis 1993. En 1995, il a été élu meilleur joueur après la victoire de la France.

For Activities G, H, J, and K, see answers below.

Allez, les Bleus!
Le Handball

G. De quoi parlent ces articles? Quel type d'informations tu penses trouver dans ces articles?

H. De quelle manière les fans français ont-ils célébré la victoire de leur équipe nationale? Est-ce que les Américains célèbrent les victoires de leurs équipes sportives de la même manière?

I. **Vrai ou faux?**

  1. Pour leur porter chance, les coéquipiers de Barthez lui touchent la tête. vrai

Cahier d'activités, p. 143, Act. 17

2. Les fans français ont surnommé leur équipe les «Rouges». faux

3. Zidane n'a pas bien joué lors de la finale de la Coupe du monde. faux

4. La finale de la Coupe du monde 1998 a eu lieu entre la France et les Etats-Unis. faux

5. Zidane a partagé son succès avec ses coéquipiers. vrai

J. Comment est-ce que le handball qu'on pratique en France diffère du handball qu'on pratique plus souvent aux Etats-Unis. A quels sports est-ce que le handball (version française) ressemble?

K. Combien de ces athlètes sont-ils connus aux Etats-Unis? D'après toi, pourquoi la presse américaine ne parle pas souvent des athlètes étrangers?

Communication for All Students

Building on Previous Skills

• Have students use the context of the article to guess the meaning of these words: **crâne** *(head, skull)*; **un coup de tête** *(head hit)*; **récidiver** *(to repeat)*; **surnommé** *(nicknamed)*; **coéquipiers** *(teammates)*.

• Have students imagine what these athletes' daily schedules might be like. Have them write out the schedule they imagine, including when they get up, eat, train, and go to bed.

Un article de magazine

Tu viens de lire des articles sur des athlètes internationaux, plus ou moins connus. Beaucoup de gens admirent les athlètes pour leur endurance, leur détermination et leur force de caractère qui leur a permis de devenir les meilleurs de leur sport. Dans cette activité, tu vas écrire un article de magazine sur un(e) athlète que tu admires ou que tu trouves intéressant(e).

Stratégie pour écrire

Of course you know that doing research is important for writing a research paper, but it can also be necessary for other kinds of writing. Whether it's a movie scene, a tourist brochure, an article, or a letter to the editor, all writing requires complete and accurate information. You may have access to more traditional research materials, such as the card catalogue and the periodicals index, or more modern ones, such as online information services and reference works stored on CD-ROM. Whatever the sources and types of information available to you, don't hesitate to do the research necessary to make your writing accurate as well as interesting.

A. Préparation

1. Choisis une personne que tu admires et au sujet de laquelle tu pourras trouver des informations.
2. Fais des recherches sur cette personne.
   a. Sélectionne des sources d'informations. Tu peux peut-être trouver ces informations dans des livres, des magazines ou des articles de journaux à la bibliothèque de ton école ou à la bibliothèque municipale.
   b. Lis toutes les informations que tu as trouvées et prends des notes ou fais des photocopies de ce que tu peux utiliser.
3. Organise les informations que tu as trouvées.
   a. Fais des catégories, comme par exemple, **Education, Entraînement** ou **Succès.**
   b. Fais un plan de ton article. Mets les catégories que tu as choisies dans l'ordre où elles apparaîtront dans ton article. Ensuite, organise les informations que tu as trouvées sous la forme de paragraphes.

B. Rédaction

1. Fais un brouillon de ton article en suivant le plan que tu as fait.
2. Vérifie que tu as bien utilisé toutes les informations que tu voulais. Consulte à nouveau les sources d'informations que tu as utilisées pour trouver des détails que tu pourrais ajouter.
3. S'il le faut, aide-toi d'un dictionnaire anglais-français pour traduire en français certaines des informations que tu as trouvées.
4. Trouve des photos pour illustrer ton article. Ecris une légende *(caption)* pour chaque photo et donne un titre à ton article.

C. Evaluation

1. Relis ton article et pose-toi les questions suivantes.
   a. Est-ce que tu as bien suivi ton plan?
   b. Est-ce que tu as trouvé des informations intéressantes pour ton article?
   c. Est-ce que tu as parlé des faits les plus importants de la vie de cet(te) athlète?
   d. Est-ce qu'il y a d'autres détails sur cet(te) athlète qui pourraient intéresser tes lecteurs?
2. Rédige la version finale de ton article en n'oubliant pas de corriger les fautes d'orthographe, de grammaire et de vocabulaire.

Teaching Resources
p. 359

PRINT
▶ Lesson Planner, p. 61
▶ Cahier d'activités, p. 156
▶ Alternative Assessment Guide, p. 27
▶ Standardized Assessment Tutor, Chapter 12

MEDIA
▶ One-Stop Planner
▶ Test Generator, Chapter 12
▶ Interactive CD-ROM Tutor, Disc 3

Process Writing

Prewriting
Teaching Suggestion

A. 2. Before students begin their research, ask them to list possible sources they are familiar with. You might also invite the school reference librarian to your class to suggest additional sources and helpful research techniques.

Writing
Visual Learners

B. 2. Have students go over their notes and underline each piece of information that pertains to a certain category (**Famille, Education,** and so on), using a different color of ink for each category. Then, have students write their rough draft, using the appropriate color of ink for each category in their article.

Portfolio

Written This activity is appropriate for students' written portfolios. For portfolio information, see *Alternative Assessment Guide,* pages iv–15.

Apply and Assess

Postwriting
Teaching Suggestion

C. 1. Have students exchange papers and notes and ask these questions about their classmate's article. If they answer no to any of the questions, they should make constructive suggestions for revisions.

Cooperative Learning

C. 2. Have students work in groups to proofread one another's article. Within each group, have students assign each member a specific proofreading task, such as spelling, vocabulary, or certain points of grammar (subject-verb agreement, noun-adjective agreement, contractions with **à** or **de,** and so on).

For **Grammaire supplémentaire** Answer Transparencies, see the *Teaching Transparencies* binder.

Grammaire supplémentaire

Première étape **Objectives** Expressing anticipation; making suppositions; expressing certainty and doubt

1 Complète les phrases suivantes avec le conditionnel et l'imparfait. **(pp. 13, 121, 347)**

1. Si je _____ (avoir) le temps, je _____ (faire) de la natation.
2. Ça m' _____ (étonner) si les Français ne _____ (gagner) pas le match.
3. S'il _____ (faire) plus de musculation, il _____ (être) plus musclé.
4. Si nous _____ (faire) plus d'entraînement, nous _____ (recevoir) une médaille d'or.
5. Si vous _____ (faire) plus d'effort, vous _____ (réussir).

2 Remplis les blancs avec la forme correcte des verbes entre parenthèses. **(pp. 133, 203, 348)**

1. Les basketteurs français? J'ai peur qu'ils _____ (se faire) battre par les Américains.
2. Ça m'étonnerait qu'il _____ (se cogner) la tête! C'est le meilleur plongeur du monde!
3. Il se peut qu'elle _____ (rater) son tir. Elle a l'air d'avoir le trac.
4. Il faudrait que tu _____ (voir) la différence entre le crawl et le papillon. Sinon, tu ne comprendras rien aux épreuves de natation!
5. Je ne pense pas que vous _____ (arriver) en finale. Vous n'avez vraiment pas de chance!
6. Je ne crois pas qu'ils _____ (pouvoir) nous battre. Nous sommes les meilleurs!

3 Complète la conversation suivante avec le futur des verbes entre parenthèses. **(p. 348)**

DOMINIQUE   J'__1__ (avoir) le trac dès que je __2__ (voir) la piscine!

BRUNO   Tu __3__ (aller) mieux dès que tu __4__ (commencer) à t'échauffer!

BENOIT   Marie-José __5__ (gagner) la plupart des épreuves dès qu'elle __6__ (apprendre) à rester calme.

BRUNO   La foule __7__ (être) en délire dès que vous __8__ (entrer)!

DOMINIQUE   Oui. Et on __9__ (jouer) l'hymne national de votre pays dès que vous __10__ (être) sur le podium!

BENOIT   Nous __11__ (battre) les Américains dès que nous __12__ (commencer) à nous concentrer sur notre entraînement.

Answers

1
1. avais, ferais
2. étonnerait, gagnaient
3. faisait, serait
4. faisions, recevrions
5. faisiez, réussiriez

2
1. se fassent
2. se cogne
3. rate
4. voies
5. arriviez
6. puissent

3
1. aurai
2. verrai
3. iras
4. commenceras
5. gagnera
6. apprendra
7. sera
8. entrerez
9. jouera
10. serez
11. battrons
12. commencerons

Grammar Resources for Chapter 12

The **Grammaire supplémentaire** activities are designed as supplemental activities for the grammatical concepts presented in the chapter. You might use them as additional practice, for review, or for assessment.

For more grammar presentations, review, and practice, refer to the following:
- Travaux pratiques de grammaire
- Grammar Tutor for Students of French

- Grammar Summary on pp. R29–R54
- Cahier d'activités
- Grammar and Vocabulary quizzes (Testing Program)
- Test Generator
- Interactive CD-ROM Tutor
- **Jeux interactifs** at <u>go.hrw.com</u>

4 Réponds en utilisant **Tu seras contente quand** et le futur du verbe qui convient. (p. 348)

EXEMPLE —Il me tarde d'aller aux Jeux olympiques!
—**Tu seras contente quand tu iras aux Jeux olympiques!**

1. Il me tarde de commencer l'entraînement!
2. Il me tarde d'entrer en compétition!
3. Il me tarde de gagner la médaille d'or!
4. Il me tarde d'être sur le podium!
5. Il me tarde de rencontrer d'autres champions!
6. Il me tarde de voir les épreuves d'athlétisme!

5 Marie et Yvonne sont aux Jeux olympiques. Marie connaît tout sur les athlètes qui y participent. Yvonne pose les questions suivantes à Marie. Réponds aux questions d'Yvonne et dis quel genre d'athlète ils sont. Utilise le superlatif dans tes phrases. (pp. 252, 348)

EXEMPLE —Est-ce qu'il joue au base-ball?
—**Oui, c'est le meilleur joueur de base-ball du monde.**

1. Il joue au basket?

2. Est-ce qu'elle nage le crawl?

3. Est-ce qu'il court?

4. Est-ce qu'elle fait de l'escrime?

Communication for All Students

Visual/Auditory Learners

5 Have students cover the questions as you read each one out loud. Next have them choose the photo that best matches the question. Then have them complete the activity, using the superlatives and answering the questions. As an extension of this activity have students use cutouts from the sports section of the newspaper or sports magazine (or their own drawings) and write an activity using this one as a model. Then have them pair off to complete each other's work. They could also extend the activity by substituting performing artists for the athletes (**c'est la meilleure chanteuse du monde**).

Answers

4 1. Tu seras contente quand tu commenceras l'entraînement.
2. Tu seras contente quand tu entreras en compétition.
3. Tu seras contente quand tu gagneras la médaille d'or.
4. Tu seras contente quand tu seras sur le podium.
5. Tu seras contente quand tu rencontreras d'autres champions.
6. Tu seras contente quand tu verras les épreuves d'athlétisme.

5 1. Oui, c'est le meilleur joueur de basket du monde.
2. Oui, c'est la meilleure nageuse du monde.
3. Oui, c'est le meilleur coureur du monde.
4. Oui, c'est la meilleure escrimeuse du monde.

Grammaire supplémentaire

WA3 FRANCOPHONE
AMERICA-12

For **Grammaire supplémentaire** Answer Transparencies, see the *Teaching Transparencies* binder.

Deuxième étape   Objectives Inquiring; expressing excitement and disappointment

6   Ces jeunes viennent de quel pays? Ecris des phrases avec le verbe **être** pour dire de quel pays ou de quelle région ils viennent. (**p. 352**)

> EXEMPLE   le Japon
> **Elle vient du Japon.**

1. l'Algérie

2. Le Canada

_____

3. La France

4. La Martinique

_____

5. Haïti

6. Les Etats-Unis

_____

Communication for All Students

Slower Pace

6   Review the use of prepositions with countries with students before doing Activity 6. Practice with them orally and then write additional examples on the board or on an overhead transparency. Have volunteer students explain their sentences and their choices of prepositions for each of the countries. Have the whole class participate in the making of a flowchart that can help guide them in selecting forms of **de** and **à** for use with countries. (are you saying what country you are from?>use a form of **de**; is the country masculine?>use **du**).

Answers

6   1. Elle vient d'Algérie.
2. Elle vient du Canada.
3. Il vient de France.
4. Elle vient de Martinique.
5. Il vient d'Haïti.
6. Il vient des Etats-Unis.

7 Chacun de ces jeunes vient du pays nommé à côté de son nom. Ecris six petites conversations en suivant le modèle donné dans l'exemple ci-dessous. (**p. 352**)

EXEMPLE   Babette / Brésil — **Moi, je viens du Brésil.**
                                — **C'est comment, la vie au Brésil?**

1. Tara / Tunisie
2. Saïd / Sénégal
3. Marco / Mexique
4. Mounia / Maroc
5. Inès / Martinique
6. Estrella / Espagne

8 Où est-ce qu'il faut aller pour faire les choses suivantes? Réponds en utilisant **il faudrait aller** et un des pays proposés ci-dessous. (**p. 352**)

la Belgique   l'Algérie   le Maroc
              la Tunisie
      l'Italie   la Suisse
      le Sénégal
                              la France
la République centrafricaine
                          le Canada
          les Etats-Unis

EXEMPLE   Pour boire du thé à la menthe, il faudrait aller...
               au Maroc.

1. Pour faire du ski, il faudrait aller…
2. Pour manger des gaufres, il faudrait aller…
3. Pour faire un safari, il faudrait aller…
4. Pour faire la cueillette des dattes, il faudrait aller…
5. Pour acheter une montre, il faudrait aller…
6. Pour manger des spaghettis, il faudrait aller…
7. Pour visiter la tour Eiffel, il faudrait aller...
8. Pour admirer les maisons du Vieux Carré en Louisiane, il faudrait aller...
9. Pour voir les beaux marchés de Dakar, il faudrait aller...
10. Pour visiter les ruines romaines de Carthage, il faudrait aller...

Review and Assess

You may wish to assign the **Grammaire supplé-mentaire** activities as additional practice or home-work after presenting material throughout the chapter. Assign Activities 2–5 after **Grammaire** (p. 348), and Activities 6–8 after **Tu te rappelles?** (p. 352). Activity 1 is a review of the conditional presented in Chapter 5.

To prepare students for the **Etape** Quizzes and Chapter Test, we suggest doing the **Grammaire supplémentaire** activities in the following order. Have students complete Activities 1–5 before taking Quiz 12-1A or 12-1B; and Activities 6–8 before Quiz 12-2A or 12-2B.

Possible answers

7
1. Moi, je viens de Tunisie.
   C'est comment, la vie en Tunisie?
2. Moi, je viens du Sénégal.
   C'est comment, la vie au Sénégal?
3. Moi, je viens du Mexique.
   C'est comment, la vie au Mexique?
4. Moi, je viens du Maroc.
   C'est comment, la vie au Maroc?
5. Moi, je viens de Martinique.
   C'est comment, la vie à la Martinique?
6. Moi, je viens d'Espagne.
   C'est comment, la vie en Espagne?

8
1. au Canada.
2. en Belgique.
3. en République centrafricaine.
4. en Algérie.
5. en Suisse.
6. en Italie.
7. en France.
8. aux Etats-Unis.
9. au Sénégal.
10. en Tunisie.

The **Mise en pratique** reviews and integrates all four skills and culture in preparation for the Chapter Test.

Teaching Resources
pp. 364–365

PRINT
▶ Lesson Planner, p. 61
▶ Listening Activities, p. 93
▶ Video Guide, pp. 75, 77–78
▶ Grammar Tutor for Students of French, Chapter 12
▶ Standardized Assessment Tutor, Chapter 12

MEDIA
▶ One-Stop Planner
▶ Video Program
   Videocassette 4, 41:40–45:10
▶ Audio Compact Discs, CD 12, Tr. 11
▶ Interactive CD-ROM Tutor, Disc 3

Teaching Suggestion

1 Have partners take turns reading parts of the article aloud to each other.

Career Path

If you have any athletes in your class, ask them if they've ever had the opportunity to travel to another city or state for a competition, or if they've ever met athletes from other countries. Have them share their experiences with the class. Sporting events often bring people together from all over the world. Ask students to imagine how the knowledge of a foreign language would be beneficial to professional athletes, coaches, and sports journalists.

Mise en pratique

internet
ADRESSE: go.hrw.com
MOT-CLE: WA3
FRANCOPHONE AMERICA-12

1 Lis cet article et réponds aux questions suivantes.

Les Jeux olympiques de l'antiquité à nos jours

Les Jeux olympiques de l'antiquité avaient lieu à Olympie en Grèce, tous les quatre ans, depuis l'an 776 av. J. C. jusqu'à leur interdiction par l'empereur Théodose Ier en 394 de notre ère. A l'origine, il n'y avait qu'une épreuve, une course de vitesse, et le vainqueur recevait une couronne de feuilles d'olivier comme récompense. D'autres épreuves de course furent ajoutées au fil du temps, ainsi que d'autres sports, comme la boxe et la lutte. Parmi les épreuves plus inhabituelles, il y avait la course en armure et la course de chars tirés non pas par des chevaux mais par deux mules. Avec le temps les récompenses devinrent plus recherchées et il y eut même des pots de vin, des cas de corruption et de boycottage.

S'inspirant des Jeux olympiques originaux, exempts de corruption, le baron français Pierre de Coubertin conçut les Jeux olympiques modernes. Il lança l'idée publiquement pour la première fois en 1892, puis passa les trois années et demie qui suivirent à rallier des soutiens. L'intérêt le plus fort se manifesta en Grèce et il fut donc décidé d'organiser les premiers Jeux olympiques à Athènes. Le terme "Olympiade" désigne la période de quatre années consécutives qui séparent deux éditions des Jeux. La première Olympiade de l'ère moderne débuta par les Jeux de 1896 à Athènes. Les Olympiades et les Jeux olympiques se calculent à partir de cette année-là, même si les Jeux n'ont pas eu lieu au cours d'une Olympiade donnée. Le terme "Olympiade" ne s'applique pas aux Jeux olympiques d'hiver.

Le premier comité international olympique (avec Pierre de Coubertin, assis à gauche)

Vrai ou faux?

1. La lutte faisait partie des premiers Jeux olympiques.   faux
2. La course de mules a fait partie des Jeux olympiques à une période donnée.   vrai
3. Pierre de Coubertin est le père des Jeux olympiques modernes.   vrai
4. Le terme « Olympiade » ne s'applique pas aux Jeux olympiques d'hiver.   vrai
5. Les sports pratiqués pendant les Jeux olympiques modernes sont les mêmes que ceux des premiers Jeux olympiques.   faux
6. Les premiers Jeux olympiques modernes ont eu lieu en 1892.   faux

---

Apply and Assess

Poetry Link

Copy the poem *L'Homme qui te ressemble* (*Listening Activities*, page 98) on a transparency and project it. Play the audio recording of the poem (Audio CD 12, Track 28), as students read along. Then, have students look back at the title of the chapter. Go over the Geography Link on page 343 of the *Annotated Teacher's Edition* and the **Note culturelle** on page 344 of the *Pupil's Edition* again. Have the class discuss how the poem reflects the spirit of the Olympics. You might do this activity in English.

2 Ecoute Marion qui montre à ses amis les photos qu'elle a prises aux Jeux olympiques. De quelle photo est-ce qu'elle parle?
See scripts and answers on p. 339H.

CD 12
Tr. 11

a.

b.

c.

d.

e.

f.

g.

h.

3 Tes camarades et toi, vous allez assister aux Jeux olympiques. Il faut que vous choisissiez à l'avance les événements que vous voulez voir pour pouvoir acheter des places. Dis à tes camarades quels sports il te tarde de voir. Ils/Elles vont parler de ce qu'ils/elles voudraient voir. Essayez de vous mettre d'accord pour pouvoir y aller tous ensemble.

4 Un magazine français va offrir un voyage aux Jeux olympiques à la personne qui écrira le meilleur essai sur la raison pour laquelle elle voudrait y aller. Ecris un essai. N'oublie pas de parler des épreuves auxquelles tu voudrais assister et de mentionner les gens que tu voudrais rencontrer. Décris comment tu imagines que ça sera.

5 **Jeu de rôle**

You and your partner are Olympic athletes. Choose the sports that you play and the countries you represent. Then, act out the following situations.

a. Imagine you're meeting each other in the Olympic village for the first time. Ask questions to find out about each other's country and interests.

b. You meet again on the last day. Tell each other how your competitions went. (One of you did very well and one of you did poorly.) Talk about your other experiences and what you enjoyed about the Games.

Review and Assess

Teaching Suggestions
- Have partners or small groups do these activities together.
- Once students have answered the questions in **Que sais-je?**, have a volunteer act as the teacher. Give the student-teacher an answer key for the questions and have him or her call on individual students to answer them at random. Encourage the student-teacher to praise the other students. (**Excellent! Bravo!**)

Possible answers

2 1. Ça doit être cool!
2. Je parie qu'il/elle va être fâché(e).
3. Je pourrai sûrement rencontrer des gens intéressants.

4 1. Ça m'étonnerait qu'ils gagnent la médaille d'or.
2. Je ne pense pas qu'il y ait d'interro.
3. Je ne suis pas certain(e) que ce soit une bonne idée.

Que sais-je?

Can you use what you've learned in this chapter?

Can you express anticipation?
p. 348

1 How would you express your anticipation if you were . . .   *Possible answers:*
1. going to watch the Olympic games?   Vivement que je sois là-bas!
2. about to be an exchange student in Switzerland?   Il me tarde d'aller en Suisse!
3. traveling to a foreign country?   Je suis vraiment impatient(e) de partir!

Can you make suppositions?
p. 348

2 What suppositions can you make about the following situations?   See answers below.
1. Your school team is going to compete in a state tournament.
2. You have to tell your best friend you've lost his/her leather jacket.
3. You're going to spend the summer working in a store.

Can you express certainty and doubt?
p. 348

3 Your friend asks you the following questions. How would you express your certainty?   *Possible answers:*

Est-ce que l'équipe de basket-ball américaine va gagner la médaille d'or?
Oui, c'est sûr.

Est-ce qu'il y a une interro de maths demain?
Oui, j'en suis sûr(e).

Est-ce que c'est une bonne idée d'étudier une langue étrangère?
Oui, j'en suis certain(e).

4 How would you express doubt about the situations in number 3?
See answers below.

Can you inquire?
p. 353

5 You've just been introduced to an exchange student from a foreign country. What questions would you ask to find out . . .
1. what life is like in that country?   C'est comment, la vie là-bas?
2. what people eat and wear there?   Qu'est-ce qu'on y mange/porte comme vêtements?
3. what is typical there?   Qu'est-ce qui est typique de chez toi?

Can you express excitement and disappointment?
p. 355

6 How would you express your excitement if . . .   *Possible answers:*
1. your school's basketball team won the state championship?   Super!
2. you got a perfect grade on a very difficult test?   J'arrive pas à y croire!
3. you received a birthday card with a $100 check inside?   Youpi!

7 How would you express your disappointment if . . .   *Possible answers:*
1. you just missed first place in a competition?   Les boules!
2. you arrived late and found that your friends had left without you?   2. Quelle angoisse!
3. you received a lower grade than you had expected on a test?   C'est pas juste.

Review and Assess

Auditory Learners
Before students attempt to answer the questions in **Que sais-je?**, read aloud some of the answers at random (**C'est vraiment le pied!**) and have students tell which functions they accomplish *(expressing excitement)*.

♞ Game
Quel sport?   Have students form small groups. In each group, one player chooses a sport. The other players ask him or her yes-no questions about the sport until one player can identify it. (**On a besoin d'un masque? On en fait en été?**) The first student to guess the player's sport takes the next turn.

Sports and equipment

les anneaux (m.)	the rings	la gymnastique	gymnastics	
l'arc (m.)	the bow	les haltères (f.)	weights	
l'aviron (m.)	rowing	l'haltérophilie (f.)	weightlifting	
la balle	the ball	le judo	judo	
le ballon	the ball	le lancer du disque	the discus throw	
les barres (f.) asymétriques	the uneven parallel bars	le lanceur	the pitcher	
le bâton	the bat	la lutte	wrestling	
la boxe	boxing	le masque	the mask	
le casque	the helmet	le panier	the basket	
la course de fond	long-distance running	le plongeoir	the diving board	
		le plongeon acrobatique	diving	
le cyclisme	cycling	plonger	to dive	
l'entraîneur (m.)	the coach	la poutre	the balance beam	
l'épée (f.)	the epee/the sword	le saut à la perche	the pole vault	
l'escrime (f.)	fencing			
l'escrimeur(-euse)	fencer	le saut en longueur	the long jump	
la flèche	the arrow	les rames (f.)	oars	
le frappeur	the batter			

la tenue	the outfit
le tir à l'arc	archery
tirer	to shoot

Expressing anticipation

Il me tarde de...	I can't wait to . . .
Je suis vraiment impatient(e) de... !	I can hardly wait to . . . !
Vivement que je... !	I just can't wait to . . . !
Dès que je serai là-bas,...	As soon as I get there, . . .
Quand je verrai...	When I see . . .

Expressing certainty and doubt

Ça, c'est sûr.	That's for sure.
Je n'en ai aucun doute.	I have no doubt of it.

Deuxième étape

Places of origin

l'Afrique (f.) du Sud	South Africa
l'Algérie (f.)	Algeria
l'Allemagne (f.)	Germany
l'Angleterre (f.)	England
la Belgique	Belgium
le Brésil	Brazil
le Canada	Canada
la Chine	China
la Côte d'Ivoire	the Republic of Côte d'Ivoire
l'Espagne (f.)	Spain
les Etats-Unis (m.)	the United States
la Guadeloupe	Guadeloupe
Haïti (m.)	Haiti
l'Italie (f.)	Italy
le Japon	Japan
le Maroc	Morocco
le Mexique	Mexico
le Niger	Niger
la République centrafricaine	the Central African Republic

la République démocratique du Congo	the Democratic Republic of Congo
la Russie	Russia
le Sénégal	Senegal
la Suisse	Switzerland
la Tunisie	Tunisia

Inquiring

Tu viens d'où?	Where are you from?
C'est comment, la vie là-bas?	What's life like there?
Qu'est-ce qu'on y... ?	What do you . . . there?
On... chez toi?	Do people . . . where you're from?
Vous avez/Il y a... chez vous?	Do you have/Are there . . . where you're from?
Qu'est-ce qui est typique de chez toi?	What's typical of where you're from?

Expressing excitement and disappointment

C'est trop cool!	That's too cool!
J'arrive pas à y croire!	I can't believe it!
C'est pas possible!	No way!
C'est vraiment le pied!	That's really neat!
Youpi!	Yippee!
Les boules!	Darn!
J'en ai vraiment marre!	I'm sick of this!
J'ai vraiment pas de chance.	I'm so unlucky.
C'est pas juste.	It's not fair.
Quelle angoisse!	This is the worst!
Qu'est-ce que je peux être nul(le)!	I just can't do anything right!

CHAPITRE 12

Circumlocution
Have students work with a partner. One student is an American tourist attending the Olympic Games in a francophone city. The other is a guide at the Olympic Village. The tourist is trying to find the location of a specific event, but can't remember the name of the sport. He or she must describe the sport, and the guide will then direct him or her to the correct location. (—Pardon, monsieur/madame, je cherche l'endroit où il y a des gens qui portent des tenues avec des masques. / —Ah, vous cherchez la salle où on fait de l'escrime? / —Oui. / —Eh bien, continuez tout droit.) Then, have partners switch roles.

Chapter 12 Assessment

▶ **Testing Program**
Chapter Test, pp. 265–270
Audio Compact Discs, CD 12, Trs. 14–16
Speaking Test, p. 300

Final Exam, pp. 279–286
Score Sheet, pp. 287–289
Listening Scripts, pp. 290–291
Answers, p. 292

Audio Compact Discs, CD 12, Trs. 17–21

▶ **Alternative Assessment Guide**
Portfolio Assessment, p. 27
Performance Assessment, p. 41
CD-ROM Assessment, p. 55

▶ **Interactive CD-ROM Tutor, Disc 3**
A toi de parler
A toi d'écrire

▶ **Standardized Assessment Tutor**
Chapter 12

▶ **One-Stop Planner, Disc 3**

Test Generator
Chapter 12

Review and Assess

Game

Dis-le! Assign at least one sport listed on this page to each student. You might include additional sports that students already know. Have students illustrate their sport(s) on one side of a large index card and write the French name of the sport on the reverse side. Then, form two teams (Team A and Team B) and have one student from each team come forward. Show the illustration on one of the cards to the student from Team A and have him or her identify the sport pictured. If the answer is correct, Team A receives a point; if the answer is incorrect, the player from Team B has the opportunity to answer. Continue until all the cards have been used. The team with the most points wins.

Reference Section

Summary of Functions

Function is another word for the way in which you use language for a specific purpose. When you find yourself in a certain situation, such as in a restaurant, in a grocery store, or at school, you'll want to place an order, or make a purchase, or talk about your class schedule. In order to communicate in French, you have to "function" in the language.

Each chapter in this book focuses on language functions. You can easily find them in boxes labeled **Comment dit-on...?** The other features in the chapter—grammar, vocabulary, and culture notes—support the functions you're learning.

Here is a list of the functions presented in the *Allez, viens!* program and their French expressions. You'll need them in order to communicate in a wide range of situations. Following each function are the numbers of the level, chapter, and page where the function was first introduced.

SOCIALIZING

Greeting people   I Ch. 1, p. 22
Bonjour.   Salut.

Saying goodbye   I Ch. 1, p. 22
Salut.   A bientôt.
Au revoir.   A demain.
A tout à l'heure.   Tchao.

Asking how people are   I Ch. 1, p. 23
(Comment) ça va?   Et toi?

Telling how you are   I Ch. 1, p. 23
Ça va.
Super!
Très bien.
Comme ci comme ça.
Bof.
Pas mal.
Pas terrible.

Expressing thanks   I Ch. 3, p. 90
Merci.   A votre service.

III Ch. 6, p. 169
Merci bien/mille fois.
Je vous remercie.
C'est vraiment très gentil de votre part.

Responding to thanks   III Ch. 6, p. 169
De rien.
Je vous en prie.
(Il n'y a) pas de quoi.
C'est tout à fait normal.

Extending invitations   I Ch. 6, p. 179
Allons...!   Tu viens?
Tu veux...?   On peut...

Accepting invitations   I Ch. 6, p. 179
Je veux bien.
Pourquoi pas?
D'accord.
Bonne idée.

Refusing invitations   I Ch. 6, p. 179
Désolé(e), je suis occupé(e).
Ça ne me dit rien.
J'ai des trucs à faire.
Désolé(e), je ne peux pas.

Identifying people   I Ch. 7, p. 203
C'est...   Voici...
Ce sont...   Voilà...

II Ch. 11, p. 313
Tu connais...?   Bien sûr. C'est...
Je ne connais pas.

Introducing people   I Ch. 7, p. 207
C'est...
Je te/vous présente...
Très heureux (heureuse).   (FORMAL)

Renewing old acquaintances   III Ch. 1, p. 9
Ça fait longtemps qu'on ne s'est pas vu(e)s.
Ça fait...
Depuis...
Je suis content(e) de te revoir.
Qu'est-ce que tu deviens?
Quoi de neuf?
Toujours la même chose!
Rien (de spécial).

Seeing someone off   I Ch. 11, p. 336
Bon voyage!   Amuse-toi bien!
Bonnes vacances!   Bonne chance!

Asking someone to convey good wishes
III Ch. 8, p. 222

> Embrasse... pour moi.
> Fais mes amitiés à...
> Salue... de ma part.
> Dis à... que je vais lui écrire.
> Dis à... que je pense à lui/elle.

Closing a letter **III Ch. 8, p. 222**

> Bien des choses à...
> Je t'embrasse bien fort.
> Grosses bises.
> Bisous à...

Welcoming someone **II Ch. 2, p. 37**

> Bienvenue chez moi/chez nous.
> Faites/Fais comme chez vous/toi.
> Vous avez/Tu as fait bon voyage?

Responding to someone's welcome **II Ch. 2, p. 37**

> Merci.   Oui, excellent.
> C'est gentil de   C'était fatigant!
>   votre/ta part.

Showing hospitality **III Ch. 6, p. 169**

> Entrez, je vous en prie.
> Ça me fait plaisir de vous voir.
> Donnez-moi votre...
> Mettez-vous à l'aise.
> Asseyez-vous.
> Je vous sers quelque chose?
> Qu'est-ce que je peux vous offrir?

Responding to hospitality **III Ch. 6, p. 169**

> Vous êtes bien   C'est gentil.
>   aimable.   Je prendrais bien...
> Moi aussi.   Vous auriez... ?

Extending good wishes **II Ch. 3, p. 79**

> Bonne fête!
> Joyeux (Bon) anniversaire!
> Bonne fête de Hanoukkah!
> Joyeux Noël!
> Bonne année!
> Meilleurs vœux!
> Félicitations!
> Bon voyage!
> Bonne route!
> Bon rétablissement!

Congratulating someone **II Ch. 5, p. 143**

> Félicitations!   Bravo!
> Chapeau!

EXCHANGING INFORMATION

Asking someone's name and giving yours
I Ch. 1, p. 24

> Tu t'appelles comment?
> Je m'appelle...

Asking and giving someone else's name
I Ch. 1, p. 24

> Il/Elle s'appelle comment?
> Il/Elle s'appelle...

Asking someone's age and giving yours
I Ch. 1, p. 25

> Tu as quel âge?   J'ai... ans.

Inquiring **III Ch. 12, p. 353**

> Tu viens d'où?
> C'est comment, la vie là-bas?
> Qu'est-ce qu'on y... ?
> On... chez toi?
> Vous avez/Il y a... chez vous?
> Qu'est-ce qui est typique de chez toi?

Asking for information (about classes)
I Ch. 2, pp. 55, 58

> Tu as quels cours... ?   Vous avez... ?
> Tu as quoi... ?   Tu as... à quelle heure?

(at a store or restaurant) **I Ch. 3, p. 94**

> C'est combien?

(about travel) **II Ch. 6, p. 172**

> A quelle heure est-ce que le train (le car) pour...
>   part?
> De quel quai... ?
> A quelle heure est-ce que vous ouvrez (fermez)?
> Combien coûte... ?
> C'est combien, l'entrée?

(about movies) **II Ch. 11, p. 320**

> Qu'est-ce qu'on joue comme films?
> Ça passe où?
> C'est avec qui?
> Ça commence à quelle heure?

(about places) **II Ch. 4, p. 102**

> Où se trouve... ?
> Qu'est-ce qu'il y a... ?
> C'est comment?

II Ch. 12, p. 348

> Qu'est-ce qu'il y a à faire... ?
> Qu'est-ce qu'il y a à voir... ?

Giving information (about classes)
I Ch. 2, p. 55

> Nous avons...   J'ai...

(about travel) **II Ch. 6, p. 172**

> Du quai...
> Je voudrais...
> Un... , s'il vous plaît.
> ... tickets, s'il vous plaît.

(about movies) **II Ch. 11, p. 320**

> On joue...   C'est avec...
> Ça passe à...   A...

(about places) II Ch. 12, p. 348
   ... se trouve...   Il y a...
   On peut...

Telling when you have class I Ch. 2, p. 58
   à... heure(s)   à... heure(s) quarante-
   à... heure(s) quinze   cinq
   à... heure(s) trente

Writing a formal letter III Ch. 5, p. 142
   Monsieur/Madame,
   En réponse à votre lettre du...
   Suite à notre conversation téléphonique,...
   Je vous prie d'agréer, Monsieur/Madame,
   l'expression de mes sentiments distingués.

Requesting information III Ch. 5, p. 142
   Pourriez-vous m'envoyer des renseignements
      sur... ?
   Je voudrais savoir...
   Vous serait-il possible de... ?

Asking for confirmation III Ch. 11, p. 316
   toujours...   ..., c'est ça?
   bien...   Si je me souviens bien,...
   ..., déjà?   Si je ne me trompe pas,...

Asking for explanations III Ch. 11, p. 323
   Qu'est-ce que c'est?
   Comment est-ce qu'on appelle ça?
   Qu'est-ce que ça veut dire,... ?
   Qu'est-ce qu'il y a dans... ?
   Comment est-ce qu'on fait... ?
   D'où vient le mot... ?
   Comment on dit... ?

Getting someone's attention I Ch. 3, p. 90
   Pardon.   Excusez-moi.

I Ch. 5, p. 151
   La carte, s'il vous   Madame!
     plaît.   Mademoiselle!
   Monsieur!

Ordering food and beverages I Ch. 5, p. 151
   Vous avez choisi?
   Vous prenez?
   Je voudrais...
   Je vais prendre... , s'il vous plaît.
   ... , s'il vous plaît.
   Donnez-moi... , s'il vous plaît.
   Apportez-moi... , s'il vous plaît.
   Vous avez... ?
   Qu'est-ce que vous avez comme... ?

Ordering and asking for details III Ch. 1, p. 18
   Vous avez décidé?
   Non, pas encore.
   Un instant, s'il vous plaît.
   Que voulez-vous comme entrée?

   Comme entrée, j'aimerais...
   Et comme boisson?
   Comment désirez-vous votre viande?
   Saignant(e).
   A point.
   Bien cuit(e).
   Qu'est-ce que vous me conseillez?
   Qu'est-ce que c'est,... ?
   ..., s'il vous plaît?
   Qu'est-ce que vous avez comme... ?

Paying the check I Ch. 5, p. 155
   L'addition, s'il vous plaît.
   Oui, tout de suite.
   Un moment, s'il vous plaît.
   Ça fait combien, s'il vous plaît?
   Ça fait... euros.
   C'est combien,... ?
   C'est... euros.

Exchanging information (about leisure activities)
I Ch. 4, p. 116
   Qu'est-ce que tu fais comme sport?
   Qu'est-ce que tu fais pour t'amuser?
   Je fais...
   Je (ne) fais (pas)...
   Je (ne) joue (pas)...

II Ch. 1, p. 12
   Qu'est-ce que tu aimes faire?
   Qu'est-ce que tu aimes comme
     musique?
   Quel(le) est ton/ta... préféré(e)?
   Qui est ton/ta... préféré(e)?

Making plans I Ch. 6, p. 173
   Qu'est-ce que tu   Je vais...
     vas faire... ?   Pas grand-chose.
   Tu vas faire quoi... ? Rien de spécial.

Arranging to meet someone I Ch. 6, p. 183
   Quand (ça)?   et quart
   tout de suite   moins le quart
   Où (ça)?   moins cinq
   devant...   midi (et demi)
   au métro...   minuit (et demi)
   chez...   vers...
   dans...   On se retrouve...
   Avec qui?   Rendez-vous...
   A quelle heure? Entendu.
   A... heures...
     et demie

III Ch. 6, p. 162
   Comment est-ce qu'on fait?
   Quand est-ce qu'on se revoit?
   A quelle heure est-ce qu'on se donne
     rendez-vous?

Inquiring about future plans   I Ch. 11, p. 329
Qu'est-ce que tu vas faire... ?
Où est-ce que tu vas aller... ?

Asking about intentions   III Ch. 5, p. 133
Qu'est-ce que tu penses faire?
Qu'est-ce que tu as l'intention de faire?
Qu'est-ce que tu comptes faire?

Asking about future plans   III Ch. 5, p. 140
Tu sais ce que tu veux faire?
Tu as des projets?
Qu'est-ce que tu veux faire plus tard?

Sharing future plans   I Ch. 11, p. 329
J'ai l'intention de...   Je vais...

Expressing intentions   III Ch. 5, p. 133
Je pense...   Je compte...
Je tiens à...   J'ai l'intention de...

Expressing conditions and possibilities
III Ch. 5, p. 133
Si... Il se peut que...
Peut-être que...   Il est possible que...

Describing and characterizing people
I Ch. 7, p. 209
Il/Elle est comment?   Il/Elle est...
Ils/Elles sont   Ils/Elles sont...
   comment?

II Ch. 1, p. 10
avoir... ans   Je suis...
J'ai...   Il/Elle est...
Il/Elle a...   Ils/Elles sont...
Ils/Elles ont...

II Ch. 12, p. 358
Il/Elle avait faim.   J'étais...
Il/Elle avait l'air...

Describing a place   II Ch. 4, p. 102
dans le nord/sud/est/ouest
plus grand(e) que
moins grand(e) que
charmant(e)
coloré(e)
vivant(e)

II Ch. 12, p. 358
Il y avait...   Il était...

Making a telephone call   I Ch. 9, p. 276
Bonjour.
Je suis bien chez... ?
C'est...
(Est-ce que)... est là, s'il vous plaît?

(Est-ce que) je peux parler à... ?
Je peux laisser un message?
Vous pouvez lui dire que j'ai téléphoné?
Ça ne répond pas.
C'est occupé.

Answering a telephone call   I Ch. 9, p. 276
Allô?
Bonjour.
Qui est à l'appareil?
Une seconde, s'il vous plaît.
Bien sûr.
Vous pouvez rappeler plus tard?
D'accord.
Ne quittez pas.

Asking others what they need   I Ch. 3, p. 82
Qu'est-ce qu'il te (vous) faut pour... ?

I Ch. 8, p. 238
De quoi est-ce que tu as besoin?
Qu'est-ce qu'il te faut?

Expressing need   I Ch. 8, p. 238
Il me faut...   J'ai besoin de...

(shopping)   I Ch. 10, p. 301
Oui, vous avez... ?
Je cherche quelque chose pour...
J'aimerais... pour aller avec...

Making purchases   II Ch. 3, p. 66
C'est combien, s'il vous plaît?
Combien coûte(nt)... ?
Combien en voulez-vous?
Je voudrais...
Je vais (en) prendre...
Ça fait combien?

Inquiring (shopping)   I Ch. 10, p. 301
(Est-ce que) je peux vous aider?
Vous désirez?
Je peux l'(les) essayer?
Je peux essayer... ?
C'est combien,... ?
Ça fait combien?
Vous avez ça en... ?

Asking which one(s)   III Ch. 4, p. 100
Quel(s)/Quelle(s)... ?
Lequel/Laquelle/Lesquels/Lesquelles?

Pointing out and identifying people and things
III Ch. 4, p. 100
Ça, c'est...   Celui avec...
Celui-là/Celle-là.   Celle qui...
Ceux-là/Celles-là.   La fille au...
Le vert.   Là-bas, le garçon qui...
Celui du...

Pointing out places and things **I Ch. 12, p. 361**

Voici...   Là, tu vois, c'est...
Regarde, voilà...   Ça, c'est...
Là, c'est...

Pointing out where things are **II Ch. 2, p. 43**

A côté de...   à gauche de
Il y a...   à droite de
en face de   près de

Asking where things are **III Ch. 2, p. 47**

Vous pourriez me dire où il y a... ?
Pardon, vous savez où se trouve... ?
Tu sais où est/sont... ?

Telling where things are **III Ch. 2, p. 47**

Par là, au bout du couloir.
Juste là, à côté de...
En bas.
En haut.
Au fond.
Au rez-de-chaussée.
Au premier étage.
A l'entrée de...
En face de...

Asking for advice (about directions)
I Ch. 12, p. 366

Comment est-ce qu'on y va?

Asking for directions **I Ch. 12, p. 371**

Pardon,... , s'il vous plaît?
Pardon,... . Où est... , s'il vous plaît?
Pardon,... . Je cherche... , s'il vous plaît.

III Ch. 2, p. 37

La route pour... , s'il vous plaît?
Comment on va à... ?
Où se trouve... ?

Giving directions **I Ch. 12, p. 371**

Vous continuez jusqu'au prochain feu rouge.
Vous tournez...
Vous allez tout droit jusqu'à...
Prenez la rue... , puis traversez la rue...
Vous passez devant...
C'est tout de suite à...

II Ch. 2, p. 49

Traversez...
Prenez...
Puis, tournez à gauche dans/sur...
Allez (continuez) tout droit.
sur la droite (gauche)

II Ch. 12, p. 348

C'est au nord/au sud/à l'est/à l'ouest de...
C'est dans le nord/le sud/l'est/l'ouest.

III Ch. 2, p. 37

Pour (aller à)... , vous suivez la... pendant à peu
    près... kilomètres.
Vous allez voir un panneau qui indique l'entrée
    de l'autoroute.
Vous allez traverser...
Après... , vous allez tomber sur...
Cette route va vous conduire au centre-ville.
Vous allez continuer tout droit, jusqu'à...

Inquiring about past events **I Ch. 9, p. 269**

Tu as passé un bon week-end?

I Ch. 9, p. 270

Qu'est-ce que tu as fait... ?
Tu es allé(e) où?
Et après?
Qu'est-ce qui s'est passé?

I Ch. 11, p. 337

Tu as passé un bon... ?
Ça s'est bien passé?
Tu t'es bien amusé(e)?

II Ch. 5, p. 139

Comment ça s'est passé?
Comment s'est passée ta journée (hier)?
Comment s'est passé ton week-end?
Comment se sont passées tes vacances?

II Ch. 6, p. 164

C'était comment?   Ça t'a plu?
Tu t'es amusé(e)?

III Ch. 1, p. 9

C'était comment, tes vacances?
Ça c'est bien passé?
Comment ça c'est passé?

Exchanging information (about vacations)
III Ch. 1, p. 10

Est-ce que tu es resté(e) ici?
Oui, je suis resté(e) ici tout le temps.
Non, je suis parti(e)...
Quand est-ce que tu y es allé(e)?
J'y suis allé(e) début/fin...
Avec qui est-ce que tu y es allé(e)?
J'y suis allé(e) seul(e)/avec...
Tu es parti(e) comment?
Je suis parti(e) en...
Où est-ce que tu as dormi?
A l'hôtel.
Chez...
Quel temps est-ce qu'il a fait?
Il a fait un temps...
Il a plu tout le temps.

Relating a series of events **I Ch. 9, p. 270**

D'abord,...   Ensuite,...
Après,...

Je suis allé(e)...
Et après ça...
Enfin,...

II Ch. 1, p. 20
Puis,...

II Ch. 4, p. 111
Après ça,...
Finalement,...
Vers... ,

Asking what things were like **II Ch. 8, p. 226**
C'était comment?
C'était tellement différent?

Describing what things were like **II Ch. 8, p. 226**
C'était...   Il y avait...
La vie était plus... ,
   moins...

Asking what a place was like **III Ch. 1, p. 12**
Qu'est-ce qu'il y avait à voir?
Qu'est-ce qu'il y avait à faire?
Il y avait… ?
Il faisait… ?

Describing what a place was like **III Ch. 1, p. 12**
Il faisait…
... est situé(e)...

Reminiscing **II Ch. 8, p. 229**
Quand j'étais petit(e),...
Quand il/elle était petit(e),...
Quand j'avais... ans,...

Telling what or whom you miss **II Ch. 8, p. 225**
Je regrette...
... me manque.
... me manquent.
Ce qui me manque, c'est...

Asking about a story **III Ch. 9, p. 266**
De quoi ça parle?
Comment est-ce que ça commence?
Comment ça se termine?

Beginning a story **II Ch. 9, p. 267**
A propos,...

Continuing a story **II Ch. 9, p. 267**
Donc,...   C'est-à-dire que...
Alors,...   ... , quoi.
A ce moment-là,...   ... , tu vois.
Bref,...

Ending a story **II Ch. 9, p. 267**
Heureusement,...
Malheureusement,...
Finalement,...

Summarizing a story **II Ch. 11, p. 326**
De quoi ça parle?
Ça parle de...
Qu'est-ce que ça raconte?
C'est l'histoire de...

III Ch. 9, p. 266
Il s'agit de...   Au début,...
A la fin,...   A ce moment-là,...
Ça se passe,...

Breaking some news **II Ch. 9, p. 263**
Tu connais la nouvelle?
Tu ne devineras jamais ce qui s'est passé.
Tu sais qui... ?
Tu sais ce que... ?
Devine qui...
Devine ce que...

III Ch. 10, p. 295
Tu savais que... ?
Tu connais la dernière?/ Tu ne connais pas la
   dernière?
J'ai entendu dire que...
Figure-toi que...
Si tu avais vu...

Showing interest **II Ch. 9, p. 263**
Raconte!
Aucune idée.
Dis vite!

III Ch. 10, p. 295
Oh là là!
Qui t'a dit ça?
Et alors?

Telling jokes **III Ch. 10, p. 297**
J'en connais une bonne.
Est-ce que tu connais l'histoire de... ?
Quelle est la différence entre... et... ?
Quel est le point commun entre... et... ?
C'est l'histoire d'un mec qui...
... et alors, il dit que...
... et l'autre lui répond...
Elle est bien bonne!
Elle est nulle, ta blague!

EXPRESSING FEELINGS AND EMOTIONS

Expressing likes and preferences about things
I Ch. 1, p. 26
J'aime (bien)...   J'aime mieux...
J'adore...   Je préfère...

I Ch. 5, p. 154
C'est...

Expressing dislikes about things I Ch. 1, p. 26
Je n'aime pas...

I Ch. 5, p. 154
C'est...

Telling what you'd like and what you'd like to do
I Ch. 3, p. 85
Je voudrais...
Je voudrais acheter...

Telling how much you like or dislike something
I Ch. 4, p. 114
Beaucoup.   Pas du tout.
Pas beaucoup.   surtout
Pas tellement.

Inquiring about likes and dislikes I Ch. 5, p. 154
Comment tu trouves ça?

Hesitating I Ch. 10, p. 310
Euh... J'hésite.
Je ne sais pas.
Il/Elle me plaît, mais il/elle est...
                          c'est...

Making a decision I Ch. 10, p. 310
Vous avez décidé de prendre... ?
Vous avez choisi?
Vous le/la/les prenez?
Je le/la/les prends.
Non, c'est trop cher.

Expressing indecision I Ch. 11, p. 329
J'hésite.
Je ne sais pas.
Je n'en sais rien.
Je n'ai rien de prévu.

III Ch. 1, p. 17
Tout me tente.
Je n'arrive pas à me décider.
J'hésite entre... et...

III Ch. 5, p. 140
Pas vraiment.
Je ne sais pas trop. Non, je me demande.
Je n'en ai aucune idée.
J'ai du mal à me décider.
Je ne sais plus ce que je veux.

Making suppositions III Ch. 7, p. 193
On pourrait sûrement...
Ça doit être...
Je parie que...
Il doit y avoir...

Expressing disbelief and doubt II Ch. 6, p. 168
Tu plaisantes!   C'est pas vrai!

Pas possible!   N'importe quoi!
Ça m'étonnerait!   Mon œil!

III Ch. 10, p. 295
Je n'en reviens pas.

Expressing doubt III Ch. 7, p. 193
Ça m'étonnerait que...
Je ne suis pas sûr(e) que...
Je ne suis pas certain(e) que...
Je ne pense pas que...

Expressing certainty III Ch. 7, p. 193
Je suis certain(e) que...
Je suis sûr(e) que...
Je sais que...
Je suis convaincu(e) que...

III Ch. 12, p. 348
Ça, c'est sûr.
Je n'en ai aucun doute.

Expressing hopes and wishes I Ch. 11, p. 329
J'ai envie de...
Je voudrais bien...

III Ch. 5, p. 140
J'aimerais bien...
Ce qui me plairait, c'est de...
Mon rêve, c'est de...

III Ch. 8, p. 225
Si seulement je pouvais,...
Si j'avais le choix,...
Si c'était possible,...
Ça serait chouette si...
Qu'est-ce que j'aimerais... !

Expressing anticipation III Ch. 12, p. 348
Il me tarde de...
Je suis vraiment impatient(e) de/d'... !
Vivement que j'arrive!
Dès que je serai là-bas,...
Quand je verrai...

Asking how someone is feeling II Ch. 2, p. 38
Pas trop fatigué(e)?
Vous n'avez pas/Tu n'as pas faim?
Vous n'avez pas/Tu n'as pas soif?

Telling how you are feeling II Ch. 2, p. 38
Non, ça va.
Si, un peu.
Si, je suis crevé(e).
Si, j'ai très faim/soif!
Si, je meurs de faim/soif!

Expressing concern for someone II Ch. 5, p. 135
Ça n'a pas l'air d'aller.
Qu'est-ce qui se passe?

Qu'est-ce qui t'arrive?
Raconte!

II Ch. 7, p. 189
Quelque chose ne va pas?
Qu'est-ce que tu as?
Tu n'as pas l'air en forme.

Sympathizing with someone **II Ch. 5, p. 141**
Oh là là!
C'est pas de chance, ça!
Pauvre vieux (vieille)!

Sharing confidences **I Ch. 9, p. 279**
J'ai un petit problème.
Je peux te parler?
Tu as une minute?

II Ch. 10, p. 286
Je ne sais pas quoi faire.
Qu'est-ce qu'il y a?
Je t'écoute.
Qu'est-ce que je peux faire?

Consoling others **I Ch. 9, p. 279**
Ne t'en fais pas!
Je t'écoute.
Ça va aller mieux!
Qu'est-ce que je peux faire?

II Ch. 5, p. 141
Courage!
T'en fais pas.
C'est pas grave.

Expressing satisfaction **II Ch. 5, p. 139**
Ça s'est très bien passé!
C'était...
   incroyable!
   super!
   génial!
Quelle journée (formidable)!
Quel week-end (formidable)!

Expressing frustration **II Ch. 5, p. 139**
Quelle journée!
Quel week-end!
J'ai passé une journée épouvantable!
C'est pas mon jour!
Tout a été de travers!

Expressing impatience **III Ch. 2, p. 40**
Mais, qu'est-ce que tu fais?
Tu peux te dépêcher?
Grouille-toi!
On n'a pas le temps!
Je suis vraiment impatient(e) de...

Expressing annoyance **III Ch. 8, p. 231**
Non mais, vous vous prenez pour qui?
Non mais, surtout, ne vous gênez pas!

Ça va pas, non?!
Ça commence à bien faire, hein?
Dites donc, ça vous gênerait de... ?

Complaining **II Ch. 7, p. 189**
Je ne me sens pas bien.
Je suis tout(e) raplapla.
J'ai mal dormi.
J'ai mal partout!

II Ch. 12, p. 354
Je crève de faim!   Je suis fatigué(e).
Je meurs de soif!   J'ai peur de...

III Ch. 8, p. 231
C'est l'horreur!
C'est insupportable, à la fin!
J'en ai ras le bol!
Je commence à en avoir marre!

Quarreling **III Ch. 6, p. 173**
Rapporteur(-euse)!
Pleurnicheur(-euse)!
Tricheur(-euse)!
Tu m'énerves, à la fin!
Tu es vraiment casse-pieds!
Tu me prends la tête!
Oh, ça va, hein?
Arrête!
Ça suffit!
Tu le fais exprès?
Mêle-toi de tes oignons!
Fiche-moi la paix!
Casse-toi!
Tant pis pour toi!
C'est toujours la même chose!
C'est lui/elle qui a commencé!
Il/Elle m'a traité(e) de... !
C'est toujours moi qui prends!

Expressing discouragement **II Ch. 7, p. 198;
II Ch. 12, p. 354**
Je n'en peux plus!
J'abandonne.
Je craque!

Offering encouragement **II Ch. 7, p. 198**
Allez!
Encore un effort!
Tu y es presque!
Courage!

Expressing disappointment **III Ch. 12, p. 355**
Les boules!
J'en ai vraiment marre!
J'ai vraiment pas de chance.
C'est pas juste.
Quelle angoisse!
Qu'est-ce que je peux être nul(le)!

Expressing excitement III Ch. 12, p. 355
> Génial!
> C'est trop cool!
> J'arrive pas à y croire!
> C'est pas possible!
> C'est vraiment le pied!
> Youpi!

Expressing astonishment III Ch. 7, p. 201
> Oh, dis donc!
> Ça alors!
> C'est pas vrai!
> Ouah!
> C'est le pied!
> Qu'est-ce que... !
> Quel... !
> Tiens! Regarde un peu!
> C'est fou comme... !
> Tu as vu comme... ?
> Je n'ai jamais vu un(e) aussi...

Expressing fear III Ch. 7, p. 202
> J'ai très peur de...   J'ai peur que...
> J'ai la frousse!

Expressing relief III Ch. 7, p. 202
> On a eu de la chance!
> Ouf! On a eu chaud!
> On l'a échappé belle!

PERSUADING

Asking for recommendations (about movies)
III Ch. 9, p. 265
> Qu'est-ce que tu as vu comme bon film?
> Qu'est-ce qu'il y a comme bons films en ce moment?

Making recommendations (about movies)
III Ch. 9, p. 265
> Tu devrais aller voir...
> Je te recommande...
> Va voir... , c'est génial comme film.
> C'est à ne pas manquer!
> N'y va pas!
> Ça ne vaut pas le coup!
> Ne va surtout pas voir...
> Evite d'aller voir...

(about food) I Ch. 5, p. 148
> Prends...   Prenez...

III Ch. 1, p. 17
> Tu devrais prendre...
> Pourquoi tu ne prends pas... ?
> Essaie...

Asking for suggestions II Ch. 1, p. 18
> Qu'est-ce qu'on fait?

II Ch. 4, p. 106
> Qu'est-ce qu'on peut faire?

Making suggestions I Ch. 4, p. 122
> On... ?

I Ch. 5, p. 145
> On va... ?
> On fait... ?
> On joue... ?

I Ch. 12, p. 366 *(how to get somewhere)*
> On peut y aller...
> On peut prendre...

II Ch. 1, p. 18
> Si tu veux, on peut...
> On pourrait...
> Tu as envie de... ?
> Ça te dit de... ?

II Ch. 4, p. 106
> On peut...
> Si on allait... ?

II Ch. 8, p. 237
> Si on achetait... ?
> Si on visitait... ?
> Si on jouait... ?

III Ch. 6, p. 161
> Ça t'intéresse de... ?
> Ça te plairait de... ?
> Tu ne voudrais pas... ?

Accepting suggestions I Ch. 4, p. 122
> D'accord.   Allons-y!
> Bonne idée.   Oui, c'est...

III Ch. 6, p. 161
> Ce serait sympa.
> Ça me plairait beaucoup.
> J'aimerais bien.

Turning down suggestions I Ch. 4, p. 122
> Non, c'est...
> Ça ne me dit rien.
> Désolé(e), mais je ne peux pas.

III Ch. 6, p. 161
> C'est gentil, mais j'ai un rendez-vous.
> Impossible, je suis pris(e).
> J'aimerais bien, mais...

Responding to suggestions II Ch. 1, p. 18
> D'accord.
> C'est une bonne/excellente idée.
> Je veux bien.
> Je ne peux pas.
> Non, je préfère...
> Pas question!
> Ça ne me dit rien.

II Ch. 8, p. 237
Bof.
Non, je ne veux pas.
Comme tu veux.

Making excuses **I Ch. 5, p. 145**
Désolé(e). J'ai des devoirs à faire.
J'ai des courses à faire.
J'ai des trucs à faire.
J'ai des tas de choses à faire.

II Ch. 10, p. 291
J'ai quelque chose à faire.
Je n'ai pas le temps.
Je suis très occupé(e).
C'est impossible.

(school) **II Ch. 5, p. 143**
..., c'est pas mon fort.
J'ai du mal à comprendre.
Je suis pas doué(e) pour...

Giving reasons **II Ch. 5, p. 143**
Je suis assez bon (bonne) en...
C'est en... que je suis le/la meilleur(e).
..., c'est mon fort!

Asking for permission **I Ch. 7, p. 213**
(Est-ce que) je peux... ?
Tu es d'accord?

III Ch. 3, p. 68
J'aimerais...
Tu veux bien que je... ?
Ça te dérange si... ?

Giving permission **I Ch. 7, p. 213**
Oui, si tu veux.
Pourquoi pas?
Oui, bien sûr.
D'accord, si tu... d'abord...

III Ch. 3, p. 68
Ça va pour cette fois.
Oui, si...

Refusing permission **I Ch. 7, p. 213**
Pas question!   Non, tu dois...
Non, c'est impossible.   Pas ce soir.

III Ch. 3, p. 68
Tu n'as pas le droit de...
Ce n'est pas possible.

Expressing obligation **III Ch. 3, p. 68**
Il faut que tu... d'abord.
Tu dois...

Reprimanding someone **II Ch. 5, p. 143**
C'est inadmissible.
Tu dois mieux travailler en classe.

Tu ne dois pas faire le clown en classe!
Ne recommence pas.

Making requests **I Ch. 3, p. 80**
Tu as... ?   Vous avez... ?

I Ch. 8, p. 240
Tu peux... ?   Tu me rapportes... ?

I Ch. 12, p. 364
Est-ce que tu peux... ?
Tu pourrais passer à... ?

III Ch. 9, p. 259
Chut!
Tais-toi!
Ne parle pas si fort.
Tu pourrais faire moins de bruit?
Vous pourriez vous taire, s'il vous plaît?
Baisse/Monte le son.

Responding to requests **I Ch. 3, p. 80**
Voilà.
Je regrette.
Je n'ai pas de...

Accepting requests **I Ch. 8, p. 240**
Pourquoi pas?
Bon, d'accord.
Je veux bien.
J'y vais tout de suite.

I Ch. 12, p. 364
D'accord.   Si tu veux.

Declining requests **I Ch. 8, p. 240**
Je ne peux pas maintenant.
Je regrette, mais je n'ai pas le temps.
J'ai des tas de choses (trucs) à faire.

I Ch. 12, p. 364
Désolé(e), mais je n'ai pas le temps.

Asking a favor **I Ch. 12, p. 364**
Est-ce que tu peux... ?
Tu me rapportes... ?
Tu pourrais passer à... ?

II Ch. 10, p. 291
Tu peux m'aider?
Tu pourrais... ?
Ça t'ennuie de... ?
Ça t'embête de... ?

Granting a favor **II Ch. 10, p. 291**
Avec plaisir.   Bien sûr que non.
Bien sûr.   Pas du tout.
Pas de problème.

Telling someone what to do **I Ch. 8, p. 240**
Rapporte-moi...   Achète(-moi)...
Prends...   N'oublie pas de...

Asking for food II Ch. 3, p. 72
Je pourrais avoir... , s'il vous (te) plaît?
Vous pourriez (tu pourrais) me passer... ?

Offering food I Ch. 8, p. 247
Tu veux... ?   Tu prends... ?
Vous voulez... ?   Encore du/de la... ?
Vous prenez ... ?

II Ch. 3, p. 72
Voilà.
Vous voulez (tu veux)... ?
Encore... ?
Tenez (tiens).

Accepting food I Ch. 8, p. 247
Oui, s'il vous (te) plaît.
Oui, avec plaisir.
Oui, j'en veux bien.

II Ch. 3, p. 72
Oui, je veux bien.

Refusing food I Ch. 8, p. 247
Non, merci.
Non, merci. Je n'ai plus faim.
Je n'en veux plus.

II Ch. 3, p. 72
Merci, ça va.
Je n'ai plus faim/soif.

Asking for advice I Ch. 9, p. 279 *(general)*
A ton avis, qu'est-ce que je fais?
Qu'est-ce que tu me conseilles?

II Ch. 10, p. 286
A ton avis, qu'est-ce que je dois faire?
Qu'est-ce que tu ferais, toi?

II Ch. 1, p. 15
Qu'est-ce que je dois... ?

III Ch. 7, p. 195
Tu crois que je devrais... ?
Tu penses qu'il vaudrait mieux... ?

(about clothes) I Ch. 10, p. 300
Je ne sais pas quoi mettre pour...
Qu'est-ce que je mets?

(about directions) I Ch. 12, p. 366
Comment est-ce qu'on y va?

(about gifts) II Ch. 3, p. 76
Tu as une idée de cadeau pour... ?
Qu'est-ce que je pourrais offrir à... ?

Giving advice I Ch. 9, p. 279
Oublie-le/-la/-les!
Téléphone-lui/-leur!

Tu devrais...
Pourquoi tu ne... pas?

I Ch. 10, p. 300
Pourquoi est-ce que tu ne mets pas... ?
Mets...

II Ch. 1, p. 15
Pense à prendre...   Prends...
N'oublie pas...

II Ch. 3, p. 76
Offre-lui (leur) ...
Tu pourrais lui (leur) offrir...
... , peut-être.

II Ch. 7, p. 197
Tu dois...   Tu ferais bien de...
Tu n'as qu'à...

II Ch. 10, p. 286
Invite-le/-la/-les.   Parle-lui/-leur.
Dis-lui/-leur que...   Ecris-lui/-leur.
Explique-lui/-leur.   Excuse-toi.

II Ch. 12, p. 356
Evite de...
Tu ne devrais pas...
Ne saute pas...

III Ch. 5, p. 140
Tu ferais mieux de...
Il faudrait que tu...
Il vaudrait mieux que...

III Ch. 7, p. 195
Je crois que ça vaut mieux.
A mon avis, c'est plus sûr.
Ce n'est pas la peine.
Je ne crois pas que ce soit utile.
Il faudrait que...
Il est très important que...
Il est essentiel que...
Il est nécessaire que...

III Ch. 8, p. 225
Si c'était moi,...
Si j'étais toi,...
A ta place,...

Justifying your recommendations II Ch. 7, p. 202
C'est bon pour toi.
Ça te fera du bien.
C'est mieux que de...

Accepting advice II Ch. 3, p. 76
Bonne idée!
C'est original.

Tu as raison.
D'accord.

Rejecting advice II Ch. 3, p. 76
C'est trop cher.
C'est banal.
Ce n'est pas son style.
Il/Elle en a déjà un(e).

II Ch. 7, p. 197
Je ne peux pas.
Non, je n'ai pas très envie.
Non, je préfère...
Pas question!
Je n'ai pas le temps.
Ce n'est pas mon truc.

Advising against something II Ch. 7, p. 202
Evite de...
Ne saute pas...
Tu ne devrais pas...

Cautioning someone III Ch. 7, p. 202
Je vous signale que...
Il serait plus prudent de...
Faites gaffe!
Faites attention!
Attention à... !
Méfiez-vous!
Ne bougez pas.

Forbidding III Ch. 3, p. 75
Il est interdit de...
Veuillez ne pas...
Prière de ne pas...
Interdiction de...
Défense de...

Reproaching someone II Ch. 10, p. 294
Tu aurais dû...
Tu aurais pu...

III Ch. 3, p. 78
Vous (ne) devriez (pas)...
Tu as tort de...
Ce n'est pas bien de...
Tu ferais mieux de ne pas...

Justifying your actions III Ch. 3, p. 78
Je suis quand même libre, non?
Tout le monde fait pareil.
Je ne suis pas le/la seul(e) à...

Rejecting others' excuses III Ch. 3, p. 78
Pense aux autres.
Ce n'est pas une raison.
Ce n'est pas parce que tout le monde... que tu
     dois le faire.

Reminding I Ch. 11, p. 333
N'oublie pas...
Tu n'as pas oublié... ?
Tu ne peux pas partir sans...
Tu prends... ?

Reassuring someone I Ch. 11, p. 333
Ne t'en fais pas.
J'ai pensé à tout.
Je n'ai rien oublié.

II Ch. 8, p. 225
Tu vas t'y faire.
Fais-toi une raison.
Tu vas te plaire ici.
Tu vas voir que...

III Ch. 2, p. 40
Ça ne va pas prendre longtemps!
Sois patient(e)!
On a largement le temps!
Il n'y a pas le feu.
Du calme, du calme.

III Ch. 4, p. 108
Crois-moi.
Je t'assure.
Fais-moi confiance.
Je ne dis pas ça pour te faire plaisir.

III Ch. 7, p. 202
Ne vous en faites pas!
N'ayez pas peur.
Calmez-vous!
Pas de panique!

Apologizing II Ch. 10, p. 294
C'est de ma faute.
Excuse-moi.
Désolé(e).
J'aurais dû...
J'aurais pu...
Tu ne m'en veux pas?

III Ch. 6, p. 164
Je m'excuse de...
Je suis vraiment désolé(e) de...
Pardonne-moi de...
Je m'en veux de...

Accepting an apology II Ch. 10, p. 294
Ça ne fait rien.
C'est pas grave.
Il n'y a pas de mal.
T'en fais pas.
Je ne t'en veux pas.

III Ch. 6, p. 164
Ne t'inquiète pas.
Ça arrive à tout le monde.

EXPRESSING ATTITUDES AND OPINIONS

Agreeing I Ch. 2, p. 54
Oui, beaucoup.
Moi aussi.
Moi non plus.

III Ch. 9, p. 257

Je suis d'accord   Tu l'as dit!
  avec toi.   Tout à fait!
Tu as raison.

III Ch. 11, p. 318
Ça, c'est sûr.

Disagreeing I Ch. 2, p. 54
Moi, non.   Moi, si.
Pas moi.   Non, pas trop.

III Ch. 9, p. 257
Pas du tout.
Tu parles!
Tu te fiches de moi?
Tu rigoles!
Tu as tort.

III Ch. 11, p. 318
Tu délires ou quoi?
N'importe quoi!

Asking for opinions I Ch. 2, p. 61
Comment tu trouves... ?
Comment tu trouves ça?

I Ch. 10, p. 306
Il/Elle me va... ?
Il/Elle te (vous) plaît... ?
Tu aimes mieux... ou... ?

III Ch. 4, p. 98
Tu n'aimes pas... ?
Elle/Il te plaît,... ?
Qu'est-ce que tu penses de... ?
Qu'en penses-tu?

III Ch. 11, p. 318
Ça te branche,... ?
Ça te plaît,... ?

Expressing opinions I Ch. 2, p. 61
C'est...

I Ch. 9, p. 269
Oui, très chouette.
Oui, excellent.
Oui, très bon.
Oui, ça a été.
Oh, pas mauvais.

C'était épouvantable.
Très mauvais.

I Ch. 11, p. 337
C'était formidable!
Non, pas vraiment.
C'était un véritable cauchemar!
Je suis embêté(e).

II Ch. 11, p. 324
C'est drôle/amusant.
C'est une belle histoire.
C'est plein de rebondissements.
Il y a du suspense.
On ne s'ennuie pas.
C'est une histoire passionnante.
Je te le/la recommande.
Il n'y a pas d'histoire.
Ça casse pas des briques.
C'est...
    trop violent.   un navet.
    trop long.   du n'importe quoi.
    déprimant.   gentillet, sans plus.
    bête.

III Ch. 4, p. 98
Je le/la trouve...
Je l'aime bien.
Elle/Il me plaît beaucoup.
C'est très bien, ça.
J'aime bien ce genre de...
Je ne l'aime pas tellement.
Elle/Il ne me plaît pas du tout.
Je trouve qu'ils/elles font...
Ça fait vraiment...

III Ch. 11, p. 318
Je trouve ça...
Si, je l'aime beaucoup.
Ça me plaît beaucoup.
Ça m'éclate.
Je n'écoute que ça.
Ça ne me branche pas trop.

Wondering what happened and offering possible explanations II Ch. 9, p. 260
Je me demande...   Je crois que...
A mon avis,...   Je parie que...
Peut-être que...

Accepting explanations II Ch. 9, p. 260
Tu as peut-être raison. Ça se voit.
C'est possible.   Evidemment.

Rejecting explanations II Ch. 9, p. 260
A mon avis, tu te trompes.
Ce n'est pas possible.
Je ne crois pas.

Asking for judgments III Ch. 9, p. 265

C'était comment?
Comment tu as trouvé ça?

Making judgments III Ch. 9, p. 265

Ça m'a beaucoup plu.
J'ai trouvé ça pas mal/amusant.
Il y avait de...
Je ne me suis pas ennuyé(e) une seconde.
Ça m'a bien fait rire.
C'est nul/lourd.
C'est un navet.
Ça n'a aucun intérêt.
Je n'ai pas du tout aimé.
Ça ne m'a pas emballé(e).
Je me suis ennuyé(e) à mourir.

Making observations III Ch. 11, p. 326

Ce qui est incroyable, c'est...
Ce qui saute aux yeux, c'est...
Ce qui me branche vraiment, c'est...
Ce que je trouve super, c'est...
Ce que j'adore/j'aime, c'est...

Giving impressions III Ch. 11, p. 326

On dirait que...
Il me semble que...
J'ai l'impression que...
Ils ont l'air de...

Making comparisons III Ch. 8, p. 232

Ce n'était pas comme ça.
Ici,... tandis que...   moins de... que
plus de... que   autant de... que...
plus... que...   moins... que...
aussi... que...

Bragging III Ch. 10, p. 287

C'est fastoche, ça!
C'est pas pour me vanter, mais moi,...
Oh, j'en ai vu d'autres.
C'est moi, le/la meilleur(e).
C'est moi qui... le mieux.

Flattering III Ch. 10, p. 287

Tu es fortiche/calé(e).
Alors là, tu m'épates!
Tu en as, du courage.
Tu es vraiment le/la meilleur(e).
Tu es le/la... le/la plus... que je connaisse.

Teasing III Ch. 10, p. 290

Tu es amoureux(-euse) ou quoi?
Non mais, tu t'es pas regardé(e)!
Réveille-toi un peu!
Tu en rates pas une, toi!
Arrête de délirer!

Responding to teasing III Ch. 10, p. 290

Lâche-moi, tu veux?
Je t'ai pas demandé ton avis.
Oh, ça va, hein!
Qu'est-ce que tu en sais?
Ben, ça peut arriver à tout le monde.
Et toi, arrête de m'embêter!

Paying a compliment (about clothing)
I Ch. 10, p. 306

C'est tout à fait ton/votre style.
Il/Elle te (vous) va très bien.
Il/Elle va très bien avec...
Je le/la/les trouve...
C'est parfait.

II Ch. 2, p. 44

Il/Elle est vraiment bien, ton/ta...
Il/Elle est cool, ton/ta...

(about food) II Ch. 3, p. 72

C'est vraiment bon!
C'était délicieux!

(about clothing) III Ch. 4, p. 108

Je te trouve très bien comme ça.
Ça fait très bien.
Que tu es... avec ça!
C'est tout à fait toi.
C'est assorti à...
Ça te va comme un gant.
Ça te va très bien!

Responding to compliments II Ch. 2, p. 44

Tu trouves?
C'est vrai? (Vraiment?)
C'est gentil!

II Ch. 3, p. 72

Ce n'est pas grand-chose.

III Ch. 4, p. 108

Ça te plaît, vraiment?
Tu crois?
Oh, c'est un vieux truc.
Oh, tu sais, je ne l'ai pas payé(e) cher.

Criticizing I Ch. 10, p. 306

Il/Elle ne te (vous) va pas du tout.
Il/Elle ne va pas du tout avec...
Il/Elle est (Ils/Elles sont) trop...
Je le/la/les trouve...

Expressing indifference II Ch. 6, p. 164

C'était...
    assez bien.
    comme ci comme ça.
    pas mal.
Mouais.
Plus ou moins.

III Ch. 9, p. 257
Je m'en fiche.
Ça m'est vraiment égal.
Peu importe.

Emphasizing likes **II Ch. 4, p. 108**
Ce que j'aime bien, c'est...
Ce que je préfère, c'est...
Ce qui me plaît, c'est (de)...

Emphasizing dislikes **II Ch. 4, p. 108**
Ce que je n'aime pas, c'est...
Ce qui m'ennuie, c'est (de)...
Ce qui ne me plaît pas, c'est (de)...

Expressing dissatisfaction **II Ch. 6, p. 164**
C'était...
    ennuyeux.
    mortel.
    nul.
    sinistre.
Sûrement pas!
Je me suis ennuyé(e).

III Ch. 1, p. 9
C'était pas terrible.
Pas trop bien.
Ça ne s'est pas très bien passé.

Expressing enthusiasm **II Ch. 6, p. 164**
C'était...
    magnifique.
    incroyable.
    superbe.
    sensass.
Ça m'a beaucoup plu.
Je me suis beaucoup amusé(e).

III Ch. 1, p. 9
C'était chouette!
Ça s'est très bien passé!
Super!

III Ch. 2, p. 45
Qu'est-ce que c'est... !
Ce que c'est bien!
C'est... comme tout!
Ça me branche!

Expressing boredom **III Ch. 2, p. 45**
Ça m'embête!
Ça me casse les pieds!
Ça m'ennuie à mourir!

This list presents vocabulary words that you've already learned in the Level 1 and Level 2 books, but may have forgotten. You may want to use them when you're working on the activities in the textbook and in the workbooks. If you can't find the words you need here, try the English-French and French-English vocabulary lists beginning on page R55.

Clothing and Accessories

un anorak	ski jacket
des baskets (f.)	sneakers
un blouson	jacket
des bottes (f.)	boots
des boucles d'oreilles (f.)	earrings
un bracelet	bracelet
un cardigan	sweater
une casquette	cap
une ceinture	belt
un chapeau	hat
des chaussettes (f.)	socks
des chaussures (f.)	shoes
une chemise	shirt (men's)
un chemisier	shirt (women's)
une cravate	tie
une écharpe	scarf
un foulard	scarf
des gants (m.)	gloves
un imperméable	raincoat
un jean	pair of jeans
une jupe	skirt
des lunettes (f.) de soleil	sunglasses
un maillot de bain	bathing suit
un manteau	coat
une montre	watch
un pantalon	(pair of) pants
un portefeuille	wallet
un pull	pullover sweater
une robe	dress
des sandales (f.)	sandals
un short	pair of shorts
un sweat-shirt	sweatshirt
un tee-shirt	T-shirt
une veste	suit jacket, blazer

Fabrics and Colors

blanc(he)(s)	white
bleu(e)(s)	blue
en cuir	leather
en coton	cotton
en jean	denim
gris(e)(s)	grey
jaune(s)	yellow
marron (inv.)	brown
noir(e)(s)	black
orange (inv.)	orange
rose(s)	pink
rouge(s)	red
vert(e)(s)	green
violet(te)(s)	purple

Describing Clothes

à la mode	in style
branché(e)(s)	cool
chic	chic
court(e)(s)	short
démodé(e)(s)	out of style
grand(e)(s)	big
horrible(s)	terrible
large(s)	baggy
mignon(ne)(s)	cute
moche(s)	ugly
petit(e)(s)	small
rétro	old-fashioned
sensass	fantastic
serré(e)(s)	tight

Family Members

le beau-père	stepfather, father-in-law
la belle-fille	stepdaughter, daughter-in-law
la belle-mère	stepmother, mother-in-law
le cousin (la cousine)	cousin
le demi-frère	half-brother/stepbrother, brother-in-law
la demi-sœur	half-sister/stepsister, sister-in-law
l'enfant (unique)	(only) child
la femme	wife

la fille	daughter
le fils	son
le frère	brother
la grand-mère	grandmother
le grand-père	grandfather
le mari	husband
la mère	mother
l'oncle (m.)	uncle
le parent	parent, relative
le père	father
la sœur	sister
la tante	aunt

Foods and Beverages

les ananas (m.)	pineapple
les avocats (m.)	avocados
la baguette	French bread
les bananes (f.)	bananas
le beurre	butter
le bœuf	beef
le café	coffee
les carottes (f.)	carrots
les céréales (f.)	cereal
les champignons	mushrooms
un chocolat chaud	hot chocolate
les citrons	lemons
un coca	cola
la confiture	jam
les crevettes (f.)	shrimp
les croissants (m.)	croissants
un croque-monsieur	toasted ham and cheese sandwich
une eau minérale	mineral water
les escargots (m.)	snails
la farine	flour
les fraises (f.)	strawberries
les frites (f.)	French fries
le fromage	cheese
le fruit	fruit
les fruits (m.) de mer	seafood
le gâteau	cake
la glace	ice cream
les gombos (m.)	okra
les goyaves (f.)	guavas
les haricots (m.)	beans
les haricots verts (m.)	green beans
un hot-dog	hot dog
les huîtres (f.)	oysters
un jus d'orange	orange juice
un jus de pomme	apple juice
un jus de raisin	grape juice
le lait	milk
les légumes	vegetables
une limonade	sparkling lemon soda
le maïs	corn
les mangues (f.)	mangoes

les noix de coco (f.)	coconuts
les œufs (m.)	eggs
les oignons (m.)	onions
les oranges (f.)	oranges
le pain	bread
les papayes (f.)	papayas
les pâtes (f.)	pasta
le pâté	pâté
les pêches (f.)	peaches
les petits pois (m.)	peas
la pizza	pizza
les poires (f.)	pears
le poisson	fish
les pommes (f.)	apples
les pommes de terre (f.)	potatoes
le porc	pork
le poulet	chicken
du raisin	grapes
une religieuse	cream puff pastry
le riz	rice
le rôti de bœuf	roast beef
la salade	salad
des salades	heads of lettuce
un sandwich	sandwich
le saucisson	salami
le sel	salt
le sucre	sugar
un steak-frites	steak and French fries
la tarte	pie
les tomates (f.)	tomatoes
la viande	meat
la volaille	poultry
le yaourt	yogurt

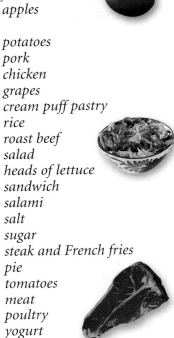

Sports

faire de l'aérobic	to do aerobics
faire du jogging	to jog
faire de la musculation	to lift weights
faire du patin à glace	to ice-skate
faire de la randonnée	to go hiking
faire du roller en ligne	to in-line skate
faire du ski	to ski
faire du ski nautique	to water-ski
faire du vélo	to bike
faire de la voile	to go sailing
jouer au foot(ball)	to play soccer
jouer au football américain	to play football
jouer au golf	to play golf
jouer au hockey	to play hockey
jouer au tennis	to play tennis
jouer au volley(-ball)	to play volleyball

This list presents extra vocabulary words you're not responsible for on tests and that you may want to use when you're working on the activities in the textbook and in the workbooks. If you can't find the words you need here, try the English-French and French-English vocabulary lists beginning on page R55.

Adjectives

calm	*calme*
cheerful	*joyeux (joyeuse)*
cultured	*cultivé(e)*
discrete	*discret (discrète)*
easy to get along with	*facile à vivre*
enthusiastic	*enthousiaste*
exasperating	*exaspérant(e)*
generous	*généreux (généreuse)*
honest	*honnête*
hypocritical	*hypocrite*
independent	*indépendant(e)*
likable	*aimable*
loves to party	*fêtard(e)*
moody	*versatile*
not with it	*pas futé(e)*
obnoxious	*pénible*
open	*ouvert(e)*
polite	*poli(e)*
pretentious	*prétentieux (prétentieuse)*
quick-witted	*vif (vive)*
reserved	*réservé(e)*
selfish	*égoïste*
sensitive	*sensible*
sincere	*sincère*
snobbish	*snob*
sociable	*sociable*
spontaneous	*spontané(e)*
talkative	*bavard(e)*
understanding	*compréhensif (compréhensive)*
weird	*bizarre*

Adventurous Activities

to fly a plane	*piloter un avion*
to go bungee jumping	*faire du saut à l'élastique*
to go mountain-climbing	*faire de l'alpinisme*
to go on a photo safari	*aller faire un safari-photo*
to go parachuting	*sauter en parachute*
to go rafting	*faire la descente d'une rivière*
to go rock-climbing	*faire de l'escalade*
to go skydiving	*sauter en chute libre*
to go spelunking	*faire de la spéléologie*
to go surfing	*faire du surf*
to race cars	*faire des courses de voitures*
to ride in a helicopter	*faire un tour en hélicoptère*

At the Beach

to build sandcastles	*faire des châteaux de sable*
to feed the seagulls	*nourrir les mouettes* (f.)
to float	*flotter*
to get sunburned	*attraper un coup de soleil*
to look for seashells	*chercher/ramasser des coquillages*
to play in the waves	*sauter/jouer dans les vagues*
to put on suntan lotion	*mettre de la crème solaire*
to sunbathe	*prendre un bain de soleil*
to walk along the shore	*se promener au bord de la mer*

Cars and Driving

accident	*un accident*
airbag	*un airbag*
antifreeze	*de l'antigel* (m.)
battery	*la batterie*
to brake	*freiner*
brake pedal	*la pédale de frein*
bumper	*le pare-chocs*
car seat	*le siège*
clutch	*la pédale d'embrayage*

dashboard	le tableau de bord
entrance ramp	l'entrée de l'autoroute (f.)
fender	l'aile (f.)
gas pedal	la pédale d'accélération
to get a ticket	avoir un P.V. (procès-verbal)
headlights	les phares (m.)
hood	le capot
horn	le klaxon
hubcap	l'enjoliveur (m.)
jack	le cric
license plate	la plaque d'immatriculation
motor	le moteur
muffler	le silencieux
parking meter	le parcmètre
radiator	le radiateur
rearview mirror	le rétroviseur
seat belt	la ceinture de sécurité
spark plugs	les bougies
speed limit	la vitesse maximale (la vitesse est limitée à...)
to stall	caler
steering wheel	le volant
sticker	un autocollant
stop sign	un stop
tow truck	une dépanneuse
traffic light	un feu (m.) rouge
transmission	la transmission
trunk	le coffre
turn signal	le clignotant
windshield wipers	les essuie-glaces (m.)
to yield	laisser la priorité/céder le passage

Clothing, Fabrics, Colors

ankle boots	des bottines (f.)
beige	beige
bell bottoms	un pattes d'eph
button	un bouton
checked	à carreaux
collar	un col
colorful	coloré(e), vif/vive
dark	foncé(e)
eyeglasses	des lunettes (f.)
flowered	à fleurs
gold	doré(e)
handkerchief	un mouchoir
khaki	kaki
lace	la dentelle
light	clair(e)
linen	en lin, en toile

loafers	des mocassins (m.)
nylon	en nylon
pajamas	un pyjama
printed	imprimé(e)
short/long sleeved	à manches courtes/longues
sleeve	une manche
slippers	des pantoufles (f.)
suede	en daim
suspenders	des bretelles (f.)
tank top	un débardeur
turquoise	turquoise
underwear	les sous-vêtements (m.)
velvet	zen velours
windbreaker	un coupe-vent
zipper	une fermeture éclair

Environment

acid rain	la pluie acide
car exhaust	l'échappement (m.)
chemical-free	sans produits chimiques
destruction of the tropical rain forest	la destruction de la forêt tropicale
droughts	les périodes (f.) de sécheresse
endangered species	les espèces (f.) en voie de disparition
erosion	l'érosion (f.) du sol
extinct animals	les espèces (f.) disparues
famine	la famine
global warming	le réchauffement de la planète
greenhouse effect	l'effet (m.) de serre
industrial waste	les déchets (m.) industriels
landfills	les décharges (f.)
melting of the polar ice caps	la fonte des glaces polaires
nuclear waste	les déchets (m.) nucléaires
organic foods	la nourriture biologique
overpopulation	la surpopulation
ozone layer	la couche d'ozone
pesticides	les pesticides (m.)
pollution	la pollution

Farm Life

barn	*une grange*
cage	*une cage*
chicken coop	*un poulailler*
fence	*une barrière, une clôture*
to get up before dawn	*se lever à l'aube*
to groom the horses	*toiletter les chevaux*
to mill cotton	*filer le coton*
pen	*un enclos*
to plant crops	*planter des cultures*
to plow the fields	*labourer les champs*
to raise cattle	*élever du bétail*
stable	*une écurie*
to take the crops to market	*aller vendre les produits agricoles au marché*
tractor	*un tracteur*
trough	*un abreuvoir* (drink), *une auge* (food)
truck	*un camion*

Foods and Beverages

asparagus	*des asperges* (f.)
bacon	*du bacon*
bland	*fade*
Brussels sprouts	*des choux* (m.) *de Bruxelles*
cabbage	*du chou*
cauliflower	*du chou-fleur*
chestnut	*un marron*
cookie	*un biscuit*
cucumber	*un concombre*
cutlet	*une escalope*
doughnut	*un beignet*
duck	*un canard*
eggplant	*une aubergine*
fried eggs	*des œufs* (m.) *au plat*
garlic	*de l'ail* (m.)
grapefruit	*un pamplemousse*
hard-boiled egg	*un œuf dur*
honey	*du miel*
hot (spicy)	*fort(e), piquant(e)*
juicy	(fruit) *juteux (-euse);* (meat) *moelleux (-euse); tendre*
lamb	*l'agneau* (m.)
liver	*du foie*
margarine	*de la margarine*
marshmallows	*des guimauves* (f.)
mayonnaise	*de la mayonnaise*
melon	*un melon*
mustard	*de la moutarde*
nuts	*des noix* (f.)
onion	*un oignon*

peanut butter	*du beurre de cacahouètes*
pepper	(spice) *du poivre;* (vegetable) *un poivron*
pickle	*un cornichon*
popcorn	*du pop-corn*
potato chips	*des chips* (f.)
raspberry	*une framboise*
salmon	*du saumon*
scrambled eggs	*des œufs brouillés*
shellfish	*des fruits de mer* (m.)
soft-boiled egg	*un œuf à la coque*
spicy	*relevé(e)*
syrup	*du sirop*
tasty	*savoureux (savoureuse)*
veal	*du veau*
watermelon	*une pastèque*
zucchini	*une courgette*

In a Restaurant

bowl	*un bol*
chef	*le chef*
to clear the plates	*enlever les assiettes*
cup	*une tasse*
fork	*une fourchette*
glass	*un verre*
host/hostess	*le maître d'hôtel*
knife	*un couteau*
napkin	*une serviette*
pepper shaker	*la poivrière*
plate	*une assiette*
to refill the glass	*remplir le verre*
reservation	*une réservation*
salt shaker	*la salière*
saucer	*la soucoupe*
serving tray	*le plateau*
spoon	*une cuillère*
tablecloth	*la nappe*
tip	*un pourboire*

Friendship

to be sorry	*être désolé(e)*
to confide in someone	*se confier à quelqu'un*
to feel guilty	*se sentir coupable*

to get along with someone	*bien s'entendre avec quelqu'un*
to help someone do something	*aider quelqu'un à faire quelque chose*
to make friends	*se faire des amis*
to meet after school	*se retrouver après l'école*
to misunderstand	*mal comprendre*
to take the first step	*faire le premier pas*
to talk with friends	*discuter avec des amis*
to trust someone	*avoir confiance en quelqu'un*

Leisure Activities

to build a fire	*faire un feu*
to collect butterflies	*faire la collection de papillons*
to collect rocks	*collectionner les/ramasser des pierres*
to collect stamps	*collectionner les timbres*
to fly a kite	*faire voler un cerf-volant*
to go to a botanical garden	*aller au jardin botanique*
to go to a concert	*aller au concert*
to go to a festival	*aller à un festival*
to go to an art exhibit	*aller voir une exposition*
to paint	*faire de la peinture*
to pick wildflowers	*cueillir des fleurs sauvages*
to play cards	*jouer aux cartes*
to play checkers	*jouer aux dames*
to play chess	*jouer aux échecs*
to rent movies	*louer des vidéos*
to ride a skateboard	*faire du skate-board*
to sew	*coudre; faire de la couture*
to sing around the campfire	*chanter autour du feu de camp*
to visit friends	*rendre visite à des amis*

Makeup and Toiletries

aftershave lotion	*la lotion après-rasage*
bath towels	*les serviettes de toilette (f.)*
blowdryer	*le séchoir à cheveux*
brush	*une brosse (à cheveux)*
comb	*un peigne*

conditioner	*l'après-shampooing (m.); le conditionneur*
cotton balls	*des boules (f.) de coton; le coton à démaquiller*
cover stick	*le correcteur de teint*
dental floss	*le fil dentaire*
deodorant	*le déodorant*
eyeshadow	*l'ombre (f.) à paupières*
foundation	*le fond de teint*
hair gel	*le gel*
hair mousse	*la mousse*
hairspray	*la laque*
hand lotion	*la crème pour les mains*
lipstick	*le rouge à lèvres*
mascara	*le mascara*

mouthwash	*le bain de bouche*
razor	*le rasoir*
rouge	*le fard à joues*
shampoo	*le shampooing*
shaving cream	*la crème à raser*
soap	*le savon*
toothbrush	*la brosse à dents*
toothpaste	*le dentifrice*
tweezers	*la pince à épiler*
washcloth	*le gant de toilette*

Musical Instruments and Equipment

acoustic guitar	*une guitare acoustique*
CD player	*un lecteur de CD*
cello	*un violoncelle*
clarinet	*une clarinette*
cymbals	*des cymbales (f.)*
electric guitar	*une guitare électrique*
harp	*une harpe*
headphones	*un casque, des écouteurs (m.)*
hit (song)	*un tube*
mandolin	*une mandoline*
oboe	*un hautbois*
speakers	*des enceintes (f.), des baffles (m.)*
trombone	*un trombone*
tuba	*un tuba*
to turn on	*allumer*
turntable	*une platine*
Walkman®	*un walkman; un baladeur*

Nature

bushes	*des buissons* (m.)
cave	*une grotte*
cliff	*une falaise*
date palm	*un dattier*
desert	*le désert*
dunes	*les dunes* (f.)
dust	*la poussière*
fields	*des champs* (m.)
insects	*les insectes* (m.)
jungle	*la jungle*
leaves	*les feuilles* (f.)
mud	*la boue*
oasis	*une oasis*
palm tree	*un palmier*
plains	*une plaine*
plateau	*un plateau*
sand	*le sable*
stream	*un ruisseau*
swamp	*un marais*
valley	*une vallée*
vines	*les plantes grimpantes* (f.)
volcano	*un volcan*
waves	*les vagues* (f.)

Professions

archaeologist	*un(e) archéologue*
athlete	*un(e) athlète*
banker	*un(e) banquier(-ière)*

businessman/
  businesswoman
	un homme d'affaires
	  (une femme d'affaires)

carpenter	*un menuisier*
commercial artist	*un(e) dessinateur(-trice)*
dancer	*un(e) danseur(-euse)*
diplomat	*un(e) diplomate*
editor	*un(e) rédacteur(-trice)*
electrician	*un(e) électricien(ne)*
fashion model	*un mannequin*
homemaker	*un homme au foyer* *(une femme au foyer)*
insurance agent	*un agent d'assurances*
judge	*un juge*

manager (of a
  company)
	le/la directeur(-trice);
	  (of a store or restaurant)
	  le/la gérant(e)

painter	*un peintre*
programmer	*un(e) programmeur(-euse)*
psychiatrist	*un(e) psychiatre*
real-estate agent	*un agent immobilier*
scientist	*un(e) scientifique, un(e)* *chercheur(-euse)*

social worker	*un(e) assistant(e)* *social(e)*
soldier	*un soldat*
surgeon	*un(e) chirurgien(ne)*
truck driver	*un routier*
veterinarian	*un(e) vétérinaire*

Sea Life and Exploration

air tank	*une bouteille de plongée*
baracuda	*un barracuda*
claws	*les pinces* (f.)
current	*le courant*
deep water	*l'eau profonde* (f.), *les hauts-fonds* (m.)
deep-sea fishing	*la pêche hauturière,* *la pêche en haute mer*
dolphin	*un dauphin*

fins (diving)	*les palmes* (f.);
	  (fish) *les nageoires*
	  (f.); (shark)
	  l'aileron (m.)

fishing line	*la ligne de pêche*
flippers	*les nageoires* (f.), *les palmes* (f.)
gills	*les ouïes* (f.), *les branchies* (f.)
high tide	*la marée haute*
piranha	*un piranha*
saltwater	*l'eau* (f.) *de mer*
scales	*les écailles* (f.)
scuba gear	*l'équipement* (m.) *de plongée*
scuba mask	*un masque de plongée*
seal	*un phoque*
shallow water	*l'eau peu profonde* (f.), *les bas-fonds* (m.)
snorkel	*un tuba*
tentacles	*les tentacules* (m.)
tropical fish	*des poissons* (m.) *tropicaux*
walrus	*un morse*
whale	*une baleine*

TV and Movies

action scenes	*les scènes (f.) d'action*
actors	*les acteurs*
actresses	*les actrices*
car chase	*une poursuite de voitures*
costumes	*les costumes (m.)*
digital sound	*le son digital*
direction	*la mise en scène*
director	*le metteur en scène, le réalisateur*
ending	*le dénouement final*
hero	*un héros*
DVD disc	*un DVD*
lighting	*la lumière*
movie soundtrack	*la bande originale d'un film*
producer	*le producteur*
scenery	*les décors (m.)*
sound effects	*le bruitage*
special effects	*les effets (m.) spéciaux*
star	*une star, une vedette*
story	*l'histoire (f.)*
stunts	*les cascades (f.)*
villain	*le méchant; le mauvais*

Wild Animals

antelope	*une antilope*
baboon	*un babouin*
bat	*une chauve-souris*
buffalo	*un buffle*
chimpanzee	*un chimpanzé*
crocodile	*un crocodile*
flamingo	*un flamant*
gazelle	*une gazelle*
gorilla	*un gorille*
gnu	*un gnou*
hyena	*une hyène*
leopard	*un léopard*
lizard	*un lézard*
ostrich	*une autruche*
panther	*une panthère*
vulture	*un vautour*

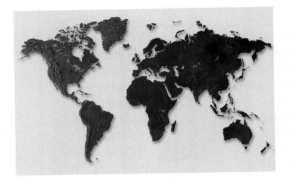

Continents

Africa	*l'Afrique (f.)*
Antarctica	*l'Antarctique (f.)*
Asia	*l'Asie (f.)*
Australia	*l'Australie (f.)*
Europe	*l'Europe (f.)*
North America	*l'Amérique (f.) du Nord*
South America	*l'Amérique (f.) du Sud*

Countries

Argentina	*l'Argentine (f.)*
Australia	*l'Australie (f.)*
Austria	*l'Autriche (f.)*
Cameroon	*le Cameroun*
Chad	*le Tchad*
Cuba	*Cuba (no article)*
Egypt	*l'Egypte (f.)*
Greece	*la Grèce*
Guinea	*la Guinée*
Holland	*la Hollande*
India	*l'Inde (f.)*
Ireland	*l'Irlande (f.)*
Israel	*Israël (m.) (no article)*
Jamaica	*la Jamaïque*
Jordan	*la Jordanie*
Lebanon	*le Liban*
Libya	*la Libye*
Luxembourg	*le Luxembourg*
Mexico	*le Mexique*
Monaco	*Monaco (f.) (no article)*
Netherlands	*les Pays-Bas (m.)*
North Korea	*la Corée du Nord*
Peru	*le Pérou*
Philippines	*les Philippines (f.)*
Poland	*la Pologne*
Portugal	*le Portugal*
Puerto Rico	*Porto Rico (no article)*
South Korea	*la Corée du Sud*
Syria	*la Syrie*
Turkey	*la Turquie*
Vietnam	*le Viêt-nam*

States

Alabama	*l'Alabama* (m.)
Alaska	*l'Alaska* (m.)
Arizona	*l'Arizona* (m.)
Arkansas	*l'Arkansas* (m.)
California	*la Californie*
Colorado	*le Colorado*
Connecticut	*le Connecticut*
Delaware	*le Delaware*
Florida	*la Floride*
Georgia	*la Géorgie*
Hawaii	*Hawaii* (no article)
Idaho	*l'Idaho* (m.)
Illinois	*l'Illinois* (m.)
Indiana	*l'Indiana* (m.)
Iowa	*l'Iowa* (m.)
Kansas	*le Kansas*
Kentucky	*le Kentucky*
Louisiana	*la Louisiane*
Maine	*le Maine*
Maryland	*le Maryland*
Massachusetts	*le Massachusetts*
Michigan	*le Michigan*
Minnesota	*le Minnesota*
Mississippi	*le Mississippi*
Missouri	*le Missouri*
Montana	*le Montana*
Nebraska	*le Nebraska*
Nevada	*le Nevada*
New Hampshire	*le New Hampshire*
New Jersey	*le New Jersey*
New Mexico	*le Nouveau-Mexique*
New York	*l'Etat de New York*
North Carolina	*la Caroline du Nord*
North Dakota	*le Dakota du Nord*
Ohio	*l'Ohio* (m.)
Oklahoma	*l'Oklahoma* (m.)
Oregon	*l'Orégon* (m.)
Pennsylvania	*la Pennsylvanie*
Rhode Island	*le Rhode Island*
South Carolina	*la Caroline du Sud*
South Dakota	*le Dakota du Sud*
Tennessee	*le Tennessee*
Texas	*le Texas*
Utah	*l'Utah* (m.)
Vermont	*le Vermont*
Virginia	*la Virginie*
Washington	*l'Etat de Washington*
West Virginia	*la Virginie-Occidentale*
Wisconsin	*le Wisconsin*
Wyoming	*le Wyoming*

Cities

Algiers	*Alger*
Brussels	*Bruxelles*
Cairo	*Le Caire*
Geneva	*Genève*
Lisbon	*Lisbonne*
London	*Londres*
Montreal	*Montréal*
Moscow	*Moscou*
New Orleans	*La Nouvelle-Orléans*
Quebec City	*Québec*
Tangier	*Tanger*
Venice	*Venise*
Vienna	*Vienne*

Other Geographical Terms

Alps	*les Alpes* (f.)
Atlantic Ocean	*l'Atlantique* (m.), *l'océan* (m.) *Atlantique*
border	*la frontière*
capital	*la capitale*
continent	*un continent*
country	*un pays*
English Channel	*la Manche*
hill	*une colline*
lake	*un lac*
latitude	*la latitude*
longitude	*la longitude*
Mediterranean Sea	*la mer Méditerranée*
North Africa	*l'Afrique* (f.) *du Nord*
the North Pole	*le pôle Nord*
ocean	*l'océan* (m.)
Pacific Ocean	*le Pacifique, l'océan* (m.) *Pacifique*
peninsula	*une presqu'île*
plain	*une plaine*
Pyrenees	*les Pyrénées* (f.)
river	*un fleuve*

Sahara desert	le désert du Sahara
sea	la mer
the South Pole	le pôle Sud
state	un état
valley	une vallée

Computers

l'ordinateur   le lecteur de CD-ROM   le CD-ROM

la souris

le clavier

CD-ROM	le CD-ROM, le disque optique compact
CD-ROM drive	le lecteur de CD-ROM, l'unité (f.) de CD-ROM
to click	cliquer
computer	l'ordinateur (m.)
delete key	la touche d'effacement
disk drive	le lecteur de disquettes, l'unité (f.) de disquettes

diskette, floppy disk	la disquette, la disquette souple
to drag	glisser, déplacer
e-mail	le courrier électronique, la messagerie électronique
file	le dossier
file/folder	le fichier
hard drive	le disque dur
homepage	la page d'accueil
Internet	Internet (m.)
keyboard	le clavier
keyword	le mot-clé
log on	l'ouverture d'une session, l'ouverture (f.) de session
modem	le modem
monitor	le moniteur
mouse	la souris
password	le mot de passe
to print	imprimer
printer	l'imprimante (f.)
to quit	quitter
to record	enregistrer
return key	la touche de retour
to save	sauvegarder, enregistrer
screen	l'écran (m.)
to search	chercher, rechercher
search engine	le moteur de recherche, l'outil (m.) de recherche
to send	envoyer
software	le logiciel
Web site	le site du Web, le site W3
World Wide Web	le World Wide Web, le Web, le W3

Sound	Letter Combination	IPA Symbol	Example
The sounds [y] and [u]	the letter **u** the letter combination **ou**	/y/ /u/	une nous
The nasal sound [ɑ̃]	the letter combination **an** the letter combination **am** the letter combination **en** the letter combination **em**	/ɑ̃/	anglais jambon comment temps
The vowel sounds [ø] and [œ]	the letter combination **eu** the letter combination **eu**	/ø/ /œ/	deux heure
The nasal sounds [ɔ̃], [ɛ̃], and [œ̃]	the letter combination **on** the letter combination **om** the letter combination **in** the letter combination **im** the letter combination **ain** the letter combination **aim** the letter combination **(i)en** the letter combination **un** the letter combination **um**	/ɔ̃/ /ɛ̃/ /œ̃/	pardon nombre cousin impossible copain faim bien lundi humble
The sounds [o] and [ɔ]	the letter combination **au** the letter combination **eau** the letter **ô** the letter **o**	/o/ /ɔ/	jaune beau rôle carotte
The vowel sounds [e] and [ɛ]	the letter combination **ez** the letter combination **er** the letter combination **ait** the letter combination **ais** the letter combination **ei** the letter **ê**	/e/ /ɛ/	apportez trouver fait français neige bête
The glides [j], [w], and [ɥ]	the letter **i** the letter combination **ill** the letter combination **oi** the letter combination **oui** the letter combination **ui**	/j/ /w/ /ɥ/	mieux maillot moi Louis huit
h, th, ch, and gn	the letter **h** the letter combination **th** the letter combination **ch** the letter combination **gn**	/ʼ/ /t/ /ʃ/ /ɲ/	les halls théâtre chocolat oignon
The **r** sound	the letter **r**	/ʀ/	rouge vert

Numbers

LES NOMBRES CARDINAUX

0	zéro	**20**	vingt	**80**	quatre-vingts
1	un(e)	**21**	vingt et un(e)	**81**	quatre-vingt-un(e)
2	deux	**22**	vingt-deux	**82**	quatre-vingt-deux
3	trois	**23**	vingt-trois	**90**	quatre-vingt-dix
4	quatre	**24**	vingt-quatre	**91**	quatre-vingt-onze
5	cinq	**25**	vingt-cinq	**92**	quatre-vingt-douze
6	six	**26**	vingt-six	**100**	cent
7	sept	**27**	vingt-sept	**101**	cent un
8	huit	**28**	vingt-huit	**200**	deux cents
9	neuf	**29**	vingt-neuf	**201**	deux cent un
10	dix	**30**	trente	**300**	trois cents
11	onze	**31**	trente et un(e)	**800**	huit cents
12	douze	**32**	trente-deux	**1.000**	mille
13	treize	**40**	quarante	**2.000**	deux mille
14	quatorze	**50**	cinquante	**3.000**	trois mille
15	quinze	**60**	soixante	**10.000**	dix mille
16	seize	**70**	soixante-dix	**19.000**	dix-neuf mille
17	dix-sept	**71**	soixante et onze	**40.000**	quarante mille
18	dix-huit	**72**	soixante-douze	**500.000**	cinq cent mille
19	dix-neuf	**73**	soixante-treize	**1.000.000**	un million

- The word **et** is used only in 21, 31, 41, 51, 61, and 71.
- **Vingt** (**trente, quarante,** and so on) **et une** is used when the number refers to a feminine noun: **trente et une cassettes.**
- The **s** is dropped from **quatre-vingts** and is not added to multiples of **cent** when these numbers are followed by another number: **quatre-vingt-cinq; deux cents,** *but* **deux cent six.** The number **mille** never takes an **s** to agree with a noun: **deux mille insectes.**
- **Un million** is followed by **de** + a noun: **un million de francs.**
- In writing numbers, a period is used in French where a comma is used in English.

LES NOMBRES ORDINAUX

1er, 1ère	premier, première	**9e**	neuvième	**17e**	dix-septième
2e	deuxième	**10e**	dixième	**18e**	dix-huitième
3e	troisième	**11e**	onzième	**19e**	dix-neuvième
4e	quatrième	**12e**	douzième	**20e**	vingtième
5e	cinquième	**13e**	treizième	**21e**	vingt et unième
6e	sixième	**14e**	quatorzième	**22e**	vingt-deuxième
7e	septième	**15e**	quinzième	**30e**	trentième
8e	huitième	**16e**	seizième	**40e**	quarantième

ADJECTIVES

REGULAR ADJECTIVES

In French, adjectives agree in gender and number with the nouns that they modify. A regular adjective has four forms: masculine singular, feminine singular, masculine plural, and feminine plural.

	Singular	Plural
MASCULINE	un homme **gourmand**	des hommes **gourmands**
FEMININE	une femme **gourmande**	des femmes **gourmandes**

When using the phrase **avoir l'air** + adjective, remember that the adjective agrees in number and gender with the subject, not with **l'air.**

Ma mère avait l'air **fâchée.**   Marc a l'air **déprimé** aujourd'hui.

ADJECTIVES THAT END IN AN UNACCENTED -E

An adjective that ends in an unaccented **-e** has one form for masculine singular and feminine singular. To form the plural of these adjectives, add an **-s** to the singular form.

	Singular	Plural
MASCULINE	un frère **pénible**	des garçons **pénibles**
FEMININE	une sœur **pénible**	des filles **pénibles**

ADJECTIVES THAT END IN -S

When the masculine singular form of an adjective ends in an **-s,** the masculine plural form does not change. The feminine forms follow the rules for regular adjectives.

	Singular	Plural
MASCULINE	un tapis **gris**	des tapis **gris**
FEMININE	une robe **grise**	des robes **grises**

ADJECTIVES THAT END IN -EUX

Adjectives that end in **-eux** do not change in the masculine plural. The feminine singular form of these adjectives is made by replacing the **-x** with **-se.** To form the feminine plural, replace the **-x** with **-ses.**

	Singular	Plural
MASCULINE	un homme **furieux**	des hommes **furieux**
FEMININE	une femme **furieuse**	des femmes **furieuses**

ADJECTIVES THAT END IN -IF

To make the feminine singular form of adjectives that end in **-if,** replace **-if** with **-ive.** To make the plural forms of these adjectives, add an **-s** to the singular forms.

	Singular	Plural
MASCULINE	un garçon **sportif**	des garçons **sportifs**
FEMININE	une fille **sportive**	des filles **sportives**

ADJECTIVES THAT END IN -IEN

To make the feminine singular and feminine plural forms of adjectives that end in **-ien** in their masculine singular form, add **-ne** and **-nes.** Add an **-s** to form the masculine plural.

	Singular	Plural
MASCULINE	un garçon **canadien**	des garçons **canadiens**
FEMININE	une fille **canadienne**	des filles **canadiennes**

ADJECTIVES THAT DOUBLE THE LAST CONSONANT

To make the adjectives **bon, gentil, gros, mignon, mortel, nul,** and **violet** agree with a feminine noun, double the last consonant and add an **-e.** To make the plural forms, add an **-s** to the singular forms. Notice that with **gros,** the masculine singular and masculine plural forms are the same.

SINGULAR					
MASCULINE	bon	gentil	gros	mignon	nul	violet
FEMININE	bonne	gentille	grosse	mignonne	nulle	violette

PLURAL					
MASCULINE	bons	gentils	gros	mignons	nuls	violets
FEMININE	bonnes	gentilles	grosses	mignonnes	nulles	violettes

INVARIABLE ADJECTIVES

Some adjectives such as **marron, orange,** and **super** are invariable.

Il me faut une montre **marron** et des baskets **orange.**

IRREGULAR ADJECTIVES

The following table summarizes the forms of the irregular adjectives **beau, nouveau,** and **vieux.**

	beau	nouveau	vieux
MASCULINE SINGULAR	un **beau** jardin	un **nouveau** lit	un **vieux** musée
BEFORE VOWEL SOUND	un **bel** homme	un **nouvel** anorak	un **vieil** imperméable
FEMININE SINGULAR	une **belle** maison	une **nouvelle** lampe	une **vieille** gare
MASCULINE PLURAL	de **beaux** jardins	de **nouveaux** lits	de **vieux** musées
FEMININE PLURAL	de **belles** maisons	de **nouvelles** lampes	de **vieilles** gares

POSITION OF ADJECTIVES

In French, adjectives are usually placed after the noun that they modify.

C'est un film **déprimant!**

However, certain adjectives are usually placed before the noun. These adjectives refer to the beauty, age, goodness, or size of the nouns they modify. Some of these adjectives are **beau (belle), bon, grand, jeune, joli, petit,** and **vieux (vieille).**

DEMONSTRATIVE ADJECTIVES

This, that, these, and *those* are demonstrative adjectives. In French, there are two masculine singular forms: **ce** and **cet.** You use **cet** before a masculine singular noun that begins with a vowel sound. Demonstrative adjectives always precede the nouns that they modify.

	Singular Before a Consonant	Singular Before a Vowel Sound	Plural
MASCULINE	ce cadre	cet imperméable	ces vases
FEMININE	cette main	cette écharpe	ces chansons

POSSESSIVE ADJECTIVES

Possessive adjectives come before the noun that they modify, and agree in number and gender with that noun. Before any singular noun that begins with a vowel sound, use the masculine singular form, **mon ami(e), ton ami(e), son ami(e).**

	Masculine Singular	**Feminine Singular**	**Masc./Fem. Singular Before a Vowel Sound**	**Masc./Fem. Plural**
my	**mon** jardin	**ma** maison	**mon** armoire	**mes** étagères
your	**ton** salon	**ta** cuisine	**ton** anorak	**tes** bottes
his, her, its	**son** tapis	**sa** lampe	**son** imperméable	**ses** mains

The possessive adjectives for *our, your,* and *their* have only two forms, singular and plural.

	Singular	**Plural**
our	**notre** jardin	**nos** armoires
your	**votre** maison	**vos** chambres
their	**leur** salon	**leurs** posters

ADJECTIVES AS NOUNS

To use an adjective as a noun, add a definite article before the adjective. The article and adjective that you use agree in number and gender with the noun that they replace.

—Tu aimes le tapis bleu ou **le gris?**
  Do you like the blue rug or the grey one?

—J'aime **le bleu.**
  I like the blue one.

—Vous préférez **les bottes noires** ou **les grises?**
  Do you prefer the black boots or the grey ones?

—Je préfère **les noires.**
  I prefer the black ones.

ADVERBS

ADVERBS OF FREQUENCY

To tell how often you do or used to do something, you use adverbs of frequency. Some adverbs of frequency are **de temps en temps** *(from time to time)*, **d'habitude** *(usually)*, **... fois par semaine** *(... time(s) a week)*, **souvent** *(often)*, **quelquefois** *(sometimes)*, **rarement** *(rarely)*, and **ne... jamais** *(never)*.

Most adverbs follow the conjugated verb. **Ne (N')... jamais** is placed around the conjugated verb. With the **passé composé**, the adverb is placed before the past participle.

> Nathalie téléphone **souvent** à ses amis.

> Je **n'ai jamais** fait de plongée.

> J'ai **beaucoup** mangé.

Adverbs made up of more than one word can be placed at the beginning or the end of a sentence.

> **D'habitude,** je ne mange pas de viande.

> Je fais des abdominaux **trois fois par semaine.**

ARTICLES

INDEFINITE ARTICLES

To refer to whole items, you use the indefinite articles **un, une,** and **des.** Remember that the indefinite articles agree in number and gender with the nouns they modify.

	Singular	Plural
MASCULINE	**un** rôti	**des** œufs
FEMININE	**une** tarte	**des** crevettes

PARTITIVE ARTICLES

To refer to only *some of* or *a portion of* an item, you use the partitive articles **du, de la,** and **de l'. Du** and **de la** modify masculine and feminine singular nouns, respectively. **De l'** is used to modify a masculine or feminine noun that begins with a vowel sound.

> Donne-moi **du** poisson, s'il te plaît.   Je voudrais **de la** mousse au chocolat.
> Tu veux **de l'**omelette, Marc?

NEGATION WITH ARTICLES

When the main verb of the sentence is negated, the indefinite and the partitive articles usually change to **de.** Definite articles remain the same after a negative verb.

> Karim prend **de l'**eau minérale.   —>   Karim ne prend pas **d'**eau minérale.
> Je vais acheter **des** fleurs.   —>   Je ne vais pas acheter **de** fleurs.
> J'ai **le** nouveau C.D. de MC Solaar. —>   Je n'ai pas **le** nouveau C.D. de MC Solaar.

THE COMPARATIVE

THE COMPARATIVE

To say that there is *more of, less of,* or *as many/much of* something in French, you use **plus de, moins de,** and **autant de** before the noun. You use **que** *(than/as)* to continue the comparison.

Il a **plus d'argent que** son frère.	*He has **more** money **than** his brother.*
Un train fait **moins de** bruit **qu'**un avion.	*A train makes **less** noise **than** an airplane.*
J'ai **autant de** livres **que** toi.	*I have **as many** books **as you.***

To compare adjectives, you use **plus, moins,** or **aussi** *(as)*. Just as with nouns, you use **que** to continue the comparison.

Janine est **plus** belle **que** Madeleine.	*Janine is **prettier than** Madeleine.*
Pierre est **moins** grand **que** son frère.	*Pierre is **shorter** (less tall) **than** his brother.*
Gisèle est **aussi** intelligente **que** Marc.	*Gisèle is **as smart as** Marc.*

To say something is *better* than something else, you use **meilleur(e).** Just as with other adjectives, **meilleur(e)** agrees in number and gender with the noun it modifies. To say something is *done better,* you use **mieux.** Since **mieux** is an adverb, it is invariable.

La vie en ville est **meilleure qu'**à la campagne.   Mon père nage **mieux que** moi.

THE SUPERLATIVE

To form the superlative in French, use the comparative forms (**plus, moins, meilleur(e)**) with the appropriate definite articles.

Pierre est **le plus grand** garçon. *(the tallest)*

Cette fille est **la plus intelligente.** *(the smartest)*

Cette glace est **la meilleure.** *(the best)*

If the adjective follows the noun, the article is placed before the noun, then repeated before the superlative construction. Notice also that in the superlative, adjectives agree in gender and number with the nouns they modify.

Mireille est **la fille la plus sportive.**

To say *in/of* after the superlative, place **de** before the collective noun.

Nous sommes **les étudiants les plus** sérieux **de** notre classe.

The definite article **le** is used with the comparative forms (**plus, moins, mieux**) to form the superlative with adverbs.

C'est Pascale qui nage **le plus vite.** *(the fastest)*

C'est Paul qui conduit **le moins vite.** *(the slowest)*

C'est moi qui parle français **le mieux.** *(the best)*

INTERROGATIVES

FORMAL AND INFORMAL QUESTIONS

To say *which* or *what,* use the appropriate form of the interrogative adjective **quel** before a noun.

	Singular	**Plural**
MASCULINE	**Quel** livre?	**Quels** films?
FEMININE	**Quelle** robe?	**Quelles** bottes?

To ask for specific kinds of information, use the following question words:

A quelle heure?	*At what time?*	**Où?**	*Where?*
Avec qui?	*With whom?*	**Quand?**	*When?*

To ask a question in a formal situation, and to ask ask formal yes-or-no questions, use the question words above followed by **est-ce que.**

A quelle heure est-ce que le train part?

Avec qui est-ce qu'on va à la bibliothèque?

Est-ce que vous avez des anoraks?

In informal situations, you may place the question words at the beginning or the end of the question. For yes-or-no questions, simply raise your voice at the end without using **est-ce que.**

Le train part **à quelle heure?**

Avec qui on va à la bibliothèque?

Tu vas acheter cette vieille maison?

INVERSION

The most formal way to ask questions is to use *inversion,* simply inverting the subject and verb and placing a hyphen between them.

Comment **allez-vous,** madame?

Pourriez-vous me dire à quelle heure le train part?

Vend-elle sa voiture?

Quel temps **fait-il?**

When you use inversion with the pronouns **il** and **elle** and a verb that ends in a vowel sound, insert a **-t-** after the verb.

Joue-t-il dans ce film?   **Va-t-elle** au stade?

NEGATION

NEGATIVE EXPRESSIONS

To make a sentence negative in French, you generally place the phrase **ne... pas** around the conjugated verb. However, there are several more specialized negative expressions that may be used as well. Like **ne... pas,** the phrases **ne... plus** *(not anymore)*, **ne... jamais** *(never)*, and **ne... rien** *(nothing)* are placed around the conjugated verb.

> Je **ne** nage **plus.**
>
> Il **n'**a **jamais** fait de randonnée pédestre.
>
> Je **n'**ai **rien** mangé hier.

When the phrase **ne... personne** *(no one)* is used in the **passé composé, personne** is placed after the past participle.

> Je **n'**ai rencontré **personne** au centre commercial.

When **rien** and **personne** are the subject of a sentence, they are placed before **ne** and the conjugated verb.

> **Personne n'**était à la porte.
>
> **Rien n'**est tombé.

As with all negative expressions, the **ne** in **ne... aucun(e)** *(not any)*, **ne... ni... ni...** *(neither . . . nor . . .)*, and **ne... nulle part** *(nowhere)* is placed before the conjugated verb. However, **aucun(e)** is placed immediately before the noun it refers to, **ni** comes immediately before each of the words it refers to, and **nulle part** is placed directly after the word it negates.

> Je **n'**ai **aucune** idée.
>
> Marie **ne** mange **ni** poisson **ni** poulet.
>
> Jacques **n'**a trouvé son livre **nulle part.**

NEGATIVE EXPRESSIONS WITH INFINITIVES

To make an infinitive negative, place the entire negative expression in front of the infinitive.

> Maman a dit de **ne pas** sortir ce soir.
>
> Il essaie de **ne rien** manger avant le dîner.
>
> Nous nous sommes promis de **ne jamais** casser.

NE... QUE

While the expression **ne... que** appears negative, it means *only*. As with the negative expressions, you place the **ne** before the conjugated verb. Place **que** immediately after the verbal expression.

> Je **n'**ai **que** deux dollars.   *I have only two dollars.*
>
> Je **ne** fais de la pêche **qu'**avec mon père.   *I go fishing only with my father.*

NOUNS

PLURAL FORMS OF NOUNS

In French, you make most nouns plural by adding an **-s** to the end of the word, unless the word already ends in **-s** or **-x**. Nouns that end in **-eau** are made plural by adding an **-x**, and nouns that end in **-al** are generally made plural by replacing the **-al** with **-aux**.

	Regular Nouns	-s or -x	-eau	-al
SINGULAR	cadre	tapis	bureau	animal
PLURAL	cadres	tapis	bureaux	animaux

PREPOSITIONS

THE PREPOSITIONS *A* AND *DE*

The preposition **à** means *to, at,* or *in,* and **de** means *from* or *of.* When **à** and **de** precede the definite articles **le** and **les,** they form the contractions **au, aux, du,** and **des.** If they precede any other definite article, there is no contraction.

Nous allons **à la** plage et au zoo.   *We're going to the beach and to the zoo.*

Tu es loin **du** marché mais près **des** musées.   *You're far from the market but near the museums.*

	Masculine Article	Feminine Article	Vowel Sound	Plural
à	à + le = **au**	à la	à l'	à + les = **aux**
de	de + le = **du**	de la	de l'	de + les = **des**

De is also used to indicate possession or ownership.

Là, c'est la boulangerie **de** ma tante.   *That's my aunt's bakery over there.*
C'est le bureau **du** prof.   *It's the teacher's desk.*

PREPOSITIONS AND PLACES

To say that you're at or going to a place, you need to use a preposition. With cities, use the preposition **à: à Paris.** One notable exception is **en Arles.** When speaking about masculine countries, use **au: au Viêt-nam.** With names of plural countries, use **aux: aux Etats-Unis.** Most countries ending in **-e** are feminine; in these cases, use **en: en Italie. Le Mexique** is an exception. If a country begins with a vowel, like **Inde,** use **en: en Inde.**

Cities	Masculine Countries	Feminine or Masculine Countries that begin with a vowel	Plural Countries
à Nantes à Paris en Arles	**au** Canada **au** Maroc **au** Mexique	**en** Italie **en** Espagne **en** Israël	**aux** Etats-Unis **aux** Philippines **aux** Pays-Bas

PRONOUNS

DEMONSTRATIVE PRONOUNS

Celui-là, celle-là, ceux-là, and **celles-là** are *demonstrative pronouns.* They mean *this one, that one, these,* or *those.* Demonstrative pronouns agree in gender and number with the noun they replace.

— **Quelles bottes** est-ce que tu préfères?　　— **Quel stylo** est-ce que tu vas acheter?

— **Celles-là.**　　— **Celui-là.**

DIRECT OBJECT PRONOUNS: *LE, LA,* AND *LES*

A direct object is a noun or pronoun that receives the action of the verb. A direct object pronoun replaces a direct object that has already been mentioned. The direct object pronoun agrees in gender and number with the noun it refers to and it is placed in front of the conjugated verb.

— Il mange **la tarte?**

— Oui, il **la** mange.

If the pronoun is the direct object of an infinitive, it precedes the infinitive.

— Tu vas attendre **le bus?**

— Oui, je vais **l'**attendre.

In an affirmative command, the direct object pronoun follows the verb and is connected to it with a hyphen. In a negative command, the pronoun precedes the verb.

— Je voudrais acheter **le pull** bleu.　　— Et **la cravate** verte?

— Achète-**le!**　　— Ne **l'**achète pas! Elle est horrible!

	Singular	**Plural**
MASCULINE	le / l'	les
FEMININE	la / l'	les

DIRECT OBJECT PRONOUNS AND THE *PASSE COMPOSE*

When using the direct object pronouns **le, la, l', les, me, te, nous,** and **vous** with the **passé composé,** you must change the spelling of the past participle to agree in number and gender with the preceding direct object pronoun.

— Tu as rangé **ta chambre?**　　— Pierre a acheté **les boissons?**

— Oui, je **l'**ai rangé**e** ce matin.　　— Non, il ne **les** a pas acheté**es.**

INTERROGATIVE PRONOUNS

Lequel, laquelle, lesquels, and **lesquelles** are called *interrogative pronouns.* You use them to ask *which one(s).* Interrogative pronouns agree in gender and number with the noun they replace.

— Je vais acheter **ce chemisier.**

— **Lequel?**

— Je trouve qu'elles sont ennuyeuses, **ces B.D.**

— **Lequelles?**

THE PRONOUN Y

The pronoun **y** replaces a phrase meaning *to, on, at,* or *in* any place that has already been mentioned and phrases beginning with prepositions of location such as **à, sur, chez, dans,** and **en + a place or thing.** Place **y** before the conjugated verb.

— Elle va **à la confiserie?**

— Oui, elle **y** va.

— On est allés **chez Gilles?**

— Oui, on **y** est allés.

If there is an infinitive in the sentence, **y** precedes the infinitive.

— Tu vas aller **à l'épicerie?**

— Oui, je vais **y** aller.

THE PRONOUN EN

The object pronoun **en** can be used to replace phrases that begin with **du, de la, de l',** or **des.** These phrases might refer to activities:

— Tu fais **de la plongée?**

— Non, je n'**en** fais pas.

or to quantities:

— Tu veux **des œufs** pour le dîner?   — Est-ce qu'il te faut **du café?**

— Oui, j'**en** veux bien.   — Non, j'**en** ai acheté hier.

Like other object pronouns, en precedes the conjugated verb. If the sentence contains an infinitive, **en** is placed between the conjugated verb and the infinitive.

— Nous avons **des crevettes?**

— Non, mais je vais **en** acheter aujourd'hui.

THE REFLEXIVE PRONOUNS

Reflexive pronouns accompany a reflexive verb, a verb whose action is done by the subject to itself. These pronouns reflect the subject, and they change, depending upon the subject of the sentence. The reflexive pronoun **se** is part of the infinitive of a reflexive verb. The verb **se laver** is conjugated below.

Subject	Reflexive Pronoun	se laver
je	me	Je **me** lave.
tu	te	Tu **te** laves.
il/elle/on	se	Il/Elle/On **se** lave.
nous	nous	Nous **nous** lavons.
vous	vous	Vous **vous** lavez.
ils/elles	se	Ils/Elles **se** lavent.

INDIRECT OBJECT PRONOUNS: *LUI* AND *LEUR*

The pronouns **lui** *(to/for him, to/for her)* and **leur** *(to/for them)* replace nouns that are indirect objects of a verb. They replace a phrase that begins with **à** or **pour** followed by a person or people.

The pronoun is placed before the conjugated verb . . .

Tu offres un cadeau **à ta mère?** —> Tu **lui** offres un cadeau?

or before an infinitive, when it is the object of that infinitive.

Je vais offrir des bonbons **à mes amis.** —> Je vais **leur** offrir des bonbons.

In affirmative commands, the pronouns follow the verb and are connected to it with a hyphen.

Offre un cadre **à ta sœur!** —> **Offre-lui** un cadre!

POSITION OF OBJECT PRONOUNS

Object pronouns like **le, la, l', les, lui, leur, me, te, nous, vous, y,** and **en** usually precede the conjugated verb in a sentence.

Tu **me** donnes un cadeau?   Mon livre? Je **l'ai** oublié à l'école.

Paul **leur** parle tout le temps.   Qui **vous** a donné ce bracelet?

In affirmative commands, the object pronoun follows the verb and is connected to it by a hyphen. In this case, **me** and **te** change to **moi** and **toi.** In negative commands, the object pronoun precedes the conjugated verb.

Téléphone-**moi** ce soir!   Donne-**le** à ta sœur!

Ne **me** donne pas de tarte!   N'**y** va pas!

When the object pronoun is the object of an infinitive, it directly precedes the infinitive.

Je voudrais **l'**inviter à la boum.   Tu aurais dû **en** acheter.

Sometimes you will have more than one object pronoun in a sentence. The following table illustrates the correct order of multiple object pronouns in the same sentence.

me	le	lui	y	en
te	la	leur		
se	l'			
nous	les			
vous				

Je **le leur** ai donné.   Ne **leur en** achète pas!

VERBS THAT TAKE A DIRECT OR INDIRECT OBJECT

These verbs take a direct object: **appeler, chercher, écouter, payer,** and **regarder.**

These verbs take an indirect object: **apprendre à, conseiller à, demander à, dire à, offrir à, parler à, permettre à, répondre à,** and **téléphoner à.**

IL/ELLE EST VERSUS C'EST

Both **il/elle est** and **c'est** can mean *he/she is*. **Il/Elle est** can be used to identify someone's profession or nationality. In this case, no article precedes the noun.

Harrison Ford? **Il est** acteur.   Céline Dion? **Elle est** québécoise.

If **c'est** is used for the same purpose, the noun must be preceded by an appropriate article.

Harrison Ford? **C'est un** acteur.   Céline Dion? **C'est une** québécoise.

When you use both an adjective and a noun, you must use **c'est.**

Céline Dion? **C'est une** chanteuse québécoise.

RELATIVE PRONOUNS: *CE QUI* AND *CE QUE*

The relative pronouns **ce qui** and **ce que** mean *what*. **Ce qui** is the subject of the verb in the clause it introduces:

Ce qui est embêtant, c'est de devoir se coucher très tôt.

Ce qui me plaît, c'est de me promener à la plage.

Ce que is the object of the verb in the clause it introduces and it is usually followed by a subject:

Ce que je n'aime pas, c'est aller à la pêche quand il pleut.

Ce que je préfère, c'est aller au cinéma le week-end.

RELATIVE PRONOUNS: *QUI, QUE,* AND *DONT*

The relative pronouns **qui** and **que** introduce clauses that give more information about a subject that you've already mentioned. **Qui** is the subject of the verb in the clause it introduces. The verb agrees with the person or object in the main clause that it refers to.

Isabelle Adjani est une actrice **qui est** très connue en France.

J'ai deux amis **qui s'appellent** Hervé et Guillaume.

Que is the direct object of the verb in the clause; therefore, it is followed by a subject. When the verb in the clause introduced by **que** is in the **passé composé,** the past participle agrees with the noun that **que** represents. Drop the **-e** from **que** before a vowel sound.

Voici le C.D. **que** je voudrais acheter.

La tente que j'ai **achetée** hier est très chouette!

La Guerre des étoiles est le film **qu'**on a vu.

You use the pronoun **dont** when you mean *whose* or *about/of/from whom* or *which*.

Tu as vu le film **dont** il parle? *(about which)*

Tu connais la fille **dont** la sœur est actrice? *(whose)*

VERBS

REGULAR -ER VERBS

To form the present tense of most **-er** verbs, drop the **-er** and add the following endings to the stem:

aimer *(to like)*		
Subject	**Stem**	**Ending**
j'		-e
tu		-es
il/elle/on		-e
	aim	
nous		-ons
vous		-ez
ils/elles		-ent

For the **nous** form of the verbs **manger, nager,** and **voyager,** only the **-r** is dropped from the infinitive; the **-e** is retained: **nous mangeons, nous nageons, nous voyageons.** For the **nous** form of **commencer,** the second **c** is changed to a **ç** in the stem: **nous commençons.**

To form the past participle of **-er** verbs, drop the **-er** from the infinitive and add **-é** to the stem (**aimer —> aimé**).

REGULAR -IR VERBS

To form the present tense of most **-ir** verbs, drop the **-ir** and add the following endings to the stem:

choisir *(to choose)*		
Subject	**Stem**	**Ending**
je		-is
tu		-is
il/elle/on		-it
	chois	
nous		-issons
vous		-issez
ils/elles		-issent

Other **-ir** verbs that follow this pattern are **finir, grandir, grossir, maigrir,** and **se nourrir.** To form the past participle of these verbs, you simply drop the **-ir** from the infinitive and add **-i** to the stem (**choisir —> choisi**).

REGULAR -RE VERBS

The present tense of most **-re** verbs is formed by dropping the **-re** and adding the following endings to the stem:

Subject	attendre *(to wait)*	
	Stem	**Ending**
j' tu il/elle/on nous vous ils/elles	attend	-s -s -(no ending) -ons -ez -ent

Other **-re** verbs that follow this pattern are **entendre, répondre,** and **perdre.** To form the past participle of these verbs, you simply drop the **-re** from the infinitive and add **-u** to the stem (**attendre —> attendu**).

VERBS LIKE *DORMIR*

These verbs follow a different pattern from the one you learned for regular **-ir** verbs. These verbs have two stems: one for the singular subjects, and another for the plural ones.

	dormir *(to sleep)*	**partir** *(to leave)*	**sortir** *(to go out, to take out)*
je tu il/elle/on	dors dors dort	pars pars part	sors sors sort
nous vous ils/elles	dormons dormez dorment	partons partez partent	sortons sortez sortent
Past Participle	dormi	parti	sorti

IRREGULAR VERBS

The verbs **avoir**, **être**, **aller**, and **faire** are irregular because they do not follow the conjugation patterns that **-er**, **-ir**, and **-re** verbs do.

	avoir *(to have)*	**être** *(to be)*
je/j'	ai	suis
tu	as	es
il/elle/on	a	est
nous	avons	sommes
vous	avez	êtes
ils/elles	ont	sont
Past Participle	eu	été

	aller *(to go)*	**faire** *(to do, make)*
je	vais	fais
tu	vas	fais
il/elle/on	va	fait
nous	allons	faisons
vous	allez	faites
ils/elles	vont	font
Past Participle	allé	fait

Devoir, **pouvoir**, and **vouloir** are also irregular. They are usually followed by an infinitive.

	devoir *(to have to, must)*	**pouvoir** *(be able to, can)*	**vouloir** *(to want)*
je	dois	peux	veux
tu	dois	peux	veux
il/elle/on	doit	peut	veut
nous	devons	pouvons	voulons
vous	devez	pouvez	voulez
ils/elles	doivent	peuvent	veulent
Past Participle	dû	pu	voulu

These verbs also have irregular forms.

	dire *(to say)*	**écrire** *(to write)*	**lire** *(to read)*
je/j'	dis	écris	lis
tu	dis	écris	lis
il/elle/on	dit	écrit	lit
nous	disons	écrivons	lisons
vous	dites	écrivez	lisez
ils/elles	disent	écrivent	lisent
Past Participle	dit	écrit	lu

	mettre *(to put, to put on, to wear)*	**prendre** *(to take, to have food or drink)*	**voir** *(to see)*
je	mets	prends	vois
tu	mets	prends	vois
il/elle/on	met	prend	voit
nous	mettons	prenons	voyons
vous	mettez	prenez	voyez
ils/elles	mettent	prennent	voient
Past Participle	mis	pris	vu

conduire *(to drive)*	
je	conduis
tu	conduis
il/elle/on	conduit
nous	conduisons
vous	conduisez
ils/elles	conduisent

The past participle of **conduire** is **conduit. Conduire** uses **avoir** as its helping verb in the **passé composé.**

connaître *(to know, to be acquainted with)*	
je	connais
tu	connais
il/elle/on	connaît
nous	connaissons
vous	connaissez
ils/elles	connaissent

The past participle of **connaître** is **connu. Connaître** uses **avoir** as its helping verb in the **passé composé.** The **passé composé** of **connaître** has a special meaning.

> **J'ai connu** Sophie au lycée. *I met Sophie (for the first time) at school.*

THE VERB *OUVRIR*

While the verb **ouvrir** ends in **-ir,** it is conjugated like a regular **-er** verb.

ouvrir *(to open)*	
j'	**ouvre**
tu	**ouvres**
il/elle/on	**ouvre**
nous	**ouvrons**
vous	**ouvrez**
ils/elles	**ouvrent**

The past participle of **ouvrir** is **ouvert. Ouvrir** uses **avoir** as its helping verb in the **passé composé.**

J'**ai ouvert** la porte pour mon père.

VERBS WITH STEM AND SPELLING CHANGES

Verbs listed in this section are not irregular, but they do have some stem and spelling changes.

	acheter *(to buy)*	**préférer** *(to prefer)*	**promener** *(to walk (an animal))*
je/j'	achète	préfère	promène
tu	achètes	préfères	promènes
il/elle/on	achète	préfère	promène
nous	achetons	préférons	promenons
vous	achetez	préférez	promenez
ils/elles	achètent	préfèrent	promènent
Past Participle	acheté	préféré	promené

The following verbs have different stems for the **nous** and **vous** forms.

	appeler *(to call)*	**essayer** *(to try)*
j'	appelle	essaie
tu	appelles	essaies
il/elle/on	appelle	essaie
nous	appelons	essayons
vous	appelez	essayez
ils/elles	appellent	essaient
Past Participle	appelé	essayé

REFLEXIVE VERBS

French verbs that require a reflexive pronoun are called *reflexive verbs*. The subject of the sentence receives the action of a reflexive verb. The reflexive pronoun must change with the subject, as shown in the table below.

se laver		
je	me	lave
tu	te	laves
il/elle/on	se	lave
nous	nous	lavons
vous	vous	lavez
ils/elles	se	lavent

To make a reflexive verb negative, place **ne... pas** around the reflexive pronoun and the verb. (**Je ne me lève pas tôt le week-end.**)

To make the **passé composé** of a reflexive verb, you use **être** as the helping verb. The past participle must agree in number and gender with the subject when there's no direct object following the verb. (**Elle s'est lavée** but **Elle s'est lavé les mains.**)

se laver			
je	me	suis	lavé(e)
tu	t'	es	lavé(e)
il/elle/on	s'	est	lavé(e)(s)
nous	nous	sommes	lavé(e)s
vous	vous	êtes	lavé(e)(s)
ils/elles	se	sont	lavé(e)s

To make a reflexive verb negative in the **passé composé**, place **ne... pas** around the reflexive pronoun and the helping verb. (**Je ne me suis pas levée tôt samedi.**)

RECIPROCAL VERBS

The pronouns **se, nous,** and **vous** may also be added to any verb to make the verb reciprocal. That is, when you add them to a verb, they mean *(to/for/at) each other.*

Ils **se** parlent souvent.	*They speak to each other often.*
Nous **nous** aimons.	*We love each other.*
Vous **vous** êtes rencontrés hier?	*Did you meet each other yesterday?*

Just as past participles agree with a reflexive pronoun that is the direct object of the verb, the same is true with reciprocal verbs. However, if the pronoun is an indirect object of the verb, there is no agreement.

Nous **nous** sommes vus hier.   *We saw each other yesterday.*

BUT

Nous **nous** sommes parlé hier.   *We talked **to** each other yesterday.*

THE IMPERATIVE (COMMANDS)

To make a request or a command of most verbs, use the **tu, nous,** or **vous** form of the present tense of the verb without the subject. Drop the final **-s** from the **tu** form of an **-er** verb.

Prends un jus de fruit!   **Allons** en colonie de vacances!

Range ta chambre!   **Faites** le plein, s'il vous plaît.

To make a command negative, simply place **ne... pas** around the verb.

Ne sors **pas** sans ton parapluie!

Place reflexive or object pronouns after the verb in a positive command or suggestion. Place a hyphen between the verb and the pronoun when writing these commands.

Dépêchons-nous!   **Grouille-toi!**

The verb **être** has irregular imperative forms.

Sois gentil! (**tu**)   **Soyons** à l'heure! (**nous**)   **Soyez** patients! (**vous**)

THE NEAR FUTURE *(LE FUTUR PROCHE)*

To say something is going to happen, use the near future (**le futur proche**). It is made up of two parts: the present tense of the verb **aller** and the infinitive of the main verb.

Je **vais faire** de la plongée demain.   *I'm going to go scuba diving tomorrow.*

To make a sentence in the **futur proche** negative, place **ne... pas** around the conjugated verb (**aller**).

Monique **ne** va **pas** lire la biographie.   *Monique isn't going to read the biography.*

THE *PASSE COMPOSE* WITH *AVOIR*

The **passé composé** of most verbs is formed with two parts: the present tense form of the helping verb **avoir** and the past participle of the main verb. To form the past participle, use the formulas below. To make a sentence negative, place **ne... pas** around the helping verb **avoir.**

Infinitive	aimer *(to love, to like)*		choisir *(to choose)*		vendre *(to sell)*	
	STEM	**ENDING**	**STEM**	**ENDING**	**STEM**	**ENDING**
Past Participle	aim aimé	-é	chois choisi	-i	vend vendu	-u
Passé Composé	**j'ai aimé**		**j'ai choisi**		**j'ai vendu**	

J'**ai mangé** au fast-food.   Nous n'**avons** pas encore **choisi** la musique.

Elle **a choisi** un anorak rouge.   Elle **n'a** pas **répondu** à sa lettre.

Some verbs have irregular past participles that do not follow the above formulas.

être	—> été	lire	—> lu	boire	—> bu
avoir	—> eu	faire	—> fait	voir	—> vu
prendre	—> pris	recevoir	—> reçu	mettre	—> mis

THE *PASSE COMPOSE* WITH *ETRE*

Some French verbs use **être** as the helping verb in the **passé composé,** including verbs of motion, like **aller, arriver, descendre, entrer, monter, partir, rentrer, retourner, revenir, sortir, tomber,** and **venir,** and verbs that indicate a state or condition, like **mourir, naître,** and **rester.** When **être** is the helping verb, the past participle has to agree in gender and number with the subject. To make a sentence negative, put **ne... pas** around the helping verb. (**Je ne suis pas allé à l'école hier.**)

aller		
je	suis	allé(e)
tu	es	allé(e)
il/elle/on	est	allé(e)(s)
nous	sommes	allé(e)s
vous	êtes	allé(e)(s)
ils/elles	sont	allé(e)s

Reflexive verbs also use **être** as their helping verb. For more information on the **passé composé** with reflexive verbs, see the heading "Reflexive Verbs," on page R50.

THE *IMPARFAIT*

To talk about what used to happen in the past or to describe what things were like, you use the **imparfait** (imperfect tense). The stem for the imperfect is the **nous** form of the verb in the present tense without **-ons** (**écrire —> nous écrivons —> écriv-**). The stem of **-ger** verbs like **manger** keeps the **-e**. The imperfect endings are listed below. To make the imperfect form negative, place **ne... pas** around the verb.

écrire		
	Stem	**Endings**
j'		-ais
tu		-ais
il/elle/on	écriv	-ait
nous		-ions
vous		-iez
ils/elles		-aient

You will often use the verbs **avoir** and **être** in the imparfait to talk about the past. The table below gives you the **imparfait** forms of both verbs. Notice that **être** uses the irregular stem **ét-.**

avoir		être	
j'	avais	j'	étais
tu	avais	tu	étais
il/elle/on	avait	il/elle/on	était
nous	avions	nous	étions
vous	aviez	vous	étiez
ils/elles	avaient	ils/elles	étaient

THE *IMPARFAIT* VS. THE *PASSE COMPOSE*

In French, there are two tenses you can use to talk about the past: the **imparfait** and the **passé composé.** The table below lists the uses of each tense.

Imparfait	Passé Composé

• to describe how things and people were in the past
    Il était petit.
• to describe general conditions or to set the scene
    Il faisait froid.
• to talk about what used to happen or to tell about repeated or habitual actions
    J'allais à l'école le samedi.
• after words that indicate a repeated action in the past, like **toujours, d'habitude, souvent, tous les jours,** and **de temps en temps**
    Je jouais souvent au foot.
• to tell what was going on when something else happened
    Je regardais la télé quand Pierre est arrivé.
• to emphasize that you were in the middle of doing something when something else happened, you can use the expression **être en train de** in the **imparfait** followed by an infinitive
    J'étais en train de manger quand Jacques est arrivé.
• to make a suggestion, you can use the expression **si on** followed by a verb in the **imparfait**
    Si on allait à la plage?
• to tell how someone seemed to be, you can use the expression **avoir l'air** in the **imparfait** followed by an adjective
    Elle avait l'air triste.
• to tell how something was or used to be, use the phrase **c'était** with an adjective
    C'était magnifique!
	• to tell what happened
	    Il est tombé.
	• after words that indicate a specific moment in the past, like **un jour, soudain, tout d'un coup, au moment où,** and **une fois**
	    Un jour, elle est partie.
	• after words that indicate in which order a series of events occurred, like **d'abord, après, ensuite, enfin,** and **finalement**
	    Ensuite, on a payé.
	• to talk about an event that occurred while another action was going on
	    Il a téléphoné quand tu dormais.

THE FUTURE TENSE *(LE FUTUR)*

To say you *will do* something, use the future tense. The future tense for most verbs is formed by adding the endings **-ai, -as, -a, -ons, -ez,** and **-ont** to the infinitive. However, if the infinitive ends in **-re,** drop the final **-e** before adding the endings. Verbs that have a spelling change in the present tense have the same change in their future stem.

Je **répondrai** à sa lettre demain.

Tu **finiras** tes devoirs samedi soir.

Il/Elle/On **achètera** un cadeau.

Nous **sortirons** ensemble la semaine prochaine.

Vous **prendrez** une décision.

Ils/Elles **choisiront** un métier.

Some irregular verbs have irregular stems in the future tense, to which are added the regular future endings.

aller —> ir-	**envoyer —> enverr-**	**savoir —> saur-**
avoir —> aur-	**être —> ser-**	**venir —> viendr-**
devenir —> deviendr-	**faire —> fer-**	**voir —> verr-**
devoir —> devr-	**pouvoir —> pourr-**	**vouloir —> voudr-**

Je **serai** très content.

Elle **aura** quinze ans.

Nous **enverrons** les lettres.

Vous **ferez** la vaisselle cette semaine.

After the prepositions **quand** *(when)* and **dès que** *(as soon as)*, use the future tense, unlike English, in which you would use the present tense.

Je serai heureux **quand je verrai** mes parents.

I'll be happy <u>when I see</u> my parents.

THE CONDITIONAL TENSE *(LE CONDITIONNEL)*

To say what you *would do* under certain circumstances, use the conditional tense. You also use the conditional tense to be polite.

J'**achèterais** une nouvelle voiture si j'avais l'argent.   *I would buy a new car if . . .*

Je **voudrais** une eau minérale.   *I would like . . .*

To form the conditional tense, you use the same stem as the future tense (usually the infinitive) and add the endings for the imperfect (**-ais, -ais, -ait, -ions, -iez, -aient**). If the infinitive ends in **-re,** drop the final **-e** before adding the endings.

Je **vendrais** ma voiture.

Tu **choisirais** la rouge.

Il/Elle/On **mangerait** du pain.

Nous **prendrions** du café.

Vous **diriez** la vérité.

Ils/Elles **achèteraient** une maison.

Verbs that have irregular stems in the future tense use the same irregular stems in the conditional tense. (See "The Future Tense.")

SI CLAUSES

To say that if one thing were so, then another thing would happen (*If I had the money, I would buy a car*), begin one clause of the sentence with **si** followed by the imperfect. The verb in the other clause should be in the conditional:

Si j'avais de l'argent, j'**achèterais** une voiture.

You may also begin your sentence with the conditional clause: J'**achèterais** une voiture si j'**avais** de l'argent.

THE SUBJUNCTIVE (LE SUBJONCTIF)

The subjunctive mood of a verb is used in clauses after certain phrases that express *obligation* (**Il faut que..**) or *will* (**vouloir que...**).

To form the present subjunctive of most verbs, drop the **-ent** from the **ils/elles** form of the present tense and add **-e, -es, -e, -ions, iez, -ent.**

disent − ent = dis + e = **dise**	Il faut que **je dise** la vérité.
mettent − ent = mett + es = **mettes**	Maman veut que **tu mettes** tes gants.
répondent − ent = répond + e = **réponde**	Je veux qu'**elle** me **réponde.**
rentrent − ent = rentr + ions = **rentrions**	Il faut que **nous rentrions** avant minuit.
sortent − ent = sort + iez = **sortiez**	Papa ne veut pas que **vous sortiez.**
finissent − ent = finiss + ent = **finissent**	Il faut qu'**ils finissent** leurs devoirs.

Some irregular verbs, like **prendre** and **venir,** have two different subjunctive stems. To form the stem for the **nous** and **vous** forms, drop the **-ons** from the present tense of the **nous** form of the verb and add the subjunctive ending. The stem for the rest of the forms comes from the **ils/elles** form of the present tense.

venons − ons = ven + ions = **venions**	Ma grand-mère veut que **nous venions** chez elle.
prenons − ons = pren + iez = **preniez**	Il faut que **vous preniez** de l'argent.
prennent − ent = prenn + e = **prenne**	Maman veut que **je prenne** mon anorak.

Other irregular verbs, such as **faire,** have one irregular stem, to which you add the subjunctive endings. The stem for faire is **fass-.** The verb **aller** has both an irregular stem and a regular stem. To form the stem for the **nous** and **vous** forms, drop the **-ons** from the present tense of the **nous** form of the verb and add the subjunctive ending. For all other forms, the stem is **aill-. Etre** and **avoir** both have irregular forms in the subjunctive.

		faire	**aller**	**être**	**avoir**
que(qu')	je(j')	fasse	aille	sois	aie
	tu	fasses	ailles	sois	aies
	il/elle	fasse	aille	soit	ait
	nous	fassions	allions	soyons	ayons
	vous	fassiez	alliez	soyez	ayez
	ils/elles	fassent	aillent	soient	aient

EXPRESSIONS REQUIRING THE SUBJUNCTIVE

Phrases requiring the use of the subjunctive express:

obligation:

Il faut qu'on **aille** au marché.

emotion:

Je suis désolé(e) que tu **sois** malade.
Je suis heureux(-euse) que...
J'ai peur que...

necessity:

Il est nécessaire que tu **fasses** ton lit.
Il est essentiel que...
Il est important que...
Il faudrait que...
Il vaudrait mieux que...

possibility:

Il est possible qu'il **soit** médecin.
Il se peut que...

will:

Je veux que tu **sois** plus patient.

doubt:

Je ne crois pas qu'il **soit** acteur.
Je ne pense pas que...
Ça m'étonnerait que...
Je ne suis pas sûr(e) que...
Je ne suis pas certain(e) que...

The indicative mood is used after expressions of *certainty*, such as **Je sais que...** and **Je suis certain(e) que...** .

THE PAST PERFECT *(LE PLUS-QUE-PARFAIT)*

To say something happened even farther in the past than another event, use the past perfect tense, or the **plus-que-parfait.** To form the **plus-que-parfait,** you use the imperfect form of the appropriate helping verb (**avoir** or **être**) and the past participle of the completed action.

Il m'a dit qu'**il avait fait** ses devoirs.	*He told me that he had done his homework.*
Tu n'as pas dit où **tu étais allé(e).**	*You didn't say where you had gone.*

The same rules for agreement of past participles in the **passé composé** apply to the **plus-que-parfait.**

Je t'ai dit que nous **étions allés** au cinéma.

THE CAUSATIVE *FAIRE*

To say you are *having something done,* use the verb **faire** with the infinitive of the action that is being done.

Je **fais laver** la voiture.	*I'm having the car washed.*

To say you *had* something done, use the **passé composé** of **faire** with the infinitive of the action that was done.

J'**ai fait tondre** la pelouse.	*I had the lawn mowed.*

If the action to be done requires a reflexive verb, the reflexive pronoun precedes the conjugated form of **faire** in the present tense. In the **passé composé,** the reflexive pronoun precedes the helping verb (**être**). In the **futur proche,** place the pronoun before the infinitive **faire.**

Pierre **se** fait couper les cheveux.	*Pierre is having his hair cut.*
Je **me** suis fait laver les cheveux.	*I had my hair washed.*
Nous allons **nous** faire friser.	*We're going to have our hair curled.*

THE PAST INFINITIVE

When you're using a verb construction that requires an infinitive and you wish to express that the action took place in the past, use the past infinitive, which is formed by using the infinitive of the helping verb and the past participle of the main verb.

Je suis désolé **d'avoir oublié** ton anniversaire.

Je m'excuse d'**être parti(e)** sans te dire au revoir.

If the past infinitive is reflexive, place the reflexive pronoun before the helping verb (**être**).

Pardonne-moi de **m'être réveillé(e)** si tard.

THE *PASSE SIMPLE*

Passé simple is a literary tense used to express a fact or an action completed in the past. It is only used in written French. The stem of regular verbs in the **passé simple** is the infinitive minus its ending, **-er, -ir,** or **-re.**

j'écout**ai**	je fin**is**	je vend**is**
tu écout**as**	tu fin**is**	tu vend**is**
il/elle/on écout**a**	il/elle/on fin**it**	il/elle/on vend**it**
nous écout**âmes**	nous fin**îmes**	nous vend**îmes**
vous écout**âtes**	vous fin**îtes**	vous vend**îtes**
ils/elles écout**èrent**	ils/elles fin**irent**	ils/elles vend**irent**

Some verbs have irregular **passé simple** forms.

	aller	avoir	être	faire	venir
je(j')	allai	eus	fus	fis	vins
tu	allas	eus	fus	fis	vins
il/elle	alla	eut	fut	fit	vint
nous	allâmes	eûmes	fûmes	fîmes	vînmes
vous	allâtes	eûtes	fûtes	fîtes	vîntes
ils/elles	allèrent	eurent	furent	firent	vinrent

This list includes both active and passive vocabulary in this textbook. Active words and phrases are those listed in boxes labeled **Vocabulaire, Comment dit-on...?, Grammaire,** and **Note de grammaire,** as well as the Vocabulaire section at the end of each chapter. You are expected to know and be able to use active vocabulary. All entries in black heavy type in this list are active. All other words are passive. Passive vocabulary is for recognition only.

The number after each entry refers to the chapter where the word or phrase is introduced. Verbs are given in the infinitive. Phrases are alphabetized by the key word(s) in the phrase. Nouns are always given with an article. If it is not clear whether the noun is masculine or feminine, m. (masculine) or f. (feminine) follows the noun. An asterisk (*) before a word beginning with h indicates an aspirate h.

The following abbreviations are used in this vocabulary: pl. (plural), pp. (past participle), and inv. (invariable).

à *to, in (a city or place),* I, 11; **A bientôt.** *See you soon.* I, 1; **A côté de...** *Next to . . . ,* II, 2; **A demain.** *See you tomorrow.* I, 1; **A point.** *Medium rare.* III, 1; **A propos,...** *By the way, . . . ,* II, 9; **A quelle heure?** *At what time?* I, 6; **A tout à l'heure!** *See you later!* I, 1; **A votre service.** *At your service; You're welcome,* I, 3; **à côté: Juste là, à côté de...** *Right there, next to . . . ,* III, 2; **à droite de** *to the right of,* II, 2; **à gauche de** *to the left of,* II, 2; **à la mode** *in style,* I, 10; **à la** *to, at,* I, 6; à réaction *jet,* III, 3; **A...** *At . . . ,* II, 11; **à la vapeur** *steamed,* III, 11
abandonner: J'abandonne. *I give up.* II, 7
l' abbaye (f.) *abbey,* III, 1
les **abdominaux** (m.): **faire des abdominaux** *to do sit-ups,* II, 7
abîmer *to damage,* III, 6
aborder *to approach,* III, 10
abriter *to shelter,* III, 7
l' Acadie (f.) *Acadia (area of Canada),* III, 11
acadien(ne) *Acadian,* III, 11
accabler *to blame,* III, 8
l' acceptation (f.) *acceptance,* III, 12
l' **accident** (m.): **avoir un accident** *to have an accident,* II, 9
l' accompagnement (m.) *side dish, sauce,* III, 2
l' **accord** (m.): **Bon, d'accord.** *Well, OK.* I, 8; **D'accord, si tu... d'abord.** *OK, if you . . . , first.* I, 7; **D'accord.** *OK.* I, 9; Faites l'accord... *Make the agreement . . . ,* III, 1; **Je ne suis pas d'accord. I**

don't agree. I, 7; **Tu es d'accord?** *Is that OK with you?* I, 7
l' **accordéon** (m.) *accordion,* III, 11
accoucher *to give birth,* III, 8
accrocher *to attach,* III, 3
Accrochez-vous! *Hang on!* III, 7
l' accueil (m.) *information desk,* III, 2
accueillant(e) *hospitable,* III, 6
accueillir *to welcome,* III, 6
acheter *to buy,* I, 9; **Achète (-moi)...** *Buy me . . . ,* I, 8; **s'acheter quelque chose** *to buy oneself something,* III, 10
l' **acteur** (m.) *actor,* III, 5
l' **actrice** (f.) *actress,* III, 5
l' actualité (f.) *the news,* III, 5
actuel(le) *present-day,* III, 11
l' **addition** (f.): **L'addition, s'il vous plaît.** *The check please.* I, 5
adorer: Ce que j'adore, c'est... *What I like/love is . . . ,* III, 11; **J'adore...** *I adore . . . ,* I, 1
l' **aérobic** (f.): **faire de l'aérobic** *to do aerobics,* I, 4; II, 7
les **aérosols** (m.): **utiliser des aérosols** *to use aerosol sprays,* III, 3
les **affaires** (f.) *business,* III, 5; femme/homme d'affaires *business woman/man,* III, 5; **partager ses affaires** *to share,* III, 3
afin de *in order to,* I, 7
affranchir *to put a stamp on,* III, 3
affreux (affreuse) *hideous,* III, 4
africain(e) (adj.) *African,* II, 11
l' **Afrique** (f.) **du Sud** *South Africa,* III, 12
l' affrontement (m.) *facing,* III, 12
âgé(e) *older,* I, 7
l' **âge** (m.): **Tu as quel âge?** *How old are you?* I, 1
l' agence de voyages (f.) *travel agency,* III, 2
l' **agent** (m.) **de police** *police officer,* III, 5

agir *to act,* III, 6; **Il s'agit de...** *It's about . . . ,* III, 9
agréer: Je vous prie d'agréer, Monsieur/Madame, l'expression de mes sentiments distingués. *Very truly yours, . . . ,* III, 5
l' **aide** (f.): à l'aide de *with the help of, using,* III, 3
aider *to help,* II, 8; **(Est-ce que) je peux vous aider?** *May I help you?* I, 10; **aider les personnes âgées** *to help elderly people,* III, 3; **Tu peux m'aider?** *Can you help me?* II, 10
ailleurs *somewhere else,* III, 1; partout ailleurs *everywhere else,* III, 3
aimable: Vous êtes bien aimable. *That's kind of you.* III, 6
aimer *to like,* I, 1; **Ce que j'aime, c'est...** *What I like/love is . . . ,* III, 11; **Ce que j'aime bien, c'est...** *What I like is . . . ,* II, 4; **Ce que je n'aime pas, c'est...** *What I don't like is . . . ,* II, 4; **J'aime bien...** *I like . . . ,* II, 1; **J'aime mieux...** *I prefer . . . ,* II, 1; **Je n'aime pas...** *I don't like . . . ,* I, 1; **Le prof ne m'aime pas.** *The teacher doesn't like me.* II, 5; **Moi, j'aime (bien)...** *I (really) like . . . ,* I, 1; **Qu'est-ce que tu aimes comme musique?** *What music do you like?* II, 1; **Qu'est-ce que tu aimes faire?** *What do you like to do?* II, 1; **Tu aimes mieux... ou... ?** *Do you prefer . . . or . . . ?* I, 10; **Tu aimes... ?** *Do you like . . . ?* I, 1; **J'aimerais bien...** *I'd really like . . . ,* III, 5; **J'aimerais...** *I'd like . . . ,* III, 3; **J'aimerais... pour aller avec...** *I'd like . . . to go with . . . ,* I, 10; **Qu'est-ce que j'aimerais... !** *I'd really like to . . . !* III, 8; **Je n'ai pas du tout aimé.** *I didn't like it at all.* III, 9

l' **aîné(e)** *the oldest child,* III, 6

l' **air** (m.): **avoir l'air...** *to seem . . . ,* II, 9; **Ça n'a pas l'air d'aller.** *Something's wrong.* II, 5; **Elle avait l'air...** *She seemed . . . ,* II, 12; **Ils ont l'air de...** *They look like . . . ,* III, 11; **mettre de l'air dans les pneus** *to put air in the tires,* III, 2; **Tu n'as pas l'air en forme.** *You don't seem too well.* II, 7

aise: Mettez-vous à l'aise. *Make yourself comfortable.* III, 6

aisément *easily,* III, 6

ajouter *to add,* III, 3

l' **album de B.D.** (m.) *comic strip book,* III, 2

l' **algèbre** (f.) *algebra,* I, 2

l' **Algérie** (f.) *Algeria,* III, 12

l' **algue** (f.) *seaweed,* III, 10

l' **Allemagne** (f.) *Germany,* III, 12

l' **allemand** (m.) *German (language),* I, 2

aller *to go,* I, 6; **l'aller simple** (m.) *a one-way ticket,* II, 6; **l'aller-retour** (m.) *a round-trip ticket,* II, 6; **aller à la pêche** *to go fishing,* II, 4; **Ça n'a pas l'air d'aller.** *Something's wrong.* II, 5; **Ça te dit d'aller...?** *What do you think about going . . . ?* II, 4; **Ça va aller mieux!** *It's going to get better!* I, 9; *It'll get better.* II, 5; **On peut y aller...** *We can go there . . . ,* I, 12; **Allez tout droit.** *Go straight ahead.* II, 2; **Allez au tableau!** *Go to the blackboard!* I, 0; **Allez!** *Come on!* II, 7; **Ça va pas, non?!** *Are you out of your mind?!* III, 8; **Ça va pour cette fois.** *OK, just this once.* III, 3; **Ça va très bien avec...** *It goes very well with . . . ,* I, 10; **N'y va pas!** *Don't go!* III, 9; **Oh, ça va, hein?** *Oh, cut it out!* III, 6; **Allons...** *Let's go . . . ,* I, 6; **Allons-y!** *Let's go!* I, 4

les **allergies** (f.): **J'ai des allergies.** *I have allergies.* II, 7

Allô? *Hello?* I, 9

les **allumettes** (f.) *matches,* II, 12

Alors,... *So . . . ,* II, 9; **Ça alors!** *How about that!* III, 7; **Et alors?** *And then?* III, 7

l' **amande** (f.) *almond,* III, 6

ambulant(e) *itinerant,* III, 6

améliorer *to improve,* III, 3

américain(e) *American (adj.),* II, 11

les **amis** (m.) *friends,* I, 1

l' **amitié** (f.) *friendship,* III, 8; **Fais mes amitiés à...** *Give my regards to . . .* III, 8

amoureux(amoureuse) *in love,* II, 9; **tomber amoureux(-euse) (de quelqu'un)** *to fall in love (with someone),* II, 9; **Tu es amoureux (-euse) ou quoi?** *Are you in love or what?* III, 10

amusant(e) *fun,* II, 11; *funny,* I, 7; **J'ai trouvé ça amusant.** *It was funny.* III, 9

les **amuse-gueule** (m.): **préparer les amuse-gueule** *to make party snacks,* II, 10

s'amuser *to have fun,* II, 4; **Qu'est-ce que tu fais pour t'amuser?** *What do you do to have fun?* I, 4; **Amuse-toi bien!** *Have fun!* I, 11; **Je me suis beaucoup amusé(e).** *I had a lot of fun.* II, 6; III, 1; **Tu t'es amusé(e)?** *Did you have fun?* II, 6

l' **ananas** (m.) *pineapple,* I, 8; II, 4

l' **ancêtre** (m./f.) *ancester,* III, 8, 11

ancien(ne) *former,* III, 2; *ancient, old,* III, 7

l' **andouille** (f.) *andouille sausage,* III, 11

l' **anglais** (m.) *English (language),* I, 1

l' **Angleterre** (f.) *England,* III, 12

l' **angoisse** (f.): **Quelle angoisse!** *This is terrible!* III, 12

l' **animateur** (l'**animatrice**) (m./f.) *host,* III, 10

les **animaux** (m.): **nourrir les animaux** *to feed the animals,* II, 12

animé(e) *lively,* II, 8

les **anneaux** (m.) *rings (in gymnastics),* III, 12

l' **année** (f.) *year,* III, 5; **Bonne année!** *Happy New Year!* II, 3

l' **anniversaire** (m.): **Joyeux (Bon) anniversaire!** *Happy birthday!* II, 3

l' **anorak** (m.) *ski jacket,* II, 1

antillais(e) *from the Antilles,* II, 11

l' **antilope** (f.) *antelope,* III, 7

l' **antre** (m.) *cave, lair,* III, 10

août *August,* I, 4

l' **appareil** (m.): **Qui est à l'appareil?** *Who's calling?* I, 9

l' **appareil-photo** (m.) *camera,* I, 11; II, 1

apparaître *to appear,* III, 10

apparenté(e) *related;* **mot apparenté** *cognate,* III, 5

s'appeler: Comment est-ce qu'on appelle ça? *What is that called?* III, 11; **Il/Elle s'appelle comment?** *What's his/her name?* I, 1; **Il/Elle s'appelle...** *His/Her name is . . . ,* I, 1; **Je m'appelle...** *My name is . . . ,* I, 1; **Tu t'appelles comment?** *What's your name?* I, 1

l' **appétit** (m.) *appetite,* III, 10

s'appliquer *to apply oneself,* III, 12

apporter *to bring,* I, 9; **Apportez-moi... , s'il vous plaît.** *Please bring me . . .* I, 5

apprendre *to learn,* I, 0; III, 8

l' **apprentissage** (m.): **faire un apprentissage** *to do an apprenticeship,* III, 5

après: Après ça... *After that . . . ,* II, 4; **Après, je suis sorti(e).** *Afterwards, I went out.* I, 9; **d'après** *from, according to,* III, 10; **Et après?** *And afterwards?* I, 9

l' **après-midi** (m.) *in the afternoon,* I, 2; **l'après-midi libre** *afternoon off,* I, 2

arabe *Arabic,* III, 6

l' **arachide** (f.) *peanut,* III, 1

l' **araignée** (f.) *spider,* III, 7

l' **arbre** (m.) *tree,* III, 7; **planter un arbre** *to plant a tree,* III, 3; **mutiler les arbres** *to deface the trees,* II, 12

l' **arc** (m.) *bow (archery),* III, 12

l' **architecte** (m./f.) *architect,* III, 5

l' **argent** (m.) *silver,* III, 6; **de l'argent** *money,* I, 11

l' **armée** (f.) *army,* III, 2

l' **armoire** (f.) *armoire/wardrobe,* II, 2

arracher *to pull,* III, 5

l' **arrêt** (m.): **arrêt de bus** *bus stop,* III, 8

arrêter: arrêter ses études *to stop one's studies,* III, 5; **Arrête!** *Stop!* III, 6; **Et toi, arrête de m'embêter!** *Stop bothering me!* III, 10

l' **arrière-grand-mère** (f.) *great-grandmother,* III, 6

l' **arrière-grand-père** (m.) *great-grandfather,* III, 6

arriver *to arrive,* II, 5; **arriver en retard à l'école** *to arrive late to school,* II, 5; **Ça peut arriver à tout le monde.** *It could happen to anyone.* III, 10; **Ça arrive à tout le monde.** *It happens to everybody.* III, 6; **J'arrive pas à y croire!** *I can't believe it.* III, 12; **Je n'arrive pas à me décider.** *I can't make up my mind.* III, 1; **Qu'est-ce qui t'arrive?** *What's wrong?* II, 5

arroser: arroser le jardin *to water the garden,* III, 3

l' **article** (m.): **article défini** *definite article,* III, 1; **article indéfini** *indefinite article,* III, 1; **article partitif** *partitive article,* III, 1

l' **artisanat** (m.): **faire de l'artisanat** *to make crafts,* III, 8

les **arts** (m.) **plastiques** *art class,* I, 2

l' **aspirateur** (m.): **passer l'aspirateur** *to vacuum,* III, 3

Asseyez-vous! *Sit down!* I, 0; III, 6

assez *sort of,* II, 9; **assez** *enough,* III, 2; **assez bien** *OK,* II, 6

l' **assiette** (f.): **l'assiette de charcuterie** *plate of pâté, ham, and cold sausage,* III, 1; **assiette de crudités** *plate of raw vegetables with vinaigrette,* III, 1; **assiette de fromages** *a selection of cheeses,* III, 1

l' **assistant(e) social(e)** *social worker*, III, 5

assister: assister à un spectacle son et lumière *to attend a sound and light show*, II, 6

associer *to associate*, III, 2

assorti: C'est assorti à... *That matches . . .*, III, 4

assure: Je t'assure. *Really.* III, 4

assurer *to insure*, III, 3

l' **atelier** (m.) *workshop*, III, 5

l' **athlétisme** (m.): **faire de l'athlétisme** *to do track and field*, I, 4

l' **atout** (m.) *asset*, III, 12

atteindre *to reach, to attain*, III, 7

attendre *to wait for*, I, 9

attention: Attention à...! *Watch out for . . . !* III, 7; **Faites attention!** *Watch out!* III, 7

attentionné: être attentionné(e) *to be considerate*, III, 3

atterrir *to land*, III, 7

attirer *to attract*, III, 6

attraper *to catch*, III, 6

au *to, at*, I, 6; *to, in (before a masculine noun)*, I, 11; **Au revoir!** *Goodbye!* I, 1; **au métro Saint-Michel** *at the Saint-Michel metro stop*, I, 6; **La fille au...** *The girl in the/with the . . .*, III, 4; **au fait** *by the way*, III, 6

l' **aubaine** (f.) *godsend*, III, 12

l' **aube** (f.) *dawn*, III, 5

l' **auberge** (f.): **l'auberge de jeunesse** *youth hostel*, II, 2

aucun(e): Ça n'a aucun intérêt. *It's not interesting.* III, 9; **Je n'en ai aucun doute.** *I have no doubt about it.* III, 12; **Aucune idée.** *No idea.* II, 9; **Je n'en ai aucune idée.** *I have no idea.* III, 5

l' **audace** (f.) *boldness*, III, 10

au-dessus *above*, III, 6

augmenter *to increase*, III, 12

l' **augure** (m.) *sign, premonition*, III, 5

aujourd'hui *today*, I, 2

aurais: J'aurais dû... *I should have . . .*, II, 10; **J'aurais pu...** *I could have . . .*, II, 10; **Tu aurais dû...** *You should have . . .*, II, 10; **Tu aurais pu...** *You could have . . .*, II, 10

auriez: Vous auriez...? *Would you have . . . ?* III, 6

aussi *also*, I, 1; **aussi... que...** *as . . . as . . .*, III, 8; **Je n'ai jamais vu un(e) aussi...** *I've never seen such a . . .*, III, 7; **Moi aussi.** *Me too.* I, 2

aussitôt *immediately*, III, 6

autant: autant de... que... *as many/as much . . . as . . .*, III, 8

l' **automne** (m.) *autumn, fall*, I, 4; **en automne** *in the fall*, I, 4

l' **autoroute** (f.) *highway*, III, 2

autour *around*, III, 10

autre: ... et l'autre lui répond... *. . . and the other one answers . . .*, III, 10; **Oh, j'en ai vu d'autres.** *I've seen/done bigger and better things.* III, 10; **Pense aux autres.** *Think about other people.* III, 3

autrefois *in the past*, III, 6

l' **autruche** (f.) *ostrich*, III, 7

avaler *to swallow*, III, 3

avancer (tu n'avances pas) *you're not going anywhere*, III, 2

avant *before*, III, 1

avancer (tu n'avances pas) *you're not going anywhere*, III, 2

avant *before*, III, 1

avare *greedy*, III, 2

avarié(e) *ruined, spoiled*, III, 2

avec: avec moi *with me*, I, 6; **Avec qui?** *With whom?* I, 6; **C'est avec qui?** *Who's in it?* II, 11; **C'est avec...** *. . . is (are) in it.* II, 11; **J'y suis allé(e) avec...** *I went with . . .*, III, 1

l' **avenir** (m.) *the future*, III, 5

avertir *to caution*, III, 7

l' **avion** (m.): **en avion** *by plane*, I, 12

l' **aviron** (m.) *rowing*, III, 12

avis: A mon avis,... *In my opinion, . . .*, II, 9; **A mon avis, c'est plus sûr.** *In my opinion, it's safer.* III, 7; **A mon avis, tu te trompes.** *In my opinion, you're mistaken.* II, 9; **A ton avis, qu'est-ce que je dois faire?** *In your opinion, what should I do?* II, 10; **A ton avis, qu'est-ce que je fais?** *In your opinion, what do I do?* I, 9

l' **avocat(e)** *lawyer*, III, 5

les **avocats** (m.) *avocados*, I, 8

avoir *to have* I, 2; **avoir (prendre) rendez-vous (avec quelqu'un)** *to have (make) a date (with someone)*, II, 9; **avoir 8 en...** *to get an 8 in . . .* II, 5; **avoir des responsabilités** *to have responsibilities*, II, 8; **avoir des soucis** *to have worries*, II, 8; **avoir faim** *to be hungry*, I, 5; **avoir l'air...** *to seem . . .*, II, 9; III, 11; **avoir le chic** *to have the knack (of doing something)*, III, 6; **avoir lieu** *to take place*, III, 12; **avoir soif** *to be thirsty*, I, 5; **avoir tendance à** *to have a tendency to*, III, 4; **avoir un accident** *to have an accident*, II, 9; **avoir... ans** *to be . . . years old*, II, 1; **Oui, vous avez...?** *Yes, do you have . . . ?* I, 10; **Qu'est-ce que vous avez comme...?** *What kind of . . . do you have?* I, 5; **Vous avez...?** *Do you have . . . ?* I, 2; **Quand j'avais... ans,...** *When I was . . . years old, . . .*, II, 8; **Si j'avais le choix,...** *If I had a choice, . . .*, III, 8; **Elle avait l'air...** *She seemed . . .*, II, 12; **Il y avait ...** *There were . . .*, III, 9

avril *April*, I, 4

B

baba *hippy*, III, 4

le **babouin** *baboon*, III, 7

le **badaud** *person who strolls*, III, 6

se bagarrer *to fight*, III, 10

la **bague** *ring*, III, 4, 10; **se faire enlever ses bagues** *to get one's braces off*, III, 10

la **baguette** *long, thin loaf of bread*, I, 12; II, 3

la **baie** *bay*, III, 10

se baigner *to go swimming*, II, 4

le **baiser** *kiss*, III, 10

baisser: *to lower*, III, 11; **Baisse le son.** *Turn down the volume.* III, 9

se balader *to take a walk*, III, 8

le **balafon** *instrument resembling a large xylophone*, III, 5

le **balcon** *balcony*, II, 2

la **balle** *ball*, III, 12

le **ballon** *ball*, III, 12

banal(e): C'est banal. *That's ordinary.* II, 3

les **bananes** (f.) *bananas*, I, 8

le **bananier** *banana tree*, II, 4

la **bande dessinée (une B.D.)** *a comic book*, II, 11; **bande élastique** *elasticized cloth bandage*, III, 3

la **banque** *bank*, I, 12

le **banquier (la banquière)** *banker*, III, 5

barbant(e) *boring*, I, 2; **C'était barbant.** *It was boring.* I, 11

la **barbe** *beard*, III, 4

barjo *nuts, crazy*, III, 12

barrer (la route) *to block (the road)*, III, 10

les **barres asymétriques** (f.) *the uneven parallel bars*, III, 12

bas *low;* **En bas.** *Downstairs.* III, 2

le **base-ball** *baseball*, I, 4; III, 12

baser sur *to base on*, III, 12

le **basket-ball** *basketball*, I, 4; III, 12

les **baskets** (f.) *sneakers*, I, 3; II, 1

la **basse** *bass (guitar)*, III, 11

le **bateau** *boat*, I, 12; **en bateau** *by boat*, I, 12; **faire du bateau** *to go boating*, I, 11

le **bâtiment** *building*, III, 8

le **bâton** *baseball bat*, III, 12; **le bâton de marche** *walking stick*, III, 3

la **batterie** *drums*, III, 11

battre *to beat*, III, 12; **se battre** *to fight*, III, 2

bavard(e) *talkative*, III, 6

bavarder *to chat*, III, 6

B.C.B.G. (abbrev. of bon chic bon genre) *preppy*, III, 4

beau *handsome*, II, 1; **Il fait beau.** *It's nice weather.* I, 4

beaucoup *A lot.* I, 4; **Pas beaucoup.** *Not very much.* I, 4

bébé *childish, stupid,* III, 2
le bec *beak,* III, 10
le beignet *donut,* III, 11
belge *Belgian,* III, 2
la Belgique *Belgium,* III, 12
belle *beautiful,* II, 1; **C'est une belle histoire.** *It's a great story.* II, 11; **On l'a échappé belle!** *That was close!* III, 7
la belle-mère *stepmother,* III, 1
le benjamin (la benjamine) *the youngest child,* III, 6
berbère *Berber,* III, 6
la berceuse *rocking chair,* III, 10
le berger *shepherd,* III, 6
le besoin: De quoi est-ce que tu as besoin? *What do you need?* I, 8; **J'ai besoin de...** *I need . . . ,* I, 8
bête *stupid,* II, 1
la bête *animal, beast,* III, 6
les bêtises (f.): **faire des bêtises** *to do silly things,* II, 8
le beurre *butter,* I, 8; II, 3
la bibliothèque *library,* I, 6; II, 2
bien: bien... *really . . .* III, 11; **Bien des choses à...** *All the best to . . . ,* III, 8; **bien se nourrir** *eat well,* II, 7; **Ça commence à bien faire, hein?** *Enough is enough!* III, 8; **Ça te fera du bien.** *It'll do you good.* II, 7; *c'est bien parce que c'est toi just because it's you,* III, 2; **Ce n'est pas bien de...** *It's not good to . . . ,* III, 3; **Ce que c'est bien!** *Isn't it great!* III, 2; **Il/Elle est vraiment bien, ton/ta...** *Your . . . is really great.* II, 2; **J'aime bien...** *I like . . . ,* II, 1; **Je ne me sens pas bien.** *I don't feel well.* II, 7; **J'en veux bien.** *I'd like some.* I, 8; **Je veux bien.** *Gladly.* I, 8; *I'd really like to.* I, 6; **Merci bien.** *Thank you so much.* III, 6; **Moi, j'aime bien...** *I really like . . . ,* I, 1; **Très bien.** *Very well.* I, 1; **Tu ferais bien de ne pas...** *You would do well not to . . . ,* III, 3; **Tu ferais bien/mieux de...** *You would do well/better to . . . ,* III, 5; **Tu veux bien que je...?** *Is it OK with you if I . . . ?* III, 3; **Bien sûr.** *Certainly,* I, 9; *Of course,* I, 3; II, 10; **Bien sûr que non.** *Of course not.* II, 10
les biens (m.) *possessions,* III, 3
bientôt: A bientôt. *See you soon.* I, 1
bienvenue: Bienvenue chez moi (chez nous). *Welcome to my home (our home).* II, 2
le bifteck *steak,* II, 3
le bijoutier *jeweller,* III, 6
les bijoux (m.) *jewelry,* III, 8
bilingue *bilingual,* III, 1, 2
le billet: billet d'avion *plane ticket,* I, 11; II, 1; **billet de train** *train ticket,* I, 11
la biographie *biography,* II, 11
la biologie *biology,* I, 2
bis *twice,* III, 4

la bise *kiss,* III, 8; **Grosses bises.** *Hugs and kisses.* III, 8
la bise *North wind,* III, 11
Bisous à... *Kisses to . . . ,* III, 8
bisque: en bisque *bisque,* III, 11
bizarre *weird,* III, 6
la blague: Elle est nulle, ta blague! *What a stupid joke!* III, 10
blanc(he) *white,* I, 3
le blé: cultiver le blé *to grow wheat,* III, 8
blesser *to wound,* III, 8
la blessure *wound,* III, 8
bleu(e) *blue,* I, 3; II, 1
blond(e) *blond,* I, 7; II, 1
le blouson *jacket,* I, 10
le blues *blues,* II, 11; III, 11
le bœuf *beef,* I, 8
Bof! *(expression of indifference),* I, 1; II, 8
boire *to drink,* III, 6
le bois *wood,* III, 1, 6
la boisson *drink, beverage,* I, 5; **Et comme boisson?** *And to drink?* III, 1; **Qu'est-ce que vous avez comme boissons?** *What do you have to drink?* I, 5
la boîte: boîte à rythmes *drum machine,* III, 11; **boîte de chocolats** *box of chocolates,* II, 3; **une boîte de** *a can of,* I, 8; *box,* III, 1; **les boîtes** (f.) *cans,* III, 3
bon(ne) *good,* I, 5; **Vous avez (Tu as) fait bon voyage?** *Did you have a good trip?* II, 2; **Bon voyage!** *Have a good trip!* I, 11; **Bon, d'accord.** *Well, OK.* I, 8; **C'est bon pour toi.** *It's good for you.* II, 7; **C'est vraiment bon!** *It's good!* II, 3; **Oui, très bon.** *Yes, very good.* I, 9; **pas bon** *not very good,* I, 5; bon chic bon genre (B.C.B.G.) *preppy,* III, 4; **bon marché** *cheap,* III, 4; **Bonne chance!** *Good luck!* I, 11; **Bonne idée.** *Good idea.* I, 4; **Bonnes vacances!** *Have a good vacation!* I, 11; **Bonne fête!** *Happy holiday! (Happy saint's day!),* II, 3; **Bonne fête de Hanoukka** *Happy Hannukah,* II, 3; **Bonne idée!** *Good idea!* II, 7; **C'est une bonne (excellente) idée.** *That's a good (excellent) idea.* II, 1; **de bonne humeur** *in a good mood,* II, 9; **Elle est bien bonne!** *That's a good one!* III, 10; Bon sang! *Darn!,* III, 2
les bonbons (m.) *candies,* II, 3
Bonjour *Hello,* I, 1
le bonnet *ski cap,* III, 3
le bord: au bord de la mer *to/at the coast,* I, 11; à bord *on board,* III, 10
bordé(e) (d'arbres) *lined (with trees),* III, 8
les bottes (f.) *boots,* I, 10; II, 1
les bottines (f.) *ankle boots,* III, 4
bouche bée *flabbergasted,* III, 10

la bouchée: bouchées doubles *double time,* III, 5
la boucherie *butcher shop,* II, 3
la boucle *buckle, loop,* III, 4, 10; **les boucles d'oreilles** (f.) *earrings,* I, 10
le boudin *blood sausage,* III, 3
bouger *to move,* III, 9; **Ne bougez pas.** *Don't move.* III, 7
la bouillabaisse *fish soup,* III, 4
bouillir *to boil,* III, 11
la boulangerie *bakery,* I, 12; II, 3
la boule *ball,* III, 6; **Les boules!** *Darn!* III, 12
la boulette (de viande) *ball (meatball),* III, 1
bouleverser *to overturn,* III, 8
la boum: faire une boum *to give a party,* II, 10
bouquiner *to read,* III, 2
La Bourse *the stock market,* III, 2; la bourse *wallet, scholarship,* III, 2, 10
bousculer *to bump into, to jostle,* III, 3
la boussole *compass,* II, 12
le bout: Par là, au bout du couloir. *Over there, at the end of the hallway.* III, 2; le bout *piece,* III, 6
la bouteille: une bouteille de *a bottle of,* I, 8
la boutique de cadeaux *gift shop,* II, 3
les boutons (m.): **avoir des boutons** *to have acne,* III, 10
la boxe *boxing,* III, 12
le bracelet *bracelet,* I, 3
le braconnier *poacher,* III, 7
branché(e) *trendy,* III, 4
brancher: Ça me branche! *I'm crazy about that!* III, 2; **Ça ne me branche pas.** *I'm not into that.* III, 11; **Ça te branche,...?** *Are you into . . . ?* III, 11; **Ce qui me branche vraiment, c'est...** *What I'm really crazy about is . . . ,* III, 11
le bras: J'ai mal au bras *My arm hurts.* II, 7
le brasero *brazier,* III, 6
la brasse *breaststroke,* III, 12
brasser *to stir,* III, 11
brave *brave,* II, 1
Bravo! *Terrific!* II, 5
Bref,... *Anyway, . . . ,* II, 9
le Brésil *Brazil,* III, 12
les bretelles (f.) *straps,* III, 3; *suspenders,* III, 4
breton(ne) *Breton, from Brittany,* III, 1
briller *to shine,* III, 6
la brique: Ça casse pas des briques. *It's not earth-shattering.* II, 11
briser *to break,* III, 3
bronzé(e) *tan, tanned,* III, 1
la brosse: les cheveux (m.) **en brosse** *a crew cut,* III, 4
se brosser: se brosser les dents *to brush one's teeth,* II, 4

le **brouillon** *rough draft*, III, 3

la brousse *the brush (bushes)*, III, 7

le bruit *noise*, III, 8; **faire du bruit** *to make noise*, III, 3; **Tu pourrais faire moins de bruit?** *Could you make less noise?* III, 9

brûler *to burn*, III, 7

la **brûlure** *burn*, III, 10

brun(e) *brunette*, I, 7; *dark brown (hair)*, II, 1

bruyant(e) *noisy*, II, 8

le **buffle** *buffalo*, III, 7

les **bulles** (f.) *speech bubbles*, III, 2

le **bureau** *office*, III, 2

le bus: en bus *by bus*, I, 12; **rater le bus** *to miss the bus*, II, 5

le **but** *goal*, III, 7

C

ça: Ça fait combien, s'il vous plaît? *How much is it, please?* I, 5; **Ça fait combien?** *How much does that make?* II, 3; **Ça fait... euros.** *It's . . . euros.* I, 5; **Ça ne me dit rien.** *That doesn't interest me.*, II, 1; **Ça se voit.** *That's obvious.* II, 9; **Ça te dit d'aller...?** *What do you think about going . . . ?* II, 4; **Ça te dit de...?** *Does . . . sound good to you?* II, 1; **Ça va.** *Fine.* I, 1; **Ça, c'est...** *This is . . .*, II, 2; **Comment ça s'est passé?** *How did it go?* II, 5; **Et après ça,...** *And after that, . . .*, I, 9; **Merci, ça va.** *No thank you, I've had enough.* II, 3; **Non, ça va.** *No, I'm fine.* II, 2; **Oui, ça a été.** *Yes, it was fine.* I, 9; **Ça te va comme un gant.** *That fits you like a glove.* III, 4

la **cacahouète** *peanut*, III, 7

cacher *to hide*, III, 6, 11

le cadeau *gift*, I, 11; **Tu as une idée de cadeau pour...?** *Have you got a gift idea for. . . ?* II, 3; **la boutique de cadeaux** *gift shop*, II, 3

le cadet (la cadette) *the younger child*, III, 6

le cadre *photo frame*, II, 3; *setting*, III, 12

le café *coffee, café*, I, 5; grains de café *coffee beans*, III, 7

la **cafetière** *coffee pot*, III, 6

le **caftan** *caftan (Oriental clothing)*, III, 6

le **cahier** *notebook*, I, 3

la **calculatrice** *calculator*, I, 3

calé: Tu es calé(e). *You're really good at that.* III, 10

le caleçon *leggings*, III, 4

le calme: Du calme, du calme. *Calm down.* III, 2; **Calmez-vous!** *Calm down!* III, 7

le **camarade (la camarade)** *friend*, III, 2

le caméscope *camcorder*, III, 7

le **camion** *truck*; un camion à réaction *a truck moving at the speed of a jet*, III, 3

la campagne: à la campagne *to/at the countryside*, I, 1

le camping: faire du camping *to go camping*, I, 11; II, 12; **terrain de camping** *campground*, II, 2

le Canada *Canada*, III, 12

canadien(ne) *Canadian* (adj.), II, 11

le **canard** *duck*, II, 12

le **canari** *canary*, I, 7

le **cancan** *gossip*, III, 10

le **caniche** *poodle*, III, 1

la **canne à pêche** *fishing pole*, II, 12

le canotage: faire du canotage *to go for a canoe ride*, II, 12

la cantine: à la cantine *at the school cafeteria*, I, 9

le **canton** *canton, department*, III, 3

la capitale *capital*, II, 4

la **capture** *catch*, III, 10

car *because*, III, 2

les **caractères gras** (m.) *bold faced characters*, III, 8

les **Caraïbes** *Caribbean*, III, 10

la **carapace** *shell*, III, 7, 10

le cardigan *sweater*, I, 10

le **Carême** *Lent*, III, 11

la **carie** *cavity*, III, 3

les carottes (f.) *carrots*, I, 8; **carottes râpées** *grated carrots with vinaigrette dressing*, III, 1

les **carreaux** (m.): à carreaux *checked*, III, 4

le carrefour: Vous continuez tout droit, jusqu'au carrefour. *Keep going straight ahead up to the intersection.* III, 2

la carte *map*, I, 0; **La carte, s'il vous plaît.** *The menu, please.* I, 5; la carte postale *postcard*, III, 1

la carte de crédit *credit card*, III, 7

les cartes (f.): **jouer aux cartes** *to play cards*, I, 4

le **cas d'urgence** *emergency*, III, 3

la **case** *hut*, III, 1

le casque *helmet*, III, 12

la **casquette** *cap*, I, 10

casser (avec quelqu'un) *to break up (with someone)*, II, 9; **Tu es vraiment casse-pieds!** *You're such a pain!* III, 6; **Casse-toi!** *Get out of here!* III, 6; **Ça casse pas des briques.** *It's not earth-shattering.* II, 11; **Ça me casse les pieds!** *That's so boring!* III, 2

se casser... *to break one's . . .*, II, 7; III, 10

la **cassette** *cassette tape*, I, 3

la cassette vidéo *videocassette*, III, 9

le **cassoulet** *bean stew*, III, 1

la **cathédrale** *cathedral*, II, 2

le cauchemar: C'était un véritable cauchemar! *It was a real nightmare!* I, 11

causer *to chat*, III, 2

CDI (Centre de documentations et d'informations) *library*, III, 11

ce que: Ce que c'est bien! *Isn't it great?* III, 2; **Ce que j'aime bien, c'est...** *What I like is . . .*, II, 4; **Ce que je n'aime pas, c'est...** *What I don't like is . . .*, II, 4; **Ce que je préfère, c'est...** *What I prefer is . . .*, II, 4; **Tu sais ce que tu veux faire?** *Do you know what you want to do?* III, 5; **Tu sais ce que...?** *Do you know what . . . ?* II, 9

ce qui: Ce qui m'ennuie, c'est(de)... *What bothers me is . . .*, II, 4; **Ce qui me plaît, c'est(de)...** *What I like is . . .*, II, 4; **Ce qui ne me plaît pas, c'est(de)...** *What I don't care for is . . .*, II, 4

céder *to give up*, III, 7

le **cèdre** *cedar*, III, 6

la ceinture *belt*, I, 10; safety *belt*, III, 3

célèbre *famous*, III, 1

célébrer *to celebrate*, III, 11

le céleri rémoulade *grated celery root with mayonnaise and vinaigrette*, III, 1

célibataire *unmarried*, III, 6

celle: Celle qui... *The woman /girl / one who . . .*, III, 4; **Celle-là.** *That one.* III, 4; **Celles-là** *Those.* III, 4

celui: Celui avec... *The man/guy/one with . . .*, III, 4; **Celui du...** *The one . . .*, III, 4; **Celui-là.** *That one.* III, 4

une **centaine** *a hundred or so*; des centaines *hundreds*, III, 5

le centre commercial *mall*, I, 6; *center*, III, 2

le **centre-ville** *downtown*, III, 2

cependant *however*, III, 12

les céréales (f.) *cereal*, II, 3

certain: Je (ne) suis (pas) certain(e) que... *I'm (not) certain that . . .*, III, 7

le **cervelas** *sausage made with pork meat and brains*, III, 1

cesser (de) *to stop, to cease (to do something)*, III, 7

C'est... *It's . . .*, I, 2; II, 11; *This is . . .*, I, 7; **C'est comment?** *What's it like?* II, 4; **Ça, c'est...** *This is . . .*, II, 2; **C'est-à-dire que...** *That is, . . .*, II, 9

ceux: Ceux-là. *Those.* III, 4

chacun(e) *each*, III, 1

la **chaîne** *channel*, III, 9

la chaîne stéréo *stereo*, II, 2

la **chaise** *chair*, I, 0

le **châle** *shawl*, III, 1

la **chaleur** *heat*, III, 6

la **chambre** *bedroom*, II, 2; **ranger ta chambre** *to pick up your room*, I, 7

le **chameau** *camel*, III, 8

les **champignons** (m.) *mushrooms*, I, 8; III, 11

les **champs** (m.) *fields*, III, 7; **les champs de canne à sucre** (m.) *sugarcane fields*, II, 4

la **chance: Bonne chance!** *Good luck!* I, 11; **C'est pas de chance, ça!** *Tough luck!* II, 5; **J'ai vraiment pas de chance.** *I'm so unlucky.* III, 12; **On a eu de la chance!** *We were lucky!* III, 7

le **chandail** *sweater*, III, 4

changer *to change*, III, 2, 4

la **chanson** *song*, II, 11

le **chant** *singing*, III, 11

chanter *to sing*, I, 9

le **chanteur** *(male) singer*, II, 11

la **chanteuse** *(female) singer*, II, 11

le **chapeau** *hat*, I, 10; **Chapeau!** *Well done!* II, 5

chaque *each*, III, 1

la **charcuterie** *delicatessen*, II, 3; **l'assiette** (f.) **de charcuterie** *plate of pâté, ham, and cold sausage*, III, 1

charmant(e) *charming*, II, 4

le **charmeur de serpents** *snake charmer*, III, 6

la **chasse** *hunting*, III, 7; **la chasse d'eau** *toilet tank*, III, 3

chasser *to hunt, to drive away*, III, 11, 7; **chasser (les idées noires)** *get that gloomy thought out of one's head*, III, 2

le **chat** *cat*, I, 7

châtain *brown (hair)*, II, 1

le **château** *castle*, III, 2; **le château fort** *fortified castle*, III, 2

chaud(e): Il fait chaud. *It's hot.* I, 4; **Ouf! On a eu chaud!** *Wow! That was a real scare!* III, 7

le **chauffeur** *driver*, III, 5

les **chaussettes** (f.) *socks*, I, 10

les **chaussures** (f.) *shoes*, I, 10

la **chauve-souris** *bat*, III, 7

la **chéchia** *typical hat worn by some Arab men*, III, 8

le **chef** *leader, chief*, III, 5

le **chef-d'œuvre** *masterpiece*, III, 6

le **chef-lieu** *county town*, III, 10

le **chemin** *path, way*, III, 10; **chemin de fer** *railway*, III, 1

la **chemise** *shirt (men's)*, I, 10

le **chemisier** *shirt (women's)*, I, 10

le **chêne** *oak*, III, 11

les **chèques** (m.) **de voyage** *traveler's checks*, II, 1

cher (**chère**): **C'est trop cher.** *It's too expensive.* I, 10; II, 3

chercher *to look for*, I, 9; **Je cherche quelque chose pour...** *I'm looking for something for . . . ,* I, 10

chéri(e) *dear*, III, 10

le **cheval** *horse*, III, 10

les **cheveux** (m.) *hair*, II, 1; III, 4

la **cheville: se fouler la cheville** *to sprain one's ankle*, II, 7

la **chèvre** *goat*, III, 8

chez: chez... *to/at . . . 's house*, I, 11; **Bienvenue chez moi (chez nous).** *Welcome to my home (our home),* II, 2; **chez le disquaire** *at the record store*, I, 12; **Faites/Fais comme chez vous/toi.** *Make yourself at home.* II, 2; **Je suis bien chez...?** *Is this . . . 's house?* I, 9; **On... chez toi?** *Do people . . . where you're from?* III, 12; **Qu'est-ce qui est typique de chez toi?** *What's typical of where you're from?* III, 12; **Vous avez/Il y a des... chez vous?** *Do you have/Are there . . . where you're from?* III, 12

chic *chic*, I, 10

le **chien** *dog*, I, 7; **promener le chien** *to walk the dog*, I, 7

le **chignon** *bun*, III, 4

la **chimie** *chemistry*, I, 2

la **Chine** *China*, III, 12

le **chiot** *puppy*, III, 9

le **chocolat** *chocolate*, I, 1; *hot chocolate*, I, 5

choisir *to choose, to pick*, I, 10; **choisir un métier** *to choose a career*, III, 5; **choisir la musique** *to choose the music*, II, 10; **Vous avez choisi?** *Have you made your selection?* III, 1

le **choix: Si j'avais le choix,...** *If I had a choice, . . . ,* III, 8

le **chômage: être au chômage** *to be unemployed*, III, 5

le **chômeur (la chômeuse)** *unemployed person*, III, 5

la **chorale** *choir*, I, 2

la **chose: C'est toujours la même chose!** *It's always the same!* III, 6; **J'ai quelque chose à faire.** *I have something else to do.* II, 10; **Quelque chose ne va pas?** *Is something wrong?* II, 7; **Bien des choses à...** *All the best to . . . ,* III, 8; **J'ai des tas de choses à faire.** *I have lots of things to do.* I, 5

le **chouchou** *teacher's pet*, III, 1

chouette *very cool*, II, 2; **Ça serait chouette si...** *It would be great if . . . ,* III, 8; **Oui, très chouette.** *Yes, very cool.* I, 9

Chut! *Shh!* III, 9

la **chute d'eau** *waterfall*, II, 4

ci-dessous *below*, III, 3; **ci-joint** *attached*, III, 5

le **ciel** *sky*, III, 2

la **cigale** *cicada*, III, 11

les **cigognes** (f.) *storks*, III, 1

les **cils** (m.) *eyelashes*, III, 4

le **cinéma** *the movies*, I, 1; *the movie theater*, I, 6

le **circuit** *tour*, III, 1; **faire un circuit des châteaux** *to tour some châteaux*, II, 6

la **circulation** *traffic*, III, 8

circuler *to circulate, to get around*, III, 3

la **cire** *wax*, III, 2

la **citation** *quotation*, III, 10

le **citoyen (la citoyenne)** *citizen*, III, 10

le **citron pressé** *lemonade*, I, 5

clair *light*, III, 4

classe *classy*, III, 4

le **classeur** *loose-leaf binder*, I, 3

le **(roman) classique** *classic*, II, 11

cligner *to blink*, III, 10

cloche *goofy*, III, 4; **Ça fait vraiment cloche.** *That looks really stupid.* III, 4

le **clou** *nail*, III, 6

le **clown: Il ne faut pas faire le clown en classe!** *You can't be goofing off in class!* II, 5

le **coca** *cola*, I, 5

le **cocotier** *coconut tree*, II, 4

le **coéquipier** *team mate*, III, 12

le **cœur** *heart*, III, 5; **J'ai mal au cœur.** *I'm sick to my stomach.* II, 7

le **coffre** *trunk*, III, 2

la **coiffe** *headdress*, III, 1

le **coiffeur (la coiffeuse)** *hair stylist*, III, 4

la **coiffure** *hairstyle*, III, 4

le **coin: au coin de** *on the corner of*, I, 12

le **col** *collar*; **à col en V** *V-necked*, III, 4

le **col roulé** *turtleneck sweater*, III, 4

la **colère** *anger*, III, 2

le **collant** *hose*, I, 10; *tights*, III, 4

collé: être collé(e) *to have detention*, II, 5

collectionner *to collect*, III, 2

le **collier** *necklace*, III, 4

le **colon** *settler*, III, 11

la **colonie: en colonie de vacances** *to/at a summer camp*, I, 11

la **colonne** *column*, III, 2

coloré(e) *colorful*, II, 4

combien: C'est combien, l'entrée? *How much is the entrance fee?* II, 6; **C'est combien,...?** *How much is . . . ?* I, 5; **Ça fait combien, s'il vous plaît?** *How much is it, please?* I, 5; **Ça fait combien?** *How much does that make?* II, 3; **Combien coûte(nt)...?** *How much is (are) . . . ?* II, 3; **Combien en voulez-vous?** *How many (much) do you want?* II, 3

la **comédie** *comedy*, III, 9; **la comédie musicale** *musical comedy*, III, 9

commander *to order*, III, 1

comme: C'est bien comme...? *Is it a nice . . . ?* III, 12; **C'est fou comme...!** *I can't believe how . . . !* III, 7; **Comme entrée, je voudrais...** *As an appetizer I would like . . . ,* III, 1; **Comme ci comme ça.** *So-so.* I, 1; **Qu'est-ce que tu fais comme sport?** *What sports do you play?* I, 4; **Qu'est-ce que vous avez comme boissons?** *What do you have to drink?* I, 5; **Qu'est-ce**

que vous avez comme...? *What kind of... do you have?* I, 5; III, 1; **Tu as vu comme...?** *Did you see how...?* III, 7; **C'est... comme tout!** *It's as... as anything!* III, 2; **Ce n'était pas comme ça.** *It wasn't like this.* III, 8

commencer *to begin, to start,* I, 9; **C'est lui/elle qui a commencé!** *He/She started it!* III, 6; **Ça commence à quelle heure?** *What time does it start?* II, 11; **Comment est-ce que ça commence?** *How does it start?* III, 9

comment *what,* I, 0; *how,* II, 5; **(Comment) ça va?** *How's it going?* I, 1; **C'est comment?** *What's it like?* II, 4; **C'était comment?** *How was it?* II, 6; III, 9; **Comment est-ce qu'on fait...?** *How do you make...?* III, 11; **Comment est-ce qu'on fait?** *How should we work this out?* III, 6; **Comment on dit...?** *How do you say...?* III, 11; **Comment tu as trouvé ça?** *How did you like it?* III, 9; **Comment tu trouves ça?** *What do you think of that/it?* I, 2; **Comment tu trouves...?** *What do you think of...?* I, 2; **Elle est comment?** *What is she like?* I, 7; **Il est comment?** *What is he like?* I, 7; **Ils/Elles sont comment?** *What are they like?* I, 7; **Tu t'appelles comment?** *What is your name?* I, 0; **Comment on va à...?** *How do you get to...?* III, 2

le **commérage** *gossip,* III, 3
la **commode** *chest of drawers,* II, 2
commun: prendre les transports en commun *to take public transportation,* III, 3
compliqué(e) *complicated,* III, 2
le **comportement** *behavior,* III, 7
se **composer de** *to be made of,* III, 1
compréhensif (compréhensive) *understanding,* III, 6
comprendre *to understand,* II, 5; **J'ai du mal à comprendre.** *I have a hard time understanding.* II, 5; **mais il comprend beaucoup de groupes ethniques** *but it's made up of many different ethnic groups,* III, 5
les **comprimés** (m.) *tablets,* III, 7
le **comptable (la comptable)** *accountant,* III, 5
compter *to count, to matter, to plan to,* III, 6; **Je compte...** *I'm planning on...,* III, 5; **Qu'est-ce que tu comptes faire?** *What do you plan to do?* III, 5
les **concerts** (m.) *concerts,* I, 1
la **concession** *a grouping of huts,* III, 5
concilier *to reconcile,* III, 12
conçu(e) *conceived of,* III, 12

la **condition** *condition;* **à condition de/que** *on the condition that,* III, 3; **se mettre en condition** *to get into shape,* II, 7
conduire *to drive,* III, 2; **conduire une voiture** *to drive a car,* II, 8; **Cette route vous conduira au centre-ville.** *This road will lead you into the center of town.* III, 2; se **conduire** *to behave,* III, 1
la **confiance: Fais-moi confiance.** *Trust me.* III, 4
confier à *to confide in,* III, 8
la **confiserie** *candy shop,* II, 3
la **confiture** *jam,* I, 8
confondre *to mix up,* III, 10
le **congé** *time off, free time,* III, 5
connais: J'en connais une bonne. *I've got a good one.* III, 10; **Je ne connais pas.** *I'm not familiar with them (him/her).* II, 11; **Tu connais la dernière?** *Have you heard the latest?* III, 10; **Tu connais la nouvelle?** *Did you hear the latest?* II, 9; **Tu connais...?** *Are you familiar with...?* II, 11
connaisse: Tu es le/la... le/la plus... que je connaisse. *You're the... -est... I know.* III, 10
connaître (pp. connu) *to know, to be familiar with,* II, 8
la **conque** *conch,* III, 10
se **consacrer** *to dedicate oneself,* III, 5
conseiller: Qu'est-ce que tu me conseilles? *What do you advise me to do?* I, 9 **Qu'est-ce que vous me conseillez?** *What do you recommend?* III, 1
le **conseiller (la conseillère)** *advisor,* III, 5; **conseillère d'orientation** *career advisor,* III, 5
les **conseils** (m.) *advice,* III, 4
consommer: consommer trop de sucre *to eat too much sugar,* II, 7
constitué(e) de *composed of,* III, 8
construire *to build,* III, 6
contenir *to contain,* III, 2
content(e) *happy,* I, 7
le **conteur** *story teller,* III, 6
continuer: Vous allez continuer cette rue jusqu'au prochain feu rouge. *You go down this street to the next light.* I, 12; **Vous continuez tout droit, jusqu'au carrefour.** *Keep going straight ahead up to the intersection.* III, 2
contraire: au contraire *on the contrary,* III, 3
convaincre *to convince,* III, 9
convaincu: Je suis convaincu(e) que... *I'm convinced that...,* III, 7
convenir *to be appropriate,* III, 1
la **copine** *friend (for a girl),* III, 10
cool *cool,* I, 2; **C'est trop cool!** *That's too cool!* III, 12; **Il/Elle est cool, ton/ta...** *Your... is cool.* II, 2
le **coquillage** *shell,* III, 10

la **coquille Saint-Jacques** *sea scallop,* III, 10
le **corail** *coral,* III, 10
corallien(ne) *coralline,* III, 10
la **corne** *horn,* III, 7; **la corne de gazelle** *"gazelle's horn", type of Morrocan pastry,* III, 6
le **correspondant (la correspondante)** *pen pal,* III, 6
correspondre *to match,* III, 2
corriger *to correct,* III, 3
costaud(e) *strong, sturdy,* III, 12
le **costume** *man's suit,* III, 4
la **côte** *cutlet; chop,* III, 1; *coast,* III, 6
le **côté: à côté de** *next to,* I, 12; II, 2; **Juste là, à côté de...** *Right there, next to...,* III, 2; **d'un côté** *on one hand;* **d'un autre côté** *on the other hand*
la **côtelette de porc pâtes** *porkchop with pasta,* III, 1
le **coton: en coton** *cotton,* I, 10
le **cou: J'ai mal au cou** *My neck hurts.* II, 7
la **couche** *layer;* **les couches superposées** *layers (of clothing),* III, 3
se **coucher** *to go to bed,* II, 4
le **coucher de soleil** *sunset,* III, 8
couler: J'ai le nez qui coule. *I've got a runny nose.* II, 7
couleur: De quelle couleur est...? *What color is...?* I, 3
le **couloir** *corridor,* III, 2
le **country** *country music,* II, 11; III, 11
le **coup** *knock,* III, 10; **le coup de cœur** *favorite,* III, 4; **le coup de soleil** *sunburn,* III, 3
la **coupe** *haircut,* III, 4; **une coupe au carré** *square cut,* III, 4
le **coupe-vent** *windbreaker, jacket,* III, 4
couper: Tu t'es fait couper les cheveux? *Did you get your hair cut?* III, 4; **se couper le doigt** *to cut one's finger,* II, 7
la **coupole** *dome,* III, 6
le **courage: Courage!** *Hang in there!* II, 5; **Tu en as, du courage.** *You've really got courage.* III, 10
courir *to run,* III, 7
la **couronne** *crown,* III, 6
le **courrier** *mail,* III, 4
le **cours** *course,* I, 2; **cours de développement personnel et social (DPS)** *health,* I, 2; **Tu as quels cours...?** *What classes do you have...?* I, 2; **au cours de** *in the course of,* III, 8
la **course de fond** *long-distance running,* III, 12
les **courses** (f.) *shopping, errands,* I, 7; **faire les courses** *to do the shopping,* I, 7
court(e) *short (objects),* I, 10; II, 1; **au court-bouillon** *boiled,* III, 11; **les cheveux courts** (m.) *short hair,* III, 4

le **couscous** *couscous (semolina like grain/typical North-African dish),* III, 6
le **cousin** *male cousin,* I, 7
la **cousine** *female cousin,* I, 7
coûte: Combien coûte(nt)...? *How much is (are)...?* II, 3
la **coutume** *custom,* III, 6
le **couturier** *fashion designer,* III, 4
la **couverture** *blanket;* **la couverture de sauvetage** *rescue blanket,* III, 3
couvrir *to cover,* III, 3
le **crabe** *crab,* III, 10
cracher *to spit (out),* III, 6
le **crâne** *skull,* III, 12
craquer: Je craque! *I'm losing it!* II, 7
la **cravate** *a tie,* I, 10
le **crayon** *pencil,* I, 3
créer *to create,* III, 1
la **crème: la crème caramel** *caramel custard,* III, 1; **la crème chantilly** *whipped cream,* III, 2; **de la crème solaire** *sunscreen,* III, 7
la **crémerie** *dairy,* II, 3
la **crêpe** *very thin pancake,* I, 5
creuser *to dig,* III, 7
crevé: avoir un pneu crevé *to have a flat tire,* III, 2; **Je suis crevé(e).** *I'm exhausted.* II, 2
crève: Je crève de faim! *I'm dying of hunger!* II, 12
la **crevette** *shrimp,* II, 3; III, 10
le **cri** *shout,* III, 8
le **cric** *car jack,* III, 2
le **crocodile** *crocodile,* III, 7
croire: J'arrive pas à y croire! *I can't believe it.* III, 12; **Crois-moi.** *Believe me.* III, 4; **Je crois que ça vaut mieux.** *I think that's better.* III, 7; **Je crois que...** *I think that...,* II, 9; **Je ne crois pas.** *I don't think so.* II, 9
croiser *to cross,* III, 10
les **croissants** (m.) *croissants,* II, 3
la **Croix Rouge** *the Red Cross,* III, 3
le **croque-monsieur** (inv.) *toasted ham and cheese sandwich,* I, 5
croyable *believable,* III, 1
les **crudités** (f.): **l'assiette de crudités** *plate of raw vegetables with vinaigrette,* III, 1
les **crustacés** (m.) *shellfish,* III, 11
la **cueillette: faire la cueillette** *to harvest (fruits),* III, 8
cueillir *to harvest,* III, 8; **cueillir des fleurs** *to pick the flowers,* III, 3
le **cuir: en cuir** *leather,* I, 10
cuire *to cook,* III, 11
la **cuisine** *kitchen,* II, 2; **faire la cuisine** *to cook,* III, 3
la **cuisinière** *cook (woman),* III, 10
cuit(e): Bien cuit(e). *Well done.* III, 1
le **cuivre** *brass, copper,* III, 8
culbuter *to knock over, to run over, to knock into,* III, 3

cultiver: cultiver le blé *to grow wheat,* III, 8
curieux (curieuse) *curious,* III, 10
le **curriculum vitae** (C.V.) *résumé,* III, 5
le **cyclisme** *cycling,* III, 12

d'abord: D'abord,... *First,...,* II, 12
d'accord: D'accord. *OK.* I, 4; II, 1; **D'accord, si tu... d'abord...** *OK, if you..., first.* I, 7; **Je ne suis pas d'accord.** *I don't agree.* I, 7; **Tu es d'accord?** *Is that OK with you?* I, 7
d'ailleurs *moreover, beside* III, 8
le **daim: en daim** *suede,* III, 4
la **dance** *dance music,* III, 11
dangereux (dangereuse) *dangerous,* II, 8
dans *in,* I, 6; **C'est dans le nord/le sud/l'est/l'ouest de...** *It's in the northern/southern/eastern/western part of...,* II, 12; **dans l'eau** *in the water,* III, 3; **Qu'est-ce qu'il y a dans...?** *What's in...?* III, 11
la **danse** *dance,* I, 2
danser *to dance,* I, 1; **danser le zouk** *to dance the zouk,* II, 4
le **danseur (la danseuse)** *dancer,* III, 6
la **datte** *date (fruit),* III, 8
le **dattier** *date palm tree,* III, 8
davantage *even more,* III, 5
de *of,* I, 0; **de l'** *some,* I, 8; **de la** *some,* I, 8; **De rien.** *You're welcome.* III, 6; **de taille moyenne** *of medium height,* II, 1; **Je n'ai pas de...** *I don't have any...,* I, 3; **Je ne fais pas de...** *I don't play/do...,* I, 4
le **débardeur** *tank top,* III, 4
débarrasser la table *to clear the table,* I, 7
les **débouchés** (m.) *job prospects,* III, 5
déboucher *to open onto,* III, 6
le **début: Au début...** *At the beginning...,* III, 9; **J'y suis allé(e) début...** *I went at the beginning of...,* III, 1
le **décalage** *gap,* III, 12
décembre *December,* I, 4
la **déception** *disappointment,* III, 3
les **déchets** (m.): **jeter (remporter) les déchets** *to throw away (to take with you) your trash,* II, 12
déchirer *to rip, to tear,* II, 5
décider: J'ai du mal à me décider. *I'm having trouble deciding.* III, 5; **Je n'arrive pas à me décider.** *I can't make up my mind.* III, 1

les **décisions** (f.): **prendre ses propres décisions** *to make up one's own mind,* III, 3
décontracté(e) *relaxed,* III, 4
le **décor** *decor/surrounding,* III, 6
décoré(e) *decorated,* III, 6
décortiquer *to shell,* III, 11
découper *to cut,* III, 2
la **découverte** *discovery,* III, 10
découvrir *to discover,* III, 2
décrire *to describe,* III, 2
décrocher *to pick up (the phone),* III, 8
déçu(e) *disappointed,* III, 5
dédaigner *to scorn,* III, 5
dedans *inside,* III, 6
le **défaut** *defect, flaw,* III, 7
Défense de... *Do not...,* III, 3
le **défi** *challenge,* III, 12
défiler *to parade,* III, 10
défoncer *to unwind,* III, 12
se **défouler** *to let off steam,* III, 12
dégoûtant *gross,* I, 5
déguisé(e) *dressed up,* III, 10
déguster *to taste, enjoy,* II, 4
dehors *outside,* III, 4
déjà *already,* I, 9; **...,déjà?** *...again?,* III, 11; **Il/Elle en a déjà un(e).** *He/She already has one (of them).* II, 3
le **déjeuner** *lunch,* I, 2
déjeuner *to have lunch,* I, 9
délicieux (délicieuse) *delicious,* I, 5; **C'était délicieux!** *That was delicious!* II, 3
délirant(e) *wild,* III, 4
délirer: Arrête de délirer! *Stop being so silly!* III, 10; **Tu délires ou quoi?** *Are you crazy or what?* III, 11
le **deltaplane: faire du deltaplane** *to hang glide,* II, 4
demain *tomorrow,* I, 2; **A demain.** *See you tomorrow.* I, 1
demander: demander la permission à tes parents *to ask your parents' permission,* II, 10; **demander pardon à (quelqu'un)** *to ask for (someone's) forgiveness,* II, 10; **Je t'ai pas demandé ton avis.** *I didn't ask your opinion.* III, 10; **demander la main de (quelqu'un)** *to ask for someone's hand for marriage,* III, 6
se **demander: Je me demande...** *I wonder...,* II, 9; III, 5
la **démarche** *move,* III, 8
démarrer *to start up,* III, 10
déménager *to move,* III, 10
la **demeure** *residence,* III, 10
demeurer *to stay,* III, 5
demie: et demie *half past,* I, 6; **demi: et demi** *half past (after midi and minuit),* I, 6; **la demi-sœur** *stepsister, halfsister,* III, 1; **le demi-tour: dans le doute faire demi-tour** *when in doubt, turn back the way you came,* III, 3

démodé(e) *out of style*, I, 10

le **dénouement** *outcome*, III, 6

la **dentelle** *lace*, III, 2

le **dentiste (la dentiste)** *dentist*, III, 5

les **dents** (f.): **J'ai mal aux dents.** *My teeth hurt.* II, 7

le **département d'outre-mer (D.O.M.)** *administrative division of France located overseas*, III, 10

dépêcher: Tu peux te dépêcher? *Can you hurry up?* III, 2; **Dépêche-toi!** *Hurry up!* III, 2

se **déplacer** *to migrate, to move around*, III, 8

déplaire *to be disliked*, III, 11

déposer *to deposit, to drop*, I, 12

le **dépotoir** *dump*, III, 3

dépourvu(e) de *without*, III, 11

déprimant(e) *depressing*, II, 11

déprimé(e) *depressed*, II, 9

Depuis... *Since . . .* , III, 1

déranger *to bother, disturb*, III, 6; **Ça te dérange si...?** *Do you mind if . . . ?* III, 3

dérivé(e) *coming from*, III, 2

dernier (dernière) *last*, III, 4

dernièrement *recently*, III, 9

dérouler *to unroll*, III, 10

derrière *behind*, I, 12

le **derviche** *dervish*, III, 6

dès que: Dès que je serai là-bas,... *As soon as I get there, . . .* , III, 12

descendre *to go down*, II, 6

désertique *deserted, bare*, III, 2

le **désinfectant** *disinfectant*, III, 7

désirer: Comment désirez-vous votre viande? *How do you like your meat cooked?* III, 1; **Vous désirez?** *What would you like?* I, 10

Désolé(e). *Sorry.* II, 10; **Désolé(e), je suis occupé(e).** *Sorry, I'm busy.* I, 6; **Désolé(e), mais je ne peux pas.** *Sorry, but I can't.* I, 4

le **dessert** *dessert*, II, 3

le **dessin animé** *cartoon*, III, 9

dessiner *to draw*, III, 4

le **dessinateur (la dessinatrice)** *commercial artist*, III, 5

dessous: ci-dessous *below*, III, 3

se **détendre** *to relax*, III, 11

la **détente** *relaxation*, III, 2

détoner *to detonate, explode*, III, 4

détruire *to destroy*, III, 7

dévalisé(e) *stripped, robbed*, III, 2

dévaliser *to rob (a store)*, III, 2

devant *in front of*, I, 6

devenir *to become*, II, 6; **Qu'est-ce que tu deviens?** *What's going on with you?* III, 1

la **devinette** *riddle*, III, 7

deviner *to guess*, III, 5; **Devine ce que...** *Guess what...*, II, 9; **Devine qui...** *Guess who . . .* , II, 9; **Tu ne devineras jamais ce qui s'est passé.** *You'll never guess what happened.* II, 9

devoir *have to, must*, III, 3; II, 7; **Ça doit être...** *It must be . . .* , III, 7; **Il doit y avoir...** *There must be . . .* , III, 7; **On doit...** *Everyone should . . .* , II, 7; **Tu crois que je devrais...?** *Do you think I should . . . ?* III, 7; **Tu devrais aller voir...** *You should go see . . .* , III, 9; **Tu devrais...** *You should . . .* , I, 9; **Tu ne devrais pas...** *You shouldn't . . .* , II, 7; **Vous (ne) devriez (pas)...** *You should(n't). . .* , III, 3

les **devoirs** (m.) *homework*, I, 2; **J'ai des devoirs à faire.** *I've got homework to do*, I, 5

dévoué(e) *dedicated*, III, 5

d'habitude *usually*, I, 4

le **diamant** *diamond*, III, 7

la **diapositive** *slide (photograpy)*, III, 7

le **dictionnaire** *dictionary*, I, 3

Dieu *God*, III, 6

la **différence: Quelle est la différence entre ... et...?** *What's the difference between . . . and . . . ?* III, 10

différencier *to differenciate*, III, 11

différer de *to differ, to be different from*, III, 10

difficile *difficult*, I, 2

le **dimanche** *on Sundays*, I, 2

la **dinde: l'escalope de dinde purée** *sliced turkey breast with mashed potatoes*, III, 1

le **dîner** *dinner*, I, 8

dîner *to have dinner*, I, 9

dingue *wild, crazy, funny*, III, 2

le **diplomate (la diplomate)** *diplomat*, III, 5

le **diplôme: obtenir son diplôme** *to get one's diploma*, III, 5

dire: dire à (quelqu'un) que... *to tell (someone) that . . .* , II, 10; **dire la vérité** *to tell the truth*, III, 3; **J'ai entendu dire que...** *I've heard that . . .* , III, 10; **Qu'est-ce que ça veut dire,...?** *What does . . . mean?* III, 11; **Vous pouvez lui dire que j'ai téléphoné?** *Can you tell her/him that I called?* I, 9; **Dis à... que je pense à lui/elle.** *Tell . . . that I'm thinking about him/her.* III, 8; **Dis à... que je vais lui écrire.** *Tell . . . that I'm going to write.* III, 8; **Dis vite!** *Let's hear it!* II, 9; **Dis-lui/-leur que...** *Tell him/her/them that . . .* , II, 10; **Oh, dis donc!** *Wow!* III, 7; **... et alors il dit que...** *So he says . . .* , III, 10; **Ça ne me dit rien.** *That doesn't interest me.* I, 4; II, 1; **Ça te dit d'aller...?** *What do you think about going . . . ?* II, 4; **Ça te dit de...?** *Does . . . sound good to you?* II, 1; **Comment on dit...?** *How do you say . . . ?* III, 11; **écouter ce qu'il/elle dit** *to listen to what he/she says*, II, 10; **Je ne t'ai pas dit?** *Didn't I tell you?* III, 10; **Qui t'a dit ça?** *Who told you that?* III, 10; **Tu l'as dit!** *You said it!* III, 9; **Dites donc, ça vous gênerait de...?** *Hey, do you think you can . . . ?* III, 8; **On dirait que...** *It looks like . . .* , III, 11; **Ça ne te dit pas trop** *It's not very appealing to you*, III, 7

diriger *to manage or direct*, III, 5

la **discothèque** *nightclub*, III, 11

discuter *to discuss*, III, 2

la **diseuse de bonne aventure** *fortuneteller*, III, 6

se **disputer (avec quelqu'un)** *to have an argument (with someone)*, II, 9

le **disquaire: chez le disquaire** *at the record store*, I, 12

le **disque compact/le C.D.** *compact disc/CD*, I, 3

se **distraire** *to entertain oneself*, III, 2

divers(e) *various*, III, 1

diviser *to divide up*, III, 1

divorcé(e) *divorced*, III, 6

le **documentaire** *documentary*, III, 9

le **doigt: se couper le doigt** *to cut one's finger*, II, 7

dommage: C'est dommage *That's a shame, that's too bad*, III, 10

Donc,... *Therefore, . . .* , II, 9; **Oh, dis donc!** *Wow!* III, 7

donner: donner à manger aux animaux *to feed the animals*, II, 6; III, 3; **Donnez-moi votre...** *Give me your . . .* , III, 6; **Donnez-moi..., s'il vous plaît.** *Please give me . . .* I, 5

doré(e) *golden*, III, 6

dormir *to sleep*, I, 1; **Où est-ce que tu as dormi?** *Where did you stay?* III, 1

le **dortoir** *dormitory*, III, 5

le **dos: J'ai mal au dos** *My back hurts.* II, 7

doter: être doté(e) de *to have, to be blessed with*, III, 10

doucement *slowly, softly*, III, 2

doué(e) *gifted*, III, 10

doux (douce) *soft*, III, 10; **l'eau douce** *fresh water*, III, 7

le **doute: Je n'en ai aucun doute.** *I have no doubt about it.* III, 12

la **douzaine: une douzaine de** *a dozen*, I, 8

le **doyen** *elder*, III, 5

le **drame** *drama*, III, 9

le **droit** *law*, **Tu n'as pas le droit de...** *You're not allowed to . . .* , III, 3

droite: à droite de *to the right of*, I, 12; II, 2; **sur la droite (gauche)** *on the right (left)*, II, 2

drôle: C'est drôle (amusant). *It's funny.* II, 11; **une drôle de machine** *a funny (peculiar) machine*, III, 3

drôlement *peculiarly, strangely;* j'allais être drôlement raisonnable *I was going to be reasonable,* III, 1

dû: J'aurais dû... *I should have . . . ,* II, 10; **Tu aurais dû...** *You should have . . . ,* II, 10

l' **eau** (f.) *water,* I, 5; **l'eau minérale** *mineral water,* I, 5; **la chute d'eau** *waterfall,* II, 4; **le sirop de fraise à l'eau** *water with strawberry syrup,* I, 5

l' **échalote** (f.) *shallot,* III, 1

l' **échange** (m.) *exchange,* III, 10

échapper *to escape,* III, 7; **On l'a échappé belle!** *That was close!* III, 7

l' **écharpe** (f.) *scarf,* I, 10; II, 1

l' **échec** (m.) *failure,* III, 8

l' **échelle** (f.) *ladder,* III, 10; **à l'échelle** *to scale,* III, 3

éclater: Ça m'éclate. *I'm wild about it.* III, 11; **éclater de rire** *to burst out laughing,* III, 10

l' **école** (f.) *school,* I, 1; **faire une école technique** *to go to a technical school,* III, 5; **l'école primaire** *elementary school,* III, 5; **l'école secondaire** *secondary school, high school,* III, 5

écologique *ecological,* III, 3

économiser *to economise, to save,* III, 3

écossais(e) *plaid,* III, 4

s'écouler *to pour out,* III, 3

écouter: écouter ce qu'il/elle dit *to listen to what he/she says,* II, 10; **écouter de la musique** *to listen to music,* I, 1; **Ecoutez!** *Listen!* I, 0; **Je n'écoute que ça.** *That's all I listen to.* III, 11; **Je t'écoute.** *I'm listening.* I, 9; II, 10

l' **écran** (m.) *screen,* III, 9

les **écrevisses** (f.) *crawfish,* III, 11

s'écrier *to exclaim,* III, 6

l' **écrivain** (m.) *writer,* III, 5

l' **écureuil** (m.) *squirrel,* II, 12

l' **édition** (f.) *publishing,* III, 5

l' **éducation** (f.) **physique et sportive (EPS)** *physical education (PE),* III, 3; I, 2

effacer *to erase,* III, 10

effilé(e) *tapering,* III, 4

l' **effort** (m.): **Encore un effort!** *One more try!* II, 7

effrayant(e) *frightening,* III, 7

égal(e) *equal,* III, 1; **de façon égale** *in an equal way, evenly,* III, 1; **Ça m'est égal.** *Whatever.* II, 8; **Ça**

m'est vraiment égal. *It's really all the same to me.* III, 9

également *also* III, 4

l' **église** (f.) *church,* II, 2

égoïste *selfish,* III, 6

élaboré(e) *elaborate,* III, 6

l' **électricien** (l'électricienne) *electrician,* III, 5

élégant(e) *elegant, sophisticated,* III, 4

l' **éléphant** (m.) *elephant,* III, 7

l' **élevage** (m.) *breeding,* III, 5

l' **élève** (m./f.) *student,* I, 2

élever *to raise,* III, 8

éliminer *to eliminate,* III, 2

elle *she or it,* I, 1

elles *they,* I, 1

éloigné(e) *distant (relative); remote,* III, 11

éloigner *to push away,* III, 5

emballé(e): Ça ne m'a pas emballé(e). *It didn't do anything for me.* III, 9

embêtant(e) *annoying,* I, 7

embêter *to pester, annoy,* III, 6; **Et toi, arrête de m'embêter!** *Stop bothering me!* III, 10; **Ça m'embête!** *That bores me!* II, 2; **Ça t'embête de...?** *Would you mind . . . ?* II, 10

l' **embouteillage** (m.) *traffic jam,* III, 8

emboutir: emboutir la voiture *to wreck the car,* III, 10

embrasser: Embrasse... pour moi. *Give . . . a kiss for me.* III, 8; **Je t'embrasse bien fort.** *Hugs and kisses.* III, 8

émérite *highly skilled,* III, 10

émincé(e) *chopped,* III, 1

émincer *to thin slice,* III, 11

l' **émission** (f.) *program,* III, 9; **l'émission de variétés** *variety show,* III, 9

emmener *to take (a person) with you,* III, 9

empêcher *to prevent, stop,* III, 12

l' **emploi** (m.) *employment,* III, 5; **bureau pour l'emploi** *unemployment office,* III, 5

employer *to use,* III, 5

emporter *to bring (with you),* II, 12

emprunter *borrow,* I, 12

l' **emprunteur** (l'emprunteuse) (m./f.) *borrower,* III, 11

en *some, of it, of them, any, none,* I, 8; **en** *to, in (before a feminine noun),* I, 11; **en laine** *wool,* III, 4; **en soie** *silk,* III, 4; **Combien en voulez-vous?** *How many (much) do you want?* II, 3; **En bas.** *Downstairs.* III, 2; **en coton** *cotton,* I, 10; **en cuir** *leather,* I, 10; **en face de** *across from,* II, 2; **En haut.** *Upstairs.* III, 2; **en jean** *denim,* I, 10; **Il/Elle en a déjà un(e).** *He/She already has one (of them).* II, 3; **Je m'en veux de...** *I feel bad for . . . ,* III, 6; **Je n'en peux plus!**

I just can't do any more! II, 7; **Je n'en veux plus.** *I don't want anymore,* I, 8; **Je ne t'en veux pas.** *No hard feelings.* II, 10; **Je suis parti(e) en...** *I went by . . . ,* III, 1; **Je vais (en) prendre...** *I'll take . . . ,* II, 3; **T'en fais pas.** *Don't worry.* II, 5; **Tu n'as pas l'air en forme.** *You don't seem too well.* II, 7; **Tu ne m'en veux pas?** *No hard feelings?* II, 10; **Vous avez ça en...?** *Do you have that in . . . ? (size, fabric, color),* I, 10; **en plein air** *outside,* III, 11

l' **enclos** (m.) *enclosure,* III, 10

encore: Encore de...? *More . . . ?* I, 8; **Encore un effort!** *One more try!* II, 7; **Encore...?** *Some more . . . ?* II, 3; **Pas encore.** *Not yet.* III, 1; **encore** *still,* III, 2

encourager *to cheer,* III, 11

l' **endroit** (m.) *place,* I, 12

l' **énergie** (f.) *energy,* III, 3

énervé(e) *annoyed,* II, 9

énerver: Tu m'énerves, à la fin! *You're bugging me!* III, 6

l' **enfant** (m./f.) *child,* I, 7; **avoir un enfant** *to have a child,* III, 5

enfermer *to lock up,* III, 6

Enfin,... *Finally, . . . ,* II, 1; II, 4; II, 9

enfoncer *to drive in (a nail),* III, 6

l' **énigme** (f.) *enigma, puzzle* III, 2

enlacer *to hug,* III, 10

enlever: enlever la neige *to shovel snow,* III, 3; **se faire enlever ses bagues** *to get one's braces off,* III, 10

l' **ennui** (m.) *boredom,* III, 6

ennuyer *to bother,* II, 8; **Ça m'ennuie à mourir!** *That bores me to death!* III, 2; **Ça t'ennuie de...?** *Would you mind . . . ?* II, 10; **Ce qui m'ennuie, c'est...** *What bores me is . . . ,* II, 4; **On ne s'ennuie pas.** *You're never bored.* II, 11; **Je me suis ennuyé(e) à mourir.** *I was bored to death.* III, 9; **Je me suis ennuyé(e).** *I was bored.* II, 6; **Je ne me suis pas ennuyé(e) une seconde.** *I wasn't bored a second.* III, 9

ennuyeux (ennuyeuse) *boring,* II, 6; **C'était ennuyeux.** *It was boring.* I, 5

enregistrer *to record,* III, 9

enseigner *to teach,* III, 5; **l'enseignement technique** *technical education,* III, 5

ensemble *together,* III, 2

Ensuite,... *Next, . . . ,* II, 1; *Then, . . . ,* II, 12

entendre: entendre le réveil *to hear the alarm clock,* II, 5; **Entendu.** *OK.* I, 6; **J'ai entendu dire que...** *I've heard that . . . ,* III, 10; **s'entendre** *to get along,* III, 6

entier (entière) *entire, whole,* III, 3

entièrement *entirely,* III, 6

entouré(e) *surrounded*, III, 10
l' entraînement (m.) *training*, III, 10
s'entraîner à... *to train for (a sport)*, II, 7
l' **entraîneur** (m.) *coach*, III, 12
entre *between*, I, 12; **Quelle est la différence entre ... et...?** *What's the difference between . . . and . . . ?* III, 10
l' entrecôte grillée *rib steak*, III, 1
l' **entrée** (f.) *first course*, II, 3; *appetizer*, III, 1, **C'est combien, l'entrée?** *How much is the entrance fee?* II, 6; **Que voulez-vous comme entrée?** *What sort of appetizer would you like?*, III, 1; **Comme entrée, j'aimerais...** *For an appetizer, I would like . . .* III, 1; **A l'entrée de...** *At the entrance to . . .* , III, 2
les entrelacs (m.) *interlacing*, III, 6
entrer *to enter*, II, 6; **entrer à l'université** *to enter the university*, III, 5
l' **enveloppe** (f.) *envelope*, I, 12
envers *towards*, III, 6
envie: J'ai envie de... *I feel like . . .* , I, 11; **Non, je n'ai pas très envie.** *No, I don't feel like it.* II, 7; **Tu as envie de...?** *Do you feel like . . . ?* II, 1
environ *about*, III, 2
envoyer: envoyer des lettres *to send letters*, I, 12; **envoyer les invitations** *to send the invitations*, II, 10; **Pourriez-vous m'envoyer des renseignements sur...?** *Could you send me information on . . . ?* III, 5
épais (épaisse) *thick*, III, 7
épater: Alors, là, tu m'épates! *I'm really impressed!* III, 10
l' **épée** (f.) *an epee/a sword*, III, 12
éperdument *hopelessly*, III, 5
épicé(e) *spicy*, III, 11
l' **épicerie** (f.) *grocery store*, I, 12
les **épices** (f.) *spices*, III, 11
les **épinards** (m.) *spinach*, III, 11
l' **épine** (f.) *thorn*, III, 10
l' **éponge** (f.) *sponge*, III, 10
épouser *to marry*, III, 6
épouvantable: avoir une journée épouvantable *to have a horrible day*, II, 5; **C'était épouvantable.** *It was horrible.* I, 9; **J'ai passé une journée épouvantable!** *I had a terrible day!* II, 5
l' **épreuve** (f.) *event (sports)*, III, 12
équilibre (tenir en équilibre) *to be balanced*, III, 6
l' **équipe** (f.) *a team*, III, 12
l' **équitation** (f.) *equestrian events*, III, 12; **faire de l'équitation** *to go horseback riding*, I, 1
l' escalier (m.) *stairs*, III, 2
l' **escalope** (f.) **de dinde purée** *sliced turkey breast with mashed potatoes*, III, 1

les **escargots** (m.) *snails*, I, 1; II, 3
l' **escrime** (f.) *fencing*, III, 12
l' **escrimeur (l'escrimeuse)** *fencer*, III, 12
Esope *Aesop*, III, 3
l' **espadon** (m.) *swordfish*, III, 10
l' **Espagne** (f.) *Spain*, III, 12
l' **espagnol** (m.) *Spanish (language)*, I, 2
les **espèces** (f.) *species*, III, 7
esquisser *to outline*, III, 6
l' **essai** (m.) *essay*, III, 11
l' **essayage** (m.) *fitting*, III, 4
essayer: Je peux essayer...? *Can I try on . . . ?* I, 10; **Je peux l'(les) essayer?** *Can I try it (them) on?* I, 10; **Essaie...** *Try . . .* , III, 1
l' **essence** (f.) *gas*, III, 2
essentiel(le): Il est essentiel que... *It's essential that . . .* , III, 7
essuyer *to wipe*, III, 1
l' **est** (m.): **dans l'est** *in the east*, II, 4; **C'est à l'est de...** *It's to the east of . . .* , II, 12
Est-ce que *(introduces a yes-or-no question)*, I, 4; **(Est-ce que) je peux...?** *May I . . . , ?* I, 7
l' **étage** (m.): **Au premier étage.** *On the second floor.* III, 2
les **étagères** (f.) *shelves*, II, 2
l' **étape** (f.) *step*, III, 3
l' **état** *state*, III, 1; **les Etats-Unis** (m.) *United States*, III, 12
l' **été** (m.) *summer*, I, 4; **en été** *in the summer*, I, 4
éteindre *to turn off/out*, III, 3; **éteindre les lumières** *to turn out the lights*, III, 3
éternuer: J'éternue beaucoup. *I'm sneezing a lot.* II, 7
l' étoffe (f.) *fabric*, III, 6
l' **étoile de mer** (f.) *starfish*, III, 10
étonné(e) *surprised*, II, 9
étonner: Ça m'étonnerait que... *I'd be surprised if . . .* , III, 7; **Ça m'étonnerait!** *That would surprise me.* II, 6; III, 10
étouffée: à l'étouffée *steamed*, III, 11
étourdi(e) *spaced-out, absent-minded*, III, 3
étrange *strange*, III, 10
étranger (étrangère) *foreign*, III, 7
l' **étranger (l'étrangère)** (m./f.) *foreigner*, III, 3
être *to be*, I, 7; **être collé(e)** *to have detention*, II, 5; **être en train de (+ infinitive)** *to be in the process of (doing something)*, II, 9; être à bout *to have had enough*, III, 11
étroit(e) *narrow*, III, 3
l' **étude** (f.) *study hall*, I, 2; **les études** (f.) *studies*, III, 5; **arrêter/finir ses études** *to stop/finish one's studies*, III, 5
étudier *to study*, I, 1
les **événements** (m.) *events*, III, 10
l' **éventail** (m.) *fan*, III, 10

évidemment *obviously*, II, 9
éviter *to avoid*, III, 3; **Évite d'aller voir...** *Avoid seeing. . . ,* III, 9; **Evite de...** *Avoid . . .* , II, 7
évoquer *to evoke*, III, 6
les **examens** (m.) *tests*, I, 1; examen d'entrée *entry exam*, III, 3
excellent(e) *excellent*, I, 5; **Oui, excellent.** *Yes, excellent.* I, 9; II, 2
s'excuser *to apologize*, II, 10; **Excuse-moi.** *Forgive me.* II, 10; **Excuse-toi.** *Apologize.* II, 10; **Je m'excuse de...** *I'm sorry for . . .* , III, 6
l' **exercice** (m.): **faire de l'exercice** *to exercise*, II, 7
exigeant(e) *demanding*, III, 5
l' **expérience** (f.) *experiment*, III, 3
expliquer: expliquer ce qui s'est passé (à quelqu'un) *to explain what happened (to someone)*, II, 10; **Explique-lui/-leur.** *Explain to him/her/them.* II, 10
l' explorateur (m.) *explorer*, III, 11
exploser *to explode*, III, 2
exprès: Tu le fais exprès? *Are you doing that on purpose?* III, 6
l' **expression** (f.) *phrase*, III, 2
l' **extrait** (m.) *excerpt*, III, 6

face: en face de *across from*, I, 12; II, 12
la **face** *face*, III, 6; faire face à *to face up to (something)*, III, 3
fâché(e) *angry*, II, 9
facile *easy*, I, 2
la **façon** *way*, III, 1; de façon égale *in an equal way, evenly*, III, 1
la **faim: avoir faim** *to be hungry*, I, 5; **Je n'ai plus faim.** *I'm not hungry anymore.* II, 3; **Si, j'ai très faim!** *Yes, I'm very hungry.* II, 2; **Vous n'avez pas/Tu n'as pas faim?** *Aren't you hungry?* II, 2
faire *to do, to make, to play*, I, 4; **faire + infinitive** *to have (something) done*, III, 4; **se faire enlever ses bagues** *to get one's braces off*, III, 10; **se faire percer les oreilles** *to have one's ears pierced*, III, 10; **se faire mal à...** *to hurt one's . . .* , II, 7; III, 10; **faire la tête** *to sulk*, II, 9; **faire le plein** *to fill it up*, III, 2; **faire les préparatifs** *to get ready*, II, 10; **Tu vas t'y faire.** *You'll get used to it.* II, 8; **fais: A ton avis, qu'est-ce que je fais?** *In your opinion, what do I do?* I, 9; **Est-ce que tu fais...?** *Do you play/do . . . ?* I, 4; **Fais-toi une raison.** *Make the*

best of it. II, 8; **Ne t'en fais pas!** *Don't worry!* I, 9; **Faites/Fais comme chez vous (toi).** *Make yourself at home.* II, 2; **Mais, qu'est-ce que tu fais?** *What are you doing?* III, 2; **Ne t'en fais pas.** *Don't worry.* I, 11; **Qu'est-ce que tu fais comme sport?** *What sports do you play?* II, 1; **Qu'est-ce que tu fais pour t'amuser?** *What do you do to have fun?* I, 4; **Qu'est-ce que tu fais quand...?** *What do you do when...?* I, 4; **Ça fait combien?** *How much does that make?* II, 3; **Ça fait vraiment...** *That looks really...,* III, 4; **Ça fait...** *It's been...,* III, 1; **Ça ne fait rien.** *It doesn't matter.* II, 10; **Comment est-ce qu'on fait?** *How should we work this out?* III, 6; **D'abord, j'ai fait...** *First, I did...,* I, 9; **Il fait beau.** *It's nice weather.* I, 4; **Il fait frais.** *It's cool.* I, 4; **Il fait froid.** *It's cold.* I, 4; **Il fait chaud.** *It's hot.* I, 4; **Qu'est-ce qu'on y fait?** *What should we do?* II, 1; **Faites gaffe!** *Look out!* III, 7; **Faites attention!** *Watch out!* III, 7; **Qu'est-ce qu'il y avait à faire?** *What was there to do?* III, 1

se faire des amis *to meet people,* III, 11

faire la fête *to party,* III, 11

faire partie de *to be part of,* III, 2

faire semblant de *to pretend to,* III, 4

le fait *fact,* III, 10; au fait *by the way,* III, 8

fameux (fameuse): pas fameux *not so great,* I, 5

fantaisiste *eccentric, whimsical,* III, 5

farci(e) (à) *stuffed (with),* III, 11

la farine *flour,* I, 8

fastoche: C'est fastoche, ça! *That's so easy!* III, 10

fastueux (fastueuse) *lavish,* III, 11

fatigant(e): C'était fatigant! *It was tiring!* II, 2

fatigué(e): Je suis fatigué(e) *I'm tired.* II, 12; **Pas trop fatigué(e)?** *(You're) not too tired?* II, 2

faudrait: Il faudrait que tu... *You should...,* III, 5; **Il faudrait que tu...** *You ought to...,* III, 7

la faune *animal life,* III, 10

faut: Il faut mieux travailler en classe. *You have to do better in class.* II, 5; **Il faut que tu... d'abord.** *First, you have to...,* III, 3; **Il me faut...** *I need...,* I, 3; **Il ne faut pas...** *One should not...,* III, 3; **Qu'est-ce qu'il te faut pour...?** *What do you need for...? (informal),* I, 3; **Il faut que tu sois...** *You must be...,* III, 3

la **faute: C'est de ma faute.** *It's my fault.* II, 10

le fauteuil *armchair,* III, 1; le fauteuil à bascule *rocking chair,* III, 10

la fée *fairy, fairy godmother,* III, 1

Félicitations! *Congratulations!* II, 3

la femme *wife,* I, 7; III, 6

la femme d'affaires *businesswoman,* III, 5

la fenêtre *window,* I, 0

la ferme *farm,* III, 1

fermer: A quelle heure est-ce que vous fermez? *When do you close?* II, 6; **Fermez la porte.** *Close the door.* I, 0

féroce *ferocious,* III, 7

le festin *feast, banquet,* III, 5

la festivité *celebration,* III, 11

la **fête: Bonne fête de Hanoukka!** *Happy Hanukkah!* II, 3; **Bonne fête!** *Happy holiday! (Happy saint's day!),* II, 3

le **feu: Il n'y a pas le feu.** *Where's the fire?* III, 2; le feu (rouge) *traffic light,* III, 3; à feu doux (cuire à feu doux) *low heat,* III, 11

la **feuille: une feuille de papier** *a sheet of paper,* I, 0; **ramasser les feuilles** *to rake leaves,* III, 3

feuilleter *to leaf through,* III, 2

le feuilleton *soap opera,* III, 9

février *February,* I, 4

les fiançailles (f.) *engagement,* III, 6

se fiancer *to get engaged,* III, 10

ficher: Je m'en fiche. *I don't give a darn.* III, 9; **Fiche-moi la paix!** *Leave me alone!* III, 6; **Tu te fiches de moi?** *Are you kidding me?* III, 9

fictif (fictive) *imaginary,* III, 10

fier (fière) *proud,* III, 10; **Tu peux être fier (fière) de toi.** *You should be proud of yourself.* II, 5

la fièvre jaune *yellow fever,* III, 7

la figue *fig,* III, 8

figurer: Figure-toi que... *Can you imagine that...,* III, 10

le fil *thread,* III, 10

le **filet de sole riz champignons** *filet of sole with rice and mushrooms,* III, 1

la fille *daughter,* I, 7

le **film: le film classique** *classic movie,* II, 11; **le film comique** *comedy,* II, 11; **le film d'action** *action movie,* II, 11; **le film d'aventures** *adventure movie,* II, 11; **le film d'horreur** *horror movie,* II, 11; **le film de science-fiction** *science-fiction movie,* II, 11; **le film policier** *detective or mystery movie,* II, 11; **le film étranger** *foreign film,* III, 9; **le film historique** *historical movie,* III, 9; **le film de guerre** *war movie,* III, 9; **le film d'espionnage** *spy movie,* III, 9; **voir un film** *to see a movie,* I, 6; **Qu'est-ce qu'il y a comme bons films en ce moment?** *What good movies are out now?* III, 9; **Qu'est-ce que tu as vu comme bons films?** *What good movies have you seen?* III, 9

le fils *son,* I, 7

fin(e) *thin,* III, 6

la **fin: A la fin...** *At the end...,* III, 9; **C'est insupportable, à la fin!** *I won't put up with this!* III, 8; **Tu m'énerves, à la fin!** *You're bugging me to death!* III, 6; **J'y suis allé(e) fin...** *I went at the end of...,* III, 1

Finalement... *Finally...,* I, 9; II, 1; II, 4; II, 9

financier (financière) *financial,* III, 2

finir: finir ses études *to finish one's studies,* III, 5

fixe *fixed,* III, 6

fixer: fixer la date *to choose the date,* II, 10

flamand(e) *Flemish,* III, 1

le flamant *flamingo,* III, 7

la Flandre *Flanders,* III, 2

la flèche *arrow,* III, 12

le fleuret *foil (sword),* III, 12

fleuri(e) *flowery,* III, 6

le fleuriste *florist's shop,* II, 3

les fleurs (f.) *flowers,* II, 3

Flûte! *Darn!,* III, 2

la flûte *flute,* III, 11

la **fois: Ça va pour cette fois.** *OK, just this once.* III, 3; **... fois par semaine** *... times a week,* I, 4; la fois *time;* à la fois *at the same time,* III, 8; **Il était une fois...** *Once upon a time...,* III, 1

foncé(e) *dark,* III, 4

foncer *to get to it (to get to doing something),* III, 3, *to rush,* III, 11

le fonceur (la fonceuse) *a "go-getter,"* III, 12

le fonctionnaire (la fonctionnaire) *government employee,* III, 5

le **fond: Au fond.** *Towards the back.* III, 2

le fond de teint *foundation (cosmetics),* III, 4

fondre (pp. fondu) *to melt,* III, 11, fondre en larmes *to break down in tears,* III, 5

le foot(ball) *soccer,* I, 1; **le football américain** *football,* I, 4

la **forêt: en forêt** *to the forest,* I, 11; **la forêt tropicale** *tropical rainforest,* II, 4

la formation *training,* III, 5

formé(e) *to be made up of,* III, 10

la **forme: Tu n'as pas l'air en forme.** *You don't seem well.* II, 7; **forme tunique** *tunic style,* III, 4

se former *to form,* III, 10

formidable: C'était formidable! *It was great!* I, 11

fort(e) *strong,* I, 7; II, 1; **Ce n'est pas mon fort.** *It's not my strong point.* II, 5; **Je t'embrasse bien fort.** *Hugs and kisses.* III, 8; fort possible *very possible,* III, 7

fortiche: Tu es fortiche. *You're really strong at that.* III, 10

fou (folle) *crazy, funny,* III, 2; **C'est fou comme...!** *I can't believe how...!* III, 7

la fougère *fern,* III, 10

la fouille *strip down,* III, 2

fouiller *to rummage around,* III, 6

le foulard *scarf,* II, 3; III, 4

la foule *crowd,* III, 8

se fouler: se fouler la cheville *to sprain one's ankle,* II, 7

la fourmi *ant,* III, 7

fourmiller *to swarm,* III, 5

fournir *to supply,* III, 7

la fourrure *fur,* III, 7

le foyer *breakroom,* III, 11

le fragment *fragment,* III, 10

les frais (m.) *fees,* III, 5

frais (fraîche): Il fait frais. *It's cool.* I, 4

les fraises (f.) *strawberries,* I, 8

le franc *franc (former monetary unit of France),* I, 3

le français *French (language),* I, 1

franchir: franchir le seuil *to walk through (clear) the door(way),* III, 5

franco-allemand(e): la frontière franco-allemande *the French-German border,* III, 1

francophone *French-speaking,* III, 1

la frange *bangs,* III, 4

frapper (à la porte) *to knock (on a door),* III, 6

le frappeur *the batter (in baseball),* III, 12

la frégate *frigate bird,* III, 10

frémir *to shiver,* III, 10

les freins (m.) *the brakes,* III, 2

le frère *brother,* I, 7

la fripe *secondhand clothes,* III, 6

frire *to fry,* III, 11

frisé(e): les cheveux frisés (m.) *curly hair,* III, 4

se friser *to curl one's hair,* III, 4

frissonner *to quiver,* III, 10

frit(e) *fried,* III, 11

les frites (f.) *French fries,* I, 1

froid(e): Il fait froid. *It's cold.* I, 4

le fromage *cheese,* I, 5; II, 3; **fromage de chèvre** *goat cheese,* III, 1

la frontière *border,* III, 1

le frottoir *washboard,* III, 11

la frousse: J'ai la frousse! *I'm scared to death!* III, 7

les fruits de mer (m.) *seafood,* II, 3

les frusques (f.) *rags,* III, 6

fuir *to run away,* III, 10

fumer *to smoke,* III, 3

furieux (furieuse) *furious,* II, 9

la fusée *rocket,* III, 2

futé(e): pas futé(e) *not with it,* III, 6

le futur *the future,* III, 1; *the future tense (of a verb),* III, 5

G

la gaffe *blunder,* III, 12; **Faites gaffe!** *Look out!* III, 7

gagner *to win,* I, 9; *to earn,* I, 9

le gant *glove,* III, 4; **Ça te va comme un gant.** *That fits you like a glove.* III, 4; **les gants** (m.) *a pair of gloves,* II, 1; III, 4

garder *to look after* I, 7

le gardien *warden, caretaker,* III, 7

la gare *train station,* II, 2

le gaspillage *waste,* III, 3

gaspiller *to waste,* III, 3

le gâteau *cake,* I, 8

gauche: à gauche *to the left,* I, 12; **à gauche de** *to the left of,* II, 2

la gaufre *waffle,* III, 2

la gazelle *gazelle,* III, 7

géant(e) *giant,* III, 7

gêné(e) *embarrassed,* II, 9

gêner: Dites donc, ça vous gênerait de...? *Hey, do you think you can...?* III, 8; **Non, mais surtout, ne vous gênez pas!** *Well just go right ahead!* III, 8; *The problems that bother me...,* III, 3

génial (e) *great,* I, 2; II, 2

le genou *knee,* II, 7

le genre: J'aime bien ce genre de... *I like this type of...,* III, 4

les gens (m.) *people,* III, 8; **les gens mal élévés** *rude people,* III, 8; **les gens pressés** *people in a hurry,* III, 8

gentil (gentille) *nice,* I, 7; **C'est gentil.** *That's nice of you.* III, 6; **C'est gentil de votre/ta part.** *That's so nice of you.* II, 2; **Merci, c'est gentil.** *Thanks, that's nice of you.* II, 3; III, 6

gentillet: gentillet, sans plus *cute (but that's all),* II, 11

la géographie *geography,* I, 2

la géométrie *geometry,* I, 2

la gestion *management,* III, 5

le gilet *vest,* III, 4

la girafe *giraffe,* III, 7

la glace *ice cream,* I, 1; **faire du patin à glace** *to ice-skate,* I, 4

le glas *toll, knell,* III, 8

le gnon *blow,* III, 3

le gnou *gnu,* III, 7

le goémon *wrack (type of seaweed),* III, 10

le golf *golf,* I, 4; **jouer au golf** *to play golf,* I, 4

le gombo *gumbo,* III, 11; **les gombos** *okra,* I, 8

la gomme *eraser,* I, 3

gommer *to erase,* III, 4

gonflable *inflatable,* III, 2

la gorge: J'ai mal à la gorge *I have a sore throat.* II, 7

le gorille *gorilla,* III, 7

le gosse (la gosse) *kid,* III, 8

gothique *Gothic,* III, 1

la gourde *canteen,* III, 7

gourmand(e) *someone who loves to eat well,* II, 1

la gousse d'ail *clove of garlic,* III, 11

le goût *taste,* III, 4; **de mauvais goût** *in poor taste,* III, 2

goûter *to taste,* III, 11

le goûter *afternoon snack,* I, 8

la goutte *drop,* III, 11

les goyaves (f.) *guavas,* I, 8

grâce: grâce à *thanks to, because of,* III, 3, 9; grâce à la pilule pousse-minute *thanks to the grow-in-a-minute pill,* III, 3; la période de grâce *grace period,* III, 12

gracieux (gracieuse) *gracious,* III, 10

grand(e) *tall, big,* I, 7; II, 1; **moins grand(e) que** *smaller than...,* II, 4; **plus grand(e) que** *bigger than...,* II, 4

grand-chose: Ce n'est pas grand-chose. *It's nothing special.* II, 3; **Pas grand-chose.** *Not much.* I, 6

la grand-mère *grandmother,* I, 7

le grand-père *grandfather,* I, 7

grandir *to grow,* I, 10

grandiose *imposing,* III, 2

la grange *barn,* III, 12

le graphisme *graphic arts,* III, 5

le gratte-ciel *skyscraper,* III, 8

le gratte-papier: carrière de gratte-papier *career as a pencil-pusher,* III, 5

grave: C'est pas grave. *It's not serious.* II, 5

gravé(e) *carved,* III, 10

la grègue *a coffeepot (Cajun),* III, 11

la grêle *hail,* III, 3

grignoter: grignoter entre les repas *snacking between meals,* II, 7

grimper *to climb,* III, 3

la grippe: J'ai la grippe. *I've got the flu.* II, 7

grippe-sou *penny pincher,* III, 2

gris(e) *grey,* I, 3

le grognement *growling,* III, 7

gros (grosse) *fat,* I, 7; *big,* III, 4; **Grosses bises.** *Hugs and kisses.* III, 8

grossir *to gain weight,* I, 10

grouiller: Grouille-toi! *Get a move on!* III, 2

le groupe *(music) group,* II, 11

le grumeau *lump,* III, 11

la Guadeloupe *Guadeloupe,* III, 12

le guépard *cheetah,* III, 7

la guêpe *wasp,* III, 12

le guichet *ticket window, booth,* III, 2

guidé(e): une visite guidée *a guided tour,* II, 6

la guitare *guitar,* III, 11

la gymnastique *gymnastics,* III, 12; **faire de la gymnastique** *to do gymnastics,* II, 7

H

habile *skillful*, III, 5
s'habiller *to get dressed*, II, 4
l' habit (m.) *cloth*, III,10
l' habitant (l'habitante) (m./f.) *inhabitant*, III, 10
habiter *to live*, III, 8, 10
l' habitude(f.): d'habitude *usually*, I, 4
habitué(e) *used to*, III, 6
hâcher *to grind*, III, 11
Haïti (m.) (no article) *Haiti*, III, 12
les haltères (m.) *barbells*, III, 12
l' haltérophilie (f.) *weightlifting*, III,12
*les hamburgers (m.) *hamburgers*, I, 1
*la hanche: sur les hanches *on the hips*, III, 3
*le hareng *herring*, III, 1
*les haricots (m.) verts *green beans*, I, 8
*le hasard: par hasard *by chance*, III, 10
*haut(e) *high*, III, 1; En haut. *Upstairs.* III, 2; *la haute couture (f.) *high fashion*, III, 4
*les hauts talons (m.) *high heels*, III, 4
*le havre de paix (m.) *haven of peace*, III, 6
hebdomadaire *weekly*, III, 11
l' hectare (m.) (abbrév. ha) *hectare (about 2 acres)*, III, 6, 11
l' herbe (f.) *grass*, III, 7
hésiter: Euh... J'hésite. *Oh, I'm not sure.* I, 10; J'hésite entre... et... *I can't decide between . . . and . . . ,* III, 1
l' heure (f.): I, 2; A quelle heure? *At what time?* I, 6; A tout à l'heure! *See you later!* I, 1; Tu as... à quelle heure? *At what time do you have . . . ?* I, 2; à... heures *at . . . o'clock*, I, 2; à... heures quarante-cinq *at . . . forty-five*, I, 2; à... heures quinze *at . . . fifteen*, I, 2; à... heures trente *at . . . thirty*, I, 2
Heureusement,... *Fortunately, . . . ,* II, 9
heureux: Très heureux (heureuse). *Pleased to meet you.* I, 7
hier *yesterday*, III, 10
l' hippocampe (m.) *seahorse*, III, 10
l' hippopotame (m.) *hippopotamus*, III, 7
*se hisser *to haul oneself up*, III, 10
l' histoire (f.) *history*, I, 2; C'est l'histoire de... *It's the story of . . . ,* II, 11; III, 9; C'est une belle histoire. *It's a great story.* II, 11; C'est une histoire passionnante. *It's an exciting story.* II, 11; Est-ce que tu connais l'histoire de... ? *Do you know the one about . . . ?* III, 10; Il n'y a pas d'histoire. *It has no plot.* II, 11; l'histoire d'amour *love story*, III, 9

l' hiver *winter*, I, 4; en hiver *in the winter*, I, 4
*le hockey *hockey*, I, 4
*le Hollandais (la Hollandaise) *Dutch person*, III, 2
*la Hollande *Holland*, III, 2
*le homard *lobster*, III, 10
l' homme d'affaires *businessman*, III, 5
*la honte: Oh la honte! *How embarrassing!* III, 11
l' horaire (m.) *schedule*, III, 6
l' horloge (f.) *clock*, III, 3; *grandfather clock*, III, 10
l' horreur (f.): C'est l'horreur! *This is just horrible!* III, 8
horrible *terrible*, I, 10
*hors *out of*, III, 4; *outside*, III, 12
*les hors-d'œuvre (m.) *hors d'œuvre*, III, 11
*le hot-dog *hot dog*, I, 5
l' hôtel (m.): A l'hôtel. *In a hotel.* III, 1
l' hôtesse (f.) *hostess*, III, 2; *flight attendant*, III, 3
*le hublot *porthole, round window of a ship*, III, 3
l' huile (f.) *the oil*, III, 2; mettre de l'huile dans le moteur *to put oil in the motor*, III, 2
les huîtres (f.) *oysters*, II, 3; III, 11
l' humeur (f): de mauvaise humeur *in a bad mood*, II, 9; de bonne humeur *in a good mood*, II, 9
l' humour (m.) *humor*, III, 2
l' hyène (f.) *hyena*, III, 7
hyper cool *super cool*, III, 4

I

ici: Ici,... tandis que... *Here, . . . whereas . . .* III, 8
l' idée (f.): Bonne idée! *Good idea!* II, 3; C'est une bonne (excellente) idée. *That's a good (excellent) idea.*, II, 1; Je n'en ai aucune idée. *I have no idea.* III, 5; Tu as une idée de cadeau pour... ? *Have you got a gift idea for. . . ?* II, 3
il *he or it*, I, 1
Il était une fois... *Once upon a time . . . ,* III, 1
il y a *there is, there are*, I, 5; il y a (adv.) *ago*, III, 8
l' île (f.) *island*, II, 4
ils *they*, I, 1
l' image (f.) *the picture*, III, 9
immense *huge*, III, 6
l' immeuble (m.) *building*, III, 8
impatient(e): Je suis vraiment impatient(e) de... ! *I can hardly wait to . . . !* III, 12; *I'm really anxious to . . . !* III, 2

impérissable *imperishable*, III, 11
l' imperméable (m.) *raincoat*, II, 1
important(e): Il est très important que... *It's very important that . . . ,* III, 7
importer: du n'importe quoi *worthless*, II, 11; N'importe quoi! *That's ridiculous!* II, 6; *Yeah, right!* III, 10; Peu importe. *It doesn't matter.* III, 9
imposant(e) *impressive*, III, 4
impossible: C'est impossible. *It's impossible.* II, 10
imprégné (e) *permeated, immersed*, III, 12
l' impression (f.): J'ai l'impression que... *I have the impression that . . . ,* III, 11
impressionner *to impress*, III, 10; impressionnant(e) *impressive*, III, 12
imprimé(e) *printed*, III, 4
impudent(e) *shameless*, III, 10
inadmissible: C'est inadmissible. *That's not acceptable.* II, 5
inattendu(e) *unexpected*, III, 3
inclu(e) *included*, III, 1
incroyable *incredible*, II, 6; C'était incroyable! *It was amazing/unbelievably bad!* II, 5; Ce qui est incroyable, c'est... *What's incredible is . . . ,* III, 11
indémodable *that will never go out of fashion*, III, 11
les indications (f.) *directions*, III, 2
indiquer *to indicate*, III, 2
l' infinitif (m.) *infinitive (of a verb)*, III, 3
l' infirmier (m.), l'infirmière (f.) *nurse*, III, 5
les informations (f.) *the news*, III, 9
l' informatique (f.) *computer science*, I, 2
l' ingénieur (m.) *engineer*, III, 5
l' ingéniosité (f.) *ingenuity*, III, 3
inouï(e) *incredible, unheard of*, III, 8
inquiet (inquiète) *worried*, II, 9
inquiéter *to cause (someone) to worry, to disturb*, III, 7
s'inquiéter: Ne t'inquiète pas! *Don't worry!* III, 6
inscrire *to write down*, III, 3
s'inscrire *to enroll*, III, 5
installer *to install*, III, 2
s'installer *to settle in*, III, 6
l' instant (m.): Un instant, s'il vous plaît. *One moment, please.* III, 1
l' instituteur (m.), l'institutrice (f.) *elementary school teacher*, III, 5
insupportable: C'est insupportable, à la fin! *I won't put up with this!* III, 8
intégré(e) *well-adjusted*, III, 3
intelligent(e): *smart*, I, 7; II, 1
l' intention (f.): J'ai l'intention de... *I intend to . . . ,* I, 11; III, 5; Qu'est-ce

que tu as l'intention de faire? *What do you intend to do?* III, 5

l' **interdiction** (f.) *ban*, III, 3; **Interdiction de... ...** *is not allowed*, III, 3

interdit(e): Il est interdit de... *It's forbidden to . . .* , III, 3

intéressant(e) *interesting*, I, 2; **Ce qui est intéressant/incroyable, c'est...** *What's interesting/ incredible is . . .* , III, 11

intéresser: Ça t'intéresse de... ? *Would you be interested in . . . ?* III, 6

l' **intérêt** (m.): **Ça n'a aucun intérêt.** *It's not interesting.* III, 9

l' **interro** (f.) *quiz*, I, 9

l' **intrigue** (f.) *plot*, III, 9

introduire *to introduce*, III, 6

inutilement *for no good reason*, III, 3

inventer *to invent*, III, 10

les **invitations** (f.): **envoyer les invitations** *to send the invitations*, II, 10

inviter *to invite*, III, 2

isolé(e) *isolated*, II, 8

s'isoler *to separate oneself, to withdraw*, III, 3

l' **Italie** (f.) *Italy*, III, 12

jaloux (jalouse) *jealous*, III, 6

le jargon *lingo*, III, 2

jamais: ne... jamais *never*, I, 4; **Je n'ai jamais vu un(e) aussi...** *I've never seen such a . . .* , III, 7

le **jambalaya** *jambalaya*, III, 11

la **jambe: J'ai mal à la jambe** *My leg hurts.* II, 7

le **jambon** *ham*, I, 5; II, 3

janvier *January*, I, 4

le **Japon** *Japan*, III, 12

le **jardin** *yard*, II, 2

jaune *yellow*, I, 3

le **jazz** *jazz*, II, 11; III, 11

je *I*, I, 1

le **jean** *(a pair of) jeans*, I, 3; II, 1; **en jean** *denim*, I, 10

jeter: jeter les déchets *to throw away your trash*, II, 12; **jeter des ordures** *to throw trash*, III, 3

le **jeu télévisé** *game show*, III, 9

le **jeudi** *on Thursdays*, I, 2

jeune *young*, I, 7; II, 1

la jeunesse *youth*, III, 5; **l'auberge (f.) de jeunesse** *youth hostel*, II, 2

les **jeux** (m.): **jouer à des jeux vidéo** *to play video games*, I, 4

le **jogging: faire du jogging** *to jog*, I, 4

le jongleur *juggler*, III, 9

jouer *to play*, I, 4; **jouer à...** *to play . . .* , I, 4; **Qu'est-ce qu'on joue comme films?** *What films are playing?* II, 11; **On joue...** *. . . is showing.* II, 11; Jouez cette scène et puis changez de rôle. *Act out this scene and then switch roles*, III, 1

le jouet *toy*, III, 3

le **jour: C'est pas mon jour!** *It's just not my day!* II, 5

le **journaliste (la journaliste)** *journalist*, III, 5

la **journée: avoir une journée épouvantable** *to have a horrible day*, II, 5; **Comment s'est passée ta journée (hier)?** *How was your day (yesterday)?* II, 5; **Quelle journée!** *What a bad day!* II, 5; **Quelle journée formidable!** *What a great day!* II, 5

joyeux (joyeuse) *cheerful*, III, 6; **Joyeux (Bon) anniversaire!** *Happy birthday!* II, 3; **Joyeux Noël!** *Merry Christmas!* II, 3

le **judo** *judo*, III, 12

le juge *judge*, III, 5

juillet *July*, I, 4

juin *June*, I, 4

les **jumeaux (-elles)** *twins*, III, 6

les **jumelles** (f.) *binoculars*, III, 7

la **jupe** *skirt*, I, 10

le **jus: le jus d'orange** *orange juice*, I, 5; **le jus de pomme** *apple juice*, I, 5

jusqu'à: Vous allez tout droit jusqu'à... *You go straight ahead until you get to . . .* , I, 12

juste: C'est pas juste. *It's not fair.* III, 12; **Juste là, à côté de...** *Right there, next to . . .* , III, 2

justement *exactly*, III, 8

le **kilo: un kilo de** *a kilogram of*, I, 8

le kilomètre *kilometer*, III, 2

le klaxon *car horn*, III, 8

-là *there (noun suffix)*, I, 3; **(Est-ce que)... est là, s'il vous plaît?** *Is . . . , there, please?* I, 9; **Là, c'est...** *Here (There) is . . .* , II, 2; **C'est comment, la vie là-bas?** *What's life like there? III, 12;* **Là-bas, le garçon qui...** *Over there, the boy who . . .* , III, 4

le jongleur *juggler*, III, 9

le **lac** *lake*, III, 3

lâcher: Lâche-moi, tu veux? *Will you give me a break?* III, 10

la **laine: en laine** *wool*, III, 4

laisser *to leave*, III, 1; **Je peux laisser un message?** *Can I leave a message?* I, 9

le **lait** *milk*, I, 8; II, 3

la **lampe** *lamp*, II, 2; **la lampe de poche** *flashlight*, II, 12

se lancer *to leap*, III, 10

le **lancer du disque** *the discus throw*, III, 12

le **lanceur** *the pitcher (baseball)*, III, 12

la langue *language*, III, 1, 2

le lanternon *lantern*, III, 6

laquelle: Laquelle? *Which one?* III, 4

large *baggy*, I, 10

largement: On a largement le temps! *We've got plenty of time!* III, 2

les **larmes** (f.) *tears*, III, 5

le **latin** *Latin*, I, 2

laver: laver la voiture *to wash the car*, I, 7; **laver les vitres** (f.) *to wash the windows*, III, 3; **se laver** *to wash oneself*, II, 4

le lecteur (la lectrice) *reader*, III, 2

la lecture *reading*, III, 2

la légende *caption*, III, 12

léger (légère) *light*, III, 3

les **légumes** (m.) *vegetables*, I, 8

lequel: Lequel? *Which one?* III, 4

le lendemain *the next day*, III, 1, 6

lesquels: Lesquels/Lesquelles? *Which ones?* III, 4

la **lessive: faire la lessive** *to do the laundry*, III, 3

la lettre *letter; lettre de motivation cover letter*, III, 5

lever: Levez la main! *Raise your hand!* I, 0; **Levez-vous!** *Stand up!* I, 0

se **lever** *to get up*, II, 4

la **librairie** *bookstore*, I, 12

libre: Je suis quand même libre, non? *I'm free, aren't I?* III, 3

lié(e) *linked*, III, 12

le lieu *place*, III, 1; avoir lieu *to take place*, III, 6

la ligne *line*, III, 1

la **limonade** *lemon soda*, I, 5

le lin *flax*, III, 4

linguistique *linguistics*, III, 2

le **lion** *lion*, III, 7

lire *to read*, I, 1

le **lit** *bed*, II, 2; **faire son lit** *to make one's bed*, III, 3

le **litre: un litre de** *a liter of*, I, 8

la **livre: une livre de** *a pound of*, I, 8

le **livre** *book*, I, 3; **le livre de poésie** *book of poetry*, II, 11

le logement *lodging*, III, 6

loger *to lodge*, III, 2

logique *logical*, III, 1

loin: loin de *far from*, I, 12

long(longue) *long*, I, 10; II, 1; **les cheveux longs** (m.) *long hair*, III, 4; **trop long** *too long*, II, 11

longtemps: Ça fait longtemps qu'on ne s'est pas vu(e)s. *It's been a long time since we've seen each other.* III, 1; **Ça ne va pas prendre longtemps!** *It's not going to take long!* III, 2

lors de *at the time of*, III, 8

lorsque *when*, III, 3

la lotion anti-moustique(s) *mosquito repellent*, III, 7

louer *to rent*, III, 11

loufoque *wild, crazy*, III, 2

le loup *wolf*, II, 12

lourd(e) *heavy*, III, 7; **C'est lourd.** *It's dull.* III, 9; **Il a fait lourd...** *It was humid . . .*, III, 1

luire *to gleam*, III, 10

les lumières (f.) *lights*, III, 3

le lundi *on Mondays*, I, 2

la lune *moon*, III, 2

les lunettes de soleil (f.) *sunglasses*, I, 10

lurette: Il y a belle lurette! *It's been ages!*, III, 1

la lutte *wrestling*, III, 12; **la lutte sans frappe** *type of wrestling specific to Senegal*, III, 5

luxuriant(e) *lavish*, III,10; *luxurious*, III, 11

le lycée *high school*, II, 2

madame (Mme) *ma'am; Mrs.* I, 1; **Madame!** *Waitress!* I, 5; **Monsieur/Madame (to start a business letter)** *Sir/Madam*, III, 5

mademoiselle (Mlle) *miss; Miss*, I, 1; **Mademoiselle!** *Waitress!* I, 5

les magasins (m.) *stores*, I, 1; **faire les magasins** *to go shopping*, I, 1

le magazine *magazine*, I, 3; **magazine télévisé** *magazine show*, III, 9

le magnétoscope *videocassette recorder, VCR*, I, 0; III, 9

magnifique *beautiful*, II, 6

mai *May*, I, 4

maigrichon(ne) *scrawny, skinny*, III, 2

maigrir *to lose weight*, I, 10

le maillot de bain *bathing suit*, I, 10

la main *hand*, I, 0; **J'ai mal à la main.** *My hand hurts.* II, 7

maintenant *now*, III, 2, 5

le maire *mayor*, III, 3

mais *but*, I, 1; **Non mais, tu t'es pas regardé(e)!** *If you could see how you look!* III, 10

le maïs *corn*, I, 8

la maison *house*, II, 2; **la Maison des jeunes et de la culture (MJC)** *recreation center*, I, 6

le maître d'hôtel *maitre d', headwaiter, host*, III, 1

majeur(e) *of-age, adult*, III, 3

mal: mal à l'aise *uncomfortable*, II, 9; **Il n'y a pas de mal.** *No harm done.* II, 10; **J'ai du mal à me décider.** *I'm having trouble deciding.* III, 5; **J'ai mal dormi.** *I didn't sleep well.* II, 7; **J'ai mal partout!** *I hurt all over!* II, 7; **J'ai mal...** *My . . . hurts.* II, 7; **J'ai trouvé ça pas mal.** *It was not bad.* III, 9; **Pas mal.** *Not bad.* I, 1; *all right*, II, 6; **se faire mal à...** *to hurt one's . . .*, II, 7; III, 10; **mal élevé(e)** *rude*, III, 8

malade: Je suis malade. *I'm sick.* II, 7

la malédiction *curse*, III, 8

le malentendu: un petit malentendu *a little misunderstanding*, II, 10

le malheur *misfortune, accident*, III, 2; **Malheureusement,...** *Unfortunately, . . .*, II, 9

malicieusement *mischievously*, III, 10

malin (maligne) *clever, shrewd, smart*, III, 3

le mammifère *mammal*, III, 2

les manches (f.): **à manches courtes/longues** *short/long-sleeved*, III, 4

manger *to eat*, I, 6; II, 7; **donner à manger aux animaux** *to feed the animals*, II, 6; III, 3 **manger mieux** *to eat better*, III, 3

les mangues (f.) *mangoes*, I, 8

manier *to handle*, III, 5

la manière *way*, III, 1; **De quelle manière...?** *In what way . . .?, How . . .?*, III, 1; **à la manière de** *the way*, III, 10

le manioc *manioc (edible root)*, III, 1

le mannequin *model*, III, 5

le manque *lack of, absence of*, III, 3; **Manque de chance...** *What bad luck!* III, 3

manquer: C'est à ne pas manquer! *Don't miss it!* III, 9; **... me manque.** *I miss . . . (singular)*, II, 8; **... me manquent.** *I miss . . . (plural)*, II, 8; **Ce qui me manque, c'est (de)...** *What I miss is . . .*, II, 8

le manteau *coat*, I, 10

le maquillage *makeup*, III, 4; **se maquiller** *to put on makeup*, III, 4

le maquis *popular Ivorian outdoor restaurant*, II, 8

le marabout *religious leader*, III, 5

le marais *marsh, swamp*, III, 11

le marbre *marble*, III, 6

marchander *to haggle over*, III, 6

la marche: rater une marche *to miss a step*, II, 5

le marché *deal*, III, 10 **marcher** *to work*, III, 2

le mardi *on Tuesdays*, I, 2

le mari *husband*, I, 7; III, 6

le mariage *marriage, wedding*, III, 6 **marié(e)** *married*, III, 6 **se marier** *to get married*, III, 5

la marionnette *puppet*, III, 2

marin(e) *marine*, III, 10

le Maroc *Morocco*, III, 12

la maroquinerie *leather-goods shop*, II, 3

la marque *brand*, III, 6 **marrant(e)** *funny*, III, 2 **marre: J'en ai vraiment marre!** *I'm sick of this!* III, 12; **Je commence à en avoir marre!** *I've just about had it!* III, 8 **marron** *brown*, I, 3; II, 1 **mars** *March*, I, 4

le masque *mask*, II, 8; III, 12 **m'as-tu-vu: être m'as-tu-vu** *to be a show off*, III, 7

le match: regarder un match *to watch a game (on TV)*, I, 6; **voir un match** *to see a game (in person)*, I, 6

les maths (f.) *math*, I, 1

les matières grasses (f.) *fat*, II, 7

le matin *in the morning*, I, 2 **mauvais(e): de mauvais goût** *in poor taste*, III, 2; **avoir une mauvaise note** *to get a bad grade*, II, 5; **de mauvaise humeur** *in a bad mood*, II, 9

le mausolée *mausoleum*, III, 6

le mec: C'est l'histoire d'un mec qui... *It's about a guy who . . .*, III, 10

le mécanicien (la mécanicienne) *mechanic*, III, 5 **méchant(e)** *mean*, I, 7

la médaille *medal*, III, 12

le médecin *doctor*, III, 5

les médicaments (m.) *medicine*, I, 12

la médina *old section of a North African city*, III, 6, 8

la méduse *jellyfish*, III, 10 **Méfiez-vous!** *Be careful!* III, 7 **meilleur(e): C'est meilleur que...** *It's better than . . .*, II, 7; **C'est moi, le/la meilleur(e).** *I'm the best.* III, 10; **Tu es vraiment le/la meilleur(e).** *You're really the best.* III, 10; **Meilleurs vœux!** *Best wishes!* II, 3

le mélange *blend*, III, 8 **mélanger** *to mix*, III, 1 **mêler** *to mix*, III, 11; **Mêle-toi de tes oignons!** *Mind your own business!* III, 6 **même: C'est toujours la même chose!** *It's always the same!* III, 6; **Toujours la même chose!** *Same old thing!* III, 1; **même** *even*; **Il y a même des sports...** *There are even sports . . .*, III, 5

la mémé *grandma*, III, 1

le ménage: faire le ménage *to do housework,* I, 1; II, 10

mener *to lead,* III, 2; mener quelqu'un par le bout du nez *to have someone wrapped around your finger,* III, 2

la menthe *mint,* III, 6

mentir *to lie,* III, 6

le menu *fixed-price menu,* III, 1

le menuisier (la menuisière) *carpenter,* III, 5

la mer *sea,* II, 4; **au bord de la mer** *to/at the coast,* I, 11

Merci. *Thank you,* I, 3; II, 2; **Merci bien/infiniment/mille fois.** *Thank you so much.* III, 6; **Merci, ça va.** *No thank you, I've had enough.* II, 3; **Non, merci.** *No, thank you.* I, 8

le mercredi *on Wednesdays,* I, 2

la mère *mother,* I, 7

mériter *to earn,* III, 1; *to deserve,* III, 10

merveilleux (merveilleuse) *marvelous,* III, 2

le message électronique *e-mail,* III, 2

la météo *the weather report,* III, 9

le métier *job, occupation,* III, 5; **choisir un métier** *to choose a career,* III, 5

le métissage *crossbreeding,* III, 4

le métro: au métro... *at the ... metro stop,* I, 6; **en métro** *by subway,* I, 12

le metteur en scène *director,* III, 9

mettre *to put, to put on, to wear,* I, 10; **Je ne sais pas quoi mettre pour...** *I don't know what to wear for...,* I, 10; **Qu'est-ce que je mets?** *What shall I wear?* I, 10; **mettre la table** *to set the table,* III, 3; **se mettre en condition** *to get into shape,* II, 7; **Mettez-vous à l'aise.** *Make yourself comfortable.* III, 6; mettre en valeur *to highlight,* III, 6; mettre l'accent sur *to put emphasis on,* III, 11

se mettre à *to start,* III, 1

meurs: Je meurs de faim (soif)! *I'm dying of hunger (thirst)!* II, 2

le Mexique *Mexico,* III, 12

le micro (le microphone) *the mike, the microphone,* III, 11

midi *noon,* I, 6

mieux: C'est moi qui... le mieux. *I ... the best.* III, 10; **Ça va aller mieux!** *It's going to get better!* I, 9; **J'aime mieux...** *I prefer...,* I, 1; **manger mieux** *to eat better,* III, 3; **Tu ferais mieux de...** *You would do better to...,* III, 5

mignon(ne) *cute,* I, 7

mijoter *to simmer,* III, 11

le milieu *middle;* au beau milieu d'un carrefour *right in the middle of an intersection,* III, 3, 10

militaire: faire son service militaire *to do one's military service,* III, 5

le millefeuille *layered pastry,* II, 3

le millénaire *millenium, thousand-year-old,* III, 4

le millier *thousand,* III, 10

mince *slender,* I, 7

mini-jupe *miniskirt,* III, 4

minuit *midnight,* I, 6

la minute: Tu as une minute? *Do you have a minute?* I, 9; II, 10

la minuterie *a kind of timer that turns off the lights after a period of time,* III, 3

minutieux (-ieuse) *meticulous,* III, 3

la mi-temps *half-time,* III, 11

les mocassins (m.) *loafers,* III, 4

moche: Je le/la/les trouve moche(s). *I think it's (they're) really tacky.* I, 10

la mode *fashion,* III, 4; **à la mode** *in style,* I, 10

moi *me,* I, 2

le moindre *the slightest,* III, 11

moins: La vie était plus... moins... *Life was more..., less...,* II, 8; **moins cinq** *five to,* I, 6; **moins de... que...** *fewer... than...,* III, 8; **moins grand(e) que** *smaller than...,* II, 4; **moins le quart** *quarter to,* I, 6; **moins... que...** *less... than...,* III, 8; **Plus ou moins.** *More or less.* II, 6; le moins d'eau *the least water, the smallest amount of water,* III, 3; moins (du moins) *at the very least,* III, 6

la moisson *harvest,* III, 1

la moitié *half,* III, 6

le moment: À ce moment-là... *At that point...,* II, 9; III, 9; **Un moment, s'il vous plaît.** *One moment, please.* I, 5

le monde *world,* III, 2

monsieur (M.) *sir; Mr.* I, 1; **Monsieur!** *Waiter!* I, 5; **Monsieur/Madame** (to start a business letter) *Sir/Madame,* III, 5

la montagne: à la montagne *to/at the mountains,* I, 11; **faire du vélo de montagne** *to go mountain-bike riding,* II, 12; **les montagnes russes** *the roller coaster,* II, 6

montagneux (montagneuse) *mountainous,* III, 6

monter *to go up,* II, 6; **monter dans une tour** *to go up in a tower,* II, 6

la montre *watch,* I, 3

montrer *to show,* I, 9

se moquer de *to tease, make fun of,* III, 10

la morale *moral,* III, 6

le moral *spirit, morale,* III, 10

le morceau: un morceau de *a piece of,* I, 8

mort(e) *dead,* III, 6

mortel(le) *deadly boring,* II, 6; III, 2; *deadly dull,* II, 6, 8

la mosquée *mosque,* II, 8

le mot *word;* écrire un mot *to write a note,* III, 2

la motivation *incentive,* III, 5

Mouais. *Yeah.* II, 6

la mouche *fly,* III, 7

la mouffette *skunk,* II, 12

la moule *mussel,* III, 12

mourir *to die,* II, 6; **Ça m'ennuie à mourir!** *That bores me to death!* III, 2; **Je me suis ennuyé(e) à mourir.** *I was bored to death.* III, 9

la moustache *mustache,* III, 4

le moustique *mosquito,* II, 4

la moutarde *mustard,* III, 2

le mouton *sheep,* III, 8

moyen(ne): de taille moyenne *of medium height,* II, 1; **le moyen** *way,* III, 2; *means;* moyen de subsistance *means of subsistence,* III, 7; **le Moyen-Age** *Middle Ages,* III, 2

la musculation: faire de la musculation *to lift weights,* II, 7

le museau *muzzle, snout,* III, 1

le musée *museum,* I, 6; II, 2

le musicien (la musicienne) *musician,* II, 11

la musique *music,* I, 2; **la musique cajun** *Cajun music,* III, 11; **la musique classique** *classical music,* II, 11; III, 11; **écouter de la musique** *to listen to music,* I, 1; **Qu'est-ce que tu aimes comme musique?** *What music do you like?* II, 1

musulman(e) *Muslim,* III, 8

mutiler: mutiler les arbres *to deface the trees,* II, 12

nager *to swim,* I, 1

la naissance *birth,* III, 6

naître *to be born,* II, 6

la natation *swimming,* III, 12; **faire de la natation** *to swim,* I, 4

la natte *braid,* III, 4

nautique: faire du ski nautique *to water ski,* I, 4

le navet: **C'est un navet.** *It stinks.* II, 11; *It's trash.* III, 9

navré(e) *sorry,* III, 6

ne: ne... pas *not,* I, 1; **ne... jamais** *never,* I, 4; **ne... pas encore** *not yet,* I, 9; **ne... aucun(e)** *no...,* III, 9; **ne... ni... ni...** *neither... nor...,* III, 9; **ne...**

nulle part *nowhere*, III, 9; **ne... personne** *no one*, III, 9; **ne... rien** *nothing*, III, 9; **ne... que** *only*, III, 9; **Tu n'as qu'à...** *All you have to do is . . .*, II, 7; III, 5

nécessaire: Il est nécessaire que... *It's necessary to . . .*, III, 7

la **nef** *nave*, III, 6

néfaste *harmful*, III, 8

la **neige: enlever la neige** *to shovel snow*, III, 3; **Il neige.** *It's snowing.* I, 4

net(te) *clean, neat*, III, 4; **net: ...sa tresse gauche avait été coupée net.** *...her braid had been sheared clean off.* III, 3

nettoyer: nettoyer la salle de bains *to clean the bathroom*, III, 3; **nettoyer le pare-brise** *to clean the windshield*, III, 2; **nettoyer le parquet** *to clean the floor*, III, 3

neuf (neuve): Quoi de neuf? *What's new?* III, 1

le **neveu** *nephew*, III, 6

le **nez: J'ai le nez qui coule.** *I've got a runny nose.* II, 7

la **nièce** *niece*, III, 6

nigaud(e) *fool, dummy, dingbat*, III, 3

le **Niger** *Niger*, III, 12

Noël: Joyeux Noël! *Merry Christmas!* II, 3

noir(e) *black*, I, 3; II, 1

les **noix de coco** (f.) *coconuts*, I, 8

le **nom** *name*, III, 2; **au nom de** *in the name of*, III, 11; **Nom d'un chien** *Darn*, III, 2

le **nombre** *number*, III, 2

non *no*, I, 1; **Moi non plus.** *Neither do I.* I, 2; **Moi, non.** *I don't.* I, 2; **Non, pas trop.** *No, not too much.* I, 2

le **nord: dans le nord** *in the north*, II, 4; **C'est au nord de...** *It's to the north of . . .*, II, 12

normal(e): C'est tout à fait normal. *You don't have to thank me.* III, 6

la **note: avoir une mauvaise note** *to get a bad grade*, II, 5

la **nouba: faire la nouba** *to party*, III, 2

la **nouille** *noodle*, III, 1

se **nourrir: bien se nourrir** *eat well*, II, 7; **nourrir les animaux** *to feed the animals*, II, 12

nous *we*, I, 1

nouveau (nouvelle) *new*, II, 2

la **nouvelle** *short story*, III, 11

novembre *November*, I, 4

la **nuit** *night*, III, 6

nul (nulle) *useless*, I, 2; *worthless*, II, 8; **C'est nul.** *It's no good.* III, 9; **Qu'est-ce que je peux être nul(le)!** *I just can't do anything right!* III, 12

O

obéir *to obey*, III, 6

obtenir: obtenir son diplôme *to get one's diploma*, III, 5; **obtenir la permission** *to get permission (to do something)*, III, 3

occupé: C'est occupé. *It's busy.* I, 9; **Désolé(e), je suis occupé(e).** *Sorry, I'm busy.* I, 6

s'**occuper de** *to take care of*, III, 8

octobre *October*, I, 4

l' **œil** (m.) (pl. **les yeux**) *eye*, II, 1; **Mon œil!** *Yeah, right!* II, 6; *No way!* III, 10

les **œufs** (m.) *eggs*, I, 8; II, 3

l' **office de tourisme** (m.) *tourist information office*, II, 2

officiel(le) *official*, III, 2

offrir (à quelqu'un) *to give (to someone)*, II, 10; **Qu'est-ce que je peux vous offrir?** *What can I offer you?* III, 6; **Qu'est-ce que je pourrais offrir à...?** *What could I give to . . . ?* II, 3; **Tu pourrais lui/leur offrir...** *You could give him/her . . .*, II, 3; **Offre-lui/-leur...** *Give him/her/them . . .*, II, 3

oh: Oh là là! *Oh no!* II, 5; *Wow!* III, 10; **Oh dis donc!** *Wow*, III, 9

l' **oignon** (m.) *onion*, I, 7

l' **oiseau** (m.) *bird*, III, 7

les **okras** (m.) *okra*, III, 11

l' **olive** (f.) *olive*, III, 8

l' **olivier** (m.) *olive tree*, III, 8

l' **ombre à paupières** (f.) *eyeshadow*, III, 4

l' **omelette** (f.) *omelet*, I, 5

on: *we, they, you, people in general*, I, 4; **On...?** *How about . . . ?* I, 4

l' **oncle** (m.) *uncle*, I, 7

l' **onglet** (m.) *prime cut of beef*, III, 1

opérer *to operate*, III, 10

opprimer *to oppress*, III, 8

l' **or** (m.) *gold*, III, 4

l' **orage** (m.) *storm*, III, 3

orange (inv.) *orange*, I, 3

les **oranges** (f.) *oranges*, I, 8

l' **ordinateur** (m.) *computer*, I, 3

ordonner *to command*, III, 10

les **ordures** (f.): **jeter des ordures** *to throw trash*, III, 3

les **oreilles** (f.): **J'ai mal aux oreilles.** *My ears hurt.* II, 7

original(e): C'est original. *That's unique.* II, 3

l' **orignal** (m.) *moose*, II, 12

orné(e) *decorated, embellished, trimmed*, III, 1

l' **orthographe** (f.) *spelling*, III, 2

l' **otarie** (f.) *seal*, III, 2

où *where*, I, 6; **D'où vient le mot...?** *Where does the word . . . come from?* III, 11; **Où ça?** *Where?* I, 6; **Où est-ce que tu vas aller...?** *Where are you going to go . . . ?* I, 11; **Où est... s'il vous plaît?** *Where is . . . , please?* II, 2; **Où se trouve...?** *Where is . . . ?* II, 4; **Tu es allé(e) où?** *Where did you go?* I, 9; **Tu viens d'où?** *Where are you from?* III, 12; **Vous pourriez me dire où il y a...?** *Could you tell me where I could find . . . ?* III, 2

Ouah! *Wow!* III, 7

oublier *to forget*, I, 9; **N'oublie pas de...** *Don't forget to . . .* I, 8; II, 1; **Oublie-le/-la/-les!** *Forget him/her/them!* I, 9; II, 10; **Je n'ai rien oublié.** *I didn't forget anything.* I, 11; **Tu n'as pas oublié...?** *You didn't forget . . . ?* I, 11

l' **ouest** (m.): **dans l'ouest** *in the west*, II, 4; **C'est à l'ouest de...** *It's to the west of . . .*, II, 12

ouf: Ouf! On a eu chaud! *Whew! That was a real scare!* III, 7

oui *yes*, I, 1

les **ouïes** (f.) *gills*, III, 10

l' **ours** (m.) *bear*, II, 12

l' **oursin** (m.) *sea urchin*, III, 10

l' **outil** (m.) *tool*, III, 2

ouvert(e) *open*, III, 2

l' **ouverture** (f.) *opening*, III, 2

l' **ouvrage** (m.) *work*, III, 10

l' **ouvrier (l'ouvrière)** *worker*, III, 5

ouvrir: A quelle heure est-ce que vous ouvrez? *When do you open?* II, 6; **Ouvrez vos livres à la page...** *Open your books to page . . .*, I, 0

P

la **page** *page*, I, 0

le **pagne** *piece of Ivorian cloth*, II, 8

la **paille** *straw*, III, 6

pailleté(e) *sequined*, III, 10

le **pain** *bread*, I, 8; II, 3; **pain au chocolat** *croissant with a chocolate filling*, II, 3

la **paix: Fiche-moi la paix!** *Leave me alone!* III, 6

le **palais** *palace*, III, 2

la **palmeraie** *palm grove*, III, 8

le **palmier** *palm tree*, II, 4

le **paludisme** *malaria*, III, 7

le **panier** *basket*, II, 8

la **panique: Pas de panique!** *Don't panic!* III, 7

panne: tomber en panne *to break down*, II, 9; **tomber en panne d'essence** *to run out of gas*, III, 2

le panneau *sign*, III, 2; **Vous allez voir un panneau qui indique l'entrée de l'autoroute.** *You'll see a sign that points out the freeway entrance.* III, 2; panneau d'interdiction *sign that indicates what is forbidden*, III, 3

les pansements (m.) *bandages*, III, 7

le pantalon *a pair of pants*, I, 10

la pantoufle *slipper*, III, 1

les papayes (f.) *papayas*, I, 8

la papeterie *stationery store*, I, 12

le papier *paper*, I, 0; III, 3; le papier glacé *glazed paper*, III, 2

le papillon *butterfly*, III, 7

Pâques *Easter*, III, 11

le paquet: un paquet de *a package/box of*, I, 8

par: Par là, au bout du couloir. *Over there, at the end of the hallway.* III, 2; **par terre** *on the ground*, III, 3; par contre *on the other hand*, III, 4; par rapport à *compared to*, III, 2

paradisiaque *heavenly*, III, 10

paraître *to appear; seem*, I, 12; Il paraît que *It is said that*, III, 2

le parapluie *umbrella*, I, 11

le parc *park*, I, 6; II, 2; **visiter un parc d'attractions** *to visit an amusement park*, II, 6

parce que *because*, I, 5; **Ce n'est pas parce que tout le monde... que tu dois le faire.** *Just because everyone else . . . doesn't mean you have to.* III, 3

le parcours *route*, III, 6

Pardon. *Pardon me.* I, 3; **demander pardon à (quelqu'un)** *to ask (someone's) forgiveness*, II, 10; **Pardon, madame.** *Excuse me, ma'am.* I, 12; **Pardon, mademoiselle. Où est... , s'il vous plaît?** *Excuse me, miss. Where is . . . please?* I, 12; **Pardon, monsieur. Je cherche... , s'il vous plaît.** *Excuse me, sir. I'm looking for . . . , please.* I, 12

pardonner à (quelqu'un) *to forgive (someone)*, II, 10; **Pardonne-moi de...** *Pardon me for . . .*, III, 6

le pare-brise: nettoyer le pare-brise *to clean the windshield*, III, 2

pareil: Tout le monde fait pareil. *Everybody does it.* III, 3

le parent *parent, relative*, I, 7

par-dessus *on top of*, III, 3

parfait(e): C'est parfait. *It's perfect.* I, 10

parier: Je parie que... *I bet that . . . ,* II, 9

parler: (Est-ce que) je peux parler à... ? *Could I speak to . . . ?* I, 9; **Je peux te parler?** *Can I talk to you?* I, 9; **parler au téléphone** *to talk on the phone*, I, 1; **Tu parles!** *No way!* III, 9; **Ça parle de...** *It's about . . . ,*

II, 11; III, 9; **De quoi ça parle?** *What's it about?* II, 11; III, 9; **Ne parle pas si fort.** *Don't speak so loudly.* III, 9; **Parle-lui/-leur.** *Talk to him/her/them.* II, 10

le parquet: nettoyer le parquet *to clean the floor*, III, 3

la part: C'est vraiment très gentil de votre part. *That's very nice of you.* III, 6

partager: partager tes affaires *to share your things*, III, 3; **partager son véhicule** *to share one's vehicle*, III, 3

partant: en partant *while leaving, on the way out*, III, 3

le participe passé *past participle (of a verb)*, III, 1

particulier(particulier) *private*, III, 8

la partie *part*, III, 1

partir *to leave*, I, 11; II, 6; **Tu ne peux pas partir sans...** *You can't leave without . . . ,* I, 11; **Je suis parti(e) en...** *I went by . . . ,* III, 1; **Non, je suis parti(e)...** *No, I went away for . . . ,* III, 1; **Tu es parti(e) comment?** *How did you get there?* III, 1; à partir de *from, starting at*, III, 3

partout: J'ai mal partout! *I hurt all over!* II, 7; partout ailleurs *everywhere else*, III, 3

parvenir à *to reach, to get to*, III, 3, 6

pas: (Il n'y a) pas de quoi. *It's nothing.* III, 6; **Pas du tout.** *Not at all.* II, 10; III, 9; **Pas mal.** *Not bad.* I, 1; **Pas mauvais** *Not bad*, I, 9; **Pas question!** *Out of the question!* I, 7; *No way!*, II, 1; **Pas super** *not so hot*, I, 2; **Pas terrible.** *Not so great.* I, 1

le pas *step*, III, 2

le passage pour piétons *pedestrian crossing*, III, 8; le passage *passage*, III, 8

le passant *passerby*, III, 9

le passé *past*, III, 1

le passeport *passport*, I, 11; II, 1

passer: Tu pourrais passer à... ? *Could you go by . . . ?* I, 12; **Vous passez devant...** *You'll pass . . . ,* 12; **Ça passe à...** *It's playing at . . . ,* II, 11; **Ça passe où?** *Where is that playing?* II, 11; **Ça se passe...** *It takes place . . . ,* III, 9; **Qu'est-ce qui se passe?** *What's going on?* II, 5; **Ça s'est bien passé?** *Did it go well?* I, 9; **Ça s'est très bien passé!** *It went really well!* II, 5; **Comment ça s'est passé?** *How did it go?* II, 5; **expliquer ce qui s'est passé (à quelqu'un)** *to explain what happened (to someone)*, II, 10; **J'ai passé une journée épouvantable!** *I had a terrible*

day! II, 5; **Qu'est-ce qui s'est passé?** *What happened?* I, 9; **Tu as passé un bon week-end?** *Did you have a good weekend?* I, 9; passer quelque chose *to give something*, III, 2

le passe-temps *leisure*, III, 11

passionnant(e): *fascinating*, I, 2; **C'est une histoire passionnante.** *It's an exciting story.* II, 11

la pastilla *Morrocan dish made with pigeon and almonds*, III, 6

la patate douce *sweet potato*, III, 11

la pâte *dough*, III, 11; mettre la main à la pâte *to get to work*, III, 5

le pâté *paté*, II, 3

les pâtes (f.) *pasta*, II, 7

patient: Sois patient(e)! *Be patient!* III, 2

le patin: faire du patin à glace *to ice-skate*, I, 4

la pâtisserie *pastry shop*, I, 12; II, 3

la patte *paw*, III, 7

les pattes (f.) *sideburns*, III, 4

le pattes d'eph *bell-bottoms*, III, 4

les paupières (f.) *the eyelids*, III, 4

pauvre: Pauvre vieille! *You poor thing!* II, 5

pavé(e) *paved*, III, 9

payer *to pay*, III, 4; **Oh, tu sais, je ne l'ai pas payé(e) cher.** *Oh, it wasn't expensive.* III, 4

le pays *country*, III, 1

le paysage *scenery, landscape*, III, 7

la peau *skin*, III, 4, 7

la pêche: aller à la pêche *to go fishing*, II, 4; la pêche au gros *deep-sea fishing*, III, 10

pêcher *to fish*, III, 8

les pêches (f.) *peaches*, I, 8

les pêcheurs (m.): **village de pêcheurs** *fishing village*, II, 4

pédestre: faire une randonnée pédestre *to go for a hike*, II, 12; cartes pédestres *maps that show hiking/walking paths*, III, 3

la peine: Ce n'est pas la peine. *It's not worth it.* III, 7

la pellicule *roll of film*, III, 7

se pelotonner *to snuggle up*, III, 10

la pelouse: tondre la pelouse *to mow the lawn*, III, 3

la peluche *plush*, III, 11

pendant: Pour (aller à)... vous suivez la... pendant à peu près... kilomètres. *To get to . . . , follow . . . for about . . . kilometers.* III, 2; pendant *during*, III, 12

le pendentif *pendant*, III, 4

pendu(e) *hanging*, III, 10

pénétrer *to enter*, III, 6

pénible *a pain in the neck*, I, 7

penser *to think*, I, 11; **J'ai pensé à tout.** *I've thought of everything.* I, 11; **Je ne pense pas que...** *I don't think that . . . ,* III, 7; **Je pense...**

I think I'll . . . , III, 5; **Pense à prendre...** *Remember to take . . .* , II, 1; **Pense aux autres.** *Think about other people.* III, 3; **Qu'en penses-tu?** *What do you think of it?* III, 4; **Qu'est-ce que tu penses de...?** *What do you think of . . .?* III, 4; *What do you say about . . .?* III, 11; **Qu'est-ce que tu penses faire?** *What do you think you'll do?* III, 5

perdre *to lose,* I, 9; II, 5; **perdre du poids** *to lose weight,* III, 10; **se perdre** *to get lost,* II, 9

le père *father,* I, 7

à une période donnée *at one time,* III, 12

la permanente *perm,* III, 4

permettre *to allow,* III, 1

le permis: passer son permis de conduire *to get one's driver's license,* III, 5

la permission: demander la permission à tes parents *to ask your parents' permission,* II, 10

le personnage *character,* III, 2

personnellement *personally,* III, 2

la peste *plague,* III, 6

petit(e) *short (height),* I, 7; II, 1; *small,* I, 10; II, 1; **petit déjeuner** *breakfast,* I, 8; **le petit-fils** *grandson,* III, 6; **la petite-fille** *granddaughter,* III, 6; **Quand il/elle était petit(e),...** *When he/she was little, . . .* , II, 8; **Quand j'étais petit(e),...** *When I was little, . . .* , II, 8

les petits pois (m.) *peas,* I, 8

peu: Peu importe. *It doesn't matter.* III, 9; **Un peu.** *A little.* II, 2

le peuple *people,* III, 7

peuplé(e) *crowded,* III, 2

peupler *to inhabit,* III, 2

la peur: J'ai peur (de la, du, des)... *I'm scared (of) . . .* , II, 12; **J'ai peur que...** *I'm afraid that . . .* , III, 7; **J'ai très peur de...** *I'm very afraid of . . .* , III, 7; **N'ayez pas peur.** *Don't be afraid.* III, 7

peut-être *maybe,* II, 3; **Peut-être que...** *Maybe . . .* , II, 9; III, 5; **Tu as peut-être raison.** *Maybe you're right.* II, 9

la pharmacie *drugstore,* I, 12

le pharmacien (la pharmacienne) *pharmacist,* III, 5

le phoque *seal,* III, 2

les photos (f.): **faire de la photo** *to do photography,* I, 4

la physique *physics,* I, 2

le piano *piano,* III, 11

la pièce *room (of a house),* II, 2; **la pièce: voir une pièce** *to see a play,* I, 6

le pied: à pied *on foot,* I, 12; **C'est le pied!** *Cool! Neat!* III, 7; **C'est vraiment le pied!** *That's really*

neat! III, 12; **J'ai mal aux pieds.** *My feet hurt.* II, 7

piétiner *to trample on,* III, 7

le piéton *pedestrian,* III, 3; **réservé aux piétons** *reserved for pedestrians,* III, 3

la pieuvre *octopus,* III, 10

piler *to pound, grind,* III, 1

le pilote *pilot,* III, 5

la pilule *pill,* III, 3; **grâce à la pilule pousse-minute** *thanks to the grow-in-a-minute pill,* III, 3

les pinces (f.): **à pinces** *pleated,* III, 4

pipelet(te) *concierge,* III, 10

le pique-nique: faire un pique-nique *to have a picnic,* I, 6; II, 6

piquer *to sting,* III, 10

la piqûre *shot,* III, 7

la piscine *swimming pool,* I, 6; II, 2

la piste *track,* III, 12

la pizza *pizza,* I, 1

la place: la place de stationnement *parking place,* III, 8; **A ta place,...** *If I were in your place, . . .* , III, 8; **la place** *square in the middle of an intersection,* III, 6

la plage *beach,* I, 1; II, 4

se plaindre *to complain,* III, 5

la plaine *field,* III, 2

plaire: Tu vas te plaire ici. *You're going to like it here.* II, 8; **Ça me plairait beaucoup.** *I'd like that a lot.* III, 6; **Ça te plairait de...** *Would you like to . . .?* III, 6; **Ce qui me plairait, c'est de...** *What I would like is to . . .* , III, 5; **Il/Elle me plaît, mais il/elle est cher/chère.** *I like it, but it's expensive.* I, 10; **Il/Elle te/vous plaît?** *Do you like it?* I, 10; **Ce qui me plaît, c'est (de)...** *What I like is . . .* , II, 4; **Ce qui ne me plaît pas, c'est (de)...** *What I don't care for is . . .* , II, 4; **s'il vous/te plaît** *please,* I, 3; **Un... s'il vous plaît.** *A . . . , please.* II, 6

plaisanter *to joke,* III, 10; **Tu plaisantes!** *You're joking!* II, 6

le plaisir: Avec plaisir. *With pleasure.* II, 10; **Ça me fait plaisir de vous voir.** *I'm happy to see you.* III, 6; **Je ne dis pas ça pour te faire plaisir.** *And I'm not just saying that.* III, 4; **Oui, avec plaisir.** *Yes, with pleasure.* I, 8

le plan *city map,* III, 2

planant(e) (musique) *spacey,* III, 11

la planche: faire de la planche à voile *to go windsurfing,* I, 11; II, 4

planter: planter un arbre *to plant a tree,* III, 3

le plastique *plastic,* III, 3

les plats (m.) **principaux** *main dishes,* III, 1; **le plat principal** *main course,* III, 1

plein(e): C'est plein de rebondissements. *It's full of plot*

twists. II, 11; **faire le plein** *to fill it up,* III, 2; **en plein air** *outdoors, in the open air,* III, 9; **à pleine vitesse** *at top speed,* III, 3

pleurer *to cry,* III, 1

Pleurnicheur(-euse)! *Crybaby!* III, 6

pleut: Il pleut. *It's raining.* I, 4

le plombier *plumber,* III, 5

la plongée: faire de la plongée avec un tuba *to snorkel,* II, 4; **faire de la plongée sous-marine** *to go scuba diving,* II, 4

le plongeoir *diving board,* III, 12

le plongeon acrobatique *diving,* III, 12

plonger *to dive,* III, 12

se plonger *to immerse oneself in,* III, 2

le plongeur (la plongeuse) *diver,* III, 12

plu (pp. of plaire): **Ça m'a beaucoup plu.** *I liked it a lot.* III, 9; **Ça t'a plu?** *Did you like it?* II, 6

plu (pp. of pleuvoir): **Il a plu.** *It rained.* III, 1

la pluie *rain,* III, 3

plus: Je n'en peux plus! *I just can't do any more!* II, 7; **Je n'en veux plus.** *I don't want anymore,* I, 8; **Je ne sais plus ce que je veux.** *I don't know what I want anymore.* III, 5; **plus tard** *later,* III, 5; **La vie était plus...** *Life was more . . .* , II, 8; **Moi non plus.** *Neither do I.* I, 2; **Non, merci. Je n'ai plus faim.** *No thanks. I'm not hungry anymore.* I, 8; **plus de... que** *more . . . than . . .* , III, 8; **plus... que** *more . . . than,* III, 8; **plus grand(e) que** *bigger than . . .* , II, 4; **Plus ou moins.** *More or less.* II, 6; **Tu es le/la... le/la plus... que je connaisse.** *You're the . . . -est . . . I know.* III, 10; **au plus** *at most,* III, 2

la plupart *most,* III, 9

plusieurs *several,* III, 10

plutôt *rather,* II, 9; **plûtot que de... *rather than . . .* ,** III, 5

les pneus (m.) *tires,* III, 2; **avoir un pneu crevé** *to have a flat tire,* III, 2

le po-boy *po-boy sandwich,* III, 11

la poêle *pan,* III, 11

poétique *poetic,* III, 10

le poids: perdre du poids *to lose weight,* III, 10

le point d'eau *watering hole,* III, 7; **A point.** *Medium rare.* III, 1; **Quel est le point commun entre...?** *What do . . . and . . . have in common?* III, 10; **le point de repère** *landmark,* III, 6

les poireaux (m.) *leeks,* III, 1

les poires (f.) *pears,* I, 8

les pois (m.): **les petits pois** (m.) *peas,* I, 8; **à pois** *polka-dotted,* III, 4

le poisson *fish,* I, 7; II, 3

la poissonnerie *fish shop,* II, 3

la poitrine *chest,* III, 5

le poivron *pepper,* III, 1

le pôle *pole,* III, 2
poli(e) *polite,* III, 3
la **pollution** *pollution,* III, 8
le polo *polo shirt,* III, 4
les **pommes** (f.) *apples,* I, 8; **les pommes de terre** (f.) *potatoes,* I, 8; les pommes mousseline (f.) *mashed potatoes,* III, 1
les **pompes** (f.)**: faire des pompes** *to do push-ups,* II, 7
le **pompiste** (la pompiste) *gas station attendant,* III, 2
le **pop** *popular, mainstream music,* II, 11
le **porc** *pork,* I, 8; III, 11; **la côtelette de porc pâtes** *porkchop with pasta,* III, 1
la **porte** *door,* I, 0
le **portefeuille** *wallet,* I, 3; II, 3
porter *to wear,* I, 10
poser: poser des questions *ask questions,* III, 1; poser sa candidature *to apply for a job,* III, 5
se poser *to land,* III, 10
posséder *to own, to have,* III, 10
la possession *possession,* III, 11
possible: Pas possible! *No way!* II, 6; **C'est pas possible!** *No way!* III, 12; **Ce n'est pas possible.** *That's not possible.* II, 9; **C'est possible.** *That's possible.* II, 9; **Il est possible que...** *It's possible that . . . ,* III, 5; **Si c'était possible,...** *If it were possible, . . . ,* III, 8; **Vous serait-il possible de...?** *Would it be possible for you to . . . ?* III, 5
postal(e): la carte postale *post card,* III, 10
la **poste** *post office,* I, 12; II, 12
le **poster** *poster,* I, 3; II, 2
le potage *soup,* III, 1
la **poterie** *pottery,* II, 8; III, 8
la potiche *oriental vase,* III, 9
la **poubelle** *trashcan,* I, 7; **sortir la poubelle** *to take out the trash,* I, 7
le pouce *inch,* III, 11
le **pouding au pain** *bread pudding,* III, 11
la **poule** *chicken,* III, 8
le **poulet** *chicken (meat),* I, 8; II, 3; **le poulet haricots verts** *roasted chicken with green beans,* III, 1
le poulpe *octopus,* III, 10
pour: Qu'est-ce qu'il te faut pour...? *What do you need for . . . ? (informal),* I, 3; **Qu'est-ce que tu fais pour t'amuser?** *What do you do to have fun?* I, 4; pour l'instant *for the moment,* III, 6
pourquoi: Pourquoi est-ce que tu ne mets pas...? *Why don't you wear . . . ?,* I, 10; **Pourquoi pas?** *Why not?* I, 6; **Pourquoi tu ne... pas?** *Why don't you . . . ?* I, 9; II, 7
pourtant *nevertheless, yet,* III, 7

pousser *to grow,* III, 3; pousser *to go too far; to push;* tu pousses *that's going a bit far,* III, 2
la **poussière: faire la poussière** *to dust,* III, 3
la **poutre** *the balance beam,* III, 12
pouvoir *to be able to, can,* I, 8; **Il se peut que...** *It might be that . . . ,* III, 5; **On peut...** *We can . . . ,* II, 4; **Je pourrais avoir...?** *May I have some . . . ?* II, 3; **Tu pourrais...?** *Could you . . . ?* II, 10; **Tu pourrais passer à...?** *Could you go by . . . ?* I, 12; **On pourrait...** *We could . . . ,* II, 1; **On pourrait sûrement...** *We'd be able to . . . for sure.* III, 7; **Vous pourriez/Tu pourrais me passer...?** *Would you pass me . . . ?,* II, 3; **Vous pourriez me dire où il y a...?** *Could you tell me where I could find . . . ?* III, 2
pratiquement *almost,* III, 10
se pratiquer *to be practiced;* un sport qui se pratique avec un ballon *a sport that is played with a ball,* III, 12
préféré: Quel est ton... préféré(e)? *What is your favorite . . . ?* II, 1; **Qui est ton/ta... préféré(e)?** *Who is your favorite . . . ?* II, 1
préférer: Ce que je préfère, c'est... *What I prefer is . . . ,* II, 4; **Je préfère** *I prefer,* II, 1
premier (première) *first,* III, 2
le **premier étage** *second floor,* II, 2
prendre *to take or to have (food or drink),* I, 5; **prendre rendez-vous (avec quelqu'un)** *to make a date (with someone),* II, 9; **Ça ne va pas prendre longtemps!** *It's not going to take long!* III, 2; **Je vais (en) prendre...** *I'll take . . . ,* II, 3; **Je vais prendre..., s'il vous plaît.** *I'm going to have . . . , please.* I, 5; **Pense à prendre...** *Remember to take . . . ,* II, 1; **prendre les transports en commun** *to take public transportation,* III, 3; **prendre ses propres décisions** *to make up one's own mind,* III, 3; **prendre des leçons de conduite** *to take driving lessons,* III, 10; **Tu devrais prendre...** *You should have . . . ,* III, 1; **Vous avez décidé de prendre...?** *Have you decided to have . . . ?* I, 10; **Je prendrais bien...** *I'd like some . . . ,* III, 6; **Prends...** *Have . . . ,* I, 5; *Get . . . ,* I, 8; **Take . . . ,** II, 1; **C'est toujours moi qui prends!** *I'm always the one who gets blamed!* III, 6; **Je le/la/les prends.** *I'll take it/them.* I, 10; **Je prends..., s'il vous plaît.** *I'll have . . . , please.* I, 5; **Tu me prends la tête!** *You're driving me crazy!* III, 6; **Tu prends...?** *Will you have . . . , ?* I, 8; *Are you having . . . ?*

I, 11; **Prenez...** *Take . . . ,* II, 2; **Non mais, vous vous prenez pour qui?** *Who do you think you are?* III, 8; **Prenez une feuille de papier.** *Take out a sheet of paper.* I, 0; **Vous le/la/les prenez?** *Are you going to take it/them?* I, 10; **Vous prenez?** *What are you having?* I, 5; **Vous prenez...?** *Will you have . . . ,* ? I, 8; **Prenez la rue..., puis traversez la rue...** *You take . . . Street, then cross . . . Street,* I, 12; prendre plaisir à *to enjoy,* III, 10; prendre soin de *to take care of,* III, 10
les **préparatifs** (m.)**: faire les préparatifs** *to get ready,* II, 10
préparer: préparer les amuse-gueule *to make party snacks,* II, 10
près: près de *close to,* I, 12; *near,* II, 2
présenter: Je te/vous présente... *I'd like you to meet . . . ,* I, 7; présenter *to introduce, to present,* III, 2
presque: Tu y es presque! *You're almost there!* II, 7; **Tu y es (On y est) presque!** *You're (we're) almost there!* II, 12
pressé(e) *in a hurry,* III, 8; **les gens pressés** *people in a hurry,* III, 8
la **pression: la pression des pneus** *the tire pressure,* III, 2; la pression *snap,* III, 4
prêt(e) *ready,* III, 2
le **prêt-à-porter** *ready-to-wear (clothes),* III, 4
le **prêteur** (la prêteuse) *lender,* III, 11
prévenir *to warn,* III, 6
prévoir *to foresee,* III, 6
prévoyant(e) *provident,* III, 5
prévu(e): Je n'ai rien de prévu. *I don't have any plans.* I, 11
prier: Entrez, je vous en prie. *Come in, please.* III, 6; **Je vous en prie.** *You're very welcome.* III, 6; **Je vous prie d'agréer, Monsieur/Madame, l'expression de mes sentiments distingués.** *Very truly yours, . . . ,* III, 5; Oh, je t'en prie! *Oh, please!,* III, 10; prier *to pray,* III, 6
la **prière: Prière de ne pas...** *Please do not . . . ,* III, 3
princier (princière) *princely,* III, 6
principal(e) *main,* III, 6
principalement *mainly,* III, 11
le **printemps** *spring,* I, 4; **au printemps** *in the spring,* I, 4
pris(e): Je suis pris(e). *I'm busy.* III, 6
privé: être privé(e) de sortie *to be "grounded",* II, 9
le prix *price,* III, 6
le **problème: J'ai un petit problème.** *I've got a problem.* I, 9; **Pas de problème.** *No problem.* II, 10
procéder *to proceed,* III, 2
prochain(e): Vous continuez cette

rue jusqu'au prochain feu rouge. *You go down this street to the next light.* I, 12; **prochain(e)** *next, upcoming,* III, 3; **la prochaine fois** *next time,* III, 3

proche *nearby,* III, 5

le producteur *producer,* III, 9

produire *to produce,* III, 11

les produits (m.) **laitiers** *dairy products,* I, 8

le prof(esseur)(la prof) *high school/college teacher,* I, 2; III, 5

la profondeur *depth,* III, 10

le programme télé *TV guide/listing,* III, 9

le programmeur (la programmeuse) *computer programmer,* III, 5

la progression *progress,* III, 2

la proie *prey,* III, 7

les projets (m.): **Tu as des projets?** *Do you have plans?* III, 5

la promenade: faire une promenade *to go for a walk,* I, 6

promener: promener le chien *to walk the dog,* I, 7; **se promener** *to go for a walk,* II, 4

promouvoir *to promote,* III, 12

prononcer *to pronounce,* III, 2

les pronostics (m.) *predictions,* III, 12

propice à *favorable to,* III, 8, 10

propos: A propos,... *By the way, . . . ,* II, 9

proposé(e) *suggested,* III, 1

proposer *to offer,* III, 2

propre *clean,* II, 8; **prendre ses propres décisions** *to make up one's own mind,* III, 3; **des qualités et des défauts propres aux humains** *good qualities and flaws characteristic of humans,* III, 7

protéger *to protect,* III, 3

les provisions (f.) *supplies,* III, 8

à proximité *close,* III, 2

prudemment: conduire prudemment *to drive safely,* III, 3

prudent(e) *careful, aware,* III, 3; **Il serait plus prudent de...** *It would be wise to . . . ,* III, 7

le psychiatre (la psychiatre) *psychiatrist,* III, 5

pu (pp. of *pouvoir*): **J'aurais pu...** *I could have . . . ,* II, 10; **Tu aurais pu...** *You could have . . . ,* II, 10

le public *public,* III, 2

la publicité (pub) *commercial,* III, 9

publicitaire *having to do with advertisement;* **le poster publicitaire** *poster serving as an advertisement,* III, 3

puis: Et puis,... *Then, . . . ,* II, 1; **Puis, tournez à gauche dans...** *Then, turn left on . . . ,* II, 2; **Vous prenez la rue... puis la rue...** *You take . . . Street, then . . . Street,* I, 12

puisque *since,* III, 1

le puits *well,* III, 8

le pull *sweater,* II, 1

le pull(-over) *pullover,* I, 3; II, 1

punir *to punish,* III, 6

qu'est-ce que: Qu'est-ce que vous avez comme spécialités? *What kind of . . . do you have?* III, 1; **Mais, qu'est-ce que tu fais?** *What are you doing?* III, 2; **Qu'est ce que tu as?** *What's wrong?,* II, 7; **Qu'est-ce qu'il y a... ?** *What is there . . . ?* II, 4; **Qu'est-ce qu'il y a à boire?** *What is there to drink?* I, 5; **Qu'est-ce qu'il y a?** *What's wrong?* II, 10; **Qu'est-ce qu'il y a dans... ?** *What's in . . . ?* III, 11; **Qu'est-ce qu'on fait?** *What should we do?* II, 1; **Qu'est-ce qu'on peut faire?** *What can we do?* II, 4; **Qu'est-ce que c'est,...?** *What is . . . ?* III, 1; **Qu'est-ce que c'est... !** *That is so . . . !* III, 2; **Qu'est-ce que c'est?** *What's that?* III, 11; **Qu'est-ce que j'aimerais... !** *I'd really like to . . . !* III, 8; **Qu'est-ce que je peux faire?** *What can I do?* I, 9; II, 10; **Qu'est-ce que tu aimes faire?** *What do you like to do?* II, 1; **Qu'est-ce que tu as fait... ?** *What did you do . . . ?* I, 9; **Qu'est-ce que tu fais... ?** *What do you do . . . ?* I, 4; **Qu'est-ce que tu vas faire... ?** *What are you going to do . . . ?* I, 6; **Qu'est-ce que vous avez comme boissons?** *What do you have to drink?* I, 5

Qu'est-ce qui: Qu'est-ce qui s'est passé? *What happened?* I, 9; **Qu'est-ce qui se passe?** *What's going on?* II, 5; **Qu'est-ce qui t'arrive?** *What's wrong?* II, 5

le quai: Du quai... *From platform . . . ,* II, 6; **De quel quai... ?** *From which platform . . . ?* II, 6

la qualité *quality,* III, 6

quand: Quand (ça)? *When?* I, 6; **Quand je verrai...** *When I see . . . ,* III, 12; **Quand est-ce que tu y es allé(e)?** *When did you go?* III, 1

quand même *at least, even so, just the same,* III, 2, 3

le quart: et quart *quarter past,* I, 6; **moins le quart** *quarter to,* I, 6

le quartier *neighborhood, quarter, district,* III, 2, 8

que: Que tu es... avec ça! *You look really . . . in that!* III, 4

quel(s): Quel(s)... *Which . . . ,* III, 4; **Quel week-end!** *What a (bad) weekend!* II, 5; **Quel week-end**

formidable! *What a great weekend!* II, 5; **Quel est ton... préféré(e)?** *What is your favorite . . . ?* II, 1; **Tu as quel âge?** *How old are you?* I, 1; **Tu as quels cours... ?** *What classes do you have . . . ?* I, 2

quelle(s): Quelle(s)... *Which . . . ,* III, 4; **Quelle journée!** *What a (bad) day!* II, 5; **Quelle journée formidable!** *What a great day!* II, 5; **Tu as... à quelle heure?** *At what time do you have . . . ?* I, 2; **Quelle barbe!** *What a drag!,* III, 8

quelque chose: J'ai quelque chose à faire. *I have something (else) to do.* II, 10; **Je cherche quelque chose pour...** *I'm looking for something for . . . ,* I, 10; **Quelque chose ne va pas?** *Is something wrong?* II, 7

quelquefois *sometimes,* I, 4

la question: Pas question! *Out of the question!* I, 7; *No way!,* II, 1

la queue de cheval *pony tail,* III, 4

qui: Avec qui? *With whom?* I, 6; **Qui est ton... préféré(e)?** *Who is your favorite . . . ?* II, 1

la quiche *quiche,* I, 5

la quinzaine (de jours) *two weeks,* III, 10

quitter *to leave;* **quitter sa famille** *to leave one's family,* III, 5; **Ne quittez pas.** *Hold on.* I, 9

quoi: (Il n'y a) pas de quoi. *It's nothing.* III, 6; **..., quoi. . . . ,** *you know.* II, 9; **De quoi ça parle?** *What's it about?* III, 9; **Je ne sais pas quoi faire.** *I don't know what to do.* II, 10; **Je ne sais pas quoi mettre pour...** *I don't know what to wear for . . . ,* I, 10; **N'importe quoi!** *That's ridiculous!* II, 6; **Tu as quoi... ?** *What do you have . . . ?* I, 2

R

raccrocher *to hang up (the phone),* III, 8

la racine *root,* III, 5

raconter *to tell;* **Raconte!** *Tell me!* II, 5; III, 10; **Qu'est-ce que ça raconte?** *What's the story?* II, 11

la radio *radio,* I, 3

raide: les cheveux raides (m.) *straight hair,* III, 4

raffiné(e) *refined,* III, 4

la raie *ray,* III, 10

le raifort *horseradish,* III, 1

le raisin *grapes,* I, 8; **les raisins secs** (m.) *raisins,* III, 11

la raison: Ce n'est pas une

raison. *That's not a reason.* III, 3; **Fais-toi une raison.** *Make the best of it.* II, 8; **Tu as raison...** *You're right...,* II, 3; III, 9

ralentir *to slow down,* III, 5

ramasser *to pick up,* III, 3; **ramasser les feuilles** *to rake leaves,* III, 3

les **rames** (f.) *oars,* III, 12

la **randonnée: faire de la randonnée** *to go hiking,* I, 11; **faire une randonnée en raquettes** *to go snow-shoeing,* II, 12; **faire une randonnée en skis** *to go cross-country skiing,* II, 12; **faire une randonnée pédestre** *to go for a hike,* II, 12

la **rangée** *row,* III, 10

ranger: ranger ta chambre *to pick up your room,* I, 7

le **rap** *rap,* II, 11; III, 11

râpé(e): les carottes râpées *grated carrots with vinaigrette dressing,* III, 1

raplapla: Je suis tout(e) raplapla. *I'm "wiped" out.* II, 7

rappeler *to remind,* III, 3; **se rappeler** *to remember,* III, 6; **Vous pouvez rappeler plus tard?** *Can you call back later?* I, 9

rapporter: Rapporte-moi... *Bring me back...,* I, 8; **Tu me rapportes...?** *Will you bring me...?* I, 8

Rapporteur(-euse)! *Tattletale!* III, 6

les **rapports** (m.) *relationship,* III, 6

se rapprocher *to get closer,* III, 3

les **raquettes** (f.): **faire une randonnée en raquettes** *to go snow-shoeing,* II, 12

rarement *rarely,* I, 4

ras: J'en ai ras le bol! *I've had it!* III, 8

rasant(e) *boring,* III, 2; **C'est rasant!** *That's boring!* III, 2

se raser *to shave,* III, 4

rassembler *to gather,* III, 10

rassurer *to reassure,* III, 4

rater: rater le bus *to miss the bus,* I, 9; II, 5; **rater un examen** *to fail a test,* I, 9; **rater une marche** *to miss a step,* II, 5; **Tu en rates pas une, toi!** *You're batting a thousand!* III, 10

ravi(e) *thrilled, delighted,* III, 1, 6

le **raton laveur** *raccoon,* II, 12

les **rayures** (f.): **à rayures** *striped,* III, 4

réaction: un camion à réaction *a truck moving at the speed of a jet,* III, 3

réagir *to react,* III, 10

la **réalisation** *production,* III, 9

réaliser (un rêve) *to achieve,* III, 10

les **rebondissements** (m.): **C'est plein de rebondissements.** *It's full of plot twists.* II, 11

recevoir: recevoir le bulletin trimestriel *to receive one's report card,* II, 5

recharger *to recharge,* III, 2

rechercher *to research, to seek information on,* III, 1

le **récif** *reef,* III, 10

la **récolte** *harvest,* III, 5

recommander: Je te le recommande. *I recommend it.* II, 11; **Je te recommande...** *I recommend...,* III, 9

recommencer: Ne recommence pas. *Don't do it again.* II, 5

récompenser *to reward,* III, 6

réconcilier: se réconcilier avec (quelqu'un) *to make up (with someone),* II, 10

reconnaissant(e) *thankful,* III, 3

reconnaître *to recognize,* III, 1

recracher: recrachées par la machine *spit out by the machine,* III, 3

la **récréation** *break,* I, 2

récrire *to rewrite,* III, 1

recycler *to recycle,* III, 3

rédiger *to write (a paper),* III, 3

redoutable *fearsome,* III, 10

réel(le) *real,* III, 10

se référer à *to refer to,* III, 2

réfléchir *to think about,* III, 2

le **reflet** *reflection,* III, 10

refréner *to restrain,* III, 5

refuser *to refuse,* III, 2

regarder: regarder la télé *to watch TV,* I, 1; **regarder un match** *to watch a game (on TV),* I, 6; **Non mais, tu t'es pas regardé(e)!** *If you could see how you look!* III, 10; **Non, merci, je regarde.** *No, thanks, I'm just looking.* I, 10; **Tiens! Regarde un peu!** *Hey! Check it out!* III, 7

le **reggae** *reggae music,* II, 11

le **régime: suivre un régime trop strict** *follow a diet that's too strict.* II, 7

la **région** *area,* III, 2

la **règle** *ruler,* I, 3; *rule,* III, 3

regretter: Je regrette. *Sorry,* I, 3; **Je regrette, mais je n'ai pas le temps.** *I'm sorry, but I don't have time.* I, 8; **Je regrette...** *I miss...,* II, 8

rejoindre *to join,* III, 11

le **relais** *relay,* III, 10

relax *relaxing,* II, 8

relever: relever *to raise, to pick up,* III, 3, 6; **relevés de terrain** (m.) *land surveys,* III, 5

la **religieuse** *cream puff pastry,* II, 3

remarquer *to notice,* III, 6

le **remerciement** *thanks;* la **note de remerciement** *thank you note,* III, 6

remercier: Je vous remercie. *Thank you.* III, 6

remonter à *to date from,* III, 11

rémoulade: le céleri rémoulade *grated celery root with mayonnaise and vinaigrette ,* III, 1

remplacer *to replace,* III, 2

remplir *to fill out, fill in,* III, 3

la **rémunération** *payment,* III, 5

le **renard** *fox,* II, 12

la **rencontre** *meeting,* III, 10

rencontrer *to meet,* I, 9; II, 9

le **rendez-vous: Rendez-vous...** *We'll meet...* I, 6; **A quelle heure est-ce qu'on se donne rendezvous?** *What time are we meeting?* III, 6; **avoir (prendre) rendezvous (avec quelqu'un)** *to have a date/make an appointment (with someone),* II, 9; **C'est gentil, mais j'ai un rendez-vous.** *That's nice of you, but I've got an appointment.* III, 6

rendre *to return something,* I, 12; **rendre les examens** *to return tests,* II, 5; **rendre** *to make;* **sans la rendre trop longue** *without making it too long,* III, 2

se rendre compte *to realize,* III, 10

renforcer *to reinforce,* 11, III

renommé(e) *renowned,* III, 12

la **renommée** *fame,* III, 1

renoncer *to give up,* III, 1

les **renseignements** (m.): **Pourriez-vous m'envoyer des renseignements sur...?** *Could you send me information on...?* III, 5

se renseigner *to get information,* III, 7

rentrer *to go back (home),* II, 6

renverser *to turn over,* III, 6

repartir *to go back,* III, 6

le **repas: sauter un repas** *to skip a meal,* II, 7

le **repassage: faire le repassage** *to do the ironing,* III, 3

repasser (son examen) *to take again,* III, 10

repeindre *to repaint,* III, 1

repérer *to spot,* III, 6

répéter *to rehearse, to practice,* I, 9; **Répétez!** *Repeat!* I, 0

le **répondeur** *answering machine,* III, 7

répondre *to answer,* I, 9; **Ça ne répond pas.** *There's no answer.* I, 9

la **réponse: En réponse à votre lettre du...** *In response to your letter of...,* III, 5

le **reportage sportif** *sportscast,* III, 9

se reposer *to relax,* III, 11

repousser: se faire repousser ses tresses *to make her braids grow back,* III, 3

le **reproche** *reproach,* III, 3; **faire des reproches** *to lecture, to scold (someone),* III, 3

la **République centrafricaine** *Central African Republic,* III, 12

la **République de Côte d'Ivoire** *the Republic of Côte d'Ivoire,* III, 12

la **République démocratique du Congo** *Democratic Republic of Congo,* III, 12

réputé(e) *known for,* III, 3, 10

la **requête** *request,* III, 5
le **requin** *shark,* III, 10
le **réservoir** *the gas tank,* III, 2
résider *to reside,* III, 6
résoudre *to resolve,* III, 3, 9
respecter: respecter la nature *to respect nature,* II, 12; **respecter tes profs et tes parents** *to respect your teachers and your parents,* III, 3
les **responsabilités** (f.): **avoir des responsabilités** *to have responsibilities,* II, 8
responsable *responsible,* III, 3
ressembler: A quoi ressemble-t-elle? *What's she like?* III, 3
ressentir *to feel,* III, 8
se resservir *to help oneself again,* III, 10
ressortir: faire ressortir *to highlight,* III, 4
le **restaurant** *restaurant,* I, 6
la **restauration** *food service; catering,* III, 5
rester *to stay,* II, 6; **Est-ce que tu es resté(e) ici?** *Did you stay here?* III, 1; **Oui, je suis resté(e) ici tout le temps.** *Yes, I stayed here the whole time.* III, 1
restitué(e): l'eau restituée à la nature *water returned to nature,* III, 3
le **résumé** *summary,* III, 9
le **rétablissement: Bon rétablissement!** *Get well soon!* II, 3
le **retard** *lateness;* être en retard *to be late,* III, 2
retenir *to hold back,* III, 2
retirer: retirer de l'argent (m.) *to withdraw money,* I, 12
retourner *to return,* II, 6
la **retraite** *retirement,* III, 5; prendre sa retraite *to retire,* III, 5
rétro (inv.) *retro,* I, 10
les **retrouvailles** (f.) *reunion,* III, 1
retrouver: On se retrouve... *We'll meet . . .* I, 6; **Où est-ce qu'on se retrouve?** *Where are we meeting?* III, 6
la **réunion** *meeting,* III, 2
se **réunir** *to get together,* III, 1
réussir son bac *to pass one's baccalaureat exam,* III, 5; réussir *to succeed,* III, 6
la **revanche:** en revanche *on the other hand,* III, 12; une revanche à prendre *to get revenge on somebody,* III, 12
rêvasser *to daydream,* III, 3
le **rêve: Mon rêve, c'est de...** *My dream is to . . ,* III, 5
rêver *to dream,* III, 2
le **réveil: entendre le réveil** *to hear the alarm clock,* II, 5
se **réveiller: Réveille-toi un peu!** *Get with it!* III, 10
revenir *to come back,* II, 6; **Je n'en reviens pas.** *I don't believe it,* III, 10

le **rêveur** (la rêveuse) *dreamer,* III, 2
réviser *to study, to review,* III, 3
revoir: Je suis content(e) de te revoir. *I'm glad to see you again.* III, 1; **Quand est-ce qu'on se revoit?** *When are we getting together?* III, 6
le **rez-de-chaussée** *first (ground) floor,* II, 2; III, 2
le **rhinocéros** *rhinoceros,* III, 7
le **rhume: J'ai un rhume.** *I've got a cold.* II, 7
ri *laughed,* III, 2
la **richesse** *wealth,* III, 6
le **rideau** *curtain,* III, 10
ridicule *ridiculous,* III, 4
rien: Ça ne fait rien. *It doesn't matter.* II, 10; **Ça ne me dit rien.** *That doesn't interest me.* I, 4; **De rien.** *You're welcome.* III, 6; **Je n'ai rien oublié.** *I didn't forget anything.* I, 11; **Rien (de spécial).** *Nothing (special).* I, 6; III, 1
rigoler *to laugh, enjoy oneself,* III, 1; **Tu rigoles!** *You're joking!* III, 9
rigolo(te) *funny, hysterical,* III, 2
ringard(e) *corny,* III, 4
le **rituel** *ritual,* III, 6
rire: Ça m'a bien fait rire. *It really made me laugh.* III, 9
la **rivière** *river,* III, 7
le **riz** *rice,* I, 8
la **robe** *dress,* I, 10; la robe de chambre *robe,* III, 10
le **robinet** *faucet,* III, 3
le **rocher** *rock,* III, 10
le **rock** *rock music,* II, 11; III, 11
le **rognon** *kidney,* III, 1
le **roi** *king,* III, 6
la **roideur** *stiffness, rigidity,* III, 4
le **rôle** *part (in movies),* III, 2
le **roller: faire du roller en ligne** *to in-line skate,* I, 4
le **roman** *novel ,* I, 3; **roman d'amour** *romance novel,* II, 11; **roman de science-fiction** *science-fiction novel,* II, 11; **roman policier (le polar)** *detective or mystery novel,* II, 11
rose *pink,* I, 3
le **rôti de bœuf** *roast beef,* II, 3
la **roue: la grande roue** *ferris wheel,* II, 6; **la roue de secours** *spare tire* III, 2
rouge *red,* I, 3
le **rouge à lèvres** *lipstick,* III, 4
le **routard** *backpacker,* III, 6
la **route: Bonne route!** *Have a good (car) trip!,* II, 3; **Cette route va vous conduire au centre-ville.** *This road will lead you into the center of town.* III, 2; **La route pour..., s'il vous plaît?** *Could you tell me how to get to . . . ?* III, 2; en route *let's go,* III, 2
roux (rousse) *redheaded,* I, 7
rude *harsh,* III, 3

la **rue** *street,* I, 12; III, 2
la **ruelle:** ruelles pavées *cobblestone alleyways,* III, 9
russe: les montagnes russes *the roller coaster,* II, 6
la **Russie** *Russia,* III, 12

le **sable** *sand,* II, 4
le **sabot** *wooden shoe, clog,* III, 1
le **sac (à dos)** *bag; backpack,* I, 3; **sac (à main)** *purse,* II, 3; III, 4
le **sac de couchage** *sleeping bag,* II, 12
sage *well-behaved (describes children),* III, 1
saignant(e) *rare.* III, 1
la **saison** *season,* III, 6
saisonnier (saisonnière) *seasonal,* III, 5
la **salade** *salad,* I, 8; **la salade verte** *green salad,* III, 1; **les salades** *heads of lettuce,* I, 8
sale *dirty,* II, 8
salé(e) *salty,* III, 11
les **saletés** (f.) *trash, junk,* III, 3
la **salle: la salle à manger** *dining room,* II, 2; **la salle de bains** *bathroom,* II, 2
le **salon** *living room,* II, 2
saluer: Salue... de ma part. *Tell . . . hi for me.* III, 8
Salut! *Hi! or Goodbye!* I, 1
le **samedi** *on Saturdays,* I, 2
les **sandales** (f.) *sandals,* I, 10
le **sandre** *pike, perch,* III, 1
le **sandwich** *sandwich,* I, 5
le **sangho** *national language of the Central African Republic,* III, 7
sangloter *to sob,* III, 5
sanguin(e) *the color of blood,* III, 10
sans *without;* sans doute *without a doubt,* III, 9; *probably,* III, 11
la **santé: C'est bon pour la santé.** *It's healthy.* II, 7
les **saucisses** (f.) *sausages,* III, 11
le **saucisson** *salami,* I, 5; II, 3
saupoudrer *to sprinkle,* III, 11
le **saut à la perche** *pole vault,* III, 12
le **saut en longueur** *long jump,* III, 12
sauter: sauter un repas *to skip a meal,* II, 7; **Ce qui saute aux yeux, c'est...** *What catches your eye is . . . ,* III, 11
sauvage *wild,* III, 2
la **savane** *savannah,* III, 7
le **savant** *scientist, inventor,* III, 3
savoir: Je voudrais savoir... *I would like to know . . .* III, 5; **Je n'en sais rien.** *I have no idea.* I, 11; **Je ne sais pas quoi faire.** *I don't know*

la stupeur *amazement*, III, 10

le style: C'est tout à fait ton style. *It looks great on you!* I, 10; **Ce n'est pas son style.** *That's not his/her style.* II, 3

le **stylo** *pen*, I, 3

le **subjonctif** *subjunctive*, III, 1

le **sucre** *sugar*, I, 8

le **sud: dans le sud** *in the south*, II, 4; **C'est au sud de...** *It's to the south of . . .*, II, 12

suffisamment *sufficiently*, III, 3

suffit: Ça suffit! *That's enough!* III, 6

le **suffixe** *suffix*, III, 2

la **Suisse** *Switzerland*, III, 12

la **suite: C'est tout de suite à...** *It's right there on the . . .*, I, 12; **J'y vais tout de suite.** *I'll go right away.* I, 8; **Suite à notre conversation téléphonique,...** *Following our telephone conversation, . . .*, III, 5; **tout de suite** *right away*, I, 6

suivant(e) *next, following*, III, 2

suivre *to follow*, II, 7; **suivre les sentiers balisés** *to follow the marked trails*, II, 12; **suivre un régime trop strict** *to follow a diet that's too strict.* II, 7; **Pour (aller à)... vous suivez la... pendant à peu près... kilomètres.** *To get to . . ., follow . . . for about . . . kilometers.* III, 2

le **sujet** *subject*, III, 2; **au sujet de** *about*, III, 10

super (adj.) *super*, I, 2; (adv.) *really, ultra-*, II, 9; **Super!** *Great!* I, 1; *Super!* III, 12; **pas super** *not so hot*, I, 2; **le super (sans plomb)** *premium (unleaded) gasoline*, III, 2

superbe *gorgeous*, II, 6

la **superficie** *surface area*, III, 1

supporter *to support*, III, 6; *to put up with*, III, 7

sur: sur la droite (gauche) *on the right (left)*, II, 2

sûr: Bien sûr. *Of course.* II, 10; **Ça, c'est sûr.** *That's for sure.* III, 11; **Je (ne) suis (pas) sûr(e) que...** *I'm (not) sure that . . .*, III, 7; **sûr(e) de soi** *confident*, III, 2

sûrement: On pourrait sûrement... *We'd be able to . . . for sure.* III, 7; **Sûrement pas!** *Definitely not!* II, 6

surmonter *to overcome*, III, 6

surnommé(e) *nicknamed*, III, 12

sursauter *to startle*, III, 10

surtout *especially*, I, 1; **Ne va surtout pas voir...** *Really, don't go see . . .*, III, 9; **Non mais, surtout, ne vous gênez pas!** *Well, just go right ahead!* III, 8

surveiller *to pay attention*, III, 3

susciter *to provoke, arouse*, III, 12

le suspense: Il y a du suspense. *It's suspenseful.* II, 11

le sweat(-shirt) *sweatshirt*, I, 3; II, 1

sympa (abbrev. of sympathique) *nice*, I, 7; II, 1

le **synthé (synthétiseur)** *synthesizer*, III, 11

le **tableau** *blackboard*, I, 0; *chart*, III, 6

le **tablier** *apron*, III, 1

la **tâche** *chore, duty, task*, III, 3; **tâche ménagère** *household chore*, III, 1

tacheté(e) *spotted*, III, 7

la **taille** *the waist*, III, 4; **en taille...** *in size...*, I, 10

le **taille-crayon** *pencil sharpener*, I, 3

le **tailleur** *tailor*, III, 5; *pantsuit*, III, 4

taire: Vous pourriez vous taire, s'il vous plaît? *Could you please be quiet?* III, 9; **Tais-toi!** *Be quiet!* III, 9

le **tam-tam** *an African drum*, II, 8

tandis que: Ici,... tandis que... *Here . . ., whereas . . .*, III, 8

tant: Tant pis pour toi! *Tough!* III, 6

tant que *as long as*, III, 1

la **tante** *aunt*, I, 7

tape-à-l'œil *gaudy*, III, 4

taper *to beat*, III, 3

le **tapis** *rug*, II, 2; III, 8

taquiner *to tease*, II, 8

tard *late*, II, 4; **plus tard** *later*, III, 5; au plus tard *at the latest*, III, 3

tarder: Il me tarde de... *I can't wait to . . .*, III, 12

le **tarif** *tariff*, III, 10

la **tarte** *pie*, I, 8; **la tarte aux pommes** *apple tart*, II, 3; **les tartes aux fruits** *fruit pies/tarts*, III, 1

la **tartine** *bread, butter, and jam*, II, 3

le tas: J'ai des tas de choses à faire. *I have lots of things to do.* I, 5

le **taux** *rate*, III, 1

le taxi: en taxi *by taxi*, I, 12

Tchao! *Bye!* I, 1

le **technicien (la technicienne)** *technician*, III, 5

le **tee-shirt** *T-shirt*, I, 3; II, 1

teint(e): les cheveux teints (m.) *dyed hair*, III, 4

le **teinturier** *dry cleaner*, III, 6

tel(le) *such*, III, 12

la **télécommande** *remote*, III, 9

le **téléphone: parler au téléphone** *to talk on the phone*, I, 1

téléphoner à (quelqu'un) *to call (someone)*, II, 10; **Téléphone-lui/-leur!** *Call him/her/them!* I, 9

le **téléviseur** *television set*, III, 9

la **télévision** *television*, I, 3; **regarder la télé(vision)** *to watch TV*, I, 1

tellement: C'était tellement différent? *Was it really so different?* II, 8; **Pas tellement.** *Not too much.* I, 4

le **temps: de temps en temps** *from time to time*, I, 4; **Je suis désolé(e), mais je n'ai pas le temps.** *Sorry, but I don't have time.* I, 12; **Il a fait un temps...** *The weather was . . .* III, 1; **On a largement le temps!** *We've got plenty of time!* III, 2; **On n'a pas le temps!** *We don't have time!* III, 2; **Quel temps fait-il?** *What's the weather like?* I, 4; **Quel temps est-ce qu'il a fait?** *What was the weather like?* III, 1

tenir: Tenez. *Here you are.* II, 3; **Tiens.** *Here you are.* II, 3; **Je tiens à...** *I really want to . . .*, III, 5; **Tiens! Regarde un peu!** *Hey! Check it out!* III, 7; **Tiens-toi bien!** *Behave yourself!*, III, 10; tenir une place importante *to have an important part*, III, 11

le **tennis** *tennis*, I, 4

la **tente** *tent*, II, 12

tenter *to tempt*, III, 11

tenu(e): les jeunes sont tenus de travailler aux champs *young people are expected to work in the fields*, III, 5

la **tenue** *outfit*, III, 12

ter *three times*, III, 4

terminer: Comment ça se termine? *How does it end?* III, 9

le **terrain de camping** *campground*, II, 2

la **terre: par terre** *on the ground*, III, 3; la terre *Earth*, III, 3; une terre inconnue *an unknown place*, III, 5; *property, land*, III, 10; en terre *made of soil, clay*, III, 8

terrible: Pas terrible. *Not so great.* I, 1; **C'était pas terrible.** *It wasn't so great.* III, 1

la **tête: faire la tête** *to sulk*, II, 9; **J'ai mal à la tête** *My head hurts.* II, 7; **Tu me prends la tête!** *You're driving me crazy!* III, 6

le **thé** *tea*, III, 6

le **théâtre** *theater*, I, 6; II, 12; **faire du théâtre** *to do drama*, I, 4

la **théière** *tea pot*, III, 6

le **thon** *tuna*, III, 1

les tickets (m.)**: Trois tickets, s'il vous plaît.** *Three (entrance) tickets, please.* II, 6

le **tien (la tienne)** *yours*, III, 10

la **tige: chaussures à tige montante** *shoes that tie above the ankle (such as hiking boots)*, III, 3

le **timbre** *stamp*, I, 12

timide *shy*, I, 7

tintinnabuler *to tinkle*, III, 10

le **tir à l'arc** *archery*, III, 12

tirer *to pull, to shoot*, III, 6, 12

la **tisane** *herbal tea*, III, 10
  tisser *to weave*, III, 10
le **tisserin** *a type of African bird*, III, 7
le tissu *fabric, cloth*, II, 8
la **toile:** en toile *linen*, III, 4; la toile *canvas*, III, 9
les **toilettes** (f.) (**les W.-C.** (m.)) *toilet, restroom*, II, 2; la toilette: faire sa toilette *to wash oneself*, III, 10
tolérant(e) *tolerant*, III, 3
les **tomates** (f.) *tomatoes*, I, 8
  tomber *to fall*, II, 5; **Après..., vous allez tomber sur...** *After..., you'll come across...*, III, 2; **tomber amoureux(-euse) (de quelqu'un)** *to fall in love (with someone)*, II, 9; **tomber en panne** *to break down*, II, 9; **tomber en panne d'essence** *to run out of gas*, III, 2; **tomber malade** *to get sick*, III, 10
le **tombeau** *grave*, III, 6
le **ton** *tone*, III, 2
  tondre: tondre la pelouse *to mow the lawn*, III, 3
  tondu(e) *closely cropped*, III, 4
  tonifier *to stimulate*, III, 11
la **tonne** *ton*, III, 2
le **tonton** *uncle (familiar)*, III, 3
la **torche** *flashlight*, III, 7
  tort: Tu as tort. *You're wrong.* III, 9; **Tu as tort de...** *You're wrong to...*, III, 3
la **tortue** *turtle*, III, 10
  tôt *early*, II, 4
  toujours: toujours...? *still...?* III, 11; **C'est toujours la même chose!** *It's always the same!* III, 6; **Toujours la même chose!** *Same old thing!* III, 1
la **tour** *tower*, II, 6
le **tour:** faire un tour sur la grande roue *to take a ride on the ferris wheel*, II, 6; **faire un tour sur les montagnes russes** *to take a ride on the roller coaster*, II, 6
le **tourbillon** *swirl*, III, 10
  tourner: Puis, tournez à gauche dans/sur... *Then, turn left on...*, II, 2; **Vous tournez...** *You turn...*, I, 12
le **tournoi** *tournament*, III, 11
  tousser *to cough*, III, 1
  tout: A tout à l'heure! *See you later!* I, 1; **Allez (continuez) tout droit.** *Go (keep going) straight ahead.* II, 2; **C'est... comme tout!** *It's as... as can be!* III, 2; **J'ai pensé à tout.** *I've thought of everything.* I, 11; **Je n'ai pas du tout aimé.** *I didn't like it at all.* III, 9; **Pas du tout.** *Not at all.* I, 4; II, 10; III, 9; **Il/Elle ne va pas du tout avec...** *It doesn't go at all with...* I, 10; **Tout a été de travers!** *Everything went wrong!* II, 5; **Tout**

me tente. *Everything looks tempting.* III, 1; **Tout à fait!** *Absolutely!* III, 9; **C'est tout à fait ton style.** *It looks great on you.* I, 10; **tout de suite** *right away*, I, 6; **C'est tout de suite à...** *It's right there on the...*, I, 12; **J'y vais tout de suite.** *I'll go right away.* I, 8; **Vous allez tout droit jusqu'à...** *You go straight ahead until you get to...*, I, 12
  tout à fait: Tout à fait! *Absolutely!* III, 9; **C'est tout à fait normal.** *You don't have to thank me.* III, 6
  tout de même *honestly*, III, 2
  tout le monde: Ça arrive à tout le monde. *It happens to everybody.* III, 6; **Ça peut arriver à tout le monde.** *It could happen to anyone.* III, 10; **Ce n'est pas parce que tout le monde... que tu dois le faire.** *Just because everyone else... doesn't mean you have to.* III, 3; **Tout le monde fait pareil.** *Everybody does it.* III, 3
  le **trac:** Tu as le trac? *Are you nervous?* III, 12
  traduit(e) *translated*, III, 1
le **train:** en train *by train*, I, 12; **être en train de** *to be in the process of (doing something)*, II, 9
  traîner *to drag*, III, 7
  traire: traire les vaches (f.) *to milk the cows*, III, 8
  traiter: Il/Elle m'a traité(e) de...! *He/She called me a...!* III, 6
la **tranche: une tranche de** *a slice of*, I, 8
  tranquille *calm*, II, 8
le **travail: trouver un travail** *to find a job*, III, 5
  travailler *to work*, I, 9; **Il faut mieux travailler en classe.** *You have to do better in class.* II, 5
les **travaux** (m.) pratiques *lab*, I, 2
  travers: Tout a été de travers! *Everything went wrong!* II, 5; travers: à travers le hublot *through the window*; III, 3; à travers *across*, III, 8
  traverser: Traversez... *Cross...*, II, 2; **Vous allez traverser...** *You cross...*, III, 2
  trébucher *to stumble, stagger*, III, 5
  trembler (de peur) *to shake (with fear)*, III, 6
la **tribu** *tribe*, III, 2
  Tricheur(-euse)! *Cheater!* III, 6
  triste *sad*, III, 6
la **trompe** *trunk*, III, 7
  se tromper: A mon avis, tu te trompes. *In my opinion, you're mistaken.* II, 9; **Si je ne me trompe pas,...?** *If I'm not mistaken,...?* III, 11

la **trompette** *trumpet*, III, 11
  trop: C'est trop cher. *It's too expensive.* II, 3; **Il/Elle est (Ils/Elles sont) trop...** *It's/They're too...*, I, 10; **Je ne sais pas trop.** *I really don't know.* III, 5; **Non, pas trop.** *No, not too much.* I, 2; **Pas trop bien.** *Not too well.* III, 1
le **trottoir** *sidewalk*, III, 8
le **trou** *hole*, III, 7
  troué(e) *hollowed out*, III, 11
le **trouillard** *coward, wimp*, III, 7
le **troupeau** *herd*, III, 7
la **trousse** *pencil case*, I, 3; **la trousse de premiers soins** *first-aid kit*, II, 12
  trouver *to find*, I, 9; **se trouve... ...is located...**, II, 12; **Ce que je trouve super, c'est (de)...** *What I think is super is...*, III, 11; **Je le/la/les trouve moche(s).** *I think it's (they're) really tacky.* I, 10; **Je trouve qu'il est...** *I think it's...*, III, 4; **Je trouve qu'ils/elles font...** *I think they look...*, III, 4; **Où se trouve...?** *Where is...?* II, 4; **Comment tu as trouvé ça?** *How did you like it?* III, 9; **J'ai trouvé ça pas mal/amusant.** *It was not bad/funny.* III, 9
le **truc** *thing*, I, 5; **Ce n'est pas mon truc.** *It's not my thing.* II, 7; **Oh, c'est un vieux truc.** *This old thing?* III, 4; **J'ai des tas de trucs à faire.** *I have lots of things to do.* I, 12; **J'ai des trucs à faire.** *I have some things to do.* I, 5; le petit truc *the little trick*, III, 3
les **truffes** (f.) *truffles*, III, 1
la **truite** *trout*, III, 1
  truquer *to cheat*, III, 8
  tu *you*, (singular, informal), I, 0
le **tuba** *snorkle*, III, 10
  tuer *to kill*, III, 7
la **Tunisie** *Tunisia*, III, 12
le **type** *guy*, III, 2
  typique: Qu'est-ce qui est typique de chez toi? *What's typical of where you're from?* III, 12

  un *a; an*, I, 3
  une *a; an*, I, 3
  uniquement *only*, III, 3
l' **urgence** (f.): cas d'urgence *emergency*, III, 3
  utile: Je ne crois pas que ce soit utile. *I don't think it's worthwhile.* III, 7
  utiliser *to use*, III, 1, 2

les vacances (f.) *vacation*, I, 1; **Bonnes vacances!** *Have a good vacation!* I, 11; **C'était comment, tes vacances?** *How was your vacation?* III, 1; **Comment se sont passées tes vacances?** *How was your vacation?* II, 5; **en colonie de vacances** *to/at a summer camp*, I, 11; **en vacances** *on vacation*, I, 4
vacciner *to vaccinate*, III, 7; **se faire vacciner** *to get vaccinated*, III, 7
vachement *really*, II, 9
vague *vague*, III, 2
la vaisselle: faire la vaisselle *to do the dishes*, I, 7
la valise *suitcase*, I, 11
la vallée *valley*, III, 2
la vanille: à la vanille *vanilla*, III, 1
se vanter *to brag*, III, 10; **C'est pas pour me vanter, mais moi...** *I'm not trying to brag, but...*, III, 10
la vapeur: à la vapeur *steamed*, III, 11
la variante *type*, III, 11
le vase *vase*, II, 3
vaudrait: Il vaudrait mieux que... *It would be better if...*, III, 5; **Tu penses qu'il vaudrait mieux...?** *Do you think it'd be better to...?* III, 7
vaut: Ça ne vaut pas le coup! *It's not worth it!* III, 9; **Je crois que ça vaut mieux.** *I think that's better.* III, 7
le vautour *vulture*, III, 7
la vedette *celebrity*, III, 10
la végétation tropicale *tropical vegetation*, III, 7
la veille *eve, the day before* III, 5
le vélo *biking*, I, 1; **à vélo** *by bike*, I, 12; **faire du vélo** *to bike*, I, 4; **faire du vélo de montagne** *to go mountain-bike riding*, II, 12
le vélomoteur *moped*, III, 8
le vendeur (la vendeuse) *salesperson*, III, 4
vendre *to sell*, I, 9
le vendredi *on Fridays*, I, 2
venir *to come*, II, 6; **celle que tu viens de lire** *the one (fable) you just read*, III, 3
le ventre: J'ai mal au ventre *My stomach hurts.* II, 7
le verbe *verb*, III, 1
vérifier *to check*, III, 2
véritable: C'était un véritable cauchemar! *It was a real nightmare!* I, 11
la vérité: dire la vérité *to tell the truth*, III, 3
le vermisseau *small worm*, III, 11

le verre *glass*, III, 3; **la bulle de verre** *the glass bubble*, III, 3
vers *about*, I, 6; **Vers...** *About (a certain time)...*, II, 4; *toward*, III, 1
versatile *moody*, III, 6
vert(e) *green*, I, 3; II, 1
la veste *suit jacket, blazer*, I, 10
les vêtements (m.) *clothes*, I, 10
le vétérinaire (la vétérinaire) *veterinarian*, III, 5
veuf (veuve) *widowed*, III, 6
veuillez: Veuillez ne pas... *Please do not...*, III, 3
la viande *meat*, I, 8; III, 11
la vidange: faire la vidange *to change the oil*, III, 2
la vidéo: faire de la vidéo *to make videos*, I, 4; **jouer à des jeux vidéo** *to play video games*, I, 4
la vidéocassette *videotape*, I, 3
le vidéoclip *music video*, III, 9
la vie: C'est comment, la vie là-bas? *What's life like there?* III, 12; **La vie était plus... moins...** *Life was more..., less...*, II, 8
le vieillard *old man*, III, 6
vieux (vieille): Pauvre vieux/vieille! *You poor thing!* II, 5
vif (vive) *quick (witted)*, III, 6
le village de pêcheurs *fishing village*, II, 4
la ville *town*, III, 2
violent: trop violent *too violent*, II, 11
violet(te) *purple*, I, 3
le violon *violin*, III, 11
le virage *turn*, III, 12
viser *to aim at, to take aim*, III, 12
la visite: une visite guidée *a guided tour*, II, 6
visiter *to visit (a place)*, I, 9; II, 6
le visiteur *visitor*, III, 2
vite *quickly* **Dis vite!** *Let's hear it!* II, 9
vitesse: à pleine vitesse *at top speed*, III, 3
les vitres (f.): **laver les vitres** *to wash the windows*, III, 3
les vitrines (f.): **faire les vitrines** *to window-shop*, I, 6
vivant(e) *lively*, II, 4
vivement: Vivement que...! *I just can't wait...!* III, 12
vivre *to live*, III, 2; **vivre: (pp. vécu) Beaucoup de Sénégalais vivent...** *Many Senegalese live...*, III, 5
les vivres (m.) *dry goods (food)*, III, 3
les vœux (m.): **Meilleurs vœux!** *Best wishes!* II, 3
Voici... *Here's...*, I, 7
Voilà. *Here it is.* II, 3; *Here*, I, 3; **Voilà...** *There's...*, I, 7; III, 12
la voie: pays en voie de développement *developing countries*, III, 3

la voile: faire de la planche à voile *to go windsurfing*, I, 11; **faire de la voile** *to go sailing*, I, 11; **le voile** *veil*, III, 8
voir: Qu'est-ce qu'il y a à voir...? *What is there to see...?* II, 12; **Qu'est-ce qu'il y avait à voir?** *What was there to see...?* III, 1; **Tu devrais aller voir...** *You should go see...*, III, 9; **Tu vas voir...** *You'll see...*, II, 8; **Va voir..., c'est génial comme film.** *Go see..., it's a great movie.* III, 9; **voir un film** *to see a movie*, I, 6; **voir un match** *to see a game (in person)*, I, 6; **voir une pièce** *to see a play*, I, 6; **...tu vois. ...you see.** II, 9; **Ça se voit.** *That's obvious.* II, 9; **Si tu avais vu...!** *If you could have seen...!* III, 10
le voisin (la voisine) *neighbor*, III, 3
le voisinage *neighborhood*, III, 11
la voiture: *car*, I, 7; **en voiture** *by car*, I, 12; **laver la voiture** *to wash the car*, I, 7; **emboutir la voiture** *to wreck the car*, III, 10
volant(e) *flying*, III, 10
le volcan *volcano*, II, 4
le volley(-ball) *volleyball*, I, 4
volontiers *sure*, III, 6
vouloir *to want*, I, 6; **Je m'en veux de...** *I feel bad that...*, III, 6; **Je ne t'en veux pas.** *No hard feelings.* II, 10; **Je veux bien.** *Gladly*, I, 12; *I'd like to.* II, 1; *I'd really like to.* I, 6; **Non, je ne veux pas.** *No, I don't want to.* II, 8; **Oui, si tu veux.** *Yes, if you want to.* I, 7; **Si tu veux, on peut...** *If you like, we can...*, II, 1; **Tu ne m'en veux pas?** *No hard feelings?* II, 10; **Tu veux bien que...** *Is it OK with you if...?* III, 3; **Je voudrais acheter...** *I'd like to buy...*, I, 3; **Je voudrais bien...** *I'd really like to...*, I, 11; **Tu ne voudrais pas...?** *Wouldn't you like to...?* III, 6
vous *you, (plural and/or formal)*, I, 1
le voyage: Bon voyage! *Have a good trip! (by plane, ship)*, I, 11; II, 3; **Vous avez/Tu as fait bon voyage?** *Did you have a good trip?* II, 2
voyager *to travel*, I, 1
le voyageur (la voyageuse) *traveller*, III, 2
le voyagiste *travel agent*, III, 6
vrai(e): C'est pas vrai! *You're kidding!* II, 6; **C'est vrai?** *Really?* II, 2
vraiment: Vraiment? *Really?* II, 2; **C'est vraiment bon!** *It's good!* II, 3; **Il/Elle est vraiment bien, ton/ta...** *Your... is really great.*

II, 2 ; **Non, pas vraiment.** *No, not really.* I, 11

le vrombissement *revving (of a motor),* III, 10

vulgaire *tasteless,* III, 4

le **week-end** *weekend; on weekends,* I, 4; **ce week-end** *this weekend,* I, 6; **Comment s'est passé ton week-end?** *How was your weekend?* II, 5

le **western** *western (movie),* II, 11

y *there,* I, 12; **Allons-y!** *Let's go!* I, 4; **Comment est-ce qu'on y va?** *How can we get there?* I, 12; **Je n'y comprends rien.** *I don't understand anything about it.* II, 5; **N'y va pas!** *Don't go!* III, 9; **On peut y aller...** *We can go there...,* I, 12; **Qu'est-ce qu'on y...?** *What do you... there?* III, 12; **Tu vas t'y faire.** *You'll get used to it.* II, 8; **y compris** *included,* III, 11

le **yaourt** *yogurt,* I, 8

les **yeux** (m.) *eyes,* II, 1

Youpi! *Yippee!* III, 12

le **zèbre** *zebra,* III, 7

zéro *a waste of time,* I, 2

le **zoo** *zoo,* I, 6; II, 6

le **zouk: danser le zouk** *to dance the zouk,* II, 4

Zut! *Darn!,* I, 3

In this vocabulary, the English definitions of all active French words in the book have been listed, followed by the French. The numbers after each entry refer to the level and chapter where the word or phrase first appears, or where it becomes an active vocabulary word. It is important to use a French word in its correct context. The use of a word can be checked easily by referring to the chapter where it appears.

French words and phrases are presented in the same way as in the French-English vocabulary.

a *un, une*, I, 3
able: We'd be able to ... for sure. *On pourrait sûrement...*, III, 7
about: About (a certain time) ... *Vers...*, II, 4; **It's about ...** *Ça parle de...*, II, 11; III, 9; **It's about ...** *Il s'agit de...*, III, 9; **It's about a guy who ...** *C'est l'histoire d'un mec qui...*, III, 10; **What's it about?** *De quoi ça parle?* II, 11; III, 9
Absolutely! *Tout à fait!* III, 9
acceptable: That's not acceptable. *C'est inadmissible.* II, 5
accident: to have an accident *avoir un accident*, II, 9
accordion *l'accordéon* (m.), III, 11
accountant *le/la comptable*, III, 5
acne: to have acne *avoir des boutons*, III, 10
across: across from *en face de*, I, 12; II, 2
action: action movie *un film d'action*, II, 11
actor *l'acteur* (m.), III, 5
actress *l'actrice* (f.), III, 5
adore: I adore ... *J'adore...*, I, 1
adventure: adventure movie *un film d'aventures*, II, 11
advise: What do you advise me to do? *Qu'est-ce que tu me conseilles?* I, 9
aerobics: to do aerobics *faire de l'aérobic*, I, 4; II, 7
aerosol: to use aerosol sprays *utiliser des aérosols*, III, 3
afraid: Don't be afraid. *N'ayez pas peur.* III, 7; **I'm afraid that ...** *J'ai peur que...*, III, 7; **I'm very afraid of ...** *J'ai très peur de...*, III, 7
African *africain(e)*, II, 11
after: After that ... *Après ça...*, II, 4, 12; **And after that, ...** *Et après ça...*, I, 9
afternoon: afternoon off *l'après-midi libre*, I, 2; **in the afternoon** *l'après-midi*, I, 2

afterwards: Afterwards, I went out. *Après, je suis sorti(e)*, I, 9; **And afterwards?** *Et après?* I, 9
again: ... again? *...déjà?*, III, 11; **Don't do it again.** *Ne recommence pas.* II, 5
agree: I don't agree. *Je ne suis pas d'accord.* I, 7; **I agree with you.** *Je suis d'accord avec toi.* III, 9
ahead: Go (keep going) straight ahead. *Allez (continuez) tout droit*, II, 2; **Well just go right ahead!** *Non mais, surtout, ne vous gênez pas!* III, 8
air: to put air in the tires *mettre de l'air dans les pneus*, III, 2
alarm: to hear the alarm clock *entendre le réveil*, II, 5
algebra *l'algèbre* (f.), I, 2
Algeria *l'Algérie* (f.), III, 12
all: All you have to do is ... *Tu n'as qu'à...*, II, 7; **I didn't like it at all.** *Je n'ai pas du tout aimé.* III, 9; **Not at all.** *Pas du tout.* I, 4; II, 10; **I don't like that at all.** *Ça ne me plaît pas du tout.* III, 11; **That's all I listen to.** *Je n'écoute que ça.* III, 11
all over: I hurt all over! *J'ai mal partout!* II, 7
all right *pas mal*, II, 6
allergies: I have allergies. *J'ai des allergies.* II, 7
allowed: You're not allowed to ... *Tu n'as pas le droit de...*, III, 3
almost: You're (We're) almost there! *Tu y es (On y est) presque!* II, 12; **You're almost there!** *Tu y es presque!* II, 7
alone: I went alone ... *J'y suis allé(e) seul(e)...*, III, 1; **Leave me alone!** *Fiche-moi la paix!* III, 6
already *déjà*, I, 9; **He/She already has one (of them).** *Il/Elle en a déjà un(e).* II, 3
also *aussi*, I, 1
always: I'm always the one who gets blamed! *C'est toujours moi qui prends!* III, 6; **It's always the same!** *C'est toujours la même chose!* III, 6

am: I am ... *Je suis...*, II, 1
amazing: It was amazing/unbelievably bad! *C'était incroyable!* II, 5
American *américain(e)*, II, 11
amusement park *un parc d'attractions*, II, 6
an *un, une*, I, 3
and *et*, I, 1
andouille sausage *l'andouille* (f.), III, 11
angry *fâché(e)*, II, 9
ankle: to sprain one's ankle *se fouler la cheville*, II, 7
annoyed *énervé(e)*, II, 9
annoying *embêtant(e)*, I, 7
answer *répondre*, I, 9; **There's no answer.** *Ça ne répond pas.* I, 9; **... and then the other one answers ...** *...et l'autre lui répond...*, III, 10
ant *la fourmi*, III, 7
anxious: I'm really anxious to ... *Je suis vraiment impatient(e) de...*, III, 2
any (of it) *en*, I, 8
any more: I don't want any more. *Je n'en veux plus.* I, 8; **I just can't do any more!** *Je n'en peux plus!* II, 7, 12
anymore: I don't know what I want anymore. *Je ne sais plus ce que je veux.* III, 5; **I'm not hungry (thirsty) anymore.** *Je n'ai plus faim (soif).* II, 3
anyone: It could happen to anyone. *Ça peut arriver à tout le monde.* III, 10
anything: I didn't forget anything. *Je n'ai rien oublié.* I, 11; **It didn't do anything for me.** *Ça ne m'a pas emballé(e).* III, 9; **I just can't do anything right!** *Qu'est-ce que je peux être nul(le)!* III, 12
Anyway, ... *Bref,...*, II, 9
apologize *s'excuser*, II, 10; **Apologize.** *Excuse-toi.* II, 10

appetizers *les entrées* (f.), III, 1; **What would you like for an appetizer?** *Que voulez-vous comme entrée?* III, 1

apples *des pommes* (f.), I, 8; **apple juice** *un jus de pomme*, I, 5; **apple tart** *la tarte aux pommes*, II, 3

appointment: **That's nice of you, but I've got an appointment.** *C'est gentil, mais j'ai un rendez-vous.* III, 6

apprenticeship: **to do an apprenticeship** *faire un apprentissage*, III, 5

April *avril*, I, 4

archery *le tir à l'arc*, III, 12

architect *l'architecte*, III, 5

are: **There is/are ...** *Il y a...* , II, 12; **They are ...** *Ils/Elles sont...* , II, 1

argument: **to have an argument (with someone)** *se disputer (avec quelqu'un)*, II, 9

arm *le bras*, II, 7

armoire: **armoire/wardrobe** *l'armoire* (f.), II, 2

around *vers*, I, 6

arrive *arriver*, II, 5; **to arrive late to school** *arriver en retard à l'école*, II, 5

arrow *la flèche*, III, 12

art class *les arts* (m.) *plastiques*, I, 2

as: **as many/as much ... as ...** *autant de... que...* , III, 8; **as ... as ...** *aussi... que...* , III, 8; **It's as ... as can be!** *C'est... comme tout!* III, 2

ask: **to ask (someone's) forgiveness** *demander pardon à (quelqu'un)*, II, 10; **to ask your parents' permission** *demander la permission à tes parents*, II, 10

at *à la, au, aux*, I, 6 II, 6; **At ...** *A...* , II, 11; **at ... fifteen (time)** *à... heures quinze*, I, 2; **at ... forty-five** *à... heures quarante-cinq*, I, 2; **at my house** *chez moi*, I, 6; **At that point, ...** *A ce moment-là,...* , II, 9; III, 9; **at the record store** *chez le disquaire*, I, 12; **At what time?** *A quelle heure?* I, 6

attend: **to attend a sound and light show** *assister à un spectacle son et lumière*, II, 6

attendant: **gas station attendant** *le/la pompiste*, III, 2

August *août*, I, 4

aunt *la tante*, I, 7

avocados *des avocats* (m.), I, 8

Avoid ... *Evite de...* , II, 12; **Avoid ...** *Evite(z) de...* , II, 7; **Avoid seeing ...** *Evite d'aller voir...* , III, 9

aware *prudent(e)*, III, 3

away: **No, I went away for ...** *Non, je suis parti(e)...* , III, 1; **Yes, right away.** *Oui, tout de suite.* I, 5

awful *sinistre*, II, 6

B

back *le dos*, II, 7; **come back** *revenir*, II, 6; **go back (home)** *rentrer*, II, 6; **Towards the back.** *Au fond.* III, 2

backpack *un sac à dos*, I, 3

bad *mauvais*, I, 5; **I feel bad that ...** *Je m'en veux de...* , III, 6; **I'm bad in computer science.** *Je suis mauvais(e) en informatique.* II, 5; **It was amazing/unbelievably bad!** *C'était incroyable!* II, 5; **It was not bad/funny.** *J'ai trouvé ça pas mal/amusant.* III, 9; **not bad** *pas mal*, I, 2, 9; **What a bad day!** *Quelle journée!* II, 5; **What a bad weekend!** *Quel week-end!* II, 5

bag *un sac*, I, 3

baggy *large*, I, 10

bakery *la boulangerie*, I, 12; II, 3

balance: **the balance beam** *la poutre*, III,12

balcony *le balcon*, II, 2

ball *la balle*, III, 12; *le ballon*, III, 12

banana tree *un bananier*, II, 4

bananas *des bananes* (f.), I, 8

bandages *les pansements* (m.), III, 7

bangs *la frange*, III, 4

bank *la banque*, I, 12

baseball *le base-ball*, III, 12; **to play baseball** *jouer au base-ball*, I, 4

basketball *le basket-ball*, I, 4; III, 12; **to play basketball** *jouer au basket (-ball)*, I, 4

baskets *des paniers* (m.), II, 8; **basket (basketball)** *le panier*, III, 12

bass (guitar) *la basse*, III, 11

bat (baseball) *le bâton*, III, 12

bathing suit *un maillot de bain*, I, 10

bathroom *la salle de bains*, II, 2

batter (baseball) *le frappeur*, III, 12

batting: **You're batting a thousand!** *Tu en rates pas une, toi!* III, 10

be *être*, I, 7; **to be in the process of (doing something)** *être en train de (+ infinitive)*, II, 9

be able to, can *pouvoir*, I, 8; **Can you ...?** *Est-ce que tu peux... ?* I, 12; **I can't.** *Je ne peux pas.* II, 7

beach *la plage*, I, 1

bear *un ours*, II, 12

beard *la barbe*, III, 4

beautiful *beau (belle)*, II, 2; *magnifique*, II, 6

because *parce que*, I, 5; **Just because everyone else ... doesn't mean you have to.** *Ce n'est pas parce que tout le monde... que tu dois le faire.* III, 3

become *devenir*, II, 6

bed *le lit*, II, 2; **to go to bed** *se coucher*, II, 4; **to make one's bed** *faire son lit*, III, 3

bedroom *la chambre*, II, 2

beef *le bœuf*, I, 8

been: **It's been ...** *Ça fait...* , III, 1

begin, to start *commencer*, I, 9

beginning: **At the beginning ...** *Au début...* , III, 9; **I went at the beginning of ...** *J'y suis allé(e) début...* , III, 1

behind *derrière*, I, 12

Belgium *la Belgique*, III, 12

believe: **Believe me.** *Crois-moi.* III, 4; **I can't believe how ...!** *C'est fou comme... !* III, 7; **I can't believe it.** *J'arrive pas à y croire!* III, 12; **I don't believe it.** *Je n'en reviens pas.* III, 10

belt *la ceinture*, I, 10

best: **All the best to ...** *Bien des choses à...* , III, 8; **Best wishes!** *Meilleurs vœux!* II, 3; **I ... the best.** *C'est moi qui... le mieux.* III, 10; **I'm the best.** *C'est moi, le/la meilleur(e).* III, 10; **Make the best of it.** *Fais-toi une raison.* II, 8; **You're really the best.** *Tu es vraiment le/la meilleur(e).* III, 10

bet: **I bet that ...** *Je parie que...* , II, 9

better: **It would be better if ...** *Il vaudrait mieux que...* , III, 5; **It'll get better.** *Ça va aller mieux.* II, 5; **It's better than ...** *C'est meilleur que...* , II, 7; **It's going to get better!** *Ça va aller mieux!* I, 9; **You have to do better in class.** *Il faut mieux travailler en classe.* II, 5; **You would do well/better to ...** *Tu ferais bien/mieux de...* , III, 5

between *entre*, I, 12

big *grand(e)*, I, 10; **big (tall)** *grand(e)*, II, 1

bigger: **bigger than ...** *plus grand(e) que*, II, 4; **I've done bigger and better things.** *Oh, j'en ai vu d'autres.* III, 10

bike *faire du vélo*, I, 4; **by bike** *à vélo*, I, 12

biking *le vélo*, I, 1

binder: **loose-leaf binder** *un classeur*, I, 3

binoculars *les jumelles* (f.), III, 7

biography *la biographie*, II, 11

biology *la biologie*, I, 2

bird *l'oiseau* (m.), III, 7

birthday: **Happy birthday!** *Joyeux (Bon) anniversaire!* II, 3

bisque *en bisque*, III, 11

black *noir(e)*, I, 3; **black** *noir*, II, 1; **black hair** *les cheveux noirs*, II, 1

blackboard *le tableau*, I, 0; **Go to the blackboard!** *Allez au tableau!*, I, 0

blamed: **I'm always the one who gets blamed!** *C'est toujours moi qui prends!* III, 6

blazer *la veste*, I, 10

bless: **Bless you!** *A tes souhaits!* II, 7

blond *blond(e)*, I, 7; **blond hair** *les cheveux blonds*, II, 1

blue *bleu(e),* I, 3; II, 1
blues (music) *le blues,* II, 11; III, 11
boat *le bateau,* I, 12; **by boat** *en bateau,* I, 12; **to go boating** *faire du bateau,* I, 12
boiled *au court-bouillon,* III, 11
book *le livre,* I, 0
bookstore *la librairie,* I, 12
boots *des bottes* (f.), I, 10; **pair of boots** *les bottes* (f.), II, 1
bored: I was bored. *Je me suis ennuyé(e).* II, 6; III, 1; **I was bored to death.** *Je me suis ennuyé(e) à mourir.* III, 9; **I wasn't bored a second.** *Je ne me suis pas ennuyé(e) une seconde.* III, 9; **You're never bored.** *On ne s'ennuie pas.* II, 11
bores: That bores me to death! *Ça m'ennuie à mourir!* III, 2; **That bores me!** *Ça m'embête!* III, 2; **What bores me...** *Ce qui m'ennuie, c'est...,* II, 4
boring *barbant(e),* I, 2; *ennuyeux (ennuyeuse),* II, 6, 8; **It was boring.** *C'était ennuyeux.* I, 5; *C'était barbant.* I, 11; **deadly boring** *mortel(le),* III, 2; **That's boring!** *C'est rasant!* III, 2; **That's so boring!** *Ça me casse les pieds!* III, 2
born: to be born *naître,* II, 6
borrow *emprunter,* I, 12
bother *ennuyer,* II, 8; **Stop bothering me!** *Et toi, arrête de m'embêter!* III, 10
bottle: a bottle of *une bouteille de,* I, 8
bow (in archery) *l'arc* (m.), III, 12
box: a package/box of *un paquet de,* I, 8
boxing *la boxe,* III, 12
bracelet *le bracelet,* I, 3
braces: to get one's braces off *se faire enlever ses bagues,* III, 10
brag: I'm not trying to brag, but... *C'est pas pour me vanter, mais moi...,* III, 10
braid *la natte,* III, 4
brakes *les freins* (m.), III, 2
brass, copper *le cuivre,* III, 8
brave *brave,* II, 1
Brazil *le Brésil,* III, 12
Brazilian (adj.) *brésilien(ne),* III, 12
bread *du pain,* I, 8; *le pain,* II, 3; **long, thin loaf of bread** *la baguette,* I, 12
bread pudding *le pouding au pain,* III, 11
break *la récréation,* I, 2; **Give me a break!** *Oh, ça va, hein!* III, 10; **Will you give me a break?** *Lâche-moi, tu veux?* III, 10; **to break one's...** *se casser le/la...,* II, 7; III, 10
break down *tomber en panne,* II, 9; **to break down (run out of gas)** *tomber en panne (d'essence),* III, 2
break up (with someone) *casser (avec quelqu'un),* II, 9
breakfast *le petit déjeuner,* I, 8

bring *apporter,* I, 9; **Bring me back...** *Rapporte-moi...,* I, 8; **Please bring me...** *Apportez-moi..., s'il vous plaît.* I, 5; **to bring (with you)** *emporter,* II, 12; **Will you bring me...?** *Tu me rapportes...?* I, 8
brother *le frère,* I, 7
brown *marron,* I, 3; II, 1; **light brown hair** *châtain,* II, 1; **dark brown hair** *les cheveux bruns,* II, 1
brunette *brun(e),* I, 7
brush (bushes) *la brousse,* III, 7; **to brush one's teeth** *se brosser les dents,* II, 4
buffalo *le buffle,* III, 7
bugging: You're bugging me! *Tu m'énerves, à la fin!* III, 6
building *l'immeuble* (m.), III, 8
bun (hairstyle) *le chignon,* III, 4
bus: by bus *en bus,* I, 12; **bus stop** *l'arrêt* (m.) *de bus,* III, 8
business: Mind your own business! *Mêle-toi de tes oignons!* III, 6; **businessman/woman** *homme/femme d'affaires,* III, 5
busy: I'm very busy. *Je suis très occupé(e).* II, 10; **It's busy.** *C'est occupé.* I, 9; **Sorry, I'm busy.** *Désolé(e), je suis occupé(e).* I, 6; *Je suis pris(e).* III, 6
but *mais,* I, 1
butcher shop *la boucherie,* II, 3
butter *du beurre,* I, 8; *le beurre,* II, 3
butterfly *le papillon,* III, 7
buy *acheter,* I, 9; **buy: Buy me...** *Achète(-moi)...,* I, 8; **How about buying...?** *Si on achetait...?* II, 8; **to buy oneself something** *s'acheter quelque chose,* III, 10
by: By the way,... *A propos,...,* II, 9
Bye! *Tchao!* I, 1

café *le café,* I, 5
cafeteria: at the school cafeteria *à la cantine,* I, 9
Cajun music *la musique cajun,* III, 11
cake *du gâteau,* I, 8
calculator *la calculatrice,* I, 3
call (someone) *téléphoner à (quelqu'un),* II, 10; **Call him/her/them!** *Téléphone-lui/-leur!* I, 9; **Can you call back later?** *Vous pouvez rappeler plus tard?* I, 9
called: Then I called... *Ensuite, j'ai téléphoné à...,* I, 9; **He/She called me a...!** *Il/Elle m'a traité(e) de...!* III, 6; **What is that called?** *Comment est-ce qu'on appelle ça?* III, 11

calling: Who's calling? *Qui est à l'appareil?* I, 9
calm *tranquille,* II, 8; **Calm down!** *Calmez-vous!* III, 7; **Calm down.** *Du calme, du calme.* III, 2
camcorder *le caméscope,* III, 7
camel *le chameau,* III, 8
camera *l'appareil-photo* (m.), I, 11; II, 1
camp: to/at a summer camp *en colonie de vacances,* I, 11
campground *le terrain de camping,* II, 2
camping: to go camping *faire du camping,* I, 11; II, 12
can: a can of *la boîte de,* I, 8
can (to be able to): *pouvoir,* I, 8; **Can I...?** *Je peux...?* III, 3; **Can I try on...?** *Je peux essayer...?* I, 10; **Can you...?** *Est-ce que tu peux...?* I, 12; **I can't because...** *Je ne peux pas parce que...* I, 5; **I can't right now.** *Je ne peux pas maintenant.* I, 8; **No, I can't.** *Non, je ne peux pas.* I, 12; II, 1, 7; **Can I talk to you?** *Je peux te parler?* II, 10; **If you like, we can...** *Si tu veux, on peut...,* II, 1; **We can...** *On peut...,* II, 4; **What can I do?** *Qu'est-ce que je peux faire?* II, 10; **What can we do?** *Qu'est-ce qu'on peut faire?* II, 4; **You can...** *On peut...,* II, 12
Canada *le Canada,* III, 12
canary *le canari,* I, 7
candies *les bonbons* (m), II, 3
candy shop *la confiserie,* II, 3
canoe: to go for a canoe ride *faire du canotage,* II, 12
cans *les boîtes* (f.), III, 3
canteen *la gourde,* III, 7
cap *la casquette,* I, 10
capital *la capitale,* II, 4
car: by car *en voiture,* I, 12; **to wash the car** *laver la voiture,* I, 7; **to wreck the car** *emboutir la voiture,* III, 10
caramel custard *la crème caramel,* III, 1
cards: to play cards *jouer aux cartes,* I, 4
care: What I don't care for is... *Ce qui ne me plaît pas, c'est...,* II, 4
career: to choose a career *choisir un métier,* III, 5
careful *prudent(e),* III, 3; **Be careful!** *Méfiez-vous!* III, 7
carrots *les carottes* (f.), I, 8; **grated carrots with vinaigrette dressing** *les carottes râpées,* III, 1
cartoon *le dessin animé,* III, 9
cartoon book *une bande dessinée (une B.D.),* II, 11
cassette tape *la cassette,* I, 3
cat *le chat,* I, 7
catches: What catches your eye is... *Ce qui saute aux yeux, c'est...,* III, 11
cathedral *la cathédrale,* II, 2
C.D. (compact disc) *un disque compact/un CD,* I, 3
celery: grated celery root with mayonnaise and vinaigrette *le céleri rémoulade,* III, 1

Central African Republic *la République centrafricaine*, III, 12
cereal *les céréales* (f.), II, 3
certain: I'm (not) certain that . . . *Je (ne) suis (pas) certain(e) que...*, III, 7
Certainly. *Bien sûr.* I, 9
chair *la chaise*, I, 0
channel (TV) *la chaîne*, III, 9
charming *charmant(e)*, II, 4
Cheater! *Tricheur(-euse)!* III, 6
check *vérifier*, III, 2; **check out: Hey! Check it out!** *Tiens! Regarde un peu!* III, 7; **The check, please.** *L'addition, s'il vous plaît.* I, 5; **traveler's checks** *les chèques* (m.) *de voyage*, II, 1
cheese *le fromage*, I, 5; II, 3; **a selection of cheeses** *l'assiette de fromages*, III, 1; **goat cheese** *fromage de chèvre*, III, 1; **toasted cheese and ham sandwich** *un croque-monsieur*, I, 5
cheetah *le guépard*, III, 7
chemistry *la chimie*, I, 2
chest: chest of drawers *la commode*, II, 2
chic *chic*, I, 10
chicken *la poule*, II, 3; III, 8
chicken *le poulet* I, 8; **chicken meat** *du poulet*, I, 8; **live chickens** *des poules*, I, 8; **roasted chicken with green beans** *le poulet haricots verts*, III, 1
child *l'enfant* (m./f.) I, 7; **to have a child** *avoir un enfant*, III, 5
childish *bébé*, III, 2
China *la Chine*, III, 12
chocolate *le chocolat*, I, 1; **box of chocolates** *la boîte de chocolats*, II, 3
choice: If I had a choice, . . . *Si j'avais le choix,...*, III, 8
choir *la chorale*, I, 2
choose *choisir*, I, 10; **to choose a career** *choisir un métier*, III, 5; **to choose the date** *fixer la date*, II, 10; **to choose the music** *choisir la musique*, II, 10
Christmas: Merry Christmas! *Joyeux Noël!* II, 3
church *l'église* (f.), II, 2
class: What classes do you have . . . ? *Tu as quels cours... ?* I, 2
classic *un (roman) classique*, II, 11; **classic movie** *un film classique*, II, 11
classical music *la musique classique*, II, 11; III, 11
classy *classe*, III, 4
clean *propre*, II, 8
clean: to clean house *faire le ménage*, I, 7; **to clean the bathroom** *nettoyer la salle de bains*, III, 3; **to clean the floor** *nettoyer le parquet*, III, 3; **to clean the windshield** *nettoyer le pare-brise*, III, 2

clear: to clear the table *débarrasser la table*, I, 7
close: That was close! *On l'a échappé belle!* III, 7
close: Close the door! *Fermez la porte!*, I, 0; **When do you close?** *A quelle heure est-ce que vous fermez?* II, 6
close to *près de*, I, 12
cloth *le tissu*, II, 8
coach *l'entraîneur* (m.), III, 12
coast: to/at the coast *au bord de la mer*, I, 11
coat *un manteau*, I, 10
coconut tree *un cocotier*, II, 4
coconuts *des noix de coco* (f.), I, 8
coffee *le café*, I, 5
cola *un coca*, I, 5
cold: I've got a cold. *J'ai un rhume.* II, 7; **It's cold.** *Il fait froid.* I, 4
color: What color is . . . ? *De quelle couleur est... ?*, I, 3
colorful *coloré(e)*, II, 4
come *venir*, II, 6; **come across: After . . . , you'll come across . . .** *Après..., vous allez tomber sur...*, III, 2; **come back** *revenir*, II, 6; **Come in, please.** *Entrez, je vous en prie.* III, 6; **Come on!** *Allez!* II, 7, 12; **Where does the word . . . come from?** *D'où vient le mot... ?* III, 11; **Will you come?** *Tu viens?* I, 6
comedy *la comédie*, III, 9; *le film comique*, II, 11
comfortable: Make yourself comfortable. *Mettez-vous à l'aise.* III, 6
comic book *une bande dessinée (une B.D.)*, II, 11; III, 2
commercial *la publicité (pub)*, III, 9
common: What do . . . and . . . have in common? *Quel est le point commun entre... et... ?* III, 10
compact disc/CD *un disque compact/un CD*, I, 3
compass *une boussole*, II, 12
competition *la compétition*, III, 12
computer *un ordinateur*, I, 3
computer science *l'informatique*, I, 2
concerts *les concerts* (m.), I, 1
Congratulations! *Félicitations!* II, 3; II, 5
conservative *sérieux (-euse)*, III, 4
considerate: to be considerate *être attentionné*, III, 3
conversation: Following our telephone conversation, . . . *Suite à notre conversation téléphonique,...*, III, 5
convinced: I'm convinced that . . . *Je suis convaincu(e) que...*, III, 7
cooked: How do you like your meat cooked? *Comment désirez-vous votre viande?* III, 1
cool *cool*, I, 2; **Cool!** *C'est le pied!* III, 7; **It's cool (outside).** *Il fait frais.* I, 4; **super cool** *hypercool*, III, 4; **That's too cool!** *C'est trop cool!* III, 12; **very cool** *chouette*, II, 2; **Yes, very cool.** *Oui, très chouette.* I, 9; I, 11;

Your . . . is cool. *Il/Elle est cool, ton/ta...*, II, 2
copper *le cuivre*, III, 8
coral *du corail*, III, 10
corn *du maïs*, I, 8
corner: on the corner of *au coin de*, I, 12
corny *ringard(e)*, III, 4
Côte d'Ivoire *la République de Côte d'Ivoire*, III, 12
cotton: in cotton *en coton*, I, 10
could: Could you . . . ? *Tu pourrais... ?* II, 10; **Could you go by . . . ?** *Tu pourrais passer à... ?* I, 12; **I could have . . .** *J'aurais pu...*, II, 10; **If I could, . . .** *Si seulement je pouvais,...*, III, 8; **We could . . .** *On pourrait...*, II, 1; **You could give him/her (them) . . .** *Tu pourrais lui (leur) offrir...*, II, 3; **You could have . . .** *Tu aurais pu...*, II, 10
country music *le country*, II, 11; III, 11
country: to/at the countryside *à la campagne*, I, 11
courage: You've really got courage. *Tu en as, du courage.* III, 10
course (school) *le cours*, I, 2; **(meal) first course** *l'entrée*, II, 3; **main course** *le plat principal*, II, 3; **Of course not.** *Bien sûr que non.* II, 10; **Of course.** *Bien sûr.* I, 3; II, 10; **Of course. They are (He/She is) . . .** *Bien sûr. C'est...*, II, 11; **Yes, of course.** *Oui, bien sûr.* I, 7
cousin *le cousin (la cousine)* I, 7
crab *le crabe*, III, 10
crafts: to make crafts *faire de l'artisanat* (m.), III, 8
crawfish *les écrevisses* (f.), III, 11
crazy (funny) *fou (folle)*, III, 2; **(wild)** *dingue*, III, 2; **Are you crazy or what?** *Tu délires ou quoi?* III, 11; **I'm crazy about that!** *Ça me branche!* III, 2; **What I'm really crazy about is . . .** *Ce qui me branche vraiment, c'est...*, III, 11; **You're driving me crazy!** *Tu me prends la tête!* III, 6
cream: cream puff pastry *la religieuse*, II, 3
credit card *la carte de crédit*, III, 7
crew: a crew cut *les cheveux en brosse* (m.), III, 4
crocodile *le crocodile*, III, 7
croissant *les croissants* (m.), II, 3; **croissant with a chocolate filling** *le pain au chocolat*, II, 3
cross: Cross . . . *Traversez...*, II, 2; **You cross . . .** *Vous traversez...*, III, 2
cross-country: to go cross-country skiing *faire une randonnée en skis*, II, 12
crowd *la foule*, III, 8
Crybaby! *Pleurnicheur(-euse)!* III, 6
curly: curly hair *les cheveux frisés* (m.), III, 4
cut: Oh, cut it out! *Oh, ça va, hein?* III, 6; **a crew cut** *les cheveux en brosse*

(m.), III, 4; **a square cut** *une coupe au carré*, III, 4; **Did you get your hair cut?** *Tu t'es fait couper les cheveux?* III, 4; **to cut one's finger** *se couper le doigt*, II, 7

cute *mignon (mignonne)*, I, 7; **cute, but that's all** *gentillet, sans plus*, II, 11

cycling *le cyclisme*, III, 12

dairy *la crémerie*, II, 3
dance *danser*, I, 1; *la danse*, I, 2; **dance music** *la dance*, III, 11; **to dance the zouk** *danser le zouk*, II, 4
dangerous *dangereux (dangereuse)*, II, 8
Darn it! *Zut!* I, 3; *Zut, alors!* III, 7; *Les boules!* III, 12
date (fruit) *la datte*, III, 8
date: to have a date/make a date (with someone) *avoir (prendre) rendez-vous (avec quelqu'un)*, II, 9
daughter *la fille*, I, 7
day: I had a terrible day! *J'ai passé une journée épouvantable!* II, 5; **It's just not my day!** *C'est pas mon jour!* II, 5; **What a bad day!** *Quelle journée!* II, 5; **What a great day!** *Quelle journée formidable!* II, 5
dead *mort(e)*, III, 6
deadly: deadly dull *mortel(le)*, II, 6; II, 8
death: I was bored to death. *Je me suis ennuyé(e) à mourir.* III, 9
December *décembre*, I, 4
decide: I can't decide between . . . and . . . *J'hésite entre... et...*, III, 1; **Have you decided to take . . . ?** *Vous avez décidé de prendre... ?* I, 10; **I'm having trouble deciding.** *J'ai du mal à me décider.* III, 5
deface: to deface the trees *mutiler les arbres*, II, 12
Definitely not! *Sûrement pas!* II, 6
delicatessen *la charcuterie*, II, 3
delicious *délicieux(-ieuse)*, I, 5; **That was delicious!** *C'était délicieux!* II, 3
Democratic Republic of Congo *la République Démocratique du Congo*, III, 12
denim: in denim *en jean*, I, 10
dentist *le/la dentiste*, III, 5
deposit *déposer*, I, 12
depressed *déprimé(e)*, II, 9
depressing *déprimant(e)*, II, 11
dessert *le dessert*, II, 3; III, 1
detective: detective or mystery movie *un film policier*, II, 11; **detective or mystery novel** *un roman policier (un polar)*, II, 11
detention: to have detention *être collé(e)*, II, 5

dictionary *le dictionnaire*, I, 3
did: First, I did . . . *D'abord, j'ai fait...*, I, 9
die *mourir*, II, 6
diet: to follow a diet that's too strict *suivre un régime trop strict*, II, 7
difference: What's the difference between . . . and . . . ? *Quelle est la différence entre ... et... ?* III, 10
different: Was it really so different? *C'était tellement/si différent?* II, 8
dining room *la salle à manger*, II, 2
dinner *le dîner*, I, 8; **to have dinner** *dîner*, I, 9
diploma: to get one's diploma *obtenir son diplôme*, III, 5
dirty *sale*, II, 8
discus: the discus throw *le lancer du disque*, III, 12
dishes: to do the dishes *faire la vaisselle*, I, 7
disinfectant *le désinfectant*, III, 7
dismissal (when school gets out) *la sortie*, I, 2
dive *plonger*, III, 12; **diving** *le plongeon acrobatique*, III, 12; **diving board** *le plongeoir*, III, 12
divorced *divorcé(e)*, III, 6
do *faire*, I, 4; **All you have to do is . . .** *Tu n'as qu'à...*, II, 7; III, 5; **Do you know what you want to do?** *Tu sais ce que tu veux faire?* III, 5; **Do you play/do . . . ?** *Est-ce que tu fais... ?* I, 4; **Don't do it again.** *Ne recommence pas.* II, 5; **I do.** *Moi, si.* I, 2; **I don't know what to do.** *Je ne sais pas quoi faire.* II, 10; **I don't play/do . . .** *Je ne fais pas de...*, I, 4; **I have errands to do.** *J'ai des courses à faire.* I, 5; **I just can't do any more!** *Je n'en peux plus!* II, 7; **I play/do . . .** *Je fais...*, I, 4; **In your opinion, what do I do?** *A ton avis, qu'est-ce que je fais?* I, 9; **It didn't do anything for me.** *Ça ne m'a pas emballé(e).* III, 9; **It'll do you good.** *Ça te fera du bien.* II, 7; **to do homework** *faire les devoirs*, I, 7; **to do the dishes** *faire la vaisselle*, I, 7; **What are you going to do . . . ?** *Qu'est-ce que tu vas faire... ?* I, 6; II, 1; *Tu vas faire quoi... ?* I, 6; **What can I do?** *Qu'est-ce que je peux faire?* I, 9; **What can we do?** *Qu'est-ce qu'on peut faire?* II, 4; **What did you do ?** *Qu'est-ce que tu as fait?* I, 9; **What do you advise me to do?** *Qu'est-ce que tu me conseilles?* I, 9; **What do you do (when) . . . ?** *Qu'est-ce que tu fais (quand)... ?* I, 4; **What do you like to do?** *Qu'est-ce que tu aimes faire?* II, 1; **What should we do?** *Qu'est-ce qu'on fait?* II, 1; **What are you doing?** *Mais, qu'est-ce que tu fais?* III, 2
doctor *médecin (m.)*, III, 5

documentary *le documentaire*, III, 9
dog *le chien*, I, 7; **to walk the dog** *promener le chien*, I, 7; *sortir le chien*, III, 3
don't: I don't. *Moi, non.* I, 2; **What I don't like is . . .** *Ce que je n'aime pas, c'est...*, II, 4; **Why don't you . . . ?** *Pourquoi tu ne... pas... ?* II, 7
done, made *fait (faire)*, I, 9
door *la porte*, I, 0
doubt: I have no doubt of it. *Je n'en ai aucun doute.* III, 12
down: to go down *descendre*, II, 6; **You go down this street to the next light.** *Vous continuez cette rue jusqu'au prochain feu rouge.* I, 12; **downstairs** *en bas*, III, 2
dozen *la douzaine de*, I, 8
drama *le drame*, III, 9; **to do drama** *faire du théâtre*, I, 4
drawers: chest of drawers *la commode*, II, 2
dream: My dream is to . . . *Mon rêve, c'est de...*, III, 5
dress *la robe*, I, 10; **to get dressed** *s'habiller*, II, 4
drink: to drink *boire*, I, 5; *la boisson*, I, 5; **And to drink?** *Et comme boisson?* III, 1; **What do you have to drink?** *Qu'est-ce que vous avez comme boissons?* I, 5; **What is there to drink?** *Qu'est-ce qu'il y a à boire?* I, 5
drive *conduire*, III, 2; **to drive a car** *conduire une voiture*, II, 8; **to drive safely** *conduire prudemment*, III, 3
driver *le chauffeur*, III, 5; **to get one's driver's license** *passer son permis de conduire*, III, 5
driving: You're driving me crazy! *Tu me prends la tête!* III, 6; **to take driving lessons** *prendre des leçons de conduite*, III, 10
drugstore *la pharmacie*, I, 12
drum (from Africa) *un tam-tam*, II, 8; **drum machine** *la boîte à rythmes*, III, 11; **drums** *la batterie*, III, 11
duck *un canard*, II, 12
dull: It's no good/dull. *C'est nul/lourd.* III, 9
dust: to dust *faire la poussière*, III, 3
dyed: dyed hair *les cheveux teints (m.)*, III, 4
dying: I'm dying of hunger! *Je crève de faim!* II, 12; **I'm dying of thirst!** *Je meurs de soif!* II, 12

early *tôt*, II, 4
earrings *des boucles d'oreilles (f.)*, I, 10

ears *les oreilles* (f.), II, 7; **to get one's ears pierced** *se faire percer les oreilles*, III, 10

earth-shattering: It's not earth-shattering. *Ça casse pas des briques.* II, 11

east: in the east *dans l'est*, II, 4; **It's to the east of ...** *C'est à l'est de...* , II, 12

eastern: It's in the eastern part of ... *C'est dans l'est de...* , II, 12

easy *facile*, I, 2; **That's so easy!** *C'est fastoche, ça!* III, 10

eat *manger*, I, 6; II, 7; **to eat too much sugar** *consommer trop de sucre*, II, 7; **someone who loves to eat** *gourmand(e)*, II, 1; **to eat better** *manger mieux*, III, 3; **to eat well** *bien se nourrir*, II, 7

eggs *des œufs* (m.), I, 8; II, 3

elderly: to help elderly people *aider les personnes âgées*, III, 3

elegant *élégant(e)*, III, 4

elementary school teacher *l'instituteur(-trice)*, III, 5

elephant *l'éléphant* (m.), III, 7

else: I have something else to do. *J'ai quelque chose à faire.* II, 10

embarrassed *gêné(e)*, II, 9

end: At the end ... *A la fin...* , III, 9; **How does it end?** *Comment ça se termine?* III, 9; **I went at the end of (month)...** *J'y suis allé(e) fin...* , III, 1; **Over there, at the end of the hallway.** *Par là, au bout du couloir.* III, 2

energy *l'énergie* (f.), III, 3

engaged: to get engaged *se fiancer*, III, 10

engineer *l'ingénieur*, III, 5

England *l'Angleterre* (f.), III, 12

English (language) *l'anglais* (m.), I, 1

enjoy *déguster*, II, 4

enough: Enough is enough! *Ça commence à bien faire, hein?* III, 8; **That's enough!** *Ça suffit!* III, 6

enter *entrer*, II, 6; **to enter the university** *entrer à l'université*, III, 5

entrance: At the entrance to ... *A l'entrée de...* , III, 2; **How much is the entrance fee?** *C'est combien, l'entrée?* II, 6

envelope *l'enveloppe* (f.), I, 12

epee (sword) *l'épée* (f.), III, 12

equestrian events *l'équitation* (f.), III, 12

eraser *la gomme*, I, 3

especially *surtout*, I, 1

essential: It's essential to ... *Il est essentiel que...* , III, 7

euro *l'euro* (m.), I, 5

evening: *le soir*, I, 2; **in the evening** *le soir*, I, 2

everybody: Everybody does it. *Tout le monde fait pareil.* III, 3; **It happens to everybody.** *Ça arrive à tout le monde.* III, 6

everyone: Everyone should ... *On doit...* II, 7; **Just because everyone else ... doesn't mean you have to.** *Ce n'est pas parce que tout le monde... que tu dois le faire.* III, 3

everything: Everything went wrong! *Tout a été de travers!* II, 5; **I've thought of everything.** *J'ai pensé à tout.* I, 11

exam *les examens* (m.), I, 1; **to pass one's baccalaureat exam** *réussir son bac*, III, 5

excellent *excellent*, I, 5, 9; II, 2

exciting: It's an exciting story. *C'est une histoire passionnante.* II, 11

excuse: Excuse me. *Excusez-moi.!* I, 3, 5; **Excuse me, ma'am. ..., please?** *Pardon, madame. ... , s'il vous plaît?* I, 12; **Excuse me, miss. Where is ..., please?** *Pardon, mademoiselle. Où est... , s'il vous plaît?* I, 12; **Excuse me, sir. I'm looking for ..., please.** *Pardon, monsieur. Je cherche... , s'il vous plaît.* I, 12

exercise *faire de l'exercice*, II, 7

exhausted: I'm exhausted. *Je suis crevé(e)*, II, 2

expensive: It's too expensive. *C'est trop cher.* II, 3; **Oh, it wasn't expensive.** *Oh, tu sais, je ne l'ai pas payé(e) cher.* III, 4

explain: Explain to him/her/them. *Explique-lui/leur.* II, 10; **to explain what happened (to someone)** *expliquer ce qui s'est passé (à quelqu'un)*, II, 10

eye *l'œil* (m.) (pl. *les yeux*), II, 1

F

fabric *le tissu*, II, 8

faded *délavé(e)*, III, 4

fail: to fail a test *rater un examen*, I, 9

fair: It's not fair. *C'est pas juste.* III, 12

fall *tomber*, II, 5; **in the fall** *en automne*, I, 4; **to fall in love (with someone)** *tomber amoureux (-euse) (de quelqu'un)*, II, 9

familiar: Are you familiar with ...? *Tu connais...?* , II, 11; **I'm not familiar with them (him/her).** *Je ne connais pas.* II, 11

fantastic *sensass (sensationnel(le))*, I, 10

far from *loin de*, I, 12

fascinating *passionnant(e)*, I, 2

fat (adj.) *gros (grosse)*, I, 7; (noun) *les matières grasses* (f.), II, 7

father *le père*, I, 7

fault: It's my fault. *C'est de ma faute.* II, 10

favorite: What is your favorite ...? *Quel(le) est ton/ta... préféré(e)?* II, 1; **Who is your favorite ...?** *Qui est ton/ta... préféré(e)?* II, 1

February *février*, I, 4

fee: How much is the entrance fee? *C'est combien, l'entrée?* II, 6

feed: to feed the animals *donner à manger aux animaux*, II, 6; III, 3; *nourrir les animaux*, II, 12

feel: Do you feel like ...? *Tu as envie de... ?* II, 1; **I don't feel like it.** *Ça ne me dit rien.* I, 6; **I don't feel well.** *Je ne me sens pas bien.* II, 7; **I feel bad for ...** *Je m'en veux de...* , III, 6; **I feel like ...** *J'ai envie de...* , I, 11; **No, I don't feel like it.** *Non, je n'ai pas très envie.* II, 7

feelings: No hard feelings. *Je ne t'en veux pas.* II, 10; **No hard feelings?** *Tu ne m'en veux pas?* II, 10

fencer *l'escrimeur(-euse)*, III, 12

fencing *l'escrime* (f.), III, 12

ferocious *féroce*, III, 7

ferris wheel *la grande roue*, II, 6

fewer: fewer ... than ... *moins de... que*, III, 8

fig *la figue*, III, 8

fight *se bagarrer*, III, 10

fill: to fill it up *faire le plein*, III, 2

film: foreign film *le film étranger*, III, 9; **roll of film** *la pellicule*, III, 7; **What films are playing?** *Qu'est-ce qu'on joue comme film?* II, 11

Finally ... *Enfin,...* , I, 9; II, 1; II, 4; II, 9 *Finalement,...* , I, 9; II, 1; II, 4; II, 9

find *trouver*, I, 9; **Could you tell me where I could find ...?** *Vous pourriez me dire où il y a... ?* III, 2; **to find a job** *trouver un travail*, III, 5

Fine. *Ça va.* I, 1; **Yes, it was fine.** *Oui, ça a été.* I, 9

finish: to finish one's studies *arrêter/finir ses études* (f.), III, 5

fire: Where's the fire? *Il n'y a pas le feu.* III, 2

first: First, ... *D'abord,...* , II, 12; **First, I did ...** *D'abord, j'ai fait...* , I, 9; **First, I'm going to ...** *D'abord, je vais...* , II, 1; **OK, if you ... first.** *D'accord, si tu... d'abord...* , I, 7

first-aid kit *une trousse de premiers soins*, II, 12; III, 7

fish *le poisson*, I, 7; II, 3; *du poisson*, I, 8; **to fish** *pêcher*, III, 8; **fish shop** *la poissonnerie*, II, 3

fishing: fishing pole *une canne à pêche*, II, 12; **fishing village** *un village de pêcheurs*, II, 4; **to go fishing** *aller à la pêche*, II, 4

fits: That fits you like a glove. *Ça te va comme un gant.* III, 4

flashlight *une lampe de poche*, II, 12; *la torche*, III, 7

flat: to have a flat tire *avoir un pneu crevé*, III, 2

floor: first (ground) floor *le rez-de-chaussée,* II, 2; **On the ground floor.** *Au rez-de-chaussée.* III, 2; **On the second floor.** *Au premier étage.* III, 2; **second floor** *le premier étage,* II, 2; **to clean the floor** *nettoyer le parquet,* III, 3

florist's shop *le fleuriste,* II, 3

flour *de la farine,* I, 8

flu: I've got the flu. *J'ai la grippe.* II, 7

flute *la flûte,* III, 11

fly *la mouche,* III, 7

folk music *le folk,* II, 11; III, 11

follow: to follow a diet that's too strict *suivre un régime trop strict,* II, 7; **to follow the marked trails** *suivre les sentiers balisés,* II, 12; **To get to . . . , follow . . . for about . . . kilometers.** *Pour (aller à)... , vous allez suivre la... pendant à peu près... kilomètres.* III, 2

following: Following our telephone conversation, . . . *Suite à notre conversation téléphonique,... ,* III, 5

foot *le pied,* II, 7; **My foot hurts.** *J'ai mal au pied.* II, 7; **on foot** *à pied,* I, 12

football: to play football *jouer au football américain,* I, 4

for: It's good for you. *C'est bon pour toi.* II, 7

forbidden: It's forbidden to . . . *Il est interdit de... ,* III, 3

foreign: foreign film *le film étranger,* III, 9

forest: to the forest *en forêt,* I, 11

forget *oublier,* I, 9; **Don't forget . . .** *N'oublie pas... ,* II, 1; *N'oublie pas de... ,* I, 8; **Forget him/her/them!** *Oublie-le/-la/-les!* I, 9; II, 10; **I didn't forget anything.** *Je n'ai rien oublié.* I, 11; **You didn't forget your . . . ?** *Tu n'as pas oublié... ?* I, 11

forgive (someone) *pardonner à (quelqu'un),* II, 10; **Forgive me.** *Excuse-moi.* II, 10

forgiveness: to ask (someone's) forgiveness *demander pardon à (quelqu'un),* II, 10

Fortunately, . . . *Heureusement,... ,* II, 9

fox *un renard,* II, 12

frame: photo frame *le cadre,* II, 3

free: I'm free, aren't I? *Je suis quand même libre, non?* III, 3

freeway: You'll see a sign that points out the freeway entrance. *Vous allez voir un panneau qui indique l'entrée de l'autoroute.* III, 2

French (language) *le français* I, 1; **French fries** *les frites* (f.), I, 1

Friday: on Fridays *le vendredi,* I, 2

fried *frit(e),* III, 11

friends *les ami(e)s ,* I, 1; **to go out with friends** *sortir avec les copains,* I, 1

from: Do people . . . where you're from? *On... chez toi?* III, 12; **Do you have/Are there . . . where you're from?** *Vous avez/Il y a des... chez vous?* III, 12; **From platform . . .** *Du quai... ,* II, 6; **Where are you from?** *Tu viens d'où?* III, 12

front: in front of *devant,* I, 6

fruit *les fruits* (m.), I, 8

fun *amusant(e),* II, 11; **Did you have fun?** *Tu t'es bien amusé(e)?* I, 11; II, 6; III, 1; **Have fun!** *Amuse-toi bien!* I, 11; **I had a lot of fun.** *Je me suis beaucoup amusé(e).* II, 6; III, 1; **What do you do to have fun?** *Qu'est-ce que tu fais pour t'amuser?* I, 4

funny *amusant(e),* I, 7; *marrant(e),* III, 2; **funny (crazy)** *fou (folle),* III, 2; **funny (hysterical)** *rigolo(te),* III, 2; **funny (wild)** *dingue,* III, 2; **It's funny.** *C'est drôle (amusant).* II, 11

furious *furieux (furieuse),* II, 9

gain: to gain weight *grossir,* I, 10

game (match) *le match,* III, 12; **game show** *le jeu télévisé,* III, 9; **to watch a game (on TV)** *regarder un match,* I, 6

gas *l'essence* (f.), III, 2; **gas station** *une station-service,* III, 2; **the gas tank** *le réservoir,* III, 2

gaudy *tape-à-l'œil,* III, 4

geography *la géographie,* I, 2

geometry *la géométrie,* I, 2

German (language) *l'allemand* (m.), I, 2; *allemand(e)* (adj.)

Germany *l'Allemagne* (f.), III, 12

get: As soon as I get there, . . . *Dès que je serai là-bas,... ,* III, 12; **Get . . .** *Prends... ,* I, 8; **Get a move on!** *Grouille-toi!* III, 2; **Get out of here!** *Casse-toi!* III, 6; **Get well soon!** *Bon rétablissement!* II, 3; **Get with it!** *Réveille-toi un peu!* III, 10; **to get up** *se lever,* II, 4; **How can I get to . . . ?** *Comment on va à... ?* III, 2; **How can we get there?** *Comment est-ce qu'on y va?* I, 12; **How did you get there?** *Tu es parti(e) comment?* III, 1; **It'll get better.** *Ça va aller mieux.* II, 5; **To get to . . . , follow . . . for about . . . kilometers.** *Pour (aller à)... , vous allez suivre la... pendant à peu près... kilomètres.* III, 2; **to get a bad grade** *avoir une mauvaise note,* II, 5; **to get an 8 in . . .** *avoir 8 en... ,* II, 5; **to get lost** *se perdre,* II, 9; **to get ready** *faire les préparatifs,* II, 10;

You'll get used to it. *Tu vas t'y faire.* II, 8

gift *le cadeau,* I, 11; **gift shop** *la boutique de cadeaux,* II, 3; **Have you got a gift idea for. . . ?** *Tu as une idée de cadeau pour... ?* II, 3

giraffe *la girafe,* III, 7

give: Give . . . a kiss for me. *Embrasse... pour moi.* III, 8; **Give . . . my regards.** *Fais mes amitiés à... ,* III, 8; **Give him/her (them) . . .** *Offre-lui (leur) ... ,* II, 3; **Give me your . . .** *Donnez-moi votre... ,* III, 6; **Please give me . . .** *Donnez-moi... , s'il vous plaît.* I, 5; **to give (to someone)** *offrir (à quelqu'un),* II, 10; **What could I give to . . . ?** *Qu'est-ce que je pourrais offrir à... ?* II, 3; **You could give him/her (them) . . .** *Tu pourrais lui (leur) offrir... ,* II, 3

give up: I give up. *J'abandonne.* II, 7

glad: I'm glad to see you again. *Je suis content(e) de te revoir.* III, 1

Gladly. *Je veux bien.* I, 8

glass *le verre,* III, 3

glove *le gant,* III, 12; **gloves** *les gants* (m.), II, 1; III, 4; **That fits you like a glove.** *Ça te va comme un gant.* III, 4

go *aller,* I, 6; **Go to the blackboard!** *Allez au tableau!,* I, 0; **Could you go by . . . ?** *Tu pourrais passer à... ?* I, 12; **Did it go well?** *Ça s'est bien passé?* I, 9; **Don't go!** *N'y va pas!* III, 9; **Go (keep going) straight ahead.** *Allez (continuez) tout droit,* II, 2; **How did it go?** *Comment ça s'est passé?* II, 5; **Let's go . . .** *Allons... ,* I, 6; **to go for a walk** *faire une promenade,* I, 6; **We can go there . . .** *On peut y aller... ,* I, 12; **Where did you go?** *Tu es allé(e) où?* I, 9; **You go down this street to the next light.** *Vous continuez cette rue jusqu'au prochain feu rouge.* I, 12

go back (home) *rentrer,* II, 6

go down *descendre,* II, 6

go out *sortir,* II, 6; **to go out with friends** *sortir avec les copains,* I, 1

go up *monter,* II, 6; **to go up in a tower** *monter dans une tour,* II, 6

go with: It doesn't go at all with . . . *Il/Elle ne va pas du tout avec... ,* I, 10; **It goes very well with . . .** *Il/Elle va très bien avec... ,* I, 10; **I'd like . . . to go with . . .** *J'aimerais... pour aller avec... ,* I, 10

goat *la chèvre,* III, 8; **goat cheese** *le fromage de chèvre,* III, 1

going: First, I'm going to . . . *D'abord, je vais... ,* II, 1; **How about going . . . ?** *Si on allait... ?* II, 4; **How's it going?** *(Comment) ça va?* I, 1; **I'm going . . .** *Je vais... ,* I, 6; **I'm going to . . .** *Je vais... ,* I, 11; **I'm**

going to have ..., please. *Je vais prendre... , s'il vous plaît.* I, 5; **What are you going to do ...?** *Qu'est-ce que tu vas faire... ?* I, 6; II, 1; **What do you think about going ...?** *Ça te dit d'aller... ?* II, 4; **What's going on?** *Qu'est-ce qui se passe?* II, 5; **What's going on with you?** *Qu'est-ce que tu deviens?* III, 1; **Where are you going to go ...?** *Où est-ce que tu vas aller... ?* I, 11; **You're going to like it here.** *Tu vas te plaire ici.* II, 8

golf *le golf,* I, 4; **to play golf** *jouer au golf,* I, 4

good *bon,* I, 5; **Did you have a good ...?** *Tu as passé un bon... ?* I, 11; **Did you have a good trip?** *Vous avez (Tu as) fait bon voyage?* II, 2; **Good idea!** *Bonne idée!* II, 3; **I've got a good one.** *J'en connais une bonne.* III, 10; **It'll do you good.** *Ça te fera du bien.* II, 7; **It's good for you.** *C'est bon pour toi.* II, 7; **It's good!** *C'est vraiment bon!* II, 3; **not very good** *pas bon,* I, 5; **pretty good** *pas mauvais,* I, 5; **That's a good (excellent) idea.** *C'est une bonne (excellente) idée.* II, 1; **That's a good one!** *Elle est bien bonne!* III, 10; **Yes, very good.** *Oui, très bon.* I, 9; **You're really strong/good at that.** *Tu es fortiche/calé(e).* III, 10

Goodbye! *Au revoir!* I, 1; *Salut!* I, 1

goofing: You can't be goofing off in class! *Il ne faut pas faire le clown en classe!* II, 5

gorgeous *superbe,* II, 6

got (to have to): All you've got to do is ... *Tu n'as qu'à... ,* III, 5; **No, you've got to ...** *Non, tu dois...,* I, 7

grade: to get a bad grade *avoir une mauvaise note,* II, 5

granddaughter *la petite-fille,* III, 6

grandfather *le grand-père,* I, 7

grandmother *la grand-mère,* I, 7

grandson *le petit-fils,* III, 6

grapes *du raisin,* I, 8

grass *l'herbe* (f.), III, 7

great *génial(e),* I, 2; II, 2; **Great!** *Super!* I, 1; *Génial!* III, 12; **Isn't it great!** *Ce que c'est bien!* III, 2; **It was great!** *C'était formidable!* I, 11; *C'était chouette!* III, 1; **It wasn't so great.** *C'était pas terrible.* III, 1; **It would be great if ...** *Ça serait chouette si... ,* III, 8; **Not so great.** *Pas terrible.* I, 1; **What a great day!** *Quelle journée formidable!* II, 5; **What a great weekend!** *Quel week-end formidable!* II, 5; **Your ... is really great.** *Il/Elle est vraiment bien, ton/ta... ,* II, 2

great-grandfather *l'arrière-grand-père* (m.), III, 6

great-grandmother *l'arrière-grand-mère,* (f.), III, 6

green *vert(e),* I, 3; II, 1; **green beans** *les haricots verts* (m.), I, 8

grey *gris(e),* I, 3

grocery store *l'épicerie* (f.), I, 12

gross *dégoûtant,* I, 5

ground: on the ground *par terre,* III, 3; **On the ground floor.** *Au rez-de-chaussée.* III, 2

grounded: to be "grounded" *être privé(e) de sortie,* II, 9

group *un groupe,* II, 11

grow *grandir,* I, 10

grow wheat *cultiver le blé,* III, 8

Guadeloupe *la Guadeloupe,* III, 12

guavas *des goyaves* (f.), I, 8

guess: Guess what ... *Devine ce que... ,* II, 9; **Guess who ...** *Devine qui... ,* II, 9; **You'll never guess what happened.** *Tu ne devineras jamais ce qui s'est passé.* II, 9

guide: TV guide/listing *le programme télé,* III, 9

guided: to take a guided tour *faire une visite guidée,* II, 6

guitar *la guitare,* III, 11

gumbo *le gombo,* III, 11

guy: It's about a guy who ... *C'est l'histoire d'un mec qui... ,* III, 10

gym *le sport,* I, 2

gymnastics *la gymnastique,* III, 12; **to do gymnastics** *faire de la gymnastique,* II, 7

had: I've really had it! *J'en ai ras le bol!* III, 8; **I've had it up to here!** *J'en ai jusque là!* III, 8; **I've just about had it!** *Je commence à en avoir marre!* III, 8

hair *les cheveux* (m.), II, 1; **black hair** *les cheveux noirs,* II, 1; **blond hair** *les cheveux blonds,* II, 1; **dark brown hair** *les cheveux bruns,* II, 1; **curly hair** *les cheveux frisés,* III, 4; **dyed hair** *les cheveux teints,* III, 4; **hair stylist** *un coiffeur (une coiffeuse),* III, 4; **long hair** *les cheveux longs,* II, 1; III, 4; **red hair** *les cheveux roux,* II, 1; **short hair** *les cheveux courts,* II, 1; III, 4; **straight hair** *les cheveux raides,* III, 4

haircut *la coupe,* III, 4

Haiti *Haïti* (m.) (no article), III, 12

half: half past *et demie,* I, 6; **half past (after midi and minuit)** *et demi,* I, 6

ham *le jambon,* I, 5; II, 3; **toasted ham and cheese sandwich** *un croque-monsieur,* (inv.) I, 5

hamburgers *les hamburgers* (m.), I, 1

hand *la main,* I, 0; II, 7

handsome *beau,* II, 1

hang: Hang in there! *Courage!* II, 5

hang glide *faire du deltaplane,* II, 4

Hanukkah: Happy Hanukkah! *Bonne fête de Hanoukka!* II, 3

happen: It could happen to anyone. *Ça peut arriver à tout le monde.* III, 10

happened: What happened? *Qu'est-ce qui s'est passé?* I, 9; **to explain what happened (to someone)** *expliquer ce qui s'est passé (à quelqu'un),* II, 10; **You'll never guess what happened.** *Tu ne devineras jamais ce qui s'est passé.* II, 9

happens: It happens to everybody. *Ça arrive à tout le monde.* III, 6

happy: Happy birthday! *Joyeux (Bon) anniversaire!* II, 3; **Happy Hanukkah!** *Bonne fête de Hanoukka!* II, 3; **Happy holiday! (Happy saint's day!)** *Bonne fête!* II, 3; **Happy New Year!** *Bonne année!* II, 3; **I'm happy to see you.** *Ça me fait plaisir de vous voir.* III, 6

hard *difficile,* I, 2; **No hard feelings.** *Je ne t'en veux pas.* II, 10; **No hard feelings?** *Tu ne m'en veux pas?* II, 10

harm: No harm done. *Il n'y a pas de mal.* II, 10

harvest: to harvest fruits *faire la cueillette,* III, 8

has: He/She has ... *Il/Elle a... ,* II, 1

hat *un chapeau,* I, 10

have *avoir,* I, 2; **have fun** *s'amuser,* II, 4; **At what time do you have ...?** *Tu as... à quelle heure?* I, 2; **Do you have ...?** *Tu as... ?* I, 3; **Do you have ...?** *Vous avez... ?* I, 2; **Do you have that in ...?** (size, fabric, color) *Vous avez ça en... ?* I, 10; **Have ...** *Prends... ,* I, 5; **Have a good trip!** (by car) *Bonne route!* II, 3; **Have a good trip!** (by plane, ship) *Bon voyage!* II, 3; **He/She has ...** *Il/Elle a... ,* II, 1; **I don't have ...** *Je n'ai pas de... ,* I, 3; **I have some things to do.** *J'ai des trucs à faire.* I, 5; **I have...** *J'ai... ,* I, 2; II, 1; **I'll have ..., please.** *Je vais prendre... , s'il vous plaît.* I, 5; **I'm going to have ..., please.** *Je vais prendre... , s'il vous plaît.* I, 5; **May I have some ...?** *Je pourrais avoir... ?* II, 3; **They have ...** *Ils/Elles ont... ,* II, 1; **to have an accident** *avoir un accident,* II, 9; **to have an argument (with someone)** *se disputer (avec quelqu'un),* II, 9; **to have done** *faire + infinitive,* III, 4; **to take or to have (food or drink)** *prendre,* I, 5; **to have a child** *avoir un enfant,* III, 5; **We have ...** *Nous avons... ,* I, 2; **What classes do you**

have . . . ? *Tu as quels cours... ?* I, 2; **What do you have . . . ?** *Tu as quoi... ?* I, 2; **What kind of . . . do you have?** *Qu'est-ce que vous avez comme... ?* I, 5; **Will you have . . . ?** *Tu prends... ?* I, 8; *Vous prenez... ?* I, 8; **Would you have . . . ?** *Vous auriez... ?* III, 6; **Yes, do you have . . . ?** *Oui, vous avez... ?* I, 10; **Why don't you have . . . ?** *Pourquoi tu ne prends pas... ?* III, 1

have to: All you have to do is . . . *Tu n'as qu'à... ,* II, 7; **First you have to . . .** *Il faut que... d'abord.* III, 3; **You have to do better in class.** *Il faut mieux travailler en classe.* II, 5; **You have to . . .** *Tu dois... ,* III, 3

having: What are you having? *Vous prenez?* I, 5

head *la tête,* II, 7

health *le cours de développement personnel et social (DPS),* I, 2

hear: Did you hear the latest? *Tu connais la nouvelle?* II, 9; **Let's hear it!** *Dis vite!* II, 9; **to hear the alarm clock** *entendre le réveil,* II, 5

heard: Have you heard the latest? *Tu connais la dernière?* III, 10; **I've heard that . . .** *J'ai entendu dire que... ,* III, 10

heavy *lourd(e),* III, 7

height: of medium height *de taille moyenne,* II, 1

Hello *Bonjour* 1; **Hello? (on the phone)** *Allô?* I, 9

helmet *le casque,* III, 12

help *aider,* II, 8; **Can you help me?** *Tu peux m'aider?* II, 10; **May I help you?** *(Est-ce que) je peux vous aider?* I, 10; **to help elderly people** *aider les personnes âgées,* III, 3

her *la,* I, 9; **her** *son/sa/ses,* I, 7; *lui,* I, 9

here: Here. *Voilà.* I, 3; **Here's . . .** *Voici...* I, 7; **Here (There) is . . .** *Là, c'est... ,* II, 2; **Here . . . , whereas . . .** *Ici,... tandis que... ,* III, 8; **Here it is.** *Voilà.* II, 3; **Here you are.** *Tenez (tiens).* II, 3

Hey! Check it out! *Tiens! Regarde un peu!* III, 7; **Hey, do you think you can . . . ?** *Dites donc, ça vous gênerait de... ?* III, 8

Hi! *Salut!* I, 1; **Tell . . . hi for me.** *Salue... de ma part.* III, 8

hideous *affreux (-euse),* III, 4

high heels *les hauts talons* (m.), III, 4

high school *le lycée,* II, 2; **high school/college teacher** *le/la professeur,* III, 5

hike: to go for a hike *faire une randonnée pédestre,* II, 12

hiking: to go hiking *faire de la randonnée,* I, 11

him *le,* I, 9; *lui,* I, 9

hippopotamus *l'hippopotame* (m.), III, 7

his *son/sa/ses,* I, 7

historical: historical movie *le film historique,* III, 9

history *l'histoire* (f.), I, 2

hockey: to play hockey *jouer au hockey,* I, 4

Hold on. *Ne quittez pas.* I, 9

holiday: Happy holiday! (Happy saint's day!) *Bonne fête!* II, 3

home: Make yourself at home. *Faites (Fais) comme chez vous (toi),* II, 2; **Welcome to my home (our home)** *Bienvenue chez moi (chez nous),* II, 2

homework *les devoirs* (m.), I, 2; **I've got homework to do.** *J'ai des devoirs à faire.* I, 5; **to do homework** *faire ses devoirs,* I, 7

horn *une corne,* III, 7

horrible: It was horrible. *C'était épouvantable.* I, 9; **This is just horrible!** *C'est l'horreur!* III, 8; **to have a horrible day** *avoir une journée épouvantable,* II, 5

horror movie *le film d'horreur,* II, 11

hors d'œuvre *les hors-d'œuvre,* III, 11

horseback: to go horseback riding *faire de l'équitation,* I, 1

hose (clothing) *un collant,* I, 10

hostel: youth hostel *l'auberge de jeunesse* (f.), II, 2

hot: hot chocolate *un chocolat,* I, 5; **hot dog** *un hot-dog,* I, 5; **It's hot.** *Il fait chaud.* I, 4; **not so hot** *pas super,* I, 2

house *la maison,* II, 2; **at my house** *chez moi,* I, 6; **Is this . . .'s house?** *Je suis bien chez... ?* I, 9; **to clean house** *faire le ménage,* I, 7; **to/at . . .'s** *chez... ,* I, 11

housework: to do housework *faire le ménage,* I, 1; II, 10

how: Could you tell me how to get to . . . ? *La route pour... , s'il vous plaît?* III, 2; **Did you see how . . . ?** *Tu as vu comme... ?* III, 7; **How about . . . ?** *On...* I, 4; **How about buying . . . ?** *Si on achetait... ?* II, 8; **How about going . . . ?** *Si on allait... ?* II, 4; **How about playing . . . ?** *Si on jouait... ?* II, 8; **How about playing baseball?** *On joue au base-ball?* I, 5; **How about skiing?** *On fait du ski?* I, 5; **How about that!** *Ça alors!* III, 7; **How about visiting . . . ?** *Si on visitait... ?* II, 8; **How can I get to . . . ?** *Comment on va à... ?* III, 2; **How did it go?** *Comment ça s'est passé?* II, 5; **How do you like it?** *Comment tu trouves ça?* I, 5; **How do you say . . . ?** *Comment on dit... ?* III, 11; **How many (much) do you want?** *Combien en voulez-vous?* II, 3; **How much does that make?** *Ça fait combien?* II, 3; **How much is (are) . . . ?** *Combien coûte(nt)... ?* II, 3; **How much is . . . ?** *C'est combien,... ?* I, 5; **How much is it?** *C'est combien?* I, 3; *Ça fait combien?* I, 10; **How much is it, please?** *Ça fait combien, s'il vous plaît?* I, 5; **How old are you?** *Tu as quel âge?* I, 1; **How was it?** *C'était comment?* II, 6; **How was your day (yesterday)?** *Comment s'est passée ta journée (hier)?* II, 5; **How was your vacation?** *Comment se sont passées tes vacances?* II, 5; **How was your weekend?** *Comment s'est passé ton week-end?* II, 5; **How's it going?** *(Comment) ça va?* I, 1; **How . . . !** *Qu'est-ce que... !* III, 6

hugs: Hugs and kisses. *Grosses bises.* III, 8; *Je t'embrasse bien fort.* III, 8

hunger: I'm dying of hunger! *Je crève de faim!* II, 12; **I'm dying of hunger!** *Je meurs de faim!* II, 2

hungry: to be hungry *avoir faim,* I, 5; **Aren't you hungry?** *Vous n'avez pas (Tu n'as pas) faim?* II, 2; **I'm not hungry anymore.** *Je n'ai plus faim.* II, 3; **No thanks. I'm not hungry anymore.** *Non, merci. Je n'ai plus faim.* I, 8; **I'm very hungry!** *J'ai très faim!* II, 2

hurry: Can you hurry up? *Tu peux te dépêcher?* III, 2; **Hurry up!** *Dépêche-toi!* III, 2; **people in a hurry** *les gens pressés,* III, 8

hurt: I hurt all over! *J'ai mal partout!* II, 7; **My . . . hurts.** *J'ai mal à... ,* II, 7; **to hurt one's . . .** *se faire mal à ... ,* II, 7; III, 10

husband *le mari,* I, 7; III, 6

hysterical (funny) *rigolo(te),* III, 2

I

I *je,* I, 0

I'd: I'd like to buy . . . *Je voudrais acheter... ,* I, 3

ice: to ice-skate *faire du patin à glace,* I, 4

ice cream *la glace,* I, 1

idea: Good idea. *Bonne idée.* I, 4; II, 3; **That's a good (excellent) idea.** *C'est une bonne (excellente) idée.* II, 1; **I have no idea.** *Je n'en sais rien.* I, 11; *Je n'en ai aucune idée.* III, 5; **No idea.** *Aucune idée.* II, 9

if: If . . . *Si... ,* III, 5; **If I could, . . .** *Si seulement je pouvais,... ,* III, 8; **If I had a choice, . . .** *Si j'avais le choix,... ,* III, 8; **If I were in your place, . . .** *A ta place,... ,* III, 8; **If I were you, . . .** *Si j'étais toi,... ,* III, 8; **If it were me, . . .** *Si c'était moi,... ,* III, 8; **OK, if you . . . first.** *D'accord, si tu... d'abord.* I, 7; **Yes, if . . .** *Oui, si... ,* III, 3

imagine: Can you imagine that...
Figure-toi que... , III, 10
impolite: impolite people *les gens* (m.)
mal élevés, III, 8
important: It's very important that...
Il est très important que... , III, 7
impossible: It's impossible. *C'est*
impossible. II, 10
impressed: I'm really impressed! *Alors,*
là, tu m'épates! III, 10
impression: I have the impression
that... *J'ai l'impression que...* ,
III, 11
in *dans,* I, 6; **...is (are) in it.** *C'est*
avec... , II, 11; **in (a city or place)**
à, I, 11; **in** (before a feminine
noun) *en,* I, 11; **in** (before a
masculine noun) *au,* I, 11; **in**
(before a plural noun) *aux,* I, 11;
In a hotel. *A l'hôtel.* III, 1; **in front**
of *devant,* I, 6; **in order to** *afin de,*
I, 7; **in the afternoon** *l'après-midi,*
I, 2; **in the evening** *le soir,* I, 2; **in**
the morning *le matin,* I, 2; **in the**
water *dans l'eau,* III, 3; **The girl in**
the/with the... *La fille au...* , III,
4; **What's in...?** *Qu'est-ce qu'il y a*
dans... ? III, 11; **Who's in it?** *C'est*
avec qui? II, 11
incredible *incroyable,* II, 6
indifference: (expression of
indifference) *Bof!* I, 1; II, 8
information: Could you send me
information on...? *Pourriez-*
vous m'envoyer des renseignements
sur... ? III, 5
insect repellent *de la lotion anti-*
moustique(s), II, 12; III, 7
intend: I intend to... *J'ai l'intention*
de... , I, 11; III, 5; **What do you**
intend to do? *Qu'est-ce que tu as*
l'intention de faire? III, 5
interest: That doesn't interest me. *Ça*
ne me dit rien. II, 1
interested: Would you be interested
in...? *Ça t'intéresse de...* ?
III, 6
interesting *intéressant,* I, 2; **It's not**
interesting. *Ça n'a aucun intérêt.*
III, 9
into: Are you into...? *Ça te branche,...* ?
III, 11; **I'm not into that.** *Ça ne*
me branche pas trop. III, 11
invite: Invite him/her/them. *Invite-*
le/la/les. II, 10
ironing: to do the ironing *faire le*
repassage, III, 3
is: He/She is... *Il/Elle est...* , II, 1; **There**
is/are... , II, 12
island *l'île* (f.), II, 4
isn't: Isn't it great! *Ce que c'est bien!*
III, 2
isolated *isolé(e),* II, 8
it *le, la,* I, 9
it's: It's... *C'est...* , I, 2; II, 11; **It's...**
euros. *Ça fait... euros.* I, 5
Italy *l'Italie* (f.), III, 12

J

jacket *le blouson,* I, 10; **ski jacket**
l'anorak (m.), II, 1
jam *de la confiture,* I, 8
jambalaya *le jambalaya,* III, 11
January *janvier,* I, 4
Japan *le Japon,* III, 12
jazz *le jazz,* II, 11; III, 11
jeans: pair of jeans *un jean,* I, 3; II, 1
jellyfish *la méduse,* III, 10
jewelry *les bijoux* (m.), III, 8
job: to find a job *trouver un travail,*
III, 5
jog *faire du jogging,* I, 4
joke: What a stupid joke! *Elle est nulle,*
ta blague! III, 10
joking: You're joking! *Tu plaisantes!* II,
6; *Tu rigoles!* III, 9
journalist *le/la journaliste,* III, 5
judo *le judo,* III, 12
July *juillet,* I, 4
June *juin,* I, 4

K

kidding: Are you kidding me? *Tu te*
fiches de moi? III, 9; **You're**
kidding! *C'est pas vrai!* II, 6
kilogram: a kilogram of *un kilo de,* I, 8
kind: That's kind of you. *Vous êtes bien*
aimable. III, 6; **What kind of... do**
you have? *Qu'est-ce que vous avez*
comme... ? I, 5, III, 1
kiss: Give... a kiss for me. *Embrasse...*
pour moi. III, 8
kisses: Hugs and kisses. *Je t'embrasse*
bien fort. III, 8; **Kisses to...** *Bisous*
à... , III, 8
kitchen *la cuisine,* II, 2
knee *le genou,* II, 7
know: Did you know that...? *Tu savais*
que... ? III, 10; **Do you know the**
one about...? *Est-ce que tu*
connais l'histoire de... ? III, 10; **Do**
you know what...? *Tu sais ce*
que... ? II, 9; **Do you know**
who...? *Tu sais qui...* ? II, 9;
I don't know what to do. *Je ne sais*
pas quoi faire. II, 10; **I don't know.**
Je ne sais pas. I, 10; **I know**
that... *Je sais que...* , III, 7; **I really**
don't know. *Je ne sais pas trop.* III,
5; **I would like to know...** *Je*
voudrais savoir... , III, 5; **What do**
you know about it? *Qu'est-ce que*
tu en sais? III, 10; **You're the...**
-est... I know. *Tu es le/la...*
le/la plus... que je connaisse. III, 10

L

lab *les travaux* (m.) *pratiques,* I, 2
lamp *la lampe,* II, 2
late *tard,* II, 4
later: Can you call back later? *Vous*
pouvez rappeler plus tard? I, 9; **See**
you later! *A tout à l'heure!* I, 1
latest: Did you hear the latest? *Tu*
connais la nouvelle? II, 9; **Have you**
heard the latest? *Tu connais la*
dernière? III, 10
Latin *le latin,* I, 2
laugh: It really made me laugh. *Ça m'a*
bien fait rire. III, 9
laundry: to do the laundry *faire la*
lessive, III, 3
lawn: to mow the lawn *tondre la*
pelouse, III, 3
lawyer *l'avocat(e),* III, 5
lead: This road will lead you into the
center of town. *Cette route va*
vous conduire au centre-ville.
III, 2
leather: leather-goods shop *la*
maroquinerie, II, 3; **in leather** *en*
cuir, I, 10
leave *partir,* I, 11; II, 6; **Can I leave a**
message? *Je peux laisser un*
message? I, 9; **Leave me alone!**
Fiche-moi la paix! III, 6; **to leave**
one's family *quitter sa famille,* III,
5; **You can't leave without...** *Tu*
ne peux pas partir sans... , I, 11
left: to the left (of) *à gauche (de),* I, 12;
II, 2
leg *la jambe,* II, 7
leggings *un caleçon,* III, 4
lemon soda *la limonade,* I, 5
lemonade *le citron pressé,* I, 5
less: less... than... *moins... que...* , III,
8; **Life was more..., less...** *La vie*
était plus... , moins... , II, 8; **More**
or less. *Plus ou moins.* II, 6
let's: Let's go... *Allons...* , I, 6; **Let's go!**
Allons-y! I, 4; **Let's hear it!** *Dis vite!*
II, 9
letter: to send letters *envoyer des lettres,*
I, 12
library *la bibliothèque,* I, 6; II, 2
license: to get one's driver's license
passer son permis de conduire, III, 5
life: Life was more..., less... *La vie*
était plus... , moins... , II, 8
lift: to lift weights *faire de la*
musculation, II, 7
lights *les lumières* (f.), III, 3
like *aimer,* I, 1; **Did you like it?** *Ça t'a*
plu? II, 6; **Do you like...?** *Tu*
aimes... ? I, 1; **Do you like it?**
Il/Elle te/vous plaît? I, 10; **Do you**
like this...? *Il/Elle te plaît,...* ? III,
4; **How did you like it?** *Comment*
tu as trouvé ça? III, 9; **How do you**

like...? *Comment tu trouves... ?* I, 10; **How do you like it?** *Comment tu trouves ça?* I, 5; **I like it a lot.** *Il/Elle me plaît beaucoup.* III, 4; **I (really) like...** *Moi, j'aime (bien)...* , I, 1; **I didn't like it at all.** *Je n'ai pas du tout aimé.* III, 9; **Don't you like...?** *Tu n'aimes pas...?* III, 4; **I don't like...** *Je n'aime pas...* , I, 1; II, 1; **I like...** *J'aime bien...* , II, 1; **I like it, but it's expensive.** *Il/Elle me plaît, mais il/elle est cher/chère.* I, 10; **I like this type of...** *J'aime bien ce genre de...* , III, 4; **I'd like...** *J'aimerais...* , III, 3; *Je voudrais...* , I, 3; II, 6; **I'd like some.** *J'en veux bien.* I, 8; **I'd like... to go with...** *J'aimerais... pour aller avec...* , I, 10; **I'd like some...** *Je prendrais bien...* , III, 6; **I'd like that a lot.** *Ça me plairait beaucoup.* III, 6; **I'd like to.** *Je veux bien.* II, 1; **I'd really like...** *J'aimerais bien...* , III, 5; **I'd really like to...** *Je voudrais bien...* , I, 11; **I'd really like to...!** *Qu'est-ce que j'aimerais...!* III, 8; **I'd really like to.** *Je veux bien.* I, 6; **If you like, we can...** *Si tu veux, on peut...* , II, 1; **Is it like here?** *C'est pareil qu'ici?* III, 12; **It looks like...** *On dirait que...* , III, 11; **It wasn't like this.** *Ce n'était pas comme ça.* III, 8; **The teacher doesn't like me.** *Le prof ne m'aime pas.* II, 5; **They look like...** *Ils ont l'air de...* , III, 11; **What are they like?** *Ils sont comment?* I, 7; **What do you like to do?** *Qu'est-ce que tu aimes faire?* II, 1; **What I don't like is...** *Ce que je n'aime pas, c'est...* , II, 4; **What I like is...** *Ce que j'aime bien, c'est...* , II, 4; *Ce qui me plaît, c'est...* , II, 4; **What I like/love is...** *Ce que j'adore/j'aime, c'est...* , III, 11; **What I would like is to...** *Ce qui me plairait, c'est de...* , III, 5; **What is he like?** *Il est comment?* I, 7; **What is she like?** *Elle est comment?* I, 7; **What music do you like?** *Qu'est-ce que tu aimes comme musique?* II, 1; **What was it like?** *C'était comment?* II, 8; **What would you like?** *Vous désirez?* I, 10; **What's life like there?** *C'est comment, la vie là-bas?* III, 12; **Would you like to...?** *Ça te plairait de...* , III, 6; **Wouldn't you like to...?** *Tu ne voudrais pas...?* III, 6; **You're going to like it here.** *Tu vas te plaire ici.* II, 8

liked: I liked it a lot. *Ça m'a beaucoup plu.* III, 9; **I really liked it.** *Ça m'a beaucoup plu.* II, 6

lion *le lion,* III, 7

listen: Listen! *Écoutez!,* I, 0; **to listen to music** *écouter de la musique,* I, 1; **to listen to what he/she says** *écouter ce qu'il/elle dit,* II, 10

listening: I'm listening. *Je t'écoute.* I, 9; II, 10

listing: TV guide/listing *le programme télé,* III, 9

liter: a liter of *un litre de,* I, 8

little: When he/she was little,... *Quand il/elle était petit(e),...* , II, 8; **When I was little,...** *Quand j'étais petit(e),...* , II, 8; **Yes, a little.** *Si, un peu,* II, 2

lively *vivant(e),* II, 4; *animé(e),* II, 8

living room *le salon,* II, 2

lobster *le homard,* III, 10

located: ...is located... *... se trouve...* , II, 12; *... est situé(e)...* , III, 1; **Where is... located?** *Où se trouve...?,* II, 12

long *long (longue),* I, 10; II, 11; **long-distance running** *la course de fond,* III, 12; **long-sleeved** *à manches longues,* III, 4; **It's been a long time since we've seen each other.** *Ça fait longtemps qu'on ne s'est pas vu(e)s.* III, 1; **It's not going to take long!** *Ça ne va pas prendre longtemps!* III, 2; **long hair** *les cheveux longs* (m.), II, 1; III, 4; **the long jump** *le saut en longueur,* III, 12

look: I think they look... *Je trouve qu'ils/elles font...* , III, 4; **I think you look very good like that.** *Je te trouve très bien comme ça.* III, 4; **If you could see how you look!** *Non mais, tu t'es pas regardé(e)!* III, 10; **Look at the map!** *Regardez la carte!,* I, 0; **Look out!** *Faites gaffe/ attention!* III, 7; **Look, here's (there's) (it's)...** *Regarde, voilà...* , I, 12; **That doesn't look good on you.** *Ça ne te (vous) va pas du tout.* I, 10; **That looks really...** *Ça fait vraiment...* , III, 4; **to look after** *garder,* III, 3; **to look after your little sister** *garder ta petite sœur,* I, 7; **to look for** *chercher,* I, 9; **You look really... in that!** *Que tu es... avec ça!* III, 4

looking: I'm looking for something for... *Je cherche quelque chose pour...* , I, 10; **No, thanks, I'm just looking.** *Non, merci, je regarde.* I, 10

looks: It looks great on you! *C'est tout à fait ton style.* I, 10; **It looks like...** *On dirait que...* , III, 11

lose *perdre,* I, 9; II, 5; III, 12; **to lose weight** *maigrir,* I, 10; *perdre du poids,* III, 10

losing: I'm losing it! *Je craque!* II, 7

lost: to get lost *se perdre,* II, 9

lot: A lot. *Beaucoup.* I, 4; **I had a lot of fun.** *Je me suis beaucoup amusé(e).* II, 6; **I liked it a lot.** *Ça m'a beaucoup plu.* III, 9; **I'd like that a lot.** *Ça me plairait beaucoup.* III, 6

lots: I have lots of things to do. *J'ai des tas de choses à faire.* I, 5

loudly: Don't speak so loudly. *Ne parle pas si fort.* III, 9

love: I love... *J'adore...* , II, 1; **love: Are you in love or what?** *Tu es amoureux (-euse) ou quoi?* III, 10; **in love** *amoureux (amoureuse),* II, 9; **to fall in love (with someone)** *tomber amoureux(-euse) (de quelqu'un),* II, 9; **What I like/love is...** *Ce que j'adore/j'aime, c'est...* , III, 11

luck: Good luck! *Bonne chance!* I, 11; **Tough luck!** *C'est pas de chance, ça!* II, 5

lucky: We were lucky! *On a eu de la chance!* III, 7

lunch *le déjeuner,* I, 2; **to have lunch** *déjeuner,* I, 9

ma'am *madame (Mme),* I, 1

madam *madame,* III, 5

made *fait (faire),* I, 9

magazine *un magazine,* I, 3; **magazine show** *le magazine télévisé,* III, 9

main dishes *les plats* (m.)*principaux,* III, 1

make *faire,* I, 4; **How do you make...?** *Comment est-ce qu'on fait...?* III, 11; **How much does that make?** *Ça fait combien?* II, 3; **Make the best of it.** *Fais-toi une raison.* II, 8; **to have (make) a date (with someone)** *avoir (prendre) rendez-vous (avec quelqu'un),* II, 9; **to make one's bed** *faire son lit,* III, 3

make up: to make up (with someone) *se réconcilier avec (quelqu'un),* II, 10; **to make up one's own mind** *prendre ses propres décisions,* III, 3

mall *le centre commercial,* I, 6

mangoes *des mangues* (f.), I, 8

many: as many/as much... as... *autant de... que...* , III, 8; **How many (much) do you want?** *Combien en voulez-vous?* II, 3

map *la carte,* I, 0

March *mars,* I, 4

married *marié(e),* III, 6; **to get married** *se marier,* III, 5

mask *le masque,* II, 8; III, 12

match (game) *le match,* III, 12

matches *les allumettes,* II, 12; **That matches...** *C'est assorti à...* , III, 4

math *les maths* (f.), I, 1

matter: It doesn't matter. *Ça ne fait rien.* II, 10; *Peu importe.* III, 9

May *mai,* I, 4

may: May I . . . ? *(Est-ce que) je peux... ?* I, 7; **May I have some . . . ?** *Je pourrais avoir... ?* II, 3; **May I help you?** *(Est-ce que) je peux vous aider?* I, 10

maybe *peut-être,* II, 3; **Maybe . . .** *Peut-être que...,* II, 9; III, 5; **Maybe you're right.** *Tu as peut-être raison.* II, 9

me *moi,* I, 2

meal *un repas,* II, 7

mean *méchant(e),* I, 7; **What does . . . mean?** *Qu'est-ce que ça veut dire,... ?* III, 11

meat *la viande,* I, 8; III, 11

mechanic *le mécanicien(la mécanicienne),* III, 5

medicine *des médicaments* (m.), I, 12

medium: of medium height *de taille moyenne,* II, 1; **Medium rare.** *A point.* III, 1

meet *rencontrer,* I, 9; II, 9; **I'd like you to meet . . .** *Je te (vous) présente...,* I, 7; **Pleased to meet you.** *Très heureux (heureuse).* I, 7; **We'll meet . . .** *On se retrouve...,* I, 6; **We'll meet . . .** *Rendez-vous...,* I, 6

meeting: What time are we meeting? *A quelle heure est-ce qu'on se donne rendez-vous?* III, 6; **Where are we meeting?** *Où est-ce qu'on se retrouve?* III, 6

menu: The menu, please. *La carte, s'il vous plaît.* I, 5

merry: Merry Christmas! *Joyeux Noël!* II, 3

message: Can I leave a message? *Je peux laisser un message?* I, 9

metro: at the . . . metro stop *au métro...,* I, 6; **metro station** *la station de métro,* III, 8

Mexico *le Mexique,* III, 12

microphone *le microphone,* III, 11

midnight *minuit,* I, 6

might: It might be that . . . *Il se peut que...,* III, 5

mike (microphone) *le micro,* III, 11

military: to do one's military service *faire son service militaire,* III, 5

milk *du lait,* I, 8; II, 3; **to milk the cows** *traire les vaches* (f.), III, 8

mind: Are you out of your mind?! *Ça va pas, non?!* III, 8; **Do you mind if . . . ?** *Ça te dérange si... ?,* III, 3; **I can't make up my mind.** *Je n'arrive pas à me décider.* III, 1; **Mind your own business!** *Mêle-toi de tes oignons!* III, 6; **to make up one's own mind** *prendre ses propres décisions,* III, 3; **Would you mind . . . ?** *Ça t'embête de... ?* II, 10; *Ça t'ennuie de... ?* II, 10

mineral water *l'eau minérale,* I, 5

miniskirt *la mini-jupe,* III, 4

minute: Do you have a minute? *Tu as une minute?* I, 9; II, 10

miss, Miss *mademoiselle (Mlle),* I, 1

miss: Don't miss it! *C'est à ne pas manquer!* III, 9; **I miss . . .** *Je regrette...,* II, 8; (plural) *... me manquent.* II, 8; (singular) *... me manque.* II, 8; **to miss a step** *rater une marche,* II, 5; **to miss the bus** *rater le bus,* I, 9; II, 5; **What I miss is . . .** *Ce qui me manque, c'est...,* II, 8

mistaken: If I'm not mistaken, . . . *Si je ne me trompe pas,...,* III, 11; **In my opinion, you're mistaken.** *A mon avis, tu te trompes.* II, 9

misunderstanding: a little misunderstanding *un petit malentendu,* II, 10

moment: One moment, please. *Un moment, s'il vous plaît.* I, 5

Monday: on Mondays *le lundi,* I, 2

money *de l'argent,* I, 11

monkey *le singe,* III, 7

mood: in a bad mood *de mauvaise humeur,* II, 9; **in a good mood** *de bonne humeur,* II, 9

moose *un orignal,* II, 12

moped *le vélomoteur,* III, 8

more: More . . . ? *Encore de... ?* I, 8; **Some more . . . ?** *Encore... ?* II, 3; **I just can't do any more!** *Je n'en peux plus!* II, 7; **Life was more . . . , less . . .** *La vie était plus..., moins...,* II, 8; **more . . . than . . .** *plus de... que...,* III, 8; **more . . . than . . .** *plus... que...,* III, 8; **More or less.** *Plus ou moins.* II, 6; **One more try!** *Encore un effort!* II, 7

morning: in the morning *le matin,* I, 2

Morocco *le Maroc,* III, 12

mosque *une mosquée,* II, 8

mosquito *un moustique,* II, 4; **mosquito repellent** *de la lotion anti-moustique(s),* II, 12; III, 7

mother *la mère,* I, 7

mountain: to go mountain-bike riding *faire du vélo de montagne,* II, 12; **to/at the mountains** *à la montagne,* I, 11

move *déménager,* III, 10; **Don't move.** *Ne bougez pas.* III, 7; **Get a move on!** *Grouille-toi!* III, 2

movie *le film,* I, 6; **the movies** *le cinéma,* I, 1; **movie theater** *le cinéma,* I, 6; **historical movie** *le film historique,* III, 9; **war movie** *le film de guerre,* III, 9; **What good movies are out?** *Qu'est-ce qu'il y a comme bons films en ce moment?* III, 9; **What good movies have you seen?** *Qu'est-ce que tu as vu comme bons films?* III, 9

mow: to mow the lawn *tondre la pelouse,* III, 3

Mr. *monsieur (M.),* I, 1

Mrs. *madame (Mme),* I, 1

much: as many/as much . . . as . . . *autant de... que...,* III, 8; **How much is (are)...?** *Combien coûte(nt)... ?* II, 3; **How much is . . . ?** *C'est combien,... ?* I, 5; **How much is it, please?** *Ça fait combien, s'il vous plaît?* I, 5; **How much is it?** *C'est combien?* I, 3; **How much is the entrance fee?** *C'est combien, l'entrée?* II, 6; **No, not too much.** *Non, pas trop.* I, 2; **Not much.** *Pas grand-chose.* I, 6; **Not too much.** *Pas tellement.* I, 4; **Not very much.** *Pas beaucoup.* I, 4; **Yes, very much.** *Oui, beaucoup.* I, 2; **I don't like that very much.** *Je n'aime pas tellement ça.* III, 11

museum *le musée,* I, 6; II, 2

mushrooms *les champignons* (m.), I, 8; III, 11

music *la musique,* I, 2; (music) **group** *un groupe,* II, 11; **classical music** *la musique classique,* II, 11; III, 11; **music video** *le vidéoclip,* III, 9; **What music do you like?** *Qu'est-ce que tu aimes comme musique?* II, 1

musical comedy *une comédie musicale,* III, 9

musician *le musicien(la musicienne),* II, 11

must: It must be . . . *Ça doit être...,* III, 7; **There must be . . .** *Il doit y avoir...,* III, 7

mustache *la moustache,* III, 4

my *mon/ma/mes,* I, 7; **It's just not my day!** *C'est pas mon jour!* II, 5

mystery: detective or mystery movie *un film policier,* II, 11

name: His/Her name is... *Il/Elle s'appelle...,* I, 1; **My name is...** *Je m'appelle...,* I, 1; **What's your name?** *Tu t'appelles comment?* I, 1

nap: to take a nap *faire la sieste,* II, 8

natural science *les sciences* (f.) *naturelles,* I, 2

near *près de,* II, 2

Neat! *C'est le pied!* III, 7; **That's really neat!** *C'est vraiment le pied!* III, 12

necessary: It's necessary that . . . *Il est nécessaire que...,* III, 7

neck *le cou,* II, 7

necklace *le collier,* III, 4

need: I need . . . *Il me faut...,* I, 3, 10; *J'ai besoin de...,* I, 8; **What do you need for . . . ?** *Qu'est-ce qu'il vous (te) faut pour... ?* I, 3, 8; **What do you need?** *De quoi est-ce que tu as besoin?; Qu'est-ce qu'il te faut?* I, 8

neither: **Neither do I.** *Moi non plus.* I, 2; III, 9

nephew *le neveu,* III, 6

never *ne... jamais,* I, 4

new *nouveau (nouvelle),* II, 2; **Happy New Year!** *Bonne année!* II, 3; **What's new?** *Quoi de neuf?* III, 1

news *les informations* (f.), III, 9

next: **Next,...** *Ensuite,...* II, 1; **next to** *à côté de,* I, 12; II, 2; **Right there, next to...** *Juste là, à côté de...,* III, 2

nice *gentil (gentille),* I, 7; *sympa,* II, 1; **It's nice weather.** *Il fait beau.* I, 4; **That would be nice.** *Ce serait sympa.* III, 6; **Thanks, that's nice of you.** *Merci, c'est gentil.* II, 3; III, 6; **That's so nice of you.** *C'est gentil de votre (ta) part,* II, 2; **That's very nice of you.** *C'est vraiment très gentil de votre part.* III, 6

niece *la nièce,* III, 6

Niger *le Niger,* III, 12

nightmare: **It was a real nightmare!** *C'était un véritable cauchemar!* I, 11

no *non,* I, 1; **No...-ing** *Défense de...,* III, 3; **It's no good.** *C'est nul* III, 9; **No way!** *C'est pas possible!* III, 12; *Mon œil!* III, 10; *Pas question!* II, 1; *Tu parles!* III, 9

noise *le bruit,* III, 8; **Could you make less noise?** *Tu pourrais faire moins de bruit?* III, 9; **to make noise** *faire du bruit,* III, 3

noisy *bruyant(e),* II, 8

none (of it) *en,* I, 8

noon *midi,* I, 6

north: **in the north** *dans le nord,* II, 4; **It's to the north of...** *C'est au nord de...,* II, 12

northern: **It's in the northern part of...** *C'est dans le nord de...,* II, 12

nose: **I've got a runny nose.** *J'ai le nez qui coule.* II, 7

not *ne... pas,* I, 1; **...is not allowed** *Interdiction de...,* III, 3; **Definitely not!** *Sûrement pas!* II, 6; **It was not bad.** *J'ai trouvé ça pas mal,* III, 9; **It's not good to...** *Ce n'est pas bien de...,* III, 3; **Not at all.** *Pas du tout.* I, 4; II, 10; III, 9; **Oh, not bad.** *Oh, pas mal.* I, 9; **not so great** *pas fameux,* I, 5; **not very good** *pas bon,* I, 5; **not yet** *ne... pas encore,* I, 9; **One should not...** *Il ne faut pas...,* III, 3; **Please do not...** *Prière de ne pas..., Veuillez ne pas...,* III, 3; **You'd do well/better not to...** *Tu ferais bien/mieux de ne pas...,* III, 3

notebook *le cahier,* I, 0

nothing: **It's nothing special.** *Ce n'est pas grand-chose.* II, 3; **It's nothing.** *(Il n'y a) pas de quoi.* III, 6; **Nothing (special).** *Rien (de spécial).* I, 6; III, 1

novel *un roman,* I, 3

November *novembre,* I, 4

nurse *l'infirmier(-ière),* III, 5

oars *les rames* (f.), III, 12

obvious: **That's obvious.** *Ça se voit.* II, 9

obviously *évidemment,* II, 9

o'clock: **at... o'clock** *à... heures,* I, 2

October *octobre,* I, 4

octopus *la pieuvre,* III, 10

of *de,* I, 0; **Of course not.** *Bien sûr que non.* II, 10; **Of course.** *Bien sûr.* I, 3; II, 10; **of it** *en,* I, 8; **of them** *en,* I, 8

off: **afternoon off** *l'après-midi libre,* I, 2

offer: **Can I offer you something?** *Je vous sers quelque chose?* III, 6; **What can I offer you?** *Qu'est-ce que je peux vous offrir?* III, 6

often *souvent,* I, 4

oh: **Oh no!** *Oh là là!* II, 5

oil *l'huile* (f.), III, 2; **to put oil in the motor** *mettre de l'huile dans le moteur,* III, 2; **to check the oil** *vérifier l'huile,* III, 2; **to change the oil** *faire la vidange,* III, 2

OK *assez bien,* II, 6; *D'accord.* I, 4; *Entendu.* I, 2; **Well, OK.** *Bon, d'accord.* I, 8; **Is it OK with you if...?** *Tu veux bien que...?,* III, 3; **Is that OK with you?** *Tu es d'accord?* I, 7

okra *des okras* (m.), III, 11; *des gombos,* I, 8

old: **How old are you?** *Tu as quel âge?* I, 1; **I am... years old.** *J'ai... ans.* I, 1; **This old thing?** *Oh, c'est un vieux truc.* III, 4; **to be... years old** *avoir... ans,* II, 1; **When I was... years old,...** *Quand j'avais... ans,...,* II, 8

old-fashioned *démodé(e),* I, 10

older *âgé(e),* I, 10

oldest: **the oldest child** *l'aîné(e),* III, 6

olive *l'olive* (f.), III, 8

omelette *l'omelette* (f.), I, 5

on: **Can I try on...?** *Je peux essayer...?* I, 10; **on foot** *à pied,* I, 12; **on (day of the week)...** *le + (day of the week),* I, 2

on the right (left) *sur la droite (gauche),* II, 2

once: **OK, just this once.** *Ça va pour cette fois.* III, 3; **once a week** *une fois par semaine,* I, 4

one: **He/She already has one (of them).** *Il/Elle en a déjà un(e).* II, 3; **That one.** *Celui-là/Celle-là,* III, 4; **The one...** *Celui du...,* III, 4; **Which one?** *Lequel/Laquelle?* III, 4;

Which ones? *Lesquels/Lesquelles?* III, 4

one-way: **a one-way ticket** *un aller simple,* II, 6

onion *l'oignon* (m.), I, 8

only *ne... que,* III, 9; **I'm not the only one who...** *Je ne suis pas le/la seul(e) à...,* III, 3

open: **Open your books to page...** *Ouvrez vos livres à la page...,* I, 0; **When do you open?** *A quelle heure est-ce que vous ouvrez?* II, 6

opinion: **I didn't ask your opinion.** *Je t'ai pas demandé ton avis.* III, 10; **In my opinion,...** *A mon avis,...,* II, 9; **In your opinion, what do I do?** *A ton avis, qu'est-ce que je fais?* I, 9; **In your opinion, what should I do?** *A ton avis, qu'est-ce que je dois faire?* II, 10

or *ou,* I, 1

orange (color) *orange,* I, 3; **orange juice** *un jus d'orange,* I, 5; **oranges** *des oranges* (f.), I, 8

ordinary: **That's ordinary.** *C'est banal.* II, 3

other: **Think about other people.** *Pense aux autres.* III, 3

ought: **You ought to...** *Il faudrait que tu...,* III, 5

our *notre, nos,* I, 7

out: **to go out** *sortir,* II, 6; **Out of the question!** *Pas question!* I, 7

outfit *la tenue,* III, 12

over there: **Over there, the boy who...** *Là-bas, le garçon qui...,* III, 4

oysters *les huîtres* (f.), II, 3; III, 11

package: **a package/box of** *un paquet de,* I, 8

page *la page,* I, 0

pain: **a pain (in the neck)** *pénible,* I, 7; **You're such a pain!** *Tu es vraiment casse-pieds!* III, 6

pair: **a pair of jeans** *un jean,* I, 3; II, 1; **of shorts** *un short,* I, 3; **of boots** *les bottes* (f.), II, 1; **of gloves** *les gants* (m.), II, 1; **of pants** *un pantalon,* I, 10; **of sneakers** *les baskets* (f.), II, 1

palm tree *un palmier,* II, 4

pancake (very thin) *la crêpe,* I, 5

panic: **Don't panic!** *Pas de panique!* III, 7

pantyhose *un collant,* III, 4

papayas *des papayes* (f.), I, 8

paper *le papier,* I, 0; III, 3; **sheets of paper** *des feuilles* (f.) *de papier,* I, 3

parallel: **the uneven parallel bars** *les barres asymétriques* (f.), III, 12

pardon: Pardon me. *Pardon*, I, 3; **Pardon me for . . .** *Pardonne-moi de... ,* III, 6
parent *le parent*, I, 7
park *le parc*, I, 6; II, 2
parking place *la place de stationnement*, III, 8
party: to give a party *faire une boum*, II, 10
pass: to pass one's baccalaureat exam *réussir son bac*, III, 5; **Would you pass . . . ?** *Vous pourriez (tu pourrais) me passer... ?,* II, 3; **You'll pass . . .** *Vous passez devant... ,* I, 12
passport *le passeport*, I, 11; II, 1; III, 7
pasta *des pâtes* (f.), II, 7
pastry *la pâtisserie*, I, 12; **pastry shop** *la pâtisserie*, I, 12; II, 3
paté *le pâté*, II, 3
patient: Be patient! *Sois patient(e)!* III, 2
peaches *des pêches* (f.), I, 8
pears *des poires* (f.), I, 8
peas *des petits pois* (m.), I, 8
pedestrian: pedestrian crossing *le passage pour piétons*, III, 8
pen *le stylo*, I, 0
pencil *un crayon*, I, 3; **pencil case** *la trousse*, I, 3; **pencil sharpener** *un taille-crayon*, I, 3
pendant *le pendentif*, III, 4
people: people in a hurry *les gens pressés*, III, 8
perfect: It's perfect. *C'est parfait.* I, 10
perm *la permanente*, III, 4
permission: to ask your parents' permission *demander la permission à tes parents*, II, 10
pharmacist *le pharmacien(la pharmacienne)*, III, 5
phone: Phone him/her/them. *Téléphone-lui/-leur.* II, 10; **to talk on the phone** *parler au téléphone*, I, 1
photo: photo frame *le cadre*, II, 3
photography: to do photography *faire de la photo*, I, 4
physical education *l'éducation* (f.) *physique et sportive (EPS)*, I, 2
physics *la physique*, I, 2
piano *le piano*, III, 11
pick *choisir*, I, 10; **to pick up your room** *ranger ta chambre*, I, 7
picnic: to have a picnic *faire un pique-nique*, I, 6; II, 6
picture *l'image* (f.), III, 9
pie *de la tarte*, I, 8; **fruit pies/tarts** *les tartes aux fruits*, III, 1
piece: a piece of *un morceau de*, I, 8
pilot *le/la pilote*, III, 5
pineapple *des ananas* (m.), I, 8; *un ananas*, II, 4
pink *rose*, I, 3
pitcher (baseball) *le lanceur*, III, 12
pizza *la pizza*, I, 1
place *l'endroit* (m.), I, 12
plaid *écossais(e)*, III, 4
plain *sobre*, III, 4

plan: What do you plan to do? *Qu'est-ce que tu comptes faire?* III, 5
plane: plane ticket *un billet d'avion*, I, 11; **by plane** *en avion*, I, 12
planning: I'm planning on . . . *Je compte... ,* III, 5
plans: Do you have plans? *Tu as des projets?* III, 5; **I don't have any plans.** *Je n'ai rien de prévu.* I, 11
plant: to plant a tree *planter un arbre*, III, 3
plastic *le plastique*, III, 3
plate: plate of pâté, ham, and cold sausage *l'assiette de charcuterie*, III, 1
platform: From platform . . . *Du quai... ,* II, 6; **From which platform . . . ?** *De quel quai... ?* II, 6
play *faire, jouer*, I, 4; **Do you play/do . . . ?** *Est-ce que tu fais... ?* I, 4; **How about playing . . . ?** *Si on jouait... ?* II, 8; **I don't play/do . . .** *Je ne fais pas de... ,* I, 4; **I play . . .** *Je joue... ,* I, 4; **I play/do . . .** *Je fais... ,* I, 4; **to play baseball** *jouer au base-ball*, I, 4; **to play basketball** *jouer au basket(-ball)*, I, 4; **to play football** *jouer au football américain*, I, 4; **to play golf** *jouer au golf*, I, 4; **to play hockey** *jouer au hockey*, I, 4; **to play soccer** *jouer au foot(ball)*, I, 4; **to play sports** *faire du sport*, I, 1; **to play tennis** *jouer au tennis*, I, 4; **to play volleyball** *jouer au volley(-ball)*, I, 4; **What sports do you play?** *Qu'est-ce que tu fais comme sport?* I, 4; II, 1
playing: It's playing at . . . *Ça passe à... ,* II, 11; **What films are playing?** *Qu'est-ce qu'on joue comme films?* II, 11; **Where is that playing?** *Ça passe où?* II, 11
please *s'il vous (te) plaît*, I, 3; **A . . . , please.** *Un(e)... s'il vous plaît.* II, 6; **Pleased to meet you.** *Très heureux (heureuse).* I, 7
pleasure: Yes, with pleasure. *Oui, avec plaisir.* I, 8; *Avec plaisir.* II, 10
pleated *à pinces*, III, 4
plenty: We've got plenty of time! *On a largement le temps!* III, 2
plot *l'intrigue* (f.), III, 9; **It has no plot.** *Il n'y a pas d'histoire.* II, 11; **It's full of plot twists.** *C'est plein de rebondissements.* II, 11
plumber *plombier* (m.), III, 5
po-boy sandwich *le po-boy*, III, 11
poetry: book of poetry *un livre de poésie*, II, 11
point: At that point . . . *A ce moment-là... ,* II, 9; III, 9; **It's not my strong point.** *Ce n'est pas mon fort.* II, 5
pole: the pole vault *le saut à la perche*, III, 12
police officer *l'agent* (m.) *de police*, III, 5; *le policier*, III, 5

polite *poli(e)*, III, 3
polka-dot *à pois*, III, 4
pollution *la pollution*, III, 8
pony tail *une queue de cheval*, III, 4
pool *la piscine*, II, 2
poor: You poor thing! *Pauvre vieux (vieille)!* II, 5
pop: popular, mainstream music *la pop*, II, 11
pork *du porc*, I, 8; III, 11; **porkchop with pasta** *la côtelette de porc pâtes*, III, 1
possible: If it were possible, . . . *Si c'était possible,... ,* III, 8; **It's possible that . . .** *Il est possible que... ,* III, 5; **That's not possible.** *Ce n'est pas possible.* II, 9; **That's possible.** *C'est possible.* II, 9; **Would it be possible for you to . . . ?** *Vous serait-il possible de... ?* III, 5
post office *la poste*, I, 12; II, 2
poster *le poster*, I, 0, 3; II, 2
potatoes *des pommes de terre* (f.), I, 8
pottery *la poterie*, II, 8; III, 8
pound: a pound of *une livre de*, I, 8
practice *répéter*, I, 9
prefer: Do you prefer . . . or . . . ? *Tu aimes mieux... ou... ?* I, 10; **I prefer** *Je préfère... ,* II, 1, 7, 8; *J'aime mieux... ,* I, 1; II, 1; **What I prefer is . . .** *Ce que je préfère, c'est... ,* II, 4
pressure: tire pressure *la pression des pneus* (m.), III, 2
prey *la proie*, III, 7
problem: I've got a problem. *J'ai un (petit) problème.* I, 9; II, 10; **No problem.** *Pas de problème.* II, 10
process: to be in the process of (doing something) *être en train de (+ infinitive)*, II, 9
public: to take public transportation *prendre les transports en commun*, III, 3
pudding: bread pudding *le pouding au pain*, III, 11
pullover (sweater) *un pull-over*, I, 3
purple *violet(te)*, I, 3
purpose: Are you doing that on purpose? *Tu le fais exprès?* III, 6
purse *le sac à main*, II, 3
push-ups: to do push-ups *faire des pompes*, II, 7
put *mettre*, I, 10; **put on (clothing)** *mettre*, I, 10; **put on makeup** *se maquiller*, III, 4; **put up: I won't put up with this!** *C'est insupportable, à la fin!* III, 8

quarter: quarter past *et quart*, I, 6; **quarter to** *moins le quart*, I, 6

question: Out of the question! *Pas question!* I, 7
quiche *la quiche,* I, 5
quiet: Be quiet! *Tais-toi!* III, 9; **Could you please be quiet?** *Vous pourriez vous taire, s'il vous plaît?* III, 9
quiz *l'interro* (f.), I, 9

raccoon *le raton laveur,* II, 12
radio *la radio,* I, 3
rain: It's raining. *Il pleut.* I, 4
raincoat *l'imperméable* (m.), II, 1
rained: It rained the whole time. *Il a plu tout le temps.* III, 1
rainforest: tropical rainforest *la forêt tropicale,* II, 4; III, 7
raise *élever,* III, 8; **Raise your hand!** *Levez la main!,* I, 0
raisins *les raisins secs,* III, 11
rake: to rake leaves *ramasser les feuilles,* III, 3
rap *le rap,* II, 11; III, 11
rare *saignant(e),* III, 1
rarely *rarement,* I, 4
rather *plutôt,* II, 9; **No, I'd rather...** *Non, je préfère...,* II, 1
read *lire,* I, 1; **read** (pp.) *lu* (pp. of *lire*), I, 9
ready: to get ready *faire les préparatifs,* II, 10
really *vachement,* II, 9; **really...** *bien...,* III, 11; **Really.** *Je t'assure.* III, 4; **Really?** *C'est vrai? (Vraiment?),* II, 2; **I (really) like...** *Moi, j'aime (bien)...,* I, 1; **I really don't know.** *Je ne sais pas trop.* III, 5; **I really liked it.** *Ça m'a beaucoup plu.* II, 6; **I'd really like...** *J'aimerais bien...,* III, 5; **I'd really like to...** *Je voudrais bien...,* I, 11; **I'd really like to.** *Je veux bien.* I, 6; **No, not really.** *Non, pas vraiment.* I, 11; **That looks really...** *Ça fait vraiment...,* III, 4; **Was it really so different?** *C'était tellement différent?* II, 8; **Your... is really great.** *Il/Elle est vraiment bien, ton/ta...,* II, 2
reason: That's no reason. *Ce n'est pas une raison.* III, 3
receive: to receive one's report card *recevoir le bulletin trimestriel,* II, 5
recommend: I recommend... *Je te recommande...,* III, 9; **I recommend it.** *Je te le recommande.* II, 11; **What do you recommend?** *Qu'est-ce que vous me conseillez?* III, 1
record: at the record store *chez le disquaire,* I, 12

recorder: videocassette recorder/VCR *le magnétoscope,* III, 9
recreation center *la Maison des jeunes et de la culture (MJC),* I, 6
recycle *recycler,* III, 3
red *rouge,* I, 3; **red hair** *les cheveux roux,* II, 1; **redheaded** *roux (rousse),* I, 7
regards: Give... my regards. *Fais mes amitiés à...,* III, 8
reggae music *le reggae,* II, 11
rehearse *répéter,* I, 9
relaxing *relax,* II, 8
remember: If I remember correctly,... *Si je me souviens bien,...,* III, 11; **Remember to take...** *Pense à prendre...,* II, 1
remote (control) *la télécommande,* III, 9
repeat: Repeat! *Répétez!,* I, 0
report card: to receive one's report card *recevoir le bulletin trimestriel,* II, 5
respect: to respect nature *respecter la nature,* II, 12; **to respect your teachers and your parents** *respecter tes profs et tes parents,* III, 3
response: In response to your letter of... *En réponse à votre lettre du...,* III, 5
responsibilities: to have responsibilities *avoir des responsabilités,* II, 8
responsible *responsable,* III, 3
restaurant *le restaurant,* I, 6
restroom *les toilettes* (f.) (*les W.-C.* (m.)), II, 2
retro *rétro,* I, 10
return *retourner,* II, 6; **to return something** *rendre,* I, 12; **to return tests** *rendre les examens,* II, 5
rhinoceros *le rhinocéros,* III, 7
rice *du riz,* I, 8
ride: to take a ride on the ferris wheel *faire un tour sur la grande roue,* II, 6; **to take a ride on the roller coaster** *faire un tour sur les montagnes russes,* II, 6
ridiculous: That's ridiculous! *N'importe quoi!* II, 6
riding: to go horseback riding *faire de l'équitation,* I, 1
right: I can't right now. *Je ne peux pas maintenant.* I, 8; **I'll go right away.** *J'y vais tout de suite.* I, 8; **It's right there on the...** *C'est tout de suite à...,* I, 12; **on the right** *sur la droite,* II, 2; **right away** *tout de suite,* I, 6; **to the right (of)** *à droite (de),* I, 12; II, 2; **Yeah, right!** *Mon œil!* II, 6; *N'importe quoi!* III, 10; **You're right.** *Tu as raison.* II, 3; III, 9; **I just can't do anything right!** *Qu'est-ce que je peux être nul(le)!* III, 12
ring: the rings (in gymnastics) *les anneaux* (m.), III, 12
rip *déchirer,* II, 5

river *la rivière,* III, 7
roast beef *le rôti de bœuf,* III, 3
rock (music) *le rock,* II, 11; III, 11
rock *le rocher,* III, 10
roll: roll of film *la pellicule,* III, 7
roller coaster *les montagnes russes,* II, 6
romance novel *un roman d'amour,* II, 11
romantic: romantic movie *une histoire* (f.) *d'amour,* II, 11
room (of a house) *la pièce,* II, 2; **to pick up your room** *ranger ta chambre,* I, 7
round-trip: a round-trip ticket *un aller-retour,* II, 6
rowing *l'aviron* (m.), III, 12
rug *le tapis,* II, 2; III, 8
ruler *la règle,* I, 3
running: long-distance running *la course de fond,* III, 12
runny: I've got a runny nose. *J'ai le nez qui coule.* II, 7
Russia *la Russie,* III, 12

safely: to drive safely *conduire prudemment,* III, 3
safer: In my opinion, it's safer. *A mon avis, c'est plus sûr.* III, 7
said: You said it! *Tu l'as dit!* III, 9
sailing: to go sailing *faire de la voile,* I, 11
salad *la salade verte,* III, 1; **salad, heads of lettuce** *de la salade,* I, 8
salami *le saucisson,* I, 5; II, 3
salesperson *le vendeur(la vendeuse),* III, 5
salt *le sel,* II, 7
salty *salé(e),* III, 11
same: It's always the same! *C'est toujours la même chose!* III, 6; **It's really all the same to me.** *Ça m'est vraiment égal.* III, 9; **Same old thing!** *Toujours la même chose!* III, 1
sand *le sable,* II, 4
sandals *les sandales* (f.), I, 10
sandwich *un sandwich,* I, 5
Saturday: on Saturdays *le samedi,* I, 2
sausages *les saucisses* (f.), III, 11
savannah *la savane,* III, 7
saxophone *le saxophone,* III, 11
say: How do you say...? *Comment on dit...?* III, 11
saying: I'm not just saying that. *Je ne dis pas ça pour te faire plaisir.* III, 4
says: So he says... *... et alors, il dit que...,* III, 10
scare: Wow! That was a real scare! *Ouf! On a eu chaud!* III, 7
scared: I'm scared (of)... *J'ai peur (de la, du, des)...,* II, 12; **I'm scared to death!** *J'ai la frousse!* III, 7

scarf *l'écharpe* (f.), I, 10; II, 1; *le foulard*, II, 3

school *l'école* (f.), I, 1; **high school** *le lycée*, II, 2

science fiction: science-fiction novel *un roman de science-fiction*, II, 11; **science-fiction movie** *un film de science-fiction*, II, 11; III, 9

score: to score ... points *marquer... points*, III, 12

screen *l'écran* (m.), III, 9

scuba dive: to go scuba diving *faire de la plongée sous-marine*, II, 4

sea *la mer*, II, 4

seahorse *l'hippocampe* (m.), III, 10

seaweed *l'algue* (f.), III, 10

second: One second, please. *Une seconde, s'il vous plaît.* I, 9

secretary *le/la secrétaire*, III, 5

see: Go see ... it's a great movie. *Va voir..., c'est génial comme film.* III, 9; **Really, don't go see ...** *Ne va surtout pas voir...*, III, 9; **See you later!** *À tout à l'heure!* I, 1; **See you soon.** *À bientôt.* I, 1; **See you tomorrow.** *À demain.* I, 1; **to go to see a game (in person)** *aller voir un match*, I, 6; **to see a movie** *voir un film*, I, 6; **to see a play** *voir une pièce*, I, 6; **What is there to see ...?** *Qu'est-ce qu'il y a à voir... ?*, II, 12; **When I see ...** *Quand je verrai...*, III, 12; **You should go see ...** *Tu devrais aller voir...*, III, 9; **You'll see that ...** *Tu vas voir que...*, II, 8

seem: to seem ... *avoir l'air...*, II, 9; III, 11; **You don't seem too well.** *Tu n'as pas l'air en forme.* II, 7

seemed: She seemed ... *Elle avait l'air...*, II, 12

seems: It seems to me that ... *Il me semble que...*, III, 11

seen (pp.) *vu* (pp. of *voir*), I, 9; **If you could have seen ...!** *Si tu avais vu...*, III, 10

selection: Have you made your selection? *Vous avez choisi?* III, 1

sell *vendre*, I, 9

send: to send letters *envoyer des lettres*, I, 12; **to send the invitations** *envoyer les invitations*, II, 10

Senegal *le Sénégal*, III, 12

sensational *sensass*, II, 6

September *septembre*, I, 4

series *la série*, III, 9

serious: It's not serious. *C'est pas grave.* II, 5

server *le serveur (la serveuse)*, III, 5

service: At your service; You're welcome. *À votre service.* I, 3

set: to set the table *mettre la table*, III, 3

shall: Shall we go to the café? *On va au café?* I, 5

shampoo: a shampoo *un shampooing*, III, 4

shape: to get into shape *se mettre en condition*, II, 7

share *partager ses affaires*, III, 3; **to share one's vehicle** *partager son véhicule*, III, 3

shark *le requin*, III, 10

shave *se raser*, III, 4

sheep *le mouton*, III, 8

sheet: a sheet of paper *la feuille de papier*, I, 0

shell *le coquillage*, III, 10

shellfish *les crustacés* (m.), III, 11

shelves *les étagères*, II, 2

Shh! *Chut!* III, 9

shirt (men's) *la chemise*, I, 10; **(women's)** *le chemisier*, I, 10

shoes *les chaussures* (f.), I, 10

shoot *tirer*, III, 12

shop: to window-shop *faire les vitrines*, I, 6

shopping *les courses* (f.), I, 7; **to do the shopping** *faire les courses*, I, 7; **to go shopping** *faire les magasins*, I, 1; **Can you do the shopping?** *Tu peux aller faire les courses?* I, 8

short (objects) *court(e)*, I, 10; **short (height)** *petit(e)*, I, 7; II, 1; **short hair** *les cheveux courts* (m.), II, 1; III, 4

shorts: (a pair of) shorts *un short*, I, 3

should: Do you think I should ...? *Tu crois que je devrais... ?* III, 7; **Everyone should ...** *On doit...*, II, 7; **I should have ...** *J'aurais dû...*, II, 10; **In your opinion, what should I do?** *À ton avis, qu'est-ce que je dois faire?* II, 10; **What do you think I should do?** *Qu'est-ce que tu me conseilles?* II, 10; **What should I ...?** *Qu'est-ce que je dois...*, II, 1; **What should I do?** *Qu'est-ce que je dois faire?* II, 12; **What should we do?** *Qu'est-ce qu'on fait?* II, 1; **You should ...** *Il faudrait que tu...*, III, 5; **You should ...** *Tu devrais...*, I, 9; II, 7; **You should be proud of yourself.** *Tu peux être fier (fière) de toi.* II, 5; **You should go see ...** *Tu devrais aller voir...*, III, 9; **You should have ... (food or drink)** *Tu devrais prendre...*, III, 1; **(ought to have)** *Tu aurais dû...*, II, 10

shouldn't: You shouldn't ... *Tu ne devrais pas...*, II, 7; *Tu ne dois pas...*, III, 3; *Vous (ne) devriez (pas)...*, III, 3; **One should not ...** *Il ne faut pas...*, III, 3

shovel: to shovel snow *enlever la neige*, III, 3

show *montrer*, I, 9; **game show** *le jeu télévisé*, III, 9; **magazine show** *le magazine télévisé*, III, 9; **sound and light show** *un spectacle son et lumière*, II, 6

showing: ... is showing. *On joue...*, II, 11

shrimp *la crevette*, II, 3; III, 10

shy *timide*, I, 7

sick: I'm sick of this! *J'en ai vraiment marre!* III, 12; **I'm sick to my stomach.** *J'ai mal au cœur.* II, 7; **I'm sick.** *Je suis malade.* II, 7

sideburns *des pattes* (f.), III, 4

sidewalk *le trottoir*, III, 8

silk *en soie*, III, 4

silly: Stop being so silly! *Arrête de délirer!* III, 10; **to do silly things** *faire des bêtises*, II, 8

simple *simple*, II, 8

Since ... *Depuis...*, III, 1

sing *chanter*, I, 9

singer *le chanteur (la chanteuse)*, II, 11

singing *le chant*, III, 11

single *célibataire*, III, 6

sir *monsieur (M.)*, I, 1; III, 5

sister *la sœur*, I, 7

sit-ups: to do sit-ups *faire des abdominaux*, II, 7

sit: Sit down. *Asseyez-vous.* III, 6

skate: to ice-skate *faire du patin à glace*, I, 4; **to in-line skate** *faire du roller en ligne*, I, 4

ski *faire du ski*, I, 4; **ski jacket** *l'anorak* (m.), II, 1; **to water ski** *faire du ski nautique*, I, 4

skiing *le ski*, I, 1

skip: Don't skip ... *Ne saute pas...*, II, 7

skipping: skipping a meal *sauter un repas*, II, 7

skirt *la jupe*, I, 10

skunk *une mouffette*, II, 12

skyscraper *le gratte-ciel*, III, 8

sleep *dormir*, I, 1; **I didn't sleep well.** *J'ai mal dormi.* II, 7

sleeping bag *un sac de couchage*, II, 12

slender *mince*, I, 7

slice: a slice of *la tranche de*, I, 8

small *petit(e)*, I, 10; III, 8

smaller: smaller than ... *moins grand(e) que*, II, 4

smart *intelligent(e)*, I, 7; II, 1

smoke *fumer*, III, 3

snack: afternoon snack *le goûter*, I, 8; **to make party snacks** *préparer les amuse-gueule*, II, 10

snacking: snacking between meals *grignoter entre les repas*, II, 7

snails *les escargots* (m.), I, 1; II, 3

snake *le serpent*, III, 7

sneakers *des baskets* (f.), I, 3; **pair of sneakers** *les baskets* (f.), II, 1

sneezing: I'm sneezing a lot. *J'éternue beaucoup.* II, 7

snorkel *faire de la plongée avec un tuba*, II, 4

snow-shoeing: to go snow-shoeing *faire une randonnée en raquettes*, II, 12

snowing: It's snowing. *Il neige.* I, 4

so: So ... *Alors,...*, II, 9; **so-so** *comme ci comme ça*, I, 1; II, 6; **not so great** *pas fameux*, I, 5; **That is so ...!** *Qu'est-ce que c'est... !* III, 2

soap opera *le feuilleton*, III, 9
soccer *le football*, I, 1; **to play soccer** *jouer au foot(ball)*, I, 4
socks *les chaussettes* (f.), I, 10
sole: filet of sole with rice and mushrooms *le filet de sole riz champignons*, III, 1
some *des*, I, 3; ; *du, de la, de l', des, en*, I, 8; **I'd like some.** *J'en veux bien.* I, 8; **Some more . . . ?** *Encore... ?* II, 3
sometimes *quelquefois*, I, 4
son *le fils*, I, 7
song *la chanson*, II, 11
soon: As soon as I get there, . . . *Dès que je serai là-bas,... ,* III, 12; **See you soon.** *A bientôt.* I, 1
sophisticated *élégant(e)*, III, 4
sorry: Sorry. *Désolé(e).* II, 10; *Je regrette.* I, 3; **I'm sorry for . . .** *Je m'excuse de... ,* II, 6
sort of *assez*, II, 9
sound *le son*, III, 9; **Does . . . sound good to you?** *Ça te dit de... ?* II, 1; **sound and light show** *un spectacle son et lumière*, II, 6
soups *les soupes* (f.), III, 11
south: in the south *dans le sud*, II, 4; **It's to the south of . . .** *C'est au sud de... ,* II, 12; **South Africa** *l'Afrique* (f.) *du Sud*, III, 12; **South African** (adj.) *sud-africain(e)*, III, 12
southern: It's in the southern part of . . . *C'est dans le sud de... ,* II, 12
Spain *l'Espagne* (f.), III, 12
Spanish (language) *l'espagnol* (m.), I, 2
speak: Could I speak to . . . ? *(Est-ce que) je peux parler à... ?* I, 9
special: It's nothing special. *Ce n'est pas grand-chose.* II, 3; **Nothing (special).** *Rien (de spécial).* I, 6; III, 1
spices *les épices* (f.), III, 11
spicy *épicé(e)*, III, 11
spider *l'araignée* (f.), III, 7
spinach *les épinards* (m.), III, 11
sports *le sport*, I, 1; **to play sports** *faire du sport*, I, 1; **What sports do you play?** *Qu'est-ce que tu fais comme sport?* I, 4; II, 1
sportscast *le reportage sportif*, III, 9
sprain: to sprain one's ankle *se fouler la cheville*, II, 7; III, 10
spring: in the spring *au printemps*, I, 4
spy flick *le film d'espionnage*, III, 9
squirrel *un écureuil*, III, 12
stadium *le stade*, I, 6
stamp *un timbre*, I, 12
stand: Stand up! *Levez-vous!*, I, 0
starfish *l'étoile* (f.) *de mer*, III, 10
start *commencer*, I, 9; **How does it start?** *Comment est-ce que ça commence?* III, 9; **What time does it start?** *Ça commence à quelle heure?* II, 11
started: He/She started it! *C'est lui/elle qui a commencé!* III, 6
stationery store *la papeterie*, I, 12

stay *rester*, II, 6; **Did you stay here?** *Est-ce que tu es resté(e) ici?* III, 1; **Where did you stay?** *Où est-ce que tu as dormi?* III, 1
stayed: Yes, I stayed here the whole time. *Oui, je suis resté(e) ici tout le temps.* III, 1
steak *le bifteck*, II, 3; **steak and French fries** *le steak-frites*, I, 5; III, 1
steamed *à la vapeur*, III, 11
stereo *la chaîne stéréo*, II, 2
still . . . *toujours... ,* III, 11
stinks: It stinks. *C'est un navet*, II, 11
stomach *le ventre*, II, 7; **I'm sick to my stomach.** *J'ai mal au cœur.* II, 7
stop: Stop! *Arrête!* III, 6; **at the . . . metro stop** *au métro... ,* I, 6; **to stop one's studies** *arrêter ses études*, III, 5
stores *les magasins* (m.), I, 1
story: It's a great story. *C'est une belle histoire.* II, 11; **It's the story of . . .** *C'est l'histoire de... ,* II, 11; III, 9; **What's the story?** *Qu'est-ce que ça raconte?* II, 11
straight: straight hair *les cheveux raides* (m.), III, 4
straight ahead: Go (keep going) straight ahead. *Allez (continuez) tout droit*, II, 2; **Keep going straight ahead up to the intersection.** *Vous allez continuer tout droit, jusqu'au carrefour.* III, 2; **You go straight ahead until you get to . . .** *Vous allez tout droit jusqu'à... ,* I, 12
strawberries *les fraises* (f.), I, 8
street: You go down this street to the next light. *Vous continuez cette rue jusqu'au prochain feu rouge.* I, 12; **You take . . . Street, then cross . . . Street.** *Prenez la rue... , puis prenez la rue... ,* I, 12
strict: to follow a diet that's too strict *suivre un régime trop strict*, II, 7
striped *à rayures*, III, 4
strong *fort(e)*, I, 7; II, 1; **It's not my strong point.** *Ce n'est pas mon fort.* II, 5; **You're really strong/ good at that.** *Tu es fortiche/calé(e).* III, 10
student *l'élève* (m./f.), I, 2
studies: to stop one's studies *arrêter ses études*, III, 5
study *étudier*, I, 1; **study hall** *l'étude* (f.), I, 2
stuffed (with) *farci(e) (à)*, III, 11
stupid *bête*, II, 1; **(childish)** *bébé*, III, 2; **What a stupid joke!** *Elle est nulle, ta blague!* III, 10; **That looks really stupid!** *Ça fait vraiment cloche!* III, 4
style: in style *très à la mode*, I, 10; **That's not his/her style.** *Ce n'est pas son style.* II, 3

subway: by subway *en métro*, I, 12
such: I've never seen such a . . . *Je n'ai jamais vu un(e) aussi... ,* III, 7
sugar *le sucre*, I, 8; **sugarcane fields** *des champs de canne à sucre*, II, 4
suit: man's suit *le costume*, III, 4; **suit jacket** *la veste*, I, 10; **Does it suit me?** *Ça me va?* I, 10; **That suits you really well.** *Ça te (vous) va très bien.* I, 10
suitcase *la valise*, I, 11
sulk *faire la tête*, II, 9
summer: in the summer *en été*, I, 4
Sunday: on Sundays *le dimanche*, I, 2
sunglasses *des lunettes de soleil* (f.), I, 10
sunscreen *de la crème solaire*, III, 7
super (adj.) *super*, I, 2; **super cool** *hypercool*, III, 4; **What I think is super is . . .** *Ce que je trouve super, c'est... ,* III, 11
sure: I'm not sure. *J'hésite.* I, 11; **I'm (not) sure that . . .** *Je (ne) suis (pas) sûr(e) que... ,* III, 7; **That's for sure.** *Ça, c'est sûr.* III, 11; **We'd be able to . . . for sure.** *On pourrait sûrement... ,* III, 7
surprise: That would surprise me. *Ça m'étonnerait!* II, 6; III, 10
surprised *étonné(e)*, II, 9; **I'd be surprised if . . .** *Ça m'étonnerait que... ,* III, 7
suspenseful: It's suspenseful. *Il y a du suspense.* II, 11
sweater *le cardigan*, I, 10; *le pull*, II, 1
sweatshirt *le sweat-shirt*, I, 3; *le sweat*, II, 1
swim *faire de la natation*, I, 4; *nager*, I, 1
swimming *la natation*, III, 12; **to go swimming** *se baigner*, II, 4; **swimming pool** *la piscine*, I, 6
Switzerland *la Suisse*, III, 12
sword *l'épée* (f.), III, 12
swordfish *l'espadon* (m.), III, 10
synthesizer *le synthé (le synthétiseur)*, III, 11

T-shirt *le tee-shirt*, I, 3; II, 1
table: to clear the table *débarrasser la table*, I, 7; **to set the table** *mettre la table*, III, 3
tacky: I think it's (they're) really tacky. *Je le/la/les trouve moche(s).* I, 10
tailor *le tailleur (la tailleuse)*, III, 5
take: Are you going to take it/them? *Vous le/la/les prenez?* I, 10; **Have you decided to take . . . ?** *Vous avez décidé de prendre... ?* I, 10; **I'll take . . .** *Je vais (en) prendre... ,* II, 3; **I'll take . . . (of**

them). *Je vais en prendre...* , II, 3; **I'll take it/them.** *Je le/la/les prends.* I, 10; **It's not going to take long!** *Ça ne va pas prendre longtemps!* III, 2; **Remember to take ...** *Pense à prendre...* , II, 1; **Take ...** *Prends...* , II, 1; *Prenez...* , II, 2; **to take; to have (food or drink)** *prendre,* I, 5; **to take pictures** *faire des photos,* I, 4; **We can take ...** *On peut prendre...* , I, 12; **You take ... Street, then cross ... Street.** *Prenez la rue...* , *puis traversez la rue...* , I, 12

take out: Take out a sheet of paper. *Prenez une feuille de papier.* I, 0; **to take out the trash** *sortir la poubelle,* I, 7

takes place: It takes place ... *Ça se passe...* , III, 9

taking: Are you taking ...? *Tu prends...?* I, 11

talk: Can I talk to you? *Je peux te parler?* I, 9; II, 10; **Talk to him/her/them.** *Parle-lui/-leur.* II, 10; **to talk on the phone** *parler au téléphone,* I, 1

tall *grand(e),* I, 7; II, 1

tank: the gas tank *le réservoir,* III, 2

tart: apple tart *la tarte aux pommes,* II, 3; **fruit pies/tarts** *les tartes aux fruits,* III, 1

taste *déguster,* II, 4; **in poor taste** *de mauvais goût,* III, 2

tasteless *vulgaire,* III, 4

Tattletale! *Rapporteur(-euse)!* III, 6

taxi: by taxi *en taxi,* I, 12

teacher *le/la professeur,* I, 0

team *l'équipe* (f.), III, 12

tear *déchirer,* II, 5

tease *taquiner,* II, 8

technical: to go to a technical school *faire une école technique,* III, 5

technician *le technicien(la technicienne),* III, 5

teeth *les dents* (f.), II, 7

television *la télévision,* I, 0; **television set** *le téléviseur,* III, 9

tell: Can you tell her/him that I called? *Vous pouvez lui dire que j'ai téléphoné?* I, 9; **Didn't I tell you?** *Je ne t'ai pas dit?* III, 10; **Tell ... hi for me.** *Salue... de ma part.* III, 8; **Tell ... that I'm going to write.** *Dis à... que je vais lui écrire.* III, 8; **Tell ... that I'm thinking about him/her.** *Dis à... que je pense à lui/elle.* III, 8; **Tell him/her/them that ...** *Dis-lui/-leur que...* , II, 10; **Tell me!** *Raconte!* II, 5; III, 10; **to tell (someone) that ...** *dire à (quelqu'un) que...* , II, 10; **to tell the truth** *dire la vérité,* III, 3

tempting: Everything looks tempting. *Tout me tente.* III, 1

tennis: to play tennis *jouer au tennis,* I, 4

tent *une tente,* II, 12

terrible *horrible,* I, 10; **I had a terrible day!** *J'ai passé une journée épouvantable!* II, 5; **This is terrible!** *Quelle angoisse!* III, 12

Terrific! *Bravo!* II, 5

tests *les examens* (m.), I, 1

than: bigger than ... *plus grand(e) que,* II, 4; **fewer ... than ...** *moins de... que...* , III, 8; **It's better than ...** *C'est meilleur que...* , II, 7; **less ... than ...** *moins... que...* , III, 8; **more ... than ...** *plus de... que...* , III, 8; *plus... que...* , III, 8; **smaller than ...** *moins grand(e) que,* II, 4

thank: You don't have to thank me. *C'est tout à fait normal.* III, 6

thank you: Thank you. *Merci.* I, 3; II, 2; *Je vous remercie.* III, 6; **Thank you so much.** *Merci bien/mille fois.* III, 6; **Yes, thank you.** *Oui, s'il vous (te) plaît.* I, 8; **No, thank you.** *Non, merci.* I, 8; **No thank you, I've had enough.** *Merci, ça va.* II, 3

thanks: No thanks. I'm not hungry anymore. *Non, merci. Je n'ai plus faim.* I, 8

that *ce, cet, cette,* I, 3; **That is so ...!** *Qu'est-ce que c'est... !* III, 2; **This/That is ...** *Ça, c'est...* , I, 12; **That is, ...** *C'est-à-dire que...* , II, 9

theater *le théâtre,* I, 6; II, 2

their *leur/leurs,* I, 7

them *les, leur,* I, 9

then: Then, ... *Ensuite,...* , II, 12; *Et puis,...* , II, 1; **And then?** *Et alors?* III, 10; **Then I called ...** *Ensuite, j'ai téléphoné à...* , I, 9

there *-là* (noun suffix), I, 3; *y,* I, 12; **Here (There) is ...** *Là, c'est...* , II, 2; **Is ... there, please?** *(Est-ce que)... est là, s'il vous plaît?* I, 9; **Over there, at the end of the hallway.** *Par là, au bout du couloir.* III, 2; **Right there, next to ...** *Juste là, à côté de...* , III, 2; **There is/are...** *Il y a...* , I, 5; II, 2; **There's ...** *Voilà...* I, 7; **What do you ... there?** *Qu'est-ce qu'on y...?* III, 12; **You're almost there!** *Tu y es presque!* II, 7

Therefore, ... *Donc,...* , II, 9

these *ces,* I, 3; **These/Those are ...** *Ce sont...* , I, 7

thing: It's not my thing. *Ce n'est pas mon truc.* II, 7; **This old thing?** *Oh, c'est un vieux truc.* III, 4

things: I have lots of things to do. *J'ai des tas de choses à faire.* I, 5; **I have some things to do.** *J'ai des trucs à faire.* I, 5

think: Do you think I should ...? *Tu crois que je devrais...?* III, 7; **Do you think it'd be better to ...?** *Tu penses qu'il vaudrait mieux...?* III, 7; **Do you think so?** *Tu trouves?* II, 2; **Hey, do you think you can ...?** *Dites donc, ça vous gênerait de...?*

III, 8; **I don't think so.** *Je ne crois pas.* II, 9; **I don't think that ...** *Je ne pense pas que...* , III, 7; **I think I'll ...** *Je pense...* , III, 5; **I think it's ...** *Je trouve qu'il est...* , III, 4; **I think it's/they're ...** *Je le/la/les trouve...* , I, 10; **I think that ...** *Je crois que...* , II, 9; **I think that's better.** *Je crois que ça vaut mieux.* III, 7; **What do you think about going ...?** *Ça te dit d'aller...?* II, 4; **What do you think I should do?** *Qu'est-ce que tu me conseilles?* II, 10; **What do you think of ...?** *Comment tu trouves...?* I, 2; *Qu'est-ce que tu penses de...?* III, 4; **What do you think of it?** *Qu'en penses-tu?* III, 4; **What do you think of that/it?** *Comment tu trouves ça?* I, 2; **What do you think you'll do?** *Qu'est-ce que tu penses faire?* III, 5; **Who do you think you are?** *Non mais, vous vous prenez pour qui?* III, 8

thirst: I'm dying of thirst! *Je meurs de soif!* II, 2

thirsty: to be thirsty *avoir soif,* I, 5; **Aren't you thirsty?** *Vous n'avez pas (Tu n'as pas) soif?* II, 2; **I'm not thirsty anymore.** *Je n'ai plus soif,* II, 3

this *ce, cet, cette,* I, 3; **This is ...** *C'est...* , I, 7; *Ça, c'est...* , II, 2; **This/That is ...** *Ça, c'est...* , I, 12

those *ces,* I, 3; **Those.** *Ceux-là/Celles-là,* III, 4; **Those are ...** *Ce sont...* , I, 7

thought: I've thought of everything. *J'ai pensé à tout.* I, 11

throat *la gorge,* II, 7

throw: to throw away your trash *jeter les déchets,* II, 12; **to throw the ball** *lancer le ballon,* III, 12; **to throw trash** *jeter des ordures,* III, 3

Thursday: on Thursdays *le jeudi,* I, 2

ticket: plane ticket *un billet d'avion,* I, 11; II, 1; **Three (entrance) tickets, please.** *Trois tickets, s'il vous plaît.* II, 6; **train ticket** *un billet de train,* I, 11

tie *la cravate,* I, 10; III, 4

tied: to be tied *être à égalité,* III, 12

tight *serré(e),* I, 10

tights *un collant,* III, 4

time: a waste of time *zéro,* I, 2; **At what time do you have ...?** *Tu as... à quelle heure?* I, 2; **At what time?** *A quelle heure?* I, 6; **from time to time** *de temps en temps,* I, 4; **I'm sorry, but I don't have time.** *Je regrette, mais je n'ai pas le temps.* I, 8; **Sorry, but I don't have time.** *Je suis désolé(e), mais je n'ai pas le temps.* I, 12; **We don't have time!** *On n'a pas le temps!* III, 2; **What time does it start?** *Ça commence à quelle heure?* II, 11; **What time does the train (the**

bus) for . . . leave? *A quelle heure est-ce que le train (le car) pour... part?* II, 6

tire *le pneu*, III, 2; **spare tire** *la roue de secours*, III, 2; **tire pressure** *la pression des pneus* (m.), III, 2; **to have a flat tire** *avoir un pneu crevé*, III, 2

tired: **I'm tired.** *Je suis fatigué(e)*, II, 12; **(You're) not too tired?** *Pas trop fatigué(e)?* II, 2

tiring: **It was tiring!** *C'était fatigant!* II, 2

to *à la* **(before a feminine noun)**, I, 6; **(a city or place)** *à*, I, 11; **(before a feminine noun)** *en*, I, 11; **(before a masculine noun)** *au*, I, 11; **(before a plural noun)** *aux*, I, 11; **five to (before an hour)** *moins cinq*, I, 6

today *aujourd'hui*, I, 2

together: **When are we getting together?** *Quand est-ce qu'on se revoit?* III, 6

toilet *les toilettes* (f.)(*les W.-C.*) (m.), II, 2

told: **Who told you that?** *Qui t'a dit ça?* III, 10

tolerant *tolérant(e)*, III, 3

tomato: **tomato salad** *la salade de tomates*, III, 1; **tomatoes** *des tomates* (f.), I, 8

tomorrow *demain*, I, 2; **See you tomorrow.** *A demain.* I, 1

tonight: **Not tonight.** *Pas ce soir.* I, 7

too: **Me too.** *Moi aussi.* I, 2; III, 9; **No, it's too expensive.** *Non, c'est trop cher.* I, 10; II, 3; **No, not too much.** *Non, pas trop.* I, 2; **Not too much.** *Pas tellement.* I, 4; **It's/They're too...** *Il/Elle est (Ils/Elles sont) trop...* , I, 10; **too violent** *trop violent(e)*, II, 11

took (pp.) *pris* (pp. of prendre), I, 9

Tough! *Tant pis pour toi!* III, 6; **Tough luck!** *C'est pas de chance, ça!* II, 5

tour: **to take a guided tour** *faire une visite guidée*, II, 6; **to tour some châteaux** *faire un circuit des châteaux*, II, 6

tourist: **tourist information office** *l'office de tourisme*, II, 2

towards: **Towards the back.** *Au fond.* III, 2

tower: **to go up in a tower** *monter dans une tour*, II, 6

track and field *l'athlétisme*, III, 12; **to do track and field** *faire de l'athlétisme*, I, 4

traffic *la circulation*, III, 8

traffic jam *l'embouteillage* (m.), III, 8

trails: **to follow the marked trails** *suivre les sentiers balisés*, II, 12

train *s'entraîner*, III, 12; **to train for (a sport)** *s'entraîner à...* , II, 7

train (locomotive): **by train** *en train*, I, 12; **train station** *la gare*, II, 2; **train ticket** *un billet de train*, I, 11

trash: **It's trash.** *C'est un navet.* III, 9; **to take out the trash** *sortir la poubelle*, I, 7; **to throw trash** *jeter des ordures*, III, 3

trashcan *la poubelle*, I, 7

travel *voyager*, I, 1

tree *l'arbre* (m.), III, 7

trip: **Did you have a good trip?** *Vous avez (Tu as) fait bon voyage?* II, 2; **Have a good trip! (by car)** *Bonne route!* II, 3; **Have a good trip! (by plane, ship)** *Bon voyage!* I, 11; II, 3

tropical rainforest *la forêt tropicale*, II, 4

trouble: **I'm having trouble deciding.** *J'ai du mal à me décider.* III, 5

truly: **Very truly yours, . . .** *Je vous prie d'agréer, Monsieur/Madame, l'expression de mes sentiments distingués.* III, 5

trumpet *la trompette*, III, 11

trunk *la trompe*, III, 7

trust: **Trust me.** *Fais-moi confiance.* III, 4

truth: **to tell the truth** *dire la vérité*, III, 3

try: **Try . . .** *Essaie...* , III, 1; **Can I try it (them) on ?** *Je peux l'(les) essayer?* I, 10; **One more try!** *Encore un effort!* II, 7

Tuesdays: **on Tuesdays** *le mardi*, I, 2

Tunisia *la Tunisie*, III, 12

turkey: **sliced turkey breast with mashed potatoes** *l'escalope de dinde purée*, III, 1

turn: **Then, turn left on . . .** *Puis, tournez à gauche dans/sur...* , II, 2; **to turn off/out** *éteindre*, III, 3; **You turn . . .** *Vous tournez...* , I, 12

turn down: **Turn down the volume.** *Baisse le son.* III, 9

turn up: **Turn up the volume.** *Monte le son.* III, 9

turtle *la tortue*, III, 10

turtleneck sweater *le col roulé*, III, 4

TV: **TV guide/listing** *le programme télé*, III, 9; **to watch TV** *regarder la télé(vision)*, I, 1

twins *les jumeaux(-elles)*, III, 6

twists: **It's full of plot twists.** *C'est plein de rebondissements.* II, 11

type: **I like this type of . . .** *J'aime bien ce genre de...* , III, 4

typical: **What's typical of where you're from?** *Qu'est-ce qui est typique de chez toi?* III, 12

ultra— (adv.) *super*, I, 2

umbrella *le parapluie*, I, 11

uncle *l'oncle* (m.), I, 7

uncomfortable (people) *mal à l'aise* (inv.), II, 9

understanding: **I have a hard time understanding.** *J'ai du mal à comprendre.* II, 5

unemployed: **to be unemployed** *être au chômage*, III, 5

Unfortunately, . . . *Malheureusement,...* , II, 9

unique: **That's unique.** *C'est original.* II, 3

United States *les Etats-Unis* (m.), III, 12

unleaded (gasoline) *sans plomb*, III, 2

unlucky: **I'm so unlucky.** *J'ai vraiment pas de chance.* III, 12

up: **to go up** *monter*, II, 6

up to: **I've had it up to here!** *J'en ai ras le bol!* III, 8

Upstairs. *En haut.* III, 2

used: **You'll get used to it.** *Tu vas t'y faire.* II, 8

useless *nul*, I, 2

usually *d'habitude*, I, 4

V-necked *à col en V*, III, 4

vacation *les vacances* (f.), I, 1; **Have a good vacation!** *Bonnes vacances!* I, 11; **How was your vacation?** *C'était comment, tes vacances?* III, 1; **on vacation** *en vacances*, I, 4

vacuum: **to vacuum** *passer l'aspirateur*, III, 3

variety show *l'émission* (f.) *de variétés*, III, 9

vase *le vase*, II, 3

VCR (videocassette recorder) *le magnétoscope*, I, 0

vegetables *les légumes* (m.), I, 8; II, 7; **plate of raw vegetables with vinaigrette** *l'assiette de crudités*, III, 1

vegetation: **tropical vegetation** *la végétation tropicale*, III, 7

very: **not very good** *pas bon*, I, 5; **very cool** *chouette*, II, 2; **Yes, very much.** *Oui, beaucoup.* I, 2

vest *le gilet*, III, 4

video: **music video** *le vidéoclip*, III, 9; **to make videos** *faire de la vidéo*, I, 4; **to play video games** *jouer à des jeux vidéo*, I, 4

videocassette *la cassette vidéo*, III, 9; **videocassette recorder/VCR** *le magnétoscope*, I, 0; III, 9

videotape *la vidéocassette*, I, 3

village: **fishing village** *un village de pêcheurs*, II, 4

violent *violent*, II, 11

violin *le violon*, III, 11

visit (a place) *visiter*, I, 9; II, 6

visiting: **How about visiting . . . ?** *Si on visitait... ?* II, 8

volcano *le volcan,* II, 4
volleyball: to play volleyball *jouer au volley(-ball),* I, 4

wait: I can hardly wait to ...! *Je suis vraiment impatient(e) de... !* III, 12; **I can't wait to ...** *Il me tarde de... ,* III, 12; **I just can't wait ...!** *Vivement que... !* III, 12
wait for *attendre,* I, 9
waiter *le serveur,* III, 5; **Waiter! Monsieur!** I, 5
waitress *la serveuse,* III, 5; **Waitress! Madame!** I, 5; *Mademoiselle!* I, 5
walk: to go for a walk *faire une promenade,* I, 6; *se promener,* II, 4; **to walk the dog** *promener le chien,* I, 7; *sortir le chien,* III, 3
wallet *le portefeuille,* I, 3; II, 3
want *vouloir,* I, 6; **Do you know what you want to do?** *Tu sais ce que tu veux faire?* III, 5; **Do you want ...?** *Vous voulez (tu veux)... ?* I, 6, II, 3; **I don't know what I want anymore.** *Je ne sais plus ce que je veux.* III, 5; **I really want to ...** *Je tiens à... ,* III, 5; **If you want.** *Si tu veux.* I, 12; **No, I don't want to.** *Non, je ne veux pas.* II, 8; **Yes, if you want to.** *Oui, si tu veux.* I, 7
war movie *le film de guerre,* III, 9
wardrobe: armoire/wardrobe *l'armoire* (f.), II, 2
warning: I'm warning you that ... *Je vous signale que... ,* III, 7
was: He was ... *Il était... ,* II, 12; **How was it?** *C'était comment?* III, 9; **I was ...** *J'étais... ,* II, 12; **It was ...** *C'était... ,* II, 6; **It was amazing/unbelievably bad!** *C'était incroyable!* II, 5; **There was/were ...** *Il y avait... ,* II, 12
wash: to wash oneself *se laver,* II, 4; **to wash the car** *laver la voiture,* I, 7; **to wash the windows** *laver les vitres,* III, 3
waste *gaspiller,* III, 3; **a waste of time** *zéro,* I, 2
watch *la montre,* I, 3
watch: to watch a game (on TV) *regarder un match,* I, 6; **to watch TV** *regarder la télé(vision),* I, 1; **Watch out for ...!** *Attention à... !* III, 7
water *l'eau* (f.), I, 5; **mineral water** *l'eau minérale,* I, 5; **to water ski** *faire du ski nautique,* I, 4; **to water the garden** *arroser le jardin,* III, 3; **Water, please.** *De l'eau, s'il vous*

plaît. III, 1; **water with strawberry syrup** *le sirop de fraise à l'eau,* I, 5
waterfall *une chute d'eau,* II, 4
watering hole *le point d'eau,* III, 7
way: a one-way ticket *un aller simple,* II, 6; **By the way, ...** *A propos,... ,* II, 9; **No way!** *C'est pas possible!* III, 12; *Mon œil!* III, 10; *Pas possible!* II, 6; *Pas question!* II, 1; *Tu parles!* III, 9
wear *mettre, porter,* I, 10; **I don't know what to wear for ...** *Je ne sais pas quoi mettre pour... ,* I, 10; **Wear ... Mets... ,** I, 10; **What shall I wear?** *Qu'est-ce que je mets?* I, 10; **Why don't you wear ...?** *Pourquoi est-ce que tu ne mets pas... ?* I, 10
weather: The weather was great. *Il a fait un temps magnifique.* III, 1; **weather report** *la météo,* III, 9; **What is the weather like?** *Quel temps est-ce qu'il fait?* I, 4; **What was the weather like?** *Quel temps est-ce qu'il a fait?* III, 1
Wednesday: on Wednesdays *le mercredi,* I, 2
weekend: Did you have a good weekend? *Tu as passé un bon week-end?* I, 9; **on weekends** *le week-end,* I, 4; **this weekend** *ce week-end,* I, 6; **What a bad weekend!** *Quel week-end!* II, 5; **What a great weekend!** *Quel week-end formidable!* II, 5
weight: to lose weight *maigrir,* I, 10; *perdre du poids,* III, 10
weightlifting *l'haltérophilie* (f.), III, 12
weights *les haltères* (m.), III, 12
welcome: At your service; You're welcome. *A votre service.* I, 3; **Welcome to my home (our home)** *Bienvenue chez moi (chez nous),* II, 2; **You're very welcome.** *Je vous en prie.* III, 6; **You're welcome.** *De rien.* III, 6
well: Did it go well? *Ça s'est bien passé?* I, 9; **It didn't go well.** *Ça ne s'est pas bien passé.* III, 1; **Get well soon!** *Bon rétablissement!* II, 3; **I don't feel well.** *Je ne me sens pas bien.* II, 7; **It went really well!** *Ça s'est très bien passé!* II, 5; **Very well.** *Très bien.* I, 1; **Well done! Chapeau!** II, 5; **well done (meat)** *bien cuit(e).* III, 1; **You don't seem too well.** *Tu n'as pas l'air en forme.* II, 7; **You would do well to ...** *Tu ferais bien de... ,* II, 7; **You would do well/better to ...** *Tu ferais bien/mieux de... ,* III, 5; **Not too well.** *Pas trop bien.* III, 1
went: Afterwards, I went out. *Après, je suis sorti(e).* I, 9; **I went ...** *Je suis allé(e)... ,* I, 9; **I went by ...** *Je suis parti(e) en... ,* III, 1; **It went really well!** *Ça s'est très bien passé!* II, 5

were: If I were in your place, ... *A ta place,... ,* III, 8; **If I were you, ...** *Si j'étais toi,... ,* III, 8; **If it were me, ...** *Si c'était moi,... ,* III, 8; **If it were possible, ...** *Si c'était possible,... ,* III, 8; **There was/were ...** *Il y avait... ,* II, 12; **There were ...** *Il y avait de... ,* III, 9
west: in the west *dans l'ouest,* II, 4; **It's to the west of ...** *C'est à l'ouest de... ,* II, 12
western: western (film) *un western,* II, 11; III, 9; **It's in the western part of ...** *C'est dans l'ouest de... ,* II, 12
what *comment,* I, 0; **What's interesting/incredible is ...** *Ce qui est intéressant/incroyable, c'est... ,* III, 11; **I don't know what to do.** *Je ne sais pas quoi faire.* II, 10; **What are you doing?** *Mais, qu'est-ce que tu fais?* II, 2; **What are you going to do ...?** *Qu'est-ce que tu vas faire... ?* I, 6; *Tu vas faire quoi... ?* I, 6; **What bothers me is ...** *Ce qui m'ennuie, c'est de... ,* II, 4; **What can we do?** *Qu'est-ce qu'on peut faire?* II, 4; **What catches your eye is ...** *Ce qui saute aux yeux, c'est... ,* III, 11; **What do you have to drink?** *Qu'est-ce que vous avez comme boissons?* I, 5; **What do you need for ...?** (formal) *Qu'est-ce qu'il vous faut pour... ?* (informal) *Qu'est-ce qu'il te faut pour... ?* I, 3; **What do you think of ...?** *Comment tu trouves... ?* I, 2; **What I don't like is ...** *Ce que je n'aime pas, c'est... ,* II, 4; **What I like is ...** *Ce qui me plaît, c'est (de)... ,* II, 4; **What is ...?** *Qu'est-ce que c'est,... ?* III, 1; **What is that called?** *Comment est-ce qu'on appelle ça?* III, 11; **What is there ...?** *Qu'est-ce qu'il y a... ?* II, 4; **What is there to drink?** *Qu'est-ce qu'il y a à boire?* I, 5; **What is your name?** *Tu t'appelles comment?* I, 0; **What's going on?** *Qu'est-ce qui se passe?* II, 5; **What's his/her name?** *Il/Elle s'appelle comment?* I, 1; **What's it like?** *C'est comment?* II, 4; **What's that?** *Qu'est-ce que c'est?* III, 11; **What's wrong?** *Qu'est-ce qui t'arrive?* II, 5
whatever: Whatever. *Ça m'est égal.* II, 8
when: When? *Quand (ça)?* I, 6; **When do you open (close)?** *A quelle heure est-ce que vous ouvrez (fermez)?* II, 6; **When did you go there?** *Quand est-ce que tu y es allé(e)?* III, 1
where: Where? *Où ça?* I, 6; **Do you know where ... are?** *Tu sais où sont... ?* III, 2; **Excuse me, could you tell me where ... is?** *Pardon, vous savez où se trouve... ?* III, 2; **Where did you go?** *Tu es allé(e)*

où? I, 9; **Where is . . . , please?** *Où est... , s'il vous plaît?* II, 2, 4; II, 12; **Where's the fire?** *Il n'y a pas le feu.* III, 2;

whereas: Here . . . whereas . . . *Ici,... tandis que... ,* III, 8

which: Which . . . *Quel(s)/Quelle(s)... ,* III, 4; **From which platform . . . ?** *De quel quai... ?* II, 6; **Which one?** *Lequel/Laquelle?* III, 4; **Which ones?** *Lesquels/Lesquelles?* III, 4

white *blanc(he),* I, 3

who: The woman/girl/one who . . . *Celle qui... ,* III, 4; **Who's calling?** *Qui est à l'appareil?* I, 9

whom: With whom? *Avec qui?* I, 6

why: Why don't you . . . ? *Pourquoi tu ne... pas?* I, 9; II, 7; **Why not?** *Pourquoi pas?* I, 6

widowed *veuf (veuve),* III, 6

wife *la femme,* I, 7; III, 6

wild *délirant(e),* III, 4; **(crazy, funny)** *dingue,* III, 2; **I'm wild about it.** *Ça m'éclate.* III, 11

win *gagner,* I, 9; III, 12

window *la fenêtre,* I, 0; **to window-shop** *faire les vitrines,* I, 6; **to wash the windows** *laver les vitres,* III, 3

windshield: to clean the windshield *nettoyer le pare-brise,* III, 2

windsurf *faire de la planche à voile,* I, 11; II, 4

winter: in the winter *en hiver,* I, 4

wiped out: I'm wiped out. *Je suis tout(e) raplapla.* II, 7

wise: It would be wise to . . . *Il serait plus prudent de... ,* III, 7

wishes: Best wishes! *Meilleurs vœux!* II, 3

with: I went with . . . *J'y suis allé(e) avec... ,* III, 1; **The girl in the/with the . . .** *La fille au... ,* III, 4; **The man/guy/one with . . .** *Celui avec... ,* III, 4; **with me** *avec moi,* I, 6; **With whom?** *Avec qui?* I, 6

withdraw: to withdraw money *retirer de l'argent* (m.), I, 12

without: You can't leave without . . . *Tu ne peux pas partir sans... ,* I, 11

wolf *un loup,* II, 12

wonder: I wonder . . . *Je me demande... ,* II, 9; III, 5

wool *en laine,* III, 4

word: Where does the word . . . come from? *D'où vient le mot... ?* III, 11

work *travailler,* I, 9

work out: How should we work this out? *Comment est-ce qu'on fait?* III, 6

worker *l'ouvrier(l'ouvrière),* III, 5

worried *inquiet (inquiète),* II, 9

worries: to have worries *avoir des soucis,* II, 8

worry: Don't worry! *Ne t'en fais pas!* I, 9; II, 5; *Ne vous en faites pas!* III, 7; **Don't worry about it!** *Ne t'inquiète pas.* III, 6

worth: It's not worth it! *Ça ne vaut pas le coup!* III, 9; *Ce n'est pas la peine.* III, 7

worthless *n'importe quoi,* II, 11; *nul (nulle),* II, 8

worthwhile: I don't think it's worthwhile. *Je ne crois pas que ce soit utile.* III, 7

would: It would be great if . . . *Ça serait chouette si... ,* III, 8; **That would be nice.** *Ce serait sympa.* III, 6; **What would you do?** *Qu'est-ce que tu ferais, toi?* II, 10; **would like: I'd like to buy . . .** *Je voudrais acheter... ,* I, 3; **Would you mind . . . ?** *Ça t'embête de... ?* II, 10; *Ça t'ennuie de... ?* II, 10; **Would you pass . . .** *Vous pourriez (tu pourrais) me passer... ,* II, 3; **Yes, I would.** *Oui, je veux bien.* II, 3; **You would do well to . . .** *Tu ferais bien de... ,* II, 7

Wow! *Oh, dis donc!* III, 7; *Ouah!* III, 7; **Wow! That was a real scare!** *Ouf! On a eu chaud!* III, 7

wreck: to wreck the car *emboutir la voiture,* III, 10

wrestling *la lutte,* III, 12

write: Write him/her/them. *Ecris-lui/-leur.* II, 10

writer *l'écrivain,* III, 5

wrong: Everything went wrong! *Tout a été de travers!* II, 5; **Is something wrong?** *Quelque chose ne va pas?*

II, 7; **Something's wrong.** *Ça n'a pas l'air d'aller.* II, 5; **What's wrong?** *Qu'est-ce qui t'arrive?* II, 5; *Qu'est ce que tu as?* II, 7; *Qu'est-ce qu'il y a?* II, 10; **You're wrong to . . .** *Tu as tort de... ,* III, 3; **You're wrong.** *Tu as tort.* III, 9

yard *le jardin,* II, 2

yeah: Yeah. *Mouais.* II, 6; **Oh yeah? Yeah, right!** *Mon œil!* II, 6

year: I am . . . years old. *J'ai... ans.* I, 1; **When I was . . . years old, . . .** *Quand j'avais... ans,... ,* II, 8

yellow *jaune,* I, 3

yes *oui,* I, 1

yet: not yet *ne... pas encore,* I, 9; III, 10

Yippee! *Youpi!* III, 12

yogurt *du yaourt,* I, 8

you *tu, vous,* I, 0; **And you?** *Et toi?* I, 1; **. . . you know.** *..., quoi.* II, 9; **. . . you see.** *..., tu vois.* II, 9

young *jeune,* I, 7; II, 1

younger: the younger child *le cadet(la cadette),* III, 6

youngest: the youngest child *le benjamin(la benjamine),* III, 6

your *ton/ta/tes,* I, 7; *votre/vos,* I, 7

yours: Very truly yours, . . . *Je vous prie d'agréer, Monsieur/Madame, l'expression de mes sentiments distingués.* III, 5

zebra *le zèbre,* III, 7

zoo *le zoo,* I, 6; II, 6

This grammar index includes topics introduced in **Allez, viens!** Levels 1, 2 and 3. The roman numeral I preceding the page numbers indicates Level 1; the Roman numeral II indicates Level 2; the Roman numeral III indicates Level 3. Page numbers in boldface type refer to **Grammaire** and **Note de grammaire** presentations. Other page numbers refer to grammar structures presented in the **Comment dit-on... ?, Tu te rappelles?, Vocabulaire,** and **A la française** sections. Page numbers beginning with R refer to the Grammar Summary in this reference section (pages R29–R54).

A

à: expressions with **jouer** I: **113;** contractions with **le, la, l',** and **les** I: **113, 177,** 360, R21; II: **48,** 190, R27; III: R35; with cities and countries I: 330, R21; II: R27; III: **352,** R35

adjectives: adjective agreement and placement I: 86, **87, 210,** R15–R17; II: **11,** R21–R23; III: R27–R29; and **de** II: **43;** as nouns I: **301,** R18; II: R24; III: R30; demonstrative I: **85,** R17; II: R23; III: R29; formation of feminine adjectives III: R27–R29; formation of plural adjective and nouns III: R27–R29; possessive I: 203, **205,** R18; II: R24; III: R30; preceding the noun II: **43,** R23; III: R30

à quelle heure: I: 58, 183, **185,** R20

adverbs: of frequency I: **134;** II: 113, 196, R25; III: R31; placement with the **passé composé** I: **272,** R18; II: R25

agreement: adjectives I: **87, 210,** R15–R17; II: **11,** R21-R23; III: R27–R29; agreement of past participles III: **11,** R47; in the **passé composé** II: **167,** R37; in the **passé composé** of reflexive verbs II: **192,** R36; III: R45; in the **passé composé** with direct object pronouns II: **293,** R28; III: R36

aller: I: 151, 173, **174,** 328, 329, R26; with an infinitive I: 174; II: 21, R40; III: 38, R46; in the **passé composé** I: 270, 338, R28; II: 140, R37

articles: definite articles **le, la, l',** and **les** I: **28,** R19; III: 19, R30; definite articles with days of the week I: **173;** indefinite articles **un, une,** and **des** I: 79, **81,** R19; II: R25; III: 19, R31; partitive articles **du, de la,** and **de l'** I: 235, **236,** 364, R19; II: 67, **73,** R25; III: 19, R31

avec qui: I: 183, **185,** R20; II: R26; III: R33

avoir: I: **55,** R26; II: **10,** R33; III: R42; **avoir besoin de** I: **238; avoir envie de** I: 329; II: 18, 197; **avoir l'air** II: **259;** expressions with II: 9, 38, 76, 135, 143, 189, 197, 354; imperfect II: 227, 296, R38; with the **passé composé** I: 269, **271,** 273, 277, 303, 338, R28; II: 136, R37; III: **11,** R46

C

ça: replacing the subject of a sentence with **il, elle,** or **ça.** III: **201**

causative faire: III: **107**

ce, cet, cette, and **ces:** I: 85, R17; II: R23; III: R29

ce que, ce qui: III: **326,** R39; See relative pronouns.

c'est: versus **il/elle est** + adjective I: **310;** II: **315,** R30; III: R39

celle-là, celles-là, celui-là, ceux-là demonstrative pronouns III: **101,** R36

cognates: I: 6–7, 27, 84, 112

commands: I: 10, 148, 151, **152,** R28; II: **15,** R40; forming commands and suggestions III: 41, R46; with object pronouns I: 151, 240, **279,** 336, R22–R23; II: R28–R30; III: 41, R50

comparative: III: **232,** R32

comparisons: II: 102, 202, 226; superlative II: 143; III: **288,** R32

conditional: II: 76, 168, 197, 202, 286, 287, 291, 356; III: **141,** R49; in the past II: 294

conduire: III: **39**

connaître: II: 263, 313, **314,** R34; **passé composé** II: **314,** R34

contractions: See **à** or **de.**

countries: prepositions with countries I: **330,** R21; II: R27; III: R35

D

de: before modified nouns II: **43,** 100, R23; contractions I: **116, 369,** R21; II: 43, R27; III: R35; expressions with **faire** I: **113;** indefinite articles (negative) I: **81;** II: R25; indicating relationship or ownership I: **204;** II: R27; III: R35; partitive article I: **236,** R19; II: R25; III: R31; with expressions of quantity I: **242**

definite articles: I: **28,** R19; III: 19

demonstrative adjectives: I: **85,** R17; II: R23; III: R29

demonstrative pronouns: III: 101

dès que with the future tense: III: **348**

devoir (irregular): I: 189, R27; II: 15, 143, **197,** 286, R31; III: 68, R42; **devrais** I: 279; II: **197,** 202

dire: I: 276, R27

direct object pronouns: I: **279, 309,** 336, R22; II: 286, 288, 324, R28; III: 46, R36

dont: relative pronouns III 265, R39

dormir: I: **334,** R26; II: R32; III: R41

E

elle(s): replacing the subject of a sentence with **il, elle,** or **ça** III: **201;** See pronouns.

emporter: II: **354,** R31

en: pronoun I: 242, 247, **248,** 333, R23; II: **66,** 196, R29; III: 46, R35; before geographic names I: **330,** R21; II: R27; III: **352,** R35

ACKNOWLEDGMENTS & CREDITS

ACKNOWLEDGMENTS

For permission to reprint copyrighted material, grateful acknowledgment is made to the following sources:

Association de Gestion des Domaines Touristiques du Vallon de la Lambrée: Advertisement, "Château Fort de Logne," from *Guide des attractions touristiques & musées, Belgique.*

Attractions et Tourisme c/o Grottes de Han: Advertisements, "Château Fort de Logne" and "Parc de Récréation Mont Mosan," from *Guide des attractions touristiques & musées, Belgique.*

Bayard Presse International: "Albert nez en l'air" and "Julie Boum" from *Albert nez en l'air* by Paul Martin, illustrated by Mario Ramos, from *Astrapi.* Copyright © by Bayard Presse International. From "Sportez-vous bien!" from *Okapi*, October 1-15, 1986. Copyright © 1986 by Bayard Presse. From "Quel rôle joue la mode dans votre vie" from *Okapi*, July 15-31, 1989. Copyright © 1989 by Bayard Presse International. From "Aimez-vous la BD?" from *Okapi*, no. 534, February 15-28, 1994. Copyright © 1994 by Bayard Presse International. "La musique est un langage universel," "La musique m'accompagne dans la vie," and "Tous aiment me voir danser" from "Quelle musique écoutez-vous?" from *Okapi*, no. 548, October 15-22, 1994. Copyright © 1994 by Bayard Presse International.

Centre Belge de la Bande Dessinée: Hours of operation from the brochure *Centre Belge de la Bande Dessinée.*

Comité Français d'Education pour la Santé: Sticker with message, "Fumer, c'est pas ma nature!"

Companhia Melhoramentos de São Paulo, Brazil and Volcano Press, Inc.: "La Tortue et le Léopard" by Rogério Andrade Barbosa, illustrated by Ciça Fittipaldi. French translation by Holt, Rinehart and Winston. Originally published in Portugese. Copyright ©1987 by Companhia Meloramentos de São Paulo; English translation copyright © 1993 by Volcano Press, Inc.

Département de l'intérieur, de l'agriculture, de l'environnement et de l'énergie, Geneva: "Aidez-nous à protéger les eaux!" from *Voyage au bout de l'eau.*

Editions Denoël: "Il faut être raisonnable" from *Les Vacances du Petit Nicolas* by Sempé and Goscinny. Copyright © 1962 by Editions Denoël.

Editions Gallimard: From "Enfance d'une fille" from *La cause des femmes* by Gisèle Halimi. Copyright © 1973 by Editions Grasset & Fasquelle.

Editions l'Harmattan: French text and illustrations from *O'gaya* by Isabelle and Henri Cadoré, illustrated by Bernadette Coléno. Copyright © 1991 by Editions L'Harmattan.

Garland Publishing, Inc.: "Froumi et Grasshopper" from *Cajun and Creole Folktales: The French Oral Tradition of South Louisiana,* collected and annotated by Barry Jean Ancelet. Copyright © 1994 by Barry Jean Ancelet.

Grand Hôtel Bristol, "L'Auberge": Adaptation of menu from restaurant "L'Auberge."

Hachette Education: "La petite maison," "Le clou de Djeha," et "Les trois femmes du roi" from *Contes et histoires du Maghreb* by Jean-Paul Tauvel. Copyright © 1975 by Hachette.

Hachette Livre: "La cuisine cajun" from "La Louisiane" from *Le guide du routard: Etats-Unis 1993/94.* Copyright © 1993 by Hachette Livre. Front cover, adaptation of "La mosquée de la kasbah," from "La place Jemaa-el-Fna," "Le minaret de la Koutoubia," "Le palais de la Bahia," adaptation from "Les souks," and from "Les tombeaux saadiens" from *Le guide du routard: Maroc, 1994-95.* Copyright © 1994 by Hachette Livre.

InterMédia Caraïbes: Text from "La Faune sous-marine de la Guadeloupe" from "Antilles Info Tourisme Guadeloupe" by Intermédia Caraïbes. Online. Available http://www.antilles-info-tourisme.com/guadeloupe.

J. C. Penney Company, Inc.: Photo from page 135 from *Celebrate Summer* catalog by J. C. Penney. Copyright © 1994 by J. C. Penney Company, Inc.

Journal L'Alsace: "A la soupe des potaches" from *Journal L'Alsace*, April 11-13, 1993. Copyright © 1993 by Journal L'Alsace.

L'Officiel des Spectacles: From "L'Ami africain," from "Le Pont de la Rivière Kwai," and from "Les Patriotes" from "Films en exclusivité" from *L'Officiel des Spectacles*, no. 2488. Copyright © by L'Officiel des Spectacles.

Christian Lacroix: From "Bazar de Christian Lacroix: automne-hiver 1994-1995," from "Christian Lacroix collection haute-couture: automne-hiver 1994/95," from "Christian Lacroix prêt-à-porter: automne-hiver 1994/95," and four illustrations by Christian Lacroix.

Le Soleil: From "Des nouveaux professionnels sur le marché" from *Le Soleil*, no. 6936, July 20, 1993. Copyright © 1993 by Le Soleil. All rights reserved. *Le Soleil* is a Senegalese daily newspaper.

Les productions La Fête: Four photographs, Scene 83, and synopsis and production information from *Fierro…L'été des secrets*, produced by Rock Demers, directed by André Melançon from a story by Rodolfo Otero, screenplay by André Melançon and Geneviève Lefebvre, stills by Jean Demers. *Fierro…L'été des secrets* is number 8 in the collection *Tales for All*. Produced by Productions La Fête, 225 Roy Street East, Suite 203, Montreal, Quebec, Canada H2W 1M5.

Librairie Gründ: "Le cimetière des éléphants" from *Légendes et contes: Contes africains* by Vladislav Stanovsk, translated into French by Dagmar Doppia. Copyright © 1992 by Aventinum, Prague; French translation copyright © 1992 by Librairie Gründ, Paris.

Madame au Foyer: "Les Tunisiennes en marche" from "Les femmes dans le monde" by Monique Roy from *Madame*, September 1994. Copyright © 1994 by Madame au Foyer.

Michelin Travel Publications: From Map No. 970, "Europe," 1994 edition. Permission No. 94-460. Copyright © 1994 by Michelin. From Map No. 409, "Belgique, Luxembourg, Belgium," 1994 edition. Permission No. 94-460. Copyright © 1994 by Michelin.

Office National du Tourisme Tunisien: Photographs and text from *Tunisie amie: Tunisie. Le pays proche.*

Parc de Récréation Mont Mosan: Advertisement, "Parc de Récréation Mont Mosan," from *Guide des attractions touristiques & musées, Belgique.*

Liliane Phung and Scoop: Four photos and text from "Mannequins d'un jour: Liliane, une vraie beauté asiatique" from *OK! Podium*, no. 34. Text copyright © by COGEDIPRESSE; photos copyright © by Fred. Gregoire.

Quelle La Source: Four photographs of clothing and accessories with descriptions from the catalog *Quelle LA Source*, Spring-Summer 1994.

Randol's Seafood & Restaurant: Logo, photographs and text from brochure *Randol's Seafood & Restaurant: Lafayette, LA.*

Swiss Council for Accident Prevention, Berne, Switzerland: From "Equipement adéquat" and front cover from *Faire des randonnées en montagne, sûrement!*

TV 7 Jours: Television listing from "Samedi, 10 septembre" from *TV 7 Jours*, September 10-16, 1992. Copyright © 1992 by TV 7 Jours.

Winstub au Cygne: Adaptation of "Le Cygne" menu.

WWF-World Wide Fund for Nature: From *Sauvegarder la nature, c'est assurer l'avenir de l'homme* and WWF Panda logo. Logo copyright © 1986 by WWF-World Wide Fund for Nature (formerly World Wildlife Fund).

WWF Suisse: Membership application for WWF from *Les Iles*, vol. 14, no. 3, September 1981.

PHOTOGRAPHY CREDITS

Abbreviations used: (t) top, (b) bottom, (l) left, (r) right, (c) center.

Rencontre culturelle students: HRW Photo/John Langford
Panorama fabric: Copyright © 1992 by Dover Publications, Inc.
All other fabric: HRW Photo/Victoria Smith.
All globes: Mountain High Maps® Copyright ©1997 Digital Wisdom, Inc.
All euros: © European Communities
Jeu de rôle masks: © PhotoSpin, Inc.

TABLE OF CONTENTS: vii (t), HRW Photo; (b), P. J. Sharpe/SuperStock; viii, © Pierre Berger/Photo Researchers, Inc.; ix, © The Purcell Team/Corbis; x (t), Eric Beggs; (b), Michael Newman/PhotoEdit; xi (t), HRW Photo/May Polycarpe; (b), © Beryl Goldberg Photography; xii, © Lineair/R. Giling/Peter Arnold, Inc.; xiii, © David Cimino/International Stock Photography; xiv, © Roberto M. Arakaki/International Stock Photography; xv, Wolfgang Kaehler Photography; xvi (t), HRW Photo; (b), Kit Kittle/Viesti Collection, Inc.; xvii, Joseph Schuyler/Stock Boston; xviii, © Bongarts Photography/SportsChrome USA; (background), HRW Photo; xix, Corbis Images; xx, Brian Seed/Stone; xxi, HRW Photo/Patrice Maurin-Berthier.

LOCATION: L'EUROPE FRANCOPHONE xviii-1, Phil Cantor/SuperStock; 2, (t), Blaine Harrington; (c), SuperStock; (b), SuperStock; 3 (t), Gary Cralle/The Image Bank; (c), SuperStock; (bl), P.& G. Bowater/The Image Bank; (br), W. Gontscharoff/SuperStock.

CHAPTER 1: 4-5, P. J. Sharpe/SuperStock; 6 (t), Jean-Marc Truchet/Stone; (cl), Barry Iverson/Woodfin Camp & Associates, Inc.; (b), Adina Tovy/Photo 20-20; 7 (tl, cl), David R. Frazier Photolibrary; (tr), Rick Lee/SuperStock; (cr), F. Bouillot/Marco Polo/Phototake; (bl), Bas van Beek/Leo de Wys, Inc.; (br), P. Halle/Marco Polo/Phototake; 8, Editions de Art Jack; 12 (l), SuperStock; (c), Shaun Egan/Stone; (r), HRW Photo/Michele Slane; 15, Catherine Ursillo/Photo Researchers, Inc.; 16 (l, c), HRW Photo/Marty Granger/Edge Productions; (r), HRW Photo/Edge Productions; 23, HRW Photo/Sam Dudgeon; 27 (l, cr), HRW Photo/Victoria Smith; (cl), HRW Photo/Sam Dudgeon; (c), HRW Photo/Marty Granger/Edge Productions; (r), Digital imagery® © 2003 PhotoDisc, Inc.

CHAPTER 2 32-33, © Pierre Berger/Photo Researchers, Inc.; 34-36 (all), HRW Photo/Patrice Maurin-Berthier; 38, Spencer Grant/PhotoEdit; 42, *Julie, Claire, Cécile: On s'éclate* by Sidney et Bom ©, 1989 Editions du Lombard, Bruxelles; 43 (l), Centre Belge de la Bande Dessinée, Bruxelles; (cl), *Les Aventures de Tintin: On a marché sur la lune* by Hergé. © 1954 Casterman, Paris-Tournai; (cr), *Les Aventures de Tintin: Le Sceptre d'Ottokar* by Hergé.

© 1975 Casterman, Paris-Tournai; (r), *L'Œuf et les Schtroumpfs* by Peyo © 1978 S.A. Editions Jean Dupuis; 44 (l, c), HRW Photo/Marty Granger/Edge Productions; (r), HRW Photo/Louis Boireau; 48 (tl), HRW Photo/Sam Dudgeon; (tr), Color Day Productions/The Image Bank; (tc), Victor Englebert; (bl), Messerschmidt/FPG; (br), F. Bouillot/Marco Polo/Phototake; 49 (l), J. Wishnetsky/Comstock; (cl), Richard Pasley Photography; (cr), F. Bouillot/Marco Polo/Phototake; (r), Victor Englebert; 50-52 *Julie, Claire, Cécile: C'est la Jungle* by Sidney et Bom © 1988 Editions du Lombard, Bruxelles; 53, HRW Photo/Sam Dudgeon; 55, HRW Photo/Patrice Maurin-Berthier; 56 (t), Richard Pasley Photography; (tc), Pierre Berger/Photo Researchers, Inc.; (c), Victor Englebert; (b), J. Wishnetsky/Comstock.

CHAPTER 3 62-63, © The Purcell Team/Corbis; 64 (tr, bl), Mark Antman/Harbrace Photo; (c, br), Blaine Harrington; 65 (t), HRW Photo/May Polycarpe; (c), Ciné-Plus Photothèque; (b), HRW Photo/Patrice Maurin-Berthier; 66 (l), HRW Photo/May Polycarpe; (cl,r), Blaine Harrington; (cr), HRW Photo/Patrice Maurin-Berthier; 71 (t), PEANUTS Reprinted by Permission United Features Syndicate; (b), Blaine Harrington; 74 (all), Blaine Harrington; 75 (all), Daniel J. Schaefer; 76 (l), HRW Photo/Louis Boireau; (c, r), HRW Photo/Marty Granger/Edge Productions; 83, HRW Photo by Sam Dudgeon; 85 (tl, tr), Digital imagery® © 2003 PhotoDisc, Inc.; (bl), HRW Photo/Victoria Smith; (br), ©Stockbyte; 87 (all), Daniel J. Schaefer; 89, Claude Martin/World Wildlife Fund; 90 (all), Daniel J. Schaefer.

CHAPTER 4 92-93, Eric Beggs; 94 (t, br), HRW Photo/Sam Dudgeon; 99 (l), HRW Photo; (r), HRW Photo/Sam Dudgeon; 102 (l), HBJ Photo/Peter Menzel; (r), Beryl Goldberg; 103 (all), HRW Photo/Marty Granger/Edge Productions; 104 (tl), Michael Newman/PhotoEdit (tr), Four By Five/SuperStock; (bl, br), HRW Photo/Sam Dudgeon; 105 (t), Cathlyn Melloan/Stone; (c), Tony Freeman/PhotoEdit; (bl), HRW Photo/Patrice Maurin-Berthier; (br), Photo 20-20; 113, HRW Photo/Sam Dudgeon; 118 (tl), © Zefa Visual Media/Index Stock Imagery, Inc.; (tr), © Telegraph Colour Library/FPG International; (remaining), HRW Photo/Sam Dudgeon.

LOCATION: L'AFRIQUE FRANCOPHONE 122-123, Gill S.J. Copeland/Nawrocki Stock Photo, Inc.; 124 (t), Gill Copeland/Nawrocki Stock Photo, Inc.; (c), SuperStock; (b), Dave G. Houser; 125 (t), Gill S.J. Copeland/Nawrocki Stock Photos; (cl), Charles G. Summers/Ron Kimball Studios; (cr), Rita Summers/Ron Kimball Studios; (bl), Cliché; (br), R. Campillo/Corbis Stock Market.

CHAPTER 5 126-127, © Beryl Goldberg Photography; 128 (t), G. Giansanti/Sygma; (c), Jason Lauré/Lauré Communications; (b), Thierry Pratt/Sygma; 129 (t), Marcus Rose/Panos Pictures; (c), Thierry Prat/Sygma; (b), HRW Photo/May Polycarpe; 130 (tl), G. Giansanti/Sygma;

(tr), HRW Photo/May Polycarpe; (bl), Marcus Rose/Panos Pictures; (br), Thierry Prat/Sygma; 131 (tl), Brian Seed/Stone; (tc, bc), SuperStock; (tr, br), Dave G. Houser; (bl), Four by Five/Superstock; 135 (l), HRW Photo/Daniel Aubry; (r), HRW Photo/May Polycarpe; 136 (t), Thierry Pratt/Sygma; (c, b), HRW Photo/Louis Boireau; 138 (all), HRW Photo/Marty Granger/Edge Productions; 139 (l), Jeff Greenberg/PhotoEdit; (cl, cr), HRW Photo/Russell Dian; (r), HRW Photo/May Polycarpe; 144-146 (background) ©PhotoSpin, Inc.

CHAPTER 6 156-157, © Lineair/R. Giling/Peter Arnold, Inc.; 158 (tl), Robert Frerck/Odyssey; (tr), © W. Walton/LPI Photo 20-20; (bl), Robert Frerck/Odyssey; (br), Elaine Little/World Photo Images; 159 (t), Noboru Komine/Photo Researchers, Inc.; (b), HRW Photo/Mark Antman; 165 (l), HRW Photo/Louis Boireau; (c, r), HRW Photo/Marty Granger/Edge Productions; 166 (both), Elaine Little/World Photo Images; 167 (t, bl), Elaine Little/World Photo Images; (br), © Createc; 168 (tl), Altitude/Peter Arnold, Inc.; (tr), Robert Frerck/Stone; (bl), John Beatty/Stone; (bc), S.A. Kaluzny; (br), Erwin C. "Budd" Nielsen/Images International; 174-176 (background), Corbis Images; 177, HRW Photo/Sam Dudgeon; 181, Beryl Goldberg; 182 (t, bl), SuperStock; (br), Panos Pictures; (br background), Blaine Harrington.

CHAPTER 7 186-187, © David Cimino/International Stock Photography; 188 (t, bl, br), HRW Photo/Patrice Maurin-Berthier; (cl, cr), Digital Stock Corporation; 189 (l, r), HRW Photo/Patrice Maurin-Berthier; (c), HRW Photo/Sam Dudgeon; 191 (tl), SuperStock; (tr), Victor Englebert; (bl), Magrus Rosshagen/Panos Pictures; (br), Jason Lauré/Lauré Communications; 197 (all), HRW Photo/Marty Granger/Edge Productions; 198 (t), ©PhotoSpin, Inc.; (c, b), SuperStock; 199 (t), SuperStock; (b), Corbis Images; 200 (tl), Corbis Images; (tcl), Christer Fredriksson/Natural Selection; (tcr, bcr), Tim Davis/Davis Lynn Images; (tr), Renee Lynn/Davis/Lynn Images; (bl, bcl), Daniel J. Cox/Natural Selection; (br), Erwin and Peggy Bauer/Natural Selection; 207, HRW Photo/Sam Dudgeon, 208 (both), HRW Photo/Sam Dudgeon; 213 (tl), SuperStock; (tc), Anup Manj Shah/Animals Animals/Earth Scenes; (tr), George Merillon/Gamma Liaison; (bl), Victor Englebert; (bc), John Giustina/The Wildlife Collection; (br), Ron Levy; 214 (l), HRW Photo/Sam Dudgeon; (cl, cr), Stephen J. Krasemann/AllStock; (r), SuperStock.

CHAPTER 8 216-217, © Roberto M. Arakaki/International Stock Photography; 218 (tl), SuperStock; (tr), Dave Bartruff; (bl), Guido Cozzi/Bruce Coleman Inc.; (br), Steve Vidler/Leo deWys, Inc.; 219 (t), Ric Ergenbright; (c), Nik Wheeler; (b), HRW Photo/Sam Dudgeon; 221 (tl), Nik Wheeler; (tr), John Elk III/Bruce Coleman Inc.; (c), Ric Ergenbright; (bl), Jason Lauré/Lauré Communications; (br), Klaus D. Francke/Peter Arnold, Inc.; 223 row 1 (l, cl,

for Artville; row 6 (l), Corbis Images; (r), ©1997 Radlund & Associates for Artville

ADDTIONAL VOCABULARY R19 (tl, bl), ©Stockbyte; (tr, br), Digital imagery® © 2003 PhotoDisc, Inc.; R20 (t, ctr), HRW Photo/Sam Dudgeon; (ctl, cbl, b), Digital imagery® © 2003 PhotoDisc, Inc.; (cbr), Letraset Phototone; R21 (tl, tc, cr, br), Digital imagery® © 2003 PhotoDisc, Inc.; (tr), HRW Photo/Michelle Bridwell; (cl), ©Stockbyte; (c), HRW Photo/Sam Dudgeon; (bl), Corbis Images; (bc), © Digital Vision; R22 (t, ctl), ©1998 Artville, LLC; (ctr), HRW Photo/Sam Dudgeon; (cbl, cbr, br), Digital imagery® © 2003 PhotoDisc, Inc.; (bl), Digital imagery® © 2003 PhotoDisc, Inc.; R23 (tl), ©Image Ideas, Inc.; (tr, cl, cr, bl), Digital imagery® © 2003 PhotoDisc, Inc.; (br), ©1997 Radlund & Associates for Artville; R24 (tl, bl, bc), Digital imagery® © 2003 PhotoDisc, Inc.; (tr), © Digital Vision; (c, cr, br), ©Stockbyte; R25 (tl, cl, c, bl, br), ©Stockbyte; (tr, cr), Corbis Images; R26 (all), Digital imagery® © 2003 PhotoDisc, Inc.

ILLUSTRATION AND CARTOGRAPHY CREDITS

Abbreviated used: (t) top, (b) bottom, (l) left, (r) right, (c) center.

All art, unless otherwise noted, by Holt, Rinehart & Winston.

FRONT MATTER: Page xxiii, MapQuest.com; xxiv, MapQuest.com; xxv, MapQuest.com; xxvi, MapQuest.com; xxvii, MapQuest.com; xxviii, MapQuest.com.

LOCATION: FRANCOPHONE EUROPE
Chapter One: Page 6-7, MapQuest.com; 10, Gilles-Marie Baur; 30, Jocelyne Bouchard. **Chapter Two:** Page 34, MapQuest.com; 37, Anne Stanley; 38, MapQuest.com; 39, Pascal Garnier; 40, Pascal Garnier; 37, Jean-Pierre Foissy; 41, Jean-Pierre Foissy; 43, Anne Stanley; 45, Ortelius Designs. **Chapter Three:** Page 68, Edson Campos; 69, Julian Willis; 70 (t), Jean-Pierre Foissy; 70 (b), Gwenneth Barth; 71 (t), Gwenneth Barth; 77, Jean-Pierre Foissy; 78, Julian Willis; 90, Julian Willis. **Chapter Four:** Page 97, Agnès Gojon; 99, Agnès Gojon; 100 (t), Pascal Pinet; 100 (c), Sylvie Rochart; 100 (b), Pierre Fouillet; 106, Jocelyne Bouchard; 107, Sylvie Rochart; 109, Agnès Gojon; 114, Agnès Gojon; 117, Jocelyne Bouchard; 120, Pierre Fouillet.

LOCATION: FRANCOPHONE AFRICA
Chapter Five: Page 122, MapQuest.com; 132, Edson Campos; 133, Jocelyne Bouchard; 134, Jocelyne Bouchard; 148, Edson Campos; 154, Jocelyne Bouchard. **Chapter Six:** Page 161, Jocelyne Bouchard; 163, Jean-Pierre Foissy; 166, Jocelyne Bouchard; 169, Sylvie Rochart; 171, Jocelyne Bouchard; 179, Jocelyne Bouchard; 184, Brian Stevens. **Chapter Seven:** Page 192, Jocelyne Bouchard; 194, Julian Willis; 201, Julian Willis; 202, Gilles-Marie Baur; 211, Julian Willis. **Chapter Eight:** Page 222, Jocelyne Bouchard; 224 (t), Jocelyne Bouchard; 224 (b), Anne Stanley; 225, Jocelyne Bouchard; 226, Bruce Roberts; 230, Jocelyne Bouchard; 231, Sylvie Rochart; 244, Pierre Fouillet.

LOCATION: FRANCOPHONE AMERICA
Chapter Nine: Page 246, MapQuest.com; 256, Jocelyne Bouchard; 257, Bruce Roberts; 258, Jocelyne Bouchard; 260, Edson Campos; 274, Sylvie Rochart. **Chapter Ten:** Page 286, Anne Stanley; 287, Anne Stanley; 289, Anne Stanley; 294, Edson Campos; 297, Jean-Pierre Foissy; 302, Anne Stanley; 304, Anne Stanley; 308, Edson Campos. **Chapter Eleven:** Page 317 (t), Bruce Roberts; 317 (b), Sylvie Rochart; 318, Jean-Pierre Foissy; 323, Gilles-Marie Baur; 328, Tim Jessell; 329, Tim Jessell; 330, Tim Jessell; 335, Bruce Roberts; 338, Edson Campos. **Chapter Twelve:** Page 345, Alain Massicotti; 346, Bernard LeDuc; 347, Alain Massicotti; 349, Bruce Roberts; 352, Anne Stanley; 353, Gilles-Marie Baur; 355, Jocelyne Bouchard.